Frommer's®

Spain 2011

by Darwin Porter & Danforth Prince

Wiley Publishing, Inc.

Published by:
Wiley Publishing, Inc.
111 River St.
Hoboken, NJ 07030-5774

ISBN 978-0-470-61435-8 (paper); ISBN 978-0-470-87718-0 (paper); ISBN 978-0-470-59487-2 (ebk); ISBN 978-0-470-59488-9 (ebk); ISBN 978-0-470-89019-6 (ebk)

Editors: Matthew Brown with Emil J. Ross
Production Editor: Heather Wilcox
Cartographer: Elizabeth Puhl
Photo Editors: Richard Fox, Alden Gewirtz
Cover Photo Editor: Richard Fox
Design and Layout by Vertigo Design
Graphics and Prepress by Wiley Indianapolis Composition Services

Front cover photo: Ceramic tiles depicting pilgrims in regional costume, Málaga, Spain ©Ken Welsh VWPics / SuperStock, Inc.

Back cover photos: *Left:* Valencian paella ©Steve Vidler / eStock Photo. *Middle:* Bullfighter in Madrid's Las Ventas bullring ©White Star Agency / AGE Fotostock, Inc. *Right:* Vineyard in Morales de Toro ©Mick Rock / Cephas Picture Library / Alamy Images.

For information on our other products and services or to obtain technical support, please contact our Customer Care Department within the U.S. at 877/762-2974, outside the U.S. at 317/572-3993 or fax 317/572-4002.

Wiley also publishes its books in a variety of electronic formats. Some content that appears in print may not be available in electronic formats.
Manufactured in the United States of America

5 4 3 2 1

CONTENTS

LIST OF MAPS

ABOUT THE AUTHORS

Veteran travel writer **Darwin Porter** wrote the first ever Frommer's guide to Spain. Back then it was called *Spain on $5 a Day*, and it became an immediate best seller in the travel book business. The only good thing about those dark days of the Franco era were the $2 hotel rooms, the $1.50 paella dinners, and the 25¢ glasses of Rioja wine. Spain has changed drastically since then, and the new *Frommer's Spain* has kept up with the developments. Porter was joined in 1982 by Spanish-speaking **Danforth Prince,** formerly of the Paris bureau of the *New York Times.* Together, they have also written such Iberian guides as *Frommer's Lisbon; Frommer's Barcelona; Frommer's Madrid;* and *Frommer's Seville, Granada & the Best of Andalusia.*

HOW TO CONTACT US

In researching this book, we discovered many wonderful places—hotels, restaurants, shops, and more. We're sure you'll find others. Please tell us about them, so we can share the information with your fellow travelers in upcoming editions. If you were disappointed with a recommendation, we'd love to know that, too. Please write to:

Frommer's Spain 2011
Wiley Publishing, Inc. • 111 River St. • Hoboken, NJ 07030-5774
frommersfeedback@wiley.com

AN ADDITIONAL NOTE

Please be advised that travel information is subject to change at any time—and this is especially true of prices. We therefore suggest that you write or call ahead for confirmation when making your travel plans. The authors, editors, and publisher cannot be held responsible for the experiences of readers while traveling. Your safety is important to us, however, so we encourage you to stay alert and be aware of your surroundings. Keep a close eye on cameras, purses, and wallets, all favorite targets of thieves and pickpockets.

FROMMER'S STAR RATINGS, ICONS & ABBREVIATIONS

Every hotel, restaurant, and attraction listing in this guide has been ranked for quality, value, service, amenities, and special features using a star-rating system. In country, state, and regional guides, we also rate towns and regions to help you narrow down your choices and budget your time accordingly. Hotels and restaurants are rated on a scale of zero (recommended) to three stars (exceptional). Attractions, shopping, nightlife, towns, and regions are rated according to the following scale: zero stars (recommended), one star (highly recommended), two stars (very highly recommended), and three stars (must-see).

In addition to the star-rating system, we also use **seven feature icons** that point you to the great deals, in-the-know advice, and unique experiences that separate travelers from tourists. Throughout the book, look for:

Special finds—those places only insiders know about

Fun facts—details that make travelers more informed and their trips more fun

Kids—best bets for kids and advice for the whole family

Special moments—those experiences that memories are made of

Overrated—places or experiences not worth your time or money

Insider tips—great ways to save time and money

Great values—where to get the best deals

The following abbreviations are used for credit cards:

AE American Express	**DISC** Discover	**V** Visa	
DC Diners Club	**MC** MasterCard		

TRAVEL RESOURCES AT FROMMERS.COM

Frommer's travel resources don't end with this guide. Frommer's website, **www.frommers. com**, has travel information on more than 4,000 destinations. We update features regularly, giving you access to the most current trip-planning information and the best airfare, lodging, and car-rental bargains. You can also listen to podcasts, connect with other Frommers.com members through our active-reader forums, share your travel photos, read blogs from guidebook editors and fellow travelers, and much more.

THE BEST OF SPAIN

S pain is one of the most diverse and visually stunning nations of Europe. As you plan your trip, you may find yourself overwhelmed by the number of fascinating sights, beautiful landscapes, and off-the-beaten-path towns to fit into your limited time. So let us give you a hand. We've scoured the country in search of the best places and experiences, and we've listed our favorites below, admittedly very personal and opinionated choices.

THE best TRAVEL EXPERIENCES

o **Sitting in *Sol* or *Sombra* at the Bullfights:** With origins as old as pagan Spain, the art of bullfighting is the expression of Iberian temperament and passions. Detractors object to the sport as cruel, bloody, and savage. Fans, however, view bullfighting as a microcosm of death, catharsis, and rebirth. If you strive to understand the bullfight, it can be one of the most evocative and memorable events in Spain. Head for the *plaza de toros* (bullring) in any major city, but particularly in Madrid, Seville, or Granada. Tickets are either *sol* (sunny side) or *sombra* (pricier, but in the shade).

o **Feasting on Tapas in the *Tascas*:** Tapas, those bite-size portions washed down with wine, beer, or sherry, are reason enough to go to Spain. Tapas bars, called *tascas*, are a quintessential Spanish experience. Originally tapas were cured ham or *chorizo* (spicy sausage). Today they are likely to be any-thing—*gambas* (deep-fried shrimp); anchovies marinated in vinegar; stuffed peppers; a cool, spicy gazpacho; or hake salad.

PREVIOUS PAGE: **A horse dressed for Feria del Caballo in Jerez.** ABOVE: **Sampling tapas in Madrid.**

Traditional flamenco.

o **Getting Caught Up in the Passions of Flamenco:** It's best heard and watched in an old tavern, in a neighborhood like Barrio de Triana in Seville. From the lowliest taberna to the poshest nightclub, you can hear the staccato foot stomping, castanet rattling, hand clapping, and sultry guitar chords. Some say its origins lie deep in Asia, but the Spanish Gypsy has given the art an original style dramatizing inner conflict and pain. Performed by a great artist, flamenco can tear your heart out with its soulful, throaty singing.

o **Seeing the Masterpieces at the Prado:** One of the world's premier art museums, the Prado is home to more than 7,000 paintings, many of them acquired by Spanish kings. The wealth of Spanish art is staggering—everything from Goya's *Naked Maja* to the celebrated *Las Meninas (The Maids of Honor)* by Velázquez (our favorite). Masterpiece after masterpiece unfolds before your eyes, including works by Hieronymus Bosch, Goya, Caravaggio, Fra Angelico, and Botticelli. See p. 160.

o **Sipping Sherry in Jerez de la Frontera:** In Spain, sherry is called *jerez*, and it's a major industry and subculture in its own right. Hispanophiles compare the complexities of sherry to those of the finest wines produced in France and make pilgrimages to the bodegas in Andalusia that ferment this amber-colored liquid. More than 100 bodegas are available for visits, tours, and tastings, opening their gates to visitors interested in a process that dates from the country's Roman occupation. See p. 334.

o **Wandering the Crooked Streets of Barcelona's Gothic Quarter:** Long before Madrid was founded, the kingdom of Catalonia was a bastion of art and architecture. Whether the Barri Gòtic, as it's called in Catalan, is truly Gothic is the subject of endless debate, but the Ciutat Vella (Old City) of Barcelona is one of the most evocative neighborhoods in Spain. Its richly textured streets, with their gurgling fountains, vintage stores, and ancient fortifications, inspired such artists as Pablo Picasso and Joan Miró (who was born here). See p. 464.

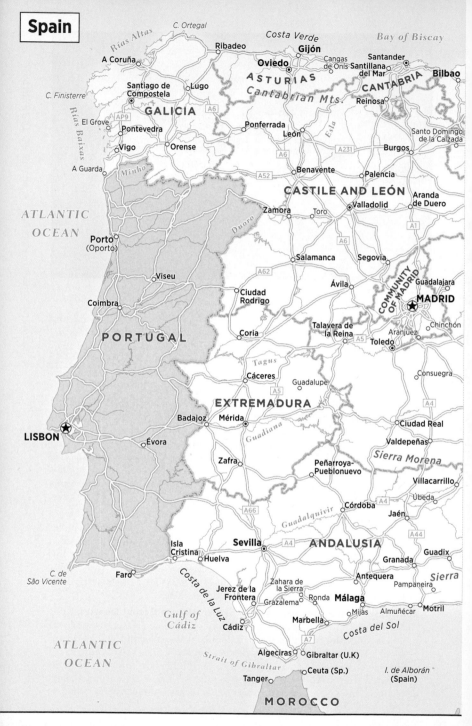

Spain

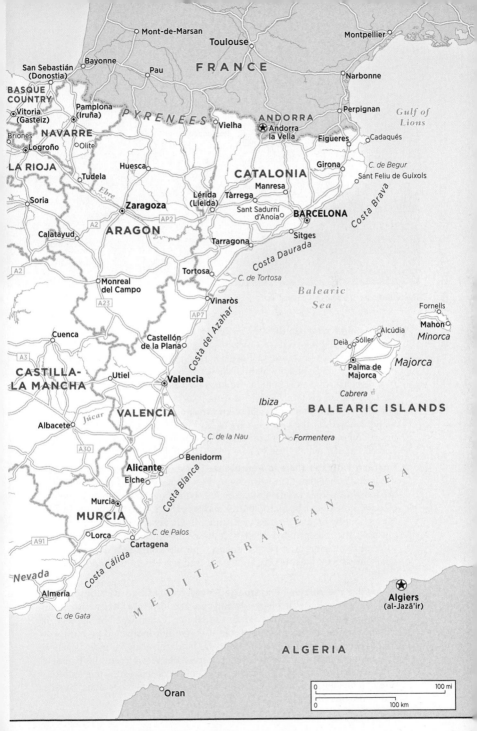

The cathedral of Santiago de Compostela.

- **Going Gaga over Gaudí:** No architect in Europe was as fantastical as Antoni Gaudí y Cornet, the foremost proponent of Catalan *modernisme* (or, in Spanish, *modernismo*). Barcelona is studded with the works of this extraordinary artist, all of which UNESCO now lists as World Trust Properties. A recluse and a celibate bachelor as well as a fervent Catalan nationalist, he lived out his fantasies in his work. Nothing is more stunning than La Sagrada Família, Barcelona's best-known landmark, a cathedral on which Gaudí labored for the last 43 years of his life. The landmark cathedral was never completed, but work on it still proceeds. If it's ever finished, "The Sacred Family" will be Europe's largest cathedral. See p. 508.

- **Running with the Bulls in Pamplona:** Okay, maybe it's smarter to watch the bulls, rather than run with them. The Fiesta de San Fermín in July is the most dangerous ritual in Spain, made even more so by copious amounts of wine consumed by participants and observers. Broadcast live on TV throughout Spain and the rest of Europe, the festival features herds of furious bulls that charge down medieval streets, at times trampling and goring some of the hundreds of people who run beside them. Few other rituals in Spain are as breathtaking or as foolhardy. And few others as memorable. See p. 596.

- **Following the Ancient Pilgrimage Route to Santiago de Compostela:** Tourism as we know it began during the Middle Ages, when thousands of European pilgrims journeyed to the shrine of Santiago (St. James), in Galicia, in northwestern Spain. Even if you're not motivated by faith, you should see some of Spain's most dramatic landscapes and grandest scenery by crossing the northern tier of the country—all the way from the Pyrenees to Santiago de Compostela. Some of the country's most stunning architecture can be viewed along the way, including gems in Roncesvalles, Burgos, and León. See p. 682.

THE best SMALL TOWNS

o **Cuenca:** Set amid a landscape of rugged limestone outcroppings at the junction of two rivers, Cuenca is a fascinating combination of medieval masonry and cantilevered balconies that seem to float above the steep gorges below. The angularity of the architecture here is said to have inspired early versions of cubism, a fact commemorated in Cuenca's Museo de Arte Abstracto Español. This museum is considered one of the finest modern art museums in Spain. See p. 227.

o **Zafra:** Zafra's 15th-century castle is the largest and best preserved in the region. It is set within the angular, stark white architecture of Zafra, which is also said to have inspired the cubists. See p. 283.

o **Baeza:** After it was wrenched away from the Moors in 1227, Baeza became a frontier town between the Christian and Moorish worlds, and a die-hard symbol of the Catholic ambition to occupy all of Iberia. Today, a wealth of architecture survives as evidence of the splendor of Iberian history. See p. 291.

o **Carmona:** Pint-size, sleepy Carmona packs a historical wallop, evoking the Roman occupation of Iberia. The town claims an architectural legacy from every occupying force since 206 B.C., when the Romans defeated the resident Carthaginian army. See p. 332.

o **Ronda:** The site appears inhospitable—a gorge slices through the town center and its twin halves are connected with bridges that are antiques in their own right. But the winding streets of this old Moorish town are perfect for wandering, and the views of the surrounding Andalusian countryside are stupendous. Ronda is also revered by bullfighting fans, for both its bullring (the oldest and most beautiful in Spain) and the region's skill in breeding the fiercest bulls in the country. See p. 346.

o **Mijas:** Wander through streets and alleys once trod by the Phoenicians, the Celts, and the Moors. Today, the town offers a welcome dose of medieval flair on the Costa del Sol, a region otherwise filled with modern, anonymous, and sometimes ugly resort hotels. See p. 408.

o **Nerja:** On the Costa del Sol at the Balcón de Europa (Balcony of Europe) lies this Mediterranean gem and its palm-shaded promenade jutting into the sea. Lined

A "hanging house" in Cuenca.

A winding alley in Mijas.

with antique iron lampposts, the village overlooks a pretty beach and fishing fleet. The resort town is on a sloping site at the foot of a wall of jagged coastal mountains. You can snuggle up in the *parador* or lodge at one of the little inns on the narrow streets. See p. 423.

o **Elche:** Although famed as a charming medieval village, Elche is best known as the excavation site of one of the premier sculptures of the Roman Empire in Iberia, *La Dama de Elche,* now exhibited in Madrid's archaeological museum. These days, you can still see date palms planted originally by the Phoenicians. A "mystery play" celebrating the Assumption of the Virgin has been performed in the village church every year since the 1300s. See p. 454.

o **Sitges:** South of Barcelona is Spain's most romantic Mediterranean beach town, with a 2.5km-long (1½-mile) sandy beach and a promenade studded with flowers and palm trees. Sitges is a town with a rich connection to art; Picasso and Dalí both spent time here. Wander its small lanes and inspect the old villas of its Casco Antiguo, the Old Quarter. When not at the beach, you can view three good art museums. Nowadays, thousands of gays and lesbians flock to Sitges, which attracts a wide spectrum of visitors of all persuasions. See p. 548.

o **Cadaqués:** The 16th-century church that dominates this town from a nearby hilltop isn't particularly noteworthy, but Cadaqués—on the Costa Brava near the French border—still charms visitors with its whitewashed, fishing-village simplicity. The azure waters of the Mediterranean appealed to surrealist master Salvador Dalí, who built a suitably bizarre villa in the adjoining hamlet of Lligat. See p. 575.

o **Santillana del Mar:** Jean-Paul Sartre called it "the prettiest village in Spain." Only 6 blocks long and just 5km (3 miles) from the sea, Santillana del Mar perfectly captures the spirit of Cantabria. It's also near the Cuevas de Altamira (Altamira Caves), often called "the Sistine Chapel of prehistoric art." Romanesque houses and mansions line the ironstone streets. People still sell fresh milk from their stable doors, as if the Middle Ages had never ended, but you can live in comfort at one of Spain's grandest *paradores,* Parador de Santillana, a converted 17th-century mansion. See p. 656.

Sitges's beachside promenade.

o **Deià:** On the island of Majorca, you'll find this lovely old village (also spelled Deyá), where the poet Robert Graves lived until his death in 1985. Following in his footsteps, artists and writers flock to this haven of natural beauty, 27km (17 miles) northwest of Palma. The views of the sea and mountains are panoramic. Gnarled and ancient olive trees dot the landscape. You can book into cozy nests of luxury like La Residencia or Es Molí. See p. 727.

THE best BEACHES

Spain may be flanked to the east by France and the Pyrenees and to the west by Portugal, but most of the country is ringed with sand, rock, and seawater. That, coupled with almost year-round sunshine, has attracted many millions of beachgoers.

o **Costa del Sol:** Stretching east from Gibraltar along the southernmost coast of Spain, the Costa del Sol is the most famous, party-hearty, overdeveloped string of beaches in Iberia. The beaches feature superb sand, and the Mediterranean waters are calm and warm throughout most of the year. But these charms have brought throngs of visitors, making this the most congested string of coastal resorts in Europe. The most important resorts here are Marbella, Torremolinos, Málaga, and Nerja. Look for soaring skyscrapers, eye-popping bikinis, sophisticated resorts and restaurants, lots of sunshine, and interminable traffic jams. See p. 386.

o **Costa Blanca:** This southeastern coast embraces the industrial city of Valencia, but its best-known resorts, Benidorm and Alicante, are packed with northern European sun-seekers every year. The surrounding scenery isn't particularly dramatic, but the water is turquoise, the sand is white, and a low annual rainfall virtually guarantees a sunny vacation. See p. 427.

o **Costa Brava:** Rockier, more serpentine, and without the long stretches of sand that mark the Costa Blanca, the cliff-edged Costa Brava extends from Barcelona to the French border. Look for the charming, sandy-bottomed coves that dot the coast. Although there are fewer undiscovered beaches

Cala'n Porter beach, on Minorca.

here than along Spain's Atlantic coast, the Costa Brava retains a sense of rocky wilderness. One of the more eccentric-looking villas along this coast belonged to the late Salvador Dalí, the region's most famous modern son, who lived much of his life near Cadaqués. See p. 554.

○ **Costa Verde:** Radically different from the dry and sunbaked coastline of Andalusia, the rocky Costa Verde (Green Coast) resembles a sunny version of Ireland's western shore. It's temperate in summer, when the rest of Spain can be unbearably hot. Much of the coast lies within the ancient province of Asturias, a region rife with Romanesque architecture and medieval pilgrimage sites—and one that has not yet been overwhelmed with tourism. Premier resorts include some districts of Santander, Gijón, and, a short distance inland, Oviedo. See p. 647.

○ **The Balearic Islands:** Just off the coast of Catalonia and a 45-minute flight from Barcelona, this rocky, sand-fringed archipelago attracts urban refugees seeking the sun, jet-set glitterati, and exhibitionists in scanty beachwear. The Mediterranean climate is warmer here than on the mainland. The city of Palma de Majorca has the greatest number of high-rises and the most crowded shorelines. Much of Ibiza is party central for young people and gay visitors during the summer. Sleepy Minorca offers more isolation. See p. 703.

THE best CASTLES & PALACES

○ **Palacio Real (Madrid):** No longer occupied by royalty, but still used for state occasions, the Royal Palace sits on the bank of the Manzanares River. It was built in the mid–18th century over the site of a former palace. It's not Versailles, but it's still mighty impressive, with around 2,000 rooms. No one has lived here since 1931, but the chandeliers, marble columns, gilded borders, paintings, and objets d'art, including Flemish tapestries and Tiepolo

The Patio de los Arrayanes at the Alhambra.

ceiling frescoes, are well preserved. The empty thrones of King Juan Carlos and Queen Sofía are among the highlights of the tour. See p. 164.

○ **Alcázar (Segovia):** Once the most impregnable castle in Spain, El Alcázar rises dramatically from a rock spur near the ancient heart of town. Isabella's marriage to Ferdinand at this foreboding site eventually led to Spain's unification. Today, it's the single most photographed and dramatic castle in Iberia. See p. 213.

○ **Palacio Real (Aranjuez):** Built at enormous expense by the Bourbon cousins of the rulers of France, the palace was designed to emulate the glories of Versailles in its 18th-century neoclassicism. The gardens are even more fascinating than the palace. The gem of the complex is the Casita del Labrador, an annex as rich and ornate as its model—Marie Antoinette's Petit Trianon at Versailles. See p. 205.

○ **Alhambra (Granada):** One of Spain's grandest sights, the Alhambra was originally conceived by the Muslims as a fortified pleasure pavilion. Its allure was instantly recognized by the Catholic monarchs after the Reconquest. Despite the presence of a decidedly European palace at its center, the setting remains one of the most exotic (and Moorish) in all of Europe. See p. 356.

○ **Alcázar (Seville):** The oldest royal residence in Europe still in use was built by Peter the Cruel (1350–69) in 1364, 78 years after the Moors left Seville. Ferdinand and Isabella once lived here. The Alcázar is one of the purest examples of the Mudéjar, or Moorish, style, and its decoration is based on that of the Alhambra in Granada. A multitude of Christian and Islamic motifs are combined architecturally in this labyrinth of gardens, halls, and courts, none more notable than the Patio de las Doncellas (Court of the Maidens). See p. 311.

THE best MUSEUMS

The spectacular Prado in Madrid is no mere museum but a travel experience. In itself, it's worth a journey to Spain. (See "The Best Travel Experiences," on p. 2.)

○ **Museo Thyssen-Bornemisza (Madrid):** Madrid's acquisition of this treasure-trove of art in the 1980s was one of the greatest coups in European art history. Amassed by a central European collector beginning around 1920 and formerly displayed in Lugano, Switzerland, its 700 canvases, with works

The interior of Seville's Alcázar.

by artists ranging from El Greco to Picasso, are arranged in chronological order. The collection rivals the legendary holdings of the queen of England herself. See p. 162.

o **Museo de Arte Abstracto Español (Cuenca):** The angular medieval architecture of the town that contains the museum is an appropriate foil for a startling collection of modern masters. A group of some of Spain's most celebrated artists settled in Cuenca in the 1950s and 1960s, and their works are displayed here. They include Fernando Zobel, Antoni Tàpies, Eduardo Chillida, Luis Feito, and Antonio Saura. See p. 229.

o **Museo-Hospital de Santa Cruz (Toledo):** Built by the archbishop of Toledo as a hospital for the poor, this is the most important museum in New Castile. It's known for its Plateresque architecture—notably its intricate facade—and for the wealth of art inside. Among its noteworthy collection of 16th- and 17th-century paintings are 18 works by El Greco, including his *Altarpiece of the Assumption,* completed in 1613 during his final period. The gallery also contains a collection of primitive paintings. See p. 196.

o **Museo Nacional de Escultura (Valladolid):** The greatest collection of gilded polychrome sculpture—an art form that reached its pinnacle in Valladolid—is on display here in the 15th-century San Gregorio College. Figures are first carved in wood and then painted with great artistry to achieve a lifelike appearance. The most remarkable exhibit is an altarpiece designed by Alonso Berruguete for the Church of San Benito. Be sure to see his *Martyrdom of St. Sebastian.* See p. 258.

o **Museo Nacional de Arte Romano (Mérida):** A museum that makes most archaeologists salivate, this modern building contains hundreds of pieces of ancient Roman sculpture discovered in and around Mérida. The Roman treasures included theaters, amphitheaters, racecourses, and hundreds of tombs full of art objects, many of which are on display here. In 1986, the well-known and award-winning architect Rafael Moneo designed this ambitious and innovative brick building. Designing the building on a grand scale, he freely borrowed from Roman motifs and daringly incorporated an ancient Roman road discovered when the foundations were dug. See p. 281.

o **Museo de Bellas Artes de Sevilla (Seville):** The Prado doesn't own all the great Spanish art in the country. Located in the early-17th-century convent of La Merced, this museum is famous for its works by such Spanish masters

The Teatre Museu Dalí in Figueres.

as Valdés Leal, Zurbarán, and Murillo. Spain's Golden Age is best exemplified by Murillo's monumental *Immaculate Conception* and Zurbarán's *Apotheosis of St. Thomas Aquinas*. See p. 316.

o **Museu Picasso (Barcelona):** Picasso, who spent many of his formative years in Barcelona, donated some 2,500 of his paintings, drawings, and engravings to launch this museum in 1970. It's second only to the Picasso Museum in Paris. Seek out his notebooks, which contain many sketches of Barcelona scenes. The pieces are arranged in roughly chronological order, so you'll discover that he completely mastered traditional representational painting before tiring of it and beginning to experiment. Watch for numerous portraits of his family, as well as examples from both his Blue Period and his Rose Period. His obsessive *Las Meninas* series—painted in 1959—offers exaggerated variations on the theme of the famous Velázquez work hanging in Madrid's Prado Museum. See p. 510.

o **Teatre Museu Dalí (Figueres):** The eccentric Salvador Dalí is showcased here as nowhere else. The surrealist artist—known for everything from lobster telephones to *Rotting Mannequin in a Taxicab*—conceived of his art partly as theater. But be warned: As Dalí's final joke, he wanted the museum to spew forth "false information." See p. 573.

THE best CATHEDRALS & CHURCHES

o **Catedral de Avila:** One of the earliest Gothic cathedrals in Castile, this rugged, plain edifice was called "a soldier's church." A brooding, granite monolith, which in some ways resembles a fortress, it is the centerpiece of a city that produced St. Teresa, the most famous mystic of the Middle Ages. The interior of the cathedral, with its High Gothic nave, is filled with notable works of art, including many Plateresque statues. See p. 224.

o **Catedral de Toledo:** Ranked among the greatest of all Gothic structures, this cathedral was built on the site of an old Arab mosque. A vast pile from the 13th to the 15th centuries, it has an interior filled with masterpieces—notably an immense polychrome retable carved in flamboyant Gothic style, and magnificent 15th- and 16th-century choir stalls. In the treasury is a splendid 16th-century silver-and-gilt monstrance, weighing about 500 pounds. See p. 195.

o **Real Monasterio de San Lorenzo de El Escorial (near Madrid):** Philip II, who commissioned this monastery in the 1530s, envisioned it as a monastic fortress against the distractions of the secular world. More awesome than beautiful, it's the world's best example of the religious devotion of

Statues at the Catedral de Toledo.

Renaissance Spain. This huge granite fortress, the burial place for Spanish kings, houses a wealth of paintings and tapestries—works by everyone from Titian to Velázquez. See p. 209.

o **Catedral de León:** Filled with more sunlight than any other cathedral in Spain, this one was begun in 1250 with a design pierced by 125 stained-glass windows and 57 oculi, the oldest of which date from the 13th century. The architectural achievement is stunning but also dangerous: Architects fear that an urgent restoration is needed to strengthen the walls to prevent collapse. The well-preserved cloisters are also worth a visit. See p. 252.

o **Catedral de Santa María (Burgos):** After its cornerstone was laid in 1221, this cathedral became the beneficiary of creative talent imported from England, Germany, and France. It is the third-largest cathedral in Spain, after Seville and Toledo. Art historians claim that among medieval religious buildings, it has the most diverse spectrum of sculpture in Gothic Spain—so diverse that a special name has been conjured up to describe it: the School of Burgos. El Cid is buried here. See p. 262.

o **Catedral de Sevilla:** The Christians are not the only occupants of Seville who considered this site holy; an enormous mosque stood here before the Reconquest. To quote the Christians who built the cathedral, they planned one "so immense that everyone, on beholding it, will take us for madmen." They succeeded. After St. Peter's in Rome and St. Paul's in London, the cathedral of this Andalusian capital is the largest in Europe. Among its most important features are the tomb of Columbus, Patio de los Naranjos (Courtyard of the Orange Trees), Giralda Tower, and Capilla Real (Royal Chapel). See p. 315.

o **Mezquita-Catedral de Córdoba:** In the 1500s, the Christian rulers of Spain tried to convert one of the largest and most elaborate mosques in the Muslim world, the Mezquita, into a Catholic cathedral. The result, a bizarre amalgam of Gothic and Muslim architecture, is an awesomely proportioned cultural compromise that defies categorization. In its 8th-century heyday, the Mezquita was the crowning Muslim architectural achievement in the West. See p. 299.

○ **Catedral de Barcelona:** Completed in 1450, this cathedral grew to represent the spiritual power of the Catalan empire. With its 81m (266-ft.) facade and flying buttresses and gargoyles, it is the Gothic Quarter's most stunning monument. The interior is in the Catalan Gothic style with slender pillars. See p. 505.

○ **Montserrat:** Since its inauguration in the 9th century by Benedictine monks, Montserrat, near Barcelona, has been the preeminent religious shrine of Catalonia and the site of the legendary statue of La Moreneta (the Black Madonna). Its glory years ended in 1812, when it was sacked by the armies of Napoleon. Today, sitting atop a 1,200m (3,937-ft.) mountain, 11km (6¾ miles) long and 5.5km (3½ miles) wide, it is one of the three most important pilgrimage sites in Spain. See p. 536.

○ **Catedralicio de Santiago de Compostela:** During the Middle Ages, this verdant city on the northwestern tip of Iberia attracted thousands of religious pilgrims who walked from as far away as Italy to seek salvation at the tomb of St. James. The cathedral itself shows the architectural influences of nearly 800 years of religious conviction, much of it financed by donations from exhausted pilgrims. Its two most stunning features are its Obradoiro facade (a baroque masterpiece) and its carved Doorway of Glory behind the facade. An enormous silver censer, called the Botafumeiro, swings from the transept during major liturgical ceremonies. See p. 684.

The monastery-fortress of El Escorial.

Córdoba's Mezquita mosque.

THE best VINEYARDS & WINERIES

Spanish wines are some of the best in the world and are remarkably afford-able here. Below is a list of bodegas that receive visitors. For more information about the 10 wine regions—and the 39 officially recognized wine-producing Denominaciones de Origen scattered across those regions—contact **Wines from Spain,** c/o the Commercial Office of Spain, 405 Lexington Ave., 44th Floor, New York, NY 10174-4499 (*©* **212/661-4959**).

Ribera del Duero

Halfway between Madrid and Santander, this region near Burgos is the fastest developing wine district in the country and the beneficiary of massive invest-ments in the past few years. Cold nights, sunny days, the highest altitudes of any wine-producing region in Spain, and fertile alkaline soil produce flavorful, award-winning wines. Among the noteworthy individual vineyards is the following:

o **Bodegas Señorío de Nava,** Nava de Roa (*©* **98-720-97-12;** www.senorio denava.es): This is one of the region's best examples of a once-sleepy and now-booming vintner. Merlot and cabernet sauvignon grapes are cultivated, as are more obscure local varieties such as Tinta del País (also known as Tempranillo) and Garnacha (or Grenache, as it's called across the border in France). Some of the wines bottled here are distributed under the brand name Vega Cubillas.

Jerez de la Frontera

This town of 200,000 (most of whose residents work in the wine trade) is sur-rounded by a sea of vineyards, which thrive in the hot, chalky soil. Ninety-five percent of the region is planted with the hardy and flavorful Palomino Fino to produce sherry, one of the most beloved products of Spain. Few other regions contain so many bodegas, any of which can be visited. See chapter 9 for more information; outstanding choices include the following:

- **Emilio Lustau,** Jerez de la Frontera (✆ **95-634-15-97;** www.emilio-lustau.com): This bodega was established in 1896 by a local lawyer, and ever since it has produced exotic forms of sherry snapped up as collectors' items by aficionados everywhere.

- **González Byass,** Jerez de la Frontera (✆ **95-635-70-00;** www.gonzalez byass.com): Flourishing since 1835, this bodega has gained enormous recognition from one of the most famous brand names and the world's best-selling sherry, Tío Pepe. It isn't as picturesque as you might hope, because modernization has added some rather bulky concrete buildings to its historic core. Nonetheless, it's one of the most visible names in the industry. See p 336.

- **Pedro Domecq,** Jerez de la Frontera (✆ **95-615-15-00;** www.casa-pedro-domecq.com): The oldest of all the large sherry houses was established in 1730 by Pedro Domecq, a young French nobleman. Its bodega contains casks whose contents were once destined for such sherry lovers as William Pitt, Lord Nelson, and the duke of Wellington. If you visit this sprawling compound, look for La Mezquita bodega, whose many-columned interior recalls the famous mosque in Córdoba.

Barrels at Pedro Domecq.

The grapes of Penedès.

Penedès

In ancient times, thousands of vessels of wine were shipped from this region of Catalonia to fuel the orgies of the Roman Empire. Much of the inspiration for the present industry was developed in the 19th century by French vintners, who found the climate and soil similar to those of Bordeaux. The region produces still wines, as well as 98% of Spain's sparkling wines (cava), which stand an excellent chance of supplanting French champagne in the minds of celebrants throughout the world. In fact, Freixenet is the largest selling sparkling wine in the world.

o **Codorníu,** Sant Sadurní d'Anoia (© **93-505-15-51;** www.codorniu.com): With a history dating from the mid-1500s, this vineyard became famous after its owner, Josep Raventós, produced Spain's first version of sparkling wine. During the harvest, more than 2.2 million pounds of grapes, collected from about 1,000 growers, are pressed daily. The company's headquarters, designed around the turn of the 20th century by Puig i Cadafalch, a contemporary of Gaudí, sits above the 31km (19 miles) of underground tunnels where the product is aged.

o **Freixenet,** Sant Sadurní d'Anoia (© **93-891-70-00;** www.freixenet.es): Codorníu's largest and most innovative competitor began in 1861 as a family-run wine business that quickly changed its production process to incorporate the radical developments in sparkling cava. Today, although still family owned, it's an awesomely efficient factory pressing vast numbers of grapes, with at least a million cases sold to the United States every year. Award-winning brand names include Cordon Negro Brut and Carta Nevada Brut. The company now operates a vineyard in California. It produces the sparkling wine Gloria Ferrer, which has won awards in the United States.

o **Miguel Torres,** Vilafranca del Penedès (© **93-817-74-00;** www.torres wines.com): This winery was established in 1870 by a local son (Jaime Torres), who returned to his native town after making a fortune trading petroleum and oil in Cuba. Today, you can see what was once the world's largest wine vat (132,000 gal.); its interior was used as the site of a banquet held in honor of the Spanish king. Thanks to generations of management by French-trained specialists, Miguel Torres is now one of the region's most sophisticated and advanced vineyards. Like the other bodegas, its location permits side trips to Barcelona, the beach resort of Sitges, and the ancient monastery of Montserrat.

La Rioja

Set in the foothills of the Pyrenees close to the French border, La Rioja turns out what most people have in mind when they think of Spanish wines. The region produced millions of gallons during the regime of the ancient Romans, and it boasts quality-control laws promulgated by a local bishop in the 9th century. Here are some of the best vineyards for a visit:

o **Herederos de Marqués de Riscal,** Elciego (© **94-560-60-00;** www. marquesderiscal.com): This vineyard was founded around 1850 by a local entrepreneur who learned winegrowing techniques in France. The modern-day enterprise still bases most of its income on the 199 hectares (492 acres) acquired by the organization's founding father. Despite several disappointing years between 1975 and 1985, it remains one of the most respected in the region.

Wines of Marqués de Riscal.

- **Bodegas Riojanas,** Cenicero (℃ **94-145-40-50;** www.bodegasriojanas. com): Set on the main street of the winegrowing hamlet of Cenicero, this century-old bodega expanded massively in the 1980s and upgraded its visitor information program. You'll be received in a mock-feudal tower where you can learn the nuances of the wine industry.

- **Bodegas Muga,** Haro (℃ **94-131-18-25;** www.bodegasmuga.com): This bodega adheres more to 19th-century old-world craftsmanship than any of its competitors do. It was founded in 1932 by Isaac Muga and his wife, Aurora Cao, who both came from a long line of families in the winemaking industry. The winery contains an assortment of old-fashioned casks made from American or French oak. Production is small, eclectic, and choice.

- **La Rioja Alta,** Haro (℃ **94-131-03-46;** www.riojalta.com): Another bodega in the winegrowing community of Haro, La Rioja Alta is set near the railway station. Founded in 1890, it has the dank and atmospheric cellars you'd expect. It was graced in 1984 by a visit from Spain's royal family. About 85% of the production at this small but quality outfit is bottled as *reservas* (aged at least 3 years) and *gran reservas* (aged at least 5 years).

Galicia

This Celtic outpost in the northwestern corner of Spain produces white wines praised by connoisseurs as the perfect accompaniment to local seafood. The marketing name for the product, appropriately, is El Vino del Mar (Sea Wine), although the Denominación de Origen includes the appellations Rias Baixas and Ribeiro. Per-capita wine consumption in Galicia is the highest in Spain; a majority of the wine produced here was formerly consumed locally. Massive investments during the 1980s changed all that.

A horse-drawn carriage at the Feria del Caballo festival.

o **Bodega Morgadio,** Albeos-Crecente (*℡* **98-826-12-12;** www.morgadio. com): This vineyard, near Pontevedra, launched the Denominación de Origen Rias Baixas in 1984. Four friends whom locals referred as "madmen" bought 28 hectares (69 acres) of land that, with the Albariño grape, they transformed into one of the most respected and award-winning vineyards in the district. Fertilizer for each year's crop comes from the bodega's own flock of sheep. The success of old-fashioned farming methods, coupled with state-of-the-art fermentation tanks, is a model of entrepreneurial courage in an otherwise economically depressed outpost of Spain.

THE best FESTIVALS

o **Autumn Festival,** Madrid (*℡* **91-720-81-83**): Held in November, the **Festival de Otoño** is the best music festival in Spain, with a lineup that attracts the best of the European and South American musical communities. The usual roster of chamber music, symphonic pieces, and orchestral works is supplemented by a program of *zarzuela* (musical comedy), as well as Arabic and Sephardic pieces composed during the Middle Ages. See p. 63.

o **Feria del Caballo,** Jerez de la Frontera (*℡* **95-633-11-50**): Few events show off Spain's equestrian traditions in such a flattering light. Costumes are appropriately ornate; riders demonstrate the stern, carefully controlled movements developed during medieval battles; and the entire city of Jerez becomes one enormous riding ring for the presentation of dressage and jumping events. Horse buying and trading are commonplace at this May event. See p. 61.

- **Las Hogueras de San Juan (St. John's Bonfires),** Alicante (© 98-120-24-06; www.hogueras.com): Bonfires blaze through the night on June 20 as a celebration of a festival revered by Celtic pagans and Romans alike—the summer solstice. Stacks of flammable objects, including discarded finery and cardboard replicas of sinners and witches, are set ablaze. The bonfire signals the beginning of 5 days of parades and 5 nights of fireworks, during which normal business comes to a virtual standstill. See p. 62.

- **Moros y Cristianos (Moors and Christians),** Alcoy, near Alicante (© 96-514-34-52): The agonizing, century-long process of evicting the Moors from Iberia is re-created during 3 days of simulated, vaudeville-style fighting between "Moors" and "Christians" every April (dates vary). Circus-style costumes worn by the Moors are as absurdly anachronistic as possible. When the Christians win, a statue of the Virgin is carried proudly through the city as proof of Alcoy's staunchly passionate role as a bastion of Christianity. See p. 61.

- **La Tomatina (Battle of the Tomatoes),** Buñol, Valencia (© 96-250-01-51; www.latomatina.es): Every year on the last Wednesday in August, nearly everyone in the town, along with thousands from neighboring towns and villages, joins this 2-hour-long tomato war (11am–1pm). The local government sponsors the festival, bringing in truckloads of tomatoes totaling more than 88,000 pounds of vegetable artillery. Local bands provide the music for dancing and singing, and there's plenty of drinking. Portable showers are installed for the participants. See p. 63.

- **La Rapa das Bestas (The Capture of the Beasts),** San Lorenzo de Sabucedo, Galicia (© 98-657-01-65; www.rapadasbestas.es): In the verdant hills of northwestern Spain, horses graze at will. On the first weekend of July, they are rounded up and herded into a corral. Here, each is branded and then released back into the wild after a few days of medical observation. For information, contact the Office of Tourism in Pontevedra. See p. 62.

- **Misteri d'Elx (Mystery of Elche),** Elche (© 96-741-11-00; www.misteridelx.com): Based on the reputed mystical powers of an ancient, black-faced statue of the Virgin, the citizens of Elche have staged a mystery play in the local church every year for more than 6 centuries. The chanting and songs that accompany the plotline are in an archaic dialect that even Castilians can barely understand. Competition is fierce for seats during the August event, and celebrations precede and follow the play. See p. 62.

A tomato fight at La Tomatina.

THE best *PARADORES*

Funded and maintained by the government, Spain's *paradores* are hostelries that showcase a building or setting of important cultural and historical interest. Some are much older and grander than others. Below are the country's most interesting and unusual. For more information, visit www.parador.es.

o **Parador de Avila** (© 92-021-13-40; www.parador.es): Built as an enlargement of a 15th-century palace (Palacio de Piedras Albas, also known as Palacio de Benavides), this *parador* features gardens that flank the northern fortifications of this well-preserved, 11th-century walled city. While only some of the comfortable, airy guest rooms are in the original palace, it's still the region's most intriguing hotel. In the *parador's* restaurant, try the roast suckling pig, a regional specialty. See p. 224.

o **Parador de Cuenca** (© 96-923-23-20; www.parador.es): This 16th-century building, once a Dominican convent, is one of the newer *paradores* in Spain. Like the medieval houses for which Cuenca is famous, the balconies here jut over rocky cliffs, overlooking swift-moving rivers below. The sight of *casas colgadas*, or "suspended houses," is unforgettable. An adjoining restaurant specializes in seasonal wild game. See p. 230.

o **Parador de Turismo de Toledo** (© 92-522-18-50; www.parador.es): Although this is a relatively modern building, the architecture subtly evokes much older models. Views from the windows, boasting faraway glimpses of the city's historic core, evoke the scenes El Greco painted in his *View of Toledo*. A swimming pool is a welcome relief in blistering Toledo. Such regional dishes as stewed partridge are featured in the hotel restaurant. See p. 199.

o **Parador Hostal San Marcos,** León (© 98-723-73-00; www.parador.es): Originally home to the Order of Santiago—a group of knights charged with protecting journeying pilgrims—the building was expanded and converted into a monastery some 400 years later. These days, set beside the Bernesga River and with a lavishly decorated church on the grounds, it's one of Spain's most deluxe *paradores*. The public areas are pure medieval grandeur: a dramatic lobby, a huge cast-iron chandelier, and stone staircases. See p. 255.

o **Parador de Zamora** (© 98-051-44-97; www.parador.es): This

The Parador de Zamora.

The Parador de Cuenca.

one-time Moorish fortress-turned-Renaissance palace is among the most beautiful and richly decorated *paradores* in Spain. A medieval aura is reflected in the details: armor, coats of arms, tapestries, and attractive four-poster beds. A swimming pool enhances the tranquil back garden. Castilian fare such as stuffed roast veal typifies the restaurant's offerings. See p. 250.

o **Parador de Cáceres** (© 92-721-17-59; www.parador.es): Live like royalty at this palace, built in the 1400s on the site of Arab fortifications. The *parador* is in the city's Old Quarter, recently declared a World Heritage Site. The spacious public areas are decorated with soft cream shades and rough-hewn ceiling beams. Venison with goat cheese and roast kid with rosemary are typical of the varied Extremaduran cuisine served in the *parador*'s restaurant. See p. 278.

o **Parador de Trujillo** (© 92-732-13-50; www.parador.es): Set in the inviting 16th-century convent of Santa Clara, this *parador* was originally built in a combination of medieval and Renaissance styles. The building was transformed into a hotel in 1984; the guest rooms are considerably more lavish than they were during their stint as nuns' cells. The cuisine is the best in town. See p. 273.

o **Parador de Mérida** (© 92-431-38-00; www.parador.es): A 16th-century building that was at various times a convent and a prison, this *parador* once hosted a meeting between the much-hated dictators of Spain (Franco) and Portugal (Salazar) in the 1960s. Mudéjar, Roman, and Visigothic elements adorn the interior in unusual but stunning juxtaposition. The inner courtyard and Mozarabic gardens add graceful notes. The kitchen serves the area's best, including gazpacho, *calderetas extremeñas* (stews), and the famous Almoharin figs. See p. 282.

Santiago de Compostela's Hostal de Los Reyes Católicos.

o **Parador de Jaén** (© 95-323-00-00; www.parador.es): In the 10th century, Muslims built this fortress on a cliff high above town. Later, Christians added Gothic vaulting and touches of luxury, which remain in place thanks to renovation by the government. Guest rooms provide sweeping views over Andalusia. A swimming pool is a welcome retreat from the burning sun. Sample such dishes as cold garlic soup and partridge salad in the panoramic restaurant. See p. 291.

o **Parador de Santillana Gil Blas,** Santillana del Mar (© 94-202-80-28; www.parador.es): This bucolic *parador* recalls the manor houses that dotted northern Spain's verdant hillsides more than 400 years ago. Composed of thick stone walls and heavy timbers, it's pleasantly isolated and elegantly countrified. A bonus is its proximity to what has been called "the Sistine Chapel of prehistoric art"—the Caves of Altamira. See p. 658.

o **Parador Molino Viejo (Parador de Gijón),** Gijón (© 98-537-05-11; www.parador.es): As the name implies, this hotel was built around the decrepit remains of a *molino,* or cider mill (and the antique presses are still at hand). Close to San Lorenzo Beach, it's the only *parador* in the northern province of Asturias. The dining room serves typical Asturian cuisine, including the famous *fabada,* a rich stew of white beans and pork. See p. 670.

o **Parador de Pontevedra** (© 98-685-58-00; www.parador.es): The building is a 16th-century Renaissance palace built on foundations at least 200 years older than that. It's famous as one of Spain's first *paradores.* Inaugurated in 1955, its success led to the amplification of the *parador* program. The hotel is still alluring today, with its delightful terrace garden and stately dining room, which serves the fresh fish and seafood for which Galicia is known. See p. 698.

- **Hostal de Los Reyes Católicos,** Santiago de Compostela (📞 **98-158-22-00;** www.parador.es): We saved the best for last—this is one of the most spectacular hotels in Europe. Originally a hospice for wayfaring pilgrims, it boasts a lavish 16th-century facade, four open-air courtyards, and a bedchamber once occupied by Franco. Today, the hotel is a virtual museum, with Gothic, Renaissance, and baroque architectural elements. It boasts four beautiful cloisters, elegant public areas, and spectacular guest rooms. See p. 687.

THE best LUXURY HOTELS

- **The Ritz Madrid** (📞 **800/237-1236** in the U.S., or 91-701-67-67; www.ritz.es): This is the most famous hotel in Spain, and arguably the best, at least for those who want the grand style of living enjoyed by aristocrats and Spanish dons at the turn of the 20th century. In the luxurious bedrooms, you can live the pre–World War I glory days of the Belle Epoque. See p. 134.

- **The Westin Palace,** Madrid (📞 **888/625-4988** in the U.S., or 91-360-80-00; www.westinpalacemadrid.com): Flawless service is the hallmark of Madrid's most distinguished hotel. Guest rooms contain antiques, gracious marble bathrooms, and elegant detailing. This Edwardian grand hotel is more relaxed than it once was, the old haughtiness of former management gone with the wind—it long ago rescinded its policy of not allowing movie stars as guests. Men still may have to wear a coat and tie, however. See p. 123.

- **Hotel Alfonso XIII,** Seville (📞 **800/221-2340** in the U.S., or 95-491-70-00; www.starwoodhotels.com): The royal family stayed here when the Infanta Elena, daughter of Juan Carlos, married in Seville in 1995. Built to house

A bedroom at the Ritz Madrid.

The formal dining room of the Hotel María Cristina.

visitors for the Iberoamerican Exposition of 1929, this grand hotel features Moorish-style rooms with doors opening onto small balconies; they overlook a Spanish courtyard with a bubbling fountain and potted palms. Set in front of the city's fabled Alcázar, the Alfonso XIII is one of Spain's most legendary hotels. See p. 321.

o **Marbella Club,** Marbella (© **800/448-8355** in the U.S., or 95-282-22-11; www.marbellaclub.com): Built during the Golden Age of the Costa del Sol (the 1950s), this bastion of chic is composed of ecologically conscious clusters of garden pavilions, bungalows, and small-scale annexes. The luxurious rooms are modeled after those displayed in a European design magazine. The Marbella Club has many competitors but remains an elite retreat. See p. 398.

o **Puente Romano,** Marbella (© **95-282-09-00;** www.puenteromano.com): On manicured and landscaped grounds facing the beach, Puente Romano evokes a highly stylized Andalusian village. Exotic bird life flutters through lush gardens planted with banana trees and other vegetation. Villas are spacious and beautifully outfitted with tasteful wood furnishings, big mirrors, and marble floors and bathrooms. During summer, flamenco dancers entertain here. See p. 398.

o **Barceló La Bobadilla,** Loja (© **95-832-18-61;** www.barcelolabobadilla. com): The most luxurious retreat in the south of Spain, this secluded oasis lies in the foothills of the Sierra Nevada, an hour's drive northeast of Málaga. Whitewashed *casas* (small individual villas) cluster around a tower and a church. Each individually designed *casa* is complete with roof terrace and balcony overlooking olive groves. Guests live in luxury within the private compound of 708 hectares (1,750 acres). See p. 419.

o **Neri,** Barcelona (© **93-304-06-55;** www.hotelneri.com): Tucked away in the Gothic quarter, this restored palace near the cathedral is the most romantic place to stay in Barcelona, ideal for honeymooners. From its creeper-covered terrace to its crystal chandeliers to its plush bedrooms, the Neri hotel is for those seeking the good life. See p. 472.

o **Hotel María Cristina,** San Sebastián (✆ **800/221-2340** in the U.S., or 94-343-76-00; www.westin.com): One of the country's great Belle Epoque treasures, this old-world seafront hotel has sheltered discriminating guests since 1912. Oriental rugs, antiques, potted palms, high ceilings, formal lounges, marble pillars, and marble floors show off a turn-of-the-20th-century glamour. The guest rooms are traditional in style, with wood furnishings and tasteful pastel fabrics. Nothing else in the Basque country quite measures up to this old charmer. See p. 623.

o **La Residencia,** Deià, Majorca (✆ **97-163-90-11;** www.hotel-la residencia.com): Set amid 12 hectares (30 acres) of citrus and olive groves, this tranquil hotel was converted from two Renaissance-era manor houses. Jasmine-scented terraces open onto panoramas of surrounding villages and mountains. Pampered guests are served a creative cuisine that features local produce. Leisure facilities include a swimming pool fed by mountain spring water. Many of the guest rooms have regal four-poster beds. The hotel is a haven from the rest of overcrowded Majorca. See p. 730.

THE best HOTEL BARGAINS

o **Hostal del Cardenal,** Toledo (✆ 92-522-49-00; www.hostaldelcardenal. com): The summer residence of Toledo's 18th-century Cardinal Lorenzano, built right into the walls of the Old City next to Bisagra Gate, this just happens to have Toledo's best restaurant. But the setting—rose gardens, cascading vines, and Moorish fountains—makes it an ideal place to stay as well. Spanish furniture and a scattering of antiques recapture the aura of Old Castile. See p. 200.

o **Hostería Real de Zamora,** Zamora (✆ 98-053-45-45; www.hosterias reales.com): Once the dreaded headquarters of the local Spanish Inquisition, this hotel today offers a far friendlier welcome. Guests enjoy coffee on the patio and the pleasures of a garden planted along the city's medieval fortifications. Imagine if these 15th-century walls could talk. See p. 250.

o **Hotel Doña María,** Seville (✆ 95-422-49-90; www.hdmaria.com): Near the fabled cathedral, this hotel boasts a rooftop terrace with unmatched

The view from the rooftop of the Hotel Doña María.

27

The Priest's Grove outside Huerto del Cura, in Elche.

views of the Andalusian capital. A private villa that dates from the 1840s, the Doña María has a swimming pool ringed with garden-style lattices and antique wrought-iron railings. Guest rooms are uniquely designed with tasteful Iberian antiques. See p. 323.

o **Husa Reina Victoria,** Ronda (✆ 95-287-12-40; www.hotelhusareina victoriaronda.com): This country-style hotel is best known as the place where the German poet Rainer Maria Rilke wrote *The Spanish Trilogy*. Its terrace, perched on a dramatic precipice, offers commanding views of the countryside. An Englishman built this Victorian charmer in 1906 to honor his recently deceased monarch, Queen Victoria. See p. 350.

o **Hotel América,** Granada (✆ 95-822-74-71; www.hotelamericagranada. com): This former private villa, within the walls of the Alhambra, is one of the most popular small hotels in Granada. Its cozy guest rooms are filled with reproductions of Andalusian antiques. Plants cascade down the white plaster walls and the ornate grillwork onto the shaded patio. Good-tasting, inexpensive meals are served in the hotel restaurant. See p. 366.

o **Hotel TRH Mijas,** Mijas (✆ 95-248-58-00; www.trhhoteles.info): The most charming affordable hotel along the Costa del Sol, the Mijas is designed in typical Andalusian style, with flowering terraces, wrought-iron accents, and sun-flooded guest rooms. Although built in the 1970s, it blends perfectly with the region's gleaming white buildings. See p. 408.

o **Huerto del Cura,** Elche (✆ 96-661-00-11; http://hotelhuertodelcura.com): From your room you'll have a panoramic view of Priest's Grove, a formidable date-palm forest. Between Alicante and Murcia, this is one of the choice addresses in the south of Spain. Guest rooms are handsomely maintained and beautifully furnished; a swimming pool separates the rooms from the palm grove. The regional cuisine in the hotel's restaurant is excellent. See p. 455.

o **Mesón Castilla,** Barcelona (✆ 93-318-21-82; www.mesoncastilla.com): This two-star charmer with an Art Nouveau facade is right in the heart of Barcelona. It is well maintained and well managed, with prices that are blessedly easy on the wallet. Comfortable rooms often come with large terraces. Only breakfast is served, but many nearby taverns serve excellent food. See p. 478

THE best RESTAURANTS

o **El Amparo,** Madrid (© 91-431-64-56): In the old days of Franco, gastronomes flocked to Jockey or Horcher. Today their savvy sons and daughters head to El Amparo, the trendiest of Madrid's gourmet restaurants. It serves haute Basque cuisine against a backdrop of cosmopolitan glamour. Patrons sample everything from cold marinated salmon with a tomato sorbet to ravioli stuffed with seafood. See p. 147.

o **Sobrino de Botín,** Madrid (© 91-366-42-17; www.botin.es): Since 1725, this restaurant has been celebrated for its roast suckling pig, prepared in a 200-year-old tile oven. Hemingway even mentioned it in *The Sun Also Rises.* The roast Segovian lamb is equally delectable. There is little subtlety of flavor here—the food is prepared according to time-tested recipes that have appealed to kings as well as Castilian peasants. The aromas waft clear across Madrid's Old Town. See p. 154.

o **José María,** Segovia (© 021-46-11-11; www.rtejosemaria.com): Foodies from Castile flock to this classic Segovian restaurant, mainly to sample two regional dishes, roast baby lamb and roast suckling pig. The roast suckling pig, praised by Ernest Hemingway, is delectable and prepared according to a century-old recipe. The lamb is not as well known, but it's equally flavorful. See p. 217.

o **Mesón Casas Colgadas,** Cuenca (© 96-922-35-09; www.mesoncasas colgadas.com): Without a doubt, this is the most spectacularly situated restaurant in Spain—a "hanging house" precariously suspended over a

Suckling pig at Sobrino de Botín, in Madrid.

The arched entrance to El Caballo Rojo.

precipice. The food is Spanish and international, with an emphasis on regional ingredients. The dishes can be ingenious, but the culinary repertoire usually includes proven classics that might have pleased your grandparents. See p. 231.

o **Chez Víctor,** Salamanca (℃ **92-321-31-23**): In the historic center of this university town, Chez Víctor is the most glamorous Continental restaurant around. Chef Victoriano Salvador gives customers terrific value for their euros with his imaginative, oft-renewed menus. The freshly prepared fish and his traditional version of roast lamb are especially tempting. Regionally rooted but modern in outlook, Salvador has a finely honed technique and isn't afraid to be inventive on occasion. See p. 247.

o **El Caballo Rojo,** Córdoba (℃ **95-747-53-75;** www.elcaballorojo.com): Begin your evening with a sherry in the popular bar, followed by a visit to the traditional dining room. Not only Andalusian dishes are served here; some classics are based on ancient Sephardic and Mozarabic specialties. Most guests begin with a soothing gazpacho and wash everything down with sangria. Finish off the meal with one of the homemade ice creams—we recommend pistachio. See p. 308.

o **Torrijos,** Valencia (℃ **96-373-29-49;** www.restaurantetorrijos.com): The Costa Levante's best restaurant, in the city that's said to have "invented" paella, this stellar restaurant serves a Mediterranean and international cuisine, and does so superbly well. Expect a flavor-filled cuisine based on the freshest of ingredients. See p. 443.

o **Jaume de Provença,** Barcelona (℃ **93-430-00-29;** www.jaumeprovenza. com): The Catalan capital has more great restaurants than even Madrid. At the western end of the Eixample district, this Catalan/French restaurant is the domain of one of the city's most talented chefs, Jaume Bargués. He serves modern interpretations of traditional Catalan and southern French cuisine— such dishes as pigs' feet with plums and truffles, or crabmeat lasagna. His personal cooking repertoire is distinctive, and he has been known to create new taste sensations when he's feeling experimental. See p. 494.

o **La Dama,** Barcelona (© **93-202-06-86;** www.ladama-restaurant.com): Among the most acclaimed restaurants in Spain, this "dame" serves one of the most refined Catalan and international cuisines along the country's east coast. Stylish and well managed, it turns out masterpieces based on the season's best in food shopping. See p. 493.

o **Botafumeiro,** Barcelona (© **93-218-42-30;** www.botafumeiro.es): The city's finest seafood is prepared here, in a glistening, modern kitchen visible from the dining room. The king of Spain is a frequent patron, enjoying paellas, *zarzuelas,* or any of the 100 or so ultrafresh seafood dishes. The chef's treatment of fish is the most intelligent and subtle in town—but don't expect such quality to come cheap. See p. 497.

o **Empordá,** Figueres (© **97-250-05-62;** www.hotelemporda.com): Although ordinary on the outside, this hotel restaurant is one of the finest on the Costa Brava. It was a favorite of Salvador Dalí, who once wrote his own cookbook. Haute Catalan cuisine is the specialty—everything from duck foie gras with Armagnac to suprême of sea bass with flan. The flavors are refined yet definite. See p. 574.

o **Akelare,** San Sebastián (© **94-321-20-52;** www.akelarre.net): The Basques are renowned for their cooking, and the owner-chef of this San Sebastián restaurant, Pedro Subijana, pioneered the school of *nueva cocina vasca* (modern Basque cuisine). His restaurant has attracted gourmets from around Europe. Subijana transforms such seemingly simple dishes as fish cooked on a griddle with garlic and parsley into something magical. No other eatery in northern Spain comes close to equaling the superb viands dispensed here. There are those (and we are among them) who consider Subijana the best chef in Spain. See p. 625.

Pea soup with ham at Akelare, in San Sebastián.

2

SPAIN IN DEPTH

T he once-accepted adage that "Europe ends at the Pyrenees" is no longer true. Today, the two countries forming the Iberian Peninsula at the southwestern end of the Continent—Spain and Portugal—are totally integrated into Europe as members of the European Union (E.U.), with democratic governments and vibrant economies of their own. In fact, Spain has the second-fastest-growing economy in the E.U.; new industries and an expanding infrastructure continue to alter its ancient landscape.

Political changes adopted after the 1975 death of Gen. Francisco Franco, Europe's remaining prewar dictator, contributed to a remarkable cultural renaissance. This rebirth has transformed Spain's two largest cities—Madrid, the capital, and Barcelona—into major artistic and intellectual centers. Amid some of the world's most innovative architecture and contemporary movements, art, literature, cinema, and fashion are constantly finding new and original expression; at night the cafes and bars hum with animated discussions on politics, the economy, and society. In every aspect of urban life, a visitor can feel the Spanish people's reawakened self-confidence and pride in their newfound prosperity.

These developments contrast with Spain's unhappy experiences last century, particularly during the devastating Civil War of 1936 to 1939, and Franco's subsequent long, iron-fisted rule. During the Franco years, political and intellectual freedoms were squelched, and Spain was snubbed by most of Europe.

Of course, Spain was previously a major world player. In the 16th century, it was the seat of a great empire; the Spanish monarchy dispatched fleets that conquered the New World, returning with its riches. Columbus sailed to America, and Balboa sailed to the Pacific Ocean; Cortés conquered Mexico for glory; and Pizarro brought Peru into the Spanish fold. The conquistadors too often revealed the dark side of the Spanish character, including brutality in the name of honor and glory, but they also represented boldness and daring.

It's difficult to visit this country without recalling its golden past: Those famous "castles in Spain" really do exist. Many Spaniards believe that Spain isn't a single country but a series of nations, united the way Yugoslavia used to be. Many groups, especially the Basques, the Catalans, and the Gallegos in the northeast, are asserting their individuality in everything from culture to language. For certain Basque separatists, that regional, "nationalistic" pride has at times taken violent turns. Castile and Andalusia, in the south, remain quintessentially Spanish. While linguistic and cultural differences are great, to the foreign visitor they are also subtle.

As the inheritors of a great and ancient civilization dating from before the Roman Empire, Spaniards inhabit a land that is not only culturally rich but also geographically varied, with wooded sierra, arid plateaus, and sandy beaches. It is this exciting variety in landscape—as well as in art, architecture, music, and cuisine—that makes Spain one of the top countries in the world to visit.

FACING PAGE: **A bullfighter in Seville.**

SPAIN TODAY

Spain has suffered severely since the fall of 2008, when it felt the pain of the rest of the world in a meltdown of the international banking system. The problems have continued into 2010, though there have been signs of growth: Unemployment remains high, but the country's debt is some 70% of the gross domestic product. Inflation is about 3.5%, an all-time low in the post-Franco era. Consumer spending remains cautious, however, because most of the new jobs being created are on short-term contracts.

In spite of the hardships, Spain is massively improving its transportation structure. The government is upgrading 7,000km (4,350 miles) of rail track to high-speed quality by late 2010. The goal is to make all major cities reachable by train from Madrid within 4 hours, or from Barcelona in 6½ hours. Already travel

THE SPECTACLE OF death

For obvious reasons, many people consider bullfighting cruel and shocking, but as Ernest Hemingway pointed out in *Death in the Afternoon,* "The bullfight is not a sport in the Anglo-Saxon sense of the word; that is, it is not an equal contest or an attempt at an equal contest between a bull and a man. Rather it is a tragedy: the death of the bull, which is played, more or less well, by the bull and the man involved and in which there is danger for the man but certain death for the bull."

When the symbolic drama of the bullfight is acted out, some believe it reaches a higher plane, the realm of art. Some people argue that it is not a public exhibition of cruelty but a highly skilled art form that requires the will to survive, courage, showmanship, and gallantry. Regardless of how you view it, the spectacle is an authentic Spanish experience and reveals much about the character of the land and its people.

The *corrida* (bullfight) season lasts from early spring to around mid-October. Fights are held in a *plaza de toros* (bullring), including the oldest ring in remote Ronda and the big-time Plaza de Toros in Madrid. Sunday is *corrida* day in most major Spanish cities, although Madrid and Barcelona may also have fights on Thursday.

Tickets fall into three classifications, and prices are based on your exposure to the famed Spanish sun: *sol* (sun), the cheapest; *sombra* (shade), the most expensive; and *sol y sombra* (a mixture of sun and shade), the medium-price range.

The *corrida* begins with a parade. For many viewers, this may be the high point of the afternoon's festivities, as all the bullfighters are clad in their *trajes de luces* (suits of lights).

Bullfights are divided into thirds *(tercios).* The first is the *tercio de capa* (cape), during which the matador tests the bull with passes and gets acquainted with the animal. The second portion, the *tercio de varas* (sticks), begins with the lance-carrying *picadores* on horseback, who weaken, or "punish," the bull by jabbing him in the shoulder area. The horses are sometimes gored, even though they wear protective padding, or the horse and rider might be tossed into the air by the now-infuriated bull. The picadores are followed by the banderilleros, whose job it is to puncture the bull with pairs of boldly colored darts.

In the final tercio de muleta, the action narrows down to the lone fighter and the bull. Gone are the fancy capes. Instead, the matador uses a small red cloth known as a muleta, which to be effective requires a bull with lowered time between Madrid and Segovia has been shortened to 2½ hours, and between Madrid to Málaga to 4½ hours. Plans are to decrease travel time between Madrid and Barcelona from 4 hours to 3 and ultimately even 2½ hours.

Madrid, the seat of government, also continues to expand and make improvements, upgrading its roads, rail links, and even its parks. The city is approaching six million inhabitants, and demands for services are increasing.

Tourism continues to dominate the economy as Spain moves into the second decade of the 21st century. Spain's vibrancy and up-and-coming changes are expected to propel it into position as a major destination alongside such front-runners as France, the United States, and Italy, even though those countries are not expected to attract the number of visitors they did during the years immediately following the millennium.

head. (The picadores and banderilleros have worked to achieve this.) Using the muleta as a lure, the matador wraps the bull around himself in various passes, the most dangerous of which is the natural; here, the matador holds the muleta in his left hand, the sword in his right. Right-hand passes pose less of a threat, since the sword can be used to spread out the muleta, making a larger target for the bull. After a number of passes, the time comes for the kill, the moment of truth.

After the bull dies, the highest official at the ring may award the matador an ear from the dead bull, or perhaps both ears, or ears and tail. For a truly extraordinary performance, the hoof is added. Spectators cheer a superlative performance by waving white hand-kerchiefs, imploring the judge to award a prize. The bullfighter may be carried away as a hero, or if he has displeased the crowd, he may be jeered and chased out of the ring by an angry mob. At a major fight, usually six bulls are killed by three matadors in one afternoon.

A *picador* lances a bull in Madrid.

Increasingly, North Americans are becoming part of the changing landscape. While many European visitors head for Spain's beach resorts, Americans occupy the number-one positions in visits to three top Spanish cities: Madrid, Barcelona, and Seville.

No longer interested in the "lager lout" image its coastal resorts earned in the 1970s and 1980s by hosting so many cheap package tours from Britain, Spain has reached out to more upscale visitors. Bargain Spain of the $5-a-day variety is now a distant memory, as prices have skyrocketed. The government is trying to lure visitors away from the overcrowded coasts (especially Majorca, the Costa del Sol, and the Costa Brava) and steer them to the country's less traveled but more historic destinations. Government *paradores* and other improved tourist facilities, better restaurants, and spruced-up attractions have sent the message.

Spain continues to change as it moves deeper into the 21st century. A drug culture and escalating crime—things virtually unheard of in Franco's day—are unfortunate signs of Spain's entry into the modern world. The most remarkable advance has been in the legal status of women, who now have access to contraception, abortion, and divorce. Sights once unimaginable now take place: an annual lesbian "kiss-in" at Madrid's Puerta del Sol, and women officiating as governors of men's prisons. Surprisingly, for a Catholic country, the birthrate continues to remain one of the lowest in the developed world, and the population is aging.

Spain's monarchy seems to be working. In 1975, when the king assumed the throne after Franco's death, he was called "Juan Carlos the Brief," implying that his reign would be short. But almost overnight he distanced himself from Franco's dark legacy and became a hardworking and serious sovereign. He staved off a coup attempt in 1981, and he and the other Spanish royals remain popular. Juan Carlos even makes do on a meager $7 million salary—less than one-tenth of what England's Queen Elizabeth II is reputed to earn in a year.

The author John Hooper, in an updated version of his 1986 bestseller, *The New Spaniards,* remains optimistic about Spain's future, in spite of its economic problems. He suggests that Spaniards not forget that "to be true to themselves

Juan Carlos I (right), the reigning king of Spain.

they may need to be different from others." Hooper believes that the new Spain will have arrived at adulthood "not on the day it ceases to be different from the rest of Europe, but on the day that it acknowledges that it is." Hooper was referring to the exotic, romantic, and varied faces of Spain that set it apart from other nations of Europe, ranging from flamenco to bullfighting and from Moorish architecture to pagan ceremonies. Nowhere—not even in Italy—are the festival and traditional, flamboyant dress more a part of annual life than in Spain, where religious processions are full of intense passion.

LOOKING BACK AT SPAIN

BARBARIAN INVASIONS, THE MOORISH KINGDOM & THE RECONQUEST Around 200 B.C., the Romans vanquished the Carthaginians and laid the foundations of the present Latin culture. Traces of Roman civilization can still be seen today. By the time of Julius Caesar, Spain (Hispania) was under Roman law and began a long period of peace and prosperity.

When Rome fell in the 5th century, Spain was overrun, first by the Vandals and then by the Visigoths from eastern Europe. The chaotic rule of the Visigothic kings lasted about 300 years, but the barbarian invaders did adopt the language of their new country and tolerated Christianity as well.

In A.D. 711, Moorish warriors led by Tarik crossed into Spain and conquered the disunited country. By 714, they controlled most of it, except for a few mountain regions around Asturias. For 8 centuries the Moors occupied their new land, which they called *al-Andalús,* or Andalusia, with Córdoba as the capital. A great intellectual center, Córdoba became the scientific capital of Europe; notable advances were made in agriculture, industry, literature, philosophy, and medicine. The Jews were welcomed by the Moors, often serving as administrators, ambassadors, and financial officers. But the Moors quarreled with one another, and soon the few Christian strongholds in the north began to advance south.

The Reconquest, the name given to the Christian efforts to rid the peninsula of the Moors, slowly reduced the size of the Muslim holdings, with Catholic monarchies forming in northern areas. The three powerful kingdoms of Aragón, Castile, and León were joined in 1469, when Ferdinand of Aragón married Isabella of Castile. The Catholic kings, as they were called, launched the final attack on the Moors and completed the Reconquest in 1492 by capturing Granada.

That same year, Columbus landed in the West Indies, laying the foundations for a far-flung empire that brought wealth and power to Spain during the 16th and 17th centuries.

The Spanish Inquisition, begun under Ferdinand and Isabella, sought to eradicate all heresy and secure the primacy of Catholicism. Non-Catholics, Jews, and Moors were mercilessly persecuted, and many were driven out of the country.

THE GOLDEN AGE & LATER DECLINE Columbus's voyage, and the conquistadors' subsequent exploration of the New World, ushered Spain into its Golden Age.

In the first half of the 16th century, Balboa discovered the Pacific Ocean, Cortés seized Mexico for Spain, Pizarro took Peru, and a Spanish ship (initially commanded by the Portuguese Magellan, who was killed during the voyage) circumnavigated the globe. The conquistadors took Catholicism to the New World and shipped cargoes of gold back to Spain. The Spanish Empire extended all the way to the Philippines. Charles V, grandson of Ferdinand and Isabella, was the most powerful prince in Europe—king of Spain and Naples, Holy Roman Emperor and lord of Germany, duke of Burgundy and the Netherlands, and ruler of the New World territories.

But much of Spain's wealth and human resources were wasted in religious and secular conflicts. First Jews, then Muslims, and finally Catholicized Moors were driven out—and with them much of the country's prosperity. When Philip II ascended the throne in 1556, Spain could indeed boast vast possessions: the New World colonies; Naples, Milan, Genoa, Sicily, and other portions of Italy; the Spanish Netherlands (modern Belgium and the Netherlands); and portions of Austria and Germany. But the seeds of decline had already been planted.

Philip, a fanatic Catholic, devoted his energies to subduing the Protestant revolt in the Netherlands and to becoming the standard-bearer for the Counter-Reformation. He tried to return England to Catholicism, first by marrying Mary I ("Bloody Mary") and later by wooing her half-sister, Elizabeth I, who rebuffed him. When, in 1588, he resorted to sending the Armada, it was ignominiously defeated; that defeat symbolized the decline of Spanish power.

In 1700, a Bourbon prince, Philip V, became king, and the country fell under the influence of France. Philip V's right to the throne was challenged by a Habsburg archduke of Austria, thus giving rise to the War of the Spanish Succession. When it ended, Spain had lost Flanders, its Italian possessions, and Gibraltar (still held by the British today).

During the 18th century, Spain's direction changed with each sovereign. Charles III (1759–88) developed the country economically and culturally. Charles IV became embroiled in wars with France, and the weakness of the Spanish monarchy allowed Napoleon to place his brother Joseph Bonaparte on the throne in 1808.

DATELINE

11th c. B.C. Phoenicians settle Spain's coasts.	**5th c.** Vandals, then Visigoths, invade Spain.
650 B.C. Greeks colonize the east.	**8th c.** Moors conquer most of Spain.
600 B.C. Celts cross the Pyrenees and settle in Spain.	**1214** More than half of Iberia is reclaimed by Catholics.
6th–3rd c. B.C. Carthaginians make Cartagena their colonial capital, driving out the Greeks.	**1469** Ferdinand of Aragón marries Isabella of Castile.
218–201 B.C. Second Punic War: Rome defeats Carthage.	**1492** Catholic monarchs seize Granada, the last Moorish stronghold. Columbus lands in the New World.
2nd c. B.C.– 2nd c. A.D. Rome controls most of Iberia. Christianity spreads.	**1519** Cortés conquers Mexico. Charles I is crowned Holy Roman Emperor, as Charles V.

THE 19TH & 20TH CENTURIES Although Britain and France had joined forces to restore the Spanish monarchy, the European conflicts encouraged Spanish colonists to rebel. Ultimately, this led the United States to free the Philippines, Puerto Rico, and Cuba from Spain in 1898.

In 1876, Spain became a constitutional monarchy. But labor unrest, disputes with the Catholic Church, and war in Morocco combined to create political chaos. Conditions eventually became so bad that the Cortés, or parliament, was dissolved in 1923, and Gen. Miguel Primo de Rivera formed a military directorate. Early in 1930, Primo de Rivera resigned, but unrest continued.

On April 14, 1931, a revolution occurred, a republic was proclaimed, and King Alfonso XIII and his family were forced to flee. Initially, the liberal constitutionalists ruled, but soon they were pushed aside by the socialists and anarchists, who adopted a constitution separating church and state, secularizing education, and containing several other radical provisions (for example, agrarian reform and the expulsion of the Jesuits).

The extreme nature of these reforms fostered the growth of the conservative Falange party (*Falange española,* or Spanish Phalanx), modeled after Italy's and Germany's fascist parties. By the 1936 elections, the country was divided equally between left and right, and political violence was common. On July 18, 1936, the army, supported by Mussolini and Hitler, tried to seize power, igniting the Spanish Civil War. Gen. Francisco Franco, coming from Morocco to Spain, led the Nationalist (rightist) forces in fighting that ravaged the country.

The popular front opposing Franco was forced to rely mainly on untrained volunteers, including a few heroic Americans called the "Lincoln brigade." (For those who want an insight into the era, Ernest Hemingway's *For Whom the Bell Tolls* is a good read.) It took time to turn untrained militias into an army fit to battle Franco's forces, and time was something the popular front didn't have.

1556 Philip II inherits the throne and launches the Counter-Reformation.

1588 England defeats the Spanish Armada.

1700 Philip V becomes king. The War of Spanish Succession follows.

1713 Treaty of Utrecht ends the war. Spain's colonies are reduced.

1759 Charles III ascends throne.

1808 Napoleon places his brother Joseph on the Spanish throne.

1813 Wellington drives the French out of Spain; the monarchy is restored.

1876 Spain becomes a constitutional monarchy.

1898 Spanish-American War leads to Spain's loss of Puerto Rico, Cuba, and the Philippines.

1923 Primo de Rivera forms a military directorate.

1930 Right-wing dictatorship ends; Primo de Rivera exiled.

1931 King Alfonso XIII abdicates; Second Republic is born.

1936–39 Civil War between the governing Popular Front and the Nationalists led by Gen. Francisco Franco.

1939 Franco establishes dictatorship, which will last 36 years.

continues

It was a war that would attract the attention of the world. By the summer of 1936, the Soviet Union was sending rubles to aid the revolution by the republicans. Even Mexico sent war materiel to the popular front. Most—but not all—of the volunteers were communists. Italy and Germany contributed war materiel to Franco's forces.

Madrid, controlled by the popular front, held out through a brutal siege that lasted for 28 months. Eventually, the government of the popular front moved to Valencia for greater safety in 1936.

But in the winter of 1936–37, Franco's forces slowly began to establish power, capturing the Basque capital of Bilbao and eventually Santander. The war shocked the world with its ruthlessness. (World War II hadn't happened yet.) Churches were burned and mass executions occurred, especially memorable in the Basque town of Guernica, which became the subject of one of Picasso's most fabled paintings.

By October 1, 1936, Franco was clearly in charge of the leadership of nationalist Spain, abolishing popular suffrage and regional autonomy—in effect, launching totalitarian rule of Spain.

The republicans were split by internal differences, and spy trials were commonplace. At the end of the first year of war, Franco held 35 of Spain's provincial capitals. In 1937, the republican forces were cut in two, and Madrid was left to fend for itself.

The last great offensive of the war began on December 23, 1938, with an attack by Franco's forces on Barcelona, which fell on January 26 after a campaign of 34 days. Republican forces fled toward France, as a succession of presidents occurred. On March 28 some 200,000 nationalist troops marched into Madrid, meeting no resistance. The war was over the next day when the rest of republican Spain surrendered. Lasting 2 years and 254 days, the war claimed some one million lives.

For memories and a sense of the Spanish Civil War, visitors can travel to El Valle de los Caídos (the Valley of the Fallen), outside El Escorial.

DATELINE *continued*

1941 Spain technically stays neutral in World War II, but Franco favors Germany.

1955 Spain joins the United Nations.

1975 Juan Carlos becomes king. Franco dies.

1978 New democratic constitution initiates reforms.

1981 Coup attempt by right-wing officers fails.

1982 Socialists gain power after 43 years of right-wing rule.

1986 Spain joins the European Community (now the European Union).

1992 Barcelona hosts the Summer Olympics.

1996 A conservative party defeats the Socialist party, ending its 13-year rule. José María Aznar is chosen prime minister.

1998 The controversial Guggenheim Museum at Bilbao is inaugurated.

2002 Spain adopts the euro as its national currency.

2003 Basque terrorists continue a campaign of terror against the government.

Although Franco adopted a neutral position during World War II, his sympathies obviously lay with Germany and Italy. Spain, although a nonbelligerent, assisted the Axis powers. This action intensified the diplomatic isolation into which the country was forced after the war's end—in fact, it was excluded from the United Nations until 1955.

Before his death in 1975, Franco selected as his successor Juan Carlos de Borbón y Borbón, son of the pretender to the Spanish throne. After 1977 elections, a new constitution was approved by the electorate and the king; it guaranteed human and civil rights, as well as free enterprise, and canceled the status of the Roman Catholic Church as the church of Spain. It also granted limited autonomy to several regions, including Catalonia and the Basque provinces, both of which, however, are still clamoring for more full-fledged autonomy.

In 1981 a group of right-wing military officers seized the Cortés and called upon Juan Carlos to establish a Francoist state. The king, however, refused, and the conspirators were arrested. The fledgling democracy overcame its first test. Its second major accomplishment—under the Socialist administration of Prime Minister Felipe González, the country's first leftist government since 1939—was to gain Spain's entry into the European Community (now European Union) in 1986.

EARLY 21ST CENTURY The shocking news for 2000 was not political but social. Spain came under increasing pressure to conform to short lunch breaks like those in the other E.U. countries. What? No 3-hour siesta? It was heresy. In spite of opposition, large companies began to cut lunch to 2 hours. Prosiesta forces in Spain cited the American custom of "power naps" as reason to retain their beloved afternoon break.

So the siesta appears to be under serious attack, perhaps as a consequence of the Spanish economy's upswing, which created more new jobs than in any other country in the E.U. More and more families are moving to the suburbs, and more women are joining the workforce. A survey has revealed that only 25% of Spaniards still take the siesta.

On other fronts, Spain moved ahead as an economic force in Latin America, where only 20 years ago Spain was a minor economic presence. Today, it is second only to the United States. The long-held monopoly of the U.S. in the region is being challenged for the first time since the Spanish-American War of 1898. In the last tally, Spaniards in 1 year poured $20 billion of investment value into Latin America.

Although there were some rough transitional periods, and a lot of older citizens were bewildered, Spain officially abandoned its time-honored peseta and went under the euro umbrella in March 2002.

2004 Al Qaeda strikes Spanish trains in the deadliest terrorist attack in Europe since World War II. José Luis Rodríguez Zapatero is elected as Socialist prime minister.

2005 Spain legalizes same-sex marriage.

2006 Basque separatist group ETA negotiates with conservative government for cease-fire. A bomb goes off at Madrid's airport; ETA claims responsibility.

2007 ETA calls an official end to cease-fire.

2009 Spain's once-buoyant economy suffers severe downturn. Unemployment reaches 17%.

During the transition period, as Spaniards struggled to adjust to the new currency, counterfeiters had a field day.

Throughout 2003, Basque terrorists, part of a separatist group (ETA), continued their campaign of terror against the government. Bombs and death tolls in 2003, including attacks in Madrid, brought the total of deaths up to 800 in this 3-decade-old campaign aimed at creating an independent Basque homeland in northern Spain and southwest France. Bombings are usually at vacation resorts, as ETA's announced aim is to disrupt Spain's main industry—tourism.

On March 11, 2004, terrorists linked to Al Qaeda exploded 10 bombs on four trains going into Madrid from the suburbs, killing 191 passengers and injuring 1,800. This was one of the deadliest terrorist attacks ever to hit Spain.

Since taking office in April 2004, Prime Minister José Luis Rodríguez Zapatero vowed to institute deep changes in social issues after 8 years of conservative rule. On the day he was confirmed as prime minister, he endorsed gay marriage. In approving the resolution in April 2005, the Spanish Parliament became the third European country to recognize gay marriage after the Netherlands and Belgium.

Rodríguez Zapatero has also made peace overtures to ETA, but after the 2006 ETA bombing at the Madrid airport, negotiations with the separatist group were stalled. Spanish Interior Minister Alfredo Pérez Rubalcaba told the press that he could not see how the peace process could resume. Indeed, in June 2007, ETA formally called an end to the cease-fire it had declared a year earlier.

Like the rest of the world, Spain's economic growth slowed sharply in 2009, as many of its companies faced financial turmoil. In the aftermath of the U.S. subprime mortgage meltdown, Spain took a big hit from more difficult financing conditions. The *New York Times* reported that unemployment in Spain hit 17% in 2009, one of the most devastating rates in years. Car sales fell by 28%.

In 2008 Zapatero was returned to power as prime minister, although with less percentage of the vote than before. His second term has been dominated by struggles with the ailing Spanish economy.

SPAIN'S ART & ARCHITECTURE

Spain's art ranges from Romanesque frescoes and El Greco's warped mannerism to Velázquez's royal portraits and Picasso's *Guernica;* its architecture, from Moorish palaces and Gothic cathedrals to Gaudí's Art Nouveau creations and Frank Gehry's metallic flower of Bilbao's Guggenheim Museum. This brief overview should help you make sense of it all.

Art

ROMANESQUE (10TH–13TH C.)

From the 8th century, most of Spain was under **Moorish** rule. The Muslims took the injunction against graven images so seriously that they produced no art in a traditional Western sense—though the remarkably intricate **geometric designs** and swooping, exaggerated letters of **Kufic inscriptions** played out in woodcarving, painted tiles, and plasterwork on Moorish palaces are decorations of the highest aesthetic order.

Madonna with Angels Playing Music (1390), by Pedro Serra, at the Museu Nacional d'Art de Catalunya.

Starting with the late-10th-century Reconquest, **Christian** Spaniards began producing art in the northern and eastern provinces. **Painting** and **mosaics** in Catalonia show the Byzantine influence of northern Italy, while **sculptures** along the northerly pilgrimage route to Compostela are related to French models, though they are often more symbolic (and primitive looking) than realistic.

Significant examples are found in **Barcelona's Museu Nacional d'Art de Catalunya.** Most of Catalonia's great Romanesque paintings were detached from their village churches in the early 20th century and are now housed in this museum. In **Catedral de Santiago de Compostela,** Pórtico de la Gloria is a 12th-century masterpiece of Romanesque sculpture.

GOTHIC (13TH–16TH C.)

The influences of Catalonia and France continued to dominate in the Gothic era—though, in painting especially, a dollop of Italian style and a dash of Flemish attention to detail were added. In this period, colors became more varied and vivid, compositions more complex, lines more fluid with movement, and features more expressive.

Significant artists and examples include **Jaime Huguet** (1415–92), the primary artist in the Catalan School, who left works in his native Barcelona's Palau Reial and Museu Nacional d'Art de Catalunya; and **Bartolomé Bermejo** (active 1474–98), the lead painter in the Italianate Valencian School, and the first Spanish painter to use oils. Some of his best early paintings are in Madrid's **Museo del Prado.**

RENAISSANCE (16TH C.)

Renaissance artists strove for greater naturalism, using techniques such as linear perspective to achieve new heights of realism. When it finally got rolling in Spain, the style had already mutated into baroque.

Significant artists include **Pedro Berruguete** (1450–1504), court painter to Ferdinand and Isabella; **Alonso Berruguete** (1488–1561), Pedro's talented son who was not only court painter to Charles V, but also the greatest native sculptor in Spain; and **El Greco** (1540–1614), Spain's most significant Renaissance artist from Crete, known for his broodingly dark colors, crowded compositions, eerily elongated figures, and a mystical touch. Toledo's churches and **Casa y Museo de El Greco** retain many of El Greco's works, as does Madrid's Museo del Prado.

BAROQUE (17TH–18TH C.)

The **baroque** was Spain's greatest artistic era, producing several painters who rank among Europe's greatest. The baroque style mixes a kind of superrealism

El Greco's *The Burial of the Count of Orgaz* (1586).

based on the use of peasant models and the *chiaroscuro* or *tenebrism* (the dramatic play of areas of harsh lighting off dark shadows) of Italy's Caravaggio with compositional complexity and explosions of dynamic fury, movement, color, and figures.

Significant artists include **José de Ribera** (1591–1652), the greatest master of *chiaroscuro* and *tenebrism* after Caravaggio; **Diego Velázquez** (1599–1660), Spain's greatest painter, a prodigy who became Philip IV's court painter at 24; **Francisco de Zurbarán** (1598–1664), Seville's master of *chiaroscuro;* and **Bartolomé Esteban Murillo** (1617–82), Zurbarán's Seville competitor. Murillo created work with a distinctly brighter, more saccharine and sentimental quality.

BOURBON ROCOCO & NEOCLASSICAL (18TH–19TH C.)

Spain's turbulent late 18th and early 19th centuries are best seen in the progression of work by the unique master **Francisco Goya** (1746–1828). His works started in the prevailing **rococo** style (a chaotic, frothy version of the baroque) but soon went off on their own track.

Spain's neoclassicism was dry, academic, and rather boring.

20TH CENTURY

Spain became an artistic hotbed again at the turn of the 20th century—even if Barcelona's own Picasso moved to Paris. Though both movements were born in France, Spanish artists were key in developing cubism and surrealism. **Cubists,** including Spaniards Picasso and Gris, accepted that the canvas is flat and painted objects from all points of view at once, rather than using optical tricks like perspective to fool viewers into seeing three dimensions; the effect is a fractured, imploded look. **Surrealists** tried to express the inner working of their minds in paint, plumbing their ids for imagery. Significant artists include **Joan Miró**

(1893–1983), greatest of the true surrealists in Spain; **Pablo Picasso** (1881–1973), the most important artist of the last century; **Juan Gris** (1887–1927), the truest of the cubists; and **Salvador Dalí** (1904–89), the most famous surrealist. Dalí's art used an intensely realistic technique to explore the very unreal worlds of dreams (nightmares, really) and paranoia in an attempt to plumb the Freudian depths of his own psyche.

Architecture

The Moors brought with them an Arabic architectural style that changed over the centuries but kept many features that give their remaining buildings, especially in Andalusia, a distinctly Eastern flair. The Moors built three major structures: mosques, alcázares, and alcazabas. **Mosques,** Islamic religious buildings, were connected to minarets, tall towers from which the muezzin would call the people to prayer. **Alcázares** were palaces built with many small courtyards and gardens with fountains and greenery. **Alcazabas** were fortresses built high atop hills and fortified like any defensive structure.

The early **Caliphate** style of Córdoba lasted from the 8th to the 11th centuries, replaced by the most austerely religious **Almohad** style in Seville in the 12th and 13th centuries.

Mezquita-Catedral de Córdoba is the best-preserved building in the Caliphate style. Of the Almohad period, the best remaining example is **Seville's Giralda Tower,** a minaret but little altered when its accompanying mosque was converted into a cathedral; the mosque and tower at **Zaragosa's Palacio de la Aljafería** have survived from the era as well. The crowning achievement of the Nasrid—of all Spanish Moorish architecture—is **Granada's Alhambra** palace and the adjacent **Generalife** gardens.

ROMANESQUE (8TH–13TH C.)

The Romanesque took its inspiration and rounded arches from ancient Rome (hence the name). Romanesque architects concentrated on building large churches with wide aisles to accommodate the pilgrims.

Although the great **Catedral de Santiago de Compostela,** the undisputed masterpiece of the style, has many baroque accretions, the floor plan is solidly Romanesque. Other good examples include **Sangüesa's Iglesia de Santa María** and **Iglesia de Santiago.**

GOTHIC (13TH–16TH C.)

Instead of dark, somber, relatively unadorned Romanesque interiors that forced the eyes of the faithful toward the altar, the Gothic interior enticed the churchgoers' gazes upward to high ceilings filled with light. The priests still conducted Mass in Latin, but now peasants could "read" the Gothic comic books of stained-glass windows.

The French style of Gothic was energetically pursued in Spain in the early to mid–13th century, first in adapting the Romanesque **Catedral de Santa María** in **Burgos,** and then in **Catedral de Toledo** and **Catedral de León,** the most ornate. Fourteenth- and fifteenth-century Gothic cathedrals include those at **Avila, Segovia, Pamplona, Barcelona,** and **Girona.** (The last is a peculiar, aisleless Catalan plan, although the interior is now baroque.) The best of the **Isabelline style** can be seen in **Valladolid** in the facades of **Iglesia de San Pablo** and **Colegio San Gregorio.**

RENAISSANCE (16TH C.)

The rules of Renaissance architecture stressed proportion, order, classical inspiration, and mathematical precision to create unified, balanced structures based on Italian models. The earliest—and most Spanish—Renaissance style (really a transitional form from Gothic) was marked by facades done in an almost Moorish intricacy and was called **Plateresque,** for it was said to resemble the work of silversmiths (*plateros*).

The best of the **Plateresque** decorates the facades of **Salamanca's Convento de San Esteban** and **Universidad.** Charles V's **Summer Palace,** built in the middle of **Granada's** Moorish **Alhambra,** is the greatest High Renaissance building in Spain. The most monumentally classical of Renaissance structures was Phillip II's **El Escorial** monastery outside Madrid, designed by Juan de Herrera (1530–97), who also started **Valladolid's Cathedral** in 1580, although the exterior was later finished in flamboyant baroque style.

BAROQUE (17TH–18TH C.)

The overall effect of the baroque is to lighten the appearance of structures and add movement of line and vibrancy to the static look of the classical Renaissance. Soon the Churriguera family of architects and their contemporaries gave rise to the overly ornate, sumptuously decorated **Churrigueresque** style.

Madrid's Plaza Mayor is the classic example of the restrained early baroque. Churrigueresque masterpieces include **Granada's Monasterio Cartuja** and **Salamanca's Plaza Mayor.** The baroque was largely used to embellish existing buildings, such as the fine, ornate facade on **Catedral de Santiago de Compostela.**

NEOCLASSICAL (18TH–19TH C.)

By the middle of the 18th century, Bourbon architects began turning to the austere simplicity and grandeur of the classical age and inaugurated the neoclassical style.

The primary neoclassical architect, **Ventura Rodríguez** (1717–85), designed the facade of **Pamplona's Cathedral** and **Madrid's grand boulevard of the Paseo del Prado.** On that boulevard is one of Spain's best neoclassical buildings, the **Museo del Prado.**

MODERNISME (20TH C.)

In Barcelona, architects such as **Lluís Domènech i Montaner** (1850–1923) and the great master **Antoni Gaudí** (1852–1926) developed one of the most appealing, idiosyncratic forms of Art Nouveau, called *modernisme.* This Catalan variant took a playful stab at building with undulating lines and colorful, broken-tile mosaics.

Identifiable features of *modernisme* include the following:

Gaudí's Casa Milà, or La Pedrera, apartment building.

- **Emphasis on the uniqueness of craft.** Like Art Nouveau practitioners in other countries, Spanish artists and architects rebelled against the era of mass production.
- **Use of organic motifs.** Asymmetrical, curvaceous designs were often based on plants and flowers.
- **Variety of mediums.** Wrought iron, stained glass, tile, and hand-painted wallpaper were some of the most popular materials.

The best of *modernisme* is in **Barcelona,** including **Gaudí's apartment buildings** along Passeig de Gràcia, and his massive unfinished cathedral, **La Sagrada Família.**

SPAIN IN BOOKS, FILMS & MUSIC
Books

ECONOMIC, POLITICAL & SOCIAL HISTORY Historically, Spain's Golden Age lasted from the late 15th to the early 17th century, a period when the country reached the height of its prestige and influence. This era is well surveyed in J. H. Elliott's *Imperial Spain 1469–1716* (New American Library).

Most accounts of the Spanish Armada's defeat are written from the English point of view. For a change of perspective, try David Howarth's *The Voyage of the Armada* (Penguin).

The story of the Spanish Inquisition is told by Edward Peters in *Inquisition* (University of California Press).

One of the best accounts of Spain's earlier history is found in Joseph F. O'Callaghan's *History of Medieval Spain* (Cornell University).

In the 20th century the focus shifts to the Spanish Civil War, recounted in Hugh Thomas's classic, *The Spanish Civil War* (Harper & Row). For a personal account of the war, read George Orwell's *Homage to Catalonia* (Harcourt Brace Jovanovich). The poet García Lorca was killed during the Civil War; the best account of his death is found in Ian Gibson's *The Assassination of Federico García Lorca* (Penguin).

If you like more contemporary history, read John Hooper's *The Spaniards* (Penguin). Hooper provides insight into the events of the post-Franco era, when the country came to grips with democracy after years of fascism.

ART & ARCHITECTURE The Moors contributed much to Spanish culture. Their distinct legacy is documented in Titus Burckhardt's *Moorish Culture in Spain* (McGraw-Hill).

Antoni Gaudí is the Spanish architect who most excites visitors' curiosity. Among the many illustrated books on his work, *Gaudí* (Escudo de Oro's "Collection Art at Spain" series) contains 150 photographs.

Spain's most famous artist was Pablo Picasso. The most controversial book about the late painter is *Picasso, Creator and Destroyer* by Arianna Stassinopoulos Huffington (Simon & Schuster).

Spain's other headline-grabbing artist was Salvador Dalí. In *Salvador Dalí: A Biography* (Dutton), author Meryle Secrest asks: Was he a mad genius or a cunning manipulator?

Andrés Segovia: An Autobiography of the Years 1893–1920 (Macmillan), with a translation by W. F. O'Brien, is worth seeking out.

Residents of Catalonia truthfully maintain that their unique language, culture, and history have been overshadowed (and squelched) by the richer and better-publicized accomplishments of Castile. Robert Hughes, a former art critic at *Time* magazine, has written an elegant testament to the glories of the capital of this region: *Barcelona* (Knopf). This book offers a well-versed and often witty articulation of the city's architectural and cultural legacy. According to the *New York Times,* the book is destined to become "a classic in the genre of urban history."

The richly illustrated *Juan de Herrera: Architect to Philip II of Spain,* by Catherine Wilkinson Zerner (Yale University Press), de-

Miguel de Cervantes.

scribes (for the first time in English) the remarkable 3-decade partnership between Herrera (1530–97) and his royal patron.

Catalan Painting: From the 19th to the Surprising 20th Century, by Joan Ainaud de Lasarte (Rizzoli), has a title that tells its theme accurately. A lavish volume written by the former director of the Art Museums of Barcelona, it contains more than 100 color plates, from Joan Miró's *The Farm* to Dalí's nightmarish prefiguration of the Spanish Civil War.

TRAVEL *Cities of Spain,* by David Gilmour (Ivan R. Dee), is a collection of perceptive essays on nine Spanish cities. Containing more literary background and historical lore than most guidebooks have space to cover, Gilmour ranges from Granada to Santiago de Compostela, from Toledo to Córdoba.

FICTION & BIOGRAPHY Denounced by some as superficial, James A. Michener's *Iberia* (Random House) remains the classic travelogue on Spain. The *Houston Post* claimed that this book "will make you fall in love with Spain."

The most famous Spanish novel is *Don Quixote* by Miguel de Cervantes. Readily available everywhere, it deals with the conflict between the ideal and the real in human nature. Despite the unparalleled fame of Miguel de Cervantes within Spanish literature, very little is known about his life. One of the most searching biographies of the literary master is Jean Canavaggio's *Cervantes,* translated from the Spanish by J. R. Jones (Norton).

Although the work of Cervantes has attained an almost mystical significance in the minds of many Spaniards, in the words of Somerset Maugham, "It would be hard to find a work so great that has so many defects." Nicholas Wollaston's *Tilting at Don Quixote* (André Deutsch Publishers) punctures any illusions that the half-crazed Don is only a matter of good and rollicking fun.

The collected works of the famed dramatist of Spain's Golden Age, Pedro Calderón de la Barca, can be read in *Plays* (University Press of Kentucky).

The major works of pre–Civil War playwright Federico García Lorca can be enjoyed in *Five Plays: Comedies and Tragicomedies* (New Directions).

Ernest Hemingway completed many works on Spain, none more notable than his novels of 1926 and 1940, respectively: *The Sun Also Rises* (Macmillan) and *For Whom the Bell Tolls* (Macmillan), the latter based on his experiences in the Spanish Civil War. Don Ernesto's *Death in the Afternoon* (various editions) remains the English-language classic on bullfighting.

For travelers to Granada and the Alhambra, the classic is *Tales of the Alhambra* (Sleepy Hollow Press) by Washington Irving.

The Life of Saint Teresa of Avila by Herself (Penguin), translated by J. M. Cohen, is said to be the third-most-widely read book in Spain, after the Bible and *Don Quixote.* Some parts are heavy going, but the rest is lively.

Isabel the Queen: Life and Times, by Peggy K. Liss (Oxford University Press), an American historian, is a vividly detailed study. It provides a "spin" on this controversial queen not often taught in Spanish history classes. One of the most influential women in history, the Catholic monarch is viewed as forging national unity through the holy terror of the Spanish Inquisition, which was launched in 1478 and resulted in the expulsion of Jews and Moors from Spain and religious intolerance in general. Even her sponsorship of Columbus, it is suggested, led to "genocide" in the Caribbean.

20TH-CENTURY VOICES Winning the Nobel Prize for Literature in 1922, Jacinto Benavente is best known for such plays as *La Boernadora* (1901)—called *The Governor's Wife* in English—and particularly for *Señora ama* (1908), or *The Lady of the House* in English, two psychological dramas taking place in a rural atmosphere. *Los intereses creados* (1907), or *The Bonds of Interest,* is hailed as his masterpiece.

The controversial Don Camilo José Cela Trulock, the Marquis of Iria Flavia, was one of the most influential Spanish writers of the 1950s, although the Franco government viewed his work as indecent. Cela's best known work, *La Colmena (The Hive),* published in 1951, featured more than 300 characters. A devotee of Spanish realism, he was sarcastic, even grotesque in print. In later years he created scandal, including a claim he could absorb a liter of water via his anus, offering to demonstrate in public.

Mercè Rodoreda, a Catalan novelist of Barcelona, wrote *La plaça del diamante,* or *The Diamond Square,* which was translated into English in 1962 as *The Time of the Doves.* It became the most acclaimed Catalan novel of all time and is the best novel dealing with the Spanish Civil War (forgive us, Ernesto).

Adept in such forms as novels, short stories, children's literature, poetry, and essays, Carmen Martín Gaite was one of the most awarded writers of her generation, dying in 2000. A major Spanish writer, Almudena Grandes, writes about life in contemporary Spain, including the 21st century. Her most celebrated work was the erotic novel *Las edades de Lulú,* translated into English.

Finally, Ana Rossetti, a Spanish poet born in Cádiz in 1950, is one of the most exuberant female voices in Spanish literature. The artist's repertoire embraces not only poetry but opera librettos, novels, and several works of prose.

Films

The first Spanish feature film, *Los Guapos del Parque (The Dandies of the Park),* directed by Segundo de Chomón, was released in 1903, 7 years after the film industry began in Barcelona.

Film studios opened in Madrid in 1920, and by 1926 Spain was producing some 30 feature films a year. Before World War II the biggest name was Florian Rey, who made both silents and talkies, his most notable work being *Le Aldea Maldita (The Damned Village)* in 1929.

After the Civil War and under Franco, Spain produced a lot of mediocre films. Even General Franco, using a pseudonym, wrote a propaganda piece called *Raza (The Race)* in 1941.

In the 1950s, Spanish film achieved world recognition, mainly because of two directors, Luís García Berlanga and Juan Antonio Bardem. Both made satirical films about social conditions in Spain, sometimes incurring the government's wrath. During the filming of *Death of a Cyclist,* in fact, Bardem was arrested and imprisoned. Upon his release, he finished the film, which won acclaim at Cannes.

Luis Buñuel became one of the biggest names in Spanish cinema, his films mirroring the social, political, and religious conflicts that tore Spain apart during most of the 20th century. In 1928, Salvador Dalí and Buñuel cooperated on the director's first movie, *Un Chien Andalou (An Andalusian Dog),* considered the most important surrealist film. Two years later, sadistic scenes in *L'Age d'Or (The Golden Age)*—again written with Dalí's help—led to riots in some movie houses. Buñuel also directed *La Mort en ce Jardin (Death in the Garden)* with Simone Signoret (1957). In 1960 he made *Viridiana,* which subsequently won the prize for best picture at Cannes, even though Franco banned the film in Spain.

In 1982 José Luis García became the first Spaniard to win an Oscar for best foreign film with *Volver a Empezar (To Begin Again),* even though local critics considered the film inferior to his earliest, *Asignatura Pendiente (Anticipated Assignation). Volver a Empezar* takes a look at an exiled writer's homecoming to Spain.

One of the biggest box-office hits in Spanish film history (and still available on DVD) is *El Crimen de Cuenca (The Crime in Cuenca),* directed by Pilar Miró, who went on to become "chief of state of television." The film, which derails Civil Guard torture, caused a furor when it was released and was suppressed until the coup attempt of 1981.

The Basque problem reached the movie screens in 1983 with *La Muerte de Mikel (Michael's Death),* which dramatizes the tortured love story of a young Basque nationalist and a transvestite from Bilbao.

The 36-year dictatorship of Franco imposed on the Spanish arts an anesthetizing effect whose aftermath is being explored cinematically today. One of the best-acclaimed examples is Vicente Aranda's steamily entertaining and psychologically insightful *Lovers* (1992). A dark, melodramatic romance set in the Franco era, it charts the changing eddies of a love triangle and the bewitching influence of a slightly over-the-hill temptress.

Hailed by some critics as a variation of the farmer's daughter tale, *Belle Epoque,* directed by Fernando Trueba and written by Rafael Azcona (in Spanish with English subtitles), won the 1993 Oscar as best foreign language film. It's a hot-blooded human comedy of a handsome innocent, a deserter from the Spanish army in the winter of 1930 to 1931, who is seduced by the four daughters of a droll old painter.

Today's *enfant terrible* is Pedro Almodóvar, whose *Woman on the Verge of a Nervous Breakdown* won an Academy Award nomination in 1990. Ostensibly, the film is the story of a woman's abandonment, but its madcap proceedings deal with everything from spiked gazpacho to Shiite terrorists. An iconoclast like Almódovar, who has publicly declared his homosexuality, flourishes in the contemporary liberal Spain, which abolished censorship in 1977.

Another Almodóvar international hit, *High Heels* (1991), is a soap opera involving a highly theatrical and highly emotional film diva who returns to Madrid and the daughter she abandoned years before. Praised by critics for "spanking his favorite ideas until they turn red with pleasure," Almodóvar plays with what has been defined as "the theatricality of the real and the authenticity of the theatrical—all in an engagingly funny combination of high and low camp." Almodóvar continued his glitz with *Kika* (1994), which he both wrote and directed. His eponymous heroine, Verónica Forqué, a beautician, is full of surprises. For example, she meets her lover-to-be, Ramón, when she's making up his presumably dead corpse. He wakes up and they fall in love—but that's only the beginning of twists and turns in this crazed soap opera.

Almodóvar has continued into the 21st century to turn out wildly popular films marked by complex narratives, using the elements of pop culture, irreverent humor, hit songs, and a vividly glossy decor. Desire, passion, family, and identity are prevalent themes in such releases as *Bad Education* in 2004 and *Volver* in 2006, the latter starring Penelope Cruz.

Other Spanish filmmakers attracting international audiences include Julio Médem, whose *Lucía y el Sexo (Sex and Lucía)*, became celebrated for its lyrical eroticism. His film *La Pelota Vasca (The Basque Ball)*, a documentary about political problems in the Basque Country, caused a furor in right-wing Madrid.

A Canadian film director, Michael Dowse, achieved renown with his British film *It's All Gone Pete Tong*, which was set in Ibiza, one of Spain's Balearic Islands. The 2004 flick was a fictional independent biopic about Frankie Wilde (played by Paul Kaye), a DJ who goes completely deaf.

Penelope Cruz won an Oscar for Best Supporting Actress in 2009 for her contribution to *Vicky Cristina Barcelona,* directed by Woody Allen and also starring Scarlett Johansson and Javier Bardém. The film, about relationship strife, shows Allen's long love for Barcelona, including his fascination with Gaudí's architecture—especially the Sagrada Família.

Music

CLASSICAL Don Odilo Cunill directs the Cor Monastic de Abadía de Montserrat in *Cants Gregorians de la Missa Per Els Fidels Missa Orbis Factor,* Gregorian chants recorded in the chapel of the monastery at Montserrat.

In the album *Andrés Segovia, España,* the late master plays guitar versions of fandangos and *tonadillas.* In a more classical vein, the same artist plays Bach, Scarlatti, and also music by the Czech composer Benda (1722–95) in *Recital Íntimo.*

The Orquesta de Conciertos de Madrid performs Falla's *El Amor Brujo* and *El Sombrero de Tres Picos.* The same group, conducted by Enrique Jorda, can be heard in Albéniz's *Suite Española* and *Dos Piezas Españoles.*

FOLK/ETHNIC Isabel Pantoja, widow of the late bullfighter, sings soulful interpretations of Andalusian ballads in *Se Me Enamora el Alma;* Rocío Jurado renders them smolderingly in *Punto de Partida* and *Canciones de España*.

Carlos Cano performs popular interpretations of Spanish Argentine tangos, habaneras, and sevillanas on *Luna de Abril*. In *Canalla,* Antonio Cortés Chiquetete is heard in 19th-century folk melodies. Felipe Campuzano gives piano interpretations of Andalusian folk music in *Cádiz: Andalucía Espiritual*.

Pasodobles Famosos, performed by the Gran Banda Taurina, is popular with older Spaniards, partly for its nostalgia value. This was the music played until very recently at every Spanish gathering, from bullfights to weddings to christenings.

Guitar master Andrés Segovia.

In *Siroca,* Paco de Lucía combines traditional flamenco guitar in its purest form with modern influences, including tangos, *bulerías,* and *tanquillos.* You can also hear Paco de Lucía on *Fantasía Flamenca,* interpreting authentic *flemencas* in a traditional manner. One of his releases, *Zyryab,* is named for the 8th-century Persian musician who brought new musical techniques to Córdoba, including (probably) the basis for the modern guitar.

The brilliance of late virtuoso Narciso Yepes can be heard on *Música Española para Guitarra,* performing traditional favorites.

CONTEMPORARY In the closing years of the 20th century, several Spanish groups rose to prominence, including Ana Belén singing contemporary love ballads in her album *A la Sombra de un León.* When a Madrid band, Radio Futura, appeared on the scene they were hailed as the "Einsteins of Spanish rock." Yet another group, Cabinet Caligari, taking their name from one of the most famous German silent films, specialized in what might be called macho Hispano pop.

One of the biggest record sellers in Spain is Joan Manuel Serrat, a singer-songwriter recording more-traditional popular music in both Catalan and Castilian.

In Madrid, traditional Spanish music is also offered by singer-songwriter Luis Eduardo Aute, who has thousands of fans in the Spanish-speaking world.

In current Spanish jazz, Tete Montoliu's recordings represent some of the best the country has to offer. All, or most, of these records are available at Spanish music stores in the United States. They are available throughout Spain as well.

Impressions

I also love the Spaniard, for he is a type in his own right, a copy of no one.
—Stendhal

In the early '80s, the pop rock Madrid group the Pistons achieved renown in the music world for their great songs, pop simplicity, and vitality. Formed in 1978, Nacha pop dominated the '80s as well. Even though they made their last record in 1988, their fame has endured.

Of course, Julio Iglesias, born in 1943 in Madrid, is the king of Spanish singers, having sold 250 million albums. He has released an astonishing 77 albums. His son, Enrique Iglesias, has followed in his father's footsteps, enjoying world renown as a Spanish pop singer and songwriter.

EATING & DRINKING IN SPAIN

Meals are an extremely important social activity in Spain, whether that means eating out late at night or having large family gatherings for lunch. Although Spain is faster paced than it once was, few Spaniards race through a meal on the way to an appointment.

The food in Spain is varied; portions are immense, but the prices, by North American standards, are high. Whenever possible, try the regional specialties, particularly when you visit the Basque Country or Galicia.

Many restaurants in Spain close on Sunday, so be sure to check ahead. Hotel dining rooms are generally open 7 days a week, and there's always something open in big cities, such as Madrid and Barcelona, or in well-touristed areas, such as the Costa del Sol. Generally, reservations are not necessary, except at popular, top-notch restaurants.

Meals

BREAKFAST In Spain, the day starts with a continental breakfast of coffee, hot chocolate, or tea, with assorted rolls, butter, and jam. Spanish breakfast might also consist of *churros* (fried fingerlike doughnuts) and hot chocolate that is very sweet and thick. However, most Spaniards simply have coffee, usually strong, served with hot milk: either a *café con leche* (half coffee, half milk) or *cortado* (a shot of espresso "cut" with a dash of milk). If you find it too strong and bitter for your taste, you might ask for a more diluted *café americano.*

LUNCH The most important meal of the day in Spain, lunch is comparable to the farm-style midday "dinner" in the United States. It usually includes three or four courses, beginning with a choice of soup or several dishes of hors d'oeuvres called *entremeses.* Often a fish or egg dish is served after this, and then a meat course with vegetables. Wine is always part of the meal. Dessert is usually pastry, custard, or assorted fruit—followed by coffee. Lunch is served from 1 to 4pm, with "rush hour" at 2pm.

TAPAS After the early-evening stroll, many Spaniards head for their favorite *tascas,* bars where they drink wine and sample assorted tapas, or snacks, such as bits of fish, eggs in mayonnaise, or olives.

Because many Spaniards eat dinner very late, they often have an extremely light breakfast, certainly coffee and perhaps a pastry. However, by 11am they are often hungry and lunch might not be until 2pm or later, so many Spaniards have a late-morning snack, often at a cafeteria. Favorite items to order are a *tortilla* (Spanish omelet with potatoes) and even a beer. Many request a large tapa served with bread.

Serrano ham tapas in Madrid.

DINNER Another extravaganza: A typical meal starts with a bowl of soup, followed by a second course, often a fish dish, and by another main course, usually veal, beef, or pork, accompanied by vegetables. Again, desserts tend to be fruit, custard, or pastries.

Naturally, if you had a heavy, late lunch and stopped off at a tapas bar or two before dinner, supper might be much lighter, perhaps some cold cuts, sausage, a bowl of soup, or even a Spanish omelet made with potatoes. Wine is always part of the meal. Afterward, you might have a demitasse and a fragrant Spanish brandy. The chic dining hour, even in one-donkey towns, is 10 or 10:30pm. (In well-touristed regions and hardworking Catalonia, you can usually dine at 8pm, but you still may find yourself alone in the restaurant.) In most middle-class establishments, people dine around 9:30pm.

The Cuisine

SOUPS & APPETIZERS Soups are usually served in big bowls. Cream soups, such as asparagus and potato, can be fine; sadly, however, they are too often made from powdered envelope soups such as Knorr and Liebig. Served year-round, chilled gazpacho, on the other hand, is tasty and particularly refreshing during the hot months. The combination is pleasant: olive oil, garlic, ground cucumbers, and raw tomatoes with a sprinkling of croutons. Spain also offers several varieties of fish soup—*sopa de pescado*—in all its provinces, and many of these are superb.

In the *paradores* (government-run hostelries) and top restaurants, as many as 15 tempting hors d'oeuvres are served. In lesser known places, avoid these *entremeses,* which often consist of last year's sardines and shards of sausage left over from the Moorish conquest.

EGGS These are served in countless ways. A Spanish omelet, a *tortilla española,* is made with potatoes and usually onions. A simple omelet is called a *tortilla francesa.* A *tortilla portuguesa* is similar to the American Spanish omelet.

FISH Spain's fish dishes tend to be outstanding and vary from province to province. One of the most common varieties is *merluza* (sweet white hake). *Langosta,* a variety of lobster, is seen everywhere—it's a treat but terribly expensive. The Portuguese in particular, but some Spaniards, too, go into raptures at the mention of *mejillones* (barnacles). Gourmets relish their sea-water taste; others find them tasteless. *Rape* (pronounced *rah*-peh) is the Spanish name for monkfish, a sweet, wide-boned ocean fish with a scallop-like texture. Also try a few dozen half-inch baby eels. They rely heavily on olive oil and garlic for their flavor, but they taste great. Squid cooked in its own ink is suggested only to those who want to go native. Charcoal-broiled sardines, however, are a culinary delight—a particular treat in the Basque provinces. Trout Navarre is one of the most popular fish dishes, usually stuffed with bacon or ham.

PAELLA You can't go to Spain without trying its celebrated paella. Flavored with saffron, paella is an aromatic rice dish usually topped with shellfish, chicken, sausage, peppers, and local spices. Served authentically, it comes steaming hot from the kitchen in a metal pan called a *paellera.* (Incidentally, what is known in the U.S. as Spanish rice isn't Spanish at all. If you ask an English-speaking waiter for Spanish rice, you'll be served paella.)

MEATS Don't expect Kansas City steak, but do try the spit-roasted suckling pig, so sweet and tender it can often be cut with a fork. The veal is also good, and the Spanish *lomo de cerdo,* loin of pork, is unmatched anywhere. Tender chicken is most often served in the major cities and towns today, and the Spanish are adept at spit-roasting it until it turns a delectable golden

Valencian paella.

brown. In more remote spots of Spain, however, "free-range" chicken is often stringy and tough.

VEGETABLES & SALADS Through more sophisticated agricultural methods, Spain now grows more of its own vegetables, which are available year-round, unlike in days of yore, when canned vegetables were used all too frequently. Both potatoes and rice are staples of the Spanish diet, the latter a prime ingredient, of course, in the famous paella originating in Valencia. Salads don't usually get much attention and are often made simply with lettuce and tomatoes.

DESSERTS The Spanish do not emphasize dessert, often opting for fresh fruit. Flan, a home-cooked egg custard, appears on all menus—sometimes with a burned-caramel sauce. Ice cream appears on nearly all menus as well. But the best bet is to ask for a basket of fruit, which you can wash at your table. Homemade pastries are usually moist and not too sweet. As a dining oddity—although it's not odd at all to Spaniards—many restaurants serve fresh orange juice for dessert.

OLIVE OIL & GARLIC Olive oil is used lavishly in Spain, the largest olive grower on the planet. You may not want it in all dishes. If you prefer your fish grilled in butter, the word is *mantequilla*. In some places, you'll be charged extra for the butter. Garlic is also an integral part of the Spanish diet, and even if you love it, you may find Spaniards love it more than you do and use it in the oddest dishes.

What to Drink

WATER It is generally safe to drink water in all major cities and tourist resorts in Spain. If you're traveling in remote areas, play it safe and drink bottled water. One of the most popular noncarbonated bottled drinks in Spain is Solares. Nearly all restaurants and hotels have it. Bubbly water is *agua mineral con gas;* noncarbonated, *agua mineral sin gas.* Note that bottled water in some areas may cost as much as the regional wine.

SOFT DRINKS In general, avoid the carbonated citrus drinks on sale everywhere. Most of them never saw an orange, much less a lemon. If you want a citrus drink, order old, reliable Schweppes. An excellent noncarbonated drink for the summer is called Tri-Naranjus, which comes in lemon and orange flavors. Your cheapest bet is a liter bottle of *gaseosa*, which comes in various flavors. In summer you should also try an *horchata*. Not to be confused with the Mexican beverage of the same name, the Spanish *horchata* is a sweet, milklike beverage made of tubers called *chufas*.

COFFEE Even if you are a dedicated coffee drinker, you may find the *café con leche* (coffee with milk) a little too strong. We suggest *leche manchada,* a little bit of strong, freshly brewed coffee in a glass that's filled with lots of frothy hot milk.

MILK In the largest cities you get bottled milk, but it loses a great deal of its flavor in the process of pasteurization. In all cases, avoid untreated milk and milk products. About the best brand of fresh milk is Lauki.

BEER Although not native to Spain, beer *(cerveza)* is now drunk everywhere. Domestic brands include San Miguel, Mahou, Aguila, and Cruz Blanca.

WINE Sherry *(vino de Jerez)* has been called "the wine with 100 souls." Drink it before dinner (try the topaz-colored *finos,* a dry and very pale sherry) or whenever you drop into some old inn or bodega for refreshment; many of them have rows of kegs with spigots. *Manzanilla,* a golden-colored, medium-dry sherry, is extremely popular. The sweet cream sherries (Harvey's Bristol Cream, for example) are favorite after-dinner wines (called *olorosos*). While the French may be disdainful of Spanish table wines, they can be truly noble, especially two leading varieties, Valdepeñas and Rioja, both from Castile. If you're not too exacting in your tastes, you can always ask for the *vino de la casa* (house wine) wherever you dine. The Ampurdán of Catalonia is heavy. From Andalusia comes the fruity Montilla. There are some good local sparkling wines (cavas) in Spain, such as Freixenet. One brand, Benjamín, comes in individual-size bottles.

Beginning in the 1990s, based partly on subsidies and incentives from the European Union, Spanish vintners have scrapped most of the country's obsolete winemaking equipment, hired new talent, and poured time and money into the improvement and promotion of wines from even high-altitude or arid regions not previously suitable for wine production. Thanks to irrigation, improved grape varieties, technological developments, and the expenditure of billions of euros, bodegas and vineyards are sprouting up throughout the country, opening their doors to visitors interested in how the stuff is grown, fermented, and bottled. These wines are now earning awards at wine competitions around the world for their quality and bouquet.

Interested in impressing a newfound Spanish friend over a wine list? Consider bypassing the usual array of Riojas, sherries, and sparkling Catalonian cavas in favor of, say, a Galician white from Rias Baixas, which some connoisseurs consider the perfect accompaniment for seafood. Among reds, make a beeline for vintages from the fastest-developing wine region of Europe, the arid, high-altitude district of Ribera del Duero, near Burgos, whose alkaline soil, cold nights, and sunny days have earned unexpected praise from winemakers (and encouraged massive investments) in the past few years.

For more information about these or any other of the 10 wine-producing regions of Spain (and the 39 officially recognized wine-producing *Denominaciones de Origen* scattered across those regions), contact **Wines from Spain,** c/o the Commercial Office of Spain, 405 Lexington Ave., 44th Floor, New York, NY 10174-0331 (© **212/661-4959**).

SANGRIA The all-time favorite refreshing drink in Spain, sangria is a red-wine punch that combines wine with oranges, lemons, seltzer, and sugar. Be careful, however; many joints that do a big tourist trade produce a sickly sweet Kool-Aid version of sangria for unsuspecting visitors.

WHISKEY & BRANDY Imported whiskeys are available at most Spanish bars but at a high price. If you're a drinker, switch to brandies and cognacs, where the Spanish reign supreme. Try Fundador, made by the Pedro Domecq family in Jerez de la Frontera. If you want a smooth cognac, ask for the "103" white label.

PLANNING YOUR TRIP TO SPAIN

G etting to Spain is relatively easy, especially for those who live in Western Europe or on the East Coast of the United States. If all your documents are in order (see "Entry Requirements," p. 64), you should clear Customs and Immigration smoothly. Increasingly, the staffs of entry ports into Spain often speak English, and they'll usually speed you on your way.

In this chapter, you'll find everything you need to plan your trip, from a sketch of Spain's various regions to tips on when to go and how to get the best airfare. For additional help in planning your trip and for more on-the-ground resources in Spain, turn to "Fast Facts," on p. 776.

WHEN TO GO

Spring and fall are ideal times to visit nearly all of Spain, with the possible exception of the Atlantic coast, which experiences heavy rains in October and November. May and October are the best months, in terms of both weather and crowds.

In summer it's hot, hot, and hotter still, with the cities in Castile (Madrid) and Andalusia (Seville and Córdoba) heating up the most. Madrid has dry heat; the average temperature can hover around 84°F (29°C) in July and 75°F (24°C) in September. Seville has the dubious reputation of being about the hottest part of Spain in July and August, often baking under average temperatures of 93°F (34°C).

Barcelona, cooler in temperature, is often quite humid. Midsummer temperatures in Majorca often reach 91°F (33°C). The overcrowded Costa Brava has temperatures around 81°F (27°C) in July and August. The Costa del Sol has an average of 77°F (25°C) in summer. The coolest spot in Spain is the Atlantic coast from San Sebastián to A Coruña, with temperatures in the 70s (21°C–26°C) in July and August.

August remains the major vacation month in Europe. The traffic from France, the Netherlands, and Germany to Spain becomes a veritable migration, and low-cost hotels along the coastal areas are virtually impossible to find. To compound the problem, many restaurants and shops also decide it's time for a vacation, thereby limiting visitors' selections for both dining and shopping.

In winter, the coast from Algeciras to Málaga is the most popular, with temperatures reaching a warm 60°F to 63°F (16°–17°C). Madrid gets cold, as low as 34°F (1°C). Majorca is warmer, usually in the 50s (low teens Celsius), but it often dips into the 40s (single digits Celsius). Some mountain resorts can experience extreme cold.

FACING PAGE: **An old *teleférico* tramway car in Fuente-Dé.**

Spain Calendar of Events

The dates given below may not be precise. Sometimes the exact days are not announced until 6 weeks before the actual festival. Check with the Tourist Office of Spain (see "Visitor Information," p. 781) if you plan to attend a specific event.

For an exhaustive list of events beyond those listed here, check http://events.frommers.com, where you'll find a searchable, up-to-the-minute roster of what's happening in cities all over the world.

JANUARY

Granada Reconquest Festival, Granada. The whole city celebrates the Christians' victory over the Moors in 1492. The highest tower at the Alhambra is open to the public on January 2. For information, contact the Tourist Office of Granada (✆ **95-824-71-28**). January 2.

Día de los Reyes (Three Kings Day), throughout Spain. Parades are held around the country on the eve of the Festival of the Epiphany. Various "kings" dispense candy to all the kids. January 6.

Día de San Antonio (St. Anthony's Day), La Puebla, Majorca. Bonfires, dancing, revelers dressed as devils, and other riotous events honor St. Anthony on the eve of his day. January 17.

FEBRUARY

Bocairente Festival of Christians and Moors, Bocairente (Valencia). Fireworks, colorful costumes, parades, and a reenactment of the struggle between Christians and Moors mark this exuberant festival. A stuffed effigy of Mohammed is blown to bits. Call ✆ **96-290-50-62** for more information. First week of February.

ARCO (Madrid's International Contemporary Art Fair), Madrid. One of the biggest draws on Spain's cultural calendar, this exhibit showcases the best in contemporary art from Europe and America. At the Nuevo Recinto Ferial Juan Carlos I, the exhibition draws galleries from throughout Europe, the Americas, Australia, and Asia, which bring with them the works of regional and internationally known artists. To buy tickets, contact Parque Ferial Juan Carlos I at ✆ **90-222-15-15.** The cost is 32€ to 63€. You can get schedules from the tourist office closer to the event's date. For more information, call ✆ **91-722-30-00** or go to www.ifema.es. Dates vary, but the event usually takes place mid-February.

Madrid Carnaval. The carnival kicks off with a big parade along Paseo de la Castellana, culminating in a masked ball at the Círculo de Bellas Artes on the following night. Fancy-dress competitions last until Ash Wednesday, when the festivities end with a tear-jerking "burial of a sardine" at the Fuente de los Pajaritos in the Casa de Campo. This is followed that evening by a concert in the Plaza Mayor. Call ✆ **91-588-16-36** or visit www.gospain.org for more information. Dates vary. Normally 40 days before Easter.

Carnavales de Cádiz, Cádiz. The oldest and best-attended carnival in Spain is a freewheeling event full of costumes, parades, strolling troubadours, and drum beating. Call ✆ **95-622-71-11** or go to www.carnavaldecadiz.com for more information. Early February or early March.

MARCH

Fallas de Valencia, Valencia. Dating from the 1400s, this fiesta centers on the burning of papier-mâché effigies of winter demons. Burnings are preceded by bullfights, fireworks, and parades. For more information, contact ✆ **96-352-17-30** or go to www.fallasfromvalencia.com. Early to mid-March.

Semana Santa (Holy Week), Seville. Although many of the country's smaller towns stage similar celebrations (especially notable in Zamora), the festivities in Seville are by far the most elaborate. From Palm Sunday until Easter Sunday, processions of hooded penitents move to the piercing wail of the *saeta,* a love song to the Virgin or Christ. *Pasos* (heavy floats) bear images of the Virgin or Christ. Make hotel reservations way in advance. Call the Seville Office of Tourism for details (✆ **95-421-00-05**). The week before Easter.

APRIL

Feria de Sevilla (Seville Fair). This is the most celebrated week of revelry in all of Spain, with all-night flamenco dancing, entertainment booths, bullfights, horseback riding, flower-decked coaches, and dancing in the streets. You'll need to reserve a hotel early for this one. For general information and exact festival dates, contact the Office of Tourism in Seville (✆ **95-421-00-05**). Second week after Easter.

Moros y Cristianos (Moors and Christians), Alcoy, near Alicante. During 3 days every April, the centuries-old battle between the Moors and the Christians is restaged with soldiers in period costumes. Naturally, the Christians who drove the Moors from Spain always win. The simulated fighting takes on almost a circuslike flair, and the costumes worn by the Moors are always absurd and anachronistic. Call ✆ **96-514-34-52** or visit www.alicantecongresos.com for more information. Late April.

MAY

Feria del Caballo, Jerez de la Frontera. The major wine festival in Andalusia honors the famous sherry of Jerez, with 5 days of processions, flamenco dancing, livestock on parade, and, of course, sherry drinking. For information, call ✆ **95-633-11-50.** Mid-May.

Festival de los Patios, Córdoba. At this famous fair, residents decorate their patios with cascades of flowers. Visitors wander from patio to patio. Call

✆ **95-749-16-77** for more information. First 2 weeks of May.

Fiesta de San Isidro, Madrid. Madrileños run wild with a 10-day celebration honoring their city's patron saint. Food fairs, Castilian folkloric events, street parades, parties, music, dances, bullfights, and other festivities mark the occasion. Make hotel reservations early. Expect crowds and traffic (and beware of pickpockets). For information, write to Oficina Municipal de Información y Turismo, Plaza Mayor 3, 28014 Madrid; or call ✆ **91-366-54-77.** May 15.

Romería del Rocío (Pilgrimage of the Virgin of the Dew), El Rocío (Huelva). The most famous pilgrimage in Andalusia attracts a million people. Fifty men carry the statue of the Virgin 15km (9⅓ miles) to Almonte for consecration. Third week of May.

JUNE

Corpus Christi, all over Spain. A major holiday on the Spanish calendar, this event is marked by big processions, especially in Toledo, Málaga, Seville, and Granada. June 2.

Veranos de la Villa, Madrid. This program presents folkloric dancing, pop music, classical music, *zarzuelas,* and flamenco at venues throughout the city. Open-air cinema is a feature in the Parque del Retiro. Ask at the tourist office for complete details. (The program changes every summer.) Sometimes admission is charged, but often these events are free. Mid-June until the end of August.

International Music and Dance Festival, Granada. Since 1952, Granada's prestigious program of dance and music has attracted international artists who perform at the Alhambra and other venues. It's a major event on Europe's cultural calendar. Reserve well in advance. For a complete schedule and tickets, contact El Festival Internacional de Música y Danza de Granada (✆ **95-822-18-44;**

www.granadafestival.org). Last week of June to first week of July.

Las Hogueras de San Juan (St. John's Bonfires), Alicante. Bonfires blaze through the night to honor the summer solstice, just as they did in Celtic and Roman times. The bonfire signals the launching of 5 days of gala celebrations with fireworks and parades. Business in Alicante comes to a standstill. Call ✆ **98-120-24-06** or go to www. hoguerassanjuan.com for more information. June 20 to June 24.

Verbena de Sant Joan, Barcelona. This traditional festival occupies all Catalans. Barcelona literally lights up—with fireworks, bonfires, and dances until dawn. The highlight of the festival is the fireworks show at Montjuïc. Late June.

JULY

La Rapa das Bestas (The Capture of the Beasts), San Lorenzo de Sabucedo, Galicia. Spain's greatest horse roundup attracts equestrian lovers from throughout Europe. Horses in the verdant hills of northwestern Spain are rounded up, branded, and medically checked before their release into the wild again. For more information, phone ✆ **98-154-63-51** or go to www.galinor.es. First weekend in July.

Festival of St. James, Santiago de Compostela. Pomp and ceremony mark this annual pilgrimage to the tomb of St. James the Apostle in Galicia. Galician folklore shows, concerts, parades, and the swinging of the *botafumeiro* (a mammoth incense burner) mark the event. July 15 to July 30.

Fiesta de San Fermín, Pamplona. Vividly described in Ernest Hemingway's novel *The Sun Also Rises,* the running of the bulls through the streets of Pamplona is the most popular celebration in Spain. It includes wine tasting, fireworks, and, of course, bullfights. Reserve many months in advance. For more information, such as a list of accommodations, contact the

Office of Tourism, Calle Eslava 1, 31002 Pamplona (✆ **84-842-04-20;** www. sanfermin.com). July 6 to July 14.

San Sebastián Jazz Festival, San Sebastián. Celebrating its 45th year in 2010, this festival brings the jazz greats of the world together in the Kursaal. Other programs take place alfresco at the Plaza de Trinidad in the Old Quarter. The Office of the San Sebastián Jazz Festival (✆ **94-348-19-00;** www. heinekenjazzaldia.com) can provide schedules and tickets. Late July.

AUGUST

Santander International Festival of Music and Dance, Santander. The repertoire includes classical music, ballet, contemporary dance, chamber music, and recitals. Most performances are staged in the Palacio de Festivales, a centrally located auditorium custom-built for this event. For further information, contact Festival Internacional de Santander (✆ **94-221-05-08;** www.festival santander.com). Throughout August.

Fiestas of Lavapiés and La Paloma, Madrid. These two fiestas begin with the Lavapiés on August 1 and continue through the hectic La Paloma celebration on August 15, the Day of the Virgen de la Paloma. During the fiestas, thousands of people race through the narrow streets. Apartment dwellers hurl buckets of cold water onto the crowds below to cool them off. There are children's games, floats, music, flamenco, and *zarzuelas,* along with street fairs. For more information, call ✆ **91-366-54-77** or go to www.gospain.org. Two weeks in early August.

Misteri d'Elx (Mystery of Elche). This sacred drama is reenacted in the 17th-century Basilica of Santa María in Elche (near Alicante). It represents the Assumption and the Crowning of the Virgin. For tickets, call the Office of Tourism in Elche (✆ **96-741-11-00**). August 11 to August 15.

Feria de Málaga (Málaga Fair). One of the longest summer fairs in southern Europe (generally lasting 10 days), this celebration kicks off with fireworks displays and is highlighted by a parade of Arabian horses pulling brightly decorated carriages. Participants are dressed in colorful Andalusian garb. Plazas rattle with castanets, and wine is dispensed by the gallon. For information, call ℂ **95-289-78-65** or visit www.andalucia.com. Always the weekend before August 19.

La Tomatina (Battle of the Tomatoes), Buñol (Valencia). This is one of the most photographed festivals in Spain, growing in popularity every year. Truckloads of tomatoes are shipped into Buñol, where they become vegetable missiles between warring towns and villages. Portable showers are brought in for the cleanup, followed by music for dancing and singing. For information, call ℂ **96-250-01-51.** Last Wednesday in August.

SEPTEMBER

Diada de Catalunya, Barcelona. This is the most significant festival in Catalonia. It celebrates the region's autonomy from the rest of Spain, following years of repression under the dictator Franco. Demonstrations and other flag-waving events take place. The *senyera,* the flag of Catalonia, is everywhere. Not your typical tourist fare, but interesting. September 11.

San Sebastián International Film Festival, San Sebastián. The premier film festival of Spain takes place in the Basque capital, often at several different theaters. Retrospectives are frequently featured, and weeklong screenings are held. For more information, call ℂ **94-348-12-12** or go to www.sansebastian festival.com. Second week in September.

Fiestas de la Merced, Barcelona. This celebration honors Nostra Senyora de la Merced, the city's patron saint, known for her compassion for animals. Beginning after dark, and after a Mass in the Iglesia de la Merced, a procession of as many as 50 "animals" (humans dressed like tigers, lions, and horses) proceeds with lots of firecrackers and sparklers to the Cathedral of Santa Eulalia, and then on to Plaza de Sant Jaume, and eventually into Les Rambles, Plaza de Catalunya, and the harborfront. For more information, call ℂ **93-486-00-98** or go to www.bcn.es. Mid-September.

OCTOBER

St. Teresa Week, Avila. *Verbenas* (carnivals), parades, singing, and dancing honor the patron saint of this walled city. October 8 to October 15.

Autumn Festival, Madrid. Both Spanish and international artists participate in this cultural program, with a series of operatic, ballet, dance, music, and theatrical performances from Strasbourg to Tokyo. This event is a premier attraction, yet tickets are reasonably priced. Make hotel reservations early. For tickets, contact Festival de Otoño, c/o Teatro de Madrid, Avenida de la Ilustración, 28013 Madrid (ℂ **91-720-81-83;** www.madrid. org). Late October to late November.

NOVEMBER

All Saints' Day, all over Spain. This public holiday is reverently celebrated, as relatives and friends lay flowers on the graves of the dead. November 1.

DECEMBER

Día de los Santos Inocentes, all over Spain. This equivalent of April Fools' Day gives people an excuse to do *loco* things. December 28.

ENTRY REQUIREMENTS

Passports

For information on how to get a passport, go to "Passports," under "Fast Facts: Spain," on p. 780; the websites listed provide downloadable passport applications as well as the current fees for processing passport applications. For up-to-date passport requirements for countries around the world, check out the **Consular Information Sheets** at the U.S. State Department website (start at http://travel.state.gov).

Visas

Visas are not needed by U.S., Canadian, Irish, Australian, New Zealand, or British citizens for visits of less than 3 months.

For information on obtaining a visa, see your consulate or embassy. For a list of embassies, see p. 777.

Customs

WHAT YOU CAN BRING INTO SPAIN

You can bring into Spain most personal effects and the following items duty-free: one portable typewriter, and one video camera or two still cameras with 10 rolls of film each; one portable radio, one tape recorder, and one laptop per person, provided they show signs of use; 400 cigarettes, or 50 cigars, or 250 grams of tobacco; and 2 liters of wine or 1 liter of liquor per person ages 18 and over. For sports equipment you are allowed fishing gear, one bicycle, skis, tennis or squash racquets, and golf clubs.

WHAT YOU CAN TAKE HOME FROM SPAIN

U.S. CITIZENS For specifics on what you can bring back and the corresponding fees, download the invaluable free pamphlet *Know Before You Go* online at **www.cbp.gov**. (Click on "Travel," and then click on "Know Before You Go.") Or contact the **U.S. Customs & Border Protection (CBP),** 1300 Pennsylvania Ave., NW, Washington, DC 20229 (✆ **877/287-8667**), and request the pamphlet.

CANADIAN CITIZENS For a clear summary of Canadian rules, write for the booklet *I Declare,* issued by the **Canada Border Services Agency** (✆ **800/461-9999** in Canada, or 204/983-3500; www.cbsa-asfc.gc.ca).

U.K. CITIZENS For information, contact **HM Revenue & Customs** at ✆ **02920/501-261** (from outside the U.K., 020/8929-0152), or consult the website at www.hmrc.gov.uk.

AUSTRALIAN CITIZENS A helpful brochure available from Australian consulates or Customs offices is *Know Before You Go.* For more information, call the **Australian Customs Service** at ✆ **1300/363-263,** or log on to www.customs.gov.au.

NEW ZEALAND CITIZENS Most questions are answered in a free pamphlet available at New Zealand consulates and Customs offices: *New Zealand Customs Guide for Travellers, Notice no. 4.* For more information, contact **New Zealand Customs,** The Customhouse, 17–21 Whitmore St., Box 2218, Wellington (✆ **04/473-6099** or 0800/428-786; www.customs.govt.nz).

Medical Requirements

Unless you're arriving from an area known to be suffering from an epidemic (particularly cholera or yellow fever), inoculations or vaccinations are not required for entry into Spain.

GETTING THERE & GETTING AROUND
Getting to Spain
BY PLANE

FROM NORTH AMERICA Flights from the U.S. East Coast to Spain take 6 to 7 hours. Spain's national carrier, **Iberia Airlines** (© 800/772-4642; www. iberia.com), has more routes into and within Spain than any other airline. It offers daily nonstop service to Madrid from New York, Chicago, and Miami. Also available are attractive rates on fly/drive packages within Iberia and Europe; they can substantially reduce the cost of both the air ticket and the car rental.

Iberia's main Spain-based competitor is **Air Europa** (© 011-34-902-401-501; www.aireuropa.com), which offers nonstop service from Newark (New Jersey) to Madrid, with continuing service to major cities within Spain. Fares are usually lower than Iberia's.

American Airlines (© 800/433-7300; www.aa.com) offers daily nonstop service to Madrid from its massive hub in Miami.

Delta (© 800/221-1212; www.delta.com) runs daily nonstop service from Atlanta (its worldwide hub) and New York (JFK) to both Madrid and Barcelona. Delta's Dream Vacation department offers independent fly/drive packages, land packages, and escorted bus tours.

Continental Airlines (© 800/231-0856; www.continental.com) offers daily nonstop flights, depending on the season, to Madrid from Newark.

AmericaWest/US Airways (© 800/622-1015; www.usairways.com) offers daily nonstop service between Philadelphia and Madrid. The carrier also has connecting flights to Philadelphia from more than 50 cities throughout the United States, Canada, and the Bahamas.

FROM THE U.K. **British Airways** (© 0844/493-0787, or 800/247-9297 in the U.S.; www.britishairways.com) and **Iberia** (© 0870/609-0500 in London; www.iberia.com) are the two major carriers flying between England and Spain. More than a dozen daily flights, on either British Airways or Iberia, depart from London's Heathrow and Gatwick airports. The Midlands is served by flights from Manchester and Birmingham, two major airports that can also be used by Scottish travelers flying to Spain. There are about seven flights a day from London to Madrid and back, and at least six to Barcelona (trip time: 2–2½ hr.). From either the Madrid airport or the Barcelona airport, you can tap into Iberia's domestic network—flying, for example, to Seville or the Costa del Sol. The best air deals on scheduled flights from England are those requiring a Saturday-night stopover.

British newspapers are filled with classified advertisements touting "slashed" fares to Spain. London's *Evening Standard* has a daily travel section, and the Sunday editions of most papers are filled with charter deals. A travel agent can advise you on the best values at the intended time of your departure.

Charter flights to specific destinations leave from most British regional airports (for example, to Málaga), bypassing the congestion at the Barcelona and Madrid airports. Figure on saving approximately 10% to 15% on regularly scheduled flight tickets. But check carefully into the restrictions and terms; read the fine print, especially in regard to cancellation penalties. One recommended company is **Trailfinders** (✆ **0845/058-5858** in London; www.trailfinders.com), which operates charters.

In London, the many bucket shops around Victoria Station and Earl's Court offer cheap fares. Make sure the company you deal with is a member of IATA, ABTA, or ATOL. These umbrella organizations will help you if anything goes wrong.

CEEFAX, the British television information service, runs details of package holidays and flights to Europe and beyond. Switch to your CEEFAX channel and you'll find travel information.

FROM AUSTRALIA From Australia, a number of options are available for your flight to Spain. The most popular is **Qantas/British Airways** (✆ **612/13-13-13;** www.quantas.com.au), which flies daily via Asia and London. Other popular and cheaper options are Qantas/Lufthansa via Asia and Frankfurt; Qantas/Air France via Asia and Paris; and Alitalia via Bangkok and Rome. The most direct option is offered by Singapore Airlines, with just one stop in Singapore. Alternatively, there are flights on Thai Airways via Bangkok and Rome, but the connections are not always good.

BY CAR

If you're touring the rest of Europe in a rented car, you might, for an added cost, be allowed to drop off your vehicle in a major city such as Madrid or Barcelona.

Highway approaches to Spain are across France on expressways. The most popular border crossing is near Biarritz, but there are 17 other border stations between Spain and France. If you plan to visit the north or west of Spain (Galicia), the Hendaye-Irún border is the most convenient frontier crossing. If you're going to Barcelona or Catalonia and along the Levante coast (Valencia), take the expressway in France to Toulouse, then the A-61 to Narbonne, and then the A-9 toward the border crossing at La Junquera. You can also take the RN-20, with a border station at Puigcerdà.

If you're driving from Britain, make sure you have a cross-Channel reservation, as traffic tends to be very heavy, especially in summer.

The major ferry crossings connect Dover and Folkestone with Dunkirk. Newhaven is connected with Dieppe, and the British city of Portsmouth with Roscoff. Taking a car on the ferry from Dover to Calais on **P & O Ferries** (✆ **0871/664-5645;** www.poferries.com) costs £45 to £50 and takes 1¼ hours. This cost includes the car and two passengers.

You can take the Chunnel, the underwater Channel Tunnel linking Britain (Folkestone) and France (Calais) by road and rail. **Eurostar** tickets, for train service between London and Paris or Brussels, are available through Rail Europe (✆ **877/272-RAIL** [272-7245]; www.raileurope.com or www.eurostar.com for information). In London, make reservations for Eurostar at ✆ **0870/518-6186.** The tunnel also accommodates passenger cars, charter buses, taxis, and motorcycles, transporting them under the English Channel from Folkestone, England, to Calais, France. It operates 24 hours a day, 365 days a year, running every 15 minutes during peak travel times, and at least once an hour at night. Tickets may be purchased at the tollbooth at the tunnel's entrance. With "Eurotunnel," gone are the days of weather-related delays, seasickness, and advance reservations.

Once you land, you'll have about a 15-hour drive to Spain.

If you plan to transport a rental car between England and France, check in advance with the rental company about license and insurance requirements and additional drop-off charges. And be aware that many car-rental companies, for insurance reasons, forbid transport of one of their vehicles over the water between England and France.

BY TRAIN

If you're already in Europe, you might want to go to Spain by train, especially if you have a Eurailpass. Even without a pass, you'll find that the cost of a train ticket is relatively moderate. Rail passengers who visit from Britain or France should make couchette and sleeper reservations as far in advance as possible, especially during the peak summer season.

Since Spain's rail tracks are of a wider gauge than those used for French trains (except for the TALGO and Trans-Europe-Express trains), you'll probably have to change trains at the border unless you're on an express train (see below). For long journeys on Spanish rails, seat and sleeper reservations are mandatory. For more information call ℂ **011-34-91-631-38-00,** or visit www.talgo.com.

The most comfortable and the fastest trains in Spain are the TER, TALGO, and Electrotren. However, you pay a supplement to ride on these fast trains. Both first- and second-class fares are sold on Spanish trains. Tickets can be purchased in the United States or Canada at the nearest office of Rail Europe or from any reputable travel agent. Confirmation of your reservation takes about a week.

If you want your car carried aboard the train, you must travel Auto-Expreso in Spain. This type of auto transport can be booked only through travel agents or rail offices once you arrive in Europe.

To go from London to Spain by rail, you'll need to transfer not only from the train but also from the rail terminus in Paris. In Paris it's worth the extra bucks to purchase a TALGO express or a "Puerta del Sol" express—that way, you can avoid having to change trains once again at the Spanish border. Trip time from London to Paris is about 6 hours; from Paris to Madrid, about 15 hours, which includes 2 hours spent in Paris just changing trains and stations. Many different rail passes are available in the United Kingdom for travel in Europe.

BY BUS

Bus travel to Spain is possible but not popular—it's quite slow. (Service from London will take 24 hr. or more.) But coach services do operate regularly from major capitals of Western Europe and, once they're in Spain, usually head for Madrid or Barcelona. The major bus line running from London to Spain is **Eurolines Limited,** 52 Grosvenor Gardens, London SW1W 0AU, U.K. (ℂ **0871/781-8181;** www.nationalexpress.com). Calls cost 10p per minute.

Getting Around Spain

BY PLANE

By European standards, domestic flights within Spain are relatively inexpensive, and considering the vast distances within the country, flying between distant points sometimes makes sense. For reservations on the national airline, Iberia, call © **800/772-4642.**

If you plan to travel to a number of cities and regions, Iberia's "Visit Spain" Air Pass can be a good deal. Sold only in conjunction with a transatlantic ticket and valid for any airport within Spain and the Canary or Balearic Islands, it requires that you choose up to four different cities in advance, in the order you'll visit them. Restrictions forbid flying immediately back to the city of departure, instead encouraging far-flung visits to widely scattered regions of the peninsula. Only one change within the preset itinerary is permitted once the ticket is issued. The dates and departure times of the actual flights, however, can be determined or changed without penalty once you arrive in Spain. The actual costs depend on what kind of ticket you are issued—consult the folks at Iberia if you're interested in a multistopover ticket and see what the best deal is at the time of your visit. Children 1 and under travel for 10% of the adult fare, and children 2 to 11 travel for 50% of the adult fare. The ticket is valid for up to 60 days after your initial transatlantic arrival in Spain.

BY CAR

A car offers the greatest flexibility while you're touring, even if you're just doing day trips from Madrid. Don't, however, plan to drive in Madrid or Barcelona for city sightseeing; they are both too congested. Theoretically, rush hour is Monday to Saturday from 8 to 10am, 1 to 2pm, and 4 to 6pm. In reality, though, it's all the time.

RENTALS Many of North America's biggest car-rental companies, including Avis, Budget, and Hertz, maintain offices throughout Spain. Although several Spanish car-rental companies exist, we've received lots of letters from readers of previous editions telling us they've had hard times resolving billing irregularities and insurance claims, so you might want to stick with the U.S.-based rental firms.

Note that tax on car rentals is a whopping 15%, so don't forget to factor that into your travel budget. Usually, prepaid rates do not include taxes, which will be collected at the rental kiosk itself. Be sure to ask explicitly what's included when you're quoted a rate.

Avis (© **800/331-1084;** www.avis.com) maintains about 100 branches throughout Spain, including about a dozen in Madrid, eight in Barcelona, a half-dozen in Seville, and four in Murcia. If you reserve and pay for your rental by telephone at least 2 weeks before your departure from North America, you'll qualify for the company's best rate, with unlimited kilometers included. You can usually get competitive rates from **Hertz** (© **800/654-3001;** www.hertz.com) and **Budget** (© **800/472-3325;** www.budget.com); it always pays to comparison shop. Budget doesn't have a drop-off charge if you pick up a car in one Spanish city and return it to another. All three companies require that drivers be at least 21 years of age and, in some cases, not older than 72. To be able to rent a car, you must have a passport and a valid driver's license; you must also have a valid credit card or a prepaid voucher. An international driver's license is not essential, but you might want to present it if you have one; it's available from any North American office of the American Automobile Association (AAA).

Two other agencies of note include **Kemwel Drive Europe** (© **877/820-0668;** www.kemwel.com) and **Auto Europe** (© **888/223-5555;** www.autoeurope.com).

Getting There & Getting Around

PLANNING YOUR TRIP TO SPAIN

Internet resources can make comparison shopping easier. **Expedia** (www.expedia.com) and **Travelocity** (www.travelocity.com) help you compare prices and locate car-rental bargains from various companies nationwide. They will even make your reservation for you once you've found the best deal.

DRIVING RULES Spaniards drive on the right side of the road. Drivers should pass on the left; local drivers sound their horns when passing another car and flash their lights at you if you're driving slowly (slowly for high-speed Spain) in the left lane. Autos coming from the right have the right of way.

Spain's express highways are known as *autopistas,* which charge a toll, and *autovías,* which don't. To exit in Spain, follow the SALIDA (exit) sign, except in Catalonia, where the exit sign says SORTIDA. On most express highways, the speed limit is 120kmph (75 mph). On other roads, speed limits range from 90kmph to 100kmph (56–62 mph). You will see many drivers far exceeding these limits.

The greatest number of accidents in Spain are recorded along the notorious Costa del Sol highway, Carretera de Cádiz.

If you must drive through a Spanish city, try to avoid morning and evening rush hours. Never park your car facing oncoming traffic, which is against the law. If you are fined by the highway patrol (*Guardia Civil de Tráfico*), you must pay on the spot. Penalties for drinking and driving are very stiff.

BREAKDOWNS These can be a serious problem. If you're driving a Spanish-made vehicle that needs parts, you'll probably be able to find them. But if you are driving a foreign-made vehicle, you may be stranded. Have the car checked before setting out on a long trek through Spain. On a major motorway you'll find strategically placed emergency phone boxes. On secondary roads, call for help by asking the operator to locate the nearest Guardia Civil, which will put you in touch with a garage that can tow you to a repair shop.

The Spanish affiliate of AAA—**Real Automóvil Club de España** (**RACE;** ✆ **90-240-45-45;** www.race.es)—can provide limited assistance in the event of a breakdown.

BY TRAIN

Spain is crisscrossed with a comprehensive network of rail lines. Hundreds of trains depart every day for points around the country, including the fast TALGO and the newer, faster AVE trains, which reduced rail time between Madrid and Seville to only 2½ hours.

If you plan to travel a great deal on the European railroads, it's worth buying a copy of the ***Thomas Cook Timetable of European Passenger Railroads.*** It's available exclusively online at www.thomascookpublishing.com.

The most economical way to travel in Spain is on Spanish State Railways (RENFE), the national railway of Spain. Most main long-distance connections are served with night express trains having first- and second-class seats as well as beds and bunks. There are also comfortable high-speed daytime trains of the TALGO, TER, and Electrotren types. You pay a general fare for these trains; bunks, beds, and certain superior-quality trains cost extra. Nevertheless, the Spanish railway is one of the most economical in Europe; in most cases, this is the best way to go.

SPANISH RAIL PASSES RENFE, the national railway of Spain, offers several discounted rail passes. You must buy these passes in the United States prior to your departure. For more information, consult a travel agent or **Rail Europe** (© **877/272-RAIL** [272-7245]; www.raileurope.com).

The **Eurail Spain Pass** entitles you to unlimited rail travel in Spain. It is available for 3 to 10 days of travel within 2 months in both first and second class. For 3 days within 2 months, the cost is 191€ in first class or 153€ in second class; for 10 days within 2 months, the charge is 391€ in first class or 313€ in second class. Children 4 to 11 pay half-fare on any of these discount passes.

The **Eurail Spain-Portugal Pass,** good for both Spain and Portugal, offers 3 to 10 days of unlimited first-class train travel in a 2-month period. Prices start at 219€ for 3 days. **Eurail Spain 'n Portugal Saverpass,** again including both Spain and Portugal, offers any 3 to 10 days unlimited, first-class train travel in a 2-month period starting at 219€ for 3 days.

The **Eurail France-Spain Pass,** good for both Spain and France, offers 4 to 10 days of unlimited train travel in a 2-month period. First-class prices start at 261€, while second-class rates are 228€.

EURAILPASS   The Eurailpass permits unlimited first-class rail travel in any country in western Europe except the British Isles (good in Ireland). Passes are available for purchase online (www.eurail.com) and at various offices/agents around the world. Travel agents and railway agents in such cities as New York, Montreal, and Los Angeles sell Eurailpasses. You can purchase them at the North American offices of CIT Travel Service, the French National Railroads, the German Federal Railroads, and the Swiss Federal Railways. It is strongly recommended that you purchase passes before you leave home as not all passes are available in Europe; also, passes purchased in Europe will cost about 20% more. Numerous options are available for travel in France.

The **Eurail Global Pass** allows you unlimited travel in 21 Eurail-affiliated countries. You can travel on any of the days within the validity period, which is available for 15 days, 21 days, 1 month, 2 months, 3 months, and some other possibilities as well. Prices for first-class adult travel are 511€ for 15 days, 662€ for 21 days, 822€ for 1 month, 1,161€ for 2 months, and 1,432€ for 3 months. Children 4 to 11 pay half-fare; those 3 and under travel for free.

A **Eurail Global Pass Saver,** also valid for first-class travel in 21 countries, offers a special deal for two or more people traveling together. This pass costs 433€ for 15 days, 562€ for 21 days, 698€ for 1 month, 986€ for 2 months, and 1,221€ for 3 months.

A **Eurail Global Youth Pass,** for those 12 to 25, allows second-class travel in 18 countries. This pass costs 332€ for 15 days, 429€ for 21 days, 535€ for 1 month, 755€ for 2 months, and 933€ for 3 months.

The **Eurail Select Pass** offers unlimited travel on the national rail networks of any 3, 4, or 5 bordering countries out of the 22 Eurail nations linked by train or ship. Two or more passengers can travel together for big discounts, getting 5, 6, 8, 10, or 15 days of rail travel within any 2-month period on the national rail networks of any three, four, or five adjoining Eurail countries linked by train or ship. A sample fare: For 5 days in 2 months you pay 211€ for three countries. **Eurail Select Pass Youth,** for travelers 25 and under, allows second-class travel within the same guidelines as Eurail Selectpass, with fees starting at 332€. **Eurail Select Pass Saver** offers discounts for two or more people traveling together, first-class travel within the same guidelines as Eurail Select Pass, with fees starting at 433€.

WHERE TO BUY RAIL PASSES Travel agents in all towns and railway agents in major North American cities sell all these tickets, but the biggest supplier is **Rail Europe** (✆ 877/272-RAIL [272-7245]; www.raileurope.com), which can also give you informational brochures.

Many different rail passes are available in the United Kingdom for travel in Britain and continental Europe. Stop in at the **International Rail Centre,** Victoria Station, London SWIV 1JY (✆ **0870/5848-848** in the U.K.). Some of the most popular passes, including Inter-Rail and Euro Youth, are offered only to travelers ages 25 and under; these allow unlimited second-class travel through most European countries.

BY BUS

Bus service in Spain is extensive, low priced, and comfortable enough for short distances. You'll rarely encounter a bus terminal in Spain. The station might be a cafe, a bar, the street in front of a hotel, or simply a spot at an intersection.

A bus may be the cheapest mode of transportation, but it's not really the best option for distances of more than 160km (100 miles). On long hauls, buses are often uncomfortable. Another major drawback might be a lack of toilet facilities, although rest stops are frequent. A bus is best for 1-day excursions outside a major tourist center such as Madrid. In the rural areas of the country, bus networks are more extensive than the railway system; they go virtually everywhere, connecting every village. In general, a bus ride between two major cities in Spain, such as from Córdoba to Seville or Madrid to Barcelona, is about two-thirds the price of a train ride and a few hours faster. (This doesn't include high-speed AVE trains.)

MONEY & COSTS

THE VALUE OF THE EURO VS. OTHER POPULAR CURRENCIES

Euro (€)	US$	UK£	C$	A$	NZ$
1€	$1.29	.85	C$1.36	A$1.47	NZ$1.81

Frommer's lists exact prices in the local currency. The currency conversions quoted above were correct at press time. However, rates fluctuate, so before departing consult a currency exchange website, such as **www.oanda.com/currency/converter** to check up-to-the-minute rates.

If there is one thing old Spaniards wax nostalgic over, it's not the police state they experienced under the dictatorship of Franco, but the prices paid back then. The **euro** became the official currency of Spain and 11 other participating countries on January 1, 1999 (for details on the euro, check out www.europa.eu), but how they miss the days when you could go into a restaurant and order a meal with wine for the equivalent of 50¢.

Regrettably, Spain is no longer a budget destination. In such major cities as Barcelona or Madrid, you can often find hotels charging the same prices as ones in London or Paris. Once you move beyond Spain's tourist meccas into regional towns, provincial capitals, and especially the countryside, the prices drop considerably. For example, it's possible to enjoy a 6-week vacation in rural Spain for about the same price that 10 days to 2 weeks could cost in Madrid.

Taken as a whole, though, Spain remains slightly below the cost-of-living index of such countries as England, Germany, Italy, and France. Unfortunately, there is a very unfavorable exchange rate in Spain when you pay in U.S. dollars, though at press time the dollar had strengthened somewhat in recent months.

Prices in Spain are generally high, but you get good value for your money. Hotels are usually clean and comfortable, and restaurants generally offer good cuisine and ample portions made with quality ingredients. Trains are fast and on time, and most service personnel treat you with respect.

In Spain, many prices for children—generally defined as ages 6 to 17—are lower than for adults. Fees for children 5 and under are generally waived.

It's always advisable to bring money in a variety of forms on a vacation: a mix of cash, credit cards, and traveler's checks. You should also exchange enough petty cash to cover airport incidentals, tipping, and transportation to your hotel before you leave home, or withdraw money upon arrival at an airport ATM.

In many international destinations, ATMs offer the best exchange rates. Avoid exchanging money at commercial exchange bureaus and hotels, which often have the highest transaction fees.

MAJOR CHANGE IN credit cards

Chip and PIN represent a change in the way that credit and debit cards are used. The program is designed to cut down on the fraudulent use of credit cards. More and more banks are issuing customers Chip and PIN versions of their debit or credit cards. In the future, more and more vendors will be asking for a four-digit personal identification or PIN, which will be entered into a keypad near the cash register. In some cases, a waiter will bring a hand-held model to your table to verify your credit card.

In the changeover in technology, some retailers have falsely concluded that they can no longer take swipe cards, or can't take signature cards that don't have PINs anymore.

For the time being both the new and old cards are used in shops, hotels, and restaurants regardless of whether they have the old credit and debit cards machines or the new Chip and PIN machines installed. Expect a lot of confusion before you arrive in Spain or elsewhere.

In the interim between traditional swipe credit cards and those with an embedded computer chip, here's what you can do to protect yourself:

o Get a four-digit PIN from your credit card's issuing bank before leaving home, or call the number on the back of each card and ask for a four-digit PIN.

o Keep an eye out for the right logo displayed in a retailer's window. You want Visa or MasterCard, not Maestro, Visa Electron, or Carte Bleue.

o Know that your Amex card will work where an Amex logo is displayed, but the card is not as widely accepted as Visa and MasterCard.

o As a last resort, make sure you have enough cash to cover your purchase.

Taxi from the airport to Puerta del Sol	25€
Public Transportation within the city	1€
Double Room at the Westin Palace (very expensive)	198€
Double Room at the Hotel Meninas (moderate)	109€
Double room at the Hostal Cervantes (inexpensive)	60€
Lunch for one, without wine, at Lhardy (expensive)	64€
Lunch for one, without wine, at La Biotika (inexpensive)	9.90€
Dinner for one, without wine, at Santceloni (very expensive)	132€
Dinner for one, without wine, at Fast Good Madrid (inexpensive)	12€
Coca-Cola in a restaurant	2.50€
Cup of coffee in a café	2.75€
Admission to the Prado	8€
Movie ticket	11€
Theater ticket	25€–80€

HEALTH
Staying Healthy

Spain should not pose any major health hazards. The rich cuisine—garlic, olive oil, and wine—may give some travelers mild diarrhea, so take along antidiarrhea medicine, moderate your eating habits, and even though the water is generally safe, drink bottled or mineral water. (Do not drink the water in mountain streams, regardless of how clear and pure it looks.) Fish and shellfish from the horrendously polluted Mediterranean should be eaten only if cooked.

If you are traveling around Spain (particularly southern Spain) over the summer, limit your exposure to the sun, especially during the first few days of your trip and, thereafter, from 11am to 2pm. Use a sunscreen with a high sun protection factor (SPF) and apply it liberally. Remember that children need more protection than adults do.

GENERAL AVAILABILITY OF HEALTHCARE

Spanish medical facilities are among the best in the world. If a medical emergency arises, your hotel staff can usually put you in touch with a reliable doctor. If not, contact the American embassy or a consulate; each one maintains a list of English-speaking doctors. Medical and hospital services aren't free, so be sure that you have appropriate insurance coverage before you travel.

Contact the **International Association for Medical Assistance to Travelers (IAMAT;** ⓒ **716/754-4883,** or 416/652-0137 in Canada; www.iamat.org) for tips on travel and health concerns in the countries you're visiting, and for lists of local, English-speaking doctors. The United States **Centers** for **Disease Control and Prevention** (𝄞 **800/CDC-INFO** [232-4636] or 404/498-1515; www.cdc.gov) provides up-to-date information on health hazards by region or country and offers tips on food safety. **Travel Health Online** (www.tripprep.com), sponsored by a consortium of travel medicine practitioners, may also offer helpful advice on traveling abroad. You can find listings of reliable medical clinics overseas at the **International Society of Travel Medicine** (www.istm.org).

In Canada, contact **Health Canada** (𝄞 **613/957-2991;** www.hc-sc.gc.ca).

What to Do If You Get Sick Away From Home

For travel abroad, you may have to pay all medical costs upfront and be reimbursed later. Medicare and Medicaid do not provide coverage for medical costs outside the U.S. Before leaving home, find out what medical services your health insurance covers. To protect yourself, consider buying medical travel insurance (see "Insurance," under "Fast Facts: Spain," on p. 778).

Very few health insurance plans pay for medical evacuation back to the U.S. (which can cost $10,000 and up). A number of companies offer medical evacuation services anywhere in the world. If you're ever hospitalized more than 150 miles from home, **MedjetAssist** (𝄞 **800/527-7478;** www.medjetassist.com) will pick you up and fly you to the hospital of your choice virtually anywhere in the world in a medically equipped and staffed aircraft 24 hours a day, 7 days a week. Annual memberships are $250 individual, $385 family; you can also purchase short-term memberships.

U.K. nationals will need a **European Health Insurance Card** (**EHIC;** 𝄞 **0845/605-0707;** www.ehic.org.uk) to receive free or reduced-cost health benefits during a visit to a European Economic Area (EEA) country (E.U. countries plus Iceland, Liechtenstein, and Norway) or Switzerland. The European Health Insurance Card replaces the E111 form, which is no longer valid. For advice, ask at your local post office.

We list **hospital** and **emergency numbers** in the "Fast Facts" sections for Madrid, Valencia, Alicante, and Barcelona (chapters 5, 11, and 12); you'll find additional emergency numbers under "Fast Facts: Spain," on p. 777.

If you suffer from a chronic illness, consult your doctor before your departure. Pack **prescription medications** in your carry-on luggage, and carry them in their original containers, with pharmacy labels—otherwise they won't make it through airport security. Carry the generic name of prescription medicines, in case a local pharmacist is unfamiliar with the brand name.

SAFETY

Spain became a victim of terror on March 11, 2004, when terrorists attacked its rail system in Madrid, slaughtering innocent people. The terrorists left 13 backpacks and gym bags in commuter trains as they pulled into three of the city's most crowded stations. Each held some 25 pounds of high explosives, with detonators wired to cellphones. As they rang, 10 of the bombs went off, causing massive carnage and the loss of 191 lives, with an additional 1,800 injured. No terrorist operation that big had ever hit Western Europe.

What can you do to protect yourself from terrorist attacks? Regrettably, very little. Spanish tourism officials at first feared massive cancellations of visitors' trips to Spain. That didn't happen. Could it be that the traveling public is learning to live under the threat of terror, knowing that you might be no safer in your home city than you would be in London, Paris, or Madrid?

The Basque separatist group, ETA, remains active in Spain. Although ETA efforts have historically been directed against police, military, and other Spanish government targets, in March 2001, ETA issued a communiqué announcing its intention to target Spanish tourist areas to harm the country's economy. Americans have not been the specific targets of ETA activities. The Spanish government is vigorously engaged in combating terrorism at home and abroad and has been able to avert many terrorist activities. Over the years, ETA has conducted many successful attacks, many of which have resulted in deaths and injuries.

In December 2006, ETA admitted to carrying out a bomb attack at the Madrid airport that killed two people. ETA claimed that the attack was not intended to harm anyone, and the group condemned the government for not evacuating the targeted building. The terrorist group had given advance warning.

U.S. tourists traveling to Spain should exercise caution and refer to the Worldwide Caution public announcements issued in the wake of the September 11, 2001, terrorist attacks in the U.S. and the March 11, 2004, train attacks in Madrid. These announcements are updated by the U.S. Department of State and are available at http://travel.state.gov.

While most of Spain has a moderate rate of crime, and the vast majority of tourists have trouble-free visits to Spain each year, the principal tourist areas have been experiencing an increase in violent crime. Madrid and Barcelona, in particular, have reported growing incidents of muggings and violent attacks, and older tourists and Asian Americans seem to be particularly at risk. Criminals frequent tourist areas and major attractions such as museums, monuments, restaurants, hotels, beach resorts, trains, train stations, airports, subways, and ATMs. In Barcelona, violent attacks have occurred near the Picasso Museum and in the Gothic Quarter, Parc Guell, Plaza Real, and Montjuïc. In Madrid, reported incidents occur in key tourist areas, including the area near the Museo del Prado and Atocha train station, and areas of Old Madrid like Sol, El Rastro flea market, and Plaza Mayor. Travelers should exercise caution; carry limited cash and credit cards; and leave extra cash, credit cards, passports, and personal documents in a safe location. Crimes have occurred at all times of day and night.

Thieves often work in teams or pairs. In most cases, one person distracts a victim while an accomplice robs you. For example, a stranger might wave a map in your face and ask for directions or "inadvertently" spill something on you. While your attention is diverted, the accomplice makes off with the valuables. Attacks can also be initiated from behind, with the victim being grabbed around the neck and choked by one assailant while others rifle through the belongings. A group of assailants may surround the victim, maybe in a crowded popular tourist area or on public transportation, and only after the group has departed does the person discover he or she has been robbed. Some attacks have been so violent that victims have needed medical attention after the attack.

Theft from parked cars is also common. Small items like luggage, cameras, or briefcases are often stolen from parked cars. Travelers are advised not to leave valuables in parked cars and to keep doors locked, windows rolled up, and valuables out of sight when driving. Unfortunately, "Good Samaritan" scams are also common. A passing car will attempt to divert the driver's attention by indicating there is a mechanical problem. If the driver stops to check the vehicle, accomplices steal from the car while the driver is looking elsewhere. Drivers should be cautious about accepting help from anyone other than a uniformed Spanish police officer or Civil Guard.

The loss or theft abroad of a passport should be reported immediately to the local police and your nearest embassy or consulate. U.S. citizens may refer to the Department of State's pamphlet, *A Safe Trip Abroad,* for ways to promote a more trouble-free journey. The pamphlet is available by mail from the Superintendent of Documents, U.S. Government Printing Office, Washington, DC 20402, or via the Internet at http://travel.state.gov/travel/tips/safety/safety_1747.html.

SPECIALIZED TRAVEL RESOURCES

In addition to the destination-specific resources listed below, visit Frommers. com for additional specialized travel resources.

Gay & Lesbian Travelers

In 1978, Spain legalized homosexuality among consenting adults. In April 1995, the parliament of Spain banned discrimination based on sexual orientation. Madrid and Barcelona are the major centers of gay life in Spain. The most popular resorts for gay travelers are Sitges (south of Barcelona), Torremolinos, and Ibiza.

The **International Gay and Lesbian Travel Association** (**IGLTA;** ☏ 800/448-8550 or 954/630-1637; www.iglta.org) is the trade association for the gay and lesbian travel industry, and offers an online directory of gay- and lesbian-friendly travel businesses and tour operators.

Many agencies offer tours and travel itineraries specifically for gay and lesbian travelers. **Above and Beyond Tours** (☏ 800/397-2681; www.above beyondtours.com) are gay Australia tour specialists. San Francisco–based **Now, Voyager** (☏ 800/255-6951; www.nowvoyager.com) offers worldwide trips and cruises. And **Olivia** (☏ 800/631-6277; www.olivia.com) offers lesbian cruises and resort vacations.

Gay.com Travel (☏ 415/834-6500; www.gay.com/travel or www.outand about.com) is an excellent online source for travel. It provides regularly updated information about gay-owned, gay-oriented, and gay-friendly lodging, dining, sightseeing, nightlife, and shopping establishments in every important destination worldwide.

The Canadian website **GayTraveler** (**www.gaytraveler.ca**) offers ideas and advice for gay travel all over the world.

The following travel guides are available at many bookstores, or you can order them from any online bookseller: *Spartacus International Gay Guide* (Bruno Gmünder Verlag; www.spartacusworld.com/gayguide) and *Odysseus: The International Gay Travel Planner,* 17th edition (Publisher Distribution Company); and the *Damron* guides (www.damron.com), with separate, annual books for gay men and lesbians.

For more gay and lesbian travel resources, visit Frommers.com.

Travelers with Disabilities

Most disabilities shouldn't stop anyone from traveling. There are more options and resources out there than ever before.

Because of Spain's many hills and endless flights of stairs, visitors with disabilities may have difficulty getting around the country, but conditions are slowly improving. Newer hotels are more sensitive to the needs of those with disabilities, and the more expensive restaurants, in general, are wheelchair accessible. However, since most places have limited, if any, facilities for people with disabilities, you might consider taking an organized tour specifically designed to accommodate travelers with disabilities.

Organizations that offer a vast range of resources and assistance to travelers with disabilities include **MossRehab** (© **800/CALL-MOSS** [225-5667]; www.mossresourcenet.org); the **American Foundation for the Blind** (**AFB;** © **800/232-5463;** www.afb.org); and **SATH** (Society for Accessible Travel & Hospitality; © **212/447-7284;** www.sath.org). **AirAmbulanceCard.com** (© **877/424-7633**) is now partnered with SATH and allows you to preselect top-notch hospitals in case of an emergency.

Access-Able Travel Source (© www.access-able.com) offers a comprehensive database on travel agents from around the world with experience in accessible travel; destination-specific access information; and links to such resources as service animals, equipment rentals, and access guides.

Many travel agencies offer customized tours and itineraries for travelers with disabilities. Among them are **Flying Wheels Travel** (© **877/451-5006** or 507/451-5005; www.flyingwheelstravel.com) and **Accessible Journeys** (© **800/846-4537** or 610/521-0339; www.disabilitytravel.com).

Flying with Disability (www.flying-with-disability.org) is a comprehensive information source on airplane travel.

Also check out the quarterly magazine *Emerging Horizons* (www.emerginghorizons.com), available by subscription.

The "Accessible Travel" link at **Mobility-Advisor.com** (www.mobility-advisor.com) offers a variety of travel resources to persons with disabilities.

British travelers should contact **Tourism for All** (© **0845/124-9971** in the U.K. only; www.tourismforall.org.uk) to access a wide range of travel information and resources for seniors and those with disabilities.

For more about organizations that offer resources to travelers with disabilities, go to Frommers.com.

Senior Travel

Members of **AARP,** 601 E St. NW, Washington, DC 20049 (© **888/687-2277;** www.aarp.org), get discounts on hotels, airfares, and car rentals. AARP offers members a wide range of benefits, including *AARP The Magazine* and a monthly newsletter. Anyone 50 or older can join.

Many reliable agencies and organizations target the 50-plus market. **Elderhostel** (© **800/454-5768;** www.exploritas.org) arranges worldwide study programs for those ages 55 and over.

Recommended publications offering travel resources and discounts for seniors include the quarterly magazine *Travel 50 & Beyond* (www.travel50and beyond.com) and the bestselling paperback *Unbelievably Good Deals and Great Adventures That You Absolutely Can't Get Unless You're Over 50 2007–2008,* 16th edition (McGraw-Hill), by Joan Rattner Heilman.

Frommers.com offers more information and resources on travel for seniors.

Female Travelers

Safety can be a concern for women exploring the world on their own. In the Franco era, solo women travelers were harassed by macho males. Spanish men are much more hip today and much more politically correct.

As always, it's good to avoid deserted streets at night. Hitchhiking is never safe, of course. Dress conservatively, especially in remote towns. If women in micro-bikinis, say, parade down the streets of Torremolinos, as many of them do, it's inevitable that they will be whistled at. Even lewd suggestions might be called out to them. One single woman we know wears a wedding band, even though she's not married. Some solo women travelers today even carry a whistle on a key chain. Others take self-defense courses to ward off a potential attack. If you're a victim of catcalls and vulgar suggestions, look straight ahead and just keep walking. If followed, seek out the nearest police officer.

Check out the award-winning website **Journeywoman** (www.journey woman.com), a "real-life" women's travel-information network where you can sign up for a free e-mail newsletter and get advice on everything from etiquette and dress to safety. The travel guide *Safety and Security for Women Who Travel* by Sheila Swan and Peter Laufer (Travelers' Tales Guides), offering common-sense tips on safe travel, was updated in 2004.

For general travel resources for women, go to Frommers.com.

SUSTAINABLE TOURISM

Eco-tourism took off in Spain in the '90s and has been gaining in popularity ever since. Growing numbers of visitors are opting for organized eco-tours or else incorporating environmental awareness during their vacations in Spain.

Spain established its first national park in 1918. Today, 4% of the Spanish land mass is devoted to national parks, including Europe's largest, **Los Picos de Europa** (p. 660), which is in Asturias in northern Spain. Spain's national parks—called *parques nacionales*—incorporate everything from wetlands to mountains.

Eco-tourism often takes the form of camping at 1,000 sites in Spain, or within accommodations that include everything from basic government-rated one-star sites to more comfortable four-star settings. Some of the campsites even rent mobile homes or bungalows. Tourist offices throughout Spain will provide data directing you to Spain's many official campgrounds, called *parques de camp-ismo*. **Vayacamping** (© 93-594-61-00; www.vayacamping.net) publishes guides and maintains a website, detailing camping possibilities throughout Spain.

For a comprehensive list of Spain's eco-tours and vacations, check out **Info Hub** (www.infohub.com), the most comprehensive guide to out-of-the-ordinary and inspiring travel ideas in Spain. The layout of the site steers you toward the style of tour that appeals to you, and then guides you to the specific website associated with the tour you want.

Highlights include self-guided trekking through the Spanish Pyrenees; flights in hot-air balloons; cycling in northern Spain; cycling in Catalonia; and birding tours through swamps and wetlands.

Ecoforest Education for Sustainability strives for minimal damage to the planet's ecosystem. The group sets up communities where participants can live, learn, and visit in a healthy, sustainable way. All food comes from vegan-organic agriculture. Ecoforest defines its locations as "paradise gardens," where volunteers can sustain themselves in ways which not only are eco-friendly, but will enhance the environment for generations to come. For additional details, contact Ecoforest Education for Sustainability, Apt. 29, Coin 29100, Málaga (© 66-922-74-47; www.ecoforest.org).

If you'd like to travel green in Spain, staying at environmentally sensitive hotels, seek out recommendations from **It's a Green Green World** (www.

itsagreengreenworld.com). Its site previews green hotels across Spain, from a *finca* (farmhouse hotel) on the island of Majorca to a small country *posada* surrounded by its own 8-hectare (20-acre) organic farm in Asturias, in northwestern Spain.

Among international chains that have taken the lead in eco-tourism in Spain is **Inter-Continental Hotels and Resorts.** It encourages its member hotels to choose methods of operation that will be the least damaging to the environment. They refer to their policies on this as the "reduce, reuse, or recycle" principal.

Travelers can make a difference in the conservation of Spain's natural habitats by learning about environmentally responsible tourism before they go. For information on the subject contact one of the following organizations: **Conservation International,** 2011 Crystal Dr., Ste. 500, Arlington, VA 22202 (✆ **800/429-5660** or 703/341-2400; www.conservation.org); **The International Ecotourism Society,** 1333 H St. NW, Ste. 300E, Washington, DC 20005 (✆ **202/506-5033;** www.ecotourism.org); or the **United Nations Environment Programme** (UNEP) 39 Quai André Citroën, Paris 75739, in France (✆ **33-1-44-37-14-50;** www.uneptie.org). If you have time to contact only one of these organizations, make it the International Ecotourism Society, the world's oldest and largest eco-tourism organization.

An admirable organization for the eco-tourist is **Leave No Trace Center for Outdoor Ethics,** P.O. Box 997, Boulder CO 80306; www.lnt.org. It has drawn up a code for outdoor travelers who want to protect the wilderness for future generations, with the aim to reduce one's impact on the environment.

For a list of even more sustainable resources, as well as tips and explanations on how to travel greener, visit www.frommers.com/planning.

SPECIAL-INTEREST TRIPS & ESCORTED TOURS

Special-Interest Trips

Spain is one of the best destinations in Europe for enjoying the outdoors. Lounging on the beach leads the list of activities for most travelers, but there's a lot more to do. Spain's mountains lure thousands of mountaineers and hikers, and fishing and hunting are long-standing Iberian obsessions. The Pyrenees of Catalonia and Aragón, plus the Guadarramas outside Madrid, attract devoted skiers in the winter. Watersports ranging from sailing to windsurfing are prime summer attractions.

In addition to sports and adventures, we detail some of the best educational and cultural programs below.

Note: The information is presented only as a preview, which you'll want to follow with your own investigation tailored to your own interests.

ACADEMIC TRIPS & LANGUAGE CLASSES

The intensive language courses at **Spanish Abroad** are designed to enable you to speak Spanish as soon as possible. Native Spanish teachers with university degrees are the teachers. For more information about these programs, contact **Spanish Abroad,** 5112 N. 40th St., Ste. 103, Phoenix, AZ 85018 (✆ **888/722-7623** or 602/778-6791; www.spanishabroad.com).

Operating in such cities as Granada, Madrid, Barcelona, and Seville, **Enforex,** Alberto Aguilera 26, 28015 Madrid (✆ **91-594-37-76;** www.enforex.

com), offers 20 Spanish language programs. Sessions last for between 1 week and a full year.

With branches in such easterly cities as Barcelona and Valencia, **Eurocentres** is one of the best language schools in Spain, suitable for beginning or advanced students. The most up-to-date computer learning programs and the best video and audio equipment are used. For additional information, contact them at 56 Eccleston Sq., London SW1V 1PH (✆ **020/7963-8450;** www.eurocentres.com).

ADVENTURE & WELLNESS TRIPS

The best name in adventure travel in Spain is **GoAbroad,** which is the source for international education and alternative travel databases. This is the site for learning about special offerings in Spain. It also provides websites so you can make contacts on your own. Programs include home stays (you're lodged with a typical family in, say, Madrid or Granada). Or else you might study Spanish within the context of a hiking pilgrimage to Santiago de Compostela, the most beautiful and historic city in northwestern Spain. For more details, contact GoAbroad at 7800 Point Meadows Dr., Ste. 218, Jacksonville, FL 32256 (✆ **720/570-1702;** www. goabroad.com).

ART TOURS

Custom tours of Spain that focus on art and architecture can be arranged, especially by **Heritage Tours** (✆ **800/378-4555** or 212/206-8400; http:// htprivatetravel.com). Founded by an architect, Joel Zack, these tours can be customized and often include guided trips through such art cities as Madrid, Toledo, Granada, Barcelona, and Bilbao. Without airfares, trips begin at around $4,000 for a 10-day jaunt.

Featuring groups ranging in size from 15 to 25 participants, **ACE Study Tours** (✆ **01223/835055;** www.acestudytours.co.uk) in Cambridge, England, offers tours led by an art historian to such cities as Barcelona and Bilbao, and to such highlights of Andalusia as Córdoba, Seville, and Granada. Eight-day trips start at $2,500 and include double occupancy in a hotel, round-trip airfare from London, plus breakfast and dinner daily.

BIKING TOURS

The leading U.S.-based outfitter is **Easy Rider Tours,** P.O. Box 228, Newburyport, MA 01950 (✆ **800/488-8332** or 978/463-6955; www.easyridertours. com). Their tours average between 48km and 81km (30–50 miles) a day; the most appealing tour follows the route trod by medieval pilgrims on their way to Santiago. The bike tours offered by **Backroads,** 801 Cedar St., Berkeley, CA 94710 (✆ **800/462-2848** or 510/527-1555; www.backroads.com), take you through the verdant countryside of Galicia and into Portugal's Minho region. One company that specializes in bike tours of Camino de Santiago is **Saranjan Tours,** P.O. Box 292, Kirkland, WA 98083 (✆ **800/858-9594;** www.saranjan.com).

Bravo Bike, c/o Montera 25–27, E-28013, Madrid (✆ **91-758-29-45;** www.bravobike.com), is a travel agency featuring organized cycling tours around Madrid. They have branched out to include other parts of Spain as well, notably the route between Salamanca to Santiago de Compostela, and the route of the conquerors in Extremadura. One of the most intriguing bike tours is the *ruta de vino* (the wine route) in La Rioja country.

In England, the **Cyclists' Touring Club,** Parklands, Railton Road, Guildford, Surrey GU2 9JX (© **0844/736-8450;** www.ctc.org.uk), charges 36€ a year for membership; part of the fee covers information and suggested cycling routes through Spain and dozens of other countries.

FOOD & WINE TRIPS

Spain Taste offers the best food and wine tours of Spain, 5-day jaunts for groups with as few as two participants or as many as six. These tours are designed for serious gastronomes. The tours take place in Catalonia, north of Barcelona, and include dinners at Michelin-starred restaurants, wine tastings, and cooking lessons with famous chefs. Tours are conducted from March to June and from September to October. For more information, contact Spain Taste, Can Valls de Moagueroles, Fogars de Montclus, Barcelona 08740 (© **93-847-51-15;** www. spaintaste.com).

Established in 2002, **Catacurian** offers 3- to 6-day cooking vacations that include classes in Catalan cuisine. Programs also feature olive-picking sessions and 1-day market visits and cooking classes within Barcelona itself. Catacurian is located in a stone house in a small village, El Masroig, in the Priorat region of Catalonia. For more information, contact Catacurian at 1717 5th St. N., St. Petersburg, FL 33704 (© **866/538-3519;** www.catacurian.com).

GOLF TOURS

In recent decades, thousands of British retirees have settled in Spain, and their presence has sparked the development of dozens of new golf courses. Although the Costa Blanca has become an increasingly popular setting for golf, more than a third of the country's approximately 160 courses lie within its southern tier, a short drive from the Costa del Sol.

Packages that include guaranteed playing time on some of the country's finest courses, as well as airfare and accommodations, can be arranged through such firms as **Golf International** (© **800/833-1389** or 212/986-9176; www.golf international.com) and **Comtours** (© **800/248-1331;** www.comtours.com).

What are the two most talked-about golf courses in Spain? The well-established **Valderrama** on the Costa del Sol, a Robert Trent Jones, Sr.–designed course carved out of an oak plantation in the 1980s; and Hyatt's **La Manga Club,** 30385 Los Belones, Cartagena, Murcia (© **96-817-50-00;** www.golf. lamangaclub.com). It's the site of three golf courses, one of which was recently remodeled by Arnold Palmer. The Ryder Cup between Spain and the United States was held in 1997 at Valderrama, Avenida Los Cortijos, 11310 Sotogrande (© **95-679-12-00;** www.valderrama.com), on the western tip of the Costa del Sol, near Gibraltar.

HIKING & WALKING TOURS

If you're drawn to the idea of combining hiking with stopovers at local inns, contact **Winetrails,** Greenways, Vann Lake, Ockley, Dorking RH5 5NT, U.K. (© **01306/712-111;** www.winetrails.co.uk). This U.K.-based company conducts 10-day treks through northern Spain's wine districts.

To venture into the more rugged countryside of Catalonia, Andalusia's valley of the Guadalquivir, or the arid and beautiful Extremaduran plains, contact **Ramblers Holidays,** Lemsford Mill, Welwyn Garden AL8 7TR, U.K. (© **01707/331-133;** www.ramblersholidays.co.uk).

HORSEBACK-RIDING TOURS

You can take a tour that winds across France and Galicia on your way to the medieval religious shrine at Santiago de Compostela in northwest Spain. Lodging, the use of a horse, and all necessary equipment are included in the price. For information and reservations, contact **Camino a Caballo,** Calle Urzáiz 91 no. 5–A, Vigo, Spain (© **98-642-59-37;** www.caminoacaballo.com).

A well-known equestrian center that conducts tours of the Alpujarras highlands is **Cabalgar,** Rutas Alternativas, Bubión, Granada (© **95-876-31-35;** www.ridingandalucia.com). The farm is best known for its weekend treks through the scrub-covered hills of southern and central Spain, although longer tours are available.

SAILING TOURS

Aventus, an agency based in Seville, offers weeklong cruises along the coast of Andalusia and the Algarve. Its three-masted, 13m (43-ft.) sailing yacht departs from the Andalusian port of Huelva. For reservations and information, contact Aventus at Calle Huelva 6, 41004 Sevilla (© **95-421-00-62;** www.alventus.com).

In northern Spain, consider a journey with **Voyages Jules Verne,** 21 Dorset Sq., London NW1 6QG, U.K. (© **020/7616-1000;** www.vjv.co.uk). Its guided vacations take in Galicia and its Portuguese neighbors Trás-os-Montes and the Minho district, as well as Porto, the second-largest city in Portugal. The trips end with a boat ride up the Douro River back into Spain.

VOLUNTEER & WORKING TRIPS

If you've been inspired to save the planet for another generation, volunteer work, combined with a vacation experience, might be the way to go. If you want to volunteer for a program, the best contact is **Plataforma del Voluntariado de España,** Calle Fuentes 10, Madrid 28013 (© **90-212-05-12;** www. plataformavoluntariado.org). This group compiles a listing, and keeps it up-to-date, of all the volunteer programs in Spain, giving you a link to the group that most closely reflects your interests.

Escorted General-Interest Tours

Escorted tours are structured group tours, with a group leader. The price usually includes everything from airfare to hotels, meals, tours, admission costs, and local transportation.

There are many escorted tour companies to choose from, each offering transportation to and within Spain, prearranged hotel space, and such extras as bilingual tour guides and lectures. Many of these tours to Spain include excursions to Morocco or Portugal.

Although escorted tours require big deposits and predetermine hotels, restaurants, and itineraries, many people derive security and peace of mind from the structure they offer. Escorted tours—whether they're navigated by bus, motorcoach, train, or boat—let travelers sit back and enjoy the trip without having to drive or worry about details. They take you to the maximum number of sights in the minimum amount of time with the least amount of hassle. They're particularly convenient for people with limited mobility and they can be a great way to make new friends.

On the downside, you'll have little opportunity for serendipitous interactions with locals. The tours can be jampacked with activities, leaving little room for individual sightseeing, whim, or adventure—plus they often focus on the heavily touristed sites, so you miss out on many a lesser-known gem.

Some of the most expensive and luxurious tours are run by **Abercrombie & Kent International** (© 800/554-7016; www.abercrombiekent.com), including deluxe 9- to 12-day tours of the Iberian Peninsula by train. Guests stay in fine hotels, ranging from a late medieval palace to the exquisite Alfonso XIII in Seville.

American Express Vacations (© 800/297-2977; www.american express.com) is one of the biggest tour operators in the world. Its offerings are comprehensive, and unescorted customized package tours are available, too.

Trafalgar Tours (© 800/854-0103; www.trafalgartours.com) offers a number of tours of Spain. One of the most popular offerings is a 16-day trip called "The Best of Spain."

Alternative Travel Group Ltd. (© 01865/315-678; www.atg-oxford. co.uk) is a British firm that organizes walking and cycling vacations, plus wine tours in Spain, Italy, and France. Tours explore the scenic countryside and medieval towns of each country.

Petrabax Tours (© 800/634-1188; www.petrabax.com) attracts those who prefer to see Spain by bus, although fly/drive packages are also offered, featuring stays in *paradores*. A number of city packages are available as well, plus an 8-day trip that tries to capture the essence of Spain, with stops ranging from Madrid to Granada.

Isramworld (© 800/223-7460; www.isram.com) sells both escorted and package tours to Spain. It can book you on bus tours as well as land and air packages. Its grandest offering is "Spanish Splendor," with a private driver and guides. Naturally, this upmarket outfitter uses only Spain's finest hotels.

STAYING CONNECTED
Telephones
To call Spain:

1. Dial the international access code: **011** from the U.S.; 00 from the U.K., Ireland, or New Zealand; or 0011 from Australia.
2. Dial the country code **34.**
3. Dial the city code, and then the number.

To make international calls: To make international calls from Spain, first dial 00 and then the country code (U.S. or Canada 1, U.K. 44, Ireland 353, Australia 61, New Zealand 64). Next you dial the area code and number. For example, if you wanted to call the British Embassy in Washington, D.C., you would dial 00-1-202-588-7800.

For directory assistance: Dial © **1003** in Spain.

For operator assistance: If you need operator assistance in making an international call, dial © **025.**

Toll-free numbers: Numbers beginning with **900** in Spain are toll-free, but calling an 800 number in the States from Spain is not toll-free. In fact, it costs the same as an overseas call.

In Spain, many smaller establishments, especially bars, discos, and a few informal restaurants, don't have phones. Furthermore, many summer-only bars and discos secure a phone for the season only, and then get a new number the next season. Many attractions, such as small churches or even minor museums, have no staff to receive inquiries from the public.

In 1998, all telephone numbers in Spain changed to a nine-digit system instead of the six- or seven-digit system used previously. Each number is now preceded by its provincial code for local, national, and international calls. For example, when calling Madrid from Madrid or from another province within Spain, telephone customers must dial © **91-482-85-80.**

More information is available on the Telefónica website (www.telefonica.es).

Cellphones

The three letters that define much of the world's wireless capabilities are GSM (Global System for Mobiles), a big, seamless network that makes for easy cross-border cellphone use throughout dozens of countries worldwide. In general reception is good.

For many, **renting** a phone is a good idea. (Even worldphone owners will have to rent new phones if they're traveling to non-GSM regions.) While you can rent a phone from any number of overseas sites, including kiosks at airports and at car-rental agencies, we suggest renting the phone before you leave home. North Americans can rent one before leaving home from **InTouch USA** (© **800/872-7626** or 703/222-7161; www.intouchglobal.com) or **RoadPost** (© **888/290-1616** or 905/272-5665; www.roadpost.com). InTouch will also, for free, advise you on whether your existing phone will work overseas.

Buying a phone can be economically attractive, as many nations have cheap prepaid phone systems. Once you arrive at your destination, stop by a local cellphone shop and get the cheapest package; you'll probably pay less than $100 for a phone and a starter calling card. Local calls may be as low as 10¢ per minute, and in many countries incoming calls are free.

Wilderness adventurers might consider renting a **satellite phone** ("satphone"). It's different from a cellphone in that it connects to satellites and works where there's no cellular signal or ground-based tower. You can rent satellite phones from RoadPost (see above). InTouch USA (see above) offers a wider range of satphones but at higher rates. Per-minute call charges can be even cheaper than roaming charges with a regular cellphone, but the phone itself is more expensive. Satphones are outrageously expensive to buy, so don't even think about it.

Internet & E-Mail
WITH YOUR OWN COMPUTER

More and more hotels, cafes, and retailers are signing on as Wi-Fi (wireless fidelity) "hot spots." Mac owners have their own networking technology: Apple AirPort. **T-Mobile Hotspot** (www.t-mobile.com/hotspot or www.t-mobile.co.uk) offers wireless connections at coffee shops nationwide. **Boingo** (www.boingo.com) and **Wayport** (www.wayport.com) have set up networks in airports and high-class hotel lobbies. iPass providers (see below) also give you access to a few hundred wireless hotel lobby setups. To locate other hot spots that provide **free wireless networks,** go to **www.jiwire.com**.

Most business-class hotels offer Wi-Fi. In addition, major Internet service providers (ISPs) have **local access numbers** around the world, allowing you to go online by placing a local call. The **iPass** network also has dial-up numbers around the world. You'll have to sign up with an iPass provider, who will then tell you how to set up your computer for your destination(s). For a list of iPass providers, go to www.ipass.com and click on "Individuals Buy Now." One solid provider is **i2roam** (© **866/811-6209** or 920/233-5863; www.i2roam.com).

Wherever you go, bring a **connection kit** of the right power and phone adapters, a spare phone cord, and a spare Ethernet network cable—or find out whether your hotel supplies them to guests.

WITHOUT YOUR OWN COMPUTER

To find cybercafes check **www.cybercaptive.com** and **www.cybercafe. com**. Cybercafes are found in all large cities in Spain, especially Madrid and Barcelona. But they do not tend to cluster in any particular neighborhoods because of competition.

In addition to formal cybercafes, most **youth hostels** and **public libraries** have Internet access. Avoid **hotel business centers** unless you're willing to pay exorbitant rates.

Most major airports now have **Internet kiosks** scattered throughout their gates. These give you basic Web access for a per-minute fee that's usually higher than cybercafe prices.

TIPS ON ACCOMMODATIONS

From castles converted into hotels to modern high-rise resorts overlooking the Mediterranean, Spain has some of the most varied hotel accommodations in the world—with equally varied price ranges. Accommodations are broadly classified as follows:

ONE- TO FIVE-STAR HOTELS The Spanish government rates hotels by according them stars. A five-star hotel is truly deluxe, with deluxe prices; a one-star hotel consists of the most modest accommodations officially recognized as a hotel by the government. A four-star hotel offers first-class accommodations; a three-star hotel is moderately priced; and a one- or two-star hotel is inexpensively priced. The government grants stars based on such amenities as elevators, private bathrooms, and air-conditioning. If a hotel is classified as a *residencia,* it means that it serves breakfast (usually) but no other meals.

HOSTALES Not to be confused with a hostel for students, a *hostal* is a modest hotel without services, where you can save money by carrying your own bags and the like. You'll know it's a *hostal* if a small s follows the capital letter H on the blue plaque by the door. *Hostales* with three stars are about the equivalent of hotels with two stars.

PENSIONS These boardinghouses are among the least expensive accommodations, but you're required to take either full board (three meals) or half-board, which is breakfast plus lunch or dinner.

CASAS HUESPEDES & FONDAS These are the cheapest places in Spain and can be recognized by the light-blue plaques at the door displaying CH and F, respectively. They are invariably basic but respectable establishments.

YOUTH HOSTELS Spain has about 140 hostels (*albergues de juventud*). In theory, travelers age 25 or under have the first chance at securing a bed for the night, but these places are certainly not limited to young people. Some of them are equipped for persons with disabilities. Most hostels impose an 11pm curfew. For information, contact **Red Española de Albergues Juveniles,** Castello 24, 28001 Madrid (© **91-522-70-07;** www.reaj.com).

PARADORES The Spanish government runs a series of unique state-owned inns called *paradores,* which now blanket the country. Deserted castles, monasteries, palaces, and other buildings have been taken over and converted into hotels. Today there are 86 *paradores* in all, and they're documented in a booklet called *Visiting the Paradores,* available at Spanish tourist offices.

At great expense, modern bathrooms, steam heat, and the like have been added to these buildings, yet classic Spanish architecture, where it existed, has been retained. Establishments are often furnished with antiques or at least good reproductions and decorative objects typical of the country.

Meals are also served in these government-owned inns. Usually, typical dishes of the region are featured. *Paradores* are likely to be overcrowded in the summer months, so advance reservations, arranged through any travel agent, are wise.

The government also operates a type of accommodations known as **albergues:** These are comparable to motels, lining the road in usually hotel-scarce areas for the convenience of passing motorists. A client is not allowed to stay in an *albergue* for more than 48 hours, and the management doesn't accept reservations.

In addition, the government runs **refugios** (refuges), mostly in remote areas, attracting hunters, fishers, and mountain climbers. Another state-sponsored establishment is the **hostería,** or specialty restaurant, such as the one at Alcalá de Henares, near Madrid. *Hosterías* don't offer rooms; they serve regional dishes at reasonable prices.

The central office for *paradores* is **Paradores de España,** Requeña 3, 28013 Madrid (© **90-254-79-79;** www.paradores.es). The U.S. representative is **Marketing Ahead,** 381 Park Ave. S., New York, NY 10016 (© **800/223-1356** or 212/686-9213; www.marketingahead.com). Travel agents can also arrange reservations.

Renting a House or an Apartment

If you rent a home or an apartment, you can save money on accommodations and dining and still take daily trips to see the surrounding area.

Apartments in Spain generally fall into two different categories: hotel *apartamentos* and *residencia apartamentos.* The hotel apartments have full facilities, with chamber service, equipped kitchenettes, and often restaurants and bars. The *residencia* apartments, also called *apartamentos turísticos,* are fully furnished with kitchenettes but lack the facilities of the hotel complexes. They are cheaper, however.

One rental company to try is **Hometours International** (© **865/690-8484** or 866/367-4668; www.budgettravel.com), which mainly handles properties in Andalusia. Call them and they'll send you a 40-page color catalog with descriptions and pictures for $5 to cover postage and handling. Units are rented for a minimum of 7 days.

Another agency is **ILC** (International Lodging Corp.; © **888/SPAIN-44** [772-4644] or 212/228-5900; www.ilcweb.com), which rents privately owned apartments, houses, and villas for a week or more. It also offers access to suites in well-known hotels for stays of a week or longer, sometimes at bargain rates. Rental units, regardless of their size, usually contain a kitchen. The company's listings cover accommodations in Madrid, Barcelona, Seville, Granada, and Majorca.

SUGGESTED
SPAIN
ITINERARIES

4

t would be a delight to get "lost" in Spain, wandering about at your leisure, discovering unspoiled villages off the beaten path. But few of us have such a generous amount of time. Vacations are getting shorter these days, and a "lean-and-mean" schedule is called for if you want to experience the best of any country in a ridiculously short amount of time.

If you're pressed for time, with only 1 week for the country, check out our "Spain in 1 Week" trip, or "Spain in 2 Weeks" if you have more time. If you've been to Spain before, especially Madrid or Barcelona, you may want to skip either of these cities, using them as gateways, and hop down to Andalusia to explore the single-most intriguing region in all of Spain. Families might want to consider the family-fun tour, with more focus on sights that appeal to kids.

Spain is so vast and so treasure-filled that it's hard to resist the temptation to pack in too much in too short a time. It's a challenging, daunting destination, and you can't even skim the surface in 1 or 2 weeks—so just go for the nuggets, such towering attractions as Madrid, Barcelona, Toledo, and Seville.

Spain ranks with Germany and France in offering Europe's best-maintained superhighways. It also boasts one of the fastest and most efficient public transportation systems in the world, especially its national rail system. Madrid stands at the hub of a vast transportation empire, with many once-remote cities now within easy reach of the capital—for example, Córdoba in 1½ hours or Seville in 2½ hours.

Our itineraries take you to some major attractions and charming towns. The pace may be a bit breathless, so skip a town or sight occasionally to have chill-out time—after all, you're on vacation. You can also peruse our review of the best of Spain in chapter 1 (p. 1) to find out what experiences or sights appeal to you and adjust the itineraries to suit your own interests.

THE REGIONS IN BRIEF

Three times the size of Illinois, with a population of approximately 40 million, Spain faces the Atlantic Ocean and the Bay of Biscay to the north and the Mediterranean Sea to the south and east. Portugal borders it on the west, and the Pyrenees separate Spain from France and the rest of Europe. The southern coastline is only a few nautical miles from the north coast of Africa. It's difficult to generalize about Spain because it is composed of so many regions—50 provinces in all—each with its own geography, history, and culture. The country's topography divides it into many regions: the Cantabrian Mountains in the north, Cuenca's mountains in the east, and the Sierra Morena in the south, which mark a high central tableland that is itself cut by hills.

MADRID & ENVIRONS Set on a high, arid plateau near the geographic center of Iberia, Madrid was created by royal decree in the 1600s, long after the much older kingdoms of León, Navarre, Aragón, and Catalonia, and long

PREVIOUS PAGE: **The gardens of the Generalife in Granada.**

after the final Moor was ousted by Catholic armies. Since its birth, all roads within Spain have radiated outward from its precincts, and as the country's most important airline and railway hub, it's likely to be your point of arrival (although many international flights and European trains now arrive in Barcelona as well).

Despite the city's increasingly unpleasant urban sprawl, paralyzing traffic jams, and skyrocketing prices, Madrid remains one of Europe's great cities. Take in the Prado, the Thyssen-Bornemisza Museum, and perhaps the Royal Palace. Walk through historic neighborhoods around the Plaza Mayor (but beware of muggers). Devote time to one of the city's great pastimes, a round of tapas tasting. Plan on at least 2 days to explore the city and another 3 for trips to the attractions beyond the capital. Perhaps as important as a visit to Madrid is a day trip to the imperial city of **Toledo,** which brims with monuments and paintings by El Greco, and is home to one of Spain's greatest cathedrals. Other worthy excursions include the Roman aqueduct at **Segovia,** such monuments as **El Escorial,** and the "hanging village" of **Cuenca** (site of a world-class museum of modern art).

OLD CASTILE & LEÓN The proud kingdoms of Castile and León in north-central Iberia are part of the core from which modern Spain developed. Some of their greatest cathedrals and monuments were erected when each was staunchly independent. But León's annexation by Queen Isabella of Castile in 1474 (5 years after her politically advantageous but unhappy marriage to Ferdinand of Aragón) irrevocably linked the two regions.

Even Spaniards are sometimes confused about the terms Old Castile (see chapter 7, p. 236) and New Castile, a modern linguistic and governmental concept that includes a territory much larger than the medieval entity known by Isabella and her subjects. Although it's easy to take a train to

Extremadura's countryside.

and from Madrid, we don't recommend that you try to see the highlights as day trips from Madrid; it's better to treat them as overnight destinations in their own right.

Highlights include **Burgos** (the ancient cradle of Castile), **Salamanca** (a medieval Castilian university town), and **León** (capital on the northern plains of the district bearing its name, and site of one of the most unusual cathedrals in Iberia). If time remains, consider an overnight stay at the extraordinary *parador* (a government-owned inn) in **Ciudad Rodrigo,** as well as trips to **Zamora,** known for its stunning Romanesque churches, and **Valladolid.**

EXTREMADURA Far from the mainstream of urbanized Spain, fascinating Extremadura lives in a time warp where hints of the Middle Ages and ancient Rome crop up unexpectedly beside sun-baked highways. Many of the conquistadors who pillaged native civilizations in the New World came from this hard, granite land.

Be prepared for hot, arid landscapes and smoking diesel trucks carrying heavy loads through this corridor between Madrid and Lisbon. You can see a lot in about 2 days, stopping off at such sites as **Guadalupe,** whose Mudéjar monastery revolves around the medieval cult of the Dark (or Black) Virgin; and **Trujillo,** where many of the monuments were built with gold sent home by native sons like Pizarro, Peru's conqueror. **Cáceres** is a beautiful, fortified city with one foot planted firmly in the Middle Ages, while **Zafra** displays greater evidence of the Moorish occupation than anywhere in Spain outside Andalusia.

ANDALUSIA In A.D. 711 Muslim armies swept into Iberia from strongholds in what is now Morocco. Since then, Spain's southernmost district has been enmeshed in the mores, art, and architecture of the Muslim world.

During the 900s, Andalucía (as it is called in Spanish) blossomed into a sophisticated society—advanced in philosophy, mathematics, and trading—that far surpassed a feudal Europe still trapped in the Dark Ages. Moorish domination ended completely in 1492, when Granada was captured by the armies of Isabella and Ferdinand, but even today the region offers echoes of this Muslim occupation. Andalusia is a dry district that isn't highly prosperous, despite such economically rejuvenating events as Seville's Expo.

The major cities of Andalusia deserve at least a week of exploration, with overnights in **Seville** (hometown of Carmen, Don Giovanni, and the barber); **Córdoba,** site of the Mezquita, one of history's most versatile religious edifices; and **Cádiz,** the seaport where thousands of ships embarked on their colonization of the New World. Perhaps greatest of all is **Granada,** a town of such impressive artistry that it inspired many of the works by the 20th-century Romantic poet Federico García Lorca.

THE COSTA DEL SOL The Costa del Sol sprawls across the southernmost edge of Spain between Algeciras to the west—a few miles from the rocky heights of British-controlled Gibraltar—and Almería to the east. Think traffic jams, suntan oil, sun-bleached high-rises, and near-naked flesh. The beaches here are some of the best in Europe, but this can also be an overly crowded, crime-filled region.

Unless you travel by car or rail from Madrid, chances are you'll arrive by plane via **Málaga,** the district's most historic city. The coast's largest resort town is distinctive, Renaissance-era **Marbella,** the centerpiece of 28km (17 miles) of beaches. Today it's a chic hangout for the tanned and wealthy. **Nerja** is just one of the booming resorts that has kept its out-of-the-way fishing-village feel. The most overcrowded and action-packed resort is **Torremolinos.** One modern development that has managed to remain distinctive is **Puerto Banús,** a neo-Moorish village curving around a sheltered marina where the wintering rich dock their yachts.

VALENCIA & THE COSTA BLANCA **Valencia,** the third-largest city in Spain, is rarely visited by foreign tourists because of the heavy industry that surrounds its inner core. More alluring are such resorts as **Alicante** and **Benidorm** or the medieval town of **Elche** (where some of the world's most famous ancient Roman statues were discovered). Unless you opt to skip Valencia completely, plan to see the city's cathedral, the exterior of its Palacio de la Generalidad, and as many of its three important museums as you can fit into a 1-day trip. For the Costa Blanca, allow as much or as little time as you want to spend on the beach.

BARCELONA & CATALONIA **Barcelona**'s history is older than that of its rival, Madrid, and its streets are filled with Gothic and medieval buildings that Spain's relatively newer capital lacks. During the 1200s it rivaled the trading prowess of such cities as Genoa and Pisa, and it became the Spanish city that most resembled other great cities of Europe. Allow yourself at least 3 days to explore the city, with stops at the Picasso Museum, the Joan Miró Foundation, the Gothic Quarter, and a crowning triumph of early *modernista* (or *modernisme*) architecture, the Eixample District, where you'll find many of Antoni Gaudí's signature works. Make time for a stroll along Les Rambles, one of the most delightful outdoor promenades in Spain.

Don't overlook Catalonia's other attractions, all within easy reach of Barcelona. A short drive to the south is **Sitges,** a stylish beach resort that

The Costa Brava, or "Wild Coast."

caters to a diverse clientele ranging from freewheeling nudists and gay party crowds to fun-seeking families. Other destinations are **Tarragona,** one of ancient Rome's district capitals; and **Montserrat,** the "Serrated Mountain," site of one of Europe's best-preserved medieval monasteries.

THE COSTA BRAVA This is Spain's other Riviera, a region with a deep sense of medieval history and a topography that's rockier and more interesting than that of the Costa del Sol. The "Wild Coast" stretches from the resort of Blanes, just north of Barcelona, along 153km (95 miles) of dangerously winding cliff-top roads that bypass peninsulas and sheltered coves on their way to the French border. Despite hordes of Spanish and northern European midsummer visitors, the Costa Brava resorts still manage to feel less congested and less spoiled than those along the Costa del Sol.

Sun worshipers usually head for the twin beachfront resorts of **Lloret de Mar** and **Tossa de Mar.** Travelers interested in the history of 20th-century painting go to **Figueres;** Salvador Dalí was born here in 1904, and a controversial and bizarre museum of his design is devoted exclusively to his surrealist works.

ARAGÓN Except for Aragón's association with Ferdinand, the unsavory, often unethical husband of Queen Isabella, few foreign visitors ever thought much about this northeastern quadrant of Iberia. A land of noteworthy Mudéjar architecture and high altitudes that guarantee cool midsummer temperatures, it's also one of the foremost bull-breeding regions of Spain.

Aragón is best visited as a stopover between Barcelona and Madrid. Stay overnight in **Zaragoza,** the district capital, and take a series of day trips to **Tarazona** ("the Toledo of Aragón"), **Calatayud,** and **Daroca,** all important Moorish and Roman military outposts. Visit **Nuévalos/Piedra,** the site of an extraordinary riverside hotel built in 1194 as a Cistercian monastery. Also worth a trip is **Sos del Rey Católico,** the rocky, relatively unspoiled village where Ferdinand was born.

NAVARRE & LA RIOJA This strategic province, one of the four original Christian kingdoms in Iberia, shares a border, and numerous historical references, with France. One of France's Renaissance kings, Henri IV "de Navarre," was linked to the province's royal family. Many Navarre customs, and some of its local dialect, reflect the influence of its passionately politicized neighbors, the Basques. Celtic pagans, Romans, Christians, and Arabs have all left architectural reminders of their presence. The province contains nine points where traffic is funneled into and out of Spain, so if you're driving or riding the train, say, from Paris to Madrid, chances are you'll get a fast overview of Navarre. The province's best-known destination is **Pamplona,** the district capital and annual host of the bull-running Fiesta de San Fermín.

One small corner of Navarre is composed of **La Rioja,** the smallest *autonomía* (semi-autonomous province) of Spain. Irrigated by the Ebro River, it produces some of the country's finest wines. If wine tasting appeals to you, head for the town of **Haro** and drop by several bodegas to sample local vintages.

THE BASQUE COUNTRY This is the native land of Europe's oldest traceable ethnic group. The Basque people have been more heavily persecuted than any other group within Spain, by Madrid regimes determined to shoehorn their unusual language and culture into that of mainstream Spain. The region of rolling peaks and fertile, sunny valleys hugs the Atlantic coast adjacent to the French border. It boasts the best regional cuisine in Spain.

Unless you want to spend more time relaxing on the beach, allow 3 leisurely days for this unusual district. Visit **San Sebastián (Donostia)** for its international glamour, **Fuenterrabía (Hondarribía)** for its medieval history, **Guernica** for a sobering reminder of the Spanish Civil War, and **Lekeitio** for its simple fishing-village charm.

CANTABRIA & ASTURIAS Positioned on Iberia's north-central coastline, these are the most verdant regions of Spain. In the Middle Ages, pilgrims passed through here on their way to **Santiago de Compostela**—a legacy evident from the wealth of Romanesque churches and abbeys in the vicinity. Come for beaches that are rainier, but much less crowded, than those along Spain's southern coasts.

Enjoy such beach resorts as **El Sardinero** and **Laredo,** as well as the rugged beauty of **Los Picos de Europa,** a dramatic mountain range that is home to rich colonies of wildlife. Sites of interest include the **Caves of Altamira** (called "the Sistine Chapel of prehistoric art," although admission is strictly regulated), the pre-Romanesque town of **Oviedo,** and the architecturally important Old Quarter of **Gijón.** The region's largest city, **Santander,** lies amid a maze of peninsulas and estuaries favored by boaters. In summer it becomes a major beach resort, although **San Sebastián** is more fashionable.

GALICIA A true Celtic outpost in northwestern Iberia, Galicia's landscape is often compared to that of rainy, windswept Ireland. Known for a spectacularly dramatic coastline, the region is wild and relatively under-populated. Spend at least 2 days here enjoying some of the most scenic drives in Iberia. Stop at historic and religious sites like **Santiago de Compostela** or the ancient Roman outpost of **Lugo.** Perhaps the region's greatest city is **A Coruña,** the point of embarkation for Spain's tragic Armada, sunk by the English army on its way to invade Britain in the late 16th century.

THE BALEARIC ISLANDS "Discovered" by English Romantics in the early 19th century, and long known as a strategic naval outpost in the western Mediterranean, these islands are sunny, subtropical, mountainous, and more verdant than the Costa del Sol. They have their pockets of style and posh, although **Majorca** and **Ibiza** are overrun in summer, especially by British and German travelers on package tours. Ibiza attracts a large gay crowd. **Minorca** is more fashionable, though more inconvenient to get to.

SPAIN IN 1 WEEK

The very title of this tour is misleading: There is no way you can see Spain in 1 week. But you can have a memorable vacation time in Madrid and see some of the highlights of Old Castile if you budget your time carefully. You can use the following itinerary to make the most out of a week in Spain, but feel free to drop a place or two to give yourself a day to relax. One week provides enough time, although barely, to introduce yourself to such attractions of Madrid as the Museo del Prado and the Museo Thyssen-Bornemisza. After 2 days, you can head for the once-royal city of Toledo, the most historic and evocative of all Spanish cities. You'll have time to take in Segovia, with its Alcázar "in the sky," and the austere monastery-fortress of El Escorial, burial place of Spanish kings.

Days 1–2 Madrid
Day 3 Toledo
Day 4 Segovia
Day 5 El Escorial
Day 6 Córdoba
Day 7 Seville

DAYS 1 & 2: Madrid ★★★

Take a flight that arrives in Madrid as early as possible. Check into your hotel and hit the nearest cafe for a pick-me-up café au lait and croissant before sightseeing. Take the Metro to Atocha or Banco de España to begin your tour of the **Museo del Prado** (p. 160), allowing at least 2 hours for a brief visit. Since you can't see it all, concentrate on the splendid array of works by Velázquez, and take in some of the works of Francisco de Goya, including his *Clothed Maja* and *Naked Maja*.

Break for lunch at **Plaza de Santa Ana,** known for its outdoor *terrazas*. This was the center of an old neighborhood for literati, attracting such Golden Age authors as Lope de Vega and Cervantes. Hemingway drank here in the 1920s.

After lunch, walk west to **Puerta del Sol,** the very center of Madrid. This is the Times Square of Madrid. Northwest of the square you can visit **Monasterio de las Descalzas Reales** (p. 157), Madrid's art-filled convent from the mid–16th century and a true treasure-trove.

After perhaps a siesta at your hotel, head for **Plaza Mayor** (p. 157), Madrid's most beautiful square and liveliest hub in the early evening. For dinner, patronize Hemingway's favorite restaurant, **Sobrino de Botín** (p. 154).

On **Day 2,** take the Metro to Atocha for a visit to **Museo Nacional Centro de Arte Reina Sofía** (p. 162), whose main attraction is one of Picasso's masterpieces, *Guernica.* Here you can also view one of the greatest collections of modern art in Spain, taking at least 2 hours. In the afternoon, view Madrid's third great art museum, **Museo Thyssen-Bornemisza** (p. 162), absorbing its many treasures. A visit will easily absorb at least 2 hours of your time.

In the early evening, join in that ritual of *tasca* hopping, going from one bar or tavern to another and sampling hot and cold tapas or small plates of Spanish appetizers, ranging from fresh anchovies to the tail of a bull. For a selection of "Our Favorite *Tascas,*" see p. 156, but you can discover plenty on your own, virtually on every street corner. After all that food and drink, you'll hardly need to order dinner. Stagger back to your hotel or else attend a flamenco show. See "Madrid After Dark" (p. 179) for the best flamenco showcases.

The Museo del Prado in Madrid.

DAY 3: Toledo ★★★

Having survived 2 days in the capital of Spain, bid *adios* and take a RENFE train to Toledo. These depart frequently from Madrid's Chamartín station (trip time: 1½ hr.).

Much of Spain's history took place behind Toledo's old walls. There is so much to see here that you need 2 days, but on a hurried visit you can visit the fortified palace, the **Alcázar,** with its army museum (p. 193); and the crowning glory of the city, the **Catedral de Toledo** (p. 195). The masterpiece of El Greco, *The Burial of the Count of Orgaz,* rests in **Iglesia de Santo Tomé** (p. 196). If time remains, see **Casa y Museo de El Greco** (p. 195), or the House and Museum of El Greco, although the artist didn't actually live here. Toledo is known for its damascene work, so pick up a souvenir before returning to Madrid by train that night. ***Note:*** At press time, the Alcázar and the El Greco House and Museum were closed for renovations; check to see if they have reopened at the time of your visit.

DAY 4: Segovia ★★★

While still based in Madrid, begin **Day 4** by taking an excursion to **Segovia,** leaving from Madrid's Chamartín station and arriving 2 hours later. The thrill of visiting the most spectacularly sited city in Spain is to view its **Alcázar** (p. 213), which rises starkly above the plain like a fairy-tale castle created by Disney. You can also view the **Cabildo Catedral de Segovia** (p. 214) and the town's architectural marvel, **Acueducto Romano** (p. 215). After lunch in Segovia, head 11km (6¾ miles) southeast to view the **Palacio Real de La Granja** (p. 218), the summer palace of the Bourbon kings. Return to Segovia and take the train back to Madrid.

The Roman aqueduct of Segovia.

DAY 5: El Escorial ★★★

Vying with Toledo as the most popular day trip from Madrid, the half monastery/half royal mausoleum of **San Lorenzo de El Escorial** (p. 207) is about an hour from Madrid's Atocha station. Felipe II constructed this mammoth complex for "God and myself," with its splendid library, palaces, and some of the world's greatest art. You can spend a full day here, breaking only for lunch, as you wander the art galleries and state apartments, including the throne room.

If you have time, make a side trip to **El Valle de los Caídos** (the **Valley of the Fallen;** p. 208), a moving and evocative monument dedicated to the *caídos,* or "fallen," who died in the Spanish Civil War in the late 1930s. Return to Madrid in the evening.

DAY 6: Córdoba ★★★

Leave Madrid early in the morning, taking the 419km (260-mile) train ride (AVE or TALGO) to Córdoba in the south, reached in 1½ to 2 hours. Córdoba was once the capital of the Islamic nation in the West. Take 2 hours to visit its **Mezquita-Catedral de Córdoba** (p. 299), the greatest Islamic masterpiece remaining in the Western world. Its stunning labyrinth of columns and red-and-white-striped arches alone is worth the visit. With remaining time you can visit **Alcázar de los Reyes Cristianos** (p. 299), a stellar example of military architecture where Ferdinand and Isabella once governed.

After lunch, take one of the frequent trains running between Córdoba and Seville. The fastest train, the AVE, takes only 45 minutes to reach Seville, where you can spend the night.

DAY 7: Seville ★★★

For a more extensive tour of Andalusia, see "Andalusia in 1 Week," p. 107. On the morning of **Day 7,** get set to experience the glories of Seville. We like to acclimate ourselves by wandering the narrow streets of **Barrio de Santa Cruz** (p. 318), the most evocative district, with its medieval streets, pocket-size plazas, and flower-filled wrought-iron balconies or tiled courtyards.

After that, head for the **Catedral de Sevilla** and **Giralda Tower** (p. 315). The cathedral is the largest Gothic building in the world and the third-largest church in Europe. After spending 1½ hours here, climb **La Giralda,** an adjacent Moorish tower erected by Islamic architects in the 12th century.

After lunch, head for the **Alcázar** (p. 311), the other great architectural monument of Seville, which lies north of the cathedral. This is the oldest royal residence in Europe still in use, dating from the 14th century. Allow 1½ hours for a hurried visit. With time remaining, visit **Museo de Bellas Artes de Sevilla** (p. 316), a converted convent housing some of Andalusia's greatest artwork, including masterpieces by El Greco and Murillo. A standard visit takes 1½ hours.

As the afternoon fades, go for a stroll through **Parque María Luisa,** which runs south along the Guadalquivir River. In summer you can rent a boat and go for a refreshing sail. After dinner in the Old Town, head for a flamenco show if you still have energy.

The next morning you can take a fast train back to Madrid for your flight home, saving the remaining wonders of Andalusia for another visit.

SPAIN IN 2 WEEKS

For this tour we head east to Barcelona, capital of Catalonia. In its own way, it is every bit as exciting as the tour of Madrid and Old Castile. Except for Madrid's "Golden Triangle" of art museums, Barcelona is an even more enthralling city than Madrid, because of its hills, bustling port life, and daring and provocative Art Nouveau architecture.

If you move fast enough, you can take in not only Barcelona but the Benedictine monastery of Montserrat, built into a jagged mountain, as well as visit Figueres to see the Salvador Dalí museum—and maybe get in some beach time at Tossa de Mar, our favorite sands in the Costa Brava.

DAYS 1 TO 7: Spain in 1 week

Follow the itineraries outlined on p. 93.

DAYS 8, 9 & 10: Barcelona ★★★

Arrive as early as you can on **Day 8** to walk the narrow cobblestone streets of the **Barri Gòtic** (p. 505), the Gothic Quarter, the single most fascinating old ghetto of any street in Europe. There is a discovery to be made at every turn. As you stroll, you'll think you're walking back into the Middle Ages. The highlight of your morning tour here will be the **Catedral de Barcelona,** dating from the 1200s and the greatest example of Catalonian Gothic architecture (p. 505).

After you see the Gothic Quarter, continue on to **Las Ramblas.** This is the most famous street in Spain, alive at all hours, day and night. Stretching from Plaça de Catalunya in the north to Plaça Portal de la Pau along the waterfront, this is a boulevard of flower vendors, booksellers, palaces, shops, and cafes—a perfect introduction to life as uniquely lived in Barcelona. At the end of the tree-lined boulevard, opening onto the waterfront, is a monument to Columbus.

Once you're at the port, walk east along **Moll de la Fusta** for its views of Barcelona port life, coming to a halt at **Parc de la Ciutadella,** where you can sit on a park bench and rest your feet.

Immediately south of the park is the waterfront and old fishermen's quarter of **Barceloneta,** ideal for a seafood lunch.

After lunch, continue north to **La Sagrada Família** (p. 508), Europe's most unconventional church. This uncompleted work is by the incomparable Antoni Gaudí (1852–1926), the leading exponent of Catalan *modernisme.*

To cap your afternoon, take the funicular to the fountains of **Montjuïc** (p. 517), where you'll see Barcelona spread out at your feet. The illuminated fountain display, **Fuentes Luminosas,** is one of the highlights of a trip to Barcelona. You can hang out here and make an evening of it, visiting the **Poble Espanyol** (p. 514), a re-created Spanish village constructed in 1929 for the World's Fair. You can also have dinner in the faux village.

On **Day 9,** visit **Museu Picasso** (p. 510), in the Gothic Quarter, allowing yourself at least 1½ hours. Stroll through the surrounding district, Barri de la Ribera, which is filled with Renaissance mansions and an intriguing collection of art galleries that surround Picasso's trove of treasures.

Days 1–7 See "Spain in 1 Week" map
Days 8–10 Barcelona
Day 11 Montserrat
Day 12 Girona & the Dalí Museum
Day 13 The Costa Brava
Day 14 Sitges and Tarragona

Before lunch you can still take in the art at **Museu Nacional d'Art de Catalunya** (p. 509), Catalonia's major art gallery, containing one of the world's greatest collections of Romanesque art. Allow 2 hours for a visit.

In the afternoon, visit the **Fundació Joan Miró** (p. 508), which owns 10,000 works, mainly paintings and sculpture, by this Catalan surrealist. To reach it, you can return to Parc de Montjuïc where, hopefully, you can watch the sun set over the skyline and port of Barcelona. Allow at least 1½ hours for visits to each of these museums.

Devote **Day 10** to all the highlights of Barcelona you've missed so far. Pay a morning visit to Gaudí's idiosyncratic park, **Parc Güell** (p. 510). Designated a World Heritage Site by UNESCO, this colorful creation of bizarre architectural monuments dates from 1922 and includes such Gaudí fantasies as the "Room of a Hundred Columns," with its 84 crooked pillars. On-site is a gingerbread-style house where Gaudí lived from 1906 to 1926. (It's been turned into a museum.) You can spend 2 hours wandering around this uncompleted park before heading back to Las Ramblas for lunch at a sidewalk cafe, where you can watch an ever-changing parade of colorful characters.

Mosaic sculptures in Barcelona's Parc Güell.

For a change of pace, after lunch visit **Palau Reial** (**Royal Palace;** p. 514), the former palace of the counts of Barcelona. Be sure to check out the Saló Del Tinell, where Isabella and Ferdinand received Columbus after his triumphant return from America. In the afternoon, head for **Tibidabo Mountain** (p. 516) for the most panoramic views of Barcelona. A funicular takes you to its summit at 488m (1,600 ft.).

Climax your tour of Barcelona by an early evening *paseo* along the **Eixample** district. Armed with a good map, take in **Plaça de Catalunya,** the geographic heart of the city, along with **Passeig de Gracia,** the boulevard of fashionable shops, and Gaudí's **La Pedrera (Casa Milà;** p. 516).

DAY 11: Montserrat ★★

Trains leave frequently from Plaça d'Espanya in Barcelona, taking you to the historic monastery of **Montserrat** (p. 536), 56km (35 miles) northwest of Barcelona. The final approach to the lofty mountaintop citadel is by aerial cableway. You can make a day out of this visit, including time spent getting there and back; a one-way trip takes an hour.

Stop in at the Montserrat tourist office (p. 538) and pick up a map to aid you in mountain walks, some of which are reached by the Santa Cova funicular. You can order lunch at Montserrat's only hotel, **Abat Cisneros** (p. 539). Time your visit so you can listen to the 50-member **Escolanía** at 1pm daily (p. 538). It's one of Europe's oldest and most renowned boys' choirs. Return to Barcelona in the evening for a stroll along Las Ramblas.

DAY 12: Girona & the Dalí Museum ★★★

On **Day 12,** rent a car in Barcelona and set out to explore the highlights of the province of Catalonia. Your first stop is the ancient city of **Girona** (p. 555), where you can book a hotel for the night.

In 2 hours, you can explore the medieval city, the most important attractions being its magnificent **Catedral** (p. 557) and its **Museu d'Art** (p. 559), the latter installed in a Romanesque and Gothic palace.

In the afternoon, drive northeast 37km (23 miles) to the little town of **Figueres** (p. 571). Here you can visit the number-one attraction in all of Catalonia, **Teatre Museu Dalí** (p. 573). The incomparable Dalí was born in this town in 1904, and he honored his birthplace by leaving a vast array of work, making this *teatro* the most visited museum in Spain, after the Prado. Many of his hallucinatory images are on display; a highlight is the Mae West Room. Return to Girona and join the locals in an early-evening *paseo* along the historic streets of the Old Town.

DAY 13: The Costa Brava ★★★

The so-called "wild coast" of Spain extends from the French border south toward Barcelona for 153km (95 miles). A drive along this rugged coast is one of the most memorable in Spain.

From Girona, check out of your hotel and drive east to our favorite resort along the coast, Tossa de Mar, a former 12th-century walled town, with good beaches, only 90km (56 miles) north of Barcelona. Check into a hotel here and get in some beach time before lunch.

In the afternoon, drive north for a visit to the most charming town along the coast, **Cadaqués** (p. 575), the last resort on the Costa Brava, 196km (122 miles) north of Barcelona. The unspoiled village is enchantment itself, fancifully dubbed "the St. Tropez of Spain." Return to Tossa de Mar for the night.

DAY 14: Sitges & Tarragona ★★

After checking out of your hotel at Tossa, head south along the coast, bypassing Barcelona to arrive at **Sitges** (p. 548) by midmorning. Although it has a strong gay patronage, this is a resort for all sexual orientations. Once it was a retreat for such artists as Salvador Dalí and Picasso. You can spend some time on the sands as well as visit museums. If you have time for only one, make it **Museu Cau Ferrat** (p. 549), where Catalan artist Santiago Rusiñol combined two 16th-century fishermen's cottages to create his house and studio, which is now a museum.

From Sitges, continue south to **Tarragona** (p. 540) for the night, a total distance from Barcelona of only 97km (60 miles). Perched on a rocky bluff above the Mediterranean, this is an ancient Roman port city. Walk its fashionable *rambles* (wide boulevards), checking out its **Catedral** (p. 542) and its **Passeig Arqueològic** (p. 543), an archway that leads to a walk along ancient ramparts built by the Romans.

Tarragona has some good restaurants serving Catalan specialties and fresh seafood. After an overnight, you can return to Barcelona in the morning for your flight back home.

SPAIN FOR FAMILIES

Spain offers many attractions that kids will enjoy. Perhaps your main concern about bringing children along is pacing yourself with museum time. After all, would you really want to go to Madrid and miss the Prado?

We suggest that you explore Madrid for 2 days with the brood in tow, and then spend a day wandering through the Old City of Toledo, which kids may think was created by Disney. After that, fly from Madrid to Barcelona for 2 days in a city filled with amusements for kids. Finally, fly from Barcelona to Seville for your final 2 days in Andalusia. In Seville, you can link up with either a flight or a fast train back to Madrid.

DAYS 1 & 2: Madrid ★★★

Arrive early in Madrid to get a running start. **Museo del Prado** (p. 160) opens at 9am, but you can get an early jump on sightseeing by heading for the adjoining **Parque del Retiro** (p. 169). With its fountains and statues, plus a large lake, this is a virtual amusement park for kids. Although your child may not be a museum buff, there are many works in the Prado that will sometimes fascinate kids long after their parents' attention has strayed—take *The Garden of Earthly Delights* by Bosch as an example. After 2 hours spent traipsing through the Prado, head for **Parque de Atracciones** (p. 171), in the Casa de Campo, for a carousel, pony rides, and even an adventure into "outer space." There are places for lunch here. In the afternoon, take in the **Zoo Aquarium de Madrid** (p. 171), with its tropical auditorium and some 3,000 animals on parade. Finally, a thrilling ride on the **Teleférico** (p. 170) is a fit ending for a busy day.

For **Day 2** in Madrid, take your brood to **Palacio Real (Royal Palace;** p. 164), with its 2,000 rooms. Your kids may have never seen a royal

A lionfish at the Zoo Aquarium de Madrid.

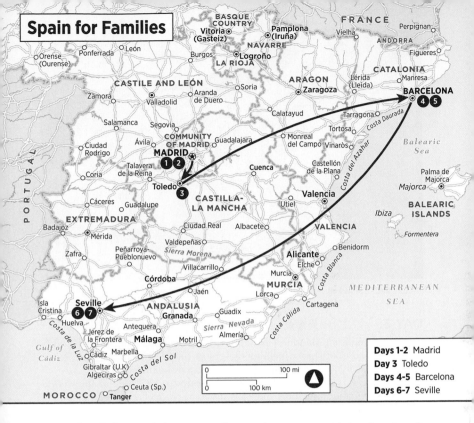

Days 1-2 Madrid
Day 3 Toledo
Days 4-5 Barcelona
Days 6-7 Seville

palace before, and this one is of particular interest, with its changing-of-the-guard ceremony, its gardens, and its collection of weaponry and armor. Allow 2 hours for a visit. If you arrived by 9 or 9:30am, you'll still have time to see **Museo de Cera de Madrid** (p. 170), the wax museum. You can easily spend an hour here and may have to drag your kids away for lunch.

For your midday meal, head for the restaurants at **Plaza Mayor** (p. 157) or on one of the side streets branching from this landmark square. This is the heart of Old Madrid, and you can easily spend 2 or 3 hours wandering its ancient streets. **Sobrino de Botín** (p. 154) is our favorite place to dine in the area. Beloved by Hemingway, it was featured in the final pages of his novel *The Sun Also Rises*.

To cap your experience, head for **Parque Warner Madrid** (© **90-202-41-00**; www.parquewarner.com), a Hollywood theme park. It's not very Spanish but is fun for all ages. You'll find it 22km (14 miles) outside Madrid on A-4 in San Martín de la Vega. You can reach it by bus no. 416 from Madrid's Estación Sur de Autobuses. Movie World charges 35€ for ages 11 to 59, 27€ for ages 5 to 10 or 60 and over. Children 4 and under are admitted free. There are all sorts of restaurants here, plus a vast array of amusements ranging from a Tom & Jerry roller-coaster ride to a Río Bravo *La Aventura*.

Toledo's Plaza Zocodover.

DAY 3: Toledo ★★★

Departing from Madrid's Chamartín station (trip time: 1½ hr.), a RENFE train heads south to the monumental city of Toledo, ancient capital of Spain. A tour of Toledo is like taking your kid into a living-history book.

Head first for the **Catedral de Toledo** (p. 195), one of the world's greatest Gothic structures and a jaw-dropping piece of architecture that will enthrall even the children.

After a visit, wander around the historic Old Town, with its narrow, twisting streets. It's a maze that's fun to get lost in. Eventually you reach **Plaza Zocodover,** the heart of the Old Town.

To avoid claustrophobia after all those labyrinthine streets, walk out of the ghetto through the San Martín sector and over to Puente San Martín, a bridge dating from 1203. As you and your brood cross the bridge, take a look back at Toledo rising on a hill before you, evoking an El Greco painting.

In the afternoon, spend about 30 minutes at **Casa y Museo de El Greco** (p. 195). Then go on a walking tour of the military fortress, the **Alcázar,** inspecting all the military weaponry (p. 193). Allow a final hour for this tour before taking one of the frequent trains back to Madrid.

DAYS 4 & 5: Barcelona ★★★

On **Day 4,** transfer to Barcelona in the east, either by train or plane. If you arrive early, you can take a 2-hour stroll through the history-rich **Barri Gòtic,** or Gothic Quarter (p. 505). Children love to wander through this maze of narrow, cobblestone streets, some dark and spooky like those in a horror movie. Drop in to visit the **Catedral de Barcelona** (p. 505). Ride the elevator leading to the roof for one of the most panoramic views of the Old City. If it's noon on a Sunday, the entire family can delight in the *sardana,* the most typical of Catalonian folk dances, performed in front of the church.

Southeast of the Barri Gòtic lies the second-most-colorful district of Barcelona, La Ribera, home to **Museu Picasso** (p. 510). Allow at least an hour for a visit and don't worry about boring the kids. Children always seem fascinated by the works of this controversial artist, even when they exclaim, "Mom, I can paint better than that."

At one of the delis in La Ribera, secure the makings of a picnic lunch and head directly southeast to **Parc de la Ciutadella** (p. 517). Here the family can enjoy the lakes, promenades, flower gardens, and wacky Cascada fountains. The highlight is **Parc Zoològic** (p. 519), the top zoo in Spain, spread over 13 hectares (32 acres), with some 7,500 animals, many of which are endangered.

After leaving the park, head west along the port of Barcelona, where you'll find the liveliest and most beautiful walk along **Moll de la Fusta.** This leads to the Plaça Portal de la Pau, at the foot of Las Ramblas (the main street of Barcelona). At the **Mirador de Colón** (p. 511), a monument to Columbus, take the elevator to the top for the most panoramic view of Barcelona's harbor.

Next, head north along **Las Ramblas.** This pedestrian-only strip extends north to Plaça de Catalunya. A stroll along this bustling avenue with its flower vendors is the highlight of a visit to Barcelona. Kids scream in delight as a man in an ostrich suit jumps out to frighten them.

To cap a very busy day, visit the mountain park of **Montjuïc** (p. 517), with its fountains, outdoor restaurants, gardens, and amusements, including an illuminated fountain display. Children enjoy wandering through the 1929 **Poble Espanyol** (p. 519), a re-created Spanish village. There are plenty of places to dine—many quite affordable—in this sprawling park south of Barcelona.

The park atop Barcelona's Montjuïc mountain.

On **Day 5,** visit **La Sagrada Família** (p. 508), the uncompleted masterpiece of the incomparable Gaudí. Take your brood up 400 steep stone steps to the towers and upper galleries (or else go up in the elevator) for a majestic view.

Still in a Gaudí frame of mind, head northwest to **Parc Güell** (p. 510), which has been likened to a surrealist Disneyland. Children take delight in the architecture, including two Hansel and Gretel–style gatehouses on Carrer d'Olot. The park still has much woodland ideal for a picnic.

After lunch, pay a visit to **L'Aquarium de Barcelona** (p. 511), the largest aquarium in Europe, with 21 glass tanks, each depicting a different marine habitat. Take your kids through the 75m (246-ft.) glass tunnel filled with sharks, stingrays, and other denizens of the deep.

Cap the day by heading for the **Parc d'Atraccions** (p. 519), a vast funfair. The park atop Tibidabo mountain is reached by funicular. First opened in 1908, the park has since modernized the rides. Automated toys are just some of the amusements at the on-site Museu d'Automates.

DAYS 6 & 7: Seville ★★★

To save precious time, we recommend that you fly from Barcelona to Seville on Iberia. (By train, the trip takes 11–12 hr.)

After checking into a hotel for 2 nights, head for the **Alcázar** (p. 311) for a 2-hour visit. This is one of the oldest royal residences in Europe. Kids delight in its construction and layout, which range from a dolls' patio to Moorish gardens with lush terraces and fountains.

Emerge in time for lunch in the **Barrio de Santa Cruz** (p. 318), the former Jewish ghetto from the Middle Ages. The most colorful place for a walk in Seville, it is filled with tiny squares, whitewashed houses, and flower-filled patios as you explore a maze of narrow alleyways. There are many taverns in the area serving lunch. The center of the old ghetto is **Plaza de Santa Cruz.** South of the square are the **Murillo Gardens,** where you can go for a stroll after eating.

Before the afternoon fades, head for **Catedral de Sevilla** (p. 315), the largest Gothic building in the world and the third-largest church in Europe. Allow an hour for the cathedral, followed by a climb up **La Giralda,** the ancient Moorish tower adjacent to the cathedral.

For **Day 7,** your final look at Seville, head for **Parque María Luisa** (p. 318). Pavilions constructed for the Spanish American Exhibition of 1929 still stand here. You can spend at least 2 pleasure-filled hours in the park, going on boat rides along the Guadalquivir River and walking along flower-bordered paths. If you can afford it, treat your brood to a horse-and-buggy ride.

Afterward, head for the landmark square, **Plaza de América** (p. 319), where you can stroll through rose gardens past water ponds and splashing fountains. Take time out to visit the **Museo de Artes y Costumbres Populares** (p. 290), a kid-pleaser with all sorts of weaponry, folklore costumes, horse saddles, and musical instruments.

For lunch, head for **Bar Giralda,** Mateos Gago 1, Barrio de Santa Cruz (© **95-422-74-35**), a tavern converted from a Muslim bathhouse across from Giralda Tower. Snag a seat on the terrace, with its panoramic view of the cathedral. Since 1934 it's been serving that kiddie favorite: *patatas a la importancia* (fried potatoes stuffed with ham and cheese). Grown-ups like them, too.

After lunch, take a bus to **Itálica** (p. 333), 9km (5½ miles) north-west of Seville. These ruins represent what was once a Roman city, founded in 206 B.C. The infamous emperors Trajan and Hadrian were both born here. The chief ruin is an elliptically shaped amphitheater that once held 25,000 spectators. Spend at least 1½ hours wandering through this city from yesterday.

Return to Seville in time for a summer night's visit to **La Cartuja** (open until midnight). Now converted into **Isla Mágica (Magic Island)**, it was the site of the 1992 World Expo. Turned into a theme park, it offers rides and shows. Its motion-picture theater offers seats that shake and shimmy like the vehicles on the screen. Magic Island is at Pabellón de España, Isla de la Cartuja, across Puente de la Barqueta (take bus no. C2 from the center).

ANDALUSIA IN 1 WEEK

Of all the provinces of Spain that merit tours in themselves, the most history-rich and evocative is Andalusia in southern Spain. It offers three of the grandest cities in all of Europe: Seville, Granada, and Córdoba, in that order.

Home of flamenco, sherry, and the country's most spectacular festivities and bullfights, Andalusia also possesses the grandest monuments, especially the Mezquita in Córdoba and the Alhambra in Granada.

After visiting the art cities of Andalusia, you can relax and wind down on its beaches strung along the Costa del Sol.

DAY 1: Córdoba & the Mezquita ★★★

The ancient Islamic center of culture in the West, Córdoba can be your gateway to Andalusia, that rich, antiquity-filled province of southern Spain. In just 1½ to 2 hours, a fast train (AVE or TALGO) from Madrid can put you in this once-great city where the Muslims ruled Spain in the Middle Ages. Check into a hotel for the night and set out to explore the glories of the **Mezquita-Catedral de Córdoba** (p. 299). Dating back 12 centuries, Córdoba's once-great mosque can easily occupy an hour and a half of your time. Discover such treasures as its Patio de los Naranjas, where orange trees grow; its Mihrab or Islamic prayer niche; and its 16th-century cathedral. Take in its labyrinth of arches and pillars, more than 850 in all.

Wander over to **Alcázar de los Reyes Cristianos** (p. 299), the former home of the Christian queens and kings such as Isabella and Ferdinand. After inspecting the fortresslike architecture inside, stroll through the beautiful gardens. Try one of the typical restaurants for lunch, our favorite being **El Caballo Rojo** (p. 308), within walking distance of the Mezquita. After lunch, wander about the **Barrio de la Judería (Jewish Quarter)** and visit its old **Sinagoga** (p. 301), dating from 1350. Allow yourself at least 1½ hours to stroll through the quarter's narrow, crooked streets flanked by whitewashed, stucco-fronted houses with flower-filled patios.

Before the afternoon fades, stop by **Palacio Museo de Viana** (p. 301), one of the few private palaces open to the public. There is no finer way to see how the grand dons of yesterday lived.

There will still be time for shopping in this city known for its crafts. Your best bet is to go to **Arte Zoco** (p. 303), an association of the best of

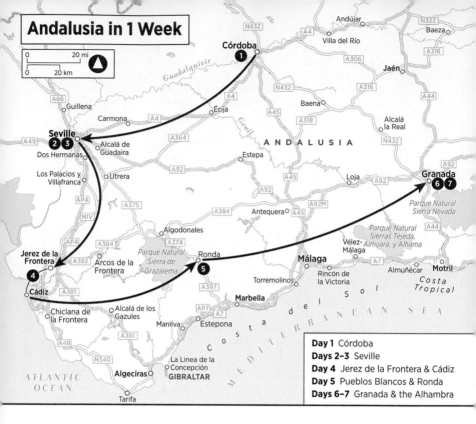

the craftspeople established in the old Jewish Quarter. A final *paseo* along the Guadalquivir River will top off the day nicely.

DAYS 2 & 3: Seville ★★★

On **Day 2,** a fast AVE train will transport you from Córdoba in the morning to the even more fabulous city of Seville. Perhaps the most charming of all Spanish destinations, this is the land of Don Juan, Carmen, and flamenco. After checking into a hotel for 2 nights, begin your tour of Seville with the **Catedral de Sevilla** and its **Giralda Tower** (p. 315). You can spend 1½ hours wandering through this great Gothic edifice before you scale La Giralda, the adjacent Moorish tower, for the city's undisputedly most panoramic view.

Next, walk to the **Alcázar** (p. 311), north of the cathedral. You can spend an hour wandering through its fabulous gardens, with its terraces, fountains, and pavilions, and then spend another hour exploring its chief attractions such as the Charles V Rooms, Salón de Embajadores, and Patio de las Doncellas.

Head for the **Barrio de Santa Cruz** (p. 318) for lunch and 2 hours of walking. Our favorite spot here for lunch is **Albahaca** (p. 368). After dining, wander at your own pace through the barrio, the former Jewish ghetto with its whitewashed houses and flower-filled balconies and patios.

To cap the afternoon, head for **Parque María Luisa** (p. 318) to wander along flower-bordered paths and where you can rent boats for rides along the Guadalquivir River. At night, enjoy a typically Andalusian dinner climaxed by a night of flamenco.

On **Day 3,** visit **Casa de Pilatos** (p. 314) in the morning. This was the 16th-century palace of the dukes of Medinaceli. Located a 7-minute walk from the cathedral, it is filled with rare treasures. Spend about 40 minutes here before proceeding to the **Museo de Bellas Artes de Sevilla** (p. 316), a treasure-trove of Andalusian art, including many works by Spanish Old Masters such as El Greco and Murillo.

Have lunch at one of the city's tapas bars before heading out of Seville for the afternoon to visit the ruins of the ancient Roman city of **Itálica** (p. 333), 9km (5½ miles) to the northwest. It can be reached by bus, which departs from the Plaza de Armas in Seville. Spend 1½ hours wandering the remains of a once-great city before returning to Seville.

For a romantic ending to your time in a romantic city, you can take one of the horse-and-buggy rides through **Barrio de Santa Cruz** (p. 318). To top your evening, catch a performance at the **Teatro de la Maestranza** (p. 332). Perhaps a Spanish *zarzuela* (operetta) will be performed. Maybe you can even see the opera *The Barber of Seville.*

DAY 4: Jerez de la Frontera & Cádiz ★★

On **Day 4,** rent a car in Seville and head south for 87km (54 miles) to the sherry-producing town of Jerez de la Frontera. Here you can tour one of the wine bodegas to see how sherry is made and end the evening with a tasting. Allow about 2 hours for a visit. For more details, see "Touring the Bodegas" (p. 335).

You can also visit **Escuela Andaluza del Arte Ecuestre** (p. 336) to see the famous dancing horses of Jerez. After a typical Andalusian lunch in Jerez, continue south to the port of **Cádiz** (p. 339), and check into a hotel for the night.

In the oldest inhabited city in the Western world, take a voyage of exploration along the historic **seaside promenades** (p. 340), where conquistadors set out to plunder the riches of the New World. Your *paseo* can end in Parque Genovés, with its exotic trees hauled in by ships sailing the Seven Seas. Visit the **Catedral de Cádiz** (p. 340) and the **Museo de Cádiz** (p. 341) before the end of the afternoon.

DAY 5: Pueblos Blancos & Ronda ★★

On **Day 5,** arm yourself with a good map and drive north from Cádiz to **Arcos de la Frontera,** where you can easily begin your journey to the town of Ronda.

Arcos is the most beautiful of the **Pueblos Blancos (White Villages)** sprinkled throughout Andalusia. The road to Ronda cuts through the Sierra de Grazalema Nature Reserve, which runs almost the entire length of the route of the Pueblos Blancos. You can have lunch in Arcos or in one of the little whitewashed towns along the way.

The road trip ends in **Ronda** (p. 346), which sits on a 150m (500-ft.) gorge spanned by a stone bridge. Spend the rest of the afternoon touring its minor sights, including some Arab baths. Overnight in Ronda.

Trained horses at the Escuela Andaluza del Arte Ecuestre.

A pool at the Generalife.

DAYS 6 & 7: Granada & the Alhambra ★★★

On **Day 6,** leave Ronda in the morning and continue your journey to the east until you reach the fabled city of **Granada** (p. 352). Book into a hotel for 2 nights. For some travelers, the experience of the Alhambra equals or tops anything discovered in Seville.

After lunch in Granada, set out to see the **Alhambra** and the **Generalife** (p. 356), the summer palace. The lavish palace, once inhabited by the rulers of the Nasrid dynasty, is the number-one attraction in all of Andalusia. That night, have dinner at the **Parador de Granada** (p. 363) the most famous *parador* in Spain. The former convent founded by the Catholic monarchs actually lies within the grounds of the Alhambra.

On **Day 7,** your final day in Granada, visit the **Catedral** and **Capilla Real** (p. 362) in the morning. The ornate Renaissance cathedral, with its Royal Chapel, was built in the flamboyant Gothic style and is the final resting place of Queen Isabella and King Ferdinand. Allow 2 hours for a visit.

Spend the rest of the morning exploring the old Arab quarter, the **Albaicín** (p. 356). On this hilly terrain, you'll find many old taverns for lunch. After a meal, pay a visit to the **Monasterio Cartuja** (p. 362), dating from the 16th century. This was the Christian answer to the Alhambra, although it is hardly as spectacular. Cap the day by shopping in the **Alcaicería,** the old Moorish silk market near the cathedral. It's filled with shops selling the arts and crafts of Granada province.

You may wish to end your day with a visit to the **Gypsy Caves of Sacromonte** (p. 371), which are overly commercialized but where the sounds of Gypsy music fill the Granadian night. First-time visitors persist in visiting these caves in spite of their touristy aura.

From Granada, you can make easy flight or rail connections back to Madrid, assuming that the capital is your departure point from Spain.

MADRID

5

nned, and built when Spain
er, and the city became the
f a great empire stretch-
umental Madrid glitters
me, or London—and it
Although it lacks the
ents of older Spanish
deur.

nd its climate is blis-
affic roars down wide
of the city's 17th-century core to
spread in recent decades.

expecting a city that looks classically Iberian. True,
buildings in the historic core look as Spanish as those you
encounter in rural towns across the plains of La Mancha. However, a great
number of the monuments and palaces mirror the architecture of France—an
oddity that reflects the link between the royal families of Spain and France.

Most striking is how the city has blossomed since Franco's demise. During
the 1980s, Madrid was the epicenter of La Movida (the movement), a resuscita-
tion of the arts after years of dictatorial creative repression. Today, despite stiff
competition from such smaller cities as Barcelona and Seville, Madrid still reigns
as the country's artistic and creative center.

PREVIOUS PAGE: **The cafes of Plaza Mayor.** ABOVE: **Rowboats in Parque del Retiro's lake.**

More world-class art is on view in the central neighborhood around the stellar Museo del Prado than within virtually any concentrated area in the world. You can see Caravaggios and Rembrandts at the Thyssen-Bornemisza; El Grecos and Velázquezes at the Prado itself; and Dalís and Mirós—not to mention Picasso's wrenching *Guernica*—at the Reina Sofía.

Regrettably, within the city limits you'll also find sprawling expanses of concrete towers, sometimes paralyzing traffic, growing street crime, and entire districts that, as in every other metropolis, bear virtually no historic or cultural interest for a temporary visitor. Many longtime visitors to the city find that its quintessential Spanish feel has subsided somewhat in the face of a Brussels-like "Europeanization" that has occurred since Spain's 1986 induction into the European Union. The city's gems remain the opulence of the Palacio Real, the bustle of El Rastro's flea market, and the sultry fever of late-night flamenco. Visitors find respite in Parque del Retiro, a vast, verdant oasis in the heart of the city, just a stone's throw from the Prado.

If your time in Spain is limited, a stopover in Madrid, coupled with day trips to its environs, can provide a primer in virtually every major period and school of Spanish art and architecture dating from the Roman occupation. No fewer than nine world-class destinations are within 161km (100 miles). They include Toledo, one of the most successful blends of medieval Arab, Jewish, and Christian cultures in the world; Segovia, site of a well-preserved ancient Roman aqueduct and monuments commemorating Queen Isabella's 1474 coronation; and Avila, the most perfectly preserved medieval fortified city in Iberia, with its 11th-century battlements and endless references to Catholicism's most down-to-earth mystic, St. Teresa. El Escorial and the palace and monuments at Aranjuez reveal the tastes and manias that inspired rulers of Spain throughout history. The neofascist monument at El Valle de los Caídos (The Valley of the Fallen) is a powerful testament to those who died in the Spanish Civil War. To see rural Iberia at its most charming, head for Chinchón, or, better yet, visit the cliff-top village of Cuenca, where a lavish homage to modern art and music has been installed. For more information on these day trips, see chapter 6, p. 190.

ORIENTATION
Arriving

BY PLANE Madrid's international airport, **Barajas** (airport code: MAD), lies 15km (9⅓ miles) east of the city center and has two terminals—one for international traffic, the other for domestic—connected by a moving sidewalk. For Barajas Airport information, call © **90-240-47-04,** or check www.aena.es.

Air-conditioned airport **buses** can take you from the arrivals terminal to a bus depot beneath the central Plaza de Colón. The fare is 2€; buses leave every 10 to 15 minutes, either to or from the airport.

By **taxi,** expect to pay 25€ and up, plus surcharges, for the trip to the airport and for baggage handling. If you take an unmetered limousine, make sure you negotiate the price in advance.

A **subway** connecting Barajas Airport and central Madrid was completed in 1999, allowing additional ground transportation options. However, the ride involves a change: Take line 8 to Nuevos Ministerios and switch to line 4; the one-way trip costs 3€.

BY TRAIN Madrid has two major railway stations: **Atocha** (Glorieta Carlos V; Metro: Atocha RENFE), for trains to and from Lisbon, Toledo, Andalusia, and Extremadura; and **Chamartín** (in the northern suburbs at Augustín de Foxá; Metro: Chamartín), for trains to and from Barcelona, Asturias, Cantabria, Castilla-León, the Basque Country, Aragón, Catalonia, Levante (Valencia), Murcia, and the French frontier. For information about connections from any of these stations, call **RENFE (Spanish Railways)** at ℂ **90-224-02-02** (daily 5am–11:50pm).

The new terminal at Barajas Airport.

For tickets, go to RENFE's main office at Alcalá 44 (ℂ **90-224-02-02** or 90-224-34-02; www.renfe.es; Metro: Banco de España). The office is open Monday to Friday 9:30am to 11:30pm.

BY BUS Madrid has at least 14 major bus terminals, including **Estación Sur de Autobuses,** Calle Méndez Alvaro 83 (ℂ **91-468-42-00;** www.estaciondeautobuses.com; Metro: Méndez Alvaro). Most buses pass through this large station.

BY CAR All highways within Spain radiate outward from Madrid. The following are the major highways into Madrid, with information on driving distances to the city:

Highways to Madrid

ROUTE	FROM	DISTANCE TO MADRID
N-I	Irún	507km (315 miles)
N-II	Barcelona	626km (389 miles)
N-III	Valencia	349km (217 miles)
N-IV	Cádiz	625km (388 miles)
N-V	Badajoz	409km (254 miles)
N-VI	Galicia	602km (374 miles)

Visitor Information

The most convenient **tourist office** is located on Duque de Medinaceli 2, Banco de España (ℂ **91-429-49-51;** www.turismomadrid.es; Metro: Antón Martín; bus no. 9, 27, 34, or 37); it's open Monday to Saturday 9am to 7pm and Sunday and holidays 9am to 3pm. Ask for a street map of the next town on your itinerary, especially if you're driving. The staff here can give you a list of hotels and *hostales*.

WEBSITES The Tourist Office of Spain (**www.spain.info**) can help you plan your trip with listings of lodging options, attractions, tour operators, and packages, plus handy tips on getting around. For the viewpoint of individual travelers, check **www.tripadvisor.com** and **www.virtualtourist.com**. The highly personal **www.madridman.com** has a home page that looks frivolous but provides a surprising amount of information, especially on cheap hostels.

City Layout

All roads lead to Madrid, which has outgrown its previous boundaries and is branching out in all directions.

MAIN ARTERIES & SQUARES Every new arrival must find the **Gran Vía,** which cuts a winding pathway across the city, beginning at **Plaza de España,** where you'll find one of Europe's tallest skyscrapers, the Edificio España. This avenue is home to the largest concentration of shops, hotels, restaurants, and movie houses in the city, with **Calle de Serrano** a close runner-up.

South of the Gran Vía lies **Puerta del Sol,** the starting point for all road distances within Spain. However, its tourism significance has declined, and today it is a prime hunting ground for pickpockets and purse snatchers. **Calle de Alcalá** begins here at Sol and runs for 4km (2½ miles).

Plaza Mayor lies at the heart of Old Madrid and is an attraction in itself, with its mix of French and Georgian architecture. (Again, be wary of thieves here, especially late at night.) Pedestrians pass beneath the arches of the huge square onto the narrow streets of Old Town, where you can find some of the capital's most intriguing restaurants and *tascas* serving tasty tapas and drinks. The colonnaded ground level of the plaza is filled with shops, many selling souvenir hats of turn-of-the-20th-century Spanish sailors or army officers.

The area south of Plaza Mayor—known as *barrios bajos*—is made up of narrow cobblestone streets lined with 16th- and 17th-century architecture. From Plaza Mayor, take **Arco de Cuchilleros,** a street packed with markets, restaurants, flamenco clubs, and taverns.

Gran Vía ends at Calle de Alcalá, and at this juncture lies the grand **Plaza de la Cibeles,** with its fountain to Cybele, "the mother of the gods," and the main post office (known as "the cathedral of post offices"). From Cibeles, the wide **Paseo de Recoletos** begins a short run north to Plaza de Colón. From this latter square rolls the serpentine central artery of Madrid: **Paseo de la Castellana,** flanked by expensive shops, apartment buildings, luxury hotels, and foreign embassies.

Heading south from Cibeles is **Paseo del Prado,** where you'll find Spain's major

---

Travel Discounts Galore

The **Madrid Card** grants access to dozens of museums, discounts on public transport, and reductions at many restaurants. Available at local tourist offices, the card costs 47€, 60€, and 74€ for 1, 2, or 3 days of use, respectively. The card also acts as a pass for 5 or 10 days of trips on the city's subway and buses. Even some participating nightclubs offer free drinks or discounts on their cover charges.

---

attraction, the Museo del Prado, as well as the Jardín Botánico (Botanical Garden). The *paseo* leads to the Atocha railway station. To the west of the garden lies **Parque del Retiro,** a magnificent park once reserved for royalty, with restaurants, nightclubs, a rose garden, and two lakes.

STREET MAPS Arm yourself with a good map before setting out. Falk maps are the best (www.omnimap.com/catalog/int/falk-map.htm), available at most newsstands and kiosks in Madrid. The free maps given away by tourist offices and hotels aren't really adequate for more than general orientation, as they don't list the maze of small streets that is Old Madrid.

The Neighborhoods in Brief

Madrid can be divided into three principal districts—Old Madrid, which holds the most tourist interest; Ensanche, the new district, often with the best shops and hotels; and the periphery, which is of little interest to visitors.

PLAZA MAYOR/PUERTA DEL SOL This is the heart of Old Madrid, often called the tourist zone. Filled with taverns and bars, it is bounded by Carrera de San Jerónimo, Calle Mayor, Cava de San Miguel, Cava Baja, and Calle de la Cruz. From Plaza Mayor, the Arco de Cuchilleros is filled with Castilian restaurants and taverns; more of these traditional spots, called *cuevas,* line the Cava de San Miguel, Cava Alta, and Cava Baja. To the west of this old district is the Manzanares River. Also in this area, Muslim Madrid is centered on the Palacio de Oriente and Las Vistillas. What is now Plaza de la Paja was actually the heart of the city and its main marketplace during the medieval period. In 1617, Plaza Mayor became the hub of Madrid, and it remains to this day the nighttime center of tourist activity, more so than Puerta del Sol.

THE SALAMANCA QUARTER Ever since Madrid's city walls came tumbling down in the 1860s, the district of Salamanca to the north has been the fashionable address. Calle de Serrano cuts through this neighborhood and is lined with stores and boutiques. The street is also home to the U.S. Embassy.

GRAN VÍA/PLAZA DE ESPAÑA Gran Vía is the city's main street, flanked by cinemas, department stores, and bank and corporate headquarters. It begins at Plaza de España, with its bronze figures of Don Quixote and his faithful squire, Sancho Panza.

ARGÜELLES/MONCLOA The university area is bounded by Pintor Rosales, Cea Bermúdez, Bravo Murillo, San Bernardo, and Conde Duque. Students haunt its famous alehouses.

CHUECA This old, decaying area north of the Gran Vía includes the main streets of Hortaleza, Infantas, Barquillo, and San Lucas. It is the center of gay nightlife, with dozens of clubs and cheap restaurants. It can be dangerous at night, although police presence is usually evident.

Madrid's main street, the Gran Vía.

CASTELLANA/RECOLETOS/PASEO DEL PRADO Not a real city district, this is Madrid's north-south axis, its name changing along the way. The Museo del Prado and some of the city's more expensive hotels are found here. Many restaurants and other hotels are located along its side streets. In summer its large medians serve as home to open-air terraces filled with animated crowds. The most famous cafe is the Gran Café de Gijón (p. 148).

GETTING AROUND

Getting around Madrid is not easy, because everything is spread out. Even many Madrileño taxi drivers (often new arrivals themselves) are unfamiliar with their own city once they're off the main boulevards.

By Subway

The Metro system is quite easy to learn and use. The fare is 1€ for a one-way trip, and the central converging point is the Puerta del Sol. The Metro operates from 6am to 2am, and you should try to avoid rush hours. For information, call ✆ **90-244-44-03** (fax 91-721-29-57; www.metromadrid.es). You can save money by purchasing a 10-trip ticket, known as a *bonos*—it costs 7.40€.

By Bus

A bus network also services the city and suburbs, with routes clearly shown at each stop on a schematic diagram. Buses are fast and efficient because they travel in special lanes. Both red and blue buses charge 1€ per ride. For 7.40€ you can purchase a 10-trip *bonos* ticket (but without transfers) for Madrid's bus system. The ticket is sold at **Empresa Municipal de Transportes,** Calle Cerro de Plata 4 (✆ **91-406-88-00** or 90-250-78-50; www.emtmadrid.es), where you can buy a guide to the bus routes. The office is open Monday to Friday from 8am to 2pm.

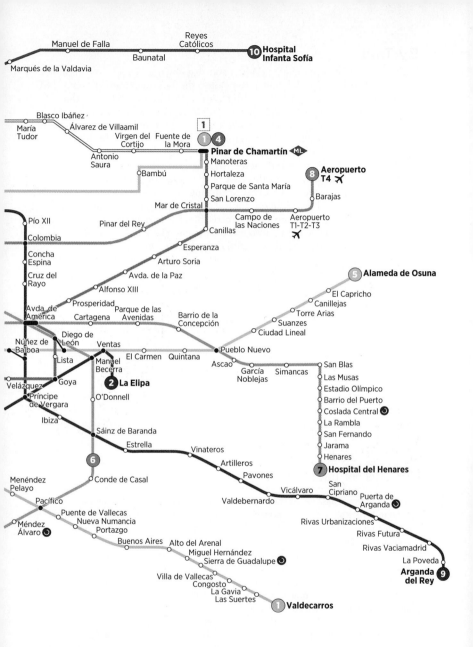

Manuel de Falla
Reyes
Católicos
Baunatal
Marqués de la Valdavia
10 Hospital
Infanta Sofía

Blasco Ibáñez
María
Tudor
Álvarez de Villaamil
Virgen del   Fuente de
Cortijo   la Mora
Antonio
Saura
Bambú
1
1 **4**
Pinar de Chamartín ◄ML►
Manoteras
Hortaleza
Parque de Santa María
San Lorenzo
8 **Aeropuerto**
T4 ✈
Barajas
Mar de Cristal
Campo de   Aeropuerto
las Naciones T1-T2-T3
✈
Pío XII
Pinar del Rey
Canillas
Colombia
Esperanza
Concha
Espina
Arturo Soria
Cruz del
Rayo
Avda. de la Paz
5 **Alameda de Osuna**
Avda. de
América
Prosperidad
Alfonso XIII
Parque de las
Cartagena   Avenidas
Barrio de la
Concepción
El Capricho
Canillejas
Torre Arias
Suanzes
Ciudad Lineal
Núñez de
Balboa
Diego de
León
Ventas
El Carmen Quintana
Pueblo Nuevo
Ascao
San Blas
Lista
Manuel
Becerra
García
Noblejas
Simancas
Las Musas
Velázquez
Goya
2 **La Elipa**
Estadio Olímpico
Príncipe
de Vergara
O'Donnell
Barrio del Puerto
Coslada Central ◉
Ibiza
Sáinz de Baranda
La Rambla
San Fernando
Estrella
Vinateros
Jarama
Henares
6
Artilleros
Pavones
7 **Hospital del Henares**
Menéndez
Pelayo
Conde de Casal
Vicálvaro
San
Cipriano
Pacífico
Valdebernardo
Puerta de
Arganda ◉
Méndez
Álvaro ◉
Puente de Vallecas
Nueva Numancia
Portazgo
Rivas Urbanizaciones
Rivas Futura
Buenos Aires
Alto del Arenal
Miguel Hernández
Sierra de Guadalupe ◉
Rivas Vaciamadrid
La Poveda
Villa de Vallecas
Congosto
La Gavia
Las Suertes
Arganda
del Rey **9**
1 **Valdecarros**

By Taxi

Cab fares are pretty reasonable. When you flag down a taxi, the meter should register 2.05€; for every kilometer thereafter, the fare increases between .98€ and 1.15€. A supplement is charged for trips to the railway station or the bullring. The ride to Barajas Airport carries a 5.50€ surcharge, and there is a 2.95€ supplement from railway stations. In addition, a 1.15€ supplement is charged on Sundays and holidays, plus a 1.18€ supplement is tacked on at night. It's customary to tip at least 10% of the fare.

Warning: Make sure the meter is turned on when you get into a taxi. Otherwise, some drivers assess the cost of the ride, and their assessment, you can be sure, is always more expensive than a metered fare.

Also, unmetered taxis hire out for the day or the afternoon. They are legitimate, but some drivers operate as gypsy cabs. Since they're not metered, they can charge high rates. They are easy to avoid—always take either a black taxi with horizontal red bands or a white one with diagonal red bands.

If you take a taxi outside the city limits, the driver is entitled to charge you twice the rate shown on the meter.

To call a taxi, dial **©** **90-250-11-30** or 90-247-82-00.

By Car

Driving in congested Madrid is a nightmare and potentially dangerous. It always feels like rush hour, although theoretically, rush hours are 8 to 10am, 1 to 2pm, and 4 to 6pm Monday to Saturday. Parking is next to impossible except in expensive garages. About the only time you can drive around Madrid with a minimum of hassle is in August, when thousands of Madrileños have taken their cars and headed for Spain's vacation oases. Save your car rentals for excursions from the capital. If you drive into Madrid from another city, ask at your hotel for the nearest garage or parking possibility and leave your vehicle there until you're ready to leave.

Discount Travel Pass

A discount travel pass for visitors called **"Abono Turístico"** is the most practical and economical way to travel by public transport in Madrid. This ticket, good for 1, 2, 3, 5, or 7 days, allows unlimited travel in its designated zones, and purchases can be made at any airport, Metro station, or tourist office. Tickets are sold for two different zones, A and T.

Zone A is good for travel on the Madrid Metro, EMT buses, and Cercanías-RENFE. **Zone T** includes the transport mentioned, plus Interurban buses in Greater Madrid, including those going to Toledo. However, this ticket is not valid for RENFE regional train services. The ticket is nontransferable and you must present your passport when purchasing it. Along with ticket instruction (in English), you are given a map of the Metro, Cercanías-RENFE routes, and a map of Madrid indicating Metro stops along with major points of interest.

For Zone A, prices are 5.20€ for 1 day, 8.80€ for 2 days, 12€ for 3 days, 18€ for 5 days, and 24€ for a week. For Zone T tickets, tariffs are 10€ for 1 day, 18€ for 2 days, 23€ for 3 days, 35€ for 5 days, and 47€ for a week. Children 10 years or younger get a 50% discount.

For more information on renting a car before you leave home, see "Getting There & Getting Around," in chapter 3, p. 65. In addition to its office at Barajas Airport (© **90-220-01-62;** www.avis.es), **Avis** has a main city office at Gran Vía 60 (© **91-548-42-04**).

[Fast FACTS] MADRID

Babysitters Most major hotels can arrange for babysitters, called *canguros* (literally, kangaroos) or *niñeras*. The concierge usually keeps a list of reliable nursemaids and will contact them for you, provided you give adequate notice. Rates vary considerably but are usually reasonable. Although many babysitters in Madrid speak English, don't count on it.

Currency Exchange The currency exchange at Chamartín railway station (Metro: Chamartín) is open 24 hours and gives the best rates. If you exchange money at a bank, ask about the commission charged. Many banks in Spain still charge a 1% to 3% commission with a minimum charge of 3€. However, branches of **Banco Santander Central Hispano** charge no commission. Branches of **El Corte Inglés,** the department store chain, offer exchange facilities with varying rates. You get the worst rates at street kiosks such as Chequepoint, Exact Change, and Cambios-

Uno. Although they're handy and charge no commission, their rates are very low. Naturally, **American Express** offices offer the best rates on their own checks. ATMs are plentiful in Madrid.

Dentists For an English-speaking dentist, contact the **U.S. Embassy,** Calle de Serrano 75 (© **91-587-22-40;** www.embusa.es), which maintains a list of dentists who offer their services to Americans abroad. For dental services, you can also consult **Unidad Médica Anglo-Americana,** Conde de Arandá 1 (© **91-435-18-23;** www.unidadmedica. com). Office hours are Monday to Friday from 9am to 8pm.

Doctors For an English-speaking doctor, contact the **U.S. Embassy,** Calle de Serrano 75 (© **91-587-22-40;** www.embusa.es).

Drugstores For a late-night pharmacy, look in the daily newspaper under *Farmacias de Guardia* to learn which drugstores are open after 8pm. Another way to find one is to go to any pharmacy, which even

if closed always posts a list of nearby pharmacies that are open late that day. Madrid has hundreds of pharmacies, but one of the most central is **Farmacia de la Paloma,** Calle de Toledo 46 (© **91-365-34-58;** Metro: Puerta del Sol or La Latina).

Embassies & Consulates See "Fast Facts," p. 777.

Emergencies A centralized number for fire, police, or ambulance services is © **112.**

Hospitals & Clinics Unidad Médica Anglo-Americana, Conde de Arandá 1 (© **91-435-18-23;** www.unidadmedica. com; Metro: Retiro), is not a hospital but a private outpatient clinic offering specialized services. This is not an emergency clinic, although someone on the staff is always available. The daily hours are 9am to 8pm. In a real medical emergency, call © **112** for an ambulance.

Internet Access Internet cafes have sprung up all over the city. Typical of these is **La Casa de**

Internet, Calle Luchana 20, corner of Calle de Francisco Rojas (☎ **91-446-80-41;** Metro: Bilbao; bus no. 40 or 147). It costs 2€ per hour and is open daily 8am to 1am.

Newspapers & Magazines The Paris-based *International Herald Tribune* is sold at most newsstands in the tourist districts, as is *USA Today,* plus the European editions of *Time* and *Newsweek. Guía del Ocio,* a small magazine sold in newsstands, has entertainment listings and addresses in Spanish. Also for readers of Spanish is *El Pais,* the leading daily newspaper, covering local news, sports, and cultural events (including movie and theater listings).

Police Dial ☎ **112.**

Post Office Madrid's central post office is in the Palacio de Comunicaciones at Plaza de la Cibeles (☎ **90-219-71-97**). Hours are Monday to Friday 8:30am to 9:30pm, Saturday 8:30am to 2pm.

Safety Because of an increasing crime rate in Madrid, the U.S. Embassy has warned visitors to leave valuables in hotel safes or other secure places before going out. Your passport may be needed, however, as the police often stop foreigners for identification checks. The embassy advises against carrying purses and suggests that you keep valuables in front pockets and carry only enough cash for the day's needs. Be aware of those around you and keep a separate record of your passport number, traveler's check numbers, and credit card numbers.

Purse snatching is common. Criminals often work in pairs, grabbing purses from pedestrians, cyclists, and even cars. A popular scam involves one robber smearing the back of the victim's clothing, perhaps with mustard, ice cream, or something worse. An accomplice then pretends to help clean up the mess, all the while picking the victim's pockets.

Every car can be a target, parked or just stopped at a light; don't leave anything in sight in your car. If a vehicle is standing still, a thief may open the door or break a window to snatch a purse or package, even from under the seat. Place valuables in the trunk when you park, and always assume that someone is watching to see whether you're putting something away for safekeeping. Keep the car locked while driving.

Taxes There are no special city taxes for tourists, except for the value-added tax (VAT, known as IVA in Spain) levied nationwide on all goods and services, ranging from 7% to 33%.

Telephone To make calls in Madrid, follow the instructions under "Staying Connected," in chapter 3, p. 83. However, for long-distance calls, especially transatlantic ones, it may be best to go to the main telephone exchange, **Locutorio Gran Vía,** Gran Vía 30. You may not be lucky enough to find an English-speaking operator, but you can fill out a simple form that will facilitate the placement of a call.

Toilets Some public restrooms are available, including those in the Parque del Retiro and on Plaza de Oriente across from the Palacio Real. Otherwise, you can go into a bar or *tasca,* but always order something. All the major department stores, such as Galerías Preciados and El Corte Inglés, have good, clean restrooms.

Transit Information For transit information (Metro and bus), call ☎ **91-580-42-60** or 90-244-44-03, or go to www.ctm-madrid.es.

WHERE TO STAY

Although expensive, Madrid's hotels are among the finest in the world. More than 50,000 hotel rooms blanket the city—from grand-luxe bedchambers fit for a prince to bunker-style beds in the hundreds of neighborhood *hostales* and *pensiones* (low-cost boardinghouses). Three-quarters of our recommendations are modern, though many guests prefer the landmarks of yesteryear, including those grand old establishments, the Ritz and the Westin Palace (ca. 1910–12).

Traditionally, hotels are clustered around the Atocha railway station and the Gran Vía. In our search for the most outstanding hotels, we've downplayed these two popular but noisy districts. The newer hotels have been built away from the center, especially on residential streets jutting from Paseo de la Castellana. Bargain seekers, however, will still find great pickings along the Gran Vía and in the Atocha district.

Note: In inexpensive hotels, be warned that you'll have to carry your bags to and from your room; don't expect bellhops or doormen to help out.

PARKING This is a serious problem, as so few hotels have garages; many buildings turned into hotels were constructed before the invention of the automobile. Street parking is rarely available, and even if it is, you run the risk of having your car broken into. If you're driving into Madrid, most hotels (and most police) will allow you to park in front of the hotel long enough to unload your luggage. Someone on the staff can usually pinpoint the location of the nearest garage in the neighborhood, often giving you a map showing the way. Parking charges given in most hotel listings are the prices these neighborhood garages charge for an average-size vehicle. You won't need a car for your time in Madrid. If you're moving on to explore the countryside, pick up your rental when you're ready to set out.

Near the Plaza de las Cortes

VERY EXPENSIVE

Hotel Villa Real ★★★ It's not on the same level as the Ritz (p. 134), but it is the first major hotel nearby to give the Westin Palace serious competition. Until 1989, the Villa Real was little more than a run-down 19th-century apartment house across a three-sided park from the Spanish parliament (Congreso de los Diputados), between Puerta del Sol and Paseo del Prado. Since then, extensive renovations have produced this stylish hotel patronized by the cognoscenti of Spain. The facade combines an odd mix of neoclassical and Aztec motifs and is guarded by footmen and doormen. Rooms at the Villa Real are more consistent in quality than those offered by its neighbor, the Westin Palace (see below), but they lack the latter's mellow charm and patina. Each unit has soundproofing, a sunken salon with leather-upholstered furniture, and built-in furniture accented with burl-wood inlays. Rooms are mostly large and bright.

Plaza de las Cortes 10, 28014 Madrid. © **91-420-37-67.** Fax 91-420-25-47. www.derbyhotels.com. 115 units. 150€–408€ double; 180€–533€ junior suite; 205€–615€ suite. AE, DC, MC, V. Parking 26€. Metro: Sevilla or Banco de España. **Amenities:** Restaurant; bar; airport transfers (75€); babysitting; concierge; room service. *In room:* A/C, TV, hair dryer, minibar, Wi-Fi (20€ per 24 hr.).

The Westin Palace ★★★ The Palace is an ornate Victorian wedding cake known as the *gran dueña* of Spanish hotels. It was inaugurated by King Alfonso XIII in 1912 and covers an entire city block. Facing the Prado and Neptune

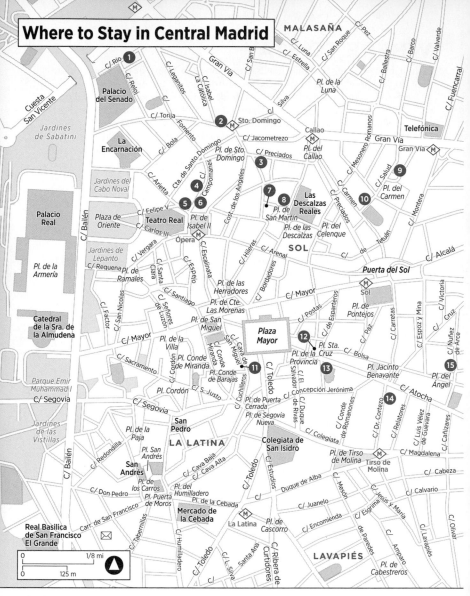

Where to Stay in Central Madrid

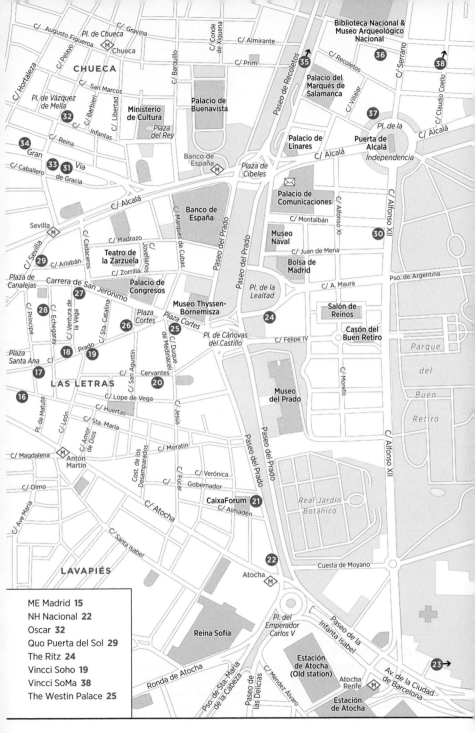

ME Madrid **15**
NH Nacional **22**
Oscar **32**
Quo Puerta del Sol **29**
The Ritz **24**
Vincci Soho **19**
Vincci SoMa **38**
The Westin Palace **25**

Fountain, it lies within walking distance of the main shopping center. Architecturally, the Palace captures the grand pre–World War I style, with an emphasis on space and comfort. Although it doesn't achieve the snob appeal of its nearby siblings, the Ritz and the Villa Real, it's one of the

📦 Telephones

The telephone area code for Madrid is 91 if you're calling from within Spain. If you're calling from the United States, dial 011, the country code (34), Madrid's city code (91), and then the local number.

largest hotels in Madrid and offers first-class service. The hotel has conservative, traditional units with plenty of space, large bathrooms, and lots of extras. Accommodations vary widely, with the best rooms located on the fourth, fifth, and sixth floors. Rooms on the side are noisy and lack views.

Plaza de las Cortes 7, 28014 Madrid. ✆ **888/625-4988** in the U.S., or 91-360-80-00. Fax 91-360-81-00. www.westinpalacemadrid.com. 468 units. 198€–558€ double; from 475€ junior suite. AE, DC, MC, V. Valet parking 35€. Metro: Banco de España. **Amenities:** 2 restaurants; bar; airport transfers (100€); babysitting; concierge; exercise room; room service; sauna. *In room:* A/C, TV, hair dryer, minibar, Wi-Fi (19€ per 24 hr.).

MODERATE

H10 Villa de la Reina ★ Overlooking Plaza Cibeles in the heart of Madrid, this sleek and modern hotel hides behind a chunky design from the early 20th century. The building has been delightfully restored, and today is a bastion of comfort and charm. Bedrooms are small to midsize and are tastefully and comfortably appointed. Many extras abound, such as scales in the bathrooms along with magnifying mirrors. We are impressed with their breakfast buffet, featuring no fewer than 60 homemade baked products. In the on-site restaurant, go for the Mediterranean cuisine or the daily chef's specials.

Gran Vía 22, 28013 Madrid. ✆ **91-523-91-01.** Fax 91-521-75-22. www.h10.es. 73 units. 145€–200€ double; 200€–340€ junior suite. AE, DC, MC, V. Nearby parking 30€. Metro: Gran Vía. **Amenities:** Restaurant; bar; room service. *In room:* A/C, TV, hair dryer, minibar, Wi-Fi (free).

Vincci Soho ★ Five traditional town houses were combined to form this chic hotel, which is stylish and minimalist yet exceedingly comfortable with its sleek avant-garde design. In the Huertas district, the hotel lies near the Prado. Rooms in the rear are not dark because they open onto a spacious courtyard. The decorator often used whimsical touches, including butterfly cutouts on the restaurant walls, to give the hotel a bright, airy feeling. Some 140 of the rooms are standard doubles, the rest being executive units (each with a balcony). The breakfast buffet is one of the best in the area, noted for its international cuisine with a Mediterranean touch.

Calle Prado 18, 28014 Madrid. ✆ **91-141-41-00.** Fax 91-141-41-01. www.vinccihoteles.com. 167 units. 124€–201€ double with breakfast. AE, DC, MC, V. Parking: 27€. Metro: Retiro. **Amenities:** Restaurant; bar; concierge; room service. *In room:* A/C, TV, hair dryer, minibar, Wi-Fi (free).

INEXPENSIVE

Hostal Cervantes 🍴 One of Madrid's most pleasant family-run hotels, the Cervantes is much appreciated by our readers, and has been for years. You'll take a tiny bird cage–style elevator to the immaculately maintained second floor of this stone-and-brick building. Each unit contains a comfortable bed and spartan furniture. No breakfast is served, but the owners, the Alfonsos, will direct you to a nearby cafe. The establishment is convenient to the Prado, Parque del Retiro, and the older sections of Madrid.

Cervantes 34, 28014 Madrid. © **91-429-83-65.** Fax 91-429-27-45. www.hostal-cervantes.com. 20 units. 60€ double; 75€ apt. MC, V. Metro: Antón Martín. *In room:* Ceiling fan, TV, hair dryer, Wi-Fi (free).

Hotel Mora This hotel can be recommended for location alone—it's across from Paseo del Prado and the Botanical Gardens. It is a fine and decent choice, especially if you want to make several visits to the Prado. The reception is bright and airy, with *trompe l'oeil* marble columns and carpets. Most of the guest rooms range from midsize to spacious, and each is comfortably and tastefully furnished, though far from lavish. Opt for a guest room opening onto the street, as these have the best views of the gardens and the magnificent Prado itself. Double-glazed windows keep down some of the noise level.

Paseo del Prado 32, 28014 Madrid. © **91-420-15-69.** Fax 91-420-05-64. www.hotelmora.com. 62 units. 83€ double; 101€ triple. AE, DC, MC, V. Nearby parking 21€. Metro: Atocha. **Amenities:** Restaurant; bar. *In room:* A/C, TV.

Near Plaza España

MODERATE

Casón del Tormes This attractive hotel is around the corner from the Royal Palace and Plaza de España. Behind a four-story red-brick facade with stone-trimmed windows, it overlooks a quiet one-way street. A long, narrow lobby floored with marble opens onto a public room. Guest rooms are generally spacious and comfortable, with color-coordinated fabrics and dark wood, including mahogany headboards. Motorists appreciate the public parking lot near the hotel.

Calle del Río 7, 28013 Madrid. © **91-541-97-46.** Fax 91-541-18-52. www.hotelcasondeltormes. com. 63 units. 60€–121€ double; 156€ triple. AE, DC, MC, V. Nearby parking 23€. Metro: Plaza de España. **Amenities:** Restaurant; bar; babysitting, room service. *In room:* A/C, TV, hair dryer, Wi-Fi (5€ per 24 hr.).

Hotel Santo Domingo ★ This stylish, carefully decorated hotel adjacent to the Gran Vía is a 2-minute walk from Plaza de España. It was inaugurated in 1994, after an older building was gutted and reconfigured into the comfortable modern structure you see today. The soundproof units are individually decorated in pastel-derived shades; each is a wee bit different from its neighbor. Some contain gold damask wall coverings, faux tortoiseshell desks, and striped satin bedspreads. The best units are the fifth-floor doubles, especially those with furnished balconies and views over the tile roofs of Old Madrid.

Plaza Santo Domingo 13, 28013 Madrid. © **91-547-98-00.** Fax 91-547-59-95. www.hotel santodomingo.net. 120 units. 75€–180€ double; 195€–305€ suite. AE, DC, MC, V. Parking 27€. Metro: Santo Domingo. **Amenities:** Restaurant; bar; babysitting; room service; Wi-Fi (free, in lobby). *In room:* A/C, TV, hair dryer, minibar.

On or Near the Gran Via

EXPENSIVE

De Las Letras ★ 🎁 This hotel with its youthful vibe was inspired by literature. A member of the stylish Epoque Hotels chain, it stands in the heart of the Gran Vía, "the main street of Madrid." Inscriptions by notable Spanish writers adorn walls in the public areas, with stone carvings and original hand-painted tiles. The wood-and-iron elevator remains from the original 1917 building. The contemporary bedrooms are painted in vivid colors such as ocher or burgundy, and most of them have wooden floors with high ceilings. Bathrooms are the latest in modern design, and each suite opens onto a terrace with a whirlpool.

Gran Vía 11, 28013 Madrid. ℂ **91-523-79-80.** Fax 91-523-79-81. www.hoteldelasletras.com. 103 units. 180€–250€ double; 270€–310€ suite. AE, DC, MC, V. Metro: Sevilla or Gran Vía. **Amenities:** Restaurant; bar; exercise room; room service; spa. *In room:* A/C, TV, hair dryer, minibar, Wi-Fi (free).

Hotel El Prado You might get the feeling this hotel is overbooked and understaffed. But it has comfortable rooms, relatively reasonable rates, and a well-scrubbed interior less than a decade old. You'll register in a somewhat claustrophobic lobby and then head upstairs to a cozy room sleekly outfitted with contemporary-looking, full-grained walls and partitions. Other than breakfast, no meals are served.

Calle Prado 11, 28014 Madrid. ℂ **91-369-02-34.** Fax 91-429-28-29. www.pradohotel.com. 48 units. 80€–205€ double. AE, DC, MC, V. Parking 23€. Metro: Antón Martín. **Amenities:** Bar; babysitting. *In room:* A/C, TV, hair dryer, minibar, Wi-Fi (free).

Hotel Urban ★★★ With a postage-stamp swimming pool open to the sky, a moonlit restaurant, and a spectacular patio, Urban is the latest in city chic, although nowhere near as spectacular as Puerta América (p. 137). Opposite the lower house of the Spanish Parliament, Urban is the creation of Catalan businessman Jordi Clos, who opened Hotel Claris in Barcelona in 1992. The lobby, for example, evokes an office-building atrium, but its grace notes are the towering sculptures from Papua, New Guinea, that are found along one wall. Rooms are luxurious and modern with dark wood furnishings and lots of dark leather. Soundproof windows block off traffic noise. At night, elegant Madrileños flood the sleek **Restaurante Europa Deco** (p. 138) to savor its Mediterranean fusion cuisine. Just below the lobby is a Museum of Egyptian Art with sculptures from the heyday of the Pharaohs.

Carrera de San Jerónimo, 28014 Madrid. ℂ **91-787-77-70.** Fax 91-787-77-99. www.derby hotels.es. 102 units. 175€–313€ double; 210€–373€ junior suite; 550€ suite. AE, DC, MC, V. Parking 26€. Metro: Sevilla. **Amenities:** Restaurant; bar; airport transfers (90€); exercise room; outdoor heated pool. *In room:* A/C, TV, minibar, Wi-Fi (20€ per 24 hr.).

MODERATE

Hotel A. Gaudí ★ In the heart of Madrid, this hotel is located in a beautifully restored turn-of-the-20th-century building that's a mondernist landmark. It was constructed in 1898 by Emilio Salas y Cortés, one of the teachers of the great Barcelona architect Gaudí. Some of the most important attractions of Madrid are within an easy walk, including the Prado, Thyssen-Bornemisza Museum, and Plaza Mayor with its rustic taverns. The guest rooms come in different sizes, each comfortably furnished and beautifully maintained. If Barcelona is not on your

Spain itinerary, you may want to sample the Catalan cuisine in the stylish on-site restaurant, Pedrera.

Gran Vía 9, 28013 Madrid. ☎ **91-531-22-22.** Fax 91-531-54-69. www.hoteles-catalonia.es. 185 units. 80€–197€ double; from 300€ suite. AE, DC, MC, V. Nearby parking 30€. Metro: Gran Vía. **Amenities:** Restaurant; bar; babysitting; exercise room; Jacuzzi; room service; sauna. *In room:* A/C, TV, hair dryer, minibar, Wi-Fi (free).

Hotel Liabeny The Liabeny, behind an austere stone facade, is in a prime location midway between the Gran Vía and Puerta del Sol. It has seven floors of comfortable, contemporary guest rooms, which are renovated and a bit pristine. They are of a good size and functionally furnished with comfortable beds and neatly organized bathrooms.

Salud 3, 28013 Madrid. ☎ **91-531-90-00.** Fax 91-532-74-21. www.liabeny.es. 220 units. 123€–150€ double; from 161€ triple. AE, DC, MC, V. Parking 17€. Metro: Plaza del Callao or Gran Vía. **Amenities:** Restaurant; bar; exercise room; room service; sauna. *In room:* A/C, TV, hair dryer, minibar, Wi-Fi (free).

INEXPENSIVE

Anaco Modest yet modern, the Anaco is just off the Gran Vía but opens onto a tree-shaded plaza. It's for those who want a clean resting place for a good price and don't expect much more. The rooms are compact and contemporary, with built-in headboards, reading lamps, and lounge chairs. Ask for one of the five terraced rooms on the top floor, which rent at no extra charge.

Tres Cruces 3, 28013 Madrid. ☎ **91-522-46-04.** Fax 91-531-64-84. www.anacohotel.com. 39 units. 60€–120€ double; 80€–150€ triple. AE, DC, MC, V. Nearby parking 30€. Metro: Gran Vía, Callao, or Puerta del Sol. **Amenities:** Restaurant; bar; babysitting; room service. *In room:* A/C, TV, hair dryer, Wi-Fi (free).

Near the Puerta del Sol

EXPENSIVE

Casa de Madrid ★★★ This small B&B lies across the street from the Royal Opera and is the most elegant B&B in Madrid. The enclave of Doña María Medina, it lies on the second floor of an 18th-century mansion. She has exquisitely decorated each bedroom with antiques, including Persian rugs. Each of the accommodations has a different theme. The simplest chamber is called the Zen room (a single). Among the most elegant units are the Spanish Room, the Indian Room, the Greek Room, and the Blue Room; the grandest is the Damascus Suite. Surely you'll agree that breakfast always tastes better when served on silver trays. The house is filled with valuable objets d'art. A stay here is like boarding with a member of Castilian aristocracy.

Calle Arrieta 2, 28013 Madrid. ☎ **91-559-57-91.** Fax 91-540-11-00. www.casademadrid.com. 17 units. 250€–285€ double; 400€ suite. Rates include continental breakfast. AE, MC, V. Nearby parking 15€. Metro: Opera. **Amenities:** Airport transfers (55€). *In room:* A/C, TV, minibar, Wi-Fi (free).

ME Madrid ★ In the Huertas district, we have stayed at this hotel throughout its many reincarnations, beginning with the Palacio de los Condes de Teba, when it was a leading stopover of the most famous matadors in Spain. It began life as a palace in 1923, lying behind an ornate stone facade, which is protected today by National Heritage (a governmental organization). It may be old on the outside, but the interior has been brought completely up-to-date, with all the latest state-of-the-art technology. Substance and style go hand in hand in the contemporary, well-maintained, and comfortable bedrooms, most of them small to midsize, although some are spacious. You can stay here in a standard double, a self-contained studio, or else some of the most glamorous suites in Madrid. Ernest Hemingway preferred to lodge in the Tower Suite.

Plaza de Santa Ana 14, 28012 Madrid. ☎ **91-701-60-00.** Fax 91-522-03-07. www.memadrid.com. 191 units. 189€–283€ standard double; 334€–358€ studio; from 434€ suite. AE, DC, MC, V. Metro: Tirso de Molina or Sol. **Amenities:** Restaurant; 2 bars; babysitting; concierge; exercise room; room service. *In room:* A/C, TV/DVD, hair dryer, minibar, MP3 docking station, Wi-Fi (free).

Quo Puerta del Sol ★ 🏨 One of Spain's most famous interior decorators played a large part in transforming this early-20th-century building into a first-rate hotel with a sleek interior of modern design, one of the best of its type in Madrid. The location is very convenient, lying between Plaza Santa Ana and Puerta del Sol. If you stay here, you'll be surrounded by some of the best restaurants and shopping in Madrid. Try for one of the top-floor rooms, each with a private patio overlooking Calle Mayor. The traditional facade conceals the high-tech amenities of the interior. An informed and efficient staff always seems ready to deal with your requests. Bedrooms are medium in size and furnished with contemporary pieces that offer both style and comfort.

Calle de Sevilla 4, 28014 Madrid. ☎ **91-532-90-49.** Fax 91-531-28-34. www.epoquehotels.com. 61 units. 150€–248€ double; 275€ suite. AE, DC, MC, V. Parking 28€. Metro: Sol. **Amenities:** Restaurant; bar; airport transfers (30€); babysitting; concierge; room service. *In room:* A/C, TV, hair dryer, minibar, Wi-Fi (free).

MODERATE

Hotel Meninas ★ 🛎 In the very center of Madrid, this little hotel was created out of a 19th-century building that was transformed into one of the better bargains in the area. During the restoration, many amenities were added, such as soundproof rooms—a good thing since the hotel lies in the center of a traffic-clogged area. The structure may be antique, but not the improvements, which range from a smoke detector system to Wi-Fi access. The bedrooms come in a range of sizes and styles, from singles to suites, and even some triples. The little hotel offers a buffet breakfast in a vaulted dining room that also has a welcoming bar with lounge.

Calle Campomanes 7, 28013 Madrid. ☎ **91-541-28-05.** Fax 91-541-28-06. www.hotelmeninas. com. 37 units. 109€–185€ double; 189€ triple; 210€ suite. AE, MC, V. Parking nearby 30€. Metro: Opera. **Amenities:** Bar; Wi-Fi (free, in lobby). *In room:* A/C, TV/DVD, hair dryer, minibar.

Hotel Preciados ★ ☺ One of Madrid's most centrally located hotels has been created from a historic 1881 structure. The original facade, entryway, grand staircase, and other architectural details have been retained, but everything else has been reconstructed from scratch for modern comfort. The five-floor hotel, which opened in 2001, is close to such landmarks as the royal palace, the opera house, and Puerta del Sol (the very center of Madrid). Children are especially welcome here; special facilities for them such as extra beds can be added to the standard rooms. There's even a kids' menu in the restaurant. Guest rooms are midsize to spacious.

Preciados 37, 28013 Madrid. ☎ **91-454-44-00.** Fax 91-454-44-01. www.preciadoshotel.com. 73 units. 90€–203€ double; 208€–350€ suite. MC, V. Parking 20€. Metro: Puerta del Sol or Santo

Domingo/Callao. **Amenities:** Restaurant; bar; airport transfers (70€); babysitting; concierge; Internet (free, in lobby); room service. *In room:* A/C, TV, hair dryer, minibar, Wi-Fi (free).

Intur Palacio San Martín ★ This used to be the American Embassy—but no more. Its developers have turned it into one of the most desirable hotels in the center of Madrid—in the vicinity of Puerta del Sol—and have retained such 19th-century architectural details as the original moldings and even the elegant wooden elevator. Constructed in 1883, it lies on a tranquil square within walking distance of such Madrid highlights as the Plaza Mayor and Plaza de Oriente. Slabs of marble, fine woods, and a beautifully crafted ceiling in the lobby remain from its days as an embassy. The midsize guest rooms have been carefully decorated and restored with many modern conveniences. Some of the better units contain Jacuzzi-style tubs.

Plaza San Martín 5, 28013 Madrid. ℭ **91-701-50-00.** Fax 91-701-50-10. www.intur.com. 94 units. 117€–220€ double; 303€–395€ suite. AE, DC, MC, V. Nearby parking 27€. Metro: Opera. **Amenities:** Restaurant; bar; airport transfers (25€); babysitting; exercise room; room service; sauna. *In room:* A/C, TV, minibar, Wi-Fi (22€ per 24 hr.).

INEXPENSIVE

Alicia ★ 🍴 The concept of this hotel chain, Room Mate, is that you're crashing at a friend's home in a trendy section of Madrid. Other "roommates" in Madrid include Oscar, Mario, or Laura. Alicia is chic yet affordable, based on the designs of Pascua Ortega, one of Spain's top decorators. It lies at the corner of the bustling Plaza de Santa Ana, close to the Prado, Reina Sofía, and Thyssen-Bornemisza museums. The small-to-midsize bedrooms have a loft aesthetic of open, flexible spaces, and many units overlooking the square have floor-to-ceiling windows. The minimalist decor and lack of some hotel services may be a drawback to certain guests, but affordable rates make this hotel a standout in pricey Madrid.

Calle del Prado 2, 28014 Madrid. ℭ **91-389-60-95.** Fax 91-369-47-95. www.room-matehotels. com. 34 units. 100€–171€ double; 173€–224€ junior suite; from 267€ duplex. AE, DC, MC, V. Metro: Puerta del Sol. **Amenities:** Restaurant; babysitting; concierge. *In room:* A/C, TV, hair dryer, minibar, Wi-Fi (free).

Hostal la Macarena 🍴 Known for its reasonable prices and praised by readers for its warm hospitality, this unpretentious hotel is run by the Ricardo González family. A 19th-century facade with Belle Epoque designs stands in ornate contrast to the chiseled simplicity of the ancient buildings facing it. The location is one of the hotel's assets: It's on a street (a noisy one) immediately behind Plaza Mayor, near one of the best clusters of *tascas* in Madrid. Guest rooms ranging from small to medium are all well kept, with modest furnishings and comfortable beds. Windows facing the street have double panes.

Cava de San Miguel 8, 28005 Madrid. ℭ **91-365-92-21.** Fax 91-364-27-57. www.silserranos.com. 20 units. 79€ double; 100€ triple. MC, V. Parking nearby 25€. Metro: Puerta del Sol, Opera, or La Latina. **Amenities:** Bar; room service. *In room:* TV, hair dryer.

Hostal la Perla Asturiana Ideal for those who want to stay in the heart of Old Madrid (1 block off Plaza Mayor and 2 blocks from Puerta del Sol), this small, family-run place welcomes you with a courteous staff at the desk 24 hours a day for security and convenience. You can socialize in the small, comfortable lobby adjacent to the reception area. Stay here for the cheap prices and location, not for grand comfort. Each of the small guest rooms comes with a comfortable bed. No breakfast is served.

Plaza de Santa Cruz 3, 28012 Madrid. ☏ **91-366-46-00.** Fax 91-366-46-08. www.perlaasturiana. com. 30 units. 42€–56€ double; 70€ triple. MC, V. Nearby parking 25€. Metro: Puerta del Sol. *In room:* A/C (in some), TV, hair dryer.

Hotel Inglés ★ You'll find this little hotel (where Virginia Woolf used to stay) on a central street lined with *tascas*. Behind the red-brick facade is a modern, impersonal hotel with contemporary, well-maintained rooms. The lobby is air-conditioned, but guest rooms are not; guests who open their windows at night are likely to hear noise from the enclosed courtyard, so light sleepers beware. Units come in a variety of shapes, most of them small; some in the back are quite dark.

Calle Echegaray 8, 28014 Madrid. ☏ **91-429-65-51.** Fax 91-420-24-23. www.hotel-ingles.net. 58 units. 118€ double; 128€ suite. AE, DC, MC, V. Parking 13€. Metro: Puerta del Sol or Sevilla. **Amenities:** Bar; concierge. *In room:* TV, hair dryer.

Hotel Plaza Mayor ★ 🎐 If you want a hotel in the very heart of historic Old Madrid, there is no better location than this little charmer, right off a famous square. The well-maintained bedrooms are rather large, and handsomely and comfortably furnished in a contemporary idiom. The best place to stay if you can afford the higher price is the Suite del Palomar, filled with luxury and imbued with charm. For the type of comfort offered, the rates are among the most affordable in Old Town. The hotel lies in what used to be the Iglesia de la Santa Cruz, a historic church that fell into disrepair until the building was recycled for another use in the 21st century. The reception staff will recommend their favorite restaurants and *tascas* in the area (if you promise not to reveal their secrets).

Calle Atocha 2, 28012 Madrid. ☏ **91-360-06-06.** Fax 91-360-06-10. www.h-plazamayor.com. 34 units. 85€–100€ double; 115€ triple. Parking 18€. Metro: La Latina. **Amenities:** Cafeteria. *In room:* A/C, TV, hair dryer, Wi-Fi (free).

Laura ★ This is a hotel of fairly recent construction—2006—although it follows the pure design of the 1800s. The interior designer created a spacious lobby and avant-garde decoration. Some guests have likened Laura to a modern hotel in New York, and the location is one of the best in town, a 2-minute walk from the heart of Plaza Mayor or a 4-minute walk from the Puerta del Sol (the Times Square of Madrid). Bedrooms are loftlike or else duplexes, each unit beautifully decorated and comfortable, even elegantly furnished, if your tastes are minimalist. We are impressed with the hotel's room amenities and the fact that the maid leaves a fresh apple on the nightstand. Each of the accommodations also comes with a minikitchen.

Travesia de Trujillos 3, 28013 Madrid. ☏ **91-701-16-70.** Fax 91-521-76-55. www.room-matehotels. com. 34 units. 117€ standard double; 139€ duplex; 170€ suite. AE, DC, MC, V. Parking 19€. Metro: Puerta del Sol. **Amenities:** Babysitting; concierge. *In room:* A/C, TV/DVD, hair dryer, kitchenette, minibar, Wi-Fi (free).

Mario 🎐 Near the opera house and the Palacio Real, this is one of the most affordable choices in the area, despite its central location. The hotel doesn't have a lot of extras, but if you're seeking a clean, decent, cheap choice in the area, consider this for a night or two. The guest rooms, though small, have modern decor along with well-maintained private bathrooms. The hotel was once a youth hostel, and a bit of that aura remains. The best and most requested room is no. 201, which is more spacious than the rest. If you don't plan to spend a lot of time in your room—preferring instead to dine out and experience the city's throbbing nightlife—consider booking here. The reception-desk staff is very helpful, especially when recommending local restaurants and decoding rail timetables.

Calle Campomanes 4, 28013 Madrid. © **91-548-85-48.** Fax 91-559-12-88. www.room-mate hoteles.com. 54 units. 134€–192€ double; 173€–214€ suite. Rates include continental breakfast. AE, DC, MC, V. Parking 20€. Metro: Opera. **Amenities:** Babysitting; concierge. *In room:* A/C, TV/ DVD, hair dryer, minibar, Wi-Fi (free).

Oscar ★★ In many ways this is the most modern and stylish of the Room Mate chain hotels sweeping across trendy Madrid. It was the personal statement of Tomás Alía, the famous interior designer, who carved the rooms from a building with a geometric design evoking Bauhaus. A haven for "fun" furniture, the hotel decorates some of its rooms with erotic wallpaper, others with very futuristic decor—for example, resembling the inside of a lava lamp. A wide variety of rooms are offered, from standard to executive doubles, even junior or regular suites. Some units have a balcony opening onto the bustling Plaza Vázquez de Mella.

Plaza Vázquez de Mella 12, 28004 Madrid. © **91-701-11-73.** Fax 91-521-87-18. www.room-mate-hotels.com. 75 units. 96€–203€ double; 160€–267€ junior suite. AE, DC, MC, V. Parking 28€. Metro: Puerta del Sol. **Amenities:** Babysitting; concierge. *In room:* A/C, TV, hair dryer, minibar, Wi-Fi (free).

Near Atocha Station
MODERATE
Hotel Cortezo Just off Calle de Atocha, which leads to the railroad station of the same name, the Cortezo is a short walk from Plaza Mayor and Puerta del Sol. Although it has been renovated many times since, it still has a lingering aura of the 1950s, when it was built. The accommodations are comfortable but simply furnished, with up-to-date plumbing. Beds are springy and the furniture is pleasantly modern; many rooms have sitting areas with desk and armchair. The public rooms match the guest rooms in freshness.

Doctor Cortezo 3, 28012 Madrid. © **91-369-01-01.** Fax 91-369-37-74. www.mediumhoteles.com. 88 units. 50€–190€ double. AE, DC, MC, V. Parking 23€. Metro: Tirso de Molina. **Amenities:** Restaurant; bar; babysitting; room service. *In room:* A/C, TV, hair dryer, minibar, Wi-Fi (free).

NH Nacional ★ This stately hotel was built around 1900 to house the hundreds of passengers flooding into Madrid through the nearby Atocha railway station. In 1997, a well-respected nationwide chain, NH Hotels, ripped out much of the building's dowdy interior, reconstructing the public areas and guest rooms with a smooth, seamless decor that takes maximum advantage of the building's tall ceilings and large spaces. Guest rooms feature modern designer decor (including avant-garde art), giving the units a welcoming ambience. Today, the Nacional is a destination for dozens of corporate conventions.

Paseo del Prado 48, 28014 Madrid. © **91-429-66-29.** Fax 91-369-15-64. www.nh-hotels.com. 214 units. 139€–212€ double; 194€–268€ suite. AE, DC, MC, V. Parking 25€. Metro: Atocha. **Amenities:** Restaurant; bar; babysitting; room service. *In room:* A/C, TV, hair dryer, minibar, Wi-Fi (17€ per 24 hr.).

INEXPENSIVE
Chic & Basic Colors ★ 🗲 A short walk from the Atocha Station, this hotel's chic and basic philosophy is no frills and no ostentation, but exquisite taste and a fun ambience. The six-floor boutique hotel draws a gay clientele, although many

straights check in, too. The hotel is divided into zones—"be yourself," where you can let your hair down; "help yourself," with free coffee and munchies; and "love yourself," where you'll find a sun terrace, chaise longues, and a shower to freshen up. Guests can adjust the intensity of light in their bedrooms to fit their moods. A "wake-up kit" is left at your modern bedroom door with a "tasty morsel" to launch your day.

Calle Atocha 113, 28012 Madrid. ✆ **91-369-28-95.** Fax 91-420-08-40. www.chicandbasic.com. 10 units. 77€–105€ double. AE, DC, MC, V. Free parking. Metro: Tirso de Molina. **Amenities:** Restaurant; bar; cafeteria; room service. In room: A/C, TV, hair dryer, Wi-Fi (free).

Near Retiro/Salamanca

VERY EXPENSIVE

Hotel Adler ★★ At the intersection of Velázquez and Goya streets, this is one of the most elegant places to stay in Madrid. You're housed in grand comfort at a location nicknamed "the golden triangle of art" (near the Prado, Reina Sofía, and the Thyssen-Bornemisza collection). The exclusive shops of Serrano are also near at hand. The classic building has been carefully restored and offers gracious comfort in a setting that evokes the 1880s but includes decidedly modern touches. The guest rooms are user-friendly: You live and sleep in ultimate comfort with luxe furnishings and totally modernized bathrooms.

Calle Velázquez 33, 28001 Madrid. ✆ **866/376-7831** in the U.S. and Canada, or 91-426-32-20. Fax 91-426-32-21. www.adlermadrid.com. 45 units. 267€–470€ double; 560€ junior suite; 680€ suite. AE, DC, MC, V. Parking 25€. Metro: Velázquez. **Amenities:** Restaurant; bar; airport transfers (105€); babysitting; bikes; concierge; room service. In room: A/C, TV/DVD, hair dryer, minibar, Wi-Fi (12€ per 24 hr.).

The Ritz ★★★ The Ritz is the most legendary hotel in Spain. With soaring ceilings and graceful columns, it offers all the luxury and pampering you'd expect from a grand hotel. Although the building has been thoroughly modernized, great effort was expended to retain its Belle Epoque character and architectural details. No other Madrid hotel, except the Palace, has a more varied history. The Ritz was built in 1908 by King Alfonso XIII with the aid of César Ritz. It looks onto the circular Plaza de la Lealtad in the center of town, facing the Prado, the Palacio de Villahermosa, and the Stock Exchange, and is near 120-hectare (297-acre) Parque del Retiro. Its facade has been designated a historic monument. The glory days of 1910 live on in the units with their roomy closets, antique furnishings, and hand-woven carpets.

Plaza de la Lealtad 5, 28014 Madrid. ✆ **800/237-1236** in the U.S. and Canada, or 91-701-67-67. Fax 91-701-67-76. www.ritz.es. 167 units. 572€–690€ double; from 1,177€ junior suite; from 2,621€ suite. AE, DC, MC, V. Parking 35€. Metro: Atocha or Banco de España. **Amenities:** Restaurant; bar; airport transfers (120€); concierge; exercise room; room service; sauna; spa. In room: A/C, TV, hair dryer, minibar, Wi-Fi (22€ per 24 hr.).

Madrid's Grandest Sunday Brunch

Every Sunday between 1:30 and 3:30pm, the celebrated Dominical Brunch is lavishly presented at the Ritz hotel (see above). Costing 80€ per person, it is the most generous spread in the city, a dazzling array of Spanish and international dishes, and champagne. Children 11 and under dine free when accompanied by an adult.

EXPENSIVE

AC Palacio del Retiro ★★ Perhaps the best-located hotel in Madrid, this well-run oasis across from Retiro Park sits close to the cultural triangle formed by the Thyssen-Bornemisza, Prado, and Reina Sofía museums. The restored building dates from the early 20th century and is a protected National Heritage monument. Its interior has been completely restored to modern tastes. Much of its elegant past can be seen in the stained-glass windows shipped in from Paris, the ceramics handmade in Talavera, the marble floors, and the Grecian columns. The midsize bedrooms are stylish and comfortable, with state-of-the-art bathrooms. Most bedrooms open onto panoramic views of Retiro Park.

Alfonso XII 14, 28014 Madrid. ✆ **91-523-74-60.** Fax 91-523-74-61. www.ac-hotels.com. 50 units. 240€–640€ double; from 820€ suite. AE, DC, MC, V. Metro: Banco de España. Parking: 8€. **Amenities:** Restaurant; bar; babysitting; concierge; exercise room; room service. *In room:* A/C, TV, hair dryer, minibar, Wi-Fi (free).

MODERATE

Ayre Gran Hotel Colón ★ East of Parque del Retiro, Gran Hotel Colón is just a few minutes from the city center by subway. Built in 1966, it offers comfortable yet reasonably priced accommodations in a modern setting. More than half of the rooms have private balconies, and all contain traditional furniture, much of it built-in. Units vary in size but most offer roomy comfort, dark wood beds, and adequate closet space. One of the Colón's founders was an interior designer, which accounts for the unusual stained-glass windows and murals in the public rooms and the paintings by Spanish artists in the lounge.

Pez Volador 1–11, 28007 Madrid. ✆ **91-400-99-00.** Fax 91-573-08-09. www.ayrehoteles.com. 360 units. 70€–197€ double; from 173€ junior suite. AE, MC, V. Parking 25€. Metro: Sáinz de Baranda. **Amenities:** Restaurant; 2 bars; exercise room; room service; sauna. *In room:* A/C, TV, hair dryer, minibar, Wi-Fi (free).

High Tech President Villamagna ★ 📇 This hotel takes the high-tech part of its name seriously. In the business district, it lies off the Paseo de la Castellana, which is the main street of New Madrid, as opposed to the Gran Vía, the main street of Old Madrid. The hotel attracts both business travelers and tourists to its six floors, two of which are devoted to meeting rooms or accommodations preferred by commercial clients. Visitors like its severe modernity on the other four floors, which are equipped with the latest technology. As the elevator lets you out, you think you might be entering a disco. Except for purple neon lights, the hall is dark. High-tech bedrooms are equipped with free laptops, a 20-inch TV, hydroshowers with a sauna, and king-size beds. There are also 28 spacious family rooms equipped with queen-size, twin, or bunk beds. The beds are among the best of any hotel in Madrid, with faux-leather headboards.

Marqués de Villamagna 4, 28001 Madrid. ✆ **91-577-19-51.** Fax 91-577-19-54. www.president castellanahotel.com. 104 units. 107€–171€ double; 160€–235€ family room. AE, DC, MC, V. Nearby parking 30€. Metro: Rubén Darío. **Amenities:** Bar; bikes. *In room:* A/C, TV, hair dryer, minibar, Wi-Fi (free).

Hospes Madrid ★★ One of the finest boutique hotels in Madrid, Hospes Madrid is housed in a restored 19th-century town house facing Puerta del Alcalá, near the city center within Plaza de la Independencia. It also lies across the street from the entrance to Retiro Park and just steps from Calle Serrano, the chic shopping artery. The rooms are spacious, featuring floor-to-ceiling windows—often overlooking the rooftops of Madrid—and the decoration, for the most part, is in muted grays and whites, with the bathrooms clad in marble. There is also a trio of bar/lounges and a remarkable on-site restaurant, **Senzone** (p. 149).

Plaza de la Independencia 3, 28001 Madrid. ✆ **91-432-29-11.** www.hospes.com. 47 units. 187€–300€ double; 423€–1,177€ suite. AE, MC, V. Parking 37€. Metro: Retiro. **Amenities:** 2 restaurants; bar; airport transfers (127€); exercise room; room service; spa. *In room:* A/C, TV, hair dryer, mini-bar, Wi-Fi (free).

Jardín de Recoletos ★ ✦ Built in 1999, this hotel welcomes its guests to the chic Salamanca district of Madrid. It is close to both the financial district and the best shops. A contemporary apartment-hotel, it stands on a quiet street close to the Plaza Colón, one of the major traffic arteries of Madrid. The inviting lobby has sleek marble floors and a stained-glass ceiling; adjacent is a combined cafe and restaurant. Most of the rooms are spacious and attractively decorated in a traditional style, with small sitting and dining areas. The accommodations come with well-equipped kitchenettes—unusual for Madrid. If you want to pay extra, you can book either a unit rated "superior" or a suite that offers a hydromassage bathroom and a big terrace.

Gil de Santivañes 6, 28001 Madrid. ✆ **91-781-16-40.** Fax 91-781-16-41. www.vphoteles.com. 43 units. 148€–209€ double; 200€–261€ suite. Rates include buffet breakfast. AE, DC, MC, V. Parking 18€. Metro: Serrano. **Amenities:** Restaurant; room service. *In room:* A/C, TV, hair dryer, kitchen-ette, minibar, Wi-Fi (free).

Vincci SoMa ★ The moment you enter this hotel (formerly the Bauzá Hotel), you notice the young bellhops wearing the words CAN I HELP YOU? embroidered in English on their uniforms. They mean it. Service here is about the best in Madrid. The fashionable hotel lies in the chic Salamanca shopping district. Modern style is combined with comfort, as reflected in the attractive public rooms and the tastefully furnished bedrooms. There is a passion for details here: The colors are muted, as is the music, and there are such thoughtful extras as a library. Except for a splash of cherry red here and there, bedrooms are mostly monochromatic and are especially noted for their sound systems. Double-paned windows help block the noise of this busy part of Madrid.

Calle Goya 79, 28001 Madrid. ✆ **91-435-75-45.** Fax 91-431-09-43. www.vinccihoteles.com. 167 units. 146€–235€ double; 205€–318€ suite. AE, DC, MC, V. Parking 23€. Metro: Goya. **Amenities:** Restaurant; bar; bikes; exercise room; room service; sauna. *In room:* A/C, TV, CD player, hair dryer, minibar, Wi-Fi (free).

INEXPENSIVE

Hotel Claridge This contemporary building beyond Parque del Retiro is about 5 minutes from the Prado by taxi or subway. The guest rooms are well organized and pleasantly styled, though small and compact. They include small, well-orga-nized bathrooms containing tub/shower combos. You can take your meals in the hotel's cafeteria and relax in the modern lounge.

Plaza Conde de Casal 6, 28007 Madrid. ✆ **91-551-94-00.** Fax 91-501-03-85. www.hotel claridgemadrid.com. 150 units. 60€–142€ double; 120€–170€ triple. AE, DC, MC, V. Parking 19€. Metro: Atocha or Conde de Casal. **Amenities:** Restaurant; bar. *In room:* A/C, TV, hair dryer, Wi-Fi (6.50€ per hour).

Chamberi

VERY EXPENSIVE

AC Santo Mauro Hotel ★★★ Reflective of its history, this hotel offers both elegance and style. It opened in 1991 in what was once a neoclassical villa built in 1894 for the duke of Santo Mauro. Set within a garden and evocative of French style, it's decorated with rich fabrics and Art Deco accents and furnishings. Staff members outnumber rooms by two to one. Each guest room contains lovely details like raw silk curtains, Persian carpets, antique prints, and parquet floors. Rooms are large and come in combinations ranging from studios to duplex suites.

Calle Zurbano 36, 28010 Madrid. ✆ **91-319-69-00.** Fax 91-308-54-77. www.ac-hotels.com. 51 units. 260€–389€ double; 371€–1,070€ suite. AE, DC, MC, V. Parking 28€. Metro: Rubén Darío or Alonso Martínez. **Amenities:** Restaurant; bar; airport transfers (100€); babysitting; concierge; exercise room; indoor heated pool; room service; sauna. *In room:* A/C, TV/DVD, CD player, hair dryer, minibar, Wi-Fi (12€ per 24 hr.).

MODERATE

Hotel Orense ★ At first glance, you might mistake this silver-and-glass tower for one of the many upscale condominium complexes surrounding it on all sides. Stylish and streamlined, with a design inaugurated in the late 1980s, it offers reproduction Oriental carpets and conservatively contemporary furniture that's comfortable, tasteful, and upscale. Accommodations, equipped along the lines of a private apartment, are appropriate for a stay of up to several weeks.

Pedro Teixeira 5, 28020 Madrid. ✆ **91-597-15-68.** Fax 91-597-12-95. www.rafaelhoteles.com. 140 units. 112€–190€ double; from 165€ suite. AE, DC, MC, V. Parking 15€. Metro: Santiago Bernabeu. **Amenities:** Restaurant; bar; room service; Wi-Fi (free, in lobby). *In room:* A/C, TV, hair dryer, minibar.

INEXPENSIVE

Hostal Residencia Don Diego ★ On the fifth floor of an elevator building, Don Diego is in a residential/commercial neighborhood that's relatively convenient to many of the city monuments. The vestibule contains an elegant winding staircase with a balustrade supported by iron griffin heads. The hotel is warm and inviting, filled with leather couches and attractively angular but comfortable furniture. Guest rooms are small, but comfortable for the price. The staff is very service-oriented and keeps the place humming efficiently.

Calle de Velázquez 45, 28001 Madrid. ✆ **91-435-07-60.** Fax 91-431-42-63. www.hostal dondiego.com. 58 units. 86€–120€ double; 110€–162€ triple. AE, DC, MC, V. Parking 28€. Metro: Velázquez. **Amenities:** Bar. *In room:* A/C, TV, hair dryer, Wi-Fi (free).

West of Chamberi

VERY EXPENSIVE

Puerta América ★★★ Nineteen architects were hired from 13 different countries, and each was granted total artistic license and a fat budget with which to play. Designers included Richard Gluckman, architect of the Andy Warhol Museum in Pittsburgh, and Norman Foster, creator of the Millennium Bridge in London. The end result has been called an architectural Tower of Babel: a showcase of wildly varied materials, colors, and shapes. There is no more avant-garde hotel in all of Europe. As the manager enigmatically puts it, "Our guests are invited to touch, to see, and even to breathe and smell." Built at a staggering cost of $92 million, Puerta América rises 12 floors in a glass-and-steel tower. The location, beside a six-lane expressway in a drab suburb 8km (5 miles) from the airport, is unexceptional; the heart of Madrid is a 15-minute taxi ride away. Each room is different, ranging from an igloo-esque space with almost no furnishings to a bedroom all in midnight black and charcoal gray.

Av. de América 41, 28002 Madrid. ✆ **91-744-54-00.** Fax 91-744-54-01. www.hotelpuert america.com. 342 units. 180€–419€ double; from 802€ suite. AE, DC, MC, V. Parking 23€. Metro: Cartagena. **Amenities:** Restaurant; bar; airport transfers (85€); concierge; exercise room; indoor heated pool; room service; spa. *In room:* A/C, TV, minibar, Wi-Fi (9€ per 24 hr.).

WHERE TO DINE

Madrid boasts the most varied cuisine and the widest choice of dining opportunities in Spain. At the fancy tourist restaurants, prices are just as high as in New York, London, or Paris, but there are lots of affordable taverns and family restaurants as well.

Many of Spain's greatest chefs have opened restaurants in Madrid, energizing the city's culinary scene. Gone are the days when mainly Madrileño food was featured, which meant Castilian specialties such as *cocido* (a chickpea-and-sausage stew) or roast suckling pig or lamb. Now you can take a culinary tour of the country while remaining in Madrid—from Andalusia with its gazpacho and braised bull's tails, to Asturias with its *fabada* (rich pork stew) and *sidra* (cider), to the Basque Country with Spain's most sophisticated cuisine. There is also a host of Galician and Mediterranean restaurants in Madrid. Amazingly, although Madrid is a landlocked city surrounded by a vast arid plain, you can order some of the freshest seafood in the country here.

One way to save money is to order the *menú del día* (menu of the day) or *cubierto* (fixed price)—both are fixed-price menus based on what is fresh at the market that day. Though these are dining bargains in Madrid, they often lack the quality of more expensive a la carte choices. Each usually includes a first course (such as fish soup or hors d'oeuvres), followed by a main dish, bread, dessert, and the house wine. You won't have a large choice. The *menú turístico* is a similar fixed-price menu, but for many it's too large, especially at lunch. It's a bargain only to those with large appetites.

In most cases, service can seem perfunctory by U.S. standards. Matter-of-fact waiters do not return to the table to ask how things are. This can seem off-putting at first, but if you observe closely, you'll see that Spanish waiters typically handle more tables than American waiters, and that they generally work quickly and efficiently. Follow the local custom and don't overtip. Theoretically, service is included in the price of the meal, but it's customary to leave an additional 10%.

Near the Plaza de las Cortes

EXPENSIVE

Restaurante Europa Deco ★★ MEDITERRANEAN Tucked away in the Urban, one of the chicest hotels in Spain (p. 128), this elegant enclave of good food attracts celebrities, politicians, and even soccer stars. The setting is stunning, with Papuan totems, golden Venetian mosaic columns, and black Brazilian granite floors. The *pijos* (the smart set) shows up here in hordes, and even serious foodies are drawn to the smashing champagne cocktails and such delights as some of Madrid's best sushi. When ordering, we gravitate to the deboned pork or to the sautéed scallops, among the chef's specialties. Joaquin de Felipe is rightly hailed as one of the city's most accomplished chefs. Perhaps you'll agree after sampling his "New Wave" gazpacho, made with fava beans and Kamone-tomato purée. His skirt steak of Iberian pig is reason enough to come back. End with one of his daily changing but always sumptuous desserts.

In the Urban Hotel, Carrera de San Jerónimo 34. ✆ **91-787-77-80.** Reservations required. Main courses 27€–40€. AE, DC, MC, V. Daily 8pm–midnight. Metro: Sevilla.

MODERATE

El Espejo ★ INTERNATIONAL Here you'll find good food and one of the most perfectly crafted Art Nouveau decors in Madrid. Upon entering, you'll find yourself in a charming cafe/bar, where many visitors linger before heading toward the spacious dining room. If the weather is good, you can sit at one of the outdoor tables and be served by uniformed waiters who carry food across the busy street to a green area flanked by trees. We prefer a table inside, within view of the tile maidens with vines and flowers entwined in their hair. Some tasty dishes that appear with regularity are lasagna with prawns and fresh vegetables; baked hake with seafood cream; and succulent sirloin steaks grilled as you like. Try profiteroles with cream and chocolate sauce for dessert.

Paseo de Recoletos 31. ✆ **91-308-23-47.** www.restauranteelespejo.com. Reservations required. Main courses 14€–23€. Fixed-price menus 37€–79€. AE, DC, MC, V. Daily 1–4pm and 9pm–midnight. Metro: Colón. Bus: 5, 27, 45, or 150.

Errota-Zar BASQUE Next to the House of Deputies and the Zarzuela Theater is Errota-Zar. The name means "old mill," a nostalgic reference to the Basque Country, home of the Olano family, owners of the restaurant. A small bar at the entrance displays a collection of fine cigars and wines, and the blue-painted walls are adorned with paintings of Basque landscapes. The restaurant has only about two dozen tables, which can easily fill up. The Basque Country has long been known as the gastronomic capital of Spain, and Errota-Zar provides a fine showcase for its cuisine.

Many Basques begin their meal with a *tortilla de bacalao* (salt cod omelet). For main dishes, sample the delights of *chuletón de buey* (oxtail with grilled vegetables), or *kokotxas de merluza en aceite* (cheeks of hake cooked in virgin olive oil). Hake cheeks may not sound appetizing, but Spaniards and many foreigners praise this fish dish. You might opt for *foie al Pedro Jiménez* (duck liver grilled and served with a sweet wine sauce). The best homemade desserts are *cuajada de la casa,* a thick yogurt made from sheep's milk; and *tarta de limón,* a lemon cake. You might also try rice ice cream in prune sauce.

Jovellanos 3, 1st Floor. ✆ **91-531-25-64.** www.errota-zar.com. Reservations recommended. Main courses 22€–58€. AE, DC, MC, V. Mon–Sat 1–4pm and 9pm–midnight. Closed Aug 15–30 and Easter. Metro: Banco España or Sevilla.

Near Plaza de la Cibeles
EXPENSIVE

El Mirador del Museo ★★ CONTINENTAL The Museo Thyssen-Bornemisza has converted its rooftop into a summer terrace dining event. You are not only rewarded with panoramic views but also presented with one of the most finely honed cuisines in the area. At lunch, gigantic umbrellas protect you from

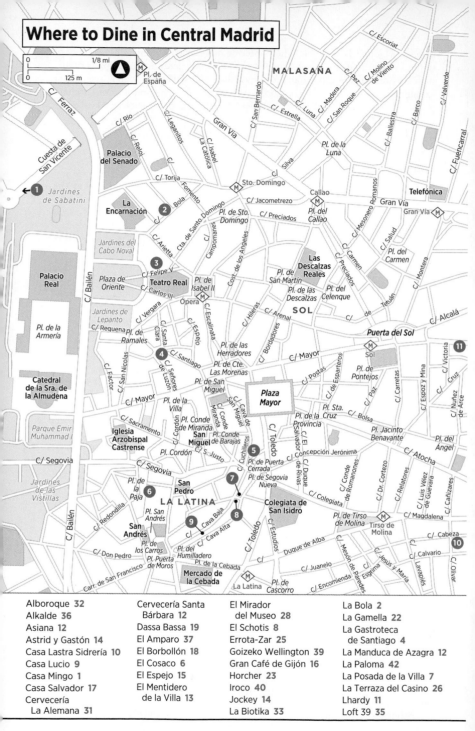

Where to Dine in Central Madrid

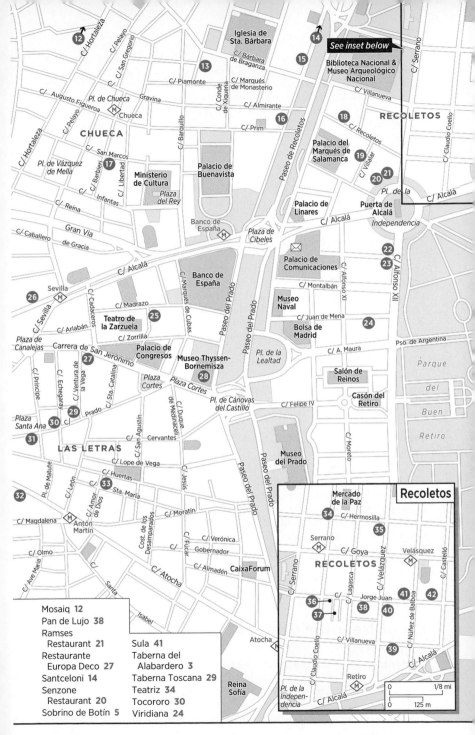

Map labels (clockwise/by area):

C/ Hortaleza
C/ Pelayo
C/ San Gregorio
Iglesia de Sta. Bárbara
C/ Bárbara de Braganza
See inset below
C/ Serrano
Biblioteca Nacional & Museo Arqueológico Nacional
C/ Piamonte
C/ Conde de Xiquena
C/ Marqués de Monasterio
C/ Villanueva
C/ Almirante
C/ Augusto Figueroa
Pl. de Chueca
Gravina
Chueca
C/ Prim
C/ Pelayo
C/ Recoletos
RECOLETOS
C/ Claudio Coello
CHUECA
C/ San Marcos
Palacio del Marqués de Salamanca
C/ Villalar
C/ Hortaleza
Pl. de Vázquez de Mella
C/ Barbieri
C/ Libertad
Ministerio de Cultura
Palacio de Buenavista
C/ Villalar
C/ Infantas
Plaza del Rey
Palacio de Linares
Puerta de Alcalá
C/ Alcalá
C/ Reina
Pl. de la
Independencia
Gran Vía
Banco de España
Plaza de Cibeles
Palacio de Comunicaciones
C/ Alfonso XI
C/ Alfonso XII
de Gracia
C/ Caballero
C/ Alcalá
Banco de España
C/ Montalbán
Sevilla
C/ Marqués de Cubas
Museo Naval
C/ Sevilla
C/ Madrazo
Teatro de la Zarzuela
C/ Cadalso
C/ Juan de Mena
Pso. de Argentina
C/ Arlabán
C/ Zorrilla
Bolsa de Madrid
Parque
Plaza de Canalejas
Carrera de San Jerónimo
Palacio de Congresos
Pl. de la Lealtad
C/ A. Maura
del
C/ Príncipe
C/ Echegaray
C/ Ventura de la Vega
C/ Sta. Catalina
Plaza Cortes
Museo Thyssen-Bornemisza
Plaza Cortes
Salón de Reinos
Buen
Prado
Pl. de Cánovas del Castillo
Casón del Retiro
Retiro
Plaza Santa Ana
C/
C/ Felipe IV
LAS LETRAS
C/ Duque de Medinaceli
Cervantes
C/ Moreto
C/ San Agustín
C/ Lope de Vega
Museo del Prado
Pl. de Matute
C/ Huertas
C/ León
C/ Amor de Dios
Sta. María
C/ Jesús
C/ Magdalena
Antón Martín
C/ Moratín
Recoletos
C/ Olmo
Cost. de los Desamparados
C/ Verónica
Mercado de la Paz
C/ Ave María
C/ Fúcar
Gobernador
C/ Hermosilla
Serrano
Santa
C/ Atocha
C/ Almadén
CaixaForum
C/ Goya
RECOLETOS
Velásquez
Isabel
C/ Serrano
C/ Lagasca
C/ Velázquez
C/ Castelló
Atocha
Jorge Juan
C/ Núñez de Balboa
Reina Sofía
C/ Villanueva
C/ Claudio Coello
Retiro
C/ Alcalá
Pl. de la Independencia
0   1/8 mi
0   125 m

141

the sun, but at night you dine under the stars. The chef displays a rare talent, a union of traditional and imaginative dishes, each platter filled with market-fresh ingredients rendered with skill. We won't soon forget the veal sirloin with cardamom-flavored vanilla pasta. You might begin with a refreshing vichyssoise with couscous. Fresh fish always appears on the menu—perhaps sea urchins for a bit of exotica. All dishes are well balanced in flavors, and the cellar is awash in fine Spanish vintages.

Paseo Prado 8. ☎ **91-429-27-32.** Reservations required. Main courses 25€–36€. AE, DC, MC, V. May–Oct Wed–Mon 8pm–1am. Closed Nov–Apr. Metro: Banco de España.

Goizeko Wellington ★★ BASQUE Normally we are not enthusiastic about hotel dining rooms, but this one is an exception. Some of the best Basque cuisine in Madrid, arguably the very best, is served within the elegant confines of the long-established Hotel Wellington. If you arrive early, have an aperitif in the swanky English Bar. Live music is presented here nightly from 7pm.

The chef specializes in what is called "High Basque" cookery, meaning only the most refined and elegant of dishes—not the more earthy cuisine enjoyed in the robust taverns of northeastern Spain. For carnivores, roast suckling pig is one of the more enduring specialties, as is freshly caught turbot. One of our all-time favorite Basque dishes is prepared with great skill here—fried pieces of codfish in a "union" with roasted red peppers. The lobster ravioli with a seafood cream sauce should win some sort of culinary award for taste and seasoning. The chef secures fresh fish flown in from the Spanish coast, and the oysters, tuna, and top-quality prawns, among other dishes, are amazingly fresh even though dished up in inland Madrid.

In the Hotel Wellington, Villanueva 34. ☎ **91-653-06-16.** www.goizekogaztelupe.com. Reservations required. Main courses 28€–42€. AE, DC, MC, V. Mon–Sat 1:30–4pm and 8:30pm–midnight. Closed 2nd and 3rd weeks in Aug. Metro: Banco de España.

MODERATE

Tocororo CUBAN This is Madrid's finest Cuban restaurant. The nostalgia is evident in the pictures of Old Havana. The waitstaff is as lively as the pop Cuban music playing on the stereo. Expect typical Caribbean dishes, such as *ropa vieja* (shredded meat served with black beans and rice) or lobster enchilada. If you prefer a simpler repast, try a selection of *empanadas y tamales* (fried potato pastries and plantain dough filled with onions and ground meat). Special house cocktails include *mojitos* (rum, mint, and a hint of sugar) and daiquiris. Winter brings live Cuban music. Discreet but pleasant, this restaurant is located in the zone of La Letras.

Calle del Prado 3 (at the corner of Echegaray). ☎ **91-369-40-00.** www.el-tocororo.com. Reservations required Thurs–Sat. Main courses 16€–22€. *Menú del día* 10€. AE, DC, MC, V. Tues–Sun 1–4pm and 8pm–midnight. Closed last 2 weeks Feb and last 2 weeks Sept. Metro: Sevilla.

On or Near the Gran Via

MODERATE

El Mentidero de la Villa ★ MEDITERRANEAN The Mentidero ("Gossip Shop" in English) is a truly multicultural experience. The owner describes the cuisine as "modern Spanish with Japanese influence and a French cooking technique." That may sound confusing, but the result is an achievement; each ingredient manages to retain its distinctive flavor. The kitchen plays with such

AN EARLY-EVENING *tapeo*

What's more fun than a pub-crawl in London or Dublin? In Madrid, it's a *tapeo,* and you can drink just as much or more than in those far northern climes. One of the unique pleasures of Madrid, a *tapeo* is the act of strolling from one bar to another to keep yourself amused and fed before the fashionable Madrileño dining hour of 10pm. In Madrid, tapas are served almost everywhere, in *tabernas, tascas,* bars, and cafes.

Although Madrid took to tapas with a passion, they may have originated in Andalusia, especially around Jerez de la Frontera, where they were traditionally served to accompany the sherry produced there. The first tapa (which means a cover or lid) was probably chorizo (a spicy sausage) or a slice of cured ham perched over the mouth of a glass to keep the flies out. Later, the government mandated bars to serve a "little something" in the way of food with each drink to dissipate the effects of the alcohol. This was important when drinking a fortified wine like sherry, as its alcohol content is more than 15% higher than normal table wines. Eating a selection of tapas as you drink will help preserve your sobriety.

Tapas can be relatively simple: toasted almonds; slices of ham, cheese, or sausage; potato omelets; or the ubiquitous olives. They can be more elaborate: a succulent veal roll; herb-flavored snails; *gambas* (shrimp); peppery *pulpo* (octopus); stuffed peppers; *anguila* (eel); *cangrejo* (crabmeat salad); *merluza* (hake) salad; and even bull testicles.

Each bar in Madrid gains a reputation for its rendition of certain favorite foods. One bar, for example, specializes in very garlicky grilled mushrooms, usually accompanied by pitchers of sangria. Another will specialize in *gambas.* Most of Madrid's chefs are men, but at tapas bars or *tascas,* the cooks are most often women—sometimes the owner's wife.

For a selection of our favorite bars, see "Our Favorite *Tascas,*" p. 156. There are literally hundreds of others, many of which you'll discover on your own during your strolls around Madrid.

adventuresome combinations as fried duck liver with caramelized eggplant; lasagna with mushrooms and duck liver; noisettes of veal with tarragon; filet steak with a sauce of mustard and brown sugar; and medallions of venison with purée of chestnut and celery. The postmodern decor includes *trompe l'oeil* ceilings, exposed wine racks, ornate columns with unusual lighting, and a handful of antique carved merry-go-round horses.

Santo Tomé 6, Plaza de las Salesas. ℭ **91-308-12-85.** www.mentiderodelavilla.es. Reservations required. Main courses 18€–30€. Fixed-price menus 60€–75€. AE, DC, MC, V. Mon–Fri 1:30–4:30pm; Mon–Sat 9pm–midnight. Closed Aug. Metro: Alonso Martínez or Chueca. Bus: 37.

Near Puerta del Sol

VERY EXPENSIVE

La Terraza del Casino ★★★ SPANISH/INTERNATIONAL The city's most imaginative chef, Ferran Adrià, isn't in Madrid. He's tending those pots and pans in the little town of Roses near Girona in Catalonia. But the innovative master of cuisine created all the dishes on the menu here and flies in regularly to see that his cooks are following his orders. His restaurant in Madrid occupies the top floor of the Casino, a historic building and a former gentlemen's club with a history going back to 1910. But the grand dons of those days didn't dine as well as you can today.

This dining hot spot provides a panoramic view of the heart of Madrid and can be reached by an elevator or by a sweeping 19th-century staircase designed to impress. The decor is classically restrained, with high ceilings and crystal chandeliers. Food critics (with whom we concur) always write about "explosions" of taste in your mouth. The exquisite food prepared with fresh seasonal ingredients reinterprets Spanish dishes. An example is *raya* (skate) in oil and saffron with parsley purée and nuts on a bed of finely diced fries. More traditional dishes are the succulent *merluza a la gallega* (Galician hake) and the *crema de la fabada asturiana* (creamed Asturian bean soup) served with *menestra* (mixed vegetables) al dente.

Alcalá 15. ✆ **91-532-12-75.** www.casinodemadrid.es. Main courses 25€–33€. AE, DC, MC, V. Mon–Fri 1:30–4pm and 9–11:45pm; Sat 9–11:45pm. Closed Aug. Metro: Sevilla or Puerta del Sol.

EXPENSIVE

Lhardy ★★ SPANISH/INTERNATIONAL This is Madrid's longest-running culinary act. Lhardy has been a Madrileño legend since opening in 1839 as a gathering place for the city's literati and political leaders. Within a dignified antique setting of marble and hardwood, steaming consommé is dispensed from silver samovars into delicate porcelain cups, and rows of croquettes, tapas, and sandwiches are served to stand-up clients who pay for their food at a cashier's kiosk near the entrance. The ground-floor deli and takeout service is open Monday to Saturday 9:30am to 3pm and 5 to 9:30pm, and Sunday 9:30am to 3pm.

The real culinary skill of the place, however, is on Lhardy's second floor, where you'll find a formal restaurant decorated in the ornate Belle Epoque style of Isabel Segunda. Specialties of the house include monkfish in lobster sauce; baked Cantabrian sea bass with fennel; partridge stew with French onions; and duck breast in a green pepper sauce.

Carrera de San Jerónimo 8. ✆ **91-521-33-85.** www.lhardy.com. Reservations recommended in the upstairs dining room. Main dishes 32€–39€. AE, DC, MC, V. Mon–Sat 1–3:30pm and 8:30–11pm. Closed Aug. Metro: Puerta del Sol.

MODERATE

Casa Lastra Sidrería ASTURIAN Some visitors come here because they've heard this establishment serves "Austrian cuisine." Actually, the food is inspired by the cuisine of Asturias, a province of Spain in the northwest. Since 1926, this tavern has attracted a devoted following, particularly among homesick Asturians. The decoration is regional, with cowbells, dried sausages, "pigtails" of garlic, and wood clogs. This restaurant and cider house (cider is the national drink of the province) is known for serving very big portions, which means you might want to skip the starters. However, if you do indulge, we recommend *fabes con almejas* (white beans with clams) and *chorizo a la sidra* (spicy Spanish sausage cooked in cider). As a main course, *merluza* (hake) is also cooked in cider. If you're here in winter, order a fabulous *fabada*—the meat, sausage, and bean casserole of the province. Goat meat is yet another specialty, as is a cheese made from a blend of milk from goats, sheep, and cows. For dessert, locals order *carbayón,* made from sweetened egg yolks and almonds. Everything is washed down with cider, which might be more potent than you think.

Calle Olivar 3. ✆ **91-369-14-82,** or 91-369-08-37 for reservations. www.casalastra.com. Reservations required. Main courses 15€–20€. AE, MC, V. Thurs–Tues 1–4pm; Thurs–Sat and Mon–Tues 8pm–midnight. Closed July. Metro: Antón Martín.

La Gastroteca de Santiago ★★ 🎁 SPANISH/INTERNATIONAL This small, coquettish space, with room for only 16 foodies, is one of the special favorites of in-the-know Madrileños, who guard its address somewhat zealously. It is typical of the new and trendy restaurants rising through Madrid, offering haute cuisine at good-value prices. La Gastroteca is a showcase for the culinary wares of its most talented chef, Juan Carlos Ramos. The menu is authentic and regional and changes frequently based on the best market conditions every week. Here you dine on well-prepared, robust fare, including terrine of pig tail, blood sausage, garlic-laden snails, and lobster or confit of goat with broad beans and mint. On Sunday, special meat-and-rice dishes are served, and the wine *carte* has more than 400 vintages (strong on burgundies). The set menu is one of the best values in Madrid, or, if you order the far more expensive sampler menu, you can enjoy a meal fit for a king (or a queen).

Plaza Santiago 1. ✆ **91-548-07-07.** www.lagastrotecadesantiago.es. Reservations required. Main courses 15€–40€; set menu 25€, sampler menu 65€. AE, MC, V. Tues–Sat 1:30–4pm and 8:30pm–midnight; Sun 1:30–4pm. Metro: Opera.

INEXPENSIVE

La Biotika ★ 🎁 VEGETARIAN Vegetarian cuisine doesn't get a lot of attention in most Madrid restaurants, but this discovery is a rare exception. Opening east of the landmark Plaza Santa Ana, it is intimate and charming. It serves the capital's best macrobiotic vegetarian cuisine, and does so exceedingly well. We always begin with one of the homemade soups, which are made fresh daily, and then have one of the large, crisp salads. The bread is also made fresh daily. A specialty is the "meatball without meat"—made with vegetables, shaped like a meatball. Tofu with zucchini and many other offerings appear daily.

Amor de Dios 3. ✆ **91-429-07-80.** www.labiotika.es. *Menú del día* 9.90€. MC, V. Daily 1–5pm. Metro: Antón Martín.

Taberna del Alabardero BASQUE/SPANISH In proximity to the Royal Palace, this little Spanish classic is known for its selection of tasty tapas, ranging from squid cooked in wine to fried potatoes dipped in hot sauce. Photographs of famous former patrons, including Nelson Rockefeller and the race-car driver Jackie Stewart, line the walls. The restaurant in the rear is said to be another of the city's best-kept secrets. Decorated in typical tavern style, it serves a savory Spanish and Basque cuisine made with market-fresh ingredients.

Felipe V no. 6. ✆ **91-547-25-77.** www.alabardero.eu. Reservations required for restaurant only. Bar: tapas 3€–12€; glass of house wine 4€. Restaurant: main courses 17€–25€. *Menú degustación* 51€. AE, DC, MC, V. Daily 1–4pm and 9pm–midnight. Metro: Opera.

Retiro/Salamanca

VERY EXPENSIVE

Santceloni ★★★ MEDITERRANEAN Santi Santamaría is ranked among the top three chefs of Spain, along with his chief rivals, Juan María Arzak and Ferran Adrià. Santamaría gets our vote as the leader of the "troika." He made his fame in his restaurant outside Barcelona. As his acclaim grew, he decided to open this branch of his fabled restaurant in Madrid. Few chefs know how to present such an enticing and imaginative Mediterranean cuisine. The cuisine is called *de mercado,* meaning that it's based on the freshest ingredients available that day in the marketplace. The same painstaking and fine care that goes into the selection of ingredients is demonstrated when the produce hits those skillets, pots, and pans. You can sample such starters as a terrine of tuna and foie gras. For main courses, you'll find well-prepared specialties including loin of roast suckling pig with fresh thyme; shoulder of lamb with candied shallots; and loin of hake with black truffles.

In the Hotel Hesperia, Paseo de la Castellana 57. © **91-210-88-40.** www.restaurantesantceloni. com. Reservations required. Main courses 37€–65€; fixed-price menus 132€–165€. AE, DC, MC, V. Mon–Fri 2–4pm; Mon–Sat 9–11pm. Closed Aug. Metro: Gregorio Marañón.

EXPENSIVE

Alkalde ★ BASQUE For decades Alkalde has been known for serving top-quality Spanish food in an old tavern setting, and it continues to do so exceedingly well. Decorated like a Basque inn, it has beamed ceilings with hams hanging from the rafters. Upstairs is a large *típico* tavern; downstairs is a maze of stone-sided cellars that are pleasantly cool in summer (although the whole place is air-conditioned).

Basque cookery is the best in Spain, and Alkalde honors that noble tradition. Begin with the cream of crabmeat soup, followed by *gambas a la plancha* (grilled shrimp). Other recommended dishes include *mero en salsa verde* (brill in green sauce), trout Alkalde, stuffed peppers, and chicken steak. The dessert specialty is *copa Cardinal* (ice cream topped with fruit).

Jorge Juan 10. © **91-576-33-59.** www.alkalderestaurante.com. Reservations required. Main courses 17€–40€. *Menú del día* 20€. AE, DC, MC, V. Daily noon–midnight. Metro: Retiro or Serrano. Bus: 20, 28, or 19.

Astrid y Gastón ★ PERUVIAN This restaurant is a posh import from Peru. Here chefs lure Madrileños away from their sushi favorites for a taste of ceviche, South American style. In a rainbow of tastes and flavors, ceviche is made with such delicacies as hake cheeks or clams flavored with cilantro, curry, and fresh lime. A real authentic Peruvian dish—though not for every taste—is corn crepes topped with suckling-pig skin and a chili-and-honey marmalade. Everything we've tasted has been harmonious in flavors, although some of the combinations may seem a bit odd for those who haven't been to Peru. Service is first-rate, and the wine list is affordably priced.

13 Paseo de la Castellana. © **91-702-62-62.** www.astridygastonmadrid.com. Reservations required. Main courses 25€–34€. MC, V. Mon–Sat 1:30–3:30pm and 8:30–11:30pm. Metro: Gregorio Marañón.

Dassa Bassa ★★ SPANISH/INTERNATIONAL Right across from Puerta de Alcalá, this hot dining ticket attracts TV and movie celebrities, models, fashionistas, and VIPs-at-large. Many magazines, including *Metropoli,* have named this Madrid's best restaurant. If anything, it has improved since those accolades. And the word is out, so getting a table may be difficult.

The place is expensive, but suitable for an extravagant night out on the town. Lighted stairs lead to a subterranean whitewashed *caveau,* where the cuisine soars to great heights. The chef is Darío Barrio, and his wife, Itziar, is the maitre d'. Barrio trained with "the master," fabled chef Ferran Adrià, hailed as Spain's greatest. Rather than being a slavish imitator, Barrio forges ahead with his own style—exemplified by the mashed potato and truffle, perhaps the finest potato dish we've ever sampled in Spain. You might enjoy a chilled almond soup poured around ginger ale gelée, or else dried codfish and trout eggs. We'd recommend the boned chunk of oxtail with wine and chocolate (yes, you read that right), based on a recipe given to the chef by his grandmother.

Villalar 7. ✆ **91-576-73-97.** www.dassabassa.com. Reservations required. Main courses 25€–30€. Fixed-price menus 65€–80€. AE, MC, V. Tues–Sat 1:30–4pm and 9–11:30pm. Closed Aug 1–21. Metro: Retiro.

El Amparo ★★ BASQUE Behind the cascading vines on El Amparo's facade is one of Madrid's most elegant gastronomic enclaves. Inside this converted carriage house, three tiers of rough-hewn wooden beams surround tables set with pink linens and glistening silver. A sloping skylight floods the interior with sun by day; at night, pinpoints of light from high-tech hanging lanterns create intimate shadows. Polite, uniformed waiters serve well-prepared nouvelle cuisine versions of cold marinated salmon with tomato sorbet; cold cream-of-vegetable-and-shrimp soup; bisque of shellfish with Armagnac; ravioli with crayfish dressed with balsamic vinegar and vanilla-scented oil; roast lamb chops with garlic purée; breast of duck; ragout of sole; roulades of lobster with soy sauce; and steamed hake with pepper sauce.

Callejón de Puigcerdà 8 (at corner of Jorge Juan). ✆ **91-431-64-56.** Reservations required. Main courses 24€–40€. AE, DC, MC, V. Mon–Fri 1:45–3:30pm; Mon–Sat 9–11:30pm. Closed Easter week. Metro: Serrano. Bus: 19, 21, or 53.

Horcher ★ GERMAN/INTERNATIONAL Horcher originated in Berlin in 1904. In 1943, prompted by a tip from a high-ranking German officer that Germany was losing the war, Herr Horcher moved his restaurant to Madrid. For years it was known as the best dining room in the city, but fierce competition has stolen that crown. Nevertheless, the restaurant is still going strong, continuing its grand European traditions, including excellent service.

You might try the skate or shrimp tartare, or the distinctive warm hake salad. The venison stew with green pepper and orange peel, and the crayfish with parsley and cucumber, are both typical of the elegant fare served with style. Spanish aristocrats often come here in autumn to sample game dishes, including venison, wild boar, and roast wild duck. Other main courses include stockfish gratiné with eggplant and veal scallops with truffles and port-wine sauce.

Alfonso XII no. 6. ✆ **91-522-07-31.** www.restaurantehorcher.com. Reservations required. Jackets and ties required for men. Main courses 25€–40€. AE, DC, MC, V. Mon–Fri 1:30–4pm; Mon–Sat 8:30pm–midnight. Metro: Retiro or Banco.

Pan de Lujo ★★ MEDITERRANEAN/ASIAN Artful and elegant, with a battery of lights that, as they change, are almost breathtaking, this big-windowed restaurant near Parque del Retiro has earned rave reviews for its interior design and its cuisine. Some areas of the floor are also lit from beneath, creating the illusion that diners and staff are bathed in patterns of light that subtly change throughout the course of a meal. Alberto Chicote, one of the city's most famous chefs, mixes Asian and Mediterranean ideas in ways that have pleased late-night Madrileños. Some of the finest of Spain's regional produce goes into the imaginative, creative dishes served here. Begin perhaps with an appetizer of paper-thin eggplant in delicate virgin olive oil resting on hummus, followed by poached red snapper with crisp baby vegetables.

Calle Jorge Juan 20. ✆ **91-436-11-00.** www.pandelujo.es. Reservations required. Main courses 18€–42€. AE, DC, MC, V. Daily 1:30–4pm and 9pm–midnight. Metro: Serrano or Retiro.

Viridiana INTERNATIONAL Viridiana—named after the 1961 Luis Buñuel film classic—is one of Madrid's established restaurants, known for the creative imagination of its chef and part owner, Abraham García, who lined the walls with stills from Buñuel films. (He is a film historian as well as a self-taught chef.) Menu specialties are contemporary adaptations of traditional recipes, and they change frequently according to availability of ingredients. Examples of the singular cooking include sauté of filet of beef with fresh porcini mushrooms; roast pigeon with pearl barley, chestnuts, and black chanterelles; and honey-glazed roast lamb with saffron couscous. The food is sublime, and the ambience invites you to relax as you enjoy dishes that dazzle the eye, notably venison and rabbit arranged on a plate with fresh greens to evoke an autumnal scene in a forest.

Juan de Mena 14. ℭ **91-523-44-78.** www.restauranteviridiana.com. Reservations recommended. Main courses 30€–37€. AE, DC, MC, V. Mon–Sat 1:30–4pm and 8:30pm–midnight. Closed Easter week. Metro: Banco de España.

MODERATE

El Borbollón BASQUE/FRENCH The welcoming Castro family presides over this little charmer lying between Calle de Serrano and Paseo de Recoletos, near both Plaza Cibeles and Plaza Colón. Since 1984 they have welcomed some of Madrid's more discerning palates. Eduardo Castro, the chef, is a local personality and a whiz in the kitchen. He is known for such dishes as a perfectly grilled *rape* (monkfish). Steak is cooked with savory green peppers, and a chateaubriand appears enticingly drenched in whiskey. Fresh turbot and hake appear regularly on the menu, and rich game dishes such as partridge are featured in the autumn. Choice cutlets of Segovian lamb are awakened with garlic cloves. Fresh flowers and bucolic art make for a soothing decor.

Calle Recoletos 7. ℭ **91-431-41-34.** www.elborbollon.es. Main courses 20€–47€; *menú completo* 55€–60€. AE, DC, MC, V. Mon–Fri 1–4pm; Mon–Sat 9pm–midnight. Metro: Retiro or Plaza Colón.

Gran Café de Gijón SPANISH If you want food and atmosphere like it was in Franco's heyday, drop in here. Each of the old European capitals has a coffeehouse that traditionally attracts the literati—in Madrid it's the Gijón, which opened in 1888 in the Belle Epoque. Artists and writers still patronize this venerated old cafe, many of them spending hours over one cup of coffee. Open windows look out onto the wide *paseo,* and a large terrace is perfect for sun worshipers and bird-watchers. Along one side of the cafe is a stand-up bar; on the lower level is a restaurant. In summer, sit in the garden to enjoy a *blanco y negro* (black coffee with ice cream) or a mixed drink.

Paseo de Recoletos 21. ℭ **91-521-54-25.** www.cafegijon.com. Reservations required for restaurant. Main courses 20€–30€. AE, DC, MC, V. Daily 7:30am–2am. Metro: Banco de España, Colón, or Recoletos.

Iroco ★ FUSION Named after a tree that grows in Africa, this welcoming restaurant in the Salamanca district has walls with botanical prints. It offers one of Madrid's prettiest outdoor eating spaces in its little central courtyard. When making a reservation (if it's a fair day), ask for a garden table in the rear.

The fusion cuisine, with a lot of inspiration from Asia, is elaborately prepared and beautifully presented. Main dishes are best accompanied by fine wines from Rioja or Ribera del Duero. For appetizers, sample the white fish salad drizzled with a Jerez (sherry) vinaigrette, or try the prawn-stuffed rolls. The vegetable tempuras are so good here that even a carnivore might be tempted.

Eggplant (aubergine) lasagna, studded with fresh mushrooms, rests under a layer of creamy mozzarella. Hake comes in an asparagus sauce, and seafood dishes are flown in fresh from Galicia.

Calle Velásquez 18. ⓒ **91-431-73-81.** Reservations required. Main courses 25€–50€. AE, MC, V. Daily 1:30–4pm and 8:30pm–midnight. Metro: Goya.

La Gamella ★★ INTERNATIONAL This restaurant occupies the 19th-century building where the Spanish philosopher Ortega y Gasset was born. The prestigious Horcher, one of the capital's legendary restaurants (p. 147), is just across the street, but the food at La Gamella is better. The russet-colored, high-ceilinged design invites customers to relax. The founder has prepared his delicate and light-textured specialties for the king and queen of Spain, as well as for Madrid's most talked-about artists and merchants, many of whom he knows and greets personally between sessions in his kitchen.

Start, perhaps, with cream of lentil soup with porcini mushrooms, and go on to such temptations as ravioli filled with pumpkin and almonds with a creamy herb sauce, or pan-seared fresh codfish in a mushroom sauce. Another specialty is baby squid stuffed with caramelized onions and served with black pasta.

Alfonso XII no. 4. ⓒ **91-532-45-09.** www.lagamella.com. Reservations required. Main courses 17€–25€. *Menú de degustación* 36€. AE, DC, MC, V. Mon–Fri 1:30–4pm and 9pm–midnight; Sat 9pm–midnight. Closed 4 days around Easter. Metro: Retiro. Bus: 19.

Loft 39 INTERNATIONAL You'll get the feeling of dining within a cozy and skillfully lit art gallery if you opt for a meal at this place, where angular lines and touches of metallic gloss seem to reflect an Iberian sense of cubism. References to art history quickly fade, however, upon presentation of dishes, which in most cases are more favorably priced than you might expect. The best examples include thin-sliced Iberian ham with tomatoes and toasted bread; tartar of tuna with guacamole, sweet onions, and caramelized soy sprouts; tempura of crab; a terrine of foie gras with rye bread and an herb-infused yogurt sauce; hake with red-curry sauce; lamb roasted at low temperatures for long periods and stuffed with apples and pine nuts; and all manner of grilled meats, including filet steaks and a very upscale version of a hamburger with a sage and mango chutney.

Calle Velázquez 39. ⓒ **91-432-43-86.** www.restauranteloft39.com. Reservations required. Main courses 16€–33€. AE, DC, MC, V. Daily 1:30–4pm and 9pm–midnight. Metro: Velázquez.

Ramses Restaurant ★ INTERNATIONAL Most patrons find the baroque decor here fascinating, owing to its great style. But the reason this place is a success is because of the refined cuisine offered by one of the city's most talented chefs, Miguel Angel Jiménez. His menu is a surprise and delight to most diners. On the ground floor, Petit offers a spectacular bar and is a venue for breakfast, lunch, or dinner. On the top floor, El Bistro offers an haute international cuisine and all that baroque decor. The menu is forever changing, but expect such creative dishes as creamy pumpkin risotto and mussels in a spicy Thai coconut curry.

Plaza de la Independencia 4. ⓒ **91-434-16-66.** Reservations required. Main courses 15€–35€. AE, DC, MC, V. Daily noon–1am. Metro: Banco de España.

Senzone Restaurant ★★ INTERNATIONAL On the ground floor of the chic Hospes Madrid (p. 135), this is a showcase restaurant for the cuisine of a young and talented chef, Francisco Morales. He is brilliantly assisted by his wife, Rut Cotroneo, one of Spain's brightest sommeliers. The dishes Morales creates are not just culinary statements but works of art, at least in presentation. He knows how to add that extraspecial taste to create a flavor sensation—for example, he dusts squid with macadamia nuts, or he serves a sea urchin broth with a silken kohrabi custard. He places his emphasis on healthful and natural foods. Arrive early and enjoy a trio of elegantly furnished bar and lounges, one a dark wood-paneled library with leather furniture and windows fronting Puerta de Alcalá. There is also a large outdoor *terraza* lit by candles.

Plaza de la Independencia 3. ☎ **91-432-29-11.** Reservations required. Main courses 10€–24€. AE, MC, V. Tues–Sat 1:30–4pm and 8:30–11pm. Metro: Retiro.

Sula ★ INTERNATIONAL In the Barrio de Salamanca, Sula is a favorite celebrity hangout in Madrid. Fortunately, the cuisine is also quite refined. The evening begins on the ground level at the tapas bar, where habitués munch chorizo croquettes (incredibly tasty) and wash them down with *cava* from the Barcelona region. Tempting starters include a cold soup of tomatoes, garlic, and bread served with quail egg and Iberian ham. Main dishes include grilled pork shoulder with essence of sesame and Parmesan shavings. Each day a dish is featured from a different region of Spain. A selection of hot dishes, such as squid with a pear aioli, or cold dishes, such as Iberian pork-shoulder carpaccio, is featured nightly. Portions are small.

Calle Jorge Juan 33. ☎ **91-781-61-97.** www.sularestaurant.com. Reservations required. Main courses 24€–30€. Mon–Sat 1:30–3:30pm and 8:30–11:30pm. Bar Mon–Sat noon to midnight. Closed Aug 3–27. Metro: Velázquez.

Chamberi
EXPENSIVE

Jockey ★★ INTERNATIONAL For decades, this deluxe culinary citadel was the premier restaurant of Spain. It's still a favorite of international celebrities, diplomats, and heads of state. The restaurant, with tables on two levels, isn't large. Wood-paneled walls and colored linens provide a cozy ambience. Against the paneling are a dozen prints of jockeys mounted on horses—hence the name.

Since Jockey's establishment, shortly after World War II, each chef who has come along has prided himself on coming up with new and creative dishes. You can still order beluga caviar from Iran, but you might settle happily for the goose-liver terrine or slices of Jabugo ham. Cold melon soup with shrimp is soothing on a hot day, especially when followed by grill-roasted young pigeon from Talavera, or by sole filets with figs in chardonnay. Some of the best of main dishes include marinated salmon with potatoes in cream; roast scallops with ham; or tender, young chicken roasted with fresh thyme. Desserts are sumptuous.

Amador de los Ríos 6. ☎ **91-310-04-11.** www.restaurantejockey.net. Reservations required. Jacket and tie required for men. Main courses 29€–40€. AE, DC, MC, V. Mon–Sat 1:30–4pm and 9pm–midnight. Closed Aug. Metro: Colón.

La Manduca de Azagra ★★ NAVARRESE/SPANISH A table here at night is one of the most sought after in Madrid. Fashionistas show up, blending in with French sophisticates, bourgeois Madrileños, and even young gay professionals. It's on the see-and-be-seen circuit. Fortunately, the cuisine is also very worthy. On the night of our last visit, cross-dressers looking like extras in a Pedro Almodóvar film shared the next table—they raved about the food, we're happy to report. We agreed with their appraisals. Incidentally, their table went for *rabo de toro,* the bull's tail; our table preferred the tender, succulently sweet roast suckling pig, prepared in the style of Segovia, and the *lomo de lubina salvaje* (wild sea bass). One of our favorite offerings here is the fried white asparagus and fresh artichokes. Each dish is a delight, carefully crafted from market-fresh ingredients. The menu bursts with freshness and originality, and the service is both polite and efficient. The wine carte is also worthy, but a bit expensive.

Sagasta 14. ✆ **91-591-01-12.** www.lamanducadeazagra.com. Reservations required. Main courses 36€–60€. AE, DC, MC, V. Mon–Sat 1:30–4pm and 9pm–midnight. Closed Aug. Metro: Alonso Martínez.

La Paloma ★ BASQUE/FRENCH This small but comfortable restaurant is the showcase for the culinary talents of chef/owner Segundo Alonso, who earned a stellar reputation at the more exclusive El Amparo. Many of his fans followed him here and have since become regulars. His restaurant is in a nostalgic old restored house with high ceilings and wooden beams. His French and Basque dishes are some of the finest of their kind in Madrid. His food is robust, and he's known for what is called "variety meats," especially pigs' trotters. Even if you have never sampled this dish before, dare to here; you might be glad you did. You could settle instead for the equally celebrated wood pigeon stuffed with foie gras. La Paloma also does an excellent lasagna with crabmeat, spinach, and leeks, as well as a fine *rabo de toro* stewed in red-wine sauce. The best fish dish is grilled turbot with tomato paste and thyme. Or try sea urchin gratinéed and served with quail eggs. For dessert, sample the fresh dates with Chantilly cream or a velvety almond mousse with cinnamon ice cream.

Jorge Juan 39. ✆ **91-576-86-92.** www.rtelapaloma.com. Reservations recommended. Main courses 20€–60€; tasting menu 60€. AE, DC, MC, V. Mon–Sat 1:30–4pm and 9pm–midnight. Metro: Velázquez or Vergara.

MODERATE

La Bola MADRILEÑA This is *the* taberna in which to savor the 19th century. Just north of the Teatro Real, it's one of the few restaurants (if not the only one) left in Madrid with a blood-red facade; at one time, nearly all fashionable restaurants were so coated. Time stands still inside this restaurant, with its traditional atmosphere, gently polite waiters, Venetian crystal, and aging velvet. Grilled sole, filet of veal, and roast veal are regularly featured. Basque-style hake and grilled salmon are well recommended. Refreshing dishes with which to begin your meal include grilled shrimp, red-pepper salad, and lobster cocktail.

Calle de la Bola 5. ✆ **91-547-69-30.** www.labola.es. Reservations required. Main courses 18€–36€. No credit cards. Mon–Sat 1–4pm and 8:30–11pm. Metro: Opera or Santo Domingo. Bus: 25 or 39.

Teatriz ★ MEDITERRANEAN/INTERNATIONAL Decorated by the famed French architect and designer Philippe Starck, this old theater is now a top-notch Italian restaurant. Theater seats have long given way to dining tables, but Starck kept many of the elements of the old theater. As you head for the restrooms, you encounter a stunning fountain of marble, silver, and gold bathed in a bluish light, making you think you're in a nightclub. The kitchen closes at midnight, but the bar remains open until 3am. The dishes are genuine and cleverly crafted. Launch yourself toward fresh mozzarella with tomatoes in virgin olive oil. For a main dish, try the Iberian pork tenderloin wrapped in Speck (dried ham), or roast rack of lamb served with sun-dried tomatoes and a rosemary gravy. Another delight is the Alaskan wild salmon drizzled with a 13-spice oil and served with an aromatic couscous.

Calle Hermosilla 15. ☎ **91-577-53-79.** Reservations recommended. Main courses 17€–25€; *menú completo* 23€ for lunch only. AE, DC, MC, V. Daily 1–4pm and 9:30pm–12:30am. Metro: Serrano.

INEXPENSIVE

Foster's Hollywood AMERICAN When your craving for Stateside food becomes overwhelming, head here. When Foster's opened its doors in 1971, it was not only the first American-style restaurant in Spain, but one of the first in Europe. Since those early days, it has expanded to 27 restaurants in Madrid, and has even opened branches in Florida. A popular hangout for both locals and visiting Yanks, it offers a choice of dining rooms, ranging from classic club to faux film studio with props. The varied menu includes Tex-Mex selections, ribs, steaks, sandwiches, freshly made salads, and, as its signature offering, hamburgers grilled over natural charcoal. The *New York Times* once claimed that it had "probably the best onion rings in the world."

Paseo de la Castellana 116–118. ☎ **91-564-63-08.** www.fostershollywood.es. Main courses 8€–19€. AE, DC, MC, V. Sun–Thurs 1–5pm and 8pm–midnight; Fri–Sat 1pm–1am. Metro: Nuevo Ministerio.

Mosaiq ★ ARABIAN This is a dining sensation in Madrid, a trio of colorfully and elegantly decorated dining rooms with low tables and such touches as pillows and hassocks in the Moroccan style. The chef, using a little exaggeration, calls his kitchen "a thousand and one delights." The cuisine is extremely well prepared, and our party worked our way through the chickpea cream with sesame oil, the shrimp brochettes, and an especially delightful "perfumed" lamb kafta. The chicken tagine (prepared with olives) is a special temptation, as is the tuna steak with fresh herbs and spices. For dessert, a variety of Arabic pastries are prepared fresh daily.

Calle Caracas 21. ☎ **91-308-44-46.** www.mosaiqrestaurante.com. Reservations required. Main courses 10€–19€. Lunch menu Mon–Fri 16€. AE, DC, MC, V. Daily 1:30–3:30pm and 9pm–midnight. Metro: Rubén Darío.

Chamartin
VERY EXPENSIVE

Zalacaín ★★★ INTERNATIONAL Outstanding in both food and decor, Zalacaín is credited with bringing nouvelle cuisine to Spain since it opened its doors back in 1973. It is reached by an illuminated walk from Paseo de la Castellana and housed at the garden end of a modern apartment complex. It's within an easy walk of such deluxe hotels as the Castellana and the Miguel Angel. The name of the restaurant comes from the intrepid hero of Basque author Pío Baroja's 1909 novel, *Zalacaín El Aventurero*. Zalacaín is small, exclusive, and expensive. It has the atmosphere of an elegant old mansion: The walls are covered with textiles, and some are decorated with Audubon-style paintings. The cuisine is innovative and based on quality produce, including beef steak in red wine with caramelized pearl onions, or grilled venison with a dried prune sauce. You can also order lobster stew with green beans or baked grouper flavored with a black truffle oil.

Alvarez de Baena 4. ☎ **91-561-48-40.** www.restaurantezalacain.com. Reservations required. Jacket and tie required for men. Main courses 29€–48€. AE, DC, MC, V. Mon–Fri 1:15–4pm; Mon–Sat 9pm–12:30am. Closed Easter week and Aug. Metro: Gregorio Marañón.

INEXPENSIVE

Fast Good Madrid ★ ✦ Ferran Adrià of Catalonia is hailed as Spain's grandest chef. In this outpost, in northeastern Madrid, in a streetside corner of the Hotel NH-Eurobuilding, he brings his take on fast food to the Spanish capital. But it's like no McDonald's you ever visited. Under translucent bubble lamps, while watching flatscreen TV, patrons sit on lavender-colored chairs in their designer jeans and sample the offerings. Note the Warhol pink–and–apple green color scheme.

The food is original in concept, simply prepared, touted as healthy, and absolutely delicious. Perhaps you'll begin with a freshly squeezed peach-and-mango juice. Cold dishes, including a green-bean salad with foie gras, are taken from a self-service buffet, while the hot dishes, such as the best french fries in town, are brought directly to your table. The fries are cooked in virgin olive oil and served in a paper cone. You can even pair them with a veal hamburger topped with tangles of fresh tarragon and mint.

Calle Padre Damián 23. ✆ **91-353-73-00.** www.fast-good.com. Main courses 5.50€–18€. AE, MC, V. Daily noon–midnight. Metro: Cuzco.

Chueca

EXPENSIVE

Asiana ★★★ 🍴 FRENCH/ASIAN Our temptation is to dine here every night—it's that special. Jaime Renedo had to persuade his mother to allow him to open this hidden-away restaurant inside her store devoted to Asian antiques in the increasingly gentrified Chueca district. After ringing the bell, you'll be shown to one of seven candlelit tables in a cellar space filled with gilt Buddhas and Ming vases. Walk-ins are not accepted, and a major credit card is needed to reserve a table at what is the most private public restaurant in town.

There is no menu. Renedo and his Japanese partner dream up multicourse feasts every night, using first-rate ingredients to concoct a daily tasting menu that is simply sublime. Two of the best specialties include ravioli stuffed with fish and potato mousse, or melon gazpacho with lobster. Fresh and tender squid is shipped in from Galicia and mated with porcini petals and a macadamia oil aioli.

Traversia de San Mateo 4. ✆ **91-310-09-65.** Reservations required. Tasting menu 90€. AE, DC, MC, V. Daily 9:30–11pm. Closed Aug. Metro: Alonzo Martínez.

MODERATE

Casa Salvador SPANISH/MADRILEÑA This is a robust, macho enclave of Madrid. The owner of this bustling restaurant configured it as a minimuseum to his hobby and passion, the Spanish art of bullfighting. Inside, near a bar that stocks an impressive collection of sherries and whiskeys, you'll find the memorabilia of years of bull watching, including photographs of great matadors beginning in the 1920s, and agrarian artifacts used in the raising and development of fighting bulls. The menu is as robust as the decor, featuring macho-size platters of oxtail in red-wine sauce; different preparations of hake (one of which is baked delectably in a salt crust); stuffed pepper, fried calamari, and shrimp entrees; and, for dessert, the local version of *arroz con leche.*

Calle Barbieri 12. ✆ **91-521-45-24.** Reservations recommended. Main courses 12€–28€. AE, DC, MC, V. Mon–Sat 1:30–4pm and 9–11:30pm. Closed 2 weeks July–Aug. Metro: Chueca.

Off the Plaza Mayor

EXPENSIVE

Sobrino de Botín ★★ SPANISH Ernest Hemingway made this restaurant famous. In the final two pages of his novel *The Sun Also Rises,* Jake invites Brett to Botín for the Segovian specialty of roast suckling pig, washed down with Rioja Alta.

As you enter, you step back to 1725, the year the restaurant was founded. You'll see an open kitchen with a charcoal hearth, hanging copper pots, an 18th-century tile oven for roasting the suckling pig, and a big pot of soup whose aroma wafts across the tables. Painter Francisco Goya was once a dishwasher here. Your host, Antonio, never loses his cool—even when he has 18 guests waiting in line for tables.

The two house specialties are roast suckling pig and roast Segovian lamb. From the a la carte menu, you might try the fish-based "quarter-of-an-hour" soup. Good main dishes include baked Cantabrian hake and filet mignon with potatoes. The dessert list features strawberries (in season) with whipped cream. You can accompany your meal with Valdepeñas or Aragón wine, although most guests order sangria.

Calle de Cuchilleros 17. ✆ **91-366-42-17.** www.botin.es. Reservations recommended. Main courses 14€–29€; fixed-price menu 40€. AE, DC, MC, V. Daily 1–4pm and 8pm–midnight. Metro: La Latina, Opera, Sol, or Tirso de Molina.

MODERATE

Casa Lucio CASTILIAN Set on a historic street whose edges once marked the perimeter of Old Madrid, this is a venerable *tasca* with all the requisite antique accessories. Dozens of cured hams hang from hand-hewn beams above the well-oiled bar. Among the clientele is a stable of sometimes surprisingly well-known public figures—perhaps even the king of Spain. The two dining rooms, each on a different floor, have whitewashed walls, tile floors, and exposed brick. A well-trained staff offers classic Castilian food, which might include Jabugo ham with broad beans, shrimp in garlic sauce, hake with green sauce, several types of roasted lamb, and a thick steak served sizzling hot on a heated platter (called *churrasco de la casa*).

Cava Baja 35. ✆ **91-365-32-52.** www.casalucio.es. Reservations required. Main courses 15€–28€. AE, DC, MC, V. Sun–Fri 1–4pm; daily 9–11:30pm. Closed Aug. Metro: La Latina.

El Schotis ★ SPANISH El Schotis was established in 1962 on one of Madrid's oldest and most historic streets. A series of large and pleasingly old-fashioned dining rooms is the setting for an animated crowd of Madrileños and foreign visitors, who receive ample portions of conservative, well-prepared vegetables, salads, soups, fish, and, above all, meat. Specialties of the house include roast baby lamb, grilled steaks and veal chops, shrimp with garlic, and fried hake in green sauce. Traditional desserts are served as well. Although one Frommer's reader found everything but the gazpacho ho-hum, this local favorite pleases thousands of diners annually. There's a bar near the entrance for tapas and before- or after-dinner drinks.

Cava Baja 11. ✆ **91-365-32-30.** Reservations recommended. Main courses 20€–28€. AE, DC, MC, V. Mon–Sat 1–4pm and 8:30pm–midnight; Sun 1–4pm. Closed Aug 15–Sept 7. Metro: Puerta del Sol or La Latina.

La Posada de la Villa SPANISH This historic inn, founded in 1642, offers a modern, more sanitized version of the earthy, grilled cuisine that fed the stonemasons who made the building's thick walls. Within a trio of dining rooms whose textured plaster and old stonework absolutely reek of Old Castile, you'll find a hardworking staff and a menu that focuses on a time-honored specialty—roasted baby lamb—that's ordered more often than anything else on the menu. Other excellent choices include different versions of hake, Madrid-style tripe, and the rich, savory stew (*cocida madrileña*) that many local residents remember fondly from childhood days. Notice that many of the chairs have brass plaques bearing the names of famous patrons—we've seen one labeled JANET JACKSON!

Cava Baja 9. ℭ **91-366-18-60.** www.posadadelavilla.com. Reservations recommended. Main courses 17€–28€. DC, MC, V. Daily 1–4pm; Mon–Sat 8pm–midnight. Closed Aug. Metro: La Latina, Tirso de Molina, or Sol.

INEXPENSIVE

El Cosaco ✔ RUSSIAN One of the few Russian restaurants in Madrid sits adjacent to one of the most charming and evocative squares in town. Inside, you'll find dining rooms outfitted with paintings and artifacts from the former Soviet Union. Menu items seem to taste best when preceded with something from a long list of vodkas, many of them from small-scale distilleries you might not immediately recognize. Items include rich and savory cold-weather dishes that seem a bit at odds with the sweltering heat of Madrid, but can be satisfying alternatives to the all-Spanish restaurants in the same neighborhood. Examples include beef stroganoff; quenelles of pikeperch with fresh dill; and thin-sliced smoked salmon or sturgeon artfully arranged with capers, chopped onions, and chopped hard-boiled eggs. The red or the white version of borscht makes a worthy starter. Blinis, stuffed with caviar or paprika-laced beef, are always excellent.

Plaza de la Paja 2. ℭ **91-365-35-48.** www.restauranteelcosaco.com. Reservations recommended. Main courses 9€–23€; menu of the day 12€. MC, V. Daily 2–4pm and 9pm–midnight. Metro: La Latina.

Lavapies

In long decay, this section south of the Plaza Mayor is being gentrified, and many of its old buildings have been restored and turned into studio flats by a rising young class of Madrileños. Side by side with these upwardly mobile locals are many immigrants from the Middle East and Morocco, among other places.

MODERATE

Alboroque ★★ SEAFOOD/SPANISH Chef Andres Madrigal delivers a market-fresh cuisine that focuses on the fresh seafood flown in from Spain's coastal ports. He has spent more than 2 decades in the kitchen, refining his take on classic Spanish cuisine, although he has imaginative ideas of his own in the various dishes served. Most of his platters are rapturously delicious, and they're offered with a smile by the friendly staff. Woth sampling are such dishes as braised rabbit with a purée of black olives or savory Castilian lamb with a merlot-infused risotto. Desserts are also sumptuous. The restaurant's rich choice of dishes contains a forever-changing but tantalizing array of appetizers.

Casa Palacio Atocha 34. ℭ **90-220-30-25.** www.alboroque.es. Reservations required. Main courses 15€–35€; *menú del día* 35€; *menú de degustación* 55€. AE, DC, MC, V. Daily noon–4pm and 9pm–midnight. Metro: Lavapiés or Embajadores.

Our Favorite *Tascas*

Don't starve while you're waiting around for Madrid's fashionable 9:30 or 10pm dinner hour. Throughout the city you'll find *tascas,* bars that serve wine and platters of tempting hot and cold tapas. Below, we've listed our favorites. Keep in mind that you can often save euros by ordering at the bar rather than occupying a table.

Casa Mingo SPANISH Casa Mingo has been known for decades for its cider, both still and bubbly. The perfect accompanying tidbit is a piece of the local Asturian *cabrales* (goat cheese), but the roast chicken is the specialty of the house, with a large number of helpings served daily. There's no formality here; customers share big tables under the vaulted ceiling in the dining room. In summer, the staff sets tables and wooden chairs out on the sidewalk. This is not so much a restaurant as a *bodega/taverna* (bar/tavern) that serves food.

Paseo de la Florida 34. ✆ **91-547-79-18.** www.casamingo.es. Main courses 2€–8€. No credit cards. Daily 11am–midnight. Metro: Principe Pío, and then 5-min. walk. Bus: 41, 46, or 75.

Cervecería La Alemana TAPAS This place earned its name because of its long-ago German clients. Opening directly onto one of the liveliest little plazas in Madrid, it clings to its turn-of-the-20th-century traditions. Young Madrileños are fond of stopping in for a mug of draft beer. You can sit at one of the tables, leisurely sipping beer or wine—the waiters make no attempt to hurry you along. To accompany your beverage, try the fried sardines or a Spanish omelet. Many of the *tascas* on this popular square are crowded and noisy—often with blaring loud music—but this one is quiet and a good place to have a conversation.

Plaza de Santa Ana 6. ✆ **91-429-70-33.** Beer 2.50€; tapas 4€–10€. MC, V. Wed–Mon 10am–2am. Metro: Tirso de Molina or Puerta del Sol. Bus: 6, 17, or 56.

Cervecería Santa Bárbara TAPAS Unique in Madrid, Cervecería Santa Bárbara is an outlet for a beer factory, and the management has done a lot to make it modern and inviting. Hanging globe lights and spinning ceiling fans create an attractive ambience, as does the black-and-white checkerboard marble floor. You go here for beer, of course: *cerveza negra* (black beer) or *cerveza dorada* (golden beer). The local brew is best accompanied by homemade potato chips or by fresh shrimp, lobster, crabmeat, or barnacles. You can either stand at the counter or go directly to one of the wooden tables for waiter service.

Plaza de Santa Bárbara 8. ✆ **91-319-04-49.** www.cerveceriasantabarbara.com. Beer 1.50€–3.50€; tapas 2.50€–14€. MC, V. Daily 8am–midnight. Metro: Alonzo Martínez. Bus: 3, 7, or 21.

Taberna Toscana TAPAS Many Madrileños begin their nightly *tasca*-crawl here. The ambience is that of a village inn far removed from 21st-century Madrid. You sit on crude country stools beneath age-darkened beams from which hang sausages, peppers, and sheaves of golden wheat. The long tiled bar is loaded with tasty tidbits, including the house specialties: *habas* (broad beans) with Spanish ham, and *chorizo* (a sausage of red peppers and pork)—almost meals in themselves. Especially delectable are the kidneys in sherry sauce and the snails in hot sauce.

Manuel Fernández y González 10. ✆ **91-429-60-31.** www.tabernatoscana.es. Beer 3€; glass of wine from 1.50€; tapas 4€–18€. MC, V. Tues–Sat noon–4pm and 8pm–midnight. Metro: Puerta del Sol or Sevilla.

SEEING THE SIGHTS
The Top Attractions

In the heart of Madrid, near the Puerta del Sol Metro stop, **Plaza Mayor ★★★** is the city's most famous square. It was known as Plaza de Arrabal in medieval times, when it stood outside the city wall. The original architect of Plaza Mayor was Juan Gómez de Mora, who worked during the reign of Philip III. Under the Habsburgs, the square rose in importance as the site of public spectacles, including the abominable *autos-da-fé*, in which heretics were burned. Bullfights, knightly tournaments, and festivals were also staged here.

Three times the buildings on the square burned—in 1631, 1672, and 1790—but each time the plaza bounced back. After the last big fire it was completely redesigned by Juan de Villanueva. Nowadays a Christmas fair is held around the equestrian statue of Philip III (dating from 1616) in the center of the square. On summer nights, the Plaza Mayor becomes the virtual living room of Madrid, as tourists sip sangria at the numerous cafes and listen to street musicians.

Monasterio de las Descalzas Reales ★★ In the mid–16th century, aristocratic women—either disappointed in love or wanting to be the "bride of Christ"—stole away to this convent to take the veil. Each brought a dowry, making this one of the richest convents in the land. By the mid–20th century, the convent sheltered mostly poor women. True, it still contained a priceless collection of art treasures, but the sisters were forbidden to auction anything, so they were literally starving. The state intervened, and the pope granted special dispensation to open the convent as a museum. Today, the public can look behind the walls of what was once a mysterious edifice on one of the most beautiful squares in Old Madrid.

The Monasterio de las Descalzas Reales.

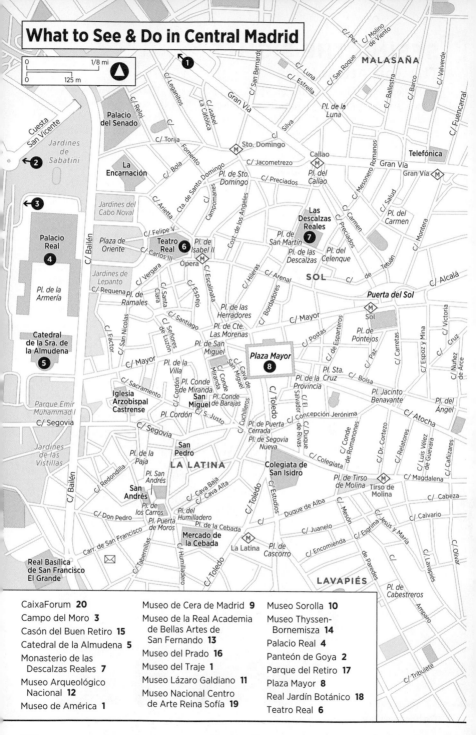

What to See & Do in Central Madrid

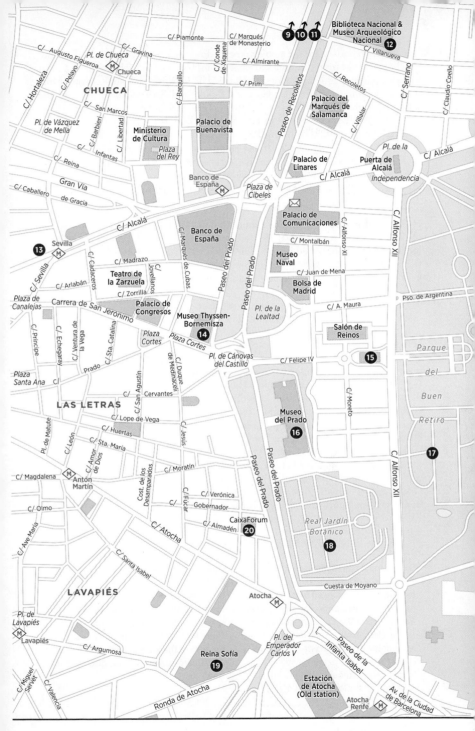

In the reliquary are the noblewomen's dowries, one of which is said to contain bits of wood from the True Cross; another, bones of St. Sebastian. The most valuable painting is Titian's *Caesar's Money*. The Flemish Hall shelters other fine works, including paintings by Hans de Beken and Bruegel the Elder. All the tapestries were based on Rubens's cartoons, displaying his chubby matrons. Be warned that the tours are not in English, but there is much to see even if you don't speak Spanish. Allot 1 hour for a visit here.

Plaza de las Descalzas Reales s/n. ☎ **91-454-88-00.** www.patrimonionacional.es. Admission 5€ adults, 2.50€ children 5–16, free for children 4 and under. Tues–Thurs and Sat 10:30am–12:45pm and 4–5:45pm; Fri 10:30am–12:45pm; Sun 11am–1:45pm. Metro: Opera. Bus: 3, 25, 39, or 148. From Plaza del Callao, off Gran Vía, walk down Postigo de San Martín to Plaza de las Descalzas Reales; the convent is on the left.

Museo del Prado ★★★ With more than 7,000 paintings, the Prado is one of the most important repositories of art in the world. It began as a royal collection and was enhanced by the Habsburgs, especially Charles V, and later by the Bourbons. For paintings of the Spanish school, the Prado has no equal; on your first visit, concentrate on the Spanish masters (Velázquez, Goya, El Greco, and Murillo).

Major Italian works are exhibited on the ground floor. You'll see art by Italian masters—Raphael, Botticelli, Mantegna, Andrea del Sarto, Fra Angelico, and Correggio. The most celebrated Italian painting here is Titian's voluptuous Venus being watched by a musician who can't keep his eyes on his work.

The Prado is a trove of the work of El Greco (ca. 1541–1614), the Crete-born artist who lived much of his life in Toledo. You can see a parade of the Greek's saints, Madonnas, and Holy Families—even a ghostly *John the Baptist*.

You'll find a splendid array of works by the incomparable Diego Velázquez (1599–1660). The museum's most famous painting, in fact, is his *Las Meninas (The Maids of Honor)*, a triumph in its use of light effects and perspective. The faces of the queen and king are reflected in the mirror in the painting itself. The artist in the foreground is Velázquez, of course.

The Flemish painter Peter Paul Rubens (1577–1640), who met Velázquez while in Spain, is represented by the peacock-blue *Garden of Love* and by *Three Graces*. Also worthy is the work of José Ribera (1591–1652), a Valencia-born artist and contemporary of Velázquez whose best painting is *Martyrdom of St. Philip*.

Goya or Not, *The Milkmaid* & *The Colossus* Are Still Great Art

Spain's most fabled museum, the Prado, shocked the art world—and visitors, too—when it announced that two of its most famous paintings, *The Milkmaid of Bordeaux* and *The Colossus,* attributed to Francisco de Goya, are not in fact the work of the Spanish master. Goya specialists agree. The paintings still hang in the Prado, although they are now "attributed" to Goya instead of "by" Goya. Want to see some real Goyas? The Prado has some 150 actual paintings by the artist. Some Goya experts question the authorship of other "supposed" Goyas, especially several portraits. There was such a market for Goyas at the turn of the 20th century that many art dealers—surprise—kept discovering "long-lost" Goyas.

Velázquez's *Las Meninas* (1656), at the Prado.

The Seville-born Bartolomé Murillo (1617–82)—often referred to as the "painter of Madonnas"—has three versions of the Immaculate Conception on display.

The Prado has an outstanding collection of the work of Hieronymus Bosch (ca. 1450–1516), the Flemish genius. *The Garden of Earthly Delights*, the best-known work of "El Bosco," is here. You'll also see his *Seven Deadly Sins* and his triptych *The Hay Wagon*. *The Triumph of Death* is by another Flemish painter, Pieter Bruegel the Elder (ca. 1525–69), who carried on Bosch's ghoulish vision.

Francisco de Goya (1746–1828) ranks along with Velázquez and El Greco in the trio of great Spanish artists. Hanging here are his unflattering portraits of his patron, Charles IV, and his family, as well as the *Clothed Maja* and the *Naked Maja*. You can see the much-reproduced *Third of May* (1808), plus a series of Goya sketches (some of which, depicting the decay of 18th-c. Spain, brought the Inquisition down on the artist) and his expressionistic "black paintings."

In a massive expansion launched by the Prado, at the cost of $92 million, the once-stuffy museum has even made room for children's workshops. Much of the expansion is buried underground. The main structure from 1785 is linked underground to the Prado's modern annex; the passageway runs beneath a garden and a plaza. The Prado has also branched out to incorporate surrounding buildings, including the Casón del Buen Retiro overlooking Parque del Retiro. It is filled with the work of 19th-century Spanish painters. The former Army Museum nearby was transferred to Toledo. The Prado grew by 50% with this expansion, the largest single growth in the 2-century history of the museum. The expansion includes several galleries, a restaurant, a lecture hall, and a gift shop. Designed by Rafael Moneo, the space blends in discreetly with the original 19th-century gallery. The expansion, among other exhibits, allows the Prado to display 1,000 Goya prints that had been in storage. Give yourself at least 3 hours here.

Paseo del Prado. ☏ **91-330-28-00.** www.museoprado.es. Admission 8€ adults, 4€ students. Free for children 17 and under, and free for all visitors on Sun. Tues–Sun 9am–8pm; holidays 9am–2pm. Call for info on guided tours. Closed Jan 1, Good Friday, May 1, and Dec 25. Metro: Atocha or Banco de España. Bus: 9, 10, 14, 19, 27, 34, 37, or 45.

Museo Nacional Centro de Arte Reina Sofía ★ What the Prado is to traditional art, this museum is to modern art: the greatest repository of 20th- to 21st-century works in Spain. Set within the echoing, futuristically renovated walls of the former General Hospital, originally built between 1776 and 1781, the museum is a sprawling, high-ceilinged showplace. Once designated "the ugliest building in Spain" by Catalan architect Oriol Bohigas, the Reina Sofía's design hangs in limbo somewhere between the 18th and the 21st centuries.

Special emphasis is paid to the great artists of 20th-century Spain: Juan Gris, Salvador Dalí, Joan Miró, and Pablo Picasso. What many critics consider Picasso's masterpiece, *Guernica,* now rests at this museum after a long and troubled history of traveling. Banned in Spain during Franco's era (Picasso refused to allow it to be displayed here, anyway), it hung until 1980 at New York's Museum of Modern Art. The fiercely antiwar painting immortalizes the town's shameful blanket bombing by the German Luftwaffe, which was fighting for Franco during the Spanish Civil War. Guernica was the cradle of the Basque nation, and Picasso's canvas made it a household name around the world.

After a $95-million expansion (2004–09), the museum now better accommodates its ever-increasing collection of contemporary art. With its latest space, Reina Sofía enters the world-class rank of modern museums, rivaling the Centre Pompidou, in Paris. The new complex is devoted to more than just paintings and includes a 450-seat auditorium for concerts and a 350,000-volume reference library. A third building contains two mammoth galleries for large-scale exhibitions. The new galleries free space for the permanent collections. If you make reservations in advance, you can also enjoy a grand lunch at the museum. A stunning restaurant, **Arola-Madrid,** is presided over by the Michelin-starred chef Sergi Arola. Allot about 1½ hours here.

Santa Isabel 52. ☎ **91-774-10-00.** www.museoreinasofia.es. Admission 6€ adults, 3€ students, free for children 17 and under. Mon–Sat 10am–9pm; Sun 10am–2:30pm. Free guided tours Mon and Wed 5pm, Sat 11am. Metro: Atocha. Bus: 6, 10, 14, 19, 26, 27, 32, 34, 36, or 37.

Museo Thyssen-Bornemisza ★★★ Until 1985, the contents of this museum overflowed the premises of a legendary villa near Lugano, Switzerland; it was a hugely popular attraction there. The collection had been laboriously amassed over a period of about 60 years by the wealthy Thyssen-Bornemisza family of Holland, Germany, and Hungary. Experts had proclaimed it one of the world's most extensive and valuable privately owned collections, rivaled only by the holdings of Queen Elizabeth II. For tax and insurance reasons, and because the collection had outgrown the boundaries of its lakeside villa, the collection was discreetly put on the market in the early 1980s, for sale to the world's major museums. Amid endless intrigue, glamorous supplicants from eight different nations came calling. Among them were Margaret Thatcher and Prince Charles; trustees of the Getty Museum in Los Angeles; the

The Colossus (1808–12), attributed to Goya.

The entrance to the Museo Thyssen-Bornemisza.

president of West Germany; and the duke of Badajoz, brother-in-law of King Carlos II. Eventually, the collection was awarded to Spain for $350 million. Controversies over the huge public cost of the acquisition raged for months. Various estimates have placed the value of this collection between $1 billion and $3 billion.

To house the collection, an 18th-century building adjacent to the Prado, the Villahermosa Palace, was fitted with appropriate lighting and security devices, and was renovated at a cost of $45 million. Rooms are arranged numerically so that by following the order of the rooms (nos. 1–48, spread out over three floors), a logical sequence of European painting can be traced from the 13th to the 20th century. The nucleus of the collection consists of 700 world-class paintings. They include works by, among others, El Greco, Velázquez, Dürer, Rembrandt, Watteau, Canaletto, Caravaggio, Hals, Memling, and Goya.

Unusual among the world's great art collections because of its eclecticism, the Thyssen group also contains 19th- and 20th-century paintings by many of the notable French Impressionists. It houses as well works by Picasso, Sargent, Kirchner, Nolde, and Kandinsky—artists who had never been well represented in Spanish museums. In addition to European paintings, major American works can be viewed here, including paintings by Thomas Cole, Winslow Homer, Jackson Pollock, Mark Rothko, Edward Hopper, Robert Rauschenberg, Stuart Davis, and Roy Lichtenstein.

Like the Prado and Reina Sofía, the museum expanded into two adjoining buildings, which allows more of the permanent collection to be shown and provides new space for temporary exhibitions. The cultural complex also contains one of Madrid's best museum restaurants, **Paradis,** specializing in the seafood and rice dishes of Catalonia. Plan to spend about 2 hours here.

Palacio de Villahermosa, Paseo del Prado 8. *©* **91-369-01-51.** www.museothyssen.org. Admission 8€ adults, 5.50€ students and seniors, free for children 11 and under. Tues–Sun 10am–7pm. Metro: Banco de España. Bus: 1, 2, 5, 9, 10, 14, 15, 20, 27, 34, 45, 51, 52, 53, 74, 146, or 150.

The Palacio Real, or Royal Palace.

Palacio Real (Royal Palace) ★★

This huge palace was begun in 1738 on the site of the Madrid Alcázar, which burned to the ground in 1734. Some of its 2,000 rooms—which that "enlightened despot" Charles III called home—are open to the public; others are still used for state business. The palace was last used as a royal residence in 1931, before King Alfonso XIII and his wife, Victoria Eugénie, fled Spain.

Highlights of a visit include the Reception Room, State Apartments, Armory, and Royal Pharmacy. The **Reception Room** and **State Apartments** should get priority here if you're rushed. They embrace a rococo room with a diamond clock; a porcelain salon; the Royal Chapel; the Banquet Room, where receptions for heads of state are still held; and the Throne Room.

The rooms are literally stuffed with art treasures and antiques—salon after salon of monumental grandeur, with no apologies for the damask, mosaics, Tiepolo ceilings, gilt and bronze, chandeliers, and paintings.

If your visit falls on the first Wednesday of the month, look for the changing-of-the-guard ceremony, which occurs at noon and is free to the public.

In the Armory, you'll see the finest collection of weaponry in Spain. Many of the items—powder flasks, shields, lances, helmets, and saddles—are from the collection of Carlos V. From here, the comprehensive tour takes you into the Royal Pharmacy. Afterward, stroll through the **Campo del Moro,** the palace gardens. Plan to spend about 1½ hours here.

Plaza de Oriente, Calle de Bailén 2. ℭ **91-454-88-00.** www.patrimonionacional.es. Admission 10€ adults, 3.50€ students and children 16 and under. Oct–Mar Mon–Sat 9:30am–5pm, Sun 9am–2pm; Apr–Sept Mon–Sat 9am–6pm, Sun 9am–3pm. Metro: Opera or Plaza de España. Bus: 3, 25, 39, or 148.

Panteón de Goya (Goya's Tomb) ★★

In a remote part of town, beyond the Norte train station, lies Goya's tomb, containing one of his masterpieces: an elaborately beautiful fresco depicting the miracles of St. Anthony on the dome and cupola of the little hermitage of San Antonio de la Florida. This has been called Goya's Sistine Chapel. Already deaf when he began the painting, Goya labored dawn to dusk for 16 weeks, painting with sponges rather than with brushes. By depicting common street life—stonemasons, prostitutes, and beggars—Goya raised the ire of the nobility, who withheld judgment until the patron, Carlos IV, viewed the painting. When the monarch approved, the formerly outrageous painting was deemed acceptable.

The tomb and fresco are in one of the twin chapels (visit the one on the right) that were built in the latter part of the 18th century. Discreetly placed mirrors will help you see the ceiling better.

Glorieta de San Antonio de la Florida 5. ℭ **91-542-07-22.** Free admission. Tues–Fri 9:30am–8pm; Sat–Sun 10am–2pm. Metro: Príncipe Pío. Bus: 41, 46, 75, or C.

THE BULLFIGHT

Madrid draws the finest matadors in Spain. If a matador hasn't proven his worth in the **Plaza Monumental de Toros de las Ventas,** Alcalá 237 (© **91-356-22-00;** www.las-ventas.com; Metro: Ventas), he hasn't been recognized as a top-flight artist. The major season begins during the Fiestas de San Isidro, patron saint of Madrid, on May 15. This is the occasion for a series of fights with talent scouts in the audience. Matadors who distinguish themselves in the ring are signed up for Majorca, Málaga, and other places.

The best place to get tickets to the bullfights (or to theater or sports events) is at the stadium's box office (Fri–Sun 10am–2pm and 5–8pm). Alternatively, you can contact one of Madrid's most competent ticket agents, **Localidades Galicia,** Plaza del Carmen 1 (© **91-531-91-31;** www.bullfightticketsmadrid.com; Metro: Puerta del Sol). It's open Tuesday to Saturday 9:30am to 1:30pm and 4:30 to 7pm, Sunday 10am to 1pm. Regardless of where you buy them, tickets to bullfights range from 16€ to 174€, depending on the event and the position of your seat within the stadium. Concierges for virtually every reputable upper-bracket hotel in Madrid can acquire tickets, through inner channels of their own, to bullfights and other sought-after entertainment. Front-row seats at the bull-fights are known as *barreras. Delanteras* (third-row seats) are available in both the *alta* (high) and the *baja* (low) sections. The cheapest seats, *filas,* afford the worst views and are in the sun *(sol)* during the entire performance. The best seats are in the shade *(sombra).* Bullfights are held on Sundays and holidays throughout most of the year, and every day during certain festivals, which tend to last around 3 weeks, usually in late spring. Starting times are adjusted according to the antici-pated hour of sundown on performance day, usually 7pm from March to October and 5pm during late autumn and early spring. Late-night fights by neophyte mat-adors are sometimes staged under spotlights on Saturday around 11pm.

Bullfighting at the Plaza Monumental de Toros de las Ventas.

If You Have More Time
MUSEUMS

CaixaForum ★ 🏛 Madrid's so-called triangle of great art—the Prado, the Thyssen-Bornemisza, and Reina Sofía—has become a quartet. Swiss architects Pierre de Meuron and Jacques Herzog, who transformed a factory into the Tate Modern in London, have taken a 1901 power station in Madrid and created an art complex. The museum, with both its permanent collection and its ever-changing exhibitions, showcases some of the most avant-garde art in Iberia.

The new museum is also home to film screenings and free concerts. The permanent collection includes stunning, often daring, paintings from the foundation's permanent archives, including works by such artists as Cindy Sherman, Anselm Kiefer, Sigmar Polke, Carlos Armorales, Roni Horn, and Ferrán García Sevilla. On top of the former electrical plant, the architects created a two-story addition in oxidized steel, making more space for galleries and a cafe overlooking Paseo del Prado.

Paseo del Prado 36. ✆ **91-330-73-00.** http://obrasocial.lacaixa.es/nuestroscentros/caixaforum-madrid/caixaforummadrid_es.html. Free admission. Daily 10am–8pm. Metro: Atocha or Banco de España.

Museo Arqueológico Nacional ★★ This stately mansion is a storehouse of artifacts from the prehistoric to the baroque. One of the prime exhibits here is the Iberian statue *The Lady of Elche,* a piece of primitive carving (4th c. B.C.) discovered on the southeastern coast of Spain. Finds from Ibiza, Paestum, and Rome are on display, including statues of Tiberius and his mother, Livia. The Islamic collection from Spain is outstanding. There are also collections of Spanish Renaissance lusterware, Talavera pottery, Retiro porcelain, and rare 16th- and 17th-century Andalusian glassware.

Many of the exhibits are treasures that were removed from churches and monasteries. A much-photographed choir stall from the palace of Palencia dates from the 14th century. Also worth a look are the reproductions of the Altamira cave paintings (chiefly of bison, horses, and boars), discovered near Santander in northern Spain in 1868.

Serrano 13. ✆ **91-577-79-12.** http://man.mcu.es. Free admission. Tues–Sat 9:30am–8pm; Sun and holidays 9:30am–3pm. Metro: Serrano or Colón. Bus: 1, 9, 19, 51, or 74.

Museo de América (Museum of the Americas) This museum, situated near the university, houses an outstanding collection of pre-Columbian, Spanish-American, and Native American art and artifacts. Various exhibits chronicle the progress of the inhabitants of the New World from the Paleolithic period to the present day. One exhibit, "Groups, Tribes, Chiefdoms, and States," focuses on the social structure of the various peoples of the Americas. Another display outlines the various religions and deities associated with them. Also included in the museum is an exhibit dedicated to communication, highlighting written as well as nonverbal expressions of art.

Av. de los Reyes Católicos 6. ✆ **91-549-26-41.** http://museodeamerica.mcu.es. Admission 3€; free for all visitors Sun. Tues–Sat 9:30am–3pm; Sun and holidays 10am–3pm. Metro: Moncloa. Bus: 1, 2, 16, 44, 46, 61, 82, 113, 132, or 133.

Museo de la Real Academia de Bellas Artes de San Fernando (Fine Arts Museum) ★ An easy stroll from Puerta del Sol, the Fine Arts Museum is located in the restored and remodeled 17th-century baroque palace of Juan

The Museo Lázaro Galdiano.

de Goyeneche. The collection—more than 1,500 paintings and 570 sculptures, ranging from the 16th century to the present—was started in 1752 during the reign of Fernando VI (1746–59). It emphasizes works by Spanish, Flemish, and Italian artists. You can see masterpieces by El Greco, Rubens, Velázquez, Zurbarán, Ribera, Cano, Coello, Murillo, Goya, and Sorolla.

Alcalá 13. ℂ **91-524-08-64.** http://rabasf.insde.es. Admission 3€ adults, 1.50€ students, free for children 17 and under; free for all visitors Wed. Tues–Fri 9am–7pm; Sat–Mon and holidays 9am–2:30pm. Metro: Puerta del Sol or Sevilla. Bus: 3, 5, 15, 20, 51, 52, 53, or 150.

Museo del Traje In Ciudad Universitaria, a 20-minute subway ride from the center, this museum displays more than 500 costumes, even frocks, from the 1700s, along with bullfighters' "suits of light." Spanish folk dress is highlighted as well, along with Chanel designs and a 1967 dress made of metal by designer Paco Rabanne. Movie scenes show fashions, including Bogie's *Casablanca* and Audrey Hepburn in Givenchy as she appeared in *Funny Face.* Attracting the most attention is Marilyn Monroe in a subway-vent–blown Travilla in *The Seven Year Itch.* Some of the exhibits are hands-on—for example, you can try on a corset or the frame of a hoop skirt, or even check out your derrière in a bustle. On-site is an excellent Basque restaurant, **Bokado.** Ever had gazpacho made with watermelon and lobster?

Av. Jean de Herrera 2. ℂ **91-550-47-00.** http://museodeltraje.mcu.es. Admission 3€, free for children 17 and under; free for all visitors Sat 2:30–7pm and all day Sun. Tues–Sat 9:30am–7pm; Sun and holidays 10am–3pm. Metro: Moncola. Bus: 46, 82, 83, 84, 132, or 133.

Museo Lázaro Galdiano ★ 🏛 Often compared to New York's Frick Museum, this house of art is a showplace for the holdings of Don José Lázaro Galdiano (1862–1947), a Gilded Age banker, writer, and collector known as "the Renaissance man of Madrid." He collected art by some of the greatest Spanish masters, including El Greco, Velázquez, Zurbarán, Ribera, Murillo, and Valdés-Leal. The Prado has its masterpieces, but the lesser works of these artists are worth viewing, too. One small painting by Goya prefigured the famous "black paintings" in the Prado. One section is devoted to works by the English portrait and landscape artists Reynolds, Gainsborough, and Constable. Italian artists are represented by Tiepolo and Guardi, among others. In addition to art, an array of goodies includes 15th-century hand-woven vestments, swords and daggers, royal seals, 16th-century crystal from Limoges, Byzantine jewelry, Italian bronzes from ancient times to the Renaissance, and medieval armor.

Calle de Serrano 122. ⓒ **91-561-6084.** www.flg.es. Admission 4€ adults, 3€ students, free for children 12 and under. Wed–Mon 10am–4:30pm. Metro: Rubén Darío. Bus: 9, 12, 16, 19, 27, 45, 51, or 150.

Museo Sorolla ★ From 1912, painter Joaquín Sorolla and his family occupied this elegant Madrileño town house off Paseo de la Castellana. His widow turned it over to the government, and it is now maintained as a memorial. Much of the house remains as Sorolla left it, right down to his stained paintbrushes and pipes. The museum wing displays a representative collection of his works.

Although Sorolla painted portraits of Spanish aristocrats, he was essentially interested in the common people, often depicting them in their native dress. On view are the artist's self-portrait and paintings of his wife and their son. Sorolla was especially fond of painting beach scenes of the Costa Blanca.

General Martínez Campos 37. ⓒ **91-310-15-84.** http://museosorolla.mcu.es. Admission 3€ adults, 1.50€ students. Tues–Sat 9:30am–8pm; Sun and holidays 10am–3pm. Metro: Iglesia, Gregorio Marañón, or Rubén Darío. Bus: 5, 7, 14, 16, 27, 40, 45, 61, 147, or 150.

A CATHEDRAL

Catedral de la Almudena Political conflicts, wars, and a simple lack of money led to incredible delays in the building of Madrid's cathedral. Construction began in 1883, but it took 110 years for this cathedral to officially open. It's named after the Virgen de la Almudena, whose icon was found during the Reconquest on this site (which, incidentally, housed Madrid's first Muslim mosque). Originally planned in the neo-Gothic style, it was subsequently changed to neoclassical by the architect Fernando Chueca. The "pop art" stained-glass windows and multicolored ceiling, along with the grand Grezing organ, graced the wedding of Prince Felipe to newscaster Doña Letizia in May 2004, the first royal wedding in nearly a century.

Calle Bailén 10. ⓒ **91-542-22-00.** Free admission. Summer daily 10am–1pm and 6–8pm; off season daily 9am–9pm. Metro: Opera.

Parks & Gardens

Casa de Campo ★ (Metro: Lago or Batán) is the former royal hunting grounds—miles of parkland lying south of the Royal Palace across the Manzanares River. You can see the gate through which the kings rode out of the palace grounds, either on horseback or in carriages, on their way to the tree-lined park. A lake contained within Casa de

The dome of the Catedral de la Almudena.

FROMMER'S favorite MADRID EXPERIENCES

Outdoor-Cafe Sitting. This is best experienced in the summertime, when Madrileños come alive on their *terrazas*. The good times can go on until dawn. From glamorous hangouts to lowly street corners, the cafe scene takes place mainly along the axis formed by Paseo de la Castellana, Paseo del Prado, and Paseo de Recoletos (which make up one continuous street).

***Tasca* Hopping.** This is the quintessential Madrid experience and the fastest way for a visitor to tap into the local scene. *Tascas* are Spanish pubs serving tapas, those tantalizing appetizers. You can go from one to the other, sampling each tavern's special dishes and wines.

Eating Around Spain. The variety of gastronomic experiences is staggering: You can literally restaurant-hop from

province to province without ever leaving Madrid.

Viewing the Works of Your Favorite Artist. Spend an afternoon at the Prado, savoring the works of your favorite Spanish artist.

Bargain Hunting at El Rastro. Madrid has one of the greatest flea markets in Europe, if not the world. Wander through its many offerings to discover that hidden treasure you've been searching for.

Enjoying a Night of Flamenco. Flamenco folk songs *(cante)* and dances *(baile)* are an integral part of the Spanish experience. Spend at least 1 night in a flamenco tavern listening to the heart-rending laments of Gypsy sorrows and dreams.

Campo is usually filled with rowers. You can have drinks and light refreshments by the water or go swimming in a city-run pool. Children will love both the zoo and the Parque de Atracciones (see "Especially for Kids," p. 170). The Casa de Campo can be visited daily from 8am to 9pm.

Parque del Retiro ★ (Metro: Retiro), originally a royal playground for the Spanish monarchs and their guests, extends over 140 hectares (346 acres). The huge palaces that once stood here were destroyed in the early 19th century; only the former dance hall, **Casón del Buen Retiro** (housing the modern works of the Prado), and the building containing the Army Museum remain. The park boasts numerous fountains and statues, plus a large lake. There are two exposition centers, the Velázquez and Crystal palaces (built to honor the Philippines in 1887), and a lakeside monument, erected in 1922 in honor of King Alfonso XII. In summer the rose gardens are worth a visit, and you'll find several places selling inexpensive snacks and drinks. The park is open daily 24 hours, but it is safest from 7am to about 8:30pm.

Real Jardín Botánico (Royal Botanical Garden) Across Calle de Alfonso XII, at the southwest corner of Parque del Retiro, lie these charming gardens. Founded in the 18th century, the gardens contain more than 104 species of trees and 3,000 types of plants. Also on the premises are an exhibition hall and a library specializing in botany.

2 Plaza de Murillo. *(C)* **91-420-30-17.** www.rjb.csic.es. Admission 2€ adults, 1€ students. Summer daily 10am–9pm; winter daily 10am–6pm; closed Christmas and New Year's Day. Metro: Atocha. Bus: 10, 14, 19, 24, 26, 27, 32, 34, 45, 57, or 140.

The Real Jardín Botánico, or Royal Botanical Garden.

Teleférico Strung high above several of Madrid's verdant parks, this aerial tramway was originally built in 1969 as part of a public fairgrounds (Parque de Atracciones, p. 171) vaguely modeled on Disneyland. Today, even for visitors not interested in the park, the Teleférico retains an allure of its own as a high-altitude method of admiring the cityscape of Madrid. The cable car departs for the 11-minute ride from Paseo Pintor Rosales at the eastern edge of **Parque del Oeste** (at the corner of Calle Marqués de Urquijo); it carries you high above two parks and railway tracks and over the Manzanares River to a spot near a picnic ground and restaurant in Casa de Campo. Weather permitting, there are good views of the Royal Palace along the way.

Paseo del Pintor Rosales. ℭ **91-541-74-50.** www.teleferico.com. 3.50€ one-way, 5.10€ round-trip. Jan Sat–Sun noon–6:30pm; Feb Sat–Sun noon–7pm; Mar Sat–Sun noon–7:30pm (shorter hours during holidays); Apr Mon–Fri noon–6:30pm, Sat–Sun noon–8pm; May Mon–Fri noon–2pm, Sat–Sun noon–8:30pm; June–July Mon–Fri noon–8pm, Sat–Sun noon–9:30pm; Aug Mon–Fri noon–2pm, Sat–Sun noon–9:30pm; Sept Sat–Sun noon–8:30pm; Oct Sat–Sun noon–7:30pm; Nov–Dec Sat–Sun noon–6pm.

Especially for Kids

Museo de Cera de Madrid (Wax Museum) ☺ The kids will enjoy seeing a lifelike wax Columbus calling on Ferdinand and Isabella, as well as Marlene Dietrich checking out Bill and Hillary Clinton. The 450 wax figures include heroes and villains of World War II. Two galleries display Romans and Arabs from the ancient days of the Iberian Peninsula; a show gives a 30-minute recap of Spanish history from the Phoenicians to the present.

Paseo de Recoletos 41. ℭ **91-319-26-49.** www.museoceramadrid.com. Admission 16€ adults and children 11 and over, 12€ children 4–10, free for children 3 and under. Mon–Fri 10am–2:30pm and 4:30–8:30pm; Sat–Sun 10am–8:30pm. Metro: Colón. Bus: 5, 27, 45, 53, or 150.

The Teleférico tram.

Parque de Atracciones ☺ The park was created in 1969 to amuse the young at heart with an array of rides and concessions. Here you'll find a toboggan slide, a carousel, pony rides, an adventure into outer space, a walk through a transparent maze, a visit to "Jungle Land," a motor-propelled series of cars disguised as a tail-wagging dachshund puppy, and a gyrating whirligig clutched in the tentacles of El Pulpo (the Octopus). The most popular rides are a pair of roller coasters named 7 Picos and Jet Star. The park has many diversions for adults too (see the listing for "Auditorio del Parque de Atracciones" under "Madrid After Dark," p. 179).

Casa de Campo. ℂ **91-463-29-00.** www.parquedeatracciones.es. Admission 29€, 21€ children 3–6, free for children 2 and under. Apr–May Tues–Fri noon–8pm, Sat–Sun noon–10pm; variable hours the rest of the year. Take the suburban train from Plaza de España and stop near the entrance to the park (Entrada de Batán). Bus: 33 or 65.

Zoo Aquarium de Madrid ☺ This modern, well-organized facility allows you to see wildlife from five continents, with about 3,000 animals on display. Most are in simulated natural habitats, with moats separating them from the public. There's a petting zoo for the kids and a show presented by the Chu-Lin band. The zoo/aquarium complex includes a 520,000-gallon tropical marine aquarium, a dolphin aquarium, and an array of colorful parrots.

Casa de Campo. ℂ **91-512-37-70.** www.zoomadrid.com. Admission 19€ adults and children 8 and over, 15€ seniors and children 3–7, free for children 2 and under. Mon–Fri 11am–6pm; Sat and holidays 10:30am–6pm. Metro: Batán or Casa de Campo. Bus: 33.

Organized Tours

A large number of agencies in Madrid book organized tours and excursions to sights and attractions both within and outside the city limits. Although it won't exactly be spontaneous, some visitors appreciate the convenience and efficiency of being able to visit so many sights in a single well-organized day.

Many of the city's hotel concierges, and all of the city's travel agents, will book anyone who asks for a guided tour of Madrid or its environs with one of Spain's largest tour operators, **Pullmantur,** Plaza de Oriente 8 (© **91-541-18-07;** www.pullmanturcruises.com). Regardless of destination and trip duration, virtually every tour departs from the Pullmantur terminal at that address. The Madrid Sightseeing Tour goes for 21€.

Toledo is the most popular full-day excursion outside the city limits. Trips cost 67€. These tours (including lunch) depart daily at 9:45am, last all day, and include ample opportunities for wandering at will through Toledo's narrow streets. You can, if you wish, take an abbreviated morning tour of Toledo, without stopping for lunch, for 55€. Tour times are at 9am and 3pm.

Another popular tour stops briefly in Toledo before it continues on to visit both the monastery at El Escorial and the Valley of the Fallen (Valle de los Caídos); it returns the same day to Madrid. With lunch included, this all-day excursion costs 95€.

The third major Pullmantur bus tour from Madrid's center to the city's surrounding attractions is a full-day guided excursion to Avila and Segovia, which takes in a heady dose of medieval and ancient Roman monuments that are really very interesting. The price per person with lunch included is 108€.

The hop-off, hop-on **Madrid Vision Bus** lets you set your own pace and itinerary. A scheduled panoramic tour lasts a half-hour, provided that you don't get off the bus. Otherwise, you can opt for an unlimited number of stops, exploring at your leisure. The Madrid Vision makes four complete tours daily, two in the morning and two in the afternoon; on Sunday and Monday buses depart in the morning only. Call © **91-779-18-88,** or visit www.madridvision.es, for departure times, which vary. You can board the bus at the Madrid tourist office at Duque de Medinaceli 2. A 1-day pass costs 47€ for adults, 7.50€ for seniors and children 7 to 16, and is free for kids 6 and under. A 2-day pass is 60€ for adults, 10€ for seniors and children 7 to 16, and is free for kids 6 and under.

SHOPPING
The Shopping Scene

Spain has always been known for its craftspeople, many of whom still work in the time-honored and labor-intensive traditions of their grandparents. It's hard to go wrong if you stick to the beautiful handcrafted objects—hand-painted tiles, ceramics, and porcelain; hand-woven rugs; handmade sweaters; and intricate embroideries. And, of course, Spain produces some of the world's finest leather. Jewelry, especially gold set with Majorca pearls, represents good value and unquestionable luxury.

Some of Madrid's art galleries are known throughout Europe for discovering and encouraging new talent. Antiques are sold in highly sophisticated retail outlets. Better suited to the budgets of many travelers are the weekly flea markets.

Spain continues to make inroads into the fashion world. Its young designers are regularly featured in the fashion magazines of Europe. Excellent shoes are available, some highly fashionable. But be advised that prices for shoes and quality clothing are generally higher in Madrid than in the United States.

GREAT SHOPPING AREAS

THE CENTER The sheer diversity of shops in Madrid's center is staggering. Their densest concentration lies immediately north of Puerta del Sol, radiating from Calle del Carmen, Calle Montera, and Calle Preciados.

CALLE MAYOR & CALLE DEL ARENAL Unlike their more stylish neighbors to the north of Puerta del Sol, shops in this district to the west tend to be small, slightly dusty enclaves of coin and stamp dealers; family-owned souvenir shops; clock makers; and sellers of military paraphernalia. An abundance of stores sell musical scores.

GRAN VIA Conceived, designed, and built in the 1910s and 1920s as a showcase for the city's best shops, hotels, and restaurants, the Gran Vía has since been eclipsed by other shopping districts. Its Art Nouveau/Art Deco glamour still survives in the hearts of most Madrileños, however. The bookshops here are among the best in the city, as are outlets for fashion, shoes, jewelry, furs, and handcrafted accessories from all regions of Spain.

EL RASTRO It's the biggest flea market in Spain, drawing collectors, dealers, buyers, and hopefuls from throughout Madrid and its suburbs. The makeshift stalls are at their most frenetic on Sunday morning. For more information, see the "Flea Markets" section, p. 177.

PLAZA MAYOR Under the arcades of the square itself are exhibitions of lithographs and oil paintings. Every weekend there's a loosely organized market for stamp and coin collectors. Within 3 or 4 blocks in every direction you'll find more than the average number of souvenir shops.

ON CALLE MARQUES Viudo de Pontejos, which runs east from Plaza Mayor, is one of the city's headquarters for the sale of cloth, thread, and buttons. Also running east, on Calle de Zaragoza, are silversmiths and jewelers. On Calle Postas, you'll find housewares, underwear, soap powders, and other household items.

NEAR THE CARRERA DE SAN JERONIMO Several blocks east of Puerta del Sol is Madrid's densest concentration of gift shops, crafts shops, and antiques dealers. Its most interesting streets include Calle del Prado, Calle de las Huertas, and Plaza de las Cortes. The neighborhood is pricey, so don't expect bargains here.

NORTHWEST MADRID A few blocks east of Parque del Oeste is an upscale neighborhood that's well stocked with luxury goods and household staples. Calle de la Princesa, its main thoroughfare, has shops selling shoes, handbags, fashion, gifts, and children's clothing. Thanks to the presence of the university nearby, there's a dense concentration of bookstores, especially on Calle Isaac Peral and Calle Fernando el Católico, several blocks north and northwest from the subway stop of Argüelles.

SALAMANCA DISTRICT It's known throughout Spain as the quintessential upper-bourgeois neighborhood, uniformly prosperous; its shops are equally exclusive. They include outlets run by interior decorators, furniture shops, fur and jewelry shops, several department stores, and design headquarters whose output ranges from the conservative to the high-tech. The main streets of this district are Calle de Serrano and Calle de Velázquez. The district lies northeast of the center of Madrid, a few blocks north of Parque del Retiro. Its most central Metro stops are Serrano and Velázquez.

The ritzy Salamanca neighborhood.

HOURS & SHIPPING

Major stores are open (in most cases) Monday to Saturday 9:30am to 8pm. Many small stores take a siesta between 1:30 and 4:30pm. Of course, there is never any set schedule, and hours can vary greatly from store to store, depending on the idiosyncrasies and schedules of the owner.

Many art and antiques dealers will crate and ship bulky objects for an additional fee. Whereas it usually pays to have heavy objects shipped by sea, it might surprise you that in some cases you can pay almost the same price to ship crated goods by airplane. Of course, it depends on the distance your crate will have to travel overland to the nearest international port, which in many cases, for the purposes of relatively small-scale shipments by individual clients, is Barcelona.

Shopping A to Z
ANTIQUES

In addition to the shop listed below, El Rastro (see "Flea Markets," p. 177) is a source of antiques.

Mercado Puerta de Toledo Located at the landmark Puerta de Toledo (Gateway to Toledo), this is an enclave of more than a dozen shops selling everything from genuine Spanish antiques to would-be antiques. You can find some good deals here in Spanish ceramics, much of it from Andalusia, and even vintage brass. Some items such as "Franco's chamber pot" are a bit fancifully labeled. Open Monday to Saturday 10:30am to 9pm, Sunday 10:30am to 2:30pm. Puerta de Toledo. ✆ **91-366-72-00.** www.centropuertadetoledo.com. Metro: Puerta de Toledo.

ART GALLERIES

Galería Kreisler ★ One successful entrepreneur on Madrid's art scene is Ohio-born Edward Kreisler, whose gallery, now run by his son, Juan, specializes in figurative and contemporary paintings, sculptures, and graphics. The gallery prides itself on occasionally displaying and selling the works of artists who are critically acclaimed and displayed in museums in Spain. Open Monday through Friday from 10:30am to 2pm and 5 to 9pm, Saturday 10:30am to 2pm. Hermosilla 8. ✆ **91-576-16-62.** www.galeriakreisler.com. Metro: Serrano. Bus: 27, 45, or 150.

Galería Soledad Lorenzo To see some of the works of major Spanish artists today, head to this brightly lit, large gallery in the Chamberí district. Painters as famous as Miguel Barceló or Antoni Tàpies have exhibited here, and the opening of a new show is often a major artistic event. Open Monday 4:30 to 8:30pm, Tuesday and Saturday 11am to 2pm and 4:30 to 8:30pm (closed evenings mid-June to mid-Sept). Orfila 5. ℂ **91-308-28-87.** www.soledadlorenzo.com. Metro: Alonso Martínez.

Juana de Aizpuru This gallery first opened in Seville in 1970 and became so successful that it moved to Madrid in 1983. Today it is one of the most prestigious galleries in the city, known for its avant-garde art and sculptures. It features not only some of Spain's best artists, but also many exciting works by international artists. Open Monday 4:30 to 8:30pm and Tuesday to Saturday 10:30am to 2pm and 4:30 to 8:30pm. Calle Barquillo 44. ℂ **91-310-55-61.** www.juanadeaizpuru. com. Closed Aug. Metro: Chuca.

CAPES

Capas Seseña Founded shortly after the turn of the 20th century, this shop manufactures and sells wool capes for both women and men. The wool comes from the mountain town of Béjar, near Salamanca. Celebrities spotted donning Seseña capes have included Picasso, Hemingway, and, more recently, Hillary Clinton and daughter Chelsea. Open Monday through Friday from 10am to 2pm and 4:30 to 8pm, Saturday from 10am to 2pm. Cruz 23. ℂ **91-531-68-40.** Metro: Sevilla or Puerta del Sol. Bus: 5, 39, 51, or 52.

CERAMICS

Antigua Casa Talavera ★ "The first house of Spanish ceramics" has wares that include regional styles from every major area of Spain, including Talavera, Toledo, Manises, Valencia, Puente del Arzobispo, Alcora, Granada, and Seville. Pitchers, dinnerware, tea sets, and vases are all handmade. Inside one of the showrooms is a selection of tiles painted with scenes from bullfights, dances, and folklore. At its present location since 1904, the shop is only a short walk from Plaza de Santo Domingo. Open Monday to Friday from 10am to 1:30pm and 5 to 8pm, Saturday from 10am to 1:30pm. Isabel la Católica 2. ℂ **91-547-34-17.** Metro: Santo Domingo. Bus: 1, 2, 44, 46, 70, 75, or 148.

CRAFTS

El Arco de los Cuchilleros Artesanía de Hoy Set within one of the 17th-century vaulted cellars of Plaza Mayor, this shop is entirely devoted to unusual craft items from throughout Spain. The merchandise is one of a kind and in most cases contemporary; it includes a changing array of pottery, leather, textiles, woodcarvings, glassware, wickerwork, papier-mâché, and silver jewelry. The hard-working owners deal directly with the artisans who produce each item, ensuring a wide inventory of handicrafts. The multilingual staff is familiar with applying for tax-free status of purchases. The shop is open daily from 11am to 8pm. Plaza Mayor 9 (basement level). ℂ **91-365-26-80.** Metro: Puerta del Sol or Opera.

DEPARTMENT STORES

El Corte Inglés ★★ This flagship of the largest department store chain in Madrid sells hundreds of souvenirs and Spanish handicrafts—damascene steel-work from Toledo, flamenco dolls, and embroidered shawls. Some astute buyers report that it also sells glamorous fashion articles, such as Pierre Balmain designs, for about a third less than in most European capitals. Services include interpreters, currency-exchange windows, and parcel delivery either to a local hotel or overseas. Open Monday through Saturday from 10am to 10pm. Preciados 3. © **91-379-80-00.** www.elcorteingles.es. Metro: Puerta del Sol.

ESPADRILLES

Cristina Castañer ★★ This is the premier shop for espadrilles in Spain, having been founded in 1927 by Luis Castañer and run today by his grandchildren. The swanky Hermès uses Castañer for its own line of espadrilles, and everybody from Marc Jacobs to Kate Spade has worn these handcrafted shoes, which today can make statements in high fashion. This small boutique occupies its original location in Madrid's premier shopping district of Salamanca. The espadrilles with ankle-wrap ribbons are a summer favorite, but this footwear comes in all shapes, sizes, and colors, from platforms to slip-ons. Open Monday to Saturday 10:30am to 8:30pm. Calle de Claudio Coello 51. © **91-578-18-90.** www.castaner.com. Metro: Serrano.

FASHION

For the man on a budget who wants to dress reasonably well, the best outlet for off-the-rack men's clothing is one of the branches of El Corte Inglés department store chain (p. 175). Most men's boutiques in Madrid are very expensive and may not be worth the investment.

Adolfo Domínguez This shop caters to fashion-conscious young men and women. Adolfo Domínguez, a designer from Galicia in northwest Spain, is known for a cool, laid-back style—too informal in the opinion of some critics. A wide selection of shoes, some quite fancy, are sold, as is sports clothing. In general, you get good value here if you don't find the style too austere. Open Monday to Saturday 10:15am to 2pm and 5 to 8:30pm. Ortega y Gasset 4. © **91-576-00-84.** www.adolfo-dominguez.com. Metro: Núñez de Balboa.

Agatha Ruiz de la Prada This designer, who reached initial fame during the *Movida* era of the 1980s, has made a comeback. She operates on the ground floor of a Chamberí salon, originally constructed by her grandfather. She is known for her stylish yet easy-to-wear informal clothing. You might want to check her out to see what the style-conscious Madrileño woman is wearing this season. Open Monday to Friday 10am to 2pm and 5 to 8pm. In August the shop is also open on Saturday 10am to 2pm. Marqués de Riscal 8. © **91-319-05-01.** www.agatharuizdelprada.com. Metro: Rubén Darío.

Herrero Piel The sheer size and buying power of this retail outlet for women's clothing make it a reasonably priced emporium for all kinds of feminine garb as well as for gentlemen's articles. The store is open Monday through Saturday from 10:30am to 8:15pm. It's also open the first Sunday of each month from noon to 8:15pm. Preciados 7. © **91-521-29-98.** Metro: Puerta del Sol or Callao.

La Maison de la Lanterne Rouge This property is a boutique and cafe, all housed within a former brothel. This was once a seedy back street but has now blossomed into a hot spot for design. Clothing is artistically arranged against a backdrop of Shanghai-inspired accents. In a country that values cutting-edge design for men and women alike, La Maison is an avant-garde showcase of fashion. Open Tuesday to Sunday noon to 3pm and 5 to 9pm. Calle Ballesta 4. © **91-310-79-61.** www.lamaison.es/habitantes/la-maison-de-la-lanterne-rouge. Metro: Gran Vía.

Zara A top name in fashion, Zara sells quality clothing, with most prices considered a good cost-to-value ratio. From party suits to office wear, her collection is wide ranging. Open Monday to Saturday 10am to 8:30pm. Princesa 45. © **91-541-09-02.** Metro: Argüelles.

FLEA MARKETS

El Rastro ★ Foremost among markets is El Rastro (translated as either "flea market" or "thieves' market"), occupying a roughly triangular district of streets and plazas a few minutes' walk south of Plaza Mayor. Its center is Plaza Cascorro and Ribera de Curtidores. The market comes alive every Sunday morning and will delight anyone attracted to a mishmash of fascinating junk interspersed with antiques, bric-a-brac, and paintings. The days of bargains largely faded with Franco himself. Today's vendors seem to know the price of everything. *Note:* Thieves are rampant here (hustling more than just antiques), so secure your wallet carefully and be alert. Plaza Cascorro and Ribera de Curtidores. Metro: La Latina. Bus: 3 or 17.

GUITARS

Guitarras Ramírez ★★ This is the premier guitar shop in Spain. It began when 12-year-old Jose Ramírez became an apprentice for the famous guitar maker Francisco González in 1870. A decade later he founded his own guitar shop, and by 1882 had created the prototype for one of the first modern guitars. Today, the outlet is run by Amalia, the great-granddaughter of the founder. Many famous musicians have ordered guitars from her, including Andrés Segovia, Eric Clapton, and even George Harrison, who used one of the Ramírez guitars to record the famous Beatles' song "Help!" Open Monday to Friday 10am to 2pm and 4:30 to 8pm, Saturday 10am to 2pm. 8 Calle de la Paz. © **91-531-42-29.** www. guitarrasramirez.com. Metro: Sol.

El Rastro flea market.

LEATHER

Loewe ★★★ Since 1846, this has been the most elegant leather store in Spain. Its gold medal–winning designers have always kept abreast of changing tastes and styles, but the inventory retains a timeless chic. The store sells luggage, handbags, and jackets for men and women (in leather or suede). Open Monday to Saturday 9:30am to 8pm. In addition to the Gran Vía location, two other branches carry much the same merchandise; they are located at Serrano 26 (© **91-577-60-56**) and at Serrano 34 (© **91-426-35-88**). The Serrano branches are open until 8:30pm. Gran Vía 8. © **91-522-68-15.** www.loewe.com. Metro: Banco de España or Gran Vía.

MARKETS

Mercado de San Miguel ★★ Just outside the walls of the Plaza Mayor, the long-dormant Beaux Arts market has come alive again after years of restoration. "It's a traditional market for the 21st-century shopper," said a publicist for the three dozen vendors sheltered under the gigantic wood-and-iron roof. The Mercado originally opened in 1916, when it evoked Les Halles in Paris. Servants and homemakers of the time flocked here to stock their houses.

Today the vendors sell everything from fresh pastas and homemade pastries to cooking utensils and even fresh fish. Consider the place a stopover for an inexpensive lunch, as it offers a cafe, a beer tavern where tapas are sold, and a pastry shop selling freshly baked apple strudel, among other goodies. Open Monday to Wednesday 10am to 10pm, Thursday to Saturday 10pm to 2am. Even at night Madrileños show up here for beer, tapas, wine, and even champagne and oysters. Plaza de San Miguel. © **91-542-49-39.** www.mercadodesanmiguel.es. Metro: Opera, Sol, or Tirso de Molina.

PERFUMES

Alvarez Gómez ★ This is a marvelously old-fashioned *perfumería*. It's been around so long it's newly fashionable again. The shop markets its own fragrances, many based on almost-long-forgotten formulas. And if you're not specifically looking for perfume, you'll find an array of unusual merchandise here, including jewelry and women's handbags and belts. Open Monday to Friday 10am to 8pm, Saturday 10am to 2pm. Castellana 111. © **91-555-59-61.** www.alvarezgomez.com. Metro: Cuzco.

Perfumería Padilla This store sells a large, competitively priced assortment of Spanish and international scents for women. It has two branches next to one another: Carmen 8 is open Monday to Saturday 10am to 2:30pm and 4:30 to 8:30pm; Carmen 7 is open Monday to Saturday 10am to 8:30pm. Calle del Carmen 7–8. © **91-521-90-70.** Metro: Puerta del Sol.

PORCELAIN

Lladró This imposing outlet is devoted almost exclusively to Lladró porcelain. The staff can usually tell you about new designs and releases the Lladró company is planning for the near future. Open Monday to Saturday 10am to 8pm. Gran Vía 46. © **91-701-04-72.** Metro: Callao.

SHOPPING MALLS

ABC Serrano Set within what used to function as the working premises of a well-known Madrileño newspaper *(ABC)*, this is a complex of about 85 upscale boutiques that emphasize fashion, housewares, cosmetics, and art objects. On the premises, you'll find cafes and restaurants, lots of potted and flowering shrubbery, and acres and acres of Spanish marble and tile. Although each of the outfitters inside is independently owned and managed, most of them maintain hours of Monday through Saturday from 10am to 10pm. Serrano 61 or Castellana 34. *©* **91-577-50-31.** www.abcserrano.com. Metro: Serrano.

MADRID AFTER DARK

Madrid abounds with dance halls, *tascas,* cafes, theaters, movie houses, and nightclubs. Because dinner is served late in Spain, nightlife doesn't really get underway until after 11pm, and it generally lasts until at least 3am—Madrileños are so fond of prowling at night that they are known around Spain as *gatos* (cats). If you arrive at 9:30pm at a club, you'll have the place all to yourself, assuming it's even open.

In most clubs, a one-drink minimum is the rule: Feel free to nurse that one drink through the entire evening's entertainment.

In summer, Madrid becomes a virtually free festival because the city sponsors a series of plays, concerts, and films. Pick up a copy of the *Guía del Ocio* (available at most newsstands) for listings of these events. This guide provides information about occasional discounts for commercial events, such as the concerts that are given in Madrid's parks. Also check the program of **Fundación Juan March,** Calle Castelló 77 (*©* **91-435-42-40;** www.march.es; Metro: Núñez de Balboa). Tapping into funds bequeathed to it by a generous financier (Sr. Juan March), it stages free concerts of Spanish and international classical music within a concert hall at its headquarters at Calle Castelló 77. In most cases, 90-minute events are presented every Monday and Saturday at noon, and every Wednesday at 7:30pm.

Flamenco in Madrid is geared mainly to prosperous tourists with fat wallets, and nightclubs are expensive. But since Madrid is preeminently a city of song and dance, you can often be entertained at very little cost—in fact, the price of a glass of wine or beer if you sit at a bar with live entertainment.

Like flamenco clubs, discos tend to be expensive, but they often open for what are erroneously called afternoon sessions (7–10pm). Although discos charge entry fees, at an afternoon session the cost might be as low as 3€, rising to 15€ and beyond for a night session—that is, beginning at 11:30pm and lasting until the early-morning hours. Therefore, if you're on a budget, go early, dance until 10pm, and then proceed to dinner. (You'll be eating at the fashionable hour.)

Nightlife is so plentiful in Madrid that the city can be roughly divided into the following "night zones."

PLAZA MAYOR/PUERTA DEL SOL The most popular areas from the standpoint of both tradition and tourist interest, these can also be dangerous, so explore them with caution, especially late at night. They are filled with tapas bars and *cuevas* (drinking caves). Here it is customary to begin a *tasca*-crawl from tavern to tavern, sampling the wine in each, along with a selection of tapas. The major streets for such a crawl are Cava de San Miguel, Cava Alta, and Cava Baja. You can order *pinchos y raciones* (tasty snacks and tidbits).

GRAN VIA This area contains mainly cinemas and theaters. Most of the after-dark action takes place on small streets branching off the Gran Vía.

PLAZA DE ISABEL II/PLAZA DE ORIENTE This is another area much frequented by tourists. Many restaurants and cafes flourish here, including the famous Café de Oriente.

CHUECA Along such streets as Hortaleza, Infantas, Barquillo, and San Lucas, this is the gay nightlife district, with dozens of clubs. Cheap restaurants, along with a few female striptease joints, are also found here. This area can be dangerous at night, so watch for pickpockets and muggers. As of late, there has been a greater police presence at night.

ARGÜELLES/MONCLOA For university students, this part of town sees most of the action. Many dance clubs are found here, along with alehouses and fast-food joints. The area is bounded by Pintor Rosales, Cea Bermúdez, Bravo Murillo, San Bernardo, and Conde Duque.

The Performing Arts

Madrid has a number of theaters, opera companies, and dance companies. To discover where and when specific cultural events are being performed, pick up a copy of *Guía del Ocio* at any city newsstand. The sheer volume of cultural offerings is staggering; for a concise summary of the highlights, see below.

Tickets to dramatic and musical events usually range in price from 6€ to 200€.

The concierges at most major hotels can usually get you tickets to specific concerts, if you are clear about your wishes. Of course, they charge a considerable markup, part of which is passed along to whichever agency originally booked the tickets.

You'll save money if you go directly to the box office. In the event your choice is sold out, you may be able to get tickets (with a reasonable markup) at **Localidades Galicia,** Plaza del Carmen 1 (*©* **91-531-91-31;** www.bullfight ticketsmadrid.com; Metro: Puerta del Sol). This agency also markets tickets to bullfights and sporting events. It is open Tuesday through Saturday 9:30am to 1:30pm and from 4:30 to 7pm, Sunday 10am to 1pm. In May, it's open daily 9am to 8pm.

MAJOR PERFORMING ARTS COMPANIES

Compañía Nacional de Nuevas Tendencias Escénicas is an avant-garde troupe that performs new and often controversial works (in Spanish) by undiscovered writers. **Compañía Nacional de Teatro Clásico,** as its name suggests, is devoted to the Spanish classics, including works by the ever-popular Lope de Vega and Tirso de Molina.

Among dance companies, **Ballet Nacional de España** is devoted exclusively to Spanish ballet. Their performances are always well attended. The national lyrical ballet company is **Ballet Lírico Nacional.**

World-renowned flamenco sensation Antonio Canales and his troupe, **Ballet Flamenco Antonio Canales,** offer spirited high-energy performances. Productions are centered on Canales's impassioned *Torero,* his interpretation of a bullfighter and the physical and emotional struggles within the man. For tickets and information, call Madrid's comprehensive ticket agency, the previously recommended **Localidades Galicia,** Plaza del Carmen 1 (*©* **91-531-91-31;** www.bullfightticketsmadrid.com). Tickets to other cultural events and virtually any event in Castile are also available here. Another agency for tickets is **Corte Inglés** (✆ **90-240-02-22** or 90-222-44-11; www.elcorteingles.es/entradas), which has satellite offices throughout Madrid.

Madrid's opera company is **Teatro Real,** and its symphony orchestra is the outstanding **Orquesta Sinfónica de Madrid.** Spain's national orchestra, widely acclaimed on the Continent, is **Orquesta Nacional de España,** which pays particular homage to Spanish composers.

CLASSICAL MUSIC

Auditorio del Parque de Atracciones The schedule of this 3,500-seat facility might include everything from punk-rock musical groups to the more highbrow warm-weather performances of visiting symphony orchestras. Check with Localidades Galicia to see what's on at the time of your visit. (See "The Performing Arts," p. 181.) Casa de Campo. Metro: Batán.

Auditorio Nacional de Música Sheathed in slabs of Spanish granite, marble, and limestone, and capped with Iberian tiles, this hall is the ultramodern home of both the National Orchestra of Spain and the National Chorus of Spain.

Standing just north of Madrid's Salamanca district, the hall ranks as a major addition to classical music venues in Europe. Inaugurated in 1988, it is devoted exclusively to performances of symphonic, choral, and chamber music. In addition to the Auditorio Principal (Hall A), whose capacity is almost 2,300, there's a hall for chamber music (Hall B), as well as a small auditorium for intimate concerts. Príncipe de Vergara 146. ✆ **91-337-01-39** or 91-337-01-40. Box office ✆ 91-337-03-07. www.auditorionacional.mcu.es. Tickets 6€–100€. Metro: Cruz del Rayo or Prosperidad.

Centro Cultural de la Villa Spanish-style ballet along with *zarzuelas* (operettas), orchestral works, and theater pieces are presented in summer at this cultural center. Tickets go on sale 5 days before the event, and performances are usually presented at two evening shows (7 and 10:30pm). Plaza de Colón. ✆ **91-480-03-00.** Tickets, depending on event, 8€–35€. Metro: Serrano or Colón.

Fundación Juan March This foundation sometimes holds free concerts at lunchtime. The advance schedule is difficult to predict, so call or visit the website for information. Calle Castelló 77. ✆ **91-435-42-40.** www.march.es. Metro: Núñez de Balboa.

Teatro Real ★★ This theater is one of the world's finest acoustic settings for opera. Its extensive state-of-the-art equipment affords elaborate stage designs and special effects. Today the building is the home of Compañía del Teatro Real, a company specializing in opera, and is a major venue for classical music. On November 19, 1850, under the reign of Queen Isabel II, the Royal Opera House opened its doors with Donizetti's *La Favorita*. Plaza Isabel II. ✆ **91-516-06-60.** www.teatro-real.es. Tickets 8€–25€. Metro: Opera.

THEATER

Madrid offers many different theater performances, useful to you only if your Spanish is very fluent. If it isn't, check the *Guía del Ocio* for performances by English-speaking companies on tour from Britain, or select a concert or subtitled movie instead.

Teatro Español This company is funded by Madrid's municipal government, its repertoire a time-tested assortment of great and/or favorite Spanish plays. The box office is open Tuesday through Sunday from 11:30am to 1:30pm and from 5pm until the show's opening. Príncipe 25. ✆ **90-210-12-12.** www.esmadrid.com. Tickets 4€–22€; 25% discount Wed. Metro: Sevilla.

Teatro Häagen-Dazs Calderón This is the largest theater in Madrid, with a seating capacity of 2,000. In the past this venue included everything from dramatic theater to flamenco, but in recent years it has taken a more serious turn by presenting mostly opera, with performances beginning most evenings at 8pm. Atocha 18. ✆ **91-420-37-97.** www.teatrohaagen-dazs.es. Tickets 5€–50€. Metro: Tirso de Molina.

Teatro Lírico Nacional de la Zarzuela Near Plaza de la Cibeles, this theater of potent nostalgia produces ballet and an occasional opera in addition to *zarzuelas*. Showtimes vary. The box office is open daily from noon to 5pm (until 8pm on show days). Jovellanos 4. ✆ **91-524-54-00.** http://teatrodelazarzuela.mcu.es. Tickets 12€–240€. Metro: Sevilla or Banco de España.

Teatro Nuevo Apolo Nuevo Apolo is the permanent home of the renowned Antología de la Zarzuela company. It is on the restored site of the old Teatro Apolo, where these musical variety shows have been performed since the 1930s. Prices and times depend on the show. The box office is open Tuesday through Sunday from 11:30am to 1:30pm and from 5pm until showtime. Plaza de Tirso de Molina 1. ✆ **91-369-06-37.** Tickets usually 21€–60€. Metro: Tirso de Molina.

Jazz & Cabaret

Café Central Off the Plaza de Santa Ana beside the famed Gran Hotel Victoria, the Café Central has a vaguely early-20th-century Art Deco interior, with an unusual series of stained-glass windows. Many customers read newspapers and talk at the marble-top tables during the day, but the ambience is far more animated during the nightly jazz sessions, which are among the best in Spain, and often draw top artists. Open Sunday through Thursday from 1:30pm to 2:30am, Friday and Saturday from 1:30pm to 3:30am; live jazz is offered daily 10pm to midnight. Beer costs 1.80€ to 2.25€. Plaza del Angel 10. ✆ **91-369-41-43.** www.cafecentralmadrid.com. Cover 7€–15€, depending on the show. Metro: Antón Martín or Puerta del Sol.

Café Jazz Populart ★ This club is known for its exciting jazz groups, which encourage the audience to dance. It specializes in Brazilian, Afro-bass, reggae,

The Teatro Real.

and new-wave African music. When the music starts, usually around 11pm, drink prices nearly double. Open Monday to Thursday 6pm to 2:30am; Friday to Saturday 6pm to 3:30am. After the music begins, beer costs 4.50€ to 6€, whiskey with soda 7€ to 11€. Calle Huertas 22. ☎ **91-429-84-07.** www.populart.es. Metro: Antón Martín or Sevilla. Bus: 6 or 60.

Clamores ★ With dozens of small tables and a huge bar in its dark and smoky interior, Clamores, which means "Noises," is the largest and one of the most popular jazz clubs in Madrid. Established in the early 1980s, it has thrived because of the diverse roster of American and Spanish jazz bands that have appeared here. The place is open daily from 6:30pm to around 3am, plus Friday and holiday evenings from 6:30pm until 4am. Daily performances are at 10pm and again at 1am. There are jam sessions Friday and Saturday night from 12:30 to 2:30am. Drinks start at around 5€ each. Albuquerque 14. ☎ **91-445-79-38.** www.salaclamores.com. Cover Tues–Sat usually 6€–27€, but varies with act. Metro: Bilbao.

Flamenco

Café de Chinitas ★ One of the best flamenco clubs in town, Café de Chinitas is set one floor above street level in a 19th-century building midway between the Opera and Gran Vía. It features an array of Gypsy flamenco artists from Madrid, Barcelona, and Andalusia, with acts changing about once a month. You can arrange for dinner before the show, although many Madrileños opt for dinner elsewhere, and then arrive for drinks and the flamenco. Open Monday through Saturday, with dinner served from 8:30pm to 2am and the show lasting from 10:15pm to 2am. Reservations are recommended. Torija 7. ☎ **91-547-15-02.** www.chinitas.com. Dinner and show 65€–80€; cover for show without dinner (but including 1 drink) 35€. Metro: Santo Domingo. Bus: 25 or 29.

Traditional flamenco dancing.

Cardamomo ★ 🎁 If you want to hear authentic flamenco away from the tourist crowds, head to this little dive. It's a no-frills flamenco club attracting a late-night crowd of young, hip Madrileños. The club patrons represent working-class Madrid. Acts feature young, rising flamenco artists. The manager told us, "We have returned flamenco to its low-life roots." Open daily 10pm to 3am. Calle Echegaray 15. ℂ **91-369-07-57.** Reservations required. Cover 15€. Metro: Puerta del Sol or Sevilla.

Casa Patas This club is one of the best places to see "true" flamenco, as opposed to the more touristy version presented at Corral de la Morería (see below). It is also a bar and restaurant, with space reserved in the rear for flamenco. Shows are presented at 10:30pm Monday to Thursday, with two shows at 9pm and mid-night on Friday and Saturday, and more frequent shows during Madrid's major fiesta month of May. The best flamenco in Madrid is found here. Proof of the pudding is that flamenco singers and dancers often hang out here after hours. Tapas—priced at 3€ to 17€—are available at the bar. The club is open Monday to Saturday from 8pm to 2:30am. Calle Cañizares 10. ℂ **91-369-04-96.** www.casapatas. com. Cover 28€–40€. Metro: Tirso de Molina or Antón Martín.

Corral de la Morería In the Old Town, the Morería ("where the Moors reside") sizzles with flamenco, but the crowd is definitely tourists. Colorfully costumed strolling performers warm up the audience around 10pm; a flamenco show follows, with at least 10 dancers. It's much cheaper to eat elsewhere first, and then pay only the one-drink minimum. Open daily 8:30pm to 2:30am. Morería 17. ℂ **91-365-84-46.** www.corraldelamoreria.com. Cover 1-drink minimum 35€; 45€–99€ with dinner. Metro: La Latina or Opera.

Las Tablas ★ 🎁 Fed up with faux flamenco on the tourist circuit and all those frilly costumes, two dancers, Antonia Moya and Marisol Navarro, opened their own little place. In a minimalist room, they perform some of the most authentic flamenco in Madrid. Sometimes the owners star in a show. This place is for flamenco devotees. Shows are held nightly at 10:30pm, and reservations are needed on weekends. Plaza de España 9. ℂ **91-542-05-20.** www.lastablasmadrid.com. Cover 24€, including first drink. Metro: Plaza de España.

THE SULTRY SOUND OF flamenco

The lights dim and the flamenco stars clatter rhythmically across the dance floor. Their lean bodies and hips shake and sway to the music. The word *flamenco* has various translations, meaning everything from "Gypsified Andalusian" to "knife," and from "blowhard" to "tough guy."

Accompanied by stylized guitar music, castanets, and the fervent clapping of the crowd, dancers are tense with emotion. Flamenco dancing, with its flash, color, and ritual, is evocative of Spanish culture, although its origins remain mysterious.

Experts disagree about where it came from, but most claim Andalusia as its seat of origin. It was the Gypsy artist who perfected both the song and the dance. Gypsies took to flamenco like "rice to paella," in the words of the historian Fernando Quiñones.

The song of flamenco represents a fatalistic attitude to life. Marxists used to say it was a deeply felt protest of the lower classes against their oppressors, but this seems unfounded. Protest or not, over the centuries rich patrons, often brash young men, liked the sound of flamenco and booked artists to stage *juergas,* or fiestas, where dancer-prostitutes became the erotic extras. By the early 17th century, flamenco was linked with pimping, prostitution, and lots and lots of drinking, both in the audience and by the artists.

By the mid–19th century, flamenco had gone legitimate and was heard in theaters and *cafés cantantes.* By the 1920s, even the pre-Franco Spanish dictator, Primo de Rivera, was singing the flamenco tunes of his native Cádiz. The poet Federico García Lorca and the composer Manuel de Falla preferred a purer form, attacking what they viewed as the degenerate and "ridiculous" burlesque of *flamenquismo,* the jazzed-up, audience-pleasing form of flamenco. The two artists launched a Flamenco Festival in Granada in 1922. Of course, in the decades since, their voices have been drowned out, and flamenco is more *flamenquismo* than ever.

In his 1995 book *Flamenco Deep Song,* Thomas Mitchell draws a parallel between flamenco's "lowlife roots" and the "orgiastic origins" of jazz. He notes that early jazz, like flamenco, was "associated with despised ethnic groups, gangsters, brothels, free-spending blue bloods, and whoopee hedonism." By disguising their origins, Mitchell notes, both jazz and flamenco have entered the musical mainstream.

Dance & Music Clubs

The Spanish dance club takes its inspiration from those of other Western capitals. In Madrid, most clubs are open from around 6 to 9pm, and then later reopen around 11pm. They generally start rocking at about midnight.

Cool This is the fave of bisexual men. With its loud colors and beautiful mirrors, it's a bit retro, a journey back to the 1970s. The best trannies and drag queens in town appear here in various acts, management calling them "more beautiful than real girls." A crowd that's mainly under 35 patronizes the joint, including a lot of visiting Brits and Yankees. Management also boasts that Madrid's "hottest" men are patrons, and you may indeed find your Urban Cowboy here. Open Friday and Saturday midnight to 6am. On Sunday from 9pm to 2am, a "Shangay Tea Dance" is presented. Isabela la Católica 6. ✆ **90-249-99-94.** Cover 15€. Metro: Santo Domingo.

Kapital This is the most sprawling, labyrinthine, and multicultural disco in Madrid. Set within what was originally a theater, it contains seven different levels, each sporting at least one bar and an ambience that's often radically different from that of the previous floor. Voyeurs of any age take heart—there's a lot to see at the Kapital, with a mixed crowd that pursues whatever form of sexuality seems appropriate at the moment. Open Thursday to Sunday midnight to 6am. Second drinks from 10€ each. Atocha 125. ✆ **91-420-29-06.** www.grupo-kapital.com. Cover 12€–15€, including 1st drink. Metro: Atocha.

Nasti The name of this indie-music venue is rather apt, attracting the grimy hipsters of Madrid to its precincts for avant-garde musical acts by both homegrown and foreign bands, even those from the States. Garage bands to punk rockers appear before stoned audiences, mostly under 35. This is definitely an underground dive, but the bartender assures us "it's a slice of the real Madrid." Open Tuesday to Sunday 11pm to 5am. Vicente Ferrer 33. ✆ **91-521-76-05.** www.nasti.es. Cover 10€. Metro: Tribunal.

Pachá This late-night club, attracting the 20-to-40 age group, has long been a fixture on the Madrid nightlife scene. In the 1930s it was a movie theater, but by the 1980s it had become a "dance cathedral." As the night grows late, milling crowds pack the precincts, and the noise level becomes deafening. Dancing to loud music and hard drinking rule the night. Open Tuesday to Sunday 11pm to 5am. Barceló 11. ✆ **91-447-01-28.** www.pacha-madrid.com. Cover 12€–15€, including 1st drink. Metro: Tribunal.

Siroco This rocking rock club heats up on weekends, offering some hot live bands plus what some patrons call the best DJs in town, young men who spin everything from hip-hop to Elvis. You need to be 18 to get in, but if you're over 30 head elsewhere; this would not be your scene. The cellar, not the main floor, is the scene of most of the action. San Dimas 3. ✆ **91-593-30-70.** www.siroco.es. Thurs–Sat 10:30pm–5am. Cover 5€–10€. Metro: San Bernardo.

Cuban Salsa

Café La Palma Live Cuban groups playing salsa dominate the agenda here. As in Paris, anything Cuban is chic in Madrid. This convivial club is one of the most happening in the capital. It's open daily from 4pm to 3am, but go after 10pm for the most action. A group made up of people mainly in their 20s and 30s is attracted here by the live music Thursday to Saturday nights. A DJ plays on Sunday. La Palma 62. ✆ **91-522-50-31.** www.cafelapalma.com. Cover 7€–19€. Metro: Noviciado.

Pubs & Bars

Bar Cock This two-floor bar attracts some of the most visible artists, actors, models, and filmmakers in Madrid. The name comes from the word *cocktail,* or so they say. The decoration is elaborate and unique, in contrast to the hip clientele, and the martinis are Madrid's best. Open Sunday to Thursday 7pm to 3am (Fri–Sat to 4am). Closed December 24 to December 31. Drinks are 5.50€ to 8€. De la Reina 16. ✆ **91-532-28-26.** www.barcock.com. Metro: Gran Vía.

Del Diego This is the perfect spot to chill out with a dry martini or a margarita. Remember Tom Cruise in the movie *Cocktail*? The bartenders here seem to imitate the character he played in that film. The bar also attracts the hottest "cougars" in town, each of these scantily dressed women eager to shatter dating stereotypes. As one beautiful, brunette cougar told us, "I begin by selecting

Ice-cream parlors *(heladerías)* have made a big comeback in Madrid, and many local young people like to hang out at these gathering places at night—not just for ice cream, since tapas and cocktails are sold as well. The most fashionable of the new *heladerías* is **Giangrossi,** Calle Alberto Aguilera 1 (✆ **91-444-01-30; www.giangrossi.es;** Metro: San Bernardo). The comfortable sofas and armchairs are made of fur, and the atmosphere is warm and welcoming. This *heladería* specializes in what it calls "artisanal ice creams," which are made on-site, in at least 40 different flavors divided among creams, chocolates, and fruits. Their shakes and sundaes are the best in town. Hours at this shop and the branches below are daily 8am to 1am. Ice cream begins at 3€ per serving. Two other branches include one at Velázquez 44 (Metro: Velázquez), and the other at Centro Comercial de la Esquina del Stadio Santiago Bernadeu (Metro: Santiago Bernadeu).

a dozen hot men, narrow it down to ten, then five, and finally one lucky man to be my soul mate for the night." In a quiet street off Gran Vía, the bar is open daily Monday to Thursday 7pm to 3am and Friday and Saturday 7pm to 3:30am (closed in Aug). Cocktails start at 6€. Reina 12. ✆ **91-523-31-06.** Metro: Gran Vía.

Glass Bar ★ In the much-recommended **Hotel Urban** (p. 128), the Glass Bar is the hottest rendezvous spot in Madrid. No other place in town makes such a dramatic use of the hotel's silica-based namesake, which is featured in everything from tables to chandeliers. The *très* cosmopolitan bar and cocktail lounge does the town's best *mojitos.* On Sunday, the bar stages a brunch buffet with champagne and cocktails (45€). Open daily 11am to 3am. Carrera de San Jerónimo 34. ✆ **91-787-77-70.** Metro: Sevilla.

La Venencia On one of the traditional *tasca* streets in Old Madrid, this tavern has a distinctive personality. It is dedicated to the art of serving Spain's finest sherry—and that's it. (Don't come in here asking for an extradry martini.) Our favorite remains Manzanilla, a delicate *vino* with just a little chill on it. To go with all that sherry, the waiters (a little rough around the edges) will serve tapas, especially those garlicky marinated olives, *majoama* (cured tuna), and blue-cheese canapés. Barrels form the decor, along with antique posters long turned tobacco-gold from the cigarette smoke. Open Sunday to Thursday 1 to 3:30pm and 7:30pm to 1:30am (Fri–Sat to 2am). Calle Echegaray 7. ☏ **91-429-73-13.** Metro: Sevilla.

Gay & Lesbian Bars

Black and White This is the major gay bar of Madrid (with a mixed crowd on weekends), located in the center of the Chueca district. A guard will open the door to a large room—painted, as you might expect, black and white. There's a disco in the basement, but the street-level bar is the premier gathering spot, featuring drag shows (beginning at 12:30am Sun–Fri), male striptease, and videos. Old movies are shown against one wall. Open Sunday to Thursday 10pm to 5am, Friday to Saturday 10pm to 6am. Beer is 7€; whiskey costs 8€. Libertad 34 at the corner of Gravina. ☏ **91-531-11-41.** www.discoblack-white.net. Metro: Chueca.

Cruising One of the landmark gay bars of Madrid, a center for raising gay consciousness and for gay cruising, this place has probably been visited at least once by every gay male in Castile. There are virtually no women inside, but always a hustler looking for a tourist john. It doesn't get crowded or lively until late at night. Open daily from 8pm to 3:30am. Beer costs from 5€; whiskey, 7€. Pérez Galdos 5. ☏ **91-521-51-43.** Metro: Chueca or Gran Vía.

Casinos

Casino Gran Madrid (☏ **91-856-11-00** or 90-090-08-10; www.casinogran madrid.es) is at Km 29 along Carretera La Coruña (the A-6 highway running btw. Madrid and A Coruña). The largest casino in Madrid, it appeals to nongamblers with a roster of dining and entertainment facilities, including two restaurants, four bars, and a nightclub. And if you happen to enjoy gambling, there are facilities for French and American roulette, blackjack, punto y banco, baccarat, and chemin de fer. Presentation of a passport at the door is essential—without it, you won't be admitted. Entrance costs 3€, although that fee is often waived for residents of some of Madrid's larger hotels who arrive with a ticket provided gratis by the hotel's management. The casino and all of its facilities are open daily from 4pm to 5am (until 6am Fri and Sat).

An a la carte restaurant in the French Gaming Room offers international cuisine, with dinners costing from 65€. A buffet in the American Gaming Room will cost 25€ to 28€. The restaurants are open daily from 9pm to 2am. The casino is about 29km (18 miles) northwest of Madrid, along the Madrid–La Coruña A-6 highway. Buses depart for the casino from Plaza de España 6 every afternoon and evening at 4:30, 6, 7:30, 9:30, and 11pm, and 12:45am. Note that between October 14 and May 14, men must wear jackets; T-shirts and tennis shoes are forbidden in any season. To enter, European visitors must present an identity card; non-European visitors must present a passport.

Summer *Terrazas*

At the first blush of spring weather, Madrileños rush outdoors to drink, talk, and sit at open-air cafes, called *terrazas,* throughout the city. The best and most expensive ones are along Paseo de la Castellana between Plaza de la Cibeles and Plaza Emilio Castelar, but there are dozens more throughout the city.

You can wander up and down the boulevard, selecting one that appeals to you; if you get bored, you can move on to another one. Sometimes these *terrazas* are called *chirinquitos.* You'll find them along other *paseos,* including the Recoletos and the Prado; both are fashionable areas but not as hip as the Castellana. For old traditional atmosphere, the terraces at Plaza Mayor win out. Plaza Santa Ana has several atmospheric choices within the Old City. Friday and Saturday are the most popular nights for drinking; many locals sit here all night. Although many *terrazas* have been around for decades, two newer ones are attracting the fashionable. The most stylish of these is the one at **Hotel Urban,** Carrera San Jerónimo 34 (© **91-787-77-70;** www.hotelurban.com). Its deck is filled with white-leather seats, and it opens onto the Gran Vía, Madrid's main street. Another stylish terraza is found by riding the elevator to the top of the avant-garde **Hotel Puerta América,** Av. de América 41 (© **91-744-54-00;** www.hotelpuertamerica.com). Here the Bar Skynight features bossa nova beats and the town's best martinis (at least that's what the bartender claims).

6

SIDE TRIPS FROM MADRID

adrid makes an ideal base for excursions because it's surrounded by some of Spain's major attractions. The day trips listed below to both New Castile and Old Castile range from 29 to 161km (18–100 miles) outside Madrid, allowing you to leave in the morning and be back by nightfall. In case you choose to stay overnight, however, we've included a selection of hotels in each town.

The satellite cities and towns around Madrid include Toledo, with its El Greco masterpieces; the wondrous El Escorial monastery; Segovia's castles that seem to float in the clouds; and the Bourbon palaces at La Granja. Cuenca, actually in La Mancha, is the longest excursion, so unless you want to spend a good part of the day getting there and back, you should consider it an overnight trip. For a selection of other cities in Old Castile—each of which is better visited on an overnight stopover rather than on a day trip from Madrid—see chapter 7.

TOLEDO ★★★

68km (42 miles) SW of Madrid, 137km (85 miles) SE of Avila

If you have only 1 day for an excursion outside Madrid, go to Toledo—a place made special by its Arab, Jewish, Christian, and even Roman and Visigothic elements. A national landmark, the city that so inspired El Greco in the 16th century has remained relatively unchanged. You can still stroll through streets barely wide enough for a man and his donkey—much less an automobile.

Surrounded on three sides by a bend in the Tagus River, Toledo stands atop a hill overlooking the arid plains of New Castile—a natural fortress in the center of the Iberian Peninsula. It was a logical choice for the capital of Spain, but it lost its political status to Madrid in the 1500s. Toledo has remained the country's religious center, as the seat of the primate of Spain.

If you're driving, the much-painted skyline of Toledo will come into view about 6km (3¾ miles) from the city. When you cross the Tagus River via 14th-century Puente San Martín, the scene is reminiscent of El Greco's moody, storm-threatened *View of Toledo,* which hangs in New York's Metropolitan Museum of Art. The artist reputedly painted that view from a hillside that is now the site of **Parador de Turismo de Toledo** (p. 199). If you arrive at the right time, you can enjoy an aperitif on the *parador's* terrace and watch one of Toledo's famous violet sunsets.

Essentials

GETTING THERE RENFE **trains** run here frequently every day. Those departing Madrid's Atocha railway station for Toledo run daily from 6:50am to 9:50pm; those leaving Toledo for Madrid run daily from 6:50am to 9:30pm. Traveling time is approximately 35 minutes on an *alta velocidad* (high-speed) train.

FACING PAGE: **The Alcázar of Toledo.**

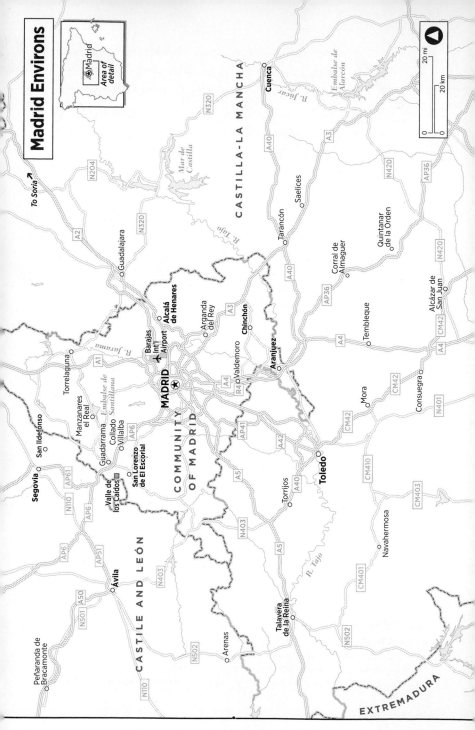

Madrid Environs

Area of detail

★ Madrid

20 mi

20 km

To Soria

CASTILLA-LA MANCHA

CASTILE AND LEÓN

COMMUNITY OF MADRID

EXTREMADURA

MADRID

Barajas Int'l Airport

Alcalá de Henares

Arganda del Rey

Chinchón

Valdemoro

Aranjuez

Guadalajara

Tarancón

Saelices

Cuenca

Corral de Almaguer

Quintanar de la Orden

Alcázar de San Juan

Tembleque

Consuegra

Mora

Toledo

Navahermosa

Torrijos

Talavera de la Reina

Arenas

Ávila

Peñaranda de Bracamonte

Segovia

San Ildefonso

Torrelaguna

Manzanares el Real

Guadarrama

Collado Villalba

San Lorenzo de El Escorial

Valle de los Caídos

Mar de Castilla

Embalse de Alarcón

Embalse de Santillana

R. Jarama

R. Tajo

R. Júcar

R. Tajo

N204

N320

N320

A2

A1

A6

AP6

N110

AP61

AP6

AP6

AP51

A50

N501

N502

N110

N403

A5

A5

N403

CM410

CM403

CM401

N502

CM401

A42

AP41

A4

R4

A4

A4

R4

A3

A3

A40

A40

A40

AP36

N320

N420

AP36

N420

CM42

N401

CM42

CM42

A4

CM42

A40

M50

N502

N501

A2

192

The fare one-way is 9.50€. For train information in Madrid, call ✆ **90-224-02-02** or 90-224-34-02 (www.renfe.es).

It's actually easier to take the **bus** from Madrid than the train. Buses are maintained by several companies, the largest of which is **Alsa** (✆ **90-242-22-42;** www.alsa.es). They depart daily, from Madrid's Estación de Plaza Elíptica, Avenida Vía Lusitana, between midnight and 11pm at 30-minute intervals. Travel time is 1 hour and 15 minutes, and a one-way transit costs 4.70€.

Once you reach Toledo, you'll be deposited at the Estación de Autobuses, which lies beside the river, about 1.2km (¾ mile) from the historic center. Although many visitors opt to walk, be ready to climb a hill. Bus nos. 5 and 6 run from the station uphill to the center, charging 1€ for the brief ride. Pay the driver directly.

By car, exit Madrid via Cibeles (Paseo del Prado) and take the N-401 south.

VISITOR INFORMATION The **tourist information office,** Plaza del Consistorio 1 (✆ **92-525-40-30;** www.toledo-turismo.com), is open daily 10am to 6pm.

Exploring Toledo

Two of the major attractions in Toledo, the fabled Alcázar and the Casa y Museo de El Greco, were closed at press time. Check with the tourist office before heading to either attraction.

Alcázar ★★★ The Alcázar, at the eastern edge of the Old City, dominates the Toledo skyline. It became world famous at the beginning of the Spanish Civil War, when it underwent a 70-day siege that almost destroyed it. Today it is being rebuilt and turned into an army museum housing such exhibits as a plastic model of what the fortress looked like after the Civil War, electronic equipment used

Toledo's skyline, with the Alcázar in the background.

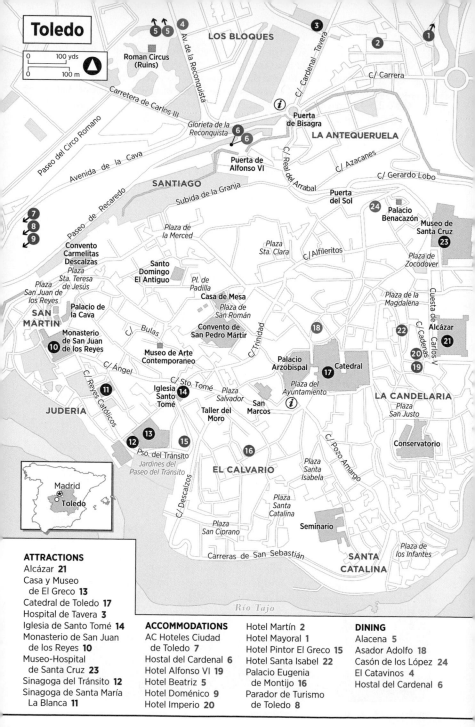

Toledo

0 — 100 yds
0 — 100 m

LOS BLOQUES

Roman Circus (Ruins)

Av. de la Reconquista

Carretera de Carlos III

C/ Cardenal Tavera

C/ Carrera

LA ANTEQUERUELA

Paseo del Circo Romano

Avenida de la Cava

Glorieta de la Reconquista

Puerta de Bisagra

Puerta de Alfonso VI

C/ Real del Arrabal

C/ Azacanes

C/ Gerardo Lobo

SANTIAGO

Subida de la Granja

Paseo de Recaredo

Puerta del Sol

Palacio Benacazón

Museo de Santa Cruz

Plaza de la Merced

Plaza Sta. Clara

C/ Alfileritos

Plaza de Zocodover

Convento Carmelitas Descalzas

Plaza Sta. Teresa de Jesús

Santo Domingo El Antiguo

Pl. de Padilla

Casa de Mesa

Plaza de San Román

Plaza de la Magdalena

Cuesta de Carlos V

Plaza San Juan de los Reyes

Palacio de la Cava

Convento de San Pedro Mártir

C/ Trinidad

Alcázar

SAN MARTÍN

C/ Bulas

Monasterio de San Juan de los Reyes

Museo de Arte Contemporaneo

Palacio Arzobispal

Catedral

C/ Cadenas

C/ Ángel

C/ Sto. Tomé

Plaza del Ayuntamiento

LA CANDELARIA

C/ Reyes Católicos

Iglesia Santo Tomé

Plaza Salvador

San Marcos

Plaza San Justo

JUDERÍA

Taller del Moro

Conservatorio

Pso. del Tránsito

Jardines del Paseo del Tránsito

EL CALVARIO

C/ Pozo Amargo

Plaza Santa Isabela

C/ Descalzos

Plaza Santa Catalina

Plaza San Ciprano

Seminario

Plaza de los Infantes

Carreras de San Sebastián

SANTA CATALINA

Río Tajo

Madrid
Toledo

during the siege, and photographs taken during the height of the battle. A walking tour gives a realistic simulation of the siege. An outstanding array of exhibits from military history is on exhibit, including El Cid's original sword. In addition, you can see the tent used by Charles V in the Tunisian desert, as well as relics of Pizarro and Cortés, and an exceptional collection of Spanish armor. Look for a piece of the cross that Columbus carried with him when he landed in the New World. The original collection was assembled by the notorious Manuel Godoy, who rose from relative poverty to become the lover of María Luisa of Parma, wife of Carlos IV. Note that at press time the museum was closed for renovations (it may reopen in late 2011); check its status before setting out.

Cuesta de Carlos V no. 2, near the Plaza de Zocodover. *C* **92-523-88-00.** Tues–Sun 9:30am–2pm.

Casa y Museo de El Greco ★ Located in Toledo's *antiguo barrio judío* (the old Jewish Quarter, a labyrinth of narrow streets on the Old Town's southwestern edge), the House of El Greco honors the master painter, although he didn't actually live here. In 1585 the artist moved into one of the run-down palace apartments belonging to the Marqués of Villena. Although he was to live at other Toledan addresses, he returned to the Villena palace in 1604 and remained there until his death. Only a small part of the original residence was saved from decay. In time, this and a neighboring house became the El Greco museum; today it's furnished with authentic period pieces.

You can visit El Greco's so-called studio, where one of his paintings hangs. The museum contains several more works, including a copy of *A View of Toledo* and three portraits, plus many paintings by various 16th- and 17th-century Spanish artists. The garden and especially the kitchen also merit attention, as does a sitting room decorated in the Moorish style.

Calle Samuel Leví s/n. *C* **92-522-40-46.** At press time, this attraction was closed for renovations. It may reopen in 2010; check its status at the time of your visit. Bus: 2.

Catedral de Toledo ★★★ Ranked among the greatest Gothic structures, the cathedral actually reflects several styles, since more than 2½ centuries elapsed during its construction (1226–1493). Many historic events transpired here, including the proclamation that Joanna the Mad and her husband, Philip the Handsome, were heirs to the throne of Spain.

Among its art treasures, the *transparente* stands out—a wall of marble and florid baroque alabaster sculpture overlooked for years because the cathedral was too poorly lit. Sculptor Narciso Tomé cut a hole in the ceiling, much to the consternation of Toledans, and now sunlight touches the high-rising angels, a *Last Supper* in alabaster, and a Virgin in ascension.

Toledo as El Greco Saw It

Wandering through the heart of Toledo is a delight. It is almost as memorable to view Toledo from afar. It still looks as El Greco painted it. For the best perspective, take the **Carretera de Circunvalación,** the road that runs 3km (1¾ miles) on the far bank of the Tagus. This road makes a circular loop of the river from the Alcántara to San Martín Bridge. Clinging to the hillsides are rustic dwellings and extensive olive groves (*cigarrales*). The *cigarrales* of the Imperial City were immortalized by Tirso de Molina, the 17th-century dramatist, in his trilogy *Los Cigarrales de Toledo.*

The 16th-century Capilla Mozárabe, containing works by Juan de Borgoña, is another curiosity of the cathedral. Mass is still held here using a Mozarabic liturgy. The Treasure Room has a 500-pound 15th-century gilded monstrance—allegedly made with gold brought back from the New World by Columbus—that is still carried through the streets of Toledo during the feast of Corpus Christi. Other highlights of the cathedral include El Greco's *Twelve Apostles* and *Spoliation of Christ* and Goya's *Arrest of Christ on the Mount of Olives.*

The cathedral shop, where you buy tickets to enter, is well organized and stocks a variety of quality souvenirs, including ceramics and damascene. Cardenal Cisneros 1. ℂ **92-522-22-41.** www.architoledo.org/cathedral/default.htm. Free admission to cathedral; Treasure Room 7€. Mon–Sat 10:30am–6:30pm; Sun 2–6pm.

Hospital de Tavera This 16th-century Greco-Roman palace, north of the medieval ramparts of Toledo, was originally built by Cardinal Tavera; it now houses a private art collection. Titian's portrait of Charles V hangs in the banquet hall. The museum owns five paintings by El Greco: *The Holy Family, The Baptism of Christ,* and portraits of St. Francis, St. Peter, and Cardinal Tavera. Ribera's *The Bearded Woman* also attracts many viewers. The library's book collection is priceless. In the nearby church is the mausoleum of Cardinal Tavera, designed by Alonso Berruguete.
Calle Cardenal Tavera 2. ℂ **92-522-04-51.** Admission 4€. Mon–Sat 10am–1:30pm and 3–5:30pm; Sun 10am–1:30pm.

Iglesia de Santo Tomé This modest little 14th-century chapel, situated on a narrow street in the old Jewish Quarter, might have been overlooked had it not possessed El Greco's masterpiece **The Burial of the Count of Orgaz** ★★★, created in 1586. *Tip:* To avoid the hordes, go when the chapel first opens.
Plaza del Conde 4, Vía Santo Tomé. ℂ **92-525-60-98.** Admission 2.30€. Daily 10am–6:45pm (closes at 5:45pm in winter). Closed Dec 25 and Jan 1.

Monasterio de San Juan de los Reyes ★ Founded by King Ferdinand and Queen Isabella to commemorate their triumph over the Portuguese at Toro in 1476, the church was started in 1477 according to the plans of architect Juan Guas. It was finished, together with the splendid cloisters, in 1504, dedicated to St. John the Evangelist, and used from the beginning by the Franciscan friars. An example of Gothic-Spanish-Flemish style, San Juan de los Reyes was restored after the damage caused during Napoleon's invasion and after its abandonment in 1835; since 1954, it has been entrusted again to the Franciscans. The church is located at the extreme western edge of the Old Town, midway between the Puente (bridge) of San Martín and the Puerta (gate) of Cambrón.
Calle Reyes Católicos 17. ℂ **92-522-38-02.** www.sanjuandelosreyes.org. Admission 2.30€ adults, 1.80€ seniors, free for children 8 and under. Winter daily 10am–6pm; summer daily 10am–7pm. Bus: 2.

Museo-Hospital de Santa Cruz ★★ Today a museum of art and sculpture, this was originally a 16th-century Spanish Renaissance hospice, founded by Cardinal Mendoza, "the third king of Spain," who helped Ferdinand and Isabella gain the throne. The facade is a stunning architectural achievement in the classical Plateresque style. The major artistic treasure inside is El Greco's *The Assumption of the Virgin,* his last known work. Paintings by Goya and Ribera are also on display along with gold items, opulent antique furnishings, Flemish

tapestries, and even Visigoth artifacts. In the museum patio you'll stumble across fragments of carved stone and sarcophagus lids. One of the major exhibits is of a large Astrolabio tapestry of the zodiac from the 1400s. In the basement you can see artifacts from archaeological digs throughout the province. During exhibitions, a guided tour costs 4€.

Calle Miguel de Cervantes 3. 📞 **92-522-14-02.** Free admission. Mon–Sat 10am–6:30pm; Sun 10am–2pm. Bus: 5 or 6. Pass beneath the granite archway on the eastern edge of Plaza de Zocodover and walk about 1 block.

Sinagoga del Tránsito ★ One block west of the El Greco home and museum stands this once-important house of worship for Toledo's large Jewish population.

The interior of the Sinagoga del Tránsito.

A 14th-century building, it is noted for its superb stucco Hebrew inscriptions, including psalms inscribed along the tops of the walls and a poetic description of the Temple on the east wall. The synagogue is the most important part of the **Museo Sefardí (Sephardic Museum),** which opened in 1971 and contains art objects as well as tombstones with Hebrew epigraphy, some dated before 1492.

Calle Samuel Leví s/n, Paseo Tansito. 📞 **92-522-36-65.** Admission 2.40€ adults, 1.20€ students, free for children 17 and under and seniors. Tues–Sat 10am–2pm and 4–6pm; Sun 10am–2pm. Closed Jan 1, May 1, June 7, Dec 24–25, and Dec 31. Bus: 2.

Sinagoga de Santa María La Blanca ★ In the late 12th century, the Jews of Toledo erected an important synagogue in the Almohada style, which employs graceful horseshoe arches and ornamental horizontal moldings. Although the synagogue had been converted into a Christian church by the early 15th century, much of the original structure remains, including the five naves and elaborate Mudéjar decorations, which are mosquelike in their effect. The synagogue lies on the western edge of the city, midway between the El Greco museum and San Juan de los Reyes.

Calle Reyes Católicos 4. 📞 **92-522-72-57.** Admission 2.30€. Apr–Sept daily 10am–6:45pm; Oct–Mar daily 10am–5:45pm. Bus: 2 or 12.

Shopping

In swashbuckling days, the swordsmiths of Toledo were renowned. They're still around and still turning out swords today. Toledo is equally renowned for its *damasquinado,* or damascene work, the Moorish art of inlaying gold, copper, or silver threads against a matte black steel backdrop. Today Toledo is filled with souvenir shops hawking damascene. The price depends on whether the item is handcrafted or machine made. Sometimes machine-made damascene is passed off as the more expensive handcrafted item, so you have to shop carefully. Bargaining is acceptable in Toledo, but if you get the price down, you can't pay with a credit card—only cash.

Marzipan (called *mazapán* locally) is often prepared by nuns and is a local specialty. Many shops in town specialize in this treat made of sweet almond paste.

The province of Toledo is also renowned for its pottery, which is sold in so many shops at competitive prices that it's almost unnecessary to recommend specific branches hawking these wares. However, over the years we've found that the large roadside emporiums on the outskirts of town on the main road to Madrid often are better bargains than the shops within the city walls, where rents are higher.

For the best deals, and if you're interested in buying a number of items, consider a trip to **Talavera la Reina,** 76km (47 miles) west of Toledo, where most of the pottery is made. Since Talavera is the province's largest city, it is hardly a picture-postcard little potter's village. Most of the shops lie along the town's main street, where store after store sells this distinctive pottery in multicolored designs.

Pottery hunters also flock to **Puente del Arzobispo,** another ceramic center, known for its green-hued pottery. From Talavera, drive west on the N-V to Oropesa, and then south for 14km (8⅔ miles) to a fortified bridge across the Tagus. In general, ceramics here are cheaper than those sold in Toledo.

Just past Oropesa at the turnoff to Lagartera is the village where the highly renowned and sought-after embroidery of La Mancha originates. Virtually every cottage in Lagartera displays samples of this free-form floral stitching, shaped into everything from skirts to tablecloths. Of course, shops in Toledo are also filled with samples of this unique embroidery.

Around since the 1920s, **Damasquinados Suárez,** Circo Romano 8 (**©** **92-528-00-27**), has manufactured damascene work in various forms, ranging from unpretentious souvenir items to art objects of rare museum-quality beauty that sell for as much as 12,000€. You'll find swords, straight-edged razors, pendants, fans, and an array of pearls. The shop is open daily from 9:30am to 7pm year-round.

Where to Stay in Toledo
EXPENSIVE

AC Hoteles Ciudad de Toledo ★★ On a beltway across the river, south of the city—follow the directions to the *parador*—this deluxe property is a member of a chain that includes the swank Santo Mauro in Madrid. Enter this epitome of luxury living at the third floor, and proceed down through the spiraling architectural design to reach the rest of the hotel. Guest rooms are spacious and luxuriously furnished, all in contemporary styling. The suites have oversize bathtubs and hydromassage.

Carretera de Circunvalación 15, 45005 Toledo. **©** **92-528-51-25.** Fax 92-528-47-00. www.ac-hotels.com. 49 units. 100€–186€ double; 165€–259€ suite. AE, DC, MC, V. Free parking. Bus: 7 or 71. **Amenities:** Restaurant; babysitting; exercise room; room service; sauna. *In room:* A/C, TV, hair dryer, minibar, Wi-Fi (12€ per 24 hr.).

Hilton Buenavista Toledo ★★★ Old-timers thought it would never happen, a Hilton in the ancient city of Toledo. It is both old and new, as the complex is integrated with a restored 16th-century palace. The location is only a 5-minute taxi ride from the historic center. If you stay here, you get the feeling that you're a pampered guest at a resort, complete with an outdoor swimming pool, a spa, and even a cigar room. The hotel is surrounded by well-manicured gardens. Bedrooms are spacious and luxuriously furnished, most of them opening onto panoramic views of Toledo. The marble-clad bathrooms are the best in town. At sunset you can head for the hotel's Tajo River Club for an exotic cocktail while watching the sun set over Toledo, a view that inspired El Greco.

Concilios de Toledo 1, 45005 Toledo. ✆ **92-528-980-00.** Fax 92-528-98-28. www1.hilton.com. 117 units. 180€–240€ double, 390€ suite. AE, DC, MC, V. Parking 10€. **Amenities:** Restaurant; bar; babysitting; exercise room; pool (outdoor); room service; spa. *In room:* A/C, TV, hair dryer, minibar, Wi-Fi (13€ per 24 hr.).

Hotel Beatriz ★★ ☺ The luxe Beatriz is the city's largest hotel, although it gives its guests personal attention. The building dates from the early 1990s but has been completely refurbished in the post-millennium, making it your best bet for up-to-date technology. Even though it lacks the atmosphere of the *parador,* that government-run hostelry is often fully booked, so you'll have a far better chance of getting in here.

The furnishings are tasteful and comfortable, and the location is only a 5-minute drive from Old Town. The facilities, including the bamboo-constructed Kiosk Bar with its great cocktails, are the best of any hotel's. **Alacena** (p. 203) is the hotel's luxurious restaurant.

Carretera de Avila, 45005 Toledo. ✆ **92-526-91-00.** Fax 92-521-58-65. www.hotelbeatriztoledo. com. 295 units. 64€–155€ double; 211€ junior suite; 300€ suite. AE, DC, MC, V. Parking 10€. **Amenities:** 2 restaurants; bar; babysitting; children's playground; outdoor pool; room service; sauna. *In room:* A/C, TV, minibar, Wi-Fi (12€ per 24 hr.).

Palacio Eugenia de Montijo ★★★ This restored palace is the only luxury hotel within the historic core. Lying only a short walk from the cathedral, it has become the most elegant choice to stay in the Toledo area, even better than the *parador* or the Hilton, minus those panoramic views. The spacious bedrooms are tasteful and luxuriously furnished, each decorated with graphic works of some of Spain's leading artists of today. The work of these artists is for sale in the shops of the hotel. Furnishings are sumptuous throughout the place. The deluxe **Restaurant Belvis** arguably is the finest hotel dining room in Toledo.

Plaza del Juego de Pelota 7, 45002 Toledo. ✆ **92-527-46-90.** Fax 92-527-46-91. www.palacio eugeniademontijo.com. 37 units. 138€–250€ double. AE, DC, MC, V. Parking 18€. **Amenities:** Restaurant; bar; room service; spa. *In room:* A/C, TV, hair dryer, minibar, Wi-Fi (free).

Parador de Turismo de Toledo ★★★ You'll have to make reservations well in advance to stay at this *parador,* which is built on the ridge of a rugged hill where El Greco is said to have painted his *View of Toledo* at a point 4km (2½ miles) from the center. That view is still here, and it is without a doubt one of the grandest in the world. The main living room/lounge, finely furnished with old chests, leather chairs, and heavy tables, leads to a sunny terrace overlooking the city. On chilly nights you can sit by the fireplace. The guest rooms are spacious and beautifully furnished with reproductions of regional antique pieces.

Cerro del Emperador, 45002 Toledo. ✆ **92-522-18-50.** Fax 92-522-51-66. www.parador.es. 76 units. 160€–197€ double; 240€–257€ suite. MC, V. Free parking. **Amenities:** Restaurant; bar; outdoor pool; room service. *In room:* A/C, TV, hair dryer, minibar, Wi-Fi (free).

MODERATE

Hostal del Cardenal ★★ 🎁 The Hostal del Cardenal features wonderful rooms (albeit not as grand as at the options listed above), and is great for an Old Toledan atmosphere. The entrance to this unusual hotel is set into the stone of the ancient city walls, a few steps from Bisagra Gate. To enter the hotel you must climb a series of terraces to the top of the crenelated walls of the ancient fortress. Here, grandly symmetrical and very imposing, is the *hostal*, the former residence of the 18th-century cardinal of Toledo, Señor Lorenzana. Just beyond the entrance, still atop the city wall, you'll find flagstone walkways, Moorish fountains, rose gardens, and cascading vines. The building has tiled walls; long, narrow salons; dignified Spanish furniture; and a smattering of antiques. Guest rooms are small to medium, each one well appointed.

Paseo de Recaredo 24, 45004 Toledo. ✆ **92-522-49-00.** Fax 92-522-29-91. www.hostaldel cardenal.com. 27 units. 105€–135€ double; 145€–170€ suite. AE, DC, MC, V. Free street parking. Bus: 5 or 6 from rail station. **Amenities:** Restaurant; bar; Wi-Fi (12€ per 24 hr., in lobby). *In room:* A/C, TV, hair dryer.

Hotel Alfonso VI Built in the early 1970s, this hotel has been kept up-to-date with frequent renovations. A few of the public rooms appear so faux Castilian they look like movie sets. It sits near a dense concentration of souvenir shops in the center of the Old City, at the southern perimeter of the Alcázar. Inside you'll discover a high-ceilinged, marble-trimmed decor with a scattering of Iberian artifacts, copies of Spanish Provincial furniture, and dozens of leather armchairs. Rooms, for the most part, are midsize, each well appointed with cushiony furnishings that include comfortable mattresses on the Spanish beds.

Calle General Moscardó 2, 45001 Toledo. ✆ **92-522-26-00.** Fax 92-521-44-58. www.hotel alfonsovi.com. 83 units. 60€–135€ double; 112€–210€ suite. AE, MC, V. Nearby parking 18€. Bus: 5 or 6. **Amenities:** Restaurant; bar; babysitting; room service. *In room:* A/C, TV, hair dryer, Wi-Fi (12€ per 24 hr.).

The Hot Dining Ticket in Toledo Province

At a point 37km (23 miles) south of Madrid and 34km (21 miles) north of Toledo lies the finest restaurant in Toledo province: El Bohío, Av. Castilla–La Mancha 81, Illescas (✆ **92-551-11-26**), with a far grander cuisine than you'll find in the city of Toledo itself. Illescas is a dusty, sleepy pueblo, but not so this citadel of fine dining. The setting is that of an upmarket Castilian tavern, with cast-iron fixtures and stained glass. Recipes in use at the time of the Spanish Civil War are given flair here, as evoked by the *sopa de ajo,* a garlicky porridge of old bread. Today chef Pepe Rodríguez reincarnates this staple, serving a glass of the regional broth with airy croutons and a dusting of pulverized garlic and paprika ice cream. The typical suckling pig is gussied up, perfectly roasted and flavored, and served with a sweetbread salad, crackling pork skins, and blood sausage along with a relish of sweet porcine cream. Rodríguez has adhered to his regional roots, what he refers to as his "taste memory," but has virtually reinvented every offering on the menu, giving dishes a lighter, airier taste. In culinary terms, it's called "recontextualized." Meals cost from 20€ to 28€. The restaurant is closed Sunday, Monday night, and throughout August. Reservations are recommended.

Hotel Doménico ★ ☺ One of the finest hotels in Toledo, Doménico is located among Los Cigarrales, the typical country houses lying south of the city and offering panoramic views. The building, although modern, is constructed in a traditional style. Launched in 1993, the hotel is only a 5-minute (3km/1¾ -mile) drive to the historic core of Toledo. Guest rooms are midsize and comfortably furnished. Some of the rooms have skylights. Second- and third-floor units have terraces opening onto breathtaking views of the city.

Cerro del Emperador, 45002 Toledo. ℂ **92-528-01-01.** Fax 92-528-01-03. www.krishoteles.com. 50 units. 50€–133€ double; 210€ suite. AE, DC, MC, V. Free parking. Bus: 7. **Amenities:** Restaurant; bar; babysitting; children's center; outdoor pool; room service, Wi-Fi (free, in lobby). *In room:* A/C, TV, hair dryer, minibar.

Hotel Mayoral In front of the walls of Toledo next to the bus station, this hotel dates from 1989. A rather formal entrance followed by a severe hallway leads to comfortable, well-furnished, midsize guest rooms with good beds and well-maintained bathrooms equipped with tub/shower combos. Most of the guest rooms have balconies with views of interior patios, although a few have a panoramic view of Toledo.

Av. de Castilla–La Mancha 3, 45003 Toledo. ℂ **92-521-60-00.** Fax 92-521-69-54. www.hoteles mayoral.com. 110 units. 118€ double. AE, MC, V. Parking 12€. Bus: 5 or 6. **Amenities:** Restaurant; bar. *In room:* A/C, TV, minibar, Wi-Fi (free).

Hotel Pintor El Greco ★ In the old Jewish Quarter, one of the most traditional and historic districts of Toledo, this hotel was converted from a typical *casa tole-dana* (house in Toledo) that had once been used as a bakery. With careful restoration, especially of its ancient facade, it was transformed into one of Toledo's best and most atmospheric small hotels—the only one to match the antique charm of Hostal del Cardenal. Decoration in both the public rooms and the bedrooms is in a traditional Castilian style. Bedrooms come in a variety of shapes and sizes, as befits a building of this age. At the doorstep of the hotel are such landmarks as the Monasterio de San Juan de los Reyes, Sinagoga de Santa María la Blanca, Sinagoga del Tránsito, Casa y Museo de El Greco, and Iglesia de Santo Tomé.

Alamillos del Tránsito 13, 45002 Toledo. ℂ **92-528-51-91.** Fax 92-521-58-19. www.hotel-pintorelgreco.com. 33 units. 112€–145€ double. AE, DC, MC, V. Parking 14€. *In room:* A/C, TV, hair dryer, minibar, Wi-Fi (free).

INEXPENSIVE

Hotel Imperio ◢ Long a budget favorite, this modest hotel lies a few yards from the Alcázar and cathedral. Built in the 1980s, the hotel has been renovated, adding more comfort to the small rooms. The furnishings are rather severe, but the renewed beds are comfortable. For the price, this is one of the city's best choices. Rooms on the second floor have balconies overlooking the street.

Cadenas 5, 45001 Toledo. ℂ **92-522-76-50.** Fax 92-525-31-83. www.terra.es/personal/himperio. 21 units. 48€ double. AE, DC, MC, V. No parking. **Amenities:** Bar. *In room:* A/C, TV.

Hotel Martín A good, serviceable choice, the two-story Martín opened in 1992 near Bisagra Gate, the main medieval doorway to the city of Toledo. It lies only a 10-minute walk from the historic center. The hotel has a homey atmosphere, with a red-brick facade, old streetlights out front, and vertical windows. The interior is decorated in wood and pastel colors; the midsize rooms are furnished comfortably. A continental breakfast is served (but is not included in the room rate).

Calle Espino 10, 45003 Toledo. ✆ **92-522-17-33.** Fax 92-522-19-18. www.hotelesmartin.com. 29 units. 55€–95€ double. MC, V. Parking 10€. **Amenities:** Bar. *In room:* A/C, TV.

Hotel Santa Isabel In a building dating from the 15th century, Santa Isabel lies in the heart of Toledo, close to the cathedral and most sights of historical interest. Opposite the Convent of Santa Isabel from which it takes its name, the hotel still has much of its original character. The interior, however, has been austerely modernized. Guest rooms, while small and spartan, are immaculately kept with comfortable beds and well-equipped bathrooms. Some units have fine views of the interior patio; others open onto the street. Overflow guests are housed in a building next door, which offers an additional 19 comparable guest rooms in a mixture of modern and antique styles.

Calle Santa Isabel 24, 45002 Toledo. ✆ **92-525-31-20.** Fax 92-525-31-36. www.santa-isabel. com. 42 units. 55€–65€ double. AE, DC, MC, V. Parking 12€. Bus: 5 or 6. **Amenities:** Wi-Fi (free, in lobby). *In room:* A/C, TV.

Where to Dine in Toledo
EXPENSIVE

Asador Adolfo ★ MEDITERRANEAN Located less than a minute's walk north of the cathedral, Asador Adolfo is one of the finest restaurants in town (although we still prefer the Hostal del Cardenal; see below). Sections of the building were first constructed during the 1400s, but the thoroughly modern kitchen has been renovated. Massive beams support the dining room ceiling, and here and there the rooms contain faded frescoes dating from the original building.

Game dishes are a house specialty, with partridge with white beans and venison consistently rating among the best anywhere. The chef often uses fruit and truffles in his dishes: roast suckling pig with green apples; roast lamb with white truffles and rosemary flowers; or bull's tail with roast apples and turnips. The house dessert is marzipan.

Calle Hombre de Palo 7. ✆ **92-522-73-21.** www.adolforestaurante.com. Reservations recommended. Main courses 25€–43€; tasting menu 75€–96€. AE, DC, MC, V. Tues–Sat 1–4pm and 8pm–midnight; Sun 1–4pm. Bus: 5 or 6.

Casón de los López ★★ CASTILIAN A short walk from Plaza de Zocodover, this charmer of a restaurant serves the lightest and most sophisticated cuisine in Toledo. Its setting alone would make it an enticing choice. In an antique building, it's a virtual museum also furnished with antiques, some from as far back as the 16th century. Castilian iron bars, Mudéjar-style wooden ceilings, Arab stucco decorations, a splashing fountain, and caged birds create the mellow atmosphere. And get this: Much of the furniture is for sale. Hope that some other diner won't buy the table out from under you when your main course is being served.

The cuisine sees us returning again and again to sample the bounty of the countryside, especially such game as hare, rabbit, partridge, and pigeon. A specialty is loin of venison with fresh, garlic-flecked spinach in a velvety-smooth mushroom cream sauce. Other dishes include red-tuna steak with asparagus or beef tenderloin with glazed onions.

Sillería 3. ✆ **90-219-83-44.** www.casontoledo.com. Reservations required. Main courses 15€–24€; fixed-price menu 39€; tasting menu 52€–69€. AE, DC, MC, V. Daily 1:30–4pm; Mon–Sat 8:30–11:30pm.

MODERATE

Alacena ★ TOLEDAN/SPANISH In the above-recommended Hotel Beatriz, this is the most elegant and comfortable restaurant in Toledo, although Hostal del Cardenal maintains a slight edge in cuisine. Using some of the area's best products and the finest produce shipped from the international markets in Madrid, Alacena hires the finest chefs in the region as well, who are dedicated to flavor, taste, and texture. The chefs prepare such specialties as stewed partridge or sirloin of deer in a sauce of fresh mushrooms. Filet of hare is yet another specialty. Sometimes the chefs feature a specialty month, such as November, when they celebrate the cuisine of Galicia province, in the northwest, shipping in turbot, hake, bullock, and goose barnacles caught off the coast of Spain. Savory Mediterranean rice dishes are another specialty. Starters may include a cream of lobster soup studded with shrimp, or a succulent salad of Iberian cured ham with duck liver.

In the Hotel Beatriz, Carretera de Avila. © **92-526-91-00.** Reservations recommended. Main courses 12€–32€; fixed-price menu 35€. AE, DC, MC, V. Mon–Sat 1:30–4pm and 8:30–11:30pm.

Hostal del Cardenal ★★ SPANISH Treat yourself to Toledo's best-known restaurant, owned by the same people who run Madrid's Sobrino de Botín (p. 154). The chef prepares regional dishes with flair and originality. Choosing from a menu very similar to that of the fabled Madrid eatery, begin with "quarter of an hour" (fish) soup or white asparagus, and then move on to curried prawns, baked hake, filet mignon, or smoked salmon. Roast suckling pig is a specialty, as is partridge in casserole. Arrive early to enjoy a sherry in the bar or in the courtyard.

Paseo de Recaredo 24. © **92-522-49-00.** Reservations required. Main courses 12€–23€. AE, DC, MC, V. Daily 1–4pm and 8:30–11:30pm. Bus: 5 or 6 from rail station.

INEXPENSIVE

El Catavinos ★ 🍴 SPANISH/CASTILIAN *Catavinos* means "wine taster" in Spanish, and indeed this charming restaurant began as a wine cellar. On the periphery of the center, a 10-minute walk from Puerta de Bisagra, the restaurant has a bar downstairs and a restaurant upstairs decorated with old photographs of Peru. In fair weather, guests often eat on the terrace. The menu is filled with regional dishes, including such delicacies as partridge salad, bell peppers with a stuffing of hare, and grilled venison-and-veal meatballs in a savory tomato sauce. The *menú de degustación* is a cornucopia of seven different plates, and desserts include a cheesecake made from goat's milk with a sweet white wine. The big drawback here is the less-than-polished staff.

Av. Reconquista 10. © **92-522-22-56.** Reservations recommended. Main courses 12€–20€; *menú de degustación* 30€ each (minimum 2 people). AE, DC, MC, V. Tues–Sat 10am–midnight; Sun noon–4pm.

Toledo After Dark

Despite the many tourists thronging its streets during the day, Toledo is quiet at night, with fewer dance clubs than you'd expect in a town of its size. If you want to hear recorded music, head for **Bar La Abadía,** Plaza San Nicolás 3 (© **92-525-11-40**), where local residents, many of them involved in the tourism industry, crowd elbow-to-elbow for pints of beer, glasses of wine, and access to the music of New York, Los Angeles, or wherever. Another spot to hit is **O'Brien's Irish Pub,** Calle Armas 12 (© **92-521-26-65**), which seems more appropriate for the streets of Dublin than for Old Toledo; a crowd in its 20s flocks here, and there's live music every Thursday at 10:30pm. A good wine-bar hangout is **Enebro,** Avenida Río Boladiez (© **92-523-47-89**).

ARANJUEZ ★★

47km (29 miles) S of Madrid, 48km (30 miles) NE of Toledo

This Castilian town, at a confluence of the Tagus and Jarama rivers, was once home to Bourbon kings in the spring and fall. With the manicured shrubbery, stately elms, fountains, and statues of the Palacio Real and surrounding compounds, Aranjuez remains a regal garden oasis in what is otherwise an unimpressive agricultural flatland known primarily for its strawberries and asparagus.

Essentials

GETTING THERE **Trains** depart about every 15 minutes from Madrid's Atocha railway station to make the 50-minute trip to Aranjuez; the one-way fare costs 3.30€. Twice a day you can take an express train from Madrid to Toledo, which makes a brief stopover at Aranjuez. This trip takes only 30 minutes. Trains run less often along the east-west route to and from Toledo (a 40-min. ride). The Aranjuez station lies about 1.6km (1 mile) outside town. For information and schedules, call © **90-224-02-02** (www.renfe. es). You can walk it in about 15 minutes, but taxis and buses line up on Calle Stuart (2 blocks from the city tourist office, in the city center). The bus that makes the run from the center of Aranjuez to the railway station is marked N–Z.

   Buses for Aranjuez depart every 30 minutes from 6:30am to 11:45pm from Madrid's Estación Sur de Autobuses, Calle Méndez Alvaro. In Madrid, call © **90-219-87-88** for information. Buses arrive in Aranjuez at the City Bus Terminal, Calle Infantas 16 (© **91-891-01-83**).

   Driving is easy and takes about 30 minutes once you reach the southern city limits of Madrid. To reach Aranjuez, follow the signs to Aranjuez and Granada, taking Highway N-IV.

VISITOR INFORMATION The **tourist information office,** Plaza de San Antonio 9 (© **91-891-04-27**; www.aranjuez.es), is open daily from 10am to 6pm.

Exploring Aranjuez

Casa del Labrador ★★ "The House of the Worker," modeled after the Petit Trianon at Versailles, was built in 1803 by Charles IV, who later abdicated in Aranjuez. The queen came here with her youthful lover, Godoy (whom she had elevated to the position of prime minister), and the feeble-minded Charles didn't seem to mind a bit. Surrounded by beautiful gardens, the "bedless" palace—it's a pavilion with no bedchambers—is lavishly furnished in the grand style of the 18th and 19th centuries. The marble floors represent some of the finest workmanship of that day; the brocaded walls emphasize the luxurious lifestyle; and the royal toilet is a sight to behold. (In those days, royalty preferred an audience.) The clock here is one of the house treasures. The *casita* lies .8km (½ mile) east of the Royal Palace; those with a car can drive directly to it through tranquil Jardín del Príncipe. **Note:** At press time the attraction was closed for renovations, with possible reopening in late 2010 or 2011; check its status before heading here.

Calle Reina, Jardín del Príncipe. ☎ **91-891-03-05.** Admission 5€ adults, 2.50€ students and children 16 and under. Apr–Sept Tues–Sun 10am–6:15pm; Oct–Mar Tues–Sun 10am–5:15pm.

Jardín de la Isla ★ After touring the Royal Palace, wander through the Garden of the Island. Spanish Impressionist Santiago Rusiñol captured its elusive quality on canvas, and one Spanish writer said that you walk here "as if softly lulled by a sweet 18th-century sonata." A number of fountains are remarkable: the "Ne Plus Ultra" fountain, the black-jasper fountain of Bacchus, the fountain of Apollo, and the ones honoring Neptune (god of the sea) and Cybele (goddess of agriculture).

You may also stroll through Jardín del Parterre, located in front of the palace. It's much better kept than the Garden of the Island, but not as romantic.

Directly northwest of the Palacio Real. No phone. Free admission. Apr–Sept daily 8am–8:30pm; Oct–Mar daily 8am–6:30pm.

Palacio Real ★★ As you enter a cobblestone courtyard, you can tell just by the size of the palace that it's going to be spectacular. Ferdinand and Isabella, Philip II, Philip V, and Charles III all made their way through here. The structure you see today dates from 1778. (The previous buildings were destroyed by fire.) Its salons show the opulence of a bygone era, with room after room of royal extravagance. Many styles are blended: Spanish, Italian, Moorish, and French. And, of course, no royal palace would be complete without a room reflecting the rage for chinoiserie that once swept over Europe. The Porcelain Salon is also of special interest. A guide (bilingual) conducts you through the huge complex. (A tip is expected.)

Plaza Palacio. ☎ **91-891-03-05.** Admission 5€ adults, 2.50€ students and children 16 and under. Tues–Sun 10am–5:15pm (until 6:15pm Apr–Sept). Bus: Routes from the rail station converge at the square and gardens at the westernmost edge of the palace.

The Jardín de la Isla (Garden of the Island).

The Palacio Real, or Royal Palace, in Aranjuez.

Where to Stay in Aranjuez

Hostal Castilla ✦ On one of the town's main streets north of the Royal Palace and gardens, the Castilla consists of the ground floor and part of the first floor of a well-preserved, early-18th-century house. Most of the accommodations overlook a courtyard with a fountain and flowers. There are excellent restaurants nearby, and the *hostal* has an arrangement with a neighboring bar to provide guests with an inexpensive lunch. This is a good location from which to explore either Madrid or Toledo on a day trip. Parking is available along the street.

Carretera Andalucía 98, 28300 Aranjuez. © **91-891-26-27.** Fax 91-891-61-33. www.hostales aranjuez.com. 19 units. 65€ double. Rates include buffet breakfast. AE, MC, V. **Amenities:** Bar. *In room:* A/C, TV, Wi-Fi (in some; free).

NH Príncipe de la Paz ★ At long last this sleepy town has a first-class hotel. Lying to the south side of the Royal Palace, the building dates from the 18th and 19th centuries. At one time, it was the intended residential palace of Manuel Godoy, who was the lover of Charles IV's queen (see Casa del Labrador, above). The original building was never completed. But its entrance forms the main reception room of the hotel today. Lying only 1km (⅔ mile) from the train station, the hotel offers midsize bedrooms that are attractively and comfortably furnished. The hotel also offers a first-class restaurant serving some of the best cuisine in town, a mixture of Castilian and international recipes.

Calle San Antonio 22, 28300 Aranjuez. © **91-809-92-22.** Fax 91-892-59-99. www.nh-hotels.com. 86 units. 86€–146€ double; 166€–220€ suite. AE, DC, MC, V. Parking 15€. **Amenities:** Restaurant; bar; concierge; exercise room; room service; sauna. *In room:* A/C, TV, Wi-Fi (17€ per 24 hr.).

Where to Dine in Aranjuez

Casa José ★★ SPANISH/INTERNATIONAL Set near Town Hall and the Church of Antonio, this well-managed restaurant occupies two ground-floor rooms of a 300-year-old house in the heart of town. It is the premier restaurant of the entire area, and local gastronomes drive for miles to dine here. The regional food is prepared with intelligence, and any of the daily offerings is well worth ordering. Look for a menu of fresh local ingredients that changes at least four times a year, with an emphasis on pork, veal, fish, chicken, and shellfish. Of special note are braised lamb chops in a fresh tomato-and-cilantro sauce, turbot roasted with fresh thyme, small lobster smoked with paprika, or grilled hake with almonds and saffron.

Calle Carretera de Andalucía 17. ☎ **91-891-14-88.** www.casajose.es. Reservations recommended. Main courses 25€–28€; fixed-price menu 58€. AE, DC, MC, V. Tues–Sun 1-4pm; Tues–Sat 9pm–midnight. Closed Aug.

El Rana Verde SPANISH "The Green Frog" lies just east of the Royal Palace, next to a small bridge spanning the Tagus. Opened in 1905 by Tomás Díaz Heredero, it is owned and run by a third-generation member of his family, Joaquin Col, who has decorated it in 1920s style. The restaurant looks like a summer house, with high-beamed ceiling and soft drooping ferns. The best tables overlook the river. As in all the restaurants of Aranjuez, asparagus is a special feature. Game, particularly partridge, quail, and pigeon, is a good choice in season, as is fish, including fried hake and fried sole. Strawberries are served with sugar, orange juice, or ice cream.

Plaza Santiago Rusiñol s/n. ☎ **91-891-13-25.** Reservations recommended. Main courses 9€–23€; fixed-price menu 17€–30€. AE, DC, MC, V. Daily 9am–11pm.

Restaurant de la Calle ★ ░ Chef Rodrigo boasts that if you aren't a serious foodie, you will be one after you dine in his simple but sublime dining room. His modest restaurant has only a plain decor, but his culinary creations certainly can't be described that way. The chef works in collaboration with a "gastro-botanist," Santiago Orts. As such, some of his produce—the freshest in town—is not only exotic but sublime. His candylike fresh dates are among the best we've ever had, even in the Sahara, and he mates them with a gamey-tasting squab breast. Everything on the menu seems to reflect the chef's imagination, even a citrus "caviar" (actually the innards of an Australian finger lime piled atop fresh, briny oysters).

Antigua Carretera de Andalucía 85. ☎ **91-891-08-07.** www.restaurantedelacalle.com. Reservations required. Main courses 17€–55€. AE, DC, MC, V. Daily 1-4pm and 7pm–midnight.

SAN LORENZO DE EL ESCORIAL ★★★

48km (30 miles) W of Madrid, 52km (32 miles) SE of Segovia

Aside from Toledo, the most important excursion from Madrid is to the austere royal monastery of San Lorenzo de El Escorial. Philip II ordered the construction of this granite-and-slate behemoth in 1563, 2 years after he moved his capital to Madrid. Once the haunt of aristocratic Spaniards, El Escorial is now a resort where hotels and restaurants flourish in the summer as hordes come to escape the heat of the capital. Aside from the appeal of its climate, the town of San Lorenzo itself is not very noteworthy. But because of the monastery's size, you might decide to spend a night or two at San Lorenzo—more if you have the time.

San Lorenzo makes a good base for visiting nearby Segovia and Avila, the royal palace at La Granja, the Valley of the Fallen—and the even more distant university city of Salamanca.

Essentials

GETTING THERE More than two dozen **trains** depart daily from Madrid's Atocha, Nuevos Ministerios, Chamartín, and Recoletos railway stations. During the summer extra coaches are added. For schedules and information, call ✆ **90-224-02-02** (www.renfe.es). A one-way fare costs 3.30€, and trip time is a little more than 1 hour.

The railway station is about a mile outside town along Carretera Estación. The Herranz bus company meets all arriving trains to shuttle passengers to and from Plaza Virgen de Gracia, about a block east of the monastery's entrance.

Empresa Herranz, Calle Del Rey 27, in El Escorial (✆ **91-890-19-15**), runs some 50 **buses** per day back and forth between Madrid and El Escorial. On Sunday, service is curtailed to 10 buses. Trip time is an hour, and the one-way fare is 5€. The same company runs one bus a day to **El Valle de los Caídos (The Valley of the Fallen).** It leaves El Escorial at 3:15pm with a return at 5:30pm. The 15-minute ride costs 11€ round-trip.

If you're driving, follow the N-VI highway (marked on some maps as A-6) from the northwest perimeter of Madrid toward Lugo, A Coruña, and San Lorenzo de El Escorial. After about a half-hour, fork left onto the C-505 heading toward San Lorenzo de El Escorial. Driving time from Madrid is about an hour.

VISITOR INFORMATION The **tourist information office,** Calle Grimaldi 4 (✆ **91-890-53-13;** www.sanlorenzoturismo.org), is open Tuesday to Saturday 10am to 2pm and 3 to 6pm, and Sunday 10am to 2pm.

Seeing the Sights

El Valle de los Caídos (The Valley of the Fallen) ★

This is Franco's El Escorial, an architectural marvel that took 2 decades to complete, dedicated to those who died in the Spanish Civil War. A gargantuan cross nearly 150m (492 ft.) high dominates the Rock of Nava, a peak of the Guadarrama Mountains. Directly under the cross is a basilica with a mosaic vault, completed in 1959. When José Antonio Primo de Rivera, the founder of the Falange party and a Nationalist hero, was buried at El Escorial, many people, especially influential monarchists, protested that he was not a royal. Infuriated, Franco decided to erect another monument—this one. Originally it was slated to honor the dead on the Nationalist side only, but the intervention of several parties led to a decision to include all the *caídos* (fallen). In time, the mausoleum claimed Franco as well; his body was interred behind the high altar.

A funicular runs from near the basilica entrance to the base of the gigantic cross on the mountaintop (where there's a superb view). The fare is 1.50€ one-way, 2.50€ round-trip; ride hours are daily from 10:30am to 6pm.

The cross of El Valle de los Caídos.

The Royal Library of El Escorial.

On the other side of the mountain is a Benedictine monastery that has some-times been dubbed "the Hilton of monasteries" because of its seeming luxury.
ⓒ **91-890-56-11.** www.patrimonionacional.es. Admission 5€ adults, 2.50€ students and chil-dren 16 and under. Apr–Sept Tues–Sun 10am–6pm; Oct–Mar Tues–Sun 10am–5pm. By bus: Tour buses from Madrid usually include an excursion to the Valley of the Fallen on their 1-day trips to El Escorial. (See "Getting There," above.) By car: Drive to the valley entrance, about 8km (5 miles) north of El Escorial in the heart of the Guadarrama Mountains. Once here, drive 6km (3¾ miles) west along a wooded road to the underground basilica.

Real Monasterio de San Lorenzo de El Escorial ★★★ This huge granite fortress houses a wealth of paintings and tapestries and serves as the burial place for Spanish kings. Intimidating both inside and out because of its sheer size and institutional look, El Escorial took 21 years to complete, a remarkably short time considering the building's bulk and the primitive construction methods of the day. After the death of the original architect, Juan Bautista de Toledo, the structure was completed by Juan de Herrera, considered the greatest architect of Renaissance Spain.

Philip II, who collected many of the paintings exhibited here in the **New Museums ★★**, did not care for El Greco but favored Titian instead. Still, you'll find El Greco's *The Martyrdom of St. Maurice,* rescued from storage, and also his *St. Peter.* Other superb works include Titian's *Last Supper* and Velázquez's *The Tunic of Joseph.*

The **Royal Library ★★** houses a priceless collection of 60,000 volumes—one of the most significant in the world. The displays range from the handwriting of St. Teresa to medieval instructions on playing chess. See, in particular, the Muslim codices and a Gothic *Cantigas* from the 13th-century reign of Alfonso X ("the Wise").

You can also visit the **Philip II Apartments ★★**; they are strictly monas-tic, and Philip called them the "cell for my humble self" in this "palace for God." Philip became a religious fanatic and requested that his bedroom be erected overlooking the altar of the 90m-high (295-ft.) basilica, which has four organs and a dome based on Michelangelo's drawings for St. Peter's. The choir contains a crucifix by Cellini. The walls of the simple Throne Room hold many ancient maps. The Apartments of the Bourbon Kings are lavishly decorated, in contrast to Philip's preference for the ascetic.

Under the church altar you'll find one of the most regal mausoleums in the world, the **Royal Pantheon** ★★★, where most of Spain's monarchs from Charles I to Alfonso XII, including Philip II, are buried. In 1993, Don Juan de Borbón, the count of Barcelona and the father of King Juan Carlos (Franco passed over the count and never allowed him to ascend the throne), was interred nearby. On a lower floor is the "Wedding Cake" tomb for children.

Allow at least 3 hours for a visit. The guided tour doesn't take you to all the sites, but you are free to explore on your own afterward.

Calle Juan de Borbón s/n. ℭ **91-890-59-03.** www.patrimonionacional.es. Comprehensive ticket 8€ adults, 4€ children, guided tour 10€. Apr–Sept Tues–Sun 10am–6pm; Oct–Mar Tues–Sun 10am–5pm.

Where to Stay in San Lorenzo de El EScorial

MODERATE

Hotel Botánico ★★ True to its name, the hotel stands in a lovely manicured garden of both indigenous and exotic shrubbery. Although the building is traditionally Castilian, the decor seems vaguely alpine, with wood paneling and beams in the reception rooms. The clean, well-lit units are large and comfortable.

Calle Timoteo Padros 16, 28200 San Lorenzo de El Escorial. ℭ **91-890-78-79.** Fax 91-890-81-58. www.labuganvilla.es. 20 units. 86€–160€ double; 158€–230€ suite. Rates include continental breakfast. AE, DC, MC, V. Free parking. **Amenities:** Restaurant; bar; room service. *In room:* A/C, TV, minibar, Wi-Fi (free).

Hotel Victoria Palace ★★ ✦ The Victoria Palace, with its view of El Escorial, is a traditional establishment that has been modernized without losing its original style and comfort. It is surrounded by beautiful gardens and has an outdoor swimming pool. The good-size guest rooms (some with private terraces) are well furnished and maintained. The rates are a bargain for a government-rated four-star hotel.

Calle Juan de Toledo 4, 28200 San Lorenzo de El Escorial. ℭ **91-896-98-90.** Fax 91-896-98-96. www.nh-hoteles.es. 87 units. 109€–150€ double; 143€–200€ suite. AE, DC, MC, V. Free parking. **Amenities:** Restaurant; bar; outdoor pool; room service; sauna. *In room:* A/C, TV, hair dryer, Wi-Fi (17€ per 24 hr.).

INEXPENSIVE

Hostal Cristina An excellent budget choice, this hotel is run by the Delgado family, which opened it in the mid-1980s. It doesn't pretend to compete with the comfort and amenities of the Victoria Palace or even the Miranda & Suizo (see below), but it has its devotees nonetheless. Some 45m (148 ft.) from the monastery, it stands in the center of town, offering clean and comfortable but simply furnished rooms. The beds have firm mattresses, and units range from small to medium. The helpful staff will direct you to the small garden. Parking is available along the street.

Juan de Toledo 6, 28200 San Lorenzo de El Escorial. ℭ **91-890-19-61.** Fax 91-890-12-04. www.hostalcristina.es. 16 units. 50€–60€ double. DC, MC, V. *In room:* TV.

Miranda & Suizo ★★ On a tree-lined street in the heart of town within easy walking distance of the monastery, this 1846 middle-bracket establishment—the oldest hotel here—ranks as a government-rated three-star hotel. It's the second choice in town, with units not quite as comfortable as those at the Victoria Palace (see above). Nevertheless, the Victorian-style building has good guest rooms, some with terraces. Many of the rooms are spacious, and each comes with a well-maintained private bathroom. The furnishings are comfortable, the beds often made of brass; sometimes you'll find fresh flowers on the tables. In summer, there is outside dining.

Calle Floridablanca 20, 28200 San Lorenzo de El Escorial. ℂ **91-890-47-11.** Fax 91-890-43-58. www.hotelmirandasuizo.com. 52 units. 95€–118€ double; 146€–155€ suite. AE, DC, MC, V. Nearby parking 15€. **Amenities:** Restaurant; bar. *In room:* A/C, TV, hair dryer, minibar, Wi-Fi (free).

Where to Dine

IN SAN LORENZO DE EL ESCORIAL

Charolés SPANISH/INTERNATIONAL The thick, solid walls of this establishment date, according to its managers, "from the monastic age"—and probably predate the town's larger and better-known monastery of El Escorial. The restaurant within was established around 1980 and has been known ever since as the best dining room in town. It has a flower-ringed outdoor terrace for use during nice weather. The cuisine doesn't quite rate a star, but chances are you'll be satisfied. The wide choice of menu items, based entirely on fresh fish and meats, includes grilled hake with green or hollandaise sauce, shellfish soup, pepper steak, a *pastel* (pie) of fresh vegetables with crayfish, and herb-flavored baby lamb chops. A strawberry or kiwi tart is a good dessert choice.

Calle Floridablanca 24. ℂ **91-890-59-75.** Reservations required. Main courses 16€–24€; fixed-price menus 45€–58€. AE, DC, MC, V. Daily 1–4pm and 9pm–midnight.

Mesón de la Cueva CASTILIAN Founded in 1768, this restaurant captures the taste of Old Castile, and it is only a short walk from the monastery. A *mesón típico* (typical Spanish bar) built around an enclosed courtyard, "the Cave" boasts such accents as stained-glass windows, antique chests, an 18th-century bullfighting collage, faded engravings, paneled doors, and iron balconies. The cooking is on target, and the portions are generous. Regional specialties include Valencian paella and *fabada asturiana* (pork sausage and beans), but the fresh trout broiled in butter is the best of all. The menu's most expensive items are Segovian roast suckling pig and roast lamb (tender inside, crisp outside). La Cueva's *tasca* (tapas bar), through a separate doorway off the courtyard, is filled with Castilians quaffing their favorite before-dinner drinks.

San Antón 4. ℂ **91-890-15-16.** www.mesonlacueva.com. Reservations recommended. Main courses 10€–24€; fixed-price menus 18€–30€. AE, MC, V. Tues–Sun 1–4pm and 9–11pm.

NEAR THE VALLEY OF THE FALLEN

Hospelería Valle de los Caídos SPANISH There aren't a lot of dining options around the Valley of the Fallen, but of the few that exist, this is a pretty good bet. Built in 1956, the building is set amid a dry but dramatic landscape halfway along the inclined access road leading to Franco's monuments, reachable only by car or bus. It's a mammoth modern structure with wide terraces and floor-to-ceiling windows. The *menú del día* usually includes such dishes as cannelloni Rossini, pork chops with potatoes, a dessert choice of flan or fruit, and wine. The typical fare of roast chicken, roast lamb, shellfish, and paella is somewhat cafeteria-style in nature.

Valle de los Caídos. ℰ **91-890-55-11.** Reservations not accepted. Fixed-price lunch 12€. No credit cards. Daily 9:30–10am, 2–3:30pm, and 9–10pm (no one accepted for dinner after 9pm). Closed Dec 15–Jan 15.

El Escorial After Dark

No longer the dead place it was during the long Franco era, the town now comes alive at night, fueled by the throngs of young people who pack the bars and taverns, especially those along Calle Rey and Calle Floridablanca.

One of the better pubs is **El Sapo Rojo,** Calle Ventura Rodríguez 7 (ℰ **91-890-91-63**), with free Internet access. Expats drop in here for a Guinness. More typically Spanish is the **Piano Bar Regina,** Floridablanca 2 (ℰ **91-890-68-43;** www.reginapianobar.com), which attracts the rowdiest crowd. It is estimated that more people get drunk here than anywhere else in town.

SEGOVIA ★★★

87km (54 miles) NW of Madrid, 68km (42 miles) NE of Avila

Less commercial than Toledo, Segovia, more than anywhere else, typifies the glory of Old Castile. Wherever you look, you'll see reminders of a golden era, whether it's the most spectacular Alcázar on the Iberian Peninsula or the well-preserved, still-functioning Roman aqueduct.

Segovia lies on the slope of the Guadarrama Mountains, where the Eresma and Clamores rivers converge. This ancient city is located in the center of the most castle-rich part of Castile. Isabella herself was proclaimed queen of Castile here in 1474.

The narrow, winding streets of this hill city must be covered on foot to fully view the Romanesque churches and 15th-century palaces along the way.

Essentials

GETTING THERE Ten **trains** leave Madrid's Chamartín railway station every day, arriving 2 hours later in Segovia, where you can board bus no. 3, departing every quarter-hour for the Plaza Mayor. The trains that leave from Chamartín first travel through Atocha station, making it closer to some travelers' hotels. A one-way rail fare costs 7€. The station at Segovia is on Paseo Obispo Quesada s/n (ℰ **90-224-02-02;** www.renfe.es), a 20-minute walk southeast of the town center.

Buses arrive and depart from **Estacionamiento Municipal de Autobuses,** Paseo de Ezequiel González 10 (ℰ **92-142-77-06**), near the corner of Avenida Fernández Ladreda and the steeply sloping Paseo Conde de Sepúlveda. There are 20 to 35 buses a day to and from Madrid (which depart from Paseo de la Florida 11; Metro: Norte), and about 4 a day traveling between Avila and Segovia. One-way tickets from Madrid cost 8€.

If you're driving, take the N-VI (on some maps it's known as the A-6), in the direction of La Coruña, northwest from Madrid, toward León and Lugo. At the junction with Rte. 110 (signposted SEGOVIA), turn northeast (AP-61 or N-603).

The cloisters of the Cabildo Catedral de Segovia.

VISITOR INFORMATION The **tourist information office,** Plaza Mayor 10 (© **92-146-03-34;** www.turismodesegovia.com), is open Monday to Saturday 9am to 2pm and 5 to 8pm.

Exploring Segovia

You'll find the best **shopping** between the Roman aqueduct, the cathedral, and the Alcázar. Head especially for **Calle de Juan Bravo, Calle Daoiz,** and **Calle Marqués del Arco.**

Alcázar ★ View the Alcázar first from below, at the junction of the Clamores and Eresma rivers. It is on the west side of Segovia, so you may not spot it when you first enter the city. But that's part of the surprise.

The castle dates from the 12th century, but a large segment containing its Moorish ceilings was destroyed by fire in 1862. Restoration has continued over the years.

Royal romance is associated with the Alcázar. Isabella first met Ferdinand here, and today you can see a facsimile of her dank bedroom. Once married, she wasn't foolish enough to surrender her royal rights, as replicas of the thrones attest—both are equally proportioned. Philip II married his fourth wife, Anne of Austria, here as well.

Walk the battlements of this once-impregnable castle, from which its occupants hurled boiling oil onto the enemy below. Ascend the hazardous stairs of the tower, originally built by Isabella's father as a prison, for a panoramic view of Segovia.

Plaza de la Reina Victoria Eugenia. © **92-146-07-59.** www.alcazardesegovia.com. Admission 4€ adults, 3€ children 6–16, free for children 5 and under. Apr–Sept daily 10am–7pm; Oct Sun–Thurs 10am–6pm, Fri–Sat 10am–7pm; Nov–Mar daily 10am–6pm. Bus: 3. Take Calle Vallejo, Calle de Velarde, Calle de Daoiz, or Paseo de Ronda.

Cabildo Catedral de Segovia ★★ Constructed between 1515 and 1558, this is the last Gothic cathedral built in Spain. Fronting the historic Plaza Mayor, it stands on the spot where Isabella I was proclaimed queen of Castile. Affectionately called *la dama de las catedrales,* it contains numerous treasures, such as the Blessed Sacrament Chapel (created by the flamboyant Churriguera), stained-glass windows, elaborately carved choir stalls, and 16th- and 17th-century paintings, including a reredos portraying the deposition of Christ from the cross by Juan de Juni. The **cloisters** ★ are older than the cathedral, dating from an earlier church that was destroyed in the so-called War of the Communeros. Inside the cathedral museum you'll find jewelry, paintings, and a collection of rare antique manuscripts.

Plaza Catedral Calle, Marqués del Arco, s/n. ℭ **92-146-22-05.** Admission to cathedral, cloisters, museum, and chapel room 3€ adults, free for children 13 and under. Late Mar to early Oct daily 9:30am–6:30pm; mid-Oct to mid-Mar daily 9:30am–5:30pm. Free admission to cathedral 9am–1:15pm Sun.

Esteban Vicente Contemporary Art Museum In the heart of the city, in a newly renovated 15th-century palace, a permanent collection of some 142 works by the abstract-expressionist artist Esteban Vicente has opened. The Spanish-born artist described himself as "an American painter, with very deep and loving Spanish roots." Born in a small town outside Segovia in 1903, he remained in Spain until 1927, eventually residing in New York, where he played a pivotal role in the development of American abstract art. Until his death in 2001, he was one of the last surviving members of the New York School, whose members included Rothko, de Kooning, and Pollock. Vicente's paintings and collages convey his sense of structure and feelings of luminous serenity with colors of astonishing vibrancy, brilliance, and range. His paintings are shown at the Metropolitan Museum of Art, the Museum of Modern Art, and the Whitney, all in New York—and now at this museum in Segovia.

Plazuela de las Bellas Artes. ℭ **92-146-20-10.** www.museoestebanvicente.es. Admission 3€ adults, 1.50€ seniors and students, free for children 11 and under; free admission for all visitors Thurs. Tues–Wed 11am–2pm and 4–7pm; Thurs–Fri 11am–2pm and 4–8pm; Sat 11am–8pm; Sun 11am–3pm.

Iglesia de la Vera Cruz Built in either the 11th or the 12th century by the Knights Templar, this is the most fascinating Romanesque church in Segovia. It stands in isolation outside the walls of the Old Town overlooking the Alcázar. Its unusual 12-sided design is believed to have been copied from the Church of the Holy Sepulchre in Jerusalem. Inside you'll find an inner temple, rising two floors, where the knights conducted nightlong vigils as part of their initiation rites.

Carretera de Zamarramala. ℭ **92-143-14-75.** Admission 2€. Apr–Sept Tues–Sun 10:30am–1:30pm and 3:30–7pm; Oct–Mar Tues–Sun 10:30am–1:30pm and 3:30–6pm. Closed Nov.

Monasterio Santa María del Parral ★ The restored "Monastery of the Grape" was established for the Hieronymites by Henry IV, a Castilian king (1425–74) known as "the Impotent." The monastery lies across the Eresma River about a half-mile north of the city. The church is a medley of styles and decoration—mainly Gothic, Renaissance, and Plateresque. The facade was never completed, and the monastery itself was abandoned when religious orders were suppressed in 1835. Today, it's been restored and is once again the domain of the *jerónimos,*

Segovia's ancient Acueducto Romano.

Hieronymus priests and brothers. Inside, a robed monk will show you the order's treasures, including a polychrome altarpiece and the alabaster tombs of the marquis of Villena and his wife—all the work of Juan Rodríguez.

Calle del Marqués de Villena (across the Eresma River). ✆ **92-143-12-98.** Free admission. Mon-Sat 10am–12:30pm and 4–6:30pm; Sun 10–11:30am and 4–6:30pm. Take Ronda de Santa Lucía, cross the Eresma River, and head down Calle del Marqués de Villena.

Roman Aqueduct (Acueducto Romano) ★★★ This architectural marvel was built by the Romans nearly 2,000 years ago. Constructed of mortarless granite, it consists of 118 arches, and in one two-tiered section it soars 29m (95 ft.) to its highest point. The Spanish call it El Puente. It spans the Plaza del Azoguejo, the old market square, stretching nearly 720m (2,362 ft.). When the Moors took Segovia in 1072, they destroyed 36 arches, which were later rebuilt under Ferdinand and Isabella in 1484.

Plaza del Azoguejo.

Where to Stay in Segovia
EXPENSIVE

Palacio San Facundo ★★ Ranking just below the *parador,* this hotel, located in the historic zone, has been massively renovated and turned into a boutique hotel. Built in the 16th century, it was the home of a former nobleman. Each room in the antique building has been modernized and individually decorated in a tasteful, comfortable style. Rooms come in various sizes as befits a home of this age. In the central atrium, underneath a glass dome, is a cafeteria.

Plaza San Facundo 4, 40001 Segovia. ✆ **92-146-30-61.** Fax 921-46-30-62. www.hotelpalacio-sanfacundo.com. 50 units. 100€–205€ double. AE, DC, MC, V. Parking 15€. **Amenities:** Cafeteria; bar; room service. *In room:* A/C, TV, hair dryer, Internet (free).

Parador de Segovia ★★★ This 20th-century tile-roofed *parador* sits on a hill 3km (1¾ miles) northeast of Segovia. Take the N-601 to get here. It is located on an estate called El Terminillo, which used to be famous for its vines and almond trees, a few of which still survive. If you have a car and can get a reservation, book here. The good-size deluxe rooms contain such extras as tiled bathrooms with tub/shower combos. Furnishings are tasteful, and large windows open onto panoramic views of the countryside. Some of the older rooms here are a bit dated, however, with lackluster decor.

The *parador* has one of the better **restaurants** in Segovia; its windows open onto a panoramic view of the mountains of Sierra de Guadarrama. A complete meal here, of either regional specialties or international dishes, costs around 30€.

Carretera Valladolid s/n (N-601), 40003 Segovia. © **92-144-37-37.** Fax 92-143-73-62. www. parador.es. 113 units. 148€–160€ double; 208€–224€ suite. AE, DC, MC, V. Covered parking 12€; free parking outside. **Amenities:** Restaurant; bar; exercise room; 2 pools (1 heated indoor, 1 outdoor); room service; sauna; outdoor tennis court (lit); Wi-Fi (free, in lobby). *In room:* A/C, TV, hair dryer, minibar.

MODERATE

Hostería Ayala Berganza ★★ 🏨 Once home to one of Spain's most famous painters, Ignacio Zuloaga (1870–1945), this converted inn now provides some of the most atmospheric lodging in Castile. Some accommodations are in the original 15th-century Castilian palace, which has been declared a historic monument. The rest of the rooms are in a modern structure completed in 1998. The hotel lies just outside the ramparts of central Segovia, a 5-minute walk to the heart of town and the cathedral. Its convenient location right next to the Romanesque church of San Millán means you are only a few minutes' walk from the aqueduct. Care and attention went into the modern guest rooms and the two suites; each is individually decorated.

Calle Carretas 5, 40001 Segovia. © **92-146-04-48.** Fax 92-146-23-77. www.hosteriaayala berganza.com. 17 units. 60€–160€ double; 150€–240€ suite. AE, DC, MC, V. Parking 10€. **Amenities:** Restaurant; bar. *In room:* A/C, TV, hair dryer, minibar, Wi-Fi (free).

Hotel Infanta Isabel ★ Named after Queen Isabel, the great-grandmother of the present king, the hotel overlooks the charming central square and is within a stone's throw of the majestic cathedral. This is where the queen would stay when on her way to the nearby summer palace of La Granja. The present owners have modernized the interior considerably, but a good deal of the building's 19th-century grandeur, such as the staircase, remains. Each room is decorated in its own style, with an eye to comfort.

Plaza Mayor, 40001 Segovia. © **92-146-13-00.** Fax 92-146-22-17. www.hotelinfantaisabel.com. 39 units. 88€–103€ double standard; 100€–114€ double superior; 170€–180€ suite. AE, DC, MC, V. Parking 14€. **Amenities:** Restaurant; bar; room service. *In room:* A/C, TV, hair dryer, minibar, Wi-Fi (free).

Hotel Los Arcos This concrete-and-glass five-story structure opened in 1987. Well run and modern, it attracts the business traveler, but tourists frequent the place in droves as well. Guest rooms are generally spacious but are furnished in a generic way that's bland except for the beautiful rug-dotted parquet floors. There are built-in furnishings and tiny bathrooms. The rooms are well kept, with good beds, although some furnishings look worn. If you don't stay here, consider dining at the hotel's **La Cocina de Segovia.**

Paseo de Ezequiel González 26, 40002 Segovia. © **92-143-74-62.** Fax 92-142-81-61. www.hotel-losarcos.com. 60 units. 59€–130€ double; 89€–165€ suite. AE, DC, MC, V. Parking 11€. **Amenities:** Restaurant; bar; exercise room; room service. *In room:* A/C, TV/DVD, hair dryer, minibar, Wi-Fi (12€ per 24 hr.).

Hotel Los Linajes ★ In the historic district of St. Stephen, at the northern edge of the Old Town, stands this hotel, the former home of a Segovian noble family. While the facade dates from the 11th century, the interior is modern, except for some Castilian decorations. Guest rooms, in a range of sizes and shapes, are comfortable, with fine beds and tidily kept tiled bathrooms. One of the best hotels in town, Los Linajes has gardens and patios where guests can enjoy a panoramic view over the city.

Doctor Velasco 9, 40003 Segovia. © **92-146-04-75.** Fax 92-146-04-79. www.loslinajes.com. 60 units. 93€–110€ double; 124€–142€ suite. AE, DC, MC, V. Parking 13€. Bus: 1. **Amenities:** Bar; room service. *In room:* A/C, TV, Wi-Fi (free).

INEXPENSIVE

Las Sirenas Standing since 1950 on the most charming old plaza in Segovia opposite the San Martín church, this hotel has been renovated several times. However, it has long since lost its Franco-era supremacy to Hotel Los Linajes (see above). Modest and well maintained, it is decorated in a conservative style. Each unit contains simple, functional furniture, good beds, and neatly kept bathrooms. However, the rooms are somewhat small. Breakfast is the only meal served, but the staff at the reception desk can direct guests to nearby cafes and *tascas.*

Juan Bravo 30, 40001 Segovia. © **92-146-26-63.** Fax 92-146-26-57. www.hotelsirenas.com. 39 units. 65€–75€ double; 86€–97€ suite. AE, DC, MC, V. Nearby parking 15€. **Amenities:** Bar; exercise room; Wi-Fi (free, in lobby). *In room:* A/C, TV.

Where to Dine in Segovia

El Bernardino ✦ CASTILIAN El Bernardino, a 3-minute walk west of the Roman aqueduct, is built like an old tavern. Lanterns hang from beamed ceilings, and the view over the red-tile rooftops of the city is delightful. There is also a summer terrace. The *menú del día* may include roast veal with potatoes, flan or ice cream, plus bread and wine. You might begin your meal with *sopa castellana* (soup made with ham, sausage, bread, egg, and garlic). The roasts are exceptional here, including roast suckling pig from a special oven and roast baby lamb. You can also order grilled rib-eye steak or stewed partridge. Even though this place has become jaded and touristic, with a rude staff, the cooks back in the kitchen consistently turn out good-tasting dishes.

Cervantes 2. © **92-146-24-77.** www.elbernardino.com. Reservations recommended. Main courses 10€–18€. AE, DC, MC, V. Daily 1–4pm and 8–11pm.

José María ★ CASTILIAN This is one of the classic restaurants of Segovia, a land known for two regional staples, *cordero asado* (roast baby lamb) and *cochinillo asado* (roast suckling pig). You have a choice of five different dining rooms, each decorated in the typical *castellano* style. The place is a bit touristy but nonetheless serves food good enough to attract hundreds of locals as well. The waiters are friendly and helpful in guiding you through the menu and wine *carte.* The chef isn't bound entirely by tradition; he offers innovative modern dishes that are forever changing based on the best of produce in any season.

Cronista Lecea 11. ☎ **02-146-11-11.** www.rtejosemaria.com. Reservations recommended. Main courses 10€–45€. AE, DC, MC, V. Daily 1–4pm and 7–11pm.

A Side Trip to La Granja

To reach La Granja, 11km (6¾ miles) southeast of Segovia, you can take a 20-minute bus ride from the center of the city. Six to 10 buses a day leave from Paseo Conde de Sepúlveda at Avenida Fernández Ladreda. A one-way fare costs 6€. For information, call ☎ **92-142-77-07.**

Palacio Real de La Granja San Ildefonso de la Granja was the summer palace of the Bourbon kings of Spain, who attempted to replicate the grandeur of Versailles in the province of Segovia. In that ambition, they fell far from the mark, as today's slightly unkempt grounds reveal. Set against the snowcapped Sierra de Guadarrama, the slate-roofed palace dominates the village that grew up around it (a summer resort these days).

The builder of La Granja was Philip V, grandson of Louis XIV and the first Bourbon king of Spain. (His body, along with that of his second queen, Isabel de Fernesio, is interred in a mausoleum in the Collegiate Church.) Philip V was born at Versailles on December 19, 1683, which may explain why he wanted to re-create that atmosphere at Segovia.

At one time a farm stood on the grounds of what is now the palace—hence its incongruous name, *la granja*, meaning "the farm." The palace was built in the first part of the 18th century. Inside you'll find valuable antiques (many in the Empire style), paintings, and a remarkable collection of Flemish tapestries, as well as tapestries based on Goya cartoons from the Royal Factory in Madrid.

Most visitors seem to find a stroll through the **gardens** more pleasing, so allow adequate time for that. The fountain statuary is a riot of cavorting gods and nymphs hiding indiscretions. The gardens are studded with chestnuts and elms. Plaza de España 17, San Ildefonso 40100 (Segovia). ☎ **92-147-00-19** or 92-147-03-28. www. patrimonionacional.es. Admission 5€ adults, 2.50€ children 5–14, free for children 4 and under. Apr–Sept Tues–Sun 10am–6pm; Oct–Mar Tues–Sat 10am–1:30pm and 3–5pm, Sun 10am–2pm.

Segovia After Dark

Just head for **Plaza Mayor, Plaza Azoguejo,** or busy **Calle Infanta Isabel** (which runs into Plaza Azoguejo). You're sure to find some fun in the scattering of simple bars and cafes that grow more crowded at night as the days grow hotter. One of our favorite bars is **Santana,** Calle Infante Isabel 18 (☎ **92-146-35-64**), where rock music throughout the night draws an under-35 crowd. Waiters serve tasty tapas, and the bar is open Thursday to Tuesday until midnight. It's always party night at **La Luna,** Puerta de la Luna 8 (☎ **92-146-26-51**). This is the town's leading disco-pub, drawing locals and visitors, usually under 35. La Luna is open daily from 4:30pm to 4am.

ALCALÁ DE HENARES

29km (18 miles) E of Madrid

History hasn't been kind to this ancient town, which once flourished with colleges, monasteries, and palaces. When a university was founded here in the 15th century, Alcalá became a cultural and intellectual center. Europe's first polyglot

Bible (supposedly with footnotes in the original Greek and Hebrew) was published here in 1517, but the town declined during the 1800s when the university moved to Madrid. Today, Alcalá is one of the main centers of North American academics in Spain, cooperating with the Fulbright Commission, Michigan State University, and Madrid's Washington Irving Center. Overall, the city has taken on new life. Commuters have turned it into a virtual suburb, dubbing it "the bedroom of Madrid."

Essentials

GETTING THERE **Trains** travel between Madrid's Atocha or Chamartín station and Alcalá de Henares every day and evening. Service is every 15 minutes (trip time: 30 min.) and one-way fare from Madrid costs 2.80€. The train station (✆ **90-224-02-02;** www.renfe.es) in Alcalá is at Paseo Estación.

    Buses from Madrid depart from Av. América 18 (Metro: América) every 15 minutes. A one-way fare is 3€. Bus service is provided by Alsa, and the Alcalá bus station is on Av. Guadalajara 36 (✆ **90-242-22-42**), 2 blocks past Calle Libreros.

    Alcalá lies adjacent to the main national highway (N-II), connecting Madrid with eastern Spain. As you leave central Madrid, follow signs for Barajas Airport and Barcelona.

VISITOR INFORMATION The **tourist information office,** Callejón de Santa María 1 (✆ **91-889-26-94;** www.turismoalcala.com), provides a map showing all the local attractions. It is open daily 10am to 2pm and 4 to 6:30pm (until 7:30pm July–Sept). It is closed on Monday in July and August.

Exploring Alcalá de Henares

Capilla de San Ildefonso Next door to the Colegio is the Capilla de San Ildefonso, the 15th-century chapel of the old university. It also houses the Italian marble tomb of Cardinal Cisneros, the founder of the original university. This chapel also has an *artesonado* (artisan's) ceiling and intricately stuccoed walls.

Plaza San Diego. ✆ **91-885-41-22** or 91-883-43-84. Admission included in tour of Colegio Mayor de San Ildefonso (see below). Hours same as Colegio.

Colegio Mayor de San Ildefonso Adjacent to the main square, Plaza de Cervantes, is the Colegio Mayor de San Ildefonso, where Lope de Vega and other famous Spaniards studied. You can see some of their names engraved on plaques in the examination room. The old university's Plateresque **facade ★** dates from 1543. From here you can walk across the Patio of Saint Thomas (from 1662) and the Patio of the Philosophers to reach the Patio of the Three Languages (from 1557), where Greek, Latin, and Hebrew were once taught. Here is the Paraninfo (great hall or old examination room), now used for special events. The hall has a Mudéjar carved-panel ceiling. The Paraninfo is entered through a restaurant, **Hostería del Estudiante** (see below).

Plaza San Diego. ✆ **91-883-43-84.** Admission 2.50€. Tours (mandatory; in Spanish or English) Mon–Fri 11am, noon, 1, and 5pm; Sat–Sun 11, 11:30am, noon, 12:30, 1, and 1:30pm.

Museo Casa Natal de Cervantes Visitors come to see the birthplace of Spain's literary giant Miguel de Cervantes, the creator of *Don Quixote,* who may have been born here in 1547. This 16th-century Castilian house was reconstructed in

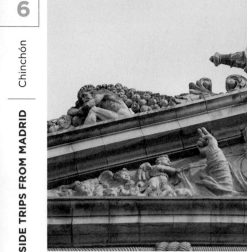

Part of the facade of the Colegio Mayor de San Ildefonso.

1956 around a beautiful little courtyard, which has a wooden gallery supported by pillars with Renaissance-style capitals, plus an old well. The house contains many Cervantes manuscripts and, of course, copies of *Don Quixote,* one of the world's most widely published books (available here in many languages).

Calle Mayor 50. (*C* **91-889-96-54.** www.museo-casa-natal-cervantes.org. Free admission. Tues–Sun 10am–6pm.

Where to Dine in Alcalá de Henares

Hostería del Estudiante ★ CASTILIAN Located within the university complex, this remarkable 1510 building is an attraction in its own right. It opened as a restaurant in 1929, and its typically Castilian recipes haven't been altered since. In the cooler months, if you arrive early, you can lounge in front of a 4.5m (15-ft.) open fireplace. Oil lamps hang from the ceiling, pigskins are filled with local wine, and rope-covered chairs and high-backed carved settees capture the spirit of the past. Run by the Spanish *parador* system, the restaurant offers a tasty (and huge) three-course set-price lunch or dinner featuring such regional specialties as roast suckling lamb, *huevos comigos* (three eggs fried with mushrooms), and Navarre-style trout. For dessert, try the cheese of La Mancha.

Calle Colegios 3. (*C* **91-888-03-30.** www.parador.es. Reservations recommended. Main courses 20€–28€; fixed-price menu 35€. AE, DC, MC, V. Mon–Sat 1–4pm and 9–11pm; Sun 1–10:30pm. Closed Aug.

CHINCHÓN ★

52km (32 miles) SE of Madrid, 26km (16 miles) NE of Aranjuez

The main attraction of Chinchón is the *cuevas* **(caves),** where Anís de Chinchón, an aniseed liqueur, is manufactured. You can buy bottles of the liqueur in Plaza Mayor, at the center of town. **Plaza Mayor ★★**, the town's main square, is the architectural highlight of Chinchón. Dominated by its church, the arcaded square is surrounded by three-story frame houses with wooden balconies. In summer, bullfights are presented on the square.

Wander along the town's steep and narrow streets, past houses with large bays and spacious carriage ways. Although closed to the public, the 15th-century **Chinchón Castle,** seat of the *conde* (count) of Chinchón, can be viewed from outside. The most interesting church, **Nuestra Señora de la Asunción,** dating from the 16th and 17th centuries, contains a painting by Goya.

GETTING THERE Chinchón is most often visited from Aranjuez (p. 204), which is a 30-minute ride away. **Buses** run seven times a day from Aranjuez, but only Monday to Friday, leaving from Calle La Fanta. Schedules tend to be erratic, so call for information (✆ **91-891-01-83**). The one-way fare is 2.50€.

You can drive from Alcalá to Toledo, bypassing Madrid by taking the C-300 in a southwesterly arc around the capital. About halfway there, follow signs to CUEVAS DE CHINCHON. Another option is to take the E-901 southeast of Madrid toward Valencia, turning southwest at the turnoff for Chinchón.

VISITOR INFORMATION The **Oficina de Información Turística Municipal** is at Plaza Mayor (✆ **91-893-53-23;** www.ciudad-chinchon.com), open daily 10am to 7pm.

Where to Stay in Chinchón

Hotel Nuevo Chinchón ✦ On the outskirts, this is one of the town's best addresses. In 1994, the owners invested lots of time and money in making it appear older and more nostalgic than it is. Low-slung and modern from the outside, it contains small bedrooms whose headboards are painted in old-fashioned folkloric patterns. The overall effect is cozy, with a low-key charm.

Urbanización Nuevo Chinchón, Carretera a Titulcia Km 1.5, 28370 Chinchón. ✆ **91-894-05-44.** Fax 91-893-51-28. www.hotelnuevochinchon.com. 17 units. 75€ double. MC, V. Free parking. **Amenities:** Restaurant; bar; babysitting; 2 pools (1 heated indoor); room service; spa. *In room:* A/C, TV, hair dryer.

Parador de Chinchón ★★★ Set near the town center, this hotel lies within the carefully restored 17th-century walls of what was originally an Augustinian convent. After a stint as both a civic jail and a courthouse, it was transformed in 1972 into a government-run *parador,* and it's the best place to stay in town. A team of architects and designers converted it handsomely, with glass-walled hallways opening onto a stone-sided courtyard. The hotel has two bars and two dining halls. Severely dignified rooms still manage to convey their ecclesiastical origins. Rooms range from small to medium, each with a quality mattress and fine linen along with a well-maintained tiled bathroom.

Av. Generalísimo 1, 28370 Chinchón. ✆ **91-894-08-36.** Fax 91-894-09-08. www.parador.es. 38 units. 100€–160€ double; 222€–304€ suite. AE, DC, MC, V. Free parking nearby. **Amenities:** Restaurant; bar; babysitting; outdoor pool; room service; Wi-Fi (free, in lobby). *In room:* A/C, TV, hair dryer, minibar.

Where to Dine in Chinchón

Mesón Cuevas del Vino ★ SPANISH/CASTILIAN This establishment is known for its wine cellars, stocked with bottles you can sample at lunch or dinner. Hanging from the rafters are hams cured by the owners, along with flavorful homemade spiced sausages. Chunks of ham and sausage cooked in oil, plus olives and crunchy bread, are served. Your meal might begin with sliced *chorizo* (Spanish sausage); blood pudding; slices of La Mancha cheese; *sopa castellana* made with garlic, ham, and eggs; or thin-sliced cured ham. Main courses place heavy emphasis on the roast suckling lamb and pig that emerge crackling from a wood-burning oven. Desserts include flan; cookies coated in cinnamon and sugar; and liquefied sweetened almonds, presented in a soupy mixture in a bowl.

Benito Hortelano 13. ℭ **91-894-02-06.** www.cuevasdelvino.com. Reservations recommended on holidays. Main courses 10€–20€. MC, V. Wed–Mon 1:30–5pm and 8–11pm.

AVILA ★★

109km (68 miles) NW of Madrid, 67km (42 miles) SW of Segovia

The ancient city of Avila is completely encircled by well-preserved 11th-century walls, which are among the most important medieval relics in Europe. The city has been declared a national landmark, and there is little wonder why. The walls aren't the only attraction, however. Avila has several Romanesque churches, Gothic palaces, and a fortified cathedral. It is among some 80 cities designated by UNESCO as World Heritage Sites.

Avila's spirit and legend are most linked to St. Teresa, who was born here in 1515. This Carmelite nun, who helped defeat the Reformation in Spain and founded a number of convents, experienced visions of the devil and angels piercing her heart with burning-hot lances. She was eventually imprisoned in Toledo.

Avila's city walls.

Many legends sprang up after her death, including the belief that a hand severed from her body could perform miracles. Finally, in 1622, she was declared a saint.

Note: Bring warm clothes if you're visiting in early spring.

Essentials

GETTING THERE More than two dozen **trains** leave daily from Madrid for Avila, about a 1½- to 2-hour trip each way. Depending on the schedule, trains depart from Chamartín, Atocha, Recoletos, and Nuevos Ministerios railway stations. The 8:32am train from Atocha, arriving in Avila at 10:43am, is a good choice, considering all there is to see. Tickets cost 6.80€ to 24€. The Avila station is at Avenida José Antonio (*©* **90-224-02-02;** www.renfe.es), 1.6km (1 mile) east of the Old City. You'll find taxis lined up in front of Avila's railway station and at the more central Plaza Santa Teresa. For taxi information, call *©* **92-035-35-45.**

Buses leave Madrid daily from Estación Sur de Autobuses at Calle Méndez Alvaro. In Avila, the bus terminal (*©* **92-022-01-54;** www.avanza bus.com) is at the corner of avenidas Madrid and Portugal, northeast of the center of town. A one-way ticket from Madrid costs 7.50€.

To drive here, exit Madrid at its northwest perimeter and head northwest on Highway N-VI (A-6) toward La Coruña, eventually forking southwest to Avila. Driving time is around 1¼ hours.

VISITOR INFORMATION The **tourist information office,** Av. Madrid 39 (*©* **92-022-59-69;** www.avilaturismo.com), is open daily 9am to 2pm and 5 to 8pm. July to September it is open Monday to Thursday 9am to 8pm, and Friday and Saturday 9am to 9pm.

Exploring Avila

Begun on orders of Alfonso VI as part of the general Reconquest of Spain from the Moors, the 11th-century **Walls of Avila ★★**, built over Roman fortifications, took 9 years to complete. Averaging 10m (33 ft.) in height, they have 88 semicircular towers and more than 2,300 battlements. Of the nine gateways, the two most famous are the St. Vincent and the Alcázar, both on the eastern side. In many respects the walls are best viewed from the west. Whichever point of view you prefer, you can drive alongside the walls' entire length of 2km (1¼ miles).

Basílica de San Vicente ★★ Outside the city walls, at the northeast corner of the medieval ramparts, this Romanesque-Gothic church in faded sandstone encompasses styles from the 12th to the 14th centuries. It consists of a huge nave and a trio of apses. The eternal struggle between good and evil is depicted on a cornice on the southern portal. The **western portal ★★**, dating from the 13th century, contains Romanesque carvings. Inside is the tomb of St. Vincent, martyred on this site in the 4th century. The tomb's medieval carvings, which depict his torture and subsequent martyrdom, are fascinating.

Plaza de San Vicente. *©* **92-025-52-30.** Admission 1.60€. Daily 10am–1:30pm and 4–6:30pm.

Carmelitas Descalzas de San José (Barefoot Carmelites of St. Joseph)

Also known as the Convento de las Madres (Convent of the Mothers), this is the first convent founded by St. Teresa, who started the Reform of Carmel in

1562. There are two churches: a primitive one, where the first Carmelite nuns took the habit; and one built by Francisco de Mora, architect for Philip III, after the saint's death. The museum displays many relics, including, of all things, St. Teresa's left clavicle.

Las Madres 4. ℭ **92-022-21-27.** Admission to museum 1€. Apr–Oct daily 10am–1:30pm and 4–7pm; Nov–Mar daily 10am–1:30pm and 3–6pm. From Plaza de Santa Teresa and its nearby Church of San Pedro, follow Calle del Duque de Alba for about 2 blocks.

Catedral de Avila ★★ Built into the old ramparts of Avila, this cold, austere cathedral and fortress (begun in 1099) bridges the gap between the Romanesque and the Gothic and, as such, enjoys a certain distinction in Spanish architecture. One local writer compared it to a granite mountain. The unusual interior is built with a mottled red-and-white stone.

Like most European cathedrals, Avila lost its purity of design through the years as new chapels and wings—one completely in the Renaissance mode— were added. A Dutch artist, Cornelius, designed the seats of the choir stalls, also in Renaissance style, and the principal chapel holds a reredos showing the life of Christ by Pedro Berruguete, Juan de Borgoña, and Santa Cruz. Behind the chapel, the tomb of Bishop Alonso de Madrigal—nicknamed "El Tostado" ("the Parched One")—because of its brownish color—is Vasco de Zarza's masterpiece. The Cathedral Museum contains a laminated gold ceiling, a 15th-century triptych, a copy of an El Greco painting, vestments, and 15th-century songbooks.

Plaza de la Catedral. ℭ **92-021-16-41.** Admission 4€ adults, free for children 9 and under. Aug–Oct daily 10am–7pm; Nov–Mar Mon–Fri 10am–5pm, Sat 10am–6pm, Sun noon–5pm; Apr–July Mon–Fri 10am–6pm, Sat 10am–7pm, Sun noon–6pm.

Convento de Santa Teresa This 17th-century convent and baroque church, 2 blocks southwest of Plaza de la Victoria, stands at the site of St. Teresa's birth. To the right of the convent, the tiny **Sala de Reliquias** exhibits some of her relics, including a finger from her right hand, the sole of one of her sandals, and a cord with which she flagellated herself.

Plaza de la Santa 2. ℭ **92-021-10-30** or 92-022-07-08. Admission 2€ (Sala de Reliquias free admission). Museum May–Sept daily 10am–1:30pm and 3:30–5:30pm; Oct–Apr Tues–Sun 10am–1:30pm and 3:30–5:30pm. Sala de Reliquias daily 9:30am–1:30pm and 3:30–7:30pm.

Where to Stay in Avila

Avila is a summer resort—a refuge from Castilian heat—but the hotels are few in number, and the Spanish book nearly all the rooms in July and August. Make your reservation in advance. **Las Cancelas** (p. 226) also rents rooms.

EXPENSIVE

Parador de Avila ★ Two blocks northwest of Plaza de la Victoria, this *parador* stands on a ridge overlooking the banks of the Adaja River. In the 15th century it was known as the Palace of Benavides; its facade forms part of the square. Through the palace's dignified entryway, most of its public lounges open onto a central courtyard with an inner gallery of columns. The refurbished guest rooms contain tasteful furnishings: stone fireplaces, polished tile floors, old chests, leather armchairs, paintings, and sculptures. The guest rooms, generally midsize, come with modern comforts, including good mattresses and tiled bathrooms.

Marqués de Camales de Chozas 2, 05001 Avila. © **92-021-13-40.** Fax 92-022-61-66. www.
parador.es. 61 units. 127€–240€ double; 286€–309€ suite. AE, DC, MC, V. Free outside parking;
garage 15€. **Amenities:** Restaurant; bar; room service. *In room:* A/C, TV, hair dryer, minibar,
Wi-Fi (free).

MODERATE

Gran Hotel Palacio de Valderrábanos ★★ Immediately adjacent to the
cathedral's front entrance, behind an entryway that is a marvel of medieval stonework, this is one of the most elegant and historic hotels of Castile. Originally
built in the 1300s as a private home by an early bishop of Avila (and a member
of the Valderrábanos family), it contains a once-fortified lookout tower (which
now houses a suite), high-beamed ceilings, and intricately chiseled stonework.
The public rooms have a somber elegance, with slightly faded baronial furniture
that adds to the old-fashioned feeling. If possible, ask for a unit overlooking the
cathedral. Guest rooms come in a variety of shapes, but each is usually midsize
and well furnished.

Plaza de la Catedral 9, 05001 Avila. © **92-021-10-23.** Fax 92-025-16-91. www.palacio
valderrabanoshotel.com. 73 units. 49€–120€ double; 140€ suite. AE, DC, MC, V. Parking 10€ per
day. Bus: 1, 2, or 3. **Amenities:** Restaurant; bar; babysitting; room service. *In room:* A/C, TV, hair
dryer, minibar, Wi-Fi (6€ per hour).

Hotel Reina Isabel ★ Cited for its elegant decoration, this 1997 hotel stands
behind a severe facade, but its tone warms considerably once you're inside. Rated
four stars by the government, it's about a 6-minute walk outside the walls of the
Old City. The interior is classically designed, with separate areas depicting various epochs in Spanish history, complete with furnishings and objets d'art from
the 14th to the 18th century, including a magnificent altarpiece from the 15th
century. The spacious guest rooms are similarly decorated and furnished with
classical motifs; they have marble floors and comfortable beds.

Paseo de la Estación 17, 05001 Avila. © **92-025-10-22.** Fax 92-025-11-73. www.reinaisabel.com.
60 units. 85€–125€ double; 165€ suite. Rates include buffet breakfast. AE, DC, MC, V. Parking 12€.
Amenities: Bar; room service; Wi-Fi (free, in lobby). *In room:* A/C, TV, hair dryer, minibar.

Palacio de Los Velada ★★★ When the Spanish chain Meliá opened this
splendid gem to guests in 1995, it quickly became the most sought-after hostelry
in the province, surpassing even the government-run *paradores*. Four centuries
ago, this palace sheltered the likes of Charles V and Philip II. Arrayed around a
central courtyard, today's hotel offers luxury.

The styling in the public rooms and the luxurious furnishings in the guest
rooms make even the *paradores* look as if they need face-lifts. Enjoying the best
location in town—right in the center near the cathedral—the hotel offers guests
the setting of a medieval palace filled with massive stones and antiques. All the
modern conveniences, including wide, comfortable beds, have been installed,
along with state-of-the-art plumbing.

Plaza de la Catedral 10, 05001 Avila. © **92-025-51-00.** Fax 92-025-49-00. www.veladahoteles.
com. 145 units. 80€–148€ double. AE, DC, MC, V. Parking 16€. **Amenities:** Restaurant; bar; Internet (free, in lobby); room service. *In room:* A/C, TV, hair dryer, minibar, Wi-Fi (free).

INEXPENSIVE

El Rastro ✦ Situated near the junction of calles Caballeros and Cepadas, this restored inn is the best choice for the bargain hunter. Few visitors know that you can spend the night at this old Castilian inn built into the city walls. The small guest rooms, basic and well maintained, include immaculate bathrooms.

Plaza del Rastro 1, 05001 Avila. ✆ **92-021-12-18.** Fax 92-025-16-26. www.elrastroavila.com. 19 units. 65€ double. AE, DC, MC, V. Free parking. **Amenities:** Restaurant; bar; Wi-Fi (free, in lobby). *In room:* A/C, TV, no phone.

Gran Hostal San Segundo This small hotel and restaurant is just outside the immense walls surrounding the historic center of Avila. The elegant 19th-century building itself has been renovated to maintain its historical charm and incorporate modern comfort. The soft salmon-hued reception rooms have high ceilings, and the midsize guest rooms are spotlessly clean, simple, and unpretentious.

San Segundo 30, 05001 Avila. ✆ **92-025-25-90.** Fax 92-025-27-90. www.hsansegundo.com. 14 units. 45€–70€ double. AE, DC, MC, V. Free street parking. **Amenities:** Restaurant; bar. *In room:* TV, hair dryer, Wi-Fi (free).

Hospedería de Bracamonte ★★ 🎁 The most tranquil spot in town is this little gem decorated in classic Castilian style. It lies 1 block north of Plaza de Victoria, the main square within the city walls. A restful and quiet oasis, it has a number of charming features, including a lovely patio and a dark wood Castilian motif throughout. Converted to a small inn in 1989, the *hostería* retains some of its aristocratic origins as the town house of Gov. Don Juan Teherán y Monjaraz. Guest rooms are spacious and have whitewashed walls; some have fireplaces and four-poster beds.

Bracamonte 6, 05001 Avila. ✆ **92-025-12-80.** Fax 92-025-38-38. www.hospederiade bracamonte.com. 23 units. 50€–73€ double. MC, V. Free street parking. **Amenities:** Restaurant; bar. *In room:* TV, minibar.

Where to Dine in Avila

MODERATE

El Molino de la Losa ★ ☺ CASTILIAN Within a 15-minute walk west of the town center, this restaurant consistently serves some of the finest food in town. It lies within a stately looking ocher-fronted building—once a 15th-century mill—that is adjacent to the historic bridge, Puente Río Adaja. Inside it has a trussed ceiling, thick walls, and elegantly rustic furnishings. If you can overlook the waitstaff, who seem to have trained in a "boot camp," you'll enjoy a really fine cuisine, including the house specialty, lamb roasted in a wooden oven from the Middle Ages. Start with Iberian ham, a plate of chorizo, or perhaps a salad of smoked salmon. The chefs also specialize in roast suckling pig and a number of good-tasting fish dishes, such as hake, which comes as a surprise in inland Avila. In the garden is a small playground for kids.

Bajada de la Losa 12. ✆ **92-021-11-01.** www.elmolinodelalosa.com. Reservations recommended. Main courses 12€–30€. AE, MC, V. Tues–Sun 1:30–4pm and 9–11pm.

Las Cancelas ★ ✦ CASTILIAN Las Cancelas is where the locals go, whereas tourists crowd into several restaurants nearby. You get good food, regional specialties, a time-mellowed Castilian ambience, and affordable prices—a rather unbeatable combination. We begin our evenings in Avila at the restaurant's tapas bar up front. Tasty tidbits, almost mystical conversations, and good wine flow freely. Later you can head back to the dining room, on a stone-columned patio where paper covers the old wooden tables. A carafe of regional wine arrives at your table as you tear off hunks of freshly baked bread and wait for seasonal dishes to emerge from the kitchen. Meats are roasted in a wood-fired oven and are the house specialties. We can never resist the *chuletón de Avila,* a mammoth T-bone steak and the chef's specialty. Platters of roast chicken, baked lamb, and other delights will also tempt you.

This Castilian inn is also one of the bargain places to stay in Avila, offering 14 small but modernized and comfortable **guest rooms,** each with private bathroom with shower, costing only 78€ for a double. Each unit has a TV, phone, and (in some cases) air-conditioning.

Cruz Viejo 6. © **92-021-22-49.** www.lascancelas.com. Reservations recommended. Main courses 13€–22€. AE, DC, MC, V. Daily 1:30–4pm and 8:30–11pm.

INEXPENSIVE

Hospedería de Bracamonte SPANISH/CASTILIAN Though parts of the building are 400 years old, every effort was made in subsequent remodelings to duplicate the original ceiling beams, rough-textured plaster, and artfully chiseled stone of the original design. The kitchen itself focuses on grills and old-fashioned roasts, many of which the regular guests might remember fondly from childhood. Examples are roasted tender baby lamb with herbs and garlic; grilled pork or veal chops; roasted chicken; all manner of steaks, cutlets, and ribs; and the occasional seafood. The largest of the restaurant's four dining rooms is usually devoted to the care and feeding of busloads of groups traveling together, so you might find a bit more intimacy in one of the three smaller dining areas.

Bracamonte 6. © **92-025-12-80.** Reservations recommended. Main courses 8€–22€. MC, V. Wed–Mon 1–4pm and 8pm–midnight.

Mesón del Rastro CASTILIAN An old inn built into the 11th-century town walls, this place serves typical Castilian dishes, with more attention given to freshness and preparation than to culinary flamboyance. Specialties include roast baby lamb (prepared at least four different ways) and tender white veal, raised in the region and known for its succulence. Dessert recipes have been passed down from Avila's nuns. Try, if you dare, the highly touted *yemas de Santa Teresa* (St. Teresa's candied egg yolk); when we dined here with travel expert Arthur Frommer himself, he found it a particularly horrible dessert—and we agree. Yet Avila residents keep praising it as a specialty. To our taste, there are far better selections on the menu. They also maintain **El Rastro,** a small hotel with 19 comfortable rooms (see above).

Plaza del Rastro 1. © **92-021-12-18.** Reservations required on weekends only. Main courses 8€–23€. AE, DC, MC, V. Daily 1–4pm and 9–11pm.

CUENCA ★★

161km (100 miles) E of Madrid, 325km (202 miles) SW of Zaragoza

This medieval town, once dominated by the Moors, is a spectacular sight with its *casas colgadas,* cliff-hanging houses set on multiple terraces that climb the impossibly steep sides of a ravine. The Júcar and Huécar rivers meet at the bottom.

Essentials

GETTING THERE **Trains** leave Madrid's Atocha railway station about four times throughout the day. Trains arrive in Cuenca's New Town at Paseo del Ferrocarril (📞 **90-224-02-02**; www.renfe.es), after a journey lasting anywhere from 2½ to 3 hours. A one-way ticket from Madrid costs 12€.

There are also about eight **buses** from Madrid every day. Buses arrive at Calle Fermín Caballero 20 (📞 **96-922-70-87** or 96-922-11-84; www.autores.net for information and schedules). A one-way fare costs 11€ to 15€.

Cuenca is the junction for several highways and about a dozen lesser roads that connect it to towns within its region. From Madrid, take the N-III to Tarancón, and then the N-400, which leads directly into Cuenca.

VISITOR INFORMATION The city **tourist information office,** Calle Alfonso VIII no. 2 (📞 **96-924-10-51**; www.cuenca.org), is open daily 9am to 8pm.

Exploring in & Around Cuenca

The chief sight of Cuenca is the **Old Town ★★** itself. Isolated from the rest of Spain, it requires a northern detour from the heavily traveled Valencia-to-Madrid road. Deep gorges give it an unreal quality, and eight old bridges, spanning two rivers, connect the ancient parts of town with the growing new sections. A footbridge is suspended over a 60m (197-ft.) drop.

Cuenca's streets are narrow and steep, often cobbled, and even the most athletic visitor will tire quickly. But you shouldn't miss it, even if you have to stop

The bridge across the Júcar gorge, leading into Cuenca.

and rest periodically. At night you're in for a special treat when the **casas colgadas** ★ are illuminated. Also, try to drive almost to the top of the castle-dominated hill. The road gets rough as you approach the end, but the view makes the effort worthwhile.

If you have the time, you can make a side trip to the not-that-enchanting **Ciudad Encantada (Enchanted City),** Carretera de la Sierra, about 40km (25 miles) to the northeast of Cuenca. Storms and underground waters have created a city here out of large rocks and boulders, shaping them into bizarre designs: a seal, an elephant, a Roman bridge. Take CU-912, turning northeast onto CU-913. Ciudad Encantada is signposted.

Catedral de Cuenca Begun in the 12th century, this Gothic cathedral was influenced by England's Norman style, becoming the only Anglo-Norman cathedral in Spain. Part of it collapsed in the 20th century, but it has been restored. A national monument filled with religious art treasures, the cathedral dominates Plaza Mayor in the center of town. The cathedral's *museo diocesano* exhibits two canvases by El Greco, a collection of Flemish tapestries (some beautifully designed), and a statue of the Virgen del Sagrario from the 1100s.

Plaza Mayor de Pío XII. Ⓒ **96-922-46-26.** Free admission to cathedral, 2€ to museum. July–Sept Mon–Fri 10am–2pm and 4–7pm, Sat 10am–7pm, Sun 10am–6:30pm; Oct–Apr daily 10:30am–2pm and 4–6pm; May–June Mon–Fri 10am–2pm and 4–7pm, Sat 10:30am–2pm and 4–7pm, Sun 10:30am–2pm and 5–6:30pm. Bus: 1 or 2.

Museo de Arte Abstracto Español ★★ North of Plaza Mayor, housed in a cliff-hanging dwelling, this ranks as one of the finest museums of its kind in Spain. It was conceived by painter Fernando Zóbel, who donated it in 1980 to the Fundación Juan March. The most outstanding abstract Spanish painters are represented, including Rafael Canogar (especially his *Toledo*), Luis Feito, Zóbel himself, Tàpies, Eduardo Chillida, Gustavo Torner, Gerardo Rueda, Sempere, Cuixart, and Antonio Saura. (See Saura's grotesque Geraldine Chaplin and also his study of Brigitte Bardot, a vision of horror, making the French actress look like an escapee from Picasso's *Guernica*.)

Calle los Canónigos s/n. Ⓒ **96-921-29-83.** www.march.es. Admission 3€ adults, 1.50€ students. Tues–Fri 11am–2pm and 4–6pm; Sat 11am–2pm and 4–8pm; Sun 11am–2:30pm. Bus: 1 or 2.

Where to Stay in Cuenca

Hotel NH Ciudad de Cuenca ★ Since you can't always get into the *parador* (see below), consider this stellar selection the second-best choice in town. In operation since the mid-1990s, it lies in a rapidly developing residential area close to Old Town. Its exterior design is severe and clinical, but its interior is filled with comfort and grace notes. The wood-floored units are comfortable and well appointed, with well-selected upholstery, comfortable beds, and fully equipped bathrooms.

○ The Hanging Houses of Cuenca

You can view one of Cuenca's most thrilling sights by walking the streets at night to admire the illuminated *casas colgadas* (hanging houses) of the town. Dating from the 14th century, these famous houses seem to hang over the deep Huécar ravine. At times they are built so close to the edge that you feel they are about to plunge over the edge.

Cuenca's *casas colgadas,* or hanging houses.

Ronda de San José 1, 16004 Cuenca. ℂ **96-923-05-02.** Fax 96-923-05-03. www.nh-hotels.com. 74 units. 66€–140€ double; 156€–180€ suite. AE, DC, MC, V. Parking 15€. Bus: 2. **Amenities:** Restaurant; bar; babysitting; exercise room; room service; sauna. *In room:* A/C, TV, hair dryer, minibar, Wi-Fi (8€ per hour).

Leonor de Aquitania Perched high on the hillside above an almost sheer drop, the hotel enjoys spectacular views of both the Old Town of Cuenca from one angle and the narrow valley rising from the harsh though beautiful precipice opposite. The reception rooms have been maintained in extremely good taste, and the hotel evokes an elegantly restrained and comfortable charm. The midsize rooms are exceedingly well cared for. The Hebrea Hermosa (Beautiful Jewish Maiden) suite is one of the most charming in this quiet medieval city.

Calle San Pedro 60, 16001 Cuenca. ℂ **96-923-10-00.** Fax 96-923-10-04. www.hotelleonor deaquitania.com. 49 units. 103€–120€ double; 178€–199€ suite. AE, DC, MC, V. **Amenities:** Restaurant; bar; babysitting; room service; Wi-Fi (free in lobby). *In room:* TV, hair dryer, minibar.

Parador de Cuenca ★★★ This government-sponsored hotel, which opened for business in 1992, occupies the dignified premises of what was originally built in 1523 as a Dominican monastery. A noteworthy example of late Gothic architecture, it lies on a hillside above Cuenca, about a half-mile northwest of the town's historic center. It is clearly the town's prestigious address. Its timeless three stories are decorated with masses of intricately chiseled 16th-century stonework (some enhanced with glass panels overlooking the river), a church, and a severely beautiful cloister. The two floors of midsize guest rooms are comfortably traditional.

Subida a San Pablo s/n, 16001 Cuenca. ☎ **96-923-23-20.** Fax 96-923-25-34. www.parador.es. 63 units. 148€–184€ double; 296€–320€ suite. AE, DC, MC, V. Parking 18€. **Amenities:** Restaurant; bar; exercise room; outdoor pool; room service; sauna; outdoor tennis court. *In room:* A/C, TV, hair dryer, minibar, Wi-Fi (.50€ per hour).

Posada de San José ★ 🛍 In its understated and unpretentious way, this is the most appealing lodging in Cuenca, perched as it is high above the gorge of the River Huécar, in Cuenca's historic core. A short walk from the cathedral, the posada sits atop a cliff overlooking the forbidding depths of a gorge. It was originally built in the 1700s by the local church as the headquarters for its choir. In 1983, the then-decrepit building was bought by Antonio and Canada-born Jennifer Cortinas and reopened as an inn. They lavished time and money on its restoration. Accommodations are comfortable and dignified, yet retain an almost monastic simplicity, with white walls, beamed ceilings, and the kind of dark, handcrafted Iberian furniture you usually associate with a monastery.

Calle Julián Romero 4, 16001 Cuenca. ☎ **96-921-13-00.** Fax 96-923-03-65. www.posadasan jose.com. 22 units, 18 with bathroom. 40€–50€ double without bathroom; 78€–157€ double with bathroom. AE, DC, MC, V. Free parking. **Amenities:** Bar. *In room:* No phone.

Where to Dine in Cuenca

El Figón de Pedro ★ CASTILIAN Set in the business section of New Town at the foot of the hills that lead you to the wonders of medieval Cuenca, this restaurant belongs to one of Spain's most celebrated restaurateurs, Mercedes Torres Ortega. Given this, and by turning a quick blind eye to the abundance of late 1960s concrete, the location is well worth a visit. The air-conditioned restaurant is relatively intimate, with 13 tables and the traditional Castilian decor of plates on walls and folkloric memorabilia. The cuisine, however, is not half as predictable. The *morteruelo* (local pâté made from partridge, pork, ham, and hare) should definitely be sampled, as should the gazpacho and *bacalao ajo arriero* (purée of cod, garlic, eggs, and olive oil).

Cervantes 13. ☎ **96-922-68-21.** www.figondepedro.com. Reservations recommended. Main courses 10€–22€. AE, DC, MC, V. Daily 1:30–4pm; Mon–Sat 9–11pm.

Mesón Casas Colgadas ★★ SPANISH/CASTILIAN/INTERNATIONAL One of the most spectacular dining rooms in Spain stands on one of the most precarious precipices in Cuenca. Established in the 1960s, it occupies a five-story, 19th-century house with sturdy supporting walls and beams. Pine balconies and windows overlook the ravine below and the hills beyond. In fact, it's the most photographed "suspended house" in town, and dinner here is worth every euro. The menu includes regional dishes and a variety of well-prepared international favorites. Drinks are served in the tavern room on street level, so even if you're not dining here, you may want to drop in for a drink and the view. You'll find the Mesón Casa Colgadas just south of the cathedral and near the Museo de Arte Abstracto Español (see above).

Canónigos s/n. ☎ **96-922-35-09.** www.mesoncasascolgadas.com. Reservations recommended. Main courses 15€–24€; fixed-price menus 27€–33€; tasting menu 40€. AE, DC, MC, V. Wed–Mon 1–4pm; Wed–Sun 9–11pm.

SORIA ★

225km (140 miles) NE of Madrid; 76km (47 miles) N of Medinaceli

This small, vibrant city on the Castilian plain is the most neglected of all the "art cities" that envelop the periphery of Madrid. Its praises were first sung by Antonio Machado (1875–1939), the famous Sevillan poet who wrote *Campos de Castilla* (1912). When he came to live in Soria, he wrote of "*Soria fría, Soria pura*" (cold Soria, pure Soria). After the death of his child bride, Leonor, Machado departed in 1912.

Soria is not only the name of the city but the name of the province over which it presides. Today the town of 40,000 is visited for its Romanesque churches, for its raucous Fiesta de San Juan in late June, and for its summer concerts and street theater. Lying on the banks of the River Duero, the town has many historic squares filled with bars offering outdoor seating. Ignore the tacky modern suburbs that surround Soria, and head instead for the historic core where the action is.

Essentials

GETTING THERE Trains leave Monday to Friday from Madrid to Soria (trip time: 3 hr.). A one-way fare costs 14€. In addition, **ALSA** (© **90-242-22-42;** www.alsa.es) runs daily **buses** to and from Madrid to Soria that take only 2½ hours, with a one-way fare costing 14€. Motorists leave Madrid heading east on the A2 to Medinaceli, at which point they cut north along N-III into Soria.

VISITOR INFORMATION The **Soria Tourist Office,** at Calle Medinaceli 2 (© **97-521-20-52;** www.turismocastillayleon.com), is open July to September 15, Monday to Thursday and Sunday 9am to 8pm; Friday and Saturday 9am to 8pm. Off-season hours are daily 9am to 2pm and 5 to 8pm.

Seeing the Sights in Soria

Allow about 2 hours (more if you plan to stop inside some churches) to explore the **Casco Viejo ★★**, the center of town. Head first for the Plaza Mayor, the main square in the heart of Old Town, and wander at your leisure through the narrow, character-filled streets branching off from here.

Ermita de San Saturio Getting to this 18th-century chapel constructed on a steep rocky hillside is part of the fun. You'll **stroll ★★** along the banks of the Duero River, traveling a pathway lined with poplars and following the footsteps of the poet Machado. He traversed the 1.5km (1 mile) to the little chapel at least once or twice a week during his stay in Soria. This is one of the most colorful and romantic walks in the province.

You begin at the Monastery of San Palo, and the footpath is marked. The shaded path leads to the cave where the holy man San Saturio (493–568) sat in meditation most of his life. He is today the patron saint of Soria. An octagonal chapel is built into the rock near where he lived, and it's covered in its interior with frescoes from the 18th century.

The view from the countryside here is panoramic. The present temple itself is baroque in style and is decorated with numerous works of art, including paintings, murals, and Gothic statues of the crucified Christ as well as the Virgin with the baby Jesus.

The precarious Ermita de San Saturio.

Paseo San Saturio. ℭ **97-518-07-03.** Free admission. July–Aug Mon–Sat 10:30am–2pm and 4:30–8:30pm; Apr–June, and Sept–Oct Mon–Sat 10:30am–2pm and 4:30–7:30pm; Nov–Mar Mon–Sat 10:30am–2pm and 4:30–6:30pm. Closed year-round Sun.

Museo Numantino ★ Founded in 1919, the museum of Numancia is filled with archaeological artifacts, many of which date from prehistoric times. From the Paleolithic age to today, the exhibits are wide ranging, with some of the most noteworthy pieces being Roman artifacts. One section on the top floor is filled with painted ceramics from the ruins of the old city of Numancia. The ruins lie 7km (4⅓ miles) northeast of Soria. The city of Numancia lives today in legend because its citizens heroically resisted invaders from Carthage for 8 months, killing themselves and burning their city when the battle turned against them.

Paseo del Espolón. ℭ **97-522-13-97.** Admission 1.20€ adults, free for children 17 and under. July–Sept Tues–Sat 10am–2pm and 5–8pm, Sun 10am–2pm; Oct–June Tues–Sat 10am–2pm and 4–7pm, Sun 10am–2pm.

San Juan de Duero On the far bank of the Duero, this church and cloister were founded by the Hospitallers of St. John of Jerusalem in the 12th century. It flourished until the 18th century. Today it is visited for its art and architecture, especially the ruins of the graceful **cloister ★**, which dates from the 12th and 13th centuries. It shows an obvious Moorish influence. Inside the church is a small museum filled with Romanesque artifacts.

Piso de las Animas. ℭ **97-523-02-18.** Admission .60€. July–Sept Tues–Sat 10am–2pm and 5–8pm; Oct–June Tues–Sat 10am–2pm and 4–7pm; Sun (year-round) 10am–2pm.

San Juan de Rabanera One of the town's Romanesque churches, this is the most harmonious in its lines. Constructed in the 12th century, it was restored in the early 20th century. The portal depicts the major events in the life of St. John. Inside, there are Gothic, even Byzantine, architectural decorations, along with Byzantine-style vaulting. Look for two intriguing crucifixes—one a Romanesque creation over the altar, the other, in the more flamboyant baroque style, in the north transept.

Plaza de San Esteban. No phone. Free admission. Irregular hours.

Santo Domingo ★ This church has one of the finest Romanesque facades in Spain, well worth a long look. The west front contains two tiers of "blind" arcades and a single, beautifully carved and **central portal** ★★, the most elegant in the entire province. The founders of this church were Alfonso VIII and his wife, Eleanor of England, and also the Duchess of Gascony. Carved scenes illustrate early chapters of Genesis and *Old Men of the Apocalypse* playing stringed instruments. The most gruesome depiction is the *Massacre of the Innocents*. The interior of the church was redone in the 16th century.

Calla Aduana Vieja. No phone. Free admission. Irregular hours (if the door is open, you can enter).

Where to Stay in Soria

Hostería Solar de Tejada ★ 👔 This is the most tranquil place to stay in town, and also the most traditional and characteristic of the region. All that, plus it's the best value. Bedrooms are furnished with a certain charm, often with wood furniture. This old house has been brought up-to-date, although the original bathrooms remain, but the plumbing has been modernized. We find the staff the most hospitable in town. Even though there's no restaurant on site, there are many dining places and cafeterias within an easy walk from the doorstep.

Claustrilla 1, 42002 Soria. ☏ **97-523-00-54.** Fax 97-523-00-54. www.hosteriasolardetejada. com. 18 units. 56€ double. MC, V. **Amenities:** Wi-Fi (free, in lobby). *In room:* A/C, TV, minibar.

Hotel Alfonso VIII ★ Despite its plain modern and unadorned facade, this offers the best accommodations right in town, though it doesn't have the charm of the more traditional Hostería Solar de Tejada (see above). It is the only government-rated four-star hotel in the center. The midsize bedrooms are done in a simple but tasteful style and have exceptionally comfortable beds. The breakfast buffet is the best in town, and the on-site restaurant, though nothing special, serves a first-class Castilian cuisine, mainly to hotel guests.

Calle de Alfonso VIII, no. 10, 42003 Soria. ☏ **97-522-62-11.** Fax 97-521-36-65. www.hotelhusa alfonsoviii.com. 81 units. 86€–125€ double. AE, DC, MC, V. Parking 15€. **Amenities:** Restaurant; bar; room service. *In room:* A/C, TV, hair dryer, minibar.

Parador Soria—Hotel Antonio Machado ★★★ We'd stay here just for the views of old Soria and the Duero River as well as the ruins of an ancient castle. The *parador* is named after the Sevillan writer Antonio Machado. Pictures of the poet and extracts from his works are found in many of the public rooms. Lying on a hilltop, enveloped by parklike grounds, this modern *parador* evokes a mountain ski lodge. Wood floors and contemporary wood furniture give a fresh aura to the place. The sleek and modern bedrooms are midsize, and many open onto views; bathrooms are state-of-the art. The on-site **restaurant** is a bit expensive but features such luxury dishes as pheasant pâté or roast suckling pig. Take Calle de Santiago to the *parador,* going by the church and burial grounds of El Espino, where Machado's teenage wife, Leonor, is buried.

Parque de Castillo, 42005 Soria. ☏ **97-524-08-00.** Fax 97-524-08-03. www.parador.es. 67 units. 148€–240€ double. AE, DC, MC, V. Free parking. **Amenities:** Restaurant; bar; room service. *In room:* A/C, TV, minibar, Wi-Fi (free).

Where to Dine in Soria

Fogón del Salvador ★★ CASTILIAN In the exact center of the Old Town, this restaurant serves first-rate regional food and has its own kind of charm, almost a throwback to Franco's Spain. It prepares an ambitious menu, including a full array of succulent grilled beefsteaks. The waiters make it clear that their beef originates from bulls, not cows. Steaks are priced by the gram. Another specialty is roasted *chuletóns,* or regional sausages. Begin perhaps with a terrine of duck liver with pistachios drizzled with olive oil. Another delectable main dish is thin-sliced carpaccio of beef with caramelized onions. The restaurant prepares the best *menú de degustación* in town.

Plaza del Salvador. € **97-523-01-94.** www.fogonsalvador.com. Reservations required. Main courses 22€–34€. Fixed-price menus 18€–40€. AE, MC, V. Daily 11am–4pm and 8pm–midnight. Closed Tues Oct 16–May 14.

Mesón Castellano ★ CASTILIAN Across from the Ayuntamiento (town hall), this is the most regional restaurant in the Old Town. It's cozy and inviting, with specialties such as veal chops *(chuletón de ternera)* cooked succulently over an open fire. Try such rural dishes as cured pork sausage eaten *con la mano* (by hand), or soaked bread crumbs fried with peppers and bacon *(migas pastoriles)*. Fish is shipped in, including hake, which can be boiled or grilled to your specifications. A good dessert is the boiled pears in a red wine sauce.

Plaza Mayor 2. € **97-521-30-45.** Reservations recommended. Main courses 22€–35€. AE, DC, MC, V. Wed–Mon 1–4pm and 9pm–1am.

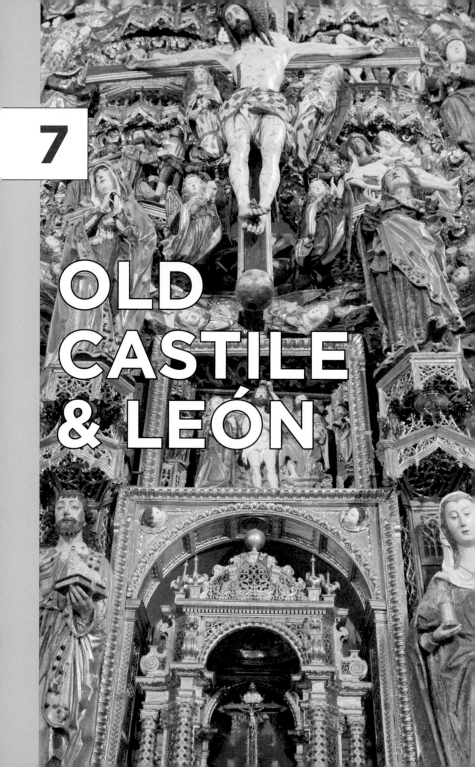

7

OLD CASTILE & LEÓN

Spain owes much to Castile, Aragón, and León, since these three kingdoms helped unify the various regions of the country. Modern Spain was conceived when Isabella of Castile married Ferdinand of Aragón in 1469. Five years later she was proclaimed queen of Castile and León. The Moors were eventually driven out of Granada, Spain was conquered, and Columbus sailed to America—all during the reign of these two Catholic monarchs.

This proud but controversial queen and her unscrupulous husband fashioned an empire whose influence extended throughout Spain, Europe, and the New World. The power once held by Old Castile shifted long ago to Madrid, but there remain many reminders of its storied past.

In the ancient kingdom of León, which was eventually annexed to Castile, you'll find Salamanca, Zamora, and the provincial capital of León. Today the region is known for its many castles.

In Old Castile, we cover the inland provincial capital of Valladolid, where Isabella married Ferdinand and where a brokenhearted Christopher Columbus died on May 19, 1506. From here we move on to Burgos, once the capital of Old Castile. Vivar, a small town nearby, produced Spain's greatest national hero, El Cid, who conquered the Moorish kingdom of Valencia.

For other destinations in the region, see chapter 6, p. 190.

CIUDAD RODRIGO ★

87km (54 miles) SW of Salamanca, 285km (177 miles) W of Madrid

A walled town dating from the Roman Empire, **Ciudad Rodrigo** is known for its 16th- and 17th-century town houses, built by the conquistadors. It was founded in the 12th century, by Count Rodrigo González, and today is a national monument. Located near the Portuguese frontier, it stands high on a hilltop and is known for the familiar silhouette of the square tower of its Alcázar. This walled part of the city is referred to as the Casco Viejo.

The ramparts were built in the 12th century along Roman foundations. Several stairways lead up to a 1.6km (1-mile) sentry path. You can wander these ramparts at leisure and then walk through the streets, along which you'll find many churches and mansions. It is not one chief monument that is the allure, but rather the city as a whole.

Plaza Mayor ★ is a showpiece of 17th-century architecture, with two Renaissance palaces. This is the city's main square.

The town's major attraction is its **Cathedral of Santa María ★** (© 92-348-14-24), which combines Romanesque and Gothic styles with a neoclassical tower. It was mostly built between 1170 and 1230, although subsequent centuries have seen more additions. It can be reached going east of

FACING PAGE: **The sculpted altar of Cartuja de Miraflores.**

Plaza Mayor through Plaza de San Salvador. The **Renaissance altar** ★ on the north aisle is an acclaimed work of ecclesiastical art; look also for the **Virgin portal** ★ at the west door, which dates from the 1200s. For 2€ you'll be admitted to the **cloisters** ★, done in a variety of architectural styles; among them is a Plateresque door. Hours are daily 10am to 1pm and 4 to 7pm.

Your transportation in Ciudad Rodrigo will be your trusty feet—walking is the only way to explore the city. Pick up a map at the tourist office (see below).

Essentials

GETTING THERE The only real way to get here is from Salamanca. Because **train** service is infrequent and the railway station is a long way from the walls of the Old City, it's easier to take the bus from Salamanca; you'll get off at the Ciudad Rodrigo station at Calle Campo de Toledo (✆ **92-346-02-17**). There are daily **buses** from Salamanca (trip time: 1 hr.). The cost is 9.90€ one-way.

The N-620 is the main road from both Salamanca and Portugal. Driving time from Salamanca is about 1¼ hours.

VISITOR INFORMATION The **tourist office,** Plaza Amayuelas 5 (✆ **92-346-05-61;** www.ciudadrodrigo.net), is open Monday to Friday 9am to 2pm and 5 to 7pm, and Saturday and Sunday from 10am to 2pm and 5 to 8pm.

SPECIAL EVENTS Ciudad Rodrigo's Carnaval festivities in February feature a running of the bulls, traditional dances, and costumes.

Where to Stay in Ciudad Rodrigo

Conde Rodrigo I Its central location next to the cathedral is a big plus for this government-rated three-star hotel; try for a room opening onto the square. The renovated rooms are small and totally devoid of style, but they're comfortable. Bathrooms have tub/shower combos. The building itself has some medieval flavor, with its thick walls of chiseled stone. Public parking is available off-street.

Plaza de San Salvador 9, 37500 Ciudad Rodrigo. ✆**92-346-14-04.** Fax 92-346-14-08. www. conderodrigo.com. 34 units. 60€–75€ double. DC, MC, V. Parking 10€. **Amenities:** Restaurant; bar. *In room:* A/C, TV, hair dryer, minibar.

Parador de Ciudad Rodrigo ★★ ☺ Now restored, this government-affiliated hostelry, on a hill overlooking Río Agueda, is easily the town's leading inn. It is constructed on the site of a 12th-century castle that was built at the command of Enrique II of Trastamara. The Torre del Homenaje defines the profile of Ciudad Rodrigo; it was once the seat of the feudal court. The *parador* has several gates and what the Spanish call *miradores*—platforms offering panoramic views. Sunset watching is a popular pastime. The Gothic entrance bears the royal coat of arms and a plaque in Gothic letters. The tastefully furnished rooms offer more style and comfort than any other hotel in town, including the Conde Rodrigo. Try for a room overlooking the garden that runs down to the Agueda River.

Plaza del Castillo 1, 37500 Ciudad Rodrigo. ✆ **92-346-01-50.** Fax 92-346-04-04. www.parador. es. 35 units. 143€–155€ double; 215€–233€ double superior. AE, DC, MC, V. Free parking. **Amenities:** Restaurant; bar; children's center; room service. *In room:* A/C, TV, hair dryer, minibar.

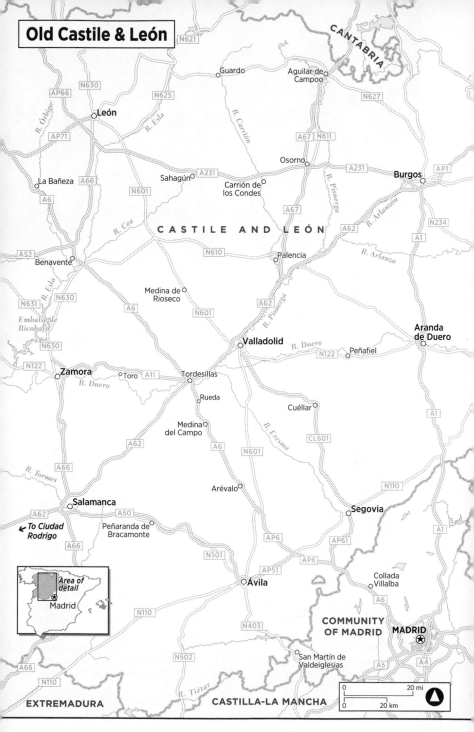

Old Castile & León

CANTABRIA

N621

AP66
N630
N625
Guardo
Aguilar de
Campoo
N627

León
R. Orbigo
R. Esla
R. Carrión
A67 N611

AP71
Osorno
A231
Burgos
AP1

La Bañeza
A66
Sahagún
A231
Carrión de
los Condes
R. Pisuerga
A62
N234

A6
N601
A67
A1

CASTILE AND LEÓN
R. Arlanzón

A52
N610
Palencia
R. Arlanza

Benavente
R. Esla

N631
N630
Medina de
Rioseco
A62
R. Pisuerga
Aranda
de Duero

Embalse de
Ricobayo
A6
N601

N630
Valladolid
R. Duero
Peñafiel

N122
N122
Peñafiel

Zamora
Toro
A11
Tordesillas
R. Duero

R. Duero
Rueda
Cuéllar
A1

Medina
del Campo
R. Eresma
CL601

A62
A6
N601

R. Tormes
Arévalo
N110

A66
Salamanca
A50
Segovia

To Ciudad
Rodrigo
A62
Peñaranda de
Bracamonte
A1

A66
N501
AP6
AP61

Area of
detail
AP51
AP6
Collada
Villalba

Madrid
Ávila
A6

N110
COMMUNITY
OF MADRID
MADRID

N403
A5
A4

N502
San Martín de
Valdeiglesias

A66
R. Tiétar
CASTILLA-LA MANCHA

N110
EXTREMADURA

0   20 mi
0   20 km

The Parador de Ciudad Rodrigo.

Where to Dine in Ciudad Rodrigo

Estoril 🦪 CASTILIAN/BASQUE This is not only one of the most centrally located restaurants in town but also one of the better dining rooms, topped only by Mayton (see below). This popular restaurant opened in 1967. The air-conditioned interior is decorated in typical regional style with a mixture of colonial and rustic accessories; there is also a covered patio with skylights. One corner is decorated with a bullfighting theme. Specialties of the house include roasted meats such as roast suckling pig, with a special emphasis on roasted goat. Seafood, including sole and hake, is presented in the Basque style. The seafood soup is particularly good. Everything is accompanied by a variety of regional wines, including Cosechero Rioja.

Calle General Pando 11. ✆ **92-348-24-81** or 92-346-05-50. www.restaurante-estoril.com. Reservations recommended. Main courses 12€–28€; fixed-price menus 12€–40€. DC, MC, V. Thurs–Tues 11am–midnight.

Mayton ★ 🦪 CASTILIAN Adjacent to Plaza Mayor, in a 12th-century building, is Mayton, one of the city's best restaurants. Its antique walls reverberate with atmosphere and legend. The dining room walls have been restored to reveal the original 12th-century rock walls. The moderately priced menu features mostly fresh fish and shellfish, done exceedingly well. Try *sopa castellana* (Castilian soup) for an appetizer, followed by *merluza* (hake) in green sauce. You can also order veal, as tender as that of Avila. Choose from more than 200 wines to accompany your meal. The place is air-conditioned.

La Colada 9. ✆ **92-346-07-20.** Reservations recommended. Main courses 10€–20€. AE, DC, MC, V. Tues–Sun 1–4pm; Tues–Sat 8pm–midnight.

SALAMANCA ★★★

204km (127 miles) NW of Madrid, 118km (73 miles) E of Portugal

This ancient city, famous for its university founded by Alfonso IX in the early 1200s, is well preserved, with turreted palaces, faded convents, Romanesque churches, and colleges that attract scholars from all over Europe. The best way to explore **Salamanca** is on foot, so arm yourself with a good map (available at the tourist office; see below) and set out to explore. Most attractions are within walking distance of the Plaza Mayor.

In its day, Salamanca was ranked with Oxford, Paris, and Bologna as one of "the four leading lights of the medieval world." Its intellectual life continues to this day, and a large invasion of American students adds to it in summer. The city's population has swelled to 180,000, but a provincial aura lingers.

Still a youthful, spirited place because of venerable Salamanca University, Salamanca has been named a World Heritage City by UNESCO.

Essentials

GETTING THERE Seven **trains** travel directly from Madrid's North station to Salamanca daily (trip time: 2½ hr.), arriving northeast of the town center on Plaza de la Estación de Ferrocarril (✆ **90-224-02-02;** www.renfe.es). The fare is 18€. More frequent are the rail connections between Salamanca, Avila, Ciudad Rodrigo, and Valladolid (around six trains each per day).

There's frequent daily **bus** service from Madrid (trip time: 2½ hr.). Salamanca's bus terminal is at Av. Filiberto Villalobos 71 (✆ **92-322-60-79**), northwest of the town center. There are also buses to Salamanca from Avila, Zamora, Valladolid, León, and Cáceres (2–13 per day, depending on the point of departure).

Salamanca isn't on a national highway, but roads converge here from such nearby cities as Avila, Valladolid, and Ciudad Rodrigo. One of the most heavily trafficked highways is the N-620, leading into Salamanca from both Barcelona and Portugal. From Madrid, take the N-VI northwest, forking off to Salamanca on the N-501.

VISITOR INFORMATION The **tourist office,** Plaza Mayor 32 (✆ **92-321-83-42;** www.aytosalamanca.es), is open Monday to Friday 9am to 2pm and 4 to 6:30pm, Saturday 10am to 6:30pm, and Sunday 10am to 2pm.

Exploring Salamanca

To start, spend as much time as you can at the **Plaza Mayor ★★★**, an 18th-century baroque square widely considered to be the most beautiful public plaza in Spain. No trip to this university town is complete unless you walk through the arcade of shops and feast your eyes on the honey-colored buildings. After this you'll understand why the *plaza mayor,* a town's main square, is an integral part of Spanish life. If it's a hot day and you want what everybody else in Plaza Mayor is drinking, stop at a cafe and order *leche helada,* a very refreshing vanilla-and-almond concoction.

Before reaching Plaza Mayor, you may want to admire the facade of the landmark **Casa de las Conchas (House of Shells) ★**, which appears as you walk north from the Patio de las Escuelas (site of the Universidad de Salamanca; see p. 244) on calles de Libreros and San Isidro. This much-photographed building is at the corner of Calle Rúa Mayor and Calle de la Compañía 2 (✆ **92-326-93-17**).

The restored 1483 house is noted for its facade of 400 simulated scallop shells. A professor of medicine at the university and a doctor at the court of Isabella created the house as a monument to Santiago de Compostela, the renowned pilgrimage site. The shell is the symbol of the Order of Santiago. You can visit the admission-free courtyard Monday to Friday 9am to 9pm, Saturday 9am to 2pm and 5 to 8pm, and Sunday 5 to 8pm.

Casa Museo Unamuno The poet and philosopher Miguel de Unamuno lived from 1900 to 1914 in this 18th-century home, located beside the university. Here he wrote many of the works that made him famous, including *San Manuel Bueno, Mártir*. You can see some of his notebooks and his library, along with many personal mementos.

Calle de Libreros 25. ℂ **92-329-44-00.** Admission 3€ adults, 1.50€ students. Tues–Fri 9:30am–1:30pm and 4–5:30pm; Sat–Sun 10:30am–1:30pm. Last tours leave 30 min. before closing time. Bus: 1.

Salamanca's main square, the Plaza Mayor.

Catedral Nueva (New Cathedral) ★★ The "new" cathedral, which dates from 1513, took more than 200 years to complete (it was finished in 1733), so the edifice represents many styles. It's classified as late Gothic, but you'll see baroque and Plateresque features as well. José Churriguera contributed some rococo elements. Its single most enthralling architectural feature is its **west front** ★★, which is divided below the windows into a quartet of wide bays corresponding to the ground plan. These bays are distinguished by pierced stonework carved as intricately as the keystones in the arches. The building has a grand gold-on-beige sandstone facade, elegant chapels, the best-decorated dome in Spain, and bas-relief columns that look like a palm-tree cluster. Unfortunately, its stained glass is severely damaged. The cathedral lies in the southern section of Old Town, about 5 blocks south of Plaza Mayor at the edge of Plaza de Anaya.

Plaza Juan XXII. ℂ **92-321-74-76.** www.catedralsalamanca.org. Free admission. Apr–Sept daily 9am–8pm; Oct–Mar daily 9am–1pm and 4–6pm only (Nov–Feb Sun 9am–1pm only). Bus: 1.

Catedral Vieja (Old Cathedral) ★★ Adjoining the New Cathedral is this older Spanish Romanesque version, begun in 1140. Its simplicity contrasts dramatically with the ornamentation of its younger but bigger counterpart. In the main apsidal chapel is an **altarpiece** ★★, painted by Nicholas of Florence in the mid–15th century, consisting of 53 beautifully decorated compartments. Even today this work of art remains fresh and vivid. After viewing the interior, stroll through the enclosed cloisters with their Gothic tombs of long-forgotten bishops.

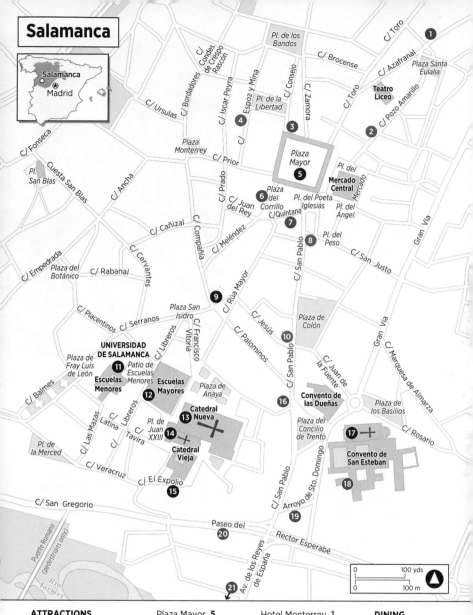

Salamanca

Salamanca
Madrid

ATTRACTIONS
Casa de las Conchas **17**
Casa Museo Unamuno **12**
Catedral Nueva **13**
Catedral Vieja **14**
Convento de San Esteban **9**
Museo de Art Nouveau-
Art Déco **15**

Plaza Mayor **5**
Universidad de
Salamanca **11**

ACCOMMODATIONS
AC Palacio de San
Esteban **18**
Hostal Plaza Mayor **6**
Hotel Don Juan **7**

Hotel Monterrey **1**
Hotel Rector **20**
Hotel San Polo **19**
NH Palacio de
Castellanos **16**
Parador de Salamanca **21**
Petit Palace Las Torres **3**

DINING
Chez Victor **4**
El Candil **2**
La Hoja Charra **10**
Río de la Plata **8**

The chapels are of special architectural interest. In the Capilla de San Martín, the frescoes date from 1242, and in the Capilla de Santa Bárbara, final exams for Salamanca University students were given. The Capilla de Santa Catalina is noted for its gargoyles.

Plaza Juan XXIII. ✆ **92-321-74-76.** www.catedralsalamanca.org. Admission 4.50€. Apr–Sept daily 10am–7:30pm; Oct–Mar daily 10am–12:30pm and 4–5:30pm. Bus: 1.

Museo de Art Nouveau–Art Déco This museum contains more than 1,500 pieces, all part of the collection of the Manuel Ramos Andrade Foundation. Dating from the late 19th century to the 1930s, the collection includes bronze and marble figurines, jewelry, furniture, paintings, and a collection of some 300 porcelain dolls. Numerous works by Emile Gallé and René Lalique are also on display.

Calle El Expolio 14. ✆ **92-312-14-25.** www.museocasalis.org. Admission 3€ adults, 2€ students, free for children 13 and under. Apr

The Universidad de Salamanca's facade.

1–Oct 15 Tues–Fri 11am–2pm and 5–9pm, Sat–Sun 11am–9pm; Oct 16–Mar 31 Tues–Fri 11am–2pm and 4–7pm, Sat–Sun 11am–8pm.

Universidad de Salamanca The oldest university in Spain was once the greatest in Europe. No other Spanish university has such a **grand entrance ★★★**. Dating from 1534, the entryway is a splendid piece of sculpture, intricate in its detail. It is said the architects carved this "doorway to heaven" in emulation of a goldsmith's art. The main medallion in the first register depicts the Catholic monarchs Isabella and Ferdinand, who supplied the cost of creating this work of art. You can visit a dim 16th-century classroom cluttered with crude wooden benches. The library upstairs can't be entered but can be viewed through a glass door, and it's an impressive sight. The university is 2 blocks from the cathedral in the southern section of Old Town.

Patio de las Escuelas 1. ✆ **92-329-44-00.** www.usal.es. Admission 4€. Mon–Sat 9:30am–1pm and 4–7pm (Sat to 6:30pm); Sun 9am–1pm. Enter from Patio de las Escuelas, a widening of Calle de Libreros.

💬 The Undaunted Fray Luis

In front of the Plateresque facade of the University of Salamanca, a statue honors Hebrew scholar Fray Luis de León. Arrested for heresy, Fray Luis was detained for 5 years before being cleared. When he returned, he began his first lecture: "As I was saying yesterday. . . ." Fray Luis's remains are kept in the chapel, which is worth a look.

Shopping

The town's two main shopping neighborhoods extend around **Calle Meléndez** and the historic borders of **Plaza Mayor.** Both areas are good bets for fashion and housewares. A *rastro,* or flea market, is held every Sunday along Avenida de Aldehuela. It's best to go before noon. Buses go here from Plaza de España, in the center of town. The best place for handicrafts is **Aertesania Duenda,** Calle San Pablo 29 (© 92-321-36-22), with one-of-a-kind items, often in wood, including music boxes and picture frames.

Where to Stay in Salamanca

EXPENSIVE

AC Palacio de San Esteban ★ This government-rated five-star hotel has been installed in the former convent dedicated to San Esteban, which dates from the 1600s. It lies within the heart of monumental Salamanca. The hotel has been totally rejuvenated but the traditional style and luxury of its architectural past have been honored. Guest rooms are midsize and attractively yet conservatively furnished; handsome bathrooms come with both tub and shower. The location is close to many sightseeing attractions, including the cathedrals.

Arroyo de Santo Domingo 3, 37001 Salamanca. © **92-326-22-96.** Fax 92-326-88-72. www.ac-hotels.com. 51 units. 90€–175€ double; 114€–210€ double superior; 180€–340€ suite. AE, DC, MC, V. Parking 11€. **Amenities:** Restaurant; bar; babysitting; exercise room; room service; sauna; Wi-Fi (free, in lobby). *In room:* A/C, TV, hair dryer, minibar.

Hotel Rector ★★ 🛎 As a little inn, this is the charmer of Salamanca, and many discerning guests prefer it to the *parador* (see below). Nothing matches it in either atmosphere or tranquillity, although the far larger NH Palacio de Castellanos (see below) remains the most substantial deluxe palace. The Rector is a mere boutique hotel. Located just beyond the Roman bridge, it was a private mansion until the owners converted it into a hotel in 1990. Guest rooms are elegantly appointed with luxury mattresses and beautifully kept bathrooms. Don't expect all the luxuries found in a full-service hotel, but the staff here is extremely professional and polite. Since this place is such a gem, you have to reserve well in advance.

Rector Esperabé 10, 37008 Salamanca. © **92-321-84-82.** Fax 92-321-40-08. www.hotelrector. com. 13 units. 160€ double; 190€ suite. AE, DC, MC, V. Parking 17€. **Amenities:** Concierge. *In room:* A/C, TV, hair dryer, minibar, MP3 docking station, Wi-Fi (free).

NH Palacio de Castellanos ★★ This deluxe hotel was built on the site of the original 15th-century Palacio de Castellanos; it lies in old Salamanca, near the Plaza Mayor, and has nice views in most directions. The good-size rooms are comfortable, contemporary, and state-of-the-art, with sleek modern furnishings, deluxe bedding, and bedside controls.

San Pablo 58–64, 37008 Salamanca. © **92-326-18-18.** Fax 92-326-18-19. www.nh-hoteles.es. 62 units. 140€ double; 170€ suite. AE, DC, MC, V. Parking 16€. **Amenities:** Bar; babysitting; room service. *In room:* A/C, TV, hair dryer, minibar, Wi-Fi (17€ per 24 hr.).

Parador de Salamanca ★★★ Situated just across the Tormes River, 1.6km (1 mile) south of the historic center, this multilevel *parador* opened in the 1980s but has been vastly altered. The new treatment divides the building into three units that are more harmonious with the landscape. All the public areas, including the lounges and dining room, were tastefully restored and redecorated. The bedrooms have never been better, and even the floors have been changed, now clad in marble and wood. Lighting and furnishings are vastly improved. The use of Spanish carpets, oil paintings, and beautiful prints make the rooms both intimate and welcoming. Many private balconies were also added. From the cafe there are panoramic views of the city.

Calle Teso de la Feria 2, 37008 Salamanca. ✆ **92-319-20-82.** Fax 92 319 20 87. www.parador. es. 110 units. 148€–176€ double; from 208€ suite. AE, DC, V. Free parking outside; 12€ garage. **Amenities:** Restaurant; bar; babysitting; exercise room; outdoor pool; room service; sauna; outdoor tennis court; Wi-Fi (free, in lobby). *In room:* A/C, TV, hair dryer, minibar.

MODERATE

Hotel Monterrey Within walking distance of the Plaza Mayor, hiding behind a golden stone facade in the neoclassical style, this 50-year-old hotel reopened early in 2005. It was completely redone in a modern style. Guest rooms are midsize to spacious, each comfortably furnished and tastefully decorated, with a tidy bathroom with tub and shower. The hotel has affiliations with a nearby spa. In lieu of its former restaurant, a cafeteria has been installed.

Calle Azafranal 21, 37002 Salamanca. ✆ **92-321-44-00.** Fax 92-321-44-00. www.hotel monterreysalamanca.com. 144 units. 75€–120€ double; 120€–150€ suite. AE, DC, MC, V. Parking 14€. **Amenities:** Bar; room service. *In room:* A/C, TV, hair dryer, minibar, Wi-Fi (free).

Hotel San Polo ★ Located in the historic center, this hotel was built on the ruins of an 11th-century church in the mid-1990s. Some of the Romanesque architectural elements have been incorporated into the contemporary building, which makes it more atmospheric. The midsize to spacious guest rooms are comfortably and tastefully furnished; many open onto views of the cathedral. The hotel is at the intersection of Paseo del Rector Esperabé and Avenida Reyes de España.

Calle Arroyo de Santodomingo 2–4, 37008 Salamanca. ✆ **92-321-11-77.** Fax 92-321-11-54. www. hotelsanpolo.com. 37 units. 50€–120€ double; 80€–180€ suite. AE, DC, MC, V. **Amenities:** Restaurant; bar; babysitting; room service. *In room:* A/C, TV, hair dryer, minibar, Wi-Fi (free).

Petit Palace Las Torres Dignified and well maintained, but with a staff that's completely lost in any language except Spanish, this hotel occupies a desirable spot near the northwest corner of the Plaza Mayor. The hotel, located in a building from 1728, was redecorated and equipped with all modern facilities. The comfortable guest rooms, although not overly large, contain excellent beds. Many of the rooms have plaza views, and bathrooms have tub/shower combos. Additional seating from the unpretentious restaurant spills outside beneath the plaza's arcades, allowing indoor/outdoor dining and lots of opportunities for people-watching.

Plaza Mayor 26 (entrance to the palace is from Calle Concejo 4), 37002 Salamanca. ✆ **92-321-21-00.** Fax 92-321-21-01. www.hthoteles.com. 53 units. 60€–120€ double; 100€–160€ suite. AE, DC, MC, V. Parking 12€. **Amenities:** Bar. *In room:* A/C, TV, hair dryer, minibar, Wi-Fi (free).

INEXPENSIVE

Hostal Plaza Mayor ✒ If you're in town mainly to sightsee and dine out, and if you don't want to spend much on a room, make this historic but relatively minimalist *hostal* your number-one choice. A modest establishment, it offers good value for clean, comfortable, small, and somewhat spartan-looking units. Each has a well-maintained private bathroom with a shower, many of which have been upgraded. The location is one of the finest in the city, right at the Plaza Mayor, opposite the church of St. Martin. The hotel has been discovered by bargain hunters; reserve months in advance.

Plaza del Corrillo 20, 37002 Salamanca. © 92-326-20-20. Fax 92-321-75-48. www.hostalplaza-mayor.es. 19 units. 50€–60€ double. MC, V. **Amenities:** Restaurant; bar; room service. *In room:* A/C, TV, Wi-Fi (free).

Hotel Don Juan ★ 👔 For the serious budget traveler, this little family hotel, right off the Plaza Mayor, is a gem. The landmark building has a completely modernized interior that is light and airy. You're given a warm welcome by the owners, the Berrocal family. Guest rooms are small but well maintained and comfortable, with tasteful decor. Equally well-maintained bathrooms have tub/shower combos. If one is available, opt for a room with a balcony overlooking the cathedral.

Calle Quintana 6, 37001 Salamanca. © **92-326-14-73.** Fax 92-326-24-75. 16 units. 62€–72€ double. MC, V. Parking 10€ nearby. **Amenities:** Bar; room service. *In room:* A/C, TV, hair dryer, minibar.

Where to Dine in Salamanca

Chez Víctor ★★ FRENCH/SPANISH/INTERNATIONAL Set within the historic center of town, this is the best, most glamorous restaurant around. Owner-chef Victoriano Salvador spent some 15 years in France learning and perfecting his craft. He returned home to open this restaurant, which won the only star Michelin has ever granted to a Salamanca restaurant. Specialties include freshly prepared fish—perhaps sea wolf in black squid sauce, broiled turbot in a hot vinaigrette sauce, or, even better, bluefin tuna steak with sesame seeds. Try the tenderloin in lemon sauce or, if it's offered, pork ribs stuffed with prunes and served with a honey-mustard sauce. Don't miss Victoriano's signature almond-bark cookies. Despite the modernity of the cuisine, the portions are ample and well suited to Spanish tastes.

Espoz y Mina 26. © **92-321-31-23.** Reservations required. Main courses 18€–28€. AE, DC, MC, V. Tues–Sun 2–3:30pm; Tues–Sat 9–11:30pm. Closed Aug.

El Candil CASTILIAN This much-patronized Castilian tavern has more than its share of devotees, often attracting a university crowd. Students of Salamanca consider it an ideal place to take their dates for the evening. That's because the food is good but also affordable. The location is in the center of town right off the Plaza Mayor. It's been in business for 6 decades, and the chefs cook as they always have, turning out regional fare that includes stuffed pimientos (a real treat) or fried *merluza* (hake) served with a side order of sweet peppers. The roast suckling pig is perfectly done and fork tender. The chefs also make some very appetizing dishes with *bacalao* (dried cod). Their *marucha* steak is one of the best items they've ever offered. As an appetizer, you might try an order of their *farinato,* a sausage made from "secret ingredients." (We tasted pork and onion.) They also do a very good *ensalada de perdiz* (partridge salad).

Ventura Ruiz Aguilera 14–16. © **92-321-72-39.** www.elcandil.info. Reservations required. Main courses 14€–23€; fixed-price menu 49€. AE, DC, MC, V. Restaurant Mon 1–4pm; Wed–Sun 1–4pm and 8–11:30pm. Bar daily 11am–midnight.

La Hoja Charra ★ CASTILIAN This fine restaurant lies in the center of town, a short walk from the landmark Plaza Mayor. The restaurant is in a narrow passage right off the main square—it occupies what was once a convent, built during the 16th century. One of the town's most outstanding chefs, Alberto López

Oliva, draws upon time-tested recipes from the province and adds an imaginative twist to each. In a setting of high ceilings and paintings, you are presented with the evening's menu. The chef uses the freshest ingredients from the market and fashions them into dishes with style, flair, and flavor. He prefers, whenever possible, to use regional produce. Among his more savory offerings are a mushroom risotto and an octopus salad with a cider vinaigrette. One of the most local dishes is lamb ribs served with fried potatoes, and a house specialty is partridge cooked in chocolate—an acquired taste for some, as are his pigs' trotters cooked with slices of apples and prawns in a balsamic vinaigrette.

Calle San Pablo 21. ✆ **92-326-40-28.** www.lahoja21.com. Reservations required. Main courses 12€–19€; fixed-price menu 33€. AE, DC, MC, V. Tues–Sat 2–4:30pm and 9–11:30pm; Sun 2–4:30pm.

Río de la Plata CASTILIAN This tiny basement restaurant, 2 blocks south of the Plaza Mayor on a small side square formed by the junction of Plaza Poeta Iglesia and Calle San Justo, has been a local dining favorite since 1958. The kitchen uses fresh ingredients, preparing a traditional but simple *cocida castellana* (Castilian stew), house-style sole, roast baby goat, many varieties of fish, and pungently flavored sausages. Although modest, the place serves good-quality dishes. Locals fill the place every night, which is endorsement enough.

Plaza del Peso 1. ✆ **92-321-90-05.** Reservations recommended. Main courses 19€–24€; *menú del día* 24€. MC, V. Tues–Sun 1:30–3:30pm and 9pm–12:30am. Closed 2 weeks in July.

Salamanca After Dark

Don't expect a large variety of nightlife options; this is a small-scale university town with an emphasis on undergraduate shenanigans. Your best bet is a stroll around the Plaza Mayor, where you'll pass cafes and bars ideal for lingering or loitering, depending on your point of view. Usually a group of singing "tuna" dressed in medieval costumes perform for free nightly at 10pm, although these students appreciate tips. You might also wander onto such neighboring medieval streets as Calle de Bordadores, Calle San Vicente, Calle Rúa Mayor, and Calle Varillas, any of which offers tucked-away spots for a quick caffeine or alcohol fix. A Salamanca disco of note is **Camelot,** Calle Bordadores 3 (✆ **92-321-21-82**). The latter occupies a stone monastery whose inhabitants 400 years ago would undoubtedly have been horrified at the goings-on here today. For a more modern spin on Salamanca's nightlife, head for **Pub Rojo y Negro,** Calle Espoz y Mina 22 (✆ **92-326-67-73**), where bouts of karaoke are interspersed with chatter, wine, whiskey, and foaming mugs of Spanish beer.

ZAMORA ★

64km (40 miles) N of Salamanca, 238km (148 miles) NW of Madrid

Little known to North American visitors, **Zamora** (pronounced Thah-*moh*-rah) is the quintessential city of Old Castile, blending ancient and modern but noted mainly for its Romanesque architecture. In fact, Zamora is often called a "Romanesque museum." A medieval frontier city, it rises starkly from the Castilian flatlands, a reminder of the era of conquering monarchs and forgotten kingdoms.

You can explore Zamora's highlights in about 4 hours. Stroll along the main square, dusty Plaza Canovas; cross the arched Romanesque bridge from the

The "Black Tapestries" of the Catedral San Salvador.

1300s; and take in at least some of the Romanesque churches—many dating from the 12th century—for which the town is known. The cathedral is the best example, but others include **Iglesia de la Magdalena,** on Rúa de los Francos, and **Parroquia de San Ildefonso,** on Calle Ramos Carrión. You might also want to look at **Iglesia de Santa María la Nueva,** on Plaza de Santa María, and **Iglesia de Santiago el Burgo,** on Calle Santa Clara.

The crowning achievement, however, at the far west end of Zamora, is the **Catedral San Salvador ★**, Plaza de la Catedral (✆ **98-053-06-44**). It is topped by a gold-and-white Eastern-looking **dome ★**. Inside, you'll find rich hangings, interesting chapels, two 15th-century Mudéjar pulpits, and intricately carved **choir stalls ★★**. Later architectural styles, including Gothic, have been added to the original Romanesque features, but this indiscriminate mixing of periods is typical of Spanish cathedrals. Inside the cloister, the Museo de la Catedral features ecclesiastical art, historical documents, church documents, and an unusual collection of **"Black Tapestries" ★★** dating from the 1400s. These priceless Flemish tapestries tell the story of the Trojan War and are called "black" because some of their subjects are people about to be decapitated. Admission to the cathedral is free, but the museum costs 3€. The museum and cathedral are open April to September, Tuesday to Sunday 11am to 2pm and 5 to 8pm. Off-season hours are Tuesday to Sunday 11am to 2pm and 4:30 to 6:30pm.

Essentials

GETTING THERE There are three **trains** to and from Madrid every day, and two to and from A Coruña (trip times: 3 hr. and 6 hr., respectively). The railway station is at Calle Alfonso Peña (✆ **90-224-02-02;** www.renfe.es), about a 15-minute walk from the edge of Old Town. Follow Avenida de las Tres Cruces northeast of the center of town. One-way fare from Madrid to Zamora is 28€ to 37€.

Ten to 23 **bus** connections a day from Salamanca make this the easiest way to get in and out of town (trip time: 1 hr.). There are seven buses a day from Madrid (trip time: 3½ hr.) for 14€ to 22€. The town's bus station lies a few paces from the railway station, at Calle Alfonso Peña 3 (*✆* **98-052-12-81**). Call *✆* **90-202-00-52** for bus schedules and price information.

Zamora is at the junction of eight different roads and highways. Most of the traffic from northern Portugal into Spain comes through here. Highways headed north to León, south to Salamanca, and east to Valladolid are especially convenient. From Madrid, take the A-6 superhighway northwest toward Valladolid, cutting west on the N-VI and west again at the turnoff onto 122.

VISITOR INFORMATION The **tourist office,** Plaza de Arias Gonzalo 20 (*✆* **98-053-36-94;** www.ayto-zamora.org), is open daily 10am to 2pm and 4 to 7pm.

SPECIAL EVENTS **Holy Week** in Zamora, the week before Easter, is a celebration throughout the country. Street processions, called *pasos,* are among the most spectacular in Spain. If you plan to visit at this time, make your hotel reservations well in advance.

Where to Stay in Zamora

Hostería Real de Zamora ★ This most charming small hotel in town, sporting walls that date from the 1400s, occupies the long-ago headquarters of Zamora's dreaded Inquisition. (Ironically, this is the former site of a Jewish-owned building reputed to have been the home of the explorer Pizarro.) Today, the outstanding historical features of the building include a medieval reservoir, a patio perfect for enjoying a cup of tea or coffee, and a verdant garden along the city's medieval fortifications. An excellent example of a tastefully modernized aristocratic villa, it stands a few steps to the west of the northern embankment of the city's much-photographed Stone Bridge. The midsize guest rooms contain good beds, and the well-maintained bathrooms are equipped with tub/shower combos. If you drive to the hotel, you'll have to rely on street parking.

Cuesta de Pizarro 7, 49027 Zamora. *✆*/fax **98-053-45-45.** www.hosteriasreales.com/hosteria4.htm. 24 units. 68€–80€ double. Rates include continental breakfast. AE, DC, MC, V. **Amenities:** Restaurant; bar; bikes; Jacuzzi. *In room:* A/C, TV, hair dryer, minibar, Wi-Fi (free).

Parador de Zamora ★★ This is the grand address for Zamora, a *parador* of tranquillity and charm. The site has always played a legendary role in Zamora. Originally fortified as an *alcazaba* by the Moors during their occupation of Zamora, it was rebuilt in 1459 by the count of Alva y Aliste. Today the structure retains the severe, high-ceilinged dignity of its 15th-century Gothic form. Set 2 blocks south of Plaza Mayor, near the junction of Plaza de Viriato and Calle Ramos Carrión, the *parador* is richly decorated with medieval armor, antique furniture, tapestries, and potted plants. In winter, glass partitions close off a large inner patio centered on an antique well; baronial fireplaces provide much-appreciated warmth. Midsize rooms are white walled, well maintained, and tastefully decorated with conservative furniture.

Plaza de Viriato 5, 49001 Zamora. *✆* **98-051-44-97.** Fax 98-053-00-63. www.parador.es. 52 units. 155€ double; 233€ double superior. AE, DC, MC, V. Hotel open-air parking 9€; garage parking 20€. **Amenities:** Restaurant; bar; outdoor pool; room service; Wi-Fi (free, in lobby). *In room:* A/C, TV, hair dryer, minibar.

Where to Dine in Zamora

El Rincón de Antonio ★★ SPANISH/INTERNATIONAL Set about a block southwest of Old Town's most visible square, Plaza Viriato, within a thick-walled 19th-century building whose angular design evokes Old Castile at its most historic, this is a well-known restaurant that somehow manages to incorporate aspects of both antique and ultracontemporary New Spain. We appreciate the old-fashioned professionalism of this place, as well as the fact that many locals come here to celebrate rites of passage. There are crowded and convivial dining areas in the main building, as well as a greenhouse-style dining extension jutting into the garden. Menu items are prepared by masterful chefs sporting years of experience in some of the most sophisticated dining venues in Spain and France, always with fresh ingredients that change with the seasons. The best examples include shrimp with garlic and mango slices; chicken with exotic wild mushrooms; and masterful versions of local ingredients, such as garbanzos, with local herbs and seasonal boletus mushrooms.

Rúa de los Francos 6. ☏ **98-053-53-70.** www.elrincondeantonio.com. Reservations recommended. Main courses 30€–40€; set menus 40€–55€. AE, DC, MC, V. Daily noon–4pm; Mon–Sat 8pm–midnight.

Serafín SPANISH/INTERNATIONAL At the northeast edge of Old Town, about a block south of the busy traffic hub of Plaza Alemania and Avenida de Alfonso IX, this air-conditioned haven with an attractive bar is a relaxing retreat from the sun. The specialties change with the season but might include the seafood soup Serafín, paella, fried hake, Iberian ham, or a savory *cocido* (stew). Regrettably, some of the staff members are ill-mannered.

Plaza Maestro Haedo 10. ☏ **98-053-14-22.** www.restauranteserafin.com. Main courses 12€–19€; fixed-price menus 18€–25€. AE, DC, MC, V. Fri–Wed 1–4:30pm and 8:30pm–midnight.

Zamora After Dark

Calle Los Herreros, also called Calle de Vinos, has more bars per square foot than any street in Zamora—about 16 in all. At each you can have a leisurely glass of wine or beer and choose from a selection of tapas. Calle Los Herreros is a narrow street at the southern end of Old Town, about 2 blocks north of the Duero River, within the shadow of the Ayuntamiento Viejo (Old Town Hall), a block south of Plaza Mayor.

LEÓN ★★

327km (203 miles) NW of Madrid, 196km (122 miles) N of Salamanca

Once the leading city of Christian Spain, this cathedral town was the capital of a centuries-old empire that declined after uniting with Castile. **León** today is the gateway from Old Castile to the northwestern routes of Galicia. It is a sprawling city, but nearly everything of interest to visitors—monuments, restaurants, and hotels—can be covered on foot once you arm yourself with a good map.

Once the heartbeat of a great kingdom, León today is a sleepy provincial city off the beaten track. But its wealth of old monuments, its top-notch accommodations, and a certain regal atmosphere make the town still feel like a capital.

Outlying mountain villages offer their own architectural gems, fine ski runs, and tasty concoctions of local trout and meat. Also, the region is particularly renowned for its soft-spoken, pristine Castilian accent. In sum, León is an excellent place to experience the tranquillity of the Spanish heartland, as well as an obligatory stop for students of medieval architecture.

Essentials

GETTING THERE León has good rail connections to the rest of Spain—seven **trains** daily from Madrid (trip time: 4–5 hr.). The station, Estación del Norte, Av. de Astorga 2 (© **90-224-02-02;** www.renfe.es), is on the western bank of the Bernesga River. Cross the bridge near Plaza de Guzmán el Bueno. A one-way ticket from Madrid ranges from 26€ to 41€.

Most of León's **buses** arrive and depart from the Estación de Autobuses, Paseo Ingeniero Sáenz de Miera (© **98-721-10-00**). Three to five buses per day link León with Zamora and Salamanca, and there are 11 per day from Madrid (trip time: 4¼ hr.). A one-way ticket on a direct regular bus from Madrid is 27€ to 41€ for the *supra* (comfortable) service. For more information about prices, call © **90-242-22-42.**

León lies at the junction of five major highways coming from five different regions of Spain. From Madrid's periphery, head northwest on the N-VI superhighway toward La Coruña. At Benavente, bear right onto the N-630.

VISITOR INFORMATION The **tourist office,** Plaza de la Regla 3 (© **98-723-70-82;** www.turismocastillayleon.com), is open Monday to Saturday 9:30am to 2pm and 4 to 7pm, and Sunday 9:30am to 5pm. From July to mid-September, the office remains open during lunch hours.

Exploring León

Catedral de León (Santa María de Regla) ★★★ The usual cathedral elements are virtually eclipsed here by the awesome **stained-glass windows** ★★★—some 125 in all (plus 57 oculi), dating from the 13th century. They are so heavy they have strained the cathedral's walls. Look for a 15th-century **altarpiece** ★ depicting the Entombment in the Capilla Mayor, as well as

---

◌ Luminous in León

In the church-building frenzy of the Middle Ages, every Gothic cathedral vied to distinguish itself with some superlative trait. Milan Cathedral was the biggest, Chartres had the most inspiring stained-glass windows, Palma de Majorca had the largest rose window, and so on.

Structurally, though, the boldest cathedral was at León. This edifice set the record for the highest proportion of window space, with stained-glass windows soaring 34m (112 ft.) to the vaulted ceiling, framed by the slenderest of columns. The windows occupied 1,672 sq. m (nearly 18,000 sq. ft.), or almost all the space where you'd expect the walls to be.

The roof is held up not by walls but by flying buttresses on the exterior. Inside, the profusion of light and the illusion of weightlessness astonish even medievalists. The architects (Juan Pérez and Maestro Enrique) who designed the cathedral in the 13th century were, in effect, precursors of architect Mies van der Rohe, 7 centuries before the age of steel girders draped with plate-glass curtain walls.

The stained glass of the Catedral de León.

a Renaissance *trascoro* (westward portion of the nave) by Juan de Badajoz. The nave dates from the 13th and 14th centuries; the Renaissance vaulting is much later. The **cloisters** ★ date in part from the 13th and 14th centuries and contain faded frescoes and Romanesque and Gothic tombs; some capitals are carved with starkly lifelike scenes. Visitors can also tour the **Museo Catedralicio Diocesano de León,** which contains valuable art and artifacts, including a 10th-century Bible, notable sculptures, and a collection of romantic images of the Virgin Mary. The cathedral is on the edge of Old Town, 7 blocks east of its most central square, Plaza de Santo Domingo.

Plaza de Regla. ✆ **98-787-57-70.** www.catedraldeleon.org. Admission to cathedral free; museum 4€; cloisters 1€. Cathedral July–Sept Mon–Sat 9:30am–2pm and 4–7:30pm; Oct–June Mon–Fri 9:30am–1:30pm and 4–7pm, Sat 9:30am–1:30pm. Museum Mon–Fri 9:30am–1:30pm and 4–7pm; Sat 9:30am–1:30pm. Bus: 4.

MUSAC (Museo de Arte Contemporáneo de Castilla y León) ★ ☺ This museum of modern art is the most avant-garde in the province. It's housed in a complex of structures decorated with stained glass, but hardly that of the caliber of the famous cathedral. The exhibitions of modern art are daring; one recent display, for example, depicted a car wreck. Most museums in the province are devoted to Spain's glorious past. This one bills itself as a "Museum of the 21st Century." In addition to its changing exhibitions of art, the museum sponsors movies and concerts, as well as a program of workshops and various activities aimed at kids.

Av. de los Reyes Leoneses 24. ✆ **98-709-00-00.** www.musac.org.es. Free admission. Tues–Fri 10am–3pm and 5–8pm, Sat and Sun 10am–3pm and 5–9pm. Bus: 7 or 11.

Real Colegiata de San Isidoro ★

This church, a short walk northwest of the cathedral, was dedicated to San Isidoro de Sevilla in 1063 and contains 23 tombs of Leoncse kings. One of the first Romanesque buildings in León and Castile, it was embellished by Ferdinand I's artists. The columns are magnificent, the capitals splendidly decorated, and the vaults covered with murals from the 12th century. Unique in Spain, the church treasury holds rare finds—a 10th-century Scandinavian ivory, an 11th-century chalice, and an important collection of 10th- to 12th-century cloths from Asia. The library museum contains many ancient manuscripts and rare books, including a Book of Job from 951, a Visigothic Bible, and a Bible from 1162, plus dozens of miniatures. Plaza San Isidoro 4. ☎ **98-787-61-61.** www.sanisidorodeleon.net. Free admission to church, 4€ to Pantheon and museum. Church

The rainbow windows of MUSAC.

daily 7am–11pm. Pantheon and museum July–Aug Mon–Sat 9am–8pm, Sun 9am–2pm; Sept–June Mon–Sat 10am–1:30pm and 4–6:30pm, Sun 10am–1:30pm. Bus: 4 or 9.

Shopping

Something about the city's architecture encourages the acquisition of old-time handicrafts made from time-honored materials like terra cotta, stone, copper, wrought iron, and leather. The Plaza de la Catedral and the streets that radiate from it are particularly rich in battered, overcrowded kiosks with this type of artifact, and part of the fun of a trip within the city's historic core involves acquiring several pieces. For a more up-to-date roster of shopping options, consider a quick march through the vast stacks within León's biggest department store, **El Corte Inglés,** Fray Luis de León 21 (☎ **98-726-31-00;** www.elcorteingles.es). Inside, look for men's and women's clothing, books, gift items, and hints of the high-fashion priorities of cities as far away as Barcelona and Madrid.

Where to Stay in León

Hotel Alfonso V ★ Although we infinitely prefer the *parador* (p. 255), this hotel in the heart of the city is less expensive and is famed for its classic contemporary decor. The pre-Franco hotel has been dramatically modernized with a stunning sculpture-filled lobby that rises seven wavy stories to a glass roof. Rooms, mostly midsize, are a study in postmodernism, fitted with French windows and excellent soundproofing. Padre Isla 1, 24002 León. ☎ **98-722-09-00.** Fax 98-722-12-44. www.lesein.es/alfonsov. 62 units. 70€ double; 125€ suite. AE, DC, MC, V. Parking 14€. **Amenities:** Restaurant; bar; babysitting; room service. *In room:* A/C, TV, hair dryer, minibar, Wi-Fi (10€ per 24 hr.).

Hotel París 🎁 Lying between the Old and New towns, this renovated hotel east of Plaza Santo Domingo lures you with Belle Epoque touches and a warm, inviting atmosphere. Guest rooms, more intimate than spacious, are comfortable. This old favorite is now better than ever. Consider it a cozy nest for your León sightseeing.

Calle Ancha 18, 24003 León. ℂ **98-723-86-00.** Fax 98-727-15-72. www.hotelparisleon.com. 55 units. 73€–78€ double; 90€–96€ triple. AE, DC, MC, V. Parking 10€. **Amenities:** Restaurant; bar; exercise room; indoor heated pool; room service; spa. *In room:* A/C, TV, hair dryer, minibar, Wi-Fi (free).

Hotel Posada Regia ★ 🏨 Completely restored, two Leonese buildings from the 14th and 19th centuries have been turned into this boutique hotel of charm and tradition. In the heart of the historic city, the main building and its equally charming annex offer a completely different decor for every room, each traditionally furnished. The use of satin and exposed-brick walls dominates, and primary, very vivid colors such as red or green are used. Expect to find antique furniture and wide beds, along with spacious bathrooms, most of which have corner bathtubs. Many romantics, especially couples, prefer the top-floor rooms under the eaves.

On site is the **Bodega Regia,** a traditional Leonese restaurant with an extensive, varied menu offering everything from conger eel to roast suckling lamb.

Regidores 11, 24003 León. ℂ **98-721-31-73.** Fax 98-721-30-31. www.regialeon.com. 36 units. 90€–120€ double. MC, V. **Amenities:** Restaurant; bar. *In room:* A/C, TV, Wi-Fi (free in most rooms).

Parador Hostal San Marcos ★★★ This 16th-century former monastery with its celebrated Plateresque facade is one of the most acclaimed *paradores* in all of Spain. The government has remodeled it at great expense, installing extravagant authentic antiques and quality reproductions as well as improving the facade. Before its monastery days, the old *hostal* put up pilgrims bound for Santiago de Compostela in the 12th century. The *parador* also contains a church with a scallop-shell facade and an archaeological museum. The good-size guest rooms are sumptuous, each with a bathroom equipped with a tub/shower combo. The *parador* is northwest of the cathedral on the outskirts of Old Town, on the east bank of the Bernesga River.

Plaza de San Marcos 7, 24001 León. ℂ **98-723-73-00.** Fax 98-723-34-58. www.parador.es. 226 units. 198€–278€ double; 634€ suite. AE, DC, MC, V. Free parking. **Amenities:** Restaurant; bar; babysitting; room service. *In room:* A/C, TV, hair dryer, minibar, Wi-Fi (free).

Where to Dine in León

Bodega Regia CASTILIAN Our favorite bodega in León is in a restored 14th-century building, an easy walk from the cathedral. A central garden patio has a rustic floor of stone and clay, emphasized by stone arches. A variety of tropical plants make for a warm, inviting atmosphere where architectural touches of the medieval period have been retained. The menu includes *embutidos de León,* a local sausage that is extremely tasty, as well as *pimientos de Bierzo con vinagre de Jerez,* red peppers grilled in a sherry-vinegar dressing. Another popular sausage is *morcilla de León y picadillo,* an exceptional treat. *Bacalao a la leonesa* is salt cod cooked with herbs and proper seasonings. *Alubias con espinaca* is an exceptional vegetable dish of white beans and spinach.

In the Posada Regia, Regidores 9–11. ℂ **98-721-31-73.** www.regialeon.com. Main courses 12€–35€. AE, DC, MC, V. Mon–Sat 1:45–4pm and 9–11:30pm. Closed 15 days in Jan and 15 days in Sept.

La Formela ★★ CASTILIAN Five minutes from the historic district and next to the Parador San Marcos, La Formela serves the finest cuisine in León and has the best service, too. Located on the second floor of the Hotel Quindós, this restaurant is warm and inviting. The owner, Jaime Quindós, is a well-known art collector and former gallery owner, and walls here are covered with contemporary paintings and a collection of antique Italian ornaments. The restaurant offers an extensive collection of wines from throughout Spain, but it is the cuisine that keeps diners happy. The menu includes *cesina de León,* one of the most delectable of local sausages, along with *revuelto de León con patatas,* sautéed fresh vegetables with potatoes. The *ciervo estofado* (venison casserole) is an alluring choice, as is *lubina a la espalda* (grilled filet of whitefish). For dessert, the chefs will prepare you a crêpe suzette or serve you *natillas caseras,* a Castilian-style pudding.

Gran Vía San Marcos 38. ☎ **98-722-45-34.** Reservations recommended. Main courses 11€–24€; fixed-price menu 20€. AE, DC, MC, V. Mon–Sat 1:30–3:30pm and 9–11:30pm.

León After Dark

Few other cities in Spain evoke the mystery of the Middle Ages like León. To best appreciate the old-fashioned eloquence of the city, after dark wander around the Plaza Mayor, the edges of which are peppered with simple cafes and bars. None is particularly different from its neighbor, but overall the effect is rich, evocative, and wonderfully conducive to conversation and romance. One of the best places for drinks is **León Antiguo,** Plaza del Cid 16 (no phone), which is open Monday to Wednesday 7pm to midnight and Thursday to Saturday 7pm to 4am. Alcoholic drinks cost 2€ to 5€.

VALLADOLID ★

201km (125 miles) NW of Madrid, 134km (83 miles) SE of León

The Catedral of Valladolid.

From the 13th century until its eventual decay in the early 17th century, Valladolid was a royal city and an intellectual center attracting saints and philosophers. Isabella and Ferdinand were married here, Philip II was born here, and Columbus died here, on May 19, 1506, broken in spirit and body after Isabella had died and Ferdinand refused to reinstate him as a governor of the Indies.

Valladolid is bitterly cold in winter, sweltering in summer. Today, after centuries of decline, the city is producing, among other things, flour, ironware, and cars. Consequently, it's polluted and noisy, and older buildings have been replaced by more modern, utilitarian ones, although many attractions remain.

From the tourist office (p. 257), you can pick up a map that marks all the major monuments. These attractions can be covered on foot, although you may want to take a taxi to the two most distant points recommended: the Museo Nacional de Escultura and the Museo Oriental.

Essentials

GETTING THERE Flights to Valladolid land at **Vallanubla Airport,** Hwy. N-601 (© **98-341-55-00**), a 15-minute taxi ride from the center of town. **Air Nostrum** (© **90-240-05-00;** www.airnostrum.es) routes daily flights to and from Barcelona.

Valladolid is well serviced by 21 daily **trains** to and from Madrid (trip time: 3–4½ hr.). The one-way fare is 15€ to 34€. Another city with train links to Valladolid is Burgos (16 trains per day). The train station (Estación del Norte), Calle Recondo s/n, by Plaza Colón (© **90-224-02-02;** www.renfe.es), is 1.6km (1 mile) south of the town's historic center, 1 block southwest of the Campo Grande park.

The **bus** station is an 8-minute walk from the railway station, at Puente Colgante (© **98-323-63-08**) on the southern edge of town. There are more than a dozen buses every day to and from Madrid (trip time: 2¼ hr.). Eight buses per day arrive from Zamora (trip time: 1¼ hr.), three buses per day from Burgos (trip time: 1½ hr.).

Valladolid lies at the center of the rectangle created by Burgos, León, Segovia, and Salamanca, and is connected to each by good highways. From Madrid, driving time is about 2¼ hours. Take superhighway A-6 northwest from Madrid, turning north on 403.

VISITOR INFORMATION The **tourist office,** inside Pabellón de Cristal, Calle Acera de Recoletos (© **98-321-93-10;** www.turismocastillayleon.com), is open in winter Monday to Saturday 9:30am to 2pm and 4 to 7pm, Sunday 9:30am to 5pm, summer daily 9am to 8pm.

Exploring Valladolid

Casa de Cervantes Now a museum, this house was once occupied by Miguel de Cervantes, author of *Don Quixote,* who did much of his writing in Valladolid and remained here for the last years of his life. Behind its white walls, the house is simply furnished, as it was in the author's day. It's located half a block south of the cathedral and 2 blocks north of the city park, Campo Grande.

Calle del Rastro s/n. © **98-330-88-10.** http://museocasacervantes.mcu.es. Admission 2.40€, 1.20€ students; free on Sun. Tues–Sat 9:30am–3pm; Sun 10am–3pm.

Catedral ★ In 1580, Philip II commissioned Juan de Herrera, architect of El Escorial, to construct this monument in the city where the latter was born. When Philip died in 1598, work came to a stop for 18 years. Alberto Churriguera resumed construction, drawing up more flamboyant plans, especially for the exterior, in unharmonious contrast to the severe lines of his predecessor's style. The classical, even sober, interior conforms more to Herrera's designs. A highlight is the 1551 altarpiece in the main apsidal chapel, the work of Juan de Juni. Art critics have commented that his polychrome figures seem "truly alive." The cathedral is in the heart of the city, east of Plaza Mayor and north of Plaza de Santa Cruz.

Plaza de Universidad 1. © **98-330-43-62.** www.catedral-valladolid.com. Free admission to cathedral; museum 3.50€. Cathedral and museum Tues–Fri 10am–1pm and 4:30–7pm; Sat–Sun 10am–2pm.

Iglesia de San Pablo Once a 17th-century Dominican monastery, San Pablo is very impressive, with its Isabelline-Gothic facade. Flanked by two towers, the main entrance supports levels of lacy stone sculpture. The church lies 6 blocks north of the cathedral, 1 block south of busy Avenida Santa Teresa. Mass is held daily, with eight Masses on Sunday.

Plaza San Pablo 4. © **98-335-17-48.** Free admission. Daily 7:30am–1:30pm and 7–9:30pm.

Museo Nacional de Escultura (National Museum of Sculpture) ★★★
Located near Plaza de San Pablo, this museum displays a magnificent collection of gilded polychrome sculpture, an art form that reached its pinnacle in Valladolid. The figures were first carved from wood, and then painted with consummate skill and grace to assume lifelike dimensions. See especially the works by Alonso Berruguete (1480–1561), son of Pedro, one of Spain's great painters. From 1527 to 1532, the younger Berruguete labored over the altar of the Convent of San Benito—a masterpiece now housed here. In particular, see his *Crucifix with the Virgin and St. John*, in Room II, and his *St. Sebastian and the Sacrifice of Isaac*, in Room III. Works by Juan de Juni and Gregorio Fernández are also displayed. After visiting the galleries, explore the two-story cloisters. The upper level is florid, with jutting gargoyles and fleurs-de-lis. See the chapel where the confessor to Isabella I (Fray Alonso de Burgos) was buried—and be horrified by the gruesome sculpture *Death*.

Colegio de San Gregorio, Calle Cadenas de San Gregorio 1–3. © **98-325-03-75.** http://museo escultura.mcu.es. Admission 3€, free for children 17 and under and adults 65 and over; free for all visitors Sun. Sept 21–Mar 20 Tues–Sat 10am–2pm and 4–6pm, Sun 10am–2pm; Mar 21–Sept 20 Tues–Sat 10am–2pm and 4–9pm, Sun 10am–2pm.

Museo Oriental Located in the Royal College of the Augustinian Fathers, near Campo Grande park, the museum has 14 rooms: 10 Chinese and 4 Filipino. It has the best collection of Asian art in Spain, with bronzes from the 7th century B.C. to the 18th century A.D.; woodcarvings; 100 fine porcelain pieces; paintings on paper and silk from the 12th century to the 19th; and ancient Chinese coins, furniture, jade, and ivory. In the Filipino section, ethnological and primitive art is represented by shields and arms. Eighteenth-century religious art can be admired in extraordinary ivories, embroideries, paintings, and silversmiths' work. Popular art of the 19th century includes bronzes, musical instruments, and statuary.

Paseo de Filipinos 7. © **98-330-68-00.** www.museo-oriental.es. Admission 3€; free for children 9 and under. Mon–Sat 10am–2pm and 4–7pm; Sun and holidays 10am–2pm.

Where to Stay in Valladolid

Felipe IV ★ When it was built, Felipe IV was one of the grandest hotels in the city, although the Olid Meliá (p. 259) now enjoys that position. Each of its midsize rooms is modernized, guaranteeing its ranking as a solidly acceptable establishment. All units have bathrooms containing tub/shower combos. A garage provides parking for motorists. The hotel is south of the busy traffic hub of Plaza de Madrid, a few blocks north of the rail station, near the eastern edge of the city park, Campo Grande.

Calle de Gamazo 16, 47004 Valladolid. © **98-330-70-00.** Fax 98-330-86-87. www.hfelipeIV. com. 127 units. 135€ double; 200€ suite. AE, DC, MC, V. Parking 15€. **Amenities:** Restaurant; exercise room; room service. *In room:* A/C, TV, hair dryer, minibar, Wi-Fi (free).

Hotel Olid Meliá ★★ Set in the heart of the historic zone about 5 blocks northwest of the cathedral, this is a modern hotel whose original construction in the early 1970s has been upgraded throughout the public areas with a post-modern gloss; the most recent renovations occurred in 2005. This is the town's leading accommodations choice, dwarfing the competition. The good-size rooms are the most comfortable in Valladolid and are furnished with antiques from all over the world.

Plaza San Miguel 10, 47003 Valladolid. © **800/336-3542** in the U.S., or 98-335-72-00. Fax 98-333-68-28. www.solmelia.com. 211 units. 102€–151€ double; 206€–291€ suite. AE, DC, MC, V. Parking 18€. **Amenities:** Restaurant; bar; babysitting; exercise room; room service. *In room:* A/C, TV, hair dryer, minibar, Wi-Fi (free).

Where to Dine in Valladolid

La Parrilla de San Lorenzo ★ 🏛 CASTILIAN/INTERNATIONAL The word for grill in Spanish is *parrilla,* and, appropriately, this restaurant serves some of the finest grilled fish and meat dishes in town. As a curiosity note, it honors St. Lawrence, who was burned to death over a grill. The *parrilla* was a late-16th-century monastery that has played many roles over the centuries before being converted into this successful restaurant. You dine in an elegant setting of gilded mirrors, wrought-iron, stained-glass windows depicting biblical themes, and stone arches—a very medieval atmosphere. You might begin with *rape*—in this case an *ensalada de rape* (monkfish salad)—with little red pimientos. The chef does an excellent capon salad as well. Duck pâté is another tantalizing appetizer. The house specialty is milk-fed lamb cooked to tender perfection in a wood oven. The bonito tuna is among the best fish offerings; it's marinated in sea salt before being lightly sautéed in virgin olive oil.

Calle Pedro Niño 1. © **98-333-50-88.** Reservations recommended. Main courses 16€–44€. AE, DC, MC, V. Daily 2–3:30pm; Mon–Sat 9pm–midnight.

Mesón Cervantes ★★ SPANISH/INTERNATIONAL Opened in 1973, this restaurant is one of the best in the city, despite rising prices and the occasionally jaded staff. The owner, Alejandro, works the dining room and is capably complemented in the kitchen by his wife, Julia, and their son, José. Two particular favorites are sole with pine nuts and seasonal river crabs. Many other fish dishes, including hake and monkfish, are available. Roast suckling pig and roast lamb are also popular. Other specialties are peppers stuffed with crabmeat; tender veal scaloppine Don Quixote, served with a piquant sauce; and *arroz con liebre* (herb-laden rice studded with chunks of roasted wild rabbit, in season). The restaurant is beside the Casa de Cervantes (p. 257), .8km (½ mile) south of the cathedral.

Calle del Rastro 6. © **98-330-61-38.** Reservations recommended. Main courses 10€–30€; fixed-price menu 40€. AE, DC, MC, V. Mon–Sat 1–4pm and 9pm–midnight. Closed Aug.

Mesón Panero ★ CASTILIAN/FRENCH The chef of this imaginative restaurant, José Ignacio Ruiz, can turn even the most austere traditional Castilian recipes into sensual experiences. Set near the water, this 1960s establishment lures diners with fresh fish, including a succulent brochette of sole, and hake with fresh asparagus. One favorite on Mondays is *cocido castellano,* the famous regional stew. Roast lamb and suckling pig are also available, plus a selection of well-chosen wines. The Mesón Panero is near the Casa de Cervantes (p. 257), a short walk from the tourist office.

Marina Escobar 1. © **98-330-70-19.** Reservations required. Main courses 23€–48€. AE, DC, MC, V. Daily 1:30–4pm; Mon–Sat 9pm–midnight. Closed Sun July–Aug.

Valladolid After Dark

There are no great clubs to recommend in Valladolid, but that doesn't mean that the city isn't a lively, bustling place when darkness falls. It's a town of bars and pubs. **Calle del Paraíso** is in itself a virtual street of bars, with action overflowing later onto the pubby **Plaza del San Miguel.** Enter the pub or bar that looks the most amusing and has the most convivial crowd, and chances are you won't go wrong. Most of these pubs and bars cater to a younger crowd, often from the university. If you're 30 or older, you might want to patronize one of the cafes along **Calle de Vincente Meliner,** especially those near Plaza Dorado.

Just off Plaza Mayor is the liveliest bar in town, **El Corcho,** Calle Correo 2 (© **98-333-08-61**), which also serves some of the tastiest Castilian tapas around. It offers a very rustic atmosphere, with 300-year-old brick walls and sawdust sprinkled over the much-used floor. Above the marble-topped bar, copperware and pig haunches are displayed. The cook rightly boasts of his *tostada de gambas* (shrimp drizzled with virgin olive oil and sprinkled over toasted bread). Other specialties include fish croquettes and Iberian ham and codfish. Tapas range in price from 2€ to 8€. Hours are daily 1 to 4pm and 8pm to midnight.

BURGOS ★★★

242km (150 miles) N of Madrid, 121km (75 miles) NE of Valladolid

Founded in the 9th century, this Gothic city in the Arlanzón River valley lives up to its reputation as the "cradle of Castile." Just as the Tuscans are credited with speaking the most perfect Italian, the citizens of Burgos, with their distinctive lisp ("El Theed" for "El Cid"), supposedly speak the most eloquent Castilian.

El Cid Campeador, Spain's greatest national hero, immortalized in the epic *El Cantar de Mío Cid,* is forever linked to Burgos. He was born near here and his remains lie in the city's grand cathedral.

Like all the great cities of Old Castile, Burgos declined seriously in the 16th century, only to be revived later. In 1936, during the Civil War, the right-wing city was Franco's Nationalist army headquarters.

Today Burgos no longer enjoys its historical glory but is a provincial city along the *meseta,* or plateau, of Spain. Dry as a desert and burning hot during the summer days, it comes alive

A 1344 depiction of El Cid.

at night and is filled with smoky cafes and dance clubs. Most of the bars, frequented by students, are in the area around the cathedral. Many of them don't start to party seriously until after 10pm, so it's a late-night town.

Essentials

GETTING THERE Burgos is well connected by **train** from Madrid (trip time: 3½ hr.), Barcelona (trip time: 8–9 hr.), the French border, and Valladolid. Fares from Madrid range from 24€ to 61€; from Barcelona, 42€ to 61€; and from Valladolid, 9€ to 27€. The Burgos railway station is at the terminus of Avenida de Conde Guadalhorce, .8km (½ mile) southwest of the center, Plaza de la Estación. To get here, head for the major traffic hub in Plaza Castilla, and then walk due south across the Arlanzón River. For train information or tickets, call © **90-224-02-02** (www.renfe.es).

Some 18 **buses** a day make the 2¾-hour trip from Madrid. A one-way fare costs 17€. The bus depot in Burgos is at Calle Miranda 4 (© **94-726-20-17;** www.alsa.es), which intersects the large Plaza de Vega, due south of (and across the river from) the cathedral.

Burgos is well connected to its neighbors by a network of highways, but its routes to and from Barcelona (trip time: 6 hr.) are especially wide and modern. The road from Barcelona changes its name several times, from the A-2 to the A-68 to the E-4, but it is a superhighway all the way. From Madrid, follow the N-I north for about 3 hours; the highway is fast but less modern than the road from Barcelona.

VISITOR INFORMATION The **tourist office,** Plaza Alonso Martínez 7 (© **94-720-31-25;** www.turismocastillayleon.com), is open July to September daily 9am to 7pm. From October to June it's open Monday to Saturday 9:30am to 2pm and 4 to 7pm, and Sunday 9:30am to 5pm.

Exploring Burgos

Casa de Cordón, the historic 15th-century palace on Plaza de Calvo Sotelo, has been restored and is now a bank. But you can still go by and take a look. History records that on April 23, 1497, Columbus met with Queen Isabella and King Ferdinand here after his second voyage to the New World. It was in this building, in 1506, that Philip the Handsome suffered a heart attack after a game of jai alai. His wife, Juana, dragged his body through the streets of Burgos, earning forever the name of Juana la Loca (the Mad).

Cartuja de Miraflores ★ Located 4km (2½ miles) east of the center of Burgos, this florid Gothic charterhouse was founded in 1441. King Juan II selected it as the royal tomb for himself and his queen, Isabel of Portugal. By 1494, the **church** ★ was finished, its sober facade belying the treasure-trove of decoration inside. The stunning attraction of the interior is the **sculptured unit** ★★★ in the apse, said to have been built with the first gold brought back from the New World. This is a masterpiece of design, and the faithful often stand here for an hour or two taking in its stunning beauty. It was the work, in the late 1400s, of Gil de Siloé, who also designed the polychrome wood altarpiece. The remains of the king and queen lie in the white marble mausoleum, designed like an eight-pointed star. The tomb's decorators gave these parents of Isabel the Catholic a fine send-off with exuberant, flamboyant Gothic decorations such as cherubs, pinnacles, canopies, and scrolls.

A detail from the altar of the Cartuja de Miraflores.

Carretera de Burgos a Cardeña Km 3. ℂ **94-725-25-86.** www.cartuja.org. Free admission. Mon–Sat 10:15am–3pm and 4–6pm; Sun 11am–3pm and 4–6pm.

Catedral de Santa María ★★★ Begun in 1221, this cathedral was one of the most celebrated in Europe. Built in diverse styles, predominantly flamboyant Gothic, it took 300 years to complete. Ornamented 15th-century bell towers flank the three main doorways by John of Cologne. The 16th-century Chapel of Condestable, behind the main altar, is one of the best examples of Isabelline-Gothic architecture, richly decorated with heraldic emblems, a sculptured filigree doorway, figures of apostles and saints, balconies, and an eight-sided-star stained-glass window.

Equally elegant are the two-story 14th-century cloisters, filled with fine Spanish Gothic sculpture. The cathedral's tapestries, including a well-known Gobelin, are rich in detail. In one of the chapels you'll see an old chest linked to the legend of El Cid—it was filled with gravel and used as collateral by the warrior to trick moneylenders. The remains of El Cid himself, together with those of his wife, Doña Ximena, lie under Santa María's octagonal, lanternlike dome. Finally, you might want to see the elaborate 16th-century Stairway of Gold in the north transept, the work of Diego de Siloé.

The cathedral is across the Arlanzón River from the railway station, midway between the river and the Citadel.

Plaza de Santa María s/n. ℂ **94-720-47-12.** www.catedraldeburgos.es. Admission to chapels, cloisters, and treasury 5€ adults, 4€ seniors, 3€ students, 1€ children 7–14, free for children 6 and under. Summer daily 9:30am–7:15pm; spring and fall daily 9:30am–1:15pm and 4–7:15pm; winter daily 10am–1:15pm and 4–6:45pm.

Monasterio de las Huelgas ★★ This cloister outside Burgos has seen a lot of action. Built in the 12th century in a richly ornamented style, it was once a summer place for Castilian royalty, as well as a retreat for nuns of royal blood. Inside, the Gothic church is built in the shape of a Latin cross. Despite unfortunate mixing of Gothic and baroque, it contains much of interest—notably some 14th- and 17th-century French tapestries. The tomb of the founder, Alfonso VIII, and of his queen, the daughter of England's Henry II, lie in the Choir Room.

Thirteenth-century doors lead to the cloisters, dating from that century and blending Gothic and Mudéjar styles. Despite severe damage to the ceiling, the remains of Persian peacock designs are visible. The beautiful Chapter Room contains the standard of the 12th-century Las Navas de Tolora (war booty taken from the Moors). The Museo de Ricas Telas is devoted to 13th-century costumes removed from tombs; these remarkably preserved textiles give you a rare peek at medieval dress.

The monastery is 1.6km (1 mile) off the Valladolid road (the turnoff is clearly marked). From Plaza Primo de Rivera in Burgos, buses for Las Huelgas leave every 20 minutes.

Calle Compás de Adentro s/n. © **94-720-16-30.** www.patrimonionacional.es. Admission 5€ adults, 2.50€ students and children 5–16. Tues–Sat 10am–1:15pm and 3:45–5:45pm; Sun 10:30am–2:15pm.

Shopping

A city as old and historic as Burgos is chockablock with emporia selling almost infinite numbers of ceramics, woodcarvings, and artifacts that include fireplace bellows crafted from leather, wood, and brass or copper. Many shops line the edges of the city's most central square, the Plaza Mayor, and the streets radiating from it. One in particular is especially worthwhile, with an appealing mixture of old and new artifacts (many from France): **Antigüedades Isla,** Calle Aparicio y Ruiz 17 (© **94-726-06-36**).

Where to Stay in Burgos

Mesón del Cid (p. 264) also rents rooms.

EXPENSIVE

Landa Palace ★★★ One of the greatest hotels of Castile, Landa Palace lies some 3km (1¾ miles) south of Burgos on N-1. A romantic getaway, it is in a handsomely restored castle from the 1300s, with later additions. Pilgrims once stopped here en route to Santiago de Compostela, in Galicia, but they wouldn't recognize the grandeur of the place today. Decorated with tasteful antiques, the lobby sets the tone with its white marble and ornate coffered ceiling. Guest rooms are spacious and cozily inviting, with antique decorations and tile floors. Marble bathrooms are state-of-the-art, with all the extras.

Carretera Madrid–Irún Km 235, 09001 Burgos. © **94-725-77-77.** Fax 94-726-46-76. www. landahotel.com. 39 units. 170€–200€ double; 230€–290€ suite. MC, V. Free parking. **Amenities:** Restaurant; bar; babysitting; exercise room; 2 heated pools (1 indoor, 1 outdoor); room service. *In room:* A/C, TV, hair dryer, minibar, Wi-Fi (free).

MODERATE

Hotel Almirante Bonifaz Book a room here more for the price than for any grand comfort. It is clean and decent, though the small rooms don't invite lingering. They are more suitable for an overnight stay. In lieu of air-conditioning, guests open their windows at night, although this subjects you to traffic noise. The hotel is near the river in the commercial part of town.

Calle Vitoria 22–24, 09004 Burgos. © **94-720-69-43.** Fax 94-725-64-04. www.almirante bonifaz.com. 79 units. 88€–150€ double. AE, DC, MC, V. Parking 11€. **Amenities:** Restaurant; bar; babysitting; room service. *In room:* A/C, TV, hair dryer, minibar (in some), Wi-Fi (free).

Hotel Rice ★★ 🎁 Located .8km (½ mile) north of the center, this is the town's leading boutique hotel. It is imbued with charm, grace, and character, almost like a London town house. Once you enter the British-style lobby, you'll feel snug, cozy, and comfortable, taking in the Queen Anne chairs, the marble surfaces, the antique cabinets, and the elegant fabrics. Guest rooms have elegant touches, with luxury mattresses and the best bathrooms in Burgos.

Av. Reyes Católicos 30, 09005 Burgos. ✆ **94-722-23-00.** Fax 94-722-35-50. www.hotelrice. com. 50 units. 48€–130€ double; from 105€ suite. AE, DC, MC, V. Parking 9€. **Amenities:** Restaurant; bar; babysitting; room service. *In room:* A/C, TV, hair dryer, minibar, Wi-Fi (free).

INEXPENSIVE

Hotel España The best budget choice in town since 1937 is a 5-minute walk southeast of the cathedral and a block south of the Plaza Mayor. It stands on a leafy promenade filled with sidewalk cafes and Castilians taking early-evening strolls. The small guest rooms lack style and imagination but are completely comfortable, with good beds and tidy bathrooms. The management is helpful to visitors. *Note:* When the España is full, they have been known to call around to other hostelries for stranded tourists.

Paseo del Espolón 32, 09003 Burgos. ✆ **94-720-63-40.** Fax 94-720-13-30. www.hotelespana. net. 69 units. 50€–72€ double. MC, V. Closed Dec 20–Jan 20. **Amenities:** Restaurant; babysitting. *In room:* TV.

Where to Dine in Burgos

The restaurants in the heart of Burgos, surrounding the cathedral, usually feature prices that soar as high as a Gothic spire. Every menu contains the roast lamb and suckling pig known throughout the area; or you might order *entremeses variados,* an appetizer sampler of many regional specialties.

Casa Ojeda ★ BURGALESE This top-notch restaurant combines excellent Burgos fare, cozy decor, attentive service, and moderate prices. Moorish tiles and low ceilings create an inviting ambience enhanced by intimate nooks, old lanterns, and intricate trelliswork. The cookery is the best in town. A la carte dishes include roast lamb, Basque-style hake, sole Harlequin, and chicken in garlic. House specialties are *alubias con chorizo y morcilla* (small white beans with spicy sausages); *sopa castellano;* spit-roasted lamb; and various kinds of fresh fish, especially hake.

Calle Vitoria 5. ✆ **94-720-90-52.** www.restauranteojeda.com. Reservations required. Main courses 16€–31€. AE, DC, MC, V. Daily 1:30–4pm; Mon–Sat 9–11:30pm.

Mesón del Cid ★ CASTILIAN In the heart of town on the most historic square, this restaurant and hotel is installed in a house-palace dating from the 15th century. It's the most centrally located place for either food or lodging. In the cozy restaurant with its traditional Castilian atmosphere, resting under handhewn beams, tables open onto views of the cathedral. For four generations the staff has been luring travelers with such dishes as Burgos-style roast suckling lamb, tenderloin of beef with wild mushrooms in a red-wine sauce, and grilled red tuna with candied tomato and crispy leeks. A good palate cleanser for dessert is the lemon-and-Spanish-champagne sorbet.

The restaurant also rents 56 well-furnished bedrooms in the traditional Castilian style. Doubles range in price from 70€ to 165€.

Plaza de Santa María 8. © **94-720-87-15.** www.mesondelcid.es. Reservations required. Main courses 16€–26€; tasting menus 30€–32€. AE, DC, MC, V. Mon–Sat 1:30–4:30pm and 8:30–11:30pm.

Mesón de los Infantes CASTILIAN/BASQUE Just below the gate (dating from the 16th c.) leading into Plaza de Santa María, this very appealing restaurant serves good food amid elegant Castilian, Burgalese, and classical decor. Many of the chef's specialties are based on recipes used in Castile for centuries. The roast suckling pig is everybody's favorite; or you can order river crabs Burgalese-style, beef tail with potatoes, or kidneys sautéed in sherry. A wide list of game is often featured, including hare, partridge, rabbit, and pigeon. Grilled steaks and roasts are also crowd pleasers. A time-honored dish that the owners are especially proud of is *olla podrida de Burgos;* it's a slow-cooked medley of red beans, ham hocks, pork sausage, and blood pudding—a meal in itself, eliminating the need for any starters unless you opt for a salad as an accompaniment.

Calle Corral de los Infantes. © **94-727-95-42.** Reservations recommended. Main courses 17€– 22€; fixed-price menus 13€–24€. AE, DC, MC, V. Daily noon–4:30pm and 8pm–midnight.

Rincón de España ✦ SPANISH This restaurant, about 1 block southwest of the cathedral, draws many discerning visitors. You can eat in the dining room or outdoors under a large awning (closed off by glass when the weather is threatening). The restaurant offers *platos combinados,* as well as a more extensive a la carte menu. Special dishes include grilled steaks, roast suckling lamb, barbecued lamb cutlets with potatoes, and roast chicken with sweet peppers. The food here is good, the portions are large, and the vegetables are fresh.

Nuño Rasura 11. © **94-720-59-55.** Reservations recommended. Main courses 10€–18€; fixed-price menus 14€–22€. AE, DC, MC, V. Daily noon–4pm and 8pm–midnight. Closed Mon–Tues night Jan–Mar.

A Side Trip to Santo Domingo de la Calzada ★

Some 68km (42 miles) east of Burgos, and easily visited on a day trip, lies Santo Domingo de la Calzada. The crowning achievement of the town, which grew as a stopover for pilgrims en route to Santiago de Compostela, is the 13th-century **cathedral ★** (© **94-134-00-33**), a national landmark. For the most part Gothic in style, it nevertheless contains a hodgepodge of architectural elements—Romanesque chapels, a Renaissance choir, and a free-standing baroque tower. St. Dominic, for whom the city is named, is buried in the crypt. A centuries-old legend is attached to the cathedral: Supposedly a rooster stood up and crowed after it had been cooked to protest the innocence of a pilgrim who had been accused of theft and sentenced to hang. To this day, a live cock and hen are kept in a cage up on the church wall, and you can often hear the rooster crowing at Mass. The cathedral is open March to December Monday to Saturday 10am to 1pm and 4 to 6:30pm (closed Jan–Feb). Admission is 3.50€ adults, 2.50€ ages 8 to 18, and free for everyone on Sunday for Mass. Motorists can reach Santo Domingo de la Calzada by following either of the traffic arteries paralleling the river, heading west from the Burgos cathedral until signs indicate N-120.

8

EXTREMADURA

T his remote region in westernmost Spain extends from the Gredos and Gata mountain ranges all the way south to Andalusia, and from Castile west to the Portuguese frontier. Spanish Extremadura (not to be confused with the Portuguese province of Extremadura) includes the provinces of Badajoz and Cáceres, and has a varied landscape of plains and mountains, meadows with holm and cork oaks, and fields of stone and lime.

The world knows Extremadura best as the land of the conquistadors. Famous sons include Cortés, Pizarro, and Balboa, as well as many less-famous but important explorers such as Francisco de Orellana and Hernando de Soto. These men were mostly driven by economic necessity, finding it hard to make a living in this dry, sun-parched province. The money they sent back to their native land financed mansions and public structures that stand today as monuments to their long-ago American adventures.

But those aren't Extremadura's only monuments to the past. Here you'll find Roman ruins in Mérida, Arabic ruins in Badajoz, and medieval palaces in Cáceres.

Extremadura is also a popular destination for outdoor fun. Spaniards come here to hunt, to enjoy the fishing and watersports popular in the many reservoirs, and to ride horseback along ancient trails. Because summer is intensely hot here, spring and fall are the best times to visit.

GUADALUPE ★★

188km (117 miles) W of Toledo, 225km (140 miles) SW of Madrid

Guadalupe lies in the province of Cáceres, 450m (1,500 ft.) above sea level. The village has a certain beauty and a lot of local color. Thanks to its famous shrine to the Virgin (also known as Our Lady of Guadalupe), it's packed with vendors and is a major outlet of the religious-souvenir industry. And it's easy to get around— everything of interest lies within a 3-minute walk of the bus drop-off point at Avenida Don Blas Pérez, also known as Carretera de Cáceres.

Around the corner and a few paces downhill is the Plaza Mayor, which contains the Town Hall (where many visitors stop in to ask questions, since there is no tourist office).

The village is best visited in spring, when the balconies of its whitewashed houses burst into bloom with flowers. Wander the twisting, narrow streets, some no more than alleyways. In fact, the buildings are so close together that in summer, you can walk in the shade of the steeply pitched sienna-colored tile roofs.

Getting There

Two **buses** operate every day to and from Madrid's Estación Sur (trip time: 3½ hr.). The road is poor, but the route through the surrounding regions is full of

FACING PAGE: **The Museo Nacional de Arte Romano in Mérida.**

savage beauty. In Guadalupe the buses park just uphill from the Town Hall. Call **Empresa La Sepulvedana,** in Madrid (*©* **91-559-89-55;** www.avanzabus. com), for schedules.

One narrow highway goes through Guadalupe. Most maps don't give it a number; look on a map in the direction of the town of Navalmoral de la Mata. From Madrid, take the winding C-401 southwest from Toledo, turning north in the direction of Navalmoral de la Mata after seeing signs for Navalmoral de la Mata and Guadalupe. Driving time from Madrid is between 3½ and 4½ hours, depending on how well you fare with the bad roads.

Exploring Guadalupe

Except for a handful of your basic souvenir shops around the Plaza Mayor, don't expect to find a lot of particularly interesting shopping in Guadalupe. The exception is the small but personalized **Cacharro Tienda,** Plaza Mayor 12 (*©* **92-715-42-67**), with an unusual collection of brass, copper, and iron.

Real Monasterio de Santa María de Guadalupe ★★ In 1325, a farmer searching for a stray cow reportedly spotted a statue of the Virgin buried in the soil. In time, this statue became venerated throughout the world, honored in Spain by Queen Isabella, Columbus, and Cervantes. Known as the Dark Virgin of Guadalupe, it is said to have been carved by St. Luke. A shrine was built to commemorate the statue, and tributes poured in from all over the world, making Guadalupe one of the wealthiest foundations in Christendom. The statue is found in the 18th-century chapel, **Camarín ★,** where a treasure-trove of riches surrounds the Virgin, including jasper, marble, and precious woods, plus nine paintings by Luca Giordano.

The church itself is noted for the wrought-iron railings in its naves and a magnificently decorated **sacristy ★★** with eight richly imaginative 17th-century

The Real Monasterio de Santa María de Guadalupe.

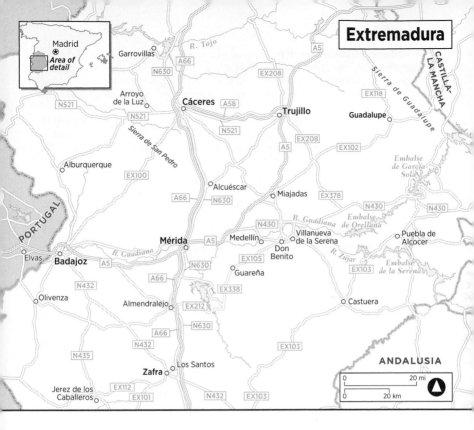

masterpieces by Francisco de Zurbarán. Don't miss the museum devoted to ecclesiastical vestments and choir books produced by 16th-century miniaturists. The 16th-century cloister is flamboyant Gothic in style, but the *pièces de résistance* are the stunning **Mudéjar cloister,** with its brick-and-tile Gothic Mudéjar shrine dating from 1405, and a **Moorish fountain** from the 14th century.

Plaza de Juan Carlos 1. ✆ **92-736-70-00.** www.monasterioguadalupe.com. Admission to museum and sacristy 4€ adults, 1.50€ children 7–14, free for children 6 and under. Daily 9:30am–1pm and 3:30–6:30pm.

Where to Stay in Guadalupe

Hospedería del Real Monasterio ★ Here's your chance to stay in an antique monastery. Once a way station for pilgrims visiting the shrine, the *hospedería* used to provide lodging in return for a small donation. Times have changed, but the prices remain moderate at this government-rated two-star hotel in the center of town. It's the second-best place to stay, after the *parador* (see below), and a whole lot cheaper. Since the place was converted from a monastery, accommodations come in various shapes and sizes, each tastefully furnished and fitted with a firm bed and well-maintained bathroom.

Plaza Juan Carlos 1, 10140 Guadalupe. ✆ **92-736-70-00.** Fax 92-736-71-77. www.monasterio guadalupe.com. 47 units. 65€ double; 87€ triple. AE, MC, V. Closed Jan 8–Feb 8. **Amenities:** Restaurant; bar. *In room:* A/C, hair dryer.

Parador de Guadalupe ★★ Located in a scenic spot in the center of the village, the area's most luxurious rooms are in a 15th-century building with a beautiful garden. Queen Isabella once stayed here, and the place was often the site of meetings between royal representatives and explorers, who signed their contracts here before setting out for the New World. The house is named after Francisco de Zurbarán, the great 17th-century painter who was born in the nearby town of Fuente de Cantos. There is a copy of a Zurbarán painting in one of the salons, along with reproduction maps and engravings—many of them valuable works of art. Most of the comfortable rooms are quite spacious.

Marqués de la Romana 12, 10140 Guadalupe. (C) **92-736-70-75.** Fax 92-736-70-76. www. parador.es. 41 units. 115€–165€ double. AE, DC, MC, V. Parking 10€. **Amenities:** Restaurant; bar; outdoor pool; room service. *In room:* A/C, TV, hair dryer, minibar.

Where to Dine in Guadalupe

Both of the hotels recommended above have good restaurants.

LAND OF THE conquistadors

It's estimated that some 15,000 Extremeños (from a total pop. of 400,000) went to seek gold in the New World. The most fabled of these adventurers were Hernán Cortés (from Medellín), who went to Mexico; Francisco Pizarro (from Trujillo), who went to Peru; Vasco Núñez de Balboa (from Jerez de los Caballeros), who landed in Panama, where he first sighted the Pacific Ocean; Hernando de Soto (from Barcarrota), who discovered the Mississippi River and explored Florida and beyond; and Francisco de Orellana (also from Trujillo), who ventured through Ecuador and the Amazon.

Thanks to these conquistadors, the names of Extremaduran villages are sprinkled through the Americas, as exemplified by the Guadalupe Mountains (Texas), Albuquerque (New Mexico), Trujillo (Peru), Mérida (Mexico), and Medellín (Colombia).

Because Extremeños faced such difficulty making a living in the harsh land of their birth, they often turned elsewhere to seek their fortune. One reason for the area's extreme poverty was that huge tracts of land, used for ranching, were owned by absentee landlords (as many still are today). These ranches are called *latifundios,* and they're often home to tenant farmers and their families, who pay the owners for the privilege of grazing a few goats or growing scanty crops in the dry climate. Worse, a system of *mayorazgo* (still in effect) decreed that all family property must be passed to the eldest son, leaving any younger sons, called *secundinos,* penniless. Not surprisingly, many of *secundinos* set sail for the New World to seek gold.

Plenty of conquistadors died or stayed in the New World, but others, who had grown rich there, returned to the land of their birth and built magnificent homes, villas, and ranches, many of which stand today. Bernal Díaz, who joined the Cortés expedition to Mexico, described the situation very bluntly. "We came here to serve God and the king," he wrote, "and to get rich."

Hostal-Restaurante 🍴 EXTREMADURAN The best place to dine in town is also a hotel that rents inexpensive rooms. The menu is regional, a delicious cuisine of Extremadura using local products whenever available. Set on the main street of town, the restaurant lies right off the landmark Plaza Mayor. Holding up to 220 diners, it has a warmly tinted classical decor and reasonable prices.

Start perhaps with gazpacho or else black thin-sliced cured ham. Roast lamb, roast goat, and roast suckling pig are the chef's main specialties, although you can also order succulently prepared lobster or calamari. The desserts, home-made daily, are most tempting.

The *hostal* offers 18 simply furnished rooms that are nonetheless comfortable and well maintained. Doubles rent for 50€ to 60€ per night.

Gregorio López 20. ✆ **972-36-73-79.** Fax 927-36-75-31. www.hostalcerezo.com. Main courses 8.50€–16€. AE, DC, MC, V. Daily 1–4pm and 8–11pm.

TRUJILLO ★

245km (152 miles) SW of Madrid, 45km (28 miles) E of Cáceres

Dating from the 13th century, the walled town of Trujillo is known for the colonizers and conquerors born here. Among its famous natives are Francisco Pizarro, the conqueror of Peru (whose family palace on the Plaza Mayor was built with gold from the New World), and Francisco de Orellana, the founder of Guayaquil, Ecuador, and the first European to explore the Amazon. Other Trujillano history-makers were Francisco de las Casas, who accompanied Hernán Cortés in his conquest of Mexico and founded the city of Trujillo in Honduras; Diego García de Paredes, who founded Trujillo in Venezuela; Nuño de Chaves, founder of Santa Cruz de la Sierra in Bolivia; and several hundred others whose names are found throughout the Americas. There is a saying that 20 American countries were born here.

Celts, Romans, Moors, and Christians have inhabited Trujillo over the centuries. The original town, lying above today's modern one, was built on a granite ledge on the hillside. It is centered on the Plaza Mayor, one of the artistic landmarks of Spain. A Moorish castle and a variety of 16th- and 17th-century palaces, manor houses, towers, churches, and arcades encircle the plaza and overlook a bronze equestrian statue of Pizarro by American artists Mary Harriman and Charles Runse. Steep, narrow streets and shadowy little corners evoke the bygone times when explorers set out from here on their history-making adventures.

Essentials

GETTING THERE There are 12 **buses** per day to and from Madrid (trip time: 3½–4½ hr.). There are also six buses running daily from Cáceres (45 min.), and five from Badajoz (2 hr.). A one-way ticket from Madrid costs 19€ to 30€; from Cáceres, 4€; and from Badajoz, 12€ to 20€. Trujillo's bus station, Calle Marqués Albayda (✆ **92-732-12-02;** www.avanzabus.com), is on the south side of town, on a side street that intersects with Calle de la Encarnación.

Trujillo lies at a network of large and small roads connecting it to Cáceres via the N-521 and to Lisbon and Madrid via the N-V superhighway. **Driving** time from Madrid is around 4 hours.

VISITOR INFORMATION The **tourist office,** on Plaza Mayor (✆ **92-732-26-77;** www.ayto-trujillo.com), is open daily 10am to 2pm and 4 to 7pm.

Exploring Trujillo's Plaza & Beyond

In the heart of Trujillo, **Plaza Mayor ★★** is one of the outstanding architectural sights of Extremadura. It's dominated by a statue honoring Francisco Pizarro, who almost single-handedly destroyed Peru's Inca civilization. The statue is an exact double of one standing in Lima. Indeed, many of the buildings on this square were financed with wealth brought back from the New World.

The square's most prominent structure is the **Ayuntamiento Viejo (Old Town Hall),** with three tiers of arches, each tier squatter than the one below.

Iglesia de San Martín stands behind the statue dedicated to Pizarro. This granite church, originally from the 15th century, was reconstructed in the 16th century in Renaissance style. Inside are an impressive nave, several tombs, and a rare 18th-century organ still in working condition.

While you're on the square, observe the unusual facade of **Casa de las Cadenas,** a 12th-century house draped with a heavy chain, a symbol meant to show that Philip II had granted the Orellana family immunity from heavy taxes.

You can then visit the **Palacio de los Duques de San Carlos,** a 16th-century ducal residence now used as a convent. Ring the bell to gain entry Monday to Saturday 9:30am to 1pm and 4:30 to 6:30pm, and Sunday 10am to 12:30pm. An entrance fee of 1.50€ is required, and a resident will show you around; appropriate dress (no shorts or bare shoulders) is required. Note the Renaissance figures sculpted on the facade. The two-level courtyard inside is even more impressive.

Palacio de la Conquista, also on the square, is one of the most grandiose mansions in Trujillo. Originally constructed by Hernán Pizarro, the present structure was built by his son-in-law to commemorate the exploits of this explorer, who accompanied his half-brother, Francisco, to Peru.

The stores that ring the Plaza Mayor have the town's best **shopping;** they stock stonework, leather, brass, copper, and ironwork.

Castillo Constructed by the Moors on the site of a Roman fortress, this castle stands at the summit of the granite hill on which Trujillo was founded. Once at the castle, you can climb its battlements and walk along the ramparts, enjoying a panoramic view of Extremadura's austere countryside. Later, you can go below and see the dungeons. It is said that the Virgin Mary appeared here in 1232, giving the Christians renewed courage to free the city from domination by the Moors. *Tip:* Many visitors find it most dramatic at sunset.

Crowning the hilltop. Admission 1.40€. June 1–Sept 30 daily 10am–2pm and 5–8:30pm; Oct 1–May 31 10am–2pm and 4–8pm.

Pizarro on horseback in the Plaza Mayor.

Iglesia de Santa María This Gothic church, with its outstanding Renaissance choir, is the largest in Trujillo, having been built over the ruins of a Moorish mosque. Ferdinand and Isabella once attended Mass here. The proudest treasure is a *retablo* (altar) with two dozen panels painted by Fernando Gallego. Also here is the tomb of Diego García de Paredes, the "Samson of Extremadura," who is said to have single-handedly defended a bridge against an attacking French army with only a gigantic sword. To reach the church, go through the gate of Plaza Mayor at Puerta de San Andrés and take Calle de las Palomas through the Old Town.

Calle de Ballesteros. ☏ **92-732-02-11.** Admission 1.40€. Apr–Sept daily 10am–2pm and 5–9pm; Oct–Mar daily 10am–2pm and 4–7pm.

Where to Stay in Trujillo

Hotel Victoria ★ 📖 This small, delightful hotel lies a 5-minute walk from the Plaza Mayor in an ornate 19th-century colonial mansion. The interior is light and airy, and the rooms surround what was once the house's courtyard. Each level is adorned with filigreed pillars and ornate wrought-iron balustrades and capitals. The accommodations are spacious, with wooden ceilings, tiled marble floors, and comfortable beds, along with modern conveniences such as private, well-equipped bathrooms.

Plaza del Campillo 22, 10200 Trujillo. ☏ **92-732-18-19.** Fax 92-732-30-84. www.hotelvictoria trujillo.es. 27 units. 80€ double; 125€ triple. AE, MC, V. Parking 10€. **Amenities:** Restaurant; bar. *In room:* A/C, TV, hair dryer.

Izán Trujillo ★ 📖 This charming hotel, from the small Spanish chain Izán, was once a monastery (with its adjoining cloisters) from the 1600s (El Convento de San Antonio). The grace note is a lovely old courtyard with a swimming pool that's simply the best place to escape the midday summer heat of Trujillo. Guest rooms come in various shapes and sizes, ranging from small to spacious. The on-site restaurant is installed in the former refectory. Like the building itself, the refectory has been handsomely converted in keeping with the spirit of the building. Regional and Spanish specialties are served, and the cookery is exceptional for the area.

Plaza del Campillo 1, Trujillo 10200. ☏ **92-745-89-00.** Fax 92-732-30-46. www.izanhoteles.es. 77 units. 85€–150€ double; 115€–190€ triple. AE, DC, MC, V. Parking 15€. **Amenities:** Restaurant; bar; outdoor pool; room service. *In room:* A/C, TV, hair dryer, minibar, Wi-Fi (free).

Las Cigüeñas Located east of the town center and convenient if you're driving, this place doesn't have the charm of the *parador* (see below), but it's cheaper. A roadside hotel with a garden, it offers functional but clean and comfortable guest rooms, which, though small, are equipped with firm mattresses and well-maintained bathrooms. You'll find Las Cigüeñas on the main highway from Madrid, about 1.6km (1 mile) before Trujillo.

Av. de Madrid s/n, 10200 Trujillo. ☏ **92-732-12-50.** Fax 92-732-13-00. www.hotelasciguenas.com. 44 units. 75€–94€ double; 90€–120€ suite. AE, DC, MC, V. Free parking. **Amenities:** Restaurant; bar; room service; Wi-Fi (free, in lobby). *In room:* A/C, TV, hair dryer, minibar.

Parador de Trujillo ★★★ Housed in the 1533 Convent of Santa Clara, this centrally located *parador,* about a block south of Avenida de la Coronación, is a gem of Trujillo-style medieval and Renaissance architecture that's been faithfully restored since being converted into a *parador* in 1984. The beautifully decorated rooms, once nuns' cells, have canopied beds and spacious bathrooms. The *parador* has been renovated with a mixture of rustic and modern furniture, and modern additions to the building (for example, a courtyard in its new section) blend seamlessly with the original convent architecture. The gardens and fruit trees of the Renaissance cloister are inviting.

Calle de Santa Beatriz de Silva 1, 10200 Trujillo. ✆ **92-732-13-50.** Fax 92-732-13-66. www. parador.es. 50 units. 143€–155€ double; 179€–215€ double superior; 229€–248€ suite. AE, DC, MC, V. Free parking. **Amenities:** Restaurant; bar; babysitting; outdoor pool; room service. *In room:* A/C, TV, hair dryer, minibar, Wi-Fi (free).

Where to Dine in Trujillo

The hotels recommended above have good restaurants serving regional cuisine.

Mesón la Troya EXTREMADURAN Locals and visitors alike are drawn to this centrally located restaurant featuring regional cuisine and doing the province proud. Have a dry sherry in the bar, which resembles the facade of a Spanish house. This cozy provincial theme continues into the dining rooms, where the white walls are decorated with ceramic plates, potted plants, and red tiles. Few people leave hungry after devouring the fixed-price menu, with its more-than-ample portions; food items change daily. Local dishes include *prueba de cerdo* (garlic-flavored pork casserole), *carne con tomate* (beef cooked in tomato sauce), and spit-roasted goat.

Plaza Mayor 10. ✆ **92-732-13-64.** Reservations not accepted. Tapas 3€–15€; fixed-price menu 16€. MC, V. Daily 1–4:30pm and 8:45–11:30pm.

Pizarro EXTREMADURAN Locals cite this central *hostal* as the best place to go for regional Extremaduran cookery at lunch. Built in 1864, the inn is set on the town's main square and is named for its famous son. The same family has owned and operated the place since 1919. Regional wines accompany meals that invariably include ham from acorn-fed pigs. You might begin with asparagus with mayonnaise sauce, and then follow with *asado de cordero* (roast lamb flavored with herbs and garlic) or Roman-style fried *merluza* (hake); roast goat is a local favorite. The kitchen's game specialty is *estofado de perdices* (partridge casserole).

Plaza Mayor 13. ✆ **92-732-02-55.** Reservations recommended. Main courses 8€–16€; *menú del día* 15€. AE, DC, MC, V. Wed–Mon 1–4pm.

CÁCERES ★★

298km (185 miles) SW of Madrid, 256km (159 miles) N of Seville

A national landmark and the capital of Extremadura, Cáceres is encircled by old city walls and has several palaces and towers, many financed by gold sent from the Americas by the conquistadors.

One of six cities in Spain designated World Heritage Sites by UNESCO, Cáceres was founded in the 1st century B.C. by the Romans as Norba Caesarina. Its present-day name is derived from *alcázares,* an Arab word meaning "fortified citadel." After the Romans, it was settled by all the cultures that have made the south of Spain the cultural melting pot of influences it is today. The contemporary city offers a unique blend of the traces these successive invaders left behind.

Essentials

GETTING THERE Cáceres has the best **rail** connections in the province, with five trains per day from Madrid (trip time: 4–5 hr.). A one-way ticket costs 25€ to 41€. There is also one train per day from Lisbon (4½ hr.); the fare ranges from 50€ to 123€.

The station in Cáceres is on Avenida Alemania (📞 **90-224-02-02**), near the main highway heading south (Carretera de Sevilla). A green-and-white bus shuttles passengers about once an hour from the railway and bus stations (across the street from one another; board the shuttle outside the bus station) to the busiest traffic junction in the new city, the Plaza de América. From there it's a 10-minute walk to the edge of the Old Town.

Bus connections to Cáceres are more frequent than railway connections. From the city bus station (📞 **92-723-25-50**) on busy Carretera de Sevilla, about .8km (½ mile) south of the city center, buses arrive and depart for Madrid (trip time: 5 hr.) and Seville (4½ hr.) every 2 to 3 hours. There's also bus transport to Guadalupe (one per day); Trujillo (six or seven a day); Mérida (four a day); Valladolid (two a day); and Córdoba (two a day). Many travelers opt to walk the short distance from the Cáceres bus station to the city center.

Driving time from Madrid is about 4 hours. Most people approach Cáceres from eastern Spain via the N-V superhighway until they reach Trujillo. Here they exit onto the N-521, driving another 45km (28 miles) west to Cáceres.

VISITOR INFORMATION The **tourist office,** Plaza Mayor s/n (📞 **92-701-08-34;** www.turismoextremadura.com), is open Monday to Friday 9am to 2pm and 4 to 6pm, and Saturday and Sunday 9:45am to 2pm. Don't expect efficiency. Things around here are slow.

Exploring the Old Town of Cáceres

The modern city lies southwest of the *barrio antiguo,* **Cáceres Viejo ★★★**, which is enclosed by massive **ramparts.** The heart of the Old City lies between Plaza de Santa María and, a few blocks to the south, Plaza San Mateo. **Plaza de Santa María ★** is an irregularly shaped, rather elongated square. On each of its sides are the honey-brown facades of buildings once inhabited by the local nobility. On a casual stroll through the city's cobblestone streets, your attention will surely be drawn to the walls that enclose the old upper town. These are a mixture of Roman and Arab engineering, and they are outstandingly preserved. About 30 towers remain from the city's medieval walls, all of them heavily restored. Originally much taller, the towers reflected the pride and independence of their builders; when Queen Isabella took control, however, she ordered them cut down to size. The largest tower is at Plaza del General Mola. Beside it stands **El Arco de la Estrella (The Arch of the Star),** constructed by Manuel Churriguera in the 18th century. To its right you'll see the Torre del Horno, a mud-brick adobe structure left from the Moorish occupation.

On the far side of Plaza de Santa María rises the **Catedral de Santa María,** basically Gothic in style although many Renaissance embellishments have been added. Completed sometime in the 1500s, this is the cathedral of Cáceres and contains the remains of many conquistadors. It has three Gothic aisles of almost equal height and a carved *retablo* at the high altar dating from the 16th century. (Insert coins to light it up.)

Cáceres Viejo, the Old City.

La Casa de los Toledo-Montezuma was built by Juan Cano de Saavedra with money from the dowry of his wife, the daughter of Montezuma. The house is set into the northern corner of the medieval ramparts, about a block to the north of Plaza de Santa María. It is now a public-records office.

Plaza Mayor is remarkably free from most of the blemishes and scars that city planning and overregulation have made so common in other historically important sites. Passing through El Arco de la Estrella (The Arch of the Star), you will catch the most advantageous angle at which to view Catedral de Santa María.

Some of the most appealing shops in Cáceres are on the streets radiating from the Plaza Mayor, with a particularly good selection of artifacts along either side of **Calle Pintores.**

Cuesta de la Compañía leads to Plaza San Mateo and the 14th-century **Iglesia de San Mateo,** which has a Plateresque portal and a rather plain nave—except for the Plateresque tombs, which add a decorative touch.

Two adjoining *plazuelas* near here embody the flavor of old Cáceres. The first of them, **Plaza de las Veletas,** on the site of the old Alcázar, has **Casa de las Veletas (Weather Vane House; ✆ 92-701-08-77)**, site of a provincial archaeological museum with priceless prehistoric and Roman pieces, along with a famous *alijibe* (Arab well). Its baroque facade, ancient Moorish cistern, five naves with horseshoe arches, and patio and paneling from the 17th century have been preserved. The museum displays Celtic and Visigothic remains, Roman and Gothic artifacts, and a numismatic collection. Admission is free. The museum is open Tuesday to Saturday 9am to 2:30pm and 4 to 7pm; on Sunday, 10am to 2:30pm. At the second *plazuela,* **San Pablo,** sits **Casa de las Cigüeñas (House of the Storks),** the only palace whose tower remains intact despite the order by Queen Isabella at the turn of the 15th century to reduce the height of all such strategic locations for military reasons. The building now serves as a military headquarters and is not open to the public.

You'll probably notice lots of storks nesting on the rooftops and bell towers in town. This is a revealing sign of how Cáceres has managed to preserve not only its landmarks but also an environmentally sound balance between people and nature.

The **Church of Santiago** was begun in the 12th century and restored in the 16th century. It has a reredos carved in 1557, by Alonso de Berruguete, and a 15th-century figure of Christ. The church is outside the ramparts, about a block to the north of Arco de Socorro. To reach it, exit the gate, enter Plaza Socorro, and then walk down Calle Godoy. The church is on your right.

If you want to see a more modern face of the region, and shop for housewares and fashion while you're at it, drive 15 minutes west of the town center to the **Centro Comercial Ruta de la Plata,** Carretera Portugal, where you'll find a scattering of boutiques, plus a number of simple snack bars and cafes.

Where to Stay in Cáceres

Hotel Extremadura This 1960s hotel offers straightforward rooms. They're a bit boxy and functionally furnished but they're well maintained and very comfortable, with good beds and immaculate bathrooms. The hotel is about .8km (½ mile) southwest of the historic center in a bustling commercial district. Prices are fair for what you get.

Av. Virgen de Guadalupe 28, 10001 Cáceres. ☎ **92-762-96-39.** Fax 92-762-92-49. www.extremadura hotel.com. 151 units. 160€ double; 195€ junior suite; 355€ suite. AE, DC, MC, V. Parking 13€. **Amenities:** Restaurant; bar; babysitting; outdoor pool; room service. *In room:* A/C, TV, hair dryer, minibar, Wi-Fi (12€ per 24 hr.).

Cáceres's Plaza Mayor.

Palacete Alameda ★★ 🍴 This old and noble house, built at the turn of the 20th century, has been completely restored and turned into the town's most romantic and inviting hotel. The original design has been preserved wherever possible, including the Venetian stucco of the central stairs (a Venetian architect was imported). For such luxury, the place is amazingly affordable. Some of the rooms are very spacious, as are the bathrooms. Modern facilities have been installed but each room is individually designed, with comfort a major consideration. On a romantic patio guests drink fresh orange juice and just-brewed coffee early in the morning. The location is idyllic, in the heart of town at the Plaza Mayor.

Calle General Margallo 45, 10003 Cáceres. ℂ/fax **92-721-16-74.** www.alamedapalacete.com. 9 units. 60€–75€ double; 85€–100€ suite. MC, V. Nearby parking 8€. *In room:* A/C, TV, no phone, Wi-Fi (free).

Parador de Cáceres ★★ At press time, this hotel was set to reopen in spring 2011, after a complete restoration. The state-operated *parador* is set within what was originally a 15th-century palace. Built in a severe style, it enjoys a tranquil location and a well-scrubbed, durable format of exposed stone, white plaster, and tile or stone floors. Pristine corridors lead to dignified rooms outfitted in a starkly appealing combination of white walls and dark-grained furniture, inspired by the austere decorative traditions of Extremadura. Modern extras that have been installed here include excellent bathrooms. Suits of armor adorn some of the public areas, giving the place a vaguely feudal feel, but the patios that open onto masses of potted plants and flowers are quite welcoming.

Calle Ancha 6, 10003 Cáceres. ℂ **92-721-17-59.** Fax 92-721-17-29. www.parador.es. 33 units. 160€–180€ double; 235€ suite. AE, DC, MC, V. Street parking free; garage parking 17€. **Amenities:** Restaurant; bar; babysitting; room service; Wi-Fi (free, in lobby). *In room:* A/C, TV, hair dryer, minibar.

Where to Dine in Cáceres

Atrio ★★★ SPANISH/CONTINENTAL Atrio serves the finest cuisine in the entire province. Even hard-to-please Michelin grants this place two stars. Situated in a shopping mall cul-de-sac, the Atrio features elegant dining-room decor. The chef steers a skillful course between rich, regional flavors and more Continental fare. The menu changes frequently to take advantage of the best of each season. Prices can exceed those indicated below if truffles are added to your dish. Service is the finest in the area—in all, it's a deluxe operation.

Av. de España 22. ℂ **92-724-29-28.** www.restauranteatrio.com. Reservations recommended. Fixed-price menus 80€–108€. AE, DC, MC, V. Daily 1:30–4pm; Mon–Sat 9pm–midnight. Closed last 2 weeks in July.

◉ The Flavor of the Land

The cuisine offered at the *parador* and at many other places in Cáceres affords a novel experience to even seasoned travelers. You might try the famous *cuchifrito,* suckling pig stewed in pepper, orange, and vinegar sauce; or *caldereta de cordero,* lamb with pepper and almonds. A more daring choice would be *jabalí a la cacereña,* wild boar marinated in red wine and herbs. The most characteristic dessert in all of Extremadura is *técula mécula,* an ancient example of the region's marzipan confectionery, which, like most things in Cáceres, has been passed down from one generation to the next for centuries.

El Figón de Eustaquio ★ EXTREMADURAN El Figón is a pleasant place serving regional cuisine that has been satisfying locals since 1948. You'll notice the four Blanco brothers, who run the place, doing practically everything. This includes preparing the amazingly varied dishes—honey soup, *solomillo* (filet of beef), and trout Extremaduran style (covered in ham), as well as typical Spanish specialties. The air-conditioned interior has a rustic decor. El Figón is west of the western ramparts of the Old City, near the intersection of Avenida Virgen de Guadalupe and Plaza San Juan.

Plaza San Juan 14. ✆ **92-724-43-62.** www.elfigondeeustaquio.com. Reservations recommended. Main courses 10€–35€; fixed-price menus 30€–45€. AE, DC, MC, V. Daily 1:30–4pm and 8pm–midnight. Closed July 1–15.

Torre de Sande ★ NOUVELLE SPANISH Set in a 15th-century palace in Plaza de San Mateo, at the city's highest point, this restaurant features a trio of separate dining rooms and a beautiful terraced garden (in use as weather permits). The view of the city from the garden is panoramic, and especially wonderful at night. The kitchen combines regional flavors and the best of modern recipes, with palate-pleasing and marvelously succulent results. Try such local dishes as *boletus con foie* (mushrooms with duck liver), *ensalada de mango y salmón* (mango and salmon salad), *solomillo de retinto* (a prized local beefsteak), or *perdiz a la cantara con salsa* (partridge stuffed with liver and truffles in a port-wine sauce). Desserts include *tapita de tres chocolates* (layer cake of three types of chocolate) and sheep's-milk pudding.

Calle de los Condes 3. ✆ **92-721-11-47.** Reservations recommended. Main courses 16€–24€. AE, DC, MC, V. Tues–Sat noon–4pm and 7pm–midnight. Closed 2 weeks in June and 2 weeks in Jan.

MÉRIDA ★

71km (44 miles) S of Cáceres, 56km (35 miles) E of Badajoz

Founded in 25 B.C., Mérida is at the intersection of the Roman roads linking Toledo with Lisbon and Salamanca with Seville. Once the capital of Lusitania (the Latin name for ancient Portugal, which included parts of southwestern Spain), Mérida was one of the most splendid cities in Iberia. It ranked as a town of major importance in the Roman Empire—in fact, it was once called a miniature Rome. Its monuments, temples, and public works make it the site of some of the finest Roman ruins in Spain, and as such it is the tourist capital of Extremadura. Old Mérida can be covered on foot—in fact, that's the only way to see it. Pay scant attention to the dull modern suburb across the Guadiana River, which skirts the town with its sluggish waters.

Essentials

GETTING THERE **Trains** depart from and arrive at the RENFE station on Calle Cardero (✆ **90-224-02-02;** www.renfe.com), about .8km (½ mile) north of the Plaza de España. Each day there are six trains to and from Cáceres (trip time: 1 hr.), five trains to and from Madrid (5–6 hr.), one to and from Seville (3 hr.), and seven to and from Badajoz (1 hr.). The fare from Madrid to Mérida is 30€ to 46€, depending on the type of train (local, morning, or night express train).

The **bus** station is on Avenida de la Libertad (✆ **92-437-14-04**), near the train station. Every day there are seven buses to and from Madrid (trip time: 5½ hr.), 6 to 12 buses to and from Seville (3 hr.), 3 buses to and from Cáceres (1 hr.), and 5 to 10 buses to and from Badajoz (1 hr.). From Mérida to Madrid, the fare is 20€ for a local bus, 36€ for an express; Mérida to Seville, 13€; Mérida to Cáceres, 11€; and Mérida to Badajoz, 9€.

To drive, take the N-V superhighway from Madrid or Lisbon. Driving time from Madrid is approximately 5 hours; from Lisbon, about 4½ hours. Park in front of the Roman theater and explore the town on foot.

VISITOR INFORMATION The **tourist office,** at Santa Eulalia 64 (© **92-433-07-22;** www.turismoextremadura.com), is open April to September Monday to Friday 9:30am to 1:45pm and 5 to 7pm, and Saturday 9:30am to 2pm. Off-season hours are Monday to Friday 9:30am to 2pm and 4 to 6pm, and Saturday and Sunday 9am to 2pm. Note that these are the *official* hours, but don't expect the staff to follow them too literally.

Exploring Mérida

The **Roman bridge** ★ over the Guadiana was the longest in Roman Spain—about half a mile—and consisted of 64 arches. It was constructed of granite under Trajan or Augustus, and then restored by the Visigoths in 686. Philip II ordered further refurbishment in 1610, and work was also done in the 19th century. The bridge crosses the river south of the center of Old Mérida, its length increased because of the way it spans two forks of the river, including an island in midstream. In 1993, it was restored yet again and turned into a pedestrian walkway. A semicircular suspension bridge was built to carry the heavy auto traffic and save the Roman bridge for future generations. Before the restoration and change, this span served as a main access road into Mérida, enduring the evolution of transportation from hooves and feet to trucks and automobiles.

Another sight of interest is the old hippodrome, or **Circus Maximus,** which could seat about 30,000 spectators for chariot races. The original Roman masonry was carted off for use in other buildings, and today the site looks more like a parking lot, though excavations have uncovered rooms that may have housed gladiators. The former circus is at the end of Avenida Extremadura on the northeastern outskirts of Old Town, about .8km (½ mile) north of the Roman bridge and a 10-minute walk east of the railway station.

Arco Trajano (Trajan's Arch) lies near the heart of the Old Town beside Calle Trajano, about a block south of the Parador Vía de la Plata. An unadorned triumphal arch, it measures 15m (49 ft.) high and 9m (30 ft.) across.

Acueducto de los Milagros is the most intact of the town's two remaining Roman aqueducts; this one brought water from Proserpina, 5km (3 miles) away. From the aqueducts, water was fed into two artificially created lakes, Cornalvo and Proserpina. The aqueduct is northwest of Old Town, lying to the right of the road to Cáceres, just beyond the railway tracks. Ten arches still stand.

The latest monument to be excavated is the **Temple of Diana** (dedicated to Caesar Augustus). Squeezed between houses on a narrow residential street, it was converted in the 17th century into the private residence of a nobleman, who used four of the original Corinthian columns in his architectural plans. The temple lies at the junction of Calle Sagasta and Calle Romero Leal, in the center of town.

While in the area, you can explore the 13th-century **Iglesia de Santa María la Mayor,** Plaza de España, on the west side of the square. It has a 16th-century chapel graced with Romanesque and Plateresque features.

A classical play at Mérida's Teatro Romano.

Alcazaba On the northern bank of the Guadiana River, beside the northern end of the Roman bridge (which it was meant to protect), stands the Alcázar, also known as the Conventual or the Alcazaba. Built in the 9th century by the Moors, who used fragments left from Roman and Visigothic occupations, the square structure was later granted to the Order of Santiago.

Plaza del Rastro, Calle Graciano s/n. ℂ **92-431-73-09.** Admission 4€. June–Sept daily 9:30am–1:45pm and 5–7:15pm; Oct–May daily 9:30am–1:45pm and 4–6:15pm.

Anfiteatro Romano ★ At the height of its glory in the 1st century B.C., this amphitheater could seat 14,000 to 15,000 spectators. Chariot races were held here, along with gladiator combats and mock sea battles, for which the arena would be flooded. Many of the seats were placed dangerously close to the bloodshed. You can visit some of the rooms that housed the wild animals and gladiators waiting to go into battle.

Calle José Ramón Melida s/n. ℂ **92-431-25-30.** Admission 7€ adults, 6€ seniors and children 9–16 (includes admission to Teatro Romano), free for children 8 and under. Daily 9:30am–1:45pm and 4–6:15pm.

Museo Arqueológico de Arte Visigodo This archaeological museum, in front of Trajan's Arch, houses a treasure-trove of artifacts left by the conquering Visigoths.

Calle Santa Julia, Plaza de España. ℂ **92-431-01-16.** Free admission. July–Sept Tues–Sat 10am–2pm and 5–7pm, Sun 10am–2pm; Oct–June Tues–Sat 10am–2pm and 4–6pm, Sun 10am–2pm.

Museo Nacional de Arte Romano ★★ Located in a modern building adjacent to the ancient Roman amphitheater, to which it is connected by an underground tunnel, this museum is acclaimed as the greatest repository of Roman artifacts in Spain. Not only does it contain more than 30,000 artifacts from Augusta Emerita, capital of the Roman province of Lusitania, but it also incorporates part of a Roman road discovered in the early 1980s during the building's construction. Many of the museum's sculptures come from the excavations of the Roman theater and amphitheater. You'll see displays of mosaics, figures, pottery, glassware, coins, and bronze objects. The museum is built of red brick in the form of a Roman basilica.

Calle José Ramón Melida s/n. © **92-431-16-90.** www.mnar.es. Admission 3€ adults, free for students and children 16 and under. Mar–Nov Tues–Sat 10am–2pm and 4–9pm, Sun 10am–2pm; Dec–Feb Tues–Sat 10am–2pm and 4–6pm, Sun 10am–2pm.

Teatro Romano ★★ This Roman theater, one of the best-preserved Roman ruins in the world, was built by Agrippa (Augustus's son-in-law) in 18 B.C. to house an audience of 6,000 people. Modeled after the great theaters of Rome, it was constructed using dry-stone methods, a remarkable achievement. During the reign of Hadrian (2nd c. A.D.), a tall stage wall was adorned with statues and colonnades. Behind the stage, today's visitors can explore excavations of various rooms. From the end of June to early July, you can also enjoy a season of classical plays.

José Ramón Melida s/n. © **92-431-25-30.** Admission 7€ adults, 6€ seniors and children 9–16 (includes admission to Anfiteatro Romano), free for children 8 and under. Daily 9:30am–1:45pm and 4–6:15pm.

Where to Stay in Mérida

Nova Roma 🦯 Lacking the old-world charm of the Parador de Mérida (see below), the 1991 Nova Roma is for those with more modern taste. Clean, comfortable, and functionally furnished, it's a good value for this heavily frequented tourist town. Guest rooms range from small to medium, and all come with firm mattress and compact bathrooms. The Nova Roma is west of the Teatro Romano and north of the Plaza de Toros (bullring).

Suárez Somonte 42, 06800 Mérida. © **92-431-12-61.** Fax 92-430-01-60. www.novaroma.com. 55 units. 90€ double. AE, DC, MC, V. Parking 13€. **Amenities:** Restaurant; bar; room service. *In room:* A/C, TV, Wi-Fi (.55€ per hour).

Parador de Mérida ★★ This *parador* is in the heart of town, on the Plaza de la Constitución, in the former Convento de los Frailes de Jesús (dating from the 16th c.). It's had a long and turbulent history and was once a prison; today a salon has been installed in the cloister, and a central garden is studded with shrubbery and flowers. Old stone stairs lead to the rooms, which come in various shapes and sizes, each beautifully kept and furnished. Bathrooms are luxurious, the best in town. In the 1960s, two dictators met here: Franco of Spain and Salazar of Portugal.

Plaza de la Constitución 3, 06800 Mérida. © **92-431-38-00.** Fax 92-431-92-08. www.parador.es. 82 units. 143€–155€ double; 251€–272€ suite. AE, DC, MC, V. Parking 19€. **Amenities:** Restaurant; bar; exercise room; outdoor pool; room service; sauna; Wi-Fi (free, in lobby). *In room:* A/C, TV, hair dryer, minibar.

Tryp Medea ★ A 15-minute walk west of the town's historic center on the opposite bank of the Guadiana River, this hotel, which opened in 1993, is equaled only by the *parador*. Lots of mirrors, stylish postmodern furniture crafted from locally made wrought iron, and numerous modern accessories decorate the rooms, many of which offer views over the historic core of Mérida. Ranging from small to medium, the units are well appointed. The accommodations on the fourth floor are equipped with a whirlpool and spacious terrace.

Av. de Portugal s/n, 06800 Mérida. © **92-437-24-00.** Fax 92-437-30-20. www.solmelia.com.
126 units. 65€–135€. AE, DC, MC, V. Free street parking; garage parking 10€. **Amenities:** Restaurant; bar; babysitting; outdoor pool; room service; sauna. *In room:* A/C, TV, hair dryer, minibar, Wi-Fi (2€ per hour).

Where to Dine in Mérida

All the hotels recommended above have good restaurants.

Altair ★★ EXTREMADURAN This restaurant, on the banks of the Guadiana River, is known for updating the province's classic dishes to appeal to the contemporary palate. A wall opening onto the river provides a vista of the famous Roman Bridge. Generous portions of tasty regional specialties predominate, including the local favorite of neighboring Castile, roast suckling pig with creamed potatoes. A roast duckling is succulently baked with honey and figs, a dish that may have originated with the Arab conquerors centuries ago. Also excellent are the baked cod and the loin of beef with fresh mushrooms. Instead of ordering a la carte, we opt for the four-course menu, which changes daily and is filled with delightful surprises. Good-quality ingredients and skillful handling of the produce bring out the flavors characterized by the cooking here.

Av. José Fernández López 7. © **92-430-45-12.** Reservations recommended. Main courses 11€–30€; fixed-price menu 69€. AE, DC, MC, V. Mon–Sat 2–4pm and Wed–Sat 8:30–11:30pm. Closed last week of Aug and 1st week of Sept.

Briz 🍴 EXTREMADURAN There is almost universal agreement, even among locals, that the dishes at Briz represent the best value in town—not only reasonable in price but very filling. Briz has been known for its Extremaduran regional dishes since 1949. Main dishes include heavily flavored lamb stew, and *perdiz* in salsa (a gamy partridge casserole), which might be preceded by an appetizer of peppery sausage mixed into a medley of artichokes. Peppery veal steak and fried filet of goat are other specialties. Strong, hearty wines accompany the dishes. The waitstaff, however, will not be awarded any prizes. You'll find Briz across from the post office.

Félix Valverde Lillo 5. © **92-431-93-07.** Main courses 12€–23€. AE, MC, V. Mon–Sat 7:30am–5pm and 7:30pm–midnight.

ZAFRA

61km (38 miles) S of Mérida, 172km (107 miles) N of Seville

One of the most interesting stopovers in lower Extremadura, the white-walled town of Zafra is filled with old Moorish streets and squares. The 1457 **castle** of the dukes of Feria, the most important in the province, boasts both a sumptuous 16th-century Herreran patio and the Sala Dorada, with its richly paneled ceiling. The place is now a government-run *parador* (see below). You'll want to spend time on the central square, the arcaded 18th-century **Plaza Mayor** ★, and on its satellite, the 16th-century **Plaza Vieja (Old Square)** ★. In addition to these two important sights in Zafra, **Nuestra Señora de la Candelaria** is a church with nine panels by Zurbarán, displayed on the *retablo* in a chapel designed by Churriguera. The church, constructed in the Gothic-Renaissance style, has a red-brick belfry. Admission is free. It's open Monday to Friday 10:30am to 1pm and 7 to 8:30pm, and Sunday 11am to 12:30pm.

Essentials

GETTING THERE Five **buses** a day arrive from Mérida; a one-way ticket costs 10€. For schedules, call **Leda** at ℂ **92-455-39-07;** for prices call ℂ **92-455-00-06,** or go to www.leda.es.

Zafra lies at the junction where the highway from Seville (E-803) splits, heading east to Mérida and Cáceres and west to Badajoz. Driving there is easy. From Mérida to Zafra, allow an hour; from Seville, allow about 2½ hours. There's also a direct road from Córdoba.

VISITOR INFORMATION The **tourist office,** at Plaza de España 8B (ℂ **92-455-10-36;** www.ayto-zafra.com), is open Monday to Friday 9:30am to 2pm and 5 to 8pm, and Saturday and Sunday 10am to 1:30pm and 6 to 8pm.

Where to Stay in Zafra

Casa Palacio Conde de la Corte ★★ Even better and more tranquil than the *parador* (see below), this town mansion was built in 1940 as the private residence of a locally famous bull breeder. Bull breeders and bullfighters from all over the province, some from as far away as Madrid, frequented this place and visited the Spanish earl's stud farm. The hotel is associated with the Huerta Honda (see below), and guests can use the facilities of that hotel as well. The bedrooms are tastefully and comfortably furnished, ranging from midsize to spacious, each with a tiled bathroom. You can live in style and comfort here.

Plaza del Pilar, Redondo 2, 06300 Zafra. ℂ **92-456-33-11.** Fax 92-456-30-72. www.condedela corte.com. 15 units. 110€–160€ standard double; 140€–200€ classic double; 160€–250€ suite. AE, MC, V. Parking nearby 8€. **Amenities:** Bar; outdoor pool; room service. *In room:* A/C, TV, hair dryer, minibar.

Huerta Honda ★ 🎁 You'll get views of the citadel and Old Town from the modern, renovated rooms of this hotel in front of the Plaza del Alcázar. Living space is a bit tight, but the beds are good and the bathrooms immaculately kept. Under the same management, the adjacent restaurant **Barbacana** (see below) is a well-recommended dining room offering Castilian cuisine.

López Asme 30, 06300 Zafra. ℂ **92-455-41-00.** Fax 92-455-25-04. www.hotelhuertahonda. com. 48 units. 85€–200€ double; 120€–240€ suite. AE, DC, MC, V. Parking 8.50€. **Amenities:** 2 restaurants; bar; outdoor heated pool; room service. *In room:* A/C, TV, hair dryer, minibar, Wi-Fi (free).

Parador de Zafra ★★ The namesake of this *parador,* which is in a restored 15th-century castle near the Plaza de España, stayed here with the dukes of Feria before his departure for the New World. The interior, beautiful but restrained, contains the chapel of the Alcázar with an octagonal Gothic dome. Although not the finest *parador* in Extremadura, the hotel is decorated with splendid taste and is quite comfortable, boasting a patio and a garden. Rooms are midsize or even spacious. Bathrooms are fairly roomy and well equipped.

Plaza Corazón de María 7, 06300 Zafra. ℂ **92-455-45-40.** Fax 92-455-10-18. www.parador.es. 45 units. 143€–272€ double; 322€–349€ suite. AE, DC, MC, V. Free parking along the Plaza Corazón de María. **Amenities:** Restaurant; bar; babysitting; outdoor pool; room service. *In room:* A/C, TV, hair dryer, minibar, Wi-Fi (free).

The Parador de Zafra.

Where to Dine in Zafra

Barbacana ★ CASTILIAN Next to the previously recommended Huerta Honda in the center of town, this is the city's most elegantly decorated restaurant. As a bonus, it just happens to serve its finest cuisine. The atmosphere is chic and sophisticated. Visitors will find the second-floor dining room more relaxed and salubrious. This restaurant has operated here for more than a decade, earning an enviable reputation throughout the region. The owner is an aficionado of the bullfight and has adorned the walls with many paintings depicting scenes from this sport. The cuisine is firmly rooted in the region, and you'll stuff yourself with well-prepared specialty after specialty. Such delicacies appear on the menu as *revuelto de trigeros* (sautéed green asparagus). From there, you can proceed to such main courses as *merluza con almejas* (hake in clam sauce) or *cochinillo* (suckling pig).

López Asme 30. ✆ **92-455-41-00.** Main courses 15€–36€; fixed-price menu 45€. MC, V. Mon-Sat 1:30–4pm and 8:30pm–midnight; Sun 1:30–4pm.

9

ANDALUSIA

T his once-great stronghold of Muslim Spain is rich in history and tradition, containing some of the country's most celebrated treasures: the world-famous Mezquita (mosque) in Córdoba, the Alhambra in Granada, and the great Gothic cathedral in Seville. It also has many smaller towns just waiting to be discovered—Ubeda, Jaén, gorge-split Ronda, Jerez de la Frontera, and the gleaming white port city of Cádiz. Give Andalusia at least a week and you'll have only skimmed the surface.

This dry, mountainous region also embraces the Costa del Sol (Málaga, Marbella, and Torremolinos), a popular coastal strip covered in the following chapter. Go to the Costa del Sol for beach resorts, nightlife, and relaxation; visit Andalusia for its architectural wonders and beauty.

Crime alert: Anyone driving south into Andalusia and the Costa del Sol should be wary of thieves. Daylight robberies are commonplace, especially in Seville, Córdoba, and Granada. It's not unusual for a car to be broken into while tourists are enjoying lunch in a restaurant. Some establishments have hired guards (a service for which you should tip, of course). Under no circumstances should you ever leave passports, traveler's checks, or other valuables unguarded in a car.

JAÉN, BAEZA & UBEDA

International tourists discovered the province of Jaén, with its three principal cities—**Jaén** (the capital), **Baeza,** and **Ubeda**—in the 1960s. For years, visitors whizzed through Jaén on the way south to Granada or bypassed it altogether on the southwest route to Córdoba and Seville. But the government improved the province's hotel outlook with excellent *paradores,* which now provide some of the finest accommodations in Andalusia.

Jaén

97km (60 miles) E of Córdoba, 97km (60 miles) N of Granada, 338km (210 miles) S of Madrid

In the center of Spain's major olive-growing district, Jaén is sandwiched between Córdoba and Granada, and has always been a gateway between Castile and Andalusia.

Jaén's bustling modern section is of little interest to visitors, but the **Moorish Old Town,** where narrow cobblestone streets hug the mountainside, is reason enough to visit. A hilltop castle, now a first-rate *parador,* dominates the city. On a clear day you can see the snow-covered peaks of the Sierra Nevada.

The city of Jaén is the center of a large province of 13,491 sq. km (5,209 sq. miles) framed by mountains: the Sierra Morena to the north, the Segura and

FACING PAGE: **The cliffside town of Ronda.**

Cazorla ranges to the east, and those of Huelma, Noalejo, and Valdepeñas to the south. To the west, plains widen into the fertile Guadalquivir Valley. Jaén province comprises three well-defined districts: the Sierra de Cazorla, a land of wild scenery; the plains of Bailén, Ajona, and Arjonilla, filled with wheat fields, vineyards, and old olive trees; and the valleys of the tributaries of the Guadalquivir.

The old walls of Jaén.

ESSENTIALS

GETTING THERE If you're driving, see location details above. You can also drive north from Granada along E-902, a distance of 93km (58 miles). If you're taking the **train** from Córdoba in the west, it takes only 1½ hours to reach Jaén from there. Four trains per day arrive from Córdoba, leaving at 8am daily and costing 9.30€ for a one-way ticket. There are four trains per day from Madrid, taking 4 to 5 hours and costing 28€ for a one-way ticket. Trains arrive in Jaén at the RENFE station on Paseo de la Estación (*©* **90-224-02-02;** www.renfe.es), north of the center of town.

If you are coming north from Granada, **Alsina Graells** runs 16 **buses** per day from Granada, taking 1½ hours and costing 7.50€ for a one-way ticket. Buses arrive in Jaén at Plaza Coca de la Piñera (*©* **90-242-22-42;** www.alsa.es), a block south of Parque de la Victoria.

VISITOR INFORMATION The **tourist office,** Calle Maestra 18 (*©* **95-323-60-32;** www.andalucia.org), is open Monday to Saturday 9am to 3pm.

EXPLORING JAÉN

Catedral de Santa María The formality and grandeur of Jaén's cathedral bears witness to the city's past importance. Begun in 1555 on the site of a former mosque and completed in 1802, it's a honey-colored blend of Gothic, baroque, and Renaissance styles, with an emphasis on the latter. The original architect was Andrés de Vandelvira (1509–75), who designed many buildings at Baeza and Ubeda. A huge dome dominates the interior with its richly carved choir stalls. The **cathedral museum ★** contains an important collection of historical objects in two underground chambers, including **paintings by Jusepe de Ribera,** the baroque painter. Its most celebrated relic is the Santo Rostro (Holy Face). According to legend, this cloth was used by Veronica to wipe Jesus' face on his way to Calvary. Evocative of Italy's Shroud of Turin, the image of Christ is said to have imprinted on the fabric. The cathedral is southwest of the Plaza de la Constitución.

Plaza de Santa María. *©* **95-323-42-33.** Free admission to cathedral; museum 3€. Cathedral daily 8:30am–1pm and 5–8pm (closes at 7pm in winter); museum Tues–Sat 9am–1pm and 5–8pm. Bus: 8, 10, or 16.

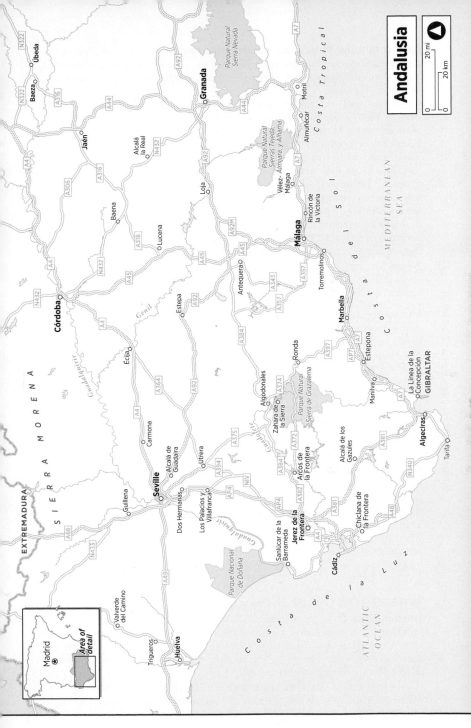

Centro Cultural Palacio de Villardompardo This is a three-in-one attraction, including some former Arab baths (known as *hamman*) and two museums, the Museo de Artes y Costumbres Populares and the Museo Internacional de Arte Naif.

Underneath the palace, near Calle San Juan and the Chapel of Saint Andrew (San Andrés), are the former **Arab baths**. They represent some of the most important Moorish architecture from the 11th century ever discovered in Spain. You can visit a warm room, a hot room, and a cold room—the last with a barrel vault and 12 star-shaped chandeliers.

The **Museo de Artes y Costumbres Populares** houses a collection of primarily 19th-century folkloric artifacts, including costumes, dolls, ceramics, and even photographs documenting former days in Andalusia. The **Museo Internacional de Arte Naif** contains a changing art exhibit featuring the work of artists from around the globe who have created professional, skilled paintings without any formal art instruction.

Plaza de Santa Luisa de Marillac s/n. © **95-324-80-68.** Free admission. Winter Tues–Fri 9:30am–8:30pm, Sat–Sun 9:30am–2:30pm; summer Tues–Fri 9am–9:30pm, Sat–Sun 9:30am–2:30pm. You must go on foot: In the Old Quarter of Jaén, follow signs indicating either BAÑOS ARABES or BARRIO DE LA MAGDALENA.

Museo de Jaén ★ An old prison has been converted to a major museum devoted to the art and culture of the Iberians, the original settlers of the peninsula well before the arrival of the Romans. Long in the making, this museum fills a large gap in the province's archaeological treasures. More than 500 ancient Iberian settlements have been identified in Jaén province, and this provincial museum can exhibit only a fraction of these valuable artifacts at one time. But what it does show is choice, including sculpture and paintings.

Paseo de la Estación 27. © **95-331-33-39.** www.museosdeandalucia.es. Admission 1.50€. Tues 2:30–8:30pm; Wed–Sat 9am–8:30pm; Sun 9am–2:30pm.

Museo Provincial ★ In this dusty, offbeat, and little-visited museum, one of the finest Spanish collections of pre-Roman artifacts is found, along with other treasures. The collection, housed in a 1547 mansion, includes Roman mosaics, a Mudéjar arch, and many ceramics from the early Iberian, Greek, and Roman periods. On the upper floor is an exhibit of Pedro Berruguete paintings, including *Christ at the Column.* Look for a paleo-Christian sarcophagus from Martos. In the most modern section stand nearly a dozen life-size Iberian sculptures that were unearthed in 1975 near the village of Porcuna. The museum is between the bus and train stations.

Paseo de la Estación 27. © **95-331-33-39.** Admission 1.50€. Tues 2:30–8:30pm; Wed–Sat 9am–8pm; Sun 9am–2:30pm.

WHERE TO STAY IN JAÉN

Husa Europa 🍴 In the commercial and historical center of Jaén, this little hotel became a winner after a massive renovation that brought everything up to date. Although the avant-garde decor is a little severe, it manages to be cozy and contemporary at the same time. The medium-size rooms have been spruced up, as have the sparkling-clean bathrooms.

Plaza de Belén 1, 23001 Jaén. © **95-322-27-04.** Fax 95-322-26-92. www.husa.es. 37 units. 59€–70€ double; 83€ triple. AE, DC, MC, V. Parking 10€. **Amenities:** Bar; bikes. *In room:* A/C, TV, hair dryer, Wi-Fi (15€ per 24 hr.).

Parador de Jaén ★★★ Five kilometers (3 miles) to the west, on the hill overlooking the city, this castle is one of the government's showplace *paradores*. In the 10th century, the castle was a Muslim fortress surrounded by high protective walls and approached only by a steep winding road. The castle is still reached by the same road; you enter through a three-story-high baronial hallway, and the polite staff will show you to your balconied midsize room (doubles only), tastefully furnished and comfortable, with canopied beds and spick-and-span tile bathrooms equipped with tub/shower combos. The most charming feature of the bedrooms is the panoramic views of mountains. Make reservations well in advance because this place fills quickly.

Castillo de Santa Catalina, 23001 Jaén. ℰ **95-323-00-00.** Fax 95-323-09-30. www.parador.es. 45 units. 126€–200€ double. DC, MC, V. Free parking. **Amenities:** Restaurant; bar; outdoor pool; room service. *In room:* A/C, TV, hair dryer, minibar, Wi-Fi (free).

WHERE TO DINE IN JAÉN

Consider having a meal in the luxurious hilltop *parador* (see above), which commands views of Jaén. It's one of the loveliest spots in the area.

Casa Antonio ★★ ANDALUSIAN Some of the best Andalusian food in the province is served here in a traditional setting. A trio of tiny dining rooms is decorated with contemporary paintings and dark wood paneling. Recommended items include mushrooms in a well-flavored cream sauce served with prawns and black olives, scallops with mashed potatoes, and a tender roast suckling pig baked with potatoes, in the Castilian style.

Calle Fermín Palma 3. ℰ **95-327-02-62.** Reservations recommended. Main courses 12€–40€. AE, DC, MC, V. Tues–Sat 1:30–4:15pm and 9–11:30pm. Closed Aug.

Casa Vicente ★ ANDALUSIAN In the historic district, this restaurant is praised locally for the quality of its tapas and its wine. The area surrounding the town is known for its vegetables, which are showcased in such dishes as *espinaca esparragada* (spinach with vegetable sauce) and *alcachofa natural* (artichokes in garlic). For a main dish, we recommend the *lomo de orsa mozárabe* (lamb in sweet-and-sour sauce) or *bacalao encebollado* (salt cod sautéed with onions and sweet peppers). Two local desserts are rice pudding and *manjarblanco mozárabe* (Moorish-style fudge).

In the Hotel Condestable, Calle Cristo Rey 3. ℰ **95-323-22-22.** Reservations recommended. Main courses 14€–20€. MC, V. Winter Thurs–Fri and Mon–Tues 1:30–4pm and 8:30–11:30pm, Sun noon–5pm; summer Mon–Sat 1:30–4pm and 5:30–11:30pm. Closed Aug.

Baeza ★★

45km (28 miles) NE of Jaén, 308km (191 miles) S of Madrid

Historic Baeza (known to the Romans as Vilvatia), with its Gothic and Plateresque buildings and cobblestone streets, is one of the best-preserved old towns in Spain. At twilight, when lanterns hanging from plastered-stone walls light the narrow streets, you might feel you've stumbled back into the 15th century. The town's heyday was in the 16th and 17th centuries. Even if you don't go inside many monuments—and, indeed, many of the most charming buildings aren't open to the public—you can still get a good idea of the architecture by strolling through the *barrio monumental* and admiring the old buildings.

ESSENTIALS

GETTING THERE The nearest major rail junction, receiving **trains** from both Madrid and most of Andalusia, is the **Estación Linares-Baeza** (✆ **90-224-02-02;** www.renfe.es), 14km (8⅔ miles) west of Baeza's center. There is one train per day from Córdoba, two per day from Madrid.

There are 20 **buses** a day from Ubeda; the ride is 15 minutes and costs 1.50€ one-way. From Jaén, there are 16 buses per day (trip time: 45 min.), costing 4.10€ one-way. For more information, call ✆ **90-242-22-42.**

To reach Baeza from Jaén (p. 287), follow Route N-321 northeast for 45km (28 miles). To get to Baeza from Madrid, follow Route N-IV south toward Seville. Take exit 292 and merge onto A-44. At exit 3, take N-332 toward Bailén/A-32/Linares. Finally, you'll have to exit onto A-6101. The town lies 308km (191 miles) south of Madrid.

VISITOR INFORMATION The **tourist office,** at the Plaza del Pópulo s/n 23440 (✆ **95-374-04-44;** www.andalucia.org), is open in winter Monday to Friday from 9am to 2:30pm and 4 to 6pm, and Saturday and Sunday from 9:30am to 3pm. Summer hours are Monday to Friday from 8:30am to 3:15pm and 4 to 7pm, Saturday and Sunday 10am to 2pm.

EXPLORING BAEZA

Baeza's main square, the **Plaza del Pópulo** ★, is a two-story open colonnade. The buildings here date in part from the 16th century, and the tourist office, where you can get a town map, is housed in one of the most interesting. Look for the fountain containing four half-effaced lions, the **Fuente de los Leones,** which may have been brought here from the Roman town of Cantulo.

Head south along the Cuesta de San Gil to reach the Gothic and Renaissance **Santa Iglesia Catedral** ★, Plaza de la Fuente de Santa María (✆ **95-374-04-44**), built in the 16th century on the foundations of an earlier mosque. Look for the **Puerta de la Luna (Moon Door),** and, in the interior, remodeled by Andrés de Vandelvira (architect of Jaén's cathedral) and his pupils, the carved wood and the brilliant painted *rejas* (iron screens). The **Gold Chapel** is especially stunning. The edifice possesses one of the most important Corpus Christi icons in Spain, *La Custodia de Baeza.* Climb the clock tower for a panoramic view of town. The cathedral is open daily October to May from 10:30am to 1pm and 4 to 6pm, June to September 10:30am to 1pm and 5 to 7pm; admission is 2€.

The colonnade of the Plaza del Pópulo.

After leaving the cathedral, continue up the Cuesta de San Felipe to the **Palacio de Jabalquinto ★** (*©* 95-374-27-75), a beautiful example of civil architecture in the flamboyant Gothic style, built by Juan Alfonso de Benavides, a relative of King Ferdinand. Its facade is filled with interesting decorative elements, and there's a simple Renaissance-style courtyard with marble columns. Inside, two lions guard the ornate baroque stairway. Visiting hours are daily 10am to 2pm and 4 to 7pm.

WHERE TO DINE IN BAEZA

Casa Juanito ★ 🎁 ANDALUSIAN Owner Juan Luis Pedro Salcedo, a devotee of the lost art of Jaén cookery, revives ancient recipes in his frequently changing specials. He runs a small olive-oil outlet, and meals are made with only his own produce. Game is served in season, and many vegetable dishes incorporate ham. Among the savory and well-prepared menu items are *habas* (beans), filet of beef with tomatoes and peppers, partridge in pastry crust, house-style cod, and venison.

In the Hotel Juanito, Plaza del Arca del Agua s/n. *©* **95-374-00-40.** Reservations required on weekends. Main courses 15€–35€. MC, V. Sun–Mon 1:30–3:30pm; Tues–Sat 1:30–3:30pm and 8–10:30pm. Closed 1st 2 weeks of July.

Vandelvira ★ 🎁 ANDALUSIAN A 16th-century former convent has been converted into this citadel of good cooking and affordable prices. Similar to a cathedral in size, the building still contains much of its original architecture and conventual furnishings. The summer terrace is one of the most popular night bars and taverns in town. The chefs have a few fish dishes, including *bacalao* (cod), but mostly their meats are the way to go. Milk-fed lamb is one of their finest options, and the veal dishes are also outstanding. One of their more exotic specialties is pigs' knuckles stuffed with *perdiz* (partridge) and spinach. They also prepare an excellent appetizer of partridge pâté with virgin olive oil.

Calle de San Francisco 14. *©* **95-374-81-72.** www.vandelvira.es. Reservations recommended. Main courses 12€–25€. AE, DC, MC, V. Sun 1:30–4pm; Tues–Sat 1:30–4pm and 8:30–11pm.

Ubeda ★★

10km (6¼ miles) NE of Jaén, 312km (194 miles) S of Madrid

A former Moorish stronghold often called the "Florence of Andalusia," Ubeda is a Spanish National Landmark and a World Heritage Site filled with golden-brown Renaissance palaces and tile-roofed whitewashed houses. The best way to discover Ubeda's charm is to wander its narrow cobblestone streets. The government long ago created a *parador* here in a renovated ducal palace—consider stopping for lunch if you're not pressed for time. Definitely allow time for a stroll through Ubeda's shops, which specialize in leather craft goods and esparto grass carpets.

ESSENTIALS

GETTING THERE The nearest **train** station is the Linares-Baeza station (*©* **90-224-02-02;** www.renfe.es). For information on trains to and from the station, refer to the Baeza section (discussed earlier).

There are 10 **buses** daily to Baeza, less than 10km (6¼ miles) away, and to Jaén. Seven buses per day go to the busy railway station at Linares-Baeza, where a train can take you virtually anywhere in Spain. Bus service to and from Córdoba, Seville, and Granada is also available. Ubeda's bus station is in the heart of the modern town, on Calle San José (© **95-375-21-57**), where signs will point you on a downhill walk to the *zona monumental.*

To drive here, turn off the Madrid-Córdoba road, head east for Linares, and then move on to Ubeda, a detour of 42km (26 miles). The turnoff is at the junction with N-322. From Jaén, the capital of the province, take N-321 northeast for 57km (35 miles).

VISITOR INFORMATION The **tourist office,** Calle Baja del Marqués 4 (© **95-377-92-04;** www.andalucia.org), is open Monday to Friday 9am to 2:45pm and 4 to 7pm (June–Sept 5–8pm), Saturday and Sunday 9:30am to 3pm.

EXPLORING UBEDA

You might begin your tour at the centrally located **Plaza de Vázquez de Molina ★★**, which is flanked by several mansions, including Casa de las Cadenas, now the Town Hall. The mansions have been decaying for centuries, but many are finally being restored.

Hospital de Santiago On the western edge of town, off Calle del Obispo Coros, stands the Hospital of Santiago, built by Andrés de Vandelvira in 1575 and still in use today. Over the main entryway is a carving of St. James "the Moorslayer" in a traditional pose on horseback. Note the monumental staircase leading upstairs from the inner patio. In the chapel are some marvelous woodcarvings. Today the hospital is a cultural venue, hosting concerts and containing a minor modern art museum.

Av. Cristo Rey. © **95-375-08-42.** Free admission. Mon–Fri 8am–3pm and 4–10pm; Sat–Sun 11am–3pm and 6–10pm.

Iglesia de San Pablo ★ This Gothic church in the center of Old Town is almost as fascinating as the Iglesia El Salvador (see below). The San Pablo church is famous for its 1511 **south portal ★** in the Isabelline style, and for its **chapels ★** decorated with beautiful wrought-iron grilles. Vandelvira himself designed the "Heads of the Dead Chapel," the most stunning. You might also seek out the richly carved Chapel of Las Mercedes, done in the florid Isabelline style.

Plaza 1 de Mayo. © **95-375-06-37.** Free admission. Mon–Sat 5:30–8:15pm; Sun 11am–1:45pm (and 7–9pm in summer).

Iglesia El Salvador ★★ One of the grandest examples of Spanish Renaissance architecture, this church was designed in 1536 by Diego de Siloé as a family chapel and mausoleum for Francisco de los Cobos, secretary of the Holy Roman Emperor Charles V. The richly embellished portal is mere window dressing for the wealth of decoration on the **interior ★** of the church, including a **sacristy ★★** designed by Andrés de Vandelvira with medallions, caryatids, *atlantes,* and coffered decorations and ornamentations. The many sculptures and altarpieces and the spectacular rose windows are also of special interest.

Calle Francisco de los Cobos. © **95-375-81-50.** Admission 2.25€ adults, 1€ children. Mon–Sat 4:30–7pm; Sun 10:45am–2pm and 4:30–7pm.

WHERE TO STAY IN UBEDA

María de Molina ★ 🏨 The *parador* (see below) is the number-one place to stay in Ubeda, but this hotel gives it serious competition. In a beautifully restored and

The dome of the Iglesia El Salvador.

once-decaying palace, the three-story hotel is in the center of the historic district. Much of the past, including stone vaulted ceilings downstairs, was retained by the modern architects. The hotel opens onto a marble-columned atrium in which chairs are placed in the center, with a skylight overhead. Wherever you look you'll find grace notes such as hand-carved wooden doors and marble arches over stairwells. In contrast, the bedrooms are thoroughly modernized, ranging from rather cramped to spacious suites. We prefer the rooms with terraces or balconies, which need to be booked well in advance. Try to have at least one dinner at the **restaurant,** enjoying not only its fine Andalusian cuisine but also its mellow ambience—particularly inviting at night.

Plaza del Ayuntamiento, 23400 Ubeda. ℂ **95-379-53-56.** Fax 95-379-36-94. www.hotel-maria-de-molina.com. 27 units. Sun–Thurs 82€ double, 105€ suite; Fri–Sat 95€ double, 116€ suite. AE, DC, MC, V. **Amenities:** Outdoor pool; room service. *In room:* A/C, TV, minibar, Wi-Fi (free).

Palacio de la Rambla ★★ 👜 The front entrance is fortress-like, with color tiles in the Mudéjar style. Inside, the cloistered courtyard has Plateresque and Renaissance-style carvings, granite columns, and forests of ivy. Eight of its rooms are open to paying guests. The spacious manorial rooms under soaring ceilings boast many of their original furnishings, but everything has been supplemented with modern conveniences. Each room is individually furnished, often with antiques, tapestries, objets d'art, and other remnants of old Spain's aristocratic life. You can still visit two incredibly formal salons, each outfitted as if awaiting a visit from Philip II.

Plaza del Marqués 1, 23400 Ubeda. ℂ **95-375-01-96.** Fax 95-375-02-67. www.palaciodela rambla.com. 8 units. 120€ double; 140€ suite. Rates include buffet breakfast. AE, MC, V. Parking 10€. Closed Jan 7–30 and July 13–Aug 6. *In room:* A/C, TV, hair dryer, minibar.

Parador de Ubeda ★★★ On the town's central square stands this 16th-century palace-turned-*parador,* which shares an old paved plaza with the Iglesia El Salvador (see above) and its dazzling facade. The formal entrance to this Renaissance palace leads to an enclosed patio, encircled by two levels of Moorish arches, where palms and potted plants sit on the tile floors. The rooms are nearly two stories high, with beamed ceilings, tall windows, and antiques and reproductions.

Plaza Vázquez de Molina 1, 23400 Ubeda. ℂ **95-375-03-45.** Fax 95-375-12-59. www.parador. es. 36 units. 144€–197€ double; 240€–257€ suite. AE, DC, MC, V. **Amenities:** Restaurant; bar; babysitting; room service; sauna; Wi-Fi (free, in lobby). *In room:* A/C, TV, hair dryer, minibar.

WHERE TO DINE IN UBEDA

Parador Restaurante ★ SPANISH/ANDALUSIAN This *parador* is the best place to dine for miles around. Although the cuisine isn't the most creative, it's made with market-fresh ingredients prepared from decades-old recipes. The menu is wide ranging. Start with a typical dish of the area, such as cold soup with almonds, delightful on a hot day. Partridge is a local favorite—appetizers might include stuffed green peppers with partridge, stewed partridge with plums, or a refreshing salad with marinated partridge. The best fish dishes are the grilled monkfish in saffron sauce and the grilled sole with garlic–and–apple vinegar sauce. Meat eaters might be tempted by regional dishes such as oxtail in red-wine sauce and stewed kid with pine nuts. The *menú del parador* is a good bet, including an appetizer plus fish or meat for a main course and then dessert. The tasting menu for two showcases four typical regional dishes nightly.

Plaza Vázquez de Molina 1. ℂ **95-375-03-45.** Reservations recommended. Main courses 10€– 22€; tasting menus 55€. AE, DC, MC, V. Daily 1:30–4pm and 8:30–11pm.

CÓRDOBA ★★★

105km (65 miles) W of Jaén, 419km (260 miles) SW of Madrid

Ten centuries ago, Córdoba was one of the greatest cities in the world, with a population of 900,000. The capital of Muslim Spain, it was Europe's largest city and a cultural and intellectual center. It flourished with public baths, mosques, a great library, and palaces. Later, greedy hordes sacked the city, tearing down ancient buildings and carting off many art treasures. Despite these assaults, Córdoba still retains traces of its former glory—enough to challenge Seville and Granada as the most fascinating city in Andalusia.

Today this provincial capital is known chiefly for its mosque, but it abounds with other artistic and architectural riches, especially its lovely homes. The old Arab and Jewish quarters are famous for their narrow streets lined with white-washed houses boasting flower-filled patios and balconies. It's perfectly acceptable to walk along, gazing into the courtyards. This isn't an invasion of privacy: The citizens of Córdoba take pride in showing off their patios as part of the city's tradition. And don't forget to bring a good pair of walking shoes, as the only way to explore the monumental heart of the city is on foot. Córdoba, which has joined the ranks of UNESCO's World Heritage Sites, is a place you'll want to spend at least a couple of days.

Essentials

GETTING THERE The train is the most convenient and most popular means of transport to Córdoba, because the city is a rail junction for routes to the rest of Andalusia and is on the vital rail link between Madrid and Seville. The most used line is the **AVE high-speed train** racing between Madrid and

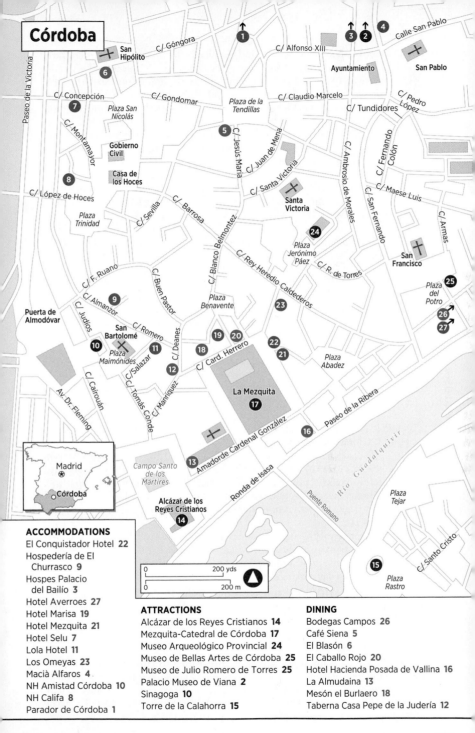

Córdoba

San Hipólito

C/ Góngora

C/ Alfonso XIII

Calle San Pablo

Ayuntamiento

San Pablo

Paseo de la Victoria

C/ Concepción

C/ Gondomar

Plaza de la Tendillas

C/ Claudio Marcelo

C/ Pedro López

C/ Tundidores

Plaza San Nícolás

C/ Montanamayor

C/ Jesús María

C/ Juan de Mena

C/ Ambrosio de Morales

C/ Fernando Colón

C/ Maese Luis

Gobierno Civil

Casa de los Hoces

C/ Santa Victoria

C/ San Fernando

C/ López de Hoces

C/ Sevilla

C/ Barrosa

Santa Victoria

C/ Armas

Plaza Trinidad

C/ F. Ruano

C/ Blanco Belmontez

Plaza Jerónimo Páez

C/ R. de Torres

San Francisco

Plaza del Potro

Puerta de Almodóvar

C/ Almanzor

C/ Buen Pastor

C/ Rey Heredio Caldederos

Plaza Benavente

Plaza Abadez

C/ Judíos

San Bartolomé

C/ Romero

C/ Déanes

C/ Card. Herrero

Plaza Maimónides

C/ Salazar

C/ Manriquez

C/ Tomás Conde

La Mezquita

Av. Dr. Fleming

C/ Cairouán

Amadorde Cardenal González

Paseo de la Ribera

Río Guadalquivir

Campo Santo de los Mártires

Plaza Tejar

Madrid

Córdoba

Alcázar de los Reyes Cristianos

Ronda de Isasa

Puente Romano

C/ Santo Cristo

Plaza Rastro

ACCOMMODATIONS

El Conquistador Hotel **22**
Hospedería de El Churrasco **9**
Hospes Palacio del Bailío **3**
Hotel Averroes **27**
Hotel Marisa **19**
Hotel Mezquita **21**
Hotel Selu **7**
Lola Hotel **11**
Los Omeyas **23**
Macià Alfaros **4**
NH Amistad Córdoba **10**
NH Califa **8**
Parador de Córdoba **1**

0   200 yds
0   200 m

ATTRACTIONS

Alcázar de los Reyes Cristianos **14**
Mezquita-Catedral de Córdoba **17**
Museo Arqueológico Provincial **24**
Museo de Bellas Artes de Córdoba **25**
Museo de Julio Romero de Torres **25**
Palacio Museo de Viana **2**
Sinagoga **10**
Torre de la Calahorra **15**

DINING

Bodegas Campos **26**
Café Siena **5**
El Blasón **6**
El Caballo Rojo **20**
Hotel Hacienda Posada de Vallina **16**
La Almudaina **13**
Mesón el Burlaero **18**
Taberna Casa Pepe de la Judería **12**

Córdoba or between Córdoba and Seville. In the Spain of today, train travel between Seville and Córdoba has been cut to just 25 minutes. That's why travelers on the most rushed of schedules visit Córdoba on a day trip while still based in Seville. Amazingly, the AVE train ride between Madrid in the north and Córdoba in the south takes just 1½ hours. There are much slower trains, but because vacation time is precious we don't recommend them.

There are between 22 and 31 trains per day arriving from Madrid, costing 57€ for a one-way ticket. A one-way ticket between Córdoba and Seville sells for 29€. If you're on the Costa del Sol and want to visit Córdoba, you can take one of the 10 to 12 trains per day from Málaga. Depending on the train, the trip takes 2 to 3 hours and costs from 20€ to 42€ for a one-way ticket.

The main train station at Córdoba is on the town's northern periphery, at Glorieta de las Tres Culturas, off Avenida de América. Bus no. 3 runs between the rail station and the historic core of the city. For rail information, call © 90-224-02-02; for AVE schedules or information call © 90-224-02-02. The RENFE advance-ticket office in Córdoba is at Ronda de los Tejares 10 (© 95-747-58-84; www.renfe.es). To reach the heart of the city from the station, head south on Avenida de Cervantes or Avenida del Gran Capitán.

Getting to this old Moorish city by **bus** is easier than ever now that **Alsina Graells Sur** (© 95-740-40-40; www.alsa.es) has taken over many smaller companies and improved service under a new network. Buses now arrive at the city's new bus station, behind the train depot on Glorieta de las Tres Culturas. The bus service has been improved to such an extent that many visitors are using it to reach Córdoba from other points within Spain, such as Granada, Madrid, or Seville. The most popular routes are between Córdoba and Seville, with 7 buses per day. The trip takes 2 hours and costs 18€ for a one-way ticket. Another popular run is between Granada and Córdoba, where eight to nine buses per day make the 3-hour run, costing 12€ for a one-way ticket.

The second-most-used terminal is operated by **Transportes Ureña** (© 95-322-01-16). Its buses arrive at the terminal on Av. de Cervantes 22, a few blocks south of the train station. If you're visiting Jaén (p. 287), you'll find a bus connection between that city and Córdoba. The trip takes 2 hours; there are seven to eight buses per day, and the cost of a one-way ticket is 10€.

If you're on the tightest of budgets, you can call **Secorbus** (© 90-222-92-92; www.socibus.es), which offers the least-expensive bus runs between Madrid and Córdoba. But the trip takes 4½ hours. There are about seven buses a day making this long haul, a one-way ticket going for 15€.

VISITOR INFORMATION The **tourist office,** Calle Torrijos 10 (© 95-735-51-79; www.andalucia.org), is open Monday to Friday 9am to 7:30pm, Saturday and Sunday 9:30am to 3pm.

Exploring Córdoba

Among Córdoba's many sights is the **Puente Romano (Roman Bridge),** dating from the time of Augustus and crossing the Guadalquivir River about 1 block south of the Mezquita. It's hardly Roman anymore because not one of its 16 supporting arches is original. The sculptor Bernabé Gómez del Río erected a statue of St. Raphael in the middle of the bridge in 1651.

The Puente Romano, or Roman Bridge, of Córdoba.

Plaza de Toros, on Gran Vía del Parque, stages its major bullfights in May, although fights are also presented at other times of the year. Watch for local announcements. Most hotels will arrange tickets for you, ranging in price (in general) from 20€ to 115€. Call ✆ **95-723-25-07** for information.

Alcázar de los Reyes Cristianos ★ Commissioned in 1328 by Alfonso XI, the Alcázar of the Christian Kings is a fine example of military architecture. Ferdinand and Isabella governed Castile from this fortress on the river as they prepared to reconquer Granada, the last Moorish stronghold in Spain. Columbus journeyed here to fill Isabella's ears with his plans for discovery.

Two blocks southwest of the Mezquita (see below), this quadrangular building is notable for powerful walls and a trio of towers—the Tower of the Lions, the Tower of Allegiance, and the Tower of the River. The Tower of the Lions contains intricately decorated ogival ceilings that are the most notable example of Gothic architecture in Andalusia. The beautiful gardens and the Moorish baths are celebrated attractions. The Patio Morisco is another lovely spot, its pavement decorated with the arms of León and Castile. A Roman sarcophagus is representative of 2nd- and 3rd-century funeral art, and the Roman mosaics are outstanding—especially a unique piece dedicated to Polyphemus and Galatea.

Caballerizas Reales. ✆ **95-742-01-51.** Admission 4€ adults (2€ for gardens), free for children 17 and under with parent. May–June Tues–Sat 10am–2pm and 5:30–7:30pm, Sun 9:30am–2:30pm; July–Sept Tues–Sat 8:30am–2:30pm; Oct–Apr Tues–Sat 10am–2pm and 4:30–6:30pm, Sun 9:30am–2:30pm. Gardens illuminated July–Sept 10pm–noon. Bus: 3 or 12.

Mezquita-Catedral de Córdoba ★★★ From the 8th century, the Mezquita was the crowning Muslim architectural achievement in the West. It's a fantastic labyrinth of red-and-white-striped arches. To the astonishment of visitors, a cathedral now sits awkwardly in the middle of the mosque, disturbing the purity of the lines. The 16th-century cathedral, a blend of many styles, is impressive in its own right, with an intricately carved ceiling and baroque choir stalls. Additional ill-conceived annexes later turned the Mezquita into an architectural

The Mezquita, as seen from afar.

oddity. Its most interesting feature is the **mihrab** ★★, a domed shrine of Byzantine mosaics that once housed the Koran. After exploring the interior, stroll through the Courtyard of the Orange Trees, which has a beautiful fountain. The hardy can climb a 16th-century tower to catch a panoramic view of Córdoba and its environs.

Calles Torrijos and Cardenal Herrero s/n (south of the train station, just north of the Roman bridge). ☎ **95-822-52-45.** Admission 8€ adults, 4€ children 13 and under. Mon–Sat 8:30am–6pm; Sun 8:30–10:15am and 2–6pm. Bus: 3.

Museo Arqueológico y Etnológico de Córdoba ★ Córdoba's archaeological museum, 2 blocks northeast of the Mezquita, is one of the most important in Spain. Housed in a palace dating from 1505, it displays artifacts left behind by the various peoples and conquerors who swept through the province. There are Paleolithic and Neolithic items, Iberian hand weapons and ceramics, and Roman sculptures, bronzes, ceramics, inscriptions, and mosaics. Especially interesting are the Visigothic artifacts. The most outstanding collection, however, is devoted to Arabic art and spans the entire Muslim occupation. Take a few minutes to relax in one of the patios with its fountains and ponds. Right next door to the museum you can view the ruins of a Roman theater, which was discovered only in 2000.

Plaza Jerónimo Páez 7, Judería. ☎ **95-735-55-17.** www.museosdeandalucia.es. Admission 1.50€. Tues 2:30–8:30pm; Wed–Sat 9am–8:30pm; Sun and public holidays 9am–2:30pm.

Museo de Bellas Artes de Córdoba ★★ This museum houses one of the finest art collections in Andalusia. It's not the Prado but could easily occupy 1½ hours of your time. The art museum is installed in the former charity hospice, Hospital de la Caridad, founded by Ferdinand and Isabella. On two separate occasions, these monarchs received Columbus here. A whole gallery is devoted to two paintings by El Greco. Works by Zurbarán are also on exhibit, as are the paintings of the deeply religious, Seville-born artist Murillo. An entire wing is

Saint Michael Killing the Dragon, at the Museo de Bellas Artes de Córdoba.

given over to the **macabre paintings** ★★ of Juan de Valdés Leal, the 17th-century artist. His paintings of John the Baptist's head on a platter include the knife (in case you didn't get the point). The museum's top floor, displaying more modern paintings, is less intriguing.

Plaza del Potro 1. ✆ **95-735-55-50.** Admission 1.50€. Tues 2:30–8:30pm, Wed–Sat 9am–8:30pm, and Sun 9am–2:30pm.

Museo de Julio Romero de Torres

Across the patio from the Museo de Bellas Artes, this museum honors Julio Romero de Torres, a Córdoba-born artist (1874–1930) who was known for his sensual portraits of women. He caused the greatest scandal with his "hyper-realistic nudes," and in 1906 the National Exhibition of Fine Arts banned his *Vivadoras del Amor.* On display here is his celebrated *Oranges and Lemons,* and other notable works such as *The Little Girl Who Sells Fuel, Sin,* and *A Dedication to the Art of the Bullfight.* A corner of Romero's Madrid studio has been reproduced in one of the rooms, displaying the paintings left unfinished at his death.

Plaza del Potro 1. ✆ **95-749-19-09.** www.museojulioromero.cordoba.es. Admission 4€. Sept 16–June 15 Tues–Fri 8:30am–7:30pm, Sat 9:30am–4:30pm, and Sun 9:30am–2:30pm; June 16–Sept 15 Tues–Sat 8:30am–2:30pm, Sun 9:30am–2:30pm.

Palacio Museo de Viana ★★ 📖 Few of Córdoba's palaces have been open to the public in the past, but that's changed with the opening of this museum. Visitors are shown into a carriage house, where the elegant vehicles of another era are displayed. Note the intricate leather decoration on the carriages and the leather wall hangings, some of which date from the period of the Reconquest. There's also a collection of leather paintings. You can wander at leisure through the **garden and patios ★★**. These patios, 14 in all, are particularly stunning. The palace is 4 blocks southeast of the Plaza de Colón, on the northeastern edge of the Old Quarter.

Plaza de Don Gome 2. ✆ **95-749-67-41.** Palace admission 6€; patios 3€. Oct–May Mon–Fri 10am–1pm and 4–6pm, Sat 10am–1pm; June 16–Sept Mon–Sat 9am–2pm. Closed June 1–15. Bus: 1.

Sinagoga In Córdoba you'll find one of Spain's three remaining pre-Inquisition synagogues, built in 1315 in the Barrio de la Judería (Jewish Quarter), 2 blocks west of the northern wall of the Mezquita (p. 299). The synagogue is noted particularly for its stuccowork; the east wall contains a large orifice where the Tabernacle was once placed (inside, the scrolls of the Pentateuch were kept). Note the various adornments of *mozárabe* patterns and Hebrew inscriptions. You can still see the balcony where women were sequestered during worship. After

---

A Caliph's Pleasure Palace: The Moorish Versailles

Conjunto Arqueológico Madinat Al-Zahra, a kind of Moorish Versailles just outside Córdoba, was constructed In the 10th century by the first caliph of al-Andalus, Abd ar-Rahman III. He named it after the favorite of his harem, nicknamed "the brilliant." Thousands of workers and animals slaved to build this mammoth pleasure palace, said to have contained 300 baths and 400 houses. Over the following years the site was plundered for building materials; in fact, it might have been viewed as a quarry for the entire region. Some of its materials, so it's claimed, went to build the Alcázar in Seville. The Royal House, rendezvous point for the ministers, has been reconstructed. The principal salon remains in fragments, though, so you have to imagine it in its majesty. Just beyond the Royal House are the ruins of a mosque constructed to face Mecca. The Berbers sacked the place in 1013.

The palace is at Carretera Palma de Río Km 8 (© **95-735-55-07;** www.museosdeandalucia.es). Admission is 1.50€. From May 1 to September 15, hours are Tuesday to Saturday 10am to 8:30pm, and Sunday 10am to 2pm; September 16 to April 30, hours are Tuesday to Saturday 10am to 6:30pm. Buses leave from Paseo de la Rivera and Avenida de la Victoria (© **90-220-17-74**).

---

the Jews were expelled from Spain, the synagogue was turned into a hospital, until it became a Catholic chapel in 1588.

Calle de los Judíos 20. © **95-720-29-28.** Admission .30€. Tues–Sat 9:30am–2pm and 3:30–5:30pm; Sun 9:30am–1:30pm. Bus: 3.

Torre de la Calahorra The Tower of Calahorra is across the river at the southern end of the Roman bridge. Commissioned by Henry II of Trastamara, in 1369, to protect him from his brother, Peter I, it now houses a town museum, Museo Vivo de Al-Andalus. Here visitors can take a self-guided tour (in English or Spanish) with headsets. One room holds wax figures of Córdoba's famous philosophers, including Maimónides. Other rooms exhibit a miniature model of the Alhambra at Granada, complete with water fountains, a miniature Mezquita, and a display of Arab musical instruments. You can climb to the top of the tower for some panoramic views of the Roman bridge, the river, and the cathedral/mosque.

Av. de la Confederación, Puente Romano. © **95-729-39-29.** www.torrecalahorra.com. Admission to museum 4.50€ adults, 3€ students and children 7 and under. Admission to Multivisión 1.20€. May–Sept daily 10am–2pm and 4:30–8:30pm; Oct–Apr daily 10am–6pm. Tours daily 11am, noon, 3, and 4pm. Bus: 16.

Shopping

In Moorish times, Córdoba was famous for its leather workers. Highly valued in 15th-century Europe, the leather was studded with gold and silver ornaments, and then painted with embossed designs (*guadamaci*). Large panels of it often served in lieu of tapestries. Today the industry has fallen into decline, and the market is filled mostly with cheap imitations. You might want to seek out the following shop, especially if you're interested in Cordovan handicrafts: **Artesanía Andaluza,** Tomás Conde 3 (no phone), near the bullfight museum, features a vast array of Cordovan handicrafts, especially filigreed silver from the mines of

Sierra Morena, and some excellently crafted embossed leather, a holdover from the Muslim heyday. Lots of junk is mixed in with the good stuff, though, so beware. The shop is open Monday to Saturday 9am to 5pm.

Córdoba has a branch of Spain's major department store, **El Corte Inglés,** at Ronda de los Tejares 30 (© **95-722-28-81;** www.elcorteingles.es). Some of the staff speak English. It's open Monday to Saturday 10am to 10pm.

Other, more standard recommendations are listed below (take bus no. 1, 3, or 7 to reach these shops).

Arte Zoco, Calle de los Judíos s/n (© **95-729-05-75**), is the largest association of craftspeople in Córdoba. Established in the Jewish Quarter in the mid-1980s, it assembles on one site the creative output of about a dozen artisans whose mediums include leather, wood, silver, crystal, terra cotta, and iron. About a half-dozen of the artisans maintain their studios on the premises, so you can visit and check out their techniques and tools. You'll find everything from new, iconoclastic, and avant-garde designs to pieces that honor centuries-old traditions. Of special interest is the revival of the Califar pottery first introduced to Córdoba during the regimes of the Muslim caliphs. The shop is open Monday to Friday 9:30am to 8pm, and Saturday and Sunday 9:30am to 2pm. The artisans' workshops and studios open and close according to the whims of their occupants, but are usually maintained Monday to Friday from 10am to 2pm and 5:30 to 8pm.

Alejandro and Carlos López Obrero run **Taller Meryan,** Calleja de Las Flores 2 (© **95-747-59-02**), on one of the most colorful streets in the city. In this 250-year-old building you can see artisans plying their crafts; although most items must be custom-ordered, some ready-made pieces are for sale, including cigarette boxes, jewel cases, attaché cases, book and folio covers, and ottoman covers. Hours are Monday to Friday 9am to 8pm, and Saturday 9am to 2pm.

Where to Stay in Córdoba

At the peak of its summer season, Córdoba has too few hotels to meet the demand, so reserve as far in advance as possible.

VERY EXPENSIVE

Hospes Palacio Del Bailío ★★★ The moment this posh palace opened in 2007, it became our favorite hotel in Córdoba. The rooms—the best in town—skillfully blend the original palatial structure, built from the 16th century, with luxurious contemporary furnishings and appointments. Design (modern and old), history, space, and light seem harmonious here. Everything from yesterday was incorporated into this new ensemble, including stables, coach houses, lofts, granaries, Roman remains, original paintings, and a splendid Moorish-style garden.

Built on the remains of Roman baths, the deluxe hotel lies in the heart of Córdoba and was declared a landmark building in 1982. Each of the units is unique, including some that open onto a view of the hotel's patios. From velvet to leather, all the pure materials used in the design are in natural colors. Some of the rooms are graced with mural paintings from the 18th and 19th centuries. Of course, we prefer the rooms with private balconies.

Ramírez de las Casas Deza 10–12, 14010 Córdoba. © **95-749-89-93.** Fax 95-749-89-94. www.fuenso.com. 53 units. 214€–353€ double; 310€–406€ junior suite; 422€–700€ suite. AE, DC, MC, V. Parking 20€. Bus: 5, 10, 11, or 13. **Amenities:** Restaurant; bar; babysitting; indoor heated pool; room service; spa. *In room:* A/C, TV, hair dryer, minibar, Wi-Fi (free).

EXPENSIVE

Macià Alfaros ★★ Near the old Arab Quarter, this modern hotel is a government-rated four-star palace rising five floors near the ruins of an ancient Roman temple, set a brisk 15-minute walk from the Mezquita. The look is vaguely Moorish, but it's merely the mock. You enter through a garage area, not an attractive debut, but the hotel improves once you're inside. A cool swimming pool is set within a courtyard. Bedrooms are small but in general have enough storage space and built-in furnishings. Architects tried for some references to old Andalusia, which are visible within the courtyard.

Alfaros 18, 14001 Córdoba. ℂ **95-749-19-20.** Fax 95-749-22-10. www.maciahoteles.com. 131 units. 60€–208€ double. AE, DC, MC, V. **Amenities:** Restaurant; bar; babysitting; exercise room; outdoor pool; room service. *In room:* A/C, TV, hair dryer, minibar, Wi-Fi (free).

Parador de Córdoba ★★ 🌿 Found inconveniently 4km (2½ miles) outside town in a suburb called El Brillante, this *parador,* named after an Arab word meaning "palm grove," offers the amenities and facilities of a luxurious resort hotel at reasonable rates. Occupying the site of a former caliphate palace, it's one of the finest *paradores* in Spain. Its most recent feature is a garden, Los Naranjos ("the orange trees"), where the first palm trees planted in Europe can be found. The spacious guest rooms have been furnished with fine dark wood pieces, and some have balconies for eating breakfast or relaxing over a drink. The dining room offers two classic Andalusian soups, both served cold. Try either *salmorejo cordobés* (vegetable soup) or *gazpacho blanco de almendras* (almond soup). To follow, try the delectable steak in green sauce.

Av. de la Arrufafa 33, 14012 Córdoba. ℂ **95-727-59-00.** Fax 95-728-04-09. www.parador.es. 94 units. 143€–179€ double; 229€–248€ suite. AE, DC, MC, V. Free parking. **Amenities:** Restaurant; bar; babysitting; children's center; concierge; exercise room; outdoor pool; room service; sauna; outdoor tennis court (lit). *In room:* A/C, TV, hair dryer, minibar, Wi-Fi (free).

MODERATE

El Conquistador Hotel ★ Built centuries ago as a private villa, this hotel—one of the most attractive in town—has been tastefully renovated. It sits opposite an unused rear entrance to the Mezquita and has triple rows of stone-trimmed windows and ornate iron balustrades. The marble-and-granite lobby opens onto an interior courtyard filled with seasonal flowers, a pair of splashing fountains, and a symmetrical stone arcade. The quality and comfort of the rooms—each with a black-and-white marble floor and a private bathroom—earn the hotel four government-granted stars. But for us, the rooms are too small.

Magistral González Francés 15, 14003 Córdoba. ℂ **95-748-11-02.** Fax 95-747-46-77. www.hotel-conquistadorcordoba.com. 132 units. 59€–169€ double. AE, DC, MC, V. Parking 15€. Bus: 3 or 16. **Amenities:** Restaurant; bar; babysitting; room service. *In room:* A/C, TV, hair dryer, minibar, Wi-Fi (8€ per hour).

Hospedería de El Churrasco ★ 🍴 In the heart of Córdoba, close to the narrow lanes of La Judería, this little inn is affiliated with El Churrasco, a well-known restaurant. The owner, Rafael Carrillo, combines his love of gastronomy and good hospitality with these two enterprises, the inn being his latest creation. The midsize, well-furnished bedrooms, each named after a Spanish artist, are decorated with Andalusian furniture and antiques. Most rooms have a "matrimonial" (double) bed, but twins are available in the superior units. On the terrace/

solarium, vistas of the Mezquita unfold. At the inn's restaurant you can enjoy grilled meats and regional Andalusian dishes.

Calle Romero 38, 14003 Córdoba. ℭ **95-729-48-08.** Fax 95-742-16-61. www.elchurrasco.com. 9 units. 130€–170€ double. AE, DC, MC, V. Parking 20€. Bus: 3. **Amenities:** Restaurant; bar; room service. *In room:* A/C, TV, hair dryer, minibar, Wi-Fi (free).

Lola Hotel ★★ If you're looking for a small and intimate boutique hotel in the shadow of the Mezquita, this is as good as it gets. The most surprising thing about this hotel, inaugurated in 2000, is that it's here at all, set behind the thick masonry walls of what was originally built as a private home in 1888. You'll register, relax, chat with your fellow guests, eat breakfast, and order drinks from the bar—all within the same cramped but convivial area: a small but cozy courtyard ringed with stone columns and open to the skies above Córdoba. At the touch of a button, an electric motor pulls a plastic canopy over the opening to shelter the furnishings from the cold and rain. Bedrooms inside are larger, more plush, and with more opulent bathrooms—each has gorgeous tile work—than you might have expected. Each bears a name popular for Muslim women during the 19th century: Aida, Aixa, Alzára, Jasmina, and Suleima.

Calle Romero 3, 14001 Córdoba. ℭ **95-720-03-05.** Fax 95-720-02-18. www.hotelconencanto lola.com. 8 units. 84€–121€ double. Rates include buffet breakfast. AE, DC, MC, V. No parking. Bus: 1, 3, or 7. *In room:* A/C, TV, minibar.

NH Amistad Córdoba ★★ In the heart of the Judería (old Jewish Quarter) a 4-minute walk from the mosque, this hotel is one of the most desirable in town. In 1992, it opened next to a synagogue that dates from 1314, after renovations combined two existing 18th-century mansions. The houses face each other and are linked by a small patio of beautiful Andalusian arches and colorful Spanish tiles. The spacious rooms come with neat bathrooms and excellent beds, and the design is a tasteful combination of wood and fabric. A more modern wing, added in 1998, has rooms that are equivalent in comfort.

Plaza de Maimónides 3, 14004 Córdoba. ℭ **95-742-03-35.** Fax 95-742-03-65. www.nh-hoteles. com. 84 units. 101€–255€ double. AE, DC, MC, V. Parking 18€. Bus: 2, 3, 5, or 6. **Amenities:** Restaurant; bar; babysitting; room service. *In room:* A/C, TV, hair dryer, minibar, Wi-Fi (18€ per 24 hr.).

NH Califa ✔ Attracting a mainly Spanish crowd, this centrally located hotel is a short walk northwest of the Mezquita. Though rather impersonal and a bit austere, it's generally a good value. It has russet-colored marble floors, velour wall coverings, a spacious lounge, and a TV that seems to broadcast soccer matches nonstop. The midsize rooms are reasonably comfortable and furnished in a functional modern style. Parking is available along the street.

Lope de Hoces 14, 14003 Córdoba. ℭ **95-729-94-00.** Fax 95-729-57-16. www.nh-hoteles.es. 65 units. 63€–137€ double; 172€ suite. AE, DC, MC, V. Parking 18€. Bus: 32. **Amenities:** Bar; babysitting; room service. *In room:* A/C, TV, hair dryer, minibar, Wi-Fi (17€ per 24 hr.).

INEXPENSIVE

Hotel Averroes ★ This hotel expanded in 1999, adding 20 more rooms after renovating the house next door, and now the two buildings are linked by an impressive patio with potted plants and wrought-iron work. With its characteristic tiled walls and classic arches, the patio is a social area with tables where you can relax after a day of sightseeing. The comfortable, medium-size rooms have marble floors, pastel walls, and good-size beds. The bus that stops in front will take you to the town center in just 15 to 20 minutes.

Campo Madre de Dios 38, 14002 Córdoba. ☏ **95-743-59-78.** Fax 95-743-59-81. www.hotel averroes.es. 79 units. 78€–103€ double; 98€–123€ junior suite. AE, DC, MC, V. Parking 9€. Bus: 3. **Amenities:** Restaurant; bar; outdoor pool; room service. *In room:* A/C, TV, hair dryer.

Hotel Marisa 🔥 In front of the Mezquita, this modest hotel is one of the most centrally located in Córdoba, not to mention one of the city's best values. Completed in the early 1970s, ongoing renovations have kept it in good shape. Most recent improvements have been to the bathrooms, where the plumbing was renewed. The rooms are small but cozily comfortable—ask for one with a balcony overlooking either the statue of the Virgin of Rosales or the Patio de los Naranjos. The architecture and furnishings are in a vaguely Andalusian style.

Cardenal Herrero 6, 14003 Córdoba. ☏ **95-747-31-42.** Fax 95-747-41-44. www.hotelmarisa cordoba.com. 28 units. 55€–75€ double. AE, DC, MC, V. Parking 15€. Bus: 3 or 16. **Amenities:** Bar; room service. *In room:* A/C.

Hotel Mezquita 🔥 This is the closest hotel to the Mezquita, facing its east side. In 1998, it was constructed on the site of two old houses, which are now connected by a patio. The decor includes tastefully arranged antiques throughout. The architecture is typically Andalusian—arches, interior patios, and hand-painted tiles, along with old mirrors and chandeliers. The small but comfortable rooms are painted pastels to contrast with the dark oak furnishings. Naturally, the rooms overlooking the Mezquita are the first to be booked.

Plaza Santa Catalina 1, 14003 Córdoba. ☏ **95-747-55-85.** Fax 95-747-62-19. www.hotelmezquita. com. 31 units. 44€–74€ double. DC, MC, V. Parking nearby 15€. Bus: 3 or 16. *In room:* A/C, TV.

Hotel Selu 🔥 Set in a commercial part of town, this well-run and very professional choice is ideal for bargain hunters. If you plan to spend most of your time sightseeing and need a hotel only for sleep and rest, you'll find the Selu well maintained, its rooms modern and comfortable. Bedrooms are midsize for the most part and furnished with a few Andalusian decorations, with perhaps a mirrored wall here and there. The accommodations are spread across three floors, and the location is close to the Judería, the Mesquita, and the town center.

Eduardo Dato 7, 14003 Córdoba. ☏ **95-747-65-00.** Fax 95-747-83-76. www.hotelselu.com. 99 units. 50€–110€. AE, DC, MC, V. Parking 16€. **Amenities:** Bar; babysitting; room service. *In room:* A/C, TV, hair dryer, minibar, Wi-Fi (9€ per 24 hr.).

Los Omeyas ★ If you want to stay in the very heart of Córdoba, you can't find a better location than this hotel nestled in the Jewish Quarter. The name comes from the Umayyad dynasty that ruled the Muslim empire of al-Andalus (the Arab tradition is still clearly visible in white marble and latticework). The hotel receives natural light through a central colonnaded patio furnished with tables. Although in no way grand, rooms are extremely comfortable and tasteful, and have modern bathrooms; those on the top floor offer a panoramic view of the ancient tower of the mosque, which is literally around the corner.

Calle Encarnación 17, 14003 Córdoba. ☏ **95-749-22-67.** Fax 95-749-16-59. www.hotel-los omeyas.com. 33 units. 57€–78€ double; 71€–92€ triple; 85€–106€ quad. AE, DC, MC, V. Parking 15€. Bus: 3 or 16. **Amenities:** Hotel restaurant nearby; bar. *In room:* A/C, TV.

Where to Dine in Córdoba

By all means, shake free of your hotel for at least one meal a day in Córdoba. The restaurants are not just places at which to have a quick bite but may combine food with flamenco—so make an evening of it.

EXPENSIVE

Bodegas Campos ★★ SPANISH/ANDALUSIAN You'll eat one of your best meals in Córdoba at this local favorite, located on a narrow cobblestone street in a residential neighborhood 10 minutes from the Mezquita. In front is one of Córdoba's hippest and most crowded tapas bars. It's filled with attractive singles—some more interested in the scene than the food. Bodegas Campos has a welcoming rustic atmosphere and has been going strong since 1908 as both a wine cellar (bodega) and a tavern. The well-chosen menu, prepared from fresh ingredients, consists of local fare like salt cod salad with orange dressing, *frituritas de la casa con salmorejo* (tiny fried fish served with thick Andalusian gazpacho), and *escabeche de perdiz* (pickled pieces of partridge). Other specialties are *merluza rellena con verduritas* (hake stuffed with julienne vegetables) and an Iberian pig's cheek casserole.

Calle de los Lineros 32. ✆ **95-749-75-00.** www.bodegascampos.com. Reservations recommended. Main courses 17€–28€. DC, MC, V. Mon–Sat 11am–midnight; Sun 11am–5pm. Closed Dec 25 and 31. Bus: 1, 3, 4, or 7.

La Almudaina ★★★ SPANISH The owners of this historic restaurant near the Alcázar deserve as much credit for their renovations of a decrepit 15th-century palace as they do for the excellent cuisine produced in their bustling kitchen. Fronting the river in the old Jewish Quarter, La Almudaina is one of the most attractive eateries in Andalusia; you can dine in one of the lace-curtained salons or on a glass-roofed central courtyard. Nearly all the chef's dishes are based on fresh produce that's purchased that day at local markets. Many foodies lead off their meals with local favorites like a tasty *salmorejo* (a soup made with bread, tomato, fresh garlic, Iberian ham, and virgin olive oil). Anglerfish filets with a frothy seafood-brandy sauce taste ultrafresh. A tenderloin of pork is cooked to perfection and served with a delicate wine sauce. A favorite dessert is Cordovan quince pastry prepared according to a 19th-century recipe.

Plaza Campos de los Santos Mártires 1. ✆ **95-747-43-42.** www.restaurantealmudaina.com. Reservations required. Set menu 35€. Main courses 15€–20€. AE, DC, MC, V. Mon–Sat 12:30–4pm and 8:30pm–midnight; Sun 12:30–4pm. Closed Sun July 15–Sept 1. Bus: 3 or 16.

Mesón el Burlaero ★ MEDITERRANEAN/ANDALUSIAN Located in a 16th-century house that belonged to the first bishops of Córdoba, this restaurant in the Jewish Quarter is in the center of the tourist area. The *mesón* offers seven dining areas, along with balconies and a central patio adorned with antique-style murals. The whole place has been lovingly restored and tastefully decorated. From the a la carte menu you can order barbecued mixed grill, filet of beef kebab, succulent lamb chops, and a grilled sirloin of *merluza* (hake).

Calle de la Hoguera 5. ✆ **95-747-27-19.** www.restauranteelburlaero.com. Reservations recommended. Main courses 12€–18€; set menus 13€–20€. MC, V. Daily 11am–4pm and 7:30pm–midnight. Bus: 3.

MODERATE

El Blasón ✦ ANDALUSIAN/MOORISH The tab, with wine, rarely exceeds 30€ at El Blasón, a restaurant in a relatively modern building near the Gran Teatro. You'll dine in any of four separate rooms, each evoking the mid–19th century, thanks to formal crystal chandeliers and a scattering of antiques. Especially appealing is an enclosed patio where ivy creeps up walls and the noises from the city outside are muffled. The cuisine is well prepared and, in some cases, described in terms that verge on the poetic. Examples are salmon with oranges from the mosque, and goose thigh in fruited wine. Braised oxtail is always a good bet, as are any of the roasted lamb dishes redolent with the scent of olive oil and herbs.

José Zorrilla 11. ⏾ **95-748-06-25.** Reservations recommended. Main courses 12€–20€; fixed-price menu 33€. AE, DC, MC, V. Sun–Thurs 11am–11:30pm; Fri–Sat 11am–12:30am. Closed in July. Bus: 3.

El Caballo Rojo ★★ SPANISH Within walking distance of the Mezquita in the Old Town, this restaurant is the most popular in Andalusia, and—with the exception of La Almudaina (see above)—the best in Córdoba. The place has a noise level no other restaurant here matches, but the skilled waiters manage to cope with all demands. Stop in the restaurant's popular bar for a predinner drink, and then take the iron-railed stairs to the upper dining room, where a typical meal might include gazpacho, a main dish of chicken, and then ice cream (often homemade pistachio) and sangria. An interesting variation on the typical gazpacho is an almond-flavored broth with apple pieces. In addition to Andalusian dishes, the chef offers both Sephardic and Mozarabic specialties, an example of the latter being monkfish prepared with pine nuts, currants, carrots, and cream. A local favorite is *rabo de toro* (stew made with the tail of a bull).

Cardinal Herrero 28, Plaza de la Hoguera. ⏾ **95-747-53-75.** www.elcaballorojo.com. Reservations required. Main courses 12€–25€; fixed-price menu 25€. AE, DC, MC, V. Daily 1–4:30pm and 8pm–midnight. Bus: 2.

Taberna Casa Pepe de la Judería ★ CORDOVAN Around the corner from the mosque, this is one of the best-located restaurants in this ancient city. It lies on the route to the Judería, the old Jewish ghetto. A series of little rooms, decorated in a typical Andalusian style, are spread over three floors. From May to October, tables are placed on the rooftop where meats such as chicken and pork are barbecued, and an Andalusian guitarist entertains. The hearty, regional fare includes combinations like cod cooked with raisins, pine nuts, and mussels that may date from recipes from the days when the Moors controlled Córdoba. The chef prepares excellent soups such as a typical Andalusian gazpacho or one made with fresh fish and shellfish. We are especially fond of the *merluza* (hake), prepared Cordovan-style with sweet peppers, garlic, and onions, as well as the baked lamb, another specialty.

Calle Romero 1. ⏾ **95-720-07-44.** Reservations recommended. Fixed-price menu 28€. MC, V. Sun–Thurs 1–4pm and 8:30–11:30pm; Fri–Sat 1–4pm and 8:30pm–midnight. Bus: 3.

INEXPENSIVE

Café Siena ✦ SPANISH The layout of Córdoba makes it far too easy to get enmeshed in the medieval neighborhood around the Mezquita, and not venture anywhere else. This big, angular, and *moderno* cafe is the most appealing of those that ring the centerpiece of Córdoba's 19th- and early-20th-century commercial core, the Plaza de las Tendillas. In nice weather, most diners and drinkers opt for an outdoor table on the square. As day turns to evening, the clientele morphs from shoppers and local office workers to night owls. The food is fairly standard, a litany of the country's favorite dishes, but the ingredients are fresh. The daily menu reflects the market shopping that morning.

Plaza de las Tendillas s/n. © **95-747-30-05.** Tapas 3€–9€; main courses 8€–16€; *menú del día* 14€. AE, DC, MC, V. Mon–Sat 9am–2am. Bus: 1, 3, 4, or 7.

Hotel Hacienda Posada de Vallina ANDALUSIAN/CORDOVAN Facing the south wall of the Mezquita, this restaurant is built on foundations that are among the oldest in Córdoba, with a history going back some 16 centuries. From a much later date are remnants of Roman columns and an old wall. The restaurant itself lies in the inner courtyard of a little hotel below the balconies and gallery of the second floor. The chef proudly calls his food *la cocina cordobesa,* and so it is. Delicious treats appear on the menu, like *salmorejo* (cold tomato soup) or artichokes vinaigrette. We also recommend the fresh baked hake served in a sauce made with clams and shrimp, and the savory oxtail. Desserts are homemade. Most main courses are priced at the lower end of the scale.

Corregidor Luis de la Cerda 83, Judería. © **95-749-87-50.** Reservations recommended. Main courses 8€–22€. AE, DC, MC. Tues 1–4pm and 8–11pm; Sun 1–4pm. Bus: 3 or 7.

Córdoba After Dark

Nighttime fun in the oldest part of Córdoba usually means visiting several tapas bars surrounding the Mezquita. Foremost among them is **Casa Pepe,** Calle Romero 1 (© **95-720-07-44**), an atmospheric old hideaway in an antique building where many generations have lifted a glass. It's open Sunday to Thursday 1 to 4pm and 8:30 to 11:30pm, Friday to Saturday 1 to 4pm and 8:30pm to midnight.

Nearby is **Casa Salinas,** Puerto de Almodóvar s/n (© **95-729-08-46**), offering glasses of sherry and plates of tapas. The bar **El Juramento,** Calle Juramento 6 (© **95-748-54-77**), is old-fashioned enough to be cozy and crowded enough to be convivial. **Bar Círculo Taurino,** Calle Manuel María Arjona 1 (© **95-747-19-53**), is small, cramped, and loaded with memorabilia from bullfights past; it's near the Plaza Colón.

Push back a thick curtain to enter dimly lit **Casa Rubio,** Puerto de Almodóvar 5 (© **95-742-08-53**), where you'll get a gruff but accommodating welcome either at the rectangular bar or in one of a pair of rooms partially covered with Andalusian tiles. We like the leafy inner courtyard where iron tables and a handful of chairs wobble only slightly on the uneven flooring. Casa Rubio is open daily 1 to 4pm and 8:30 to 11:30pm.

For the city's most popular flamenco club head for **Mesón Flamenco La Bulería,** Pedro López 3 (© **95-748-38-39**), close to the Plaza de la Corredera on the outskirts of the old part of town. This is one of the most reasonably priced flamenco shows in Andalusia, considering the class of its talent. The cover of 15€ includes your first drink. Most shows start nightly around 10:30pm. The club is generally closed from December to February. For more formal entertainment, check out the listings at the city's theatrical grande dame, the early 1900s **Gran Teatro de Córdoba,** Av. Gran Capitán 3 (© **95-748-02-37;** www.teatro cordoba.com), site of most of the ballet, opera, chamber music, and symphony performances in town.

SEVILLE ★★★

549km (341 miles) SW of Madrid, 217km (135 miles) NW of Málaga

Sometimes a city becomes famous simply for its beauty and romance. Seville (Sevilla in Spanish), the capital of Andalusia, is such a place. In spite of its sultry summer heat and its many problems, such as high unemployment and street crime, it remains one of the most charming Spanish cities. Don Juan and Carmen—aided by Mozart and Bizet—have given Seville a romantic reputation. Because of the acclaim of *Don Giovanni* and *Carmen,* not to mention *The Barber of Seville,* debunkers have risen to challenge this reputation. But if a visitor can see only two Spanish cities in a lifetime, they should be Seville and Toledo.

All the images associated with Andalusia—orange trees, mantillas, lovesick toreros, flower-filled patios, and castanet-rattling Gypsies—come to life in Seville. But it's not just a tourist city; it's a substantial river port, and it contains some of the most important artistic works and architectural monuments in Spain.

Unlike other Spanish cities, Seville has fared rather well under most of its conquerors—the Romans, Moors, and Christians. Rulers from Pedro the Cruel to Ferdinand and Isabella held court here. When Spain entered its 16th-century golden age, Seville funneled gold from the New World into the rest of the country, and Columbus docked here after his journey to America.

Be warned, however, that driving here is a nightmare: Seville was planned for the horse and buggy rather than for the car, and nearly all its streets run one-way toward the Guadalquivir River. Locating a hard-to-find restaurant or a hidden little square will require patience and luck.

Essentials

GETTING THERE Seville's **Aeropuerto San Pablo,** Calle Almirante Lobo (© **95-444-90-00;** www.aena.es), is served by **Iberia** (© **800/772-4642** in the U.S., or 90-240-05-00 toll-free in Spain; www.iberia.com), which flies several times a day between Madrid (and elsewhere via Madrid) and Seville. It also flies several times a week to and from Alicante, Grand Canary Island, Lisbon, Barcelona, Palma de Majorca, Tenerife, Santiago de Compostela, and (once a week) Zaragoza. The airport lies about 9.6km (6 miles) from the center of the city, along the highway leading to Carmona. A bus run by **Amarillos Tour S.A.** (© **90-221-03-17**) meets all incoming flights and transports you into the center of Seville for 3€.

Train service into Seville is centralized into the **Estación Santa Justa,** Av. Kansas City s/n (© **90-224-02-02** for information and reservations; www.renfe.es). Bus nos. C1 and C2 take you from this train station to the bus station at Prado de San Sebastián, and bus no. EA runs to and from the airport. The high-speed AVE train has reduced travel time from Madrid to Seville to 2½ hours. The train makes 20 trips daily, with a stop in Córdoba, and costs 78€. A total of 37 trains a day connect Seville and Córdoba; the AVE train takes 45 minutes and costs 29€. Eleven trains a day run to Málaga, taking 3 hours; there are also four trains per day to Granada (3 hr.).

Although Seville confusingly has several satellite **bus** stations servicing small towns and nearby villages of Andalusia, most buses arrive and depart from the city's largest bus terminal, on the southeast edge of the Old City, at Prado de San Sebastián, Calle José María Osborne 11 (© **95-441-71-18**).

Several companies make frequent runs to and from Córdoba (trip time: 2½ hr.), Málaga (3½ hr.), Granada (4 hr.), and Madrid (8 hr.). For information and ticket prices, call Alsina Graells at ✆ **95-441-88-11.** A newer bus station is at Plaza de Armas (✆ **95-490-80-40**), but it usually services destinations beyond Andalusia, including Portugal.

Seville is 549km (341 miles) southwest of Madrid and 217km (135 miles) northwest of Málaga. Several major highways converge on Seville, connecting it with the rest of Spain and Portugal. During periods of heavy holiday traffic, the N-V (E-90) from Madrid through Extremadura—which, at Mérida, connects with the southbound N-630 (E-803)—is usually less congested than the N-IV (E-5) through eastern Andalusia.

VISITOR INFORMATION The tourist office, **Oficina de Información del Turismo,** at Av. de la Constitución 21B (✆ **95-478-75-78;** www.andalucia. org), is open Monday to Friday 9am to 7:30pm, Saturday and Sunday 9:30am to 3pm.

SPECIAL EVENTS The most popular times to visit Seville are during the **April Fair**—the most famous *feria* in Spain, with bullfights, flamenco, and folklore on parade—and during **Holy Week,** when wooden figures, called *pasos,* are paraded through streets by robed penitents. See "Spain Calendar of Events," p. 60, and contact the tourist office (see above) for more information.

FAST FACTS There's a **U.S. consulate** at Plaza Nueva 8 (✆ **95-421-87-51**), open Monday to Friday 10am to 1pm. For **medical emergencies,** go to the Virgen del Rocío, Av. Manuel Siurot s/n (✆ **95-501-20-00**), about 2km (1¼ miles) from the city center.

Warning: With its massive unemployment, the city has been hit by a crime wave in recent years. María Luisa Park is especially dangerous, as is the highway leading to Jerez de la Frontera and Cádiz. Dangling cameras and purses are especially vulnerable. Don't leave cars unguarded with your luggage inside. Regrettably, some daring attacks are made when passengers stop for traffic signals—as happens in some U.S. cities.

If you need a **cab,** call Tele Taxi at ✆ **95-462-22-22** or Radio Taxi at ✆ **95-458-36-05.** Cabs are metered and charge 1€ per kilometer at night and .85€ during the day.

Seeing the Sights in Seville

The only way to explore Seville is on foot, with a good map in hand—but remember to be alert for muggers.

THE TOP ATTRACTIONS

Alcázar ★★★ Pedro the Cruel built this magnificent 14th-century Mudéjar palace north of the cathedral. It's the oldest royal residence in Europe still in use: On visits to Seville, King Juan Carlos and Queen Sofía stay here. From the Dolls' Court to the Maidens' Court through the domed Ambassadors' Room, it contains some of the finest work of Sevillian artisans. In many ways it evokes the Alhambra at Granada. Ferdinand and Isabella, who at one time lived in the Alcázar and influenced its architectural evolution, welcomed Columbus here on his return from America. On the top floor, the Oratory of the Catholic Monarchs has a fine altar in polychrome tiles made by Pisano in 1504. The well-kept **gardens ★,**

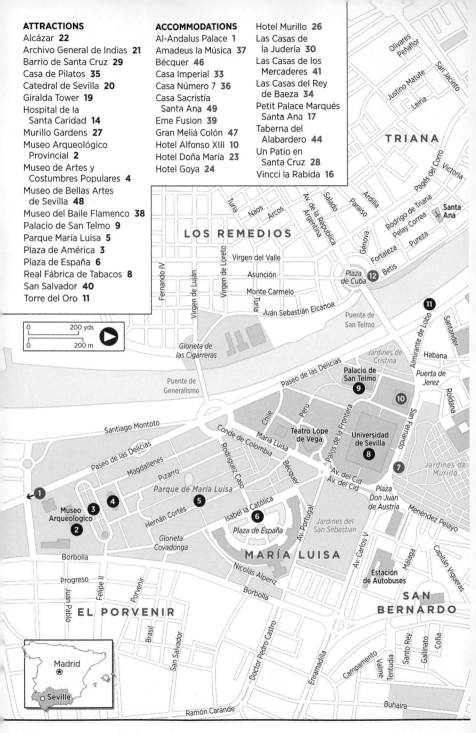

ATTRACTIONS

Alcázar **22**
Archivo General de Indias **21**
Barrio de Santa Cruz **29**
Casa de Pilatos **35**
Catedral de Sevilla **20**
Giralda Tower **19**
Hospital de la
  Santa Caridad **14**
Murillo Gardens **27**
Museo Arqueológico
  Provincial **2**
Museo de Artes y
  Costumbres Populares **4**
Museo de Bellas Artes
  de Sevilla **48**
Museo del Baile Flamenco **38**
Palacio de San Telmo **9**
Parque María Luisa **5**
Plaza de América **3**
Plaza de España **6**
Real Fábrica de Tabacos **8**
San Salvador **40**
Torre del Oro **11**

ACCOMMODATIONS

Al-Andalus Palace **1**
Amadeus la Música **37**
Bécquer **46**
Casa Imperial **33**
Casa Número 7 **36**
Casa Sacristía
  Santa Ana **49**
Eme Fusion **39**
Gran Meliá Colón **47**
Hotel Alfonso XIII **10**
Hotel Doña María **23**
Hotel Goya **24**
Hotel Murillo **26**
Las Casas de
  la Judería **30**
Las Casas de los
  Mercaderes **41**
Las Casas del Rey
  de Baeza **34**
Petit Palace Marqués
  Santa Ana **17**
Taberna del
  Alabardero **44**
Un Patio en
  Santa Cruz **28**
Vincci la Rabida **16**

Seville

Río Guadalquivir

Descubrimientos

Estación de Autobuses

Antigua Estación de Córdoba

Museo de Bellas Artes 48

Plaza San Laureano

Puente del Cacherro

Puente de la Cartuja

Puente de Isabel II

CENTRO

San Lorenzo

ARENAL

Plaza de Toros

Plaza Nueva

Hospital de la Caridad 14

Archivo de Indias 21

Catedral

Alcázar

SANTA CRUZ

Palacio de Lebrija

Palacio Arzobispal

Salvador

Anunciación

Plaza de la Encarnación

Palacio de las Dueñas

Iglesia de San Luis

Iglesia de San Marcos

Casa de Pilatos 35

San Leandro

Plaza Ponce de León

San Esteban

LA CALZADA

Jardines del Valle

Ayuntamiento

Pl. del Triunfo

Pl. Virgen de Los Reyes

Santa Cruz

San José

Alameda de Hercules 49

San José

The mosaic interior of Seville's Alcázar fortress.

filled with beautiful flowers, shrubbery, and fruit trees, are alone worth the visit. Plan to spend about 1½ hours here.

Plaza del Triunfo s/n. ℂ **95-450-23-23.** www.patronato-alcazarsevilla.es. Admission 7.50€. Oct–Mar Tues–Sun 9:30am–5pm; Apr–Sept Tues–Sun 9:30am–7pm.

Archivo General de Indias The great architect of Philip II's El Escorial (see "San Lorenzo de El Escorial," p. 207), Juan de Herrera, was also the architect of this building next to the cathedral, originally the Lonja (Stock Exchange). Construction on the Archivo General de Indias lasted from 1584 to 1646. In the 17th century it was headquarters for the Academy of Seville, founded in part by the great Spanish artist Murillo. In 1785, during the reign of Charles III, the building was turned over for use as a general records office for the Indies. That led to today's Archivo General de Indias, said to contain some four million antique documents, even letters exchanged between patron Queen Isabella and explorer Columbus (his, detailing his discoveries and impressions). These very rare documents are locked in air-conditioned storage to keep them from disintegrating. Special permission has to be acquired before examining some of them. On display in glass cases are fascinating documents in which the dreams of the early explorers come alive. Give yourself about an hour here.

Av. de la Constitución. ℂ **95-450-05-28.** www.mcu.es. Free admission. Mon–Sat 9am–4pm; Sun 10am–2pm.

Casa de Pilatos ★★ This 16th-century Andalusian palace of the dukes of Medinaceli recaptures the splendor of the past, combining Gothic, Mudéjar, and Plateresque styles in its courtyards, fountains, and salons. According to tradition, this is a reproduction of Pilate's House in Jerusalem. Don't miss the two old carriages or the rooms filled with Greek and Roman statues. The collection of paintings includes works by Carreño, Pantoja de la Cruz, Sebastiano del Piombo, Lucas Jordán, Batalloli, Pacheco, and Goya. The museum's first floor is seen by guided tour only, but the ground floor, patios, and gardens are self-guided. The

A courtyard statue at Casa de Pilatos.

palace is about a 7-minute walk northeast of the cathedral on the northern edge of Barrio de Santa Cruz, in a warren of labyrinthine streets whose traffic is funneled through nearby Calle de Aguilas. Plan to spend 45 minutes here.

Plaza Pilatos 1. Ⓒ **95-422-52-98.** Museum 8€; patio and gardens 5€. June–Sept daily 9am–7pm; Oct–May daily 9am–6pm.

Catedral de Sevilla and Giralda Tower ★★★ The largest Gothic building in the world and the third-largest church in Europe, after St. Peter's in Rome and St. Paul's in London, the Catedral de Sevilla was designed by builders with a stated goal—that "those who come after us will take us for madmen." Construction began in the late 1400s on the site of an ancient mosque and took centuries to complete. The cathedral is said to contain the remains of Columbus, with his tomb mounted on four statues.

Works of art abound here, many of them architectural, such as the 15th-century stained-glass windows, the iron screens *(rejas)* closing off the chapels, the elaborate 15th-century choir stalls, and the Gothic reredos above the main altar. During Corpus Christi and Immaculate Conception observances, altar boys with castanets dance in front of the high altar. In the treasury are works by Goya, Murillo, and Zurbarán, as well as a touch of the macabre in a display of skulls. After touring the dark interior, you emerge into

A detail from the altar of the Catedral de Sevilla.

315

the sunlight of the Patio of Orange Trees, with its fresh citrus scents and chirping birds.

La Giralda, a Moorish tower next to the cathedral, is the city's most famous monument—it conjures up Seville. Erected as a minaret in the 12th century, it has seen later additions, such as 16th-century bells. A climb to the top is the walk of a lifetime. There are no steps—you ascend a seemingly endless ramp. If you can make it to the top, you'll have a dazzling view of Seville. Entrance is through the cathedral. Allot about 1½ hours here.

Av. de la Constitución s/n. ✆ **95-421-49-71.** www.catedraldesevilla.es. Cathedral and tower 8€ adults, 2€ students 25 and under, free for children 11 and under, free for all Sun. Sept–June Mon–Sat 11am–5pm, Sun 2:30–6pm; July–Aug Mon–Sat 9:30am–4pm.

Hospital de la Santa Caridad ★ This 17th-century hospital is intricately linked to the legend of Miguel Manara, portrayed by Dumas and Mérimée as the scandalous Don Juan. It was once thought that he built the institution to atone for his sins, but this has been disproved. The death of Manara's beautiful young wife in 1661 caused him such grief that he retired from society and entered the "Charity Brotherhood," burying corpses of the sick and diseased as well as condemned and executed criminals. Today the members of this brotherhood continue to look after the poor, the old, and invalids who have nowhere else to turn. Nuns will show you through the festive orange-and-sienna courtyard. The baroque chapel contains works by the 17th-century Spanish painters Murillo and Valdés-Leal. As you leave the chapel, look over the exit door for the macabre picture of an archbishop being devoured by maggots. Plan to spend about 45 minutes here.

Calle Temprado 3. ✆ **95-422-32-32.** www.santa-caridad.es. Admission 5€ adults, free for children 11 and under. Mon–Sat 9am–1:30pm and 3:30–7:30pm; Sun 9am–1pm.

Museo de Bellas Artes de Sevilla ★★ This lovely old convent off Calle de Alfonso XII houses one of Spain's most important art collections. A whole

---

DNA Enters the Debate over Columbus's Bones

DNA samples from 500-year-old bone slivers could contradict the Dominican Republic's competing claim that Columbus was buried in Santo Domingo, and not in Seville. Scientists in 2006 confirmed that "at least some of the explorer's remains" were buried in Seville. But the debate still rages. It is entirely possible that some of Columbus's remains could have been buried in the Dominican Republic; his body was moved several times after his death. A forensic team compared DNA from the bones buried in Seville with DNA from the remains known to be from Columbus's brother Diego. "There was an absolute matchup," geneticists said.

These claims were refuted by Juan Bautista Mieses, the director of the Columbus Lighthouse in Santo Domingo, where the explorer's alleged remains rest. He has, however, turned down requests to take DNA samples. "We Christians believe that one does not bother the dead," Mieses said.

The Torre del Oro.

gallery is devoted to two paintings by El Greco, and works by Zurbarán are on exhibit; however, the devoutly religious paintings of Seville-born Murillo are the highlight. An entire wing is given over to macabre paintings by the 17th-century artist Valdés-Leal. His painting of John the Baptist's head on a platter includes the knife. The top floor, which displays modern paintings, is less interesting. Thirty minutes is enough time to see this museum.

Plaza del Museo 9. **ⓒ 95-478-65-00.** www.museosdeandalucia.es. Admission 1.50€. Tues 2:30–8pm; Wed–Sat 9am–8:30pm; Sun 9am–2:30pm. Bus: C3 or C4.

Museo del Baile Flamenco In the heart of Seville, this museum is best visited before you enjoy the nightly flamenco shows. That way, you'll better appreciate the artistry of this Gypsy dance. The museum has exhibits relating to every subject from the mysterious origins of the dance to flamenco stars and their lives. In this museum, the deepest roots of flamenco meet the latest multimedia technology. It's not all history, as museumgoers can witness the latest developments in modern flamenco as well. Allot about a half-hour to see this museum.

Calle Manuel Rojas Marcos 3. **ⓒ 95-434-03-11.** www.museoflamenco.com. Admission 10€ adults, 6€ children. Daily 9am–7pm.

Torre del Oro The 12-sided Tower of Gold, dating from the 13th century, overlooks the Guadalquivir River. Originally it was covered with gold tiles, but someone long ago made off with them. The tower has been restored and turned into a

Ｏ *Olé:* A Day at the Bullfight

From Easter to late summer, some of the best bullfighters in Spain appear at the **Maestranza bullring,** on Paseo de Colón (**ⓒ 95-450-13-82;** www.plazadetorosdelamaestranza.com). One of the leading bullrings, the stadium attracts matadors whose fights often get television and newspaper coverage throughout Iberia. Unless there's a special festival going on, bullfights *(corridas)* occur on Sunday; the best are staged during April Fair celebrations. Tickets tend to be pricey and should be purchased in advance at the ticket office *(despacho de entradas)* on Calle Adriano, beside the Maestranza. You'll find many unofficial ticket-vending kiosks placed strategically along the main shopping street, Calle Sierpes, but they charge a 20% commission—or a lot more if they think they can get it.

A matador facing down a bull at Seville's Maestranza bullring.

maritime museum, the Museo Náutico, displaying drawings and engravings of the port of Seville in its golden heyday. Twenty minutes should be sufficient here.

Paseo de Cristóbal Colón. 🕐 **95-422-24-19.** Admission 1€; free Tues. Tues–Fri 10am–2pm; Sat–Sun 11am–2pm. Closed Aug.

MORE ATTRACTIONS

Barrio de Santa Cruz ★★★ What was once a ghetto for Spanish Jews—who were forced out of Spain in the late 15th century in the wake of the Inquisition—is today the most colorful district of Seville. Near the old walls of the Alcázar, winding medieval streets, with names like Vida (Life) and Muerte (Death), open onto pocket-size plazas. Flower-filled balconies with draping bougainvillea and potted geraniums jut over this labyrinth, shading you from the hot Andalusian summer sun. Feel free to look through numerous wrought-iron gates into patios filled with fountains and plants. In the evening it's common to see Sevillians sitting outside drinking icy sangria under the glow of lanterns.

To enter the Barrio Santa Cruz, turn right after leaving the Patio de Banderas exit of the Alcázar. Turn right again at Plaza de la Alianza, going down Calle Rodrigo Caro to Plaza de Doña Elvira. **Note:** Use caution when strolling through the area, particularly at night; many robberies have occurred here.

Parque Maria Luisa ★★ This park, dedicated to María Luisa, sister of Isabella II, was once the grounds of the **Palacio de San Telmo.** The palace, whose baroque facade is visible behind the deluxe Alfonso XIII Hotel, today houses a seminary. The former private royal park is now open to the public. In 1929, Seville was to host the Spanish American Exhibition, and many pavilions from around the world were erected here. The worldwide Depression put a damper on the exhibition, but the pavilions still stand.

Running south along the Guadalquivir River, the park attracts those who want to ride boats, walk along flower-bordered paths, jog, or bicycle. The most romantic way to traverse the park is by rented horse and carriage, but this can be expensive, depending on negotiation with the driver.

Warning: Exercise caution while walking through this park—many muggings have been reported.

Plaza de America A landmark Sevillian square, the Plaza de América represents city planning at its best: Here you can walk through gardens planted with roses, enjoying the lily ponds and the fountains and feeling the protective shade of the palms. And here you'll find a trio of elaborate buildings left over from the world exhibition that never materialized—in the center, the home of the government headquarters of Andalusia; on either side, two minor museums worth visiting only if you have time to spare.

The **Museo Arqueológico Provincial** (© 95-478-64-74) contains many artifacts from prehistoric times and the days of the Romans, Visigoths, and Moors. It's open Wednesday through Saturday from 9am to 8pm, Tuesday 3 to 8pm, and Sunday 9am to 2pm. Admission is 1.50€ for adults and free for students and children. Bus nos. 30, 31, and 34 stop there. Nearby is the **Museo de Artes y Costumbres Populares** (© 95-471-23-91; www.museosdeandalucia.es). In a Mudéjar pavilion opposite the Museo Arqueológico, this is Seville's museum of folklore artifacts. On its ground floor you see remnants of traditional occupations, including, among others, a forge, a baker's oven, a wine press, and a tanner's shop. More interesting on this floor, though, is the stunning collection of ceramics. The upstairs is devoted to such exhibitions as the court dress of the 19th century, as well as 18th-century fabrics and embroideries from the factories of Seville. One from Murillo, *Children Eating Grapes,* is particularly evocative. Gold works and a varied collection of paintings and musical instruments are also displayed on this floor. It's open Tuesday 2:30 to 8:30pm, Wednesday to Saturday 9am to 8:30pm, and Sunday 9am to 2:30pm. Admission is 1.50€ for adults and free for children and students.

Plaza de España The major building left from the exhibition at the Parque María Luisa (see above) is the half-moon-shaped Renaissance-style structure set on this landmark square. The architect, Aníbal González, not only designed but supervised the building of this immense structure; today it's a government office building. At a canal here you can rent rowboats for excursions into the park, or you can cross bridges spanning the canal. Set into a curved wall are alcoves focusing on the characteristics of Spain's 50 provinces, as depicted in tile murals.

Real Fabrica de Tabacos When Carmen waltzed out of the tobacco factory in the first act of Bizet's opera, she made its 18th-century original in Seville world famous. This old tobacco factory was constructed from 1750 to 1766, and 100 years later it employed 10,000 *cigarreras,* of which Carmen was one in the opera. (She rolled cigars on her thighs.) In the 19th century, these tobacco women made up the largest female workforce in Spain. In fact, many visitors arriving today ask guides to take them to "Carmen's tobacco factory." The building, located on Calle San Fernando near the city's landmark luxury hotel, the Alfonso XIII (p. 321), is the second largest in Spain. But the Real Fábrica de Tabacos is now part of the Universidad de Sevilla. Look for signs of its former role in the bas-reliefs of tobacco plants and Indians over the main entrances. You'll also see bas-reliefs of Columbus and Cortés. Then you can wander through the grounds for a look at student life, Sevillian-style. The factory is directly south of the Alcázar gardens.

Shopping

ART One of the most respected galleries in Seville, **Rafael Ortiz,** Marmolles 12 (✆ **95-421-48-74;** www.galeriarafaelortiz.com), specializes in contemporary paintings, usually from Iberian artists. Exhibitions change frequently and inventories sell out quickly. It's open Monday to Saturday 10am to 1:30pm and 4:30 to 8pm.

BOOKS Close to Seville's university, **Librería Vértice,** San Fernando 33 (✆ **95-421-16-54;** www.libreriavertice.com), stocks books in a variety of languages. The polyglot inventory ranges from the academic to Spanish romances of the soap opera genre. It's open Monday to Friday 9:30am to 2pm and 5 to 8:30pm, and Saturday 11am to 2pm. In July and August, hours are Monday to Wednesday 9am to 2:30pm and 6 to 8:30pm, and Thursday and Friday 9am to 3pm.

CERAMICS Near the cathedral, **El Postigo,** Arfe s/n (✆ **95-456-00-13**), has a wide selection of Andalusian ceramics. Some of the pieces are much too big to fit into your suitcase; others—especially the hand-painted tiles—make charming souvenirs that can easily be transported. It's open Monday to Saturday 10am to 2pm (also 5–8:30pm Mon–Fri). Near the town hall, **Martian,** Calle Sierpes 74 (✆ **95-421-34-13**), sells a wide array of painted tiles and ceramics: vases, plates, cups, serving dishes, and statues, all made in or near Seville. Many of the pieces use ancient Andalusian geometric patterns. Other floral motifs are rooted in Spanish traditions of the 18th century. Martian is open Monday to Saturday 10am to 2pm and 5 to 8:30pm.

DEPARTMENT STORES **El Corte Inglés,** Plaza Duque de la Victoria, 13B (✆ **95-459-70-00;** www.elcorteingles.es), is the best of the several department stores clustered in Seville's commercial center. It features multilingual translators and rack after rack of every conceivable kind of merchandise for the well-stocked home, kitchen, and closet. If you're in the market for the brightly colored *feria* costumes worn by young girls during Seville's holidays, there's an impressive selection of the traditional regional fashion, along with all the latest designer fashions for every day. It's open Monday to Saturday 10am to 8pm.

FASHION See also "Department Stores," above. **Iconos,** Av. de la Constitución 21A (✆ **95-422-14-08**), is an idiosyncratic boutique loaded with fashion accessories for everyone from teenage girls to mature women. Silk scarves, costume jewelry, and an assortment of T-shirts with logos lettered in varying degrees of taste—they're all here. Iconos is open Monday to Saturday from 10am to 9pm, Sunday from noon to 5pm. Head for **Victorio & Lucchino,** Sierpes 87 (✆ **95-422-79-51;** www.victorioylucchino.com), for chic upscale fashions sold Monday to Saturday 10:30am to 1:30pm and 5:30 to 8:30pm.

Where to Stay in Seville

During Holy Week and the Seville Fair, hotels often double, even triple, their rates. Price increases are often not announced until the last minute. If you're going to be in Seville at these times, arrive with an ironclad reservation and an agreement about the price before checking in.

VERY EXPENSIVE

Al-Andalus Palace ★★ No hotel in Seville has a more avant-garde design than this palace, just 5 minutes from the center in the Heliópolis district, an upmarket residential area. The front public rooms are suspended by cable, and the glass facade reflects both the blue skies of Seville and the marble floors. The large guest rooms are elegantly appointed, with big windows; some have balconies. The decor and furnishings are minimalist—functional but modern. Many accommodations have small living rooms and suites with their own breakfast bars.

Av. Palmera s/n, 41012 Seville. © **95-423-06-00.** Fax 95-423-19-12. www.hoteles-silken.com. 623 units. 250€ double; 1,284€ suite. AE, DC, MC, V. Parking 13€. Bus: 34. **Amenities:** 5 restaurants; 2 bars; babysitting; concierge; outdoor pool; room service; spa. *In room:* A/C, TV, hair dryer, minibar, Wi-Fi (free).

Eme Fusion ★★★ A cluster of fourteen 18th- and 19th-century town houses have been linked together into a harmonious whole that has been beautifully restored with many Andalusian architectural details still intact. Face to face with La Giralda, it enjoys one of the best locations in Seville. Shaded courtyards and a panoramic rooftop pool terrace provide just some of its allure. Each unit is individually decorated with an elegant decor that at times is rather monastic, with unpolished stucco walls and inky-black Andalusian grass rugs. The suites and two superior doubles open onto private terraces with Jacuzzis. Most of the public space is taken over with dining and drinking facilities, the best of which is **Santo,** serving a contemporary Mediterranean cuisine.

Calle de los Alemanes 27, 41004 Sevilla. © **95-456-00-00.** www.emecatedralhotel.com. 60 units. 200€–500€ double; 750€–950€ suite. AE, DC, MC, V. Bus: C5. **Amenities:** 4 restaurants; 2 bars; concierge; exercise room; pool (outdoor); room service; spa. *In room:* A/C, TV, hair dryer, minibar, Wi-Fi (free).

Hotel Alfonso XIII ★★★ Located at a corner of the gardens fronting the Alcázar, this rococo building is one of Spain's three or four most legendary hotels, and Seville's premier address. This splendid palace dwarfs the competition and is now a Westin hotel. Built in the Mudéjar/Andalusian-revival style as a shelter for patrons of the Ibero-American Exposition of 1929, and named after the then-king of Spain, it reigns as an ornate and expensive bastion of glamour. Its rooms and hallways glitter with hand-painted tiles, acres of marble and mahogany, antique furniture embellished with intricately embossed leather, and a spaciousness that's nothing short of majestic.

San Fernando 2, 41004 Seville. © **800/221-2340** in the U.S. and Canada, or 95-491-70-00. Fax 95-491-70-99. www.starwoodhotels.com. 146 units. 350€–650€ double; from 700€ suite. AE, DC, MC, V. Parking 17€. **Amenities:** 2 restaurants; 3 bars; airport transfers (75€); babysitting; concierge; exercise room; outdoor saltwater pool; room service; outdoor tennis court (lit). *In room:* A/C, TV, hair dryer, minibar, Wi-Fi (3€ per hour).

EXPENSIVE

Casa Imperial ★★★ This hotel, in the historic center near Casa Pilatos, was launched in the mid-1990s. The building dates from the 15th century, when it housed the butler to the Marquis of Tarifa. The interior is refined, and there are four Andalusian patios adorned with exotic plants. The beamed ceilings are original, and sparkling chandeliers hang from the ceilings. The rooms are large—many have small kitchens and ample terraces. Bathrooms are tastefully decorated with showers and luxurious tubs, some of which are antiques.

Calle Imperial 29, 41003 Seville. ℰ **95-450-03-00.** Fax 95-450-03-30. www.casaimperial.com. 24 units. 169€–341€ double; 246€–415€ junior suite. AE, DC, MC, V. Limited free parking, otherwise 25€. Bus: 24 or 27. **Amenities:** Restaurant; bar; babysitting; room service. In room: A/C, TV, hair dryer, minibar, Wi-Fi (free).

Casa Número 7 ★★ 🍴 This is as close as you can get to staying in an elegant private home in Seville. Next to the Santa Cruz barrio, the little inn is in a beautiful, sensitively restored 19th-century mansion where you live in style, with a butler to serve you breakfast. Small in size, Casa Número 7 is big on style and grace notes, recapturing the aura of Old Seville. It portrays itself, with justification, as a civilized oasis in the midst of a bustling city. The building envelops an old atrium and is filled with such touches as family photographs, Oriental area rugs, a marble fireplace, and floral-print love seats. Rooms are individually decorated in Old Sevillano style, with impeccable taste and an eye to comfort. Our favorite is the spacious Yellow Room, with its "Juliet balcony" overlooking the street.

Vírgenes 7, 41004 Seville. ℰ **95-422-15-81.** Fax 95-421-45-27. www.casanumero7.com. 6 units. 177€–280€ double. Rates include continental breakfast. AE, MC, V. Parking nearby 15€. Bus: 10, 15, 24, or 32. **Amenities:** Bar. In room: A/C, hair dryer.

Gran Meliá Colón ★★ This hotel opened more than 80 years ago and became a landmark over the years, celebrated for its neo-baroque designs. The good news is that it's been restored, reopening in 2009 with its original dome crowning the open and airy lobby. The hotel in Seville's Old Quarter has been pushed into the 21st century, with a sensory-rejuvenation spa, a solarium terrace, a hydromassage swimming pool, and lots of high-tech gadgets. Traditional decoration and contemporary aesthetics combine in the midsize to spacious bedrooms, which have a minimalist ambience.

Canalejas 1, 41001 Seville. ℰ **95-450-55-99.** Fax 95-422-09-38. www.gran-melia-colon.com. 146 units. 169€–269€ double, from 460€ suite. AE, DC, MC, V. Parking 22€. **Amenities:** Restaurant; bar; babysitting; health club; pool (heated indoor); room service; spa. In room: A/C, TV, CD player, hair dryer, minibar, MP3 docking station, Wi-Fi (4.50€ per hour).

Las Casas del Rey de Baeza ★ Less luxurious (and more expensive) than its sibling, Las Casas de la Judería (p. 324), this antique hotel close to the Casa de Pilatos is still a winning choice with its stone floors and 19th-century Andalusian architecture. A hotel since 1998, it has an interior patio surrounded by a cozy coterie of rooms and a long Andalusian balcony. Some of the beautifully furnished rooms have living rooms, and the decor is finely honed in marble and wood with comfortable furnishings.

Calle Santiago, Plaza Jesús de la Redención 2, 41003 Seville. ℰ **95-456-14-96.** Fax 95-456-14-41. www.fuenso.com. 41 units. 117€–310€ double; 214€–520€ suite. AE, DC, MC, V. Parking 18€. Bus: 10, 15, 20, or 32. **Amenities:** Restaurant; bar; babysitting; exercise room; outdoor heated pool; room service; spa. In room: A/C, TV, hair dryer, minibar, Wi-Fi (free).

Vincci La Rabida ★ 🍴 This restored *palacio* in the Barrio del Arenal neighborhood, near the cathedral, was erected in the typical Andalusian style of the 18th century. The hotel is only a short walk from many of the city's major attractions, including its main shopping district. The restored bedrooms are handsomely, even elegantly, furnished in a typical Andalusian manner. Best are the two suites with large balconies overlooking Seville and offering panoramic views of the cathedral and the Giralda Tower. The suites also have a separate sitting room and a Jacuzzi. The hotel's restaurant features a traditional Sevillian cuisine, with such well-prepared dishes as red tuna with soy sauce and honey, Iberian pork tenderloin, and a boned bull's tail. A special feature here is an outdoor sun terrace with a hot tub. To get the best deals, book on the website.

Calle Castelar 24, 41001 Sevilla. ℂ **95-450-12-80.** Fax 95-421-66-00. www.vinccihoteles.com. 83 units. 135€–450€ double; 253€–500€ family room/suite. AE, DC, MC, V. Parking 15€. Bus: AC, C5, or 43. **Amenities:** Restaurant; bar; room service. *In room:* A/C, TV, hair dryer, minibar, Wi-Fi (free).

MODERATE

Alcoba del Rey de Sevilla ★ 👜 This small boutique hotel, in a little palace dating from the 13th century, is inspired by the Seville of al-Andalus in the city's splendid heyday. Its architectural structure is based on handmade materials used here 8 centuries ago. Rooms open onto a central Andalusian patio. Each midsize bedroom not only contains an exotic name—Princess Zaida or Rumaykiyya, for example—but also has a unique decor including horseshoe arches, silk fabrics, carved headboards, king-size beds with canopy, and the scent of cedar furnishings. The stuccoed bathrooms are a special feature with much use made of marble. As a surprise, guests can buy everything they see in the hotel, even the beds and furnishings.

Calle Bécquer, 41009 Seville. ℂ **95-491-58-00.** Fax 95-491-56-75. www.alcobadelrey.com. 15 units. 130€–271€ double. AE, DC, MC, V. Parking 16€. Bus: C1, C2, or 32. *In room:* A/C, TV, hair dryer, Wi-Fi (free).

Bécquer 🦋 A short walk from the action of the Seville bullring and only 2 blocks from the river, Bécquer is on a street full of cafes where you can order tapas and enjoy Andalusian wine. The Museo de Bellas Artes is also nearby. Built in the 1970s, the hotel was enlarged and much renovated. It occupies the site of a former mansion and retains many objets d'art rescued before that building was demolished. You register in a modern lobby before being shown to one of the functionally furnished rooms—a good value in a pricey city, as most units are at the lower end of the price scale.

Calle Reyes Católicos 4, 41001 Seville. ℂ **95-422-89-00.** Fax 95-421-44-00. www.hotelbecquer. com. 141 units. 105€–210€ double; 250€–324€ suite. AE, DC, MC, V. Parking 15€. Bus: C1, C2, or C4. **Amenities:** Restaurant; 2 bars; babysitting; outdoor rooftop pool; room service; spa. *In room:* A/C, TV, hair dryer, minibar, Wi-Fi (free).

Casa Sacristía Santa Ana ★ 👜 A former 18th-century sacristy has been successfully converted into a government-designated three-star hotel in the historic center of Seville, near Plaza de La Alameda. This country-chic modern establishment has all the contemporary gadgetry and plumbing, but still maintains a certain Andalusian architectural purity. All the midsize rooms are decorated in a romantic style, and are meticulously decorated and designed for both comfort and style.

Alameda de Hércules 22, 41022 Seville. ℂ **95-491-57-22.** Fax 95-490-53-16. http://sacristiade santaana.com. 25 units. 60€–200€ double; 150€–300€ junior suite. MC, V. **Amenities:** Restaurant; bar; room service. *In room:* A/C, TV, minibar, Wi-Fi (free).

Hotel Doña María ★ ☺ Highlights here include the Iberian antiques in the stone lobby and upper hallways and a location a few steps from the cathedral, which allows for dramatic views from the rooftop terrace. An ornate neoclassical entryway is offset with a pure white facade and iron balconies, which hint at the building's origin in the 1840s as a private villa. Amid the flowering plants on the upper floor you'll find garden-style lattices and antique wrought-iron railings. Room sizes range from small to large enough for the entire family, and some have four-poster beds, while others have a handful of antique reproductions. Light sleepers might find the noise of the church bells jarring. There are a garden courtyard and a rooftop pool.

Don Remondo 19, 41004 Seville. © **95-422-49-90.** Fax 95-421-95-46. www.hdmaria.com. 64 units. 96€–294€ double. AE, DC, MC, V. Parking 20€. **Amenities:** 2 bars; outdoor pool; room service. *In room:* A/C, TV, hair dryer, minibar, Wi-Fi (free).

Hotel San Gil ★★ 🏨 This landmark building from 1901, in a setting of towering palm trees, captures some of the colonial style of Old Seville. As a guest, you can enjoy an aura of Old Andalusia while taking advantage of modern amenities. Located near the historic Macarena Wall and the Santa Cruz barrio, the hotel has a rooftop swimming pool that opens onto vistas of the surrounding cityscape. Inside, the hotel is richly endowed with Old Andalusian styling, including an elaborate use of tiles. Bedrooms are midsize for the most part and decorated in creamy colors with light wooden furnishings.

Parras 28, 41002 Seville. © **95-490-68-11.** Fax 95-490-69-39. www.sevillahotelsangil.com. 60 units. 67€–211€ double; 117€–233€ junior suite. Rates include continental breakfast. AE, DC, MC, V. Parking 15€. Bus: C3, 2, 13, or 14. **Amenities:** Restaurant; bar; babysitting; outdoor pool; room service; Wi-Fi (free, in lobby). *In room:* A/C, TV, hair dryer, kitchenette (in some), minibar.

Las Casas de la Judería ★★ 🏆 In the Santa Cruz district, this hotel is installed in a palace from the 1600s once owned by the duke of Beja, a great character in the history of Spain's aristocracy and known as the patron of Cervantes. Within easy walking distance of the cathedral and other sights, the building has been a hotel since 1991. It's now one of the best places to stay in Seville, offering excellent bang for your euro. All the rooms, medium in size, are individually decorated and furnished in an antique style, sometimes with four-poster beds; all have balconies, some facing street scenes and others opening onto one of the four interior patios. Many units have living rooms, and all the suites contain whirlpool tubs.

Plaza Santa María la Blanca, Callejón de Dos Hermanas 7, 41004 Seville. © **95-441-51-50.** Fax 95-442-21-70. www.casasypalacios.com. 118 units. 128€–265€ double; 385€ junior suite. AE, DC, MC, V. Parking 15€. Bus: 21 or 23. **Amenities:** Restaurant; bar; babysitting; concierge; outdoor pool; room service; Wi-Fi (free, in lobby). *In room:* A/C, TV, hair dryer, minibar.

Las Casas de los Mercaderes ★ 🎁 Charming and historic, this boutique-style hotel was built in the 18th century (with alterations in the 19th c.) as a patio-centered three-story private home that's about as Sevillian as you can get. Today, the patio that for many generations remained open to the sky is covered with a Victorian-inspired glass-and-iron canopy, allowing the courtyard to be plushly furnished with kilim carpets and wicker chairs that gracefully show off a ring of delicate granite columns. Bedrooms are cozy and relatively plush, with big curtains, carpets, and hand-carved furniture resting on marble floors. The cathedral lies within a 4-minute walk, and the staff is attentive.

Calle Alvarez Quintero 9–13, 41004 Seville. © **95-422-58-58.** Fax 95-422-98-84. www.casas ypalacios.com. 47 units. 91€–128€ double. Parking 18€ per day. AE, DC, MC, V. Bus: 21, 23, 41, or 42. **Amenities:** 2 bars; babysitting; room service. *In room:* A/C, TV, hair dryer, minibar.

Petit Palace Marqués Santa Ana ★★ In the Arenal sector, within walking distance of the Cathedral, this chain hotel occupies a building dating from the 19th century. It was taken over and sensitively restored to receive modern guests. The midsize bedrooms, updated and designed for comfort, are decorated in a very contemporary style and have lots of conveniences such as trouser presses and hydroshowers.

Jimios 9–11, 41002 Sevilla. © **95-422-18-12.** Fax 95-422-89-93. www.hotelmarquessantaana. com. 57 units. 150€ double, 170€ triple, 190€ quad. AE, DC, MC, V. Parking 15€. Bus: C5. Tram: Plaza Nueva. **Amenities:** Breakfast room. *In room:* A/C, TV, minibar, Wi-Fi (free).

Taberna del Alabardero ★★ 🎁 This tavern now houses one of the most charming places to stay in the city. Close to the bullring and a 5-minute walk from the cathedral, this restored 19th-century mansion has a spectacular central patio and a romantic atmosphere. The units on the third floor have balconies overlooking street scenes as well as whirlpool tubs. All the rooms are spacious and comfortable, each individually decorated in a specific regional style.

Zaragoza 20, 41001 Seville. © **95-450-27-21.** Fax 95-456-36-66. www.tabernadelalabardero. es. 7 units. 130€–250€ double; 150€–290€ junior suite. Rates include continental breakfast. AE, DC, MC, V. Parking 15€. Bus: 21, 25, 30, or 43. **Amenities:** Restaurant; bar; babysitting; room service. *In room:* A/C, TV/DVD, hair dryer, minibar, Wi-Fi (free).

INEXPENSIVE

Amadeus la Música ★ 🎁 In the Santa Cruz district, this family-run small hotel honors Mozart with a musical theme throughout. Instruments line some of the walls, and there are pianos in some rooms. An 18th-century manor house was totally renovated and adapted to receive today's guests, although the Sevillian style was left intact. María Guerrero and her helpful daughters are the gracious hosts. Designer bedrooms are midsize to spacious, created with your comfort in mind. Breakfast is served on the roof terrace, opening onto views of Giralda Tower in the distance.

Calle Farnesio 6, Barrio de Santa Cruz, 41004 Sevilla. © **95-450-14-33.** Fax 95-450-00-19. www. hotelamadeussevilla.com. 14 units. 82€–117€ double; 145€ junior suite. AE, DC, MC, V. Nearby parking 15€. Bus: C3, C4, 1, or 21. **Amenities:** Babysitting. *In room:* A/C, TV, hair dryer, minibar, Wi-Fi (free).

Hotel Goya Its location, in a narrow-fronted town house in the oldest part of the barrio, is one of the Goya's strongest virtues, but the building's gold-and-white facade, ornate iron railings, and picture-postcard demeanor are all noteworthy as well. The rooms are cozy and simple. Guests congregate in the marble-floored ground-level salon, where a skylight floods the couches and comfortable chairs with sunlight. No meals are served. Reserve well in advance. Parking is often available along the street.

Mateus Gago 31, 41004 Seville. © **95-421-11-70.** Fax 95-456-29-88. www.hostalgoyasevilla.com. 19 units. 55€–95€ double. MC, V. Bus: 10, 12, 41, or 42. *In room:* A/C, TV.

Hotel Murillo Tucked away on a narrow street in the heart of Santa Cruz, this *residencia* (named after the artist who used to live in this district) is very close to the gardens of the Alcázar. Inside, the lounges harbor some fine architectural characteristics and antique reproductions; behind a grilled screen is a retreat for drinks. Many of the rooms are cheerless and gloomy, so have a look before checking in. You can reach this *residencia* from the Menéndez y Pelayo, a wide avenue west of the Parque María Luisa, where a sign leads you through the **Murillo Gardens** on the left. Motorists should try to park in the Plaza de Santa Cruz. Then walk 2 blocks to the hotel, which will send a bellhop back to the car to pick up your suitcases. *Tip:* If there are two in your party, station a guard at the car, and if you're going out at night, instead of strolling through the streets of the Old Quarter, call for an inexpensive taxi to take you—it's less romantic but a lot safer.

Calle Lope de Rueda 7–9, 41004 Seville. ☎ **95-421-60-95.** Fax 95-421-96-16. www.hotelmurillo. com. 57 units. 75€–100€ double; 93€–125€ triple. AE, DC, MC, V. Parking 15€ nearby. Bus: 21 or 23. **Amenities:** Wi-Fi (free, in lobby). *In room:* A/C, TV, hair dryer.

Un Patio en Santa Cruz ★ 🍴 In the historic Old Town, a traditional Sevillian house from the early 19th century has been beautifully restored and made into a modern hotel. Exceptional features are a plant-filled white-marble patio and a panoramic terrace with bar opening onto a view of the Giralda. Even though the facade is traditional, the interior is strikingly contemporary, offering reasonably priced bedrooms that are well furnished and cozy with double-glazed windows. The hotel is on a pedestrian street, within walking distance of the cathedral and Alcázar. The rooms on the top floor have direct access to the roof terrace.

Calle Doncellas 15, 41004 Seville. ☎ **95-453-94-13.** Fax 95-453-94-61. www.patiosantacruz. com. 13 units. 70€–128€ double; 78€–138€ triple. AE, DC, MC, V. Parking 15€. Bus: 21 or 22. **Amenities:** Bar; babysitting; room service. *In room:* A/C, TV, Wi-Fi (free).

Where to Stay Nearby

El Palacio de San Benito ★★★ 🏠 The most exclusive B&B in southern Spain, this treasure lies in a stunningly converted palace that represents the epitome of luxury living as practiced by Spanish dons in the 14th and 15th centuries. You'll need a car to reach the little Moorish town of **Cazalla de la Sierra,** a 75km (47-mile) drive north of the center of Seville. Seville's best-known decorator, Manuel Morales de Jódar, is responsible for the restoration of the palace and for its decoration. Various tapestries from Aubusson in France and from Brussels decorate the palace. The library, with its Carrara marble fireplace, evokes the best of 19th-century Victoriana. The bedrooms are sumptuous and beautifully furnished, most often with 17th- and 18th-century pieces.

Cazalla de la Sierra, 41370 Seville. ☎ **95-488-33-36.** Fax 95-488-31-62. www.palaciodesan benito.com. 9 units. 90€–210€ double. Rates include buffet breakfast. AE, DC, DISC, MC, V. Parking 15€. **Amenities:** Restaurant; bar; outdoor pool; room service. *In room:* A/C, TV, hair dryer, minibar, Wi-Fi (free).

Hacienda Benazuza/El Bulli Hotel ★★★ 🏠 On a hillside above the agrarian hamlet of **Sanlúcar la Mayor,** 19km (12 miles) south of Seville, this legendary manor house is surrounded by 16 hectares (40 acres) of olive groves and farmland. Basque-born entrepreneur Rafael Elejabeitia bought the property and spent millions to transform it into one of Andalusia's most historic hotels. All but a few of the rooms are in the estate's main building, each individually furnished with Andalusian antiques and Moorish trappings. The **kitchen** is run by Ferran Adrià, the famous Catalonian chef who is hailed as one of the top two or three best chefs in the country. He's rarely on the premises, but his recipes and cooking style are used.

Calle Virgen de las Nieves s/n, 41800 Sanlúcar la Mayor, Seville. ☎ **95-570-33-44.** Fax 95-570-34-10. www.elbullihotel.com. 44 units. 350€–490€ double; 455€–570€ junior suite; 820€–1,440€

suite. AE, DC, MC, V. Free parking. Closed Nov 1–Mar 17. From Seville, follow the signs for Huelva and head south on the A-49 Hwy., taking exit 16. **Amenities:** 3 restaurants; 2 bars; babysitting; Jacuzzi; outdoor pool; room service; sauna; outdoor tennis court (lit). *In room:* A/C, TV, hair dryer, minibar, Wi-Fi (free).

Where to Dine in Seville

VERY EXPENSIVE

Egaña Oriza ★★★ BASQUE/INTERNATIONAL Seville's most stylish restaurant is within the conservatory of a restored mansion adjacent to the Murillo Gardens. Its reputation stems in large part from a game-heavy menu in a region otherwise devoted to seafood. The restaurant was opened by Basque-born owner/chef José Mari Egaña, who combines his passion for hunting with his flair for cooking. Many of the ingredients have been trapped or shot within Andalusia. The view from the dining room encompasses a garden and a wall that formed part of the fortifications of Muslim Seville. Specialties depend on the season but might include ostrich carpaccio, gazpacho with prawns, steak with foie gras in grape sauce, casserole of wild boar with cherries and raisins, duck *quenelles* in a potato nest with apple purée, and woodcock flamed in Spanish brandy.

San Fernando 41. © **95-422-72-11.** www.restauranteoriza.com. Reservations required. Main courses 22€–56€. AE, DC, MC, V. Mon–Sat 1:30–3:30pm and 8:30–11:30pm. Closed Aug. Bus: 21 or 23.

La Isla ★ SPANISH/ANDALUSIAN La Isla consists of two large Andalusian dining rooms (thick plaster walls, tile floors, and taurine memorabilia). The seafood is trucked or flown in from either Galicia or Huelva, one of Andalusia's major ports, and is always fresh. The menu is filled with well-prepared delights, beginning with a starter such as monkfish and shrimp soup, followed by such mains as grilled red mullet or baked filet of sole in a cream sauce. Succulent steaks can be grilled with ham and mushrooms or else served covered with red peppers and onions. The restaurant, a short walk from the cathedral, is within a very old building erected, the owners say, on foundations laid by the ancient Romans.

Arfe 25. © **95-421-26-31.** www.restaurantelaisla.com. Reservations recommended. Main courses 22€–38€. AE, DC, MC, V. Daily 1:30–5:30pm and 8pm–midnight. Closed Aug. Bus: 21, 25, 41, or 42.

EXPENSIVE

Enrique Becerra ★ ANDALUSIAN Near the cathedral and Plaza Nueva, this popular tapas bar and dining spot has a cozy, intimate setting that makes you feel welcome and appreciated. While perusing the menu, you can sip dry Tío Pepe and nibble herb-cured olives with lemon peel. The cookery pleases gourmets and gourmands with such dishes as Norwegian salmon garnished with fresh herbs, swordfish in a pale dry sherry, or lamb meatballs flavored with mint. The lemon sorbet with champagne is a good way to end your meal. The ice-cold sangria is great for hot summer days. The wine list is one of Seville's best.

Gamazo 2. © **95-421-30-49.** www.enriquebecerra.com. Reservations recommended. Main courses 8.50€–24€; fixed-price menus 42€–55€. AE, DC, MC, V. Mon–Sat 1–4:30pm and 8pm–midnight (closed Sat July–Aug). Bus: 21, 25, 30, or 40.

Hostería del Laurel ★ 🏠 ANDALUSIAN This hidden treasure is tucked in one of the most charming buildings on tiny, difficult-to-find Plaza de los Venerables, in Barrio de Santa Cruz. When the 19th-century playwright José Zorrilla rewrote Tirso de Molina's original *Don Juan,* he used the Hostería del

Luarel as one of the settings for his rewrite. It has iron-barred windows stuffed with plants. Inside, amid Andalusian tiles, beamed ceilings, and more plants, you'll enjoy good regional cooking. The *hostería* has some of the best and freshest tapas in town, our favorite being a *zarzuelita de mariscos* (shellfish cocktail) appetizer or fried anchovies. The catch of the day is flown in, and fish can be either grilled or fried. The chefs also turn out one of the town's best seafood-studded paellas.

Plaza de los Venerables 5. ☏ **95-422-02-95.** www.hosteriadellaurel.com. Reservations recommended. Main courses 12€–35€. AE, DC, MC, V. Daily noon–4pm and 8pm–midnight. Bus: 21, 23, 41, or 42.

Taberna del Alabardero ★★ ANDALUSIAN One of Seville's most prestigious restaurants occupies a 19th-century town house 3 blocks from the cathedral. Famous as the dining choice of nearly every politician and diplomat who visits Seville, it has hosted the king and queen of Spain, the Spanish president and members of his cabinet, and dozens of well-connected but merely affluent visitors. Amid a collection of European antiques and oil paintings, you'll dine in any of two main rooms or three private ones, and perhaps precede your meal with a drink or tapas on the flowering patio. There's a garden in back with additional tables. Tantalizing menu items include spicy peppers stuffed with pulverized thigh of bull, Andalusian fish (*urta*) on a compote of aromatic tomatoes with coriander, cod filet with essence of red peppers, and Iberian beefsteak with foie gras and green peppers.

Calle Zaragoza 20, 41001 Seville. ☏ **95-450-27-21.** www.tabernadelalabardero.es. Reservations recommended. Main courses 20€–30€. AE, DC, MC, V. Daily 1:30–4:30pm and 8:30pm–midnight. Closed Aug. Bus: 21, 25, 30, or 43.

MODERATE

Barbiana ★★ ANDALUSIAN/SEAFOOD Close to the Plaza Nueva in the heart of Seville, this is one of the city's best fish restaurants. Chefs endeavor to secure the freshest seafood, even though Seville is inland. In the classic Andalusian architectural tradition, a tapas bar is up front. In the rear is a cluster of rustically decorated dining rooms. The trick here is not to consume so much wine and tapas in the front that you are too stuffed to enjoy the main courses. If you visit for lunch, you can try the chef's specialty, seafood with rice (not available in the evening). We've sampled many items on the menu, none better than *ortiguilla,* a sea anemone quick-fried in oil, and the *tortillitas de camarones,* chickpea fritters with bits of chopped shrimp and fresh scallions. If you're going to order shellfish, the specialty here, get it *a la plancha* (fresh from the grill). Fresh fish is also available grilled with a zesty sauce, or deep-fried. We always keep an eye out for the *sargo* (rockfish), which is grilled and flavored with garlic juice and served with sweet roasted red peppers.

Calle Albareda 11. ☏ **95-422-44-02.** www.restaurantebarbiana.com. Reservations recommended. Main courses 12€–21€. AE, DC, MC, V. Mon–Sat noon–5pm and 8pm–midnight; Sun 8pm–midnight. Bus: 21, 25, 30, or 40.

Casa Cuesta ★ 🍴 SPANISH/ANDALUSIAN This is a fine choice in Triana, the pottery-making district across the river from the medieval core of Old Seville. The venue, which dates from 1880, is warm and old-fashioned. With its geometric tile work, checkerboard-patterned marble floors, high ceilings, and ornate 19th-century bar, Casa Cuesta is a great place for lunch or dinner, or just for drinks and some tapas. The biggest of the dining-room tables is round and features a rough-hewed tree trunk rising from its center to support part of the massive ceiling and a wrought-iron lighting fixture. The well-prepared Spanish food includes cured Iberian ham, fried meats and fish, *raciones* (servings) of potato salad flavored lightly with olive oil, and a variety of fried meats and fish. For a starter, we recommend *salmorejo,* a thick Cordovan version of gazpacho. The ambience in Triana is less touristy and a bit more workaday than its counterparts across the river.

Calle Castilla 1, Triana. (**95-433-33-35.** www.casacuesta.net. Reservations recommended. Main courses 12€–24€. MC, V. Daily noon–midnight. Bus: B2 or 43.

Mesón Don Raimundo ANDALUSIAN Near the cathedral and the landmark Virgen de los Reyes, this restaurant is not only one of the best in the heavily trodden tourist district, but also one of the most convenient lunch spots for sightseers. It is tucked away in an alleyway—a bit hard to find—off Calle Argote de Molina. Very cozy, with dark wooden furnishings, it evokes an old convent. The wine cellar is choice, and the welcome is warm. Dishes have a real taste of Andalusia, exemplified by the ribs of wild boar baked to perfection over firewood. Sherry from nearby Jerez de la Frontera flavors a sauce for the beef tenderloin. Some of the dishes display a Moorish influence, including the Mozarabic-style wild duck braised in sherry. In fall look for the perfectly seasoned pheasant. Fish also appears; our favorite is the filet of sea bass with fresh prawns, lots of garlic and olive oil, and pine nuts.

Calle Argote de Molina 26, Santa Cruz. (**95-422-33-55.** www.mesondonraimundo.com. Reservations recommended. Main courses 16€–26€. MC, V. Daily 11:30am–4pm and 7:30pm–2am. Bus: 21, 23, or 25.

Porta Coeli ★★ MEDITERRANEAN With one of Seville's most sophisticated decors, Porta Coeli offers the finest hotel dining in the city. Even if you're not a hotel guest, consider reserving one of the 15 beautifully laid tables set against a backdrop of tapestry-hung walls. The flavor combinations are contemporary, and rely on fresh ingredients. The menu boasts a wide variety of dishes featuring duck with fried white beans and ham. Another savory offering is *ensalada de bacalao con tomate* (salt cod salad with tomatoes) and *arroz marinero con bogavante* (rice with crayfish). The locals rave about the *corazón de solomillo al foie con zetas al vino* (beef heart with liver and mushroom in red-wine sauce), though this might be an acquired taste. For dessert, nothing beats the luscious napoleon with fresh fruit.

In the Hesperia Sevilla, Eduardo Dato 49. (**95-454-83-00.** Reservations recommended. Main courses 12€–32€. AE, DC, MC, V. Mon–Sat 1:30–4pm and 9pm–midnight. Closed Aug. Bus: 23.

Río Grande ANDALUSIAN This classic Sevillian restaurant is named for the Guadalquivir River, which its panoramic windows overlook. It sits near the Plaza de Cuba, in front of the Torre del Oro, and some diners come here just for the view of the city monuments. Most dishes are priced at the lower end of the scale. A meal might include stuffed sweet-pepper *flamenca,* fish-and-seafood soup seaman's-style, salmon, chicken-and-shellfish paella, bull's tail Andalusian-style, or garlic chicken. A selection of fresh shellfish is brought in daily. Large terraces contain a snack bar, the Río Grande Pub, and a bingo room. You can often watch sports events such as soccer on the river in this pleasant (and English-speaking) spot.

Calle Betis s/n. (**95-427-39-56.** www.riogrande-sevilla.com. Reservations recommended. Main courses 15€–23€. AE, DC, MC, V. Daily 1–4pm and 8pm–midnight. Bus: C3.

INEXPENSIVE

Fogón de Leña ★ ANDALUSIAN Close to Old Town, this landmark wins new fans every year. Converted from an old building, it has a main door that's intricately carved and crafted, and its roof is red tiled in the traditional style. The two-story interior has a decor of antique tiles and typical Andalusian artifacts. At the entrance is the mounted head of the last bull killed by the famous matador José Luis Vásquez. You can savor such dishes as *chuletón de buey* (ox steak) or *carne con chimichurri* (steak with chopped parsley and garlic dressing in virgin olive oil). Desserts are freshly made every day, including traditional puddings and tasty tarts, most often with fresh fruit.

Santo Domingo de la Calzada 13. 🕿 **95-453-17-10.** www.elfogon.com. Reservations required. Main courses 12€–20€. AE, DC, MC, V. Daily 1–4:30pm and 8:30pm–midnight. Closed last 2 weeks in Aug. Bus: 24, 27, or 32.

Seville After Dark

When the sun goes down, think sherry, wine, and tapas. After a couple of drinks get you going, you might venture to a flamenco club or even try to learn the intricate steps of one of southern Spain's most addictive dances, Las Sevillanas.

DRINKS & TAPAS Tapas are said to have originated in Andalusia, and the old-fashioned **Casa Román,** Plaza de los Venerables 1 (🕿 **95-422-84-83**), in the Barrio de Santa Cruz, looks as if it has been dishing them up since day one. (It's actually been around since 1934.) Definitely include this place on your *tasca*-hopping through the Old Quarter. It's open Monday to Friday 9:30am to 4pm and 7pm to midnight, Saturday and Sunday 11am to 4pm and 7:30pm to midnight. Tapas are priced from 3.50€.

As you make the rounds of tapas bars, you'll discover *pata negra* ham, made from the black-hoofed Iberian breed of pig of the same name. Surely one of the world's great hams, it has a sweet, subtle flavor, not salty like Virginia ham. Pigs here are fed on acorns.

El Rinconcillo, Gerona 42 (🕿 **95-422-31-83;** www.elrinconcillo. es), at the northern edge of Barrio de Santa Cruz, has a 1930s ambience, partly because of its real age and partly because of its owners' refusal to change one iota of the decor. It may actually be the oldest bar in Seville, dating from 1670. Amid dim lighting, heavy ceiling beams, and marble-topped tables, you can enjoy a beer or a full meal along with the rest of the easygoing crowd. The bartender will mark your tab in chalk on a well-worn wooden countertop. El Rinconcillo is especially known for its salads, omelets, hams, and selection of cheeses. Look for the Art Nouveau tile murals. It's open Thursday to Tuesday from 1pm to 1:30am. A complete meal will cost around 30€.

The best seafood tapas in town are served at **La Alicantina,** Plaza del Salvador 2 (🕿 **95-422-61-22**), amid the glazed-tile decor typical of Seville. Both the bar and the sidewalk tables always overflow with patrons. The owner serves generous portions of clams marinara, fried squid, grilled shrimp, fried cod, and clams in béchamel sauce. La Alicantina, about 5 blocks north of the cathedral, is open September to June daily noon to midnight; July and August daily 10:30am to 4pm and 8pm to 1am. Tapas range upward from 3.50€.

At the northern end of Murillo Gardens, opening onto a quiet square with flower boxes and an ornate iron railing, **Modesto,** Cano y Cueto 5 (© **95-441-68-11;** www.modestorestaurantes.com), also serves fabulous seafood tapas. In the bar you can choose your appetizers just by pointing. Upstairs there's a good-value restaurant. Modesto is open daily from 8pm to 2am. Tapas are priced from 3.50€.

In the Arenal district, **Buddha del Mar ★**, Plaza del Región s/n (© **95-408-90-95**), is a three-floor complex filled with an attractive crowd of mostly young people who patronize its Balinese terrace and nightclub, its chill-out bar, or its top-rate restaurant. The smell of incense and an exotic decor greet you. Buddha del Mar is open Monday to Saturday 9pm to 6am. Tapas range from 6€ to 15€.

FLAMENCO When the moon is high in Seville and the scent of orange blossoms is in the air, it's time to wander the alleyways of Santa Cruz in pursuit of the sound of castanets. Or, to be on the safe side, take a taxi. A showcase for Spanish folk song and dance, **El Patio Sevillano,** Paseo de Cristóbal Colón 11 (© **95-421-41-20;** www.elpatiosevillano.com), is a showcase for Spanish folk song and dance performed by exotically costumed dancers. The presentation includes a wide variety of Andalusian flamenco and songs, as well as classical pieces by such composers as de Falla, Albéniz, Granados, and Chueca. Two shows, at 7 and 9:30pm, are presented nightly. The cover of 37€ includes your first drink.

Consider a visit to **Tablao Los Gallos,** Plaza de Santa Cruz 11 (© **95-421-69-81;** www.tablaolosgallos.com), a reputable nightclub where male and female performers stamp, clap, and exude rigidly controlled Iberian passion on a small stage in front of appreciative observers. A cover charge of 30€ includes the first drink. No meals are served, and reservations are a good idea. Two shows are presented nightly, the first from 8 to 10pm, the second from 10:30pm to 12:30am. Its leading competitor, charging roughly the same prices with more or less the same program, is **El Arenal,** Calle Rodó 7 (© **95-421-64-92;** www.tablaoelarenal.com), where you'll sit at tiny, cramped tables with barely enough room to clap—but you will clap, because of the smoldering emotions conveyed in the performances here.

Torres Macarena ★, in the Calle Torrijiano 29 (© **95-437-23-84;** www.torresmacarena.com), is the major *peña*, or music hall, in Seville. Founded in 1974, it offers a 120-seat venue. Performances are without any kind of sound system—only the voices and instruments as they are heard naturally. Performances happen on a small stage combined with a bar or in a courtyard that also has a stage. These performances are impromptu, but here you can listen to the sounds of some of the best flamenco in the city. Torres Macarena is open Monday to Saturday 9pm to 2am.

GAY NIGHTLIFE Seville has a large gay and lesbian population, much of it composed of foreigners, including Americans, Germans, and British, and Andalusians who fled here for a better life, escaping less tolerant towns and villages. Gay life thrives in such bars as **Isbiliyya Café-Bar,** Paseo de Colón (© **95-421-04-60**), which is usually open daily 5pm to 4am. The bar is found across the street from Puente Isabel II, near Bar Capote. Outdoor tables are a magnet in summer.

THE PERFORMING ARTS To keep abreast of what's happening in the arts and after dark in Seville, pick up a copy of the free monthly leaflet *El Giraldillo*, or consult the listings in the local press, *Correo de Andalucía, Sudoeste, Nueva Andalucía,* or *ABC Sevilla.* Everything is listed here, from jazz to classical music concerts and from art exhibits to dance events. You can also call a cultural hot line at ✆ **010** to find out what's happening. Most of the staff at the other end speak English.

Keep an eye out for classical concerts that are sometimes presented in the cathedral of Seville, the church of **San Salvador,** and the Conservatorio Superior de Música at Jesús del Gran Poder. Variety productions, including some plays for the kids, are presented at **Teatro Alameda,** Crédito (✆ **95-490-01-64**). The venerable **Teatro Lope de Vega,** Avenida María Luisa (✆ **95-459-08-67;** www.teatrolopedevega.org), is the setting for ballet performances and classical concerts, among other events. Near Parque María Luisa, this is the leading stage of Seville, but performances are in Spanish.

It wasn't until the 1990s that Seville got its own opera house, but **Teatro de la Maestranza,** Paseo de Colón 22 (✆ **95-422-33-44;** www. teatromaestranza.com), quickly became one of the world's premier venues for operatic performances. Naturally, the focus is on works inspired by Seville, including Verdi's *La Forza del Destino* or Mozart's *Marriage of Figaro,* although jazz, classical music, and even the quintessentially Spanish *zarzuelas* (operettas) are also performed here. The opera house may be visited only during performances. Tickets (which vary in price, depending on the event staged) can be purchased daily from 10am to 2pm and 6 to 9pm at the box office in front of the theater.

Side Trips from Seville

CARMONA ★ An easy hour-long bus trip from the main terminal in Seville, Carmona is an ancient city dating from Neolithic times. Thirty-four kilometers (21 miles) east of Seville, it grew in power and prestige under the Moors, establishing ties with Castile in 1252.

Surrounded by fortified walls, Carmona has three Moorish fortresses—one a *parador,* and the other two the Alcázar de la Puerta de Córdoba and Alcázar de la Puerta de Sevilla. The top attraction is **Seville Gate,** with its double Moorish arch opposite St. Peter's Church. Note, too, Córdoba Gate, on Calle Santa María de Gracia, which was attached to the ancient Roman walls in the 17th century.

The town itself is a virtual national landmark, filled with narrow streets, whitewashed walls, and Renaissance mansions. **Plaza San Fernando** is the most important square, with many elegant 17th-century houses. The most important church is dedicated to Santa María and stands on Calle Martín López. You enter a Moorish patio before exploring the interior and its 15th-century white vaulting.

In the area known as Jorge Bonsor (named for the original discoverer of the ruins) is a Roman amphitheater as well as a Roman necropolis containing the remains of 1,000 families who lived in and around Carmona 2,000 years ago. Of the two important tombs, the Elephant Vault consists of three dining rooms and a kitchen. The other, the Servilia Tomb, was the size of a nobleman's villa. On-site is **Museo Arqueológico** (✆ **95-423-**

9

ANDALUSIA | Seville

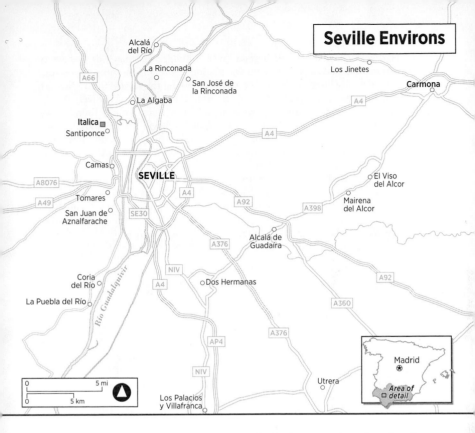

24-01; www.museociudad.carmona.org), displaying artifacts found at the site. From September 1 to June 15, hours are Tuesday to Sunday 11am to 7pm, Monday 11am to 2pm; from June 16 to August 31, Monday to Friday 10am to 2pm and 6:30 to 8:30pm, Saturday and Sunday 9:30am to 2pm. Admission is 3€ for adults and free for students and children.

If you're driving to Carmona, exit from Seville's eastern periphery onto the N-V superhighway, follow the signs to the airport, and then proceed to Carmona on the road to Madrid. The Carmona turnoff is clearly marked.

If you want to stay overnight, try **Casa de Carmona ★★**, Plaza de Lasso 1, 41410 Carmona (© **95-419-10-00;** fax 95-419-01-89; www. casadecarmona.com), one of the most elegant hotels in Andalusia. It was built as the home of the Lasso family during the 1500s. Several years ago, a team of entrepreneurs turned it into a luxury hotel but retained the marble columns, massive masonry, and graceful proportions of the original. Each of the 32 units is a cozy enclave of opulent furnishings, with a theme inspired by ancient Rome, medieval Andalusia, or Renaissance Spain. Rates are 120€ to 200€ for a double, 700€ to 900€ for a suite.

ITALICA Lovers of Roman history will flock to Itálica (© **95-562-22-66**), the ruins of an ancient city northwest of Seville on the major road to Lisbon, near the small town of Santiponce.

After the battle of Ilipa, Publius Cornelius Scipio Africanus founded Itálica in 206 B.C. Two of the most famous Roman emperors, Trajan and

333

Hadrian, were born here. Indeed, master builder Hadrian was to have a major influence on his hometown. During his reign, the **amphitheater,** the ruins of which can be seen today, was among the largest in the Roman Empire. Lead pipes that carried water from the Guadalquivir River still remain. A small **museum** displays some of the Roman statuary found here, although the finest pieces have been shipped to Seville. Many mosaics, depicting beasts, gods, and birds, are on exhibit, and others are constantly being discovered. The ruins, including a Roman theater, can be explored for 1.50€. The site is open April to September Tuesday to Saturday 8:30am to 8:30pm and Sunday 10am to 4pm. From October to March, it's open Tuesday to Saturday 9am to 6:30pm and Sunday from 10am to 4pm.

If you're driving, exit from the northwest periphery of Seville, and follow the signs for Highway E-803 in the direction of Zafra and Lisbon. A bus marked M-172 goes to Itália, and departures are from the Estación de Autobuses at Plaza de Armas. Buses depart every hour for the 30-minute trip.

JEREZ DE LA FRONTERA ★

87km (54 miles) S of Seville, 593km (368 miles) SW of Madrid, 34km (21 miles) NE of Cádiz

The charming little Andalusian town of Jerez de la Frontera made a name for itself in England for the thousands of casks of golden sherry it has shipped there over the centuries. Nearly 3,000 years old, Jerez is nonetheless a modern, progressive town with wide boulevards, although it does have an intriguing Old Quarter. Busloads of visitors pour in every year to get free drinks at one of the bodegas where wine is aged and bottled.

The name of the town—which is also the Spanish word for sherry—is pronounced Heh-*res* or Heh-*reth,* in Andalusian or Castilian Spanish, respectively. The French and the Moors called it various names, including Heres and Scheris, which the English corrupted to Sherry.

Essentials

GETTING THERE Iberia offers **flights** to Jerez daily from Barcelona and Zaragoza; four daily flights from Madrid; and several flights a week to and from Germany, London, and, in the summer, Grand Canary Island. The airport at Carretera Jerez-Sevilla is about 11km (6¾ miles) northeast of the city center (follow the signs to Seville). Call ✆ **95-615-00-00** (www.aena.es) for information.

Most visitors arrive by one of 15 **trains** per day from Seville, taking 1¼ hours and costing 8.40€ one-way. Trains from Madrid also arrive daily (trip time: 4 hr.). A ticket from Madrid to Jerez on the ALVIA costs 65€, and the trip takes 4½ hours. The railway station in Jerez is at the Plaza de la Estación s/n (✆ **90-224-02-02;** www.renfe.es), at the eastern end of Calle Medina.

Bus connections are more frequent than train connections, and the location of the bus terminal is more convenient. You'll find it on Calle Cartuja at the corner of Calle Madre de Dios, a 12-minute walk east of the Alcázar. About 17 buses arrive daily from Cádiz (1 hr. away) and three buses per day travel from Ronda (2¾ hr.). Seven buses a day arrive from Seville (1½ hr.). Call ✆ **95-633-96-66** for more information.

Jerez lies on the highway (E-5) connecting Seville with Cádiz, Algeciras, Gibraltar, and the ferryboat landing for Tangier, Morocco. There's also an overland road connecting Jerez with Granada and Málaga.

VISITOR INFORMATION The **tourist office** is at Alameda Cristina s/n (© **95-633-88-74;** www.turismojerez.com). It's open in winter Monday to Friday 9am to 3pm and 4:30 to 6:30pm, Saturday and Sunday 9:30am to 2:30pm; in summer Monday to Friday 9am to 3pm and 5 to 7pm, Saturday and Sunday 9:30am to 2:30pm. The English-speaking staff can provide directions, transportation suggestions, open hours, and so on for any bodega you might want to visit. You'll also be given a map pinpointing the location of various bodegas.

Exploring the Area
TOURING THE BODEGAS ★★

Jerez is not surrounded by vineyards as you might expect. Instead, the vineyards lie to the north and west in the "Sherry Triangle" marked by Jerez, Sanlúcar de Barrameda, and El Puerto de Santa María (the latter two towns are on the coast). This is where top-quality *albariza* soil is found, the highest quality containing an average of 60% chalk, which is ideal for the cultivation of grapes used in sherry production, principally the white Palomino de Jerez. The best time to visit is September. However, you can count on the finest in hospitality year-round since Jerez is widely known for the warm welcome it bestows.

In and around Jerez there must be more than 100 bodegas where you not only see how sherries are made, bottled, and aged, but also get free samples. Among the most famous producers are Sandeman, Pedro Domecq, and González Byass, the maker of Tío Pepe. On a typical visit to a bodega, you'll be shown through several buildings in which sherry and brandy are manufactured. In one building, you'll see grapes being pressed and sorted; in another, the bottling

A barrel of Tio Pepe sherry from González Byass.

process; in a third, thousands of large oak casks. Then it's on to an attractive bar where various sherries—amber, dark gold, cream, red, sweet, and velvety—can be sampled. *Tip:* If either is offered, try the very dry La Ina sherry or the Fundador brandy, one of the most popular in the world. Note, however, that these drinks are more potent than you might expect!

Most bodegas are open Monday to Friday from 10:30am to 1:30pm. Regrettably, many of them are closed much of August, but they reopen by the third week of the month to prepare for the wine festival in early September.

Of the dozens of bodegas you can visit, the most popular are listed below. Some charge an admission fee and require a reservation.

Williams & Humbert Limited, Carretera Nacional IV Km 641.75, Puerto Santa María (© **95-635-34-05;** www.williams-humbert.com), offers tours from 9am to 3pm Monday to Friday, charging 10€. Their premium brands include the world-famous Dry Sack Medium Sherry, Canasta Cream, Fino Pando, and Manzanilla Alegría, in addition to Gran Duque de Alba Gran Reserva Brandy. It's wise to reserve in advance.

Another famous name is **González Byass,** Manuel María González 12 (© **95-635-70-16;** www.gonzalezbyass.com); admission is 8€, and reservations are required. Tours in English depart at 11:30am, 12:30, 1:30, 2, 3:30, 4:30, and 5:30pm daily. Equally famous is **Domecq,** Calle San Luis (© **95-633-96-34;** www.alvarodomecq.com). Reservations are required, and admission is 7€. Tours

---

The Dancing Horses of Jerez

A rival of sorts to Vienna's famous Spanish Riding School is the **Escuela Andaluza del Arte Ecuestre (Andalusian School of Equestrian Art),** Av. Duque de Abrantes s/n (© **95-631-96-35;** www. realescuela.org). In fact, the long, hard schooling that brings horse and rider into perfect harmony originated in this province. The Viennese school was started with Hispano-Arab horses sent from this region, the same breeds you can see today. Every Thursday at noon, crowds come to admire the **Dancing Horses of Jerez** ★★ as they perform in a show that includes local folklore. Lanes 1 and 2 (the lanes are rows for seating) sell for 24€, and lanes 3 to 7 go for 18€. When performances aren't scheduled, you can visit the stables and tack room, observing as the elegant horses are being trained. Hours are Monday to Wednesday and Friday from 10am to 2pm, and admission is 10€ adults, 6€ children and seniors. On the grounds

of the school you can visit **Museo del Enganche,** the harness museum, which displays antique carriages. Entrance is 4€. Bus no. 18 goes here.

start at 10 and 11am, noon, and 2pm Monday to Friday (Sat tours May–Sept at noon and 2pm).

Since many people go to Jerez specifically to visit a bodega, August or weekend closings can be very disappointing. If this happens to you, make a trip to the nearby village of Lebrija, about halfway between Jerez and Seville, 14km (8⅔ miles) west of the main highway. A good spot to get a glimpse of rural Spain, Lebrija is a local winemaking center where some very fine sherries originate. At one small bodega, **Juan García,** the owner courteously escorts visitors around. There are several other bodegas in Lebrija, and the locals will gladly point them out to you. It's all very casual, and much more informal than in Jerez.

Where to Stay in Jerez de la Frontera

EXPENSIVE

Barceló Montecastillo ★★★ Giving the NH Avenida Jerez (see below) serious competition is this deluxe country club in the rolling hills of the sherry *campiña* (wine country). The area's most tranquil retreat, it has rooms with balconies overlooking the plush, scenic landscape. The hotel, a 10-minute ride from the center of Jerez, is elegantly furnished and professionally run. The spacious rooms are decorated in a provincial French style with elegant fabrics, beautiful linens, and large beds.

Carretera de Arcos, 11406 Jerez de la Frontera. (C) **95-615-12-00.** Fax 95-615-12-09. www.barcelomontecastillo.com. 170 units. 76€–250€ double; from 255€ suite. Rates include buffet breakfast. AE, DC, MC, V. Free parking. **Amenities:** 3 restaurants; bar; babysitting; exercise room; 18-hole golf course; 3 pools (2 outdoor, 1 heated indoor); spa; outdoor tennis court (lit); Wi-Fi (free, in lobby). *In room:* A/C, TV, hair dryer, minibar.

Guadalete ★ In a tranquil, exclusive area north of Jerez, this first-class hotel is a 15-minute walk from the historic core. It may not be as good as the Sherry Park (see below), but it is still one of the town's leading hotels, often hosting business travelers dealing with the sherry industry. A marble-floored lobby, spacious and contemporary public rooms, and palm-tree gardens give this place somewhat of a resort aura. The medium to spacious rooms have state-of-the-art bathrooms with tub/shower combos. The hotel is decorated with original watercolors and lithographs painted by local artists in the 1970s.

Av. Duque de Abrantes 50, 11407 Jerez de la Frontera. (C) **95-618-22-88.** Fax 95-618-22-93. www.hotelguadalete.com. 137 units. 69€–429€ double. Rates include breakfast. AE, MC, V. Free parking. **Amenities:** Restaurant; bar; babysitting; Jacuzzi; outdoor pool; room service; sauna. *In room:* A/C, TV/DVD, hair dryer, minibar, Wi-Fi (free).

Hipotel Sherry Park ★★ Especially noted for its setting within a palm-fringed garden whose tiled borders attract many sun-loving guests, this is one of the best modern hotels in Jerez. It's located on a wide boulevard north of the historic center of town and contains a marble-floored lobby, modern public rooms, and fairly standard but comfortable guest rooms. The uniformed staff lays out a copious breakfast buffet and serves drinks at several hideaways, both indoors and within the garden.

Av. Alcalde Alvaro Domecq 11 bis, 11405 Jerez de la Frontera. (C) **95-631-76-14.** Fax 95-631-13-00. www.hipotels.com. 174 units. 50€–250€ double; 251€–345€ suite. AE, DC, MC, V. Free parking. **Amenities:** 3 restaurants; bar; babysitting; exercise room; 2 pools (1 heated indoor); room service; sauna; Wi-Fi (free, in lobby). *In room:* A/C, TV, hair dryer, minibar.

NH Avenida Jerez ★★ Very close to the commercial heart of Jerez, this hotel occupies a modern balconied structure and is the best hotel within the center of Jerez itself, although Barceló Montecastillo (see above), on the outskirts, is a serious challenger. Inside, cool polished stone floors, leather armchairs, and a variety of potted plants create a restful haven. The good-size rooms are discreetly contemporary and decorated in neutral colors, with big windows and comfortable beds.

Av. Alcalde Alvaro Domecq 10, 11405 Jerez de la Frontera. ℂ **95-634-74-11.** Fax 95-633-72-96. www.nh-hoteles.es. 95 units. 99€–218€ double. AE, DC, MC, V. Parking 14€. **Amenities:** Restaurant; bar; babysitting; room service. *In room:* A/C, TV, hair dryer, minibar, Wi-Fi (17€ per 24 hr.) in some.

MODERATE

La Cueva Park ☺ This charming hotel, in a century-old building 6.5km (4 miles) from the center of town, attracts motorists. It's also a convenient .8km (½ mile) from the bus station. The architecture is typical of Andalusia, with a tiled roof overhanging thick brick walls. Gardens surround the hotel. All the units are medium in size and comfortably furnished. There are nine white-walled bungalow-style apartments classified as suites, each with its own cooking area, living room, and terrace.

Carretera de Arcos Km 7, Apartado 536, 11406 Jerez de la Frontera. ℂ **95-618-91-20.** Fax 95-618-91-21. www.hotellacueva.com. 53 units. 70€–100€ double; 200€–330€ suite. AE, DC, MC, V. Free parking. **Amenities:** Restaurant; bar; children's center; Jacuzzi; outdoor pool; room service. *In room:* A/C, TV, hair dryer, minibar, Wi-Fi (3€ per hour).

INEXPENSIVE

El Coloso 🥄 Located a few steps from the Plaza de las Angustias in the historic center, this is one of the best bargains in town, modest but worth recommending. The decor is in the conventional local style, with whitewashed walls and a trio of Andalusian-style patios with balconies opening onto street scenes of Jerez. The hotel opened in 1969, and its rooms have been renovated many times since and are well maintained. Breakfast is the only meal served.

Calle Pedro Alonso 13, 11402 Jerez de la Frontera. ℂ /fax **95-634-90-08.** www.elcolosohotel. com. 26 units. 55€–95€ double. AE, MC, V. Parking 8€. *In room:* A/C, TV, hair dryer.

Hotel Avila One of the better bargains in Jerez, the Avila is a modern building erected in 1968 and renovated in 1987. It's near the post office and the Plaza del Arenal, in the commercial center of town. Its rooms are clean, comfortable, and well maintained, although not special in any way. The beds, however, are quite comfortable and the bathrooms are well equipped.

Calle Avila 3, 11401 Jerez de la Frontera. ℂ **95-633-48-08.** Fax 95-633-68-07. www.hotelavila. com. 33 units. 57€–123€ double. DC, MC, V. Parking 8€–10€ nearby. **Amenities:** Bar; Internet (free, in lobby). *In room:* A/C, TV, hair dryer.

Where to Dine in Jerez de la Frontera

El Bosque ★ SPANISH/INTERNATIONAL Located less than 1.6km (1 mile) northeast of the city center, El Bosque opened after World War II and is still the city's most elegant restaurant. A favorite of the sherry-producing aristocracy, it retains a strong emphasis on bullfighting memorabilia, which makes up most of the decor. Get the excellent *rabo de toro* (oxtail stew) if you want to dine like a native. You could also begin with a soothing gazpacho, and then try one of the fried-fish dishes, such as hake prepared Seville-style. Rice with king prawns and baby shrimp omelets are popular. Desserts are usually good, especially the pistachio ice cream.

Av. Alcalde Alvaro Domecq 26. ℭ **95-630-70-30.** Reservations required. Main courses 18€–25€; *menú degustación* 26€–35€. AE, DC, MC, V. Mon–Sat 1:30–5pm and Tues–Sat 8:30pm–midnight.

Gaitán ANDALUSIAN/BASQUE Small, well-orchestrated, and cozy, this restaurant—within a pair of cozy dining rooms in the historic core of Jerez, a short walk from the Puerta Santa María—continues to impress longtime clients. Come here for tasty versions of squid in its own ink; braised oxtail in a spicy sauce; roasted veal with a cognac-flavored foie gras sauce; peppers stuffed with mince cod and two sauces; and hake served with "Pedro Ximenes" sauce, concocted from a local sherry.

Calle Gaitán 3. ℭ **95-634-58-59.** www.restaurantegaitan.es. Reservations recommended. Main courses 10€–16€; fixed-price menu 20€. AE, DC, MC, V. Daily 1–4:30pm and 8:30–11:30pm.

Mesa Redonda ★★ 🍴 TRADITIONAL SPANISH This restaurant is a rare treat. Owner José Valdestino sought out traditional recipes once served in the homes of the aristocratic sherry dons of Jerez. He serves them in a setting that's like a private residence, complete with a library filled with old recipe books and literature about food and wine. The 10 tables fill quickly, and the menu is ever changing. Try the deboned oxtail with potato topping, a marvelous version of potato salad infused with sherry vinegar and topped with strips of Ibérico ham; braised monkfish with broad beans in sherry sauce; or fried mackerel in an almond sauce. For dessert, there's nothing finer than the lemon-and-almond cake.

Manuel de la Quintana 3. ℭ **95-634-00-69.** Reservations required. Main courses 11€–16€. Set menu 26€–35€. AE, DC, MC, V. Mon–Sat 1:30–4pm and 9–11:30pm. Closed last week in July and 1st 3 weeks in Aug.

CÁDIZ ★

122km (76 miles) S of Seville, 625km (388 miles) SW of Madrid

Cádiz is the oldest inhabited city in the Western world, founded in 1100 B.C. This modern, bustling Atlantic port is a kind of Spanish Marseille, a melting pot of Americans, Africans, and Europeans who are docking or passing through. The Old Quarter teems with local characters, little dives, and seaport alleys. But despite its thriving life, the city isn't of major interest to visitors except in terms of the diverse cultures that have shaped it. Phoenicians, Arabs, Visigoths, Romans, and Carthaginians all passed through Cádiz and left their imprints. Throughout the ages, this ancient port city has enjoyed varying states of prosperity, especially after the discovery of the New World.

At the end of a peninsula, Cádiz separates the Bay of Cádiz from the Atlantic, and from numerous sea walls around the town you have views of the ocean. It was here that Columbus set out on his second voyage.

Essentials

GETTING THERE Twelve daily **trains** arrive from Seville (trip time: 2 hr.), Jerez de la Frontera (40 min.), and Córdoba (3 hr.). A one-way fare from Seville costs 12€, from Córdoba 28€ to 45€, and from Jerez 4.55€. The train station is on Avenida del Puerto, Plaza de Sevilla 1 (*©* **90-224-02-02;** www.renfe. es), on the southeast border of the main port.

Three daily nonstop **buses** run from Madrid to Cádiz. Trip time is 7¾ hours and a one-way ticket costs 24€. The bus from Madrid is run by **Secorbus** (*©* **95-625-74-15;** www.socibus.es), at Avenida José León de Carranza (N-20). Arrivals are at the rate of 11 to 14 per day, taking 2 hours and costing 13€ for a one-way ticket. These buses arrive at a terminal on the north side of town, a few blocks west of the main port.

Driving from Seville, the A-4 (also called E-5), a toll road, or N-IV, a toll-free road running beside it, will bring you into Cádiz.

VISITOR INFORMATION The **tourist office,** Av. Ramón de la Carranza s/n (*©* **95-620-31-91;** www.andalucia.org), is open during the summer Monday to Friday 9am to 8pm and Saturday to Sunday 10am to 2pm, and during the winter Monday to Friday 9am to 7:30pm and Saturday to Sunday 10am to 1:30pm.

Exploring Cádiz

A stroll along its **seaside promenades** ★★ is reason enough to visit Cádiz. The port city's *paseo* runs around the Old Town and along the sometimes turbulent Atlantic Ocean. There is no better way to get an understanding of the city and its relationship to the sea, on which Cádiz has always relied for its life and its commerce. You can only imagine what the port must have looked like when Spanish vessels departed this harbor to plunder the riches of the New World.

The southern and western promenades overlook the ocean. Those *paseos* lead to the famous public gardens of Cádiz, including **Parque Genovés 2** ★, with its exotic trees and plants brought in from all over the world. Chattering monkeys are always on hand to offer a greeting. Summer concerts are presented here, and the park also has a palm garden, just like the type enjoyed in the oases of North Africa across the sea.

From Parque del Genovés, follow Avenida Duque de Nájera to **Playa de la Caleta,** one of the Cádiz's most popular beaches. At the northern end of this bay stands **Castillo de Santa Catalina** (*©* **95-622-63-33**). It was built in 1598 and for many decades was the port's main citadel. Except for the views, there isn't that much to see here, but it's open for guided visits that depart every half-hour. In summer it's open daily 10:30am to 8pm, in winter only Sunday and Monday 10:30am to 6pm. No admission is charged.

Catedral de Cádiz This gold-domed baroque peacock by architect Vicente Acero has a neoclassical interior dominated by an outstanding apse. Construction began in 1720 but the cathedral wasn't completed until 1838. The tomb of Cádiz-born composer Manuel de Falla (1876–1946) lies in a splendid crypt. Haydn composed *Seven Last Words* for this cathedral, the last great cathedral erected in Spain that was financed by riches from the New World. It is still laden with treasures that include the Custodia del Millón, a monstrance set with a million precious stones. On-site is a museum filled with art and more treasures. Much of the gold, silver, and precious jewels on show here came from the New World.

Cádiz's promenade along the sea.

Note Enrique de Arfe's processional cross, which is carried through the streets in the annual Corpus Christi parades.

Next door is the church, **Iglesia de Santa Cruz,** Plaza Fray Félix (© **95-628-77-04**), which was the original cathedral, built in the 1200s. The invading British destroyed this *catedral vieja* in 1592 but it has been rebuilt. The church is open Tuesday to Thursday and Saturday 10am to 1pm and 5:30 to 8:30pm, Friday 9am to 1:30pm and 5:30 to 8pm, and Sunday 10:30am to 1pm and 6:15 to 7:30pm. Admission is free.

In back of the cathedral, properly called La Catedral de San Salvador, are found the unimpressive ruins of what was once a mammoth **Teatro Romano** (© **95-620-33-68**), entered by way of Campo del Sur. It is open daily from 10am to 2pm; admission is free.

A waterfall in the Parque Genovés 2.

Plaza Catedral. © **95-628-61-54.** Admission 4€. Tues–Fri 10am–1:30pm and 4:30–6:30pm; Sat 10am–1pm.

Museo de Cádiz ★ This museum is housed in two buildings, one a former Franciscan convent, the other a contemporary structure. It has three sections, two devoted to archaeology and fine arts, plus an ethnological collection. Among the ancient relics, the most intriguing collection is a series of two 5th-century-B.C.

A portrait of Saint Bruno by Zurbarán, in the Museo de Cádiz.

Phoenician **sarcophagi** ★ carved into human likenesses. Depicting both a man and a woman, these tombs were copied by Greek artists after Egyptian models. There is also an intriguing collection of rare Phoenician jewelry and (mostly) headless Roman statues. The Fine Arts Department is rich in 17th-century Spanish painting and is known especially for its works by **Zurbarán.** Dating from the peak of his mastery between 1630 and 1640, these 21 magnificent **paintings** ★★ of angels, saints, and monks were brought here from a Carthusian monastery in Jerez de la Frontera and are today the pride of Cádiz. Zurbarán was at his best when painting his *Quartet of Evangelists.* Murillo and Ribera are among the other Spanish Old Masters represented. In the ethnological section, the folklore of the province lives again in the Tía Norica puppet theater, with its props and characters that have delighted young and old for years.

Plaza de Mina s/n. © **95-620-33-68.** www.museosdeandalucia.es. Admission 1.50€. Tues 2:30–8:30pm; Wed–Sat 9am–8:30pm; Sun 9am–2:30pm. Bus: L2, 1, 3, 5, or 8.

Where to Stay in Cádiz

Cádiz has a number of inexpensive accommodations, some of which are quite poor. For a moderate price, though, you can afford some of the finest lodgings in the city. Note that rooms are scarce during the February Carnaval season.

Hospedería Las Cortes de Cádiz ★ 🎁 This hotel opened in 2003 within a patrician merchant's house that was built in 1859 with profits generated from trade with Spain's New World colonies. The hotel's centerpiece is a graceful three-story courtyard lined with stone columns and capped with a skylight. Each of the bedrooms evokes late-19th-century Cádiz, with a variety of mostly monochromatic color schemes that include a courageous use of vibrant pinks, blues, and buttercup yellow. Each of the other rooms is named for a historical event or person significant to the history of Cádiz. A favorite of ours is La Caleta, which has a mirador-style glassed-in balcony overlooking the busy pedestrian traffic on the street below. This was the Old Town's first hotel to combine a historic core with modern-day conveniences.

Calle San Francisco 9, 11004 Cádiz. ✆ **95-622-04-89.** Fax 95-621-26-68. www.hotellascortes. com. 36 units. 70€–138€ double. Rates include buffet breakfast. AE, MC, V. Parking 19€ per day. Bus: 2 or 7. **Amenities:** Restaurant; bar; exercise room; Jacuzzi; room service; Wi-Fi (free, in lobby). *In room:* A/C, TV, hair dryer, minibar.

Hotel Puertatierra ★ Opened in 1993, this city-center hotel is close to the financial and shopping section of town. Its midsize bedrooms are furnished with modern pieces, color-coordinated fabrics, and often painted provincial wooden furniture. This neoclassical hotel stands less than 100m (328 ft.) from Santa María del Mar beach.

Av. de Andalucía 34, 11008 Cádiz. ✆ **95-627-21-11.** Fax 95-625-03-11. www.hotelesmonte.com. 98 units. 66€–159€ double. DC, MC, V. Parking 12€. Bus: 1, 2, or 7. **Amenities:** Restaurant; bar; babysitting; room service. *In room:* A/C, TV, hair dryer, minibar, Wi-Fi (free).

Where to Dine in Cádiz

Achuri ★ BASQUE/ANDALUSIAN Achuri, a block behind the Palace of Congress in the historic district, is one of the best-loved restaurants in this old port city. It's been in the same family for half a century, earning a fine reputation. The interior is in a typical Mediterranean-port style, white stucco walls adorned with paintings interspersed with windows letting in plenty of sunshine. The menu includes fresh anchovies in virgin olive oil with a green-leaf salad, *merluza al achuri* (hake casserole with green asparagus sauce), and *pardo al brandy* (red snapper in brandy sauce). Another excellent dish is *bacalao en rosa verde* (salt cod in tomato-and-vegetable sauce).

Calle Plocia 7. ✆ **95-625-36-13.** Reservations recommended. Main courses 11€–18€. AE, MC, V. Daily 10am–4:30pm; Thurs–Sat 8pm–midnight. Closed Dec 23–Jan 8. Bus: L2.

El Faro ★★★ SEAFOOD/ANDALUSIAN Since its founding in 1964, this has been among Old Town's best and most respected restaurants, featuring a busy tapas bar near the Mudéjar entrance. El Faro is justified in claiming that it's the best restaurant in the province, thanks to the devotion, skill, and talent of its owner. It is decorated with tile work and marble. Tables are elaborately decorated and set with crisp napery, and lots of cutlery, crystal, and flowers. The waitstaff is the best in Cádiz. Tempting specialties include fresh fish and shellfish based on the catch of the day. We prefer ours baked in a salt crust that seals in the aroma and juices. Begin perhaps with the seafood soup and follow with, say, the roulades of sole with fresh spinach, hake with green sauce, or an especially delectable monkfish with strips of Serrano ham.

Calle San Félix 15. ✆ **95-621-10-68.** www.elfarodecadiz.com. Reservations recommended. Main courses 17€–25€; fixed-price menu 45€–63€. AE, DC, MC, V. Daily 1–4:30pm and 8:30pm–midnight. Bus: 2 or 7.

El Ventorillo del Chato ★ 🏨 ANDALUSIAN El Chato ("pug nose") is the nickname of the original founder of this inn, which was launched in 1780 on the isthmus linking the port city to the mainland. While technically under house arrest, the Spanish king, Fernando VII, came here for food, drink, and sex with the local prostitutes. It is a low-slung, whitewashed, and boxy-looking building that's perched beside the roaring highway (CA-33) stretching from New Cádiz toward the suburb of San Fernando. Inside the restaurant, you'll find a thick-walled shelter of enormous charm, with a wood-burning stove, flowers, and a collection of 19th-century antiques. The food is excellent. Try the *arroz del señorito* (a paella of shellfish that has been taken from the shells and cleaned before cooking), *arroz negro con chocos* (squid with rice colored by its own ink), or *dorada en berenjena confitada al vino tinto* (gilthead sea bream with eggplant cooked with red-wine sauce).

Carretera de Cádiz a San Fernando Km 2. © **95-625-00-25.** Reservations recommended. Main courses 14€–30€; tasting menu 45€. AE, DC, MC, V. Daily 1–4pm and 9pm–midnight.

Cádiz After Dark

In Cádiz, the city's role as a beach resort deeply affects the way night owls party after dark. In winter, when cold winds blow in from the Atlantic across the Bahía de Cádiz, nightclubbers find shelter in Old Town, especially in its northernmost quadrant, the neighborhood radiating outward from the **Plaza de San Francisco.** Here, within a labyrinth of impossibly narrow streets, cubbyhole tapas bars get going around 10pm and roar until 4am.

For an early tapas adventure, you can head for **Casa Manteca,** Corralón de los Carros 66 (© **95-621-36-03**), the best-known tavern in the Barrio La Viña. Over the years this was the preferred hangout for local bullfighters and flamenco singers and dancers. Its sherry comes from the vineyards of neighboring Sanlúcar de Barrameda. Dig into the fresh anchovies, regional sausages, caviar, and the best-tasting *chacina* (Iberian ham) in town. Most tapas range from 1.50€ to 3.50€. Hours are Tuesday to Sunday noon to 4pm and 8pm to 1am.

In summer (late May to late Sept), nightlife moves to the beachfronts, especially the Playa Victoria. Beginning around 2:30am, there's a migration to nightclubs that include **Barabass,** Calle Muñoz Arenillas 4–6 (© **95-607-90-26;** www.barabass.es), very close to Glorieta Ingeniero La Cierva and the Playa Victoria Hotel. It's known for theme parties that vary with the night of the week. These might revolve around Brazilian (Love in Ipanema) or Dominican (Merengue Madness) music, or "Mol Cool" house and garage music.

COSTA DE LA LUZ ★

Isla Cristina: 55km (34 miles) W of Huelva, 649km (403 miles) SW of Madrid; Tarifa: 95km (59 miles) SE of Cádiz, 691km (429 miles) SW of Madrid

West of Cádiz, near Huelva and the Portuguese frontier, is the rapidly developing Costa de la Luz (Coast of Light), which hopes to pick up the overflow from Costa del Sol. The Luz coast stretches from the mouth of the Guadiana River, forming the boundary with Portugal, to Tarifa Point, on the Straits of Gibraltar. Dotting the coast are long stretches of sand, pine trees, fishing cottages, and lazy whitewashed villages.

The Huelva district forms the northwestern half of the Costa de la Luz. The southern half stretches from Tarifa to Sanlúcar de Barrameda, the spot from which Magellan embarked in 1519 on his voyage around the globe. Columbus also made this the home port for his third journey to the New World. Sanlúcar today is widely known in Andalusia for its local sherry, Manzanilla, which you can order at any of the city's bodegas.

If you make it to **Sanlúcar,** you'll find the **tourist office** at Calzada de Ejército s/n (© **95-636-61-10**), just a block inland from the beach. It's open Monday to Friday 10am to 2pm and Saturday and Sunday 10am to 2pm and 6 to 8pm. Don't count on a great deal of guidance, however. To travel between the northern and southern portions of the Costa de la Luz, you must go inland to

Seville, since no roads go across the Coto Doñana and the marshland near the mouth of the Guadalquivir.

Essentials

GETTING THERE **Transportes Generales Comes,** Calle Batalla del Salado 19 (© **95-668-40-38;** www.tgcomes.es), has good **bus** links from nearby towns and key points in Andalusia. When its office is closed, you can purchase tickets directly from the driver. There are five buses a day from Cádiz, which take 2 hours and cost 8.50€ for a one-way ticket. There are even four daily buses from Seville, which cost 18€ and take 3 hours.

FRS Ferries (© **95-668-18-30;** www.frs.es) make the run between Tarifa and Tangier. Departures are daily 9am to 11pm; the trip takes only 45 minutes. Returns from Morocco are at 7am and 9pm (Morocco time). A round-trip passage costs 74€ for adults and 40€ for children.

Tarifa is the southernmost point on the E-5 (also known as the N-340). From Cádiz it's a 106km (65-mile) drive southeast, from Algeciras a 23km (14-mile) drive southwest.

VISITOR INFORMATION The **Tarifa Tourist Office,** on Paseo de la Alameda s/n (© **95-668-09-93;** www.aytotarifa.com), is open June to September Monday to Friday 10am to 9pm, Saturday and Sunday 10am to 2pm and 6 to 8pm. From October to May hours are Monday to Friday 10am to 2pm and 5 to 7pm, Saturday 10am to 2pm.

Exploring the Costa de la Luz

At Huelva, a large statue on the west bank of the river commemorates the departure of Christopher Columbus on his third voyage of discovery. About 7km (4⅔ miles) up on the east bank of the Tinto River, a monument marks the exact spot where his ships were anchored while they were being loaded with supplies before departure.

South of Huelva is the **Monasterio de la Rábida,** Palos de la Frontera (© **95-935-04-11;** www.monasteriodelarabida.com), in whose little white chapel Columbus prayed for success on the eve of his voyage. Even without its connections to Columbus, the monastery would be worth a visit for its paintings and frescoes. A guide (bilingual) will show you around the Mudéjar chapel and a large portion of the old monastery, which is open March to July and September to October, Tuesday to Sunday 10am to 1pm and 3 to 7pm; in August, hours are Tuesday to Sunday 10am to 1pm and 5 to 8pm; and from November to February, Tuesday to Sunday 10am to 1pm and 4 to 6:45pm. Admission is 3€ or 1.50€ for children 11 and under. The monastery is on the east bank of the Tinto. Take bus no. 1 from Huelva.

Where to Stay & Dine on the Costa de la Luz

Accommodations are severely limited along the Costa de la Luz in summer, so it's crucial to arrive with a reservation. You can stay at a government-run *parador* east of Huelva in Mazagón (see below), or in Ayamonte, near the Portuguese border. Where you're unlikely to want to stay overnight is the dreary industrial port of Huelva itself.

Ayamonte was built on the slopes of a hill on which a castle stood. It's full of beach high-rises, which, for the most part, contain vacation apartments for

Spaniards in July and August. Most of these visitors come from Huelva, Seville, and Madrid, so the Costa de la Luz is more Spanish in flavor than the overrun and more international Costa del Sol.

Ayamonte has clean, wide sandy beaches and mostly calm waves. Portions of the beaches are even calmer because of sandbars 50 to 100m (164–328 ft.) from the shore, which become virtual islands at low tide. The nearest beaches to Ayamonte are miles away, at Isla Canela and Moral.

Parador de Ayamonte ★★ ⚓ One of the leading accommodations in Ayamonte is this *parador* that opened in 1966. Commanding a sweeping view of the river and the surrounding towns along its banks—sunsets are memorable here—the *parador* is about 30m (100 ft.) above sea level on the site of the old castle of Ayamonte. It was built in a severe modern style and boasts Nordic-inspired furnishings. Most rooms are medium size and comfortably appointed.

Av. de la Constitución s/n, 21400 Ayamonte. © **95-932-07-00.** Fax 95-902-20-19. www.parador. es. 54 units. 104€–178€ double; 188€–229€ suite. AE, DC, MC, V. Free parking. From the center of Ayamonte, signs for the *parador* lead you up a winding road to the hilltop, about 1km (⅔ mile) southeast of the center. **Amenities:** 2 restaurants; bar; babysitting; outdoor pool; room service. *In room:* A/C, TV, hair dryer, minibar, Wi-Fi (free).

Parador de Mazagón ★★ One of the best accommodations in the area is 23km (14 miles) west of Huelva and 6km (3¾ miles) from the center of Mazagón. The *parador* was constructed on a pine-grove cliff overlooking a sandy beach. A rambling 1960s structure, it has comfortable, spacious rooms with balconies and terraces overlooking an expansive garden. Pine groves slope down to the white-sand beach at Mazagón, which is a small village with a number of restaurants. We prefer to stay in this village outside Huelva rather than at one of the more impersonal hotels within the city center. Even if you're just driving and exploring the area, consider a stop here for lunch. The chef specializes in regional dishes, including stuffed baby squid.

Carretera de San Juan del Puerto a Matalascañas s/n, 21130 Mazagón. © **95-953-63-00.** Fax 95-953-62-28. www.parador.es. 63 units. 148€–171€ double; 222€–257€ suite. AE, DC, MC, V. Free parking. Exit from Magazón's eastern sector, following the signs to the town of Matalas-cañas. Take the coast road (Hwy. 442) to the *parador.* **Amenities:** Restaurant; bar; babysitting; children's center; exercise room; Jacuzzi; 2 heated pools (1 outdoor, 1 indoor); room service; sauna; outdoor tennis court (lit); Wi-Fi (free, in lobby). *In room:* A/C, TV, hair dryer, minibar.

RONDA ★★

102km (63 miles) NE of Algeciras, 97km (60 miles) W of Málaga, 147km (91 miles) SE of Seville, 591km (367 miles) S of Madrid

This little town high in the Serranía de Ronda Mountains (698m/2,290 ft. above sea level) is one of the oldest and most aristocratic places in Spain. The main tourist attraction is a 150m (492-ft.) gorge, spanned by a Roman stone bridge, the Puente San Miguel, over the Guadalevín River. On both sides of this hole-in-the-earth are cliff-hanging houses, which look as if the slightest push will send them into the chasm.

Ronda is an incredible sight. The once-difficult road here is now a wide highway with guardrails. The town and the surrounding mountains were legendary hide-outs for bandits and smugglers, but today the Guardia Civil has just about put an end to that occupation. The gorge divides the town into an older part, the Moorish and aristocratic quarter, and the newer section south of the gorge, built principally after the Reconquest. The Old Quarter is by far the more fascinating; it contains narrow, rough streets and buildings with a marked Moorish influence. (Look for the minaret.) After the lazy resort living of the Costa del Sol, make a side excursion to Ronda; its unique beauty and refreshing mountain air are a tonic.

Tip: Note that local children may attach themselves to you as guides. For a few euros, it might be worthwhile to hire one, since it's difficult to weave your way in and out of the narrow streets.

Essentials

GETTING THERE Most visitors take a **train** to the main station at Avenida La Victoria (© **95-287-16-73** or 90-224-02-02; www.renfe.es). Three trains arrive from Granada per day. The trip takes 3 hours and costs 12€ one-way. You can also visit Ronda from the Costa del Sol, where one daily train makes the 2-hour trip from Málaga to Ronda, costing 9.50€ one-way. Two trains daily connect Ronda and Madrid. The trip takes 4½ hours and costs 62€ one-way.

The main **bus** station is at Plaza Concepción García Redondo s/n (© **95-218-70-61**). There are five buses a day from Seville, taking 2½ hours and costing 15€ one-way. There is also service from Málaga, taking 2½ hours and costing 13€ one-way. Also on the Costa del Sol, Marbella runs five buses per day to Ronda, taking 1 hour and costing 10€ one-way.

Major highways circle Ronda, but you'll have to take winding, circuitous, and secondary routes to drive into the town itself. From Seville, take N-334 southwest. When you reach the small town of El Arahal, continue south into Ronda along C-339. If you're in Granada, take N-342 west to the junction with N-332, and then take N-332 southwest to the junction with C-339, which eventually winds its way southeast into Ronda. If you're on the Costa del Sol, you can reach Ronda from Málaga traveling northwest via the scenic C-344, or from Marbella northwest on C-339.

VISITOR INFORMATION The **tourist office,** Paseo de Blas Infante s/n (© **95-218-71-19;** www.turismoderonda.es), is open Monday to Friday 9am to 7:30pm, and Saturday and Sunday 10am to 2pm.

Exploring Ronda

The still-functioning **Baños Arabes** are reached from the turnoff to Puente San Miguel. Dating from the 13th century, the baths have glass-roof windows and hump-shaped cupolas. They're generally open Tuesday through Sunday from 9:30am to 2pm and 4 to 6pm. Admission is free, but you should tip the caretaker who shows you around.

Palacio de Mondragón, Plaza de Mondragón (© **95-287-84-50**), was once the 14th-century private home of the Moorish king, Abomelic. But after the Reconquista, it was renovated to receive King Ferdinand and Queen Isabella, who stayed here. Inside you can see a trio of courtyards and a collection of Moorish mosaics. There is also a beautiful carved wooden ceiling. A small museum houses artifacts devoted to regional archaeology. Better than the museum is the restored Mudéjar courtyard where you can take in a panoramic view of El Tajo with the

The Baños Arabes, or Arab Baths, of Ronda.

Serranía de Ronda looming in the background. Flanked by two Mudéjar towers, the building now has a baroque facade. It's open Monday through Friday from 10am to 6pm, and Saturday and Sunday 10am to 3pm; admission is 2€, free for children 13 and under.

Casa del Rey Moro, Cuesta del Santo Domingo (© **95-218-72-00;** www.casadelreymoro.com), is misnamed, as this House of the Moorish King was actually built in 1709. However, it's believed to have been constructed over Moorish foundations. From the garden you can take an underground stairway, called La Mina, which leads you to the river, a distance of 365 steps. Christian slaves cut these steps in the 14th century to guarantee a steady water supply, in case Ronda came under siege. The house itself (not the main attraction) is being turned into a luxury hotel. The site is open daily 10am to 7pm, charging 4€ for adults or 2€ for children.

Ronda has the oldest bullring in Spain. Built in 1785, the **Plaza de Toros ★★** is the setting for the yearly Corrida Goyesca, in honor of Ronda native son Pedro Romero, one of the greatest bullfighters of all time. The bullring is a work of architectural beauty, built of limestone with double arches and 136 Tuscan-like columns. The town is still talking about the music video Madonna and entourage staged here in 1994. If you want to know more about Ronda bullfighting, head for the **Museo Taurino,** Calle Virgen de la Paz (© **95-287-41-32;** www.rmcr.org), reached through the ring. It's open daily March to October 10am to 8pm and November to February 10am to 6pm. Admission is 6€. Exhibits document the exploits of the noted Romero family. Francesco invented the killing sword and the muleta, and his grandson Pedro (1754–1839) killed 5,600 bulls during his 30-year career. Pedro was the inspiration for Goya's famous *Tauromaquia* series. There are also exhibits devoted to Cayetano Ordóñez, the matador immortalized by Hemingway in *The Sun Also Rises.*

PREHISTORIC cave paintings

Near Benaoján, the **Cueva de la Pileta** ★ (© **95-216-73-43;** www.cuevadelapileta. org), 25km (16 miles) southwest of Ronda, has been compared to the Caves of Altamira in northern Spain, where prehistoric paintings were discovered toward the end of the 19th century. In a wild area known as the Serranía de Ronda, José Bullón Lobato, grandfather of the present owners, discovered this cave in 1905. More than a mile in length and filled with oddly and beautifully shaped stalagmites and stalactites, the cave also contained five fossilized human skeletons and two animal skeletons.

In the mysterious darkness, **prehistoric paintings** depict animals in yellow, red, black, and ocher, as well as mysterious symbols. One of the highlights of the tour is a trip to the chamber of the fish, which contains a wall painting of a great black seal-like creature about 1m (3¼ ft.) long. This chamber, the innermost heart of the cave, ends in a precipice that drops vertically nearly 75m (246 ft.). In the valley just below the cave lives a guide who'll conduct you around the chambers, carrying artificial light to illuminate the paintings. (Tours in English or Spanish.) Plan to spend at least an hour here. Tours are given daily from 10am to 1pm and 4 to 6pm (Nov to mid-Apr 10am–1pm and 4–5pm). Admission, including the hour-long tour, is 8€ adults, 4.50€ children 10 to 13, and 4€ children 5 to 9.

It's easiest to get here by car from Ronda, but you can also take the train to Benaoján. The cave, whose entrance is at least 6.5km (4 miles) uphill, is in the rocky foothills of the Sierra de Libar, midway between two tiny villages: Jimera de Libar and Benaoján. Ronda and the cave are in parallel valleys, separated by a steep range of hills. Reaching the cave requires a rather complicated detour to either the south or the north of Ronda, and then doubling back.

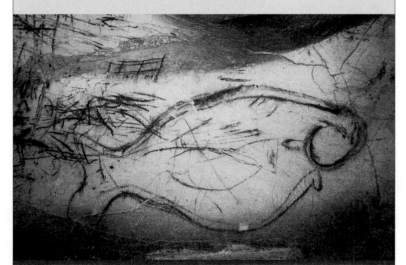

Where to Stay in Ronda

EXPENSIVE

El Juncal ★★ 🛏 Tiny, quirky, and delightful, this is a real discovery. Manuel María López and Lola Jiménez, who also operate Ronda's Michelin-starred restaurant, Tragabuches (p. 352), are the entrepreneurs who created this gem of an inn. A 5-minute ride from the town center, it is surrounded by vineyards. An old Spanish *finca* (a kind of farmhouse) has been beautifully converted with furniture by Philippe Starck, contemporary rugs, even antique lace. The comfortable, midsize bedrooms have cool parquet flooring and modern decor. The double rooms and suites are spread over two stories, some with private terraces or patios. Each unit is individually decorated. A lovely swimming pool is set in landscaped gardens. Although it's not as good as Tragabuches, there is an on-site Spanish **restaurant** with a fixed-price menu and fine regional wines.

Carretera El Burgo Km 1, 29400 Ronda. ℂ **95-216-11-70.** Fax 95-216-11-60. www.eljuncal.com. 9 units. 124€–172€ double; 209€–250€ suite. AE, DC, MC, V. Free parking. **Amenities:** Restaurant; babysitting; Jacuzzi; outdoor pool; room service; sauna; Wi-Fi (free, in lobby). *In room:* A/C, TV, hair dryer.

Parador de Ronda ★★★ This *parador* has the grandest accommodations in the area. It sits on a high cliff overlooking the fantastic gorge that cuts a swath more than 150m (492 ft.) deep and 90m (295 ft.) wide through the center of this mountain town. Stretching along the edge of the gorge to a bridge, the Puente Nuevo, the *parador* is surrounded by a footpath with scenic views of the gorge and the Guadalevín River below. The good-size rooms are beautifully furnished; many open onto balconies with views of the peaks surrounding Ronda.

Plaza de España s/n, 29400 Ronda. ℂ **95-287-75-00.** Fax 95-287-81-88. www.parador.es. 78 units. 160€–197€ double; 256€–274€ suite. AE, DC, MC, V. Parking 10€. **Amenities:** Restaurant; bar; outdoor pool; room service. *In room:* A/C, TV, hair dryer, minibar (in some), Wi-Fi (free).

MODERATE

Husa Reina Victoria ★ On the eastern periphery of town, this country-style hotel dates from 1906, when it was built by an Englishman in honor of Queen Victoria. It's near the bullring and has terraces that hang right over a 147m (482-ft.) precipice. Hemingway frequently visited, but the Reina Victoria is known best as the place where poet Rainer Maria Rilke wrote *The Spanish Trilogy.* His third-floor room has been set aside as a museum with first editions, manuscripts, photographs, and even a framed copy of his hotel bill. Its gardens and terraces have an enduring appeal, as does the Victorian architecture with towering chimneys and sloping roofs. The rooms are big and airy, some with living rooms and many with private terraces.

Paseo Doctor Fleming 25, 29400 Ronda. ℂ **95-287-12-40.** Fax 95-287-10-75. www.hotelhusa reinavictoriaronda.com. 89 units. 85€–150€ double; 165€–190€ suite. AE, DC, MC, V. Free parking. **Amenities:** Restaurant; bar; babysitting; outdoor pool; room service. *In room:* A/C, TV, hair dryer, minibar.

INEXPENSIVE

Hotel Don Miguel ★ ⬕ From the narrow street leading to it, this hotel presents a severely dignified white facade very similar to that of its neighbors. From the back, however, some of its rooms look out over the river gorge of a steep ravine.

Set a few steps east of the Plaza de España, and composed of several interconnected houses, it offers a vine-strewn patio above the river, a modernized interior accented with exposed brick and varnished pine, and renovated and comfortable small rooms. Overflow guests are housed in a building (no. 13) across the street. Rooms here have the same dramatic views and are comparable to those in the main building.

Calle Villanueva 4, 29400 Ronda. © **95-287-77-22.** Fax 95-287-83-77. www.dmiguel.com. 30 units. 85€–100€ double. Rates include continental breakfast. AE, DC, MC, V. Parking 9€. **Amenities:** Restaurant. *In room:* A/C, TV.

Hotel San Gabriel ★★ 🏩 This charming 1736 mansion—also called Su Casa en Ronda—stands in the historic core a 5-minute walk from the gorge. The building was painstakingly renovated by the owner and his sons and daughter, who give guests Ronda's warmest welcome. Inside, all is stylish and homelike, filled with antiques, stained-glass windows, a Spanish-style billiards table, a *cine* salon (with seats taken from the city's old theater), and even an old library. Each room is spacious and well appointed, all with exterior views and individual decoration. Try for no. 15, a cozy top-floor nest on two levels.

Marqués de Moctezuma 19 (just off Calle Armiñán), 29400 Ronda. © **95-219-03-92.** Fax 95-219-01-17. www.hotelsangabriel.com. 16 units. 82€–130€ double; 103€–190€ suite. AE, MC, V. Closed Jan 1–9, July 19–31, and Dec 21–31. **Amenities:** Bar; Wi-Fi (free, in lobby). *In room:* A/C, TV, hair dryer, minibar.

La Rondeña 🦐 A 2-minute walk from the gorge and next to the Plaza de Toros (the bullring), this two-story family-style house attracts bargain hunters. The small bedrooms are relatively simple but comfortable—however, at these prices, you can't expect dramatic views of the gorge. Rooms do open onto the landscaped grounds and the Sierras in the distance. Every nook and cranny of the public areas have been decorated in a typical Andalusian style. The on-site **restaurant** offers typical dishes from the mountains of Ronda. Tables are placed on a covered terrace where live music can sometimes be heard. The government-rated, three-star hotel lies between Puente Nuevo (the new bridge)—overlooking the Tajo River—and Paseo de blas Infante gardens.

José Aparicio 3, 29400 Ronda. © **95-287-34-88.** Fax 95-287-99-03. 16 units. 75€–90€. Rates include continental breakfast. AE, DC, MC, V. Parking 15€. **Amenities:** Restaurant; bar; Wi-Fi (free, in lobby). *In room:* A/C, TV, hair dryer.

Maestranza ★ 🦐 This modern hotel grew up on the site of a villa once inhabited by Pedro Romero, a legendary bullfighter. In the center of town, it faces the oldest bullring in the world. Today all traces of the former villa are gone. In its place is one of the best and most contemporary hotels in town. The bedrooms are small to midsize, but have been designed for comfort, with modern furnishings, carpets, and draperies. The public rooms are tastefully furnished, and the helpful staff provides excellent service. Clients can use the facilities of a private country club nearby, with a swimming pool and tennis courts.

Calle Virgen de la Paz 24, 29400 Ronda. © **95-218-70-72.** Fax 95-219-01-70. www.hotel maestranza.com. 54 units. 70€–115€ double; 100€–147€ suite. AE, DC, MC, V. Parking 10€. **Amenities:** Restaurant; bar; babysitting; room service. *In room:* A/C, TV, hair dryer, minibar, Wi-Fi (10€ per 24 hr.).

Where to Dine in Ronda

Casa Santa Pola INTERNATIONAL/ANDALUSIAN Constructed in the 19th century but altered and rebuilt over the years, this building on the outskirts of the city opens onto views of the gorge. It's composed of three levels built onto the mountainside; access is through the third floor. The interior is a mix of Moorish, rococo, and contemporary, with a decor of antique ornaments, wooden floors, archways, terra-cotta walls, and red bistro-style tablecloths. Many of the meals are cooked in a traditional brick oven. Excellent dishes include *cochinillo* (roast suckling pig), *lomo asado* (grilled filet beefsteak), and the savory *rabo de toro* (roast oxtail). Desserts are homemade and traditional to the area. Anticipate unexpected closings on at least 1 day a week (it could vary, perhaps Mon or Tues).

Cuesta Santo Domingo 3. © **95-287-92-08.** Main courses 18€–26€; set menu 17€–60€. AE, DC, MC, V. Daily 11:30am–5pm and 7:30–11pm.

Restaurante Pedro Romero SPANISH/ANDALUSIAN Named after the famed bullfighter, this restaurant attracts aficionados of that sport. It's opposite the bullring and on bullfighting days it's almost impossible to get a table. While seated under a stuffed bull's head, surrounded by photographs of young matadors, you might begin your meal with the classic garlic soup, and then follow with a well-prepared array of meat or poultry dishes.

Virgen de la Paz 18. © **95-287-11-10.** www.rpedroromero.com. Reservations required on day of *corrida* and Fri–Sat. Main courses 17€–22€; *menú del día* 17€. AE, DC, MC, V. Daily 12:30–4pm and 7:30–11pm. Closed Sun night and Mon June–Aug.

Tragabuches ★★★ MODERN SPANISH/ANDALUSIAN This restaurant serves the finest and most creative cuisine in Ronda. There are two dining rooms, each with stylish, contemporary decor. Against a typical backdrop of white walls, tables are decked out with pastel cloths and seat covers. The inventive menu is likely to feature well-crafted dishes like *cochinillo asado* (grilled suckling pig) or *rape en salsa de vinagreta, pulpo y verdura* (monkfish in a vinaigrette sauce with octopus and fresh vegetables). Begin, perhaps, with a cheese taco or the tasty liver pâté.

José Aparicio 1 (btw. Plaza de España and Plaza de Toros). © **95-219-02-91.** www.tragabuches. com. Reservations recommended on weekends. Main courses 12€–25€; set menu 74€. AE, DC, MC, V. Sun 1:30–3:30pm; Mon–Sat 1:30–3:30pm and 8:30–10:30pm.

GRANADA ★★★

415km (258 miles) S of Madrid, 122km (76 miles) NE of Málaga

About 660m (2,165 ft.) above sea level in the foothills of the snowcapped Sierra Nevada, Granada sprawls over two main hills, the Alhambra and the Albaicín, and is crossed by two rivers, the Genil and the Darro. This former stronghold of Moorish Spain is full of romance and folklore. Washington Irving (*Tales of the Alhambra*) used the symbol of this city, the pomegranate (*granada*), to conjure up a spirit of romance. In fact, the name probably derives from the Moorish word *Karnattah*. Some historians have suggested that it comes from Garnatha Alyehud, the name of an old Jewish ghetto.

Washington Irving may have helped publicize the glories of Granada to the English-speaking world, but in Spain the city is known for its ties to Federico

García Lorca. Born in 1898, this Spanish poet/dramatist, whose masterpiece was *The House of Bernarda Alba,* was shot dead by soldiers in 1936 in the first months of the Spanish Civil War. During Franco's rule, García Lorca's works were banned in Spain, but they are now honored not only in Granada, his hometown, but also throughout the country.

Cuesta de Gomérez is one of the most important streets in Granada. It climbs uphill from the Plaza Nueva, the center of the modern city, to the Alhambra. At the Plaza Nueva, the east-west artery, Calle de los Reyes Católicos, goes to the heart of the 19th-century city and the cathedral towers. Granada's main street is the Gran Vía de Colón, the principal north-south artery.

Calle de los Reyes Católicos and the Gran Vía de Colón meet at circular Plaza de Isabel la Católica, graced by a bronze statue of the queen offering Columbus the Santa Fe agreement, which granted the rights to the epochal voyage to the New World. Going west, Calle de los Reyes Católicos passes near the cathedral and other major sights in downtown Granada. The street runs to Puerta Real, the commercial hub of Granada, with many stores, hotels, cafes, and restaurants.

Essentials

GETTING THERE **Iberia** flies to Granada from Barcelona and Madrid, and several times a week from Palma de Majorca. Three planes a day land from Barcelona (trip time: 1 hr.); four planes fly in from Madrid, taking only half an hour. Granada's **Federico García Lorca Airport** *(aeropuerto nacional)* is 16km (10 miles) west of the center of town on Carretera Málaga; call ☎ **90-240-47-04** for information. Other than a minor tourist-information booth and an ATM, there are few services here. A convenient Iberia ticketing office is located 2 blocks east of the cathedral, at Plaza Isabel Católica 2 (☎ **90-240-05-00**). A bus departs several times daily connecting this office with the airport; the one-way fare is 7€. The bus runs Monday to Saturday at 8:15, 9:15am, and 5:30pm; and on Sunday at 5:30 and 7pm. Trip time is 45 minutes. Taxis line up outside the terminals at the airport, charging about 25€ to take you to your hotel in the city center.

The **train** station is **Estación de RENFE de Granada,** Av. Andaluces s/n (☎ **90-243-23-43;** www.renfe.es). Granada is well linked with the most important Spanish cities, especially those of Andalusia. Four trains per day arrive from Seville, taking 4 to 5 hours, depending on the train, and costing 22€ for a one-way ticket. From Madrid, two daily trains arrive in Granada, taking 4½ hours and costing 64€. From Barcelona, there is a daily train, taking 12 to 13 hours and costing 60€ one-way.

Granada is served by far more **buses** than trains. It has links to virtually all the major towns and cities in Andalusia, and even to Madrid. The main bus terminal is **Estación de Autobuses de Granada,** Carretera de Jaén s/n (☎ **95-818-54-80**). One of the most heavily used bus routes is the one between Seville and Granada. Ten buses run per day, costing 34€ for a one-way ticket. The trip is 3 hours. You can also reach Granada in 3 hours on one of nine daily buses from Córdoba; cost is 14€ for a one-way ticket. If you're on the Costa del Sol, the run is just 2 hours, costing 12€ per one-way ticket. This is a very popular routing, with 19 buses going back and forth between Granada and the coast per day. For bus information, contact **Alsina Graells** (☎ **95-818-54-80;** www.alsa.es).

Granada is connected by superhighway to Madrid, Málaga, and Seville. Many sightseers prefer to make the drive from Madrid to Granada in 2 days, rather than 1. If that is your plan, Jaén (p. 287) makes a perfect stopover.

VISITOR INFORMATION The **Patronato Provincial de Turismo de Granada,** Plaza de Mariana Pineda 10 bajo (*©* **95-824-71-46;** www.tur granada.es), is open Monday to Friday 9am to 8pm, Saturday 10am to 7pm, and Sunday 10am to 3pm. The **Tourist Information Office of Junta de Andalucía,** Calle de Santa Ana 4 (*©* **95-857-52-02;** www.andalucia.org), is open Monday to Friday 9am to 7:30pm, Saturday and Sunday 9:30am to 3pm.

Exploring Granada

Try to spend some time walking around Old Granada. Plan on about 3 hours to see the most interesting sights.

The Puerta de Elvira is the gate through which Ferdinand and Isabella made their triumphant entry into Granada in 1492. It was once a grisly place where the rotting heads of executed criminals hung from its portals. The quarter surrounding the gate was the Arab section *(morería)* until all the Arabs were driven out of the city after the Reconquest.

One of the most fascinating streets is Calle de Elvira; west of it, the Albaicín, or old Arab Quarter, rises on a hill. In the 17th and 18th centuries,

Strolling Andalusia's Most Romantic Street

The most-walked street in Granada is **Carrera del Darro,** running north along the Darro River. It was discovered by the Romantic artists of the 19th century; many of their etchings (subsequently engraved) of scenes along this street were widely circulated, doing much to spread the fame of Granada throughout Europe. You can still find some of these old engravings in the musty antiques shops. Carrera del Darro ends at Paseo de los Tristes (Ave. of the Sad Ones), so named for the funeral corteges that used to go by here on the way to the cemetery.

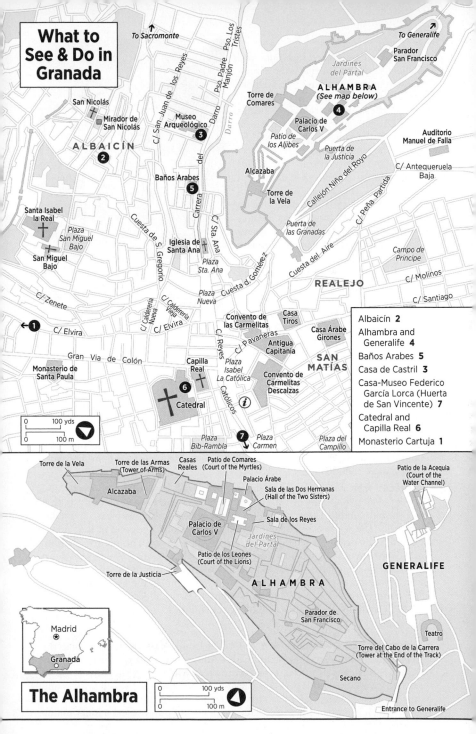

What to See & Do in Granada

To Sacromonte

Pso. Los Tristes

Pso. Padre Manjón

C/ San Juan de los Reyes

San Nicolás

Mirador de San Nicolás

Museo Arqueológico **3**

Darro del Carrera

Darro

ALBAICÍN 2

Baños Arabes **5**

Santa Isabel la Real

Plaza San Miguel Bajo

San Miguel Bajo

Cuesta de S. Gregorio

Iglesia de Santa Ana

Plaza Sta. Ana

C/ Sta. Ana

C/ Zenete

C/ Caldereria Vieja

C/ Caldereria Nueva

← **1** C/ Elvira

C/ Elvira

Gran Via de Colón

Monasterio de Santa Paula

Capilla Real **6**

Catedral

C/ Reyes

Plaza Isabel La Católica

C/ Reyes Católicos

Plaza Bib-Rambla

7 Plaza Carmen

To Generalife

Parador San Francisco

Torre de Comares

ALHAMBRA *(See map below)* **4**

Palacio de Carlos V

Patio de los Aljibes

Puerta de la Justicia

Alcazaba

Torre de la Vela

Puerta de las Granadas

Callejón Niño del Royo

Auditorio Manuel de Falla

C/ Antequeruela Baja

C/ Peña Partida

Jardines del Partal

Cuesta del Aire

REALEJO

Campo de Principe

C/ Molinos

C/ Santiago

Cuesta d. Gomérez

Plaza Nueva

Convento de las Carmelitas

Casa Tiros

C/ Pavaneras

Antigua Capitania

Casa Árabe Girones

SAN MATÍAS

Convento de Carmelitas Descalzas

Plaza del Campillo

Albaicín **2**

Alhambra and Generalife **4**

Baños Arabes **5**

Casa de Castril **3**

Casa-Museo Federico García Lorca (Huerta de San Vincente) **7**

Catedral and Capilla Real **6**

Monasterio Cartuja **1**

---

0 — 100 yds
0 — 100 m

The Alhambra

Torre de la Vela

Torre de las Armas (Tower of Arms)

Casas Reales

Patio de Comares (Court of the Myrtles)

Palacio Árabe

Sala de las Dos Hermanas (Hall of the Two Sisters)

Alcazaba

Palacio de Carlos V

Sala de los Reyes

Patio de la Acequia (Court of the Water Channel)

Jardines del Partal

Patio de los Leones (Court of the Lions)

Torre de la Justicia

ALHAMBRA

GENERALIFE

Parador de San Francisco

Teatro

Torre del Cabo de la Carrera (Tower at the End of the Track)

Secano

Entrance to Generalife

Madrid ⊛

Granada ○

0 — 100 yds
0 — 100 m

many artisans occupied the shops and ateliers along this street and those radiating from it. Come here if you're looking for **antiques.** On Calle de Elvira is the Iglesia de San Andrés, begun in 1528, with its Mudéjar bell tower. Much of the church was destroyed by fire in the early 19th century, but several interesting paintings and sculptures remain. Another old church in this area is the Iglesia de Santiago, constructed in 1501 and dedicated to St. James, patron saint of Spain. Built on the site of an Arab mosque, it was damaged in an 1884 earthquake. The church contains the tomb of architect Diego de Siloé (1495–1563), who did much to change the face of the city.

Despite its name, the oldest square is **Plaza Nueva,** which, under the Muslims, was the site of the wood-cutters' bridge. The Darro was covered

Houses of the Albaicín.

over here, but its waters still flow underneath the square (which in Franco's time was named Plaza del General Franco). On the east side of Plaza Nueva is the 16th-century Iglesia de Santa Ana, built by Siloé. Inside its five-nave interior you can see a Churrigueresque reredos and coffered ceiling.

The *corrida* isn't really very popular here, but if you want to check out the bullfights anyway, they're usually limited to the week of the Fiesta de Corpus Christi, May 29 to June 6, or Día de la Cruz (Day of the Cross), observed on May 3. There's also a fight on the last Sunday in September. The Plaza de Toros, the bullring, is on Avenida de Doctor Olóriz, close to the soccer stadium. For more information, call the tourist office.

Albaicín ★★ This old Arab Quarter, on one of Granada's two main hills, doesn't belong to the city of 19th-century buildings and wide boulevards. Both it and the surrounding Gypsy caves of Sacromonte are holdovers from a more distant past. The Albaicín once flourished as the residential section of the Moors, but it fell into decline when the Christians drove them out. This narrow labyrinth of crooked streets escaped the fate that befell much of Granada: being torn down in the name of progress. Preserved are its alleyways, cisterns, fountains, plazas, whitewashed houses, villas, and the decaying remnants of the old city gate. Here and there you can catch a glimpse of a private patio filled with fountains and plants, a traditional, elegant way of life that continues.

Bus: 31 or 32.

Alhambra and Generalife ★★★ One of Europe's greatest attractions, the stunningly beautiful and celebrated **Calat Alhambra (Red Castle)** is perhaps the most remarkable fortress ever constructed. Muslim architecture in Spain reached its apogee at this pleasure palace once occupied by Nasrid princes and their harems. Although later Moorish occupants turned the Alhambra into a lavish palace, it was originally constructed for defensive purposes on a rocky hilltop outcropping above the Darro River. The modern city of Granada was built across the river from the Alhambra, about .8km (½ mile) from its western foundations.

When you first see the Alhambra, its somewhat somber exterior may surprise you. The true delights of this Moorish palace lie within. Tickets are sold in the office at the Entrada del Generalife y de la Alhambra. Enter through the incongruous 14th-century **Puerta de la Justicia (Gateway of Justice)** ★. Most visitors don't need an expensive guide but will be content to stroll through the richly ornamented open-air rooms, with their lacelike walls and courtyards with fountains. Many of the Arabic inscriptions translate to "Only Allah is conqueror."

The tour begins in the **Mexuar,** also known as Palacio Nazaríes (Palace of the Nasrids), which is the first of the trio of palaces that compose the Alhambra. This was the main council chamber where the sultan's chief ministers met. The largest of these chambers was the Hall of the Mexuar, which Spanish rulers converted to a Catholic chapel in the 1600s. From this chapel a panoramic view spreads over the rooftops of the Albaicín.

Pass through another chamber of the sultan's ministers, the Cuarto Dorado (Golden Room), and you'll find yourself in the small but beautiful **Patio del Mexuar.** Constructed in 1365, this is where the sultan sat on giant cushions and listened to the petitions of his subjects, or met privately with his chief ministers. The windows here are surrounded by panels and richly decorated with tiles and stucco.

The Palace of the Nasrids, Mexuar, was constructed around two courtyards, the **Patio de los Arrayanes (Court of the Myrtles)** and the **Patio de los Leonares (Court of the Lions)** ★★★. The latter was the royal residence.

The Court of the Myrtles contains a narrow reflecting pool banked by myrtle trees. Note the decorative and rather rare tiles, which are arguably the finest in the Alhambra. Behind it is the **Salón de Embajadores (Hall of the Ambassadors),** with an elaborately carved throne room that was built between 1334 and 1354. The crowning cedar wood dome of this salon evokes the seven heavens of the Muslim cosmos. Here bay windows open onto **panoramic vistas** ★★ of the enveloping countryside.

An opening off the Court of the Myrtles leads to the greatest architectural achievement of the Alhambra, the Patio de los Leonares (Court of Lions), constructed by Muhammad V. At its center is Andalusia's finest fountain, which rests on 12 marble lions. These marble lions represent the hours of the day, the

The detailed mosaic work of the Alhambra.

months of the year, and the signs of the zodiac. Legend claims that water flowed from the mouth of a different lion each hour of the day. This courtyard is lined with arcades supported by 124 (count them) slender marble columns. This was the heart of the palace, the most private section where the sultan enjoyed his harem, which included both male and female beauties.

At the back of the Leones courtyard is the **Sala de los Abencerrajes ★**, named for a noble family whose members were rivals of the last emir, Boabdil. This hall has a richly adorned honeycombed ceiling. To get rid of his rivals, Boabdil invited them to a banquet. In the middle of the banquet, his guards entered and massacred his guests.

Opening onto the Court of Lions are other salons of intrigue, notably the Hall of the Two Sisters, **Sala de las Dos Hermanas,** where the sultan kept his "favorite" of the moment. The Hall of the Two Sisters takes its name from the two large white marble slabs, each identical, in the pavement. Boabdil's stern, unforgiving mother, Ayesha, once inhabited the Hall of the Two Sisters. This salon has a honeycomb dome and is celebrated as the finest example of Spanish Islamic architecture in the world.

The nearby **Sala de los Reyes (Hall of Kings)** was the great banquet hall of the Alhambra, site of parties, orgies, and feasts. Its ceiling paintings are on leather and date from the 1300s. Eunuchs guarded the harem, but not always well. According to legend, one sultan beheaded 36 Moorish princes here because one of them was suspected of being intimate with his favorite.

A gallery leads to the **Patio de la Reja (Court of the Window Grille).** This is where Washington Irving lived in furnished rooms, and where he began to write his famous book *Tales of the Alhambra.* The best-known tale is the legend of Zayda, Zorayda, and Zorahayda, the three beautiful princesses who fell in love with three captured Spanish soldiers outside the Torre de las Infantas. Irving credits the French with saving the Alhambra for posterity, but in fact they were responsible for blowing up seven of the towers in 1812, and it was a Spanish soldier who cut the fuse before more damage could be done. When the duke of

Wellington arrived a few years later, he chased out the chickens, the Gypsies, and the transient beggars who were using the Alhambra as a tenement and set up housekeeping here himself.

Before you proceed to the Emperor Charles V's palace, look at some other gems around the Court of Lions, including the **Baños Reales (Royal Baths),** with their lavish, multicolored decorations. Light enters through star-shaped apertures. To the immediate east of the baths lies the **Daraxa Garden,** and to its immediate south the lovely and resplendent **Mirador de Daraxa,** the sultana's private balcony onto Granada.

To the immediate southeast of these attractions are the **Jardines del Partal ★★** and their perimeter towers. These beautiful gardens occupy a space that once was the kitchen garden, filled with milling servants preparing the sultan's banquets. These gardens are dominated by the **Torre de Las Damas (Ladies' Tower).** This tower and its pavilion, with its five-arched porticoes, are all that are left of the once-famous Palacio del Partal, the oldest palace at the Alhambra. Of less interest are the perimeter towers, including the Mihrab Tower, a former Nasrid oratory; Torre de las Infantas (Tower of the Princesses); and Torre de la Cautiva (Tower of the Captive). Like the Damas tower, these towers were also once sumptuously decorated inside; today only some decoration remains.

Finally you can move to the immediate southwest to visit **Emperor Charles V's Palace (Palacio de Carlos V) ★,** where the Holy Roman emperor lived. Charles may have been horrified when he saw a cathedral placed in the middle of the great mosque at Córdoba, but he's also responsible for some architectural confusion in Granada. He literally built a Renaissance palace in the middle of this Moorish stronghold. It's quite beautiful, but terribly out of place in such a

The Jardines del Partal at the Alhambra.

setting—Charles V did not consider the Nasrid palaces grand enough. In 1526 he ordered Pedro Machuca, a student of Michelangelo, to design him a fitting royal residence. He financed the palace by levying a tax on the Muslims. In spite of its incongruous location, the final result is one of the purest examples of classical Renaissance in Spain.

The square exterior opens to reveal a magnificent, circular, two-story courtyard that is open to the sky. Inside the palace are two museums. The first, **Museo de la Alhambra** (© **95-822-75-27**), is a museum of Hispano-Muslim Art, its salons opening onto the Myrtle and Mexuar courts. They display artifacts retrieved from the Alcázar, including fragments of sculpture, as well as unusual braziers and even perfume burners used in the harems. The most outstanding exhibit is a **blue amphora** ★ that is 132 centimeters (52 in.) high. This precious object stood for years in the Hall of the Two Sisters. Also look for an ablutions basin dating from the 10th century and adorned with lions chasing stags and an ibex. The museum is open Tuesday to Saturday 9am to 7:15pm and Sunday 9am to 5:45pm.

The palace also houses the **Museo Bellas Artes en la Alhambra** (© **95-822-14-49**), open Tuesday to Saturday 9am to 8pm and Sunday 9am to noon. Of minor interest, it displays mostly religious paintings and sculpture from the 16th to the 18th century.

Before leaving the Alhambra precincts, try to see the **Alcazaba,** which dates from the 9th century and is the oldest part of the complex. This rugged fortress from the Middle Ages was built for defensive purposes. For a spectacular **view** ★★, climb the **Torre de la Vela (Watchtower).** You look into the lower town onto Plaza Nueva, and you can also see the snowcapped Sierra Nevada in the distance. From the tower you can also view the Generalife (see below), the "Gypsy hill" of Sacromonte.

Exit from the Alhambra via the Puerta de la Justicia, and then circumnavigate the Alhambra's southern foundations until you reach the gardens of the summer palace, where Paseo de los Cipreses quickly leads you to the main building of the **Generalife** ★★, built in the 13th century to overlook the Alhambra and set on 30 lush hectares (74 acres). The sultans used to spend their summers in this palace (pronounced Heh-neh-rah-*lee*-feh), safely locked away with their harems. Don't expect an Alhambra in miniature: The Generalife was always meant to be a retreat, even from the splendors of the Alhambra. Lying north of the Alhambra, this country estate of the Nasrid emirs was begun in the 13th

Walking to the Alhambra

Many visitors opt to take a taxi or the bus to the Alhambra, but some hardy souls enjoy the uphill climb from the cathedral at the Plaza de la Lonja. (Signs indicate the winding roads and the steps that lead to the Alhambra.) If you decide to walk, enter the Alhambra via the Cuesta de Gomérez, which, although steep, is the quickest and shortest pedestrian route. It begins at the Plaza Nueva, about 4 blocks east of the cathedral, and goes steeply uphill to the Puerta de las Granadas, the first of two gates to the Alhambra. The second, another 183m (600 ft.) uphill, is the Puerta de la Justicia, which accepts 90% of the touristic visits to the Alhambra. *Caution:* Beware of self-styled guides milling around the parking lot; they may just be interested in picking your pocket.

century, but the palace and gardens have been much altered over the years. The palace is mainly noted for its beautiful courtyards, including **Patio de Polo,** where the visitors of yore would arrive on horseback.

The highlight of the Generalife is its **gardens** ★★★, begun in the 13th century but much modified over the years. Originally, they contained orchards and pastures for domestic animals. Of special note is **Escalera del Agua (the Water Staircase),** with water flowing gently down. An enclosed Oriental garden, **Patio de la Acequía,** was constructed around a long pool, with rows of water jets making graceful arches above it. The **Patio de la Sultana** (also called the Patio de los Cipreses) was the secret rendezvous point for Zoraxda, wife of Sultan Abu Hasan, and her lover, the chief of the Abencerrajes.

Palacio de Carlos V. ✆ **90-244-12-21.** www.alhambra-patronato.es. Comprehensive ticket, including Alhambra and Generalife, 12€; Museo Bellas Artes 1.50€; Museo de la Alhambra free; garden visits 6€; illuminated visits 12€. Mar–Oct daily 8:30am–8pm, floodlit visits Tues–Sat 10pm–midnight; Nov–Feb daily 8:30am–6pm, floodlit visits Fri–Sat 8–10pm. Bus: 30 or 32.

Baños Arabes It's remarkable that these "baths of the walnut tree," as they were known by the Moors, escaped destruction during the reign of the Reyes Católicos (Ferdinand and Isabella). Among the oldest buildings still standing in Granada, and among the best-preserved Muslim baths in Spain, they predate the Alhambra. Visigothic and Roman building materials are supposed to have gone into their construction.

Carrera del Darro 31. ✆ **95-802-78-00.** Free admission. Tues–Sat 10am–2pm. Bus: 31 or 32.

Casa de Castril This building has always been one of the most handsome Renaissance palaces in Granada. The Plateresque facade of 1539 has been attributed to Diego de Siloé. In 1869, it was converted into a museum with a collection of minor artifacts found in the area. The most outstanding exhibit here is a collection of Egyptian alabaster vases that were dug up in a necropolis in Almuñécar. Look especially for the figure of a bull from Arjona. There is also a selection of decorative Moorish art that the Moors left behind as they retreated from Granada.

Museo Arqueológico, Carrera del Darro 41–43. ✆ **95-857-54-08.** Admission 1.50€. Tues 2:30–8:30pm; Wed–Sat 9am–8:30pm; Sun 9am–2:30pm. Bus: 31 or 32.

Casa-Museo Federico García Lorca (Huerta de San Vicente) ★ 🎁 Poet/

dramatist Federico García Lorca, author of *Blood Wedding, The House of Bernarda Alba,* and *A Poet in New York,* spent many happy summers with his family here at their vacation home. He moved to Granada in 1909, when he was a dreamy-eyed schoolboy and was endlessly fascinated with the city's life, including the Alhambra and the Gypsies, whom he later described compassionately in his *Gypsy Ballads.* The house is decorated with green trim and grillwork and filled with family memorabilia such as furniture and portraits. You can look out at the Alhambra from one of its balconies. You may inspect the poet's upstairs bedroom and see his oak desk stained with ink. Look for the white stool that he carried to the terrace to watch the sun set over Granada. The house is in the Fuentevaqueros section of Granada, near the airport.

Calle de la Virgen Blanca s/n, Parque Federico García Lorca. ✆ **95-825-84-66.** www.huerta desanvicente.com. Admission 3€. Apr–June Tues–Sun 10am–12:30pm and 5–7:30pm; July–Aug Tues–Sun 10am–2:30pm; Sept Tues–Sun 10am–12:30pm and 5–7:30pm; Oct–Mar Tues–Sun 10am–12:30pm and 4–6:30pm. Bus: 6.

Catedral and Capilla Real ★★ This richly ornate Renaissance cathedral with its spectacular altar is one of the country's architectural highlights, acclaimed for its beautiful facade and gold-and-white interior. It was begun in 1521 and completed in 1714. Behind the cathedral (entered separately) is the flamboyant Gothic **Royal Chapel** ★★, where the remains of Queen Isabella and her husband, Ferdinand, lie. It was their wish to be buried in recaptured Granada, not Castile or Aragón. The coffins are remarkably tiny—a reminder of how short they must have been. Accenting the tombs is a wrought-iron grille, itself a masterpiece. Occupying much larger tombs are the remains of their daughter, Joanna the Mad, and her husband, Philip the Handsome. In the sacristy you can view Isabella's personal **art collection** ★★, including works by Rogier Van der Weyden and various Spanish and Italian masters such as Botticelli. The cathedral is in the center of Granada off two prominent streets, Gran Vía de Colón and Calle de San Jerónimo. The Capilla Real abuts the cathedral's eastern edge.

Plaza de la Lonja, Gran Vía de Colón 5. ℂ **95-822-29-59.** www.capillarealgranada.com. Cathedral 3.50€; chapel 3.50€. Daily 10:30am–1:30pm and 3:30–6:30pm (4–8pm in summer). Bus: 6, 9, or 11.

Monasterio Cartuja ★ This 16th-century monastery, off the Albaicín on the outskirts of Granada, is sometimes called the "Christian answer to the Alhambra" because of its ornate stucco and marble and the baroque Churrigueresque fantasy in the sacristy. Its most notable paintings are by Bocanegra, its outstanding sculpture by Mora. The church of this Carthusian monastery was decorated with baroque stucco in the 17th century, and its 18th-century sacristy is an excellent example of latter-day baroque style. Napoleon's armies killed St. Bruno here, and La Cartuja is said to be the only monument of its kind in the world. Sometimes one of the Carthusian monks will take you on a guided tour.

Paseo de Cartujar s/n. ℂ **95-816-19-32.** Admission 3.50€. Daily 10am–1pm and 4–8pm (closes at 6pm in winter). Bus: 8 from cathedral.

Shopping

Alcaicería, once the Moorish silk market, is next to the cathedral in the lower city. The narrow streets of this rebuilt village of shops are filled with vendors selling the arts and crafts of Granada province. For the souvenir hunter, the Alcaicería offers one of the most splendid assortments in Spain of tiles, castanets, and wire figures of Don Quixote chasing windmills. Lots of Spanish jewelry can be found here, comparing favorably with the finest Toledan work. For the window-shopper in particular, it makes a pleasant stroll.

Handicrafts stores virtually line the main shopping arteries, especially those centered on Puerta Real, including Gran Vía de Colón, Reyes Católicos, and Angel Ganivet. For the best selection of antiques stores, mainly selling furnishings of Andalusia, browse the shops along Cuesta de Elvira.

Where to Stay in Granada

EXPENSIVE

AC Palacio de Santa Paula ★★★ One of Granada's grandest and most unusual hotels opened in 2001 behind the very large, sienna-colored facade of what had been built in the 19th century as Jerónimos Convent. Inside, you'll find one of the most imaginative combinations of modern and antique architecture in Spain, a brilliantly schizophrenic integration of buildings that incorporates a 15th-century medieval cloister, two 14th-century Arab houses, a deconsecrated baroque chapel, and many high-ceilinged vestiges of Granada's Catholic Reconquista. All these structures are interlinked with a sophisticated, ultramodern shell of glass, steel, aluminum, and polished stone. Even the simplest units are hypermodern, soothing, comfortable, and well designed, with soundproof windows protecting sleepers from the busy traffic of the Gran Vía de Colón. Somewhat more upscale units and suites occupy the site of the Moorish houses and the cloister. Scattered throughout the premises are a half-dozen imaginative suites.

Gran Vía de Colón 31, 18001 Granada. ✆ **95-880-57-40.** Fax 95-880-57-41. www.ac-hotels.com. 75 units. 140€–327€ double; from 217€ suite. AE, DC, MC, V. Parking 15€ per day. Bus: 3, 6, 8, or 11. **Amenities:** Restaurant; babysitting; exercise room; room service; sauna. *In room:* A/C, TV, minibar, Wi-Fi (12€ per 24 hr.).

Hotel Alhambra Palace Evoking a Moorish fortress complete with a crenellated roofline, a crowning dome, geometric tile work, and the suggestion of a minaret, this legendary hotel is a good choice. It was built by Duke San Pedro de Galatino in 1910 in a secluded spot just a 10-minute walk from the Alhambra. The private rooms don't live up to the drama of the public areas. Most units are spacious and quite comfortable, but a few small ones are in need of restoration. Try for one with a balcony opening onto a view of the city of Granada, but avoid the court rooms, whose windows lack double-glazing.

Plaza Arquitecto García de Paredes 1, 18009 Granada. ✆ **95-822-14-68.** Fax 95-822-64-04. www.h-alhambrapalace.es. 126 units. 136€–190€ double; from 260€ suite. AE, DC, MC, V. Free parking. Bus: 30. **Amenities:** Restaurant; bar; babysitting; room service. *In room:* A/C, TV, hair dryer, minibar, Wi-Fi (20€ per 24 hr.).

Parador de Granada ★★★ The most famous *parador* in Spain—and the hardest to get into—is within the grounds of the Alhambra. It's rich with Mudéjar- and Arab-inspired architectural touches, including splashing fountains, wraparound loggias, gardens laden with wisteria, and aromatic herbs. Unfortunately, it is consistently booked, so reserve as far as possible in advance. The decor is tasteful, and the rich Andalusian ambience evokes a lot of history. From the terrace you have views of the Generalife gardens and the Sacromonte caves. The guest rooms are roomy and comfortable. Ask for a unit in the older section, which is furnished with antiques; rooms in the more modern wing are less inspired.

Real de la Alhambra s/n, 18009 Granada. ✆ **95-822-14-40.** Fax 95-822-22-64. www.parador. es. 36 units. 249€–349€ double; 601€ suite. AE, DC, MC, V. Free parking. Bus: 30. **Amenities:** Restaurant; bar; room service. *In room:* A/C, TV, hair dryer, minibar, Wi-Fi (free).

Room Mate Migueletes ★★ This is the best-accessorized and plushest of the crop of boutique hotels that has opened within medieval houses of the Albaicín. Although it has a three-star government rating, it contains many accessories associated with four-star hotels. The structure was built in 1642 and used by the local police force (then known as Los Migueletes, for the weapons they carried) throughout most of the 1800s. After collapsing into a virtual ruin, it was rescued by Norway-born Karl Otto Skogland and his wife, Lise. Some of the rooms, especially the spectacular suite, feel baronial, thanks to high ceilings and majestic proportions. All bedrooms are different in size and layout, some opening onto the interior courtyard, whereas others have a view of the Alhambra.

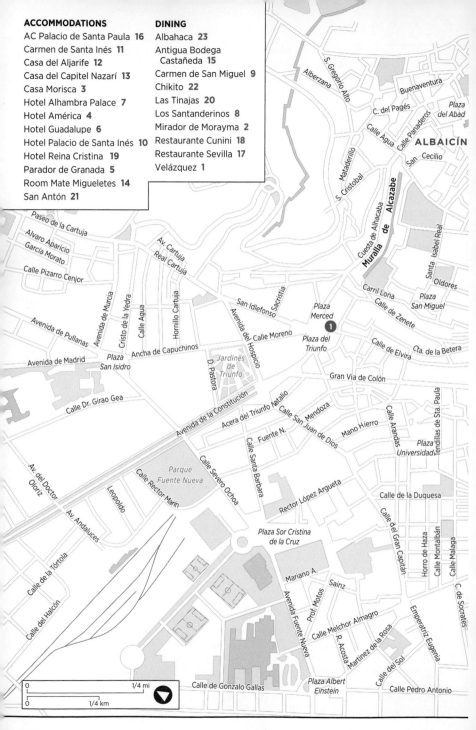

ACCOMMODATIONS
AC Palacio de Santa Paula **16**
Carmen de Santa Inés **11**
Casa del Aljarife **12**
Casa del Capitel Nazarí **13**
Casa Morisca **3**
Hotel Alhambra Palace **7**
Hotel América **4**
Hotel Guadalupe **6**
Hotel Palacio de Santa Inés **10**
Hotel Reina Cristina **19**
Parador de Granada **5**
Room Mate Migueletes **14**
San Antón **21**

DINING
Albahaca **23**
Antigua Bodega
  Castañeda **15**
Carmen de San Miguel **9**
Chikito **22**
Las Tinajas **20**
Los Santanderinos **8**
Mirador de Morayma **2**
Restaurante Cunini **18**
Restaurante Sevilla **17**
Velázquez **1**

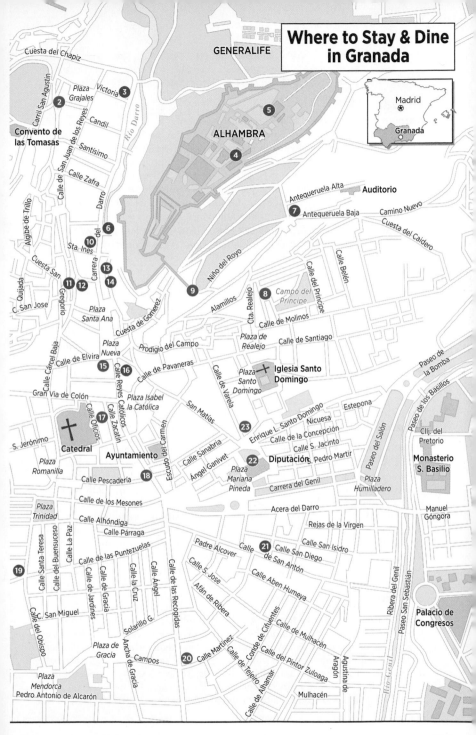

Where to Stay & Dine in Granada

GENERALIFE

Madrid

Granada

Cuesta del Chapiz

Plaza Grajales

Victoria ③

② Carril San Agustín

Calle de San Juan de los Reyes

Candil

Convento de las Tomasas

Santísimo

Calle Zafra

Río Darro

Algibe de Trillo

Darro

⑥

Sta. Ines

⑩

Carrera del

⑬

⑭

Cuesta San

⑪ ⑫

C. San José

C. Quijada

Gregorio

Plaza Santa Ana

Cuesta de Gomerez

Plaza Nueva

Prodigio del Campo

Calle Cárcel Baja

Calle de Elvira

⑮ ⑯

Calle Reyes Católicos

Calle Zacatín

Plaza Isabel la Católica

Gran Via de Colón

Calle de Pavaneras

San Matías

Plaza Santo Domingo

⑰

Calle Oficios

Catedral

S. Jerónimo

Ayuntamiento

Plaza Romanilla

Calle Pescadería

⑱

Calle de los Mesones

Plaza Trinidad

Calle Alhóndiga

Calle Párraga

Calle Santa Teresa

Calle del Buensuceso

Calle La Paz

Calle de las Puntezuelas

⑲

Calle de Gracia

Calle de Jardines

Calle la Cruz

Calle Ángel

Calle de las Recogidas

Solarillo G.

C. San Miguel

Calle del Obispo

Plaza de Gracia

Ancha de Gracia

⑳

Plaza Mendorca

Pedro Antonio de Alcarón

ALHAMBRA

④

⑤

Antequeruela Alta

Auditorio

⑦ Antequeruela Baja

Camino Nuevo

Cuesta del Caidero

Calle Belén

Niño del Royo

⑨

Alamillos

Cta. Realejo

⑧ Campo del Príncipe

Calle del Príncipe

Calle de Molinos

Plaza de Realejo

Calle de Santiago

Iglesia Santo Domingo

Calle de Varela

⑳

Enrique L. Santo Domingo

Nicuesa

Estepona

Calle de la Concepción

Calle S. Jacinto

Calle Sanabría

Ángel Ganivet

⑳

Plaza Mariana Pineda

Diputación

Pedro Martir

Paseo del Salón

Carrera del Genil

Plaza Humilladero

Acera del Darro

Rejas de la Virgen

Padre Alcover

Calle

⑳ Calle San Diego

de San Antón

Calle San Isidro

Calle S. José

Afán de Ribera

Calle Aben Humeya

Conde de Cifuentes

Calle de Mulhacén

⑳ Calle Martínez

Calle de Tejeiro

Calle del Pintor Zuloaga

Agustina de Aragón

Mulhacén

Calle de Alhamar

Paseo de la Bomba

Paseo de los Basillos

Cllj. del Pretorio

Monasterio S. Basilio

Ribera del Genil

Paseo San Sebastián

Río Genil

Manuel Góngora

Palacio de Congresos

Calle Benelua 11, 18010 Granada. © **95-821-07-00.** Fax 95-821-07-02. www.casamigueletes. com. 25 units. 96€–199€ double; 154€–229€ junior suite; 221€–349€ suite. AE, DC, MC, V. Parking 15€ per night. Bus: 30, 31, or 32. *In room:* A/C, TV, hair dryer, minibar, Wi-Fi (free).

MODERATE

Carmen de Santa Inés ★ ✦ Graciously restored, Carmen de Santa Inés will house you stylishly, comfortably, and affordably. Lying in the historical Albaicín section, this was an old Moorish house on a quiet street. Much of that past has been retained, including original wooden beams, a private patio, Arab fountains, a marble staircase, and columns—all very romantic. Bedrooms are small but filled with comfort and character. If you've got a few extra euros to spare, book "El Mirador," with its balcony terrace opening onto panoramic views of the Alhambra and the cityscape. There is no elevator, and only breakfast is served.

Placeta de Porras 7, 18018 Granada. © **95-822-63-80.** Fax 95-822-44-04. 9 units. www.carmen desantaines.com. 65€–140€ double; 150€–225€ suite. AE, DC, MC, V. Parking 31€. Bus: 30, 31, or 32. *In room:* A/C, TV, hair dryer, minibar.

Casa Morisca ★★ 📖 We thought we couldn't top the charms of the two Ineses: Carmen de Santa Inés and Hotel Palacio de Santa Inés (see above and below, respectively). Then we slept at Casa Morisca and fell in love again, fickle us. Located in the historic lower district of Albayzin, at the foot of the Alhambra, this house dates from the end of the 15th century. In the patio you can still see the remains of a Moorish pool and galleries supported by pilasters and columns. The interior was kept and restored, although the facade was given a 17th-century overlay. Bedrooms are individually decorated in an old style but with all modern comforts.

Cuesta de la Victoria 9, 18010 Granada. © **95-822-11-00.** Fax 95-821-57-96. www.hotelcasa morisca.com. 14 units. 90€–148€ double; 150€–198€ suite. AE, DC, MC, V. Free parking. Bus: 31 or 32. **Amenities:** Room service. *In room:* A/C, TV, hair dryer, minibar, Wi-Fi (free).

Hotel América ★★ ✦ This is one of only two hotels on the actual grounds of the Alhambra, the other being the much more expensive (and much better-accessorized) Parador de Granada (p. 363). Hotel América was built in the mid–19th century as a private home and then transformed in 1928 into the intimate, small-scale Victorian-era hotel you see today. There's a courtyard in back that's festooned with grapevines and dotted with blue-and-white ceramic tiles. Antiques, curios, and photos of past literati who have stayed here abound. Although small, the rooms are comfortably and decently furnished and well maintained.

Real de la Alhambra 53, 18009 Granada. © **95-822-74-71.** Fax 95-822-74-70. www.hotel americagranada.com. 17 units. 70€–140€ double; 150€ suite. MC, V. Nearby parking 15€. Bus: 30 or 32. **Amenities:** Restaurant. *In room:* A/C, hair dryer, Wi-Fi (free).

Hotel Palacio de Santa Inés ★★ This *casa antigua,* consisting of two small Mudéjar buildings constructed in the first third of the 16th century, is one of the most enchanting places to stay in Granada. It's in the colorful Albaicín district, about a 5-minute walk from the Alhambra. The painstakingly restored little palace was in complete ruins until the mid-1990s. Today it's a lovely, graceful inn, even a bit luxe. A 16th-century courtyard, time-aged wood-beamed ceilings, and silver chandeliers take you back to yesterday. The rooms are medium size, some have small sitting rooms, and several open onto views of Granada. Much of the furniture is antique.

Cuesta de Santa Inés 9, 18010 Granada. ✆ **95-822-23-62.** Fax 95-822-24-65. www.palacio santaines.com. 35 units. 80€–170€ double; 150€–250€ suite. AE, DC, MC, V. Parking 19€. Bus: 30 or 32. *In room:* A/C, TV, hair dryer, minibar.

Hotel Reina Cristina In the center of the city, a 3-minute walk from the cathedral in a renovated 19th-century mansion called a *casa granadina,* this hotel had a role in a dark moment of Granada's history. Here, the right-wing forces of Generalísimo Franco abducted one of the nation's greatest writers and Granada's favorite son, the poet/playwright Federico García Lorca. He was taken 3km (1¾ miles) away and executed. The family-operated hotel now exudes grace, charm, and tranquillity, and the service is helpful. All the small rooms have undergone extensive renovation, although many of the original furnishings remain.

Calle Tablas 4, 18002 Granada. ✆ **95-825-32-11.** Fax 95-825-57-28. www.hotelreinacristina.com. 58 units. 138€ per person double; 168€ per person triple. Rates include buffet breakfast. AE, DC, MC, V. Parking 16€. Bus: 5. **Amenities:** Restaurant; bar; room service. *In room:* A/C, TV, hair dryer, minibar, Wi-Fi (free).

San Antón ★ Across the Río Genil from the Palacio de Congresos, this first-class modern hotel caters to both vacationers and commercial clients. Rising eight floors, it is a typical city hotel with architecturally straight lines graced with panoramic windows. From here you can walk to many of the sights. Bedrooms are well furnished with modern wooden pieces, and are midsize for the most part. When reserving, request accommodations in the -01 or -03 series, as these are upper-floor chambers opening onto the Alhambra.

San Antón 74, 18005 Granada. ✆ **95-852-01-00.** Fax 95-852-19-45. www.hotelsananton granada.com. 189 units. 55€–250€ double; 70€–270€ suite. AE, DC, MC, V. Nearby parking 18€. Bus: 3. **Amenities:** Restaurant; bar; outdoor pool; room service. *In room:* A/C, TV, minibar, Wi-Fi (free).

INEXPENSIVE

Casa del Aljarife ★ 🎒 In the Albaicín district 4 blocks from the Plaza Santa Ana, this little nugget is known only to a few discerning travelers. In a renovated 17th-century structure, it has a large patio with trees and a Moorish fountain with views of the Alhambra. A family concern, the *casa* is well cared for and has a welcoming atmosphere. Each medium-size or spacious room has a distinct, Andalusian style. Owner Christian Most is gracious, apologizing for the lack of luxuries by pointing out that "everything you need" is virtually outside the door.

Placeta de la Cruz Verde 2, 18010 Granada. ✆/fax **95-822-24-25.** www.casadelaljarife.com. 4 units. 91€ double; 116€ triple. MC, V. Nearby parking 20€. Bus: 3 or 33. *In room:* A/C.

Casa del Capitel Nazarí ★ 🔗 This is one of at least four boutique hotels that opened during the early millennium within the cramped but evocative medieval neighborhood known as the Albaicín, a few steps uphill from the Plaza Nueva. Situated within a private, patio-centered home built at least 400 years ago, and the beneficiary of a river of funds spent on renovations and modern comforts (like plumbing), it's a cozy, appealing mixture of antique and modern. The well-furnished and rather small bedrooms are accented with hand-hewn antiques, including wooden beams in the old Spanish style. Accommodations are spread over three floors, and from the main courtyard you can access all the units.

Cuesta Aceituneros 6, 18010 Granada. ℂ **95-821-52-60.** Fax 95-821-58-06. www.hotelcasa capitel.com. 17 units. 68€–110€ double. DC, MC, V. Parking 20€ per day. Bus: 31 or 32. *In room:* A/C, TV, hair dryer, minibar.

Hotel Guadalupe This building sits beside a road leading up to the Alhambra. Rising five floors, Hotel Guadalupe uses lots of marble and stonework to add architectural character. Built in 1969, the hotel is rated three stars by the government. Its major drawback is that it's an oasis for the tour-bus set. Nonetheless, it remains one of the better choices in this price range, enhanced by its rustic arches, a beamed lobby, marble floors, and a fireplace. The better units lie within the hotel's main core, while the less desirable ones are in an annex a few yards away. Furnishings evoke a large, low-key country hotel.

Paseo de la Sabica s/n, 18009 Granada. ℂ **95-822-34-23.** Fax 95-822-37-98. www.hotel guadalupe.es. 58 units. 65€–111€ double. AE, DC, MC, V. Parking 15€. Bus: 30 or 32. **Amenities:** Restaurant; bar; babysitting; room service. *In room:* A/C, TV, hair dryer, minibar, Wi-Fi (free).

Where to Dine in Granada
EXPENSIVE

Carmen de San Miguel ANDALUSIAN Located on the hill leading up to the Alhambra, this likable restaurant offers spectacular views over the city center. Meals are served in a glassed-in dining room and patio-style terrace, where the banks of flowers are changed seasonally. Specialties include grilled hake, a pâté of partridge with a vinaigrette sauce, Iberian ham with Manchego cheese, and a casserole of monkfish and fresh clams. The food, although good, doesn't quite match the view. The wines are from throughout the country, with a strong selection of Riojas.

Plaza de Torres Bermejas 3. ℂ **95-822-67-23.** www.carmensanmiguel.com. Reservations recommended. Main courses 10€–24€; *menú degustación* 55€. AE, DC, MC, V. Mon–Sat 1:30–4pm and 8:30–11:30pm; winter Sun 1:30–4pm. Bus: 30 or 32.

Los Santanderinos ★★ SPANISH/ANDALUSIAN This is arguably the best restaurant in Granada, located in the new part of town. It is a genuinely wonderful dining choice—don't be disappointed by its location on a banal-looking expanse of concrete, within a modern-day apartment complex. Inside, the venue contains a small tapas bar near the entrance, an immaculate and formal dining room that's packed with members of the local bourgeoisie and business community, and an attentive staff.

Chef Jesús Diego Díaz prepares dishes that include green asparagus "in the style of Santanderinos," which is artfully interspersed with Iberian ham, shavings of cheese, and ingredients we couldn't even guess at. Tasty main courses include stuffed squid covered with a squid-ink-based black sauce, as well as a medley of beef, lamb, and other fish dishes. Come here for the food and the insight into modern-day, nontouristic Granada.

Albahaca 1 (Urbanización Jardín de la Reina, near the Puente del Genil). ℂ **95-812-83-35.** www. lossantanderinos.com. Main courses 14€–24€. MC, V. Mon–Sat 1–3:30pm; Tues–Sat 8–11:30pm. Bus: 1 or 3.

MODERATE

Albahaca ★ ▮▮ SPANISH/ANDALUSIAN You'd have to be in Granada for quite a while to discover this local favorite, a little *mesón* (inn) in a century-old building. Owner Javier Jiménez seats 28 diners at eight tables in an old-fashioned restaurant decorated in a rustic style with bare white walls. The traditional dishes served are unpretentious and tasty, especially the *salmorejo* (creamy tomato gazpacho) and *ensalada de dos salsas* (a green salad with two dressings). The stuffed salmon is marvelous, as is *pastel de berenjena con salmón marinado* (layered pastry with eggplant and marinated salmon). For dessert, we recommend the velvety yogurt mousse.

Calle Varela 17. ✆ **95-822-49-23.** Reservations recommended on weekends. Main courses 9€–16€; *menú del día* 15€. MC, V. Tues–Sat 1:30–4pm and 8:30–11pm; Sun 1–4pm. Closed Aug. Bus: C, 8, or 13.

Chikito SPANISH Chikito is across from the famous tree-shaded square where García Lorca met with other members of El Rinconcillo (The Little Corner), a group of young men who brought a brief but dazzling cultural renaissance to their hometown in the 1920s. The cafe where they met has now changed its name, and today is a bar/restaurant. In fair weather, guests enjoy drinks and snacks on tables placed in the square; in winter they retreat inside to the tapas bar. Specialties include *sopa sevillana,* shrimp cocktail, Basque hake, baked tuna, oxtail, *zarzuela,* grilled swordfish, and Argentine-style veal steak.

Plaza del Campilio 9. ✆ **95-822-33-64.** www.restaurantechikito.com. Reservations recommended. Main courses 11€–32€; fixed-price menu 22€–25€. AE, DC, MC, V. Thurs–Tues 1–4pm and 8–11:30pm. Bus: 1, 2, or 7.

Las Tinajas ★ ANDALUSIAN This restaurant, a short walk from the cathedral, is named for the huge amphorae depicted on its facade. For more than 3 decades it has been the culinary showcase of José Alvarez. The decor is classical Andalusian, with wood walls adorned with ceramic tiles and pictures of Old Granada. Diners are surrounded by antique ornaments interspersed with modern elements and fixtures. There's a convivial but crowded bar where locals and visitors alike order Andalusian wines and a wide variety of delicious tapas. You're sure to admire the chef's direct style of cooking, which emphasizes fresh ingredients and local recipes. Try the sirloin steak with mushrooms and Jabugo ham in sherry sauce, or loin of lamb stuffed with an assortment of nuts and a hint of mint. Sea bass comes stuffed with prawns. The best starters—when featured—are the artichoke hearts stuffed with broad beans and crispy ham.

Martínez Campos 17. ✆ **95-825-43-93.** www.restaurantelastinajas.com. Reservations recommended. Main courses 12€–25€. AE, DC, MC, V. Daily noon–5pm and 8pm–midnight. Closed July 15–Aug 15. Bus: 4 or 6.

Restaurante Cunini SEAFOOD/SPANISH The array of seafood specialties served at Cunini, perhaps 100 options in all, starts with the tapas offered at the long, stand-up bar. Many guests move on, after a drink or two, to the paneled ground-floor restaurant. Meals often begin with soup—perhaps *sopa sevillana* (with ham, shrimp, and whitefish). Also popular is a deep-fry of small fish, called a *fritura Cunini,* with other specialties including rice with seafood, *zarzuela* (seafood stew), smoked salmon, and grilled shrimp. The Plaza de la Pescadería is adjacent to the Gran Vía de Colón just below the cathedral. Outdoor tables fill part of a lovely old square, and they are protected with canvas canopies from the wind and rain.

Plaza de la Pescadería 14. ✆ **95-826-75-87.** http://cuninigranada.iespana.es. Reservations recommended. Main courses 14€–32€; fixed-price menu 20€. AE, DC, MC, V. Tues–Sat noon–4pm and 8pm–midnight; Sun noon–4pm. Bus: 5 or 11.

Velázquez ANDALUSIAN/GRANADINO This restaurant was founded in 1989 by the Gastronomic Society of Andalusia. Named for Spain's greatest Golden Age artist, it lies near two landmark squares, Puerta de Elvira and Plaza del Triunfo. The decor is in the typical Spanish style with a wood-beamed dining room upstairs and hams hanging from the ceiling at the bodega on the ground floor. Foodies who like to eat well and affordably, but not flashily, appreciate the chef's brand of cooking. Offerings change with the seasons, and every autumn a delectable pâté of pheasant liver is featured as an appetizer. One of the chef's signature dishes has Moroccan overtones: honey-coated baked lamb. Also in the Moroccan style is oven-baked lamb flavored with mint. Fish fanciers will also like the braised medallions of monkfish *(lomitos de rape)*.

Emilio Orozco 1, Triunfo. ✆ **95-828-01-09.** Reservations recommended. Main courses 10€–24€. MC, V. Mon–Sat 1–4pm and 8–11:30pm. Closed Aug. Bus: 3, 10, or 20.

INEXPENSIVE

Antigua Bodega Castañeda ★ 🏮 ANDALUSIAN An increasing number of discerning visitors are going to Andalusia wanting to dine in *típico* joints that rarely see a foreigner. Our nomination for the most rustic local bodega in Granada is the Castañeda. It's been here for more than a century and is the oldest of its type in the colorful Albaicín barrio, only a 10-minute walk from the Alhambra, just off the Plaza Nueva. A convivial spot, it's crowded with locals who know they can get tasty but unpretentious food at low, low prices. Tapas win high praise—there are 18 stuffed versions of the humble potato alone. Other meals include a variety of thick stews served in traditional clay bowls, ideal if visiting on a cold day. You can order a *tabla ibérica,* a selection of small dishes featuring cheese, ham, crab, shrimp, and venison.

Calle Elvira 5. ✆ **95-822-63-62.** Main courses 10€–16€. AE, MC, V. Daily 12:30–5pm and 8pm–1:30am. Bus: 30, 31, or 33.

Mirador de Morayma ANDALUSIAN/SPANISH Don't expect subtlety or big-city sophistication here—what you'll get are generous portions of good cooking and a deep pride in the region's rural traditions. Facing the Alhambra in an antique Renaissance-era house in the Albaicín, this is a large, rambling restaurant with a half-dozen dining rooms and three outdoor terraces. According to tradition, Morayma, the wife of Boabdil, last of the Muslim kings, was born here. The hardworking staff prepares dishes like gazpacho, roasted goat in wine sauce, slabs of beefsteak with a sauce of aromatic herbs, grilled Spanish sausages, and roasted lamb.

Calle Pianista García Carrillo 2. ✆ **95-822-82-90.** Reservations recommended. Main courses 12€–24€. AE, MC, V. Daily 1:30–3:30pm and 8:30–11:30pm; Sun 1:30–3:30pm. Bus: 31 or 32.

Restaurante Sevilla ANDALUSIAN/SPANISH Attracting a mixed crowd of all ages, the Sevilla is definitely *típico,* but with an upbeat elegance. The "great broads" and "fabulous studs" of the '50s and '60s who came here included Ava Gardner, Marlon Brando, Salvador Dalí, Andrés Segovia, Gene Kelly, and Ingrid Bergman. Even before them, the place was discovered by García Lorca, a patron in the 1930s, and Manuel de Falla. Most dishes are at the lower end of the price scale. The manager claimed that the most frequently ordered dinner for decades was gazpacho and later included Andalusian veal with fresh vegetables, topped off by flan, plus crusty homemade bread and the wine of Valdepeñas. To break the gazpacho monotony, try *sopa virule,* made with pine nuts and chicken breast. For a main course, we recommend the *cordero a la pastoril* (lamb with herbs and paprika). The best dessert is bananas flambé. You can dine inside, which is pleasantly decorated, or on the terrace. The restaurant is opposite the Royal Chapel, near the Plaza Isabel Católica.

Calle Oficios 12. (℃ **95-822-12-23.** www.restaurantesevilla.es. Reservations recommended. Main courses 12€–24€. *Menú de degustación* 36€. AE, DC, MC, V. Tues–Sat 1–4:30pm and 8–11:30pm. Bus: 32 or 39.

Granada After Dark

DRINKS & TAPAS A good place to begin your night is along the Campo del Príncipe, where at least seven old-fashioned tapas bars do a rollicking business during the cool of the evening.

One of the most popular tapas bars in Granada (at least with us) is **El Agua Casa de Vinos,** Calle Algibe de Trillo 7 (℃ **95-822-43-56**), a well-maintained bar with an adjoining restaurant in a small garden in the heart of the Albaicín. Everyone agrees that the cooling nighttime breezes show off this convivial spot to its best advantage. Don't expect full-fledged platters; its strength is small-scale portions of cheeses, pâtés, and salads, which go especially well with glasses of wine and beer. An equally historic spot with a verdant patio loaded with plants and shrubs is **Bar Pilar del Toro,** Calle Hospital de Santa Ana 12 (℃ **95-822-54-70;** www.pilardeltoro.es), near the cathedral and the Plaza Nueva. An even larger competitor, **La Gran Taberna,** Plaza Nueva 12 (℃ **95-822-88-46**), is a modern and irreverent site that attracts coffee and wine tasters as well as lovers of sliced Serrano ham, fondues, and liqueurs.

THE GYPSY CAVES OF SACROMONTE ✋ These inhabited Gypsy caves are the subject of much controversy. Admittedly, they're a tourist trap, one of the most obviously commercial and shadowy rackets in Spain. Still, the caves are a potent enough attraction if you follow some rules.

Once, thousands of Gypsies lived on the "Holy Mountain," so named because of several Christians martyred here. However, many of the caves were heavily damaged by rain in 1962, forcing hundreds of the occupants to seek shelter elsewhere. Nearly all the Gypsies remaining are in one way or another involved with tourism. (Some don't even live here—they commute from modern apartments in the city.)

When evening settles over Granada, loads of visitors descend on these caves near the Albaicín, the old Arab section. In every cave, you'll hear the rattle of castanets and the strumming of guitars, while everybody in the Gypsy family struts his or her stuff. Popularly known as the *zambra,* this is intriguing entertainment only if you have an appreciation for the grotesque. Whenever a Gypsy boy or girl shows genuine talent, he or she is often grabbed up and hustled off to the more expensive clubs. Those left at home can be rather pathetic in their attempts to entertain.

One of the main reasons to go is to see the caves themselves. If you expect primitive living, you may be in for a surprise—many are quite comfortable, with conveniences like telephones and electricity. Often they're decorated with copper and ceramic items—and the inhabitants need no encouragement to sell them to you.

White Gypsy caves in Sacromonte.

If you want to see the caves, you can walk up the hill by yourself. Your approach will already be advertised before you get here. Attempts will be made to lure you inside one or another of the caves—and to get money from you. Alternatively, you can book an organized tour arranged by one of the travel agencies in Granada. Even at the end of one of these group outings—with all expenses theoretically paid in advance—there's likely to be an attempt by the cave dwellers to extract more money from you. As soon as the *zambra* ends, hurry out of the cave as quickly as possible. Many readers have been critical of these tours.

A visit to the caves is almost always included as part of the morning and (more frequently) afternoon city tours offered every day by such companies as **Grana Visión** (✆ **90233;** www.granavision.com). Night tours of the caves (when they are at their most eerie, most evocative, and most larcenous) are usually offered only to those who can assemble a group of 10 or more. This might have changed by the time of your visit, so phone a reputable tour operator such as Grana Visión to learn if any new options are available.

CLUBS If you eventually tire of bodega crawling, you might be tempted as the night progresses to go dancing in the town's most popular disco: **Granada 10,** Calle Carcel Baja 10 (✆ **95-822-41-26**), open Monday to Friday 12:30 to 5am, Saturday and Sunday 12:30 to 7am. A cover charge of 10€ includes the first drink.

At **Camborio,** Camino del Sacromonte 48 (✆ **95-822-12-15**), the best DJs in Granada spin music on the dance floors, including a rooftop patio with some of the best nighttime panoramas of the Alhambra. A lively under-30 crowd of both locals and foreigners frequents the place. A cover charge of 10€ is charged only on Friday and Saturday nights. The club is open Tuesday to Saturday from 11pm until daybreak. You can either walk up from the Plaza Nueva in about 20 minutes, or catch a night bus (no. 31), which climbs the hill every night until 2am.

La Industrial Copera, Paz 7, Carretera de la Armilla (© **95-825-84-49;** www.industrialcopera.net), features a huge dance floor under pulsating, glowing lights. The DJs here are the best in town. Techno music is the main entertainment for the beautiful young people of Granada, who range in age here from late teens to early 30s. The club is open nightly from 10:30pm to 4am, charging 12€ to 20€ cover.

A DRIVING TOUR OF THE PUEBLOS BLANCOS

The brilliantly whitewashed villages and towns of inland Andalusia are called Pueblos Blancos (white towns). These are archetypal towns and villages that dot the steep slopes of the mountains, which extend north of Gibraltar. They occupy that part of Andalusia that lies between the Atlantic in the west and the Mediterranean extending eastward. One of the most traveled routes through the towns is the road that stretches from Arcos de la Frontera all the way to Ronda in the east.

Many towns have "de la Frontera" as part of their name, an ancient reference to the frontier towns that formed a boundary between Christian-held territories and Muslim towns and villages in the Middle Ages. Although the Catholic troops eventually triumphed, it is often the Moorish influence that makes these towns architecturally interesting, with their labyrinths of narrow, cobblestone streets, their fortress-like walls, and their little whitewashed houses with the characteristic wrought-iron grilles.

The drive outlined below passes by some of the great scenic landscapes of Spain, various thickly wooded areas that are often the home to some rare botanical species, including the Spanish fir, *Abies pinsap,* which grows in only four locations at more than 1,000m (3,281 ft.). As you drive along you'll approach limestone slopes that rise as high as 6,640m (21,785 ft.). Castle ruins and old church bell towers also form part of the landscape. For those who have been across the sea to North Africa, much of the landscape of the Pueblos Blancos will evoke Morocco. The white towns sprawl across the provinces of Cádiz and Málaga, lying east of Seville.

The ideal time to drive through the Pueblos Blancos is spring, when the wildflowers in the valleys burst into bloom. Fall is another good time. Allow at least a day for Ronda, covered in detail on p. 346. You can pass through the other villages on this tour, admiring the life and the architecture, and then moving on. The best hotels and restaurants along the entire stretch of the Pueblos Blancos are found in Ronda and Arcos de la Frontera. Elsewhere, accommodations and restaurants are very limited, although we have included some recommendations along the way.

These whitewashed villages are fairly close together, so driving times, as indicated below, are short. From Seville, you can begin your tour by heading to the Pueblos Blancos along A-4, which becomes N-IV. Continue southeast along N-IV until you come to the turnoff for C-343. At this point, our first stopover on the tour, Arcos de la Frontera, will be signposted. Follow C-343 south into Arcos de la Frontera. The first part of the tour from Arcos to Ronda can be done in 1 day, with an overnight in Ronda.

The second part of the tour, from Ronda to Jerez de la Frontera in the west, can also be done in a day. However, those with more time can extend this tour to 3 or 4 days. In the towns along the way, we have recommended the best places to stay and dine: If you find a place that enchants you and your schedule allows it, you can stop over rather than pressing on to Ronda.

Arcos de la Frontera ★★

Along with Ronda, this old Arab town is a highlight of the Pueblos Blancos and the center of the best inns along the route. Now a National Historic Monument, Arcos de la Frontera was built in the form of an amphitheater. The major attraction here is the village itself. Wander at leisure and don't worry about skipping a particular monument. Nearly all that interests the casual visitor will be found in the elevated **Medina (Old Town) ★★**, which towers over the flatlands. The Old Town is huddled against the crenellated castle walls. You park your car below and walk up until you reach the site built on a crag overlooking a loop in the Guadalete River.

At the main square, Plaza del Cabildo, you can pick up a map at the **tourist office** (© **95-670-22-64;** www.ayuntamientoarcos.org), open Monday to Saturday from 10am to 2:30pm and 4 to 8pm; Sunday from 10am to 1:30pm. Start your visit at the **Balcón de Arcos,** at the same square. Don't miss the **view ★★** from this rectangular esplanade overhanging a deep river cleft. You can see a Moorish castle, but it's privately owned and not open to the public. The main church on this square is **Iglesia de Santa María,** constructed in 1732 in a blend of Renaissance, Gothic, and baroque styles. Its **western facade ★**, in the Plateresque style, is its most stunning achievement. The interior is a mix of many styles—Plateresque, Gothic, Mudéjar, and baroque. Look for the beautiful star-vaulting and a late Renaissance altarpiece. It's open Monday to Friday from 10am to 1pm and 4 to 7pm. Admission is 1.50€.

The hilltop town of Arcos de la Frontera.

Down the main street heading out of Plaza del Cabildo is **Iglesia de San Pedro,** with its baroque bell tower. It is on the other side of the cliff and approached through a charming maze of narrow alleys evocative of Tangier. You can climb the tower, but with few guardrails, it's not for those with vertigo. Paintings here include *Dolorosa* by Pacheco, the tutor of the great Velázquez, and works by Zurbarán and Ribera. It's open Monday to Saturday from 10:30am to 2pm. Admission is 1€.

WHERE TO STAY IN ARCOS DE LA FRONTERA

Cortijo Fain ★ ☺ A real discovery, this 17th-century farmhouse has been turned into a hacienda hotel lying 3km (1¾ miles) southeast of Arcos near the hamlet of Algar (reached via CA-52). Draped with purple bougainvillea, the house is warm and inviting with arches, white walls, a stone footpath, and Andalusian courtyards. Last renovated in 2006, the inn offers large bedrooms that are comfortably and rather charmingly furnished. The setting is in a vast olive grove, and the inn has a swimming pool and a library. You can explore the countryside on a horseback ride arranged by the inn.

Carretera Arcos-Algar Km 3, 11630 Arcos de la Frontera. ℂ **95-670-41-31.** Fax 95-671-79-32. www.arcosgardens.com. 9 units. 113€–160€ double; 119€–170€ suite. Rates include buffet breakfast. AE, DC, MC, V. Free parking. **Amenities:** Restaurant; bar; bikes; children's center; concierge; 18-hole golf course; 1 outdoor pool; room service; spa; outdoor tennis court (lit); Wi-Fi (free, in lobby). *In room:* A/C, TV, hair dryer, minibar.

El Convento Near Santa María Church, this was originally Convento Las Mercedarías, but it was turned into an inn in 1987 and has been renovated several times since. The hotel is reached via a tiny cobblestone alleyway in back of the Parador Casa del Corregidor (see below). In a classic style, with a red-tile roof and wrought-iron grilles, the hotel is a snug nest. It is furnished with rustic wooden pieces and is beautifully maintained. Its bedrooms are midsize, inviting, and comfortable enough to make you want to linger.

Maldonado 2, 11630 Arcos de la Frontera. ℂ **95-670-23-33.** Fax 95-670-41-28. www.hotelel convento.es. 11 units. 75€–90€ double. AE, DC, MC, V. Parking 10€ nearby. **Amenities:** Bar; room service. *In room:* A/C, TV, hair dryer.

Marqués de Torresoto At the center of Arcos, at the landmark Plaza del Cabildo, this is a converted palace dating from the 17th century, with its original chapel still intact. It was a private family home built by a local nobleman, Marqués de Torresoto. Turned into a hotel in 1994, it is graced with interior patios, corridors, columns, and arches in the typical Andalusian style. Rooms, mostly small, are a bit minimalist, evocative of a monastery, with white walls and wooden furniture.

Marqués de Torresoto 4, 11630 Arcos de la Frontera. ℂ **95-670-07-17.** Fax 95-670-42-05. www. hotelmarquesdetorresoto.com. 15 units. 60€–100€ double; 90€–130€ suite. MC, V. Parking 5€ nearby. **Amenities:** Restaurant; bar; babysitting; room service. *In room:* A/C, TV, hair dryer.

Parador Casa del Corregidor ★★ In the old part of the city, this is the kind of first-class place that's more typical of Ronda than of the other Pueblos Blancos. Originally the house of the *corregidor* (king's magistrate), it dates from the 18th century. From its balconies are panoramic views of the Guadalete River and the plains and farms beyond. Evocative of a chalet, the inn rises three floors with outside corridors, wooden columns, and a big terrace with a vista. The midsize bedrooms are traditionally and comfortably furnished, matching the style of the house. Many open onto views, and each comes with a small, tiled bathroom. The on-site **restaurant** serves dishes typical of the Sierra region (there's that oxtail again), but there are many other good options, including pork in a red-wine and fresh tomato sauce.

Plaza del Cabildo s/n, 11630 Arcos de la Frontera. © **95-670-05-00.** Fax 95-670-11-16. www. parador.es. 24 units. 143€–186€ double. AE, DC, MC, V. Free parking nearby. **Amenities:** Restaurant; bar; room service. *In room:* A/C, TV, hair dryer, minibar (in some); Wi-Fi (free).

WHERE TO DINE IN ARCOS DE LA FRONTERA

El Lago ANDALUSIAN   This is a reliable choice, serving predictable but good food. The setting is rustic with wooden columns, a bar, heavy furniture, and the typical white walls. The service is friendly, efficient, and welcoming. Chefs turn out classic recipes like oven-baked lamb flavored with garlic and fresh herbs. One casserole is made of fresh tomatoes and the extraordinarily delicious Jabugo ham. A tenderloin of beef appears with a zesty pepper sauce. The home-baked bread is fresh and aromatic, and the soups are filling and tasty.

Carretera A-382 Este Km 1. © **95-670-11-17.** Reservations recommended. Main courses 11€–21€; fixed-price menu 12€. AE, DC, MC, V. Daily 1–5pm and 8pm–midnight. Closed Sun June–Aug.

Zahara de la Sierra ★

From Arcos de la Frontera, take the A-383 northeast, following the signs to Algodonales. Once you reach this town, head south at the junction with CA-531 to Zahara de la Sierra, the most perfect of the province's fortified hilltop *pueblos*. Trip time from Arcos is about 35 minutes, and the distance is 51km (32 miles).

Zahara lies in the heart of the **Natural Park Sierra de Grazalema ★★**, a 50,590-hectare (125,000-acre) park. An important reserve for griffon vultures, among other creatures, the park is studded with pine trees and oak forests. The **Parque Natural Information Office** (© **95-612-31-14;** www.zaharadela sierra.es) lies at Calle San Juan (the eastern end of the main street). Hours are daily from 9am to 2pm and Monday to Saturday from 4 to 7pm. It dispenses information and maps for those who'd like to go for walks in the park. There are five major routes in the park, and for most you'll need to seek permission at the office, which also organizes horseback riding, canoeing, and bike trips.

The white village of Zahara itself zigzags up the foot of a rock topped by a reconstructed *castillo*. Houses covered in characteristic red tiles huddle up to the ruined castle. Count on a 15- to 20-minute climb to reach what was once a 10th-century Muslim fortress constructed on Roman foundations 511m (1,677 ft.) above sea level. You can visit the Moorish castle, which is always open and offers **panoramic views ★** of the surrounding countryside.

The cobbled main street, Calle San Juan, links the two most important churches, **Iglesia San Juan** and **Iglesia Santa María de la Mesa.** The latter is an 18th-century baroque church worth a look inside (if it's open). It displays an impressive *retablo* with a 16th-century image of the Madonna. The best time to be here is in June for the Corpus Christi celebration (annual dates vary). Streets and walls seem to disappear under a mass of flowers and greenery.

WHERE TO STAY & DINE IN ZAHARA DE LA SIERRA

Arco de la Villa   In business since 1998, this rural inn is a rustic stone house resting under a low roof and set near a promontory in front of the castle. It's

Zahara de la Sierra, as seen from afar.

modern and minimally decorated with whitewashed walls and light wooden furnishings. It's a safe, well-maintained nest that, despite its modesty, is the best place to stay in Zahara. Bedrooms are small and simply but comfortably furnished, with little tile bathrooms with tub/shower combos. A reasonably good meal, costing 20€, is served in the on-site **restaurant** if you're just passing through Zahara and need lunch.

Paseo Nazarí s/n, 11688 Zahara de la Sierra. ✆ **95-612-32-30.** Fax 95-612-32-44. 17 units. 59€ double. DC, MC, V. Free parking. **Amenities:** Restaurant; bar; room service. *In room:* A/C, TV.

Los Tadeos This inn, launched at the beginning of the 21st century, is a family-run business that's located in a two-story structure outside town, near the municipal swimming pool. Its **restaurant** is more popular than its hotel rooms. Tables are placed on the terrace, and the food is typically Andalusian and budget priced, depending on the menu featured that day (fixed-price menus 9€–20€). Bedrooms are comfortable but small, each with a little tiled bathroom with tub and shower. They're decorated rustically, soberly, and simply. The best, and the most expensive, open onto private balconies with views.

Paseo de la Fuente, 11688 Zahara de la Sierra. ✆ **95-612-30-86.** 10 units. 50€–55€ double. MC, V. Free parking. **Amenities:** Restaurant; bar. *In room:* A/C, TV, Wi-Fi (free).

Marqués de Zahara This rural inn is a 17th-century structure, a former private home that has been converted to receive guests on its three floors. The location is central, and the decoration is very rustic with heavy curtains and dark colors. Furnishings are a bit of a disappointment, rather flea-markety, but they're comfortable enough for a night. Each of the small rooms comes with a shower-only bathroom, and the most expensive doubles contain private balconies. The handsomest feature is an attractive courtyard and delightful **bar and dining room,** where even nonguests can enjoy regional meals usually costing under 20€.

Calle San Juan 3, 11688 Zahara de la Sierra. ✆ **95-612-30-61.** Fax 95-612-32-68. www.marques dezahara.com. 10 units. 50€ double. Rates include continental breakfast. AE, DC, MC, V. Free parking. **Amenities:** Restaurant; bar. *In room:* A/C, TV, Wi-Fi (free).

Olvera

From Zahara, return to CA-531 and follow the signs north to A-382. Once on A-382 head northeast to the village of Olvera. The distance between towns is only 24km (15 miles), usually taking only 15 minutes.

Olvera's two chief monuments are its castle and its cathedral, but even better is the view of the town and surrounding countryside. Olvera comes at you like an explosion of little whitewashed houses tumbling down a hill crowned by the twin towers of its church and ancient castle. Climb the hill by walking up the town's long main street.

In the town's Muslim heyday, **El Castillo de Olvera,** Plaza de la Iglesia 3, was one of the most impregnable fortresses in Andalusia. But even such a mighty bastion fell to the troops of King Alfonso XI in 1327. After the citadel was conquered, the castle and the surrounding village became part of the feudal estate of Pérez de Guzmán, a local nobleman. As late as the 19th century, the castle was still in private hands, the home of the dukes of Osuna. The castle is open Tuesday to Sunday from 10:30am to 2pm and 4 to 6pm. Admission is 3€, and tickets can be purchased at the tourist office.

The village is known for its handicrafts, and you can see little shops on the narrow streets selling *esparto* and other hand-woven straw products. Foodies may want to stock up on Olvera's pure virgin olive oil, which is among the best in Andalusia.

The **Oficina de Turismo,** Plaza del Ayuntamiento 1 (© **95-612-08-16;** www.olvera.es), has what little information is needed. Hours are Tuesday to Sunday from 10:30am to 2pm and 4 to 6pm. It's open at other times as well, so check locally.

WHERE TO STAY IN OLVERA

Hotel-Mesón Fuente del Pino Standing at the entrance to town, this large two-story house was turned into a hotel in 1992 and last renovated in 2006. It is one of the town's better addresses, ideal for a 1-night stopover. Extravagantly decorated in its public rooms, it is imbued with a real Andalusian aura with its flowery curtains, local tiles, wooden furniture, and whitewashed walls. Bedrooms are small and simply furnished. The on-site **restaurant** serves a varied cuisine based on regional products.

Av. Julián Besteiro s/n, 11690 Olvera. © **95-613-02-32.** Fax 95-613-13-99. 32 units. 55€–65€ double. MC, V. Free parking. **Amenities:** Restaurant; bar; outdoor pool. *In room:* A/C, TV, Wi-Fi (free).

Sierra y Cal Near Parque Entre Caminos, a 10-minute walk from the center, this large two-story hotel has been going strong since 1989. The rooms here are small and fairly standard, but are well maintained and reasonably comfortable. Expect tile floors, iron frames, and whitewashed walls. There is a tea salon plus a terrace with a view. Guests will find an affordable **restaurant** on-site that specializes in regional dishes (see below).

Av. Nuestra Señora de los Remedios 2, 11690 Olvera. © **95-613-05-42.** Fax 95-613-05-83. www.tugasa.com. 34 units. 59€ double; 85€ suite. AE, DC, MC, V. Free parking. **Amenities:** Restaurant; bar; outdoor pool. *In room:* A/C, TV.

WHERE TO DINE IN OLVERA

Lirios ANDALUSIAN In front of the local hospital in the newer part of town, this is one of the best places for regional Andalusian platters. Typical of the area is a casserole made from locally grown asparagus. They also do a peppery baked veal that's quite tasty, as is their garlic-flavored and perfectly roasted suckling pig. Though the restaurant is located inland, the kitchen manages to get fresh fish. Often it is served *a la sal,* which means it was cooked coated in salt, the skin removed at the last minute. The salt coating seals in the juices. Desserts are rather standard.

Av. Julián Besteiro 54. ✆ **95-613-03-75.** Reservations recommended. Main courses 8€–20€; fixed-price menus 15€–50€. DC, MC, V. Wed–Mon 9am–midnight.

Sierra y Cal ★ ANDALUSIAN In the hotel of the same name (see above), this rustically decorated restaurant serves the finest food in the area. It is open to nonguests as well, most of whom are passing through Olvera for the day and stopping for lunch. It takes market-fresh ingredients and with a minimum of artifice transforms them into flavorful dishes. Start, perhaps, with the house specialty, a bowl of *pega con bolos,* asparagus soup with homemade bread. Enticing fish dishes include sole in meunière sauce and trout in a sauce made with fresh prawns and ham. Diners will delight in a tender and juicy Iberian sirloin of beef prepared with sausages.

Av. Nuestra Señora de los Remedios 2. ✆ **95-613-05-42.** Reservations recommended. Main courses 11€–22€. AE, DC, MC, V. Daily 1–3:30pm and 8–10:30pm.

Setenil de las Bodegas ★★

From Olvera, follow the signs to CA-4222, which will take you southeast to Setenil de las Bodegas. This winding road stretches for 13km (8 miles), taking you by olive groves and farming valleys. You'll pass through the town of **Torre Alhaquime** after 4km (2½ miles). Allow 15 to 30 minutes for this trip.

Setenil is one of the most bizarre of the Pueblos Blancos. The Río Trejo carved itself through the tufa rock to make room for the town, which is literally crammed into clefs of rock, its cavelike streets formed from the overhanging ledge of a gorge. Houses rise two or three floors, using the natural rock as their roofs. One street is actually a tunnel.

Other than the town itself, there are no specific attractions. The 16th-century Gothic church, **Iglesia La Encarnación,** stands on a rock in the center of the village next to an Arab tower, and the ruins of a **Muslim castle** are nearby. Another building, the **Ayuntamiento (town hall),** boasts a magnificent Mudéjar *artesonado* ceiling. **Calle Herreria** is the oldest street in town, its houses wedged into the massive rock.

Chances are you'll press on and not spend the night. However, if you do, there is one place to stay, the **Hotel El Almendral,** Setenil de Las Bodegas, 11692 (✆ **95-613-40-29;** fax 95-613-44-44; www.tugasa.com). This is a little *pensión* (boardinghouse) nestled under rock ridges. The 28 small rooms are simply furnished with wooden pieces, including decent beds. The on-site restaurant serves simple meals. The hotel charges 59€ for a double room.

Continuing on to Ronda

To reach Ronda, the capital of the Pueblos Blancos, return to CA-4222 and head southeast, following the signs. The route will become CA-4211 as you continue south by the town of Arriate and then change to MA-428, which takes you into Ronda. In all, this is a distance of only 18km (11 miles), taking about 15 to 20 minutes. Spend at least 1 night in Ronda before continuing the driving tour the

The town of Setenil, set into the rock.

next day. Or you can end the tour in Ronda if you feel you're going blind from seeing too many white villages glistening in the bright Andalusian sun. For more on Ronda, including its sights and where to stay and dine, see p. 346.

Grazalema ★

After visiting Ronda, head to the village of Grazalema by taking A-376 northwest. At the junction with A-372, follow signs southwest to Grazalema. Travel time for the 33km (21-mile) drive is about a half-hour.

This is the whitest of the white towns—perhaps a *pueblo blanquísimo* (extraordinarily white town). It's also one of the best centers for exploring the **Parque Natural** of the Sierra de Grazalema. This charming village nestles under the craggy peak of San Cristóbal at 1,525m (5,003 ft.). As you wander its sloping, narrow streets, you'll pass house after house filled with summery flowers.

On the main square is the **Grazalema Parque Natural Information Office,** Plaza de España (✆ 95-671-60-63), open Monday to Friday from 10am to 2pm and 4 to 9pm, Saturday and Sunday from 10am to 9pm. Information is provided here about walks in the park and local activities like horseback riding.

Towering limestone crags overlook the town. For the best panoramic view, climb to a belvedere near the 18th-century chapel of San José.

The town has two beautiful old churches, **Iglesia de la Aurora,** on Plaza de España, and the nearby **Iglesia de la Encarnación.** Both date from the 17th century.

Grazalema is also known for its local products, especially pure wool blankets and rugs. A 5-minute walk from Plaza de España is **Artesanía Textil de Grazalema,** Carretera de Ronda (✆ 95-613-20-08). At this small factory, open to the public, you can buy blankets and ponchos that are made from local wool using hand-operated looms and antique machinery. It also sells souvenirs, handicrafts, and traditional gifts. It's open Monday to Friday from 8am to 2pm and 3 to 6:30pm. Closed in August.

WHERE TO STAY IN GRAZALEMA

Casa de las Piedras The building housing this inn dates from the 19th century. It stands on one of the oldest streets of the little town, only 50m (164 ft.) from the central square. It is a traditional Andalusian house spread across two floors. The bedrooms themselves are small and simple yet with a certain comfort, containing whitewashed walls, small lamps, a desk, and heavy wooden beds. The hotel's **dining room** is one of the best in town (see below).

Las Piedras 32, 11610 Grazalema. ℭ/fax **95-613-20-14.** www.casadelaspiedras.net. 32 units, 16 without bathrooms. 50€ double. DC, MC, V. **Amenities:** Restaurant.

Hotel El Horcajo ★ ☺ Set on a working estate in the Grazalema Parque Natural, this is a traditional Spanish colonial–style farmhouse with whitewashed walls and iron grilles at the windows. The building dates from the 19th century, and the bedrooms have been installed in what were once stables. The main country house, still with its vaulted arches and wood beamed ceilings, is more than 170 years old. It has retained much of its original character and offers an intimate family atmosphere. The very sober but cozy bedrooms are furnished with tiles and light wooden pieces. Constructed near the main building are 10 family units with a large double bed plus two single beds upstairs. These are built in a traditional style that blends in with the older structures. Many accommodations open onto a private terrace overlooking the estate. Rooms are decorated with locally crafted materials, and there is a comfortable lounge for guests. Typical local food is served, including some produce grown on the estate.

Carretera Ronda, 29400 Grazalema. ℭ **95-218-40-80.** Fax 95-218-41-71. www.elhorcajo.com. 24 units. 66€–82€ double; 84€–107€ triple; 112€–145€ quad. AE, MC, V. **Amenities:** Restaurant; outdoor pool; room service. *In room:* A/C, TV, hair dryer.

Villa Turística de Grazalema ☺ One of the finest accommodations is found in this big chalet, built country-style across two floors with white walls and wooden columns. Dating from 1990, it lies across the valley from the center of Grazalema. It's really a complex with semidetached apartments that sleep from two to six guests. Most of the rooms open onto vistas of Grazalema or the *sierra* beyond. Families often book these rooms, especially during the summer season—the noise level may be uncomfortably high at that time. Bedrooms are small and furnished with light wooden pieces, tile floors, and summery colors. Regional specialties are served at the villa's restaurant.

El Olivar s/n, 11610 Grazalema. ℭ **95-613-21-36.** Fax 95-613-22-13. www.tugasa.com. 24 units. 59€ double. MC, V. Free parking. **Amenities:** Restaurant; outdoor pool. *In room:* A/C, TV, hair dryer.

WHERE TO DINE IN GRAZALEMA

Cádiz El Chico ANDALUSIAN The best restaurant in town stands right on the main square. In an antique building, it's typically decorated, even using blankets made in town. The simplified classic cuisine is inexpensive and good. There are some unusual dishes on the menu, notably *tagarnina* soup (made with an edible kind of cactus). Shoulder of lamb is studded with garlic and cooked over firewood. Oven-baked deer is another signature dish, most often served in a red-wine sauce. Of course, you'll also find that Andalusian favorite, oxtail. Desserts are simple.

Plaza de España 8. ℭ **95-613-20-27.** Reservations recommended. Main courses 7€–19€. AE, MC, V. Daily 1–4pm and 8–11pm.

Casa de las Piedras ANDALUSIAN In the above-recommended hotel, near the central square, authentic, full-flavored regional dishes are presented in a 19th-century house. It's decorated in (what else?) a typical Andalusian regional style. Under beamed ceilings, you sit at wooden tables on wooden chairs. Perhaps you'll begin with *Grazalema* (tomato) soup and follow with the delicious shredded veal with vegetables. Sea bass is perfectly sautéed and served with a mass of home-cut french fries. A signature dish is the oven-baked wild boar with spices. Prices are extremely reasonable considering the quality of the food and the generous portions.

Las Piedras 32. ✆ **95-613-20-14.** www.casadelaspiedras.net. Reservations recommended. Main courses 8€–23€. DC, MC, V. Sept–June Tues–Sun 1:30–3:30pm and 7:30–10pm; July–Aug daily 1:30–3:30pm and 7:30–10pm.

Gaucín

From Grazalema, take A-374 southwest to Ubrique. From here, get on A-373 south. The route will curve east to Cortez de la Frontera. Once you reach this town, continue along the same A-373 south to Algatocín. At this point, connect with the A-369 and follow it southwest until you connect with the A-377 into Gaucín (look for signs). Allow at least an hour for the 63km (39-mile) trip.

This whitewashed mountain town is perched on a ridge below a former Muslim fortress, which opens onto a panoramic vista of the countryside. Many expats—Brits in particular—live here.

At the eastern edge of the village, head up to the **Castillo del Aguila,** the Moorish castle. From its battlements, you can look out over the countryside and on a clear day see all the way to the Rock of Gibraltar. It's open daily from 11am to 1pm and 4 to 6pm. Admission is free.

The best place to stay and dine is **La Fructuosa,** Calle Convento 67, 29480 Gaucín (✆ **95-215-10-72;** fax 95-215-15-80; www.lafructuosa.com), in the center of Gaucín. Its bedrooms are simply but comfortably furnished, each with a tiled bathroom. Rooms go for 88€ to 98€ double. The hotel restaurant, serving meals for 18€, is open Wednesday to Saturday 8 to 10pm. The style of cooking is typically Andalusian, and portions are generous.

Jimena de la Frontera ★

To reach this white town from Gaucín, take the winding A-369 out of town, traveling southwest for some 30 minutes, a distance of 23km (14 miles). Enveloped by Los Alcornocales Natural Park, Jimena was built 200m (656 ft.) above sea level. It lies so close to San Roque on the Costa del Sol and its string of beaches that it gets a lot of visitors on day trips, especially from the exclusive golf and polo belt of the coast. Chic Sotorgrande, an upmarket resort, is just a short drive to the south.

You enter Jimena through a gateway of three arches. Over the years the town has known many rulers, from the Phoenicians and Romans to the Moors and ultimately the Christian armies.

It's a delight to walk the steep and narrow cobblestone streets of Jimena, one of the more stunning of the Pueblos Blancos. It takes about 15 minutes to ascend to the highest point, the castle-fortress built on Roman ruins. Today the **Castillo-Fortaleza** is in ruins but is still impressive. Inside the castle enclosure, you can take in one of the most panoramic **views** ★ of the Costa del Sol, including the Rock of Gibraltar and the port of Algeciras, where ferries depart for Morocco.

Visitors with more time will find that Jimena is the gateway to the **Parque Natural de los Alcornocales** ★★, stretching south to the Mediterranean and north to one of the white towns, El Bosque. The park is named for its cork oaks (*alcornocales*), which are among the largest in the world, but is also home to the gall and the holm oak as well as wild olive trees. Creatures such as the Egyptian mongoose, the royal eagle, eagle owls, lion buzzards, and the roebuck also inhabit the park. The park is one of the most heavily forested in Spain and will give you a sense of what Iberia used to look like before being deforested.

At one of the tourist offices in one of the Pueblos Blancos that actually has tourist offices, inquire about a booklet, *Junta de Andalucía,* detailing eight walks through the park, ranging from 2 to 7km (1¼–4⅓ miles).

WHERE TO DINE IN JIMENA DE LA FRONTERA

Restaurante El Anon INTERNATIONAL/ANDALUSIAN An American citizen, Suzana Odell, opened this place in 1979. Serving a savory and affordable cuisine, the restaurant lies in the Hostal El Anon, a series of small houses and stables blended seamlessly together. There is an inviting Andalusian courtyard along with a comfortable restaurant and a rooftop pool. The style is rustic with wooden furniture, antique ceramics, and copper ornaments. Parts of the building are 3 centuries old. Begin, perhaps, with the kidney pâté and follow with the freshly arrived catch of the day, hauled up from the Costa del Sol; many savvy locals prefer it just with olive oil and lemon. Local chicken is tantalizingly prepared with grapes, and a tender sirloin of beef appears on a platter with a blue-cheese sauce.

The *hostal's* 14 comfortably furnished **bedrooms** are priced at 65€ for a double, including breakfast.

Calle Consuelo 36. ✆ **95-664-01-13.** www.hostalanon.com. Reservations recommended. Main courses 13€–23€. DC, MC, V. Thurs–Tues 1–3:30pm and 8–11:30pm. Closed 2 weeks in late June.

Medina Sidonia

From Jimena, take C-333 northwest until you come to the junction with A-375 heading southwest to the junction with A-381. Once on A-381, continue northwest into Medina Sidonia. This 86km (53-mile) trip takes about an hour.

This village has seen better days, but wandering its cobbled and narrow streets is still an evocative experience, a bit like stepping back into the Middle Ages. Start at the central square, **Plaza de España.** The most impressive architecture here is the Renaissance facade of the 17th-century **Ayuntamiento (town hall).**

Nearby is the town's second-most-beautiful square, **Plaza Iglesia Mayor.** Here you can visit **Iglesia Santa María La Coronada,** open daily from 10am to 2pm and 4 to 8pm; admission is 2.50€. Built on the foundations of a former mosque, it is celebrated for its stunning *retablo* ★★, standing 15m (49 ft.) high. The *retablo* depicts scenes from the life of Jesus and is a piece of master work in polychrome wood achieved by the artisans of the Middle Ages.

After the church you can visit the **Roman Sewers** (www.medinasidonia.com), entered at Calle Ortega 10. They're open daily from 10am to 2pm and 4 to 8pm, and admission is 3€. The sewers date from the 1st century A.D. With the same ticket, you can also see the ruins of a well-preserved **Roman road** nearby.

More Moorish architecture is seen in a trio of gates, the best preserved of which is **Arco de la Pastora,** lying close to the Carretera de Jerez.

For information about the area, head to the local **tourist office,** Plaza Iglesia Mayor (© **95-641-24-04**), open daily from 10am to 2pm and 4 to 8pm.

If you find yourself in Media for lunch, consider stopping at **Venta La Duquesa** (© **95-641-08-36;** www.duquesa.com), lying along A-393 3km (1¾ miles) to the southeast. The food is good and well prepared, without rising to any spectacular heights. Try the loin of pork, which is well spiced and tasty, or a more local dish, partridge baked with onions and mushrooms. Main courses cost 12€ to 18€.

Vejer de la Frontera ★

From Medina Sidonia, follow the C-393 south to Vejer de la Frontera, a distance of 26km (16 miles), usually taking 20 minutes. This is one of the more dazzling Pueblos Blancos. Like most of the other towns we've visited, this Pueblo Blanco also reflects its Moorish history.

Vejer, still partially walled, lies in a deep cleft between two hills on the road between Tarifa (southernmost point in Spain) and the port of Cádiz, 10km (6¼ miles) inland. Dominated by its castle and a Gothic church, it looks like a town you'd find in the Greek islands.

For orientation, head to the **tourist office** at Calle Marqués de Tamarón 10 (© **95-645-01-91;** www.vejerdelafrontera.es). Hours are June to August Monday to Friday from 9am to 2pm and 6:30 to 8pm. In August it is also open on Saturday from 10:30am to 2pm. In other months, it keeps no set hours.

You can skip most of the monuments and simply enjoy the beauty of the town. Or else you can duck into **Iglesia del Divino Salvador,** the major church, lying in back of the tourist office. Its doors may or may not be open. It's a mix of styles, including Romanesque, Mudéjar, and Gothic.

Castillo Moro (the Moorish castle) is reached by heading down Calle Ramón y Cajal from the church. The castle keeps such erratic, changing hours it's best to inquire at the tourist office. Over the years it's been altered drastically, but as of 1000 B.C., it is known to have been some sort of fortress, standing watch over the fishing grounds and factories along the coast for the approach of an enemy vessel by sea. The site was also used by the Phoenicians and Carthaginians long before the coming of the Romans. Even if you can't see the castle, you can admire the **panoramic view ★**.

WHERE TO STAY & DINE IN VEJER DE LA FRONTERA

El Cobijo de Vejer This Moorish-style house with an Andalusian courtyard is a much-restored 250-year-old building. Its flower-filled patio is a delight, and it has individually decorated bedrooms that are midsize and vary in quality. The best units open onto vistas of the town and countryside. Each comes with a tiled bathroom with shower. Some of the accommodations also come with small kitchen units and private sitting rooms.

Calle San Filmo 7, 11150 Vejer de la Frontera. © **95-645-50-23.** Fax 95-645-17-20. www.elcobijo. com. 7 units. 60€–95€ double. Rates include continental breakfast. DC, MC, V. Free parking. *In room:* A/C, TV, fridge.

Hotel Convento de San Francisco ★ Once a convent for the Clarias order, this restored 17th-century structure is on the smaller of the town's two main

A plaza in Vejer de la Frontera.

squares. Within its intact, ancient stone walls, you'll enjoy the rustic charm and comfort provided by its antique furnishings. Bedrooms are midsize, and each is equipped with a small tiled bathroom. The former chapel holds a cafeteria serving one of the best breakfasts in town. The **restaurant** is also an excellent choice for regional specialties; a complete lunch or dinner costs 16€ to 25€.

La Plazuela, 11150 Vejer de la Frontera. **95-645-10-01.** Fax 95-645-10-04. www.tugasa.com. 25 units. 66€ double. AE, DC, MC, V. Free parking. **Amenities:** Restaurant; bar. *In room:* A/C, TV, hair dryer.

Continuing on to the Sherry Triangle

After your tour of Vejer, you can take N-340 northwest. At the junction with N-IV, continue northeast into Jerez de la Frontera. The distance from Vejer to Jerez is 62km (39 miles). The trip takes 45 minutes. Once in Jerez, you'll be in the center of the sherry-producing district of Andalusia, the Sherry Triangle.

Three cities make up this region: **Jerez de la Frontera** and the port cities of **El Puerto de Santa María** and **Sanlúcar de Barrameda.** If you have time to visit only one, make it Jerez because it has the best bodegas where you can see how sherry is produced and taste samples.

Jerez also gets the nod because it is a great equestrian center, known for its Carthusian horses, and it is also one of the best places to hear authentic flamenco.

Visitors flock to Sanlúcar de Barrameda for its beaches and also for its sherry bodegas. Those arriving at Puerto de Santa María find a dilapidated but intriguing little fishing port with lovely beaches nearby. Columbus once lived here. It deserves at least a day as you visit its sherry and brandy bodegas and sample its *marisco* (shellfish) bars along the water.

THE COSTA
DEL SOL

10

T he mild winter climate and almost-guaranteed summer sunshine have made this stretch of Mediterranean shoreline, known as the Costa del Sol, a year-round attraction. From the harbor city of Algeciras, it stretches east to the port city of Almería. You'll find poor to fair beaches, sandy coves, whitewashed houses, olive trees, lots of new apartment houses, fishing boats, golf courses, souvenir stands, fast-food outlets, and widely varied flora and fauna.

This coastal strip, quite frankly, no longer enjoys the chic reputation it had in Franco's day. It's overbuilt and spoiled, though you can still find pockets of posh (including **Puerto Banús,** with its yacht-clogged harbor). One advantage of the area is that, thanks to European Union money, it's easier to get around now than ever before. The infamous N-340 highway from Málaga to Estepona has become a fast, safe, six-lane road. (In days of yore, it was the most dangerous highway in Spain.)

For those traveling long distances along the coast, a new toll expressway with four lanes—called **Autopista del Sol**—has greatly relieved the traffic situation.

The coast is even better for **golf** than for beaches. The best resorts are **Los Monteros** (© 95-277-17-00; www.monteros.com), in Marbella, which has the leading course; **Hotel Atalaya Park,** in Estepona (© 95-288-90-00; www.atalaya-park.es); and **Golf Hotel Guadalmina,** in Marbella (© 95-288-22-11; www.hotelguadalmina.com). To learn more, pick up a copy of the monthly magazine *Costa Golf* at any newsstand. Many golfers prefer to play a different course at every hotel. Usually, if you notify your hotel reception desk a day in advance, a staff member will arrange a tee time.

Water-skiing and windsurfing are available in every resort, and all types of boats can be rented from kiosks at the main beaches. You don't have to search hard for these outfitters—chances are they'll find you.

From June to October the coast is mobbed, so make sure you have a reservation in advance. And keep in mind that October 12 is a national holiday—so make doubly sure of your reservations if you're coming then. At other times, innkeepers are likely to roll out the red carpet.

Many restaurants close around October 15 for a much-needed vacation. Remember, too, that many supermarkets and other facilities are closed on Sunday.

ALGECIRAS

679km (422 miles) S of Madrid, 132km (82 miles) W of Málaga

Not really a destination in and of itself, Algeciras is the jumping-off point for Africa—it's only 3 hours to Tangier, Morocco. If you're planning an excursion, there's an inexpensive baggage-storage depot at the ferry terminal. Algeciras is also a base for day trips to **Gibraltar.** For information, check with the Gibraltar

Tourist Office, Casemates Square (© **0035/074-950**). It's open Monday to Friday from 9am to 4:30pm, Saturday from 10am to 3pm, and Sunday from 10am to 1pm. If you don't have time to visit "the Rock," you can at least see it from Algeciras—it's only 10km (6¼ miles) away.

Sailing past the rock of Gibraltar.

Essentials

GETTING THERE The local RENFE office is at Calle Juan de la Cierva (© **90-224-02-02**; www.renfe. es). From Madrid, two **trains** daily make the 5½-hour trip; the fare is 66€. From Málaga, you have to transfer in Bobadilla; the fare is 20€. The trip takes 4 hours and 50 minutes and runs along most of the Costa del Sol, including Marbella and Torremolinos.

Various independent **bus companies** serve Algeciras. **Empresa Portillo,** Calle San Bernardo 1 (© **90-214-31-44;** www.ctsa-portillo. com), 1½ blocks to the right when you exit the port complex, runs nearly 20 buses a day along the Costa del Sol to Algeciras from Málaga. It also sends six buses a day to Córdoba (trip time: 6 hr.) and two buses a day to Granada (trip time: 5 hr.). To make connections to or from Seville, use **Line Sur,** Calle San Bernardo s/n (© **95-498-82-22;** www.linesur.com). Eight buses a day go to Jerez de la Frontera, and 11 to Seville. **Transportes Generales Comes,** Calle San Bernardo 1 (© **90-219-92-08;** www.tgcomes.es), sells tickets to **La Línea,** the border station for the approach to Gibraltar.

Most visitors in Algeciras plan to cross to Tangier, Morocco. **Ferries** leave every hour on the hour daily from 6am to 10pm. A ticket costs 37€ per person. To transport a car costs 125€. The trip takes 1½ hours. *Tip:* An express service that runs four times a day 6am to 6:30pm and takes only 30 minutes costs the same as the regular ferry. For more information, contact **Acciona Trasmediterránea** (© **90-245-46-45;** www.trasmediterranea. es). There's an inexpensive, secured baggage storage depot at the ferry terminal if you want to store your things.

Carretera de Cádiz (E-15/N-340) runs from Málaga west to Algeciras. If you're driving south from Seville (or Madrid), take highway N-IV to Cádiz, and then connect with the N-340/E-5 southwest to Algeciras.

VISITOR INFORMATION The **tourist office** at Juan de la Cierva (© **95-678-41-31;** www.andalucia.org) is open Monday to Friday 9am to 7:30pm, Saturday and Sunday 9:30am to 3pm.

Where to Stay in Algeciras

AC Algeciras ★ ✦ Algeciras has a lot of seedy joints where you can lay your head. This newly constructed hotel isn't one of them. It's the most modern and

The Costa del Sol

up-to-date in town. In front of the Puerto Marítimo, it lies only 1km (⅔ mile) from the city center. The rooms are severe-modern yet comfortable, and the hotel is well maintained. Accommodations are midsize to spacious, with large agreeable bathrooms. Most of the rooms open onto panoramic views of Gibraltar. The decorator of this hotel was in love with chocolate. Most guests are in Algeciras just to wait for the ferry to Tangier.

Calle Hermanos Portilla s/n, 11204 Algeciras. ✆ **95-663-50-60.** Fax 95-663-30-61. www.ac-hotels.com. 108 units. 70€–112€ double; 104€–126€ suite. AE, DC, MC, V. Parking 13€. **Amenities:** Restaurant; babysitting; exercise room; room service; sauna; Wi-Fi (free, in lobby). *In room:* A/C, TV, hair dryer, minibar.

Hotel Al-Mar ★ The government-rated three-star Al-Mar is one of the best choices in town, with renovated rooms and good, continual maintenance of the property. It's near the port, where the ferries leave for Ceuta and Tangier. This large hotel boasts blue-and-white Sevillian and Moorish decor. The midsize guest rooms are well maintained, furnished in an Andalusian style, with good beds and bathrooms with tub/shower combos. A fourth-floor drawing room provides a panoramic view of the Rock.

Av. de la Marina 2–3, 11201 Algeciras. ✆ **95-665-46-61.** Fax 95-665-45-01. www.hotelalmar.com. 192 units. 87€–94€ double; 88€–95€ suite. Rates include buffet breakfast. AE, DC, MC, V. Parking 7.50€. **Amenities:** Restaurant; bar; Wi-Fi (free, in lobby). *In room:* A/C, TV.

beaches: **THE GOOD, THE BAD & THE UGLY**

We'd like to report that the Costa del Sol is a paradise for swimmers. Surprisingly, it isn't, although it was the allure of beaches that originally put the "sol" in the Costa del Sol beginning in the 1950s.

The worst beaches—mainly pebbles and shingles—are at Nerja, Málaga, and Almuñécar. Moving westward, you encounter the gritty, grayish sands of Torremolinos. The best beaches here are at El Bajondillo and La Carihuela (which borders an old fishing village). Another good stretch of beach is along the meandering strip between Carvajal, Los Boliches, and Fuengirola. In addition, two good beaches—El Fuerte and La Fontanilla—lie on either side of Marbella. However, all these beaches tend to be overcrowded, especially in July and August. Crowding is worst on Sundays, May through October, when beaches are overrun with family picnickers as well as sunbathers.

All public beaches in Spain are free. Don't expect changing facilities—there might be cold showers on the major beaches, but that's it.

Although it's not sanctioned or technically allowed by the govern- ment, many women go topless on the beaches. If you indulge, you will be subject to arrest by the Guardia Civil. If you want to bare it all, head for the Costa Natura, about 3km (1¾ miles) west of Estepona. This is the site of the only official nudist colony along the Costa del Sol.

Hotel Reina Cristina ★ In its own park on the southern outskirts of the city (a 10-min. walk south of the rail and bus stations), this is the town's leading hotel, having hosted over the years everyone from Sir Winston Churchill to Cole Porter, along with a lot of World War II spies. A Victorian building accented with turrets, ornate railings, and a facade painted with pastels, the Reina Cristina offers a view of the faraway Rock of Gibraltar. On the premises are a small English-language library and a semitropical garden. The comfortable, high-ceilinged rooms have excellent furnishings, including comfortable beds and bathrooms.

Paseo de la Conferencia s/n, 11207 Algeciras. © **95-660-26-22.** Fax 95-660-33-23. www. reinacristina.es. 188 units. 70€–150€ double. Rates include buffet breakfast. AE, DC, MC, V. Free parking. **Amenities:** Restaurant; 2 bars; exercise room; 2 freshwater pools (1 heated indoor, 1 outdoor); room service; sauna; 2 outdoor tennis courts; Wi-Fi (free, in lobby). *In room:* A/C, TV, hair dryer (in some).

Where to Dine in Algeciras

Because Algeciras is not distinguished for its restaurants, many visitors dine at their hotels instead of taking a chance at the dreary little spots along the waterfront.

Montes SPANISH/ANDALUSIAN This is no more than a little portside eatery, but it's the most popular and the most serviceable joint in town. Throughout the afternoon and deep into the night, the casual diner is filled with foreign travelers, most of whom are either returning from or going to Morocco on one of the fer- ries. You can fill up on nearly 30 varieties of freshly made tapas, most of them fish or vegetable based. The fresh catch of the day is always featured on the menu, usually fried, although it can be stewed. One of the chef's specialties is a very filling paella studded with shellfish. Among the meat dishes, the baby beef roast is the perennial favorite.

Calle Juan Morrison 27. ℭ **95-665-42-07.** Main courses 12€–18€. AE, DC, MC, V. Daily noon–5pm and 7pm–midnight.

ESTEPONA

85km (53 miles) W of Málaga, 639km (397 miles) S of Madrid, 46km (29 miles) E of Algeciras

A town of Roman origin, Estepona is a budding beach resort, less developed than Marbella or Torremolinos and more likable for that reason. Estepona contains an interesting 15th-century parish church, with the ruins of an old aqueduct nearby (at Salduba). Its recreational port is an attraction, as are its **beaches:** Costa Natura, N-340 Km 257, the first legal nude beach of its kind along the Costa del Sol; La Rada, 3km (1¾ miles) long; and El Cristo, only 550m (1,804 ft.) long. After the sun goes down, stroll along the Paseo Marítimo, a broad avenue with gardens on one side, beach on the other.

In summer, the cheapest places to eat in Estepona are the *chiringuitos,* little dining areas set up by local fishers and their families right on the beach. Naturally they feature seafood, including sole and sardine kabobs grilled over an open fire. You can usually order a fresh salad and fried potatoes; desserts are simple.

After your siesta, head for the tapas bars. You'll find most of them—called *freidurías* (fried-fish bars)—at the corner of Calle de los Reyes and La Terraza. Tables spill onto the sidewalks in summer. *Gambas a la plancha* (shrimp) are the favorite (but not the cheapest) tapas to order.

A beachside market in Estepona.

Essentials

GETTING THERE The nearest rail links are in Fuenginola. However, Estepona is on the **bus** route from Algeciras to Málaga. If you're driving, head east from Algeciras along the E-5/N-340.

VISITOR INFORMATION The **tourist office,** Av. San Lorenzo 1 (✆ **95-280-20-02;** www.estepona.es), is open Monday to Friday 9am to 8pm, Saturday 10am to 1:30pm.

Where to Stay in Estepona

Estepona is known for having some of the most expensive and most luxurious resorts along the coast.

VERY EXPENSIVE

Kempinski Hotel Bahía Estepona ★★★ ☺ One of the most luxurious retreats in this part of the Costa del Sol, this modern resort hotel allows you to enjoy a lush, elegant lifestyle. Between the main coastal route and the beach, the Kempinski borrowed heavily from nearby Morocco to create this oasis of charm and grace with hanging gardens adding a dramatic touch. A member of the Leading Hotels of the World, the property opens onto beautifully landscaped and luxuriant palm-studded gardens fronting the ocean. Bedrooms are airy and spacious, with balconies or private terraces overlooking the sea. After a multimillion-dollar renovation, the rooms and suites now have exquisite interiors with warm tones and state-of-the-art amenities.

Carretera de Cádiz Km 159, Playa el Padrón, 29680 Estepona. ✆ **95-280-95-00.** Fax 95-280-95-50. www.kempinski-spain.com. 148 units. 180€–440€ double; 400€–700€ junior suite; from 700€ suite. AE, DC, MC, V. Free parking outside; 12€ garage. **Amenities:** 4 restaurants; 3 bars; babysitting; children's center; concierge; exercise room; 4 pools (1 heated indoor); room service; spa; outdoor unlit tennis court; extensive watersports equipment/rentals. *In room:* A/C, TV, hair dryer, minibar, Wi-Fi (20€ per 24 hr.).

Las Dunas ★★★ One of the Costa del Sol's great resorts, Las Dunas attracts fashionable Europeans looking to be pampered. Site of a world-class spa, this five-star government-rated hotel is constructed in a U-shape, evocative of a gigantic hacienda. It stands in the midst of gardens and fountains; regrettably, the beach nearby is mediocre. Suites outnumber standard doubles, and most units have balconies overlooking the Mediterranean. All are sumptuously comfortable and equipped with roomy bathrooms. You'll find one of the Costa del Sol's best restaurants here (see "El Lido," below).

Urbanización La Boladilla Baja-Noreste, Carretera de Cádiz Km 163.5, 29689 Estepona. ✆ **95-280-94-00.** Fax 95-280-94-06. www.las-dunas.com. 88 units. 470€–720€ junior suite; from 570€ suite. Rates include buffet breakfast. AE, DC, MC, V. Free parking. **Amenities:** 3 restaurants; bar; babysitting; bikes; concierge; health club; 2 outdoor pools; room service; spa; limited watersports equipment rental. *In room:* A/C, TV (TV/DVD in some), CD player in some, hair dryer, minibar, movie library, Wi-Fi (free).

EXPENSIVE

Atalaya Park Golf Hotel & Resort ★★ ☺ Midway between Estepona and Marbella, this modern resort complex attracts sports and nature lovers. Its tranquil beachside location sits amid 8 hectares (20 acres) of subtropical gardens. Spacious rooms, furnished in elegant modern style, are well maintained and inviting. Guests have complimentary use of the hotel's extensive sports facilities, including two magnificent golf courses. Many northern Europeans check in and almost never leave the grounds.

Carretera de Cádiz Km 168.5, 29688 Estepona. **☎ 95-288-90-00.** Fax 95-288-90-02. www. atalaya-park.es. 475 units. 121€–284€ double; 168€–320€ suite; 500€ bungalow. Rates include buffet breakfast. AE, DC, MC, V. Free parking. **Amenities:** 3 restaurants; 3 bars; babysitting; bikes; children's center; exercise room; 2 18-hole golf courses; 6 freshwater pools (2 heated indoor); room service; sauna; 9 outdoor tennis courts (6 lit); extensive watersports equipment/ rentals; Wi-Fi (free, in lobby). *In room:* A/C, TV, hair dryer, minibar.

MODERATE

El Paraíso Costa del Sol ★ The impressive El Paraíso Costa del Sol is the leading moderately priced establishment in town. Located between Marbella and Estepona in front of Costalita Beach, this modern building, constructed in the 1980s, is 12km (7½ miles) from the center of Estepona. The most notable element of the bedrooms is that they open onto balconies fronting the Mediterranean. Otherwise, expect midsize to fairly spacious accommodations furnished in a typical resort style—comfortable but not special. Guests can indulge in many activities in the area, including golf nearby. The best feature here is the panoramic bar on the seventh floor with a nudist sunning terrace. The hotel also has a children's play area, although it's hardly a reason to check in if you have kids.

Urbanización El Paraíso, Noreste, Carretera de Cádiz Km 167, 29688 Estepona. **☎ 800/465-9936** in the U.S., or 95-288-30-00. Fax 95-288-20-19. www.hoteltrhparaisocostadelsol.com. 176 units. 125€–185€ double; 205€–265€ suite. AE, DC, MC, V. Free parking. **Amenities:** 2 restaurants; 4 bars; babysitting; Jacuzzi; 2 freshwater pools (1 heated indoor); room service; sauna; Wi-Fi (free, in lobby). *In room:* A/C, TV, hair dryer, minibar.

INEXPENSIVE

Buenavista This comfortable if modest little *residencia* beside the coastal road opened in the 1970s. The tiny rooms are likely to be noisy in summer because of heavy traffic nearby. Beds are comfortable but the bathrooms are small yet neat. Buses from Marbella stop nearby.

Av. de España 180, 29680 Estepona. **☎ 95-280-01-37.** Fax 95-280-55-93. www.buena vistaestepona.com. 38 units. 50€–70€ double. DC, MC, V. *In room:* TV.

Where to Dine in Estepona

El Lido ★★★ INTERNATIONAL In the deluxe Las Dunas hotel (see above) you'll find one of the grandest and most elegant restaurants along the Costa del Sol. Panoramic views, a mammoth crystal chandelier, and romantic piano tunes set the tone at this octagonal restaurant with floor-to-ceiling windows opening onto a sheltered terrace. Expect nothing but culinary delights on the ever-changing menu. Some of the dishes evoke the Pacific Rim; others draw upon inspiration from Europe. Only the finest products are used: duck from Nantes, lamb from Provence, beef and veal from Spain's Basque Country, or tender and delectable chicken from Bresse (in our view, Europe's best). Picture it: sea bass carpaccio in a basil vinaigrette, fresh lobster in delicate saffron sauce, veal sweetbreads with *fines herbes*.

Urbanización La Boladilla Baja-Noreste, Carretera de Cádiz Km 163.5. **☎ 95-280-94-00.** Reservations recommended. Main courses 20€–42€. AE, DC, MC, V. Tues–Sat 1:30–4pm and 8–11pm. Closed mid-Jan to mid-Feb.

La Alcaría de Ramos ★ 🎁 SPANISH This country retreat has been decorated in the style of an old summer house along the Spanish coast. There's a beautiful terrace garden where customers may dine as weather permits. The chef and owner, José Ramos, has won many national gastronomic competitions and has been creating intriguing variations on traditional recipes since the early 1990s. He will regale you with such dishes as *tortas de patatas* (potato cakes—yes, potato cakes, and how good they are!). Try also his *crepes de aguacate con gambas* (avocado crepes with shrimp) and his *pato asado con puré de manzana y col roja* (grilled duck with apple purée and red cabbage).

Urbanización El Paraíso Vista al Mar 1, N-340 Km 167. 📞 **95-288-61-78.** www.laalcariaderamos. es. Reservations recommended. Main courses 15€–25€. MC, V. Mon–Sat 7:30pm–midnight.

PUERTO BANÚS

8km (5 miles) E of Marbella, 782km (486 miles) S of Madrid

A favorite resort for international celebrities, the coastal village of Puerto Banús was created almost overnight in the traditional Mediterranean style. It's a dreamy place, the very image of what a Costa del Sol fishing village should look like but rarely does. Yachts can be moored nearly at your doorstep. Along the harborfront you'll find an array of expensive bars and restaurants. Wandering through the quiet back streets, you'll pass archways and patios with grilles.

To reach the town, you can take one of 15 buses that run daily from Marbella, or you can drive east from Marbella along the E-15.

Where to Stay in Puerto Banús

H10 Andalucía Plaza ★★ A 1970s structure that was looking tired has been given a complete makeover, emerging as a true 21st-century hotel with a lot of eco-minded upgrades such as solar panels and keycard-activated electricity. The hotel also has been restylized and made more glamorous opposite the Puerto Banús marina. Today the stunning modern decor is avant-garde, with decorative

The chic harbor at Puerto Banús.

elements ranging from silver-and-gold-accented walls to oversize portraits of models and movie stars such as Marilyn Monroe. We prefer the rooms in the West Wing, which have been renovated the most. Here you'll find underground bedrooms that have a modern, stylized decor and come in a wide range: from standard and superior doubles to standard and superior junior suites. Guests have free admission to the Marbella Casino next to the hotel. An underground walkway cuts under the busy streets and puts you on the beach after a 10-minute walk.

Urbanización Nueva Andalucía, Puerto Banús, 29600 Marbella. © **95-281-20-00.** Fax 95-281-47-92. www.h10hotels.com. 400 units. 101€–135€ double; 160€–415€ junior suite. Free parking. **Amenities:** 2 restaurants; 2 bars; exercise room; 3 pools (1 indoor); room service; spa; Wi-Fi (free, in lobby). *In room:* A/C, TV, hair dryer, minibar.

Park Plaza Suites Hotel ★ Yachties often stay here when they need a break from their boat. This sleekly modern hotel lies near the harbor, offering elegant accommodations in spacious double rooms or in glamorous but expensive suites. The rooms are attractively and comfortably furnished. Many restaurants and nightclubs are accessible from here.

Paseo Marítimo de Benabola, 29660 Puerto Banús. © **95-290-90-00.** Fax 95-281-28-46. www.parkplazasuiteshotel.com. 50 units. 194€–377€ double; 264€–713€ suite. Rates include buffet breakfast. DC, MC, V. Parking 24€. **Amenities:** Restaurant; bar; exercise room; Jacuzzi; room service; Wi-Fi (free, in lobby). *In room:* A/C, TV, hair dryer, minibar.

Where to Dine in Puerto Banús

Antonio ★ SEAFOOD/INTERNATIONAL There's no better place to sit and watch Puerto Banús's chic port life than this longtime favorite. Opt for a table on the terrace (if the weather's right) and watch a parade of beautiful people who believe in traveling the world in style.

The first-class cuisine here lives up to the setting, which has lots of modern paintings on the wall, an abundance of greenery, and predominant decorative colors of black and white. The chef, Juan Trujillo, knows how to balance colors, textures, and flavors, creating such delicious fare as the best filet mignon we've tasted in the area, well-flavored pork chops with fries and vegetables, and a tender, moist loin of veal. Paella is big here, as is fried fish, which usually consists of sprats, squid, mullet, and whitebait, all of it deep-fried and served with pink sauce, tartar sauce, or peppery mayonnaise (whichever you prefer). Platters of this deep-fried fish are especially good when accompanied with roasted peppers and onions, served cold with vinaigrette, as a cold salad.

Muelle de Ribera. © **95-281-35-36.** Reservations required. Main courses 25€–34€. AE, DC, MC, V. Daily 1–4pm and 7:30–11pm (until 12:30am Aug–Sept).

Dalli's Pasta Factory 🦪 PASTA The meals here, consisting of pasta, pasta, and more pasta served with garlic bread and a carafe of house wine, are a great bargain in pricey Puerto Banús. In a setting that's a cross between high-tech and Art Deco, you can order nutmeg-flavored ravioli with spinach filling, *penne all'arrabbiata,* lasagna, and several kinds of spaghetti. More filling are the chicken cacciatore and scaloppine of chicken and veal. They are served with—guess what?—a side dish of pasta. The owners, incidentally, are a trio of Roman-born brothers who were reared in England and educated in California.

Muelle de Rivera. © **95-281-86-23.** Pastas 10€–18€; meat platters 16€–24€. AE, MC, V. Daily 1:30–4pm and 7pm–midnight.

MARBELLA ★

60km (37 miles) W of Málaga, 45km (28 miles) W of Torremolinos, 80km (50 miles) E of Gibraltar, 76km (47 miles) E of Algeciras, 600km (373 miles) S of Madrid

Although it's packed with tourists and only slightly less popular than Torremolinos, Marbella is still the nicest resort town along the Costa del Sol, with some of the region's best upscale resorts coexisting with budget hotels. Despite the hordes, Marbella remains what it always has been, a pleasant Andalusian town at the foot of the Sierra Blanca. Traces of its past survive in its palatial town hall, medieval ruins, and ancient Moorish walls. Marbella's most charming area is the **Old Quarter** of narrow cobblestone streets and Moorish houses centered on Plaza de los Naranjos.

The biggest attractions in Marbella, however, are **El Fuerte** and **La Fontanilla,** the two main beaches. There are other, more secluded beaches, but you need your own transportation to get there. A long-ago visitor, Queen Isabella, is said to have exclaimed, *"¡Qué mar tan bello!"* ("What a beautiful sea!"), and the name stuck.

Essentials

GETTING THERE The main **bus** link is between Málaga and Marbella, with the **Empresa Portillo** (✆ 90-214-31-44; www.ctsa-portillo.com) running 14 buses a day. The trip takes 1 hour and 25 minutes and costs 5.15€ one-way. Madrid and Barcelona each have three daily buses to Marbella. The bus station is located on the outskirts of Marbella on Avenida Trapiche, a 5-minute ride from the center of town.

If you're driving, Marbella is the first major resort as you head east on the N-340/E-15 from Algeciras.

VISITOR INFORMATION The **tourist office,** Glorieta de la Fontanilla s/n (✆ 95-277-14-42; www.marbella.es), is open Monday to Friday 9:30am to 9pm, Saturday 10am to 2pm. Another tourist office with the same hours is on the Plaza de los Naranjos (✆ 95-277-46-93).

Shopping

Some other Andalusian village may inspire you to buy handicrafts (particularly pottery, woodcarvings, or wrought iron), but Marbella's international glamour might incite in you so much insecurity about your wardrobe that you'll want to rush out to accessorize. Should you suddenly feel underdressed, head for Old Town, where there are many fashion outlets.

If art is your passion, tour the galleries that pepper the town. You'll spot high-rolling investors picking up contemporary treasures on shopping sprees. One of Marbella's most appealing art galleries lies in the Old Town: **Galleria d'Arte Van Gestel,** Plaza General Franco 11 (✆ 95-277-48-19). And if your search for fine art carries over to **Puerto Banús,** consider the contemporary artwork displayed at **Sammer Gallery,** Av. de Julio Iglesias 3, Las Terrazas de Banús, Local 10–16 (✆ 95-281-29-95). If you'd like to purchase some of Andalusia's regional ceramics, your best bet is **Cerámica San Nicolás,** Plaza de la Iglesia 1 (✆ 95-277-05-46).

On Saturday morning, forget the shops and head with the locals to **Nueva Andalucía flea market.** Everything is likely to be on sale, from Spanish leather goods to local pottery and embroideries.

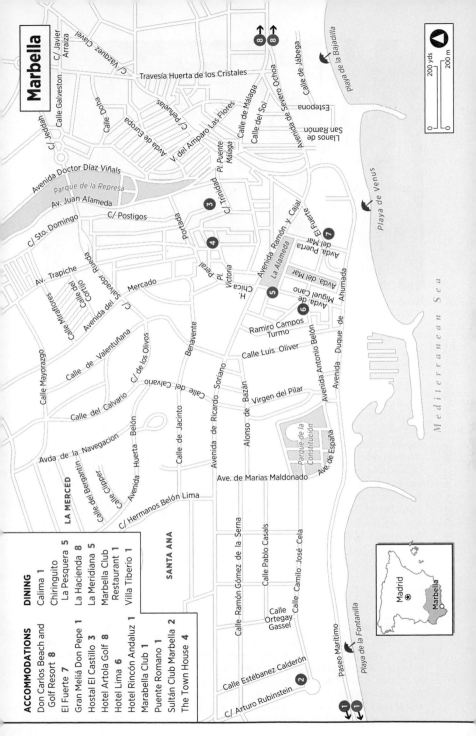

Marbella

ACCOMMODATIONS
Don Carlos Beach and
Golf Resort **8**
El Fuerte **7**
Gran Meliá Don Pepe **1**
Hostal El Castillo **3**
Hotel Artola Golf **8**
Hotel Lima **6**
Hotel Rincón Andaluz **1**
Marbella Club **1**
Puente Romano **1**
Sultán Club Marbella **2**
The Town House **4**

DINING
Calima **1**
Chiringuito
La Pesquera **5**
La Hacienda **8**
La Meridiana **5**
Marbella Club
Restaurant **1**
Villa Tiberio **1**

Mediterranean Sea

Madrid
Marbella

200 yds
200 m

Marbella's beachside promenade.

Where to Stay in Marbella

Because the setting is ideal, some of the best hotels along the Costa del Sol are in Marbella.

VERY EXPENSIVE

Marbella Club ★★★ This is the grande dame of all Costa del Sol resorts. Until a few equally chic hotels were built along the Costa del Sol, the snobbish Marbella Club reigned almost without equal as the exclusive hangout of aristocrats and tycoons. Established in 1954, the resort sprawls over a landscaped property that slopes from its roadside reception area down to the private beach. Composed of small, ecologically friendly clusters of garden pavilions, bungalows, and small-scale annexes, the Marbella Club has some of the loveliest gardens along the coast. Hotel rooms along the Costa del Sol don't come much better than these varied and spacious choices, often with canopy beds. Rooms have private balconies or terraces. The clientele is discreet, international, elegant, and appreciative of the resort's small scale and superb service.

Bulevar Príncipe Alfonso von Hohenlohe, 29600 Marbella. ⓒ **800/448-8355** in the U.S., or 95-282-22-11. Fax 95-282-98-84. www.marbellaclub.com. 121 units. 290€–920€ double; from 410€ suite. AE, DC, MC, V. Free parking. **Amenities:** 2 restaurants; bar; babysitting; bikes; concierge; 18-hole golf course; 3 pools (1 indoor); room service; state-of-the-art spa. *In room:* A/C, TV, hair dryer, minibar, Wi-Fi (free).

Puente Romano ★★ Devotees rank this resort right up there with the Marbella Club, but we'll give it the runner-up prize. This hotel was originally built as a cluster of vacation apartments, which influenced the attention to detail and the surrounding landscaping. In the early 1970s, a group of entrepreneurs transformed it into one of the most unusual hotels in the south of Spain. Although it sits close to the frenetic coastal highway midway between Marbella and Puerto Banús, and some critics have dismissed it as "more flash than class," it still enjoys a loyal following. Inside the complex, arbor-covered walkways lead past cascading water, masses of vines, and a subtropical garden. The spacious Andalusian-Mediterranean accommodations have semisheltered balconies.

Carretera de Cádiz Km 177, 29600 Marbella. *☎* **95-282-09-00.** Fax 95-277-57-66. www. puenteromano.com. 285 units. 227€–426€ double; from 406€ suite. AE, DC, MC, V. Limited free parking. **Amenities:** 3 restaurants; 2 bars; babysitting; children's center; concierge; 18-hole golf course (nearby); state-of-the-art health club; 3 outdoor freshwater pools; room service; sauna; 10 outdoor tennis courts (lit); extensive watersports equipment/rentals. *In room:* A/C, TV, DVD player (in some), CD player (in some), hair dryer, minibar, Wi-Fi (19€ per 24 hr.).

EXPENSIVE

Don Carlos Beach and Golf Resort ★★★ One of the most dramatic hotels on the coast, the Don Carlos rises on a set of angled stilts above a pine forest. Between the hotel and its manicured beach—the best in Marbella—are 4 hectares (9¾ acres) of award-winning gardens. With cascades of water and thousands of subtropical plants, they require a full-time staff of 22 gardeners. The hotel's low-lying terraces attract high-powered conferences from throughout Europe. Each of the roomy accommodations has lacquered furniture.

Carretera de Cádiz Km 192, 29604 Marbella. *☎* **95-276-88-00.** Fax 95-283-34-29. www.hotel-doncarlos.com. 243 units. 144€–392€ double; 293€–1,094€ suite. Rates include buffet breakfast. AE, DC, MC, V. Free parking. **Amenities:** 2 restaurants; 2 bars; babysitting; exercise room; 2 outdoor freshwater pools; room service; spa; 12 outdoor tennis courts (lit). *In room:* A/C, TV, CD player, hair dryer, minibar, movie library, Wi-Fi (15€ per 24 hr.).

El Fuerte ★★ ☺ We'd give the edge to Gran Meliá Don Pepe (see below), but of the hotels within Marbella proper, this resort is in a neck-to-neck race for supremacy with the similarly named Fuerte Miramar. Fronting a good sandy beach, the hotel opened back in Marbella's jet-setting heyday. It is surrounded by some of the best-maintained and most beautiful hotel gardens along the coast. Decorators have been busy here, matching the draperies and adding splashes of color in the various wallpapers. There is lush carpeting, creamy tones, and much use of comfortable wooden furniture. Rooms, for the most part, are midsize, although some are spacious. A **beach restaurant** specializes in grilled fish based on the catch of the day. The staff here is helpful, and the amenities are excellent.

Av. del Fuerte, 29600 Marbella. *☎* **800/448-8355** in the U.S., or 95-286-15-00. Fax 95-282-44-11. www.fuertehoteles.com. 263 units. 101€–342€ double; from 220€ suite. AE, DC, MC, V. Parking 10€. **Amenities:** 2 restaurants; bar; airport transfers; babysitting; 18-hole golf course (nearby); health club; 2 freshwater pools (1 heated indoor); room service; sauna; outdoor tennis court (lit). *In room:* A/C, TV, hair dryer, minibar, Wi-Fi (in some; 12€ per 24 hr.).

Gran Meliá Don Pepe ★★ Located on the beach a short stroll from the town center, this chain-run hotel is one of Marbella's best resorts, offering taste, elegance, and grand comfort. The hotel is known for its spacious, beautiful rooms opening onto views of the Mediterranean, as well as for its tropical gardens and fine dining. Most of the accommodations have a terrace or balcony with a sea view. At night, the hotel features shows and live music—often flamenco. Guests get free entrance to the Casino de Marbella.

José Meliá, 29602 Marbella. *☎* **95-277-03-00.** Fax 95-277-99-54. www.solmelia.com. 201 units. 143€–480€ double; from 512€ suite. AE, DC, MC, V. Parking 20€. **Amenities:** 4 restaurants; 2 bars; babysitting; bikes; small health club; Jacuzzi; 3 pools (1 heated indoor); room service; sauna; 2 outdoor tennis courts (lit); Wi-Fi (4€ per hour, in lobby). *In room:* A/C, TV, hair dryer, kitchenette (in some), minibar.

Sultán Club Marbella ★ On the outskirts of Marbella a 10-minute drive from the center, this apartment-hotel is in the residential district of Milla de Oro, just a short walk to the beach. It opened in 1997 and is meant to evoke luxury living such as the sultans of old enjoyed. The interior brims with tropical plants and fountains. The apartments contain one or two bedrooms, each with a large balcony, a small dining room, and a fully equipped kitchen.

Calle Arturo Rubinstein, 29600 Marbella. ✆ **95-277-15-62.** Fax 95-277-55-58. www.monarquehoteles.es. 76 units. 107€–255€ 1-bedroom apt.; 136€–321€ 2-bedroom apt. AE, DC, MC, V. Parking 15€. **Amenities:** Restaurant; bar; babysitting; exercise room; 2 freshwater heated pools (1 indoor); room service; spa; Wi-Fi (free, in lobby). *In room:* A/C, TV, hair dryer.

Vincci Selección Estrella del Mar ★★★ A sumptuous retreat for the hedonist, this deluxe hotel lies outside Marbella in a tony section known as Elvira-Las Chapas, which is near one of the best beaches along the Costa del Sol. It lies 8km (5 miles) from the center of Marbella and is built in a modern Mediterranean style that shows a distinct Arab influence. The resort complex is graced with gardens and fountains studded with pine trees and a quartet of swimming pools.

Unlike many hotels along the coast that are indistinguishable, this one is imbued with a unique character. The decorative objects came from Lebanon, Egypt, and India, and are combined with Art Deco elements along with ornamental tiles. Bedrooms are spacious and furnished with great modern style, using for the most part canopied beds. The superior doubles contain a sitting-room area with a sofa or two armchairs. All the rooms have a large terrace opening onto the sea.

Urbanización Estrella del Mar, A-7 Km 190.5, 29604 Marbella. ✆ **95-105-39-70.** Fax 95-105-39-80. www.vinccihoteles.com. 137 units. 140€–208€ double; 265€–525€ suite. AE, DC, MC, V. Free parking. **Amenities:** 3 restaurants; 2 bars; babysitting; bike rentals; exercise room; 4 outdoor pools; room service; water sports (rentals). *In room:* A/C, TV, hair dryer, minibar, Wi-Fi (free).

MODERATE

Hotel Artola Golf ★ Located between Fuengirola and Marbella, .8km (½ mile) from the beach, this charming place was originally an old staging post for travelers en route to Gibraltar. In the 1970s it was converted into an inn. The architecture is typically Andalusian, with a stucco-and-wood facade under a terra-cotta roof. A garden and patio surround the building. The interior has retained some of its historical aura with colorful tiles plus decorative wooden wall panels and beams. The midsize rooms are comfortably furnished and tastefully decorated, often with Moorish details.

Carretera de Cádiz Km 194, 29600 Marbella. ✆ **95-283-13-90.** Fax 95-283-04-50. www.hotelartola.com. 31 units. 90€–115€ double; 140€–165€ suite. AE, MC, V. Free parking. **Amenities:** Restaurant; bar; babysitting; 9-hole golf course; outdoor pool; room service; Wi-Fi (free, in lobby). *In room:* A/C (in some), TV.

Hotel Rincón Andaluz ★ ☺ In a stylish area of Marbella 1km (⅔ mile) from Puerto Banús, this government-rated four-star hotel is meant to evoke a *pueblo andaluz* (Andalusian village). The resort lies only 500m (1,640 ft.) from a good beach. Located in a park, the low-level, rustic-style buildings form an ideal retreat. The large rooms are tastefully decorated and fully equipped, and all units have at least a small living room (those in the suites are larger). Ground-floor rooms have direct access to the gardens; others open onto balconies.

Carretera de Cádiz Km 173, 29660 Marbella. © **95-281-15-17.** Fax 95-281-41-80. www.hotel rinconandaluz.com. 315 units. 60€–140€ double; from 210€ suite. Rates include buffet breakfast. AE, DC, MC, V. Free parking. **Amenities:** Restaurant; 2 bars; children's center; 3 freshwater outdoor pools (1 heated); room service; Wi-Fi (free, in lobby). *In room:* A/C, TV, hair dryer, minibar.

The Town House ★★ 👪 Deep in the heart of Old Town, this former private home has been tastefully converted into the town's most romantic-looking boutique hotel. Of all the hotels in Marbella, this one comes the closest to evoking life in a private town house from yesterday, yet it has been completely modernized with today's comforts. The day begins with morning coffee on the roof terrace and comes to an end with a cold drink, perhaps a cocktail, on that same terrace as the sun sets. The house lies some 300m (984 ft.) from the boardwalk along the beach (which extends all the way to Puerto Banús, incidentally). The midsize bedrooms were designed with exquisite care, with antique objects combined with contemporary design. Some of the objects you might admire, such as candleholders or pictures, can be purchased.

Plaza Tetuán, Calle Alderete 7, 29600 Marbella. © /fax **95-290-17-91.** www.townhouse.nu. 9 units. 110€–130€ double. MC, V. **Amenities:** Bar; room service. *In room:* A/C, TV.

INEXPENSIVE

Hostal El Castillo At the foot of the castle in the narrow streets of Old Town, this small hotel opens onto a minuscule triangular area used by the adjoining convent and school as a playground. There's a small, covered courtyard. The spartan rooms are scrubbed clean and have well-maintained bathrooms. No breakfast is served, and the staff speaks only a little English.

Plaza San Bernabé 2, 29601 Marbella. © **95-277-17-39.** Fax 95-282-11-98. www.hotelelcastillo. com. 26 units. 38€–52€ double. MC, V. *In room:* A/C, TV.

Hotel Lima 🍴 Tucked in a residential area right off the N-340/E-15 and near the beach, the Lima is more secluded than other hotels nearby. The modern structure features plain rooms with Spanish provincial furnishings and private balconies.

Av. Antonio Belón, 29600 Marbella. © **95-277-05-00.** Fax 95-286-30-91. www.hotellima marbella.com. 64 units. 62€–96€ double. AE, DC, MC, V. Parking 13€. **Amenities:** Restaurant; babysitting; room service. *In room:* A/C, TV, hair dryer, minibar, Wi-Fi (12€ per 24 hr.).

Where to Stay Near Marbella

Castillo de Monda ★ 👪 In 1996, a group of entrepreneurs transformed the crumbling ruins of an 8th-century Moorish fortress into this showplace, which lies in a sleepy "white" village 12km (7½ miles) north of Marbella. El Castillo de Monda adds a soothing note of calm and quiet to a region that grows glitzier by the year. Rooms are beautifully maintained, generous in size, and traditionally furnished.

El Castillo s/n, 29110 Monda (Málaga). © **95-245-71-42.** Fax 95-245-73-36. www.castillode monda.es. 28 units. 114€–224€ double; 210€–260€ suite. MC, V. Free parking. **Amenities:** Restaurant; bar; babysitting; outdoor pool; room service; Wi-Fi (free, in lobby). *In room:* A/C, TV/DVD, hair dryer.

Refugio del Juanar ★ 👪 The former hunting lodge of King Alfonso XIII has been turned into this hotel and restaurant, an ideal retreat from Marbella. Over the years it has attracted both aristocrats and politicians, including Charles de Gaulle. The *refugio* lies 4km (2½ miles) from the town of Ojén, which is 10km (6¼ miles) north of Marbella. In the heart of the Sierra Blanca, the inn stands at the southern edge of a mountainous wilderness, Serranía de Ronda, which is inhabited by wild ibex.

Bedrooms are rather standard but comfortable, each midsize. An old-fashioned, Spanish hacienda style prevails, with iron headboards and flowery fabrics. A log fire roars downstairs in winter, and six of the accommodations have their own fireplaces.

Sierra Blanca s/n, 29610 Ojén. ✆ **95-288-10-00.** Fax 95-288-10-01. www.juanar.com. 26 units. 75€–135€ double; 185€–200€ suite. AE, DC, MC, V. **Amenities:** Restaurant; bar; outdoor pool; room service; outdoor tennis court; Wi-Fi (free, in lobby). *In room:* TV, hair dryer, minibar.

Where to Dine in Marbella

EXPENSIVE

Calima ★★★ ANDALUSIAN/INTERNATIONAL Dani García is the most exciting and innovative chef in Marbella. An example of his inventiveness: He injects liquid nitrogen into olives. When they explode, they become popcornlike morsels, which he then serves with fresh lobster salad. Or he'll take wild baby shrimp and lay them on a slate heated to 300°F (149°C), which he garnishes with an olive oil emulsion and fennel dust. But, for the most part, he is not some mad scientist in a lab. Instead, he keeps his menu local, relying on the famous products of the region, not only the regional olive oil but such delights as Andalusian *jamón* (ham) and sherry from Jerez. Meals are enjoyed on a large terrace overlooking the ocean. The fresh Mediterranean and Atlantic seafood is the best we've sampled along the coast. We also have nothing but praise for García's cold soups, homemade pastries, and impressive wine selection. After dinner, you can head for the piano bar, El Almirante, with live music and regular shows in season.

In the Gran Meliá Don Pepe (p. 399). Calle José Meliá. ✆ **95-276-42-52.** Reservations required. Main courses 22€–38€. AE, DC, MC, V. Tues–Sat 1:30–3:30pm and 8:30–10:30pm.

La Hacienda ★★★ INTERNATIONAL La Hacienda, a tranquil choice 13km (8 miles) east of Marbella, serves some of the best food along the Costa del Sol. In cooler months you can dine in the rustic tavern before an open fireplace. In fair weather, meals are served on a patio partially encircled by open Romanesque arches. Appetizers often include foie gras with lentils and lobster croquettes. For a main dish, try roast guinea hen with cream, minced raisins, and port; or beef carpaccio with duck liver. The flavorful food is prepared with the freshest ingredients and presented with style. An iced soufflé finishes the meal nicely.

Urbanización Hacienda Las Chapas, Carretera de Cádiz Km 193. ✆ **95-283-12-67.** www.restaurantelahacienda.com. Reservations recommended. Main courses 20€–30€; fixed-price menu 50€–60€. AE, DC, MC, V. Summer daily 8:30pm–midnight; winter Wed–Sun 1–3:30pm and 8:30–11:30pm. Closed Nov 12–Dec 7.

La Meridiana ★★★ ITALIAN/INTERNATIONAL If it's not the most sophisticated restaurant along the Costa del Sol, La Meridiana certainly is the most romantic—with its garden terrace—and arguably serves the best cuisine as well. A sweep of a glass-enclosed porch has been added to the original restaurant. **La Notte** (p. 405), a nightclub, is on a nearby terrace and is a hot spot along the coast for late-night revelers. The menu of Italian and Andalusian specialties changes four times yearly. Some of the most tantalizing items likely to be featured on the menu include wild sea bass seasoned with thyme and served with a prawn sauce, or else roast monkfish with a red-pepper preserve on a bed of onion purée. You might also order the house specialty, roast duck flambé in Calvados with truffles, fried onions, dates, and dried figs.

Camino de la Cruz s/n. © **95-277-61-90.** www.lameridiana.es. Reservations required. Main courses 14€–28€. AE, DC, MC, V. Daily 8pm–midnight.

Marbella Club Restaurant ★★ INTERNATIONAL Our favorite meals here have been on the terrace in good weather. Lunch is traditionally an overflowing buffet served in the beach club. You dine amid blooming flowers, flickering candles, and strains of live music—perhaps a Spanish classical guitarist, a small chamber orchestra playing 19th-century classics, or a South American vocalist. Menu items, inspired by European cuisines, change with the season. You might begin with a lobster cocktail with diced mango and honey truffle dressing or else spicy coconut soup with lemongrass. Specialties include beef entrecôte with a mushroom pepper sauce, or seared tuna with shiitake fried rolls and ginger dressing.

In the Marbella Club (p. 398), Bulevar Príncipe Alfonso von Hohenlohe s/n. © **95-282-22-11.** www.marbellaclub.com. Reservations recommended. Main courses 27€–45€. AE, DC, MC, V. Summer daily 9pm–12:30am; winter daily 8:30–11:30pm.

Villa Tiberio ★ ITALIAN/INTERNATIONAL Villa Tiberio's proximity to the upscale Marbella Club (a 5-min. walk away; p. 398) ensures a flow of visitors from that elite hotel. In what was originally built as a private villa during the 1960s, it serves the most innovative Italian food in the region and attracts the many north European expatriates living nearby. Appetizers include thinly sliced smoked beef with fresh avocados and oil-and-lemon dressing, and *fungi fantasía* (a large wild mushroom stuffed with seafood and lobster sauce). Especially tempting is the *pappardelle alla Sandro*—large flat noodles studded with chunks of lobster, tomato, and garlic. Other versions come with cream, caviar, and smoked salmon. Main dishes include sea bass with cherry tomatoes, basil, and black truffle oil; duck baked with orange and Curaçao liqueur; and *osso buco* (braised veal shanks).

Carretera de Cádiz Km 178.5. © **95-277-17-99.** www.villatiberio.com. Reservations recommended. Main courses 18€–28€; fixed-price menus 52€–58€. AE, DC, MC, V. Mon–Sat 7:30pm–12:30am.

MODERATE

Casa de la Era ★ 🏮 ANDALUSIAN This little discovery outside Marbella is in a rustic house, very much in the style of an old hacienda with internal patios decorated with plants, trees, and flowers. Wooden furniture only adds to the old-fashioned look, as do hanging hams and ceramics used for decoration. In addition, the restaurant offers a beautiful terrace. On a full night the place is a whirl of color and activity. The charming waiters rather proudly bring out the chef's specialties.

Some of the best of the chef's specialties include noodles with angler fish and baby clams, as well as baby goat from the mountains above Málaga. Codfish is a savory dish here when cooked in a spicy fresh tomato sauce. Other delectable

A MARBELLA *tasca* CRAWL

To really rub shoulders with the locals and experience a taste of Spain, take your meals in the tapas bars. Marbella boasts more hole-in-the-wall tapas bars than virtually any other resort town in southern Spain. Even if you set out with a specific place in mind, you'll likely be distracted en route by a newer, older, bigger, smaller, brighter, or just more interesting joint you want to try. That's half the fun.

Prices and hours are remarkably consistent: The coffeehouse that opens at 7am will switch to wine and tapas when the first patron asks for it (sometimes shortly after breakfast), and then continue through the day dispensing wine, sherry, and, more recently, bottles of beer. On average, tapas cost 3€ to 10€, but some foreign visitors configure them into *platos combinados.*

Tapas served along the Costa del Sol are principally Andalusian in origin, with an emphasis on seafood. The most famous plate, *fritura malagueña,* consists of fried fish based on the catch of the day. Sometimes *ajo blanco,* a garlicky local version of gazpacho made with almonds, is served, especially in summer. Fried squid or octopus is another favorite, as are little Spanish-style herb-flavored meatballs. *Tortilla* (an omelet, often with potatoes) is the most popular egg dish. Other well-known tapas include pungent tuna,

grilled shrimp, *piquillos rellenos* (red peppers stuffed with fish), *bacalao* (salt cod), and mushrooms sautéed in olive oil and garlic.

Tapas bars line many of the narrow streets of Marbella's historic core, with rich pickings around Calle del Perral and, to a somewhat lesser extent, Calle Miguel Cana. In August especially, when you want to escape wall-to-wall people and the heat and noise of the Old Town, head for one of the shoreline restaurants and tapas bars called *chiringuitos.* All serve local specialties, and you can order a full meal, a snack, tapas, or a drink. One of our favorites is **Los Sardinales,** Playa de los Alicates (✆ **95-283-70-12**), which serves some of the best sangria in the area. Another favorite is **Chiringuito La Pesquera,** Playa Marbellamar (✆ **95-277-03-38**), where you can order a plate of fresh grilled sardines.

delights include free-range chicken stewed with Montilla wine and fresh garlic, or else rabbit pan-cooked with fresh thyme and served with an almond sauce.

Finca El Chorraero, Carretera de Ojén Km 0.5. ℭ **95-277-06-25.** www.casadelaera.com. Reservations recommended. Main courses 12€–24€. AE, DC, MC, V. Sept–June Mon–Sat 1–4pm and 8–11pm; July–Aug 8–11pm.

Marbella After Dark

There's more international wealth hanging out in the watering holes of Marbella, and a wider choice of glam (or pseudoglam) discos, than virtually anywhere else in the south of Spain. Foremost among these is the chic **Olivia Valere,** in the Carretera Istan, N-340 Km 0.8 (ℭ **95-282-88-61;** www.oliviavalere.com); it's open Friday and Saturday from midnight to 7am with a cover of 30€. A fashionable place to rendezvous at night, **La Notte,** Camino de la Cruz s/n (ℭ **95-277-76-25**), stands next to the swank La Meridiana restaurant (p. 402). Decorated in a Marrakesh style, La Notte offers a terrace and an elegant atmosphere with rich decoration. Live music and shows are presented here during its nightly hours from 12:30 to 4am. It is closed from November 1 to December 21.

If you're in the heart of historic Marbella, enjoy a night in the bodegas and taverns of Old Town. Conveniently located adjacent to one of the town's widest thoroughfares is **Bodega La Venensia,** Plaza de los Olivos s/n (ℭ **95-277-99-63**). Its wide choice of sherries, wines, and tapas draws lots of chattering patrons. One with a particularly large assortment of wines is **Vinacoteca,** Plaza Joaquín Gómez Agüera 2 (ℭ **95-277-52-03**). Dedicated to offering as many Spanish wines as possible, it provides the opportunity to compare the vintages produced in the surrounding region.

The best flamenco club in town is **Tablao Flamenco Ana María,** Av. Severo Ochoa 24 (ℭ **95-277-56-46**). We think it's the most authentic place for foreign visitors with a limited knowledge of Spanish. The long, often-crowded bar area sells tapas, wine, sherry, and a selection of more international libations. On the stage, singers, dancers, and musicians perform flamenco and popular songs. This is late-night entertainment—the doors don't open until 11:30pm, and the crowd really gets going between midnight and 3am. Drink prices start at 25€, including cover.

Seven kilometers (4⅓ miles) west of Marbella, near Puerto Banús, **Casino Nueva Andalucía Marbella,** Bajo Hotel Andalucía Plaza, Urbanización Nueva Andalucía (ℭ **95-281-40-00;** www.casinomarbella.com), is on the lobby level of the Bajo Hotel Andalucía Plaza resort complex at Urbanización Nueva. Unlike the region's competing casino, at the Hotel Torrequebrada, the Marbella does not offer cabaret or nightclub shows. The focus is on gambling, and mobs of visitors from northern Europe come here. Individual games include French and American roulette, blackjack, punto y banco, craps, and chemin de fer. Hours are daily noon to 5am for coin machines, daily 8pm to 5am for the main body of the casino. Admission is 5€.

You can dine before or after gambling in the **Casino Restaurant,** a few steps above the gaming floor. Jackets are not required for men, but shorts and T-shirts will be frowned upon. The casino is open daily from 8pm to 2 or 4am. A passport is required for admission.

FUENGIROLA & LOS BOLICHES

32km (20 miles) W of Málaga, 104km (65 miles) E of Algeciras, 574km (357 miles) S of Madrid

The fishing towns of Fuengirola and Los Boliches lie halfway between the more famous resorts of Marbella and Torremolinos. A promenade along the water stretches some 4km (2½ miles). Less-developed Los Boliches is just .8km (½ mile) from Fuengirola.

These towns don't have the facilities or drama of Torremolinos and Marbella, but except for two major luxury hotels, Fuengirola and Los Boliches are cheaper. This has attracted hordes of budget-conscious European tourists.

Santa Amalja, Carvajal, and **Las Gaviotas,** the best beaches, are broad, clean, and sandy. Everybody goes to the big **flea market** at Fuengirola on Tuesday. It's the largest along the coast. Many British retirees who live in the holiday apartments nearby attend this sprawling market, later stopping in at one of the Irish or British pubs for a pint, just like they used to do back in their home country.

Essentials

GETTING THERE Fuengirola is on the main Costa del Sol **bus** route from either Algeciras in the west or Málaga in the east. Call **Empresa Portillo,** Av. Condes de San Isidro s/n, in Fuengirola (✆ **90-214-31-44;** www.ctsa-portillo.com). The one-way fare is 1.75€ from Málaga to Fuengirola or 9.30€ one-way from Algeciras to Fuengirola. If you're driving from Marbella, take the N-340/E-15 east.

VISITOR INFORMATION The **tourist office,** Paseo Jesús Santos Rein 6 (✆ **95-246-76-25;** www.fuengirola.org), is open Monday to Friday 9:30am to 2pm and 5 to 7pm, and Saturday 9:30am to 1:30pm.

Where to Stay Around Fuengirola & Los Boliches

Gran Hotel Guadalpin Byblos ★★★ ☺ In spite of its address, this pocket of posh is closer to Fuengirola than to Mijas, having been constructed in a spectacular garden of fountains, swaying palms, and stately cypress trees. It's an oasis of calm in a relatively traffic-free area overlooking two 18-hole golf courses. The exquisite luxury hotel is a blend of Moorish and Western architecture, with Seville-style patios and the sound of fountains once enjoyed by the sultans of Granada. For spa devotees, this is the best choice along the coast, the staff specializing in thalassotherapy, using seawater and seaweed administered in a Roman-inspired marble temple. The resort lies within walking distance of a good beach. Bedrooms are among the most luxurious along the coast. Spacious and beautifully furnished family rooms and suites can hold two to five persons.

Urbanización Mijas-Golf, Mijas Costa, 29640 Mijas. ✆ **95-247-30-50.** Fax 95-247-67-83. www. granhotelguadalpin.com. 144 units. 107€–200€ double; 149€–220€ junior suite; from 214€ suite. AE, DC, MC, V. Parking 15€. **Amenities:** 3 restaurants; 3 bars; airport transfers (69€); babysitting; bikes; children's center; concierge; 2 18-hole golf courses; 5 freshwater pools (3 heated indoor); room service; spa; 4 outdoor tennis courts (lit). *In room:* A/C, TV, hair dryer, minibar, Wi-Fi (12€ per 24 hr.).

Las Pirámides This resort, a favorite of northern Europeans and tour groups, is a citylike compound about 46m (151 ft.) from the beach. The government-rated four-star resort consists of two buildings connected by a hall, each with 10 floors. All the rooms are good size and have slick modern styling as well as terraces. Bathrooms contain tub/shower combos. On the beach, guests enjoy a wide range of watersports, including pedal boating, water-skiing, windsurfing, parasailing, boating, and fishing. The reception desk at the hotel can also point you to the best golf courses in the area, and horseback riding is available near the hotel. You can also rent bikes nearby.

Calle Miguel Márquez 43, 29640 Fuengirola. © **95-247-06-00.** Fax 95-258-32-97. www.hotel-laspiramides.com. 320 units. 122€–167€ double; 148€–182€ suite. AE, MC, V. Parking 15€. **Amenities:** 2 restaurants; 5 bars; babysitting; exercise room; Jacuzzi; 2 freshwater pools (1 heated indoor); room service; sauna; extensive watersports equipment/rentals; Wi-Fi (6€ per hour, in lobby). *In room:* A/C, TV, hair dryer, minibar.

Villa de Laredo ★ 🎁 With a panoramic site on the waterfront promenade, this good-value inn lies a block east of the main port. One of the more modern hotels in town, it benefits from a central location without even attempting to equal the luxury offered on the periphery by such resorts as Byblos Andaluz. Bedrooms are newly styled and comfortably furnished, containing small bathrooms. Try for one of the rooms with a small terrace opening onto the seafront promenade. The featured attraction of the villa is its rooftop pool, opening onto views of the Paseo Marítimo.

Paseo Marítimo Rey de España 42, 29640 Fuengirola. © **95-247-76-89.** Fax 95-247-79-50. 74 units. 79€–150€ double. Rates include continental breakfast. AE, DC, MC, V. **Amenities:** Restaurant; bar; outdoor pool; room service. *In room:* A/C, TV, hair dryer, minibar, Wi-Fi (free).

Where to Dine Around Fuengirola & Los Boliches

La Langosta ★ INTERNATIONAL/SEAFOOD Just a stone's throw from Fuengirola and 2 blocks from the beach, La Langosta is one of the best restaurants in the area. The Art Deco dining room is a welcome relief from the ever-present Iberian rustic style of so many other restaurants. The menu features a variety of seafood, as well as Spanish dishes like *gazpacho andaluz* and prawns in a curry sauce. Lobster is prepared thermidor style or virtually any other way you want. Mussels come in a savory saffron cream sauce. Sometimes the best plate to order is the simplest: grilled Dover sole with boiled potatoes and fresh butter. The staff is particularly well trained and helpful.

Calle Francisco Cano 1, Los Boliches. © **95-247-50-49.** www.restaurantelalangosta.net. Main courses 13€–29€; tasting menu 39€. AE, DC, MC, V. Mon–Sat 7–11:30pm. Closed Dec–Jan.

Restaurant Guy Massey ★ INTERNATIONAL A respected British chef opened a restaurant in Pueblo López, close to the harborfront, taking over the premises of an antique house that, prior to his tenure, had established a reputation as a home-away-from-home for English-speaking expatriates. Today, within a sun-flooded dining room that's outfitted like a rustic and cozy Iberian tavern, Guy Massey prepares a flavorful roster of dishes based on fresh market ingredients and a skillful blend of Iberian and English traditions. The dinner menu is stylish and esoteric, including foie gras on toast with Calvados-infused peach marmalade as a starter. In the main-dish specialties, harmony of flavor reigns. Try the salmon filet with rosemary and creamy spinach, or roast quail in a tomato tarragon dressing with wild mushrooms. Other delights are the duck confit on braised cabbage in a hazelnut jus, or pheasant breast with a pomegranate dressing. A succulent rack of lamb appears in a red-wine jus with a carpaccio of beetroot.

Rotonda de la Luina, Pueblo López. ℭ **68-917-94-92.** www.guymassey.es. Reservations recommended. Main courses 16€–45€; fixed-price menus 40€–75€. DC, MC, V. Mon–Sat noon–3pm and 7pm–midnight. Closed Jan–Feb.

MIJAS ★

30km (19 miles) W of Málaga, 585km (364 miles) S of Madrid

Just 8km (5 miles) north of coastal road N-340/E-15, this village is known as "White Mijas" because of its marble-white Andalusian-style houses. Mijas is at the foot of a mountain range near the turnoff to Fuengirola, and from its lofty height—450m (1,476 ft.) above sea level—you get a panoramic view of the Mediterranean.

Celts, Phoenicians, and Moors preceded today's intrepid tourists to Mijas. The town itself, rather than a specific monument, is the attraction. The easiest way to get around its cobblestone streets is to rent a burro taxi. If you consider Mijas overrun with souvenir shops, head for the park at the top of Cuesta de la Villa, where you'll see the ruins of a **Moorish fortress** dating from 833. If you're in town for a fiesta, you'll attend events in the country's only square bullring (bullsquare?).

There's frequent bus service to Mijas from the terminal at Fuengirola, 30 minutes away. To drive from Fuengirola, take the Mijas road north.

Where to Stay in & Around Mijas

The Beach House ★ 🎁 A stay here is like being a private guest in a Mediterranean villa. This is a gracious, somewhat offbeat way to live in Mijas if you don't want a standard hotel. It's good to have a car as the beaches, restaurants, and nightlife of the resort of Fuengirola are about a 10-minute drive to the south. In the cooler weather, guests lounge around the fireplace. In summer they can be found around the sparkling pool or at the bougainvillea-draped bar. Bedrooms are modern and minimalist, each tastefully and comfortably furnished. The most expensive doubles open onto views of the Mediterranean in the distance.

Urbanización El Chaparral, N-340 Km 203, 29648 Mijas-Costa. ℭ /fax **95-249-45-40.** www.beachhouse.nu. 10 units. 125€–175€ double. Rates include breakfast. AE, DC, MC, V. **Amenities:** Restaurant; outdoor pool; room service. *In room:* A/C, TV, Internet (in some; free).

Hotel TRH Mijas ★★ One of the most inviting hotels on the Costa del Sol dates from 1970, when it was built on steeply sloping land in the center of town. This Andalusian-inspired block of white walls and flowering terraces is sun flooded and comfortable. There are sweeping views over the Mediterranean from most of the public areas and the tiny but comfortable rooms. The staff is tactful and hardworking.

Urbanización Tamisa 2, 29650 Mijas. ℭ **95-248-58-00.** Fax 95-248-58-25. www.trhhoteles.info. 204 units. 100€–160€ double; 180€–280€ suite. DC, MC, V. Free parking. **Amenities:** Restaurant; bar; babysitting; exercise room; Jacuzzi; outdoor freshwater pool; room service; sauna; outdoor tennis court; Wi-Fi (free, in lobby). *In room:* A/C, TV, hair dryer.

La Cala Resort ★★ Golfers journey to Mijas just to stay at this stylishly contemporary inland resort. The two golf courses at La Cala are its main attraction, including La Cala North (par 73) and La Cala South (par 72). Both were

A "burro taxi" in Mijas.

designed by the noted golf architect Cabell B. Robinson, who cited the Costa del Sol terrain as his most challenging project. Even if you're not a golfer, this is one of the finest hotels in the area, unless you prefer to be right on the sea rather than 7km (4⅓ miles) away. Accommodations are midsize to spacious, attractively furnished in a contemporary mode, with superb bathrooms. Every unit opens onto a large balcony overlooking the fairways and greens and the Mijas hills beyond. The food here, a medley of Spanish and Continental dishes, is first-rate and uses quality ingredients.

La Cala de Mijas, 29649 Mijas. ⓒ **95-266-90-00.** Fax 95-266-90-13. www.lacala.com. 107 units. 142€–235€ double; 207€–270€ junior suite. AE, DC, MC, V. **Amenities:** 2 restaurants; bar; airport transfers (80€); babysitting; exercise room; 3 18-hole golf courses; 2 freshwater heated pools (1 indoor); room service; spa; 2 outdoor tennis courts (lit); Wi-Fi (free, in lobby). *In room:* A/C, TV, hair dryer, minibar.

Where to Dine in Mijas

El Padrastro ★ INTERNATIONAL Part of the fun of dining at the town's best restaurant is getting here. You go to the cliff side of town and, if you're athletic, walk up 77 steps; alternatively, you can take the elevator to the highest point. El Padrastro serves international cuisine on its covered terraces with panoramic views of the coast. You can choose whether to eat inexpensively (stick with the regional dishes) or elaborately (break the bank and go for the chateaubriand with a bottle of the best Spanish wine).

Av. del Compás 20–22. ⓒ **95-248-50-00.** Reservations recommended. Main courses 20€–27€. AE, DC, MC, V. Sun–Fri 12:30–4pm and 7–11:30pm.

TORREMOLINOS

15km (9⅓ miles) W of Málaga, 122km (76 miles) E of Algeciras, 568km (353 miles) S of Madrid

This Mediterranean beach resort is the most famous in Spain. It's known as a melting pot for international visitors, mostly Europeans and Americans. Many relax here after a whirlwind tour of Europe—the living is easy, the people are fun, and there are no historical monuments to visit. Once a sleepy fishing village, Torremolinos has been engulfed in cement-walled resort hotels. Prices are on the rise, but it remains one of Europe's vacation bargains.

Essentials

GETTING THERE The nearby Málaga airport (p. 414) serves Torremolinos, and frequent **trains** also run from the terminal at Málaga. For train information,

Beachfront hotels in Torremolinos.

call ℰ **90-224-02-02,** or log on to www.renfe.es. **Buses** run frequently between Málaga and Torremolinos; call ℰ **90-214-31-44** for schedules.

If you're driving, take the N-340/E-15 west from Málaga or the N-340/E-15 east from Marbella.

VISITOR INFORMATION The **tourist information office** is at Plaza Independencia (ℰ **95-237-42-31**). It's open daily 8am to 3pm (in winter Mon–Fri 9:30am–2:30pm).

Where to Stay in Torremolinos
MODERATE

Hotel Cervantes ★ The government-rated four-star Cervantes, located in a shopping center, is a 7-minute walk from the beach. It has a garden and is adjacent to a maze of patios and narrow streets of boutiques and open-air cafes. Rooms have modern furniture and spacious terraces; many have balconies with sea views. In midsummer this hotel is likely to be booked with tour groups from northern Europe, many of whom can be seen sunning themselves on the hotel's rooftop terrace. A special feature in summer is the luncheon buffet and barbecue by the pool.

Calle las Mercedes s/n, 29620 Torremolinos. ℰ **95-238-40-33.** Fax 95-238-48-57. www.hotasa cervantes.com. 397 units. 52€–175€ double. Rates include buffet breakfast. AE, DC, MC, V. Parking 15€. **Amenities:** Restaurant; 2 bars; babysitting; exercise room; 2 freshwater pools (1 heated indoor); room service; sauna. *In room:* A/C, TV, hair dryer, Wi-Fi (10€ per 24 hr.).

Hotel Tropicana & Beach Club ★ This government-rated four-star hotel stands right on a beach at the beginning of the La Carihuela coastal strip. Boasting its own beach club, Tropicana is desirable mainly because it's removed from the summer hysteria in the heart of Torremolinos. In honor of its namesake, a tropical motif dominates. Some decorators tried to give a little flair to the comfortably furnished and midsize bedrooms. Most of the rooms open onto private balconies with sea views. Many seafood restaurants are only a 5-minute stroll from the hotel's door, or else you can patronize the Tropicana's **Restaurante Mango,** with its terrace facing the sea.

Trópico 6, 29620 Torremolinos. © **95-238-66-00.** Fax 95-238-05-68. www.hotel-tropicana.net. 84 units. 50€–210€ double. Rates include continental breakfast. AE, DC, MC, V. Free parking. **Amenities:** Restaurant; bar; babysitting; outdoor freshwater pool; room service; Wi-Fi (free, in lobby). *In room:* A/C, TV, fridge, hair dryer.

Meliá Costa del Sol ★ Centrally located, this hotel lies on the seafront along Playa de Bajondillo, a 10-minute walk from the shopping area of Torremolinos. The midsize rooms are modern and well maintained, and each has a well-kept bathroom. However, the hotel is popular with package-tour groups, so you may not feel a part of things if you come alone.

Paseo Marítimo 11, 29620 Torremolinos. © **95-238-66-77.** Fax 95-238-64-17. www.melia costadelsol.solmelia.com. 540 units. 78€–225€ double; 138€–299€ junior suite; 298€–530€ suite. Rates include buffet breakfast. AE, MC, V. Free parking. **Amenities:** 2 restaurants; 2 bars; babysitting; bikes; concierge; health club; outdoor freshwater pool; room service; spa. *In room:* A/C, TV, hair dryer, minibar, Wi-Fi (free).

Roc Lago Rojo ★ 🏨 In the heart of the fishing village of La Carihuela, Roc Lago Rojo is the area's finest place to stay. It's only 45m (148 ft.) from the beach and has its own gardens and sunbathing terraces. Built in the 1970s and renovated in 2006, it offers tastefully decorated studio-style rooms, all of which have terraces with views. In the late evening there is disco dancing.

Miami 5, 29620 Torremolinos. © **95-238-76-66.** Fax 95-238-08-91. www.roc-hotels.com. 144 units. 66€–155€ double. Rates include buffet breakfast. AE, DC, MC, V. Parking 15€. **Amenities:** Restaurant; bar; babysitting; outdoor freshwater pool; Wi-Fi (4€ per hour, in lobby). *In room:* A/C, TV.

INEXPENSIVE

Hotel El Pozo 🗲 This hotel isn't for light sleepers—it's in one of the liveliest sections of town, a short walk from the train station. It's usually filled with budget travelers, including many students from northern Europe. The lobby level has professional French billiards, heavy Spanish furniture, and a view of a small courtyard. From your window or terrace you can view the promenades below. The small rooms are furnished in a simple, functional style—nothing special, but the price is right.

Casablanca 2, 29620 Torremolinos. © **95-238-06-22.** Fax 95-238-71-17. www.hotelelpozo.com. 28 units. 49€–79€ double. DC, MC, V. Parking 8€. **Amenities:** Bar; Wi-Fi (free, in lobby). *In room:* A/C, TV.

Hotel Los Jazmines Located on one of the best beaches in Torremolinos, Los Jazmines faces a plaza at the foot of the shady Avenida del Lido. Sun-seekers will find it replete with terraces, lawns, and an irregularly shaped swimming pool. The small rooms (all doubles) seem a bit impersonal, but have little balconies and compact bathrooms. From here it's a good hike up the hill to the town center.

Av. de Lido 6, 29620 Torremolinos. © **95-238-50-33.** Fax 95-237-27-02. www.hotellosjazmines. com. 100 units. 55€–95€ double. AE, DC, MC, V. **Amenities:** Restaurant; bar; outdoor freshwater pool. *In room:* A/C, TV.

Miami ★ 🍴 The Miami, near the Carihuela section, might remind you of a 1920s Hollywood movie star's home. High walls and private gardens surround the property. Fuchsia and bougainvillea climb over the rear patio's arches, and a tile terrace is used for sunbathing and refreshments. The country-style living room contains a walk-in fireplace, and the compact rooms are furnished in a traditional, comfortable style. Each has a balcony. Breakfast is the only meal served.

Calle Aladino 14, 29620 Torremolinos. ☎ **95-238-52-55.** www.residencia-miami.com. 26 units. 40€–64€ double. Rates include continental breakfast. No credit cards. Free parking. **Amenities:** Bar; outdoor freshwater pool. *In room:* A/C.

Where to Dine

A good spot to try in **Torremolinos** is the food court at La Nogalera, the major gathering place between the coast road and the beach. Head down Calle del Cauce to this compound of modern whitewashed Andalusian buildings. Open to pedestrian traffic only, it's a maze of passageways, courtyards, and patios for eating and drinking. You can find everything from sandwiches to pizza to Belgian waffles to scrambled eggs.

If you want to get away from the high-rises and honky-tonks, head to nearby **La Carihuela.** In the old fishing village on the western outskirts of Torremolinos, you'll find some great bargain restaurants. Walk down toward the sea to reach the village.

Casa Juan ★ SEAFOOD In a modern-looking building in La Carihuela, this seafood restaurant is about 1.6km (1 mile) west of Torremolinos's center. Menu items include selections from a lavish display of fish and shellfish prominently positioned near the entrance. You might try *mariscada de mariscos* (shellfish), a fried platter of mixed fish, cod, kabobs of meat or fish, or paella. Of special note is *lubina a la sal*—sea bass packed in layers of roughly textured salt, broken open at your table and deboned in front of you. When the restaurant gets busy, as it often does, the staff is likely to rush around hysterically—something many local fans think adds to its charm.

Calle San Gines 18–20. ☎ **95-237-35-12.** www.losmellizos.info. Reservations recommended. Main courses 12€–42€. AE, DC, MC, V. Tues–Sun 12:30–4:30pm and 7:30–11:30pm. Closed Dec.

Figón de Montemar ★ SPANISH/ANDALUSIAN One of the better restaurants in the area, Figón de Montemar lies near the beach, and like so many others it's decorated with glass, tiles, and various nautical paraphernalia. Its chefs call its cuisine *cocina de mercado,* which means its menus are based on what was good and fresh at the market that day, including the daily seafood catch. From the mountains in the distance comes lamb that is perfectly roasted and seasoned with garlic and spices and served with a mint sauce. *Merluza* (hake) is baked with fresh spices, and fresh codfish is prepared in a delightful red sauce. Want something more adventurous? You can also order oxtail, a local specialty.

Av. Espada 101. ☎ **95-237-26-88.** Reservations recommended. Main courses 14€–24€. Set menus 15€–25€. AE, DC, MC, V. Mon noon–1:30pm; Tues–Sat noon–1:30pm and 5:30–8pm. Closed Jan 10–Feb 10.

IN BENALMÁDENA-COSTA

Where Torremolinos ends and Benalmádena-Costa to the west begins is hard to say. The two resorts seem to merge. Benalmádena offers some of the better restaurants in the area.

Mar de Alborán ★★ BASQUE/ANDALUSIAN This restaurant's elegantly airy decor is appropriate for its location near the sea, just a short walk from the resort's Puerto Marina. It serves the specialties of both Andalusia and the Basque region of northern Spain. The imaginative chef is fond of harmonious pairings of ingredients, as evoked by the small squid braised in baby onions or the king shrimp tails with a touch of sherry served on black rice. Especially good is Iberian breast of pork braised in red wine and served with tempura vegetables, or the escalope of duck liver with Málaga wine and an apple stew. The restaurant's game dishes (available in season) are renowned. Dessert might be a frothy peach mousse with purée of fruit and dark-chocolate sauce.

Alay 5. ℃ **95-244-64-27.** Reservations recommended. Main courses 14€–26€. AE, DC, MC, V. Sun 1:30–4pm; Tues–Fri 1:30–4pm and 8:30pm–midnight; Sat 8:30pm–midnight. Closed Dec 22–Jan 22.

Ventorrillo de la Perra ★ 🏠ANDALUSIAN/SPANISH This inn, from 1785, is one of the oldest restaurants we've found along the Costa del Sol. It's the way the Costa del Sol used to be before the invading hordes conquered it.

You can eat on a shaded patio, ideal on a summer day, or head for the intimate dining room with its cozy bar. Andalusian cured hams hang from the ceiling. You may think you know what gazpacho is until you order *gazpacuelo malagueño,* which is actually served warm. It's a combination of both rice and potatoes, enlivened with fresh shrimp. Another typical soup specialty is *ajo blanco,* a cold almond soup, heavy on the garlic. Almonds appear again in a sauce with your order of rabbit *(conejo).* Lamb appears frequently on the menu, as does fresh fish based on the day's catch.

Av. Constitución 115 Km 13, Arroyo de la Miel. ℃ **95-244-19-66.** www.ventorrillodelaperra. es. Reservations recommended. Main courses 12€–28€. AE, DC, MC, V. Tues–Sun 1–4pm and 8pm–midnight.

Torremolinos After Dark

Torremolinos has more nightlife than any other spot along the Costa del Sol. The earliest action is always at the bars, which stay lively most of the night, serving drinks and tapas. Sometimes it seems that in Torremolinos there are more bars than people, so you shouldn't have trouble finding one you like. Note that some bars are open during the day as well.

La Bodega, San Miguel 40 (℃ **95-238-73-37**), relies on its colorful clientele and the quality of its tapas to draw customers, who seem to rank this place above the dozens of other *tascas* in this popular tourist zone. Many guests come here for lunch or dinner, making a satisfying meal from the plentiful bar food. You'll be lucky if you find space at one of the small tables, but once you begin to order—platters of fried squid, pungent tuna, grilled shrimp, tiny brochettes of sole—you might not be able to stop. Most tapas cost 2€. A beer costs 1.50€ to 2.50€, a hard drink at least 3.50€ to 4€. La Bodega is open daily from 12:30 to 5pm and 7:30pm to midnight.

Ready to dance off all those tapas? **El Palladium,** Palma de Mallorca (℃ **95-238-42-89**), a well-designed nightclub in the town center, is one of the most convivial in Torremolinos. Strobes, spotlights, and a loud sound system set the scene. There's even a swimming pool. Expect to pay 3.50€ or more for a drink; cover is 10€, including one drink after 11pm. The club is open from 11pm to 6am in summer months only.

For flamenco, albeit of a touristy kind, head for **Taberna Flamenca Pepe López,** Plaza de la Gamba Alegre (✆ **95-238-12-84**), in the center of Torremolinos. In an old house (at least old in the Torremolinos sense), this is a tavern-style joint with darkened wood furnishings. Many of the artists come from the *boîtes* of Seville and Granada, and they perform nightly at 10pm April to October. Shows are substantially reduced during the cooler months, and confined mainly to the weekends—call to confirm first. A 28€ cover includes your first drink and the show.

Gay men and women from throughout northern Europe are almost always in residence in Torremolinos; if you want to meet some of them, consider having a drink or two at **Abadia,** La Nogalera 521 (no phone), open daily 6pm to dawn.

One of the Costa del Sol's major casinos, **Casino Torrequebrada,** Avenida del Sol, Benalmádena-Costa (✆ **95-257-73-00;** www.casinotorrequebrada. net), is on the lobby level of the Hotel Torrequebrada. It has tables devoted to blackjack, chemin de fer, punto y banco, and two kinds of roulette. The casino is open daily from 9pm to 5am. The nightclub offers a flamenco show year-round at 10:30pm Tuesday to Saturday nights; in midsummer, there might be more glitz and more frequent shows (ask when you get there or call). Nightclub acts begin at 10:30pm (Las Vegas revue) and 11:30pm (Spanish revue). The restaurant is open nightly from 9:30pm to midnight. Casino admission is 3€. Bring your passport to be admitted.

MÁLAGA ★

548km (341 miles) S of Madrid, 132km (82 miles) E of Algeciras

Málaga is a bustling commercial and residential center whose economy does not depend exclusively on tourism. Its chief attraction is the mild off-season climate. Summer can be sticky.

Málaga's most famous citizen was Pablo Picasso, born in 1881 at Plaza de la Merced, in the city center. The artist unfortunately left little of his spirit—and only a small selection of his work—in his birthplace.

Essentials

GETTING THERE Travelers from North America must transfer for Málaga in Madrid or Barcelona. From within Europe, some airlines (including British Airways from London) offer nonstop flights to Málaga. **Iberia** has frequent service. Flights can be booked through Iberia's reservations line (✆ **800/772-4642** in the U.S., or 90-240-05-00 in Spain; www.iberia.com).

At least five **trains** a day arrive in Málaga from Madrid (trip time: 2½ hr.). Three trains a day connect Seville and Málaga (trip time: 3 hr.). For ticket prices and rail information in Málaga, contact RENFE (✆ **90-224-02-02;** www.renfe.es).

Buses from all over Spain arrive at the terminal on the Paseo de los Tilos, behind the RENFE offices. Buses run to all the major Spanish cities, including eight buses per day from Madrid (trip time: 7 hr.), five per day from Córdoba (trip time: 3 hr.), and 10 per day from Seville (trip time: 3 hr.). Call ✆ **90-242-22-42** in Málaga for bus information.

An interior courtyard of Málaga's Alcazaba palace.

From resorts in the west (such as Torremolinos and Marbella), you can drive east along the N-340/E-15 to Málaga. If you're in the east at the end of the Costa del Sol (Almería), take the N-340/E-15 west to Málaga, with a stopover at Nerja.

VISITOR INFORMATION The **tourist office,** at Plaza de la Marina 11 (*©* **95-212-20-20;** www.malagaturismo.com), is open Monday to Friday 9am to 7pm and Saturday and Sunday 10am to 7pm.

SPECIAL EVENTS The most festive time in Málaga is the first week in August, when the city celebrates its Reconquest by Ferdinand and Isabella in 1487. The big *feria* (**fair**) is an occasion for parades and bullfights. A major tree-shaded boulevard, the Paseo del Parque, is transformed into a fairground featuring amusements and restaurants.

Exploring Málaga

Unlike the rest of the Costa del Sol, Málaga has several historical sites of interest to the average visitor.

Alcazaba ★ The remains of this ancient Moorish palace are within easy walking distance of the city center, off the Paseo del Parque. Plenty of signs point the way up the hill. The fortress was erected in the 9th or 10th century, although there have been later additions and reconstructions. Ferdinand and Isabella stayed here when they reconquered the city. With orange trees and purple bougainvillea making the grounds even more beautiful, the view overlooking the city and the bay is among the most panoramic on the Costa del Sol.

Plaza de la Aduana, Alcazabilla. *©* **95-212-20-20.** Admission 2€. Museum Tues–Sun 8:30am–8pm. Bus: 4, 18, 19, 24, or 135.

Castillo de Gibralfaro On a hill overlooking Málaga and the Mediterranean are the ruins of an ancient Moorish castle-fortress of unknown origin. It is near the government-run *parador* and might easily be tied in with a luncheon visit.

The outer walls of the Alcazaba.

Warning: Do not walk to Gibralfaro Castle from town. Readers have reported muggings along the way, and the area around the castle is dangerous. Take the bus from the cathedral (see below).

Cerro de Gibralfaro. Admission 2€. Daylight hours. Microbus: 35, leaving hourly from cathedral.

Contemporáneo de Málaga ★ This contemporary arts center lies in a renovated old wholesalers' market and stages the best array of temporary art exhibitions in town, many showcasing the works of international artists such as Alex Katz and Louise Bourgeois. It always has a permanent exhibition. The museum also focuses some of its exhibitions on up-and-coming Spanish artists, and it also displays photographic studies in its vast exhibition space. Skip it if you have time only for Museo Picasso Málaga, but try to see it if you can, as this is the major cultural center of modern art in the south of Spain.

Alemania s/n. *©* **95-212-00-55.** www.cacmalaga.org. Free admission. Mid-June to mid-Sept Tues–Sun 10am–2pm and 5–9pm; off season Tues–Sun 10am–2pm and 5–8pm.

Fundación Picasso A well-told tale concerns the birth of Picasso: In October 1891, when the artist was born, he was unable to draw breath until his uncle blew cigar smoke into his lungs. Whether this rather harsh entry into the world had any effect on his work is mere speculation. What cannot be denied is the effect he was to have on the world. He was born in a five-story building in the heart of Málaga's historic quarter; this is where he spent the first 17 months of his life. Today, the house is both headquarters of the Picasso Foundation and a library for art historians. The Picasso family lived on the second floor, called Casa Natal. Regrettably, the original furnishings are long gone. What you'll see today is a permanent exhibit of Picasso ceramics, sculpture, and engravings. The museum mounts temporary exhibitions featuring avant-garde works from Picasso's time.

Plaza de la Merced 15. *©* **95-206-02-15.** www.fundacionpicasso.es. Admission 1€. Mon–Sat 10am–8pm; Sun 10am–2pm.

Málaga Cathedral This 16th-century Renaissance cathedral in Málaga's center, built on the site of a great mosque, suffered damage during the Spanish Civil War. However, it remains vast and impressive, reflecting changing styles of interior architecture. Its most notable attributes are the richly ornamented choir stalls by Ortiz, Mena, and Michael. The cathedral has been declared a national monument.

Plaza Obispo. *©* **95-221-59-17.** Admission 3.50€. Mon–Sat 10am–6:30pm. Closed holidays. Bus: 14, 18, 19, or 24.

Museo Picasso Málaga ★★★ In the Old Quarter of the city, a short walk from Picasso's birthplace, this museum displays some of his important works. The museum, which opened in 2003, combines a restored 16th-century Mudéjar palace, Palacio de Buenvista, with a series of modernist buildings that evoke the Pueblos Blancos in the hills above Málaga. The Spanish dictator Franco detested Picasso, his politics, and his "degenerate art," and refused the artist's offer to send paintings from France to Málaga in the 1950s. Ultimately, the collection here was made possible by two of Picasso's heirs: his son Paulo's wife, Christine Ruiz-Picasso; and Bernard, Christine and Paulo's son. Many of the artworks are virtual family heirlooms, including paintings depicting one of the artist's wives, such as *Olga Kokhlova with Mantilla,* or one of his lovers, *Jacqueline Seated.* Basically, this is the art Picasso gave to his family or else the art he wanted to keep for himself—in all, more than 200 paintings, drawings, sculpture, ceramics, and graphics. Some other notable works on display—many of them never on public view before—include *Bust of a Woman with Arms Crossed Behind Her Head, Woman in an Armchair,* and *The Eyes of the Artist.* There is also a memorable painting of Picasso's son, done in 1923.

San Agustín 8. *©* **95-212-76-00.** www.museopicassomalaga.org. Combined permanent collection and exhibitions 8€; half-price for seniors, students, and children 11–16; free for children 10 and under. Tues–Thurs 10am–8pm; Fri–Sat 10am–9pm; Sun 10am–8pm.

Shopping

The region around Málaga produces artfully rustic pottery, which makes a nice gift or souvenir. A handful of appealing outlets are scattered throughout the city's historic core. Another offering, **Ceramica Las Vistillas,** Carretera Mijas Km 2 (*©* **95-245-13-63;** www.ceramicalasvistillas.com), is about 2km (1¼ miles) from Málaga's center.

Where to Stay in Málaga

For such a large city in a resort area, Málaga has a surprising lack of hotels. Book well in advance, especially if you want to stay in a *parador.*

EXPENSIVE

AC Málaga Palacio ★ The leading hotel in the town center, the Palacio opens onto a tree-lined esplanade near the cathedral and the harbor. Most balconies offer views of the port, and below you can see horses pulling century-old carriages. The midsize rooms are traditionally furnished and have firm beds and good bathrooms. The street-floor lounges mix antiques with more modern furnishings. One Toronto couple writes that the breakfast buffet is excellent, but you "can't get a hot cup of coffee here no matter how you try."

Cortina del Muelle 1, 29015 Málaga. *©* **95-221-51-85.** Fax 95-222-51-00. www.ac-hotels.com. 214 units. 130€–186€ double; 195€–375€ suite. AE, DC, MC, V. Parking 25€ nearby. Bus: 4, 18, 19, or 24. **Amenities:** Restaurant; bar; babysitting; concierge; exercise room; outdoor pool; room service; sauna. *In room:* A/C, TV, hair dryer, minibar, Wi-Fi (12€ per 24 hr.).

Parador de Málaga-Gibralfaro ★★ Restored in 1994, this is one of Spain's oldest, most tradition-heavy *paradores*. It enjoys a scenic location high on a plateau near an old fortified castle. Overlooking the city and the Mediterranean, it has views of the bullring, mountains, and beaches. Rooms have private entrances, living room areas, and wide glass doors opening onto private sun terraces. The **restaurant** (p. 421), notable for its views, serves Spanish cuisine.

Castillo de Gibralfaro s/n, 29016 Málaga. ✆ **95-222-19-02.** Fax 95-222-19-04. www.parador.es. 38 units. 160€–223€ double. AE, DC, MC, V. Free parking. Take the coastal road, Paseo de Reding, which becomes Av. de Pries, and then Paseo de Sancha. Turn left onto Camino Nuevo and follow the small signs. **Amenities:** Restaurant; bar; outdoor pool; room service. *In room:* A/C, TV, hair dryer, minibar, Wi-Fi (free).

Tryp Guadalmar ★ ☺ Drenched in sunlight, this nine-story modern hotel sits across from a private beach that's 3km (1¾ miles) west of the center of Málaga. The hotel benefited from a radical renovation in 1996 and a takeover by the well-respected Tryp chain. Accommodations are spacious, airy, and simply furnished; each room has a private seaview balcony. Families check in here to use the beach in front, one of the safest in the area. The staff plans activities for children from June to September, including swimming lessons. An air of anonymity prevails as the staff struggles with the comings and goings of large numbers of vacationers.

Calle Mobydick 2, Urbanización Guadalmar, 29004 Málaga. ✆ **95-223-17-03.** Fax 95-224-03-85. www.solmelia.com. 196 units. 83€–175€ double; 195€–320€ junior suite. Children 11 and under stay half-price in parent's room. AE, DC, MC, V. Free parking. **Amenities:** 2 restaurants; 3 bars; babysitting; exercise room; Jacuzzi; 2 freshwater pools (1 heated indoor); room service; sauna; outdoor tennis court. *In room:* A/C, TV, hair dryer, minibar, Wi-Fi (6€ per 12 hr.).

MODERATE

Hotel los Naranjos 🏅 The well-maintained Hotel los Naranjos is one of the more reasonably priced choices in the city. It's 1.6km (1 mile) from the heart of town on the eastern side of Málaga, past the Plaza de Toros (bullring), and near the best beach in Málaga, the Baños del Carmen. The hotel offers midsize, contemporary rooms. Breakfast (which costs extra) is the only meal served.

Paseo de Sancha 35, 29016 Málaga. ✆ **95-222-43-16.** Fax 95-222-59-75. www.hotel-los-naranjos.com. 41 units. 102€–150€ double; 160€ suite. AE, DC, MC, V. Parking 13€. Bus: 11. **Amenities:** Restaurant; bar; room service. *In room:* A/C, TV, hair dryer, minibar, Wi-Fi (free).

Parador de Málaga Golf ★★ A tasteful resort hotel created by the Spanish government, this hacienda-style *parador* is flanked by a golf course on one side and the Mediterranean on another. It's less than 3km (1¾ miles) from the airport, 11km (6¾ miles) from Málaga, and 4km (2½ miles) from Torremolinos. Rooms have private balconies with water views. The furnishings are attractive, the beds excellent. This restaurant has an indoor/outdoor dining room and a refined country-club atmosphere.

Carretera de Málaga, Torremolinos, 29080 Apartado 324, Málaga. ✆ **95-238-12-55.** Fax 95-238-89-63. www.parador.es. 60 units. 160€–209€ double; 240€–273€ suite. AE, DC, MC, V. Free parking. **Amenities:** Restaurant; bar; babysitting; 18-hole golf course; outdoor pool; room service; spa; outdoor tennis court (lit); Wi-Fi (free, in lobby). *In room:* A/C, TV, hair dryer, minibar.

Room Mate Loala ★ 🏅 A stylish hotel that is great value lies only a 10-minute walk from Málaga's famous Picasso Museum. Its sleek black-and-white interiors, all geometric patterns and etched glass, are in a chic Art Deco style, though certain antique pieces have been added to give the little boutique hotel more character. The designer wasn't afraid to use color—we're talking lavender and acid green. Bedrooms are midsize and tastefully and comfortably furnished, set around a tranquil courtyard with a gushing fountain. This is where you can take your breakfast or else chill out. The hotel has a small rooftop pool with a sun terrace where you can see the mountains in the distance.

Casa de Campos, 29001 Málaga. ☎ **952-779-300.** Fax 952-228-265. www.room-matehotels. com. 50 units. 95€–165€ double. AE, DC, MC, V. **Amenities:** Cafeteria; bar; pool (outdoor); room service. *In room:* A/C, TV, hair dryer, minibar, MP3 docking station, Wi-Fi (free).

INEXPENSIVE

El Cenachero Opened in 1969, this modest little hotel is 5 blocks from the park near the harbor. The nicely carpeted rooms are simply and functionally furnished; half have showers, the rest full bathrooms. No meals are served.

Barroso 5, 29001 Málaga. ☎ **95-222-40-88.** 14 units. 50€ double. No credit cards. Bus: 4 or 14. *In room:* TV.

Hostal Derby ★ ✦ Forget about beach locations and all that. This is one of those Franco-era stopovers that's suitable for those who want value and merely a decent place to lay their head for the night. A fourth-floor boardinghouse, it's in the heart of town, on a main square directly north of the train station. Some of the rather basic, cramped rooms have excellent views of the Mediterranean and the port of Málaga. Most units have only a shower. No breakfast is served, and the hotel is very light on extras.

San Juan de Dios 1, 29015 Málaga. ☎ **95-222-13-01.** 16 units, 12 with bathroom. 50€ double with sink; 53€–57€ double with bathroom. No credit cards. Bus: 7, 9, 12, 14, 15, 16, or 17. **Amenities:** Lounge.

Hotel Residencia Carlos V This hotel is in a central location near the cathedral, with an interesting facade decorated with wrought-iron balconies and *miradores* (viewing stations). It's a reliable, conservative choice. The small rooms are furnished in a no-frills style, but are well maintained and equipped with adequate bathrooms.

Cister 10, 29015 Málaga. ☎ **95-221-51-20.** Fax 95-221-51-29. www.hotel-carlosvmalaga.com. 50 units. 54€–71€ double. AE, DC, MC, V. Parking 10€. Bus: 3 from the rail station. *In room:* A/C, TV.

Luxurious Places to Stay Near Málaga

Barceló La Bobadilla ★★★ ☺ An hour's drive northeast of Málaga, La Bobadilla is one of the most luxurious retreats in southern Spain. It is a secluded oasis in the foothills of the Sierra Nevada near the town of Loja, which is 71km (44 miles) north of Málaga. La Bobadilla is a 21km (13-mile) drive from Loja. The hotel complex is built like an Andalusian village, a cluster of whitewashed *casas* constructed around a tower and a white church. Every *casa* has a roof terrace and a balcony overlooking the olive grove–studded district. Each unit is sumptuous and individually designed, from the least expensive double to the most expensive King's Suite. The hotel village stands on a hillside, on 404 hectares (998 acres) of private, unspoiled grounds.

Finca La Bobadilla, Apartado 144E, 18300 Loja (Granada). ☎ **95-832-18-61.** Fax 95-832-18-10. www.barcelolabobadilla.com. 70 units. 212€–419€ double; 242€–925€ suite. Rates include buffet

Málaga's main street, Calle Larios.

breakfast. AE, DC, MC, V. Free parking. From the Málaga airport, follow signs toward Granada, but at Km 175 continue through the village of Salinas. Take road marked SALINAS/RUTE; after 3km (1¾ miles), follow signposts for hotel to the entrance. **Amenities:** 2 restaurants; bar; babysitting; bikes; children's center; concierge; exercise room; 2 pools (1 heated indoor); room service; spa; 2 outdoor unlit tennis courts. *In room:* A/C, TV/DVD, hair dryer, minibar, Wi-Fi (free).

Villa Padierna/Thermas de Carratraca Hotel & Spa ★★★ Throughout the Franco era and for a few years into the new millennium, this once-imperial villa functioned as a low-rent inn, with an impeccable historic pedigree but without any pretensions of glamour. (It had originally been built in 1830 by Ferdinand VII for the entertainment of guests who included, among others, the Empress Eugénie and Lord Byron.) All that changed in 2007 when it reopened as a government-rated five-star deluxe enclave of plush. Positioned in the center of this small spa town (pop. 1,000), with direct access to the healing waters of the source favored by the ancient Romans and the Arab caliphs who replaced them, it retained many of the architectural grace notes of its original construction, including antique wooden doors. These lead into a posh boutique hotel outfitted with plushly comfortable furniture inspired by French styles of the late 19th century. Large numbers of clients overnighting at this place opt for at least some of the spa treatments with waters from the springs.

Calle Antonio Riobbo 11, 29551 Málaga. ☏ **95-248-95-42.** Fax 95-248-95-44. www.thermas decarratraca.com. 43 units. 220€–280€ double; 275€–400€ junior suites and suites. AE, DC, MC, V. Lies 30km (18 miles) north of Málaga, on A-357. Parking 10€. **Amenities:** Restaurant; bar; concierge; room service; spa. *In room:* A/C, TV, hair dryer, Wi-Fi (free).

Where to Dine in & Around Málaga
EXPENSIVE

Café de París ★★ FRENCH/SPANISH Café de París, Málaga's best restaurant, is in La Malagueta, the district surrounding the Plaza de Toros (bullring). Proprietor José García Cortés worked at many important dining rooms before carving out his own niche. His son, José Carlos García, is the chef. Much of Cortés's cuisine has been adapted from classic French dishes to please the

Andalusian palate. You might be served crepes gratinés filled with baby eels, or local whitefish baked in a salt crust. Stroganoff is given a Spanish twist with the use of ox meat. Save room for the creative desserts, such as citrus-flavored sorbet made with champagne or custard-apple mousse.

Vélez Málaga 8. ✆ **95-222-50-43.** www.rcafedeparis.com. Reservations required. Main courses 18€–28€; *menú del día* 45€. AE, DC, MC, V. Tues–Sat 1:30–3:30pm and 8:30–11pm. Closed July 1–15. Bus: 13.

Escuela de Hostelería ★ 🎁 MEDITERRANEAN We were surprised and pleased to discover this restaurant that's part of a hotel and catering school housed in a villa from the 1800s. It's 8km (5 miles) outside Málaga and 3km (1¾ miles) from the international airport. In business since the early 1990s, this place is mainly patronized by discerning locals with a taste for good food. The menu changes monthly. Freshly caught *merluza* is perfectly prepared with zesty mussels and mushrooms in a parsley-laced sauce. In autumn, loin of deer might appear on the menu with a chestnut purée. Other tempting dishes include sautéed filet of beef with a broccoli purée, green asparagus, and truffle juice, or lightly smoked sea bass cooked with a white wine and ginger sauce. The villa is old but the dining room adjoining it is modern, opening onto a garden.

Finca La Cónsula, Churriana. ✆ **95-243-60-26.** Reservations required. Main courses 16€–28€. AE, DC, MC, V. Mon–Fri 1–4pm. Closed Aug.

MODERATE

Adolfo ★ INTERNATIONAL/ANDALUSIAN Along the ocean-bordering Paseo Marítimo, this restaurant has been one of the best and most reliable in Málaga ever since opening to instant success in the mid-1990s. The decor is regional, with hardwood floors and exposed brick walls. Backed up by an excellent wine list strong on Andalusian vintages, the restaurant has a friendly, helpful staff. Well worth ordering are such daily specials as hake in a green sauce and duck glazed with a sweet wine. The big favorite here, often ordered on festive occasions, is *cochinillo* (roast suckling pig) flavored with garden herbs. Two other delicious choices are stewed anglerfish with prawns and wild mushrooms and roast baby kid in a rosemary-flavored honey sauce.

Paseo Marítimo Pablo Ruiz Picasso 12. ✆ **95-260-19-14.** www.restauranteadolfo.com. Reservations recommended. Main courses 10€–24€; fixed-price menu 45€. AE, DC, MC, V. Mon–Sat 1:30–4pm and 8:30–11pm. Closed June.

El Chinitas ★ SPANISH/MEDITERRANEAN In the heart of Málaga, a short walk from the tourist office, is this well-established restaurant. Many regular patrons consume a round of tapas and drinks at the associated Bar Orellana next door (which maintains the same hours, minus the midafternoon closing), and then head to Chinitas for a meal. The place is often filled with locals—always a good sign. The menu changes but might include a mixed fish fry, grilled red mullet, shrimp cocktail, grilled sirloin, or shellfish soup. The service manages to be both fast and attentive.

Moreno Monroy 4. ✆ **95-221-09-72.** www.elchinitas.com. Reservations recommended. Main courses 10€–20€. DC, MC, V. Daily 1–4pm and 8pm–midnight.

Parador de Málaga-Gibralfaro SPANISH This government-owned restaurant, on a mountainside high above the city, is especially notable for its view. You can look down into the heart of the Málaga bullring, among other sights. Meals are served in the attractive dining room or under the arches of two wide terraces with views of the coast. Featured dishes include *hors d'oeuvres parador*—your entire table covered with tiny dishes full of tasty tidbits. Two other specialties are an omelet of *chanquetes,* tiny whitefish popular in this part of the country, and chicken Villaroi. Otherwise, the quality of the food varies greatly.

Castillo de Gibralfaro. © **95-222-19-02.** Main courses 12€–26€. AE, DC, MC, V. Daily 1–4pm and 8:30–11pm. Microbus: 35.

INEXPENSIVE

Refectorium SPANISH Located behind the Málaga bullring, this place becomes hectic during any bullfight, filling up with fans and often, after the fight, with the matadors too. The cuisine has an old-fashioned flair, and the servings are generous. Try a typical Málaga soup, *ajo blanco con uvas* (cold almond soup flavored with garlic and garnished with big muscatel grapes). Another classic opener is garlicky mushrooms with bits of ham. The fresh seafood is a delight, including *rape* and angler; lamb might be served with a saffron-flavored tomato sauce. Desserts are like the ones Mama made, including rice pudding.

Calle Cervantes 8. © **95-221-89-90.** Reservations recommended on weekends and at bullfights. Main courses 15€–35€. AE, DC, MC, V. Tues–Sat 1–5pm and 8pm–midnight.

Málaga After Dark

The fun of nightlife in Málaga is just wandering, although there are a few standout destinations. More than just about any other city in the region, Málaga offers night owls the chance to stroll a labyrinth of inner city streets, drinking wine at any convenient *tasca* and talking with friends and new acquaintances.

Start out along the town's main thoroughfare, **Calle Larios,** adjacent to the city's port. Off Calle Larios, you can gravitate to any of the *tascas,* discos, and pubs lining the edges of the **Calle Granada.**

If you want to eat well and cheaply, do as the locals do and head for the taverns below. Don't expect a refined experience, but the food is some of the most enjoyable and least expensive in Málaga. You can easily fill up on two or three orders of tapas because portions are extremely generous.

Nearby, an all-pedestrian street, **Calle Compagnía,** and a square, the **Plaza Uncibaj,** are home to simpler *tascas.* Completely unpretentious (and in some cases without any discernible name), they serve glasses of wine and tapas similar to those available from their neighbors.

A rock venue, **ZZ Pub,** 6 Tejón y Rodríguez (© **95-244-15-95;** www.zzpub.es), is a favorite hangout for university students drawn here to see local bands play. Sometimes the Málaga newspaper, *El Sur,* publishes details. DJs rule the night at other times.

The main theater in the province is **Teatro Cervantes,** Ramos Marin s/n (© **95-222-41-00;** www.teatrocervantes.es), which opened its doors in the second half of the 19th century. Reopened in 1987 after a long closure by Queen Sofía, this is an elegant yet austere building. Its programs include plays in Spanish, as well as a number of concerts and flamenco entertainment of interest to all. The major performances of the Málaga Symphony Orchestra are staged here in winter. The theater is open from mid-September to the end of June; its box office is open Monday to Friday 10am to 2pm and 5:30 to 8:30pm, and Saturday 5:30 to 8:30pm.

The Balcón de Europa.

NERJA ★★

52km (32 miles) E of Málaga, 168km (104 miles) W of Almería, 548km (341 miles) S of Madrid

Nerja is known for its good beaches and small coves, its seclusion, its narrow streets and courtyards, and its whitewashed, flat-roofed houses. Nearby is one of Spain's greatest attractions, the Cave of Nerja (see below).

At the mouth of the Chillar River, Nerja gets its name from the Arabic word *narixa*, meaning "bountiful spring." Its most dramatic spot is the **Balcón de Europa ★★**, a palm-shaded promenade that juts into the Mediterranean. The walkway was built in 1885 in honor of a visit from the Spanish King Alfonso XIII in the wake of an earthquake that had shattered part of nearby Málaga. The phrase "Balcón de Europa" (Balcony of Europe) is said to have been coined by the king during one of the speeches he made in Nerja praising the beauty of the panorama around him. To reach the best beaches, head west from the Balcón and follow the shoreline.

Essentials

GETTING THERE At least 19 **buses** per day make the 1-hour trip from Málaga to Nerja, costing 3.85€ one-way. Service is provided by Alsina Graells. From Almería, there are seven buses running to Nerja (trip time: 3½ hr.), costing 12€ for a one-way ticket. Call the bus station, Av. Pescia s/n (**(✆ 95-252-15-04;** www.alsa.es), for information and schedules.

If you're driving, head along the N-340/E-15 east from Málaga, or take the N-340/E-15 west from Almería.

VISITOR INFORMATION The **tourist office,** at Calle Carmen 1 (**(✆ 95-252-15-31;** www.nerja.org), is open Monday to Saturday 10am to 2pm and 5 to 9pm, Sunday 10am to 2pm.

SPECIAL EVENTS A **cultural festival** takes place here in July. In the past it has drawn leading artists, musicians, and dancers from around the world.

Exploring Cueva de Nerja

The most popular outing from Málaga and Nerja is to the **Cueva de Nerja (Cave of Nerja) ★★**, Carretera de Maro s/n (**(✆ 95-252-95-20;** www. cuevadenerja.es). Scientists believe this prehistoric stalactite and stalagmite cave was inhabited from 25,000 to 2000 B.C. It was undiscovered until 1959, when a handful of boys found it by chance. When it was fully opened, it revealed a wealth of treasures left from the days of the cave dwellers, including Paleolithic paintings. They depict horses and deer, but at press time the room with cave paintings was not open to the public. You can walk through stupendous galleries where ceilings soar to a height of 60m (197 ft.).

The cave is in the hills near Nerja. From here you get panoramic views of the countryside and sea. It's open daily 10am to 2pm and 4 to 6:30pm (until 7:30pm July–Aug). Admission is 8.50€ adults, 4.50€ children 6 to 12, free for children 5 and under. Buses to the cave leave from Muelle de Heredia in Málaga hourly from 7am to 8:15pm. Return buses run every 2 hours until 8:15pm. The journey takes about 1 hour.

Where to Stay in Nerja

EXPENSIVE

Parador de Nerja ★★ This government-owned and -rated four-star hotel is on the outskirts of town, a 5-minute walk from the center. On the edge of a cliff, next to the sea, the hotel centers on a flower-filled courtyard with splashing fountain. The spacious rooms are furnished in understated but tasteful style, with midsize bathrooms.

Calle Almuñécar 8, 29780 Nerja. ✆ **95-252-00-50.** Fax 95-252-19-97. www.parador.es. 98 units. 148€–223€ double; 296€–342€ suite. AE, DC, MC, V. Free parking. **Amenities:** Restaurant; bar; babysitting; outdoor freshwater pool; room service; outdoor tennis court; Wi-Fi (free, in lobby). *In room:* A/C, TV, hair dryer, minibar.

MODERATE

Carabeo ★ 🎁 There is no more tranquil oasis in Nerja than this little inn, one of our favorite stopovers along the coast—and it's very affordable as well. A boutique hotel of charm and sophistication, Carabeo lies in the old sector of town in a typical Andalusian house, but it's also within an easy walk of the center and a 5-minute walk to a good beach. Taste and care have gone into the comfortable furnishings, and the place is filled with antiques and original art. The bedrooms are generally spacious, each with a small bathroom. Units are individually furnished, with well-chosen fabrics—in all, the British owners have created a rather homey feel. The five nicest rooms open onto views of the sea. These seaview bedrooms also contain a terrace large enough to shelter sun beds and a small table for breakfast.

Hernando de Carabeo 34, 29780 Nerja. ✆ **95-252-54-44.** Fax 95-252-17-34. www.hotelcarabeo. com. 12 units. 80€–130€ double; 110€–145€ junior suite; 135€–180€ suite. Rates include continental breakfast. AE, DC, MC, V. Children 11 and under not accepted. **Amenities:** Restaurant; bar; exercise room; outdoor pool; room service; sauna. *In room:* A/C, TV, hair dryer, minibar.

Hotel Balcón de Europa Occupying the best position in town, at the edge of the Balcón de Europa, this 1970s hotel offers guest rooms with private balconies overlooking the water and the rocks. At a private beach nearby, parasol-shielded tables are a peaceful place to enjoy the vista. The comfortable, midsize rooms have modern furniture and firm beds. There's a private garage a few steps away.

Paseo Balcón de Europa 1, 29780 Nerja. ✆ **95-252-08-00.** Fax 95-252-44-90. www.hotel-balconeuropa.com. 110 units. 98€–198€ double; 183€–235€ suite. AE, DC, MC, V. Parking 12€.

The Cueva de Nerja.

Amenities: 2 restaurants; bar; babysitting; outdoor freshwater heated pool; room service; sauna. *In room:* A/C, TV, hair dryer, minibar, Wi-Fi (9€ per 24 hr.).

Plaza Cavana ★ 📖 In the center of town, just behind the Balcón de Europa and a short walk from the beach, this two-story hotel is imbued with old-fashioned Andalusian charm. It lies behind a typical white facade with wooden balconies. The lobby has a classic decor with marble floors, and there is a garden patio where guests can relax. Rooms are elegant, spacious, and comfortable, and open onto balconies with either sea or mountain views.

Plaza Cavana 10, 29780 Nerja. © **95-252-40-00.** Fax 95-252-40-08. www.hotelplazacavana. com. 39 units. 75€–145€ double. AE, DC, MC, V. Parking 12€. **Amenities:** Restaurant; bar; exercise room; Jacuzzi; 2 freshwater pools (1 heated indoor); sauna; Wi-Fi (free, in lobby). *In room:* A/C, TV, hair dryer, minibar.

INEXPENSIVE

Hostalana 🌶 This simple inn calls itself a *hostal,* but it's more like a B&B, and one of the best bargains in a town where prices continue to rise dramatically. One of the town's more modern structures, it is still built in the old style and looks older than it is. Lying only 100m (328 ft.) from the landmark Balcón de Europa, it is run by a friendly couple who welcome you into their home. Bedrooms are simply furnished yet comfortable, the most desirable unit having a big bathroom with Jacuzzi.

Calle La Cruz, 29780 Nerja. © **95-252-30-43.** www.nerjalodging.com. 17 units. 32€–51€ double. MC, V. *In room:* A/C, TV, no phone.

Hostal Miguel The family-run Miguel is a pleasant, unpretentious inn on a quiet back street about a 3-minute walk from the Balcón de Europa, across from the well-known Pepe Rico Restaurant (see below). The simply furnished, somewhat small rooms have been renovated to add more Andalusian flavor. Breakfast is the only meal served, usually on a lovely roof terrace with a view of the mountains and sea. From July 15 to September 15, a minimum stay of 2 nights is required.

Almirante Ferrándiz 31, 29780 Nerja. © **95-252-15-23.** www.hostalmiguel.com. 9 units. 35€–52€ double. MC, V. *In room:* Ceiling fan, fridge, no phone.

Paraíso del Mar ★ 🏨 Next door to the more upmarket Parador de Nerja, this little hacienda also offers a panoramic view of the coastline. The former home of a wealthy expatriate has been turned into this comfortable villa near the edge of a cliff opening onto the fabled Balcón de Europa. Bedrooms are tastefully furnished but not luxurious. Most people request a seaview room; the rooms in the rear that lack views make up for it by being larger or including a Jacuzzi. You can also absorb the sea view from one of the hotel's public terraces.

Prolongación del Carabeo 22, 29780 Nerja. © **95-252-16-21.** Fax 95-252-23-09. www.hotel-paraisodelmar.es. 16 units. 85€–140€ double; 126€–170€ suite. AE, DC, MC, V. Parking 12€. **Amenities:** Bar; airport transfers (70€); bikes; Jacuzzi; outdoor freshwater pool; sauna; limited watersports rentals. *In room:* A/C, TV, hair dryer, minibar.

Where to Dine in Nerja

Casa Luque 🍴 INTERNATIONAL With its impressive canopied and balconied facade near the heart of town, Casa Luque looks like a dignified private villa. The interior has an Andalusian courtyard, and in summer there's a seaview terrace. Dishes are tasty, and portions are generous. Meals change according to the season and might include such palate-pleasing dishes as duck magret with honey and a kalamansi sauce (a bitter lemon-based sauce), or roast turkey suprême with a potato cake.

Plaza Cavana 2. © **95-252-10-04.** www.casaluque.com. Reservations recommended. Main courses 10€–22€. DC, MC, V. Mon–Tues and Thurs–Sat 1:30–3pm and 8–11pm; Sun 8–11pm.

Pepe Rico Restaurant ★ INTERNATIONAL Opened in 1966, Pepe Rico is one of Nerja's finest restaurants. Dine in a tavern room or alfresco on the patio. The specialty of the day, which might be a Spanish, German, Swedish, or French dish, ranges from almond-and-garlic soup to duck in wine. The impressive list of hors d'oeuvres includes smoked swordfish, salmon mousse, and prawns *pil-pil* (with hot chile peppers). Main dishes include filet of sole, roast leg of lamb, prawns Café de Paris, and steak dishes. Considering the quality of the food, the prices are reasonable.

Almirante Ferrándiz 28. © **95-252-02-47.** www.peperico.info. Reservations recommended. Main courses 12€–25€; fixed-price menu 11€–25€ at lunch, 25€ at dinner. MC, V. Mon–Sat 12:30–3pm and 7–11pm. Closed 2 weeks in Dec and 1 week in Jan.

Restaurante Rey Alfonso ★ SPANISH/INTERNATIONAL Few visitors to the Balcón de Europa realize they're standing directly above one of the most unusual restaurants in town. The menu and decor don't hold many surprises, but the close-up view of the crashing waves makes dining here worthwhile. Have a drink at the bar if you don't want a full meal. Specialties include a well-prepared *paella valenciana,* Cuban-style rice, five preparations of sole (from grilled to meunière), several versions of tournedos and entrecôte, crayfish in whiskey sauce, and crêpes suzette for dessert. You enter from the bottom of a flight of stairs that skirts the rocky base of a late-19th-century *mirador* (viewing station), which juts seaward as an extension of the town's main square.

Paseo Balcón de Europa s/n. © **95-252-09-58.** Reservations recommended. Main courses 10€–18€. MC, V. Mon–Sat noon–3pm and 7–11pm. Closed 4 weeks Jan–Feb.

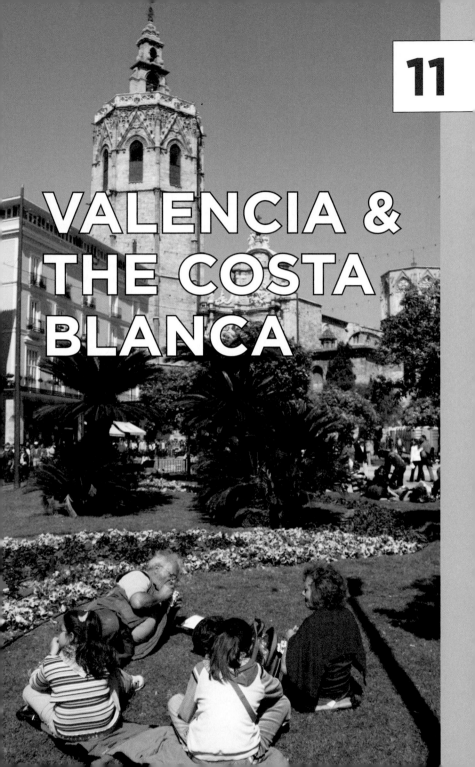

VALENCIA & THE COSTA BLANCA

S pain's third-largest city, Valencia—celebrated for oranges and paella—lies in the midst of a *huerta,* a fertile crescent of alluvial plain that's irrigated by a centuries-old system. The area is a breadbasket of Spain, a place where "the soil never sleeps."

For such a major city, Valencia is relatively unexplored by tourists, even though it has some rewarding treasures, including a wealth of baroque architecture, fine museums, good cuisine, and a proud, if troubled, history.

The **Costa Blanca (White Coast)** begins rather unappealingly at Valencia but improves considerably as it winds its way south toward Alicante. The overbuilt route south is dotted with fishing ports and resorts known chiefly to Spanish and other European vacationers. The success of **Benidorm** began in the 1960s, when this fishing village was transformed into an international resort. **Alicante,** the official capital of the Costa Blanca, enjoys a reputation as a winter resort because of its mild climate. **Murcia** is inland but it's on the main road to the Costa del Sol, so hordes of motorists pass through it.

VALENCIA ★★

351km (218 miles) SE of Madrid, 361km (224 miles) SW of Barcelona, 650km (404 miles) NE of Málaga

Valencia's charms—or lack thereof—are much debated. Some claim that the city where El Cid faced the Moors is one of the most beautiful on the Mediterranean. Others write it off as drab, provincial, and industrial. The truth lies somewhere in between. This Mediterranean port is in the midst of a Bilbao-type renewal. Valencia's answer to Bilbao's Guggenheim is the jaw-dropping City of Arts and Sciences.

Set amid orange trees and rice paddies, Valencia's reputation as a romantic city seems more justified by its past than by its present. Hidden between modern office buildings and monotonous apartment houses, remnants of an illustrious past do remain. However, floods and war have been cruel to Valencia, forcing Valencianos to tear down buildings that today would be architectural treasures.

Valencia has a strong cultural tradition. Its most famous son was writer Vicente Blasco Ibáñez, best known for his novel about bullfighting, *Blood and Sand,* and for his World War I novel, *The Four Horsemen of the Apocalypse.* Both were filmed twice in Hollywood, with Rudolph Valentino starring in the first version of each. Joaquín Sorolla, the famous Spanish Impressionist, was another native of Valencia. You can see his works at a museum dedicated to him in Madrid.

Essentials

GETTING THERE Iberia flies to Valencia from Barcelona, Madrid, Málaga, and many other cities. There are also flights between Palma de Majorca and Valencia. For flight information contact the **Iberia Airlines** office, Calle

PREVIOUS PAGE: **Picnicking in front of the Catedral of Valencia.**

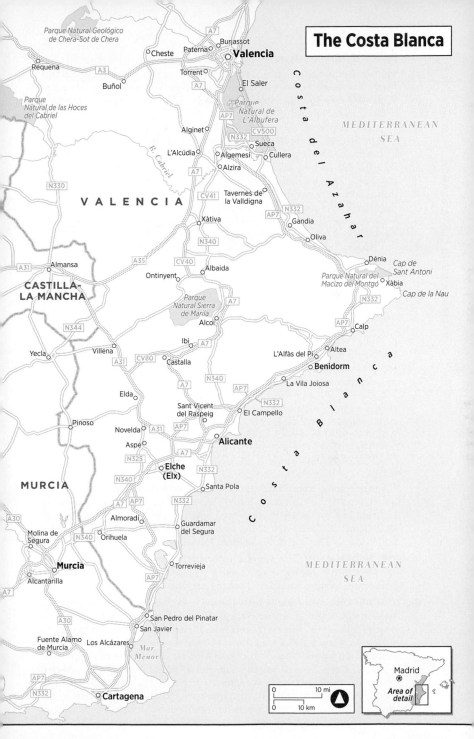

The Costa Blanca

Paz 14 (☎ **90-240-05-00;** www.iberia.com). You'll land 15km (9⅓ miles) southwest of the city. To travel between the airport and the city center, take Metro line 3 or 5; a one-way ticket costs 1.40€. For more information call ☎ **90-046-10-46.** A taxi (☎ **96-370-33-33**) from the airport to the town center goes for around 15€.

Trains run to Valencia from all parts of Spain. Estación del Norte (North Station), Calle Játiva 2, is close to the heart of the city, making it a convenient arrival point. Its information office on Calle Renfe (☎ **90-224-02-02;** www.renfe.es) is open Monday to Friday 8am to 9pm. From Barcelona, 15 trains—including the TALGO, which takes 3½ hours—arrive daily. Fourteen trains daily connect Madrid with Valencia. The new Alaris high-speed train travels at 221kmph (137 mph) and has shaved travel time between Madrid and Valencia to less than 3½ hours. From Málaga, on the Costa del Sol, the trip takes 9 hours.

Buses arrive at Valencia's Estació Terminal d'Autobuses, Av. de Menéndez Pidal 13 (☎ **96-346-62-66**), about a 30-minute walk northwest of the city's center. Take bus no. 8 from the Plaza del Ayuntamiento. Thirteen buses a day, at least one every hour, run from Madrid (trip time: 4 hr.), 10 buses from Barcelona (trip time: 5 hr.), and five buses from Málaga (trip time: 8 hr.).

You can take a **ferry** to and from the Balearic Islands (see chapter 20, p. 703). Ferries to Palma de Majorca take 6 hours. Ferries leave Valencia for Ibiza at midnight Tuesday to Sunday from March to September. In winter, there is one ferry per week. Travel agents in Valencia sell tickets, or you can buy them from the Trasmediterránea office at the port, Estació Marítim (☎ **90-245-46-45;** www.trasmediterranea.es), on the day of your departure. To reach the port, take bus no. 4 or 19 from the Plaza del Ayuntamiento. Ferries from Majorca to Valencia leave from Estació Marítim 2. Call ☎ **90-245-46-45** for details.

The easiest route if you're driving is the express highway (E-15) south from Barcelona. You can also use a national highway, E-901, from Madrid northwest of Valencia. From Alicante, take the E-15 express highway north. If you're coming from Andalusia, the roads are longer, more difficult, and not connected by express highways. You can drive from Málaga north to Granada and cut across southeastern Spain on the 342, which links with the 340 into Murcia. From there, take the road to Alicante for an easy drive into Valencia. The Barcelona-Valencia toll is 24€.

VISITOR INFORMATION The **tourist information office** is at Calle Paz 48 (☎ **96-398-64-22;** www.comunitatvalenciana.com). It's open Monday to Friday 9am to 8pm, Saturday 10am to 8pm, and Sunday 10am to 2pm.

GETTING AROUND Most **local buses** leave from Plaza del Ayuntamiento 22. You can buy tickets at any newsstand. The one-way fare is 1.25€; a 10-ride booklet sells for 6€. Bus no. 8 runs from Plaza del Ayuntamiento to the bus station at Avenida Menéndez Pidal. A bus map is available at the EMT office, Calle Correo Viejo 5. It's open Monday to Friday 9am to 2pm and 4:30 to 7:30pm. For bus information, call ☎ **96-315-85-15.** The **Metro** system (☎ **90-046-10-46;** www.metrovalencia.es) is more efficient than the bus. It covers the Old Town rather well and also branches out to the outskirts. You can purchase tickets from automatic machines in any station; the cost ranges from 1.40€ for one zone to 1.90€ for two zones. A *bonometro,*

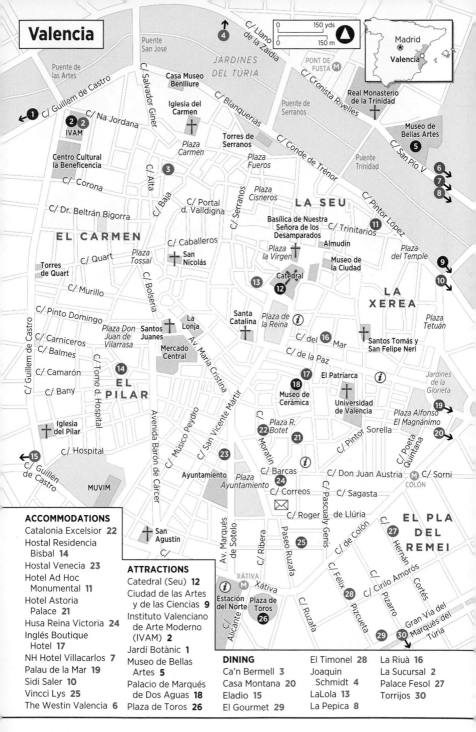

Valencia

C/ Llano de la Zaidia

Puente San José

JARDINES DEL TÚRIA

PONT DE FUSTA M

C/ Cronista Rivelles

Real Monasterio de la Trinidad

Puente de Serranos

Casa Museo Benlliure

Iglesia del Carmen

C/ Blanquerias

Museo de Bellas Artes **5**

C/ San Pío V

C/ Salvador Giner

C/ Na Jordana

IVAM

Plaza Carmen

Torres de Serranos

Plaza Fueros

C/ Conde de Trénor

Puente Trinidad

6
7
8

C/ Guillem de Castro

Centro Cultural la Beneficencia

C/ Corona

C/ Alta

C/ Baja

Plaza Cisneros

LA SEU

C/ Pintor López

C/ Dr. Beltrán Bigorra

C/ Portal d. Valldigna

C/ Serranos

Basílica de Nuestra Señora de los Desamparados

C/ Trinitarios

11

Almudín

Plaza del Temple

9
10

EL CARMEN

C/ Caballeros

C/ Quart

Plaza Tossal

San Nicolás

Plaza la Virgen

Museo de la Ciudad

LA XEREA

Torres de Quart

C/ Murillo

C/ Bolseria

Catedral

13

12

Plaza del Temple

Plaza Tetuán

C/ Pinto Domingo

Santa Catalina

Plaza de la Reina

i

Plaza Don Juan de Vilarrasa

Santos Juanes

La Lonja

Av. María Cristina

C/ del Mar **16**

Santos Tomás y San Felipe Neri

C/ Carniceros

C/ Balmes

Mercado Central

C/ de la Paz

C/ Guillem de Castro

C/ Camarón

C/ Tomo d. Hospital

EL PILAR

14

17

El Patriarca

i

Jardines de la Glorieta

C/ Bany

Museo de Cerámica

18

Universidad de Valencia

Plaza Alfonso El Magnánimo

19

Iglesia del Pilar

Avenida Barón de Cárcer

C/ Músico Peydro

C/ San Vicente Mártir

Plaza R. Botet

22

21

C/ Pintor Sorella

C/ Poeta Quintana

20

15

C/ Guillem de Castro

C/ Hospital

MUVIM

23

Ayuntamiento

Plaza Ayuntamiento

C/ Barcas

24

C/ Correos

i

C/ Don Juan Austria

M C/ Sorni

COLÓN

San Agustín

C/

Av. Marqués de Sotelo

C/ Ribera

Paseo Ruzafa

C/ Roger de Llúria

C/ Pascual y Genís

C/ Sagasta

EL PLA DEL REMEI

C/ de Colón

27

Hernán

C/ Cirilo Amorós

Cortés

25

XÁTIVA M

Xátiva

Estación del Norte

i

Plaza de Toros

26

C/ Félix Pizcueta

C/ Pizarro

Gran Via del Marqués del Túria

C/ Alicante

C/ Ruzafa

28

29

30

Madrid ✱

Valencia ✱

0 — 150 yds
0 — 150 m

ACCOMMODATIONS
Catalonia Excelsior **22**
Hostal Residencia Bisbal **14**
Hostal Venecia **23**
Hotel Ad Hoc Monumental **11**
Hotel Astoria Palace **21**
Husa Reina Victoria **24**
Inglés Boutique Hotel **17**
NH Hotel Villacarlos **7**
Palau de la Mar **19**
Sidi Saler **10**
Vincci Lys **25**
The Westin Valencia **6**

ATTRACTIONS
Catedral (Seu) **12**
Ciudad de las Artes y de las Ciencias **9**
Instituto Valenciano de Arte Moderno (IVAM) **2**
Jardí Botànic **1**
Museo de Bellas Artes **5**
Palacio de Marqués de Dos Aguas **18**
Plaza de Toros **26**

DINING
Ca'n Bermell **3**
Casa Montana **20**
Eladio **15**
El Gourmet **29**

El Timonel **28**
Joaquin Schmidt **4**
LaLola **13**
La Pepica **8**

La Riuà **16**
La Sucursal **2**
Palace Fesol **27**
Torrijos **30**

431

The Plaza de Toros bullring.

good for 10 trips in the zones indicated, is a better deal, selling for 6.50€ for one zone or 9.30€ for two zones.

If you need a taxi, call © **96-370-33-33.**

SPECIAL EVENTS **Fallas de San José,** honoring the arrival of spring and the memory of St. Joseph, is held March 15 to March 19. It is a time for parades, street dancing, fireworks, and bullfights. Neighborhoods compete to see who can erect the most intricate and satirical papier-mâché effigy, or *ninot.* Some 300 *ninots* then appear in the street parades. The festival ends with *la nit del foc,* or "fire night," when effigies are burned. Historically, this inferno was to exorcise social problems and bring luck to farmers in the coming summer.

FAST FACTS In a medical emergency, call © **112;** or go to the **Hospital Clínico Universitario,** Av. Blasco Ibáñez 17 (© **96-386-26-00**).

Don't be surprised if you see signs in a language that's not Spanish or Catalan. It is **Valenciano,** a dialect of Catalan. Often you'll be handed a "bilingual" menu in Castilian Spanish and in Valenciano. Many citizens of Valencia are not caught up in this cultural resurgence and view the promotion of the dialect as possibly damaging to the city's economic goals. Most street names appear in Valenciano.

There are many Internet cafes in Valencia, the most reliable of which is **Work Center,** open 24 hours at Xátiva 19 (© **96-112-08-30**), in front of the bullring and Estación del Norte.

Exploring Valencia

Corridas (bullfights) are staged for a week during the *fallas* observances in March. Today locals seem more interested in soccer than in bullfighting. Nevertheless, Valencia's **Plaza de Toros,** one of the largest rings in Spain, is adjacent to the rail station at Calle de Xátiva 28 (© **96-351-93-15**).

As a respite from the heat, retreat to the **Jardí Botànic,** Calle Quart 80 (© **96-315-68-00;** www.jardibotanic.org), which was founded by the University of Valencia in 1567. For 2 centuries it was an orchard for medicinal plants, and botany classes are still offered. Today it boasts one of the most important collections of varied tree life and palms in Europe. In all, nearly 45,000 international species are displayed. Admission is 2€ (free for children 6 and under). Hours are daily May to August 10am to 9pm, April and September 10am to 8pm, March and October 10am to 7pm, and November to February 10am to 6pm (Metro: Turia and Angel Guimerà).

Catedral (Seu) ★ For 500 years, this cathedral has claimed to possess the Holy Grail, the chalice Jesus used at the Last Supper; it's on display in a side chapel. The subject of countless legends, the Grail was said to have been used by Joseph of Arimathea to collect Jesus' blood as it dripped from the cross. It looms large in Sir Thomas Malory's *Morte d'Arthur,* Tennyson's *Idylls of the King,* and Wagner's *Parsifal.*

Although this 1262 cathedral represents a number of styles, including Romanesque and baroque, Gothic predominates. Its huge arches have been restored, and in back is a handsome domed basilica. It was built on the site of a mosque torn down by the Catholic monarchs.

After seeing the cathedral, you can scale an incomplete 47m-high (154-ft.) Gothic tower known as **Miguelete** ★ (Micalet in local dialect). It affords a panoramic view of the city and the fertile *huerta* beyond. Or visit the **Museo de la Catedral,** where works by Goya and Zurbarán are on exhibit.

Plaza de la Reina. © **96-391-81-27.** www.catedraldevalencia.es. Free admission to cathedral; to Miguelete 2.50€; to Museo de la Catedral 3.50€. Cathedral daily 7:30am–1pm and 4:30–8:30pm; Miguelete Mon–Fri 10am–12:30pm and 5:30–6:30pm, Sun 10am–1pm and 5–6:30pm; Museo de la Catedral Mon–Fri 10am–1pm and 4–7pm. Bus: 9, 27, 70, or 71.

The facade of the Catedral of Valencia.

Biking around the Ciudad de las Artes y de las Ciencias.

Ciudad de las Artes y de las Ciencias (City of the Arts and the Sciences) ★★★ In a bid to rival Seville's Expo and Barcelona's redeveloped port, Valencia competes with what has been billed "the largest urban complex in Europe for cultural, educational, and leisure expansion." It's in the southern part of the city, on a 36-hectare (89-acre) site in a carefully landscaped park of lush greenery and peaceful lagoons. The goal of the complex is to make learning fun. The state-of-the-art educational center consists of four main buildings:

L'Hemisferic ★: Designed by award-winning architect Santiago Calatrava, this building offers documentaries and an exploration of the universe. A laser show (with changing programs) runs on a 47-sq.-m (506-sq.-ft.) concave IMAX screen, with the soundtrack in four languages, and six-channel stereo.

Museo de las Ciencias Príncipe Felipe ★: Devoted to science and discovery, the building takes the form of a vast roof supported by a transparent glazed north facade and an opaque south facade. At the center, the visitor can look, touch, and feel in this "museum of sensations." The museum is filled with special exhibitions demonstrating the high technology of companies in the 21st century.

L'Oceanografic: Eight hectares (20 acres) of the complex are devoted to lagoons and leisure pavilions arranged into an underwater city that re-creates marine habitats from every ocean. There's also a dolphinarium for aquatic shows and a miniport for playing with remote-controlled boats. Submarine glass walkways connect the areas. An underwater restaurant is on-site.

Palacio de las Artes: A seemingly weightless 45m-high (148-ft.) glass-and-metal construction contains one outdoor and two indoor auditoriums. All three have the latest technology for the performance of plays, opera, and music.

Av. Autopista del Saler 1, 3, 5, 7. ✆ **90-210-00-31.** www.cac.es. Admission to L'Hemisferic 7.50€; 5.80€ children 12 and under, students, and seniors. Admission to L'Oceanografic 24€ adults; 18€ children 12 and under, students, and seniors. Admission to Museo de las Ciencias Príncipe Felipe 7.50€ adults; 5.80€ children 16 and under, students, and seniors. L'Hemisferic daily 10am–9pm. Museo de las Ciencias Príncipe Felipe and L'Oceanografic daily 10am–7pm (9pm July–Sept). Bus: 19, 35, 40, or 95 to Centro Comercio de Saler.

Instituto Valenciano de Arte Moderno (IVAM) ★★ This contemporary art center jump-started a renaissance of art in Valencia. The giant complex consists of two sites: an ultramodern building and a 13th-century former convent. Its opening gained Valencia prime status among the world's art capitals.

Julio González Centre is named for the avant-garde Spanish artist whose paintings, sculptures, and drawings form the nucleus of the permanent collection. Much influenced by Picasso, González was a pioneer in iron sculpture. His work in turn exerted a profound influence on the American sculptor David Smith, among others.

The other site is the nearby **Center del Carmen,** the old convent, with cloisters from the 14th and 16th centuries. It devotes three halls to changing exhibits of contemporary art. Permanent displays include works of Ignacio Pinazo, whose paintings and drawings mark the beginning of modernism in Valencia. The institute is on the western edge of Old Town, near the **Torres de Quart,** 15th-century towers that guard the entrance to the city.

Calle Guillém Castro 118. © **96-386-30-00.** www.ivam.es. Admission 2€ adults, free for children 9 and under. Tues–Sun 10am–8pm. Bus: 5.

Museo de Bellas Artes ★ This treasure house of paintings and sculptures, which stands on the north bank of the Turia River, contains a strong collection of Flemish and native Valencian art. Of particular note are those by the 14th- and 15th-century **Valencian "primitives"** ★★. The most celebrated painting is a 1640 self-portrait by Velázquez, and a whole room is devoted to Goya. Other artists exhibited include Bosch, Morales, El Greco *(St. John the Baptist),* Ribera, Murillo, Pinturicchio, and Sorolla. Of special interest is a salon displaying the works of contemporary Valencian painters and an important sculpture by Mariano Benlliure. The ground-floor archaeological collection encompasses early Iberian, Roman (including an altar to a pagan emperor), and Christian finds.

San Pío V 9. © **96-387-03-00.** www.museobellasartesvalencia.gva.es. Free admission. Tues–Sun 10am–8pm. Bus: 1, 5, 6, 8, 16, 26, 29, 36, 79, or 95. Metro: Alameda.

Palacio de Marqués de Dos Aguas ★ This landmark palace houses the famous Museo Nacional de Cerámica, with one of the grandest collections of ceramics in Spain. The vast collection offers everything from lizards on plates to frogs riding the backs of lambs. In addition, there is a Gallery of Humorists, with caricatures of everybody from Einstein on down. In the case of this palace, the building—a bizarre mixture of rococo and Churrigueresque—competes with the exhibits. Ignacio Vergara, in the 18th century, carved the figures of *Dos Aguas* (Two Waters), the palace's namesake. Its history goes back to 1496, although the building's current look is predominantly 19th century. After you get your fill of art, a carriage museum and an armor room downstairs offer variety.

Poeta Querol 2. © **96-351-63-92.** http://mnceramica.mcu.es. Admission 3€. Tues–Sun 10am–2pm; Tues–Sat 4–8pm. Metro: Plaza de los Pinazo.

Beaches & Boating

BEACHES Valencia boasts more than 2.8km (1¾ miles) of beaches, with excellent facilities. The **Arenas** and **Malvarrosa** beaches are just minutes from the city center. Adjoining these beaches is the seafront promenade, **Paseo Marítimo,** where you can walk, jog, sunbathe, or roller-skate. The beaches to the north and south of the port, Playa de la Punta and Playa de Levante, are too polluted for swimming. However, if you head south you'll reach **El Saler,** where you'll see the European blue flag waving; it's awarded for clear waters and golden sands.

BOATING Club Náutico Valencia, Camí del Canal 91 (© **96-367-90-11;** www.rcnauticovalencia.com), has a sailing school that rents boats for scuba diving and snorkeling. It maintains a full yacht-service facility.

Shopping

You haven't seen Valencia until you've headed for the 1920s **Mercado Central,** on the Plaza del Mercado in the heart of the city. It stands across the street from **La Lonja,** the silk exchange that dates from 1482 and is one of the most splendid examples of secular Gothic architecture in Spain. After a visit to this "central market," you'll never want to shop in a supermarket again. The market lies in a grand railway station–like building, with stained glass no less. It sells everything: blood sausage, ungracefully nude *poulets,* saffron, bomba rice for paella, even Marcona almonds. To see the women of Valencia shop for food is reason enough to go.

If you're in Valencia on a Sunday morning, head for the open-air market at **Plaza Redonda** (literally "round square"). Found near the cathedral, it hawks traditional Valencian handicrafts, including ceramics, ironwork, silver items, and inlaid marquetry. Vendors also sell crafts from other regions of Spain, even Morocco. The best shopping streets include **Plaza del Ayuntamiento, Calle Don Juan de Austria, Calle Colón,** and the streets thereabouts. For a peek at what aging Valencian *duennas* are storing in their cellars and attics, head for the *rastro* (flea market), on Avenida de Suecia near the soccer stadium, beginning around 8:30am every Sunday. The city's largest department store, **El Corte**

LEFT: **The Paseo Marítimo.** ABOVE: **A fish vendor at the Mercado Central, Valencia's central market.**

Inglés, Calle Pintor Sorolla 26 (© **96-315-95-00**), sells a wide array of anything you might want, including local handicrafts, crystal and porcelain, and other luxury items.

The **Mercado de Colón** ★ in the heart of the city is a Gaudí-inspired fantasy that's a hub of many modern cafes, restaurants, crafts shops, and flower stalls. The market hall dates from 1916 when it opened in the center of Eixample, the city's most exclusive and residential area. Influenced by the celebrated architect Gaudí, the market was called "an epiphany of *Modernista* architecture and a fusion of historicism and modernism." Several streets around the market also attract the crowds, notably a locally famous chocolatier, **Cacao Sampaka,** 19 Calle Conde de Salvatierra (© **96-353-40-62;** www.cacaosampaka.com). Ever had a balsamic vinegar–flavored bonbon?

Valencia is home to some of Spain's best pottery. The region produces Lladró porcelain, Manises stoneware, and glassware. Local craftspeople take pride in their *azulejos*—brightly colored ceramic tiles, first developed during the Muslim occupation of Andalusia. Some of the best of Valencian crafts are sold at **Nela,** 2 Calle San Vicente (© **96-392-30-23**).

One of the best outlets for women's fashion along the eastern coast of Spain is **Linda Vuela a Río,** Gran Vía Marqués del Turia 31 (© **96-351-77-46**).

For more avant-garde fashion, head for **Tonuca,** Calle Félix Pizcueta 20 (© **96-394-05-55**). On the cutting edge, Tonuca Belloch-Burguera is the most avant-garde Valencian designer.

Everything from Chinese painted mirrors to Moroccan poufs is sold at a center for interior design, **Zara Home,** Carrer Jorge Juan 15 (© **96-351-32-52**).

On a street filled with antiques dealers, two of the best art galleries in Valencia are within walking distance of each other: **My Name's Lolita,** Carrer Avellanas 7 (© **96-391-13-72;** www.mynameslolita.com), and **Galeria Valle Orti,** Carrer Avellanas 22 (© **96-392-33-77;** www.valleorti.com).

One worthy detour is to **Manises,** 9km (5⅔ miles) west of Valencia. It's known as a center for ceramics and for its *azulejos.* As a pottery center, Manises dates from the Middle Ages. Representatives from all the major kingdoms of Europe came here to purchase wares, which are characterized by their distinctive blue-and-white patterns. The town is packed with ceramics factories and retail outlets. From the center of Valencia, several buses run frequently to Manises.

Another good stop for the serious shopper is nearby **Paterna,** about 6.5km (4 miles) northwest of Valencia off C-234. (It's signposted all the way.) It has dozens of pottery stores with prices far below those in the center of Valencia.

Continuing farther north to the province of Castellón, you'll find the towns of **Alcora** and **Onda.** They're justly celebrated for their pottery, much of which is reasonably priced because the "middleperson" is often eliminated. In addition to pottery, several shops in Onda sell some of the best-crafted *azulejos* in this part of Spain. **Alcora** is 19km (12 miles) northwest of Castellón de la Plana along the C-232; **Onda,** 15km (9⅓ miles) west along the C-223.

In the city of Valencia itself, head for **Lladró,** Calle Poeta Querol 9 (© **96-351-16-25**), where prices are consistent with those at other retail outlets. Or seek out the shop adjacent to the factory, **Casa de Lladró,** Carretera de Alborraya s/n, in the suburb of Tavernas Blanques (© **90-021-10-10;** www. lladro.com), 5km (3 miles) north of the city center. The factory retail outlet sells slightly damaged or irregular pieces at lower prices. To visit the factory itself, call 1 month in advance.

Where to Stay in Valencia

In July and August, when Valencia can be uncomfortably hot and humid, some hoteliers lower prices significantly if business is slow. It never hurts to ask.

EXPENSIVE

Hilton Valencia ★★★ This upscale hotel lies immediately adjacent to the city's convention center, about 3km (1¾ miles) east of the town's historic core. Opened in 2007, this 29-story glass-and-dark-metal tower is the tallest building in Valencia, and, as such, is visible from most neighborhoods of the city. Bedrooms are medium to large in size, well accessorized, and plush, with big-windowed views, tasteful contemporary furnishings, and warm tones of beige and salmon. Bathrooms are sheathed in marble, and each room has a writing table. There are two restaurants on-site: **Azahar** (for breakfast, lunch, and dinner) and the more posh and cutting-edge **Bice,** a branch of a well-known Italian chain with outposts scattered across Europe.

Av. Cortes Valencianas 52, 46015 Valencia. **(?) 96-303-00-00.** Fax 96-303-00-01. www.hilton. com. 304 units. 145€–439€ double; from 285€ suite. AE, DC, MC, V. Valet parking 23€. Metro: Benifarri. **Amenities:** 2 restaurants; 2 bars; babysitting; concierge; health club; indoor heated pool; room service; spa. *In room:* A/C, TV, hair dryer, minibar, Wi-Fi (12€ per hour).

Hotel Astoria Palace ★ On a small, charming square in the heart of town, this modern business hotel offers some of the best-furnished public and private rooms in Valencia. A favorite of such Spanish stars as opera singer Montserrat Caballé, bullfighter Manuel Benítez ("El Cordobés"), and an impressive roster of writers and politicians, the Astoria is plush, well managed, and appealing. Many of the tastefully furnished guest rooms overlook a sculpture of Grecian maidens and swans in the square outside. The highest prices are for the three premium floors, which have a private lounge and separate check-in. The hotel is 5 short blocks south of the cathedral.

Plaza Rodrigo Botet 5, 46002 Valencia. **(?) 96-398-10-00.** Fax 96-398-10-11. www.hotel-astoria-palace.com. 204 units. 100€–356€ double; 150€–407€ junior suite; 180€–814€ suite. AE, DC, MC, V. Parking 15€ nearby. Bus: 9, 10, 27, 70, or 71. **Amenities:** Restaurant; bar; fitness room; Jacuzzi; room service; sauna. *In room:* A/C, TV, hair dryer, minibar, Wi-Fi (16€ per 24 hr.).

Palau de la Mar ★★★ For those who appreciate good taste and elegant comfort, Palau de la Mar is the finest place to stay in Valencia. In a restored *palacio* built in the 1800s, this stylish boutique hotel lies in the heart of the city. The perfect blend of antique and modern contrasts heavily carved doors and intricate ironwork with steel, glass, and creamy white textiles. Elegance, art, and design are happily combined here. The chief asset is a stunningly designed interior patio with a luxuriant garden. The bedrooms are cozy retreats, with crisp white bed linens set off against dark wood floors. And at last, a hotel that offers complimentary access to the minibars.

Calle Navarro Reverter 14–16, 46004 Valencia. **(?) 96-316-28-84.** Fax 96-316-28-85. www.fuenso. com. 66 units. 123€–350€ double; 379€–450€ junior suite. AE, DC, MC, V. Parking 25€. Metro: Colón. **Amenities:** Restaurant; bar; babysitting; state-of-the-art health club & sauna; indoor heated pool; room service. *In room:* A/C, TV/DVD, minibar, Wi-Fi (free).

Sidi Saler If it's summer, and you want a location right on the beach, head for the coastal strip 12km (7½ miles) south of Valencia at Playa El Saler, one of the best sandy beaches in the area. Open year-round, and built in 1975, this hotel is at its best in the warm months. A golf course is close at hand should you grow bored with the sands. Standard guest rooms (doubles) are midsize, and most of them have a midsize balcony overlooking the sea. The junior suites are even better, each with a large balcony and a separate living room as well. Furnishings are modern but traditional in styling. Well-maintained bathrooms come with tubs and showers. If you don't want to travel far afield for your meals, you'll find good dining on-site, with not only Valencian paella but also an array of regional and international dishes.

Playa el Saler, 46012 Valencia. © **96-161-04-11.** Fax 96-161-08-38. www.hotelessidi.es. 276 units. 120€–332€ double; 191€–492€ junior suite; 362€–1,032€ suite. AE, DC, MC, V. Free parking. **Amenities:** 2 restaurants; 2 bars; babysitting; bikes; exercise room; 2 pools (1 heated indoor, 1 outdoor); room service; sauna; 2 outdoor tennis courts; Wi-Fi (17€ per 24 hr.). *In room:* A/C, TV, hair dryer, minibar.

Vincci Lys ★ Just a 4-minute walk from the train station, this centrally located hotel, completely restored, is one of the best bets for those who want to drop anchor at the very heart of Valencia. Located on a pedestrian-only street lined with cafes, it offers modern, functional space geared to the vacationer and the business traveler alike. Guest rooms are light, airy, and spacious, each with a well-maintained private bathroom. Nearly two dozen of the accommodations have private balconies opening onto cityscapes. Some of the guest rooms are designed especially for women travelers. The on-site restaurant, **Almudí,** is a winning choice, serving traditional Valencian dishes such as paella and using locally grown products whenever possible.

Martínez Cubells 5, 46002 Valencia. © **96-350-95-50.** Fax 96-350-95-52. www.vinccihoteles. com. 101 units. 110€–300€ double; 211€–655€ junior suite; 420€–755€ suite. AE, DC, MC, V. Parking 27€. Bus: 4, 6, 8, 16, 35, or 36. **Amenities:** Restaurant; bar; concierge; room service. *In room:* A/C, TV, hair dryer, minibar, Wi-Fi (10€ per 24 hr.).

The Westin Valencia ★★★ The major hotel in the region occupies the radically restored and almost unimaginably worked-over premises of what was originally built in 1917 as a textile mill, and which later functioned, during the Franco era, as a police and fire station. It reopened as a Westin in 2006 and is now considered by many to be the best hotel in Valencia, a three-story palace that's outfitted with dignity, comfort, and good taste. Bedrooms, decorated in warm tones of brown, evoke a vaguely Art Deco feeling, while public areas are plush, contemporary, and baronial. It lies close to the historic core of the city, within a 20-minute walk from the port.

Amadeo de Saboya 16, 46010 Valencia. © **96-362-59-00.** Fax 96-362-59-09. www.westin. com/valencia. 135 units. 135€–270€ double; from 305€ suite. AE, DC, MC, V. Parking 20€. Metro: Aragón or Alameda. **Amenities:** 2 restaurants; 3 bars; babysitting; bikes; concierge; health club; indoor heated pool; room service; spa. *In room:* A/C, TV, movie library, hair dryer, minibar, Wi-Fi (5.50€ per hour).

MODERATE

Catalonia Excelsior ★ 🍴 This 1930s building has been sensitively restored and turned into one of the most welcoming and affordable hotels in the central part of town. The public rooms of the seven-floor structure are refreshing, especially the Art Deco–style restaurant with its adjacent bar. A spiral marble stairwell climbs to a mellow salon—paneled in dark cherry wood—that opens onto a terrace. Guest rooms range from small to midsize and have new carpeting and very comfortable beds, often with brass headboards. The other furnishings are comfortable as well.

Barcelonina 5, 46002 Valencia. ✆ **96-351-46-12.** Fax 96-352-34-78. www.hoteles-catalonia.es. 81 units. 59€–165€ double. AE, DC, V. Nearby parking 19€. **Amenities:** Bar. *In room:* A/C, TV, hair dryer, minibar, Wi-Fi (free).

Hotel Ad Hoc Monumental ★ 📖 The owner, Luis García Alarcón, an antiques dealer, is the inspiration behind this choice government-rated three-star hotel in a sensitively restored building from the 1880s. Occupying a bull's-eye position—in fact, it's one of Valencia's best-located hotels—it lies near the old source of the Turía River between the Torres Serranos (1391) and Civil Government (1763) buildings. Guest rooms, many with exposed brick walls, are soundproofed against traffic noise and are simply but tastefully furnished. Don't judge the hotel by its facade, which is rather impersonal and ordinary. The building's interior will warm your heart. Note that the hotel's location on a small street is difficult to reach if you're driving because of a series of one-way streets.

Boix 4, 46003 Valencia. ✆ **96-391-91-40.** Fax 96-391-36-67. www.adhochoteles.com. 28 units. 80€–220€ double; 165€–260€ triple. AE, DC, MC, V. Parking 17€. **Amenities:** Restaurant; room service. *In room:* A/C, TV, hair dryer, Wi-Fi (free).

Husa Reina Victoria ★ Restored after a long slumber, the Reina Victoria enjoys a reputation as the most architecturally glamorous hotel in Valencia. Built in 1913, the hotel has welcomed many distinguished guests, including Alfonso XIII and the hotel's namesake Queen Victoria herself, as well as Dalí, Manolete, Picasso, Falla, García Lorca, and Miró. Brimming with neoclassical detailing and wrought-iron accents, it overlooks the flower gardens and fountains of Valencia's central square, Plaza del País Valenciano. Room sizes range from small to medium (only a few are really spacious) and have midsize bathrooms. The hotel is in the heart of town, a 5-minute walk from the railway station.

Barcas 4, 46002 Valencia. ✆ **96-352-04-87.** Fax 96-352-27-21. www.husareinavictoria.com. 96 units. 67€–210€ double; 180€–245€ triple. AE, DC, MC, V. Parking 17€. Bus: 4, 6, 7, 8, 14, or 27. **Amenities:** Restaurant; bar; room service. *In room:* A/C, TV, hair dryer, minibar.

Inglés Boutique Hotel ★★ This turn-of-the-20th-century hotel, the former palace of the duke and duchess of Cardona, has aged well. In the heart of Old Valencia, it stands opposite another Churrigueresque palace. Guest rooms vary in size. Most overlook the tree-lined street and offer comforts such as sofa beds with fine linens and immaculately kept bathrooms. Ask for a room with a view of one of the city's many palaces. The service is discreet and polite.

Marqués de Dos Aguas 6, 46002 Valencia. ✆ **96-351-64-26.** Fax 93-272-41-49. www.hotel-inglesboutique.com. 63 units. 75€–220€ double. AE, DC, MC, V. Parking 22€. Bus: 6, 9, 31, or 32. **Amenities:** Restaurant; bar; bikes; room service. *In room:* A/C, TV, hair dryer, minibar, Wi-Fi (6.50€ per hour).

NH Hotel Villacarlos Located close to the river, this hotel is within easy walking distance of most of the city's monuments. Following Barcelona's lead, Valencia has been keen to adopt the new, and the Hotel Villacarlos is a prime example. It has a simple postmodern facade that makes the reception area's bright orange decor all the more surprising. Abstract paintings in orange and blue (the hotel's color scheme) adorn the walls—remember your sunglasses if you have a headache. In the guest rooms, however, the blue and orange are kept to a minimum. The furniture is functional and new, including comfortable beds and full-length mirrors.

Av. del Puerto 60, 46023 Valencia. ✆ **96-337-50-25.** Fax 96-337-50-74. www.nh-hotels.com. 51 units. Mon–Thurs 65€–155€ double; Fri–Sun 80€ double. AE, DC, MC, V. Parking 15€. Bus: 1, 2, 3, or 4. **Amenities:** Restaurant; bikes. *In room:* A/C, TV, hair dryer, minibar, Wi-Fi (11€ per 24 hr.).

INEXPENSIVE

Hostal Residencia Bisbal Conveniently located in the Old Town, this husband-and-wife operation offers simply furnished rooms. They're a bit small, but tidy and comfortable. No meals are served, and the hotel offers no real luxuries, but you'll find many bars and restaurants nearby. The English-speaking staff is very helpful.

Pie de la Cruz 9, 46001 Valencia. ✆ **96-391-70-84.** Fax 96-392-37-37. 10 units. 60€ double; 78€ triple. AE, MC, V. Parking nearby 17€. Bus: 8, 27, 29, or 81. *In room:* No phone.

Hostal Venecia ★ ✦ In the city center, around the corner from the town hall, this government-rated two-star hotel is one of the most affordable. You don't get frills here, but you are rewarded with an immaculate hotel with well-maintained and comfortable guest rooms. The rooms have a rather minimalist decor. Each comes with a small bathroom. In spite of its simplicity, the Venecia has won several awards from Spanish hotel guides.

En Lop 5, 46002 Valencia. ✆ **96-352-42-67.** Fax 96-352-44-21. www.hotelvenecia.com. 54 units. 61€–120€ double. AE, MC, V. Parking nearby 22€. Bus: 19, 35, 70, or 71. *In room:* A/C, TV, hair dryer, Wi-Fi (free).

Where to Dine in Valencia

If you gravitate to hotel dining, you will find that some of the best cuisine is served at the Hilton Valencia (p. 438) at its two superb restaurants, **Azahar** and **Bice,** the latter, with its Italian cuisine, being far superior. Another winning choice is the restaurant **Almudí,** serving one of the city's fine cuisines at Vincci Lys (p. 439).

EXPENSIVE

Eladio ★★ SPANISH/INTERNATIONAL Borrowing from culinary concepts he learned during his apprenticeship in Switzerland, Eladio Rodríguez prepares flavorful cuisine based on seasonal ingredients. The menu changes daily depending on what is fresh and available. Some diners particularly praise his shellfish and fish from his native Galicia, which might include hake, monkfish, or sea wolf, prepared as simply or as elaborately as you want. Many customers order fish grilled simply over charcoal and served with garlic butter sauce. Other noteworthy dishes include baby-squid salad, hake with clams in a green sauce, sirloin-steak stroganoff flambé with vodka, and a lobster and anglerfish stew. The setting is calm and pleasant.

Calle Chiva 40. ✆ **96-384-22-44.** www.restauranteeladio.es. Reservations recommended. Main courses 20€–27€. AE, DC, MC, V. Mon–Sat 1–4pm; Tues–Sat 9–11:30pm. Closed Aug. Bus: 3, 70, or 72.

Joaquín Schmidt ★★ ☺ MEDITERRANEAN Of German parents but born in Madrid, chef Joaquín Schmidt Río-Valle is becoming one of the best known chefs in Valencia. His restaurant shines brightly because of his philosophy of "preparing each menu as if I'm cooking for cherished friends." With an impressive wine list to back up his culinary creations, his food always rises above the merely routine or even the merely competent. From his menu surprises, anticipate an explosion of unexpected aromas and tastes. All dishes are prepared using only extra-virgin olive oils, the best of balsamic vinegars, and special salts he imports from Brittany and Great Britain.

Calle Visitación N7. ☎ **96-340-17-10.** www.joaquinschmidt.com. Reservations required. Fixed-price menus 40€, 45€, and 56€. Children's menu 25€. AE, MC, V. Tues–Sat 1:30–3:30pm; Mon–Sat 9–11pm.

La Pepica ★ SEAFOOD/VALENCIAN This old Hemingway haunt, established in 1898, looks a little worse for wear, but it's still going strong. Royalty no longer dines here, and don Ernesto is long gone, but the same recipes that used to entice such personages are still practiced with skill at this typical old Valencian hideaway. The place remains famous for its paella dishes. The favorite rice dish is made with fresh lobster, but this, of course, is the most expensive selection. Grilled or fried seafood share equal billing with the various kinds of paella. The chef is skilled at preparing calamari, among other dishes. Finish off with one of the desserts of the region, including flan, pudding, or fresh-fruit tart.

El Paseo Neptuno 6–8, La Playa de las Arenas. ☎ **96-371-03-66.** www.lapepica.com. Reservations recommended. Main courses 24€–50€; tasting menu 40€ with wine. AE, DC, MC, V. Daily 1–4pm; Mon–Sat 8:30–11pm. Closed last 2 weeks of Nov. Bus: 1, 2, 19, 20, 21, 22, 30, 31, or 81.

La Sucursal ★★ VALENCIAN Located within the Instituto Valenciano de Arte Moderno (IVAM; p. 435), this restaurant is in the Barrio Antiguo, the ancient quarter of this historic city. With a minimalist decor, it invites you to innovative cuisine and an impressive wine list of regional vintages (such as a fruity red *ceremonia* made from a blend of cabernet sauvignon and tempranillo grapes). The chef is known for his soupy rice dishes prepared in deep pots instead of in paella pans. Of these dishes, the specialty that wins local raves is *arroz caldoso de bogavante,* made with bits of lobster and seasoned with saffron and paprika. Unusual dishes include a carpaccio made of deer and an "octopus cake" seasoned with brie and fresh herbs. You can also order a loin of beef in a rosemary *jus* sauce, followed by a platter featuring cheese made from both sheep and goat milk from the nearby mountains of Espadán. Begin with cauliflower mousse with shellfish "air" (a kind of lather), or try the house foie gras, and finish with a smooth-tasting sorbet made of fresh quince. You

---

Insider's Tips on Drinks & Tapas

To be a true Valenciano, you have to head for the increasingly chic Barrio del Carmen to visit **Sant Jaume**, a cafe at Carrer Cavalleros 51 (☎ **96-391-24-01**), and have a drink of *agua de Valencia.* It's a mixture of orange juice, Cointreau, and cava. The drink is said "to cure all that ails you," so it's appropriate that the building itself used to be a former apothecary. An easy-to-miss tapas bar, beloved by local foodies, is **Ca'n Bermell,** Santo Tomas 18 (☎ **96-391-02-88**). The city's most famous drink, *horchata,* made with ground tiger nuts, is best at **Horchatería El Siglo,** Plaza Santa Catalina 11 (☎ **96-391-84-66**).

can also order a winning pistachio sorbet, or even a beet compote with fresh cheese ice cream and seasonal berries.

La Sucursal, Guillén de Castro 118. ℭ **96-374-66-65.** www.restaurantelasucursal.com. Reservations required. Main courses 25€–29€. AE, DC, MC, V. Mon–Fri 1–3:30pm; Mon–Sat 8:30–11:30pm. Closed 1 week in Aug.

Torrijos ★★★ MEDITERRANEAN/INTERNATIONAL This stellar restaurant serves the best cuisine in Valencia. The menu, described by owner and chef Josep Quintana as "Mediterranean," displays the knowledge of French and German cooking he acquired while working in Switzerland. Specialties include rice dishes—in particular, paella. Rice with *rape* (monkfish) and artichokes is excellent, as is rice with king prawns. Fish from the Mediterranean and the Atlantic feature heavily on the menu. Señor Quintana also makes delicious foie gras. Wine buffs should note that there are some 25,000 quality bottles in his cellar. The restaurant is centrally located in the Barrio Ruzafa.

Calle Dr. Sumsi 4. ℭ **96-373-29-49.** www.restaurantetorrijos.com. Reservations required. Main courses 21€–30€. Fixed-price menus 50€, 80€, and 95€. AE, DC, MC, V. Tues–Sat 1–3:45pm and 9–11:30pm. Closed Jan 6–15, 1 week at Easter, and Aug 15–Sept 15. Metro: Colón.

MODERATE

Ca'n Bermell ★ 🍴 VALENCIAN In a lovely old 1600s building, this restaurant lies in the Barrio del Carmen, Valencia's oldest district. In such a beautiful tavern setting, Emilio Bermell has built up a reputation as one of the best chefs in the city. Each day he goes to the sprawling marketplace to select only the best local ingredients, which he later fashions into carefully crafted and good-tasting dishes, such as honeycombs stuffed with foie gras. Dig into his first tempting specialty, a superb mushroom salad made with fresh fruit from the region. For a main course, we suggest cod, which is stuffed with onions and served with a tangy green-pepper sauce. Duck breast served with a Rioja wine sauce is immensely appealing as well.

Calle Santo Tomás 18. ℭ **96-391-02-88.** Reservations recommended. Main courses 8€–20€. AE, DC, MC, V. Tues–Sat 1:30–3pm; Mon–Sat 8:30–11pm. Closed Aug. Metro: Angel Guimerà.

Casa Montana ★★ TAPAS An institution since 1836, this bodega serves the tastiest tapas in Valencia. Locals and visiting foodies convene not just for the tapas but also for the inexpensive wines by the glass. We always head here with a party so we can sample a little bit of everything, including anchovies from Santoña, cooked fava beans, codfish croquettes, and Valencia *clochinas* (mussels). Grilled sardines come straight from the boats in Castellón. Another favorite of ours is *titaina,* prepared with tuna, fresh tomatoes, peppers, and pine nuts. Sometimes epicureans from Barcelona drive down here just for lunch.

Calle José Benlliure 69. ℭ **96-367-23-14.** www.emilianobodega.com. Reservations not necessary. Tapas 5€–20€; fixed-price 5-course lunch 25€. MC, V. Mon–Sat noon–3:30pm and 8–11:30pm; Sun 12:30–3:30pm.

El Timonel ★ MEDITERRANEAN/SEAFOOD Since 1997, discerning diners have headed for the domain of chef/owner Jaime Sauz, whose restaurant lies 2 blocks east of the Plaza de Toros. The comfortable, cozy interior is decorated like a yacht, evocative of the chef's use of fresh fish and seafood. Expect bass, flounder, red mullet, and a delectable local white fish called *lliva.* The fish is usually grilled. Señor Sauz believes if the product is fresh enough, it doesn't have to be mucked up with a lot of sauces. One of the best dishes is *dorada a la sal*, gilthead sea bream baked in a coating of salt to seal in its juices. Rice dishes blended with seafood (similar to paella) have always been one of the mainstays of the local diet, and excellent ones are served here—none better than *arroz de bogavante*, or rice with prawns and lobster. For meat eaters, we recommend *chuletón de buey* (breaded oxtail steaks) or *chuleticas de cordero lechal* (small spring lamb cutlets).

Félix Pizcueta 13. ☎ **96-352-63-00.** www.eltimonel.com. Reservations recommended. Main courses 20€–29€. AE, DC, MC, V. Tues-Sun 1:30–4:30pm and 8:15–11:30pm. Metro: Corte Inglés.

LaLola ★ MEDITERRANEAN/INTERNATIONAL In the rapidly rising neighborhood of Barrio del Carmen, this is one of the most imaginative restaurants in Valencia. Its minimalist and chicly modern decor employs a massive use of black, red, and white. Prepare your palate for a parade of sunny flavors. The starters are creative and eclectic, including ice cream made with virgin olive oil over a tomato-and-olive sauce. The eager-to-please staff will tempt you with such delightful main courses as codfish with caramelized saffron and honey, or else an extremely appealing Argentine baby beef loin with watermelon sorbet and *jamón serrano* (cured ham). We also recommend grilled sea bass with green pepper and a cauliflower purée or grilled pork steak with a mushroom purée.

Subida del Toledano 8. ☎ **96-391-80-45.** www.lalolarestaurante.com. Reservations required. Main courses 17€–22€; fixed-price lunch menu 12€; fixed-price gourmet dinner 45€. MC, V. Mon-Sat 2–4pm and 9pm–2am; Sun 2–4pm. Bus: 2, 4, 6, or 7.

La Riuà ★ 🎒 VALENCIAN Set in Valencia's historic core, a short walk from Plaza de la Reina and the cathedral, this well-managed restaurant has done a booming business with local residents ever since it opened in 1982. There's no outdoor terrace (the congestion of the urban neighborhood prevents that), but you'll get a good view of traditional local decorative styles from the tiles and ceramics that adorn the walls of its cozy dining rooms. The menu is a lexicon of traditional Valenciano dishes, including virtually every kind of fish (grilled, fried, or baked, in some cases within a salt crust) that exists in the western Mediterranean. There are well-flavored versions of paella, and fish that's served with three distinctly different seasoned rices, such as one flavored with squid ink. Meats include *chuletas* (spicy sausages), roasted pork, and tender, well-flavored veal. Locals appreciate stewed octopus *(pulpitos guisados)*, a dish that many of them remember from their childhood. The restaurant's name, incidentally, translates from the Valenciano dialect as "the spot where the river meets the sea."

Calle del Mar 27. ☎ **96-391-45-71.** Reservations recommended. Main courses 13€–25€. AE, DC, MC, V. Mon-Sat 2–4:15pm and 9–11pm. Closed Aug and Easter. Bus: 4.

INEXPENSIVE

El Gourmet SPANISH/INTERNATIONAL This restaurant is an honest establishment where well-trained waiters serve good-quality, reasonably priced food. Set in the center of Valencia, it serves up such dishes as hake with clams, partridge with herbs in puff pastry, oxtail stew, fried filets of veal or pork, scrambled eggs with eggplant and shrimp, and seasonal vegetables.

Calle Taquígrafo Martí 3. ☎ **96-395-25-09.** Reservations recommended. Main courses 14€–17€; fixed-priced menu 27€. AE, DC, MC, V. Tues-Sat 1–4pm and 9–11:30pm; Sun 1–4pm. Closed Easter week and Aug. Metro: Colón.

Palace Fesol ★ 🍴 MEDITERRANEAN/VALENCIAN This has been a lunch-time favorite since 1909. In the years after World War I, the Palace Fesol became famous for its namesake specialty, lima beans. Today many more excellent dishes grace the menu at the "bean palace," with typical Valencian paella high on the list at lunch. You can also order several chicken dishes served with rice. Other selections include grilled catch of the day, baby hake, baby lamb cutlets, and chateaubriand. Photos of film stars, bullfighters, and other celebrities line the walls. The restaurant is cooled by old-fashioned ceiling fans and decorated with beamed ceilings, lanterns, and a hand-painted tile mosaic.

Hernán Cortés 7. ✆ **96-352-93-23.** www.palacefesol.com. Reservations recommended. Main courses 22€–28€. AE, DC, MC, V. Tues–Sun 1–4pm and 9–11pm. Closed Sat–Sun July–Aug. Bus: 5. Metro: Colón.

Valencia After Dark

Where you go at night in Valencia depends on when you visit. The best area in the cooler months is historic **Barrio Carmen,** in the city center. Valencia is famous for its *marcha* (nightlife) and for its bohemian bars. **Calle Alta** is a good street on which to start your *tasca* bar–crawl, as is the historic core around **Plaza del Ayuntamiento.** Some of the most evocative *tascas* don't even have clear signs—your best bet is to jump into and out of whichever ones appeal to you.

A longtime local favorite is **Barcas,** Barcas 7 (✆ **96-352-12-33**), among banks and office buildings in the heart of town directly north of Estación del Norte. It serves drinks and tapas (including small servings of paella) at the stand-up bar. You could conceivably stop here for your first cup of coffee at 7am and for your final nightcap at 1am. In the evening there is often live music. The establishment is more popular as a bar than as a restaurant. It's open daily from 7am to 1am. Drink prices start at 1.50€, and tapas cost 4€.

In the Barrio del Carmen, **Disco City,** 16 Calle Pintor Zariñena (✆ **96-391-41-51**), is a dance club with a black-on-black decor and a wall of mirrors lining the dance floor. It attracts the under-30 crowd, who come here to dance to funk, soul, and R&B. It's definitely for late-nighters: The scene doesn't get rolling until 3am. Cover is usually 15€.

In summer, the emphasis switches to the beach, Playa de Malvarrosa. Valencia is hot and steamy, and the cool night sea breezes are especially welcome. Everyone from teens to 40-somethings congregates around open-air bars, which play music, often have dance floors, and are open from late May to September. Drinks usually cost 3€ to 5€. There are also discos in this part of town, one of which is the **Akuarela Playa** (✆ **96-385-93-85;** www.akuarela.es), Calle Eugenia Viñes 152. Cover is 10€ to 13€, and drinks are several euros more than in the open-air bars.

Valencia is Spain's third-biggest city and, after Madrid and Barcelona, the country's biggest gay center. Most of the action is in the historic center in the **Barrio Carmen,** particularly along Calle Quart. Valencia is a progressive, liberal city, and visitors need have no fear about being "out" on the street. For more information, interested parties can contact **Lambda,** Vivons 26 (✆**96-334-21-91;** www.lambdavalencia.org). There are many clubs, bars, coffee shops, saunas, hotels, and restaurants from which to choose. The best publication for what's happening, and when, is Madrid-based *Shangay,* distributed free in gay establishments.

As in many cities, gay men have to some degree elbowed lesbian interests out of the way. As in the rest of Spain, the night starts late, and 10pm is considered quite early. One of the best places to go is **Café de la Seu,** Calle Santo Caliz 7 (© **96-391-57-15;** www.cafedelaseu.com). All shades of pinkdom can have a relaxing drink for 2€ to 5€ daily from 6pm to 2am. Go-go dancers evoking the '60s and drag shows make for lively evenings at **Venial,** Quart 26 (© **96-391-73-56;** www.venialvalencia.com), with a cover that can vary with the event. Hot, sweaty bodies—many of them available—turn up here for Latino nights on Thursdays, house nights on Friday and Saturday, and just X-rated gay fun on Sunday. The dance floor is one of the most active in town. Take bus no. N4.

Much more highbrow than the nocturnal activities above, the **Palau de la Música** ★★, Paseo de la Alameda 30 (© **96-357-50-20;** www.palaude valencia.com; Metro: Alameda), presents an impressive array of 200-plus programs a year. Between September and October, the prestigious Valencia Orchestra is in residence. The fantastic hall seats 1,793 guests and has wonderful acoustics. After a concert here, Placido Domingo claimed that "Palau is a Stradivarius." Held up by 10 porticoed pillars, the dome evokes a greenhouse; designer José María de Paredes won the national prize awarded annually for architecture. The most prestigious orchestras in the world, as well as directors and soloists, appear here. An on-site art gallery is open daily from 10:30am to 1:30pm and 5:30 to 9pm. Ticket prices vary depending on the program but are generally in the 10€-to-80€ range.

Palau de les Arts Reina Sofía ★★★, Autopista del Saler 1 (© **96-197-58-00;** www.lesarts.com), is the grand opera house of Valencia. It's housed in a futuristic, helmet-shaped building that is part of the City of the Arts and the Sciences (p. 434), a dazzling complex of polished glass. This dramatic structure has helped transform Valencia from a neglected port city into a cool resort. Some of the world's most prestigious opera companies perform here. Tickets, costing from 20€ to 175€, are sold at the box office Monday to Friday noon to 8pm. The box office also opens 3 hours before the start of a performance.

BENIDORM

43km (27 miles) NE of Alicante, 135km (84 miles) S of Valencia

Before tourists discovered its 6km (3¾ miles) of beaches, Benidorm was a tiny fishing village. Now, summer vacationers pour in, and a new concrete hotel seems to be built every day. With its heavy northern European influence, Benidorm has become the most overrun beach town east of Torremolinos. It has both ardent fans and determined detractors.

According to an 1890s guidebook, Benidorm was a "very tranquil place where drunkenness was unknown." Change overcame the resort by the 1970s and 1980s, when it attracted a rowdy, beer-drinking crowd. Today, some 180,000 people a day visit the long beach strip.

After the bad press of the past, city officials are trying to clean up Benidorm and make it more of an upmarket (rather than package-tour) destination. Aiguera Park and its amphitheater exemplify the change. It offers such free cultural activities as dancing, jazz, soul music, and even a Russian choir.

Despite efforts to upgrade its image, Benidorm still has high-rises and economical package tourists. In winter, pensioners from all over Europe, even Russia, fill the villas and small hotels. In summer, however, the place takes on a much more youthful aura. The resort has two fine white-sand beaches.

Essentials

GETTING THERE From Alicante, there are hourly **train** departures for Benidorm. **Buses** from Valencia and Alicante leave almost hourly, too.

If you're driving, take the E-15 expressway south from Valencia or north from Alicante. The one-way toll from Alicante to Benidorm is 7.20€; the one-way toll from Valencia to Benidorm is 12€.

VISITOR INFORMATION The **tourist information office** is at Av. Martínez Alejos 16 (© **96-585-13-11;** www.benidorm.org). It's open Monday to Friday 9am to 8pm, and Saturday 10am to 1:30pm and 4:30 to 7pm.

Where to Stay in Benidorm

Make sure you reserve a room in advance between mid-June and September. If you arrive without a reservation, you'll be out of luck. During this time hotel managers often slap the full-board requirement onto their rates. To beat this, book one of the rare *residencias,* which serve only breakfast.

Belroy ★★ A few steps from the port, this centrally located first-class hotel is not quite in the same league as Meliá Benidorm (see below), but it is the most daringly modern and sophisticated at the resort. Each of its spacious bedrooms is furnished in a minimalist style, almost Japanese in simplicity, and each unit opens onto a panoramic view. The hotel lies only 50m (164 ft.) from Levante Beach and a 5-minute walk from the center of Benidorm. Pale pastel walls, travertine floors, and advanced modern lighting and technology are found throughout. As the sun sets, guests gather on Alaire Terrace. The hotel also shelters one of the Benidorm's finest restaurants, **Kataria Gastronómica** (see below).

Av. Mediterráneo 13, 03503 Benidorm. © **96-585-02-03.** Fax 96-586-37-32. www.belroy.es. 125 units. 90€–250€ double. Rates include buffet breakfast. AE, DC, MC, V. Parking 15€. **Amenities:** 2 restaurants; bar; babysitting; exercise room; Jacuzzi; 2 freshwater heated pools (1 indoor); room service; sauna. *In room:* A/C, TV, hair dryer, minibar, Wi-Fi (free).

Gran Hotel Delfín ★ About 3km (1¾ miles) west of the town center, away from the traffic-clogged mayhem that sometimes overwhelms central Benidorm, this 1960s hotel is located beside the very popular Poniente Beach. The hotel caters to a sun-loving crowd of vacationers who appreciate its airy spaciousness and lack of formality. Guest rooms are sparsely decorated, with masonry floors and much-used furniture, some in a darkly stained Iberian style. Nonetheless, the accommodations are quite comfortable with tiled bathrooms.

Playa de Poniente (La Cala), 03502 Benidorm. © **96-585-34-00.** Fax 96-585-71-54. www.granhoteldelfin.com. 92 units. 96€–275€ double. Rates include breakfast and dinner. AE, DC, MC, V. Free parking. Closed Nov–Mar. **Amenities:** Restaurant; bar; babysitting; outdoor freshwater pool; room service; 1 outdoor tennis court (lit for night play); Wi-Fi (free, in lobby). *In room:* A/C, TV, hair dryer, minibar.

Hotel RH Canfali A seaside villa between Playa de Levante and Playa de Poniente, the Canfali is one of the best small hotels in town. Originally built in 1950, it was enlarged in 1992. Its location is a scene-stealer—on a low cliff at the end of the esplanade, with a staircase winding down to the beach. The best rooms have balconies with sea views. Although the hotel is spacious and comfortable, its decor is undistinguished and its guest rooms are merely functional. Terraces overlooking the sea are perfect spots for morning coffee.

Plaza de San Jaime 5, 03501 Benidorm. © **96-585-08-18.** Fax 96-585-00-66. www.hotelesrh. com. 38 units. 60€–110€ double. Rates include full board when you stay a minimum of 7 nights. AE, DC, MC, V. No parking. **Amenities:** Restaurant; bar. *In room:* A/C, TV.

Meliá Benidorm ★★ The resort's only luxe hotel, this member of a first-rate Spanish chain dominates the accommodations scene—and is rather mammoth in size. Located only 500m (1,640 ft.) from the Playa de Levante, it is surrounded by a large, well-landscaped park. All guest rooms are midsize to large, each comfortably and tastefully furnished. Both the regular and junior suites occupying the top floors of the building's two towers come with circular bathtub and hydromassage shower.

The hotel also offers two of the best **dining facilities** in town, using market-fresh and first-rate ingredients, with a special emphasis on lavish buffet spreads.

Av. Severo Ochoa 1, 03500 Benidorm. © **96-681-37-10.** Fax 96-680-21-69. www.solmelia.com. 526 units. 90€–195€ double; 197€–300€ junior suite; 260€–420€ regular suite. AE, DC, MC, V. Parking 15€. **Amenities:** 2 restaurants; bar; exercise room; Jacuzzi; 2 heated freshwater pools (1 indoor); room service; sauna; Wi-Fi (free, in lobby). *In room:* A/C, TV, hair dryer, minibar.

Where to Dine in Benidorm

Kataria Gastronómica ★★ MEDITERRANEAN This restaurant not only has the most glamorously modern setting at the resort but also has the finest cuisine. Benidorm is a bit of a gastronomic wasteland, so this deluxe restaurant is a wonderful option. With its large windows, the restaurant is flooded with light, and the kitchen also has a window so you can see what the chefs are up to. They are busy turning out creative and surprising delicacies, such as baked hake stuffed with sea urchins, prawns, and a caviar sauce. You might start with caramelized foie gras with mango strips and fresh tomato. Dishes are carefully presented and full of flavor. A dessert selection might be a small French toast with honey along with pumpkin ice cream.

In Hotel Belroy, Av. del Mediterráneo 13. © **96-683-13-72.** www.katariagastronomica.com. Reservations required. Main courses 15€–30€. AE, DC, MC, V. Daily 1:30–3:30pm; Mon–Sat 8–11:30pm; Sun 7–11pm.

Benidorm After Dark

The best nightclub in the region is **Benidorm Palace,** Carretera Dr. Severo Ochoa 13, Rincón de Loix (© **96-585-16-60;** www.benidorm-palace.com). The cover (including one drink) is a steep 23€ to 53€, but the place features the latest music, a large dance floor, and the biggest stage in Europe (40m/131 ft. wide). The stage fills with 50 international artists, often entertaining an audience of 1,500. Shows have ranged from "Hurrah for Hollywood" to Russian dancers. Always count on glamorous dancing women as part of the show. There are expansive bars and ample seating. The club is open Tuesday to Saturday from 10pm to 2am; shows start at 10pm. Drinks cost 4€.

Casino Mediterráneo, N-332 Km 141.5 (© **90-233-21-41;** www. casinomediterraneo.es), offers gambling in a modern building surrounded by the rolling hills of the Costa Blanca. Most visitors come to try their hand at roulette (French and American), blackjack, and *boules.* An on-site restaurant serves a la carte Spanish meals ranging from 30€ to 50€ per person every evening from 9pm to 2am. The casino is open daily 4pm to 4am. It's about 4km (2½ miles) from Benidorm, beside the highway to Alicante. Casino admission is 2€ and requires a passport.

ALICANTE ★

81km (50 miles) N of Murcia, 40km (25 miles) S of Benidorm, 172km (107 miles) S of Valencia, 417km (259 miles) SE of Madrid

Alicante (Alacant), capital of the Costa Blanca, is popular in both summer and winter. Many consider it the best all-around city in Spain. As you amble about its esplanades, you almost feel as if you are in Africa: Women in caftans and peddlers hawking carvings from Senegal or elsewhere often populate the waterfront.

San Juan, the largest beach in Alicante, is a short distance from the capital. It's lined with villas, hotels, and restaurants. The bay of Alicante has two capes, and on the bay is **Postiguet Beach.** The bay stretches all the way to the **Cape of Santa Pola,** a town with two good beaches, a 14th-century castle, and several seafood restaurants.

Essentials

GETTING THERE Alicante's **Internacional El Altet Airport** (℡ 96-691-90-00) is 19km (12 miles) from the city. There are as many as 11 daily flights from Madrid, about 3 flights per week from Seville, and 3 flights per week from Barcelona. Fifteen buses daily connect the city to the airport; the fare is 2.60€. The **Iberia Airlines** ticket office (℡ 90-240-05-00; www.iberia. com) is at the airport.

Twelve **trains** a day make the 2-hour trip from Valencia. Eight trains a day come from Barcelona (trip time: 3–6 hr.), and 12 a day from Madrid (trip time: 4 hr.). The RENFE office is at **Estación Alicante,** Avenida Salamanca (℡ 90-224-02-02; www.renfe.es).

Different **bus** lines from various parts of the coast converge at the terminus, Calle Portugal 17 (℡ 96-513-07-00). There is almost hourly service from Benidorm (p. 446) and from Valencia (trip time: 4 hr.). Buses also run from Madrid, a 5- to 6-hour trip.

To drive here, take the E-15 expressway south along the coast from Valencia. The expressway and N-340 run northeast from Murcia.

VISITOR INFORMATION The **tourist information office** is at Rambla de Mendez Núñez (℡ 96-520-00-00; www.comunitatvalenciana.com). It's open Monday to Friday 9am to 8pm, Saturday 10am to 8pm, and Sunday 10am to 2pm.

FAST FACTS For medical assistance, go to the **Hospital General,** Calle Maestro Alonso 109 (℡ 96-593-83-00). In an emergency, dial ℡ **091;** to reach the city police, call ℡ **96-514-95-00.**

Exploring Alicante

With its wide, palm-lined avenues, this town was made for walking—and that's just what you'll do! The magnificent **Esplanada d'Espanya ★,** extending around part of the yacht harbor, includes a promenade of mosaic sidewalks under the palms. All the boulevards are clean and lined with unlimited shopping options.

The Esplanada d'Espanya promenade.

At Alicante's leading department store, El Corte Inglés, you can find bargains without being trampled by mobs, as in Madrid. Alicante is known for its parks, gardens, and lines of palm trees, and it boasts several old plazas, some paved with marble.

High on a hill, the stately **Castell de Santa Bárbara** (© **96-526-31-31**) towers over the bay and provincial capital. The Greeks called the fort Akra Leuka (White Peak). Its original defenses, erected by the Carthaginians in 400 B.C., were later used by the Romans and the Arabs. The fortress's grand scale is evident in its moats, drawbridges, tunneled entrances, guardrooms, cisterns, underground storerooms, hospitals, batteries, powder stores, barracks, high breastworks, and deep dungeons, as well as Matanza Tower and the Keep. From the top of the castle is a panoramic view over land and sea. The castle is accessible by road or by elevator. Board the elevator at the Explanada d'Espanya; admission by elevator is 3€. In summer the castle is open daily from 10am to 8pm; in winter, daily from 9am to 7pm.

It is also possible to drive to the top. A paved road off Avenida Vásquez de Mella leads directly to a parking lot beside the castle. If you drive, admission is free.

On the slopes of Castillo de Santa Bárbara behind the cathedral is the **Barrio de Santa Cruz** ★. Forming part of the **Villa Vieja (Old Quarter),** it is a colorful section with wrought-iron window grilles, flowers, and a view of the entire harbor.

Alicante isn't all ancient. Facing Iglesia Santa María is the **Museu de Arte del Siglo XX Asegurada** ★, Plaza de Santa María 3 (© **96-514-07-68**). Housed in the city's oldest building, it contains modern art. Constructed as a granary in 1685, the restored building features works by Miró, Calder, Cocteau, Vasarély, Dalí, Picasso, and Tàpies. Other notable artists include Braque, Chagall, Giacometti, Kandinsky, and Zadkine. You'll also see a musical score by Manuel de Falla. The museum was formed in 1977 with the donation of a private collection by the painter and sculptor Eusebio Sempere, whose works are on display. It

The Castell de Santa Bárbara.

is open year-round Tuesday to Saturday 10am to 2pm and 4 to 8pm, and Sunday 10:30am to 2:30pm. From October to May, the Tuesday-through-Saturday evening hours are 5 to 9pm. Admission is free.

Shopping

Despite the hurly-burly of tourism that unfolds around you at almost every street corner, there are many worthwhile shopping opportunities. Some of the best involve handmade artifacts—ceramics, hand-tooled leather, woodcarvings, ornamental boxes, candleholders, and small-scale mosaics. One of the best all-purpose shops is **Fran Holuba,** Calle Jaime Segarra 16 (℃ **96-524-45-95**), which carries examples of each of the major artisanal forms described above. For general merchandise, head for the town's largest department store, **El Corte Inglés,** Av. Maison Nave 53 (℃ **96-592-50-01**).

Where to Stay in Alicante
EXPENSIVE

Hotel Meliá Alicante ★ ☺ Built in 1973 on a spit of landfill jutting into the Mediterranean, this massive beachfront hotel almost dwarfs every other establishment in town. Midsize guest rooms are painted in sunny colors and have balconies, usually with sweeping panoramas of sailboats in the nearby marina or over the beach. The public rooms are contemporary, with lots of marble. The hotel is midway between the main harbor and the very popular El Postiguet beach. Its most spectacular feature is its first-class restaurant on the 26th floor, opening onto one of Alicante's most panoramic views of the sea and the cityscape.

Plaza del Puerto 3, 03001 Alicante. ℃ **800/336-3542** in the U.S., or 96-520-50-00. Fax 96-514-26-33. www.solmelia.com. 545 units. 92€–169€ double; 202€–222€ suite. AE, DC, MC, V. Parking 20€. **Amenities:** 2 restaurants; 2 bars; babysitting; children's programs; exercise room; health club; 2 freshwater pools (1 heated indoor, 1 outdoor); room service; sauna; spa; Wi-Fi (free). *In room:* A/C, TV, hair dryer, minibar.

MODERATE

Abba Centrum Alicante Hotel This eight-floor modern hotel is one of the most convenient in Alicante, 320m (1,050 ft.) from the harbor and convenient to both the rail and the bus depots. Opening in 1992, it underwent massive renovations in 2005, retaining its contemporary ambience and inviting quality. Its guest rooms are midsize for the most part and attractively decorated and furnished, each adjoined by a well-maintained bathroom. The on-site **restaurant** is a good choice for its fresh Mediterranean fish platters, rice dishes, and grilled meats. Some of its food is inspired by Basque cuisine.

Calle Pinto Lorenzo Casanova 33, 03003 Alicante. ✆ **96-513-04-40.** Fax 96-592-83-23. www.abbahoteles.com. 150 units. 77€–99€ double; 162€–227€ suite. AE, DC, MC, V. Parking 13€. **Amenities:** Restaurant; bar; concierge; exercise room; room service; sauna; Wi-Fi (5€ per 45 min.). *In room:* A/C, TV, minibar.

Hotel Residencia Leuka 🏊 The Leuka is best booked for the weekend, when it offers good value and is free of packs of businesspeople. Although it's about a 15-minute walk from the sea, it is close to the train station and two of the city's main thoroughfares. Guests have easy access to almost all destinations by bus. The 10-story building has an anonymous 1970s facade. However, all the rooms have good-size balconies, and units above the third floor offer wonderful views of the castle. The rooms' decor is quite plain, but accommodations are spacious and reasonably comfortable.

Calle Segura 23, 03004 Alicante. ✆ **96-520-27-44.** Fax 96-514-12-22. www.hotelleuka.com. 106 units. Mon–Thurs 60€ double; Fri–Sun 54€ double. AE, DC, MC, V. Parking 12€. Bus: 22. **Amenities:** Restaurant; bar; room service. *In room:* A/C, TV, hair dryer, minibar.

INEXPENSIVE

Hostal Les Monges Palace 🏊 A building dating from 1912 and a hotel since 1989 has been restored and turned into a good stopover in the oldest and most historic district of the inner city. A family-run B&B-type hotel, it offers small and rather simply but comfortably furnished guest rooms. Each tastefully, elegantly decorated unit is equipped with traditional, old-style furnishings. All of them contain antiques and paintings, making this hotel exceptional compared to the standard *moderno* choices in the area. The suite is special in that its furnishings are Japanese, and its bathroom offers both a private Jacuzzi and a sauna.

Calle San Agustín 4, 03002 Alicante. ✆ **96-521-50-46.** Fax 96-514-71-89. www.lesmonges.net. 23 units. 44€–60€ double; 100€ suite. DC, MC, V. Parking 10€. **Amenities:** Bar. *In room:* A/C, TV, hair dryer, minibar, Wi-Fi (7€ per 24 hr.).

Hostal Portugal The two-story Portugal is 1 block from the bus station, about 4 blocks from the train station, and a 3-minute walk from the harbor. The small rooms, furnished in tasteful modern style, are immaculate but basic. Some face an interior courtyard; those opening onto the outside have a small private terrace and lots of sunlight. Guests in units with private bathrooms and showers will find their rooms a bit cramped but serviceable. For those who share, the corridor bathrooms are adequate.

Calle Portugal 26, 03003 Alicante. ✆ **96-592-92-44.** www.pensionportugal.es. 20 units, 8 with private bathroom. 40€ double with shared bathroom; 46€ double with private bathroom. No credit cards. No parking. **Amenities:** Wi-Fi (free, in lobby). *In room:* A/C, TV, no phone.

A Hotel Outside Alicante

Hotel Ferrero ★★ This romantic villa outside Alicante has been restored and turned into a boutique hotel of much charm and grace. For a hotel of only a dozen rooms, it offers some of the facilities of a deluxe hotel, including a swimming pool and spa. A top tennis star, Juan Carlos Ferrero of Spain, purchased the property and restored the 19th-century house to its former glory after investing some $12 million. The hotel, 58km (36 miles) north of Alicante, lies behind a periwinkle exterior, with a light-drenched modern interior containing luxuriously furnished bedrooms.

Carretera Ontinyent-Villena Km 16, Boicairent 46880 Valencia. ℂ **96-235-51-75.** www.hotel ferrero.com. 12 units. 195€–290€ double, 290€–340€ junior suite; 340€–390€ suite. AE, DC, MC, V. **Amenities:** Restaurant; bar; pool (outdoor); room service; spa; 2 tennis courts. *In room:* A/C, TV/DVD, minibar, Wi-Fi (free).

Where to Dine in Alicante

The characteristic dish of Alicante is rice, served many different ways. The most typical sauce is aioli, a kind of mayonnaise made from oil, egg yolks, and garlic. Dessert selections are the most varied on the Costa Blanca; *turrón de Alicante* (Spanish nougat) is the most popular.

Dársena ★ SPANISH This is a famous waterfront restaurant along the Costa Blanca, celebrated for offering a staggering 140 different paellas. Everything you thought didn't go into paella goes into the different versions here, even cauliflower, chicken livers, and lamb kidneys. You can opt for one of the more conventional paellas, which include succulent morsels like shellfish; in fact, you can work up a big appetite just reading the long menu. We'd recommend that you start by ordering an appetizer: *fritura de la Bahía*, a crisp, fried local fish (similar to red mullet), or *boquerón* (fresh anchovies). Try the velvety smooth crab soup flavored with Armagnac, or a refreshing tart composed of tuna and fresh spinach. One of the more memorable paellas is *arroz con bacalao y costar de ajo*, which is made with salt cod, thinly sliced garlic, and potatoes, the medley crowned by a light, airy egg crust.

Marina Deportiva, Muelle de Levante 6. ℂ **96-520-75-89.** www.darsena.com. Reservations required at lunch. Main courses 15€–30€; set-price menu 43€–62€. AE, DC, MC, V. Daily 1:30–4:30pm and Mon–Sat 8:30–11:30pm.

Nou Manolín ★ 🍴 TAPAS/SPANISH This is the kind of discovery locals will tell you about if they like you. The place is fabled locally for its array of some 50 tapas served daily, everything from shrimp in garlic sauce to batter-fried fresh anchovies. When he established it in 1972, the founder of this restaurant named it after an almost-forgotten neighborhood bar (El Manolín), which his grandfather had maintained before the Spanish Civil War. Nou Manolín's street level contains a busy bar area, but diners usually gravitate to the upstairs dining room, where tiled walls and uniformed waiters contribute to the ambience of an elegant *tasca*. Menu items focus mainly on paellas, but include many kinds of fish cooked in a salt crust, several kinds of stew, fresh shellfish, and a wide selection of Iberian wines. An unusual rice dish is *arroz con kokotxas*, which is made with fresh cod "cheeks"—that is, the arrowhead-shaped flesh of the lower jaw. It has a gelatinous texture. The rice is also studded with such fresh vegetables as sweet red peppers, artichokes, cauliflowers, and green beans.

Calle Villegas 3. ℂ **96-520-03-68.** www.noumanolin.com. Reservations recommended. Main courses 20€–32€. AE, DC, MC, V. Daily 1:15–4pm and 8:15pm–1:15am.

Restaurante El Jumillano SPANISH This place has changed so little you might think one of Franco's soldiers will stroll into this time capsule. This was a humble wine bar when it opened in 1936 near the Old City. The original wine-and-tapas bar is still going strong, but the food has improved immeasurably. Today the original owner's sons (Juan José and Miguel Pérez Mejías) offer a cornucopia of succulent food, including fresh fish laid out in the dining room on the sun-bleached planks of an antique fishing boat. Many menu items are derived from locally inspired recipes. The specialties include a "festival of canapés," slices of cured ham served with fresh melon, shellfish soup with mussels, Alicante stew, pigs' trotters, a savory filet of beef seasoned with garlic, and a full gamut of grilled hake, sea bass, and shellfish.

César Elhuezabal 64. (℗ **96-521-29-64.** www.restaurantejumillano.com. Reservations recommended. Main courses 18€–30€. AE, DC, MC, V. Mon–Sat 1–4pm and 8pm–midnight; Sun noon–4pm. Closed Sun July–Sept. Bus: D or F.

Restaurante La Ereta ★★ LEVANTE It not only enjoys the most scenic and tranquil location in Alicante, right next to the castle in the Parque de la Ereta but also serves some of the best cuisine, with lots of Valencian specialties including rice dishes. While you're gazing out at the sea, you can enjoy both traditional cookery and a creative cuisine served by a formally attired staff. Instead of the usual tomato-based Andalusian gazpacho, you get a version with avocados. In elegant though minimalist surroundings, you can feast off main dishes that include paella or cod with cuttlefish. *El jefe de cocina* (the head chef), Daniel Frias, prepares tasting menus that are the best in Alicante province, and he is known for his deft handling of seafood and his market-fresh ingredients.

Parque de la Ereta. (℗ **96-514-32-50.** www.laereta.es. Reservations required. Tasting menus 48€–56€. MC, V. Tues–Sat 2–3:30pm and 9–11pm. Closed Jan 10–31.

Alicante After Dark

A town devoted to the pursuit of hot times, Alicante never lacks a bar. You can find alcohol and socializing at almost any time of the day or night. One of the town's densest concentrations of watering holes lies adjacent to the port. Night owls wander from one bar to the next along the length of **Muelle del Puerto** (a stretch of pavement also known as the Explanada d'Espanya). There are at least 20 spots that rock through the night. The most popular and visible are **Bar Potato,** where tapas are consumed with something approaching vigor, and **Puerto di Rana.** Their addresses are all Muelle del Puerto s/n, and they have no phones. Also consider the bar at one of our favorite restaurants, **Dársena** (see above).

Alternatively, walk through the narrow streets of Alicante's **Casco Antiguo.** Streets particularly rich in bodegas and *tavernas* include **Calle Laboradores, Calle Cien Fuegos,** and **Plaza Santísima Faz.** We usually prefer to wander aimlessly through this district, popping in and out wherever we feel most comfortable. If you want to plan ahead, consider **El Mesón,** at Calle Laboradores 23.

ELCHE ★

21km (13 miles) SW of Alicante, 56km (35 miles) NE of Murcia, 406km (252 miles) SE of Madrid

Sandwiched between Alicante and Murcia, the little town of Elche (Elx) is famous for its age-old mystery play, lush groves of date palms, and shoe and sandal making.

The 600,000-tree Palm Grove.

On August 14 and 15 for the past 6 centuries, the **Misteri d'Elx (Mystery of Elche)** has celebrated the Assumption of the Virgin. It is reputedly the oldest dramatic liturgy in Europe. Songs are performed in an ancient form of Catalan. Admission is free, but it's hard to get a seat unless you book in advance through the tourist office (see "Essentials," below). The play takes place at the Church of Santa María, which dates from the 17th century.

Unless you visit at the time of the mystery play, the town's **Palm Grove** ★★ holds the most appeal. The 600,000-tree palm forest is unrivaled in Europe. It's said that Phoenician (or perhaps Greek) seafarers originally planted the trees. A thousand years ago, the Moors created the irrigation system that still maintains the palms. Stroll through the **Huerto del Cura (Priest's Grove)** ★★, open daily from 9am to 6pm, to see the palm garden and collection of tropical flowers and cactuses. In the garden, look for the **Palmera del Cura (Priest's Palm)** from the 1840s, with seven branches sprouting from its trunk. In the grove you will see one of the most famous ladies of Spain, *La Dama de Elche.* This is a replica—the original 500 B.C. limestone bust, made by the Iberians and discovered in 1897, is on display in the National Archaeological Museum in Madrid.

Essentials

GETTING THERE The central train station is Estación Parque, Avenida del Ferrocarril. **Trains** arrive almost hourly from Alicante. Call ✆ **90-224-02-02,** or visit www.renfe.es, for schedules.

The bus station (✆ **96-661-50-50**) is at Avenida de la Libertat. **Buses** travel between Alicante and Elche on the hour.

Take the N-340 highway from Alicante and proceed southwest if you're driving.

VISITOR INFORMATION The **tourist information office** is at Parque Municipal s/n, 3203 Elche, Alicante (✆ **96-665-81-95;** www.turismedelx.com). It's open Monday to Saturday 10am to 7pm, Sunday 10am to 2pm.

Where to Stay in Elche

Huerto del Cura ★★ 🎁 Staying here is a unique experience. Huerto del Cura is in the Priest's Grove, so you'll have panoramic views of the palm trees from your room. The privately owned *parador* consists of a number of immaculately kept cabins in the grove. Each is well furnished and roomy, with efficiently organized, tiled bathrooms. Service is impeccable.

Porta de La Morera 14, 03203 Elche. ℂ **96-661-00-11.** Fax 96-661-20-60. www.hotelhuerto delcura.com. 82 units. 84€–132€ double; 120€–164€ suite. AE, DC, MC, V. Free parking. **Amenities:** Restaurant; bar; exercise room; outdoor pool; room service. *In room:* A/C, TV, hair dryer, minibar, Wi-Fi (free).

Where to Dine in Elche

Parque Municipal INTERNATIONAL A large open-air restaurant and cafe in the middle of a public park, Parque Municipal is a good place to go for decent food and relaxed service. Many regional dishes appear on the menu; try one of the savory rice dishes as a main course, followed by "cake of Elche." Two specialties are paella and Mediterranean sea bass, sailor's style (prepared as a stew).

Paseo La Estación s/n. ℂ **96-545-34-15.** Reservations recommended. Main courses 10€–19€; fixed-price menus 16€–24€. AE, DC, MC, V. Daily 9am–11pm.

Restaurante La Finca ★ MEDITERRANEAN In the countryside near the Elche football (soccer) stadium, this restaurant lies 2km (1¼ miles) south of town along the Carretera de El Alted. La Finca opened in 1984, and its good food has attracted customers ever since. The menu changes frequently, based on the season and what's fresh. Both fish and meat are prepared in creative ways, although time-tested recipes are used as well. Try tuna-stuffed peppers or veal kidneys with potatoes. Chocolate mousse might be available for dessert.

Partida de Perleta, Poligano 1–7. ℂ **96-545-60-07.** www.lafinca.es. Reservations recommended. Main courses 23€–28€; fixed-price menus 52€–80€. AE, MC, V. Tues–Sat 1:30–4pm and 8:30pm–12:30am; Sun 1–4pm. Closed 2 weeks in Jan, 3 weeks in Nov.

12

BARCELONA

Blessed with rich and fertile soil, an excellent harbor, and a hardworking population, Barcelona has always prospered. When Madrid was still a dusty Castilian backwater, Barcelona was a powerful, diverse capital, influenced by the Mediterranean empires that conquered it. Carthage, Rome, and Charlemagne-era France overran Catalonia, and each left an indelible mark on the region's identity.

The Catalan people have clung fiercely to their unique culture and language, both of which Franco systematically tried to eradicate. But Catalonia has endured, becoming a semiautonomous region of Spain (with Catalan its official language). And Barcelona, the region's lodestar, has truly come into its own. The city's most powerful monuments open a window onto its history: the intricately carved edifices of the medieval Gothic Quarter; the curvilinear *modernismo* (Catalan Art Nouveau) that inspired Gaudí's Sagrada Família; and the seminal works of Picasso and Miró, in museums that mark Barcelona as a crucial incubator for 20th-century art. And an array of parks, restaurants, nightlife (Barcelona is a *big* bar town), and shopping possibilities, plus nearby wineries, ensure that you'll be entertained round-the-clock. It makes for some serious sightseeing; you'll need plenty of time to take it all in—in fact, almost as much time as it takes to see Madrid.

CATALONIAN CULTURE

Barcelona has always thrived on contact and commerce with countries beyond Spain's borders. From its earliest days, the city has been linked more closely to France and the rest of Europe than to Iberia. Each of the military and financial empires that swept through Catalonia left its cultural imprint.

Language

Catalonia lies midway between France and Castilian Spain. The province is united by a common language, **Catalan.** Modern linguists attribute the earliest division of Catalan from Castilian to two phenomena. The first was the cultural links and trade ties between ancient Barcina and the neighboring Roman colony of Provence, which shaped the Catalan tongue along Provençal and Languedocian models. The second major event was the invasion of the eastern Pyrenees by Charlemagne in the late 800s, and the designation of Catalonia as a Frankish march (buffer zone) between Christian Europe and Moorish-dominated Iberia.

Although Catalan is closely related to Castilian Spanish, even those travelers who are fluent in Spanish are occasionally confronted with unfamiliar words in Barcelona. Don't be surprised if maps or brochures have addresses in Spanish, but you find signs in Catalan on the street. Today, Catalan is the most widely spoken nonnational language in Europe.

PREVIOUS PAGE: **The Palau de la Música Catalana.**

Architecture

Like many other cities in Spain, Barcelona claims its share of Neolithic dolmens and ruins from the Roman and Moorish periods. Monuments survive from the Middle Ages, when the Romanesque solidity of no-nonsense barrel vaults, narrow windows, and fortified design were widely used.

In the 11th and 12th centuries, religious fervor swept through Europe, and pilgrims began to flock to Barcelona on their way west to Santiago de Compostela, bringing with them French building styles and the need for new and larger churches. The style that emerged, called Catalonian Gothic, had softer lines and more elaborate ornamentation than traditional Gothic. It used ogival (pointed) arches, intricate stone carvings, large interior columns, exterior buttresses, and vast rose windows set with colored glass. One of Barcelona's purest and most-loved examples of this style is the **Church of Santa María del Mar,** north of the city's harbor.

The Barcelona best remembered by visitors, however, is the Barcelona of *modernismo,* an Art Nouveau movement that from about 1890 to 1910 put the city on the architectural map. It blends pre-Raphaelite voluptuousness with Catalonian romanticism, lacing them heavily with curved lines and organic forms easily recognized in nature.

The movement's most famous architect was Antoni Gaudí. The chimneys of his buildings look like half-melted mounds of chocolate twisted into erratic spirals; his horizontal lines flow over vertical supports. Some of Gaudí's most distinctive creations include Casa Milà, Casa Batlló, Parc Güell, and the landmark **Temple Expiatori de la Sagrada Família** (left incomplete at his death).

Other modernist architects of this era looked for inspiration to medieval models. Examples include Domènech i Montaner and Puig i Cadafalch, whose elegant mansions and concert halls seemed perfectly suited to the enlightened prosperity of the 19th-century Catalonian bourgeoisie. A 19th-century economic boom neatly coincided with the profusion of geniuses who suddenly emerged in the building business. Entrepreneurs who had made their fortunes in the fields and mines of the New World commissioned beautiful and elaborate villas in Barcelona and nearby Sitges.

Initiated in 1858, the expansion of Barcelona into the northern **Eixample district** laid the groundwork for the *modernismo* architects' designs. The gridlike streets in the Eixample were intersected by broad diagonals. Although opposed by local landowners and never endowed with the detail of the original design, it provided a carefully planned, elegant path in which a growing city could showcase its finest buildings.

Consistent with the general artistic stagnation in Spain during the Franco era (1939–75), the 1950s saw a tremendous increase in the number of anonymous housing projects around the periphery of Barcelona. Since the death of Franco, a cultural renaissance has ensued: New and more creative designs for buildings are again being executed.

Art

From the cave paintings discovered at Lérida to several true giants of the 20th century—Picasso, Dalí, and Miró—Catalonia has had a long and significant artistic tradition. It is the Spanish center of the plastic arts.

The first art movement to attract attention in Barcelona was **Catalonian Gothic sculpture,** which held sway from the 13th to the 15th century and

A detail of Gaudí's Sagrada Família.

produced such renowned masters as Bartomeu and Pere Johan. Sculptors working with Italian masters brought the Renaissance to Barcelona, but few great Catalonian legacies remain from this period. The rise of baroque art in the 17th and 18th centuries saw Catalonia filled with several impressive examples, but nothing worth a special pilgrimage.

In the neoclassical period of the 18th century, Catalonia, and particularly Barcelona, awoke from an artistic slumber. Art schools opened and foreign painters arrived, exerting considerable influence. The 19th century produced many Catalonian artists who followed the general European trends of the time without forging any major creative breakthroughs.

The 20th century brought renewed artistic ferment in Barcelona, as reflected by the arrival of Málaga-born **Pablo Picasso.** (The Catalan capital today is the site of a major Picasso museum.) The great surrealist painters of the Spanish school, **Joan Miró** (who also has a museum in Barcelona) and **Salvador Dalí** (whose fantastical museum is along the Costa Brava, north of Barcelona), also came to the Catalonian capital.

Today, many Barcelona artists are making major names for themselves, and their works are sold in the most prestigious galleries of the Western world. Outstanding among these is sculptor Susana Solano, who ranks among the most renowned names in Spanish contemporary art.

ORIENTATION
Arriving

BY PLANE Most travelers to Barcelona fly to Madrid and change planes there, although there are direct flights to Barcelona on American. **Iberia** (② 800/772-4642; www.iberia.com) offers many daily shuttle flights between Barcelona and Madrid—at 15-minute intervals during peak hours on weekdays—plus service from Valencia, Granada, Seville, and Bilbao. Generally cheaper than Iberia, both **Air Europa** (② 90-240-15-01; www.air-europa.com) and **Spanair** (② 90-213-14-15; www.spanair.es) run shuttles between Madrid and Barcelona. Shuttle schedules depend on demand, with more frequent service in the early morning and late afternoon. For more information on flying into Madrid, refer to "Getting There & Getting Around," p. 65.

American Airlines (② 800/433-7300; www.aa.com) has launched nonstop daily flights between New York's Kennedy Airport and Barcelona.

The Eixample district.

The flight leaves JFK at 7pm and arrives in Barcelona the following day, at 9:10am. A flight departs Barcelona daily at 11:10am, arriving in New York at 1:45pm.

The Barcelona airport, **El Prat de Llobregat,** 08820 Prat de Llobregat (*©* **90-240-47-04;** www.aena.es), is 12km (7½ miles) southwest of the city.

In 2009 Barcelona opened **Terminal T1,** a $1.7-billion structure shaped like an aluminum sword. It is anticipated that the terminal will greet 30 million passengers annually, doubling the airport's previous capacity. It's eco-friendly, with solar-powered water heaters and other features, and it also has a spa, fitness center, hairdresser, and even beds for rent, plus some 80 shops and restaurants.

The route to the center of town is carefully signposted. A train runs between the airport and Barcelona's Estació Central de Barcelona-Sants every day from 6:10am (the first airport departure) to 10:45pm (from Sants) or 11:50pm (the last city departure). The 20-minute trip costs 3.50€. If your hotel is near Plaça de España, you might opt for an **Aerobús** (*©* **93-415-60-20**). It runs daily every 12 minutes between 6am and 1am from the airport, and till 12:30am from the Plaça de Catalunya. The fare is 5€ single trip, 8.65€ round-trip. A taxi from the airport into central Barcelona costs 20€ to 27€.

BY TRAIN A train called the **Trenhotel** provides rail service between Paris and Barcelona in 12 hours. For many other routes from the rest of Europe, you change trains at Port Bou, on the France-Spain border. Most trains issue seat and sleeper reservations. Trains arrive at the **Estació de França,** Avenida Marqués de L'Argentera (Metro: Barceloneta, L3), from points throughout Spain as well as from international cities. High-speed trains now link Madrid with Barcelona, with some 25 daily connections leaving from both Madrid and Barcelona. The fast nonstop services between Spain's two leading cities take 2 hours and 38 minutes, with those stopping en route taking 45 minutes longer. The trains are spacious and comfortable; even seats in tourist class are reclining. Small TV screens and radio channels are provided at every seat.

From Seville, two trains make the 10-hour trip to Barcelona. There is also an AVE train from Seville to Barcelona taking 5 hours and 40 minutes. Some 15 trains a day arrive in Barcelona from Valencia in just 3 hours.

The modernized 1929 station has a huge screen with updated information on train departures and arrivals, personalized ticket dispatching, a passenger-attention center, a tourism information center, showers, internal baggage control, a first-aid center, and centers for hotel reservations and car rentals. It is much more than a departure point: The station also has an elegant restaurant, a cafeteria, a book-and-record store, a jazz club, and even a disco. Estació de França is steps from Ciutadella Park, the zoo, and the port, and is near Vila Olímpica. RENFE also has a terminal at **Estació Central de Barcelona-Sants,** Plaça de Països Catalanes (Metro: Sants-Estació). For general RENFE information, call © **90-224-02-02,** or log on to www.renfe.es.

BY BUS Bus travel to Barcelona is possible but not popular—it's pretty slow. Barcelona's Estació del Nord is the arrival and departure point for **Alsa** (© **90-242-22-42;** www.alsa.es) buses to and from southern France and Italy. Alsa also operates 27 buses per day to and from Madrid (trip time: 8½ hr.). A one-way ticket from Madrid costs 28€ to 50€.

Linebús (© **90-233-55-33;** www.linebus.com) offers six trips a week to and from Paris. **Eurolines Viagens,** Carrer Viriato (© **90-240-50-40;** www.eurolines.es), operates seven buses a week to and from Frankfurt and another five per week to and from Marseille.

For bus travel to the beach resorts along the Costa Brava (p. 554), go to **Sarfa,** Estació del Nord (© **90-230-20-25;** www.sarfa.com). Trip time is usually 1 hour and 20 minutes.

BY CAR From **France** (the usual European road approach to Barcelona), the major access route is at the eastern end of the **Pyrenees.** You have a choice of the express highway (E-15) or the more scenic coastal road. But be warned: If you take the coastal road in July and August, you will often encounter bumper-to-bumper traffic. You can also approach Barcelona via **Toulouse.** Cross the border into Spain at **Puigcerdà** (where there are frontier stations), near the principality of Andorra. From there, take the N-152 to Barcelona.

From **Madrid,** take the N-2 to Zaragoza, and then the A-2 to El Vendrell, followed by the A-7 freeway to Barcelona. From the **Costa Blanca** or **Costa del Sol,** follow E-15 north from Valencia along the eastern Mediterranean coast.

BY FERRY Trasmediterránea, Moll Sant Bertran s/n (© **90-245-46-45;** www.trasmediterranea.es), operates daily trips to and from the Balearic Islands of Majorca (trip time: 8 hr.) and Minorca (8 hr.). In summer, it's important to have a reservation as far in advance as possible.

Visitor Information

Barcelona has two types of tourist offices. The local government office deals with Spain in general and Catalunya in particular, with basic information about

Barcelona. This organization has an office at the airport, **El Prat de Llobregat** (Terminal A ✆ **93-478-47-04,** Terminal B ✆ 93-478-05-65), which you'll pass as you clear Customs. Hours are daily 9am to 9pm. There is another large office in the center of Barcelona at the **Palau de Rubert,** Passeig de Gràcia 107 (✆ **93-238-80-91;** www.gencat.net), where there are often exhibitions. It's open Monday to Saturday 10am to 7pm; Sunday and holidays 10am to 2pm.

The other organization, **Oficina de Informació de Turisme de Barcelona,** Plaça de Catalunya 17-S (✆ **93-285-38-34;** www.barcelona turisme.com), deals exclusively with the city of Barcelona. This is also where you can get detailed information about the city and the Barcelona Card for tourist discounts. The office is open daily 9am to 9pm. The same organization has an office at the **Estació Central de Barcelona-Sants** (Sants railway station), Plaça de Països Catalanes (✆ **90-224-02-02;** Metro: Sants-Estació). In summer, it is open daily from 8am to 8pm; off season, it is open Monday to Friday 8am to 8pm, and Saturday and Sunday 8am to 2pm.

City Layout

MAIN SQUARES, STREETS & ARTERIES Plaça de Catalunya (Plaza de Cataluña in Spanish) is the city's heart; the world-famous **Rambles (Las Ramblas)** are its arteries. Las Ramblas begins at the Plaça Portal de la Pau, with its 49m-high (161-ft.) monument to Columbus, and stretches north to the Plaça de Catalunya. Along this wide promenade you'll find bookshops and newsstands, stalls selling birds and flowers, and benches or cafe tables, where you can sit and watch the passing parade.

At the end of the Rambles is the **Barri Xinés** (**Barrio Chino** or **Chinese Quarter**). It has long enjoyed notoriety as a haven of prostitution and drugs. Still a dangerous district, it is best viewed during the day, if at all.

Off the Rambles lies **Plaça Reial (Plaza Real),** the most harmoniously proportioned square in Barcelona. Come here on Sunday morning to see the stamp and coin collectors peddle their wares.

The major wide boulevards of Barcelona are the **Avinguda (Avenida) Diagonal** and **Passeig (Paseo) de Colom,** as well as the elegant shopping street, **Passeig de Gràcia.**

A short walk from the Rambles will take you to the **Passeig del Moll de la Fusta,** a waterfront promenade developed in the 1990s. It's home to some of the best (but not the cheapest) restaurants in Barcelona. If you can't afford the prices, come here at least for a drink in the open air and a view of the harbor.

To the east is the old port, **La Barceloneta,** which dates from the 18th century. This strip of land between the port and the sea has traditionally been a good place for seafood. **Barri Gòtic (Barrio Gótico** or **Gothic Quarter)** is east of the Rambles. This is the site of the city's oldest buildings, including the cathedral.

North of Plaça de Catalunya, the **Eixample** unfolds. An area of wide boulevards, it contains two major roads that lead out of Barcelona: Avinguda Diagonal and Gran Vía de les Corts Catalanes. Another major neighborhood, working-class **Gràcia,** is north of the Eixample.

Montjuïc, one of the city's mountains, begins at Plaça d'Espanya, a traffic rotary, beyond which are Barcelona's famous fountains. Montjuïc was the setting for the principal events of the 1992 Summer Olympic Games. The other mountain is **Tibidabo,** in the northwest, which boasts great views of the city and the Mediterranean. It has an amusement park.

FINDING AN ADDRESS/MAPS Finding a Barcelona address can be a problem. The city abounds with long boulevards and a complicated maze of narrow, twisting streets. Knowing the street number, if there is one, is essential. The designation s/n (*sin número*) means that the building has no number. It's crucial to learn the cross street if you're seeking a specific address.

The rule about street numbers is that there is no rule. On most streets, numbering begins on one side, runs up that side until the end, and then runs in the opposite direction on the other side. Number 40 might be opposite 408. But there are many exceptions. Sometimes street numbers on buildings in the older quarters have been obscured by the patina of time.

Arm yourself with a good map before setting out. The best map for exploring Barcelona, published by **Falk,** is available at most bookstores and newsstands, such as those found along the Rambles.

The Neighborhoods in Brief

BARRI GÒTIC This section rises to the north of Passeig de Colom, with its **Columbus Monument.** Its eastern border is a major artery, Vía Laietana, which begins at La Barceloneta at Plaça d'Antoni López and runs north to Plaça d'Urquinaona. Las Ramblas forms the western border of the Gothic Quarter, and on the northern edge is the Ronda de Sant Pere, which intersects with **Plaça de Catalunya** and the **Passeig de Gràcia.** The heart of this medieval quarter is the **Plaça de Sant Jaume,** which was a major crossroads in the old Roman city. Many of the structures in the old section are ancient, including the ruins of a Roman temple dedicated to Augustus. Antiques stores, restaurants, cafes, museums, some hotels, and bookstores fill the area today. It is also the headquarters of the **Generalitat,** seat of the Catalan government.

THE barcelona card

An ideal way to appreciate Barcelona better and save money at the same time is with the Barcelona Card. It's definitely a bargain if you stay in the city for more than an afternoon and do any sightseeing at all. For adults, it costs 26€ for 2 days or 35€ for 3 days. For children ages 4 to 12, the card costs 22€ for 2 days and 27€ for 3 days.

The 24-hour card covers the Metro or bus, and unlimited travel on all public transport. Culture vultures who hold the card can get discounts of 10% to 100% in 29 museums. Eleven theaters and shows grant a 10% to 25% discount, which also applies at 15 leisure and night venues. You also get a 12% discount at 23 leading stores. Finally, there is a 10% discount in 15 restaurants. The cards specify where they can be used. They're for sale at the tourist offices at the airport, at Sants station, and in the Plaça de Catalunya. (See "Visitor Information," above, or go to www.barcelonaturisme. com.)

The Plaça de Catalunya.

LAS RAMBLAS (LES RAMBLES) Also commonly known as **La Rambla,** the most famous promenade in Spain, ranking with Madrid's Paseo del Prado, was once a drainage channel. These days, street entertainers, flower vendors, news vendors, cafe patrons, and strollers flow along its length. The gradual 1.5km (1-mile) descent toward the sea has often been called a metaphor for life because its bustling action combines cosmopolitanism and crude vitality.

Las Ramblas actually consists of five sections, each a particular *rambla*—Rambla de Canaletes, Rambla dels Estudis, Rambla de Sant Josep, Rambla dels Caputxins, and Rambla de Santa Mónica. The shaded pedestrian esplanade runs from the Plaça de Catalunya to the port—all the way to the Columbus Monument. Along the way you'll pass the **Gran Teatre del Liceu,** on Rambla dels Caputxins, one of the most magnificent opera houses in the world until it caught fire in 1994 and had to be rebuilt. Miró created a sidewalk mosaic at the Plaça de la Boquería. During the stagnation of the Franco era, this street grew seedier and seedier, but the opening of the Ramada Renaissance hotel and the restoration of many buildings have brought energy and hope for the street.

BARRI XINÉS Despite the name ("Chinese Quarter"), this isn't Chinatown—historians are unsure how the neighborhood got its name. For decades it's had an unsavory reputation. Petty thieves, prostitutes, drug dealers, and purse snatchers are just some of the neighborhood characters. Nighttime is dangerous, so exercise caution; still, most visitors like to take a quick look to see what all the excitement is about. Just off Las Ramblas, the area is primarily between the waterfront and Carrer de l'Hospital. Although Barri Xinés has a long way to go, an urban renewal program has led to the destruction of some of the seedier parts of the barrio. The opening of the **Museu d'Art Contemporani** at Plaça dels Angels has led to a revitalization of the area and the opening of a lot more art galleries. The official name Barcelona has given to this district is **El Raval.**

BARRI DE LA RIBERA Another neighborhood that stagnated for years but is now well into a renaissance, the Barri de la Ribera is adjacent to the Barri Gòtic, going east to Passeig de Picasso, which borders the Parc de la Ciutadella. The centerpiece of this district is the **Museu Picasso,** housed in the 15th-century Palau Agüilar, Montcada 15. Numerous art galleries have opened around the museum, and the Old Quarter is fashionable. Many mansions in this area were built during one of Barcelona's major maritime expansions, principally in the 1200s and 1300s. Most of these grand homes still stand along **Carrer de Montcada** and other nearby streets.

LA BARCELONETA & THE HARBORFRONT Although Barcelona has a long sea-going tradition, its waterfront was in decay for years. Today, the waterfront promenade, **Passeig del Moll de la Fusta,** bursts with activity. The best way to get a bird's-eye view of the area is to take an elevator to the top of the Columbus Monument in Plaça Portal de la Pau.

Near the monument were the **Reials Drassanes,** or royal shipyards, a booming place during the Middle Ages. Years before Columbus landed in the New World, ships sailed around the world from here, flying the traditional yellow-and-red flag of Catalonia.

To the east is a mainly artificial peninsula, **La Barceloneta (Little Barcelona).** Formerly a fishing district dating primarily from the 18th century, it's now filled with seafood restaurants. The blocks here are long and surprisingly narrow—architects planned them that way so that each room in every building fronted a street. Many bus lines terminate at the Passeig Nacional, site of the **Barcelona Aquarium.**

THE EIXAMPLE To the north of the Plaça de Catalunya is the Eixample, or Ensanche, the section of Barcelona that grew beyond the old medieval walls. This great period of enlargement (*eixample* in Catalan) occurred mainly in the 19th century. Avenues form a grid of perpendicular streets, cut across by a majestic boulevard—**Passeig de Gràcia,** a posh shopping street ideal for leisurely promenades. The area's main traffic artery is **Avinguda Diagonal,** which links the expressway and the heart of the congested city.

The Eixample was the center of Barcelona's *modernismo* movement, and it possesses some of the most original buildings any architect ever designed. Gaudí's Sagrada Família is one of the major attractions.

MONTJUÏC & TIBIDABO Montjuïc, called Hill of the Jews after a Jewish necropolis here, gained prominence in 1929 as the site of the World's Fair and again in 1992 as the site of the Summer Olympic Games. Its major attractions are the Joan Miró museum, the Olympic installations, and the **Poble Espanyol (Spanish Village),** a 2-hectare (5-acre) site constructed for the World's Fair. Examples of Spanish art and architecture are on display against the backdrop of a traditional Spanish village. Tibidabo (503m/1,650 ft.) is where you should go for your final look at Barcelona. On a clear day you can see the mountains of Majorca, some 209km (130 miles) away. Reached by train, tram, and cable car, Tibidabo is the most popular Sunday excursion in Barcelona.

PEDRALBES Pedralbes is where wealthy Barcelonans live in either stylish blocks of apartment houses, 19th-century villas behind ornamental fences, or stunning *modernismo* structures. Set in a park, the **Palau de Pedralbes** (Av. Diagonal 686) was constructed in the 1920s as a gift from the city to Alfonso XIII, the grandfather of King Juan Carlos. Today it has a new life,

Waterfront dining in Barceloneta.

housing a museum of carriages and European paintings called the **Colecció Cambó.**

VILA OLÍMPICA This seafront property contains the tallest buildings in the city. The revitalized site, in the post–Olympic Games era, is the setting for many imported-car showrooms, designer clothing stores, restaurants, and business offices. The "village" was where the athletes lived during the 1992 games. A miniature city has taken shape, complete with banks, art galleries, nightclubs, bars, and even pastry shops.

GETTING AROUND

To save money on public transportation, buy a card that's good for 10 trips. **Tarjeta T-10,** for 7.70€, is good for the Metro and the bus. Passes (*abonos temporales*) are available at **Transports Metropolitans de Barcelona,** Plaça de la Universitat. It's open Monday to Friday 8am to 8pm (© **93-138-70-74;** www. tmb.net).

To save money on sightseeing tours year-round, ride on **Bus Turistic,** which passes by 24 of the most popular sights. You can get on or off the bus as you please, and the price covers the Tibidabo funicular and the Montjuïc cable car and funicular. Tickets, which can be purchased on the bus or at the tourist office at Plaça de Catalunya, cost 21€ for 1 day, 27€ for 2 days; for children, it's 17€ for 1 day and 21€ for 2 days.

By Subway

Barcelona's Metro system consists of six main lines; it crisscrosses the city more frequently and with greater efficiency than the bus network. Two commuter trains run between the city and the suburbs. Service operates Sunday to Thursday from

5am to midnight, Friday and Saturday from 5am to 2am. The one-way fare is 1.35€. Each Metro station entrance is marked with a red diamond. The major station for all subway lines is **Plaça de Catalunya.**

By Bus

Some 190 bus lines traverse the city and, not surprisingly, you don't want to ride them at rush hour. The driver issues a ticket as you board at the front. Most buses operate daily from 5:30am to 10pm; some night buses go along the principal arteries from 11pm to 4am. Buses are color coded—red ones cut through the city center during the day, and yellow ones operate at night. The one-way fare is 1.35€.

By Taxi

Each yellow-and-black taxi bears the letters SP *(Servicio Público)* on its front and rear. A lit green light on the roof and a LIBRE sign in the window indicate the taxi is free to pick up passengers. The basic rate begins at 2€. Check to make sure you're not paying the fare of a previously departed passenger; taxi drivers have been known to "forget" to turn back the meter. Each additional kilometer in slow-moving traffic costs 1€. Supplements might apply—1€ for a large suitcase placed in the trunk, for instance. Rides to the airport sometimes carry a supplement of 3.10€. For a taxi, contact **Radio Taxi** (✆ **93-303-30-33;** www.radiotaxi033.com).

By Car

Driving in congested Barcelona is frustrating and potentially dangerous. Besides, it's unlikely you'd ever find a place to park. Try other means of getting around. Save your car rentals for excursions and for when you're ready to move on.

All three of the major U.S.-based car-rental firms are represented in Barcelona, both at the airport and (except for Budget) downtown. **Avis,** Calle Corcega 293–295 (✆ **93-237-56-80;** www.avis.es), is open Monday to Friday 8am to 9pm, Saturday 8am to 8pm, and Sunday 8am to 1pm. Remember that it's usually cheaper and easier to arrange your car rental before leaving the United States. For more information on car rentals in Spain, see "Getting There & Getting Around," p. 65.

By Funicular & Rail Links

At some point in your journey, you may want to visit Tibidabo or Montjuïc (or both). A train called **Tramvía Blau (Blue Streetcar)** goes from Plaça Kennedy to the bottom of the funicular to Tibidabo. It operates every 15 to 20 minutes from 10am to 6pm on weekends only. The fare is 2.70€ one-way, 4.10€ round-trip. During the week, buses run from the Plaça Kennedy to the bottom of the funicular from approximately 10am to 6pm daily. The bus costs 1.35€ one-way.

At the end of the run, you can go the rest of the way by funicular to the top, at 503m (1,650 ft.), for a stunning panoramic view of Barcelona. The funicular operates only when the Fun Fair at Tibidabo is open. Opening times vary according to the time of year and the weather conditions. As a rule, the funicular starts operating 20 minutes before the Fun Fair opens and then every half-hour. During peak visiting hours, it runs every 15 minutes. The cost is 2€ one-way, 3€ round-trip.

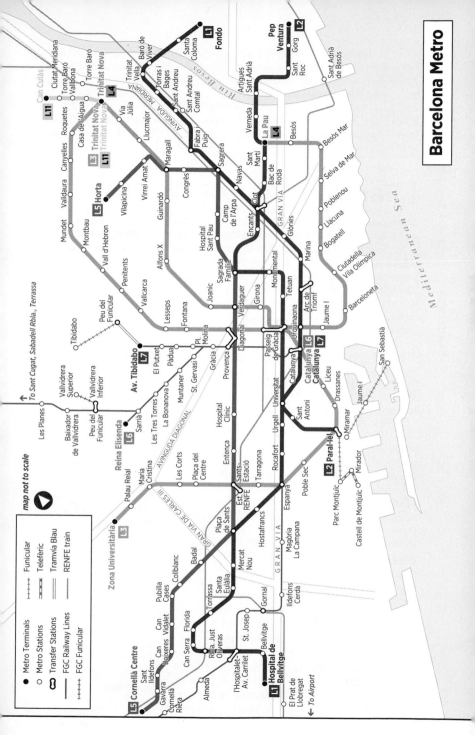

Barcelona Metro

469

The **Tibibus** (☎ **93-211-79-42**) goes from the Plaça de Catalunya (in the city center) to Tibidabo from June 24 to September 15 on Saturday and Sunday. It runs every 30 minutes from 11am to 6:30pm and sometimes 8:30pm, depending on when the park closes. The one-way fare is 2.50€. To reach Montjuïc, the site of the 1992 Olympics, take the **Montjuïc funicular** (☎ **93-318-70-74**). It links with subway lines 2 and 3 at Paral.lel. The funicular runs daily 10am to 7pm in April, May, and October; 10am to 9pm June to September; and 10am to 6pm November to March.

[FastFACTS] BARCELONA

Consulates For information on embassies, see p. 777, "Fast Facts." The **U.S. Consulate,** Reina Elisenda 23 (☎ **93-280-22-27;** train: Reina Elisenda), is open Monday to Friday 9am to 1pm. The **Canadian Consulate,** Plaça de Catalunya 9 (☎ **93-412-72-36;** Metro: Plaça de Catalunya), is open Monday to Friday 9am to 12:30pm. The **U.K. Consulate,** Av. Diagonal 477 (☎ **93-366-62-00;** Metro: Hospital Clínic), is open Monday to Friday 8:30am to 1:30pm. The **Australian Consulate** is at Plaza gal-al Placídia 1-3, 1st Floor (☎ **93-490-90-13;** bus: 22 or 24), and is open Monday to Friday 10am to noon.

Currency Exchange Most banks exchange currency Monday to Friday 8:30am to 2pm and—in the downtown area, except in the summer—on Saturday 8:30am to 1pm and 4 to 8pm. A major *oficina de cambio* (exchange office) is at the Estació Central de Barcelona-Sants, the principal rail station. It's

open Monday to Saturday 8:30am to 10pm, Sunday 8:30am to 2pm and 4:30 to 10pm. Exchange offices at Barcelona's airport are open daily 6:30am to 11pm.

Dentists Call **Clínica Dental Beonadex,** Passeig Bonanova 69, 3rd Floor (☎ **93-418-44-33**), for an appointment. It's open Monday from 3 to 9pm, Tuesday to Friday from 8am to 3pm.

Doctors See "Hospitals," below.

Drugstores The most centrally located one is **Farmacia Manuel Nadal i Casas,** La Rambla 121 (☎ **93-317-49-42;** Metro: Plaça de Catalunya). It's open daily 9am to 10pm. Pharmacies take turns staying open late at night. Those that aren't open post the names and addresses of pharmacies in the area that are.

Emergencies To report a fire, call ☎ **080;** to call an ambulance, ☎ **061;** to call the police, ☎ **091.**

Hospitals Barcelona has many hospitals and clinics,

including **Hospital Clínic** (☎ **93-227-54-00**) and **Hospital de la Santa Creu i Sant Pau,** at the intersection of Carrer Cartagena and Carrer Sant Antoni María Claret (☎ **93-291-90-00;** Metro: Hospital de Sant Pau).

Internet Access Internet cafes are found throughout Barcelona. Charging only 2€ per hour, **Cybercafe Coffee & Bit,** Carrer de Fluvià 40 (☎ **93-266-45-64;** www.barcelona-coffeebit.com; Metro: Selva de Mar), is open daily 9am to 1am.

Newspapers & Magazines The *International Herald-Tribune* is sold at major hotels and nearly all the news kiosks along Las Ramblas. Sometimes you can buy *USA Today* or one of the London newspapers, such as the *Times.* Barcelona's leading daily newspapers, which often list cultural events, are *El Periódico* and *La Vanguardia.*

Police In an emergency, call ☎ **092.**

Post Office The main post office is at Plaça d'Antoni López (© **93-486-80-50;** www.correos. es; Metro: Jaume I). It's open Monday to Friday 8:30am to 9:30pm and Saturday 8:30am to 2pm for sending letters and telegrams.

Safety Be particularly careful with cameras, purses, and wallets, all favorite targets of thieves and pickpockets in Barcelona,

particularly on the world-famous Ramblas. The southern part of Las Ramblas, near the waterfront, is the most dangerous section, especially at night. Proceed with caution.

Taxis See "Getting Around," above.

Telephone Dial © 11818 (www.telefonica.es) for national information. For elsewhere in Spain, dial © 1409. Most local calls cost .40€. Hotels impose

surcharges on phone calls, especially long distance, either in Spain or abroad. There is no longer a central telephone office, but calls can be made in comfort and security from phone centers on Las Ramblas.

Transit Information
For general **RENFE (train)** information, dial © **90-224-02-02** (www.renfe. es).

WHERE TO STAY

Barcelona may be one of the most expensive cities in Spain, but prices at Barcelona's first-class and deluxe hotels are completely in line with those in other major European cities—and they even look reasonable compared with prices in Paris and London.

Safety is an important factor when choosing a hotel. Some of the least expensive hotels are not in good locations. A popular area for budget-conscious travelers is the **Barri Gòtic (Gothic Quarter),** in the heart of town. You'll live and eat less expensively here than in any other part of Barcelona, but you should be careful when returning to your hotel late at night.

More modern, but more expensive, accommodations can be found north of the Barri Gòtic in the **Eixample district,** centered on the Metro stops Plaça de Catalunya and Universitat. Many buildings are in the *modernismo* style, from the first 2 decades of the 20th century—and sometimes the elevators and plumbing are of the same vintage. The Eixample is a desirable and safe neighborhood, especially along its wide boulevards. Noise is the only problem you might encounter.

Farther north, above the Avinguda Diagonal, you'll enter the **Gràcia** area, where you can enjoy distinctively Catalan neighborhood life. The main attractions are a bit distant but can be reached easily by public transportation.

Many of Barcelona's hotels were built before the invention of the automobile, and even those that weren't rarely found space for a garage. When parking is available at the hotel, the price is indicated; otherwise, the hotel staff will direct you to a garage. Expect to pay upwards of 16€ for 24 hours, and if you do have a car, you might as well park it and leave it there, because we never recommend driving around the city.

Ciutat Vella (Barri Gòtic, El Raval & La Ribera)

The Ciutat Vella (Old City) forms the monumental center of Barcelona, taking in Las Ramblas, Plaça de Sant Jaume, Vía Laietana, Passeig Nacional, and Passeig de Colom. It contains some of the city's best hotel bargains. Most of the glamorous, and more expensive, hotels are here.

VERY EXPENSIVE

Hotel Murmuri ★★ In the heart of Barcelona, this small hotel has emerged as another hipster address in a city already blessed with plenty of urban hotel chic. It's got all the elements for today's modern traveler, right down to the efficient black-clad staff, a chic Asian restaurant, and even a cocktail bar often filled with young beauties from South America. In the midsize to spacious bedrooms, you can adjust the lighting to fit your mood. Accommodations have tasteful furnishings in neutral tones and twin or queen-size beds overlooking a pedestrian street. Soundproof double-glazed windows protect you from the traffic noises.

Rambla de Catalunya 104, 08008 Barcelona. ☏ **93-550-06-00.** www.murmuri.com. 7 units. 450€–510€ double; 630€–730€ suite. AE, MC, V. Parking 24€. Metro: Diagonal. **Amenities:** Restaurant; bar; concierge; room service. *In room:* A/C, TV, hair dryer, MP3 docking station, Wi-Fi (15€ per 24 hr.).

Le Meridien Barcelona ★★★ Originally built in 1956, but massively restored in 2007, this is the finest hotel in Old Town, as the roster of famous guests (such as Madonna) can surely attest. It's superior in comfort to its two closest rivals in the area, the Colón and the Rivoli Ramblas (and it's also more expensive). Guest rooms are spacious and comfortable, with extralarge beds; bathrooms have heated floors. All rooms come with double-glazed windows, but that doesn't fully block out noise from Las Ramblas. The Renaissance Club, an executive floor popular with businesspeople, provides extra luxuries.

Las Ramblas 111, 08002 Barcelona. ☏ **800/543-4300** in the U.S., or 93-318-62-00. Fax 93-301-77-76. www.meridienbarcelona.com. 233 units. 253€–395€ double; 480€–2,100€ suite. AE, DC, MC, V. Parking 37€. Metro: Liceu or Plaça de Catalunya. **Amenities:** Restaurant; bar; babysitting; concierge; room service; Wi-Fi (free, in lobby). *In room:* A/C, TV, hair dryer, minibar.

Neri ★★★ 🎒 This worthy hotel in the Gothic barrio is a real charmer—a hidden gem buried deep within a labyrinth of streets. Lying at the Plaça Felip Neri close to the cathedral, the palace housing the Neri dates from the 17th century. It's a romantic and fashionable address. Stone floors and walls set off crystal chandeliers and velvet couches, a contrast in textures. The plush bedrooms are inviting, with silk draperies, rough-stone bathroom walls, rustic wooden tables, shot-silk pillowcases, and throw rugs. A rooftop garden is rich with jasmine and creepers. The on-site restaurant serves a savory Catalan cuisine, including delights such as loin of venison with chopped figs and pomegranates.

Sant Sever 5, Barri Gòtic, 08002 Barcelona. ☏ **93-304-06-55.** Fax 93-304-03-37. www.hotel-neri.com. 22 units. 195€–360€ double; 235€–395€ junior suite. AE, DC, MC, V. Public parking nearby 25€. Metro: Jaume or Liceu. **Amenities:** Restaurant; airport transfers (65€); babysitting; concierge; room service. *In room:* A/C, TV/DVD, CD player, hair dryer, minibar, Wi-Fi (free).

EXPENSIVE

Casa Camper ★★ 🎒 A family of cobblers has gone from making footwear to housing guests in an agreeable Zen-like ambience attired in fire-engine red. Most of the rooms are whimsical in decor, a kind of hippie chic, and playfully outfitted with hammocks as well as beds. It's an odd hybrid of indulgence and asceticism, its owners declaring it not just a place to stay but a sensibility to embrace. The New Age inn lies in a renovated 19th-century commercial building in increasingly trendy El Raval. Rooms are a bit austere for our tastes, and come with separate sleeping and living spaces. The roof terrace beckons with its hammocks for siesta-taking. Each floor has a suite with a large living room linked to a bedroom through a pocket door. An on-site cafeteria provides a round-the-clock complimentary spread of snacks, including fruit, hot soup, and sandwiches. A famous Camper shoe boutique is within walking distance.

Carrer Elisabets 11, 08001 Barcelona. **①** **93-342-62-80.** Fax 93-342-75-63. www.casacamper. com. 25 units. 179€–265€ double; 202€–295€ suite. AE, MC, V. Parking nearby 30€. Metro: Plaça de Catalunya. **Amenities:** Bar; airport transfers (66€); babysitting; bikes; room service. *In room:* A/C, TV, hair dryer, Wi-Fi (free).

Duquesa de Cardona ★★★ A marvelous example of recycling antique buildings, this structure, whose origins lie in the 16th century, has been given a new lease on life as an elegant boutique hotel. The palace was mainly constructed in the 1800s, though many stylings smack of Art Deco. Located at the maritime promenade, Moll de la Fusta, the hotel's backdrop is the historic Gothic Quarter. From its rooms you can enjoy a panoramic view of Montjuïc, as well as the Christopher Columbus monument and the Olympic Port. Ideal for honeymooners, many of the midsize bedrooms have a romantic feel, plus sleek, contemporary bathrooms. We recommend paying the extra euros for the harborfront rooms, as the rear rooms are cramped. The public lounges are stylish, and the Mediterranean restaurant, with its original marble tiles, not only has a chic look but also serves a savory cuisine.

Passeig Colom 12, 08002 Barcelona. **①** **866/376-7831** in the U.S. and Canada, or 93-268-90-90. Fax 93-268-29-31. www.hduquesadecardona.com. 40 units. 230€–270€ double; 290€–420€ junior suite. AE, DC, MC, V. Parking 30€. Metro: Jaume I or Drassanes. **Amenities:** Restaurant; babysitting; concierge; room service. *In room:* A/C, TV, hair dryer, minibar, Wi-Fi (9€ per hour).

H1898 ★★★ The location is on the most bustling stretch of the Ramblas, but the elegant rooms inside, evoking a colonial yacht club, are soundproof. The owners re-created the opulence of Spain in the 1800s but with 21st-century conveniences. The hotel takes its name from the year Spain lost the Philippines to the United States; the impressive building was converted from the former headquarters of the Philippines Tobacco Company. The rooftop terrace and lap pool have been called "the most decadent spot in Barcelona." The hotel offers five levels of rooms, ranging from "classic" to the most spacious—known as "privilege." If money is no object, book one of three dramatic colonial suites with a Jacuzzi, a swimming pool, and a private garden opening onto Las Ramblas.

Rambla 109, 08003 Barcelona. **①** **93-552-95-52.** Fax 93-552-95-52. www.hotel1898.com. 169 units. 169€–326€ double; 1,300€–1,500€ colonial suite. AE, DC, MC, V. Free parking. Metro: Plaça de Catalunya. **Amenities:** Restaurant; bar; concierge; exercise room; 2 heated pools (1 indoor); spa. *In room:* A/C, TV, hair dryer, minibar, MP3 docking station, Wi-Fi (free).

MODERATE

Casanova BCN Hotel ★ In this most stylish of Spain's cities, only a stylish hotel would do. The lobby is painted the color of a pistachio ice-cream cone, and in the courtyard is a garden spa. Such design elements, along with a fusion-cuisine restaurant that blends Catalan with Mexican food, have turned this 18th-century limestone residence into a hotel with theatrical flair. Whimsical lighting fixtures and sculptural chairs add to the avant-garde look. The bedrooms come in a number of sizes and designs, beginning with standard doubles and going up to junior suites that are a study of both minimalism and comfort. Expect plush beds and hardwood floors, with some units opening onto a private balcony.

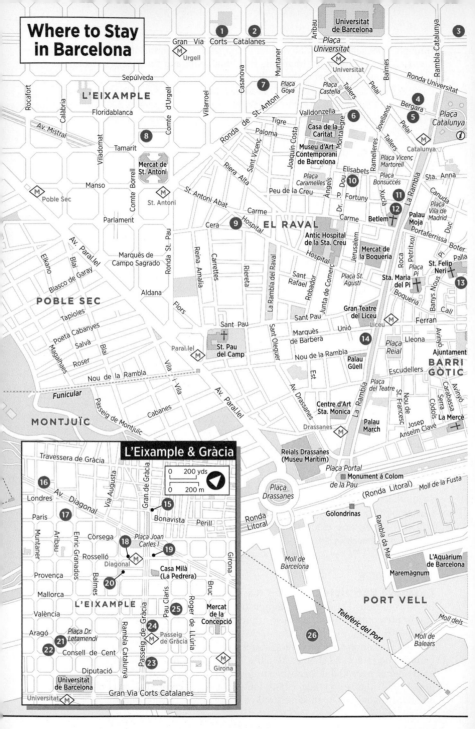

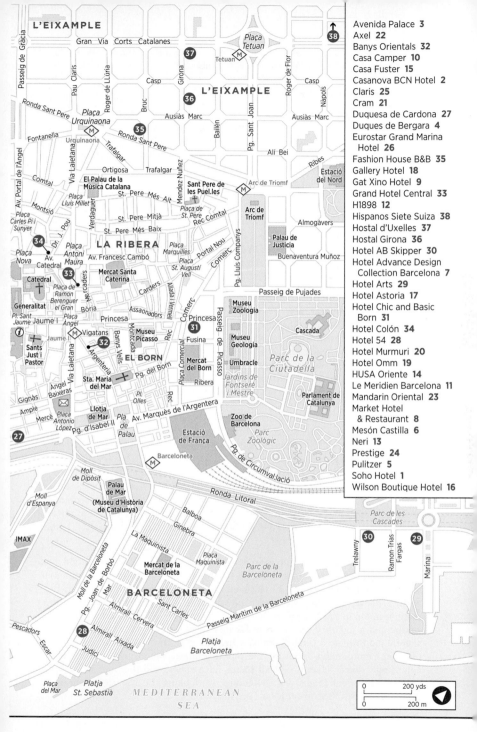

Gran Vía de les Corts Catalanes 559, 08011 Barcelona. ☎ **93-396-48-00.** Fax 93-396-48-10. www.casanovabcnhotel.com. 124 units. 133€–253€ double; 240€–358€ junior suite. MC, V. Parking 30€. Metro: Universitat. **Amenities:** Restaurant; bar; room service; spa. *In room:* A/C, TV, hair dryer, minibar, Wi-Fi (15€ per 24 hr.).

Duques de Bergara ★ This upscale hotel occupies an 1899 town house built for the duke of Bergara. In 1998, the original five-story structure more than doubled in size with the addition of a new seven-story tower. Guest rooms throughout have the same conservative, traditional comforts. Each has large, comfortable beds with first-rate mattresses, elegant fabrics, and good lighting. Public areas contain most of the paneling, stained glass, and decorative accessories originally installed by *modernismo* architect Emilio Salas i Cortes, a professor of the movement's greatest luminary, Gaudí. In the reception area, look for stained-glass panels displaying the heraldic coat of arms of the building's original occupant and namesake, the duke of Bergara.

Bergara 11, 08002 Barcelona. ☎ **93-301-51-51.** Fax 93-317-34-42. www.hoteles-catalonia.com. 151 units. 109€–245€ double; 146€–295€ triple. AE, DC, MC, V. Public parking nearby 40€. Metro: Plaça de Catalunya. **Amenities:** Restaurant; bar; babysitting; concierge; outdoor heated pool; room service. *In room:* A/C, TV, hair dryer, minibar, Wi-Fi (free).

Grand Hotel Central ★★ This hip hotel in the heart of El Born was created out of a 1920s office building. Boasting one of the most helpful staffs in Barcelona, it offers as a special feature a small rooftop terrace with a plunge pool. The bedrooms are a bit Zen, with limed oak furniture and walls painted taupe. The rooms have a sophisticated color scheme of tobacco, chocolate, and pewter. The location is between the Santa Caterina market and the 13th-century cathedral. Opt for one of the sixth-floor doubles that don't face traffic-clogged Vía Laietana.

The generous buffet breakfasts offer a tasty assortment of regional cheese, homemade pastries, and delightful finger sandwiches. The on-site restaurant, **Avalon,** offers not only midafternoon tapas but also the imaginative dishes of chef Ramón Freixa. His take on Catalan cuisine is one of the best in the district. Try his black sesame-encrusted langoustines with fresh corn.

Vía Laietana 30, 08003 Barcelona. ☎ **93-295-79-00.** Fax 93-268-12-15. www.grandhotelcentral. com. 147 units. 165€–290€ double; 208€–765€ suite. AE, MC, V. Parking 30€. Metro: Barceloneta. **Amenities:** Restaurant; bar; airport transfers (90€); babysitting; concierge; exercise room; rooftop heated pool; room service; Wi-Fi (14€ per 24 hr., in lobby). *In room:* A/C, TV/DVD, CD player, hair dryer, minibar.

Hotel Colón ★★ The Colón is an appropriate choice if you plan to spend a lot of time exploring Barcelona's medieval neighborhoods, as have such luminaries as Jane Fonda, Sophia Loren, Ernest Hemingway, Tennessee Williams, Jean-Paul Sartre, and W. Somerset Maugham. Blessed with what might be the most dramatic location in the city, opposite the main entrance to the cathedral, this hotel sits behind a dignified neoclassical facade. Inside, you'll find conservative and slightly old-fashioned public rooms, a helpful staff, and good-size guest rooms filled with comfortable furniture. Despite recent renovations, the units retain an appealingly dowdy charm. Not all rooms have views, and the ones in back are quieter. Sixth-floor rooms with balconies overlooking the square are the most desirable. Some of the lower rooms are rather dark.

Av. de la Catedral 7, 08002 Barcelona. ☏ **93-301-14-04.** Fax 93-317-29-15. www.hotelcolon.es. 145 units. 118€–245€ double; from 230€ suite. AE, DC, MC, V. No parking. Metro: Urquinaona. Bus: 17, 19, or 45. **Amenities:** Restaurant; bar; babysitting; concierge; room service; Wi-Fi (11€ per 24 hr., in lobby). *In room:* A/C, TV/DVD, hair dryer, minibar.

HUSA Oriente Right on the bustling Ramblas, this hotel, a government-rated three-star, was once one of the original "grand hotels" of Barcelona. On the site of a Franciscan monastery, the hotel dates from 1842. It was so prominent in its day that it attracted the likes of Toscanini and Maria Callas. It even became part of Hollywood legend when Errol Flynn checked in. He became so drunk he passed out in the bar. The manager ordered two bartenders to carry him upstairs, where they were instructed to strip the swashbuckling star. The manager then sent word to guests down below that they could see the star in the nude. They filed in one by one for the viewing all night. When Flynn woke up with a hangover the next morning, he was none the wiser. Renovations have improved the hotel, but it lacks the character of its former glory, today attracting mainly frugal travelers. Rooms are simply though comfortably furnished. You get the basics with relatively modern pieces, but little more.

Las Ramblas 45, 08002 Barcelona. ☏ **93-302-25-58.** Fax 93-412-38-19. www.hotelhusaoriente. com. 142 units. 96€–246€ double. AE, MC, V. Parking 30€. Metro: Liceu. **Amenities:** Restaurant; bar; concierge. *In room:* A/C, TV, Wi-Fi (11€ per 24 hr.).

Soho Hotel ★★ Innovative and minimalist, this nugget of a boutique hotel was the creation of some of Europe's best designers and architects, notably the award-winning Barcelona-born Alfredo Arribas. Interior design touches were also added by Franc Aleu, who reproduces various parts of the human body on the walls. Look for other such designer frills as globelike lamps by the late Verner Panton. The beds offer super comfort, as do the natty glassed-in bathrooms; the best accommodations are on the seventh floor, complete with wood-decked terraces. Rooms on the lower level can be noisy because of heavy Gran Vía traffic. On an August day, the cool rooftop plunge pool is idyllic.

Gran Vía 543. ☏ **93-552-96-10.** Fax 93-552-96-11. www.hotelsohobarcelona.com. 51 units. 133€–294€ double. MC, V. Parking 22€. Metro: Plaça de Catalunya. **Amenities:** Bar; outdoor heated pool. *In room:* A/C, TV, hair dryer, minibar, Wi-Fi (free).

INEXPENSIVE

Banys Orientals ★ 🏨 Its location in El Born at the doorway to the Barri Gòtic is a compelling reason to stay here in the most historic part of Barcelona—but this boutique hotel has more compelling reasons than that. For quality and comfort, at an affordable price, it's a feverishly cool choice. Hipsters and fashionistas often prefer it. An 1800s once-private mansion has been given a radical modernist makeover, with dark hardwood floors, shiny marble bathrooms, and some high-ceilinged suites with their private patios. On the ground level is **Senyor Parellada,** a classic Barcelona restaurant serving Catalan cuisine.

Argentería 37, 08003 Barcelona. ☏ **93-268-84-60.** Fax 93-268-84-61. www.hotelbanys orientals.com. 43 units. 100€ double; 130€ suite. AE, DC, MC, V. Nearby parking 20€. Metro: Jaume I. **Amenities:** Restaurant; room service. *In room:* A/C, TV, hair dryer, Wi-Fi (free).

Gat Xino Hotel ★ 🦊 This budget hotel is part of a pioneering chain that gives face-lifts to hostels, turning them into comfortable oases that rent at affordable prices. "Gat" is Catalan for cat, incidentally. One of the chic color schemes involves acid apple greens combined with black trim, and the overall look is modern and inviting. There's a roof terrace, for siestas in the sun and for the daily Mediterranean-style buffet at lunchtime. The Gat is just a 2-minute walk from Las Ramblas.

Calle Hospital 149–155, 08001 Barcelona. ✆ **93-324-88-33.** Fax 93-324-88-34. www.gatrooms. com. 35 units. 75€–90€ double; 95€–130€ suite. AE, DC, MC, V. Parking 25€. Metro: Liceu. **Amenities:** Bikes. *In room:* A/C, TV, Wi-Fi (6.50€ per hour).

Hotel Chic and Basic Born ★ 🎁🛏 Hip Barcelona, from fashionistas to paparazzi, goes here to chill out. It's a rather daring spot, especially those glass shower stalls in the middle of the bedrooms, but this is a hotel where it's okay to flaunt it. Right in the center of the Born-Ribera nighttime scene, it is a choice address, with individually designed rooms that range from small (basic yet comfortable) to more luxurious. Note that most accommodations are on the inexpensive side of the range given below. The **White Bar,** with its albino decor, is increasingly a chic rendezvous at night.

Carrer Princesa 50, 08010 Barcelona. ✆ **93-295-45-62.** www.chicandbasic.com. 31 units. 96€– 255€. AE, DC, MC, V. Free parking. Metro: Jaume I. **Amenities:** Restaurant; bar; room service. *In room:* A/C, TV, hair dryer, minibar, Wi-Fi (free).

Market Hotel & Restaurant ★ 🛏 This quiet, stylish hotel, charging affordable prices, lies in a tranquil neighborhood about a 15- to 20-minute walk to the center. The hotel takes its name from the neighboring San Antonio Market, the first market to open outside the city walls in the Eixample district. The hotel is cosmopolitan and full of character with sophisticated decorative touches and comfort, including polished hardwood floors, Asian lacquered furnishings, and bathrooms in black tile. The accommodations are large, and some of them open onto private terraces. An exceedingly good **Catalan restaurant** lies downstairs.

Passatge Sant Antoni Abad 10 (at the corner of Comte Borrell), 08015 Barcelona. ✆ **93-325-12-05.** Fax 93-425-29-65. www.markethotel.com.es. 46 units. 85€ double; 117€ junior suite. AE, DC, MC, V. Nearby parking 25€. Metro: Sant Antoni. **Amenities:** Restaurant; bar; room service. *In room:* A/C, TV, hair dryer, minibar, Wi-Fi (free).

Mesón Castilla ★ 🍴 This government-rated two-star hotel, a former apartment building, has a Castilian facade with a wealth of Art Nouveau detailing. Owned and operated by the Spanish hotel chain HUSA, the Castilla is charming and well maintained, and it certainly has a fantastic location, right in the center of the city close to Las Ramblas. Its nearest rival is the Regencia Colón, to which it is comparable in atmosphere and government ratings. It is far superior to the Cortés and the Continental. The midsize rooms are comfortable—beds have ornate Catalan-style headboards—and some open onto large terraces.

Valldoncella 5, 08001 Barcelona. ✆ **93-318-21-82.** Fax 93-412-40-20. www.mesoncastilla.com. 56 units. 107€–165€ double; 128€–192€ triple. Rates include continental breakfast. AE, DC, MC, V. Parking 23€. Metro: Plaça de Catalunya or Universitat. **Amenities:** Babysitting; room service; Wi-Fi (free, in lobby). *In room:* A/C, TV, hair dryer, minibar.

Eixample

VERY EXPENSIVE

Avenida Palace ★ In an enviable 19th-century neighborhood filled with elegant shops and apartment buildings, this hotel is behind a pair of mock fortified towers. Despite its relative modernity (it dates from 1952), it evokes an old-world sense of charm, partly because of the attentive staff and scattering of flowers and antiques. Guest rooms are solidly traditional and quiet. The soundproof rooms range from midsize to spacious, with comfortable beds and mostly wood furnishings.

Gran Vía de les Corts Catalanes 605 (at Passeig de Gràcia), 08007 Barcelona. © **93-301-96-00.** Fax 93-318-12-34. www.avenidapalace.com. 151 units. 205€–363€ double; 465€–768€ suite. AE, DC, MC, V. Parking 20€. Metro: Passeig de Gràcia. **Amenities:** Restaurant; bar; airport transfers (95€); babysitting; concierge; Internet (free, in lobby); room service; sauna. *In room:* A/C, TV, hair dryer, minibar, Wi-Fi (22€ per 24 hr.).

Casa Fuster ★★★ 🛅 In one of the city's grandest *modernista* buildings, a former private home for the Fuster family has—thanks to an $80-million investment—turned into one of Barcelona's finest addresses. When it was first built, in 1908, Casa Fuster was the most expensive residence in the city because of the high-quality marble used. Today it is a government-rated five-star deluxe hostelry. The glory days of the Belle Epoque live again in the palette of magenta, mauve, and taupe. Many of the beautifully furnished bedrooms contain private balconies that open onto Passeig de Gràcia. The **Vienna Café,** once a meeting place for the literati, is open once again.

Passeig de Gràcia 132, 08008 Barcelona. © **93-255-30-00.** Fax 93-255-30-02. www.hotel casafuster.com. 96 units. 267€–798€ double; 454€–945€ junior suite; 642€–2,940€ suite. AE, DC, MC, V. Parking 33€. Metro: Diagonal. **Amenities:** Restaurant; bar; babysitting; concierge; exercise room; Jacuzzi; outdoor heated pool; room service; sauna; Wi-Fi (free, in lobby). *In room:* A/C, TV, hair dryer, minibar.

Claris ★★ This postmodern lodging at the north end of town is a posh, government-rated five-star property. It incorporates vast quantities of teak, marble, steel, and glass behind the facade of a landmark 19th-century building (Verdruna Palace). Opened in 1992 (in time for the Olympics), it's a seven-story structure with a swimming pool and garden on its roof. There's a museum of Egyptian antiquities from the owner's collection on the second floor. The blue-violet guest rooms contain state-of-the-art electronic accessories as well as unusual art objects—Turkish kilims, English antiques, Hindu sculptures, Egyptian stone carvings, and engravings. The spacious, soundproof rooms are among the most opulent in town, with wood marquetry and paneling, custom furnishings, and some of the city's most sumptuous beds.

Carrer de Pau Claris 150, 08009 Barcelona. © **800/888-4747** in the U.S., or 93-487-62-62. Fax 93-215-79-70. www.hotelclaris.com. 124 units. 170€–481€ double; 280€–1,210€ suite. AE, DC, MC, V. Parking 25€. Metro: Passeig de Gràcia. **Amenities:** 2 restaurants; 2 bars; babysitting; concierge; exercise room; outdoor heated pool; room service; sauna. *In room:* A/C, TV, hair dryer, minibar, Wi-Fi (17€ per 24 hr.).

Hotel Omm In the fashionable Passeig de Gràcia district, Grupo Tragaluz, owner of some of Barcelona's finest gourmet restaurants, operates this nugget of a hotel. The Omm features one of the most sophisticated modern designs in the city, the work of some of Spain's best architects and interior designers. The hotel was designed so that guests could enjoy the view of Gaudí's La Pedrera, opposite the hotel. La Pedrera is considered one of the Catalan architect's most celebrated masterpieces (p. 516). The smooth textures and light tones of the hotel rooms create a tranquil, comfortable, and relaxing atmosphere. As part of the trendy design, bathrooms are open to sunlight. Varnished aluminum cabinets set a high tone for the interior decor. Special features include a rooftop pool and **Moo** (p. 494), one of Barcelona's finest hotel dining rooms.

Rosello 265, 08008 Barcelona. ✆ **93-445-40-00.** Fax 93-445-40-04. www.hotelomm.es. 59 units. 215€–400€ double; 515€–700€ suite. AE, DC, MC, V. Parking 32€. Metro: Diagonal. **Amenities:** Restaurant; bar; babysitting; concierge; rooftop heated pool; room service; spa. *In room:* A/C, TV, CD player, hair dryer, minibar, Wi-Fi (free).

Mandarin Oriental ★★★ This chain hotel took a relatively dull 1950s building and transformed it into one of the deluxe citadels of Barcelona. Its luxuriously furnished and equipped guest rooms (including some 52 exquisitely designed suites) are among the most lavish in the city. The Mandarin also boasts one of Barcelona's most elegant spas. Many of the units overlook the hotel's gardens, which can be viewed from private terraces. Other deluxe rooms overlook the Passeig de Gràcia. A special feature of the hotel is a panoramic rooftop terrace with dipping pool, and alfresco dining is also a highlight.

Passeig de Gràcia, 08007 Barcelona. ✆ **93-151-88-88.** Fax 93-151-88-89. www.mandarin oriental.com/barcelona. 98 units. 355€–535€ double, from 655€ suite. AE, DC, MC, V. Parking 15€. **Amenities:** Restaurants; bar; airport transfers (150€); exercise room; room service. *In room:* A/C, TV/DVD, hair dryer, minibar, Wi-Fi (20€ per 24 hr.).

EXPENSIVE

Hispanos Siete Suiza ★ 🎁 This is a fantastic little discovery lying about a block from the landmark Sagrada Família and its nearby Metro stop. Every detail of the hotel seems to have been planned well in advance. Units are like little apartments or junior suites, each with a completely equipped kitchen and such features as daily cleaning and a hydromassage shower. On site is a sophisticated restaurant, **Cúpula,** serving an inventive international cuisine.

Sicilia 255, 08025 Barcelona. ✆ **93-208-20-51.** Fax 93-208-20-52. www.hispanos7suiza.com. 19 units. 210€–270€ double; 240€–300€ triple; 270€–330€ quad; 420€–500€ royal suite. Rates include continental breakfast. AE, MC, V. Parking 25€. Metro: Sagrada Família. **Amenities:** Restaurant; bar; room service. *In room:* A/C, TV, hair dryer, kitchen, minibar.

Prestige ★★ Even the likes of Madonna might be satisfied with this oh-so-hip address in Barcelona. The elegant and restored 19th-century facade along Passeig de Gràcia provides no hint of the minimalist retreat to be found inside. You're far removed from the hustle and bustle of Barcelona once you enter, yet you're located in the very heart of the city, convenient to art, culture, shopping, and leisure activities. Model-like fashionistas meet in the chic Zeroom Breakfast Bar and Library for blood-red, fresh-squeezed orange juice, and "simply divine coffee, darling." Think of the hotel's infamous "Ask Me" service as a genie in a bottle, providing whatever assistance you require, such as information about the city. Public rooms are graced with Asian touches like bamboo planters and an Eastern-vibe garden. Bedrooms are Japanese inspired, sleekly elegant, and spacious.

Passeig de Gràcia 62, 08007 Barcelona. ✆ **93-272-41-80.** Fax 93-272-41-81. www.prestige paseodegracia.com. 45 units. 109€–301€ double; 149€–341€ superior double; 226€–528€ junior suite. AE, DC, MC, V. Parking 26€. Metro: Diagonal. **Amenities:** Bar; babysitting; concierge; exercise room; room service. *In room:* A/C, TV, hair dryer, minibar, Wi-Fi (free).

Pulitzer ★★ 🏨 With its high-concept modern design, attractive guest rooms, and immensely welcoming sense of comfort, this fashionable boutique hotel is our favorite hotel in an area that is too often marred by stark commercial lodging with no heart. Pulitzer, located right off the heartbeat Plaça de Catalunya, boasts a rooftop bar that opens onto panoramic views of Las Ramblas and the Gothic Quarter. White-leather sofas and black-marble trim grace the public areas, and there are such touches as a comprehensive library and private patio. The bedrooms are decorated in tones of charcoal gray, squid-ink black, and stark white, and some of them are a bit cramped. But even the humblest abode here has a bit of flair, with leather, silk, glamorous fabrics, and state-of-the-art bathrooms.

Bergata 8, 08002 Barcelona. © **93-481-67-67.** Fax 93-481-64-64. www.hotelpulitzer.es. 91 units. 109€–250€ standard double; 139€–275€ superior double. AE, DC, MC, V. Parking 25€. Metro: Plaça de Catalunya. **Amenities:** Restaurant; bar; airport transfers (80€); babysitting; concierge; exercise room; access to nearby health club; room service; spa. *In room:* A/C, TV, hair dryer, minibar, Wi-Fi (free).

MODERATE

Axel ★ 🏨 Your heart doesn't have to be young and gay to check in here, but it certainly helps. Cutting-edge architectural designs and a liberal, cosmopolitan atmosphere prevail at this chic bastion of comfort and charm. It was awarded "Best Hotel" in 2005 by *outTraveler* magazine, and that award-winning standard of hospitality still prevails today. Hotel-savvy travelers, and not just gay ones, view Axel as a cherished, unique address. You might meet Mr. Right at the rooftop pool and sun deck, or perhaps in the hip cocktail bar or lobby restaurant. The designers of the hotel weren't afraid to use splashes of scarlet against a mellow background of whites and neutrals. Bedrooms are midsize and soundproof, with king-size beds. Squashy pillows and many fine touches, even erotic art, set a romantic tone.

Aribau 33, 08011 Barcelona. © **93-323-93-93.** Fax 93-323-93-94. www.axelhotels.com. 66 units. 96€–234€ double; 115€–269€ superior double; 261€–353€ suite. AE, DC, MC, V. Parking 20€. Metro: Universitat. **Amenities:** Restaurant; 2 bars; exercise room; Jacuzzi; outdoor heated pool; room service; sauna. *In room:* A/C, TV, hair dryer, Wi-Fi (6€ per 24 hr.).

Cram ★ 🏨 Don't judge this hotel by its name. A hip crowd of guests, most of whom are in their 30s and 40s, seeks out this hot address, with its textured red-leather walls, glossy black surfaces, and whimsical touches like UFO-shaped chairs. Opened in 2005, this gem is housed in a restored and architecturally beautiful building from the 19th century. The team of architects respected the facade but turned the interior into a modern palace of convenience and comfort. The bedrooms are high quality with mirrored walls, amber-wood floors, and sophisticated color schemes such as mustard yellow and saffron. The location is good, too, right in the center of Barcelona, just 4 blocks from the Passeig de Gràcia and an easy walk from Las Ramblas. To the delight of both guests and nonguests, the 130-year-old restaurant **Gaig** has taken up residence here as well.

Aribau 54, 08011 Barcelona. © **93-216-77-00.** Fax 93-216-77-07. www.hotelcram.com. 67 units. 143€–278€ double; 200€–430€ executive and privilege units; 286€–515€ suite. Rates include buffet breakfast. AE, MC, V. Parking 15€. Metro: Universitat. **Amenities:** Restaurant; bar; concierge; outdoor pool; room service; spa. *In room:* A/C, TV/DVD, movie library, hair dryer, Wi-Fi (free).

Hotel Advance Design Collection Barcelona ★ 📷 In the heart of Barcelona, only a 3-minute walk from the Ramblas, this hotel was created from a restored 19th-century structure in the Eixample historic district. Its guest rooms and facilities live up to the hotel's namesake. The stylish bedrooms with tasteful furnishings are comfortable and spacious. The entire hotel, in fact, is sleek and sophsiticated throughout. Thirty of its bedrooms open onto private balconies overlooking the action of this bustling city, and six open onto their own private terraces. *Note:* The hotel bills itself as gay-friendly.

Calle Sepúlveda 180, 08011 Barcelona. 🕐 **93-289-28-92.** Fax 93-289-30-24. www.hotel advance.com. 36 units. 149€–333€ double; 503€ triple. Rates include breakfast. AE, MC, V. Metro: Urgell. *In room:* A/C, TV, hair dryer, minibar, Wi-Fi (free).

INEXPENSIVE

Fashion House B&B ★ 📷 B&Bs aren't typical Barcelona accommodations, but this boutique hotel may be a trendsetter. The gay-friendly house is situated in the heart of the Eixample, a few minutes' walk from La Pedrera and only 3 blocks off Plaça de Catalunya. In a restored 19th-century building, Fashion House has been converted to receive and house guests in comfort. Decorated with stucco and friezes, the B&B evokes a homey aura. Bedrooms are attractively furnished, each cheerily decorated with pastels, and the finest units open onto little verandas. The most spacious of the accommodations is La Suite, a self-catering apartment big enough for a family. In summer, breakfast is served on a communal terrace.

Bruc 13 Principal, 08010 Barcelona. 🕐 **63-790-40-44.** Fax 93-165-15-60. www.bcn-fashion-house.com. 8 units. 55€–102€ double; 75€–122€ triple; 95€–140€ suite. MC, V. Parking 25€. Metro: Urquinaona. *In room:* A/C, TV (in suite only), kitchenette (in suite only).

Hostal d'Uxelles ★ 📷 One of the better small hotels in the Eixample, this charmer offers totally redesigned bedrooms that are both comfortable and tastefully decorated. The most desirable accommodations have their own balcony or private patio. Art Deco wood paneling is used in places along with such romantic flourishes as Cupid's bow draperies above some beds.

Gran Vía de les Corts Catalanes 667, 08010 Barcelona. 🕐 **93-265-25-60.** Fax 93-232-85-67. www.hotelduxelles.com. 30 units. 90€–102€ double; 111€–123€ triple; 145€–161€ quad. AE, DC, MC, V. No parking. Metro: Girona or Tetuan. **Amenities:** Room service. *In room:* TV, ceiling fan.

Hostal Girona ★ 🛥 Imbued with atmosphere and character, this modestly priced *hostal* dates from the 1860s, when the *moderniste* architect Ildefons Cerada designed it. Today it's a nostalgic choice and has been completely restored and made suitable to receive guests. However, some of its units still lack a private bathroom. Bedrooms are simply but comfortably furnished, and several contain small private balconies opening onto the street or onto a tranquil rear courtyard.

Carrer Girona 24 (piso 1, puerta 1), 08010 Barcelona. 🕐 **93-265-02-59.** Fax 93-265-85-32. www.hostalgirona.com. 19 units (10 with private bathroom). 60€–85€ double without bathroom, 85€ double with bathroom. AE, DC, MC, V. Nearby parking 20€. Metro: Girona or Urquinaona. **Amenities:** Concierge. *In room:* A/C, TV, Internet (free).

Hotel Astoria ★ 🛥 One of our favorite hotels, and an excellent value, the Astoria is near the upper part of the Ramblas and the Diagonal. Built in 1952, it has an Art Deco facade that makes it appear older than it is. The high ceilings, geometric designs, and brass-studded detail in the public rooms could be

Moorish or Andalusian. Modernist sculpture fills the lounge where guests meet each other over coffee. The comfortable, midsize guest rooms are soundproof and contain slick louvered closets and glistening white paint.

París 203, 08036 Barcelona. ☎ **93-209-83-11.** Fax 93-202-30-08. www.derbyhotels.es. 117 units. 90€–140€ double; 215€–265€ suite. AE, DC, MC, V. Nearby parking 25€. Metro: Diagonal. **Amenities:** Restaurant; bar; exercise room; outdoor pool; room service; sauna. *In room:* A/C, TV, hair dryer, minibar, Wi-Fi (free).

Norte Diagonal

EXPENSIVE

Gallery Hotel ★ 🛎 This is a winning, modern choice lying between the Passeig de Gràcia and Rambla de Catalunya. The name, Gallery, comes from its location close to a district of major art galleries. The stylishly decorated hotel lies in the upper district of the Eixample, just below the Diagonal. Guest rooms are midsize for the most part and tastefully furnished. The on-site restaurant is known for its savory Mediterranean cuisine.

Calle Rosello 249, 08008 Barcelona. ☎ **93-415-99-11.** Fax 93-415-91-84. www.galleryhotel. com. 115 units. 165€–280€ double; 251€–406€ suite. AE, DC, MC, V. Parking 25€. Metro: Diagonal. **Amenities:** Restaurant; bar; babysitting; exercise room; room service; sauna. *In room:* A/C, TV, fax, hair dryer, minibar, Wi-Fi (free).

INEXPENSIVE

Wilson Boutique Hotel This comfortable hotel stands in an architecturally rich neighborhood. The small lobby isn't indicative of the rest of the building; the second floor opens into a large, sunny lounge. The guest rooms are well kept, generally spacious, and furnished in a modern minimalist style with parquet floors.

Av. Diagonal 568, 08021 Barcelona. ☎ **93-209-25-11.** Fax 93-200-83-70. www.wilsonbcn.com. 53 units. 95€–100€ double; 150€–200€ suite. AE, DC, MC, V. Parking 25€. Metro: Diagonal. **Amenities:** Bar. *In room:* A/C, TV, hair dryer, minibar, Wi-Fi (free).

Moll de Barcelona

EXPENSIVE

Eurostar Grand Marina Hotel ★★ No, it's not New York's iconic Guggenheim Museum, although its circular, upside-down wedding cake design evokes that famous building. Next to Barcelona's World Trade Center, the hotel naturally attracts businesspeople, bankers, and conventioneers, although it's equally suitable as a holiday hotel. It lies at the end of a long pier that juts into the Barcelona harbor. Some of the most panoramic views of water and cityscape can be seen from the hotel's windows. The Gothic Quarter is about a 20-minute walk away, although most guests take a taxi. The eight-floor hotel offers spacious, well-furnished guest rooms, with private terraces in some units. Elegant decoration, soothing colors, and luxurious woods and fabrics characterize the hotel. Guest rooms feature high-tech audiovisual equipment and top-notch bathrooms.

Moll de Barcelona s/n, 08039 Barcelona. ☎ **93-603-90-00.** Fax 93-603-90-90. www.grand marinahotel.com. 278 units. 150€–280€ double; 240€–350€ junior suite; from 290€ suite. AE, DC, MC, V. Parking 25€. Metro: Drassanes. **Amenities:** Restaurant; bar; babysitting; concierge; exercise room; Jacuzzi; small outdoor heated pool; room service; sauna; Wi-Fi (free, in lobby). *In room:* A/C, TV, hair dryer, minibar.

W Barcelona ★★★ As you look at this sail-shaped glass tower, you'll think you're in Dubai. Actually, the city's most architecturally dramatic hotel rises in the trendy beachside sector called Barceloneta. It's the first Barcelona hotel with direct access to the beach, and also the first big hotel on the Passeig de Joan de Borbó, which is a fast-rising waterfront district of shops, bars, and nightclubs. The designer was the famed Spanish architect Ricardo Bofill. The sleek, modern, spacious, and luxuriously furnished bedrooms open onto panoramic sea views. From its infinity pool, terraces, and cabanas to its first-class spa and gym, the hotel is one of the best equipped in Barcelona, complete with a rooftop bar and a gourmet restaurant.

Plaça de la Rosa del Vents 1 (Passeig de Joan de Borbó), 08039 Barcelona. ✆ **93-295-28-00.** Fax 93-295-28-00. www.w-barcelona.com. 473 units. 280€–350€ double, 420€–620€ suite. AE, DC, MC, V. Free parking. Metro: Barceloneta. **Amenities:** Restaurant; 2 bars; exercise room; infinity pool; room service; spa. *In room:* A/C, TV/DVD player, hair dryer, minibar, Wi-Fi (free).

MODERATE

Hotel 54 ★ In the increasingly fashionable fishing quarter of Barceloneta, this boutique hotel has been installed in an old building of the Association of Fishermen, offering panoramic views of the harbor and skyline. It stands in front of Port Vell, close to Playa San Sebastián and within an easy walk of Las Ramblas. After a major restoration, the hotel is now elegantly modern. There are such trendy decorative touches as neon mood lighting and green-glass sinks in the bathrooms. Bedrooms have a lighting system allowing you to "personalize" your choice of color.

Passeig Joan de Borbó 54, 08003 Barcelona. ✆ **93-225-00-54.** Fax 93-225-00-80. www. bestwesternhotel54.com/eng. 28 units. 135€–150€ double. MC, V. Nearby parking 20€. Metro: Barceloneta. **Amenities:** Bar; room service. *In room:* A/C, TV, hair dryer, minibar, Wi-Fi (free).

Vila Olímpica
VERY EXPENSIVE

Hotel Arts ★★★ This hotel occupies 33 floors of one of the highest buildings in Spain, and one of Barcelona's only skyscrapers. (The upper floors of the 44-floor postmodern tower contain the private condominiums of some of the country's most gossiped-about aristocrats and financiers.) The hotel is about 2.5km (1½ miles) southwest of Barcelona's historic core, near the sea and the Olympic Village. Its decor is contemporary and elegant. The spacious, well-equipped guest rooms have built-in furnishings, generous desk space, and large, sumptuous beds. Clad in pink marble, the deluxe bathrooms come with fluffy robes, dual basins, and phones. Views take in the skyline and the Mediterranean, and the hotel possesses the city's only beachfront pool. The young staff is polite and hardworking, the product of months of Ritz-Carlton training.

Carrer de la Marina 19–21, 08005 Barcelona. ✆ **800/241-3333** in the U.S., or 93-221-10-00. Fax 93-221-10-70. www.ritzcarlton.com. 483 units. 221€–605€ double; 370€–2,600€ suite. AE, DC, MC, V. Parking 35€. Metro: Ciutadella–Vila Olímpica. **Amenities:** 5 restaurants; 2 bars; children's programs; concierge; exercise room; outdoor heated pool; room service; spa. *In room:* A/C, TV, hair dryer, minibar, Wi-Fi (free).

EXPENSIVE

Pullman Barcelona Skipper ★ Lying only 50m (164 ft.) from the beach, this hotel is imbued with a stylish contemporary design, opening onto a view of a private interior garden. It stands next to the Arts Hotel at Port Olímpic. There are many luxurious touches and a lot of high-tech gadgets. Your bathtub, if you request it, can be filled with flower petals or salts. Showers have the effect of rain; the rooms are soundproof, the beds draped in Egyptian cotton, and entire floors are reserved for nonsmokers. The executive junior suites are decorated in the style of modern yacht cabins, with a conceptual Japanese minimalism, evoking the spaciousness of a New York City loft.

Litoral 10, 08005 Barcelona. © **93-221-65-65.** www.pullman-barcelona-skipper.com. 150 units. 180€–585€ double, from 800€ executive junior suite; from 1,500€ suite. AE, DC, MC, V. Parking 26€. Metro: Ciutadella-Vila Olímpica. **Amenities:** Restaurant; bar; airport transfers (116€); babysitting; bikes; concierge; health club; 2 pools (outdoor); room service; spa. *In room:* A/C, TV, TV/DVD player, CD player, hair dryer, minibar, Wi-Fi (free).

Near the Airport
EXPENSIVE

Hesperia Tower ★★ The famous British architect Richard Rogers, who won the Pritzker Prize for architecture, created this high-tech modernist hotel with his trademark exoskeletal design. At 107m (351 ft.), the hotel is one of the tallest buildings in Catalonia, lying closer to the airport than to the city center. On its peak, it looks as if a spaceship has landed, but it's actually the deluxe 55-seat **Evo Restaurant,** presided over by Santi Santamaría, who has previously enjoyed Michelin stars for a creative cuisine. The bedrooms are dramatically furnished; you get the feeling of being on a luxurious ocean liner sailing the high seas.

Gran Vía 144, L'Hospitalet de Llobregat, 08907 Barcelona. © **93-413-50-00.** www.hesperia. com/hotels/hesperia-tower. 280 units. 139€–332€ double; 229€–583€ suite. AE, DC, MC, V. **Amenities:** 3 restaurants; 2 bars; free airport transfers; babysitting; concierge; health club; indoor heated pool; room service; spa. *In room:* A/C, TV, hair dryer, minibar, Wi-Fi (free).

WHERE TO DINE

If money is no object, you'll find some of the grandest culinary experiences in Europe here. Diverse Catalan cuisine reaches its pinnacle in Barcelona, but you don't get just Catalan fare—the city is rich in the cuisines of all the major regions of Spain, including Castile and Andalusia. Because of Barcelona's proximity to France, many of the finer restaurants serve French or French-inspired dishes.

At the other end of the spectrum, finding an affordable restaurant in Barcelona is easier than finding an inexpensive hotel. *Note:* Reservations are seldom needed, except in the most expensive and popular places. The **Barri Gòtic** offers the cheapest meals. There are many budget restaurants in and around the **Carrer de Montcada,** site of the Picasso museum. Dining rooms in the **Eixample** tend to be more formal and expensive, but less adventurous.

Ciutat Vella (Barri Gòtic, El Raval & La Ribera)
VERY EXPENSIVE

ABaC ★★ INTERNATIONAL One of the leading chefs of Barcelona, Xavier Pellicer follows his own culinary path, creating a *cuisine d'auteur* based on his imagination. This means a menu of dishes you've had nowhere else. All this is served at a minimalist restaurant attracting some of the most serious foodies of Barcelona. When you arrive here, you never know what you'll be served, but chances are you'll like it. His savory cooking, a balance of flavor and harmonious combinations, charms most palates. Pellicer isn't afraid to take chances with his dishes. Perhaps sometimes he doesn't quite hit the mark, but no one faults his creativity. Tempting dishes might include fennel-infused ravioli with seafood or roasted sea bass with sweet pimientos, or even Iberian roast suckling pig.

Carrer del Rec 7989 © **93-319-66-00.** www.abacbarcelona.com. Reservations required. Main courses 30€–55€. Tasting menu 100€. Tues–Sat 1:30–3:30pm; Mon–Sat 8:30–10:30pm. Metro: Barceloneta or Jaume I.

Ca L'Isidre ★ CATALAN Okay, the location is seedy and potentially dangerous at night—the restaurant's clientele arrives by taxi. Inaugurated in 1970, this little dive has attracted everybody from the king and queen of Spain to singer Julio Iglesias. Epicureans, the cognoscenti, and just plain lovers of good food make their way here to what the restaurant's more ardent devotees call the finest food in Barcelona.

The family-owned restaurant, located in Raval, hires chefs that pay special attention to seasonal products, which means that the menu changes daily. For starters, try, if featured, lobster gazpacho with "fruits of the sea," or else the yellowfin tuna tartare with salmon eggs. The chef wins our admiration with some of his specialties, notably pigs' trotters stuffed with porcini mushrooms, truffles, and duck liver; or the roast baby goat with pearl onions and white wine. Another good dish is baked monkfish in a truffle vinaigrette.

Les Flors 12. © **93-441-11-39.** www.calisidre.com. Reservations required. Main courses 22€–48€. AE, DC, MC, V. Mon–Sat 1:30–4pm and 8:30–11pm. Closed 3 weeks in Aug. Metro: Paral.lel.

Casa Leopoldo ★ 📖 SEAFOOD/MEDITERRANEAN An excursion through the somewhat seedy streets of the Barri Xinés is part of the Casa Leopoldo experience. At night it's safer to come by taxi. This colorful restaurant, founded in 1929, serves some of the freshest seafood in town to a loyal clientele. There's a popular stand-up tapas bar in front, as well as two dining rooms. Some serious foodies, who have been dining here for decades, launch their repast with scrambled eggs with young garlic and meaty prawns. Our favorite dishes over the years have remained more or less the same: perfectly grilled turbot, small Norwegian lobsters sautéed with clams, and truly savory oxtail stew.

Sant Rafael 24. © **93-441-30-14.** www.casaleopoldo.com. Reservations required. Main courses 45€–70€; tasting menu 50€. AE, DC, MC, V. Tues–Sun 1:30–4pm; Tues–Sat 9–11pm. Closed 1 week in Jan, 1 week at Easter, and Aug 4–Sept 4. Metro: Liceu or Paral.lel.

EXPENSIVE

Espai Sucre ★★ 📖 DESSERTS Espai Sucre (literally, "Sugar Space") is Barcelona's most unusual dining room, with a minimalist decor and seating for 30. For the dessert lover, it is like entering a heaven created by the sugar fairy. The desserts here are original creations. "Salad" is likely to be small cubes of spicy milk pudding resting on matchsticks of green apple with baby arugula leaves, peppery caramel, dabs of lime kefir and lemon curd, and toffee. A tiny phyllo pyramid, no bigger than a pencil eraser, conceals a filling of lemon and rosemary marmalade. Ever had a soup of litchi, celery, apple, and eucalyptus? If some of the concoctions frighten your palate, you'll find comfort in the more familiar—vanilla cream with coffee sorbet and caramelized banana. Every dessert comes with a recommendation for the appropriate wine to accompany it.

There is a short list of so-called "salty" dishes for those who want to cool it with the sugar. Actually, they're quite good and imaginatively prepared, including the likes of ginger couscous with pumpkin and grilled stingray, or artichoke cream with poached quail egg and Serrano ham. The lentil stew with foie gras is first-rate, as are the spicy veal "cheeks" with green apples.

Princesa 53. ✆ **93-268-16-30.** www.espaisucre.com. Reservations required. Tasting menus 45€–50€; 3-dessert platter 30€; 5-dessert platter 40€. DC, MC, V. Tues–Thurs 9–11:30pm; Fri–Sat 8:30–11:30pm. Closed Dec 24 to 1st week of Jan. Metro: Arco de Triompho or Jaume I.

Restaurant Hofmann ★★ CATALAN/FRENCH/INTERNATIONAL This restaurant is one of the most famous in Barcelona, partly because of its creative cuisine. The culinary and entrepreneurial force behind it is German/Catalan Mey Hofmann. Menu items change every 2 months and often include French ingredients. Some of the chef's most notable dishes, which frequently turn up on the menu, include turbot stuffed with mushrooms, lobster-studded risotto, or duck liver with grapes. A marvelous dessert is caramel-coated nut ice cream.

Granada del Penedes 14. ✆ **93-218-71-65.** www.hofmann-bcn.com. Reservations recommended. Main courses 23€–45€. AE, DC, MC, V. Mon–Fri 1:30–3:15pm and 9–11:15pm. Metro: Diagonale.

MODERATE

Comerç 24 ★ 🎁 CATALAN/ASIAN/ITALIAN View a dining visit here as an opportunity to experience the culinary vision of a rare aesthete and artist. The chef and owner is Carles Abellan, who has given his imaginative, distinctive interpretation to all the longtime favorite dishes of Catalonia. With his avant-garde and minimalist design, he offers a soothing backdrop for his cuisine. The restaurant lies close to the waterfront along Barceloneta, the Parc de la Ciutadella, and the old Gothic barrio. The chef uses fresh seasonal ingredients, balanced sauces, and bold but never outrageous combinations, and he believes in split-second timing. Perhaps you'll sample his fresh salmon "perfumed" with vanilla and served with yogurt. Other vibrant, earthy dishes include a veal entrecote with wasabi sauce or ravioli with cuttlefish and fresh morels. Believe it or not, Abellan serves an old-fashioned snack that Catalan children used to be offered, a combination of chocolate, salt, and bread flavored with olive oil. It's surprisingly good, but who would dare order it except a food writer on assignment?

Carrer Comerç 24, La Ribera. ✆ **93-319-21-02.** www.comerc24.com. Reservations required. Main courses 12€–36€; tasting menu 62€. MC, V. Tues–Sat 1:30–3:30pm and 8:30–11:30pm. Closed 10 days in Aug, 10 days in Dec. Metro: Arco de Triompho or Estación de Francia.

Els Quatre Gats 🍴 CATALAN This has been a Barcelona legend since 1897. The "Four Cats" (in Catalan slang, "just a few people") was a favorite of Picasso, Rusiñol, and other artists, who once hung their works on its walls. On a narrow cobblestone street in the Barri Gòtic near the cathedral, the *fin de siècle* cafe has been the setting for piano concerts by Isaac Albéniz and Ernie Granados, and murals by Ramón Casas. It was a base for members of the *modernismo* movement and figured in the city's intellectual and bohemian life.

Today the restored bar is a popular meeting place. The fixed-price meal is one of the better bargains in town, considering the locale. The unpretentious Catalan cooking here is called *cucina de mercat* (based on whatever looks fresh at the market). The constantly changing menu reflects the seasons. For starters, you

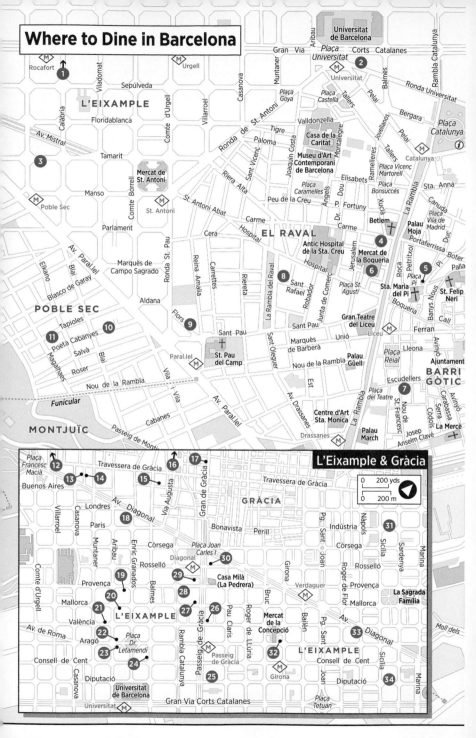

Where to Dine in Barcelona

Universitat de Barcelona
Plaça Universitat
Gran Via Corts Catalanes
Rocafort
Urgell
Sepúlveda
Viladomat
Muntaner
Balmes
Ronda Universitat
Rambla Catalunya

L'EIXAMPLE
Floridablanca
Comte d'Urgell
Villarroel
Casanova
Plaça Goya
Plaça Castella
Tallers
Pelai
Bergara
Plaça Catalunya

Av. Mistral
Tamarit
Calàbria
Valldonzella
Ronda de St. Antoni
Sant Antoni
Tigre
Paloma
Joaquín Costa
Casa de la Caritat
Museu d'Art Contemporani de Barcelona
Elisabets
Plaça Vicenç Martorell
Tallers
Sta. Anna

Manso
Comte Borrell
Mercat de St. Antoni
St. Antoni
Poble Sec
Parlament

Riera Alta
Sant Vicenç
Riera Baixa
Plaça Caramelles
Àngels
Dr. Dou
P. Fortuny
Plaça Bonsuccés
Xuclà
Canuda
Plaça Vila de Madrid
Duc

St. Antoni Abat
Carme
Hospital
EL RAVAL
Carme
Betlem
Palau Moja
Portaferrissa
Boter
Palla

Marquès de Campo Sagrado
Cera
Antic Hospital de la Sta. Creu
Hospital
Mercat de la Boqueria
Jerusalem
Roca
Petritxol
Plaça Pi
Sta. Maria del Pi
Banys Nous
St. Felip Neri

POBLE SEC
Av. Paral·lel
Elkano
Blai
Blasco de Garay
Marquès de Barberà
Nou de la Rambla
Palau Güell
Plaça Reial
Ajuntament
BARRI GÒTIC

Tapioles
Poeta Cabanyes
Salvà
Blai
Roser
Magallhaes
Vila i Vila
St. Pau
Gran Teatre del Liceu
Liceu
Ferran
Lleona
Avinyó
Carabassa
Serra
Codols
La Mercè

Nou de la Rambla
Funicular
Cabanes
Passeig de Montj
Av. Paral·lel
Est
Av. Drassanes
Centre d'Art Sta. Monica
Palau March
Plaça del Teatre
Nou de St. Francesc
Josep Anselm Clavé

MONTJUÏC
Drassanes

L'Eixample & Gràcia

Plaça Francesc Macià
Travessera de Gràcia
Gran de Gràcia
Travessera de Gràcia
GRÀCIA

0   200 yds
0   200 m

Buenos Aires
Av. Diagonal
Via Augusta
Bonavista
Perill
Pg. Sant Joan
Indústria
Nàpols
Sicília
Sardenya
Marina

Villarroel
Casanova
Londres
Paris
Muntaner
Aribau
Enric Granados
Còrsega
Rosselló
Plaça Joan Carles I
Diagonal
Casa Milà (La Pedrera)
Girona
Roger de Flor
Còrsega
Rosselló
Provença
La Sagrada Família

Comte d'Urgell
Provença
Balmes
L'EIXAMPLE
Mallorca
València
Plaça Dr. Letamendi
Aragó
Rambla Catalunya
Pau Claris
Roger de Llúria
Bruc
Mercat de la Concepció
Bailèn
Mallorca
Diagonal
Sicília
L'EIXAMPLE

Av. de Roma
Consell de Cent
Diputació
Universitat de Barcelona
Passeig de Gràcia
Verdaguer
Girona
Consell de Cent
Diputació

Universitat
Gran Via Corts Catalanes
Plaça Tetuan

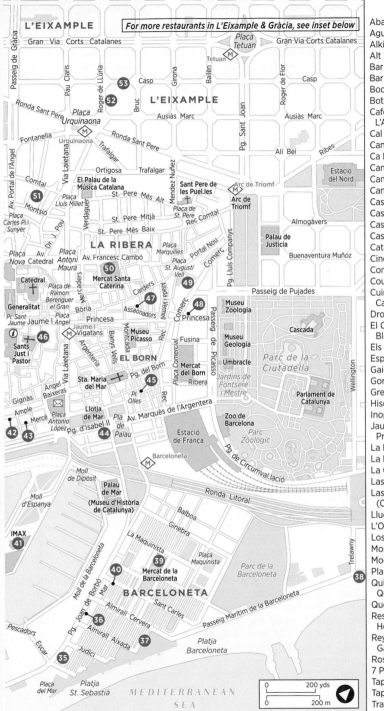

might try the onion soup au gratin with egg and Parmesan cheese. We'd recommend such specialties as artichoke hearts sautéed with bacon and pork sausage, or else salt cod loin flavored with an aioli sauce, or even Mediterranean sea bass stuffed with red pepper and served with a garlic vinaigrette.

Montsió 3. © **93-302-41-40.** www.4gats.com. Reservations required Sat–Sun. Main courses 12€–28€. AE, DC, MC, V. Daily 10am–1am. Metro: Plaça de Catalunya.

La Gardunya CATALAN This is the most famous restaurant in Barcelona's covered food market, La Boqueria. Originally conceived as a hotel, it has concentrated on food since the 1970s. Battered, somewhat ramshackle, and a bit claustrophobic, it's fashionable with an artistic set that might have been designated as bohemian in an earlier era. It's near the back of the market, so you'll pass endless rows of fresh produce, cheese, and meats before you reach it. You can dine downstairs near a crowded bar, or upstairs, which is a bit more formal. Food is ultrafresh—the chefs certainly don't have to travel far for the ingredients. You might try "hors d'oeuvres of the sea," cannelloni Rossini, grilled hake with herbs, *rape marinera,* paella, brochettes of veal, filet steak with green peppercorns, seafood rice, or *zarzuela* (stew) of fresh fish with spices.

Carrer Jerusalem 18. © **93-302-43-23.** www.lagardunya.com. Reservations recommended. Main courses 13€–30€; fixed-price lunch 15€; fixed-price dinner 22€. AE, DC, MC, V. Mon–Sat noon–5pm and 8pm–midnight. Metro: Liceu.

Quo Vadis ★ SPANISH/CATALAN/CONTINENTAL Elegant and impeccable, this is one of the finest restaurants in Barcelona. In a century-old building near the open stalls of the Boqueria food market, it was established in 1948 and has been a discreet but thriving business ever since. The three paneled dining rooms exude conservative charm. Culinary creations include roast suckling pig, fried gooseliver with prunes, filet of *toro* (bull) with wine sauce, and a variety of grilled or flambéed fish. There's a wide choice of desserts made with seasonal fruits imported from all over Spain.

Carme 7. © **93-302-40-72.** www.restaurantquovadis.com. Reservations recommended. Main courses 21€–35€. AE, MC, V. Mon–Sat 1:15–4pm and 8:30–11:30pm. Metro: Liceu or Plaça de Catalunya.

INEXPENSIVE

Café de L'Academia ★ 🍴 CATALAN/MEDITERRANEAN In the center of the Barri Gòtic a short walk from Plaça Sant Jaume, this 15-table (20–25 in summer) restaurant looks expensive but is really one of the most affordable, as well as the best, in the medieval city. The building dates from the 15th century, but the restaurant was founded in 1987. Owner Jordí Casteldi offers you an elegant atmosphere in a setting of brown stone walls and ancient wooden columns. At a small bar you can peruse the menu and study the wines offered. Dishes of this quality usually cost three times as much in Barcelona. The chef is proud of his "kitchen of the market," suggesting that only the freshest ingredients from the day's shopping are featured. Try such delights as *lassanye de butifarra i ceps* (lasagna with Catalan sausage and flap mushrooms), *bacalla gratinado i musselina de carofes* (salt cod gratiné with an artichoke mousse), or *terrina d'berengeras amb fortmage de cabra* (terrine of eggplant with goat cheese).

Carrer Lledó 1 (Barri Gòtic), Plaça Sant Just. © **93-319-82-53.** Reservations required. Main courses 10€–18€; fixed-price menu (lunch only) 14€. AE, MC, V. Mon–Fri 1:30–5pm and 8:30pm–1am. Closed last 2 weeks of Aug. Metro: Jaume I.

Cuines Santa Caterina ★ 👖 ASIAN/MEDITERRANEAN/ITALIAN In the Santa Caterina market, top architects Enric Miralles and Benedetta Tagliabue created this soaring space with an open kitchen, a tapas bar, and chunky wooden tables. It's especially lively at lunchtime, when locals shout their orders after reading the scrawls on a chalkboard. With its different types of kitchens, ranging from Asia to Italy, this fusion cuisine is served against a backdrop that includes columns of light, ficus trees planted in between tables, and one wall composed of shelves stacked with wine, olive oil, and various vinegars. The food comes directly from the market, so it's very fresh. Many dishes are suitable for vegetarians, especially those fresh green asparagus emerging from the grill or the delicious salads made, say, of melted cheese, nuts, and dates. The sushi tastes fresh and is prepared in the best tradition of Japan. A juice bar hawks vegetable and fruit drinks. From Thai green curry to grilled goat kid chops, the dishes are tasty and appealing. One diner called the chocolate cake "dangerously dark and brooding."

Mercado de Santa Caterina, Av. Francesc Cambó 17, La Ribera. 🕐 **93-268-99-18.** www.cuines santacaterina.com. Reservations not required. Main courses 8€–22€. MC, V. Daily 1–4pm and 8–11:30pm. Metro: Jaume I.

Los Caracoles CATALAN "The Snails" (as it translates into English) was founded back in 1835 in the heart of the Gothic Quarter near the Rambles, and the tantalizing aroma of roasting chicken still wafts through this seedy street after all these years. The founding Bofarull family is still in charge of this time-mellowed favorite, which is seemingly visited by every tourist in town. Even though Los Caracoles hasn't been acclaimed the best restaurant in Barcelona since the time of the American Civil War, it remains a bastion of local culture and a favorite of old-time locals who mingle with diners from everywhere from Japan to the Yukon territories. The food on the menu at this old favorite—which was featured in the inaugural edition of *Spain on $5 a Day* and recommended for many years—has never been altered. Try such dishes as grilled langoustines, fried small squid, or else chicken and ham croquettes. For longtime visitors to Barcelona, maybe the memories are also an important lure.

Escudellers 14. 🕐 **93-301-20-41.** www.loscaracoles.es. Reservations recommended. Main courses 8€–30€. AE, DC, MC, V. Daily 1:15pm–midnight. Metro: Drassanes.

Pla de la Garsa ★ 🐟 SPANISH/FRENCH/CATALAN In Barrio Ribera close to the cathedral, this historic building is fully renovated but retains some 19th-century fittings, such as a cast-iron spiral staircase used to reach another dining area upstairs. However, the ground floor is more interesting. Here you'll encounter the owner, Ignacio Sulle, an antiques collector who has filled his establishment with an intriguing collection of objets d'art. His restaurant boasts one of the city's best wine lists and features a daily array of traditional Catalan and Mediterranean favorites. Begin with one of the pâtés, especially the goose, or a confit of duck thighs. You can also order meat and fish pâtés. One surprise is a terrine with black olives and anchovies. For a main course you can order perfectly seasoned beef bourguignon or confit leg of duck with kidney beans. The cheese selection is one of the finest we've found in town, especially bountiful in Catalan goat cheese, including Serrat Gros from the Pyrenees.

Assaonadors 13. 🕐 **93-315-24-13.** www.pladelagarsa.com. Reservations recommended for weekends. Main courses 9€–22€. AE, MC, V. Daily 8pm–1am. Metro: Jaume I.

Tapaç 24 ★★ TAPAS If you're like us and prefer at times to compose an entire meal of just tapas, you can find no better choice in Barcelona than this chef-driven bistro. It was created by Carles Abellan, who worked at El Bulli (p. 563), acclaimed as the top—or one of the top—restaurants of Spain. First-rate produce, such as purple-tinged artichokes, is transformed into tantalizing treats—one foodie called them "swoon inducing." You can stop in for breakfast, lunch, or dinner at this nonstop kitchen. Try the cod omelet with beans and regional peppers, the truffled grilled-cheese sandwich of mozzarella and Iberian ham, or perhaps the silken anchovies spread on slices of Requeson cheese. Ever had cooked duck eggs broken up over french fries for lunch?

Carrer de la Disputació 269. ⑦ **93-488-09-77.** Reservations not required. Tapas 4€–15€. MC, V. Mon–Sat 8am–midnight. Metro: Tetuan.

Eixample
VERY EXPENSIVE

Can Ravell ★ 🍴 CATALAN There's a good reason that the most serious Barcelona foodies covet this secret address and pray that no guidebook writer will ever discover it. Founded in 1929 by Ignasy Ravell, it started as a food store and still is, more or less. Although the joint is in the heart of Barcelona, you'd never know it was there if you were just strolling along the street. Tucked away on the second floor of a deli, you reach it by going through a kitchen and shimmying up a spiral staircase. Some of the freshest food in the city is served here and the chef, Jesus Benavente, prepares heavenly food, adjusting his menu to take advantage of the best on the market in any given season. We don't know what will be featured at the time of your visit, but we recall with fondness roast lamb with pearl onions, pigs' trotters stuffed with shrimp, and veal steak with foie gras. The restaurant also boasts a fine wine collection, with more than 10,000 bottles in the cellar, including cavas and champagnes.

Aragó 313. ⑦ **93-457-51-14.** www.ravell.com. Reservations required. Main courses 15€–50€. AE, DC, MC, V. Tues–Wed 10am–9pm; Thurs–Sat 10am–11pm. Metro: Gerona.

Drolma ★★★ INTERNATIONAL Since 1999, Drolma has been one of Barcelona's best haute cuisine restaurants. Fermí Puig is one of Spain's most celebrated chefs, and his culinary showcase can be found here in the Hotel Majestic. The restaurant's name is Sanskrit for Buddha's female side. He might as well have called his restaurant "Majestic," as the food certainly is. Only the freshest ingredients go into his carefully balanced cookery based on the market's seasonal bounty. We especially like the personal spin he gives to seasonal dishes along with the luxurious foodstuffs presented nightly. What diner could not love the chef who presents pheasant-stuffed cannelloni in a velvety foie gras sauce, the dish delicately sprinkled with rare black truffle? His wild turbot is enhanced with fresh mushrooms from the Catalan countryside. The prawns with fresh asparagus tips in a virgin olive oil sauce emphasize the natural flavor of each ingredient; though simple, this dish is, in a word, divine. The lamb is aromatically grilled with fresh herbs, giving the meat a pungent and refreshing dimension. The baked goat with potatoes and mushrooms is bold yet delicate in flavor.

In the Hotel Majestic, Passeig de Gràcia 68-70. ⑦ **93-496-77-10.** www.drolmarestaurant.cat. Reservations required. Main courses 39€–84€. AE, DC, MC, V. Mon–Sat 1–3:30pm and 8:30–11pm. Closed for lunch in Aug. Metro: Passeig de Gràcia.

Gaig ★★★ CATALAN Carlos Gaig is one of the media darlings of Barcelona. He's also a superb chef who now runs an outstanding restaurant whose origins go back to 1869, when it opened elsewhere. He is a fourth-generation family member running the place, and he is always searching for the best produce in any season. He takes classic recipes, often from Catalonia, and gives them a modern twist. He's always concerned with taste, aroma, and aesthetics. Try such specialties as grilled monkfish with fresh, locally grown herbs; filet of veal with pine nuts and prunes; or even partridge with fresh mushrooms. His roast pork is also a winning dish. We prefer the tasting menu, which always contains delightful surprises.

Aragó. ✆ **93-429-10-17.** www.restaurantgaig.com. Reservations required. Main courses 30€–50€; tasting menu 85€. AE, DC, MC, V. Mon–Sat 1:30–3:30pm and 9–11pm; Sun 9–11pm. Metro: Passeig de Gràcia.

La Dama ★★★ CATALAN/INTERNATIONAL This is one of the few restaurants in Barcelona that deserves, and gets, a Michelin star. In a grand early-20th-century building, this stylish and well-managed restaurant serves a clientele of local residents and civic dignitaries. You take an Art Nouveau elevator (or the sinuous stairs) up one flight to reach the dining room. The most enticing specialties include sea bass suprême with chanterelles and an orange vinaigrette; lobster gratin on a bed of spinach; beef tenderloin with foie gras in a port-wine sauce; and deboned pigs' trotters stuffed with mushrooms and truffles. The building, designed by Manuel Sayrach and built in 1918, is 3 blocks west of the intersection of Avinguda Diagonal and Passeig de Gràcia.

Diagonal 423. ✆ **93-202-06-86.** www.ladama-restaurant.com. Reservations required. Main courses 19€–47€; tasting menu 65€–98€. AE, DC, MC, V. Daily 1:30–3:30pm and 8:30–11:30pm. Metro: Provença.

EXPENSIVE

Casa Calvet ★ MEDITERRANEAN This is one of the most visible and sought-after restaurants of the Eixample district, with a reputation and cachet that has attracted everyone from the mayor of Barcelona to Queen Sofía and her daughter, the Infanta Cristina. It is on the ground floor of one of the great modernist apartment buildings of Barcelona, a stained-glass and wood-trimmed fantasy designed by Antoni Gaudí in 1899. Menu items are artful and sophisticated, reflecting influences from both Catalonia and France. An array of well-crafted specialties include grilled scallops with crispy potatoes, leeks, and turnips in asparagus oil; and a casserole of rock fish with fresh mussels and prawns. A couple of unusual offerings include sirloin of veal with pumpkin and a mushroom sauce, and duck liver in port wine with a raspberry sauce.

Carrer Casp 48. ✆ **93-412-40-12.** www.casacalvet.es. Reservations recommended. Main courses 25€–32€; tasting menus 40€–75€. AE, DC, MC, V. Mon–Sat 1–3:30pm and 8:30–11pm. Metro: Passeig de Gràcia.

Coure ★★ CATALAN/INTERNATIONAL In the Gràcia district, Coure offers the best-tasting menu in Barcelona. Chef-owner Albert Ventura prepares an elegant setting that seems to attract nearly all of Barcelona. Expect some wonderful taste sensations if you dine here. The chef's cooking reveals a control over a fertile imagination, and we applaud his harmonious flavors and combinations of ingredients. One specialty is *carpaccio de pies de cerdo,* combining pigs' trotters with oysters. That may frighten you away, but many gourmets throughout the city rave about the dish. Less challenging delights to your palate might be the fresh sea bass with soupy rice or else fresh tuna flavored with lime and served with smoked eggplant. An exotic specialty is hare stuffed with foie gras, chocolate, and fresh mushrooms.

Pasaje Marimón 20. ✆ **93-200-75-32.** Main courses 20€–24€; fixed-price lunch 45€. Tasting menu 45€. V. Tues–Sat 1:30–3:30pm and 8:30–11:30pm. Closed Easter week and 3 weeks in Aug. Metro: Hospital Clínic.

Hisop ★★ 🎁 CATALAN On the northern tier of the Eixample sector, young men Oriol Ivern and Guillem Pla are in the vanguard of gifted chefs revolutionizing Spanish—and ultimately European—cuisine. They dare, dare, and then *dare* some more. The decor is hip, stylish, minimalist, and dominated by a sleek red-and-black gloss. Their philosophy is to take the recipes of the past and give them an entirely contemporary interpretation. Their signature dish is a rosy pigeon breast served with pear purée and tomato confit. The pigeon comes with different peppers (ranging from Jamaican to Szechuan) and different salts (ranging from red to *fleur de sel*). You more or less get to season to taste. Duck liver comes with the unusual accompaniments of beets and mangoes. Fresh scallops are tossed with pumpkin flowers, and John Dory appears on your platter with truffles. Locally caught squid is made even more delectable with a green pesto made from wild arugula and a white salsify purée. Drizzled on this is an orange-flavored sweet-pepper oil. And who makes a better chocolate Madeleine soaked in rose syrup and served with strawberry-pepper ice cream?

Pasaje Marimon 9. ✆ **93-241-32-33.** www.hisop.com. Reservations required. Main courses 23€–25€. AE, DC, MC, V. Mon–Fri 1:30–3:30pm and 9–11pm; Sat 9–11pm. Closed 1 week in Aug. Metro: Hospital Clínic.

Jaume de Provença ★★★ CATALAN/FRENCH A few steps from the Estació Central de Barcelona–Sants railway station, at the western end of the Eixample, this is a small, cozy restaurant with rustic decor. It is the only restaurant along the Diagonal that can compare to La Dama (see above). Named after its owner and chef, Jaume Bargués, it features modern interpretations of traditional Catalan and southern French cuisine. Both warm and cold appetizers tempt you, including an especially delightful truffle-stuffed ravioli with a mushroom cream sauce. Radiantly authentic flavors come out in such dishes as sole stuffed with crab, thyme, and lemon, or else veal filet in a sauce of truffles and Madeira.

Provença 88. ✆ **93-430-00-29.** www.jaumeprovenza.com. Reservations recommended. Main courses 11€–32€; fixed-price menu 49€. AE, DC, MC, V. Tues–Sun 1–3:45pm; Tues–Sat 9–11:15pm. Closed Easter week and Aug. Metro: Entença.

Moo ★★★ MEDITERRANEAN When you win the lottery, you can fly to Barcelona just to dine with the famed Roca brothers at their swank restaurant in the chic Hotel Omm. Style and substance meet in this design-centric enclave of sublime food, where steel and slate dead-end into a glassed-in bamboo garden. You'll be mooing with praise for the brothers' creativity in the kitchen where they approach a kind of culinary genius night after night, making Moo Barcelona's most innovative restaurant. One habitué told us, "I come here once or twice a month and never know exactly what I'm eating . . . and I'm much too cool to ask.

I just thrill at the taste sensations." The Roca brothers create flavors that actually evoke the aroma of the *vino* being served, an amazing achievement. For example, salad Verdejo, named after the white Rueda grape, brought out the wine's delicate, grassy flavoring by combining tender lamb's lettuce, fresh fennel and chervil, mango, and rhubarb, with a tantalizing drizzle of dill oil. Their lobster with licorice curry (you read that right) might sound ghastly but is in fact a celestial dish. Baby goat is slow-cooked in a rosemary-honey glaze and served on a "cloud" of goat's-milk foam.

In the Hotel Omm (p. 479), Rosselló 265. ✆ **93-445-40-00.** www.hotelomm.es. Reservations required. Main courses 19€–26€; fixed-price menus 55€–100€. AE, DC, MC, V. Mon–Sat 1:30–4pm and 8:30–11pm. Metro: Diagonal.

MODERATE

Alkimia ★★ 🍴 CATALAN So you think a "fried egg" for an appetizer sounds a bit dull? You won't after you taste this starter here. In the Eixample sector, Chef Jordi Vilà stretches the fundamental boundaries of Catalan cuisine, which might begin with the above-mentioned fried egg. Actually, it is composed of a ring of cauliflower cream studded with candied lemon and caramelized onion. The so-called yolk is a scoop of unsweetened egg-yolk ice cream with a dollop of Sevruga caviar. Vilà calls his pioneering cuisine "deconstructivism," in that it breaks down a traditional recipe into components before it is reinterpreted in creative ways. The rice in the dish is actually creamed and ringed with black squid ink. You can also try other imaginative delights such as red mullet in garlic oil with a yogurt and cucumber-apple chutney, monkfish with cauliflower purée and black-olive jam, or glazed veal shank with seasonal mushrooms.

Calle Industria 79. ✆ **93-207-61-15.** Reservations required. Main dishes 9€–19€. Fixed-price menus 35€–74€. DC, MC, V. Mon–Fri 1:30–3:30pm and 8:30–10:30pm. Closed 3 weeks in Aug. Metro: Sagrada Família.

Cata 181 ★★ 🍴 CATALAN/TAPAS All dishes here are tapas-size, and how innovative they seem until you learn that many of the recipes are based on time-tested favorites from Grandmother Catalonia's cupboard. Take the pigs' trotters with walnuts and fresh figs, accompanied by a scoop of honey ice cream. Sweetened pigs'-foot flan in some variation has been served in Catalonia for centuries. Another startling but flavor-filled dish is squid stuffed with minced pork and served with an almond-flavored chocolate sauce. A savory rice dish is served with fresh asparagus and black truffles, and ravioli come stuffed with codfish and minced smoked ham. A Catalan favorite, cannelloni is presented in a truffle-studded béchamel sauce. Three squares of fresh and succulent rare tuna are crowned with savory mustard. The restaurant is mainly a tapas bar celebrated for both its extraordinary wine list and its cuisine.

Calle Valencia 181. ✆ **93-323-68-18.** www.cata181.com. Reservations required. Tasting menu 34€ for 9 dishes, 45€ for 11 dishes; tapas 8€–11€. AE, DC, MC, V. Sun–Fri 1pm–midnight; Sat 8pm–12:30am. Closed 3 weeks in Aug. Metro: Passeig de Gràcia or Hospital Clínic.

Cinc Sentits ★★★ MEDITERRANEAN Cinc Sentits in Catalan means five senses, and chef Jordi Artal appeals to all of them. Yes, his cuisine is that special. In the fashionable Eixample sector, the restaurant, with its cream-colored walls and intimate black banquettes, is a chic rendezvous. For an appetizer, the plate-stacked foie gras, along with a wedge of pastry and sugar-glazed beets sprinkled with balsamic vinegar, is a perfect marriage of sweet and savory, with textures that run the gamut from a velvety smoothness to a sharp crunch. The delicately pan-seared lobster is served with white-garlic soup, and crisp duck breast is accentuated with a Priorat wine sauce and accompanied by a sherry-enhanced sweet-potato purée. Dishes are subtle and perfectly seasoned, and the wine cellar offers some delightful bottles.

Aribau 58. © **93-323-94-90.** www.cincsentits.com. Reservations required. Main courses 10€–25€; tasting menu 65€. AE, DC, MC, V. Tues–Sat 1:30–3:30pm and 8:30–11pm. Closed Aug 8–31. Metro: Passeig de Gràcia.

El Caballito Blanco SEAFOOD/INTERNATIONAL The "Little White Horse" is a Barcelona standby famous for seafood and popular with the locals. The fluorescent-lit dining area does not offer much atmosphere, but the food is good, varied, and relatively inexpensive (unless you order lobster or other expensive shellfish). Located in the Passeig de Gràcia area, the restaurant features a huge selection, including monkfish, mussels marinara, and shrimp with garlic. If you don't want fish, try the grilled lamb cutlets. Several different pâtés and salads are offered. There's a bar to the left of the dining area.

Mallorca 196. © **93-453-10-33.** Main courses 18€–31€. AE, MC, V. Tues–Sun 1–3:45pm; Tues–Sat 9–10:45pm. Closed Aug. Metro: Hospital Clínic or Diagonal.

Gresca ★★ 🍴 CATALAN/INTERNATIONAL This small restaurant, a real discovery, is the creation of Chef Rafael Peña, who fine-tuned his culinary skills under Ferran Adrià, often hailed as the world's greatest chef. In this modern setting, a chic crowd of foodies is lured to taste the offerings of the highly talented and imaginative Peña. Food-smart Catalans, with palates that came into maturity long after the dullness of the Franco era, can be seen ordering some of the chef's more experimental dishes—fresh calves' liver with plantains and licorice, for example. The octopus carpaccio is a surefire winner, and so is the black *bultifarra* (a regional sausage popular in Catalonia). Here it's served with fried potatoes. We also recall with great fondness those seared scallops with fresh shrimp, as well as one specialty, tender beef cheeks braised in Rioja wine. A delectable ham comes with strips of fast-fried calamari.

Carrer Provenza 230. © **93-451-61-93.** Reservations required. Main courses 15€–30€; fixed-price menu 45€. MC, V. Daily 1:30–3:30pm; Mon–Sat 8:30–11pm. Metro: Plaça de Catalunya or Hospital Clínic.

L'Olive ★ CATALAN/MEDITERRANEAN You assume that this two-floor restaurant is named for the olive that figures so prominently into its cuisine, but actually it's named for the owner, Josep Olive. The building is designed in modern Catalan style. The tables are topped in marble, the floors impeccably polished. There are sections on both floors where it's possible to have some privacy, and overall the feeling is one of elegance with a touch of intimacy. You won't be disappointed by anything on the menu, especially *bacalla llauna* (raw salt cod), *filet de vedella al vi negre al forn* (baked veal filets in a red-wine sauce), or *salsa maigret* of duck with strawberry sauce. Monkfish flavored with roasted garlic is always a palate pleaser. You can finish with *crema catalana* (a flan) or one of the delicious Catalan pastries.

Calle Balmes 47 (corner of Concéjo de Ciento). © **93-452-19-90.** www.rte-olive.com. Reservations recommended. Main courses 15€–29€. AE, DC, MC, V. Daily 1–4pm; Mon–Sat 8:30pm–midnight. Metro: Passeig de Gràcia.

Rosalert ★ CATALAN/SEAFOOD At the corner of Carrer Napols close to La Sagrada Família, this restaurant (a typical setting of hardwood floors and tile-covered walls) has been the domain of Jordi Alert for more than 4 decades. He specializes in *comida de mar a la plancha,* or grilled seafood. His seafood and crustaceans are grilled on a heated iron plate without any additives. There is no more impressive glass tank of live shellfish in Barcelona. You choose your meal, which is extracted with a net and thrown on the grill. Of course, you find all the typical offerings, such as tiny octopus, succulent mussels, fat shrimp, squid, fresh oysters, and langoustines. If you're daring, you can order such unusual seafood as *dátiles* ("dates" in English), a delicious shellfish whose shape resembles a date. Begin with one of the freshly made tapas, such as salt cod in vinaigrette or broad beans laced with garlic and virgin olive oil. Your best bet might be the *parrillada,* assorted grilled fish and shellfish. One of the best offerings is turbot cooked on the grill with potatoes and fresh mushrooms.

Av. Diagonal 301. ✆ **93-207-10-19.** Reservations recommended. Main courses 20€–50€. AE, DC, MC, V. Tues–Sat noon–5pm and 8pm–2am; Sun noon–5pm. Closed 10 days in Jan and Aug. Metro: Verdaguer/Sagrada Família.

INEXPENSIVE

La Dentelliére ★ 🍴 MEDITERRANEAN Charming and steeped in the French aesthetic, this bistro is imbued with a modern, elegant decor. Inside, you'll find a small corner of provincial France, thanks to the dedicated effort of Evelyne Ramelot, the French writer who owns the place. After an aperitif at the sophisticated cocktail bar, you can order from an imaginative menu that includes a lasagna made from strips of salted cod, peppers, and tomato sauce; and a delectable carpaccio of filet of beef with pistachios, lemon juice, vinaigrette, and Parmesan cheese. The wine list is particularly imaginative, with worthy vintages mostly from France and Spain.

Calle Ample 165. ✆ **93-319-68-21.** Reservations recommended. Main courses 9€–14€; set-price dinner 16€. MC, V. Daily 7:30pm–midnight. Metro: Diagonal or Jaume I.

Tragaluz ★ MEDITERRANEAN Named after the turn-of-the-20th-century modernist building that contains it, this well-respected restaurant offers three very contemporary-looking beige dining rooms on separate floors. Menu items are derived from fresh ingredients that vary with the season. Depending on the month of your visit, you might find terrine of duck liver, Santurce-style hake (with garlic and herbs), filet of sole stuffed with red peppers, or beef tenderloin in a Rioja-wine sauce. One of the best desserts is a semisoft slice of deliberately underbaked chocolate cake. Diners seeking low-fat dishes will find solace here, as will vegetarians: The vegetables served are the best and freshest in the market that day. The Tragaluz chefs are adept at taking local products and turning them into flavorful, carefully prepared dishes, most of which are at the lower end of the price scale.

Pasaje Concepción 5, Eixample. ✆ **93-487-06-21.** www.grupotragaluz.com. Reservations recommended. Main courses 13€–30€. AE, DC, MC, V. Daily 1:30–4pm; Sun–Wed 8:30pm–midnight (Thurs–Sat to 1am). Metro: Diagonal or Provença.

Norte Diagonal

VERY EXPENSIVE

Botafumeiro ★★★ SEAFOOD Although the competition is strong, this classic *marisquería* consistently puts Barcelona's finest seafood on the table. Much of the allure comes from the attention of the white-jacketed staff. International businesspeople often rendezvous here, and the king of Spain is sometimes a patron. Menu items include fresh seafood prepared in a glistening, modern kitchen partly visible from the dining room. The establishment prides itself on its fresh and saltwater fish, clams, mussels, lobster, crayfish, scallops, and several varieties of crustaceans that you may have never seen before. Stored live in holding tanks or in enormous crates near the entrance, many of the creatures are flown in daily from Galicia, home of owner Moncho Neira. With 100 or so fish dishes, the menu lists only four or five meat dishes, including three kinds of steak, veal, and a traditional version of pork with turnips. The wine list offers a wide array of cavas from Catalonia and highly drinkable choices from Galicia.

Gran de Gràcia 81. ☎ **93-218-42-30.** www.botafumeiro.es. Reservations recommended for dining rooms. Main courses 26€–60€. AE, DC, MC, V. Daily 1pm–1am. Metro: Fontana.

Lasarte ★★★ BASQUE One of the most sought-after reservations in Barcelona is at this 35-seat restaurant, the showcase for one of Europe's most acclaimed chefs, Martín Berasategui. In a hotel, the restaurant itself is low-key yet elegant, inspired by the prevalent modernist style of the city. The creative cuisine of Berasategui, who is known for his superfresh ingredients, has made him a media darling. He earns those accolades.

His dishes will keep your taste buds twitching with curiosity—and pleasure. Every day the food options are rousing. We didn't know that roast sole with stewed lentils and potatoes with red pepper could taste this good. He makes what one food critic called the best roasted wood pigeon in the world. You might start with his foie gras and smoked eel, or else take delight in his scallop sandwich with creamy raw celery. None of these dishes sound all that startling; the magic is what Berasategui does with the simplest of ingredients.

If the price is too high in this citadel, consider eating in his adjoining annex, **Loidi,** where a Berasategui-inspired four-course fixed-price menu goes for only 40€.

In the Hotel Condes de Barcelona, Mallorca 259. ☎ **93-445-00-00.** www.condesdebarcelona. com. Reservations required. Tasting menu 95€. AE, DC, MC, V. Tues–Sat 1:30–3:30pm and 8:30–11pm. Closed Aug. Metro: Provença.

EXPENSIVE

Gorría ★ 🍴 BASQUE/NAVARRE If you're a devotee of the cookery of both Navarre and the coastal Basque Country, in northern Spain, as we are, then make a date in Barcelona to head for this quite wonderful discovery. Built on two levels, the restaurant has been in business since the mid-1970s, lying only 200m (656 ft.) from La Sagrada Família and just 50m (164 ft.) from Plaza de Toros (the bullring). Javier Gorría learned to cook from his more famous father, the chef Fermin Gorría, and Javier is as good as his old man. At this location in the Eixample, Gorría holds forth nightly, tempting your taste buds with his creations. He pampers his regular clientele, mainly homesick expats from Navarre and the Basque Country, with memories of home. No dish is finer than the herb-flavored baby lamb baked in a wood-fired oven. The classic Basque dish, hake, comes in a garlic-laced green-herb sauce with fresh mussels and perfectly cooked asparagus on the side. His grilled turbot is fresh and straightforward, perfection itself with its flavoring of garlic, virgin olive oil, and a dash of vinegar. Braised pork also emerges from the wood-fired oven.

Moll de la Fusta & Barceloneta

EXPENSIVE

Can Costa ★ SEAFOOD This is one of the oldest seafood restaurants in this seafaring town. Established in the late 1930s, it has two busy dining rooms, a practiced staff, and an outdoor terrace, although a warehouse blocks the view of the harbor. Fresh seafood prepared according to traditional recipes rules the menu. It includes the best baby squid in town—sautéed in a flash so that it has a nearly grilled flavor, almost never overcooked or rubbery. A long-standing chef's specialty is *fideuá de peix,* a relative of the classic Valencian shellfish paella, with noodles instead of rice. Other temptations on the menu include grilled lobster with lemon sauce, baked monkfish, and grilled king prawns. Desserts are made fresh daily.

Passeig Don Joan de Borbò 70. ✆ **93-221-59-03.** www.cancosta.com. Reservations recommended. Main courses 15€–33€. MC, V. Daily 12:30–4pm; Thurs-Tues 8–11:30pm. Metro: Barceloneta.

Can Solé CATALAN/SEAFOOD In Barceloneta at the harbor, Can Solé still honors the traditions of this former fishing village. Many of the seafood joints here are too touristy for our tastes, but this one is authentic and delivers good value. The decor is rustic and a bit raffish, with wine barrels, lots of noise, and excellent food. Begin with the sweet tiny clams or the cod cakes, or perhaps fried small octopus legs or else cabbage hearts with tuna fish. Little langoustines are an eternal but expensive favorite. Everything is aromatically perfumed with fresh garlic. You might also sample one of the seafood-rich dishes. Desserts are so good they're worth saving room for, especially the orange pudding and the praline ice cream. Most main courses are on the low end of the price range given below.

Carrer Sant Carles 4. ✆ **93-221-50-12.** www.restaurantcansole.com. Reservations required. Main courses 11€–48€. AE, DC, MC, V. Tues–Sun 1:30–4pm; Tues–Sat 8:30–11pm. Closed 2 weeks Aug. Metro: Barceloneta.

Lluçanes ★★ SEAFOOD This barrio, once the haunt of fishermen and washerwomen, is looking up, thanks at least partly to this upscale restaurant. A chic clientele shows up nightly to sample some of the best seafood in Barcelona, the creation of its skilled chef, Angel Pascual. This Michelin-starred restaurant occupies an upstairs corner of the local market and is graced with a large open-to-view kitchen (no secrets here). Against a backdrop of an industrial decor, some of the most savory and freshest seafood in Barcelona is served. *Suquet,* a flavor-filled Catalan shellfish stew, is served daily, and it's a classic—perhaps the finest you'll be served in Barcelona. An array of other freshly caught fish dishes are also prepared to perfection. The chef loves the expensive truffle, and this morsel appears in everything from soups to desserts. The artisanal breads come from the ground-floor market.

Place de la Font, Mercat de la Barceloneta. ✆ **93-224-25-25.** www.restaurantllucanes.com. Main courses 32€–56€. AE, MC, V. Daily 1:30–3:30pm and 8:30–10:30pm. Metro: Barceloneta.

Mondo ★ SEAFOOD Barcelona epicureans flock to this restaurant with panoramic views of the Mediterranean, knowing they can get the best seafood in

Barcelona. A terrace overlooks the harbor. In cooler weather, you can dine inside, enjoying the chic interior of red and white, with lots of leather sofas. On a summer night, the terrace is one of the most romantic places to dine in the city. Here's your chance to sample some seafood you may never have encountered—take *espardenyas,* for example. These fresh sea cucumbers are served with virgin olive oil and fresh garlic—that's it. They're highly valued by connoisseurs, as are the raw Carril clams. Our favorite are the *cigalas,* or langoustines. Many of the fresh fish dishes are grilled *(a la plancha).* The chefs also work their magic in such dishes as turbot with crispy skin, served with zucchini flowers stuffed with grilled vegetable and shiitake mushrooms; and in the grilled rib of lamb with mashed celery and apple.

Imax Building, Moll d'Espanya, Maremagnum. © **93-222-39-11.** www.mondobcn.com. Reservations required. Main courses 24€–38€. MC, V. Wed–Sun 1–4pm and 8–11pm. Metro: Drassanes.

7 Portes ★ SEAFOOD This is a lunchtime favorite for businesspeople (the Stock Exchange is across the way) and an evening favorite for many in-the-know diners who have made it their preferred restaurant in Catalonia. Festive and elegant, it's been going since 1836, making it one of the oldest restaurants in Barcelona. Regional dishes include fresh herring with onions and potatoes, a different paella daily (sometimes with shellfish, for example, or with rabbit), and a wide array of fresh fish. You might order succulent oysters, or sample an herb-laden stew of black beans with pork or of white beans with sausage. Portions are enormous. The restaurant's name means "Seven Doors," and it really does have seven doors. Waiters wear the long white aprons of the Belle Epoque era.

Passeig d'Isabel II no. 14. © **93-319-30-33.** www.7portes.com. Reservations required. Main courses 16€–30€. AE, DC, MC, V. Daily 1pm–1am. Metro: Barceloneta.

MODERATE

Agua ★ MEDITERRANEAN/ITALIAN It bustles, it's hip, and it serves well-prepared fish and shellfish in a hypermodern setting overlooking the beach. A terrace beckons anyone who wants an in-your-face view of the water, but if the wind is blowing with a bit too much chill, you can retreat into the big-windowed blue-and-yellow dining room. Here, amid display cases showing the catch of the day, you can order heaping portions of meats and fish to be grilled over an open fire. Examples include excellent grilled chicken, fish, shrimp, crayfish, and an especially succulent stuffed squid. Most of them are served with as little culinary fanfare and as few sauces as possible, allowing the freshness and flavor of the raw ingredients to shine through the chargrilled coatings. Risottos, some of them studded with fresh clams and herbs, are usually winners, with many versions suitable for vegetarians.

Passeig Marítim de la Barceloneta 30 (Port Marítim). © **93-225-12-72.** www.aguadeltragaluz. com. Reservations recommended. Main courses 15€–35€. AE, MC, V. Mon–Fri 1–4pm and 8:30–11:30pm; Sat–Sun 1–4:30pm and 8:30pm–12:30am. Metro: Ciutadella.

Cal Pep ★ 🍴 CATALAN One of the dining secrets of Barcelona, Cal Pep lies close to the Picasso Museum and is a slice of local life. On a tiny postage stamp square, it's generally packed, and the food is some of the tastiest in the Old Town. There's actually a real Pep, and he's a great host, going around to see that everybody is one happy family. At the back is a small dining room, but most patrons like to occupy one of the counter seats up front. From the pans in the rear emerges a selection of perfectly cooked dishes. Try the fried artichokes or the mixed medley of seafood that includes small sardines. Tiny clams come swimming in a well-seasoned broth given extra spice by a sprinkling of hot peppers. A delectable tuna dish comes with a sesame sauce, and fresh salmon is flavored with such herbs as basil—sublime.

Plaça des les Olles 8. © **93-310-79-61.** www.calpep.com. Reservations required. Main courses 15€–28€. AE, MC, V. Mon 8–11:30pm; Tues–Fri 1–4pm and 8–11:30pm; Sat 1–4pm. Closed Aug. Metro: Barceloneta or Jaume I.

Can Majó ★★ SEAFOOD Located close to the harbor, this is one of the best seafood restaurants in Barcelona. In summer, one of the most desirable tables at the port is found on the terrace of this restaurant. The decoration inside is in rustic tavern-style, most inviting. Art lines the walls, and the staff exudes a hospitable, friendly aura as they give excellent, if sometimes-rushed, service. The food plows fairly familiar ground, but when it's good, it can be very good indeed. The fish is very fresh—just brought in that morning. Now almost into its 4th decade, the restaurant still serves some of the best *sopa de pescado y marisco* (fish and shellfish soup) in the area. Its sautéed squid is a heavenly meal in itself or, in the words of one diner: "A day without calamari is a day in hell." *Bacalao* (dried cod) appears in a savory green sauce with baby clams still in their shells. The paellas are as good as those served in the famed restaurants of Valencia, and the lobster bouillabaisse is extremely gratifying.

Almirall Aixada 23, Barceloneta. © **93-221-54-55.** www.canmajo.es. Reservations recommended. Main courses 11€–32€. AE, DC, MC, V. Tues–Sun 1–3:30pm; Tues–Sat 8–11:30pm. Metro: Barceloneta.

Paral.lel

MODERATE

Tapioles 53 ★★★ 🏠 MEDITERRANEAN/ASIAN This is the great dining secret of Barcelona, but it's hard to get a reservation unless you book well in advance. The former personal chef of media tycoon Rupert Murdoch, Australia native Sarah Stothart has only six tables. There's no sign out front—"We like to keep it hidden"—and the atmosphere is very exclusive, even though the prices are amazingly affordable. Her menus change nightly and, in our view, are the best dining deal in town.

The atmosphere is personal, intimate, and relaxed, and the decor is the creation of famed Barcelona designer Ricardo Feriche. The restaurant was created out of an old umbrella factory. The menus are short but choice, with fresh ingredients gathered every morning at the Santa Caterina market. No chef seems to care as much about the freshness of her ingredients as Stothart; she even picks figs from her parents' garden and has been known to gather wild mushrooms from the forests around Barcelona. The sea salt on every table is collected from the natural salt pans of Greece.

There's no printed menu. The chef arrives at your table and explains what she's cooked for that day. While watching her prepare your order in the open-to-view kitchen, you can sample her own homemade bread. Try such dishes as fresh goat-cheese and spinach gnocchi with sage butter; duck confit with marmalade of pineapple, apple, and pear; or perhaps Thai-spiced minced pork in large lettuce leaves with a spicy chili sauce.

Carrer Tapioles 53. © **93-329-22-38.** www.tapioles53.com. Reservations required. Fixed-price menus 27€–36€. MC, V. Tues–Sat 9pm–midnight. Metro: Poble Sec or Paral.lel.

On the Outskirts
VERY EXPENSIVE
El Racó de Can Fabes ★★★ MEDITERRANEAN/INTERNATIONAL This is one of the greatest restaurants of Spain—maybe *the* greatest. If you don't mind the 30-minute drive or the 45-minute train ride from Barcelona, a distance of 52km (32 miles), you will be transported to a gourmet citadel housed in a 3-century-old building in the center of the Catalan village of 1,700 people. Santi Santamaría and Angels Serra, who founded the restaurant in 1981, seemed immune to press acclaim, continuing to show their discipline and craftsmanship in spite of all the raves. They don't let a single platter reach their dining room without their keen-eyed approval. This Michelin three-star restaurant (its highest rating) is run with exquisite care and dedication. The restaurant is refined and elegant yet retains a rustic atmosphere. A heavenly concoction is spicy foie gras with Sauterne and a coulis (essence) of sweet red and green peppers. Two different preparations of crayfish, each one a delight, come both raw and cooked. Roast pigeon is prepared according to the season and the "mood of the chef." For dessert, there's nothing finer than their "Festival de Chocolate."

Sant Joan 6, Sant Ceoloni. ✆ **93-867-28-51.** www.canfabes.com. Reservations required. Main courses 45€–65€; fixed-price menus 149€–250€. AE, DC, MC, V. Wed-Sun 1:30–3:30pm; Wed-Sat 8:30–10:30pm. Closed Jan 2-31. Take any France-bound RENFE train from the Passeig de Gràcia station, and disembark at Sant Ceoloni.

Our Favorite *Tascas*
The bars listed below are known for their tapas; for more recommendations, see the "Barcelona After Dark" section, p. 527.

Alt Heidelberg GERMAN/TAPAS A Barcelona institution since the 1930s, Alt Heidelberg serves German beer on tap, a good selection of German sausages, and Spanish tapas. You can also order full meals—sauerkraut garni is a specialty.

Ronda Universitat 5. ✆ **93-318-10-32.** Tapas 3€–7€; combination plates 8€–14€. MC, V. Daily 8:30am-1:45am. Metro: Universitat.

Bar del Pi TAPAS One of the most famous bars in the Barri Gòtic, this establishment is midway between two medieval squares opening onto the church of Pi. Tapas are limited; most visitors come to drink coffee, beer, or wine. You can sit inside, at one of the cramped bentwood tables, or stand at the crowded bar. In warm weather, take a table beneath the single plane tree on the landmark square. The plaza usually draws an interesting group of young bohemian sorts and travelers.

Plaça Sant Josep Oriol 1. ✆ **93-302-21-23.** www.bardelpi.com. Tapas 2€–8€. MC, V. Tues-Sat 9am-11pm; Sun 10am-10pm (closed Sun July–Aug). Closed mid-Jan to mid-Feb. Metro: Liceu.

Bar Turó TAPAS In an affluent residential neighborhood north of Old Town, Bar Turó serves some of the best tapas in Barcelona. In summer you can sit outside or retreat to the narrow confines of the bar. You select from about 20 kinds of tapas, including Russian salad, fried squid, and Serrano ham.

Tenor Viñas 1. ✆ **93-200-69-53.** Tapas 2€–10€. MC, V. Mon-Fri 10am-midnight; Sat 9am-midnight; Sun 10am-4pm. Metro: Hospital Clínic.

Bodegueta TAPAS Founded in 1942, this old wine tavern specializes in Catalan sausage. Wash it down with an inexpensive Spanish wine. Beer costs 1.50€; wine goes for 1.80€.

Rambla de Catalunya 100. ℂ **93-215-48-94.** Tapas 4€–16€. V. Mon–Sat 7am–1:45am; Sun 6:30pm–1:15am. Metro: Diagonal.

Casa Alfonso TAPAS Spaniards love their ham, which comes in many forms. The best of the best is *jamón Jabugo,* the only one sold at this traditional establishment. Entire hams hang from steel braces. They're taken down, carved, and trimmed before you into paper-thin slices. This particular form of cured ham, generically called *jamón Serrano,* comes from pigs fed acorns in Huelva, in deepest Andalusia. Devotees of all things porcine will ascend to piggy-flavored heaven.

Roger de Lluria 6. ℂ **93-301-97-83.** www.casaalfonso.com. Tapas 6€–12€. AE, DC, MC, V. Mon–Tues 9am–midnight; Wed–Sat 9am–1am. Metro: Urquinaona.

Casa Tejada TAPAS Covered with rough stucco and decorated with hanging hams, Casa Tejada (established in 1964) offers some of the best tapas. Arranged behind a glass display case, they include such dishes as marinated fresh tuna, German-style potato salad, authentic Serrano ham, and five preparations of squid (including one that's stuffed). For variety, quantity, and quality, this place is hard to beat. There's outdoor dining in summer.

Tenor Viñas 3. ℂ **93-200-73-41.** Tapas 3€–21€. MC, V. Mon–Fri 7am–1:30am; Sat 9am–2am; Sun 9am–12:30pm. Metro: Muntaner or Hospital Clínic.

Inopia ★★ TAPAS This is the most sought-after tapas bar in Barcelona. It was opened by Albert Adrià, acclaimed as one of the world's greatest chefs. Albert also operates the finest chocolate shop in Barcelona, Cacao Sampaka. Local hipsters crowd into this place at night, and it's standing-room only. In the Sant Antoni sector of town, he serves the best *patatas bravas* (home fries in hot sauce and aioli) that we've ever had in Barcelona, and wait until you taste those garlic-laced chicken wings. The handsome staff (in Hugo Boss clothing) will bring you your selection of tapas that feature *manzanillas* stuffed with anchovies, our favorite. We predict you'll go wild for the sardine sandwich or for the addictive Russian salad of tuna and potatoes. There is also great wine, costing from 3€ a glass.

Carrer Tamarit 104. ℂ **93-424-52-31.** www.barinopia.com. Tapas 2.50€–15€. AE, MC, V. Mon–Fri 7–11pm; Sat 1–3:30pm and 7–11pm. Metro: Poble Sec.

A Wine Taster's Secret Address

It doesn't get much better in Barcelona than an afternoon spent on the terrace of **La Vinya del Senyor,** Plaça Santa María 5 (ℂ 93-310-33-79), taking in the glorious Gothic facade of Santa María del Mar. Imagine, for example, 13 Priorats, 31 Riojas, and more than a dozen vintages of the legendary Vega Sicilia. In all, there are more than 300 wines and selected cavas, sherries, and *moscatells,* and the list is constantly rotated so you can always expect a surprise on the *carte.* If you don't want a bottle, you'll find some two dozen wines offered by the glass, including a sublime 1994 Jané Ventura cabernet sauvignon. Tantalizing tapas are served, including walnut rolls drizzled in olive oil, cured Iberian ham, and French cheese. Tapas cost from 2€ to 9€. American Express, Diners Club, MasterCard, and Visa are accepted. Hours are Sunday to Thursday from noon to 1:30am and Friday and Saturday until 2am (Metro: Jaume I or Barceloneta).

Chocolate at a Tapas Bar?

We always come back to Barcelona for a slice of the best chocolate cake in the world. Master *pâtissier* Carles Mampel won the Lyon Press Award for the best chocolate cake in 2005, and he hasn't changed the recipe since. We've never tasted chocolate cake any better since then, so we assume this chocolatier is still the king. You can enjoy a slice of that cake at **bubo & bubo bar** ★★★, at Caputxes 10 (✆ **93-268-72-24;** www.bubo.ws), which is not only the greatest confectioner in Barcelona but also a new-wave tapas bar near Basílica Santa María del Mar in the heart of El Born.

Even if you don't like chocolate, you can sample his carrot jelly swirled with coconut mousse and served with litchi ice cream topped with a hazelnut crunch. Of course, there are glittering macaroons and chocolate confections, even sugar-encrusted marshmallow bonbons. We bit into one of these chocolate bonbons to discover it was a curious savory flavor like tomato bread. They cost 1€ each.

Adjoining is the minimalist **bubo bar,** which we think serves the best tapas in town, including grilled eggplant with a feta-cheese salad laced with pine nuts, or a *tortilla española* (egg and potatoes) stuck on a fanciful straw. Tapas average 2€ to 4€, unless you want something expensive and fancy.

For dessert, return to the pastry shop and ask them for a takeout box containing the best and most delicate Sacher torte in town. Find a bench somewhere and watch city life pass you by.

Las Campanas (Casa Marcos) TAPAS From the street (there's no sign), Las Campanas looks like a storehouse for cured hams and wine bottles. Patrons flock to the long, stand-up bar for chorizo pinioned between two pieces of bread. Sausages are usually eaten with beer or red wine. The place opened in 1952, and nothing has changed since. A tape recorder plays nostalgic favorites.

Mercé 21. ✆ **93-315-06-09.** Tapas 1.50€–8.50€. No credit cards. Thurs–Tues 1–4pm and 8pm–2am. Metro: Jaume I.

Quimet & Quimet ★ TAPAS/CHEESE This is a great tapas bar, especially for cheese—it offers the finest selection in Barcelona. Built at the turn of the 20th century, the tavern in the Poble Sec sector is still run by the fifth generation of Quimets. Their wine cellar is one of the best stocked of any tapas bar, and their cheese selection is varied. One night we sampled four on the same plate, including *nevat,* a tangy goat cheese; *cabrales,* an intense Spanish blue; *zamorano,* a hardy, nutty sheep's-milk cheese; and *torta del Casar,* a soft, creamy farm cheese. Of course, you can order other delights such as mussels with tomato confit and caviar, razor clams, and even sturgeon.

Poeta Cabanyes 25. ✆ **93-442-31-42.** Tapas 3€–12€. MC, V. Mon–Fri noon–4:30pm and 7–10:30pm; Sat noon–4pm. Metro: Paral.lel.

Rey de la Gamba SHELLFISH The "King of Prawns" could also be called the House of Mussels, since it sells more of that shellfish. In the 18th-century fishing village of Barceloneta, this place packs them in, especially on weekends. A wide array of seafood accompanies cured ham—the combination is a tradition.

Moll de Mestral 23–25. ✆ **93-221-00-12.** www.elreydelagamba.com. Main courses 9€–50€. MC, V. Tues–Sun 11am–2am. Closed mid-Jan to mid-Feb. Metro: Calle Marina or Ciutadella.

SEEING THE SIGHTS

Spain's second-largest city is also its most cosmopolitan and avant-garde. Barcelona is filled with landmark buildings and world-class museums offering many sightseeing opportunities. These include Antoni Gaudí's Sagrada Família, Museu Picasso, Barcelona's Gothic cathedral, and Las Ramblas, the famous tree-lined promenade cutting through the heart of the Old Quarter.

Sightseeing Suggestions for First-Time Visitors

IF YOU HAVE 1 DAY Spend the morning exploring the Barri Gòtic. In the afternoon visit Antoni Gaudí's unfinished masterpiece, La Sagrada Família, before returning to the heart of the city for a walk down Las Ramblas. To cap your day, take the funicular to the fountains at Montjuïc or go to the top of Tibidabo for a panoramic view of Barcelona and its harbor.

IF YOU HAVE 2 DAYS On Day 2, visit the Museu Picasso in the Gothic Quarter. Then stroll through the surrounding district, the Barri de la Ribera, which is filled with Renaissance mansions and is the site of the gorgeous Church of Santa María del Mar. Follow this with a ride to the top of the Columbus Monument for a panoramic view of the harborfront. Have a seafood lunch at La Barceloneta and, in the afternoon, stroll up Las Ramblas again. Explore Montjuïc and visit the Museu d'Art de Catalunya if time remains. End the day with a meal at Los Caracoles, a famous restaurant in the Old City, just off Las Ramblas.

IF YOU HAVE 3 DAYS On Day 3, make a pilgrimage to the monastery of Montserrat, about 45 minutes outside Barcelona, to see the venerated Black Madonna and a host of artistic and scenic attractions. Try to time your visit to hear the 50-member boys' choir.

IF YOU HAVE 4 OR 5 DAYS On Day 4, take a morning walk along the harborfront, or in the modernist Eixample section of Barcelona. Have lunch on the pier. In the afternoon visit Montjuïc again to tour the Fundació Joan Miró and walk through the Poble Espanyol, a miniature village with reproductions of regional architecture, created for the 1929 World's Fair. On Day 5, take another excursion from the city. If you're interested in history, visit the former Roman city of Tarragona to the south. If you want to unwind on a beach, head south to Sitges.

The Top Attractions

One of Barcelona's greatest attractions is not a single sight but an entire neighborhood, the **Barri Gòtic (Gothic Quarter)** ★★. This is the old aristocratic quarter, parts of which have survived from the Middle Ages. Spend at least 2 or 3 hours exploring its narrow streets and squares, which continue to form a vibrant, lively neighborhood. Start by walking up the Carrer del Carme, east of Las Ramblas. A nighttime stroll adds drama, but exercise caution—safety is an issue here. The buildings are austere and sober for the most part, the cathedral being the crowning achievement. Roman ruins and the vestiges of 3rd-century walls add further interest. Consult your map; this area is intricately detailed and filled with many attractions that are easy to miss.

Catedral de Barcelona ★★★ Barcelona's cathedral is a celebrated example of Catalonian Gothic architecture. Construction began at the end of the 13th

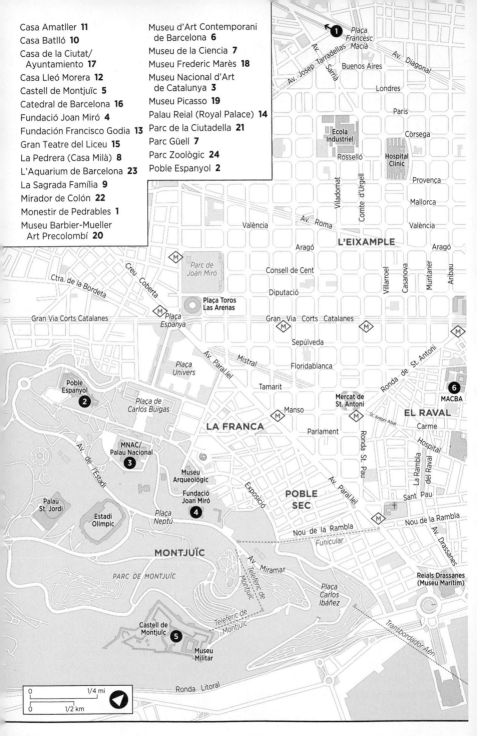

Casa Amatller **11**
Casa Batlló **10**
Casa de la Ciutat/
    Ayuntamiento **17**
Casa Lleó Morera **12**
Castell de Montjuïc **5**
Catedral de Barcelona **16**
Fundació Joan Miró **4**
Fundación Francisco Godia **13**
Gran Teatre del Liceu **15**
La Pedrera (Casa Milà) **8**
L'Aquarium de Barcelona **23**
La Sagrada Família **9**
Mirador de Colón **22**
Monestir de Pedrables **1**
Museu Barbier-Mueller
    Art Precolombí **20**

Museu d'Art Contemporani
    de Barcelona **6**
Museu de la Ciencia **7**
Museu Frederic Marès **18**
Museu Nacional d'Art
    de Catalunya **3**
Museu Picasso **19**
Palau Reial (Royal Palace) **14**
Parc de la Ciutadella **21**
Parc Güell **7**
Parc Zoològic **24**
Poble Espanyol **2**

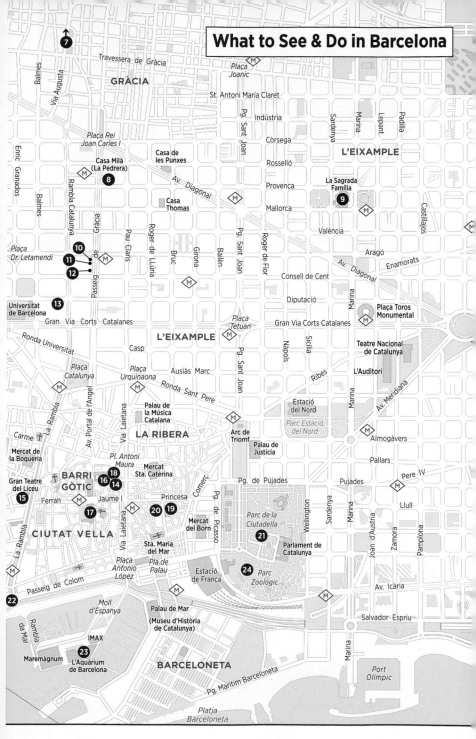

What to See & Do in Barcelona

The Barri Gòtic.

The Catedral de Barcelona.

century and was nearly completed in the mid–15th century (although the west facade dates from the 19th c.). The three naves, cleaned and illuminated, have splendid Gothic details. With its large bell towers, blending of medieval and Renaissance styles, beautiful **cloister** ★, high altar, side chapels, handsomely sculptured choir, and Gothic arches, this ranks as one of the most impressive cathedrals in Spain. Vaulted galleries in the cloister, enhanced by forged iron grilles, surround a garden of magnolias, medlars, and palm trees. The historian Cirici called this "the loveliest oasis in Barcelona." The cloister, illuminated on Saturday and during fiestas, also contains a museum of medieval art. Its most notable work is the 15th-century *La Pietat* of Bartolomé Bermejo. You can take an elevator to the roof, where you will have a wonderful view of Gothic Barcelona, but only Monday to Saturday from 10:30am to 12:15pm and 5:15 to 7pm. At noon on Sunday, you can watch the sardana, a Catalonian folk dance, performed in front of the cathedral. Allow about an hour here.

Plaça de la Seu s/n. 🕐 **93-315-15-54.** www.catedralbcn.org. Free admission to cathedral; to museum 1€. Global ticket to museum, choir, rooftop terraces, and towers 5€. Cathedral daily 8am–12:45pm and 5:15–7:30pm; cloister museum daily 10am–12:30pm and 5:15–7pm. Metro: Jaume I.

Fundació Joan Miró ★ Born in 1893, Joan Miró was one of Spain's greatest artists, known for his whimsical abstract forms and brilliant colors. Some 10,000 works by the Catalan surrealist, including paintings, graphics, and sculptures, are collected here. The building has been greatly expanded in recent years, following the design of Catalan architect Josep Lluís Sert, a close friend of Miró's. An exhibition in a modern wing charts Miró's artistic evolution, from his first drawings, at the age of 8, to his last works. The museum frequently mounts temporary exhibitions of contemporary art. Give yourself about 30 minutes here.

Plaça de Neptú, Parc de Montjuïc. 🕐 **93-443-94-70.** www.bcn.fjmiro.es. Admission 8€ adults, 6€ students, free for children 14 and under. July–Sept Tues–Wed and Fri–Sat 10am–8pm, Thurs 10am–9:30pm, Sun 10am–2:30pm; Oct–June Tues–Wed and Fri–Sat 10am–7pm, Thurs 10am–9:30pm, Sun 10am–2:30pm. Bus: 50 (at Plaça d'Espanya) or 55.

La Sagrada Família ★★ Gaudí's incomplete masterpiece is one of the country's more idiosyncratic creations—if you have time to see only one Catalan landmark, make it this one. Begun in 1882 and incomplete at the architect's death in 1926, this incredible cathedral—the Church of the Holy Family—is a bizarre wonder. The languid, amorphous structure embodies the essence of Gaudí's style, which some have described as "Art Nouveau run wild." Admission includes a 20-minute video presentation. Work continues on the structure, with a completion date projected for 2025. At press time, the cathedral's roof was scheduled to be fully completed by the end of 2010. Plan to spend an hour here.

Entrance from Carrer de Sardenya or Carrer de la Marina. ✆ **93-207-30-31.** www.sagradafamilia. org. Admission 11€; elevator to the top (about 60m/200 ft.) 3€. Oct–Mar daily 9am–6pm; Apr–Sept daily 9am–8pm. Closed Christmas Day, Dec 26, New Year's Day, and Jan 6. Metro: Sagrada Família.

Museu Nacional d'Art de Catalunya ★★★ This museum, which underwent massive renovations, is the major depository of Catalan art, both antique and modern. The National Art Museum of Catalonia is perhaps the most important center for Romanesque art in the world. More than 100 pieces, including sculptures, icons, and frescoes, are on display. The highlight is the collection of murals from various Romanesque churches. The frescoes and murals are displayed in apses much like those in the churches in which they were found. They're in sequential order, giving the viewer a tour of Romanesque art from its primitive beginnings to the more advanced late Romanesque and early Gothic eras. The contents of the former Museu d'Art Modern are also on display here and feature an impressive collection of late-19th- and early-20th-century Catalan works by such artists as Ramon Casa and Pau Gargallo. Allot 1½ hours for a visit here.

Palau Nacional, Parc de Montjuïc. ✆ **93-622-03-76.** www.mnac.es. Admission 8.50€ adults, 6€ ages 15–20, free for children 14 and under. Tues–Sat 10am–7pm; Sun 10am–2:30pm. Metro: Espanya (line 1 or 3).

The Fundació Joan Miró.

Museu Picasso ★ Two old palaces on a medieval street contain this museum of the work of Pablo Picasso (1881–1973). He donated some 2,500 of his paintings, engravings, and drawings to the museum in 1970. Picasso was particularly fond of Barcelona, where he spent much of his youth. In fact, some of the paintings were done when he was only 9. One portrait, dating from 1896, depicts his stern aunt, Tía Pepa. Another, completed when Picasso was 16, depicts *Science and Charity.* (His father was the model for the doctor.) Many works, especially the early paintings, show the artist's debts to van Gogh, El Greco, and Rembrandt; a famous series, *Las Meninas* (1957), is said to "impersonate" the work of Velázquez. The *La Vie* drawings from the Blue Period are perhaps the most interesting. His notebooks contain many sketches of Barcelona scenes. Because the works are arranged in rough chronological order, you can get a wonderful sense of Picasso's development and watch as he discovered a trend or had a new idea, mastered it, grew bored with it, and then was off to something new. Additional space in a medieval mansion is used for temporary exhibitions. Allot 1½ hours for a visit here.

Montcada 15–19. ℂ **93-256-30-00.** www.museupicasso.bcn.es. Admission to permanent exhibits 9€ adults, 6€ students and ages 16–25; free for children 15 and under. Tues–Sun 10am–8pm. Metro: Jaume I (line 4).

Parc Güell ★★ Gaudí began this idiosyncratic park as a real estate venture for a friend, the well-known Catalan industrialist Count Eusebi Güell, but it was never completed. Although only two houses were constructed, it makes for an interesting excursion. The city took over the property in 1926 and turned it into a public park. One of the houses, **Casa-Museu Gaudí,** Carrer del Carmel 23, contains models, furniture, drawings, and other memorabilia of the architect. (Ramón Berenguer, not Gaudí, designed the house.) Admission to the house is 4€. It's open October to March daily 10am to 6:45pm, April to September daily 10am to 8:45pm. Gaudí completed several of the public areas, which today look like a surrealist Disneyland, complete with a mosaic pagoda and lizard fountain spitting water. Gaudí had planned to make this a model community of 60 dwellings, arranged somewhat like a Greek theater. A central grand plaza was built above a market, as well as an undulating bench decorated with ceramic fragments. The bizarre Doric columns of the would-be market are hollow, part of Gaudí's drainage system. One hour should be sufficient here.

Calle de Olot. ℂ **93-219-38-11.** www.casamuseugaudi.org. Free admission. May–Sept daily 10am–9pm; Oct–Apr daily 10am–6pm. Bus: 24, 25, 31, 74, 92, or 116. Metro: Lesseps.

If You Have More Time

Fundación Francisco Godia 🎁 In the heart of Barcelona, this museum showcases the famous art collection of Francisco Godia Sales, the Catalan art collector and entrepreneur. Godia (1921–90) amassed one of the greatest private collections of art in the country. As a collector, he showed exquisite taste and great artistic sensibility.

Godia acquired works by some of the most important artists of the 20th century, including Julio González, María Blanchard, Joan Ponç, Antoni Tàpies, and Manolo Hugué, the latter a great friend of Picasso. From its earliest stages, Godia realized the artistic importance of Catalan *modernismo* and collected works by painters like Santiago Rusiñol and Ramon Casas. Godia also dipped deeper into

A mosaic sculpture at Gaudí's Parc Güell.

The Mirador de Colón in the distance.

the past, acquiring works, for example, of two of the most important artists of the 17th century: Jacob van Ruysdael and Luca Giordano.

Carrer Valencia 284. ✆ **93-272-31-80.** www.fundacionfgodia.org. Admission 5€ adults, 3€ children 5–16 and students, free for children 4 and under. Mon–Sat 10am–2pm and 4–7pm; Sun 10am–2pm. Metro: Passeig de Gràcia.

L'Aquarium de Barcelona One of the most impressive testimonials to sea life anywhere opened in 1996 in Barcelona's Port Vell, a 10-minute walk from the bottom of Las Ramblas. The largest aquarium in Europe, it contains 21 glass tanks positioned along either side of a wide, curving corridor. Each tank depicts a different marine habitat, with emphasis on everything from multicolored fish and corals to seagoing worms to sharks. The highlight is a huge "oceanarium" representative of the Mediterranean as a self-sustaining ecosystem. You view it from the inside of a glass-roofed, glass-sided tunnel that runs along its entire length, making fish, eels, and sharks appear to swim around you.

Port Vell. ✆ **93-221-74-74.** www.aquariumbcn.com. Admission 17€ adults, 12€ children 4–12 and students, free for children 3 and under. July–Aug Mon–Fri 9:30am–9pm, Sat–Sun 9:30am–11pm; June and Sept Mon–Fri 9:30am–9pm, Sat–Sun 9:30am–9:30pm; Oct–May daily 9:30am–9pm. Metro: Drassanes or Barceloneta. Bus: 14, 17, 19, 36, 38, 40, or 45.

Mirador de Colón This monument to Christopher Columbus was erected at the Barcelona harbor on the occasion of the Universal Exhibition of 1888. It consists of three parts, the first being a circular structure raised by four stairways (6m/20 ft. wide) and eight iron heraldic lions. On the plinth are eight bronze bas-reliefs depicting Columbus's principal feats. (The originals were destroyed; these are copies.) The second part is the base of the column, consisting of an eight-sided polygon, four sides of which act as buttresses; each side contains sculptures. The third part is the 50m (164-ft.) column, which is Corinthian in style. The capital boasts representations of Europe, Asia, Africa, and America—linked together. Finally, over a princely crown and a hemisphere recalling the newly discovered part of the globe, is a 7.5m-high (25-ft.) bronze statue of Columbus—pointing, ostensibly, to the New World—by Rafael Ataché. Inside the iron column, an elevator ascends to the *mirador*. From here, a panoramic view of Barcelona and its harbor unfolds.

Portal de la Pau. ✆ **93-302-52-24.** Admission 2.50€ adults, 1.50€ children 4–12, free for children 3 and under. June–Sept daily 10am–1:30pm and 4:30–7:30pm; Oct–May daily 10am–2pm and 3:30–7:30pm. Closed Jan 1, Oct 12, and Dec 25–26. Metro: Drassanes. Bus: 14, 36, 38, 40, 45, 57, 59, 64, 91, or 157.

Monestir de Pedralbes ★ One of the oldest buildings in Pedralbes (the city's wealthiest residential area) is this monastery founded in 1326 by Elisenda de Montcada, queen of Jaume II. Still a convent, the establishment is the mausoleum of the queen, who is buried in its Gothic church. Walk through the cloisters, with nearly two dozen arches on each side, rising three stories high. A small chapel contains the chief treasure of the monastery, murals by Ferrer Bassa, who was the major artist of Catalonia in the 1300s.

Among the outstanding works of art are Fra Angelico's *The Virgin of Humility* and 20 paintings from the early German Renaissance period. Italian Renaissance paintings range from the end of the 15th century to the middle of the 16th century.

FROMMER'S favorite BARCELONA EXPERIENCES

Walking Through the Barri Gòtic. You'll pass through 15 centuries of history in one labyrinthine district.

Watching the Sardana. The national dance of Catalonia is performed at noon on Sunday at the Plaça de San Jaume in front of the cathedral.

Riding to the Top of Montjuïc. Barcelona spreads out at your feet. This stop will provide enough amusement to fill a day.

Soaking Up Designer Bar Culture. Bars of all shapes and sizes are the chic places to go at night—Barcelona has more than any other city in Spain. Catalan design is paramount.

Drinking Cava in a Xampanyería. Enjoy a glass of bubbly, Barcelona style. The wines are excellent, and Catalans swear that their cavas taste better than French champagne.

Touring Barcelona's Harbor. Stroll from the pier in front of the Columbus Monument to the breakwater.

Exploring the Museu Picasso. Examine the evolution, from the age of 9, of the world's greatest 20th-century artist.

Marveling at La Sagrada Família. Gaudí's "sand-castle cathedral" is a testimony to the architect's talent and religious belief.

Visiting Poble Espanyol. Artificial village, to be sure, but it gives you a chance to see the architecture of all of Spain without leaving Barcelona.

The courtyard of the Monastir de Pedralbes.

Baixada del Monestir 9. ℭ **93-203-94-08.** www.museuhistoria.bcn.es. Admission 6€ adults, 4€ students and seniors 65 and over, free for children 16 and under. Mon–Fri 10am–2pm; Tues and Thurs 4–6pm. Metro: Reina Elisenda. Bus: 22, 63, 64, 75, or 78.

Museu Barbier-Mueller Art Precolombí ★★ Inaugurated by Queen Sofía in 1997, this is one of the most important collections of pre-Columbian art in the world. In the restored Palacio Nadal, which was built during the Middle Ages, the collection contains almost 6,000 pieces of tribal and ancient art. Josef Mueller (1887–1977) acquired the first pieces by 1908. Pre-Columbian cultures created religious, funerary, and ornamental objects of great stylistic variety with relatively simple means. Stone sculpture and ceramic objects are especially outstanding. For example, the Olmecs, who settled on the Gulf of Mexico at the beginning of the 1st millennium B.C., executed monumental sculpture in stone and magnificent figures in jade. Many exhibits focus on the Mayan culture, the most homogenous and widespread of its time, dating from 1000 B.C. Mayan artisans mastered painting, ceramics, and sculpture. Note the work by the pottery makers of the Lower Amazon.

Carrer de Montcada 12–14. ℭ **93-310-45-16.** www.barbier-mueller.ch. Admission 3€ adults, 1.50€ students, free for children 15 and under. Free to all 1st Sun of the month. Tues–Fri 11am–7pm; Sat 10am–7pm; Sun and holidays 10am–3pm. Metro: Jaume I. Bus: 14, 17, 19, 39, 40, 45, or 51. Tourist bus: Ruta Sur (Azul).

Museu d'Art Contemporani de Barcelona ★ A soaring white edifice in the once-shabby but rebounding Raval district, the Museum of Contemporary Art is to Barcelona what the Pompidou Center is to Paris. Designed by the American architect Richard Meier, the building is a work of art itself, manipulating sunlight to offer brilliant, natural interior lighting. On display in the 6,875 sq. m (74,000 sq. ft.) of exhibit space is the work of modern luminaries Tàpies, Klee, Miró, and many others. The museum has a library, bookshop, and cafeteria.

Plaça dels Angels 1. ℭ **93-412-08-10.** www.macba.es. Admission 3€ adults, 2€ students, free for children 14 and under and seniors 65 and over. Mon and Wed–Fri 11am–7:30pm; Sat 10am–8pm; Sun 10am–3pm. Metro: Plaça de Catalunya.

Museu Frederic Marès ★★ One of the biggest repositories of medieval sculpture in the region is the Frederic Marès Museum, just behind the cathedral. It's in an ancient palace with impressive interior courtyards, chiseled stone, and soaring ceilings, an ideal setting for the hundreds of polychrome sculptures. The sculpture section dates from pre-Roman times to the 20th century. In the same building is the Museu Sentimental, a collection of everyday items that help illustrate life in Barcelona during the past 2 centuries. The ticket price includes admission to both museums.

Plaça de Sant Iu 5-6. ℰ **93-256-35-00.** www.museumares.bcn.es. Admission 4.20€ adults, 2.40€ students, free for children 15 and under. Tues–Sat 10am–7pm; Sun 10am–3pm. Metro: Jaume I. Bus: 17, 19, or 45.

Palau Reial (Royal Palace) ★ The former palace of the counts of Barcelona, this later became the residence of the kings of Aragón. It is believed that Isabella and Ferdinand received Columbus here when he returned from his first voyage to the New World. Here, some say, the monarchs got their first look at a Native American. The Saló del Tinell, a banquet hall with a wood-paneled ceiling held up by half a dozen arches, dates from the 14th century. Rising five stories above the hall is the Torre del Reí Martí, a series of porticoed galleries.

Plaça del Rei. ℰ **93-315-11-11.** Admission 6€. Summer Tues–Sat 10am–8pm; off season Tues–Sat 10am–2pm and 4–7pm; year-round Sun 10am–3pm. Metro: Jaume I. Bus: 16, 17, 19, 22, 40, or 45.

Poble Espanyol ★☺ In this re-created Spanish village, built for the 1929 World's Fair, regional architectural styles are reproduced. From the Levant to Galicia, 115 life-size reproductions of buildings and monuments represent the 10th to the 20th centuries. At the entrance, for example, stands a facsimile of the gateway to the walled city of Avila. The center of the village has an outdoor cafe where you can sit and have drinks. Numerous shops sell provincial crafts and souvenir items, and in some of them you can see artists at work printing fabric and blowing glass. Since the 1992 Olympics, the village has included 14 restaurants and one disco. Many families delight in the faux Spanish atmosphere, but the more discriminating find it a bit of a tourist trap—overly commercialized and somewhat cheesy. It's a matter of personal taste. You'll find lots of mediocre places to eat here.

Av. Marqués de Comillas 13, Parc de Montjuïc. ℰ **93-508-63-00.** www.poble-espanyol.com. Admission 8.50€ adults, 5.50€ children 7–12, free for children 6 and under. Mon 9am–8pm; Tues–Thurs 9am–2pm; Fri 9am–4am; Sat 9am–5pm; Sun 9am–midnight. Metro: Espanya. Bus: 13 or 50.

MORE ARCHITECTURAL HIGHLIGHTS

Architecture enthusiasts will find a wealth of fascinating sights in Barcelona. Primary among them, of course, are the fantastical creations of Antoni Gaudí and his *modernismo* cohorts.

Casa Amatller Constructed in a cubical design with a Dutch gable, this building was created by Puig i Cadafalch in 1900. It stands in sharp contrast to its neighbor, the Gaudí-designed Casa Batlló (see below). The architecture of the Casa Amatller, imposed on an older structure, is a vision of ceramic, wrought iron, and sculptures. The structure combines grace notes of Flemish Gothic—especially on the finish of the facade—with elements of Catalan architecture. The gable outside is in the Flemish style. Inside, be sure to view the original Gothic Revival interior, now the headquarters of the Institut Amatller d'Art Hispanic. Only the library is open to the public.

Casa Batlló Next door to the Casa Amatller, Casa Batlló was designed by Gaudí in 1905. Using sensuous curves in iron and stone, the architect gave the facade a lavish baroque exuberance. The balconies have been compared to "sculpted waves." The upper part of the facade evokes animal forms, and delicate tiles spread across the design. The downstairs building is the headquarters of an insurance company. Many tourists walk inside for a view of Gaudí's interior, which is basically as he designed it. This is a place of business, so be discreet.

Passeig de Gràcia 43. © **93-216-03-06.** www.casabatllo.es. Admission 17€ adults, 13€ children 5–16 and students, free for children 4 and under. Daily 9am–8pm. Metro: Passeig de Gràcia.

Casa de la Ciutat/Ayuntamiento Constructed at the end of the 14th century, the building that houses the municipal government is one of the best examples of Gothic civil architecture in the Catalan Mediterranean style. Across the landmark square from the Palau de la Generalitat, it has been endlessly renovated and changed. Behind a neoclassical facade, the building has a splendid courtyard and staircase. Its major architectural highlights are the 15th-century Salón de Ciento (Room of the 100 Jurors) and the black marble Salón de las Crónicas (Room of the Chronicles). The Salón de Ciento, in particular, represents a medley of styles.

Plaça de Sant Jaume. © **93-402-70-00.** Free admission. Sun 10am–1:30pm. Metro: Jaume I or Liceu.

Casa Lleó Morera Between the Carrer del Consell de Cent and the Carrer d' Aragó stands one of the most famous buildings of the *modernismo* movement. It is one of the trio of structures called the Mançana de la Discòrdia (Block of Discord), an allusion to the mythical judgment of Paris. Three of Barcelona's most famous *modernismo* architects, including Gaudí, competed with their works

Casa Amatller (left) and Casa Batlló (right).

The rooftop sculptures of La Pedrera.

Barcelona as seen from Tibidabo Mountain.

along this block. Florid Casa Lleó, designed by Domènech i Montaner in 1905, was revolutionary in its day. That assessment still stands. The building is private, and the interior is closed to the public.

Passeig de Gràcia 35. No phone. Metro: Passeig de Gràcia.

La Pedrera (Casa Milà) ★★ When locals first took a gander at this architectural masterpiece by Antoni Gaudí, they ridiculed it, nicknaming it "the Quarry" because of its fortresslike appearance. Today, a more sympathetic generation views it as one of the most outstanding examples of *modernista* architecture. Constructed between 1906 and 1912, the building was declared a World Heritage Site by UNESCO in 1984. Currently, the structure houses the office of Fundació Caixa Catalunya, but guests are allowed to wander about the patios and the Espai Gaudí (loft and roof). Visitors may also go inside the Pedrera Apartment, allowing them to see how an apartment might have looked at the turn of the 20th century. Gaudí's sinuous, rippling facade stands in sharp contrast to the neoclassical structures that make up the neighborhood. For many visitors, the roof, with its centurion-like chimneys, is the highlight of the tour; it also offers some of the most panoramic vistas of Barcelona, including views of Sagrada Família.

Provença 261–265. ✆ **93-484-59-00.** Admission 9.50€ adults, 6€ seniors and students, free for children 11 and under. Daily 10am–8pm. Metro: Diagonal.

BULLFIGHTING

Catalans do not pursue this art form, or sport, with as much fervor as Castilians do. Nevertheless, you may want to attend a *corrida* (bullfight) in Barcelona. Bullfights are held from March 19 to October 12, usually on Sunday at 6:30pm at **Plaça de Toros Monumental,** Gran Vía de les Corts Catalanes (✆ **93-215-95-70**). Tickets cost 19€ to 98€.

PARKS & GARDENS

Barcelona isn't just museums; much of its life takes place outside, in its unique parks and gardens. **Tibidabo Mountain** ★, north of the port, offers the finest panoramic view of Barcelona. A funicular takes you up 488m (1,600 ft.) to the summit. The ideal time to visit this summit (the culmination of the Sierra de

Collserola) is at sunset, when the city lights are on. At the time of the Olympics, a 255m (837-ft.) communications tower, Mirador Torre de Collserola (© **93-406-93-54;** www.torredecollserola.com), was built. Although attacked by traditionalists for destroying the natural beauty of the mountain, Torre de Collserola offers the most panoramic views in all of Catalonia. It costs 5€ to go up the tower. From Plaça de Catalunya, take the subway to Penintents on line 3, and then take bus no. 73 to Avinguda del Tibidabo, where you can board a special bus to the funicular. Hop aboard to scale the mountain. The funicular runs daily when the park is open. The fare is 2€ one-way, 3€ round-trip.

In the southern part of the city, the mountain park of **Montjuïc** has splashing fountains, gardens, outdoor restaurants, and museums, making for quite an outing. A re-created Spanish village, the Poble Espanyol (p. 514), and the Joan Miró museum (p. 508) are also in the park. There are many walks and vantage points from which to view the Barcelona skyline.

An illuminated fountain display, **Fuentes Luminosas,** is on view at Plaça de la Font Magica, near the Plaça d'Espanya. October to May, it is shown from 8 to 11pm every Saturday and Sunday; June to September, it is shown from 9pm to midnight on Thursday, Saturday, and Sunday.

To reach the top, take the bus named PARC DE MONTJUÏC from Plaça d'Espanya or the Montjuïc funicular. The funicular is open daily 9am to 10pm. In winter it operates daily from 9am to 8pm. The round-trip fare is 8.30€.

Parc de la Ciutadella, Av. Wellington s/n (© **93-225-67-80**), is named Park of the Citadel because it is the site of a former fortress. After Philip V won the War of the Spanish Succession (Barcelona was on the losing side), he got his revenge: He ordered that the "traitorous" residential suburb be leveled. In its place rose a citadel. In the mid–19th century it too, was leveled, but some architectural evidence survives in a governor's palace and an arsenal.

The Fuentes Luminosas.

Today lakes, gardens, and promenades fill most of the park, which also holds a **zoo** (p. 519). Gaudí contributed to the monumental fountain in the park when he was a student; the lampposts are also his. The park is open daily in March 10am to 6pm; April 10am to 7pm; May to August 10am to 8pm; September 10am to 6pm; and October to February 10am to 5pm. Admission is free. To reach the park, take the Metro to Ciutadella.

Parc de Joan Miró, near the Plaça de Espanya, is dedicated to one of Catalonia's most famous artists. It dates to the 1990s and occupies an entire block. One of Barcelona's most popular parks, it is often called Parc de l'Escorxador (slaughterhouse), a reference to its former occupant. Its main features are an esplanade and a pond from which rises a giant sculpture by Miró, *Woman and Bird.* Palm, pine,

FROM TOP: **The gardens of the Parc de la Ciutadella; the atrium of Cosmocaixa, the science museum.**

and eucalyptus trees, as well as playgrounds and pergolas, complete the picture. To reach the park, take the Metro to Espanya. It is open throughout the day.

ESPECIALLY FOR KIDS

The Catalan people have great affection for children, and although many of the attractions of Barcelona are for adults, an array of amusements are designed for the young—and the young at heart.

Children from 3 to 7 years old have their own place at the **Cosmocaixa, Museu de la Ciencia,** Teodor Roviralta 47–51 (✆ **93-212-60-50;** www.fundacio.lacaixa.es). "Clik del Nens" is a science playground where children can walk on a giant piano, make bubbles, lift a hippopotamus, and enter an air tunnel.

They observe, experiment, and examine nature in a specially created environment. Special 1-hour guided sessions take place daily.

At the **Poble Espanyol,** Marqués de Comillas, Parc de Montjuïc (ⓒ **93-508-63-00;** www.poble-espanyol.com), kids find a Spanish version of Disneyland. Frequent fiestas enliven the place, and it's fun for everybody, young and old. (See "If You Have More Time," p. 510.)

Only an hour's drive from Barcelona and most often visited from the city of Tarragona (p. 540), **Port Aventura** (ⓒ **97-777-90-90;** www.porta ventura.es) lies at Autovéia Salou/Vila-Seca Km 2, outside the town of Salou, which is 11km (6¾ miles) south of Reus, reached after a 13km (8-mile) drive northwest of Tarragona. This park promises "the adventure of one's life" in a series of dangerous-appearing rides, plus steam-engine trips, water slides, and simulated boat trips through places as exotic as the American West or Polynesia. Admission is 44€ adults, 35€ children 4 to 10, free for children 3 and under. From July 1 to September 2, it is open daily from 10am to midnight; off-season hours are Saturday to Sunday from 10am to 7pm.

Parc d'Atraccions (Tibidabo) On top of Tibidabo, this park combines tradition with modernity in rides dating from the beginning of the 20th century to 1990s novelties. In summer the place takes on a carnival-like atmosphere.

Plaça Tibidabo 3–4, Cumbre del Tibidabo. ⓒ **93-211-79-42.** www.tibidabo.es. Ticket for all rides: 25€ adults, 9€ seniors 60 and over and children up to 1.2m (4 ft.) in height, free for children 3 and under. May–June Sat–Sun noon–9pm; July–Sept Wed–Sun noon–10pm; off season Sat–Sun and holidays noon–6pm. Bus: 58 to Av. del Tibidabo to Tramvía Blau, and then funicular.

Parc Zoològic ★ Modern, with barless enclosures, this ranks as Spain's top zoo. The setting itself is interesting, in a century-old garden spread over 13 hectares (32 acres) of Ciutadella Park. The splendid park contains around 7,500 animals belonging to some 500 species from all over the world. The fabled albino gorilla, Snowflake (Copito de Nieve), died in 2003; his three surviving offspring

An elephant at the Parc Zoològic.

include a male and two females. There is a large collection of other primates, all in danger of extinction. The collection includes the titis, the world's smallest monkeys. Other endangered species are the Sumatran tiger, the Sri Lanka leopard, and the cheetah. The main entrances to the zoo are on Ciutadella Park and Wellington.

Parc de la Ciutadella. ℐ **90-245-75-45.** www.zoobarcelona.com. Admission 16€ adults, 9.60€ students and children 3–12, 8€ seniors, free for children 2 and under. Summer daily 10am–7pm; off season daily 10am–6pm. Metro: Ciutadella, Barceloneta, or Arc de Triomf. Bus: 14, 17, 36, 39, 40, 41, 45, 51, 57, 59, 100, 141, or 157.

Organized Tours

Pullmantur, Gran Vía de les Corts Catalanes 645 (www.spanish-fiestas.com/madrid/tours.htm; Metro: Plaça de Catalunya), offers a number of tours and excursions with English-speaking guides. For a preview of the city, you can take a morning tour. They depart from the company's terminal at 9:30am and take in the cathedral, the Gothic Quarter, the monument to Columbus, the Spanish Village, and the Olympic Stadium. Tickets cost 60€. An afternoon tour leaves at 3:30pm and visits some of the most outstanding architecture in the Eixample, including Gaudí's La Sagrada Família. The tour includes Parc Güell and a stop at the Picasso Museum. The cost is 60€.

Pullmantur also offers several excursions outside Barcelona. The daily tour of the monastery of Montserrat includes a visit to the Royal Basilica to view the famous sculpture of the Black Virgin. This tour, which costs 74€, departs at 9:30am and returns at 2:30pm to the company's terminal. A full-day Girona-Figueres tour includes a visit to Girona's cathedral and its Jewish Quarter, plus a trip to the Dalí museum. This excursion, which costs 153€, leaves Barcelona at 8:30am and returns at approximately 6:30pm (June–Sept Tues and Thurs). Call ahead—a minimum number of participants is required.

Another company that offers tours of Barcelona and the surrounding countryside is **Julia Travel,** Ronda Universitat 5 (ℐ **93-317-64-54;** www.juliatravel.com). "Barcelona Artística" focuses on the city's artistic significance. The tour passes Domènech i Montaner's Casa Lleó Morera and takes in many of Gaudí's brilliant buildings, including Casa Milà (La Pedrera) and La Sagrada Família. Included is a visit to the Museu Picasso, depending on the day of your tour. The tour leaves at 3:30pm and returns at 7pm; the cost is 43€.

ACTIVE PURSUITS
An Outstanding Fitness Center

The city's main fitness center is adjacent to the Olympic Stadium in an indoor/outdoor complex whose main attractions are its two beautifully designed swimming pools. Built for the 1992 Summer Olympics, the facility contains a health club and gym. It's open to the public; a full day's pass costs 9.65€. For the address and hours, see the Piscina Bernardo Picornell review in "Swimming," below.

Golf

One of the city's best courses, **Club de Golf Vallromanes,** Afueras s/n, Vallromanes, Barcelona (ℐ **93-572-90-64;** www.clubdegolfvallromanes.com), is 20 minutes north of the center by car. Nonmembers who reserve tee times in advance are welcome to play. The greens fee is 100€ on weekdays, 160€ on weekends. The club is open Wednesday to Monday 8am to 9pm.

Real Club de Golf El Prat, Plans de Bonvilar 17, 08227 (© **93-728-10-00;** www.rcgep.com), is a prestigious club that allows nonmembers to play on two conditions: They must have a handicap issued by the governing golf body in their home country, and they must prove membership in a golf club at home. The club has two 18-hole par-72 courses. Greens fees are 114€ Monday to Friday. Weekends are for members only after noon. Nonmembers' greens fees are 228€ unless you play with a guest; then there is a 50% discount. From Barcelona, follow Avinguda Once de Septiembre past the airport to Barrio de San Cosme. From there, follow the signs along Carrer Prat to the golf course.

Swimming

Most city residents head to the beaches near the Vila Olímpica or Sitges when they feel like swimming. If you're looking for an uncrowded pool, you'll find one at the **Esportiu Piscina DeStampa,** Carrer Rosic 12, in the Hospitalet district (© **93-334-56-00**). It's open Monday to Friday from 7:30am to 10pm, Saturday from 10am to 2pm and 4 to 8pm, and Sunday from 10am to 2pm. Weekday admission is 3.30€; Saturday and Sunday, it's 3.50€.

A much better choice, however, allows you to swim where some Olympic events took place: **Piscina Bernardo Picornell,** Av. de Estadi 30–40, on Montjuïc (©**93-423-40-41;** www.picornell.cat). Adjacent to the Olympic Stadium, it incorporates two of the best swimming pools in Spain (one indoors, one outdoors). They're open to the public Monday to Friday 7am to midnight, Saturday 7am to 9pm, and Sunday 7am to 4pm. Admission costs 9.65€ in winter, 5.30€ in summer, and allows use of whichever pool is open, plus the gymnasium, the sauna, and the whirlpools. Bus no. 50 makes frequent runs from Plaça d'Espanya.

Along the Passeig de Gràcia.

SHOPPING

For fashion and style, Barcelonans look more to Paris and their own sense of design than to Madrid. *Moda joven* (young fashion) is all the rage.

If your time and budget are limited, you may want to patronize Barcelona's major department store, **El Corte Inglés,** for an overview of Catalan merchandise at reasonable prices. Barcelona is filled with boutiques, but clothing is expensive, even though the city has been a textile center for centuries.

Markets (p. 525) are very popular and suitable places to search for good buys.

The Barcelona Shopping Scene

If you're a window-shopper, stroll along the **Passeig de Gràcia** from the Avinguda Diagonal to the Plaça de Catalunya. Along the way, you'll see some of the most elegant and expensive shops in Barcelona, plus an assortment of splendid turn-of-the-20th-century buildings and cafes, many with outdoor tables. Another prime spot is the **Rambla de Catalunya** (upper Rambles).

Yet another shopping destination is the **Mercat de la Boqueria,** Rambla 91 (no phone), near Carrer del Carme. Here you'll see a wide array of straw bags and regional products, along with a handsome display of the food you're likely to eat later: fruits, vegetables (artfully displayed), breads, cheeses, meats, and fish. Vendors sell their wares Monday to Saturday 8am to 8pm.

In the **Old Quarter,** not far from Plaça de Catalunya, the principal shopping streets are all five Ramblas, plus Carrer del Pi, Carrer de la Palla, and Avinguda Portal de l'Angel, to cite some major thoroughfares. Moving north in the **Eixample,** you'll walk through Passeig de Catalunya, Passeig de Gràcia, and Rambla de Catalunya. Even farther north, **Avinguda Diagonal** is a major shopping boulevard. Other prominent shopping streets include Bori i Fontesta, Vía Augusta, Carrer Muntaner, Travessera de Gràcia, and Carrer de Balmes.

In general, shopping hours are Monday to Saturday 9am to 8pm. Smaller shops may close from 1:30 to 4pm.

Watch for sales (*rebajas,* or *rebaixes* in Catalan) in mid-January, late July, and August. Stores getting rid of their winter or summer stock often offer heavy discounts.

Shopping A to Z

Prices in Barcelona tend to be slightly lower than in London, Paris, and Rome.

You'll find stylish, attractively designed **clothing** and **shoes. Decorative objects** are often good buys. In the city of Miró, Tàpies, and Picasso, **art** is a major business and the reason for visits by gallery owners from around the world. You'll find dozens of galleries, especially in the Barri Gòtic and around the Picasso Museum. Barcelona is also noted for its **flea markets,** where good purchases are always available if you search hard enough.

Antiques abound, but rising prices have put many of them beyond the means of the average shopper. However, the list below includes some shops where you can at least look. Most shoppers from abroad settle happily for handicrafts, and the city is rich in offerings ranging from pottery to handmade furniture. Barcelona has been in the business of creating and designing **jewelry** since the 17th century, and its offerings and prices are of the widest possible range.

What follows is a very limited selection of some of the hundreds of shops in Barcelona.

ANTIQUES

Antigüedades Artur Ramón ★★ One of the finest antiques and art dealers in Barcelona can be found at this three-level emporium. Set on a narrow flagstone-covered street near Plaça del Pi (the center of the antiques district), it stands opposite a tiny square, the Placeta al Carrer de la Palla. The store, which has been operated by four generations of men named Artur Ramón, also operates branches nearby and is known for its 19th- and 20th-century painting, sculpture, drawings and engravings, and 18th- and 19th-century decorative arts and objets d'art, along with rare ceramics, porcelain, and glassware. Prices are high, as you'd expect for items of quality and lasting value. Open Tuesday to Friday 10am to 1:30pm and 5 to 8pm, Saturday 10am to 1:30pm. Palla 23. © **93-302-59-70.** www.arturamon.com. Metro: Jaume I.

El Bulevard dels Antiquaris ★★ This 70-unit complex adjacent to one of the town's most aristocratic avenues has a huge collection of art and antiques assembled in a series of boutiques. There's a cafe/bar on the upper level. Hours are Monday to Saturday 10:30am to 8:30pm; closed Saturday during July and August. Some boutiques keep shorter hours. Passeig de Gràcia 55. © **93-215-44-99.** www.bulevarddelsantiquaris.com. Metro: Passeig de Gràcia. Bus: 22, 24, or 26.

BOOKS

LAIE The best selection of English-language books, including travel maps and guides, is at LAIE, a block from the Gran Vía de les Corts Catalanes. It's open Monday to Friday from 10am to 9pm, Saturday from 10:30am to 9pm. The bookshop has an upstairs cafe with international newspapers and a little terrace. It serves breakfast, lunch (salad bar), and dinner. The cafe is open Monday from 9am to 9pm and Tuesday to Saturday from 9am to 1am. The shop schedules cultural events, including art exhibits and literary presentations. Pau Claris 85. © **93-302-73-10.** www.laie.es. Metro: Plaça de Catalunya or Urquinaona. Bus: 22 or 28.

CHOCOLATES

Cacao Sampaka ★★ Albert Adrià, the brother of Ferran Adrià (hailed by some as the world's greatest chef) is Spain's most famous chocolatier. The chocolates that emerge from his bakeries are the most acclaimed in Spain. Of course, you expect chocolate truffles, but not such imaginative concoctions as the pudding-like *chocolat a la taza,* made with cinnamon-flecked milk and even speckles of hot pepper. He uses some of the finest sweetmeats on the market, including liqueurs and digestives, even fresh flowers and herbs. On-site is a bar/cafe where you can order hot, creamy chocolate along with rich pastries and sandwiches "to die for," as some customers claim. Monday to Saturday 9am to 9:15pm; closed Sunday. Consell de Cent 292. © **93-272-08-33.** www.cacaosampaka.com. Metro: Passeig de Gràcia.

DEPARTMENT STORES

El Corte Inglés ★ One of the local representatives of the largest and most glamorous department store chain in Spain, this branch sells a wide variety of merchandise. It ranges from Spanish handicrafts to high-fashion items, from Catalan records to food. The store has restaurants and cafes and offers consumer-related services, such as a travel agent. One department will mail your purchases home. Not only that, but you can have shoes reheeled, hair and beauty treatments, and food and drink at the rooftop cafe. Open Monday to Saturday 10am to 10pm. El Corte Inglés has other Barcelona locations: Av. Diagonal 617–619

(☎ 93-366-71-00; Metro: María Cristina) and Av. Diagonal 471 (☎ 93-493-48-00; Metro: Hospital Clínic). Plaça de Catalunya 14. ☎ **93-306-38-00**. www.el corteingles.es. Metro: Plaça de Catalunya.

DESIGNER HOUSEWARES

Vinçón ★★ Fernando Amat's Vinçón is the best store of its kind in the city, with 10,000 products—everything from household items to the finest in Spanish contemporary furnishings. Its mission is to purvey good design, period. Housed in the former home of artist Ramón Casas—a contemporary of Picasso's during his Barcelona stint—the showroom is filled with the best Spain has. The always-creative window displays alone are worth the trek: Expect *anything*. Open Monday to Saturday from 10am to 8:30pm. Passeig de Gràcia 96. ☎ **93-215-60-50**. www.vincon.com. Metro: Diagonal.

FABRICS & WEAVINGS

Coses de Casa Appealing fabrics and weavings are displayed in this 19th-century store, called simply "Household Items." Many are hand-woven in Majorca, their boldly geometric patterns inspired by Arab motifs of centuries ago. The fabric, for the most part, is 50% cotton, 50% linen; much of it would make excellent upholstery material. Open Monday to Friday from 10am to 2pm and 4:30 to 8pm, Saturday from 10am to 2pm and 5 to 8pm. Plaça de Sant Josep Oriol 5. ☎ **93-302-73-28**. www.cosesdecasa.com. Metro: Jaume I or Eliceo.

FASHION

Adolfo Domínguez ★ This shop, one of many outlets spread across Spain and Europe, displays fashion that has earned for the store the appellation "the Spanish Armani." There's one big difference: Domínguez's suits for both women and men, unlike Armani's, are designed for those with hips. They cover all ages at their stores, including the youth market. As one fashion critic said of their offerings, "They are austere but not strict, forgivingly cut in urbane earth tones." Open Monday to Saturday from 10am to 8:30pm. Passeig de Gràcia 32. ☎ **93-487-41-70**. www.adolfo-dominguez.com. Metro: Passeig de Gràcia.

Groc ★ One of the most stylish shops in Barcelona, Groc is expensive but filled with high-quality men's and women's apparel made from the finest natural fibers. The men's store is downstairs, the women's store one flight up. Open Monday to Saturday from 10am to 2pm and 4:30 to 8:30pm. Rambla de Catalunya 100. ☎ **93-215-77-78**. Metro: Diagonal.

Zara ★★ Begun in the 1970s by Amancio Ortega (now the richest man in Spain), the fashion house of Zara launched a worldwide revolution with an aim to allow every woman to dress up like a movie star—but at an affordable price. It now has stores in some 65 countries, but its major outlets are in Barcelona, the most central one of which is recommended below. The atmosphere is tumultuous here, and there is very little customer service, but the merchandise is of high quality and stunning in design. Open Monday to Saturday 10am to 9pm. Av. Puerta del Angel 24. ☎ **93-317-65-86**. www.zara.com. Metro: Plaça de Catalunya.

GALLERIES

Art Picasso Here you can get good lithographic reproductions of works by Picasso, Miró, and Dalí, as well as T-shirts emblazoned with the masters' designs. Tiles often carry their provocatively painted scenes. Open daily from 10am to 8pm; summer hours 9:30am to 8pm. Tapinería 10. ☎ **93-268-32-40**. Metro: Jaume I.

Sala Parés ★★ Established in 1840, this is a Barcelona institution. The Maragall family recognizes and promotes the work of Spanish and Catalán painters and sculptors, many of whom have gone on to acclaim. Paintings are displayed in a two-story amphitheater, with high-tech steel balconies supported by a quartet of steel columns evocative of Gaudí. Exhibitions of the most avant-garde art in Barcelona change about every 3 weeks. Open Monday to Saturday from 10:30am to 2pm and 4:30 to 8:30pm; Sunday (only in winter) 11:30am to 3pm. Petritxol 5. © **93-318-70-08.** www.salapares.com. Metro: Plaça de Catalunya.

LEATHER

Loewe ★★ Barcelona's biggest branch of this prestigious Spanish leather-goods chain is in one of the best-known *modernismo* buildings in the city. Everything is top-notch, from the elegant showroom to the expensive merchandise to the helpful salespeople. The company exports its goods to branches throughout Asia, Europe, and North America. Open Monday to Saturday from 10am to 8:30pm. Passeig de Gràcia 35. © **93-216-04-00.** www.loewe.com. Metro: Passeig de Gràcia.

MARKETS

El Encants antiques market is held every Monday, Wednesday, Friday, and Saturday in Plaça de les Glòries Catalanes (Metro: Glòries). Go anytime during the day to survey the selection.

Coins and postage stamps are traded and sold in **Plaça Reial** on Sunday from 10am to 8pm. It's off the southern flank of Las Ramblas (Metro: Drassanes). A book and coin market is held at the Ronda Sant Antoni every Sunday from 10am to 2pm (Metro: Universitat).

MUSIC

Casa Beethoven Established in 1880, this store carries the most complete collection of sheet music in town. The collection naturally focuses on the works of Spanish and Catalan composers. Music lovers might make some rare discoveries. Open Monday to Friday from 9am to 2pm and 4 to 8pm; Saturday from 9am to 1:30pm and 5 to 8pm. Las Ramblas 97. © **93-301-48-26.** www.casabeethoven. com. Metro: Liceu.

PORCELAIN

Kastoria This large store near the cathedral is an authorized Lladró dealer and stocks a big selection of the famous porcelain. It also carries many kinds of leather goods, including purses, suitcases, coats, and jackets. Open Monday to Saturday from 10am to 7pm; Sunday from 10am to 2pm. Av. Catedral 6–8. © **93-310-04-11.** www.kastoria.com. Metro: Plaça de Catalunya or Jaume I.

POTTERY

Itaca Here you'll find a wide array of handmade pottery from Catalonia and other parts of Spain, plus Portugal and Morocco. The merchandise has been selected for its basic purity, integrity, and simplicity. Open Monday to Saturday from 10am to 8:30pm. Carrer Ferran 26. © **93-301-30-44.** Metro: Liceu.

SHOES

La Manuel Alpargatera ★ This is the most famous workshop in Catalonia for making espadrilles, opening its workshop right after the Spanish Civil War in 1940. Lying in the Gothic Quarter, it is still going strong. Shoes are still made of natural materials such as hemp, jute, cotton, and linen. Espadrilles have been around for 4,000 years, but today they are more stylish than ever, including an *espadenya* with ribbon ankle-ties. You can also buy platform-wedge espadrilles or even pancake-flat espadrilles. Patrons have included everyone from the pope to Michael Douglas and Catherine Zeta-Jones stopping off here en route to their vacation home in Majorca. In days gone by, Salvador Dalí was a faithful customer. Open Monday to Saturday 9:30am to 1:30pm and 4:30 to 8pm. Calle Avinyó. ℂ **93-301-01-72.** www.lamanual.net. Metro: Jaume I or Barceloneta.

An alleyway in the Poble Espanyol.

SHOPPING CENTERS & MALLS

The landscape has exploded since the mid-1980s with the construction of several American-style shopping malls. Some are too far from the city's historic core to be convenient for most foreign visitors, but here's a description of some of the city's best.

Centre Comercial Barcelona Glòries Built in 1995, this three-story emporium of the good life is the largest shopping center in downtown Barcelona. It's based on the California model but is crammed into a distinctly urban neighborhood. It has more than 100 shops, some posh, others much less so. Although there's a typical shopping mall anonymity to some aspects of this place, you'll be able to find almost anything you might have forgotten while packing. Open Monday to Saturday from 10am to 10pm. Av. Diagonal 208. ℂ **93-486-04-04.** www.lesglories.com. Metro: Glòries.

Diagonal Center (L'Illa Diagonal) This two-story mall contains stores devoted to luxury products, as well as a scattering of bars, cafes, and simple but cheerful restaurants favored by office workers and shoppers. It has about half the number of shops offered by the Centre Comercial Barcelona Glòries (see above). Built in the early 1990s, it even has an area devoted to video games where teenagers can make as much electronic noise as they want while their guardians shop. Open Monday to Saturday from 10am to 9:30pm. Av. Diagonal 557. ℂ **93-444-00-00.** www.lilla.com. Metro: María Cristina.

Maremagnum The best thing about this place is its position adjacent to the waterfront on Barcelona's historic seacoast; it's also well suited to outdoor promenades. Built in the early 1990s near the Columbus Monument, it contains many shops, 12 cinemas, an IMAX, and a wide variety of restaurants, pubs, and discos catering to a very young crowd. Nightlife here begins at 11pm, lasting until dawn. You might get the idea that only a few of the people who come here are interested in shopping. Open daily from 10am to 10pm. Moll d'Espanya s/n. ℂ **93-225-81-00.** www.maremagnum.es. Metro: Drassanes or Barceloneta.

Poble Espanyol This is not technically a shopping mall but a "village." (See p. 514.) About 35 stores sell typical folk crafts from every part of Spain: glassware, leather goods, pottery, paintings, carvings, and so forth. Store hours vary, but you can visit anytime during the day. Marqués de Comillas 13, Parc de Montjuïc. ℂ **93-508-63-31.** www.poble-espanyol.com. Metro: Espanya. Bus: 13 or 50.

BARCELONA AFTER DARK

Barcelona comes alive at night with a staggering array of diversions. There is something to interest almost everyone and to fit most pocketbooks. The **funicular ride** to Tibidabo and the illuminated **fountains** of Montjuïc are especially popular, and fashionable **clubs** operate in nearly every major district of the city. For families, the **amusement parks** are the busiest venues.

Locals sometimes opt for an evening in the *tascas* **(taverns),** or perhaps settle in for a bottle of wine at a cafe, an easy and inexpensive way to spend an evening people-watching. Serious drinking in pubs and cafes begins by 10 or 11pm. But for the most fashionable bars and discos, Barcelonans delay their entrances until at least 1am.

Your best source of local information is a little magazine called *Guía del Ocio,* which previews "La Semana de Barcelona" ("This Week in Barcelona"). It's in Spanish, but most of its listings should be comprehensible to those who don't speak Spanish. Almost every news kiosk along Las Ramblas carries the publication.

Nightlife begins for many Barcelonans with a **promenade** *(paseo)* along Las Ramblas in the early evening, usually from 5 to 7pm. Then things quiet down a bit until a second surge of energy brings out the crowds again, from 9pm to midnight. After that the esplanade clears out quite a bit, but it's always lively.

If you're very young, you might want to check out the nightlife scene at **Maremagnum** (see "Shopping Centers & Malls," above).

If you've been scared off by press reports about Las Ramblas between the Plaça de Catalunya and the Columbus Monument, you should know that the area's really been cleaned up in recent years. Still, you will feel safer along the Rambla de Catalunya, in the Eixample, north of the Plaça de Catalunya. This street and its offshoots are lively at night, with many cafes and bars. During the Franco era the center of club life was the cabaret-packed district near the south of Las Ramblas, but the area is known for nighttime muggings—use caution if you go there.

Cultural events are also big in the Catalonian repertoire, and old-fashioned **dance halls** survive in some places. Although **disco** has waned in some parts of the world, it is still going strong in Barcelona. Decaying movie houses, abandoned garages, and long-closed vaudeville theaters have been taken over and restored as nightlife venues.

Flamenco isn't the rage here that it is in Seville and Madrid, but it still has its devotees. The city is also filled with **jazz** aficionados. Best of all, the old tradition of the **music hall** with vaudeville lives on.

The Performing Arts

Culture is deeply ingrained in the Catalan soul, and the performing arts are strong. In fact, some performances take place on the street, especially along Las Ramblas. Crowds often gather around a singer or a mime. A city square will suddenly come alive on Saturday night with a spontaneous festival; "tempestuous, surging, irrepressible life and brio," is how the writer Rose MacCauley described it.

Long a city of the arts, Barcelona experienced a cultural decline during the Franco years, but now it is filled once again with the best opera, symphonic, and choral music. At the venues listed here, unless otherwise specified, ticket prices depend on the event.

A mosaic in the Palau de la Música Catalana.

CLASSICAL MUSIC

La Casa dels Músics Pianist Luis de Arquer has established a small chamber company in his 19th-century Gràcia home. Here in an intimate atmosphere, small-scale productions of *opera buffa* and *bel canto* are presented, usually beginning at 9pm (but you must call to confirm that presentations will take place and to make reservations). For the true music lover, this could be your most charming evening in Barcelona. Carrer Encarnació 25. © **93-284-99-20.** www.lacasadelsmusics. com. Tickets 20€. Metro: Fontana or Joanic.

Palau de la Música Catalana ★ In a city chock-full of architectural highlights, this one stands out. In 1908 Lluís Domènech i Montaner, a Catalan architect, designed this structure using stained glass, ceramics, statuary, and ornate lamps, among other elements. It stands today, restored, as a classic example of *modernismo*. Concerts and leading recitals take place here. Open daily from 10am to 3:30pm. The box office is open Monday to Saturday from 10am to 9pm, Sunday 1 hour before concerts. Sant Francesc de Paula 2. © **93-295-72-00.** www.palaumusica. org. Metro: Urquinaona.

FLAMENCO

El Tablao de Carmen ★ This club presents a highly rated flamenco cabaret in the re-created village. You can go early and explore the village, and even have dinner. This place has long been a tourist favorite. The club is open Tuesday to Sunday from 8pm to around 1am (weeknights), often until 2 or 3am on weekends, depending on business. The first show is always at 7:45pm; the second show is at 10pm. Reservations are recommended. Poble Espanyol de Montjuïc. © **93-325-68-95.** www.tablaodecarmen.com. Dinner and show 69€; drink and show 35€. Metro: Espanya.

Los Tarantos ★ Established in 1963, this is the oldest flamenco club in Barcelona, with a rigid allegiance to the tenets of Andalusian flamenco. Its roster of artists changes regularly. They often come from Seville or Córdoba, stamping out their well-rehearsed passions in ways that make the audience appreciate the nuances of Spain's most intensely controlled dance idiom. No food is served. The place resembles a cabaret theater, where up to 120 people at a time can drink, talk quietly, and savor a dance that combines elements of medieval Christian and Muslim traditions. The club is open daily 8 to 11:30pm. Each show lasts around an hour. Shows are held Monday to Saturday at 8:30, 9:30, and 10:30pm. Plaça Reial 17. ✆ **93-319-17-89.** Cover 6€. Metro: Liceu.

Tablao Flamenco Cordobés At the southern end of Las Ramblas, a short walk from the harborfront, you'll hear the strum of the guitar, the rhythmic clapping of hands, and the haunting sound of the flamenco, a tradition here since 1968. Head upstairs to an Andalusian-style room where performances take place with the traditional *cuadro flamenco*—singers, dancers, and guitarist. Cordobés is said to be the city's best flamenco showcase. Most of the year they have three shows starting at 8:15, 10, and 11:30pm, but if you want to have dinner, shows are at 7, 8:30, and 10pm. Reservations are required. Las Ramblas 35. ✆ **93-317-57-11.** www.tablaocordobes.com. Dinner and show 68€; 1 drink and show 37€. Metro: Drassanes.

THEATER

Theater is presented in the Catalan language and therefore will not be of interest to most visitors. For those who do speak the language, or perhaps are fluent in Spanish (though you're still unlikely to understand much), here are some recommendations.

Gran Teatre del Liceu ★★★ This monument to Belle Epoque extravagance, a 2,700-seat opera house, is one of the grandest theaters in the world. It was designed by the Catalan architect Josep Oriol Mestves. On January 31, 1994, fire gutted the opera house, shocking Catalonians, many of whom regarded this place as the very citadel of their culture. The government immediately vowed to rebuild, and the new Liceu was reopened in 1999, well before the millennium deadline set by the cultural czars. La Rambla 51-54. ✆ **93-485-99-13** or 93-485-99-00. www.liceubarcelona.com. Metro: Liceu.

The Gran Teatre del Liceu.

Mercat de Los Flors Housed in a building constructed for the 1929 International Exhibition at Montjuïc, this is the other major Catalan theater. Peter Brook first used it as a theater for a 1983 presentation of *Carmen*. The theater focuses on innovators in drama, dance, and music, as well as European modern dance companies. Lleida 59. ✆ **93-426-18-75.** www.mercatflors.org. Tickets 9€–30€. Metro: Espanya or Pueblo Seco.

Teatre Nacional de Catalunya Josep María Flotats heads this major company. The actor-director trained in the tradition of theater repertory, working in Paris at Théâtre de la Villa and the Comédie Française. His company presents both classic and contemporary plays. The theater is closed in August. Plaça de les Arts 1. ✆ **93-306-57-00.** www.tnc.es. Tickets 12€–32€. Metro: Glòries.

Cabaret, Jazz & More

Barcelona Pipa Club If you find the Harlem Jazz Club (see below) small, wait until you get to the "Pipe Club." Long beloved by jazz aficionados, this is for true devotees. Ring the buzzer and you'll be admitted (at least we hope you will). Climb two flights in a run-down building. This is hardly a trendy nightclub, with five rooms decorated with displays or photographs of pipes. Music ranges from New Orleans jazz to blues. The club and its comfortable bar are open daily from 6pm to 3am. Plaça Reial 3. ☎ **93-301-11-65.** www.bpipaclub.com. Metro: Liceu.

Harlem Jazz Club ★ On a nice street in the Ciutat Vella, this is one of Barcelona's oldest and finest jazz clubs. It's also one of the smallest, with just a handful of tables. No matter how many times you've heard "Black Orpheus" or "The Girl from Ipanema," they sound new here. Music is viewed with a certain reverence; no one talks when the performers are on. Live jazz, blues, tango, Brazilian music—the sounds are always fresh. Open Tuesday to Thursday and Sunday from 8pm to 4am (until 5am Fri–Sat). Live music begins at 10:30pm Tuesday to Thursday and Sunday, and at 11:30pm on Friday and Saturday. The second set is at midnight (1am Fri–Sat). Closed 2 weeks in August. Comtessa de Sobradiel 8. ☎ **93-310-07-55.** www.harlemjazzclub.es. 1-drink minimum. Metro: Jaume I or Liceu.

Jamboree ★★ In the heart of the Barri Gòtic, this has long been one of the city's premier locations for good blues and jazz, although it doesn't feature jazz every night. Sometimes a world-class performer will appear here, but most likely it'll be a younger group. The crowd knows its stuff and demands only the best talent. On our last visit, we were entertained by an evening of Chicago blues. You might find that a Latin dance band has been scheduled. Open daily from 8:30pm to 5am; shows are at 9 and 11pm. Plaça Reial 17. ☎ **93-319-17-89.** www.masimas.com. Cover 10€–12€. Metro: Liceu.

Luz de Gas This theater and cabaret has the hottest Latino jazz on weekends. On weeknights there is cabaret. The place is an Art Nouveau delight, with colored glass lamps and enough voluptuous nudes to please Rubens himself. The club was once an entire theater, and its original seating has been turned into different areas, each with its own bar. The lower two levels open onto the dance floor and stage. If you'd like to talk, head for the top tier, which has a glass enclosure. Call to see what the lineup is on any given night: jazz, pop, soul, rhythm and blues, or anything else. Open Sunday and Monday 11pm to 4am, Tuesday 11pm to 4:30am, Wednesday 11pm to 5am, Thursday 11pm to 5:30am, Friday and Saturday 11pm to 5:45am. Carrer de Muntaner 246. ☎ **93-209-77-11.** www.luzde gas.com. Cover (includes 1 drink) 15€. Bus: 6, 27, 32, or 34.

Dance Clubs & Discos

La Paloma Those feeling nostalgic may want to drop in on Barcelona's most famous dance hall. Remember the fox trot? The mambo? If not, learn about them here, along with the tango, the cha-cha, and the bolero. Live orchestras provide the music. The ornate old hall is open Thursday to Sunday. Matinees are from 6 to 9:30pm; night dances are from 11:30pm to 5am. Drink prices start at 3.50€. Tigre 27. ☎ **93-301-68-97.** Cover 8€. Metro: Universitat.

Mojito Club Named after Ernest Hemingway's favorite drink, this club rocks with a Latin beat. Every night here is like Carnaval in Rio. The nickname for the club is S&S (samba and salsa). An international crowd frequents the joint,

Cafes along La Rambla.

including a lot of visiting South Americans. Open Tuesday to Sunday 11pm to 4:30am. Carrer Rosselló 217. ✆ **93-237-65-28.** www.mojitobcn.com. Cover 10€. Metro: Diagonal.

Razzmatazz The name is appropriate. This multilevel club in a converted warehouse is actually five clubs in one, including everything from Razz Club to Lo*Li*Ta to The Loft. Each club within the club has its own music. A large crowd of university students favors the place. One entrance fee covers admission to all clubs, but mixed cocktails are expensive, hovering around 8€. Open Friday and Saturday 1 to 5am. Carrer Pamplona 88. ✆ **93-320-82-00.** www.salarazzmatazz. com. 8€–30€ (except for special concerts). Metro: Bogatell.

Cafes

Integral to the time-honored tradition of Catalonia is the cafe, where everything from politics to art is debated in the traditional format of a *tertulia*, a semiformalized combined argument and conversation. Picasso once frequented some of these cafes, as did many Catalan leaders in the dark days of the Franco era.

Café de la Opera Located across from the Liceu opera house, this is Barcelona's most famous cafe, having opened more than a century ago. It has remained the favorite stopover not only for operagoers and performers but for those strolling along Las Ramblas. Since it opens at 8:30am daily, many locals come here for a traditional breakfast. At any time of the day you can enjoy tapas, drinks, and people-watching. La Rambla 74. ✆ **93-317-75-85.** www.cafeoperabcn.com. Metro: Liceu.

Café Zurich At the top of Las Ramblas, this is a traditional meeting point in Barcelona; it's also a great place to watch the passing parade along Catalonia's most fabled boulevard. If the weather is fair, opt for an outdoor table, enjoying the excellent tapas (all kinds), the cold beer, and the gaiety. Launched in the early 1920s, it's been going strong ever since, with its dark wood furnishings and columns. Try one of the little sandwiches here—called *bocadillos*. Those with the Serrano ham are especially good. The cafe is open November to April daily 8am to 11pm, May to October 8am to 1am. Plaça de Catalunya 1. ✆ **93-317-91-53.** Metro: Plaça de Catalunya.

The Best Ham Sandwich in the World

It's served along Las Ramblas—at **Café Viena,** La Rambla del Estudis 115 (⌕ **93-317-14-92**), to be exact. With its plastic menus and *hamburguesas,* the cafe doesn't appear special, in spite of its interior of wrought iron and marble. But step right up and order a beer from the porcelain-and-brass tap as well as a *flauta d'ibéric jabugo,* which English-speaking people call a ham roll or sandwich. Prepare yourself for a taste sensation.

The *flauta* (flute) itself resembles a long roll or small sub and has a crisp crust and a tender, chewy interior. It encases a slice of the famous salt-cured ham from the famous Iberian black pig whose diet includes ripe acorns. These pigs are raised in Jabugo, near Seville. Their meat is like prosciutto but so much better.

Costing 7€ a serving, a ham sandwich doesn't come better than this, and we've sampled them all over the world.

Bars & Pubs

Cocktail Bar Boadas This intimate, conservative bar is usually filled with regulars. Established in 1933, it is near the top of Las Ramblas. Many visitors stop in for a predinner drink and snack before wandering to one of the district's many restaurants. The bar stocks a wide array of Caribbean rums, Russian vodkas, and English gins, and the skilled bartenders know how to mix them all. The place is especially well known for its daiquiris. The dress code is formal and slightly conservative. Open daily from noon to 2am (till 3am Fri–Sat). Tallers 1. ⌕ **93-318-88-26.** Metro: Plaça de Catalunya.

Dirty Dick's An English-style pub in a residential part of town, Dirty Dick's has lots of dark paneling and exposed brick, with banquettes for quiet conversation. If you sit at the bar, you'll be faced with a tempting array of tiny sandwiches that taste as good as they look. The pub is at the crossing of Vía Augusta, a main thoroughfare through the district. Open daily 6pm to 2:30am. Taberna Inglesa, Carrer Marc Aureli 2. ⌕ **93-200-89-52.** Metro: Muntaner.

Dry Martini This is increasingly becoming a chic rendezvous for a late-night drink. A laid-back crowd shows up, often locals and an occasional tourist. The well-mixed cocktails make this a venue worth seeking out. The bartender has a number of drink specials. It's a great place to sit and talk as you watch nighttime Barcelona pass by your table. Open Monday to Friday 1pm to 2:30am, Saturday and Sunday 6:30pm to 3am. Aribau 162–166. ⌕ **93-217-50-72.** www.drymartinibcn. com. Metro: Diagonal.

El Born Facing a rustic-looking square, this former fish store has been cleverly converted. There are a few tables near the front, but our preferred spot is the inner room, decorated with rattan furniture and modern paintings. The music might be anything from Louis Armstrong to classic rock 'n' roll. The room is somewhat cramped, but you'll find a simple, tasty collection of fish, meat, and vegetable dishes, all carefully laid out. A full dinner, without wine, costs around 18€ to 25€. Beer and wine are quite cheap. Open Monday to Saturday 6pm to 2am (until 3am Fri–Sat). Passeig del Born 26. ⌕ **93-319-53-33.** Metro: Jaume I or Barceloneta.

Schilling A young and stylish crowd can be seen crossing Plaça Reial, with its Gaudí lampposts, heading for this old cafe to sample its drinks, succulent pastas, savory tapas, and panini. Forsaking Barcelona's fabled modernism, Schilling gleefully lingers in another era, with its iron columns, marble tables, and wall of wine bottles. A large gay crowd often dominates the night along with some hip, supposedly straight young things and a few aging pensioners. On one visit, we noted three models that would give Jennifer Lopez competition and at least two young Catalan versions of Brad Pitt. A waiter confided to us, "We're famous for our slow service." His appraisal was right on the mark. Open Monday to Thursday from 10am to 2:30am, Friday and Saturday from 10am to 3am, and Sunday from noon to 2am. Carrer Ferran 23. © **93-317-67-87.** www.cafeschilling.com. Metro: Liceu.

Champagne Bars

The Catalans call their own version of sparkling wine cava. In Catalan, champagne bars are called *xampanyerías*. The Spanish wines are often excellent, and some consider them better than their French counterparts. With more than 50 Spanish companies producing cava, and each bottling up to a dozen grades of wine, the best way to learn about Spanish champagne is to visit the vineyard or to sample the products at a *xampanyería*.

Champagne bars usually open at 7pm and stay open into the wee hours of the morning. They serve tapas ranging from caviar to smoked fish to frozen chocolate truffles. Most establishments sell only a limited array of house cavas by the glass, and more esoteric varieties by the bottle. You'll be offered a choice of *brut* (slightly sweeter) or *brut nature*. The most acclaimed brands include Mont-Marçal, Gramona, Mestres, Parxet, Torello, and Recaredo.

El Xampanyet This little champagne bar, our favorite in Barcelona, has been operated by the same family since the 1930s. When the Picasso Museum opened nearby, its popularity was assured. On the ancient street, the tavern is adorned with colored tiles, antique curios, marble tables, and barrels. With your sparkling wine, you can order fresh anchovies in vinegar or other tapas. If you don't want the cava, you can order fresh cider at the old-fashioned zinc bar. Open Tuesday to Saturday noon to 4pm and 6 to 11:30pm; Sunday 11am to 4pm. Closed in August. Carrer Montcada 22. © **93-319-70-03.** Metro: Jaume I.

Xampú Xampany At the corner of the Plaça de Tetuan, this *xampanyería* offers a variety of hors d'oeuvres in addition to wine. Abstract paintings, touches of high tech, and bouquets of flowers break up the pastel color scheme. Open Monday to Saturday from 8pm to 1:30am. Gran Via de les Corts Catalanes 702. © **93-265-04-83.** Metro: Girona or Tetuan.

Gay & Lesbian Bars

Café Miranda In this Eixample nightclub, drag queens and kings sing and entertain you between courses. As one journalist puts it, "The cafe offers plenty of ways to be *louche,* but flirt with care—your eyes may deceive you." The club is decorated in what is known locally as "*artista* kitsch," meaning faux leopard skin and lots of red, black, and gold decor. Main courses are reasonably priced, ranging from 15€ to 18€. The place draws both a gay and a straight crowd that seems to enjoy the spectacle equally. Is it retro? You'd better believe that. Shows are from 10:30pm nightly until closing (times vary). Casanova 30. © **93-453-52-49.** Metro: Hospital Clínic.

Dboy ★★ This late-night club is arguably the hottest gay bar in Barcelona. If you show up (go late), you'll see Barcelona's handsomest guys dancing with their shirts off. The club technically closes at 5am, but often it's going strong long after the rooster has crowed. The gay ambience (pun intended) is about the liveliest in the city. Sometimes live performances make the atmosphere sizzle; otherwise DJs rule, including on theme nights. Open Thursday to Saturday midnight to 5am. Ronda Sant-Pere 19–21. ℂ **93-318-06-86.** www.dboyclub.com. Metro: Diagonal.

Metro Still one of the most popular gay discos in Barcelona, Metro attracts a diverse crowd—from young fashion victims to more rough-and-ready macho types. One dance floor plays contemporary house and dance music, and the other traditional Spanish music mixed with Spanish pop. This is a good opportunity to watch men of all ages dance Las Sevillanas in pairs with surprising grace. The gay press in Barcelona quite accurately dubs the back room here as a "notorious, lascivious labyrinth of lust." One interesting feature appears in the bathrooms, where videos have been installed in quite unexpected places. Open Sunday and Tuesday to Thursday midnight to 5am; Friday and Saturday midnight to 6am; Monday 1 to 5am. Sepúlveda 185. ℂ**93-323-52-27.** www.metrodiscobcn.com. Cover 15€. Metro: Universitat.

For Camp & Drag

El Cangrejo (The Crab) Launched in 1902, this very retro transvestite cabaret still packs them in, ringing with music, laughter, and kitsch. Every patron, from honeymooners (straight ones, that is) to same-sex couples, fill the tables to catch the show of the rhinestone-and-sequin-spangled stars. One journalist called the decor a combination of "lemon meringue pie and paella Valenciana." Open Tuesday to Sunday 9pm to 4am. Calle Montserrat 9. ℂ**93-301-29-78.** Cover 25€. Metro: Drassanes.

La Concha (The Shell) Just to let you in on how campy this dive is, it is dedicated to drag icon Sara Montiel, that 1960s favorite whose photographs fill the walls from floor to ceiling. A gay or gay-friendly crowd frequents the joint. Expect a Moroccan gay-kitsch aura in this Barrio Chino joint where the streets are none too safe at night. There's a small dance floor where sometimes a live band plays for dancers (of all sexual persuasions) who hit the tiles with various renditions of the tango, fox trot, and perhaps flamenco. Open daily 4pm to 4:30am. Calle Guardia. ℂ**93-302-41-18.** Metro: Drassanes.

○ Piaf, Drag Queens & a Walk on the Wild Side

Do you long to check out the seedy part of Barcelona brought so vividly to life by writers such as Jean Genet? Much of it is gone forever, but *la Vida* nostalgically lives on in pockets like the **Bar Pastis,** Carrer Santa Mónica 4 (ℂ 93-318-79-80; Metro: Drassanes).

Valencianos Carme Pericás and Joaquín Ballester opened this tiny bar just off the southern end of Las Ramblas in 1947. They made it a shrine to Edith Piaf, and her songs play on an old phonograph in back of the bar. The decor consists mostly of paintings by Ballester, who had a dark, rather morbid vision of the world.

Outside the window, check out the view—usually a parade of transvestite hookers. The crowd is likely to include almost anyone, especially people who used to be called bohemians. The bar features live music: French music on Sunday, tango on Tuesday, and *canta autor* on Wednesday, in which the performer both writes and sings his own songs. Open Tuesday to Thursday from 7:30pm to 2:30am; Friday, Saturday, and Sunday until 3am.

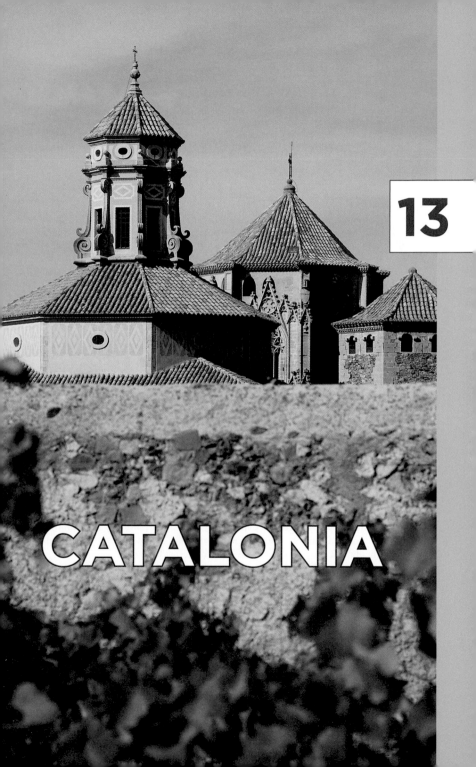

CATALONIA

You can take several noteworthy day trips from Barcelona. The most popular is to the Benedictine monastery of Montserrat, northwest of Barcelona. To the south, the Roman city of Tarragona has been neglected by visitors but is particularly interesting to those who appreciate ancient history. Beach lovers, and gays and lesbians, should head for the resort town of Sitges.

About six million people live in Catalonia, and twice that many visit every year. It's one of Europe's playgrounds, with its beaches along the **Costa Brava** (p. 554) and the **Costa Dorada,** centered on Sitges. Tarragona is the capital of its own province, and Barcelona is the political, economic, and cultural center of Catalonia.

The province of Catalonia forms a triangle bordered by the French frontier to the north, the Mediterranean Sea to the east, and the province of Aragón to the west. The northern coastline is rugged, whereas the Costa Dorada is flatter, with sandy beaches and a mild, sunny climate.

Pilgrims may go to Montserrat for its scenery and religious associations, and history buffs to Tarragona for its Roman ruins, but just plain folks head to the Costa Dorada for fun. Named for its strips of golden sand, this seashore extends along the coastlines of Barcelona and Tarragona provinces. One popular stretch is **La Maresme,** extending 64km (40 miles) from Río Tordera to Barcelona. Allow at least 2½ hours to cover it without stops. The Tarragonese coastline extends from Barcelona to the Ebro River, a distance of 193km (120 miles); a trip along it will take a full day. Highlights along this coast include **Costa de Garraf,** a series of creeks skirted by the corniche after Castelldefels, Sitges, and Tarragona. One of the coast's most beautiful stretches is **Cape Salou,** south of Tarragona in a setting of pine woods.

We begin our tour through this history-rich part of Catalonia inland at the Sierra de Montserrat, which has more spectacular views than any coastal location. Wagner used it as the setting for his opera *Parsifal.* The serrated outline made by the sierra's steep cliffs led the Catalonians to call it *montserrat* (saw-toothed mountain). Today it remains the religious center of Catalonia. Thousands of pilgrims annually visit the town's monastery with its Black Virgin.

The **Monestir de Poblet** in Tarragona is the other major monastery of Catalonia. It, too, is a world-class attraction.

MONTSERRAT ★★

56km (35 miles) NW of Barcelona, 592km (368 miles) E of Madrid

The monastery at **Montserrat,** which sits atop a 1,200m-high (3,937-ft.) mountain, 11km (6¾ miles) long and 5.5km (3½ miles) wide, is one of the most important pilgrimage spots in Spain. It ranks alongside Zaragoza and Santiago de Compostela. Thousands travel here every year to see and touch the medieval

PREVIOUS PAGE: **The Monestir de Poblet.**

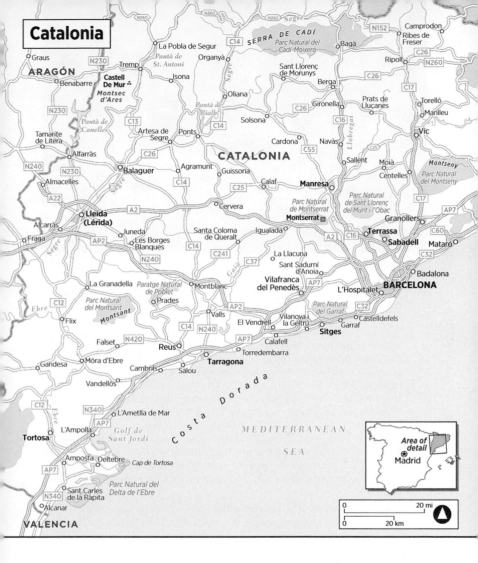

statue of La Moreneta (the Black Virgin), the patron saint of Catalonia. Many newly married couples flock here for her blessing.

Avoid visiting on Sunday, if possible, as thousands of locals pour in, especially if the weather is nice. Remember that the winds blow cold up here even in summer, so visitors should bring along warm sweaters, jackets, or coats. In winter, thermal underwear might not be a bad idea.

Essentials

GETTING THERE The best and most exciting way to get to Montserrat is via the Catalan railway, **Ferrocarrils de la Generalitat de Catalunya** (Manresa line), with 12 trains a day leaving from the Plaça d'Espanya in Barcelona.

The monastery at Montserrat.

The central office is at Plaça de Catalunya 1 (© **93-205-15-15;** www.fgc. es). The train connects with an aerial cableway (Aeri de Montserrat), which is included in the fare of 18€ round-trip.

The train, with its funicular tie-in, has taken over as the preferred means of transport. However, a long-distance **bus** service is provided by **Autocars Julià** in Barcelona. Daily service from Barcelona to Montserrat is generally available, with departures near the Estació Central de Barcelona-Sants on Plaça de Països Catalanes. One bus makes the trip at 9:15am, returning at 5pm (6pm July–Aug); the round-trip ticket costs 12€. On Saturday and Sunday the round-trip fare is 13€. Contact Autocars Julià at Santa Eulàlia 236 (© **93-402-69-00;** www.autocaresjulia.es).

To drive to Montserrat, take the N-2 southwest of Barcelona toward Tarragona, turning west at the junction with the N-11. The signposts and exit to Montserrat will be on your right. From the main road, it's 15km (9⅓ miles) up to the monastery through eerie rock formations and dramatic scenery.

VISITOR INFORMATION The **tourist office,** at Plaça de la Creu (© **93-877-77-01;** www.montserratvisita.com), is open daily from 9am to 5:30pm.

Exploring Montserrat

One of the monastery's noted attractions is the 50-member **Escolanía ★★,** one of the oldest and most renowned boys' choirs in Europe, dating from the 13th century. At 1pm daily you can hear them singing "Salve Regina" and the "Virolai" (hymn of Montserrat) in the basilica. The basilica is open daily from 8 to 10:30am and noon to 6:30pm. Admission is free. To view the **Black Virgin,** a statue from the 12th or 13th century, enter the church through a side door to the right.

At the Plaça de Santa María you can also visit the **Museu de Montserrat** (© **93-877-77-77**), known for its ecclesiastical paintings, including works by Caravaggio and El Greco. Modern Spanish and Catalan artists are also represented; you'll want to see Picasso's early *El Viejo Pescador* (1895). Works by Dalí and such French Impressionists as Monet, Sisley, and Degas are shown. The collection of ancient artifacts is quite interesting; make sure to look for the crocodile mummy, which is at least 2,000 years old. The museum is open Monday to Friday from 10am to 5:45pm, charging 6.50€ adults, 5.50€ seniors, free for students and children 17 and under.

The 9-minute **funicular ride** to the 1,236m-high (4,055-ft.) peak, Sant Joan, makes for a panoramic trip. The funicular operates about every 20 minutes daily from 9am to 5:30pm in low season and to 7pm in summer. The cost is 8.50€ round-trip. From the peak, you'll see not only the whole of Catalonia but also the Pyrenees and the islands of Majorca and Ibiza.

You can also make an excursion to **Santa Cova (Holy Grotto),** the alleged site of the discovery of the Black Virgin. The grotto dates from the 17th century and was built in the shape of a cross. You go halfway by funicular, but must complete the trip on foot. The grotto is open daily from 10am to 1pm and 4 to 7pm. The funicular operates April through October, every 20 minutes daily from 10am to 5:45pm; and November through March, daily from 11am to 4:45pm. Note that it closes between 1 and 2pm. The round-trip fare is 3.50€.

Where to Stay & Dine in Montserrat

Few people spend the night here, but most visitors want at least one meal. If you don't want to spend a lot, buy a picnic in Barcelona or ask your hotel to pack a meal.

Abat Cisneros ★ This modern hotel on the main square of Montserrat offers few pretensions and a history of family management since 1958. The small rooms are simple and clean, with comfortable beds and generous bathrooms. Many regional dishes of Catalonia are served at the in-house restaurant. The hotel's name is derived from a title given to the head of any Benedictine monastery during the Middle Ages.

Plaça de Monestir, 08199 Montserrat. **€ 93-877-77-01.** Fax 93-877-77-24. www.barcelona hotels.es. 86 units. 107€ double. Rates include continental breakfast. AE, DC, MC, V. Parking 7€. **Amenities:** Restaurant; bar; Wi-Fi (free, in lobby). *In room:* TV.

TARRAGONA ★★

97km (60 miles) S of Barcelona, 554km (344 miles) E of Madrid

The ancient Roman port city of **Tarragona,** on a rocky bluff above the Mediterranean, is one of the grandest but most neglected sightseeing centers in Spain. Despite its Roman and medieval remains, it's merely the second-oldest city of Catalonia.

The Romans captured Tarragona in 218 B.C., and during their rule the city sheltered one million people behind 64km-long (40-mile) city walls. One of the four capitals of Catalonia when it was an ancient principality, and once the home of Julius Caesar, Tarragona today consists of an old quarter filled with interesting buildings, particularly the houses with connecting balconies. The upper walled town is mainly medieval, the town below newer.

In the new town, walk along the main artery, **Ramble Nova,** a fashionable wide boulevard. Running parallel with Ramble Nova to the east is the **Ramble Vella,** which marks the beginning of the Old Town. The city has a bullring, good hotels, and even beaches. The Romans were the first to designate Tarragona a resort town.

A JOURNEY TO andorra

You might never have heard of the tiny principality of **Andorra ★★**, sandwiched between Spain and France high in the eastern Pyrenees. Charlemagne gave this country its independence in A.D. 784, and with amused condescension, Napoleon let Andorra keep its autonomy. The principality is now ruled by two co-princes, the president of France and the Spanish archbishop of La Seu d'Urgell.

Less than 464 sq. km (179 sq. miles) in size, Andorra is a storybook land of breathtaking scenery—cavernous valleys, snowcapped peaks, rugged pastureland, and deep gorges. It's long been popular for summer excursions and is also a winter ski resort.

Because of its isolation, Andorra retained one of Europe's most insular peasant cultures until as late as 1945. But since the 1950s, tourists have increased from a trickle to a flood—12 million every year, in fact. This has wreaked havoc on Andorra's traditional way of life and turned much of the country into one vast shopping center. Andorrans live almost entirely on earnings from tax-free shopping, along with the thriving ski market in the winter months.

Most people make their base in **Andorra-la-Vella** (in Spanish, Andorra-la-Vieja), or in the adjoining town, **Les Escaldes,** where there are plenty of shops, bars, and hotels. Shuttles run between the towns, but most shop-

pers prefer to walk. Many of the major hotels and restaurants line the main street of Andorra-la-Vella (Av. Meritxell) or the main street of Les Escaldes (Av. Carlemany).

But unless you've come just to shop, you'll want to leave the capital for a look at this tiny principality. Two nearby villages, **La Massana** and **Ordino,** can be visited by car or by bus (leaving about every 30 min. from the station in Andorra-la-Vella). Buses cross the country from south to north and vice versa. The drive to Andorra takes you through some of the finest mountain scenery in Europe, with a backdrop of peaks, vineyards, and rushing brooks. From Barcelona, drive via Puigcerdà to La Seu d'Urgell. From here on the C-145, it's a quick 10km (6¼ miles) to the border of this principality, one of the world's smallest countries.

Although no one ever accused the Pyrenees of being more dramatic than the Alps, they are, in fact, far more rugged. The climate of dry air is brisk in

After seeing the attractions listed below, cap off your day with a stroll along the **Balcó del Mediterráni (Balcony of the Mediterranean),** where the vistas are especially beautiful at sunset.

Essentials

GETTING THERE Daily, 43 **trains** make the 1- to 1¼-hour trip to and from the Barcelona-Sants station. There are no direct trains between Madrid and Tarragona; from Madrid, you have to go first to Barcelona, where you change trains for Tarragona. In Tarragona, the RENFE office is in the train station, Plaza Pedrera s/n (© **90-224-02-02;** www.renfe.es).

From Barcelona, there are 10 **buses** per day to Tarragona (trip time: 1½ hr.); from Valencia, 10 buses (trip time: 3½ hr.); and from Alicante, 6 buses (trip time: 6½ hr.). Call © **97-722-91-26** in Tarragona for more information.

winter, and some of Europe's best skiing can be found here. Abundant snow usually lasts from November to April. **Pas de la Casa-Grau Roig** is the oldest resort, located just within the French border. Along with a slalom course, it has 18 trails for advanced skiers, some tame slopes for neophytes, and 25 lifts. The largest complex is **Soldeu-El Tarter,** with 28 slopes, 22 ski lifts, and a 12km (7½-mile) cross-country course. The resort of **Pals** features 20 trails, 14 lifts, and a forest slalom course. **Arinsal** offers 25 slopes serving both the experienced skier and the beginner. But the most beautiful and dramatic resort of all is **Ordino Arcalis,** with 11 lifts and 16 slopes. Many British visitors flock here in winter, as Andorran ski packages are, in general, far more reasonable than those offered in Switzerland or Austria.

Warning: Border guards check very carefully for undeclared goods.

To drive, take the A-2 southwest from Barcelona to the A-7, and then take the N-340. The route is well marked. This is a fast toll road. The one-way cost of the toll road from Barcelona to Tarragona is 9€.

VISITOR INFORMATION The **tourist office,** at Calle Major 39 (© **97-725-07-95;** www.tarragonaturisme.es), is open April to October Monday to Saturday 10am to 9pm, Sunday 10am to 2pm; off-season hours are Monday to Saturday 10am to 2pm and 4 to 7pm, Sunday 10am to 2pm.

Exploring Tarragona

Amfiteatre Romà At the foot of Miracle Park and dramatically carved from a cliff that rises from the beach, this Roman amphitheater recalls the 2nd century, when thousands gathered here for amusement.

Parc del Milagro. ✆ **97-724-25-79.** www.museutgn.org. Admission 3€ adults, 1.50€ students and seniors, free for children 16 and under. Easter–Sept 30 Tues–Sat 9am–9pm, Sun 9am–3pm; Oct 1 to the week before Easter Tues–Sat 9am–5pm, Sun 10am–3pm. Closed Christmas Day, Dec 26, New Year's Day, and Jan 6. Bus: 2.

Catedral ★ At the highest point of Tarragona is this 12th-century cathedral, whose architecture represents the transition from Romanesque to Gothic. It has an enormous vaulted entrance, fine stained-glass windows, Romanesque cloisters, and an open choir. In the main apse, observe the altarpiece of St. Thecla, patron of Tarragona, carved by Pere Joan in 1430. Two flamboyant Gothic doors open into the *chevet*. The east gallery is the **Museu Diocesà,** with a collection of Catalan art.

Plaça de la Seu. ✆ **97-723-86-85.** Cathedral and museum 3.80€. Mar 16–May 30 Mon–Sat 10am–1pm and 4–7pm; June 1–Oct 15 Mon–Sat 10am–7pm; Oct 16–Nov 15 Mon–Sat 10am–5pm; Nov 16–Mar 15 Mon–Sat 10am–2pm. Bus: 1.

Museu D'Art Modern de Tarragona ★ This museum was launched by the acquisition of all the works of the sculptor Julio Antonio that had been kept by his sisters. Since then the bequests have grown to take in many more Catalan artists, especially the painter Josep Sancho I Piqué and sculptors Santiago Costa I Vaqué and Salvador Martorell I Ollé. The museum was formed by combining three ancient buildings in the Old Town. It also displays a rich collection of photographs by some of the nation's best photographers.

Santa Anna 8. ✆ **97-723-50-32.** www.altanet.org/MAMT. Free admission. Tues–Fri 10am–8pm; Sat 10am–3pm.

Museu Nacional Arqueològic Overlooking the sea, the Archaeology Museum houses a collection of Roman relics—mosaics, ceramics, coins, silver, sculpture, and more. The outstanding attraction here is the mosaic *Head of Medusa* **★★**, with its penetrating stare.

Plaça del Rei 5. ✆ **97-723-62-09.** www.mnat.es. Admission 2.40€. June–Sept Tues–Sat 9:30am–8:30pm, Sun 10am–2pm; Oct–May Tues–Sat 9:30am–6pm, Sun 10am–2pm. Bus: 8.

An outer wall of Tarragona's Amfiteatre Romà.

CATALONIA REMEMBERS pablo casals

Fleeing from Franco and the fascist regime, the world's greatest cellist, Pablo Casals, left his homeland in 1939. Today his body has been returned to El Vendrell, 72km (45 miles) south of Barcelona, where he is remembered by a museum in his honor. The museum is installed in the renovated house where he lived until he went into self-imposed exile.

The 17 rooms are filled with Casals memorabilia, including his first cello, photographs and films of his performances, the Peace Medal awarded him by the United Nations in 1971, and photographs of the artist with such famous men as John F. Kennedy, who awarded him the Medal of Freedom.

Casals died in Puerto Rico in 1973 at the age of 96, and he was finally returned to his beloved Catalonia in 1979, where he is buried at El Vendrell graveyard.

Casa Pau Casals is located at Av. Palfuriana 59–61, in El Vendrell

(© **97-768-42-76;** www.paucasals. org). From September 16 to June 14, it's open Tuesday to Friday 10am to 2pm and 4 to 6pm, Saturday 10am to 2pm and 4 to 7pm, and Sunday 10am to 2pm. From June 15 to September 15, it's open Tuesday to Saturday 10am to 2pm and 5 to 9pm, and Sunday 10am to 2pm. Admission is 6€ for adults and 3€ for children. Allow 1 hour.

To reach El Vendrell from Barcelona, head southwest along A-19 until you come to C-246. Continue along this route, which will lead you into El Vendrell.

Passeig Arqueològic ★ At the far end of the Plaça del Pallol, an archway leads to this .8km (½-mile) walkway along the ancient ramparts, built by the Romans on top of gigantic boulders. The ramparts have been much altered over the years, especially in medieval times and in the 1600s. There are scenic views from many points along the way.

El Portal del Roser. © **97-724-57-96.** www.museutgn.com. Admission 3€. Oct–Mar Tues–Sat 9am–5pm, Sun and holidays 10am–3pm; Apr–Sept Tues–Sat 9am–9pm, Sun and holidays 9am–3pm. Bus: 2.

Shopping

You'll find a scattering of handicrafts shops throughout Tarragona's historic core, with a particularly dense concentration along the Ramble Nova. Any of them might provide a handcrafted souvenir of your visit. But for the densest concentration of shops and boutiques, head for the **Centro Comercial Parc Central,** on Avinguda Roma. Although the focus here is a supermarket, the center has at least 40 other stores selling whatever clothing, sundries, and household goods you might need.

Nearby Theme Park Thrills

A 10-minute ride from the heart of Barcelona, **Port Aventura Amusement Park,** Port Aventura (© **97-777-90-90;** www.portaventura.es), is Spain's biggest theme park. Universal Studios acquired a prime stake in it and plans to make it even larger. The park's vast 810 hectares (2,000 acres) will be expanded to become Europe's largest entertainment center, possibly within the next decade.

Since its inauguration in 1995, it has become one of the Mediterranean's favorite family destinations.

The park is a microcosm of five distinct worlds, with full-scale re-creations of classic villages ranging from Polynesia to Mexico, from China to the old American West. It also offers a thrilling variety of roller coaster and white-water rides, all centered on a lake you can travel via the deck of a Chinese junk.

The park is open daily from March 27 to June 17, 10am to 8pm (it often closes at 7pm). In summer it is open daily from 10am to midnight. From September 12 to January 6 it is open daily 10am to 7pm. It's closed at other times. Admission costs 44€ adults, 35€ children 4 to 10; free for children 3 and under. The fee includes all shows and rides.

Some 50% of the trains on the Barcelona-Sitges-Tarragona line stop at Port Aventura. From Barcelona, the one-way trip takes 50 minutes and costs 7€. A taxi from the center of Tarragona to Port Aventura costs about 16€ one-way.

Where to Stay in Tarragona

Ciutat de Tarragona ★ Within the city, the sleek, modern hotel is the best Tarragona has to offer. The well-equipped, modern rooms are neat and stream-lined. The location, in the bull's-eye center, means you can walk to most of the attractions in the historic core. The beaches, however, are about a 10-minute stroll from the hotel. Parc de la Ciutat, next to the hotel, is a good location for walking or jogging. The hotel also has the best facilities of any in-town competitor, including a small swimming pool among other features. The restaurant menu offers both international and traditional Catalonian specialties.

Plaça Imperial Tarraco 5, 43005 Tarragon. ✆ **977/25-09-99.** Fax 977/25-06-99. www.sbhotels. es. 158 units. 66€–155€ double; from 190€ junior suite. AE, DC, MC, V. **Amenities:** Restaurant; bar; exercise room; pool (outdoor); room service. *In room:* A/C, TV, hair dryer, minibar, Wi-Fi (free).

Hotel Astari Travelers in search of peace and quiet on the Mediterranean come to the Astari, which opened in 1959. This resort hotel on the Barcelona road offers fresh and airy (though rather plain) accommodations. Most guest rooms are small, but each comes with a good bed and a well-maintained bathroom. The Astari has long balconies and terraces, one favorite spot being the outer flagstone terrace with its umbrella-shaded tables set among willows, orange trees, and geranium bushes. This is the only hotel in Tarragona with garage space for each guest's car.

Vía Augusta 95, 43003 Tarragona. ✆ **97-723-69-00.** Fax 97-723-69-11. www.hotelastari.com. 81 units. 72€–95€ double. AE, DC, MC, V. Parking 8€. Bus: 1. **Amenities:** Restaurant; bar; outdoor pool; room service. *In room:* A/C, TV, CD player, hair dryer, minibar, Wi-Fi (free).

Hotel Lauria ★ Less than a half-block north of the town's popular seaside promenade (Passeig de les Palmeres), beside the tree-lined *rambla,* this government-rated three-star hotel offers unpretentious clean rooms, each of which has been modernized. The rooms range from small to medium and are comfortably furnished. The rooms in back open onto views of the sea.

Rambla Nova 20, 43004 Tarragona. ✆ **97-723-67-12.** Fax 97-723-67-00. www.hlauria.es. 72 units. 64€–75€ double. AE, DC, MC, V. Parking 10€. Bus: 1. **Amenities:** Bar; outdoor pool; room service. *In room:* A/C, TV, hair dryer, Wi-Fi (10€ per 24 hr.).

Husa Imperial Tarraco ★★ About .4km (¼ mile) south of the cathedral, atop an oceanfront cliff whose panoramas include a sweeping view of both the sea and the Roman ruins, this hotel is among the finest in town. It was designed in the form of a crescent and has guest rooms that may angle out to sea and almost always include small balconies. The rooms, all with neat bathrooms, contain uncomplicated plain modern furniture. The public rooms display lots of polished white marble, Oriental carpets, and leather furniture. The staff responds well to the demands of both traveling businesspeople and art lovers on sightseeing excursions.

Passeig Palmeras/Rambla Vella, 43003 Tarragona. ℂ **97-723-30-40.** Fax 97-721-65-66. www. husa.es. 170 units. 69€–174€ double; 170€–210€ suite. Rates include continental breakfast. AE, DC, MC, V. Free parking. Bus: 1. **Amenities:** Restaurant; bar; babysitting; concierge; outdoor pool; room service; outdoor tennis court; Wi-Fi (10€ per hour, in lobby). *In room:* A/C, TV, hair dryer, minibar.

Where to Dine in Tarragona

Barquet ★ CATALAN/SEAFOOD Just a 5-minute walk from the cathedral, this restaurant specializes in seafood and shellfish rice prepared in the Catalan style. It opened in 1950 in the cellar of a relatively modern building and today is run by the third generation of its original owners. Within a pair of nautical-themed dining rooms, you can enjoy *sopa de pescados* (fish soup) Tarragona style, *romesco* (ragout) of sea bass with herbs, an assemblage of fried finned creatures called *fideos rossejats,* and several preparations of sole and hake. If you're not interested in seafood, grilled veal, chicken, or beef are offered. The list of Spanish and Catalan wines will complement any meal. The staff is well trained, polite, and proud of its Catalan antecedents.

Calle Gasometro 16. ℂ **97-724-00-23.** Reservations recommended. Main courses 26€–35€; *menú de degustación* 36€–50€. DC, MC, V. Mon–Sat 1–3:30pm; Tues–Sat 9–10:30pm. Closed Aug 15–Sept 15.

Les Coques ★ 🍴 MEDITERRANEAN Positioned within an antique building whose ocher walls, wood paneling, and exposed masonry evoke a well-established and prosperous country inn, this is a real discovery in the historic core of old Tarragona. Sophisticated Les Coques specializes in fare from both land and sea and does so exceedingly well. The specialties depend on whatever is good

The Balcó del Mediterráni.

that season. For example, their selection of mushrooms, called *zetas*, can be prepared in almost any style and have a marvelously woodsy taste. They also prepare the best grilled miniature octopus in town, and a wide array of roasts, grills, and stews. Among the meat selections are sirloin steak with Calvados and wild mushrooms, or roast baby goat with Rancio wine and foie gras sauce.

Calle San Llorenç. ✆ **97-722-83-00.** Reservations required. Main courses 13€–33€. DC, MC, V. Mon–Sat 1–3:45pm; Thurs–Sat and Mon–Tues 9pm–2:45am.

Les Voltes ★ ☗ MEDITERRANEAN This excellent restaurant lies within the vaults of Roman Circus Maximus. Chiseled stone from 2,300 years ago blends harmoniously with thick plate glass and polished steel surfaces. A large 250-seat restaurant, Les Voltes offers a kitchen of skilled chefs turning out a flavorful and well-seasoned Mediterranean cuisine. The menu features time-tested favorites such as succulent baked lamb from the neighboring hills. *Rape* (monkfish) deserves special billing, served with roasted garlic in a cockle-and-mussel sauce. Showing sure-handed spicing, the peppery loin of veal is served with broiled eggplant.

Carrer Trinquet Vell 12. ✆ **97-723-06-51.** Reservations recommended. Main courses 12€–28€. MC, V. Tues–Sun 1–3:30pm (July–Aug closed Sun at lunch); Tues–Sat 8:30–11:30pm. Closed 2 weeks in Jan and 2 weeks in July.

Sol-Ric CATALAN/INTERNATIONAL Many guests remember the attentive service here long after memories of the good cuisine have faded. Dating from 1859, the place has a rustic ambience replete with antique farm implements hanging from the walls. There's an outdoor terrace, as well as a central fireplace, usually blazing in winter. The chef prepares oven-baked hake with potatoes, tournedos with Roquefort, seafood stew, and several exotic fish dishes, among other specialties.

Vía Augusta 227. ✆ **97-723-20-32.** Main courses 20€–40€; fixed-price menus 12€–46€. AE, MC, V. Tues–Sun 1–4pm; Tues–Sat 8:30–11pm. Closed Dec 20–Jan 30.

Tarragona After Dark

Rambla Nova contains a handful of sleepy-looking bars, any of which will serve a cup of coffee or bottle of beer throughout the day and evening.

You might try the cafe/bar **Pla La Seu,** Plaza de la Seu 5 (✆ **97-723-04-07**), which lies close to the cathedral. You can sit outside enjoying a drink while taking in the facade. In summer, live jazz is presented on Saturday and Sunday.

Concerts and theatrical productions are staged in the city's cultural centerpiece, **Teatro Metropol,** Rambla Nova 46 (✆ **97-724-47-95**). Because of the language barrier, you might skip theatrical events presented in Catalan in favor of musical and dance presentations.

Side Trips from Tarragona

If you rent a car, you can visit two attractions within a 30- to 45-minute drive from Tarragona. The first stop is the **Monestir de Poblet ★★★**, Plaça Corona d'Aragó 11, E-43448 Poblet (✆ **97-787-00-89;** www.poblet.cat), 47km (29 miles) northwest of Tarragona, one of the most intriguing monasteries in Spain. Its most exciting features are the oddly designed tombs of the old kings of Aragón and Catalonia. Constructed in the 12th and 13th centuries and still in use, Poblet's cathedral-like church reflects both Romanesque and Gothic architectural styles.

THE beaches OF THE COSTA DORADA

Running along the entire coastline of the province of Tarragona, for some 211km (131 miles) from Cunit as far as Les Cases d'Alcanar, is a series of excellent beaches and impressive cliffs, along with beautiful pine-covered headlands. In the city of Tarragona itself is **El Milagre** beach, and a little farther north are the beaches of **L'Arrabassade, Savinosa, dels Capellans,** and **Llarga.** At the end of the latter stands **La Punta de la Mora,** which has a 16th-century watchtower. The small towns of **Altafulla** and **Torredembarra,** both complete with castles, stand next to these beaches and are the location of many hotels.

Farther north again are the two magnificent beaches of **Comarruga** and **Sant Salvador.** The first is particularly cosmopolitan; the second is more secluded. Last come the beaches of **Calafell, Segur,** and **Cunit,** all with modern tourist complexes. You'll also find the small towns of **Creixell, Sant Vicenç de Calders,** and **Clarà,** which are backed by wooded hills.

South of Tarragona, the coastline forms a wide arc that stretches for miles and includes **La Piñeda** beach. **El Recó** beach fronts the **Cape of Salou,** where, among its coves, hills, and hidden-away corners, many hotels are located. The natural port of Salou is nowadays a center for international tourism.

Continuing south toward Valencia, you next come to **Cambrils,** a maritime town with an excellent beach and an important fishing port. In the background stand the impressive Colldejou and Llaberia mountains. Farther south are the beaches of **Montroig** and **L'Hospitalet,** as well as the small town of **L'Ametlla de Mar,** with its small fishing port.

After passing the Balaguer massif, you eventually reach the delta of the River Ebro, a wide lowland area covering more than 483km (300 miles), opening like a fan into the sea. This is an area of rice fields crisscrossed by branches of the Ebro and by an enormous number of irrigation channels. There are also some lagoons that, because of their immense size, are ideal hunting and fishing grounds. Moreover, there are some beaches over several miles in length and others in small hidden estuaries. Two important towns in the region are **Amposta,** on the Ebro itself, and **Sant Carles de la Ràpita,** a 19th-century port town favored by King Carlos III.

The Costa Dorada extends to its most southwesterly point at the plain of **Alcanar,** a large area given over to the cultivation of oranges and other similar crops. Its beaches, along with the small hamlet of **Les Cases d'Alcanar,** mark the end of the Tarragona section of the Costa Dorada.

Cistercian monks still live here, passing their days writing, studying, working a printing press, farming, and helping restore the building, which suffered heavy damage during the 1835 revolution. Admission to the monastery costs 6€ adults, 3.50€ children 13 and under and students. March 15 to October 12, it's open Monday to Saturday 10am to 12:30pm and 3 to 6pm; October 13 to March 14, it's open daily 10:30am to 12:30pm and 3 to 5:30pm. Except for Monday, when no guide service is available, visits to the monastery usually include tours, mostly in Spanish but with occasional English translations. They depart at 75-minute intervals during the monastery's open hours.

About 4.8km (3 miles) farther along, you can explore an unspoiled medieval Spanish town, **Montblanch.** At its entrance, a map pinpoints the principal artistic and architectural treasures—and there are many. Walk, don't drive, along the narrow, winding streets.

SITGES ★★

40km (25 miles) S of Barcelona, 596km (370 miles) E of Madrid

Sitges is one of the most popular resorts of southern Europe, the brightest spot on the Costa Dorada. It's especially crowded in summer, mostly with affluent, young northern Europeans, many of them gay. For years the resort drew largely prosperous middle-class industrialists from Barcelona, but those staid days have gone; Sitges is as swinging today as Benidorm and Torremolinos down the coast.

Sitges has long been known as a city of culture, thanks in part to resident artist, playwright, and bohemian mystic Santiago Rusiñol. The 19th-century *modernismo* (aka *modernisme*) movement began largely at Sitges, and the town remained the scene of artistic encounters and demonstrations long after the movement waned. Sitges continued as a resort of artists, attracting such giants as Salvador Dalí and poet Federico García Lorca. The Spanish Civil War (1936–39) erased what has come to be called the Golden Age of Sitges. Although other artists and writers arrived in the decades to follow, none had the name or the impact of those who had gone before.

Essentials

GETTING THERE RENFE (www.renfe.es) runs **trains** from Barcelona-Sants to Sitges; the 30-minute trip costs 3.50€. Call ✆ **93-490-02-02** in Barcelona for information about schedules. Four trains leave Barcelona per hour.

Sitges is a 45-minute drive from Barcelona along the C-246, a coastal road. An express highway, the A-7, opened in 1991. The coastal road is more scenic, but it can be extremely slow on weekends because of the heavy traffic, as all of Barcelona seemingly heads for the beaches.

VISITOR INFORMATION The **tourist office** is at Carrer Sinea Morera 1 (✆ **93-894-50-04;** www.sitges.com). From July to September 15, it's open daily 9am to 8pm; September 16 to June, hours are Monday to Friday 9am to 2pm and 4 to 6:30pm.

SPECIAL EVENTS The **Carnaval** at Sitges is one of the outstanding events on the Catalan calendar. For more than a century, the town has celebrated the days before the beginning of Lent. Fancy dress, floats, feathered outfits, and sequins all make this an exciting event. The party begins on the Thursday before Lent, with the arrival of the king of the Carnestoltes, and ends on Ash Wednesday, with the "Burial of a Sardine." Activities reach their jubilant best on Sant Bonaventura, where gays and lesbians hold their own celebrations.

Fun on & off the Beach

The old part of Sitges used to be a fortified medieval enclosure. The castle is now the seat of the town government. The local parish church, called **La Punta (the Point)** and built next to the sea on top of a promontory, presides over an extensive maritime esplanade, where people parade in the early evening. Behind the church are the Museu Cau Ferrat (p. 549) and the Museu Maricel (p. 549).

Sitges's seaside.

Most people are here to hit the beach. The beaches have showers, bathing cabins, and stalls; kiosks rent motorboats and watersports equipment. Beaches on the eastern end and those inside the town center are the most peaceful—for example, **Aiguadoiç** and **Els Balomins. Playa San Sebastián, Fragata Beach,** and the **"Beach of the Boats"** (below the church and next to the yacht club) are the area's family beaches. A young, happening crowd heads for the **Playa de la Ribera,** to the west.

All along the coast, women can and certainly do go topless. Farther west are the most solitary beaches, where the scene grows racier, especially along the **Playas del Muerto,** where two tiny nude beaches lie between Sitges and Vilanova i la Geltrú. A shuttle bus runs between the cathedral and Golf Terramar. From Golf Terramar, go along the road to the club L'Atlántida, and then walk along the railway. The first beach draws nudists of every sexual persuasion, and the second is almost solely gay. Be advised that lots of action takes place in the woods in back of these beaches.

Museums in Sitges

Beaches aside, Sitges has some choice museums, which really shouldn't be missed. The museums reviewed below keep the same seasonal hours.

Museu Cau Ferrat The Catalan artist Santiago Rusiñol combined two 16th-century cottages to make this house, where he lived and worked; upon his death in 1931 he willed it to Sitges along with his art collection. More than anyone else, Rusiñol made Sitges a popular resort. The museum collection includes two paintings by El Greco and several small Picassos, including *The Bullfight.* A number of Rusiñol's works are on display.

Carrer del Fonollar. ✆ **93-894-03-64.** Admission 3.50€ adults, 1.75€ students, free for children 5 and under. Combination ticket for the 3 museums listed in this section: 6.40€ adults, 3.50€ students and children 6 and under. June 15–Sept 30 Tues–Sat 9:30am–2pm and 4–7pm, Sun 10am–3pm; Oct 1–June 14 Tues–Sat 9:30am–2pm and 3:30–6:30pm, Sun 10am–3pm.

Museu Maricel Opened by the king and queen of Spain, the Museu Maricel contains art donated by Dr. Jesús Pérez Rosales. The palace, owned by American Charles Deering when it was built right after World War I, is made up of two parts connected by a small bridge. The museum has a good collection of Gothic and Romantic paintings and sculptures, as well as many fine Catalan ceramics.

Playa San Sebastián beach.

There are three noteworthy works by Santiago Rebull and an allegorical painting of World War I by José María Sert.

Carrer del Fonallar. ℭ **93-894-03-64.** Admission 3.50€ adults, 1.75€ students, free for children 5 and under. Admission included in combination ticket. (See Museu Cau Ferrat, above, for opening times.)

Museu Romàntic ("Can Llopis") This museum re-creates the daily life of a Sitges land-owning family in the 18th and 19th centuries. The family rooms, furniture, and household objects are most interesting. You'll find wine cellars downstairs and an important collection of antique dolls upstairs.

Sant Gaudenci 1. ℭ **93-894-29-69.** Admission (including guided tour) 3.50€ adults, 1.75€ students, free for children 5 and under. Admission included in combination ticket. (See Museu Cau Ferrat, above, for opening times.)

Where to Stay in Sitges

In spite of a building spree, Sitges just can't handle the large numbers of tourists who flock here in July and August. By mid-October just about everything—including hotels, restaurants, and bars—slows down considerably or closes altogether.

EXPENSIVE

Meliá Gran Sitges ★ Designed with steeply sloping sides reminiscent of a pair of interconnected Aztec pyramids, this hotel dates from 1992, when it housed spectators and participants in the Barcelona Olympics. The hotel has a marble lobby with what feels like the largest window in Spain, overlooking a view of the mountains. Each midsize room comes with a large furnished veranda for sunbathing, and each bathroom has a tub/shower combo. Many guests are here to participate in the conferences and conventions held frequently in the battery of high-tech convention facilities. The hotel is about a 15-minute walk east of the center of Sitges, near the access roads leading to Barcelona.

Joan Salvat Papasseit 38, 08870 Sitges. ℭ **800/336-3542** in the U.S., or 93-811-08-11. Fax 93-894-90-34. www.solmelia.com. 307 units. 99€–235€ double; 179€–441€ suite. Rates include continental breakfast. AE, DC, MC, V. Parking 13€. **Amenities:** Restaurant; bar; babysitting; bikes; exercise room; Jacuzzi; 2 freshwater heated pools (1 indoor); room service; sauna. *In room:* A/C, TV, hair dryer, minibar, Wi-Fi (4€ per hour).

San Sebastián Playa ★★ The best choice in Sitges, opposite San Sebastián beach, this government-rated four-star hotel with its wedding-cake facade has been in operation since 1990. The functional Art Deco interior is the most beautifully decorated of any hotel in Sitges. A lot of attention has gone into the guest rooms, which are spacious and comfortable, with modernized bathrooms. Each has a balcony opening onto the sea.

Calle Port Alegre 53, 08870 Sitges. ℭ **93-894-86-76.** Fax 93-894-04-30. www.hotelsan sebastian.com. 51 units. 170€–341€ double; 273€–475€ suite. Rates include continental breakfast. AE, DC, MC, V. Parking 16€. **Amenities:** Restaurant; bar; babysitting; outdoor pool; room service. *In room:* A/C, TV, hair dryer, minibar, Wi-Fi (free).

Subur Marítim ★ In a residential area on the seafront facing a good beach, this government-rated four-star Best Western hotel is only a 5-minute walk from the center. It's a winning choice, made up of a traditional Catalan building and a more modern functional structure. The interior is cozy, with a traditional Catalan decor of wood fittings and cast-iron adornments on doors and windows. The amply sized rooms are comfortably furnished and tastefully decorated, each with a balcony and neatly kept bathroom.

Passeig Marítim, 08870 Sitges. ℭ **800/528-1234** in the U.S., or 93-894-15-50. Fax 93-894-04-27. www.hotelsuburmaritim.com. 42 units. 74€–191€ double; 123€–413€ suite. Rates include buffet breakfast. AE, DC, MC, V. Free parking. **Amenities:** Restaurant; bar; babysitting; bikes; outdoor freshwater pool; room service. *In room:* A/C, TV, hair dryer, minibar, Wi-Fi (free).

Terramar ★ Facing the beach in a residential area of Sitges, about .8km (½ mile) from the center, this modern resort hotel with its balconied front evokes a many-tiered yacht. The interior, however, is designed in a classical Mediterranean style with marble floors and white walls. The spacious guest rooms are comfortable, with carpeted floors and colorful wall coverings.

Passeig Marítim 80, 08870 Sitges. ℭ **93-894-00-50.** Fax 93-894-56-04. www.hotelterramar.com. 209 units. 120€–175€ double; 165€–210€ suite. Rates include breakfast buffet. AE, DC, MC, V. Free parking. Closed Nov–Apr. Bus: 1. **Amenities:** 2 restaurants; bar; babysitting; children's center; outdoor freshwater pool; room service; 2 outdoor tennis courts. *In room:* A/C, TV, hair dryer, minibar.

MODERATE

Hotel Romàntic de Sitges ★ 🎁 Composed of three beautifully restored 19th-century villas, this hotel is only a short walk from the beach and the train station. The romantic bar is an international rendezvous, and the public rooms are filled with artwork. You can have breakfast in the dining room or in a garden filled with mulberry trees. The guest rooms, reached by stairs, range from small to medium and are well maintained, with good beds and bathrooms with shower stalls. Overflow guests are housed in a nearby annex, Hotel de la Renaixença.

Carrer de Sant Isidre 33, 08870 Sitges. ℭ **93-894-83-75.** Fax 93-811-41-29. www.hotelromantic. com. 60 units. 98€–125€ double. Rates include continental breakfast. AE, MC, V. Parking nearby 25€. Closed Oct 15–Apr 6. **Amenities:** Bar; babysitting. *In room:* Hair dryer.

Hotel Subur This old-time favorite stands in a prominent position in the center of town on the seafront. The first hotel built in Sitges (in 1916), the Subur was torn down and reconstructed in 1960, and was last renovated in 1992. Its small rooms are well furnished, its bathrooms well equipped. Balconies open onto the Mediterranean. Unlike some others in the area, the hotel remains open year-round.

Passeig de la Ribera s/n, 08870 Sitges. ℭ **93-894-00-66.** Fax 93-894-69-86. www.hotel-subur.com. 95 units. 62€–133€ double; 84€–179€ triple. Rates include continental breakfast. AE, DC, MC, V. Parking 25€. **Amenities:** Restaurant; bar; babysitting; room service. *In room:* A/C, TV, minibar, Wi-Fi (free).

INEXPENSIVE

El Galeón A leading choice only a short walk from both the beach and the Plaça d'Espanya, this well-styled hostelry blends a bit of the old Spain with the new. The small public rooms feel cozy; the good-size guest rooms, accented with wood grain, have a more streamlined air. Each unit comes with a comfortable bed, plus a simple but adequate bathroom.

Sant Francesc 44, 08870 Sitges. (*C*) **93-894-13-79.** Fax 93-894-63-35. www.hotelsitges.com. 74 units. 75€ double. Rates include continental breakfast. MC, V. Parking 15€. Closed Oct 20–Apr. **Amenities:** Restaurant; bar; outdoor freshwater pool; Wi-Fi (free, in lobby). *In room:* A/C, TV.

Hotel El Cid El Cid's exterior suggests Castile, and inside, appropriately enough, you'll find beamed ceilings, natural stone walls, heavy wrought-iron chandeliers, and leather chairs. The same theme is carried out in the rear dining room and in the pleasantly furnished guest rooms, which, though small, are still quite comfortable, with fine beds and bathrooms. Breakfast is the only meal served. El Cid is off the Passeig de Vilanova, in the center of town.

San José 39 bis, 08870 Sitges. (*C*) **93-894-18-42.** Fax 93-894-63-35. www.hotelsitges.com. 77 units. 55€–85€ double. Rates include continental breakfast. MC, V. Closed Nov–Apr. **Amenities:** Bar; babysitting; outdoor freshwater pool. *In room:* No phone.

Hotel El Xalet ★ 👔 Right in the town center, this little charmer (the name is pronounced like "chalet") is about a 10-minute stroll from the nearest good beach. A happy blend of contemporary comfort and traditional styling, the modernist building is from the early 20th century, with both Gothic and Art Nouveau architectural adornments. Passersby may think it's a Gothic church because of its ornate stonework, intricate carvings, and towering spires. Antique mosaics and marble decorate the lobby and reception area. Grace notes are the small pool in the hotel's well-manicured gardens and an inviting roof terrace where you can order breakfast. The small to midsize guest rooms, done in pastel shades of salmon and yellow, are comfortably furnished. The summer-only **restaurant** serves succulent Catalonia specialties.

Isla de Cuba 21, 08870 Sitges. (*C*) **93-811-00-70.** Fax 93-894-55-79. www.elxalet.com. 12 units. 60€–100€ double; 80€–125€ suite. Rates include continental breakfast. AE, DC, MC, V. **Amenities:** Restaurant; outdoor pool. *In room:* A/C, TV, hair dryer, minibar.

Where to Dine in Sitges

El Velero ★ SEAFOOD This is one of Sitges's leading restaurants, positioned along the beachfront promenade. The most desirable tables are found on the glass greenhouse terrace, opening onto the esplanade, though the restaurant inside is more glamorous. Try a soup, such as clam and truffle or whitefish, followed by a main dish such as paella marinara (with seafood), suprême of salmon in pine nut sauce, or locally line-caught *dorada* that's prepared in several different ways. The chef tells us that it's especially good when grilled and served with a garlic-and-parsley sauce.

Passeig de la Ribera 38. (*C*) **93-894-20-51.** www.restaurantevelero.com. Reservations required. Main courses 18€–36€. AE, DC, MC, V. Wed–Sun 1:30–4pm; Tues–Sat 8:30–11:30pm.

Fragata ★ SEAFOOD Though its simple interior offers little more than well-scrubbed floors, tables with crisp napery, and air-conditioning, some of the most delectable seafood specialties in town are served here, and hundreds of loyal customers come to appreciate the authentic cuisine. Specialties include seafood soup, a mixed grill of fresh fish, cod salad, mussels marinara, several preparations of squid and octopus, plus flavorful meat dishes such as grilled lamb cutlets.

Passeig de la Ribera 1. ② **93-894-10-86.** www.restaurantefragata.com. Reservations recommended. Main dishes 18€–30€. AE, DC, MC, V. Daily 1:30–4:30pm and 8:30–11:30pm.

Mare Nostrum SEAFOOD This landmark dates from 1950, when it opened in what had been a private home in the 1890s. The dining room has a waterfront view, and in warm weather, tables are placed outside. The menu includes a full range of seafood dishes, among them grilled fish specialties and steamed hake with champagne. The fish soup is particularly delectable. The chef prepares seven different rice dishes nightly. Next door, the restaurant's cafe serves ice cream, milkshakes, sandwiches, tapas, and three varieties of sangria, including one with champagne and fruit.

Passeig de la Ribera 60. ② **93-894-33-93.** www.restaurantmarenostrum.com. Reservations required. Main courses 15€–25€. AE, DC, MC, V. Thurs–Tues 1–4pm; Thurs–Sat and Mon 8–11pm. Closed Dec 15–Feb 1.

Sitges After Dark

One of the best ways to pass an evening in Sitges is to walk the waterfront esplanade, have a leisurely dinner, and then retire at about 11pm to one of the open-air cafes for a nightcap and some serious people-watching.

If you're straight, you may have to hunt to find a bar that isn't predominantly gay. There are so many gay bars, in fact, that a map is distributed pinpointing their locales. Nine of them are concentrated on **Carrer Sant Bonaventura** in the center of town, a 5-minute walk from the beach (near the Museu Romàntic).

Mediterráneo, Sant Bonaventura 6 (no phone), is the largest gay disco/bar. Located in a restored 1690s house just east of the Plaça d'Espanya, it sports a formal Iberian garden and sleek modern styling. Upstairs are pool tables and a covered terrace. On summer nights, the place is overflowing.

The sexiest bar in town is the aptly named **Man Bar,** Sant Bonaventura 19 (no phone). It's the raunchiest gay watering hole along the eastern coast of Spain, and has a hard industrial feel, with chains and metal bars. Its dark lighting creates a cruisy atmosphere. Patrons are encouraged to "play" in the rear dark room. Leather, rubber, and uniforms are the dress of choice, except on underwear nights when clients must wear suitable underwear or else go naked. The bar closes in winter, but is open nightly the rest of the year from 10pm to 3:30am.

Other gay bars include **Bourbon's,** Sant Bonaventura 13 (② **93-894-33-47;** www.bourbonsbar.com), with a predominantly youngish crowd. **El Horno,** Joan Tarrida 6 (② **93-894-09-09**), with slight leather overtones that grow more prominent as the night progresses, opens earlier, at 5:30pm, and also features a dark room.

Another of the town's most popular nightspots is **Ricky's Disco,** Sant Pau 25 (② **93-894-96-81**), which charges a cover of 10€ to 12€. This place caters to an international mix of gay and straight visitors. It's set back from the beach on a narrow street noted for its inexpensive restaurants and folkloric color. **Trailer,** Angel Vidal 36 (② **93-894-04-01;** www.trailerdisco.com), is the best place to end the night. Its foam parties are infamous along the coast. The 10€ cover includes a drink. It closes at 6am.

14

GIRONA & THE COSTA BRAVA

C osta Brava, the so-called "Wild Coast," is a 153km (95-mile) stretch of coastline—the northernmost Mediterranean seafront in Spain—beginning north of Barcelona at Blanes and stretching toward the French border. Visit this area in May, June, September, or October, and avoid July and August, when tour groups from northern Europe book virtually all the hotel rooms.

Undiscovered little fishing villages along the coast long ago bloomed into resort towns. **Tossa de Mar** is the most delightful of them. **Lloret de Mar** is immensely popular but too commercial and overdeveloped for many tastes. The most unspoiled spot is remote **Cadaqués.** Some of the smaller villages make excellent stops.

If you want to visit the Costa Brava but simply can't secure a room in high season, consider taking a day trip by car from Barcelona or booking one of the daily organized tours that leave from that city. Allow plenty of time for the drive. In summer, traffic jams can be fierce and the roads between towns difficult and winding.

If you visit the coast in summer without a hotel reservation, you'll stand a fair chance of getting a room in **Girona,** the capital of the province and one of the most interesting medieval cities in Spain.

GIRONA ★★

97km (60 miles) NE of Barcelona, 90km (56 miles) S of Perpignan, France

Founded by the Romans, **Girona** is one of the most important historical sites in Spain. Later, it became a Moorish stronghold. Later still, it reputedly withstood three invasions by Napoleon's troops (1809). For that and other past sieges, Girona is often called "the City of a Thousand Sieges."

Split by the Onyar River, this sleepy medieval city attracts crowds of tourists darting inland from the Costa Brava for the day. For orientation purposes, go to the ancient stone footbridge across the Onyar. From here, you'll have the finest view. Bring good walking shoes, as the only way to discover the particular charm of this medieval city is on foot. You can wander for hours through the **Call,** the labyrinthine old quarter, with its narrow, steep alleyways and lanes and its ancient stone houses, which form a rampart chain along the Onyar.

Essentials

GETTING THERE More than 25 **trains** per day run between Girona and Barcelona from 6:10am to 9:30pm, including one TALGO. Trip time is 60 to 90 minutes, depending on the train. Tickets can run from 7€ to 24€ one-way. Trains arrive in Girona at the Plaça Espanya (© **90-224-02-02** for information; www.renfe.es).

FACING PAGE: **The high bluffs of Lloret de Mar.**

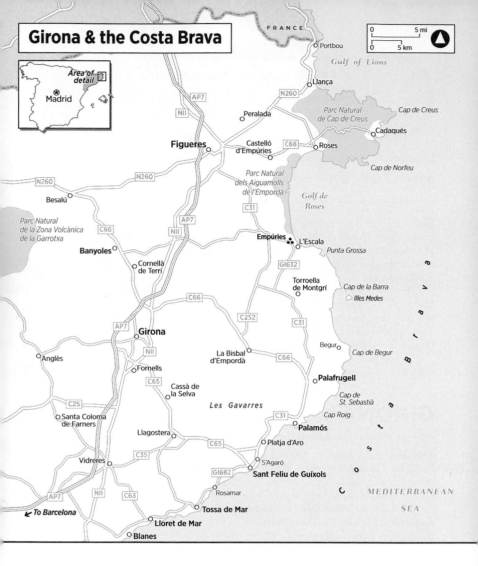

Girona & the Costa Brava

FRANCE

Portbou

Gulf of Lions

Llançà

Parc Natural de Cap de Creus

Cap de Creus

Peralada

Cadaqués

Figueres

Castelló d'Empúries

Roses

Cap de Norfeu

Parc Natural dels Aiguamolls de l'Empordà

Golf de Roses

Besalú

Parc Natural de la Zona Volcànica de la Garrotxa

Banyoles

Empúries

L'Escala

Punta Grossa

Cornellà de Terri

Torroella de Montgrí

Cap de la Barra

Illes Medes

Girona

Anglès

La Bisbal d'Empordà

Begur

Cap de Begur

Fornells

Palafrugell

Cassà de la Selva

Cap de St. Sebastià

Les Gavarres

Cap Roig

Santa Coloma de Farners

Palamós

Llagostera

Platja d'Aro

Vidreres

S'Agaró

Rosamar

Sant Feliu de Guíxols

← To Barcelona

Tossa de Mar

MEDITERRANEAN SEA

Lloret de Mar

Blanes

Area of detail

Madrid

From the Costa Brava, you can take one of the SARFA **buses** (© 97-220-17-96 in Girona; www.sarfa.com) to Girona (7:15–8:15am). Three per day depart from Tossa de Mar. (See "Tossa de Mar," p. 568.) Barcelona Bus (© 97-220-24-32 in Girona; www.barcelonabus.com) also operates express buses between Girona and Barcelona at the rate of 6 to 13 runs per day, depending on the season and demand.

From Barcelona or the French border, drivers connect with the main north-south route (A-7), taking the turnoff to Girona. From Barcelona, take the A-2 north to reach the A-7.

VISITOR INFORMATION The **tourist office** at Rambla de la Libertat (© 97-222-65-75; www.ajuntament.gi) is open Monday to Friday 8am to 8pm, Saturday 8am to 2pm and 4 to 8pm, and Sunday 9am to 2pm.

Exploring the Medieval City

Banys Arabs These 12th-century Arab baths, an example of Romanesque civic architecture, are in the Old Quarter of the city. Visit the **caldarium** (hot bath), with its paved floor, and the **frigidarium** (cold bath), with its central octagonal pool surrounded by pillars that support a prismlike structure in the overhead window. Although the Moorish baths were heavily restored in 1929, they give you an idea of what the ancient ones were like.

Carrer Ferran el Católic. ⓒ **97-221-32-62.** www. banysarabs.org. Admission 2€ adults, 1€ students. Apr–Sept Mon–Sat 10am–7pm, Sun 10am–2pm; Oct–Mar Mon–Sat 10am–2pm. Closed Jan 1, Jan 6, Easter, and Dec 25–26.

Catedral ★★ Girona's major attraction is its magnificent cathedral, reached by climbing a 17th-century baroque staircase of 90 steep steps. The 14th-century cathedral represents many architectural styles, including Gothic and Romanesque, but most notably Catalan baroque. The facade you see as you climb those long stairs dates from the 17th and 18th centuries; from a cornice on top rises a bell tower crowned by a dome with a bronze angel weather vane. Go through the cathedral's main door and enter the nave, which at 23m (75 ft.) is the broadest in the world of Gothic architecture.

FROM TOP: **The alleys of the Call; the Banys Arabs.**

The *Tapestry of the Creation*, in Girona's cathedral.

The cathedral contains many works of art, displayed for the most part in its museum. Its prize exhibit is the *Tapestry of the Creation*, a unique piece of 11th- or 12th-century Romanesque embroidery depicting humans and animals in the Garden of Eden. The other major work displayed is one of the world's rarest manuscripts—the 10th-century *Códex del Beatus*, which contains an illustrated commentary on the Book of the Apocalypse. From the cathedral's **Chapel of Hope**, a door leads to a **Romanesque cloister** from the 12th and 13th centuries, with an unusual trapezoidal layout. The cloister gallery, with a double colonnade, has a series of biblical scenes, the prize jewel of Catalan Romanesque art. From the cloister you can view the 12th-century **Torre de Carlemany (Charlemagne's Tower).**

Plaça de la Catedral. ☏ **97-221-58-14.** www.catedraldegirona.org. Free admission to cathedral; cloister and museum 5€ adults, 3€ students and children 16 and under. Cathedral: Daily 9am–1pm and during cloister and museum visiting hours. Cloister and museum: July–Sept Tues–Sat 10am–8pm, Sun 10am–2pm; Oct–Feb Tues–Sat 10am–2pm and 4–6pm, Sun 10am–2pm; Mar–June Tues–Sat 10am–2pm and 4–7pm, Sun 10am–2pm.

Església de Sant Feliu This 14th- to 17th-century church was built over what may have been the tomb of Feliu of Africa, martyred during Diocletian's persecution at the beginning of the 4th century. Important in the architectural history of Catalonia, the church has pillars and arches in the Romanesque style and a Gothic central nave. The **bell tower**—one of the Girona skyline's most characteristic features—has eight pinnacles and one central tower, each supported on a solid octagonal base. The interior contains some exceptional works, including a 16th-century **altarpiece** and a 14th-century alabaster *Reclining Christo.* Notice the eight pagan and Christian **sarcophagi** set in the presbytery walls, the two oldest of which are from the 2nd century A.D. One shows Pluto carrying Persephone to the depths of the earth.

Pujada de Sant Feliu. ☏ **97-220-14-07.** www.esglesiasantfeliu.com. Free admission. Mon–Sat 7am–12:30pm and 4–6:30pm; Sun and holidays 4–6:30pm.

Museu Arqueològic Housed in a Romanesque church and cloister from the 11th and 12th centuries, this museum illustrates the history of the country from the Paleolithic to the Visigothic periods, using artifacts discovered in nearby excavations. The monastery itself ranks as one of the best examples of Catalan Romanesque architecture. In the cloister, note some Hebrew inscriptions from gravestones of the old Jewish cemetery.

Sant Pere de Galligants, Santa Llúcia 1. ✆ **97-220-26-32.** www.mac.cat. Admission 2.30€ adults, 1.50€ students, free for seniors and children 15 and under. Sun (year-round) 10am–2pm; Oct–May Tues–Sat 10am–2pm and 4–6pm; June–Sept Tues–Sat 10:30am–1:30pm and 4–7pm.

Museu d'Art ★ In a former Romanesque and Gothic Episcopal palace (Palau Episcopal) next to the cathedral, this museum displays artworks spanning 10 centuries (once housed in the old Diocesan Museum and the Provincial Museum). Stop in the throne room to view the **altarpiece of Sant Pere of Púbol,** by Bernat Martorell, and the **altarpiece of Sant Miguel de Crüilles,** by Luis Borrassa. Both of these works, from the 15th century, are exemplary of Catalan Gothic painting. The museum is also proud of its **altar stone** of Sant Pere de Roda, from the 10th and 11th centuries; this work in wood and stone, depicting figures and legends, was once embossed in silver. The 12th-century *Crüilles Timber* is a unique piece of Romanesque polychrome wood. *Our Lady of Besalù,* from the 15th century, is one of the best Virgins carved in alabaster.

Pujada de la Catedral 12. ✆ **97-220-38-34.** www.museuart.com. Admission 2€ adults; 1.50€ students, children 17 and under, and seniors 65 and over. Mar–Sept Tues–Sat 10am–7pm, Sun 10am–2pm; Oct–Feb Tues–Sat 10am–6pm, Sun 10am–2pm. Closed Jan 1, Jan 6, and Dec 25–26.

Museu del Cinema ★ Film buffs flock to this museum, the only one of its kind in Spain. It houses the Tomàs Mallol collection of some 25,000 cinema artifacts, going all the way to films shot as late as 1970. Many objects are from the "pre-cinema" era, others from the early days of film. The museum even owns the original camera of the pioneering Lumière brothers. Fixed images such as photographs, posters, engravings, drawings, and paintings are exhibited along with some 800 films of various styles and periods. A library holds film-related publications.

Sèquia 1. ✆ **97-241-27-77.** www.museudelcinema.org. Admission 4€ adults, 2€ students, free for children 16 and under. May–Sept Tues–Sun 10am–8pm; Oct–Apr Tues–Fri 10am–6pm, Sat 10am–8pm, Sun 11am–3pm.

Museu d'Història de la Ciutat Housed in the old 18th-century Capuchin Convent de Sant Antoni, this collection dates from the time of Puig d'en Roca (Catalonia's oldest prehistoric site) to the present. It includes Girona's (and Spain's) first electric streetlights. Additional displays of tools, technical materials, and the accouterments of passing lifestyles make up a kind of municipal résumé. From the original Capuchin convent, there remains the cemetery used for drying corpses before mummifying them (one of three of this type left in the world).

Carrer de la Força 27. ✆ **97-222-22-29.** Admission 3€ adults, 2€ students and seniors, free for children 16 and under. Tues–Sat 10am–2pm and 5–7pm; Sun 10am–2pm.

Shopping

Consistent with its role as an international seaside resort, Girona has a network of shops selling everything from sportswear to formalwear. The most appealing shopping street is **Carrer Santa Clara.** At **Adolfo Domínguez,** Carrer Santa Clara 36 (✆ **97-220-43-65**), the styles of men's and women's clothing derive from Spanish and other European designs. For men's and women's sportswear, try

Tommy, Rambla de la Libertat 28 (☎ **97-222-36-93**). Finally, consider **Zara,** Carrer Joan Maragall 25 (☎ **97-222-13-05**), a stylish but affordable emporium for both men and women.

If handicrafts appeal to you, consider a 32km (20-mile) eastward trek from Girona to the hamlet of **La Bispal,** more or less midway between Girona and the town of Palamos. (From Girona, follow the signs pointing to Palamos.) Here, in rows of simple shops, dozens of artisans display and sell artfully rustic ceramics, some of which are too bulky to ship, while others can be packed in your carry-on luggage.

Where to Stay in Girona

MODERATE

Ciutat de Girona ★ 🖋 Bedecked in marble, this modern hotel blends in with Girona's traditional Catalan architecture. But inside, its bedrooms are among the most up-to-date in town, equipped with the latest technology, ranging from Wi-Fi to satellite TV. The bedrooms are midsize to spacious and furnished in a Japanese minimalist style. The good on-site restaurant, **Blanc,** is decorated with hundreds of multicolored glass bottles. The cuisine is Mediterranean style.

Calle Nord 2, 17001 Girona. ☎ **97-248-3038.** Fax 97-248-3026. www.hotel-ciutatdegirona. com. 44 units. 150€–202€. Rates include buffet breakfast. AE, DC, MC, V. Parking 21€. **Amenities:** Restaurant; bar; room service; Wi-Fi (free, in lobby). *In room:* A/C, TV, CD player, fridge, hair dryer, minibar.

Hotel Carlemany ★ In a commercial area only 10 minutes from the historic core, this 1995 hotel is the city's best. A favorite of business travelers, it's contemporary with an ultramodern design and a cavernous interior of marble, polished wood, Oriental carpets, and tropical plants. The midsize to spacious rooms are soundproof and airy.

Plaça Miguel Santaló, 17002 Girona. ☎ **97-221-12-12.** Fax 97-221-49-94. www.carlemany.es. 90 units. 120€ double; 315€ suite. AE, MC, V. Parking 20€. **Amenities:** Restaurant; bar; babysitting; Internet (free, in lobby); room service. *In room:* A/C, TV, hair dryer, minibar, Wi-Fi (13€ per 24 hr.).

Hotel Historic ★★★ 🏠 This hideaway boutique hotel, often a retreat for Spanish movie stars, is our favorite nest in the area. In this undiscovered gem, you'll find grand comfort and personalized attention. The inn, which opens onto views of a Gothic-vaulted cathedral, was formed from a 9th-century house that incorporated parts of a Roman wall and a 3rd-century aqueduct. The hotel offers a standard room or a private apartment—choose according to your needs. Rooms are spacious and well furnished, and each one is tastefully decorated. Modern plumbing, with tubs and showers, has been installed throughout the ancient structure. Most units have balconies. The **restaurant** serves first-rate Catalan dishes.

Carrer Bellmirall 4A, 17004 Girona. ☎ **97-222-35-83.** Fax 97-220-09-32. www.hotelhistoric.com. 15 units. 115€ double; 150€ junior suite; 300€ apt. AE, DC, MC, V. Free parking on adjoining plaza. **Amenities:** Restaurant; room service. *In room:* A/C, TV, minibar.

Meliá Girona ★ This modern and functional runner-up to the Hotel Historic (see above) is a member of the large Spanish chain opened in 1990, and it attracts mostly business travelers. About 20 minutes from the resorts of the Costa Brava, it's often used as emergency accommodations in summer when the beach hotels are packed. Its decor lacks a personal touch, but the guest rooms are spacious and comfortable.

Calle Barcelona 112, 17003 Girona. ℂ **97-240-05-00.** Fax 97-224-32-33. www.solmelia.com. 112 units. 85€–129€ double; 164€–189€ suite. AE, DC, MC, V. Parking 15€. **Amenities:** Restaurant; bar; exercise room; Jacuzzi; room service; sauna. *In room:* A/C, TV, hair dryer, minibar, Wi-Fi (free).

INEXPENSIVE

Bellmirall ★ 🍴 Across the Onyar River, this little discovery lies in the heart of the old Jewish ghetto. It's one of the best values in the Old Town. The building itself, much restored and altered over the years, dates originally from the 14th century. Christina Vach took control of the venerated old building, restored it, and converted it to a hotel. She has succeeded admirably in her task. Guest rooms are small to midsize and are decorated in part with antiques set against brick walls. In summer, it's possible to order breakfast outside in the courtyard.

Carrer Bellmirall 3, 17004 Girona. ℂ **97-220-40-09.** 7 units. 75€–85€ double; 90€–100€ triple. Rates include continental breakfast. No credit cards. Free parking (hotel provides permit). Closed Jan–Feb. *In room:* No phone.

Condal 🍴 Near the rail and bus stations west of the Old Town, this 1960s hotel is, in the words of one frequent visitor, "aggressively simple." As such, it's recommended for bargain hunters only. The lounge and reception area is small, and no meals are served—but these are minor concerns. The small guest rooms are clean and functional, and some open onto pleasant views. The attendants speak only a little English, but they're more than willing to try.

Joan Maragall 10, 17002 Girona. ℂ/fax **97-220-44-62.** www.hotelcondalgirona.com. 28 units. 69€ double. AE, DC, MC, V. Parking 16€. *In room:* A/C, TV, hair dryer, Wi-Fi (free).

Hotel Peninsular Devoid of any significant architectural character, this modest hotel provides clean but unremarkable accommodations near the cathedral and the river. The small rooms, which benefited from a 1990 renovation, are scattered over five floors. The hotel is better for short-term stopovers than for prolonged stays. Breakfast is the only meal served.

Av. Sant Francesc 6, 17001 Girona. ℂ **90-273-45-41.** Fax 97-221-04-92. www.novarahotels.com. 45 units. 74€–101€ double. AE, DC, MC, V. Parking 15€ nearby. **Amenities:** Bar; room service. *In room:* TV, hair dryer, Wi-Fi (free).

Hotel Ultonia This small hotel lies a short walk from the Plaça de la Independencia. Since the late 1950s it has been a favorite with business travelers, but today it attracts more tourists because it's close to the historic district. The compact rooms are furnished in a modern style, with comfortable beds. Double-glazed windows keep out the noise. Some of the rooms opening onto the avenue have tiny balconies. In just about 10 minutes, you can cross the Onyar River into the medieval quarter. Guests can enjoy a breakfast buffet (not included in the rates quoted below), but no other meals are served.

Av. Jaume I no. 22, 17001 Girona. ℂ **97-220-38-50.** Fax 97-220-33-34. www.hotelhusaultonia.com. 45 units. 77€–95€ double. AE, DC, MC, V. Nearby parking 15€. **Amenities:** Wi-Fi (3€ per hour, in lobby). *In room:* A/C, TV, minibar.

Places to Stay Near Girona

Hostal de la Gavina ★★★ This is the grandest address in the northeast corridor of Spain. Since it opened in the early 1980s, the Hostal de la Gavina has attracted the rich and glamorous, including King Juan Carlos, Elizabeth Taylor, and a host of celebrities from northern Europe. It's on a peninsula jutting seaward from the center of S'Agaro, within a thick-walled Iberian villa built as the home of the Ansesa family (the hotel's owners) in 1932. Most of the accommodations are in the resort's main building, which has been enlarged and modified. The spacious guest rooms are the most sumptuous in the area, with elegant appointments and deluxe fabrics.

Plaça de la Rosaleda, 17248 S'Agaro (Girona). ✆ **97-232-11-00.** Fax 97-232-15-73. www.lagavina. com. 74 units. 171€–353€ double; 251€–850€ suite. AE, DC, MC, V. Free parking outside; garage 20€. Closed Nov–Apr. **Amenities:** 2 restaurants; 2 bars; babysitting; bikes; health club; 2 pools (1 heated indoor, 1 saltwater outdoor); room service; spa; 2 outdoor tennis courts. *In room:* A/C, TV, hair dryer, minibar, Wi-Fi (free).

Mas de Torrent ★★★ An hour's drive north of Barcelona and a 15-minute drive from the beaches of the Costa Brava, this member of Relais & Châteaux was elegantly created from a 1751 farmstead (*masía*). In the hamlet of Torrent, Mas de Torrent is one of the most artful and best hotels in Spain. Try for one of the 10 rooms in the original farmhouse, with its massive beams and spacious bathrooms with deep tubs and power showers. The rooms in the newer, bungalow-style annex are just as comfortable but lack the mellow old atmosphere. If you can afford it, the suites are the way to go here; each has a private terrace with an individual pool heated with solar panels. From the rooms' stone balconies, visitors can enjoy vistas of the countryside, with Catalonian vineyards in the distance.

Afueras de Torrent, Torrent 17123 Girona. ✆ **97-230-32-92.** Fax 97-230-32-93. www.mas torrent.com. 39 units. 310€–445€ double; 375€–690€ suite. Rates include buffet breakfast. AE, DC, MC, V. Free parking. 37km (23 miles) north of Girona. **Amenities:** 2 restaurants; 2 bars; babysitting; bikes; state-of-the-art health club; 2 freshwater pools (1 heated indoor); room service; spa; outdoor tennis court. *In room:* A/C, TV/DVD, hair dryer, minibar, Wi-Fi (free).

Where to Dine in Girona

Albereda ★★ CATALAN This elegant, classically decorated restaurant in a building from 1848 is the most expensive—and the best—place to dine within the city center. Forgotten herbs, surprising tastes, and colorful vegetables are just part of the vibrant cookery. The menu is adjusted to take advantage of the best shopping at the open-air markets in any season. All the dishes, including starters, main courses, and desserts, are carefully crafted, appearing as "works of art" on your palate. Some dishes that display a pleasing regional accent include whitefish ravioli with a creamy wild-mushroom sauce; confit of cod with asparagus and rice on an aioli sauce of garlic with pesto; and cannelloni stuffed with crabmeat. An old-fashioned, time-tested staple is Girona-style veal steak cooked with truffles in a salt crust.

Albereda 7. ✆ **97-222-6002.** www.restaurantalbereda.com. Reservations required. Fixed-price menus 32€, 40€, 50€, and 60€. AE, DC, MC, V. Tues–Sun 1–4pm and 9–11pm. Closed 2 weeks in Aug.

Casa Marieta ★ CATALAN This is the oldest and most historic restaurant in Girona, with walls of photographs that celebrate the town's modernist movement as well as the opening of its first narrow-gauge railway—in this case between Girona and nearby St. Feliu de Guixols. Set in the heart of town, it specializes in regional Catalan cuisine that's completely dependent on whatever is available at local markets. The best examples include chicken with shrimp, roast lamb, duck with pears, filet steak with flap mushrooms, and fresh grilled fish. A noteworthy regional specialty is a casserole-style *trinxat*, made from rice, ham, cabbage, and potatoes; another is scrambled eggs prepared with pork sausage and prawns. Dessert might include a deliberately undercooked, marvelous slice of white-chocolate cake with house-made ice cream. The restaurant contains five different dining areas, most of them permeated with an Art Nouveau theme, some with stained-glass windows and high-backed banquettes.

Plaça Independencia 5–6. ✆ **97-220-10-16.** www.casamarieta.com. Reservations recommended. Main courses 13€–20€. MC, V. Tues–Sun 1–3:30pm and 8–10:30pm. Closed Feb 8–28.

El Celler de Can Roca ★★★ CATALAN/INTERNATIONAL About 2km (1¼ miles) from the center of town, this is the best of the wave of modern restaurants that have collectively transformed Girona into one of the more fashionable cities of Spain. It was established in 1987 by a trio of brothers (Joán, Jodi, and Josep) whose grandparents first launched the family into the restaurant business in the 1920s. In 2007, the venue moved into dignified newer premises. Cuisine here is about as elegant, upscale, and creative as you're likely to find anywhere in Catalonia, changing according to the seasons and the inspiration of the chef. Oysters with cava or several variations of foie gras might begin your meal, or perhaps you'll start with shrimp soup or a salad of seasonal mushrooms with truffles. Main courses might include codfish braised with spinach, or turbot with goat's milk in a potato shell with mint.

Can Sunyer 48. ✆ **97-222-21-57.** www.cellercanroca.com. Reservations recommended. Main courses 20€–50€; fixed-price menus 80€–125€. AE, DC, MC, V. Tues–Sat 1–4pm and 9–11pm. Closed Dec 24–Jan 15 and 2 weeks in Aug.

NEARBY PLACES TO DINE

El Bulli ★★★ SPANISH/CATALAN Chef Ferran Adrià is hailed as the most exciting chef in Spain. The press has dubbed him the "Salvador Dalí of the kitchen" because of his creative approach to cookery. Joël Robuchon, often called the world's finest chef before his retirement in Paris, has announced that Adrià is worthy of that title. Adrià operates his luxe eatery in the little hamlet of Roses, but many of the most discerning palates in Catalonia seek out this restaurant. Michelin grants it three stars, an accolade most often reserved for the top restaurant of Paris. El Bulli, which means "innovative" in Spanish, lives up to its name. Most guests order a 12-course tasting menu finer than any you'll be served in Barcelona's top restaurants. You never know what's going to appear, but you can expect the most delightful surprises, based on the season's finest produce. One dish alone should give Adrià culinary immortality: his lasagna of calamari. *Travel + Leisure* has hailed El Bulli as "the world's most outrageously creative kitchen," and we concur.

Cala Montjoi, Roses. ✆ **97-215-04-57.** www.elbulli.com. Reservations required. Main courses 32€–42€; *menú de degustación* 215€. AE, DC, MC, V. July–Sept daily 8–10:30pm; Oct–June Wed–Sun 8–10:30pm. From Girona, take N-I north to Figueres, and then Rte. 260 east to Roses, a total of 56km (35 miles).

Sant Pau ★★★ CATALAN/CONTINENTAL The owner of this world-class restaurant has been the subject of feature articles in women's magazines throughout the Spanish-speaking world. She's Carme Ruscalleda, Spain's leading female chef, whose restaurant in the town of Sant Pol de Mar earned a third Michelin star. Established in 1988, it has evolved from a relatively simple delicatessen into one of the culinary landmarks of Spain, replete with the associated fanfare and celebrity-watching. A location midway between Girona (50km/31 miles) and Barcelona (45km/28 miles) helps attract the urban-hipster and grand bourgeois clientele. The setting is a once-private villa on the main street of St. Pol de Mar, near the railway station.

Inside, the setting is restrained, with immaculate contemporary decor and ever-so-polite service. Menu items are noted for the way they pique the intellect as well as the palate. They change frequently, but might include Norwegian lobster with a black-olive froth; boneless scorpion fish with crispy skin, strawberries, and a broth concocted from the fish bones; consommé of squid and duck with the duck's "spicy spleen," kombu seaweed, and the squid's gelatinized ink; stingray without its cartilage, served with roasted apples, citrus juice, pink pepper oil, and the stingray's own deep-fried cartilage; and roasted rabbit with hazelnuts, eggplant, and zucchini.

Carrer Nou 10, in St. Pol de Mar. ☎ **93-760-06-62.** www.ruscalleda.com. Reservations required. Main courses 40€–50€; tasting menu 144€. AE, DC, MC, V. Tues–Wed and Fri–Sun 1–3:30pm; Tues–Sat 9–11pm. From Girona, take N-I about 55km (34 miles) south. Closed for 3 weeks in May and 3 weeks in Nov.

Girona After Dark

Central Girona has a good number of tapas bars and cafes, some of which don't have easily distinguishable names. Many are scattered along **La Rambla,** around the edges of the keynote **Plaça de Independencia,** and within the antique boundaries of the **Plaça Ferrán el Católic.** Moving at a leisurely pace from one to another is considered something of an art form in the sultry heat of Girona's early evenings. Appealing for its crowded conviviality and its impressive roster of shellfish and seafood tapas is **Bar Boira,** Plaça de Independencia 17 (☎ **97-222-29-33**).

Beginning around 11pm, you might want to drop into one or another of the town's discos, the most popular of which is **Disco/Sala de Fiestas Platea,** Jeroni Real de Fontclara 4 (☎ **97-222-72-88**). In the city's oldest core (in a narrow alley just behind Girona's main post office), it's open Wednesday to Sunday from 11pm to 5am.

One of the most appealing things to do in Girona after dark, at least between June and September, is to cross the river into the verdant precincts of **Parque de la Devesa,** an artfully landscaped terrain of stately trees, flowering shrubs, kiosk-style refreshment stands, and open-air bars.

LLORET DE MAR

100km (62 miles) S of the French border, 68km (42 miles) N of Barcelona

Although it has a good half moon–shaped sandy beach, Lloret de Mar is neither chic nor sophisticated, and most people who come here are Europeans on inexpensive package tours. The competition for cheap rooms is fierce.

Lloret de Mar's seaside.

Lloret de Mar has grown at a phenomenal rate, from a small fishing village with just a few hotels to a bustling resort with more hotels than anyone can count. The accommodations are typical of those in other Costa Brava towns, running the gamut from impersonal modern box-type structures to vintage flowerpot-adorned whitewashed buildings on the narrow streets of the Old Town. There are even a few pockets of posh. The area has rich vegetation, attractive scenery, and a mild climate.

Essentials

GETTING THERE From Barcelona, take a **train** to Blanes, and then take a **bus** 8km (5 miles) to Lloret. If you drive, head north from Barcelona along the A-19.

VISITOR INFORMATION The **tourist office,** at Passeig Camprodóni Arrieta 1–2 (*©* **97-236-47-35;** es.lloretdemar.org), is open June to September Monday to Saturday 9am to 8pm, Sunday 10am to 1pm and 4 to 7pm; and October to May Monday to Saturday 9am to 1pm and 4 to 7pm.

Where to Stay in Lloret de Mar

Many of the hotels—particularly the government-rated three-star places—are booked solid by tour groups. Here are some possibilities for those who reserve in advance.

Guitart Monterrey ★★ ☺ This hotel opened in 1940 when the world was at war, but it shut down in 2007 and was completely restored from top to bottom. Reopening in 2008, it's never been better and is now one of the most desirable places to stay along the coast for those seeking a country club atmosphere in a large park, a town center, and beaches. The interior areas have large windows and panoramic views. Guest rooms are spacious and luxuriously decorated, many large enough to contain a lounge area. A lot of the accommodations also open onto private balconies. The restaurants and bars are among the best of any hotel in town, and kids are especially welcomed, with much entertainment provided for them. The **Grand Casino Costa Brava** opened near the hotel at the end of 2009. Designed by the prestigious architect Fermín Vázquez, it is one of the grandest casinos in Spain.

Carretera de Tossa, 17310 Lloret de Mar. ✆ **97-234-60-54.** Fax 97-236-35-12. www.ghmonterrey. com. 200 units. 86€–200€ double; 231€–535€ suite. AE, DC, MC, V. Parking 15€. Closed Oct–Mar. **Amenities:** 3 restaurants; 4 bars; babysitting; bikes; children's center; health club; 2 freshwater pools (1 heated indoor); room service; spa; 3 outdoor tennis courts; extensive watersports equipment/rental. In room: A/C, TV, CD player (in some), hair dryer, Wi-Fi (free).

Hostal Roger de Flor ★ This much-enlarged older hotel, some of which is reminiscent of a private villa, is a pleasant diversion from the aging slabs of concrete filling other sections of the resort. Set at the eastern edge of town, it offers the most pleasant and panoramic views of any hotel. Potted geraniums, climbing bougainvillea, and evenly spaced rows of palms add elegance to the combination of new and old architecture. The midsize rooms are high ceilinged, modern, and excellently furnished. The public rooms contain plenty of exposed wood and spill onto a partially covered terrace.

Turó de l'Estelat s/n, 17310 Lloret de Mar. ✆ **97-236-48-00.** Fax 97-237-16-37. www.husa rogerdeflor.com. 100 units. 130€–210€ double; 170€–270€ suite. Rates include buffet breakfast. AE, DC, MC, V. Free parking. **Amenities:** Restaurant; 2 bars; babysitting; exercise room; outdoor saltwater pool; room service; 2 outdoor tennis courts. In room: TV, hair dryer, minibar.

Hotel Excelsior This hotel attracts a beach-oriented clientele from Spain and northern Europe. The Excelsior sits almost directly on the beach, rising six floors above the esplanade. All but a handful of the rooms offer either frontal or lateral views of the sea. The furniture is modern but uninspiring. During midsummer, half-board is obligatory. Even though the hotel is modest, one of the Costa Brava's greatest restaurants, **Les Petxines,** is located here.

Passeig Mossèn Jacinto Verdaguer 16, 17310 Lloret de Mar. ✆ **97-236-41-37.** Fax 97-237-16-54. www.bestwesternhotelexcelsior.com. 45 units. 45€–150€ double. MC, V. Parking 15€. **Amenities:** Restaurant; babysitting; exercise room; Jacuzzi; sauna. In room: A/C, TV, Wi-Fi (free).

Hotel Santa Marta ★ 👔 This tranquil hotel, a short walk above a crescent-shaped bay favored by swimmers, is nestled in a sun-flooded grove of pines. Both public and guest rooms are attractively paneled and traditionally furnished. The spacious guest rooms offer private balconies overlooking the sea or a pleasant garden. The neighborhood is quiet but desirable, about 2km (1¼ miles) west of the commercial center of town. The **restaurant** (see below) features Catalan cuisine with an international flair, as well as a sweeping view of the sea.

Playa de Santa Cristina, 17310 Lloret de Mar. ✆ **97-236-49-04.** Fax 97-236-92-80. www.hsta marta.com. 78 units. 228€–350€ double. AE, DC, MC, V. Free parking. Closed Nov 9–Feb 12. **Amenities:** 2 restaurants; 2 bars; babysitting; Jacuzzi; outdoor freshwater pool; room service; sauna; 2 outdoor tennis courts. In room: A/C, TV, hair dryer, minibar, Wi-Fi (free).

Rigat Park Hotel ★★ This is a pocket of tranquillity and luxury lying 2km (1¼ miles) from the center of Lloret de Mar on the magnificent Playa de Fanals, one of the best beaches along the Costa Brava. This cozy enclave of Mediterranean plushness is surrounded by a garden of pine and eucalyptus. It looks like a private home of charm and grace. The most desirable of the rooms, all well furnished, are those opening onto the seafront, of course. In the evening, the hotel restaurant is a romantic place to dine by candlelight on an open terrace cooled by sea breezes.

Playa de Fanals, 17310 Lloret de Mar. ☎ **97-236-52-00.** Fax 97-237-04-11. www.rigat.com. 78 units. 203€–363€ double; 342€–475€ suite. AE, DC, MC, V. Free parking. Closed Dec–Feb. **Amenities:** Restaurant; bar; exercise room; Jacuzzi; 2 freshwater pools (1 heated indoor, 1 outdoor); room service; sauna; Wi-Fi (free, in lobby). *In room:* A/C, TV, hair dryer, minibar.

Where to Dine in & Around Lloret de Mar

For grand hotel dining, **Les Petxines** at the Hotel Excelsior (see above) offers a deluxe international cuisine in a formal setting.

El Trull SEAFOOD This restaurant attracts hordes of Spaniards who appreciate the beautiful scenery of the 3km (1¾-mile) trek north of Lloret into the hills. Set in the modern suburb of Urbanización Playa Canyelles, and known for its enduring popularity, El Trull positions its tables within view of a well-kept garden and a (sometimes-crowded) pool. The food is some of the best in the neighborhood. Among the best menu items are Galician-style octopus with potatoes stewed in olive oil; grilled sea cucumbers; and grilled hake with Jerusalem artichokes and chanterelle mushrooms and truffles.

Cala Canyelles s/n. ☎ **97-236-49-28.** www.eltrull.com. Main courses 11€–42€; fixed-price menu 58€. AE, DC, MC, V. Daily 1–4pm and 8–11pm.

Restaurante Santa Marta ★ INTERNATIONAL/CATALAN Set in the recommended 40-year-old hotel about 2km (1¼ miles) west of the commercial center of town, this pleasantly sunny enclave offers well-prepared food and a sweeping view of the beaches and the sea. Menu specialties vary with the season but might include pâté of wild mushrooms in a special sauce; sirloin of veal from Girona flavored with port and served with duck liver; John Dory on a bed of mushrooms; or cod en papillote with seasonal vegetables.

In the Hotel Santa Marta, Playa de Santa Cristina. ☎ **97-236-49-04.** Reservations recommended. Main courses 20€–40€. AE, DC, MC, V. Daily 1:30–3:30pm and 8:30–10:30pm. Closed Nov 9–Feb 12.

Lloret de Mar After Dark

At the **Casino Lloret de Mar,** Carrer Esports 1 (☎ **97-236-61-16;** www. casino-lloret.com), games of chance include French and American roulette, blackjack, and chemin de fer. There's a restaurant, buffet dining room, bar-boîte, and dance club, along with a pool. The casino is southwest of Lloret de Mar, beside the coastal road leading to Blanes and Barcelona. Drive or take a taxi at night and bring your passport for entry. Hours are Sunday through Thursday from 7pm to 3am, Friday and Saturday from 7pm to 4am. (The casino closes 30 min. later in summer.) Admission is free.

The dance club **Hollywood,** Carretera de Tossa (☎ **97-236-74-63;** www. discohollywood.es), at the edge of town on the corner of Carrer Girona, is open nightly 10pm to 5am.

TOSSA DE MAR ★★

90km (56 miles) N of Barcelona, 12km (7½ miles) NE of Lloret de Mar

The gleaming white town of Tossa de Mar, with its 12th-century walls, labyrinthine Old Quarter, fishing boats, and fairly good sand beaches, is perhaps the most attractive base for a Costa Brava vacation. It seems to have more *joie de vivre* than its competitors.

In the 18th and 19th centuries, Tossa survived as a port center, growing rich on the cork industry. But that declined in the 20th century, and many of its citizens immigrated to America. In the 1950s, thanks in part to the Ava Gardner movie *Pandora and the Flying Dutchman,* tourists began to discover the charms of Tossa, and a new industry was born.

To experience these charms, walk through the 12th-century walled town, known as **Vila Vella,** built on the site of a Roman villa from the 1st century A.D. Enter through the Torre de les Hores.

Tossa was once a secret haunt for artists and writers—Marc Chagall called it a "blue paradise." It has two main beaches, **Mar Gran** and **La Bauma.** The coast near Tossa, north and south, offers even more possibilities.

One of the few resorts that has withstood exploitation and retained most of its allure, Tossa enjoys a broad base of international visitors—so many that in summer it's next to impossible to find a room unless reservations are made far in advance.

Essentials

GETTING THERE Direct **bus** service is offered from Blanes and Lloret de Mar. Tossa de Mar is also on the main Barcelona-Palafruggel route. Service from Barcelona is daily from 8:15am to 8:15pm and takes 1½ hours. For information, call ℂ **90-226-06-06** or 93-265-65-08.

To drive, head north from Barcelona along the A-19.

Tossa de Mar.

VISITOR INFORMATION The **tourist office** is at Av. El Pelegrí 25 (© **97-234-01-08;** www.infotossa.com). April, May, and October, it's open Monday to Saturday 10am to 2pm and 4 to 8pm; November to March, Monday to Saturday 10am to 1pm and 4 to 7pm; June to September, Monday to Saturday 9am to 9pm, and Sunday 10am to 2pm and 5 to 8pm.

Where to Stay in Tossa de Mar

VERY EXPENSIVE

Gran Hotel Reymar ★ A triumph of engineering a 10-minute walk southeast of the historic walls—the hotel occupies a position on a jagged rock above the sea edge—this graceful building was constructed in the 1960s and has been renovated several times since. The Reymar has several levels of expansive terraces ideal for sunbathing away from the crowds below. Each good-size guest room has a mix of modern wood-grained and painted furniture, a balcony, and a sea view.

Playa de Mar Menuda, 17320 Tossa de Mar. © **97-234-03-12.** Fax 97-234-15-04. www.best westernghreymar.com. 166 units. 188€–290€ double; 254€–417€ suite. Rates include buffet breakfast. AE, DC, MC, V. Parking 14€. Closed Nov–Apr 17. **Amenities:** Restaurant; 3 bars; babysitting; children's center; exercise room; Jacuzzi; outdoor freshwater pool; room service; sauna; outdoor tennis court. *In room:* A/C, TV, hair dryer, minibar, Wi-Fi (3€ per hour).

MODERATE

Best Western Mar Menuda ★★ 📖 This hotel is a gem, a real Costa Brava hideaway surviving amid tawdry tourist traps and fast-food joints. Its terrace is the area's most panoramic, overlooking the sea and the architectural highlights of the town. The guest rooms range from midsize to spacious, each tastefully furnished and containing a good-size bathroom. The staff is helpful in arranging many watersports, such as scuba diving, windsurfing, and sailing. The cuisine served here is first-class.

Playa de Mar Menuda, 17320 Tossa de Mar. © **800/528-1234** in the U.S., or 97-234-10-00. Fax 97-234-00-87. www.bestwestern.com. 50 units. 75€–194€ double; 90€–227€ suite. Rates include buffet breakfast. AE, DC, MC, V. Free parking. Closed Nov–Dec. **Amenities:** Restaurant; bar; babysitting; children's playground; outdoor freshwater pool; room service. *In room:* A/C, TV, hair dryer, Wi-Fi (free).

Hotel Diana ★ Set back from the esplanade, this government-rated two-star hotel is a former villa designed in part by students of Gaudí. It boasts the most elegant fireplace on the Costa Brava. An inner patio—with towering palms, vines, flowers, and fountains—is almost as popular with guests as the sandy front-yard beach. The spacious rooms contain fine traditional furnishings and modern bathrooms; many open onto private balconies.

Plaça de Espanya 6, 17320 Tossa de Mar. © **97-234-18-86.** Fax 97-234-11-03. www.diana-hotel. com. 21 units. 80€–140€ double; 108€–192€ triple. Rates include buffet breakfast. AE, DC, MC, V. Parking nearby 9€. Closed Nov–Mar 15. **Amenities:** Restaurant; bar; room service. *In room:* A/C, TV, hair dryer, minibar.

INEXPENSIVE

Canaima ☺ Lacking the charm of Hotel Diana (see above), this little inn is the bargain of Tossa de Mar. It lies in a tranquil zone in a residential area 150m (492 ft.) from the beach. The palm trees in this sector of Tossa evoke a real Mediterranean setting. Built in 1963, the hotel bounced back with a series of postmillennium restorations. Most of the midsize guest rooms, each with a tiled bathroom, have a balcony opening onto a view. Since some of the units have three beds, the Canaima is also a family favorite.

Av. La Palma 24, 17320 Tossa de Mar. ℂ **97-234-09-95.** Fax 97-234-09-95. www.hotelcanaima. com. 17 units. 55€–75€ double. Rates include continental breakfast. MC, V. Parking 6€. Closed Oct–Mar. **Amenities:** Terrace bar. *In room:* No phone.

Hotel Cap d'Or ★ 🛏 Perched on the waterfront on a quiet edge of town, this 1790s building nestles against the stone walls and towers of the village castle. Built of rugged stone itself, the Cap d'Or is a combination of old country inn and seaside hotel. The guest rooms come in different shapes and sizes but are decently maintained, each with a good bed and a small bathroom. Although the hotel is a bed-and-breakfast, it does have a terrace on the promenade offering a quick meal.

Passeig de Vila Vella 1, 17320 Tossa de Mar. ℂ/fax **97-234-00-81.** www.hotelcapdor.com. 11 units. 77€–96€ per person double. Rates include buffet breakfast. MC, V. Parking nearby 23€. Closed Nov–Mar. **Amenities:** Restaurant; bar. *In room:* A/C, TV, hair dryer, Wi-Fi (free).

Hotel Neptuno The popular Neptuno sits on a quiet residential hillside northwest of Vila Vella, somewhat removed from the seaside promenade and the bustle of Tossa de Mar's inner core. Built in the 1960s, the hotel was enlarged in the late 1980s. Inside, antiques are mixed with modern furniture. The beamed-ceiling dining room is rustic. The guest rooms are tastefully lighthearted and modern, each with a good bed and a small bathroom. This place is a longtime favorite with northern Europeans, who often book it solid during July and August.

La Guardia 52, 17320 Tossa de Mar. ℂ **97-234-01-43.** Fax 97-234-19-33. www.ghthotels.com. 124 units. 44€–130€ double. Rates include buffet breakfast. AE, DC, MC, V. Parking 16€. Closed mid-Oct to Apr. **Amenities:** Restaurant; bar; outdoor freshwater pool; Wi-Fi (free, in lobby). *In room:* A/C, hair dryer, TV.

Hotel Tonet Opened in the early 1960s, in the earliest days of the region's tourist boom, this family-run pension is one of the Tossa's oldest. Renovated since then, it's on a central plaza surrounded by narrow streets and maintains the ambience of a country inn, with upper-floor terraces where you can relax amid potted vines and other plants. The small guest rooms are rustic, with wooden headboards and simple furniture. The Tonet maintains its own brand of Catalan charm.

Plaça de l'Església 1, 17320 Tossa de Mar. ℂ **97-234-02-37.** Fax 97-234-30-96. www.hoteltonet. com. 36 units. 65€ double. Rates include continental breakfast. AE, DC, MC, V. Nearby parking 10€. **Amenities:** Bar; Internet (free, in lobby). *In room:* TV, no phone.

Where to Dine in Tossa de Mar

Bahía ★ CATALAN Adjacent to the sea, Bahía is well known for a much-awarded chef and a history of feeding hungry vacationers since 1953. Menu favorites are, for the most part, based on time-honored Catalan traditions and include *simitomba* (a grilled platter of fish), *brandade* of cod, baked monkfish, and an array of grilled fish—including *salmonete* (red mullet), *dorada* (gilthead sea bream), and *calamares* (squid)—depending on what's available.

Passeig del Mar 29. ℂ **97-234-03-22.** Reservations recommended. Main courses 12€–40€. AE, DC, MC, V. Daily 1–4pm and 8pm–midnight.

La Cuina de Can Simón ★★★ CATALAN Nine of the most sought-after dining tables in Tossa de Mar are within this charming, cozy, and intimate establishment. During the colder months, a fire might be burning in the stately looking fireplace. The antique, elegantly rustic, stone-sided dining room was originally built in 1741. Its small size allows the hardworking staff to prepare some extremely esoteric courses. Most diners select the *menú gastronómico,* consisting of six refined, brilliantly realized small courses. Expect a seductive, modern repertoire that displays unerring technique and imaginative flavors. Courses, adjusted seasonally, include a minicassoulet of shellfish; oven-roasted duckling with sweet-and-sour sauce; crayfish-stuffed ravioli with caviar and truffle oil; or monkfish suprême with scalloped potatoes and golden-fried sweet onions. The artfully arranged platter of ice cream, pastries, sauces, tarts, and seasonal red fruits is a perfect ending.

Portal 24. ℂ **97-234-12-69.** www.lacuinadecansimon.es. Reservations required. Main courses 21€–48€. AE, DC, MC, V. Daily 1–3pm and 8–10:30pm. Closed Jan 15–Feb 15 and 2 weeks in Nov.

FIGUERES

219km (136 miles) N of Barcelona, 37km (23 miles) E of Girona

In the heart of Catalonia, Figueres once played a role in Spanish history. Philip V wed María Luisa of Savoy here in 1701 in the church of San Pedro, thereby paving the way for the War of the Spanish Succession. But there are two reasons for visiting Figueres today: one of the best restaurants in Spain and the Dalí Museum.

Essentials

GETTING THERE RENFE (ℂ **90-224-02-02;** www.renfe.com) has hourly **train** service between Barcelona and Figueres. All trains between Barcelona and France stop here. It's better and faster to take the train if you're coming from Barcelona. But if you're in Cadaqués (p. 575), four daily SARFA **buses** (ℂ **97-225-87-13**) make the 45-minute trip.

Figueres is a 40-minute drive from Cadaqués. Take the excellent north-south highway, the A-7, either south from the French border at La Jonquera or north from Barcelona, exiting at the major turnoff to Figueres.

VISITOR INFORMATION The **tourist office** is at the Plaça del Sol (ℂ **97-250-31-55;** www.figueresciutat.com). From July to September, the office is open Monday to Saturday 9am to 8pm and Sunday 10am to 3pm; from November to Easter, hours are Monday to Friday 9am to 3pm; and from Easter to June and October, hours are Monday to Friday 9am to 3pm and 4 to 7pm, and Saturday 10am to 2pm and 3:30 to 6:30pm.

The whimsical roof of the Teatre Museu Dalí.

THE MAD, MAD WORLD OF salvador dalí

Salvador Dalí (1904–89) became one of the leading exponents of surrealism, depicting irrational imagery of dreams and delirium in a unique, meticulously detailed style. Famous for his eccentricity, he was called "outrageous, talented, relentlessly self-promoting, and unfailingly quotable." Until his death at age 84, he was the last survivor of the three famous *enfants terribles* of Spain. (The poet García Lorca and the filmmaker Luis Buñuel were the other two.)

For all his international renown, Dalí was born in Figueres and died in Figueres. Most of his works are in the eponymous Theater-Museum there, built by the artist himself around the former theater where his first exhibition was held. Dalí was also buried in the Theater-Museum, next door to the church that witnessed both his christening and his funeral—the first and last acts of a perfectly planned scenario.

Salvador Felipe Jacinto Dalí i Domènech, the son of a highly respected notary, was born on May 11, 1904, in a house on Carrer Monturiol in Figueres. In 1922, he registered at the School of Fine Arts in Madrid and went to live at the prestigious Residencia de Estudiantes. There his friendship with García Lorca and Buñuel had a more enduring effect on his artistic future than his studies at the school. As a result of his undisciplined behavior and the attitude of his father, who clashed with the Primo de Rivera dictatorship over a matter related to elections, the young Dalí spent a month in prison.

In the summer of 1929, the artist René Magritte, along with the poet Paul Eluard and his wife, Gala, came to stay at Cadaqués, and their visit caused sweeping changes in Dalí's life. The young painter became enamored of Eluard's wife; Dalí left his family and fled with Gala to Paris, where he became an enthusiastic member of the surrealist movement. Some of his most famous paintings—*The Great Masturbator, Lugubrious Game,* and

Visiting Dalí

Castell de Púbol ★★ For additional insights into the often bizarre aesthetic sensibilities of Spain's most famous surrealist, consider a 40km (25-mile) trek from Figueres eastward along Highway C-252, following the signs to Parlava. In the village of Púbol, whose permanent population almost never exceeds 200, you'll find the Castell de Púbol. Dating from 1000, it was in partial ruins when Dalí bought it as a residence for his estranged wife, Gala, in 1970, on the condition that he'd come over only when she invited him. (She almost never did.) After her death in 1982, Dalí moved in for 2 years, proceeding to other residences in 1984 after his bedroom mysteriously caught fire one night. Quieter, more serious, and much less surrealistically showy than the houses in Port Lligat and Figueres, the castle is noteworthy for its severe Gothic and Romanesque dignity, and for furniture and decor that reflect the tastes of the surrealist master. (Don't expect a lot of paintings—that's the specialty of the museum at Figueres; see below.) Carrer Gala Salvador Dalí s/n. ✆ **97-248-86-55.** www.salvador-dali.org. Admission 7€ adults, 5€ students, free for children 8 and under. June 15–Sept 15 daily 10am–8pm; Mar 13–June 14 and Sept 16–Nov 1 Tues–Sun 10am–6pm.

Portrait of Paul Eluard—date from his life at Port Lligat, the small Costa Brava town where he lived and worked off and on during the 1930s.

Following Dalí's break with the tenets of the surrealist movement, his work underwent a radical change, with a return to classicism and what he called his mystical and nuclear phase. He became one of the most fashionable painters in the United States and seemed so intent on self-promotion that the surrealist poet André Breton baptized him with the anagram "Avida Dollars." Dalí wrote a partly fictitious autobiography titled *The Secret Life of Salvador Dalí*, and *Hidden Faces*, a novel containing autobiographical elements. These two short literary digressions earned him still greater prestige and wealth, as did his collaborations in the world of cinema (such as the dream set for Alfred Hitchcock's *Spellbound*, 1945) and in those of theater, opera, and ballet.

On August 8, 1958, Dalí and Gala were married according to the rites of the Catholic church in a ceremony performed in the strictest secrecy at the shrine of Els Angels, just a few miles from Girona.

During the 1960s, Dalí painted some very large works, such as *The Battle of Tetuán,* and *Perpignan Railway Station,* a veritable revelation of his paranoid-critical method that relates this center of Dalí's mythological universe to his obsession with painter Jean-François Millet's *The Angelus.*

In 1979, Dalí's health began to decline, and he retired to Port Lligat in a state of depression. When Gala died, he moved to Púbol, where, obsessed by the theory of catastrophes, he painted his last works until he suffered severe burns in a fire that nearly cost him his life. Upon recovery, he moved to the Torre Galatea, a building he had bought as an extension to the museum in Figueres. Here he lived for 5 more years, hardly ever leaving his room, until his death in 1989.

Teatre Museu Dalí ★★★ The internationally known Dalí was as famous for his flamboyance and exhibitionism as he was for his surrealist and often erotic imagery. At the Figueres museum, in the center of town beside the Rambla, you'll find his paintings, watercolors, gouaches, charcoals, pastels, prints, and sculptures, many rendered with seductive and meticulously detailed imagery. His wide-ranging subject matter encompassed such repulsive issues as putrefaction and castration. You'll see, for instance, *The Happy Horse,* a grotesque and lurid purple beast the artist painted during one of his long exiles at Port Lligat. A tour of the museum is an experience. When a catalog was prepared, Dalí said with a perfectly straight face, "It is necessary that all of the people who come out of the museum have false information."

Plaça de Gala-Dalí 5. ✆ **97-267-75-00.** www.salvador-dali.org. Admission 11€ adults, 8€ students and seniors 65 and over, free for children 9 and under. Mar–June and Oct daily 9:30am–5:45pm; Nov–Feb daily 10:30am–5:45pm; July–Sept daily 9am–7:45pm.

Where to Stay & Dine in Figueres

Durán ★ CATALAN This popular place for a top-notch meal in the provinces once claimed Dalí as a loyal patron. You might start with the Catalan salad made with radishes, boiled egg, ham pâté, tuna fish, tomato, and fresh salad greens. Other specialties are steak with Roquefort, *zarzuela* (fish stew), and *filetes de lenguado a la naranja* (sole in orange sauce). Like the Empordá (see below), the Durán specializes in game. If it's available, try the grilled rabbit on a plank, served with white wine. The french fries here, unlike those in most of Spain, are crisp and excellent. Finish off with a rich dessert or at least an espresso. You can also stay at the Durán, in one of its 65 well-furnished rooms, each with bathroom, air-conditioning, and TV. A double goes for 94€ to 125€.

Carrer Lasauca 5, 17600 Figueres. ℂ **97-250-12-50.** Fax 97-267-70-46. www.hotelduran.com. Reservations required. Main courses 14€–29€. AE, DC, MC, V. Daily 12:30–4pm and 8:30–11pm.

Empordá ★★★ CATALAN You might have your finest meal in the area at this restaurant. Don't judge the place by its ordinary appearance; there's nothing ordinary about the cuisine, as all the food-loving French who cross the border to dine here can attest. This family-run restaurant, .8km (½ mile) north of the town center, gained an early reputation among U.S. military personnel in the area for subtly prepared game and fish dishes. Salvador Dalí (who wrote his own cookbook) and Josep Pla, perhaps the country's greatest 20th-century writer, were fans. The appetizers are the finest along the Costa Brava, including duck foie gras with Armagnac, warm pâté of *rape* (monkfish) with garlic mousseline, and fish soup with fennel. The outstanding fish and seafood dishes include cuttlefish in Catalan sauce, suprême of sea bass with flan made with fennel and anchovy, and brochette of grilled baby squids in vinaigrette. Among the meat selections are the chef's special *lieure à la royale* (hare), beef filet in red-wine sauce with onion marmalade, and goose in a delectable mushroom sauce. You can also stay in one of the 42 midsize rooms here, each with air-conditioning and TV. Doubles run 102€ to 134€, while suites are 160€ to 197€.

Av. Salvador Dalí 170. ℂ **97-250-05-62.** www.hotelemporda.com. Reservations required. Main courses 15€–36€; fixed-price menu 31€. AE, DC, MC, V. Daily 12:45–3:30pm and 8:30–10:30pm.

Hotel Pirineos This pleasant hotel near the main road leading to the center of town is a 5-minute walk from the Dalí museum. Many of the comfortable but small rooms have balconies. Furnishings are rather plain, although the beds are good and the bathrooms are neat. The hotel was last renovated in 2005 and has been well maintained ever since.

Av. Salvador Dalí 68, 17600 Figueres. ℂ **97-250-03-12.** Fax 97-250-07-66. www.hotel pirineospelegri.com. 56 units. 62€–78€ double. AE, DC, MC, V. Parking 10€. **Amenities:** 2 restaurants; bar. *In room:* A/C, TV, Wi-Fi (free).

Hotel President Since 1970, this has been one of the most desirable hotels in town because of its location in the town's center, a 5-minute walk from the Dalí museum. An austere exterior belies the welcoming comfort inside. The midsize guest rooms are neutrally decorated, with comfortable beds and tiled bathrooms.

Av. Salvador Dalí 82, 17600 Figueres. ℂ **97-250-17-00.** Fax 97-250-19-97. www.hotelpresident. info. 76 units. 85€–95€ double. DC, MC, V. Free parking. **Amenities:** Restaurant; bar; room service. *In room:* A/C, TV, hair dryer.

Cadaqués's waterfront.

Hotel Ronda 🛥 A 10-minute walk from the Dalí museum, this hotel has been welcoming travelers since the 1970s. You are housed in comfort (at a very low price) in a typically Catalan building with an unpretentious facade; the building has conventional Mediterranean-style white walls, ample balconies, and simple decorations. The small guest rooms are clean and simple, each with a plain bathroom. The hotel is popular with budget-minded Europeans, so reservations in summer are highly recommended.

Ronda Barcelona 104, 17600 Figueres. 📞 **97-250-39-11.** Fax 97-250-16-82. www.hotelronda. com. 52 units. 60€–100€ double. AE, MC, V. Parking 9.50€. **Amenities:** Restaurant; bar. *In room:* A/C, TV, hair dryer, Wi-Fi (free).

CADAQUÉS ★★

196km (122 miles) N of Barcelona, 31km (19 miles) E of Figueres

Cadaqués is still unspoiled and remote, despite the publicity it received when Salvador Dalí lived in the next-door village of Lligat (in a split-level house surmounted by a giant egg). The last resort on the Costa Brava before the French border, Cadaqués is reached by a small road winding over the mountains from Rosas, the nearest major center. When you get to Cadaqués, you really feel off the beaten path. The village winds around half a dozen small coves, with a narrow street running along the water's edge. This street has no railing, so exercise caution.

Scenically, Cadaqués is a knockout: crystal-blue water, fishing boats on the sandy beaches, old whitewashed houses, narrow twisting streets, and a 16th-century parish up on a hill.

Essentials

GETTING THERE Three to four **buses** per day run from Figueres to Cadaqués. Trip time is 1¼ hours. The service is operated by SARFA (📞 **97-225-87-13**). Driving from Barcelona, follow the A-7 northeast until you come to the town of Figueres, where you'll see signs leading east to Cadaqués.

VISITOR INFORMATION The **tourist office,** Cotxe 2 (📞 **97-225-83-15**), is open Monday to Saturday 9am to 2pm and 3 to 8pm, and Sunday 10:30am to 1pm.

Where to Stay in Cadaqués

Hostal S'Aguarda 🎣 On the road winding above Cadaqués on the way to Port Lligat, this *hostal* has a panoramic view of the village's harbor and medieval church. Each of the modern, airy rooms opens onto a flower-decked terrace. They have tiled floors and simple furniture, along with well-equipped bathrooms.

Carretera de Port Lligat 30, 17488 Cadaqués. ℂ **97-225-80-82.** Fax 97-225-10-57. www.hotelsaguarda.com. 28 units. 50€–148€ double. AE, DC, MC, V. Free parking. Closed Nov. **Amenities:** Bar; outdoor freshwater pool; room service. *In room:* A/C, TV, hair dryer.

Hotel Playa Sol In a relatively quiet section of the port along the bay, this 1950s hotel offers the best view of the stone church at the distant edge of the harbor. The balconied building is constructed of brick and terra-cotta tiles. The small rooms are comfortably furnished. The hotel doesn't have an official restaurant, but it does offer lunch from June 15 to September 15.

Platja Planch 3, 17488 Cadaqués. ℂ **97-225-81-00.** Fax 97-225-80-54. www.playasol.com. 50 units. 73€–191€ double. AE, DC, MC, V. Parking 10€–14€. Closed Nov 9–Feb 12. **Amenities:** Bar; bikes; Jacuzzi; outdoor freshwater pool; room service; outdoor tennis court. *In room:* A/C, TV, hair dryer, Wi-Fi (free).

Llane Petit 🎣 This little inn of considerable charm is located below the better-known Hotel Rocamar and opens right onto the beach. A hospitable place, it offers decent-size guest rooms and well-maintained bathrooms. All accommodations open onto small terraces. The owners keep the hotel under constant renovation during the slow months so that it is always fresh when the summer hordes descend. The hotel's small dinner-only restaurant is recommended, as the cuisine is well prepared and most affordable.

Doctor Bartomeus 37, 17488 Cadaqués. ℂ **97-225-10-20.** Fax 97-225-87-78. www.llanepetit.com. 37 units. 60€–150€ double. DC, MC, V. Free parking. Closed Nov 3–Feb 5. **Amenities:** Bar; outdoor freshwater pool; room service. *In room:* A/C, TV, Wi-Fi (free).

Rocamar ☺ At the beach, this government-rated three-star hotel is one of the better choices in town, attracting a fun-loving crowd of young northern Europeans in summer. All the accommodations are well furnished, with rustic yet comfortable pieces; the small bathrooms are adequate. The rooms in front have balconies opening onto the sea, while those in back have balconies with views of the mountains and beyond. The hotel is known for its good food served at affordable prices.

Doctor Bartomeus, 17488 Cadaqués. ℂ **97-225-81-50.** Fax 97-225-86-50. www.rocamar.com. 70 units. 74€–220€ double; 150€–321€ suite. Rates include buffet breakfast. AE, DC, MC, V. Free parking. **Amenities:** Restaurant; bar; babysitting; children's playground; Jacuzzi; 2 freshwater pools (1 heated indoor, 1 outdoor); room service; sauna; outdoor tennis court; Wi-Fi (free, in lobby). *In room:* A/C, TV, hair dryer.

Where to Dine in Cadaqués

The summer town of Cadaqués sees restaurants come and go, some hardly surviving for one season. Many guests in summer wander the back streets looking for a little eatery. There are several along Calle Miguel Rosset off Plaça Frederic Rahola. Cadaqués doesn't have a world-class restaurant as of yet.

Canshelabi CATALAN/MOROCCAN "Shelabi," the owner's nickname, has brought a little enclave of North Africa to this oasis. He prepares a number of

Catalan dishes for local palates, but his heart lies in his Moroccan specialties. He makes some of the best tajines along the coast. This is a couscous stew served in a ceramic "chimney pot," and it tastes authentically North African. In the afternoon, as the beach lovers head back to their hotels, many stop in here for a sweet mint tea just like that served in the Casbah.

Calle Riera 9. (© **97-225-89-00.** Reservations not needed. Main courses 17€–28€. MC, V. Daily 11am–2am.

Cadaqués After Dark

The distinctive **L'Hostal,** Paseo 8A (© **97-225-80-00**), has attracted some of the most glamorous names in the art and music worlds. Some music critics have called it the second-best jazz club in Europe, and it certainly rates as the best club along the coast. It's a Dixieland bar par excellence, run by the most sophisticated entrepreneurial team in town. Habitués remember when Salvador Dalí escorted Mick Jagger here, much to the delight of Colombian writer Gabriel García Márquez. In fact, the bar's logo was designed by Dalí himself. Heightening the ambience are the dripping candles, the high ceilings, and the heavy Spanish furniture. The best music is usually performed late at night. The club is open daily from 11am to 5am. Entrance is free.

Sights in & Around Cadaqués

The landmark of Cadaqués is the **Església de Santa María,** Calle Eliseu Meifren, a 16th-century Gothic church with a baroque altar. It is one of the most easterly churches in Spain. It stands in the old section of town, dominating the narrow hilly streets. Hours are not written in stone. Usually it can be visited daily from 9am to 5pm, but don't count on that.

Museo de Cadaqués, Carrer de Narcis Monturiol 15 (© **97-225-88-77**), displays rotating art exhibits, most often spinning around the incomparable Dalí. It is open mid-June to September daily 11am to 1:30pm and 4 to 8:30pm, charging 5€ for adults, 3.50€ for students and children.

From this museum it is only a half-hour walk to **Casa-Museo Salvador Dalí,** in Port Lligat (© **97-225-10-15;** www.salvador-dali.org), 3km (1¾ miles) from the town center along the beach. This was Dalí's summer house where he lived with Gala, his muse and spouse. Famous friends were frequent visitors, including poet Federico García Lorca and the filmmaker Luis Buñuel. This museum forms part of the "Dalí triangle," which includes the Teatre Museu Dalí at Figueres (p. 573) and the castle at Púbol (p. 572). Only two Dalí works remain in the house, including a lip-shaped sofa and a pop-art miniature of Granada's Alhambra. Overlooking the beach, the fisherman's house has amusing little white-chimney pots and two egg-shaped towers. Hours are mid-June to mid-September, daily 9:30am to 9pm. From mid-September to November and mid-March to mid-June, hours are Tuesday to Sunday 10:30am to 6pm. Admission is 10€ for adults or 8€ for children, students, and seniors. Reservations are mandatory to visit the museum.

15

ARAGÓN

Landlocked Aragón, along with Navarre, forms the northeastern quadrant of Spain. It is an ancient land composed of three provinces: Zaragoza; remote Teruel, which is farther south; and Huesca, in the north as you move toward the Pyrenees. These are also the names of the provinces' three major cities.

Most of Aragón constitutes terra incognita for the average tourist—which is unfortunate, since it is one of the most history-rich regions of the country. You can visit it as an extension of your trip to Castile to the west, or as a segment of your trek through Catalonia to the east. Huesca, close to the mountains, is ideal for a summer visit—unlike most of Aragón, especially the fiercely hot southern section, which has Spain's worst climate. Winter is often bitterly cold, but spring and autumn are ideal.

Aragón is known best for two former residents: Catherine of Aragón, who foolishly married Henry VIII of England; and Catherine's father, Ferdinand of Aragón, whose marriage to Isabella, queen of Castile and León in the 15th century, led to the unification of Spain.

Aragón also prides itself on its exceptional Mudéjar architecture and on its bullfighting tradition. In September many villages in the region have their own festivals, when bulls run through the streets. What they don't have is the good promotion that Hemingway gave the festival at Pamplona, in the neighboring province of Navarre. On the other hand, they aren't plagued with wine-drunk tourists—the curse of the Pamplona festival. In folklore, Aragón is known for the *jota*, a bounding, leaping dance performed by men and women since at least the 1700s.

Aragón's capital, **Zaragoza,** is the most visited destination in the region because it lies on the main route between Madrid and Barcelona. If you're driving from Madrid to Barcelona (or vice versa), make a detour to Zaragoza. If Aragón interests you while there, stick around to explore this ancient land.

ZARAGOZA ★★

322km (200 miles) NE of Madrid, 306km (190 miles) W of Barcelona

Zaragoza (pronounced Thah-rah-*goh*-thah) lies halfway between Madrid and Barcelona. This provincial capital, the seat of the ancient kingdom of Aragón, is a bustling, prosperous, commercial city of wide boulevards and arcades.

Zaragoza has not one but two cathedrals and, like Santiago de Compostela in Galicia, was a major pilgrimage center. According to legend, the Virgin Mary appeared to St. James, patron saint of Spain, on the banks of the Ebro River and ordered him to build a church there.

Zaragoza is at the center of a rich *huerta*, or plain. Its history dates from the time of the Romans, who called it Caesar Augusta. Today, Zaragoza is a city of more than 750,000 people, just less than 75% of the entire population of Aragón.

FACING PAGE: **The gardens of the Monasterio de Piedra.**

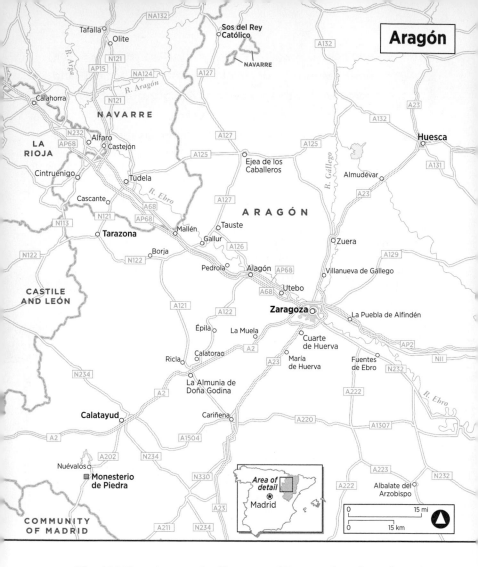

The 40,000 students at the University of Zaragoza have livened up this once-staid city. Cafes, theaters, restaurants, music bars, and *tascas* (tapas bars) have boomed in recent years, and more monuments have been restored and opened to the public.

Essentials

GETTING THERE Iberia (© 90-240-05-00; www.iberia.com/us) has direct **flights** to Zaragoza from Madrid and Barcelona. From the airport in Zaragoza, you can get a bus to the Plaza de San Francisco.

A total of 28 **trains** arrive daily from Barcelona (trip time: 3½–4½ hr.) and 17 from Madrid (3 hr.). Trains pull into Estación Zaragoza-Delcias, Calle Rioja 33 (© 90-224-02-02).

There is one direct **bus** a day between Zaragoza and Barcelona (3½ hr.).
By car, Zaragoza is easily reached on the E-90 (A-2) east from Madrid
or west from Barcelona.

VISITOR INFORMATION The **tourist office,** Plaza del Pilar s/n (*©* **90-214-
20-08;** www.turismozaragoza.com), is open daily April to October 9am to
9pm, and November to March 10am to 8pm.

SPECIAL EVENTS One of the city's big festivities is the **Fiesta de la Virgen del
Pilar,** held the week of October 12, with top-name bullfighters, religious
processions, and general merriment.

Seeing the Sights in Zaragoza

Basílica de Nuestra Señora del Pilar ★ This 16th- and 17th-century basilica on the bank of the Ebro River has an almost Asian style with its domes and
towers. Thousands of the faithful travel here annually to pay homage to the tiny
statue of the *Virgen del Pilar* in the Holy Chapel. The name of the cathedral,
El Pilar, comes from the pillar upon which the Virgin is supposed to have stood
when she asked Santiago (St. James) to build the church. During the second
week of October, the church is a backdrop for an important festival devoted to
Our Lady of the Pillar, with parades, bullfights, fireworks, flower offerings, and
street dancing. Also of interest within the church are frescoes painted by Goya,
who was born nearby.

You can also visit the **Museo del Pilar,** which houses the jewelry collection used to adorn the Pilar statue as well as sketches by Goya and other artists,
including both Bayeu brothers. Much of the collection is ancient.

Plaza de las Catedrales. *©* **97-629-95-64.** Free admission to cathedral; museum 1.50€. Cathedral Tues–Sun 7am–8:30pm; museum daily 9am–2pm and 4–6pm. Bus: 22 or 23.

La Seo del Salvador ★★ This Gothic-Mudéjar church, built between 1380
and 1550, is more impressive than El Pilar (see above). It has a rich baroque
and Plateresque facade and is a particularly fine example of Aragonese Gothic

The dome of La Seo del Salvador.

architecture. Among its more important features are the main altar and a fine collection of French and Flemish tapestries from the 15th to the 17th centuries, which are housed in the adjacent museum. The baroque cupolas in the Temple of Pilar were decorated by Goya and Bayeu.

Plaza de la Seo. ☎ **97-629-12-311.** Museum 3€. Nov–Apr Tues–Sun 10am–2pm and 4–6pm; May–Oct Tues–Sun 10am–2pm and 4–7pm. Bus: 21, 22, 29, 32, 35, 36, 43, 44, or 45.

Museo de Zaragoza This museum is installed in a 1908 building with 10 ground-floor rooms devoted to exhibits from the prehistoric to the Muslim periods. The Roman legacy (nos. 4–8) has sculptures (including a bust of Augustus), mosaics, and ceramics. The fine-arts section includes paintings by Goya (no. 20); you can see one of his self-portraits there. In the next room, you'll find his drawings, *Los Caprichos (The Whims)*. Also displayed is a Goya portrait of Carlos IV and his wife. The museum is directly north of Paseo de Marino Moreno.

Plaza de los Sitios 6. ☎ **97-622-21-81.** Free admission. Tues–Sat 9am–2pm and 5–8pm; Sun 10am–2pm. Bus: 30, 35, or 40.

Museo Pablo Gargallo This museum honors sculptor Pablo Gargallo, born in Maella in 1881. It is installed in a beautiful Aragonese Renaissance–style palace (1659) that was declared a national monument in 1963. Gargallo, influential in the art world of the 1920s, is represented by 100 original works, ranging from *Dr. Petit's Fireplace* (1904) to *Great Prophet*, a bronze piece from 1933. The museum is located in the center, a 5-minute walk south of El Pilar.

Plaza de San Felipe 3. ☎ **97-672-49-22.** Free admission. Tues–Sat 10am–2pm and 5–9pm; Sun 10am–2pm. Bus: 35 or 36.

Where to Stay in Zaragoza

EXPENSIVE

Boston ★★ This hotel, which opened in 1992, lies in the heart of Zaragoza's modern business district, a 15-minute walk from the medieval neighborhoods that most visitors want to explore. Named in honor of Boston, Massachusetts, where the building's architect earned his degree, it's the city's best hotel and one of the tallest buildings in town. Throughout, the style is ultramodern, even futuristic, strongly infused with postmodern design and American ideas. The guest rooms are the town's finest—usually spacious, with modern comforts and well-maintained bathrooms.

Av. de las Torres 28, 50008 Zaragoza. ☎ **97-659-91-92.** Fax 97-659-74-10. www.hotelboston.es. 312 units. 120€–275€ double; 250€–300€ junior suite; 600€–800€ suite. AE, DC, MC, V. Parking 20€. Bus: 29. **Amenities:** Restaurant; bar; babysitting; exercise room; room service; sauna. *In room:* A/C, TV, hair dryer, minibar, Wi-Fi (free).

Hiberus ★★ This deluxe property lies next to the trade fair site on the edge of Zaragoza, a short ride from the center of the city. Its well maintained and beautifully furnished bedrooms open onto panoramic views of the River Ebro. The government-rated five-star property lies in well-landscaped garden areas with palm-tree-shaded squares and terraces. The breakfast buffet is among the most generous in town. The hotel's gourmet restaurant, **Celebris,** serves an avant-garde cuisine, based on traditional products, and in summer you can dine on the outdoor terrace.

Paseo De los Puentes 2, 50018 Zaragoza. ☏ **87-654-20-08.** Fax 87-654-20-09. www.pala foxhoteles.com. 176 units. 260€–365€ double; 475€ suite. AE, DC, MC, V. Parking 16€. **Amenities:** 2 restaurants; bar; cafe; exercise room; pool (outdoor); room service; spa. *In room:* A/C, TV, minibar, Wi-Fi (free).

Hotel Palafox ★ One of the top hotels in town, the Palafox looks somewhat like an apartment house. It was inaugurated in 1982 and rates five stars from the government. A favorite of business travelers, it frequently hosts local events such as fashion shows. The midsize rooms have sleek traditional styling and are well maintained and comfortable, with quality beds.

Calle Casa Jiménez s/n, 50004 Zaragoza. ☏ **97-623-77-00.** Fax 97-623-47-05. www.palafox hoteles.com. 179 units. 100€–223€ double; 200€–342€ suite. AE, MC, V. Parking 21€. Bus: 22, 30, or 40. **Amenities:** Restaurant; bar; babysitting; exercise room; outdoor pool; room service; sauna. *In room:* A/C, TV, fax, hair dryer, minibar, Wi-Fi (6.50€ per hour).

NH Gran Hotel ★ 🎁 Nearly a kilometer (½ mile) south of the cathedral, behind one of the most beautiful Hispano–Art Deco facades in town, this hotel is the most historic and charming in Zaragoza and a good value. Established by King Alfonso XIII in 1929, the Gran has an array of public areas and conference facilities. Guest rooms have been restored into a neutral, standard international style, and all have neatly kept bathrooms with tub/shower combos. A favorite of the business community, the hotel offers excellent service. Hemingway and one of his biographers, A. E. Hotchner, stayed at the Gran when they were in Zaragoza.

Joaquín Costa 5, 50001 Zaragoza. ☏ **97-622-19-01.** Fax 97-623-67-13. www.nh-hoteles.com. 134 units. 90€–196€ double; from 139€ junior suite; from 298€ suite. AE, DC, MC, V. Parking 16€. **Amenities:** Restaurant; bar; babysitting; exercise room; room service; sauna. *In room:* A/C, TV, hair dryer, minibar, Wi-Fi (22€ per 24 hr.).

MODERATE

Hesperia Zaragoza This hotel in the historic center, a 5-minute walk from the basilica of El Pilar, has welcomed guests since 1994. A plain, modern exterior opens to reveal a marble-floor lobby where you'll encounter an efficient staff. There is no great stylishness here, but your comfort is ensured. The guest rooms are small but well furnished and inviting.

Conde de Aranda 48, 50003 Zaragoza. ☏ **97-628-45-00.** Fax 97-628-27-17. www.hesperia-zaragoza.com. 86 units. 62€–155€ double. AE, DC, MC, V. Parking 13€. **Amenities:** Restaurant; bar; babysitting; room service. *In room:* A/C, TV, fax, hair dryer, minibar, Wi-Fi (free).

Husa Vía Romana ★ 🏨 This is a real find in the Old Town, a government-rated three-star hotel that is welcoming and comfortable, especially if you want to cover Zaragoza on foot. The 1988 hotel has been beautifully restored, with a well-trained staff and inviting midsize rooms with good furnishings and comfortable beds. For some reason, this hotel is fully booked in October, but you can easily make a reservation during other months.

Calle de Don Jaime I nos. 54–56, 50001 Zaragoza. ☏ **97-639-82-15.** Fax 97-629-05-11. www. husa.es. 66 units. 60€–180€ double. AE, DC, MC, V. Parking 15€ nearby. **Amenities:** Restaurant; bar; room service. *In room:* A/C, TV, hair dryer, minibar, Wi-Fi (15€ per 24 hr.).

INEXPENSIVE

Hotel Gran Vía ⚓ This hotel on the Paseo Gran Vía, near the Church of Santa Engracia and close to the main shopping district, lacks character but it is modern, welcoming, and comfortable, with bedrooms at very reasonable prices. You don't get a lot of frills here, as the rooms are small and functional, but the white walls, carpeted floors, excellent beds, and tidy bathrooms make for a restful stopover.

Calle Gran Vía 38, 50005 Zaragoza. 🕾 **97-622-92-13.** Fax 97-622-07-07. www.granviahotel. com. 47 units. 99€ double. AE, DC, MC, V. Parking 16€. **Amenities:** Bar; room service. *In room:* A/C, TV, hair dryer, minibar.

Hotel Las Torres ⚓ This budget hotel takes its name from its balcony views of El Pilar. Directly opposite the cathedral of Zaragoza, it is a good choice if you're not too demanding. Bedrooms are small but well equipped and decently maintained with comfortable, motel-standard furniture. You can find better hotels than this in town, but not one this conveniently located. *Take note:* Light sleepers beware—those church bells sound every 15 minutes throughout the night.

Plaza del Pilar 11, 50003 Zaragoza. 🕾 **97-639-42-50.** Fax 97-639-42-54. www.hotellastorres. com. 69€–79€ double. AE, DC, MC, V. Parking 14€. **Amenities:** Cafeteria. *In room:* A/C, TV, hair dryer, Wi-Fi (free).

Zenit Don Yo ⚓ Of course, you have to check out this place because of its intriguing name. Right in the center of town at the Plaza de Aragón and Plaza de la Independencia, it is a favorite among local journalists and draws a large repeat clientele among the business communities of Madrid and Barcelona. The hotel offers quiet, personal service, but it's not strong on atmosphere. The midsize rooms are well furnished, though not particularly stylish, but you'll find them to be well maintained and relaxing, with especially good beds. For comfort and good value, Don Yo is an appealing choice.

Juan Bruil 4–6, 50001 Zaragoza. 🕾 **97-622-67-41.** Fax 97-621-99-56. www.zenithoteles.com. 147 units. 70€–80€ double; from 102€ junior suite. AE, DC, MC, V. Parking 13€. **Amenities:** Restaurant; bar; room service. *In room:* A/C, TV, fax, hair dryer, minibar, Wi-Fi (free).

Where to Dine in Zaragoza

La Mar ★★ SEAFOOD This is the top seafood restaurant in town. Service is leisurely, but if you're in the mood for a prolonged meal, the menu might include a full range of seasonal vegetables, peppers stuffed with seafood mousse, *dorada* (gilthead sea bream) cooked in a salt crust, baked sea bream, turbot with clams, grilled hake or monkfish, grilled squid, shellfish soup, or shellfish rice. If you're not in the mood for fish, try the grilled beefsteak with several choices of sauce.

Plaza Aragón 12. 🕾 **97-621-22-64.** www.restaurantelamar.com. Reservations recommended. Main courses 17€–32€; fixed-price menu 65€. AE, DC, MC, V. Mon–Sat 1:30–3:30pm and 9–11:30pm.

La Rinconada de Lorenzo ★ ARAGONESE One of the best in town, this restaurant offers such unusual dishes as fried rabbit with snails. Oven-roasted lamb or lamb hock can be ordered in advance, but lamb skewers are always available. The chef prepares several versions of *migas* (fried bread crumbs) flavored with a number of ingredients, including grapes and ham. Even though Zaragoza is inland, fresh fish is always on the menu: hake, grilled sole, sea bream, and salmon, for example. Veal is featured on the menu with wild boar and veal ribs, as well as veal meatballs served in a bean stew. Desserts are all homemade. Regional wines make fine accompaniments.

Calle La Salle 3. ✆ **97-655-51-08.** www.larinconadadelorenzo.com. Reservations required. Main courses 6€–16€; fixed-price menu 20€–30€. AE, DC, MC, V. Mon–Sat noon–4pm and daily 8–11:30pm (closed Mon July–Aug). Bus: 20, 30, 35, 40, 41, or 45.

Los Borrachos SPANISH/FRENCH Committed to preserving an old-fashioned kind of service, this restaurant occupies a formal set of dining rooms near the heart of town. Menu items may include a combination platter of hake with lobster, wild boar with wine sauce, filet of beef with a pepper-cognac sauce, roasted pheasant, and an asparagus mousse accented with strips of Serrano ham. This restaurant's name, incidentally, translates as "the Drunkards," taken from the characters in a famous Velázquez painting.

Paseo de Sagasta 64. ✆ **97-627-50-36.** Reservations recommended. Main courses 18€–24€; tasting menu 30€–40€. DC, MC, V. Tues–Sat 1–4pm and 9pm–midnight.

Risko Mar BASQUE/NAVARRESE One of Zaragoza's most consistently reliable restaurants occupies a 1970s building that sits in the heart of the city's busiest commercial zone, a short walk from El Corte Inglés department store and lots of other shops and boutiques. Within a pair of wood-paneled, red-toned dining rooms, you'll rub elbows with a busy workaday crowd of Spaniards, some of whom memorized the menu long ago and simply tell the waiters what they feel like eating that day. The best items include fresh fish, pork, veal, and beefsteaks, as well as a popular version of roasted suckling lamb prepared with herbs, vegetables, and drippings. *Merluza Risko Mar* (house-style hake served with fresh clams, baby eels, and green sauce) is a justifiably celebrated house specialty.

Calle Francisco de Vitoria 16–18. ✆ **97-622-50-53.** Reservations recommended. Main courses 20€–46€; *menú de degustación* 40€. AE, DC, MC, V. Daily 1:30–3:30pm; Mon–Sat 9–11:30pm. Closed 2 weeks at Easter. Bus: 33.

Zaragoza After Dark

Zaragoza seems sleepy and low-key until after around 11pm, when things perk up. A good place to begin an evening's bar- and pub-crawl is Plaza Santa Cruz.

A popular tapas bar worth a visit is **Casa Luis,** Romea 8 (✆ **97-629-11-67**), whose array of shellfish tapas includes oysters, shrimp, and razor clams in little bundles. It's open most of the year (closed in June and last 3 weeks of Nov) Tuesday to Sunday 1 to 4pm and 8pm to midnight. A glass of house wine costs 1.50€, and the tapas range from 1.50€ to 5€.

If you want to just barhop and try different *tascas,* most of which aren't even identified with signs, consider a promenade along Calle Dr. Cerrada (near Plaza Pamplona), nearby Calle Dr. Casas, or Calle La Paz.

Other hot spots around town include **Bull McCabe's,** Calle Cádiz 7 (✆ **97-622-50-16;** www.bullmccabes.net), hailed by its patrons as the best Irish pub in Aragón. It's spread across two floors, hawking pizza and sports on big TV screens. It closes down at 2:30am every morning. McCabe's is for boys who like girls; boys who like boys should head to **Mick Havanna,** Calle Ramón Pignatelli 7 (✆ **97-628-44-50**), with its long bar peopled by hotties and its zebra-striped wallpaper. Open daily 5pm to 2am.

TARAZONA

88km (55 miles) W of Zaragoza, 293km (182 miles) NE of Madrid

To call Tarazona the "Toledo of Aragón" may be a bit much, but it does deserve the name "Mudéjar City." Located about halfway along the principal route connecting Zaragoza to the province of Soria, it is laid out in tiers above the quays of the Queiles River. Once the kings of Aragón lived here, and before that, the city was known to the Romans. You can walk through the old barrio with its tall facades and narrow medieval streets.

A relief on the facade of Tarazona's Ayuntamiento.

Essentials

GETTING THERE From Zaragoza, six **buses** leave daily for Tarazona. Trip time is 1 hour, and a one-way fare costs 6.50€. For bus information and schedules, contact Therpasa (✆ **97-622-57-23;** www.therpasa.es). If you're driving, head west from Zaragoza along the A-68, connecting with the N-122 to Tarazona.

VISITOR INFORMATION The tourist office, at Plaza San Francisco 1 (✆ **97-664-00-74;** www.tarazona.org), is open daily 9am to 1:30pm and 4:30 to 7pm.

Exploring Tarazona

Tarazona's major attraction is its Gothic **cathedral,** begun in 1152 but essentially reconstructed in the 15th and 16th centuries. The Aragonese Mudéjar style is still much in evidence, especially in the lantern tower and belfry. You can, of course, view the cathedral from the outside, but the interior is closed indefinitely due to ongoing restoration.

The town is also known for its 16th-century **Ayuntamiento (Town Hall),** which has reliefs across its facade depicting Ferdinand and Isabella retaking Granada. The monument stands on the Plaza de España in the older upper part of town, on a hill overlooking the river. Take the Ruta Turística, a scenic walk, from here up to the church of **Santa Magdalena,** with a Mudéjar tower that forms the chief landmark of the town's skyline; its mirador opens onto a panoramic view. Continuing up the hill, you reach **La Concepción,** another church with a narrow brick tower.

Where to Stay & Dine in Tarazona

Brujas de Bécquer Nearly a kilometer (½ mile) southeast of town beside the road leading to Zaragoza, you'll find this unpretentious modern hotel, built in 1972 and renovated several times since. Guest rooms are modest but comfortable and bathrooms are neatly kept with shower stalls. The dining room serves delicious fixed-price meals, and reservations are almost never needed. The hotel, incidentally, was named in honor of a 19th-century Seville-born patriot and poet (Gustavo Adolfo Bécquer) who praised the beauties of Aragón in some of his writing.

Teresa Cajal 30, 50500 Tarazona. 🕿 **97-664-04-04.** Fax 97-664-01-98. www.hotelbrujas.com. 56 units. 60€–75€ double. AE, DC, MC, V. Parking garage 9€. **Amenities:** Restaurant. *In room:* A/C, TV, hair dryer, Wi-Fi (free).

Condes de Visconti ★ At long last a hotel has stolen the thunder from the long-reigning Brujas de Bécquer (see above). This is now the finest and most elegant nest in town, installed in a restored palace whose origins date from the 16th century. The decoration is often whimsical, even elegant, a medley of modern and traditional. Many of the spacious bedrooms are decorated in the romantic style, with draped beds. Objects of art and designer lamps, among other touches, add a certain glamour.

Calle Visconti 15, 50500 Tarazona. 🕿 **97-664-0074.** Fax 97-664-1858. www.condesdevisconti. com. 15 units. 90€ double. AE, DC, MC, V. **Amenities:** Restaurant; bar; room service. *In room:* A/C, TV, hair dryer.

NUÉVALOS/PIEDRA

118km (73 miles) W of Zaragoza, 230km (143 miles) E of Madrid

The town of Nuévalos, with its one paved road, isn't much of a lure, but thousands of visitors from all over the world flock to the **Monasterio de Piedra** (see below).

Getting There

From Madrid, **train** connections reach Alhama de Aragón. Take a taxi from there to the monastery. Driving from Zaragoza, head southwest on the N-II through Calatayud. At the little town of Ateca, take the left turnoff, which is marked for Nuévalos and the Monasterio de Piedra, and continue for 23km (14 miles). If you're driving from Madrid, take the N-II and turn east at the spa town of Alhama de Aragón.

Touring the Monastery

Nuévalos's major attraction is the **Monasterio de Piedra** ★★ (🕿 **97-684-90-11;** www.monasteriopiedra.com), dubbed "the garden district" of Aragón. Though *piedra* means "rock" in Spanish, the district is a virtual Garden of Eden—it even has a 60m (197-ft.) waterfall. It was here in 1194 that Cistercian monks built a charterhouse on the banks of the Piedra River. The monks departed in 1835, but their former quarters are now a hotel (see below).

Two pathways, marked in blue or red, meander through the grounds, and views are offered from any number of levels. Tunnels and stairways dating from the 19th century are the work of Juan Federico Mutadas, who created the park. Slippery steps lead down to an iris grotto, just one of many quiet, secluded retreats. It is said the original monks inhabited the site because

The gardens of the Monasterio de Piedra.

they wanted a "foretaste of paradise." To be honest, they were escaping the court intrigues at the powerful Monestir de Poblet in Tarragona province. The monastery at Piedra is only 3km (1¾ miles) from the hillside village of Nuévalos. You can wander through the grounds daily April to October 10am to 1:15pm and 3 to 7pm. During the rest of the year daily hours are 10am to 1:15pm and 3 to 6pm. Admission is 13€ adults, 9€ children.

Where to Stay & Dine

Monasterio de Piedra ★★ 🎁 This is one of the showplaces of Aragón. The grounds include a beautiful garden with small log bridges and masses of flowering plants and trees. The beautifully maintained guest rooms, which you should reserve well in advance, have phones and TVs but no other in-room amenities. Some open onto terraces, and all contain neatly kept bathrooms. Guests and nonguests dine here.

50210 Nuévalos. © **97-684-90-11.** Fax 97-684-90-54. www.monasteriopiedra.com. 61 units. 105€–157€ double. Rates include buffet breakfast and admission to the monastery. AE, DC, MC, V. Free parking. **Amenities:** 3 restaurants; 3 bars; outdoor pool; room service. *In room:* TV, hair dryer.

SOS DEL REY CATÓLICO ★

422km (262 miles) N of Madrid, 60km (37 miles) SW of Pamplona

The most visited town in northern Aragón is Sos del Rey Católico, so named because it was the birthplace of Ferdinand, the Catholic king, in 1452. Locals will point out the Palacio de Sada, where the king is said to have been born. The kings of Aragón fortified this village on the Navarre border with a thick wall. Much of that medieval character has been preserved—enough so that the village has been declared a national monument. The town is more interesting than its minor monuments, and you can wander its narrow, cobbled streets, stopping any place you fancy.

Getting There

From Zaragoza to Sos, a 1½-hour ride away, there is a daily **bus** at 7pm, returning at 7am the next morning. To drive from Zaragoza, take the N-330 to Huesca. Continue on the N-330 to Jaca, and then bear west on the N-240 toward Pamplona. Turn south at the cutoff to Sangüesa.

Where to Stay & Dine

Parador de Sos del Rey Católico ★★ This member of the government-owned *parador* network is unusual because of the care that was taken to blend a six-story building into its medieval setting. Built in 1975, it's composed mostly of stone and wood timbers, with lots of interior paneling and antique-looking accessories. Despite its location in the heart of the village, sweeping views open from some of the windows onto the nearby countryside. Guest rooms vary, but all have quality beds and are well maintained and beautifully furnished. Aragonese food is served in the restaurant.

Sainz de Vicuña 1, 50680 Sos del Rey Católico. © **94-888-80-11.** Fax 94-888-81-00. www.parador.es. 58 units. 127€–172€ double; 254€–274€ junior suite. AE, DC, MC, V. Free parking. Closed Jan to mid-Feb. **Amenities:** Restaurant; bar; room service. *In room:* A/C, TV, hair dryer, minibar, Wi-Fi (2€ per hour).

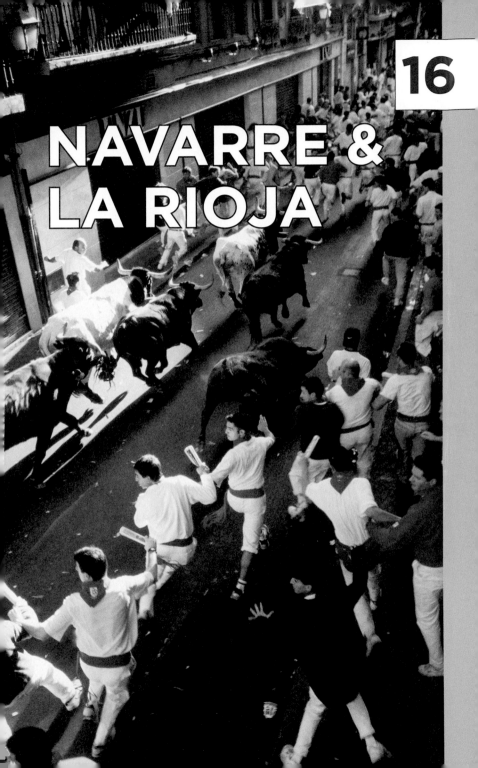

NAVARRE &
LA RIOJA

The ancient land of Navarre (Navarra in Spanish, Nafarroa in Basque) shares a 130km (82-mile) frontier with France, with nine crossing points. This province with a strong Basque tradition is an important link between Iberia and the rest of the Continent.

As a border region, Navarre has seen its share of conflict, and to this day the remains of lonely castles and fortified walled towns bear witness to that. But somehow this kingdom, one of the most ancient on the peninsula, has managed to preserve its own government and identity. Romans, Christians, Muslims, and Jews have all left their stamp on Navarre, and its architecture is as diverse as its landscape. It is also a province rich in folklore. Pagan rites were blended with Christian traditions to form a mythology that lives on today in Navarre's many festivals. Dancers and singers wear the famous red berets, the *jota* is the province's most celebrated folk dance, and its best-known sport is *pelota*—sometimes called jai alai in other parts of the world.

Navarre is also rich in natural attractions, but most foreign visitors miss them when they come in July to see the **Fiesta de San Fermín** and the running of the bulls through the streets of Pamplona, Navarre's capital and major city. Even if you do visit for the festival, try to explore some of the panoramic Pyrenean landscape.

Adjoining Navarre is **La Rioja,** the smallest region of mainland Spain—bordered not only by Navarre but also by Castile and Aragón. Extending along the Ebro River, this province has far greater influence than its tiny dimensions would suggest because it is one of the most important winegrowing districts in Europe. The land is generally split into two sections: Rioja Alta, which gets a lot of rainfall and has a mild climate; and Rioja Baja, which is much hotter and more arid, like Aragón. The capital of the province is Logroño, a city of some 200,000 that links the two regions.

The most-visited towns are **Logroño** and **Haro,** the latter known for its wineries. **Santo Domingo de la Calzada** was a major stop on the ancient pilgrims' route en route to Santiago de Compostela, while **Nájera** once served as capital for the kings of Navarre. Now little more than a village, it lies along the Najerilla River.

PAMPLONA ★

90km (56 miles) SE of San Sebastián, 385km (239 miles) NE of Madrid, 168km (104 miles) NE of Zaragoza

Ernest Hemingway's descriptions of the running of the bulls in his 1927 novel, *The Sun Also Rises,* made **Pamplona** known throughout the world. The book's glamour remains undiminished for the crowds who read it and then rush off to Pamplona to see the *encierros* (bull running) during the Fiesta de San Fermín. Attempts to outlaw this world-famous ceremony have failed so far, and it remains a superstar attraction, particularly among bullfighting aficionados. The riotous

PREVIOUS PAGE: **The running of the bulls in Pamplona.**

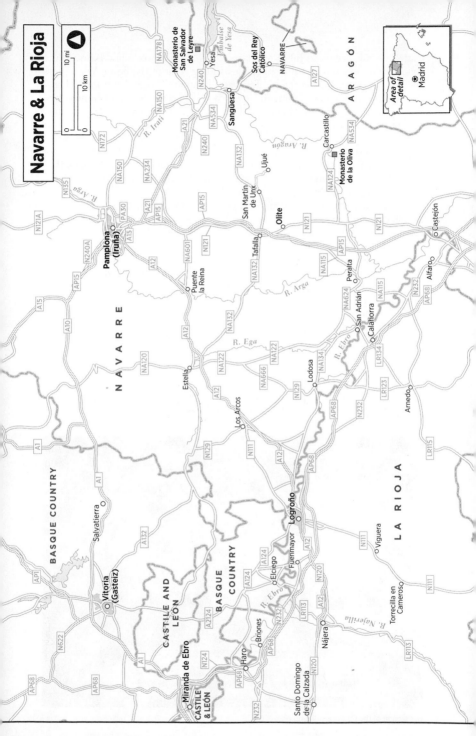

Navarre & La Rioja

591

festival usually begins on July 6 and lasts to July 14. Fireworks and Basque flute concerts are only some of the spectacles adding color to the fiesta. Wine flows and people party nonstop for the festival's duration. Those who want to know they'll have a bed after watching the *encierro* should **reserve a year in advance** at one of the city's handful of hotels or boardinghouses, or lodge in San Sebastián or another neighboring town.

But Pamplona is more than just a city where an annual festival takes place. Long the most significant town in Spain's Pyrenean region, it was also a major stopover for those traveling either of two frontier roads: the Roncesvalles Pass or the Velate Pass. Once a fortified city, it was for centuries the capital of the ancient kingdom of Navarre.

In its historic core, the Pamplona of legend lives on, but the city has been engulfed by modern real-estate development. The saving grace of new Pamplona is La Taconera, a spacious green swath of fountain-filled gardens and parkland west of the Old Quarter where you will see students from the University of Navarre.

Pamplona became the capital of Navarre in the 10th century. Its Golden Age was during the reign of Charles III (called "the Noble"), who gave it its cathedral, where he was eventually buried. Over the years, the city has been the scene of many battles, with various factions struggling for control. Those who lived in the Old Quarter, the Navarrería, wanted to be allied with Castile, whereas those on the outskirts favored a French connection. Castile eventually won out, although some citizens of Navarre today want Pamplona to be part of a newly created country of the Basque lands.

Essentials

GETTING THERE Pamplona is the air hub of the Navarre region. The city is served by four to six weekday Iberia **flights** (www.iberia.com/us) from both

The facade of the Catedral of Pamplona.

Madrid and Barcelona; international connections can be made from either city. Arrivals are at **Aeropuerto de Noaín** (© **90-240-47-04**), 6.5km (4 miles) from the city center and accessible only by taxi for about 13€.

Four RENFE **trains** a day arrive from Madrid (trip time: 3½–4 hr.) and three from Barcelona (trip time: 4 hr.). Pamplona also has three daily train connections from San Sebastián to the north (trip time: 1¼ hr.) and four daily from Zaragoza to the south (trip time: 1½ hr.). For information, call © **90-224-02-02**, or go to www.renfe.es.

Buses connect Pamplona with several major Spanish cities: four per day from Barcelona (trip time: 5½ hr.), eight per day from Zaragoza (trip time: 2 hr.), and seven per day from San Sebastián (trip time: 1 hr.). Instead of calling for information, you'll have to consult the bulletin board's list of destinations at the **Estación de Autobuses,** at Calle Conde Olivetto (corner of Calle Yanguas and Miranda). Nearly 20 privately owned bus companies converge here, in a mass of confusion.

The A-15 Navarra national highway begins on the outskirts of Pamplona and runs south to join A-68, midway between Zaragoza and Logroño. N-240 connects San Sebastián with Pamplona.

VISITOR INFORMATION The **tourist office,** at Calle Eslava 1 (© **84-842-04-20;** www.pamplona.es), is open Monday to Friday 10am to 7pm, Saturday 10am to 2pm and 4 to 7pm, and Sunday 10am to 2pm.

Exploring Pamplona

The heart of Pamplona is the **Plaza del Castillo,** formerly the bullring, built in 1847. Today it is the seat of the autonomous provincial government. This elegant tree-lined *paseo* becomes a virtual communal bedroom during the Festival of San Fermín.

The narrow streets of the Old Quarter extend from three sides of the square. The present bullring, the **Plaza de Toros,** is just east and south of this square alongside Paseo Hemingway. Running parallel to the east of the square is **Calle Estafeta,** a narrow street that is the site of the running of the bulls. With its bars and *tascas,* it attracts university students and is lively year-round. During the festival it is the most frequented place in town next to the Plaza del Castillo. The bulls also run through the barricaded streets of Santo Domingo and Mercaderes.

Catedral ★ This is the most important sight in Pamplona, dating from the late 14th century on the site of a former Romanesque basilica. The present facade, a mix of neoclassical and baroque, was the work of Ventura Rodríguez, architect to Charles III. The interior is Gothic with lots of fan vaulting. At the center is the alabaster tomb of Charles III and his Castilian wife, Queen Leonor, done in 1416 by Flemish sculptor Janin de Lomme. The 14th- and 15th-century Gothic cloisters are a highlight of the cathedral. The Barbazán Chapel, off the east gallery, is noted for its vaulting. The Museo Diocesano, housed in the cathedral's refectory and kitchen, displays religious objects, spanning the era from the Middle Ages to the Renaissance.

Calle Curia/Calle Dormitalería. © **94-822-29-90.** www.catedraldepamplona.com. Free admission to cathedral; museum 4.40€. Mon–Fri 10am–1:30pm and 4-7pm; Sat 10:30am–1:30pm.

Museo de Navarra ★ The major museum of Pamplona is housed in a 16th-century hospital, Nuestra Señora de la Misericordia, close to the river. Its rich

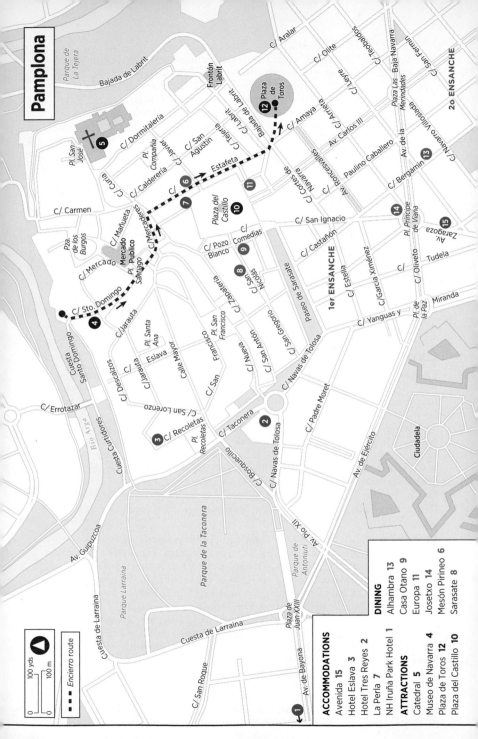

Pamplona

ACCOMMODATIONS
Avenida **15**
Hotel Eslava **3**
Hotel Tres Reyes **2**
La Perla **7**
NH Iruña Park Hotel **1**

ATTRACTIONS
Catedral **5**
Museo de Navarra **4**
Plaza de Toros **12**
Plaza del Castillo **10**

DINING
Alhambra **13**
Casa Otano **9**
Europa **11**
Josetxo **14**
Mesón Pirineo **6**
Sarasate **8**

Encierro route

100 yds
100 m

collections of Roman artifacts include some 2nd-century mosaics. Also on exhibit is Romanesque art, plus an important Goya portrait of the Marqués de San Adrián. Gothic and Renaissance paintings are on the second floor. Murals from the 13th century are another highlight.

Cuesta de Santo Domingo 47. ✆ **94-842-64-92.** www.cfnavarra.es. Admission 2€ adults, 1€ students and seniors, free for children 15 and under. Tues–Sat 9:30am–2pm and 5–7pm; Sun 11am–2pm.

ATTENDING A *PELOTA* MATCH

While in Pamplona, you might want to head about 6km (3¾ miles) outside town to **Frontón Euskal–Jai Berri** (✆ **94-833-11-59**), along Avenida de Francia, to check out a professional *pelota* (jai alai) match. Game times are Saturday at 4pm and some Sundays and regional and national holidays. Four matches are usually played on game days, and tickets can be purchased anytime during the sets. Admission to the bleachers is 12€ to 15€. We recommend leaving the betting to the experts.

Shopping

You'll find lots of Navarrese handicrafts in kiosks scattered through the Old Town, but for a particularly well-inventoried outlet, head for **Echeve,** Calle Mercaderes 14 (✆ **94-822-42-15**). It sells such handcrafted items as vests, ceramics, hats, woodcarvings, and *botas* (wineskins), which locals use to squirt wine, with great dexterity, into their open mouths. A roughly equivalent competitor is **Las Tres ZZZ,** Calle Comedias 7 (✆ **94-822-44-38;** www.lastreszzz.com), which sells wineskins, neckerchiefs, and wide belts known as *gerrikos,* favored by weight lifters and sports enthusiasts who feel twinges in their backs when they're called upon to perform heavy-duty lifting.

Professional *pelota,* or jai alai.

THE RUNNING OF THE bulls

Beginning at noon on July 6 and continuing nonstop to July 14, the **Fiesta de San Fermín** is one of the most popular events in Europe, drawing thousands of tourists who severely overtax Pamplona's limited facilities.

Get up early (or don't go to bed at all) because the bulls run every day at 8am sharp. To watch, be in position behind the barricades along Calle Estafeta no later than 6am. Only the able-bodied and sober should plan to run.

There simply aren't enough beds or bullfight tickets to go around, and scalpers have a field day. Technically, tickets for a good seat in the ring go on sale at 8pm the night before the corrida (bullfight), and tickets for standing room go on sale at 4pm the day of the bullfight. But all the tickets are sold out, and since it is impossible to get them through travel agents beforehand, tourists have to use scalpers.

The fiesta draws half a million visitors, many of whom camp in the city parks. Temporary facilities are set up, but there are never enough beds. Hotel reservations should be confirmed at least 6 months beforehand—the tourist office will not make any recommendations during the festival. If you look respectable, some Pamplónicos may

rent you a room. Be aware, however, that they may gouge you for the highest price they think you'll pay, and your room might turn out to be a dirty floor shared with others in a slumlike part of the city. Many young visitors sleep on the grounds of the Ciudadela and Plaza Fueros traffic ring, but muggings can occur. Longtime visitors to Pamplona advise that it's better to sleep in a group, on top of your belongings, and during the day. If you can't find a room, check your valuables at the bus station on Calle Conde Oliveto (where there are showers—free, but cold).

As for bars and restaurants, ignore all the times given in the listings on p. 598. Most establishments operate round-the-clock during the festival. Some people go to the festival not to watch the bulls but to pick pockets. Also, don't take needless risks, such as leaping from a building in the hope friends below will catch you. Many people do this, and not all are caught.

If you're looking for fashion or accessories, head for a boutique called **Zara,** Av. Carlos III no. 7 (© **94-822-75-04**).

Where to Stay in Pamplona

During the Fiesta de San Fermín, prices are three to four times higher than those listed below. In some instances, a hotel commits itself to prices it will charge at *Fiesta* (the original name of *The Sun Also Rises* when it was first published in Britain). Other owners charge pretty much what they want. Therefore, agree on the price when making a reservation—that is, if you've been able to get a reservation in the first place.

EXPENSIVE

Hotel Tres Reyes ★ A short walk west of Old Town, just 2 blocks north of the ancient citadel, this is one of the finest hotels in Pamplona, surpassed only by Iruña Park (see below). It provides tasteful, airy rooms with contemporary furnishings, lots of sunlight, and private bathrooms equipped with tub/shower combos. Many rooms have balconies, and all are welcome refuges from the intensity of the local festivities.

Jardines de la Taconera 1, 31001 Pamplona. © **94-822-66-00.** Fax 94-822-29-30. www.hotel-3reyes.com. 160 units. 170€–599€ double; 471€–790€ suite. AE, DC, MC, V. Parking 20€ indoors; free outside. **Amenities:** Restaurant; bar; babysitting; exercise room; outdoor pool; room service; sauna. *In room:* A/C, TV, hair dryer, minibar, Wi-Fi (12€ per 24 hr.).

NH Iruña Park Hotel ★★ A short walk west of Parque de la Ciudadela in the suburbs, this is the largest and best hotel in town, often the site of conventions. A large staff maintains the blandly furnished but comfortable guest rooms, and bathrooms are well equipped. Public areas are modern and glossy, with deep armchairs and big windows.

Arcadio María Larraona 1, 31008 Pamplona. © **94-819-71-19.** Fax 94-817-23-87. www.nh-hoteles. com. 225 units. 129€–391€ double; 212€–576€ suite. AE, DC, MC, V. Parking 16€. **Amenities:** Restaurant; bar; babysitting; room service. *In room:* A/C, TV, hair dryer, minibar, Wi-Fi (17€ per 24 hr.).

MODERATE

Avenida ★ 🛅 One of the best inns in town, this small, well-run place opened in 1989. The midsize guest rooms have furnishings that tend toward the sleek and modern, and local watercolors add a warm touch. Some units—slightly larger with a small balcony—are even better than the government's three-star rating suggests.

Zaragoza 5, 31003 Pamplona. © **94-824-54-54.** Fax 94-823-23-23. www.hotelavenida.biz. 24 units. 59€–145€ double. AE, DC, MC, V. Parking 12€. **Amenities:** Restaurant; bar; room service. *In room:* A/C, TV, hair dryer, minibar, Wi-Fi (free).

Hotel Eslava ★ 🛅 Right off the Plaza de Recoletas, and a 10-minute walk from the bus station, this renovated hotel manages to combine the spirits of old and new Spain. Its small living room resembles the drawing room of a distinguished Spanish house. The average-size guest rooms are tastefully decorated; some have balconies with views of the city walls and the vistas beyond. All come with comfortable beds and spick-and-span bathrooms.

Plaza Virgen de la O 7 (corner with Calle Recoletas 20), 31001 Pamplona. © **94-822-22-70.** Fax 94-822-51-57. www.hotel-eslava.com. 28 units. 69€–145€ double. AE, DC, MC, V. Bus: 3, 4, 9, or 16. **Amenities:** Bar. *In room:* TV, Wi-Fi (free).

La Perla ★ Opened in 1880 and last renovated in 2007, the hotel has been radically altered, its bedrooms reduced in number and made larger when La Perla went from 67 bedrooms to only 44. During the festival it becomes *the* place to stay, because it opens onto the main square of Pamplona and overlooks Calle Estafeta, the straightaway of the *encierro* through which the bulls run. The rooms are furnished with contemporary, comfortable pieces. In days of yore the hotel sheltered everybody from Ernest Hemingway to U.S. Sen. Henry Cabot Lodge.

Plaza del Castillo 1, 31001 Pamplona. ☏ **94-822-30-00.** Fax 94-822-23-24. www.granhotel laperla.com. 44 units. 160€–325€ double; 475€ suite. AE, DC, MC, V. Parking 29€. **Amenities:** Restaurant; bar; room service. *In room:* A/C, TV, minibar, Wi-Fi (free).

Where to Dine in Pamplona

EXPENSIVE

Alhambra ★ NAVARRESE/SPANISH One of the best-known and most stable restaurants in Pamplona, and just a 15-minute walk from the cathedral, Alhambra dates from the end of World War II. Set within two paneled dining rooms, it features a complete selection of local wines and regional specialties. Main courses likely to tempt you are roast baby lamb sweetbreads, duck liver with glazed onion, or roast venison in a sweet-and-sour raisin sauce. The spiciest dish on the menu is codfish *pil-pil* in a fiery pepper sauce. Two other well-prepared fish dishes include baked turbot with fried garlic in a sweet wine vinegar sauce or monkfish with crunchy almonds and soy vinaigrette.

Calle Bergamín 7. ☏ **94-824-50-07.** www.restaurantealhambra.es. Reservations recommended. Main courses 19€–28€; fixed-price menus 45€–56€. AE, DC, MC, V. Mon–Sat 1–3pm and 9–11pm.

Europa ★★★ BASQUE/SPANISH Located in the center of Pamplona near Plaza del Castillo, this, along with Josetxo (see below), is the best restaurant in the entire region. Both have Michelin stars, which are rarely doled out in this part of Europe. The chef and culinary artist is Pamplona-born Pilar Idoate, who prepares a seasonal menu. Examples of Europa's cuisine include young lamb roasted in its own sauce and accompanied by a sweetbreads kebab; or carpaccio of sirloin steak stuffed with mushrooms. Another regional dish is grilled turbot with refried sweet-and-sour chardonnay vinegar. A spectacular dessert is mango with black chocolate over a mango carpaccio with clove-flavored ice cream.

Calle Espoz y Mina 11. ☏ **94-822-18-00.** www.hreuropa.com. Reservations recommended. Main courses 20€–28€; fixed-price menus 45€–62€. AE, DC, MC, V. Mon–Sat 1–3:30pm and 9–11:30pm. Closed Easter.

Josetxo ★★★ BASQUE The finest and grandest restaurant in town, Josetxo is run by a civic-minded local family with more than 30 years' experience in the restaurant trade. The chef has a magic combination: inventiveness and solid technique, backed up by the very freshest ingredients. Specialties vary with the seasons but might include pigeon braised in its jus with foie gras and potato purée, or grilled monkfish with bacon ribbons, Norwegian lobster, and chive cream. Dessert might be a chocolate truffle tart layered with orange-flavored cream. The restaurant is beside a busy traffic circle, 4 blocks south of the Plaza del Castillo.

Plaza Príncipe de Viana 1. ☏ **94-822-20-97.** www.restaurantejosetxo.com. Reservations recommended on weekends. Main courses 18€–34€. AE, DC, MC, V. Mon–Sat 1:30–3:30pm and 9–11pm. Closed Holy Week and Aug.

MODERATE

Casa Otano NAVARRESE/SPANISH In the oldest part of town, on a narrow street that empties into the Plaza de Castillo, this is a busy and popular tavern-style restaurant with three dining rooms and a reputation for feeding generations of Pamplona residents since the 1950s. The menu includes house-style hake (baked with garlic, green sauce, herbs, and clams), many kinds of succulent grilled meats and fish, chicken roasted in sherry sauce, and thick cuts of delicious pork chops.

Calle San Nicolás 5. © **94-822-70-36.** www.casaotano.com. Reservations recommended on weekends. Main courses 12€–30€. AE, DC, MC, V. Daily 1–4pm; Mon–Sat 9–11:30pm.

INEXPENSIVE

Mesón Pirineo 🍴 NAVARRESE This dive is the best place in town for hearty appetites. The portions of Basque specialties are huge. After stuffing you, the friendly waiters even offer you a regional liqueur on the house. Many typical specialties of the area are offered, including game in season, especially quail. The most filling dish is a hearty bean stew that a Basque grandmother might have prepared for a family on a winter's day. Duck confit is another regularly featured dish, and beef dishes are usually tender and filled with flavor.

Estafeta 41. © **94-822-20-45.** Reservations not needed. Main courses 8€–32€; fixed-price menu (Mon–Fri) 16€. MC, V. Daily 1–4pm; Mon–Sat 8–10:30pm.

Sarasate VEGETARIAN Above a fish market, this favorite of students of Pamplona serves the best vegetable platters in town, including vegan or gluten-free offerings for those who desire that. Only the freshest vegetables from the bountiful countryside are used. Start with one of the soothing mixed fresh-fruit juices (the pomegranate is heavenly), and follow with a selection of well-prepared dishes that make lavish use of fresh salad greens as well as beans and other produce. During the running of the bulls, the chefs even offer meat, poultry, and seafood. This is mainly a lunch eatery, but it does serve dinner 2 nights a week.

Calle San Nicolás 32. © **94-822-57-27.** www.restaurantesarasate.com. Reservations not needed. Fixed-price menu 11€. V. Daily 1–4pm; Fri–Sat 8:30–11pm.

Pamplona After Dark

In a city famous for bulls running through its streets, there's something consistent about the local habit of wandering through the city, particularly within the historic *casco antiguo*. Three streets in particular—**Calle San Nicolás, Calle Estafeta,** and **Calle de Jarauta**—are lined with *tascas*, bars, bodegas, and pubs. Lots of them don't have signs, so wander in and out of whichever strikes your fancy.

The town's most popular club is **Marengo,** Av. Bayona 2 (© **94-826-55-42**), a huge nightspot where a crowd in their 20s and 30s dances the night away to recorded music. Your dress code must pass inspection by a team of hardened doormen before you are allowed inside. Tickets to enter cost 15€, and hours are Thursday to Saturday 11pm to 6am.

Looking for a dance club where you can let off some late-night steam? Head for Pamplona's most popular disco, **Reverendos,** Monasterio de Velate 5 (© **94-826-15-93;** www.reverendos.com), where 20- and 30-somethings dance, flirt, and drink till all hours. The cover charge is 10€, which includes the price of a drink.

Dating from 1888, the Art Deco **Café Iruña,** Plaza del Castillo 44 (© **94-822-20-64;** www.cafeiruna.com), has an outdoor terrace that's popular in summer. The winter crowd is likely to congregate around the bar, ordering combination plates and snacks in addition to drinks. The place thrives as a cafe/bar daily from 9am to 9:30pm, but it becomes more of a restaurant during the lunch hour. Platters of hot food are served to local office workers and day laborers. The *menú del día* (menu of the day) is 13€. A full lunch, served daily from 1 to 3:30pm, costs 10€ to 12€.

Cafetería El Molino, Bayona 13 (© **94-825-10-90**), centrally located in the commercial Barrio San Juan, doubles as a popular tapas bar. Late in the evening, the action really heats up. The huge assortment of tapas includes fried shrimp, squid, anchovies, fish croquettes, and Russian salad. Most tapas don't exceed 2€, although some of the more expensive ones go for 3€. It's open Monday to Saturday (except Wed) 8am to 2am, and Sunday from 10am to midnight.

OLITE ★

44km (27 miles) S of Pamplona, 369km (229 miles) N of Madrid

A historic city, Olite sits in a rich agricultural belt with a Mediterranean climate of short winters and long, hot summers. Cornfields and vineyards, along with large villages, pepper the countryside. Olite is also the center of a winemaking industry carried on by cooperative cellars. These wine merchants hold a local festival each year in mid-September.

Essentials

GETTING THERE Four **trains** per day run from Pamplona to Olite, taking 40 minutes one-way. For rail information, call © **90-224-02-02.**

Two **bus** companies, **Conda** (© **94-822-10-26;** www.condasa.com) and **La Tafallesa** (© **94-822-28-86**), run from Pamplona to Olite at the rate of 7 to 12 buses per day. The trip takes 35 to 45 minutes.

By car, take the A-15 expressway south from Pamplona.

VISITOR INFORMATION The **tourist office,** at Plaza Teobaldos (© **94-874-17-03;** www.turismo.navarra.es), is open during the high season Monday to Saturday 10am to 2pm and 4 to 7pm, and Sunday 10am to 2pm. Low-season hours are weekdays from 10am to 5pm and weekends from 10am to 2pm.

Exploring Olite

In the 15th century, this Gothic town was a favorite address of the kings of Navarre. Charles III put Olite on the map, ordering that the **Palacio Real** (© **94-874-00-35**), Plaza Carlos III el Noble, be built in 1406. The towers and lookouts make visiting it an adventure. April through September, hours are daily 10am to 7pm (to 8pm in July and Aug); October to March, hours are daily 10am to 6pm. Admission is 3.10€ adults; 1.60€ children 5 to 16, students, and seniors; free for children 4 and under. It's closed December 25, January 1, and January 6.

Next to the castle stands a Gothic church, **Iglesia de Santa María la Real,** with a splendid 12th-century doorway decorated with flowers.

Where to Stay in Olite

Parador de Olite ★★ This state-run *parador* in the center of town is in one of the wings of the Palacio Real (see above). Surrounded by watchtowers, thick walls, and massive buttresses, the building is one of the most impressive sights in town. Only 16 accommodations, however, are in the *parador's* medieval core, and they go for a premium over their comfortable counterparts, which are in a new wing, added in 1963, when the castle became a *parador*. Regardless of their location in the compound, the rooms are dignified and quite comfortable, each with a well-equipped bathroom.

Plaza de los Teobaldos 2, 31390 Olite. © **94-874-00-00.** Fax 94-874-02-01. www.parador.es. 43 units. 173€–220€ double. AE, DC, MC, V. **Amenities:** Restaurant; bar; room service; Wi-Fi (free, in lobby). *In room:* A/C, TV, hair dryer, minibar.

Where to Dine

Tubal ★★★ NAVARRESE Instead of dining in Olite, we suggest you drive directly north 15 to 20 minutes to Tafalla, lying on the AP-15 leading to Pamplona. In this restaurant on the main square, you'll meet Atxen Jiménez, the grande dame of Navarre gastronomy. Foodies from miles around flock to her dining room, the kitchen run by her talented son Nicolás. Tubal has been called "the Garden of Eden" for fresh vegetables, including nutty cardoons, Spain's best asparagus, and scarlet *piquillo* peppers, not to mention fava beans and artichokes. Start with Jabugo ham or natural goose pâté and go on to pigeon in its own juices or roast suckling lamb. Even though Tafalla is inland, you get some of the best and freshest fish dishes in the province, including grilled sea bass with a tomato-and-onion sauce or grilled hake with black mushrooms.

Plaza de Navarra 4. © **94-870-08-52.** Reservations required. www.restaurantetubal.com. Main courses 14€–28€. AE, DC, MC, V. Tues–Sun noon–3:30pm and Tues–Sat 8-10:30pm. Closed Aug 21–Sept 4.

Olite's Palacio Real.

Rustic Lodgings in the Navarre Countryside

If you have some time to spend in the area, consider a rental at one of the government-sponsored home stays, ranging from rooms in old farmhouses in the mountains to simple lodgings in homes in the region's small hamlets. Sometimes fully equipped apartments are available. In nearly all cases, these lodgings are extremely reasonable in price and very affordable for families who'd like to experience the great out-doors in this often-overlooked part of Spain. Called *casas rurales,* the lodgings are documented in detail in a helpful guide called *Guía de Alojamientos de Turismo Rural.* These guides are distributed free at any of the tourist offices in Navarre, including the one at Pamplona. For more information, call the office at ℂ **94-829-13-27** (www.navarra seleccion.com), where some staff members speak English.

Side Trips to Ujue & a Historic Monastery

High up on a mountain of the same name, a short drive east along a secondary road from Olite, **Ujúe** seems plucked from the Middle Ages. Built as a defensive town, it has cobbled streets and stone houses clustered around its fortress **Church of Santa María,** dating from the 12th to the 14th century. The heart of King Charles II ("the Bad") was placed to rest here. The church towers open onto views of the countryside, extending to Olite in the west and the Pyrenees in the east.

On the Sunday after St. Mark's Day (Apr 25), Ujúe is an important pilgrimage center for the people of the area, many of whom, barefoot and wearing tunics, carry large crosses. They come to Ujúe to worship Santa María, depicted on a Romanesque statue dating from 1190. It was plated in silver during the second half of the 15th century.

If you have a car, you might also check out the **Monasterio de la Oliva** ★ (ℂ **94-872-50-06**), 34km (21 miles) south of Olite. It was founded by King García Ramírez in 1164 and is an excellent example of Cistercian architecture. This monastery, one of the first to be constructed by French monks outside France, once had great influence; today the most notable feature is its 14th-century Gothic cloisters. The late-12th-century church is even more impressive than the cloisters. It has a distinguished portal and two rose windows. Pillars and pointed arches fill its interior. It's open daily from 9:30am to 12:30pm and 3:30 to 6pm. Guided visits are available.

TUDELA ★

84km (52 miles) S of Pamplona, 316km (196 miles) N of Madrid

In the center of the food belt of the Ribera, or Ebro Valley, with a population of only 30,000, the ancient city of Tudela is the second largest in Navarre. Situated on the right bank of the Ebro, it had a long history as a city where Jews, Arabs, and Christians lived and worked together. The Muslims made it a dependency of the Caliphate at Córdoba, a period of domination that lasted until 1119. The city had a large Moorish quarter, the *morería,* and many old brick houses are in the Mudéjar style. King Sancho VII ("the Strong"), who defeated the Saracens, chose Tudela as his favorite residence in 1251. It has been a bishopric since the 18th century.

Essentials

GETTING THERE Tudela lies on the southern rail line south of Pamplona. Two **RENFE trains** (✆ **90-224-02-02;** www.renfe.es) pass through here, one connecting La Rioja to Zaragoza via Castejón de Ebro. The other train links Zaragoza with Vitoria-Gasteiz via Pamplona. Schedules are subject to change, so call ahead.

Conda buses (✆ **94-882-03-42;** www.condasa.com) go to Tudela from Pamplona at the rate of 8 to 10 buses per day (trip time: 1¼ hr.). If you're driving, take A-15 south from Pamplona.

VISITOR INFORMATION The **tourist office,** at Calle Juicio 4 (✆ **94-884-80-58;** www.turismo.navarra.es), is open Monday to Friday 9:30am to 2pm and 4 to 8pm, Saturday 10am to 2pm and 4 to 8pm, and Sunday 10am to 2pm. The office closes at 7pm in February and March.

Touring Tudela's Cathedral

Begin your exploration at the central Plaza de los Fueros, from where you can wander through a maze of narrow alleys laid out during the Moorish occupation.

At the square called Plaza Vieja, Tudela's most important monument, **Catedral de Santa María ★**, is open Monday to Saturday 10am to 1:30pm and 4 to 7pm, and Sunday 10am to 1pm. Admission is 3€. Constructed in the 12th and 13th centuries, its facade has an outstanding work of art, the *Doorway of the Last Judgment,* with about 120 groups of figures. Creation is depicted, but the artisans were truly inspired in showing the horrors of hell. The church contains many Gothic works of art, such as choir stalls from the 1500s. Several chapels are richly decorated, including one dedicated to Our Lady of Hope, with masterpieces from the 15th century. The main altar contains an exceptional *retablo* painted by Pedro Díaz de Oviedo. The small but choice cloisters are the highlight of the tour, however, and cost 1€ to enter. Dating from the 12th and 13th centuries, they contain many Romanesque arches. Capitals on the columns include scenes from the New Testament.

The Catedral de Santa María's *Doorway of the Last Judgment.*

Where to Stay & Dine in Tudela

Tudela Bardenas ★ This is one of the best choices for an overnight stopover. Directly in front of the bullring (Plaza de Toros), this hotel was built in the 1930s and tripled in size by 1992. Today it is modern and functional, with a polite and helpful staff. Rooms, though a bit boxy and standardized, are nevertheless comfortable and have well-maintained bathrooms.

The in-house **restaurant** is one of the best in the city. It draws a lively crowd, especially before and after bullfights, and serves well-prepared food. It offers typical fresh products of the Ribera region, along with magnificent fish and grilled meat. Try the omelet with cod or the baked monkfish. You can also order beefsteak, followed by homemade pastries and desserts. Sample such wines as Viña Magaña. Reservations are recommended.

Av. Zaragoza 60, 31500 Tudela. ☎ **94-841-08-02.** Fax 94-841-09-72. www.tudelabardenas. com. 46 units. 60€–98€ double; 98€–118€ triple. AE, DC, MC, V. Parking 13€. **Amenities:** Restaurant; babysitting. *In room:* A/C, TV, hair dryer, minibar, Wi-Fi (free).

SANGÜESA ★

407km (253 miles) N of Madrid, 47km (29 miles) SE of Pamplona

Sangüesa is on the left bank of the Aragón River, at the Aragonese frontier. A monumental town in its own right, Sangüesa can also serve as a base for excursions in the area, including visits to some of Navarre's major attractions, such as **Javier Castle** and the monastery at **Leyre.**

Long known to the Romans, Sangüesa was later involved in the battle against Muslim domination in the 10th century. It has seen many wars, including occupation by supporters of Archduke Charles of Austria in 1710 and many a skirmish during the Carlist struggles of the 19th century. On several occasions it has been the seat of Navarre's parliament. Pilgrims crossing northern Spain to Santiago de Compostela stopped at Sangüesa.

Essentials

GETTING THERE Three **buses** bound for Sangüesa leave from Pamplona daily (trip time: 45 min.); for information, call ☎ **94-887-02-09.** If you're driving from Pamplona, take the secondary road N-240 to Sangüesa.

VISITOR INFORMATION The **tourist office,** at Calle Mayor 2 (☎ **94-887-14-11;** www.turismo.navarra.es), is open Easter to September, Monday to Saturday 10am to 2pm and 4 to 7pm; October to Easter, hours are Monday to Friday 10am to 5pm, and Saturday and Sunday 10am to 2pm.

Visiting Sangüesa's Churches

Iglesia de Santa María ★, on Calle Mayor (☎ **94-887-01-32**), stands at the far end of town beside the river. Begun in the 12th century, it has a doorway from the 12th and 13th centuries that is an outstanding work of Romanesque art. The south portal, filled with remarkably carved sculptures, is Santa María's most outstanding feature. The vestry contains a 1.5m-high (5-ft.) processional monstrance from the 15th century. The church is open daily 10am to 1:30pm and 4:30 to 6:30pm; admission is free.

The nearby **Iglesia de Santiago,** on Calle Santrago 18 (☎ **94-887-01-32**), is a late traditional Romanesque structure from the 12th and 13th centuries.

It has a battlement-type tower and contains an impressive array of Gothic sculptures, discovered under the church only in 1964. Look for the bizarre statue of St. James atop a big conch. The church is open 30 minutes before Mass Monday to Friday at 8:30pm, Sunday noon and 8pm; admission is free.

Where to Stay & Dine in Sangüesa

If after visiting the town you want to spend the night in the area, you can check in at the hotel reviewed below; or you can drive 15km (9⅓ miles) south to one of the most charming towns of Aragón, Sos del Rey Católico (p. 588). It features an excellent *parador* (p. 588).

Hotel Yamaguchi The best place to stay among extremely limited choices is this hotel, .4km (¼ mile) outside town on the road to Javier. The small rooms are functional, modern, clean, and comfortable, each with a good bed and a neatly kept bathroom. The many Navarrese dishes served in the restaurant include lamb stew and steak. You can also sample award-winning wines from local wine cellars.

Carretera de Javier s/n, 31400 Sangüesa. ℂ **94-887-01-27.** Fax 94-887-07-00. www.hotel yamaguchi.com. 40 units. 63€–70€ double; 73€–80€ triple. AE, DC, MC, V. Free parking. **Amenities:** Restaurant; bar. *In room:* A/C, TV.

Side Trips to Leyre & Javier Castle

LEYRE The **Monasterio de San Salvador of Leyre** ★ (ℂ 94-888-40-11; www.monasteriodeleyre.com) is 16km (10 miles) east of Sangüesa, perched on the side of a mountain of the same name, overlooking the Yesa Dam. Of major historic and artistic interest, the main body of the monastery was constructed from the 11th to the 15th century on the site of a primitive pre-Romanesque church; in time, it became the spiritual center of Navarre. Many kings, including Sancho III, made it their pantheon. Its **crypt,** consecrated in 1057, ranks as one of the country's major works of Romanesque art.

When the church was reconstructed by the Cistercians in the 13th century, the bays of the old Romanesque church were retained. The outstanding and richly adorned 12th-century west portal is called the **Porta Speciosa** and is covered with intricate carvings. In one section, Jesus and his disciples are depicted atop mythical creatures. Some of the other artistic treasures of this once-great monastery are displayed at the Museo de Navarra in Pamplona.

The monastery is 4km (2½ miles) from Yesa, which itself is on N-240, the major road linking Pamplona, Sangüesa, and Huesca. Take the N-240 into Yesa, and then follow an uphill road marked LEYRE to the monastery. Visits are possible daily from 10:15am to 2pm and 4 to 7pm. Admission is 2€ for adults and .50€ for children 6 to 12.

At Leyre you'll also find one of the most unusual accommodations in Navarre, the **Hospedería de Leyre,** Monasterio de Leyre, 31410 Yesa (ℂ **94-888-41-00;** www.hotelhospederiadeleyre.com). This two-star inn with 30 units (all with bathrooms) was created from the annexes constructed by the Benedictines in the 1700s. Guest rooms open onto views of the Yesa Reservoir. The rate is 70€ to 85€ for a double room, and parking is free. The hotel **restaurant,** which serves good Navarrese food in a rustic setting, is open daily 8:30 to 10am, 1 to 3:30pm, and 8 to 10pm. The Hospedería is closed from December 10 to March 1.

The Castillo de Javier, outside Sangüesa.

JAVIER CASTLE The second major excursion possible in the area is to **Castillo de Javier** ★ (© 94-888-40-24; www.santuariodejavier.org), 8km (5 miles) from Sangüesa. The castle dates from the 11th century, but owes its present look to restoration work carried out in 1952. Francisco Javier (Xavier), patron of Navarre, was born here on April 7, 1506. Along with Ignatius Loyola, he founded the order of the Society of Jesus (the Jesuits) in the mid–16th century. The castle houses a magnificent 13th-century crucifix, and thousands of the faithful congregate at Javier on two consecutive Sundays in March. This is the most popular pilgrimage in Navarre. Known as the Javierada, it pays homage to Francisco Javier, who was canonized in 1622.

During your visit to the castle, view the oratory, the guard chamber, the great hall, and the saint's bedroom. The castle teems with interesting art, including a 15th-century fresco called the *Dance of Death.* To drive to the castle, take the N-240 to Yesa and then follow an unmarked road that's signposted CASTILLO DE JAVIER. The castle is open daily from 10am to 1:30pm and 3:30 to 7pm in summer (until 6pm in winter). Admission is 2€ for adults and 1€ for children.

For food and lodging, go to the tranquil **Hotel El Mesón,** Plaza de Javier, 31411 Javier (© 94-888-40-35; fax 94-888-42-26; www.hotel meson.com), right in the center of the hamlet of Javier on the same unmarked road the castle is on. Management rents eight comfortably furnished rooms, but the hotel is closed from December 15 to February. Doubles go for 75€, and parking is free. The hotel's restaurant offers the best food in the area, with a fixed-price menu going for 20€.

LOGROÑO ★

330km (205 miles) N of Madrid, 92km (57 miles) W of Pamplona

The capital of the province of La Rioja, Logroño is also the major distribution center for the area's wines and agricultural products. Because La Rioja is so small, Logroño can serve as your base for touring the province's major attractions. Although much of Logroño is modern and dull, its Old Quarter is known to the pilgrims crossing this region to visit the tomb of St. James at Santiago de Compostela. Encased in medieval walls, the Old Quarter can be explored in about 1½ hours. Its most typical and beautiful streets are **Muro Francisco de la Mata** and **Breton de los Herreros.**

Essentials

GETTING THERE There are four daily **RENFE trains** (© 90-224-02-02; www.renfe.es) from Barcelona (trip time: 4–5 hr.) and one per day from Madrid (trip time: 3¾ hr.). From Bilbao in the north, two trains arrive per day (trip time: 2½–3¼ hr.).

Five **buses** arrive daily from Pamplona (trip time: 1 hr.) and five from Madrid (trip time: 5 hr.). For information, call © **94-123-59-83.**

If you're driving, take N-111 southwest from Pamplona or A-68 northwest from Zaragoza.

VISITOR INFORMATION The **tourist office,** at Calle Portales 50 (© **94-127-33-53;** www.logroturismo.org), is usually open Monday to Saturday 10am to 2pm and 4:30 to 7:30pm, and Sunday 10am to 2pm. From July to September the office is open daily 9am to 2pm and 5 to 8pm.

Exploring Logroño

Catedral de Santa María de la Redonda, Plaza del Mercado (© **94-125-76-11**), has vaulting from the 1400s, although the baroque facade dates from 1742. Inside, you can visit its 1762 Chapel of Our Lady of the Angels, built in an octagonal shape with rococo adornments. Constructed on top of an earlier Romanesque church, today's cathedral is known for its broad naves and twin towers. Admission is free. It's open Monday to Saturday 8am to 1:30pm and 6:30 to 8:45pm, and Sunday 9am to 2pm and 6:30 to 8:45pm.

From the square on which the cathedral sits, walk up Calle de la Sagasta until you reach the 12th-century **Iglesia de Santa María de Palacio,** on Marqués de San Nicolás, once part of a royal palace. The palace part dates from 1130, when Alfonso VII offered his residence to the Order of the Holy Sepulchre. Most of what he left is long gone, of course, but there remains a pyramid-shaped spire from the 13th century.

Walk through the heart of Logroño, exploring the gardens of the broad **Paseo del Espolón.** In the late afternoon, all the residents turn out for their *paseo,* or stroll.

While in Logroño, you can visit **Bodegas Olarra,** Polígono de Cantabria s/n (© **90-213-10-44;** www.bodegasolarra.es), open Monday to Friday from 9am to 1pm and 3 to 7pm. It produces wines under the Otonal and Olarra labels. Admission is free, but reserve a tour at least 2 weeks in advance. Bodegas Olarra is closed in August and during the Wine Harvest Festival.

A Special Event

About a third of all Rioja wine production comes from the Najerilla River's valleys. From September 20 to September 26, the **Wine Harvest Festival** (© **94-129-12-60**) takes place throughout the region of La Rioja. Barefoot locals stomp upon grapes spilling from oak casks, and area vineyards showcase their wares. Other activities include dances, parades, music, and bullfights.

A Superstar Architect Designs a Luxury Hotel

The architect Frank Gehry became even more famous than he already was when he designed the Guggenheim Museum in Bilbao. He also designed the luxury hotel **Marqués de Riscal ★★★**, Calle Torrea 1 (✆ **94-518-08-80;** www.luxurycollection.com/marquesderiscal), at Elciego 01340. It's 26km (16 miles) northwest of Logroño, and about 129km (80 miles) south of Bilbao, in the heart of the Rioja wine region. The 43-room "new style" hotel, part of the Starwood organization, has many of the architectural characteristics of the Guggenheim Museum. The roof, for example, is constructed from curved plates of titanium suspended at different angles and tinted silver, gold, and rose. The design of the exterior of the hotel is meant to evoke a "grapevine just before the fruit is harvested." The elegant rooms are all about windows; there are even window seats that follow the zigzagging contours of the exterior glass. The architect said he wanted "to make the view part of the room." The hotel is very pricey, charging 320€ to 842€ for a double, with suites costing 480€ to 1,315€. A Michelin-starred restaurant is on-site, as is an indoor heated swimming pool, a fitness center, and even a spa offering "wine treatment therapies."

Where to Stay in Logroño

Hotel Murrieta ✦ At the western border of the historic part of town, a block north of the Gran Vía, is this 1980s hotel offering midsize, comfortable, pristine rooms at a relatively good rate. Units contain private, well-maintained bathrooms.

Marqués de Murrieta 1, 26005 Logroño. ✆ **94-122-41-50.** Fax 94-122-32-13. www.pretur.es. 104 units. 110€ double; 120€ triple. AE, DC, MC, V. Parking 14€. **Amenities:** Restaurant; bar; room service; Wi-Fi (free, in lobby). *In room:* A/C, TV, hair dryer, minibar.

La Numantina 🖋 This rather simple hotel, one of the best bargains in town, is on a street central to both the historic core and the commercial district. Its small and basic rooms are clean and reasonably comfortable, each with a good bed and a tidy bathroom with shower. No breakfast is served, but you can buy pastries at a shop across the street.

Calle Sagasta 4, 26001 Logroño. © **94-125-14-11.** Fax 94-125-16-45. www.hostalnumantina.com. 17 units. 55€ double. MC, V. Closed Dec 22–Jan 7. *In room:* A/C, TV.

Tryp Bracos ★ According to many wine merchants who come here frequently on business, this landmark government-rated four-star hotel is the finest in town. Logroño's toniest address has an elegant reception hall and the most helpful staff in town. The street on which it's located is one of the best known in the city, and although it used to lie outside the walls, Logroño has now expanded here. The midsize rooms are handsomely furnished, if rather monotonous in style. Many good restaurants and cafes are within an easy walk.

Bretón de los Herreros 29, 26001 Logroño. © **94-122-66-08.** Fax 94-122-67-54. www.husa.es. 71 units. 100€–130€ double; from 121€ suite. AE, DC, MC, V. Parking 18€. **Amenities:** Restaurant; bar; babysitting; room service. *In room:* A/C, TV, hair dryer, minibar, Wi-Fi (free).

Where to Dine in Logroño

Asador Emilio ★ LOGRONESE An ample bar greets you as you enter Asador Emilio, which serves primarily roasts, especially goat and beef. In air-conditioned comfort, you can also enjoy peppers stuffed with cod, or baked hake. From the well-stocked wine cellar come some of the finest Rioja wines. Asador Emilio is south of the Old Town, directly west of the major boulevard, Vara de Rey.

República Argentina 8. © **94-125-88-44.** www.asadoremilio.com/marcos.htm. Reservations recommended. Main courses 19€–28€; set menus 25€. AE, DC, MC, V. Mon–Sat 1:30–4pm and 9–11:30pm. Closed Aug.

Juan & Juan 🖋 LOGRONESE There are many other better-rated restaurants in Logroño—and a lot more expensive ones—but we find ourselves returning again and again to this intimate restaurant. The brothers Juan Manuel and Juan Marcos welcome guests into their little enclave, plying them with an array of tasty local specialties, backed up by an affordable selection of local wines. The portions are generous, the dishes well prepared, including such specialties as *lomo a la plancha* (loin of pork), roast goat, or tender, succulent lamb flavored with garlic.

Calle Albornoz 5. © **94-122-99-83.** Reservations not necessary. Fixed-price dinner menu 10€–12€; fixed-price lunch menu 9€–15€; dinner entrees 15€–25€. MC, V. Tues–Sun 1:30–4pm; Tues–Sat 9–11pm.

HARO ★

359km (223 miles) N of Madrid, 48km (30 miles) NE of Logroño

Center of the wine tours of the Rioja Alta district, the region around Haro has been compared to Tuscany. Come here to taste the wine at the bodegas, as international wine merchants do year-round (but especially after the autumn harvest).

16

NAVARRE & LA RIOJA | Haro

Essentials

GETTING THERE Four to five **RENFE trains** (☎ 90-224-02-02; www.renfe. es) run daily from Logroño (trip time: 45 min.). There are also two to three connections per day from Zaragoza (trip time: 3–3½ hr.). Six to seven **buses** per day run to Haro from Logroño (trip time: 45 min.–1 hr.). For information, call ☎ **94-123-59-83.** If you're driving, follow the A-68 expressway (south of Logroño) northwest to the turnoff for Haro.

VISITOR INFORMATION The **tourist office,** at Plaza Monseñor Florentino Rodríguez s/n (☎ **94-130-33-66**), is open October to June Tuesday to Sunday 10am to 2pm, and Saturday 4 to 7pm; and July to September Tuesday to Saturday 10am to 2pm and 4:30 to 7:30pm, and Sunday 10am to 2pm.

SPECIAL EVENTS Every June 29, the **Battle of Wine** erupts. It's an amusing, mock-medieval brawl in which opposing teams splatter each other using wineskins filled with the output from local vineyards.

Exploring Haro & Visiting the Bodegas

The town itself deserves a look before you head for the bodegas. The Old Quarter is filled with mansions, some from the 16th century; the most interesting ones lie along **Calleja del Castillo.** At the center of the Old Quarter is the town's major architectural landmark, **Iglesia de Santo Tomás,** Plaza de la Iglesia. Distinguished by its wedding-cake tower and Plateresque south portal, the 16th-century church has a Gothic interior.

You could spend up to 3 days touring the wineries in town, but chances are that a few visits will satisfy your curiosity. **Bodegas Muga,** Av. Vizcaya s/n (☎ **94-131-04-98**), near the rail station, offers tours (usually in Spanish) of its wine cellars. A tour in English is offered Monday to Friday at 11am. The winery is closed at Easter and August 1 to August 15.

Finally, pay a visit to **Rioja Alta,** Av. Vizcaya s/n (☎ **94-131-03-46**), not far from Muga. It's open Monday to Friday from 10am to 2pm. Visits must be arranged in advance.

If you arrive in Haro in August or the first 2 weeks in September, when many of the bodegas are closed, settle instead for drinking wine in the *tascas* that line the streets between Parroquia and Plaza de la Paz. After a night spent there, you'll forget all about the bodega tours. Some of the finest wines in Spain are sold at these *tascas,* along with tapas—all at bargain prices.

Where to Stay in Haro

Hotel Ciudad De Haro Nearly a kilometer (½ mile) southeast of the city on the highway, this Haro hotel should be your second choice (Los Agustinos, below, should be your first). The small but comfortable rooms are attractively furnished, many with impressive views. Ample parking facilities are available.

Carretera N-124 Km 41 s/n, 26200 Haro. ☎ **94-131-12-13.** Fax 94-131-17-21. www.ciudadeharo. com. 59 units. 70€–190€ double; 132€–220€ suite. AE, DC, MC, V. Free parking. **Amenities:** Restaurant; bar; exercise room; Jacuzzi; outdoor pool; room service. *In room:* A/C, TV, hair dryer, minibar, Wi-Fi (free).

Los Agustinos ★★ This former Augustinian convent is now a government-rated four-star hotel in the center of Haro. Since its restoration and reopening in 1990, it has become the most desirable place to stay in a town that has always had too few accommodations. Owned by a Basque chain of hotels, it is in a "zone of tranquillity" (pedestrian zone). Rooms are well appointed and comfortable, each equipped with a good bed.

Calle San Agustín 2, 26200 Haro. ✆ **94-131-13-08.** Fax 94-130-31-48. www.aranzazu-hoteles. com. 62 units. 123€ double. AE, DC, MC, V. Parking 15€. **Amenities:** Restaurant; bar; babysitting; exercise room; room service. *In room:* A/C, TV, hair dryer, Wi-Fi (free).

Where to Dine in Haro

Beethoven I, II, y III ★ 🎁 NAVARRESE/BASQUE Haro's premier restaurant in the center of town is actually three air-conditioned restaurants adjacent to each other. All offer good food and value, and the wine cellars are among the finest in the area. They're justifiably famous for their platters of wild mushrooms, which chef María Angeles Frenso raises herself. Try the stuffed filet of sole, vegetable stew, or wild pheasant, and finish it off with an apple tart.

Santo Tomás 3-5. ✆ **94-131-11-81.** www.restaurantebeethoven.com. Reservations required in summer. Main courses 16€–30€. MC, V. Wed–Mon 1:30–4pm; Wed–Sun 8:30–11:30pm.

Terete ★ 🎁 NAVARRESE This place has been an *horno asado* (restaurant specializing in roasts) since 1867 and is beloved by locals for its roast suckling pig. The service is discreet, the food savory and succulent—the kitchen has had a long time to learn the secrets of roasting meats. The dishes are all prepared according to traditional regional recipes. When the fresh asparagus comes in, that is reason enough to dine here. The local peaches in season make the best dessert. Naturally, the finest of Rioja wines are served. Terete is in the center of Haro.

Lucrecia Arana 17. ✆ **94-131-00-23.** www.terete.es. Reservations recommended. Fixed-price menu 35€. DC, MC, V. Tues–Sun 1:15–4pm; Tues–Sat 8:30–11pm. Closed July 1–15 and Oct 15–31.

The cellars of Bodegas Muga.

17

THE BASQUE COUNTRY

The Basque people are the oldest traceable ethnic group in Europe. Their language, Euskera (also spelled Euskara, Uskara, or Eskuara, depending on the dialect), predates any of the commonly spoken Romance languages; its origins, like those of the Basque race itself, are lost in obscurity. There are many competing theories. One is that the Basques are descended from the original Iberians, who lived in Spain before the arrival of the Celts some 3,500 years ago. Conqueror after conqueror, Roman to Visigoth to Moor, may have driven these people into the Pyrenees, where they stayed and carved out a life for themselves—filled with tradition and customs practiced to this day.

The region is called Euskadi, which in Basque means "collection of Basques." In a very narrow sense it refers to three provinces of Spain: Guipúzcoa (whose capital, **San Sebastián,** the number-one sightseeing destination in Euskadi, features La Concha, one of Spain's best-loved stretches of sand); Viscaya (whose capital is the industrial city of **Bilbao**); and Alava (with its capital at **Vitoria**). But to Basque nationalists who dream of forging a new nation that will one day unite all the Basque lands, Euskadi also refers to the northern part of Navarre and three provinces in France, including the famed resort of Biarritz.

The three Spanish Basque provinces occupy the eastern part of the Cantabrian Mountains, between the Pyrenees and the valley of the Nervión. They maintained a large degree of independence until the 19th century, when they finally gave in to control from Castile, which continued to recognize their ancient rights and privileges until 1876.

Geographically, the Basque Country straddles the western foothills of the Pyrenees, so the Basque people live in both France and Spain—but mostly in the latter. During the Spanish Civil War (1936–39), the Basques were on the Republican side defeated by Franco. Oppression during the Franco years has led to deep-seated resentment against the policies of Madrid. The Basque separatist movement, ETA (*Euskadi ta Askatasuna,* or Basque Nation and Liberty) and the French organization Enbata (Ocean Wind) engaged unsuccessfully in guerrilla activity in 1968 to secure a united Basque state.

Many Basque nationalists still fervently wish that the Basque people could be united into one autonomous state instead of being divided between France and Spain.

The riddle of the Basque language has puzzled linguists and ethnologists for years; its grammar, syntax, and vocabulary are unrelated to those of any other European language. Although on the wane since the beginning of this century, the Basque language is now enjoying a modest renaissance; it's taught in schools, and autonomous TV stations in the region broadcast in the language.

FACING PAGE: **Cai Guo-Qiang's installation,** *Inopportune: Stage One,* **in the atrium of the Guggenheim.**

Basques wear a *boina,* a beret of red, blue, or white wool, as a badge of pride and a political statement. You may see nationalist graffiti as you travel, slogans such as EUSKADI TA ASKATASUNA (Basque Nation and Liberty). Although the separatist movement is still simmering, you'll find most of the people friendly and welcoming. Politics rarely intrude on vacationers in this beautiful corner of Spain.

VITORIA ★

66km (41 miles) S of Bilbao, 114km (71 miles) SW of San Sebastián, 351km (218 miles) N of Madrid

Quiet and sleepy until the early 1980s, Vitoria was chosen as headquarters of the Basque region's autonomous government. In honor of that occasion, it revived the name Gasteiz, by which it was known when founded in 1181 by King Sancho of Navarre. Far more enduring, however, has been the name Vitoria, a battle site revered by the English. On June 21, 1813, Wellington vanquished the occupying forces of Napoleon. A statue dedicated to the Iron Duke stands today on the neoclassical Plaza de la Virgen Blanca.

Shortly after its founding, the city became a rich center for the wool and iron trades, and this wealth paid for the fine churches and palaces in the medieval quarter. Many of the city's buildings are made of gray-gold stone. Local university students keep the taverns rowdy until the wee hours.

Essentials

GETTING THERE The **Aeropuerto Vitoria-Foronda** (✆ 90-240-47-04) is 8km (5 miles) northwest of the town center and has direct air links to Madrid on **Iberia Airlines** (✆ 90-240-05-00; www.iberia.com).

From San Sebastián, eight **RENFE trains** (✆ 90-224-02-02; www.renfe.es) daily make the 1¾-hour trip to Vitoria.

Roughly eight **buses** daily make the 1½-hour trip from San Sebastián. Eight to 12 buses daily make the 1-hour trip from Bilbao. Call ✆ 94-525-84-00 for more information and schedules.

Take the E-5 north from Madrid to Burgos, cutting northwest until you see the turnoff for Vitoria. (Note that along its more northerly stretches, this superhighway is identified as both E-5 and A-1.)

VISITOR INFORMATION The **tourist office,** at Plaza General Loma 1 (✆ 94-516-15-98; www.vitoria-gasteiz.org/turismo), is usually open Monday to Saturday 10am to 7pm and Sunday 11am to 2pm. From July to October hours are extended—daily 9:30am to 7:30pm.

SPECIAL EVENTS One of the major jazz festivals in the north of Spain takes place here annually in mid-July. It's the weeklong **Festival de Jazz de Vitoria-Gasteiz** (✆ 94-514-19-19; www.jazzvitoria.com). For the big-name performers, tickets range from 15€ to 40€, but spontaneous entertainment takes place on the street for free, although donations are appreciated.

Exploring Vitoria

The most important sight in Vitoria is the **medieval district ★,** whose Gothic buildings were constructed on a series of steps and terraces. Most of the streets, arranged in concentric ovals, are named after medieval artisan guilds. The

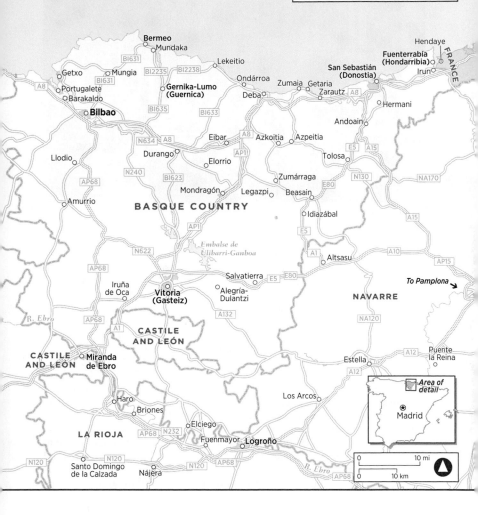

The Basque Country

Bay of Biscay

northern end is marked by the Catedral de Santa María, its southern flank by the Iglesia de San Miguel.

One of the most intriguing streets in the barrio is **Calle Cuchillaría,** which contains many medieval buildings. You can enter the courtyard at no. 24, **Casa del Cordón,** which was constructed in different stages from the 13th to the 16th century. Number 58, **Bendana Palace,** built in the 15th century, has a fine ornate staircase set into its courtyard.

Catedral de Santa María (the "old" cathedral), Calle Fray Zacaras (© **94-525-51-35;** www.catedralvitoria.com), was built in the 14th century in the Gothic style. It contains a good art collection, with paintings that imitate

The medieval district of Vitoria.

various schools, including those of Van Dyck, Caravaggio, and Rubens, as well as several tombs carved in a highly decorated Plateresque style. Santa María is at the northern edge of the Old Town. The cathedral is closed for general visits not arranged in advance because of upcoming renovations, which may last for several years to come. However, you can call the number above and ask to be included in a group, as only group visits are allowed. Such tours are possible daily 11am to 1pm and 5 to 7pm by appointment only, for 5€. Groups can be spontaneously formed if enough people are interested. For more details, contact the tourist office (p. 614).

This cathedral is not to be confused with the town's enormous neo-Gothic "new cathedral," **Catedral María Inmaculada,** Calle Monseñor, Cadena y Eleta s/n (© **94-518-19-18**), just north of the Jardines la Florida. This cathedral is from the 20th century and can be skipped, although on-site is its **Museo Diocesano de Arte Sagrado** (© **94-525-06-31**), a small but choice collection of ecclesiastical paintings gathered from various churches, including a minor work by El Greco. The cathedral is open Monday to Saturday 11am to 2pm, charging no admission. The museum can be visited Tuesday to Friday 10am to 2pm and 4:30 to 6:30pm, Saturday 10am to 2pm, and Sunday 11am to 2pm. There is no charge for admission.

The major historic square is **Plaza de la Virgen Blanca,** a short walk south of the medieval quarter. Its neoclassical balconies overlook a statue of Wellington. The square is named after the late Gothic polychrome statue of the Virgen Blanca (the town's patron), which adorns the portico of the 13th-century **Church of San Miguel** at the square's upper edge. The 17th-century altarpiece inside was carved by Gregorio Fernández. The church is open Monday through Friday from 11am to 3pm.

At **Plaza de España** (also known as Plaza Nueva), a satellite square a short walk away, the student population of Vitoria congregates to drink.

The **Museo de Arqueología de Alava,** Calle de la Correría 116 (© **94-518-19-22**), behind a half-timbered facade, exhibits pottery shards and statues unearthed from digs in the area. Some of these date from Celto-Iberian days; others are from the Roman era. The museum is open Tuesday to Friday 10am to 2pm and 4 to 6:30pm, Saturday 10am to 2pm, and Sunday 11am to 2pm. Admission is free.

Museo de Bellas Artes de Alava, Palacio de Agustín, Paseo de Fray Francisco 8 (✆ **94-518-19-18**), has a collection of several unusual weapons, a *Crucifixion* and portraits of Saints Peter and Paul by José Ribera, and a triptych by the Master of Avila. This museum also contains a fine selection of Spanish art dating from the 18th and 19th centuries and a collection that traces the development of Basque art from 1850 to 1950. It's open Tuesday to Friday 10am to 2pm and 4 to 6:30pm, Saturday from 10am to 2pm, and Sunday from 11am to 2pm. Admission is free.

Where to Stay in Vitoria

MODERATE

Barceló Hotel Gasteiz ★ On the eastern flank of the broad, tree-lined boulevard that circumnavigates Old Town, this is the most modern hotel around. Built in 1982, it was completely renovated in 1994. Although not architecturally distinguished, it serves as the preferred meeting place for the city's business community, offering good-size, conservative rooms with uncomplicated furnishings, and a series of comfortable (albeit undramatic) public rooms.

Av. Gasteiz 45, 01008 Vitoria. ✆ **94-522-81-00.** Fax 94-522-62-58. www.barcelogasteiz.com. 150 units. 65€–135€ double; 105€–145€ suite. AE, DC, MC, V. Parking 17€. **Amenities:** Restaurant; bar; Internet (free, in lobby); room service. *In room:* A/C, TV, hair dryer, minibar, Wi-Fi (12€ per 24 hr.).

Hotel General Alava ★ Named after a local hero—a Spanish general who won an important battle against the French in 1815—this hotel is one of the best and most comfortably furnished in town. The guest rooms range from small to midsize, each fitted with a small tiled bathroom with a shower stall. Built in 1975, the hotel attracts scores of business travelers from throughout Spain. It is a 10-minute walk west of the town center, near the junction of Calle Chile.

Gasteiz 79, 01009 Vitoria. ✆ **94-521-50-00.** Fax 94-524-83-95. www.ac-hotels.com. 113 units. 80€–185€ double. AE, DC, MC, V. Parking 15€. **Amenities:** Restaurant; bar; exercise room; sauna. *In room:* A/C, TV, hair dryer, minibar, Wi-Fi (10€ per 24 hr.).

INEXPENSIVE

Achuri This attractively priced, modern hotel provides a friendly welcome. A short walk from the train station, it offers tidy and comfortably furnished but small guest rooms and well-equipped bathrooms. Breakfast is the only meal available (and is not included in the room rates), but you'll find several places serving food in the vicinity.

Rioja 11, 01005 Vitoria. ✆ **94-525-58-00.** Fax 94-526-40-74. 40 units. 55€ double; 65€ triple. AE, DC, MC, V. **Amenities:** Bar. *In room:* A/C, TV.

Hotel Dato ★ 🛏 Located 3 blocks south of the southern extremity of the Old Town, in the pedestrian zone, this hotel offers the best budget accommodations in Vitoria. It's known for its original regional decor, making the hotel a virtual small museum. The rooms, ranging from small to midsize, are well decorated, often with quite a bit of style. No breakfast is served.

Calle Eduardo Dato 28, 01005 Vitoria. ✆ **94-514-72-30.** Fax 94-523-23-20. www.hoteldato. com. 14 units. 48€–60€ double; 62€–68€ triple. AE, DC, MC, V. Parking 10€. *In room:* TV, hair dryer, Wi-Fi (free).

Where to Dine in Vitoria

Tasca-hopping before dinner with the consumption of small glasses (*chiquiteos*) of beer or wine at many bars and taverns is very popular and fun for visitors to Vitoria. A number of places can be found on **Avenida de Gasteiz.**

El Portalón ★★ BASQUE   This is the finest restaurant in town. It was built in the late 1400s as a tavern and post office near what at the time was one of the only bridges leading in and out of Vitoria. Rich with a sense of history, the restaurant prides itself on serving extremely fresh fish from the nearby Gulf of Biscay, always prepared in traditional style. Cream and butter are rarely used. Some of the finest menu items are baked hake with fresh vegetables or lamb trotters slowly cooked in a red pepper sauce. Roast suckling pig is another specialty, as is grilled sirloin steak with thinly sliced sautéed potatoes.

Correría 151. © **94-514-27-55.** www.restauranteelportalon.com. Reservations recommended. Main courses 15€–25€; fixed-price menu 35€–59€. AE, DC, MC, V. Daily 1:30–3:30pm and 9–11pm. Closed Aug 9–Sept 4.

Mesa BASQUE   For price and value, this ranks as one of the most worthwhile restaurants in town. You can try a number of Basque specialties, none better than the notable *merluza* (hake), the fish so beloved by Basque chefs. Fresh fish and a well-chosen selection of meats are presented nightly, and the service is attentive. The setting is solid, sober, and severely dignified, with white walls and wood trim, and tables and chairs stained dark in the Iberian style.

Chile 1. © **94-522-84-94.** Reservations recommended. Main courses 10€–15€; fixed-price menus 21€–33€. AE, MC, V. Thurs–Tues 1–3:30pm and 9–11:30pm. Closed Aug 11–Sept 4.

SAN SEBASTIÁN ★★

21km (13 miles) W of the French border, 483km (300 miles) N of Madrid, 100km (62 miles) E of Bilbao

San Sebastián (Donostia, in the Basque language) is the summer capital of Spain, and here the Belle Epoque lives on. Ideally situated on a choice spot on the Bay of Biscay, it's surrounded by green mountains. From June to September, the population swells as hundreds of Spanish bureaucrats escape the heat and head for this tasteful resort—it has few of the tawdry trappings associated with major beachfront cities. San Sebastián is an ideal base for trips to some of the Basque Country's most fascinating towns.

Queen Isabella II put San Sebastián on the map as a resort when she spent the summer of 1845 here. In time, it became the summer residence of the royal court. On July 8, 1912, Queen María Cristina inaugurated the grand hotel named after her, and the resort became very fashionable. In what's now the city hall, built in 1887, a casino opened, and European aristocrats gambled in safety here during World War I.

San Sebastián is the capital of Guipúzcoa province, the smallest in Spain, tucked in the far northeastern corner bordering France. It's said that Guipúzcoa has preserved Basque customs better than any other province. Half of the *donostiarras*—residents of San Sebastián—speak Euskera. The city is a major seat of Basque nationalism, so be advised that protests, sometimes violent, are frequent.

San Sebastián contains an old quarter, **La Parte Vieja,** with narrow streets, hidden plazas, and medieval houses, but it is primarily a modern city of elegant shops, wide boulevards, sidewalk cafes, and restaurants.

La Concha is the city's most famous beach—especially in July and August, when it seems as if half the populations of Spain and France spend their days under striped canopies or in the cool waters of the bay. Shell-shaped La Concha has a promenade, where crowds mill during the evening. The adjoining beach is **Playa de Ondarreta**. The climate here is decidedly more Atlantic than Mediterranean.

San Sebastián has a good, though insufficient, choice of hotels in summer, plus many excellent restaurants, most of which are expensive. Its chief drawback is overcrowding in July and August. Bullfights, art and film festivals, sporting events, and cultural activities keep San Sebastián hopping during summer.

Essentials

GETTING THERE From Madrid, **Iberia Airlines** (☏ 90-240-05-00; www.iberia.com) offers three to six daily flights to San Sebastián, plus three daily flights from Barcelona. The domestic airport is at nearby Fuenterrabía. From Fuenterrabía, buses run to the center of San Sebastián every 20 minutes Monday to Saturday from 6:45am to 9:05pm, and Sunday every 30 minutes from 7:40am to 9:05pm. Tickets are 4€. Contact **Interbus** (☏ 94-364-13-02) for more information.

From Madrid, **RENFE** runs **trains** to the French border at Irún, many of which stop in San Sebastián (a 6- to 8-hr. trip). RENFE also provides 9-hour overnight train service from Barcelona to San Sebastián and on to Bilbao. For RENFE information, call ☏ 90-224-02-02, or log on to www.renfe.es.

San Sebastián is well linked by a **bus** network to many of Spain's major cities, although if you're in Madrid, it's more convenient to take a train. **Continental Auto,** Av. de Sancho el Sabio 31 (☏ 94-346-90-74; www.alsa.es), runs seven to nine daily buses from Madrid, taking 6 hours and costing 32€. **Vibasa,** Po. De Vizcaya 16 (☏ 94-345-75-00; www.vibasa.es), operates three buses from Barcelona, a 7-hour trip costing 29€ one-way. Finally, **Transportes PESA,** Av. de Sancho el Sabio 33 (☏ 90-210-12-10; www.pesa.net), runs buses from Bilbao every 30 minutes during the day, taking 1¼ hours and costing 15€ one-way.

Driving from Madrid, take the N-I toll road north to Burgos, and then follow A-1 to Miranda de Ebro. From here, continue on the A-68 north to Bilbao and then the A-8 east to San Sebastián. From Pamplona, take the A-15 north to the N-I route, which leads right into San Sebastián.

VISITOR INFORMATION The **tourist office** is at Boulevard 8 (☏ 94-348-11-66; www.sansebastianturismo.com). From June to September, it's open Monday to Saturday 8am to 8pm, Sunday 10am to 2pm; off-season hours are Monday to Saturday 9am to 1:30pm and 3:30 to 7pm, Sunday 10am to 2pm.

SPECIAL EVENTS Two weeklong events draw visitors from around the world. In mid-August, San Sebastián stages its annual party, **Aste Nagusia,** a joyous celebration of traditional Basque music and dance, along with fireworks, cooking competitions, and sports events. In mid-September, the San Sebastián **International Film Festival** draws luminaries from America and Europe. The actual dates of these festivals vary from year to year, so check with the tourist office (see above). In the second half of July, San Sebastián hosts a jazz festival, **Jazzaldia**.

One of San Sebastián's city beaches.

Exploring & Enjoying San Sebastián

San Sebastián means beach time, excellent Basque food, and strolling along the **Paseo de la Concha.** The monuments, such as they are, can easily be viewed before lunch.

Museo de San Telmo, Plaza Zuloaga 1 (✆ **94-348-15-80;** www.museo santelmo.com), housed in a 16th-century Dominican monastery, contains an impressive collection of Basque artifacts from prehistoric times. The museum includes works by Zuloaga (*Torreillos en Turégano,* for example), Golden Age artists such as El Greco and Ribera, and a large number of Basque painters. Located in the Old Town at the base of Monte Urgull, the museum is open Tuesday to Saturday 10:30am to 1:30pm and 4 to 7:30pm, Sunday from 10:30am to 2pm. Admission is free. *Note:* This museum was closed for renovations at press time; check its status before heading here.

The wide promenade **Paseo Nuevo** almost encircles Monte Urgull, one of the two mountains between which San Sebastián is nestled. (Monte Igueldo is the other one.) A ride along this promenade opens onto panoramic vistas of the Bay of Biscay. The *paseo* comes to an end at **Palacio del Mar ★**, Plaza Carlos, Blasco de Imaz s/n (✆ **94-344-00-99;** www.aquariumss.com), an oceanographic museum/aquarium. Like most cutting-edge aquariums, it boasts a mesmerizing collection of huge tanks containing myriad marine species. A transparent underwater walkway allows a 360-degree view of sharks, rays, and other fish as they swim around you. A maritime museum upstairs presents a fascinating synopsis of humankind's precarious relationship with the sea through the ages, with historical displays of fishing gear, naval artifacts, and marine fossils. Here you can also see the skeleton of the next-to-last whale caught in the Bay of Biscay, in 1878. The museum is open October 1 through April 2 Monday to Friday 10am to 7pm, Saturday and Sunday 10am to 8pm; April 3 through June 30 and September Monday to Friday 10am to 8pm, Saturday and Sunday 10am to 9pm; and Easter week and July 1 through August 31 10am to 10pm. Admission is 12€ adults, 8€ students, and free for children 4 and under.

Other sights include the **Palacio de Miramar** (✆ **94-321-90-22**), which stands on its own hill opening onto La Concha. In the background is the residential district of Antiguo. Queen María Cristina, after whom the grandest hotel in the north of Spain is named, opened this palace in 1893, but by the turbulent 1930s, it had fallen into disrepair. The city council took it over in 1971. You can visit daily from 8am to 9pm. Because you can't go inside the palace, you must settle for a look at the lawns and gardens. The palace stands on land splitting the two major beaches of San Sebastián: Playa de la Concha and Playa de Ondarreta.

Palacio de Ayete was constructed by the duke of Bailéen in 1878 and became the summer home of King Alfonso XIII and his queen, María Cristina, until their own Palacio de Miramar (see above) was completed. With 75,000 sq. m (807,300 sq. ft.) of parkland, the palace served as the summer home of Franco from 1940 until 1975. The residence remains closed to the public. However, you can wander through the beautiful grounds daily in summer from 8am to 9pm, and in the off season from 8am to 7pm. To reach it, take bus no. 19 to Ayete from Plaza de Guipúzcoa.

Museo Chillida-Leku, Caserío Zabalaga 66, Jáuregui Barrio, Hernani (✆ **94-333-60-06;** www.eduardo-chillida.com), is devoted to the artwork of Eduardo Chillida, a sculptor legendary in the Basque world; his work appears in many of the world's museums. He's best known for his monumental steel *Comb of the Wind* rising from the rocks at the far end of the Bay of Biscay. A 10-minute drive from the heart of San Sebastián, the museum lies in the little mountain town of Hernani. The hillside around the museum is studded with some 40 Chillida monoliths set among beech trees, oaks, and magnolias. In the center of the property is a farmhouse from the 1500s, which the artist designed to display some of his smaller pieces. These include hanging paper "gravitations" (not quite a collage, but not a mobile, either), translucent alabaster sculpture,

and stone blocks that evoke the Mayan culture, as well as "jigsaw" sculptures of metal and marble. The aging sculptor referred to his museum as a "cathedral." Surprisingly and virtually unheard-of in an art museum, he firmly believed that his sculpture "should be touched" by visitors. Hours in July and August are Monday to Saturday 10:30am to 8pm and Sunday 10:30am to 3pm; hours from September to June are Wednesday to Monday 10:30am to 3pm. The museum is closed December 25 and January 1. Admission is 8.50€ adults, 6.50€ students and seniors, and free for those 9 and under. Guided visits are an additional 5.50€. Take bus no. G2 from San Sebastián.

Finally, for the best view of the city, ride the funicular to the top of

Sculptures of the Museo Chillida-Leku.

The underwater walkway of the Palacio del Mar.

Monte Igueldo ★★★ (© **94-321-02-11**), where, from a gazebo, you can take in a panoramic view of the bay and the Cantabrian coastline. From July to October, the funicular runs Monday to Friday 10am to 9pm, Saturday and Sunday 10am to 10pm. From April to June, it runs Monday to Friday 10am to 8pm, Saturday and Sunday 10am to 9pm. Round-trip fare is 2.50€ adults, 1.40€ children 7 and under. It's also possible to drive up. In spring, the air is rich with the scent of honeysuckle. The funicular is closed from November to March.

Shopping

Your immersion into Basque culture will probably prompt you to buy handicrafts and accessories from the region. One of the best outlets is **Txapela,** Calle Puerto 8 (© **94-342-02-43**). It sells souvenirs and the rough cotton shirts for which the Basques are famous. If you're looking for a *boina* (beret) or any other form of headgear, consider a visit to the venerable shelves of San Sebastián's oldest hat manufacturer, **Ponsol,** Calle Narrica 4 (© **94-342-08-76**). For virtually anything else in the city, try the length of the most congested shopping district, **Parte Vieja,** where dozens of merchants hawk everything from T-shirts to cameras to film.

Where to Stay in San Sebastián

If you book well in advance, you'll find many good hotel values. However, in the high season, most hoteliers insist you take at least half-board (breakfast plus one meal).

VERY EXPENSIVE

Hotel María Cristina ★★★ One of the most spectacular Belle Epoque hotels in Spain, enviably positioned in the heart of town midway between the bay and Río Urumea, this is the town's top choice. The Cristina opened in 1912 behind a facade of chiseled stone and ornate ironwork. The crowd is likely to include movie stars and film directors; this is where the glitterati stay during San Sebastián's film festival. The public rooms are opulent with ormolu, mahogany, onyx, exotic marbles, and rosewood marquetry. The spacious guest rooms are appropriately lavish, with luxury beds and bathrooms with tub/shower combos.

Calle Oquendo 1, 20004 San Sebastián. © **800/221-2340** in the U.S., or 94-343-76-00. Fax 94-343-76-76. www.westin.com. 136 units. 240€–395€ double; from 530€ suite. AE, DC, MC, V. Parking 24€. **Amenities:** Restaurant; bar; babysitting; concierge; exercise room; indoor heated pool; room service; spa. *In room:* A/C, TV, hair dryer, minibar, Wi-Fi (17€ per 24 hr.).

EXPENSIVE

Barceló Costa Vasca ★★ A large red-brick hotel rated four stars by the government, the Costa Vasca is 10 minutes from Ondarreta Beach, and a 5-minute drive (or 10 min. on foot) from the center of town. The interior of the hotel is modern and businesslike, with plenty of space for conferences and banquets; it's ideal for the individual traveler, too. The decor is tasteful but discreet. The rooms are good-size and comfortably furnished; many of the accommodations have balconies.

Av. de Pío Baroja 15, 20008 San Sebastián. © **94-331-79-50.** Fax 94-321-24-28. www.barcelo. com. 203 units. 62€–167€ double; 216€–345€ suite. AE, DC, MC, V. Free parking outside; 15€ garage. **Amenities:** Restaurant; bar; babysitting; bikes; outdoor pool; room service. *In room:* A/C, TV, hair dryer, minibar, Wi-Fi (free).

Londres y de Inglaterra ★ Beside the northern edge of Playa de la Concha, the town's most popular beach, this 19th-century hotel is one of the most stylish in town. It's not as plush as the María Cristina but is significantly more affordable. The views from many of the balconies encompass the beach and some rocky offshore islands. The traditional-style public rooms contain deep armchairs and big windows. Renovated in recent years, the hotel has good-size guest rooms with a vaguely English decor and modern bathrooms.

Zubieta 2, 20007 San Sebastián. © **94-344-07-70.** Fax 94-344-04-91. www.hlondres.com. 148 units. 120€–293€ double. AE, DC, MC, V. Nearby parking 23€. **Amenities:** Restaurant; bar; room service. *In room:* A/C, TV, hair dryer, minibar, Wi-Fi (free).

Monte Igueldo ★ This first-class hotel is perched like a castle on top of the mountain overlooking San Sebastián, a 10-minute drive from the center of town. The public rooms, guest rooms, and main terrace all boast panoramic coastal views. The streamlined, modern guest rooms have private balconies and the furnishings are standardized but reasonably comfortable.

Paseo del Faro 134, Monte Igueldo, 20008 San Sebastián. © **94-321-02-11.** Fax 94-321-50-28. www.monteigueldo.com. 125 units. 126€–155€ double; 191€–210€ triple. AE, DC, MC, V. Free parking. Bus: Igueldo. **Amenities:** Restaurant; bar; outdoor pool; room service. *In room:* TV, hair dryer.

Villa Soro ★★ On the edge of the historic core of the city, Villa Soro, a *fin de siècle* mansion, has been turned into a small hotel imbued with atmosphere, comfort, and charm. Much of its period architecture was retained in a major restoration, including its sweeping staircase and its curved French doors. The hotel still has its original hardwood floors and is filled with many antiques. Bedrooms and bathrooms, however, are completely up-to-date with modern furnishings. Each unit is individually decorated with plush fabrics and rare woods, as well as paintings from local artists. The dining room lies in the former *serre*, or winter garden. Ask for a room in the original house, although the newly built additions are just as comfortable.

Avenida Ategorrieta 61, 20013 San Sebastián. © **943-297-970.** Fax 943-297-971. www.villa soro.com. 25 units. 225€–288€ double. AE, DC, MC, V. **Amenities:** Breakfast room; free bikes; room service. *In room:* A/C, TV/DVD, hair dryer, minibar, Wi-Fi (free).

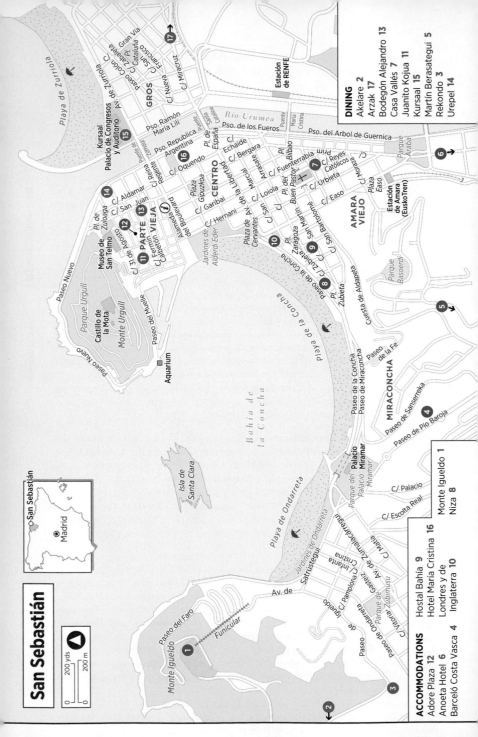

San Sebastián

San Sebastián
Madrid

0 200 yds
0 200 m

Playa de Zurriola

GROS

C/ Miracruz
C/ Nueva
Gran Vía
C/ Cataluña
Pl. de Zabieta
Paseo Colón
Francisco
C/ San Francisco
Av. de Zurriola

Estación
de RENFE

Kursaal
Palacio de Congresos
y Auditorio **15**

Pso. Ramón
María Lili

Pso. República
Argentina **16**

Río Urumea

Pso. de los Fueros

Pso. del Arbol de Guernica

Parque
Araba

6

C/ Aldamar **14**

C/ San Juan **13**

Pl. de
Zuloaga **12**

Museo de
San Telmo

C/ 31 de Agosto

C/ Fermín
Calbetón

**PARTE
VIEJA** **11**

Alameda
del Boulevard

C/ Garibai

C/ Hernani

C/ Oquendo

C/ Reina
Regente

Puente Zurriola
Puente Santa Catalina
Puente María Cristina

Pl. de
España

C/ Echalde
C/ Bergara

Plaza
Gipuzkoa

CENTRO

C/ Loiola

Av. de la Libertad

C/ Marcial
C/ Arrasate

C/ Fuenterrabia **7**

C/ Reyes
Católicos

C/ Prim

C/ San Martín
Av. Buen Pastor
C/ San Bartolomé

Pl. del
Buen Pastor

C/ Urbieta

C/ Easo

Plaza
Easo

Estación
de Amara
(EuskoTren)

**AMARA
VIEJO**

C/ Moraza

Plaza
Easo

Parque
Basoerdi

5

Jardines de
Alderdi Eder

Plaza de
Cervantes

Pl.
Zaragoza

Pl. de
Zubieta

Pl.
Zubieta

10
9
8

Cuesta de Aldapeta

Parque
Basoerdi

Paseo Nuevo

Parque
Urgull

Paseo Urgull

Castillo de
la Mota

Monte Urgull

Paseo del Muelle

Aquarium

Bahía de
la Concha

Playa de la Concha

Isla de
Santa Clara

Paseo de la Concha
Paseo de Miraconcha

Paseo
de la Fe

MIRACONCHA

Paseo de Sanserreka

Paseo de Pío Baroja

4

Palacio
Miramar

Palacio
Miramar

Parque de
Palacio Miramar

C/ Palacio

C/ Escolta Real

Monte Igueldo **1**
Niza 8

Paseo del Faro

Monte Igueldo

Funicular

1

Playa de Ondarreta

Jardines de
Ondarreta

Av. de
Satrústegui

Paseo de Ondarreta

C/ Infanta
Cristina

Av. de Zumalacárregui

Pl. de
Pamplona

C/ Victoria
Eugenia
C/ María
Cristina

Gaztelugaitz

Paseo
de
Igueldo

3

2

ACCOMMODATIONS
Adore Plaza **12**
Anoeta Hotel **6**
Barceló Costa Vasca **4**
Hostal Bahía **9**
Hotel María Cristina **16**
Londres y de
Inglaterra **10**
Monte Igueldo **1**
Niza **8**

DINING
Akelare **2**
Arzak **17**
Bodegón Alejandro **13**
Casa Vallés **7**
Juanito Kojua **11**
Kursaal **15**
Martín Berasategui **5**
Rekondo **3**
Urepel **14**

624

MODERATE

Anoeta Hotel Close to the sports arena and a 5-minute drive from the town center, this government-rated three-star hotel is named for the old village that once stood here but was long ago absorbed by the growing boundaries of San Sebastián. Anoeta features cherrywood, marble fittings, and a modern decor behind its brick facade. With a welcoming atmosphere, it's one of the better choices in the midprice range. The guest rooms are generally small but quite inviting, with comfortable beds and wooden furniture.

Paseo de Anoeta 30, 20014 San Sebastián. ℂ **94-345-14-99.** Fax 94-345-20-36. www.hotel anoeta.com. 26 units. 85€–118€ double; 114€–145€ suite. AE, DC, MC, V. Parking 8€. Bus: 26 or 28. **Amenities:** Restaurant; bar; babysitting. *In room:* A/C, TV, hair dryer, minibar, Wi-Fi (free).

Niza ★ 🛏 This little hotel, opening onto the Playa de la Concha, offers real character and a great location. Its small public rooms have modern furnishings, while the public lounges hold antiques. In direct contrast are the rather basic guest rooms, with wooden headboards, white walls, and wall-to-wall carpeting; 18 units open onto ocean views.

Zubieta 56, 20007 San Sebastián. ℂ **94-342-66-63.** Fax 94-344-12-51. www.hotelniza.com. 40 units. 123€–145€ double. AE, DC, MC, V. Nearby parking 15€. Bus: 5 or 6. **Amenities:** Restaurant; bar; babysitting; room service. *In room:* A/C (in most units), TV, hair dryer, Wi-Fi (free).

INEXPENSIVE

Adore Plaza ⚜ Among the most affordable local hotels, this well-run and well-maintained establishment is one of the resort's bargains. It offers handsomely decorated and comfortable guest rooms. Every four units share hallway facilities. In the heart of the Old Town, next to La Concha and Zurriola beaches, the hotel offers spacious guest rooms in double or triple size.

Plaza de la Constitución 6, 20003 San Sebastián. ℂ **94-342-22-70.** www.adoreplaza.com. 9 units. 20€–30€ per person double; 18€–27€ per person triple. MC, V. *In room:* A/C, TV.

Hostal Bahía ⚜ A good-value hotel a block from the beach, the Bahía features guest rooms of varying sizes: Some are large enough to contain sofas and armchairs; others fall into the cubicle category. Many North Americans stay here and take public transportation to Pamplona for the running of the bulls.

Calle San Martín 54B, 20007 San Sebastián. ℂ **94-346-92-11.** Fax 94-346-39-14. www.hostal bahia.com. 55 units. 49€–139€ double. Rates include continental breakfast. DC, MC, V. Nearby parking 15€. Bus: 5, 6, 7, 8, or 9. **Amenities:** Bar. *In room:* TV, hair dryer, Wi-Fi (free).

Where to Dine in San Sebastián

EXPENSIVE

Akelare ★★★ BASQUE Opened in 1974 on the western edge of San Sebastián in a hexagonal villa, Akelare became a must for serious foodies when owner/chef Pedro Subijana won the 1983 National Prize for Gastronomy as the best chef in Spain. His preparations have influenced a generation of chefs and defined the entire philosophy of *la nueva cocina vasca* (modern Basque cuisine). Inside, a sweeping view through large windows encompasses the mists and raging currents of the Bay of Biscay far below. The plushly upholstered modern decor, with a hospitable fireplace, is an appropriate foil for dishes inspired by the Basque *caseríos* (farmsteads).

The perfect beginning to any meal is puff pastry filled with anchovy filets, accompanied by a glass of chilled *fino* sherry. Traditional dishes might include fish cooked on a griddle with garlic and parsley; beans with bacon, chorizo, and pork ribs; baked rice with clams; or a special *marmitako* (fisherman's stew). Fresh market ingredients and regional recipes inspire such dishes as sautéed duck liver, fish and shellfish soup, lobster salad flavored with cider vinegar, and roast suckling pig. The name of the restaurant, incidentally, translates from the Basque as "Witches' Sabbath."

Paseo del Padre Orkolaga 56. © **94-321-20-52.** www.akelarre.net. Reservations highly recommended. Main courses 36€–67€; tasting menu 135€. AE, DC, MC, V. Wed–Sun 1–3:30pm; Wed–Sat 8:30–11pm. Closed Feb and Sept 27–Oct 15, Mon–Tues Jan–June, and Mon July–Dec.

Arzak ★★★ BASQUE One of the most famous restaurants in the Basque world, this legendary place occupies the lavishly renovated childhood home of owner/chef Juan Mari Arzak. Well known in San Sebastián for his role in preparing a meal for Queen Elizabeth II of Britain, Arzak combines staples of the Basque culinary legacy with many new creations of his own. Begin with a selection of fresh oysters or natural foie gras. Crayfish is regularly featured as an appetizer, as is the chef's special *sopa de pescado* (fish soup). For a main course, consider *merluza* (hake) in vinaigrette with onions and small squid. On the back of the menu is a list of classic dishes that have won the most praise among visitors—everything from stuffed sweet peppers with fish mousse to pheasant to partridge. The orange flan with cream just might be the best dessert you've ever had. The restaurant is on the main road leading from the center of town to the French border.

Alto de Miracruz 21. © **94-328-55-93.** www.arzak.es. Reservations required. Main courses 48€–72€; tasting menu 165€, excluding drinks. AE, DC, MC, V. Tues–Sat 1:30–3pm and 8:30–11pm. Closed June 18–July 5 and Nov 5–25.

Kursaal ★ BASQUE In the sparkling Palacio de Congresos, between Playa Zurriola and the River Urumea, this establishment has dining on two levels, with the haute cuisine served on the upper floor. On the ground floor is a gastropub with a livelier atmosphere. Most of the cuisine here, inspired by the recipes of Martín Berasategui (see below), is postmodern. Crisp-skinned Iberian suckling pig is served with its stewed ears and an apple cream sauce; spider-crab meat comes with an anchovy sauce and cauliflower cream. The fish of the day is roasted in its skin and served with strips of eggplant (aubergine). Some of the more daring dishes include herb-roasted boned rack of veal with a coffee sauce, pumpkin cream, and orange blossoms, or else cod confit in virgin olive oil on a bed of leeks with potato couscous and coriander sauce.

Zurriola Pasealekua 1, Gros. © **94-300-31-62.** www.restaurantekursaal.com. Reservations required. Main courses 25€–50€. AE, DC, MC, V. Wed–Sun 1–3:30pm; Thurs–Sat 8:30–10:30pm.

Martín Berasategui ★★★ BASQUE Just when you thought the dining situation in San Sebastián couldn't stand any more starred chefs, along comes Martín Berasategui, whose cooking excites food critics throughout Europe. Trained by his mother, who cooked for local fishers, Berasategui opened his restaurant on the outskirts of town. His cuisine is subtle and pure, and he uses butter and cream for desserts only. The hors d'oeuvres are among the best in the region—from a curl of cider-marinated mackerel with fried anchovies in olive oil to morsels of rare tuna belly grilled over wooden charcoal. Starters include a rich lobster soup with barnacles. Other imaginative dishes: scallops and a sea urchin custard with soy sprouts, coffee cream, cinnamon, and curry; and roast Dover sole with clam oil, citrus flavors, black mint, and a dry tangerine and nut powder. Other selections include oysters with watercress, arugula, and green apple dressed in lemon grass and served with fennel cream or *mille-feuille* of smoked eel, foie gras, and spring onions.

Loidi Kalea 4, Lasarte. ℂ **94-336-64-71.** www.martinberasategui.com. Reservations required. Main courses 32€–50€. AE, DC, MC, V. Wed–Sat 1–3:30pm and 8:30–11pm; Sun 1–3:30pm. Closed Dec 15–Jan 17.

MODERATE

Bodegón Alejandro ★ 🏠 BASQUE In a pair of pale-yellow dining rooms accented with tiles and a sense of nostalgia, this bodega-style restaurant focuses exclusively on a fixed-price menu whose composition changes virtually every day. Many of the ingredients come from the nearby marketplace, reflecting the seasonality and bounty of the Basque Country. Menu items are based on old recipes, which have been adapted to modern palates. Specialties, for example, might include a stewed and glazed veal tail served with a potato-and-bacon terrine along with roasted pepper *jus,* or else roasted lamb with butternut pumpkin cream and sheep's-milk foam. Any of a rotating series of pastries and cakes are highly caloric but eminently satisfying desserts.

Calle Fermín Calbetón 4. ℂ **94-342-71-58.** www.bodegonalejandro.com. Reservations recommended on weekends. Fixed-price menu 34€. AE, DC, MC, V. Wed–Sun 1–3:30pm; Wed–Sat 8:30–10:30pm. Closed Dec 23–Jan 15.

Juanito Kojua ★ BASQUE/SEAFOOD This little seafood restaurant in the Old Town has no decor to speak of, but it's famous throughout Spain. There are two dining areas on the main floor, behind a narrow bar (perfect for an appetizer while you're waiting for your table), and one downstairs. All are air-conditioned in summer. The fish served here is sparkling fresh and well prepared, as evoked by such dishes as sole grilled in butter and served with a lemon sauce, as well as tasty jewfish with sautéed potatoes. The chef also has a penchant for well-seasoned meat dishes, our favorite being a succulent grilled veal chop served with a garden-fresh green salad.

Puerto 14. ℂ **94-342-01-80.** www.juanitokojua.com. Reservations recommended. Main courses 17€–24€; fixed-price menus 30€–52€. AE, MC, V. Tues–Sun 1–3:30pm; Wed–Sun 8–11pm. Closed 3 weeks in Feb and 2 weeks in June.

Rekondo BASQUE This is one of the most substantial restaurants in town, lying within an antique stone house on the western outskirts of town, 4km (2½ miles) from the center. The setting is a trio of formally decorated dining rooms. Menu items include grilled chops and steaks, preparations of hake and flounder, and spicy garlic-laced versions of squid. The food is usually accompanied by any of a very large choice of vintages from around Europe. The chefs don't tax their imaginations but prepare reliable fare based on time-tested recipes.

Paseo Igueldo 57. ℂ **94-321-29-07.** www.rekondo.com. Reservations recommended. Main courses 25€–34€. AE, DC, MC, V. Thurs–Tues 1–3:30pm; Thurs–Mon 8:30–11pm. Closed 2 weeks in June and 3 weeks in Nov.

Urepel ★★ BASQUE/INTERNATIONAL Urepel is near the mouth of the Urumea River, at the edge of the Old Town. Its interior isn't as elegant as those of the restaurants above, but fans of this place aren't bothered by that at all. They come for the food. The restaurant is the domain of Tero Almandoz, one of the outstanding chefs in the north of Spain. Deftly handled seafood dominates the menu and is often served with delicate sauces. The main courses are enhanced by an emphasis on perfectly prepared vegetables. *Rape, dorada* (gilthead sea bream), and raviolis of *cigalas* (crayfish) are likely to turn up on the menu. You can also order goose or duck, somewhat rare in San Sebastián. A local food critic got so carried away by the dessert cart and its presentation that she claimed, "It would take Velázquez to arrange a pastry so artfully"—an indication of how highly regarded this place is. We prefer it in the evening instead of at midday, when many of the tables are reserved by local businesspeople and government officials.

Paseo de Salamanca 3. ✆ **94-342-40-40.** www.urepel.net. Reservations required. Main courses 22€–35€; tasting menu 50€–85€. AE, DC, MC, V. Mon and Wed–Sat 1–3:30pm and 8:30–11pm. Closed Easter week, July 1–23, and Dec 24–Jan 6.

INEXPENSIVE

Casa Vallés ✦ SPANISH Established in 1942 on an all-pedestrian street near the cathedral, this restaurant has survived government coups, civil wars, and the ongoing blur of locals who have come in for daily sustenance. You'll find a bustling tapas bar on the ground floor, where small plates of fish, vegetable, and meat-based tapas cost from 1.80€ to 3.25€ each. There's a simple but dignified-looking paneled dining area upstairs. Menu items include lots of fresh fish, as well as succulent meats—veal, steak, pork, and chicken—that you can ask to have grilled over charcoal. Hake, sole, and filet of eel are among the most popular fish, but since the menu is huge, and since a long list of seasonally based specials is often added to the menu, most tastes are abundantly satisfied.

Reyes Católicos 10. ✆ **94-345-22-10.** www.barvalles.com. Main courses 6€–23€; fixed-price menu 23€. AE, DC, MC, V. Restaurant Thurs–Tues 1–3pm; Thurs–Mon 8:30–11pm. Bar daily 8:30am–11pm. Closed 2 weeks in late May.

San Sebastián After Dark

The best evening entertainment in San Sebastián is to go **tapas tasting** in the Old Quarter. Throughout the rest of Spain this is known as a *tapeo,* or tapas-crawl. In San Sebastián it's called a *poteo-ir-de-pintxos,* or searching out morsels on toothpicks. In most of the Basque Country, the tapas-eating ritual is different than in the rest of Spain. A platter of tapas *(pintxos)* is placed on the bar, and patrons spear the tasty morsels with toothpicks; when they're done, servers tally up the toothpicks to determine how much is owed. A pale, dry white wine, known as *xacoli,* is usually consumed chilled in a plain highball glass.

Groups of young people often spend their evenings on some 20 streets in the Old Town, each leading toward Monte Urgull, the port, or La Brecha marketplace. **Alameda del Bulevar** is the most upscale of these streets, and **Calle Fermín Calvetón** is one of the most popular.

Bar Asador Ganbara, Calle San Jerónimo 21 (✆ **94-342-25-75**), is decorated with flair in light-colored wood and is a tapas lover's delight. The dishes are well prepared from market-fresh ingredients. Try the house specialty, *tartaleta de chagurro* (grilled crab pie). Also sample the spider crab and prawns with mayonnaise or *hojaldre de chistorra* (garlic sausage). In addition to its bar service, the establishment runs a restaurant in a separate section. The bar is open Tuesday to Sunday 11am to 3:15pm and 6 to 11:45pm. The restaurant is open Tuesday to Sunday 1 to 3:15pm and 8 to 11:15pm. Calle San Jerónimo runs at a right angle to Calle Fermín Calvetón.

The tasty tapas served at **Casa Alcalde,** Mayor 19 (✆ **94-342-62-16**), just a 5-minute walk from Parque Alderdi Eder, are thinly sliced ham, cheese, and shellfish dishes. You can also have full meals in a small restaurant at the back, daily from 10am to 4pm and 6 to 11pm. The variety of tapas and wines offered at **Casa Vallés,** Reyes Católicos 10 (✆ **94-345-22-10;** www.barvalles. com), seems endless. Go to hang out with the locals and feast on tidbits guaranteed to spoil your dinner. Located in the center of town behind the cathedral, it is open daily from 8:30 to 11:30pm (closed the last 2 weeks of Dec).

Many locals say that **La Cepa,** 31 de Agosto 7–9 (✆ **94-343-19-73;** www.barlacepa.com), on the northern edge of Old Town, serves perhaps the best tapas. The Jabugo ham is one proof of this claim. Try the grilled squid or the omelet of salt cod and green pepper. You can also order dinner here. La Cepa is open Wednesday through Monday from 11am to midnight. At **Aloña/Berri,** Berminghan 24, Nuevo Gros (✆ **94-329-08-18;** www.alonaberri.com), you can feast on the delights of silky salt-cod *brandade,* pigeon in pastry, and anchovies in red-pepper cream. It is open Tuesday to Saturday 10:30am to 4pm and 7 to 11pm, Sunday 10:30am to 4pm.

San Sebastián has other nightlife possibilities, but they dim when compared with a *tapeo.* Nevertheless, if disco isn't too retro for you, head for **Kabutzia,** Muelle (✆ **94-342-97-85;** www.lakabutzia.com), where the cover and one drink cost 15€. The club opens at 8pm, with variable closing times, depending on business.

San Sebastián's only venue for gambling is the **Casino de San Sebastián,** Mayor 1 (✆ **94-342-92-14;** www.casinokursaal.com). The casino requires minimum bets of 1€ to 50€ for the roulette tables. For the blackjack tables, it requires 5€, or 2.50€ on Sunday. Entrance costs 4€ per person after 10:30pm and requires an ID card with photo or a passport. Jackets and ties for men are not required. From September 16 to June 14, the casino is open Sunday to Friday from 4pm to 4am (until 5am Sat and holidays); from June 15 to September 15, it's open daily from 4pm to 5am.

The big cultural center is the concert hall, **Kursaal Centre,** Av. de Zurriola 1 (✆ **94-300-30-00;** www.kursaal.org), a daringly modern avant-garde building strategically positioned on the Bay of Concha. A cultural, sporting, and leisure center, it is the venue for almost any major event: "Basque Dixieland" band, a big salsa band from Madrid, or gospel singers from America's deep South.

The Kursaal, along with the Guggenheim museum in Bilboa, has helped put the Basque Country on the cultural map of Europe. Many tradition-minded locals objected to the glaringly modern structure, feeling that it was at odds with the city's essential Belle Epoque architecture. All of San Sebastián's major festivals, including the September film festival, are staged here. There is a 1,800-seat theater for plays, music, dance, and *zarzuela* performances. Even if no major event is staged here during your visit to San Sebastián, you can take a guided tour for 2€ (Fri –Sun at 1:30pm).

FUENTERRABÍA ★

23km (14 miles) E of San Sebastián, 510km (317 miles) N of Madrid, 18km (11 miles) W of St-Jean-de-Luz (France)

A big seaside resort and fishing port near the French frontier, Fuenterrabía (Hondarribía in Basque) was, in theory, supposed to guard Spain against frequent attacks over the centuries and has performed that task with varying degrees of success.

Essentials

GETTING THERE Fuenterrabía doesn't have a **train** station but is serviced by the station in nearby Irún (© **90-224-02-02;** www.renfe.es). Buses depart Irún's Plaza de San Juan for Fuentarrabía at 10- to 15-minute intervals. Irún is the end of the line for trains in northern Spain. East of Irún, you must board French trains.

Buses run every 20 minutes from Plaza Guipúzcoa in San Sebastián to Fuenterrabía, 30 to 45 minutes away. Call © **94-364-13-02** for information. By car, take A-8 east to the French border, turning toward the coast at the exit sign for Fuenterrabía.

VISITOR INFORMATION The **tourist office,** at Calle Javier Ugarte 6 (© **94-364-54-58;** www.bidasoaturismo.com), is open July to August, Monday 4 to 8pm and Tuesday to Friday 10am to 8pm; off-season hours are Monday to Friday 9am to 1:30pm and 4 to 6:30pm, Saturday 10am to 2pm and 3 to 8pm, and Sunday 10am to 2pm.

Exploring Fuenterrabía & Environs

The most interesting part of town is the **medieval quarter** in the upper market, where some of the villas date from the early 17th century. The fishing district in the lower part of town is called **La Marina;** old homes, painted boats, and marine atmosphere there attract many visitors. Because restaurants in Fuenterrabía tend to be very expensive, you may want to fill up here on seafood tapas in the many taverns along the waterfront. The beach at Fuenterrabía is wide and sandy, and many prefer it to the more famous ones at San Sebastián.

Wander for an hour or two around the Old Quarter, taking in Calle Mayor, Calle Tiendas y Pampinot, and Calle Obispo. **Castillo de Carlos V,** standing at the Plaza de las Armas, has been turned into one of the smallest and most desirable *paradores* in Spain. (See Parador de Hondarribía, below.) It's hard to get a

Boats docked in La Marina.

room here unless you reserve well in advance, but you can visit the well-stocked bar over the entrance hall.

Sancho Abarca, a king of Navarre in the 10th century, is supposed to have founded the original castle that stood on this spot, but the present look owes more to Charles V in the 16th century. You can still see battle scars on the castle dating from the time of the Napoleonic invasion of Spain.

The most impressive church in the Old Quarter is **Iglesia de Santa María,** a Gothic structure that was vastly restored in the 17th century and given a baroque tower.

If you have a car, you can take some interesting trips in the area, especially to **Cabo Higuer,** a promontory with panoramic views, reached by going 4km (2½ miles) north. Leave by the harbor and beach road. You can see the French coast and the town of Hendaye from this cape.

Where to Stay in Fuenterrabía

Jáuregui Opened in 1981 in the center of the old village, this is a good choice for moderately priced accommodations. The modern interior boasts comfortable accessories, and the hotel has a garage—a definite plus, since parking in Fuenterrabía is virtually impossible. Each room is small but well furnished and maintained; thoughtful extras include a shoeshine machine on each floor. Breakfast is the only meal served (not included in the rates quoted below).

Zuloaga 5, 20280 Hondarribia. ☏ **94-364-14-00.** Fax 94-364-44-04. www.hoteljauregui.com. 42 units. 70€–155€ double; 102€–197€ apt. AE, MC, V. Parking 12€. **Amenities:** Restaurant; bar; babysitting; room service. *In room:* A/C, TV, hair dryer, minibar, Wi-Fi (free).

Parador de Hondarribía ★★ This beautifully restored 10th-century castle, on a hill in the center of the Old Town, was once used by Emperor Charles V as a border fortification. The building is impressive, and so are the taste and imagination of the restoration. Antiques, old weapons, and standards hang from the high vaulted ceilings, and some of the comfortable provincial-style rooms open onto the Bay of Biscay. Units range from small to midsize, each with a well-maintained bathroom. Breakfast (not included in the rates) is the only meal served. It's best to reserve a room here well in advance.

Plaza de Armas, 20280 Hondarribia. ☏ **94-364-55-00.** Fax 94-364-21-53. www.parador.es. 36 units. 222€–298€ double; 410€ suite. AE, DC, MC, V. Parking 15€. **Amenities:** Bar; room service; Wi-Fi (free, in lobby). *In room:* TV, hair dryer, minibar.

Río Bidasoa ★ Five minutes from the center of town and only 5km (3 miles) west of the French border, this was an old mansion remodeled to become the modern hotel you see today. It's surrounded by one of the most beautiful gardens in the area. The exterior is crisp and white, with balustrades trimmed in wood. The rooms are midsize to spacious and furnished in contrasting styles (even in the same room).

Sunset in the Basque Country

You can head west out of town along the **Jaizkibel Road ★★**, which many motorists prefer at sunset. After going 5km (3 miles), you'll reach the shrine of the Virgin of Guadalupe, where another panoramic view unfolds. From here, you can see the French Basque coast. If you continue on this road, you will come to the little fishing village of Pasai Donibane, 18km (11 miles) away.

Nafarroa Behera 1, 20280 Hondarribía. ℂ **94-364-54-08.** Fax 94-364-51-70. www.hotelrio bidasoa.com. 44 units. 100€–177€ double; 130€–208€ suite. AE, DC, MC, V. Free parking. **Amenities:** Restaurant; bar; babysitting; outdoor pool; room service. *In room:* A/C, TV, hair dryer, minibar, Wi-Fi (free).

Where to Dine in Fuenterrabía

Ramón Roteta ★★ BASQUE Named after its owner/founder, this attractive restaurant is one of Europe's most consistently respected purveyors of traditional Basque cuisine. Contained in what was a 1920s villa, it's on the southern outskirts of town, near the local *parador* and the city limits of Irún. Menu specialties include a terrine of green vegetables and fish served with red-pepper vinaigrette, baked sea crabs with tiny potatoes and onions, and fresh pasta with seafood. The dessert specialty is a mandarin-orange tart flavored with rose petals. The villa is surrounded by a pleasantly unstructured garden you can appreciate from a table on the terrace.

Calle Irún 2. ℂ **94-364-16-93.** www.roteta.com. Reservations recommended. Main courses 18€–34€; tasting menu 55€–70€. AE, DC, MC, V. Wed–Mon 1–3:30pm; Wed–Sat and Mon 8:30–11:30pm. Closed 1 week in Nov.

Sebastián BASQUE In the oldest district of Fuenterrabía, close to the castle, this restaurant offers modern cuisine using top-notch ingredients appropriate to the season. The two floors of the restaurant feature thick masonry walls, hung with an array of 18th-century paintings. Try one of the specialties: foie gras of duckling Basque style, terrine of fresh mushrooms, or medallions of sole and salmon with seafood sauce. Fresh hake is another specialty, coming with clams and green sauce, or else baked and served with baked potatoes.

Mayor 9–11. ℂ **94-364-01-67.** www.sebastianhondarribia.com. Reservations required. Main courses 19€–24€; tasting menu 40€. AE, DC, DISC, MC, V. Tues–Sun 1–3:30pm; Tues–Sat 8–11pm. Closed Feb 1–15.

GUERNICA

428km (266 miles) N of Madrid, 84km (52 miles) W of San Sebastián

The subject of Picasso's most famous painting (returned to Spain from the Museum of Modern Art in New York and now displayed at the Reina Sofía Museum in Madrid), Guernica (Gernika, in Basque), the spiritual home of the Basques and the seat of Basque nationalism, was destroyed in a Nazi air raid on April 26, 1937, during the Spanish Civil War. It was the site of a revered oak tree under whose branches Basques had elected their officials since medieval times. No one knows how many died during the 3½-hour attack—estimates range from 200 to 2,000. The bombers reduced the town to rubble, but a mighty symbol of independence was born. Although activists around the world attempted to rally support for the embattled Spanish Republicans, governments everywhere, including that of the United States, left the Spaniards to fend for themselves, refusing to supply them with arms.

The town has been attractively rebuilt close to its former style. A church bell chimes softly, and laughing children play in the street. In the midst of this peace, however, you'll suddenly come upon a sign: SOUVENIRS . . . REMEMBER.

The stained-glass ceiling of the Casa de Juntas, depicting Guernica's oak tree.

The former Basque parliament, **Casa de Juntas** (**Juntetxea;** ✆ **94-625-11-38**), is the principal attraction in town. It contains a historical display of Guernica and is open June to September daily 10am to 2pm and 4 to 7pm, October to May daily 10am to 2pm and 4 to 6pm. Admission is free. Outside are the remains of the ancient communal oak tree, symbol of Basque independence; it wasn't uprooted by Hitler's bombs. From the train station, head up Calle Urioste. **Fundación Museo de la Paz de Guernica,** Foru Plaza 1 (✆ **94-627-02-13;** www.museodelapaz.org), contains a permanent exhibition of the bombing as depicted in photographs in 1937 and in artifacts, including bomb fragments bearing Luftwaffe markings. We learn that the tragic bombing on a market day (greater casualties that way) began at 4pm and lasted for 1 to 3 hours, as Nazi bombers unloaded thousand-pound bombs and thousands of incendiary projectiles on the helpless Basque populace. On one wall of the museum is a framed letter from President Roman Herzog of Germany, dated March 27, 1997, acknowledging German responsibility for the indefensible act of aerial bombardment and calling for reconciliation and peace. Copies of Picasso's working drawings for *Guernica* are also displayed.

July and August, the museum is open Tuesday to Saturday from 10am to 8pm, and Sunday 10am to 3pm; September to June, it's open Tuesday to Saturday from 10am to 2pm and 4 to 7pm, Sunday from 10am to 2pm. Admission is 4€ for adults, 2€ for students and seniors, and free for kids 10 and under.

Essentials

GETTING THERE **Bizkaibus,** at Calle Iparraguirre 4, runs buses to Bilbao, with connections to Guernica. For information, call ✆ **90-222-22-65.**

If you're driving, from Bilbao head east along the A-8 superhighway; cut north on the 6315 and follow the signs for Guernica. From San Sebastián, drive west along A-8, and cut north on the 6315. A more scenic but slightly longer route involves driving west from San Sebastián on the A-8, and branching off on the coastal road to Ondárroa. Continue on as the road turns south and follow the signs to Guernica.

VISITOR INFORMATION The **tourist office** is at Calle Artekalea 8 (✆ **94-625-58-92;** www.gernika-lumo.net). In summer hours are Monday to Saturday 10am to 7pm, Sunday 10am to 2pm; off season, it is open Monday to Saturday 10am to 2pm and 4 to 7pm, Sunday 10am to 2pm.

Where to Stay in Guernica

Boliña This little place is modesty itself but provides a decent shelter for those who come to Guernica wanting to absorb its regional atmosphere. It's a small, contemporary structure with simply furnished rooms, each with a tiny bathroom. The staff is helpful and inviting, although English is hardly the native tongue around here.

Barrenkale 3, 48300 Guernica. ℂ **94-625-03-00.** Fax 94-625-03-04. www.hotelbolina.net. 16 units. 40€–49€ double. AE, DC, MC, V. No parking. **Amenities:** Restaurant; bar. *In room:* TV.

Hotel Gernika Because so many pilgrims flock to this scene of the notorious air-raid massacre at the dawn of World War II, the town finally has a first-rate hotel. It's not the Ritz, but it's suitable for its relatively modest comfort. Guest rooms are midsize and comfortably furnished, each with a small, tiled bathroom. Breakfast is served but there is no on-site restaurant. Several good dining options lie close at hand.

Carlos Gangoiti 17, 48300 Guernica. ℂ **94-625-03-50.** Fax 94-625-58-74. www.hotel-gernika. com. 40 units. 80€ double. Free parking. AE, DC, MC, V. **Amenities:** Bar; babysitting; Internet (free, in lobby); room service. *In room:* A/C, hair dryer, Wi-Fi (free).

Where to Dine in Guernica

Baserri Maitea ★ 🏛 BASQUE This is a 3-century-old Basque *caserío* (farmhouse) skillfully converted to entertain diners with its imaginative home cookery. We know of no other place in the area that offers such a sense of Basque tradition and food. Wooden beams hold the place together, the decorative notes sounded by strings of garlic and red peppers grown in the countryside. The young pigeon in a caramelized glaze is a delight, as is the milk-fed lamb roasted in a wood-fired oven. From that same oven emerges a beautifully roasted *besugo* (sea bream). Look also for the catch of the day—on our last visit it was a white fish called *raya,* caught in Basque waters and served with the aromatic green sauce so beloved by locals.

Barrio Atxondoa s/n, Forua. ℂ **94-625-34-08.** Reservations recommended. Main courses 22€–30€. AE, MC, V. Daily 1–3:30pm; Fri–Sat 9–11pm.

BILBAO ★

396km (246 miles) N of Madrid, 100km (62 miles) W of San Sebastián

Bilbao, Spain's sixth-largest city and biggest port, has been described as an ugly, gray, decaying, smokestack city. But it has a number of interesting secrets to reveal, as well as good food. It serves as a rail hub from which to explore some of the Basque Country. Most of the city's sights can be viewed in a day or two. Many visitors flock here to see the controversial $100-million Guggenheim Museum, designed by American architect Frank Gehry and called "the beast" by some locals because of its bizarre shape. From afar, it resembles a gargantuan sculpture, with a "tumbling-boxes" profile and a 131m-long (430-ft.) ship gallery.

As the industrial center of the north and the Basque people's political capital, Bilbao prospers through shipping, shipbuilding, steel making, and banking. Its commercial heart, bursting with skyscrapers and sky cranes, hums with activity. The metropolitan area has the highest population (around 450,000) in the Basque region; including the suburbs and surrounding towns, Bilbao is home to over a million inhabitants.

Bilbao has a wide-open feeling, extending more than 8km (5 miles) across the valley of the Nervión River, one of Spain's most polluted waterways. Since some buildings still wear a layer of grime, visitors may compare Bilbao to the sooty postindustrial sprawl of an English port town. Bilbao was badly hit by the 1970s economic crisis, leading to closures of shipyards and steelworks. It has benefited greatly from a $1.5-billion reconversion grant, of which the Guggenheim project is one of the main beneficiaries. The Guggenheim Museum is a symbol of Basque economic revival, and locals hope it will lead to continued revitalization of their city. Positive development includes a flashy new Metro system, designed by Englishman Sir Norman Foster, as well as a new airport terminal, the work of Spanish architect Santiago Calatrava.

Bilbao was established by charter on June 15, 1300, which converted it from a village (*pueblo*), ruled by local feudal duke Don Diego López de Haro, into a city. Aided by water power and the transportation potential of the Nervión River, it grew and grew, most of its fame and glory coming during the industrial expansion of the 19th century. Many of the city's grand homes and villas for industrialists were constructed then, particularly in the wealthy suburb of Neguri. The most famous son of Bilbao was Miguel de Unamuno, the writer/educator more closely associated with Salamanca.

Essentials

GETTING THERE **Bilbao Airport** (© 90-240-47-04; www.aena.es) is 8km (5 miles) north of the city, near the town of Erandio. Flights arrive from Madrid, Barcelona, Alicante, Arrecife, Fuenteventura, Las Palmas, Málaga, Palma, Santiago de Compostela, Sevilla, Tenerife, Valencia, Vigo, Brussels, Frankfurt, Lisbon, London, Milan, Paris, and Zurich. **Iberia**'s main booking office in Bilbao is at the airport (© 90-240-05-00; www.iberia.com), open daily from 5am to 10pm. From the airport into town, take bus no. A3247 to the heart of the city for 3€.

The **RENFE train** station, Estación de Abando (© 90-224-02-02; www.renfe.es), is on Plaza Circular 2, just off Plaza de España. From here, you can catch short-distance trains within the metropolitan area of Bilbao, and long-distance trains to most parts of Spain. Two trains per day run to and from Madrid (trip time: 7 hr. on the afternoon train, 9 hr. on the night train). Two trains per day run to and from Barcelona (trip time: 9½ hr.), and one train per day goes to and from Galicia (trip time: 12 hr.). There are also two night trains per week to and from the Mediterranean Coast: one toward Alicante and Valencia (daily during the summer months), and the other toward Málaga (three times a week in summer).

PESA, at the Estación de Buses de Garillano (© 90-210-12-10; www.pesa.net), operates more than a dozen **buses** per day to and from San Sebastián (trip time: 1¼ hr.). **Continental Auto,** Calle Gurtubay 1 (© 94-427-42-00; www.alsa.es), has nine buses per day from Madrid (trip time: 5 hr.). If you'd like to explore either Lekeitio or Guernica (p. 632) by bus, use the services of **Bizkaibus** (© 90-222-22-65). Fifteen buses per day go to Lekeitio Monday to Saturday and two on Sunday. Trip time is 45 minutes. Ten buses run each weekday to Guernica (trip time: 45 min.). On weekends, only five buses per day go to Guernica. For general bus information, call © **94-439-50-77.**

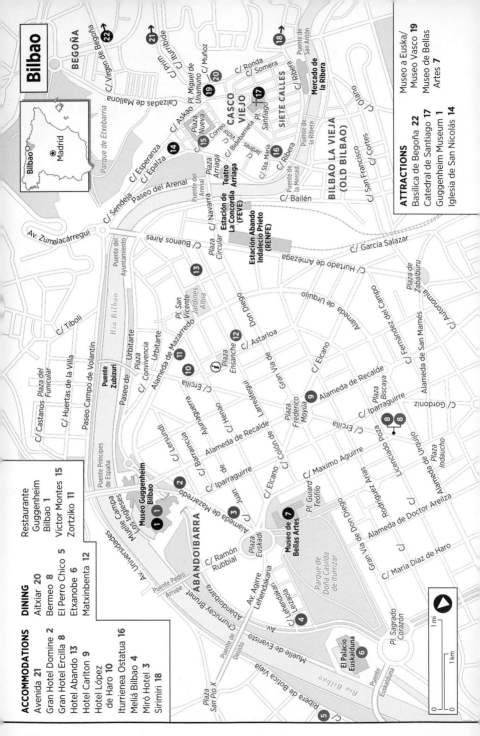

Bilbao

ACCOMMODATIONS
Avenida **21**
Gran Hotel Domine **2**
Gran Hotel Ercilla **8**
Hotel Abando **13**
Hotel Carlton **9**
Hotel López de Haro **10**
Iturrienea Ostatua **16**
Meliá Bilbao **4**
Miró Hotel **3**
Sirimiri **18**

DINING
Aitxiar **20**
Bermeo **8**
El Perro Chico **5**
Etxanobe **6**
Matxinbenta **12**
Restaurante Guggenheim Bilbao **1**
Victor Montes **15**
Zortziko **11**

ATTRACTIONS
Basílica de Begoña **22**
Catedral de Santiago **17**
Guggenheim Museum **1**
Iglesia de San Nicolás **14**
Museo a Euska/ Museo Vasco **19**
Museo de Bellas Artes **7**

Bilbao is beside the A-8, linking the cities of Spain's northern Atlantic seacoast to western France. It is connected by superhighway to both Barcelona and Madrid.

VISITOR INFORMATION The **tourist office,** at Plaza Ensanche 11 (© **94-479-57-60;** www.bilbao.net), is open Monday to Friday 9am to 2pm and 4 to 7:30pm.

SPECIAL EVENTS Festivals often fill the calendar, the biggest and most widely publicized being **La Semana Grande,** dedicated to the Virgin of Begoña and lasting from mid-August to early September. During the celebration, the Nervión River is the site of many flotillas and regattas. July 25 brings the festival of Bilbao's patron saint, **Santiago (St. James);** July 31 is the holiday devoted to the region's patron saint, **St. Ignatius.**

Exploring Bilbao

The **Nervión River** meanders through Bilbao, whose historic core was built inside one of its loops, with water protecting it on three sides. Most of the important shops, banks, and tourist facilities are a short walk from the **Gran Vía,** running east-west through the heart of town. The Old Quarter is east of the modern commercial center, across the river.

THE TOP ATTRACTIONS

Guggenheim Museum ★★★ The biggest attraction in Bilbao is the Guggenheim Museum, at the intersection of the bridge called Puente de la Salvé and the Nervión River. The 104,700-sq.-m (1,126,980-sq.-ft.) colossus is the focal point of a $1.5-billion redevelopment plan for the city. The internationally acclaimed Frank Gehry design features a 50m-high (164-ft.) atrium—more than 1½ times the height of the rotunda of Frank Lloyd Wright's Guggenheim Museum in New York. Stretching under the aforementioned bridge and incorporating it in its design, the museum reanimates the promenade with a towering roof reminiscent of a blossoming metallic flower.

The Guggenheim isn't an encyclopedic museum, such as the Met in New York City. This museum features the works of some of the most towering artists of the latter half of the 20th century—including Picasso, Robert Motherwell, Robert Rauschenberg, Clyfford Still, Antoni Tàpies, Andy Warhol, Ives Klein, and Willem de Koonig. The beginning of the collection is marked by a 1952 Mark Rothko work, *Untitled.* Recent European art is also exhibited along with an array of works by young Basque and Spanish artists. Artwork lent by the Guggenheims in New York and Venice rotates, and Bilbao hosts temporary exhibits traveling here from New York.

Although some disgruntled Basque locals still call the museum "the colossal Californian cauliflower" or "a cheese factory," many architectural critics from around the world, including Paul Goldberger of the *New York Times,* have hailed Frank Gehry's unique structure as the first great building of the 21st century. The structure is said to have been inspired by the Fritz Lang film classic *Metropolis* and is viewed as a homage to Bilbao's industrial past and commitment to its future. The massive museum is clad in shimmering titanium, which many observers find sexy and unmistakably elegant. The building takes up 24,000 sq. m (258,330 sq. ft.) in the former dockyards beside the Nervión River; about half of that space is devoted to the exhibition halls. The museum has virtually abolished

LEFT: **A spider sculpture outside the Guggenheim Museum.** RIGHT: **A bust in the Museo de Bellas Artes.**

right angles and flat walls. As one critic put it, "It was as if Gehry were working in pastry rather than concrete or steel."

Calle Abandoibarra 2. ☏ **94-435-90-80.** www.guggenheim-bilbao.es. Admission 13€ adults, 7.50€ seniors and students, free for children 11 and under. Sept–June Tues–Sun 10am–8pm; July–Aug daily 10am–8pm. Closed Jan 1 and Dec 25. Bus: 1, 10, 13, or 18.

Museo a Euska/Museo Vasco Devoted to Basque archaeology, ethnology, and history, this museum is in the center of the Old Quarter, south of Calle Esperanza Ascao, housed in a centuries-old Jesuit cloister. Some of the exhibits showcase Basque commercial life during the 16th century. You can see everything from ship models to shipbuilding tools, along with reconstructions of rooms illustrating political and social life. Basque gravestones are also on view. In addition, you'll see the equipment used to play the popular Basque game of *pelota* (jai alai).

Plaza Miguel de Unamuno 4. ☏ **94-415-54-23.** Fax 94-479-06-08. http://euskal-museoa.org. Admission 3€ adults, 1.50€ children 10–16 and students, free for children 9 and under; free for all on Thurs. Tues–Sat 11am–5pm; Sun 11am–2pm.

Parking-Lot Robberies

Regrettably, the lot where many patrons to the Guggenheim Museum park is the scene of countless car robberies. The lot is not run by the museum, and the museum is in no way responsible for the thefts that take place there. But many visitors stop off at the Guggenheim in cars filled with luggage, intending to spend the night elsewhere along the Basque coast.

Even if luggage is locked in the trunk, these thefts in broad daylight are commonplace. In most cases, the police seem to offer little assistance, and the lot appears unguarded. Be warned that **your property is at great risk if you leave your car in the lot** while you spend 2 or 3 hours enjoying the museum. Consider arriving by bus or taxi instead.

Museo de Bellas Artes ★ This is another of Spain's important art museums, containing both medieval and modern works, including paintings by Velázquez, Goya, Zurbarán, and El Greco. Among the works of non-Spanish artists are *The Money Changers,* by the Flemish painter Quentin Massys, and *The Lamentation Over Christ,* by Anthony van Dyck. In its modern wing, the museum contains works by Gauguin, Picasso, Léger, Sorolla, and Mary Cassatt. The gallery is particularly strong in 19th- and 20th-century Basque artists, the foremost of whom is the modern sculptor Eduardo Chillida, who created a massive piece titled *Monument to Iron.* You can also walk in the English-inspired gardens around the museum, 4 blocks south of the Old Quarter.

Plaza del Museo 2. ℂ **94-439-60-60.** www.museobilbao.com. Admission 5.50€ adults, 4€ seniors and students, free for children 11 and under; free for all on Wed. Tues–Sun 10am–8pm.

EXPLORING THE CASCO VIEJO (OLD QUARTER) ★

Despite the fact that Bilbao was established around 1300, it has curiously few medieval monuments. On the east side of the Nervión River, it does have an intriguing Old Quarter, the site of its most interesting bars and restaurants. The custom is to come to the Old Quarter at night and barhop, ordering small cups of beer or wine. A small glass of wine is called a *chiquiteo*.

The Old Quarter of Bilbao is connected to the much larger modern section on the opposite bank by four bridges. A few paces north of the Old Quarter's center are **graceful arches,** 64 in all, enclosing the Plaza Nueva, also called the Plaza de los Mártires, completed in 1830.

The entire barrio has been declared a national landmark. The barrio was originally defined by an area around seven streets, but it long ago spilled beyond that limitation. Its most important church is **Iglesia de San Nicolás** (ℂ **94-416-34-24**). Behind this church you'll find an elevator on Calle Esperanza Ascao, which, if working, carries sightseers to the upper town. It is open daily from 10:30am to 12:30pm and 3:30 to 8pm. You can also climb 64 steps from the Plaza Unamuno. From here it's a short walk to the **Basílica de Begoña** (ℂ **94-412-70-91**), built largely in the early 1500s. Inside the dimly lit church is a brightly illuminated depiction of the Virgin, the patroness of the province, dressed in long, flowing robes. Also displayed are some enormous paintings by Luca Giordano. Hours are daily 10:30am to 2pm and 5:30 to 8:30pm. While in the Old Quarter, you might visit the **Catedral de Santiago,** Plaza Santiago (ℂ **94-432-01-25**), which was built in the 14th century and then restored in the 16th century after a fire. The cathedral's facade was rebuilt in the 19th century. It is open daily 11am to 1pm and 4 to 6:30pm. On Sunday you may take in the **flea market,** starting at 8am, on the streets of the Old Quarter.

To reach the Old Quarter on foot, the only way to explore it, take the Puente del Arenal from the Gran Vía, Bilbao's main street.

Shopping

Many visitors like to return from the Basque Country with a chic beret, which locals call *txapelas*. The best selection is found at **Sombreros Gorostiaga,** Calle Victor 9 (ℂ **94-416-12-76**), a family-owned business since 1857. They also sell woolen caps and hunting caps. If you'd like to purchase Basque artisanal products, head for **Basandere,** Iparraguirre Kalea 4 (ℂ **94-423-63-86**), near the Guggenheim Museum. Their crafts are of high quality, and every 3 months they stage exhibitions by local artists. In addition, the shop sells gourmet Basque food items.

A plaza in Bilbao's Casco Viejo.

There are lots of art galleries to explore in Bilbao. One of them, **Sala Rekalde,** Recalde Zumarkalea 30 (✆ **94-406-87-55**), is within walking distance of the Guggenheim. The **Gran Hotel Domine,** Alameda de Mazarredo 61 (✆ **94-425-33-00;** www.hoteles-silken.com), also has a small art gallery across from the Guggenheim.

Where to Stay in Bilbao

EXPENSIVE

Gran Hotel Domine ★★★ No other hotel in Bilbao has the whimsical design of this charmer. Facing the Guggenheim Museum, it is a government-rated five-star establishment. The mansion reflects the design and conceptual wit of Javier Mariscal, who created the 1992 Olympic mascot Cobi in Barcelona. A famous architect, Iñaki Aurreroextea, provided the setting. The exterior is created from polished stone, with black glass windows cantilevered out from the facade of odd angles, reflecting the architecture of Frank Gehry's Guggenheim Bilbao. Mariscal called his concept "a colorist microcosmos." Each floor has its own color scheme, ranging from ochers to blues to reds, even such "box of chocolate" tones as vanilla, cocoa, and caramel. On the seventh floor, a wooden deck opens onto a panoramic view of the Guggenheim and of Bilbao itself.

Alameda de Mazarredo 61, El Ensanche, 48009 Bilbao. ✆ **94-425-33-00.** Fax 94-425-33-01. www.granhoteldominebilbao.com. 135 units. 117€–208€ double; 310€–428€ suite. AE, DC, MC, V. Parking 18€. Metro: Moyua. Bus: 38 or 48. **Amenities:** Restaurant; bar; airport transfers (46€); concierge; exercise room; room service; sauna. *In room:* A/C, TV, hair dryer, minibar, Wi-Fi (free).

Gran Hotel Ercilla ★ Soaring high above the buildings surrounding it in the heart of Bilbao's business district, this is a tastefully decorated bastion of attentive service and good living. The midsize to spacious guest rooms are conservative and comfortably furnished. The Ercilla is one of Bilbao's most desirable hotels, the usual preference of Spanish politicians and journalists.

Ercilla 37–39, 48011 Bilbao. ✆ **94-470-57-00.** Fax 94-443-93-35. www.hotelercilla.es. 325 units. 74€–267€ double; 269€–497€ suite. AE, DC, MC, V. Parking 18€. **Amenities:** Restaurant; bar; babysitting; exercise room; Jacuzzi; room service; sauna. *In room:* A/C, TV, hair dryer, minibar, Wi-Fi (16€ per 24 hr.).

Hotel Carlton ★★ Returned to its former glory, this is the grande dame of all Bilbao hotels, long the leader before anyone ever heard of the Guggenheim Museum. Today you are likely to see such celebrities as Chelsea Clinton or Pierce Brosnan. In days of yore, it was Albert Einstein or Ernest Hemingway. During the Civil War, the hotel was the seat of the Basque government. The lobby, with its magnificent stained glass, sets the 1919 style (the year it was built). The spacious guest rooms are the epitome of traditional style and taste, each with a luxurious bathroom. The building has been declared a historic, artistic, and cultural monument. At the **Artagan Restaurant,** classic Basque haute cuisine is served.

Moyúa Plaza 2, 48009 Bilbao. ✆ **94-416-22-00.** Fax 94-416-46-28. www.aranzazu-hoteles. com. 143 units. 90€–267€ double; from 321€ junior suite. AE, DC, MC, V. Parking 22€. Metro: Moyúa. **Amenities:** Restaurant; bar; exercise room; room service; sauna. *In room:* A/C, TV, hair dryer, minibar, Wi-Fi (free).

Hotel López de Haro ★★★ This refined palace of pleasure is the ultimate in luxury living in the greater Bilbao area. Behind a discreet facade of chiseled gray stone, this 1990 hotel is filled with English touches and features marble flooring, hardwood paneling, and a uniformed staff. The comfortable midsize guest rooms contain flowered or striped upholstery, modern bathrooms, and wall-to-wall carpeting or hardwood floors.

Obispo Orueta 2–4, 48009 Bilbao. ✆ **94-423-55-00.** Fax 94-423-45-00. www.hotellopezdeharo. com. 53 units. 96€–164€ double; from 250€ suite. AE, MC, V. Parking 19€. **Amenities:** Restaurant; bar; babysitting; room service. *In room:* A/C, TV, hair dryer, minibar, Wi-Fi (15€ per 24 hr.).

Meliá Bilbao ★ This hotel stands on the site of the former headquarters of the shipping industry in Bilbao. In honor of that role, the architect, Ricardo Legorreta, built this huge building to evoke an ocean liner of tomorrow. He said he was inspired by the work of Eduardo Chillida (1920–2002), a Basque sculptor. Often filled with art lovers, the public rooms of the hotel are decorated with a stunning collection of modern art as well as Spanish ship models. In the heart of the business district, the hotel offers midsize to spacious bedrooms furnished in a luxurious style, with all the comforts including marble bathtubs. The bedroom views are panoramic, though the hotel doesn't approach the charm of the Carlton or even the Grand Hotel Domine Bilbao.

Calle Leizaola 29, El Ensanche, 48001 Bilbao. ✆ **94-428-00-00.** Fax 94-428-00-01. www.sol melia.com. 210 units. 99€–210€ double; from 249€ suite. AE, DC, MC, V. Parking 23€. **Amenities:** Restaurant; bar; concierge; exercise room; outdoor heated pool; room service; sauna. *In room:* A/C, TV, hair dryer, minibar, Wi-Fi (15€ per 24 hr.).

Miró Hotel ★★ 📖 Fans of Antonio Miró (called the Calvin Klein of Spain) are checking into Bilbao's first boutique hotel. Just steps from the Guggenheim, it offers old-fashioned European service but with an idiosyncratic 21st-century decor. With its black carpeted floors and black marble bathrooms, it is rather minimalist but elegant. It effectively uses light to create a cozy ambience or places white-velvet curtains in unexpected places, such as a bathroom. Rooms, decorated in a minimalist style, come in a wide range of sizes from standard doubles to deluxe suites. In the **Bar Miró,** you might find international art collectors and occasionally hear live jazz.

Alameda Mazarredo 77, 48009 Bilbao. © **94-661-18-80.** Fax 94-425-51-82. www.mirohotel bilbao.com. 50 units. 114€–145€ double; 140€–201€ junior suite. AE, DC, MC, V. Parking 18€. **Amenities:** Bar; babysitting; exercise room; room service; spa. *In room:* A/C, TV/DVD, CD player (in some), hair dryer, minibar, Wi-Fi (free).

MODERATE

Avenida For those who want to be away from the center and don't mind a bus or taxi ride or two, this is a welcoming choice. It's in the Barrio de Begoña, near one of the major religious monuments of Bilbao, the Basílica de Begoña. The hotel was built in the late 1950s, and its small rooms, furnished in a functional modern style, are well kept and maintained. During special fairs in Bilbao, rates increase by at least 10%.

Zumalacárregui 40, 48006 Bilbao. © **94-412-43-00.** Fax 94-411-46-17. www.bchoteles.com. 189 units. 90€–190€ double; from 150€ junior suite. Rates include breakfast. AE, DC, MC, V. Parking 16€. Metro: Santutxu. **Amenities:** Restaurant; bar; babysitting; exercise room; indoor heated pool; room service; spa. *In room:* A/C, TV, hair dryer, minibar, Wi-Fi (free).

Hotel Abando ★ This government-rated four-star hotel isn't in the same class as the López de Haro (see above), but it's a first-class property. The hotel is in the city center, offering an array of well-furnished rooms with comfortable beds. If you don't want to go out at night, you can enjoy top Basque and international cuisine at the **restaurant.**

Colón de Larreautegui 9, 48001 Bilbao. © **94-423-62-00.** Fax 94-424-55-26. www.aranzazu-hoteles.com. 143 units. 80€–160€ double; 203€ suite. AE, DC, MC, V. Parking 16€. All buses to Estación de Abando. **Amenities:** Restaurant; bar; babysitting; bikes; exercise room; room service; sauna. *In room:* A/C, TV, hair dryer, minibar, Wi-Fi (6€ per hour).

INEXPENSIVE

Iturrienea Ostatua ★★ 🛏 In the Old Quarter, far removed from the impersonal, sleek, and commercial hotels of Bilbao, this beautifully restored town house with wooden beams and 19th-century stone floors is a good bet for those seeking an authentically old-fashioned experience (read: no air-conditioning). Adorning the walls are works of sculpture and scenes of historic Bilbao life. Two Basque sculptors, Jesus Chueca and Roberto Atance, handpicked the lighting and original furnishings. Even curators from famous museums, who could afford four- or five-star luxury, book here for the best deal in town. For sheer friendliness, personality, and charisma, this cozy nest has no equal. One downside: The front rooms tend to be noisy.

Santa María 14, 48005 Bilbao. © **94-416-15-00.** Fax 94-415-89-29. www.iturrieneaostatua.com. 21 units. 60€–80€ double; 80€–96€ triple. DC, MC, V. Parking 16€. Metro: Casco Viejo. **Amenities:** Bar. *In room:* TV, Wi-Fi (free).

Sirimiri 🍴 One of the best of the inexpensive choices, this little hotel lies in a restored 19th-century building in the center of the city. Most bedrooms are rather spacious, each with a well-maintained private bathroom. Furnishings are modern and comfortable. Guests meet fellow guests in the lounge, and the staff (many of whom speak English) is one of the town's most efficient.

Plaza de la Encarnación, 48006 Bilbao. © **94-430-07-59.** Fax 94-433-08-75. www.hotel sirimiri.es. 28 units. Summer 80€–90€ double; off-season 60€–70€ double. AE, MC, V. **Amenities:** Breakfast room; exercise room; room service; sauna. *In room:* TV.

Where to Dine in Bilbao

EXPENSIVE

Bermeo ★★★ BASQUE One of the best hotel restaurants in all of Spain, and one of the finest representatives of Basque cuisine anywhere in the world, Bermeo caters to the Basque world's most influential politicians, writers, and social luminaries. Within the modern walls of one of Bilbao's tallest hotels, the restaurant is decorated with glowing wood panels, crisp linens, and copies of 19th-century antiques. Service from the formal, uniformed staff is impeccable. Menu items change with the seasons but might include a salad of lettuce hearts in saffron dressing with smoked salmon, homemade foie gras with essence of bay leaves, fresh thistles sautéed with ham, five preparations of cod, stewed partridge with glazed shallots, or duckling filets with green peppercorns. For dessert, try the truffled figs or a slice of bilberry pie with cream.

In the Gran Hotel Ercilla (p. 640), Ercilla 37–39. ℂ **94-470-57-00.** Reservations required. Main courses 16€–29€; tasting menu 45€. AE, DC, MC, V. Mon–Fri 1–3:30pm, 8:30–11:30pm; Sat 8:30–11:30pm; Sun 1–3:30pm.

Etxanobe ★★ BASQUE/INTERNATIONAL In the gleaming Palacio Euskalduna, this postmodern restaurant is the hottest dining ticket in Bilbao today. Part of the far-reaching waterfront development project, this bastion of grand cuisine is a showcase for the culinary talents of Fernando Canales. One Bilbao gourmet, whose tastes we respect, says he literally "swoons over" the innovative, tasty dishes emerging from the Canales kitchen. The bountiful cuisine is made from only the freshest of ingredients and handled with precision and skill by the kitchen staff. Try the grilled codfish with leeks, roasted scallops in a leek vinaigrette sauce, or boiled hake with seaweed cream. Other delectable dishes include poached eggs with beef kidneys and foie gras or codfish in a licorice *pil-pil* sauce with fresh pumpkin.

Av. de Abandoibarra 4. ℂ **94-442-10-71.** www.etxanobe.com. Reservations required. Main courses 17€–32€; tasting menu 60€. AE, DC, MC, V. Mon–Sat 1:30–3:30pm and 8:30–11:30pm (Fri–Sat until midnight). Closed Aug 1–15.

Restaurante Guggenheim Bilbao ★★ INTERNATIONAL/BASQUE This museum is home not only to a world-class art collection but also to a world-class restaurant carved out of this architectural curiosity. The *chef de cuisine,* Bixenta Arrieta, is a master of *nueva cocina vasca,* and his fisherman's stew in an herb-laced green broth is award winning, as is his white salt cod with tomatoes stuffed with baby squid and black rice (colored by the squid's ink). Diners make selections from the "menu of the sea" (*del mar*) or the "menu of the countryside" (*del campo*). Begin, perhaps, with a lobster salad or duck-stuffed cannelloni. A wide selection of Basque wines is served.

Abandoibarra Etorbidea 2. ℂ **94-423-93-33.** www.restauranteguggenheim.com. Reservations required (as far in advance as possible). Main courses 25€–36€; tasting menus 62€–72€. AE, DC, MC, V. Tues–Sun 1:30–3:15pm; Wed–Sat 9–10:30pm. Closed 2 weeks at Christmas. Metro: Moyúa. Bus: 1, 10, 13, or 18.

Zortziko ★★★ BASQUE/CONTINENTAL This bastion of refined cuisine ranks near the top of all the Basque Country's restaurants. In a multiroom, vaguely French setting furnished in late Victorian style, you'll find a formal environment. Lunches tend to focus on business discussions among clients; dinners tend to be more leisurely and recreational. One of the most unusual dining areas is the wine cellar, where the only table is reserved, sometimes many days in advance, by diners who appreciate being surrounded by valuable vintages. It's more likely, however, that your table will be on the restaurant's street level. In a city where the restaurant competition is fierce, this kitchen emerges at the very top. Menu items include most of the traditional Basque staples, like pigeon breast or sea bass marinated and roasted in red Rioja wine. The tasting menu presents a wide variety of imaginative dishes including roast suckling pig flavored with cinnamon oil, or guinea fowl with the tantalizing addition of truffle juice.

Alameda de Mazarredo 17. © **94-423-97-43.** www.zortziko.es. Reservations recommended. Main courses 20€–39€; fixed-price menu 85€. AE, DC, MC, V. Tues–Sat 1–3:30pm and 9–11:30pm. Metro: Abando.

MODERATE

El Perro Chico ★ 🍴 BASQUE In our view, this is the most underappreciated restaurant in Bilbao. It's true that the decor doesn't win any *Architectural Digest* awards; it could easily be turned into a Gypsy den for telling fortunes. But patrons come here for the cuisine, an array of Basque classics. Frank Gehry considers it his favorite Bilbao dining room. Start, perhaps, with the grilled fresh anchovies with a green sauce, or long green peppers, which are fried and perfectly salted. Fresh tuna comes with a black-squid-ink sauce that's rich and delectable. Other temptations include roast duck in orange sauce served with seasonal vegetables or codfish au gratin topped with a béchamel sauce.

Aretxaga 2. © **94-415-05-19.** Reservations required. Main courses 8€–27€. MC, V. Tues–Sat 1:30–3pm and 9:15–11pm.

Matxinbenta ★ BASQUE Serving some of the finest Basque food in the city since the 1950s, this restaurant is popular for business lunches or dinners, in spite of its often-rude staff. Specialties include fresh tuna in piquant tomato sauce, and a local ratatouille known as *piperada*. You can order veal cutlets cooked in port wine, and finish with a mint-flavored fresh-fruit cocktail. Matxinbenta contains three dining rooms, each with contemporary furniture, potted plants, and lots of exposed wood. It's a block north of the Gran Vía, adjacent to Bilbao's most visible department store, El Corte Inglés.

Ledesma 26. © **94-424-84-95.** Reservations required on weekends. Main courses 12€–24€; *menú del día* 30€. AE, DC, MC, V. Daily 1–4pm; Mon–Sat 8–11:30pm.

INEXPENSIVE

Aitxiar 🐟 BASQUE Well respected for its good food, low prices, and utter lack of pretension, this restaurant in the Old Quarter serves Basque cuisine in two dining rooms in a house built in the 1930s. Expect a decor that includes lots of exposed stone and wood, a somewhat hysterical waitstaff, strong flavors, and lots of regional pride. Menu items include potato soup with chunks of fresh tuna, and an array of fish hauled in that morning from nearby waters. Two of the most appealing fish dishes are hake, which tastes marvelous in an herb-infused green sauce, and cod, prepared in at least two versions. Baby squid is a savory choice, as are the spicy sausages *(chuletas)*, which are best consumed as an appetizer.

Calle María Muñoz 8. © **94-415-09-17.** Main courses 12€–25€; set lunch menu 9€–50€. AE, MC, V. Tues–Sun 1–3:30pm and 8:30–11:30pm. Metro: Plaza Unamuno.

Víctor Montes ★ 🎁 BASQUE/SPANISH In the heart of Bilbao's oldest neighborhood, this restaurant maintains a handful of battered dining rooms—some upstairs—where closely packed tables, racks of wine, and frantic waiters create a sense of good-natured hysteria, especially at lunchtime. Expect copious portions of old-fashioned roasts, stews, soups, and salads, usually with an emphasis on fresh vegetables and seafood such as grilled squid or fresh fava beans with nuggets of cod. Many locals, especially those in a hurry, tend to bypass a dining table altogether, opting for one or more *raciones* of tapas. Lined up atop the bar, the small plates taste wonderful when accompanied with sherry, wine, or beer.

Plaza Nueva 8. ℂ **94-415-70-67.** www.victormontesbilbao.com. Reservations recommended for full meals; not necessary for tapas bar. Tapas from 1.50€; main courses 8€–22€; fixed-price menus 35€–52€. MC, V. Daily 11am–11pm. Metro: Casco Viejo.

Bilbao After Dark

Basque cuisine is the finest in Spain, featuring *pintxos* (pronounced *peen-chohs*)—tapas. The best place for tapas bars is **Calle Licenciado Poza,** between Alameda del Doctor Areilza and Calle Iparraguirre. Favorites include **Atlanta,** Calle Rodríguez Arias 28 (ℂ **94-427-64-72**), famous locally for its *jamón Serrano* (cured ham) sandwiches.

Café Bar Bilbao, Plaza Nueva 6 (ℂ **94-415-16-71**), has two tapas we delight in: silky anchovies (fresh, of course) wrapped around green olives, and *bacalao al pil-pil* (salt cod with garlic emulsion).

During your nights in Bilbao, you can wander through the Casco Viejo's narrow alleyways, two of which (**Calle Pozas** and **Calle Barrencalle**) are dotted with all manner of bars, *tascas,* and bodegas. After a drink or two, you might opt to go out dancing, or at least visit any of three popular discos to watch how it's done in the Basque Country. Favorites include **Disco-Pub Crystal,** Plaza Venezuela 1 (ℂ **94-424-25-08**).

If you want to go gay, head for **High Club,** Naja 5 (no phone), where loud music and hot men rule the night. "We're young, we're queer, and we can now marry in Spain," said a newly liberated young bartender. Porno, most often from Los Angeles, is featured upstairs.

On Friday and Saturday nights from 6:30pm to 6:30am, the bar that's jumping is **Cotton Club,** Calle Gregorio de la Revilla 25 (ℂ **94-410-49-51**), named after its early ancestor in New York's Harlem. More than 30,000 beer caps form part of the decor. A DJ spins the latest tunes for the mingling throngs in their 20s and 30s. The atmosphere is less hectic when the club is open Sunday from 6:30pm to 3am and Monday and Thursday from 4:30pm to 3am. Beer begins at 3€, whiskey at 5.50€, and there's no cover.

The major cultural venue in Bilbao is the **Teatro Arriaga,** Plaza Arriaga s/n (ℂ **94-416-35-33;** www.teatroarriaga.com), on the banks of the Nervión River. This is the setting for world-class opera, classical music concerts, ballet, and even *zarzuelas* (comic operas). Announcements of cultural events at the time of your visit are available at the tourist office. (See "Visitor Information," earlier in this section.)

18

CANTABRIA & ASTURIAS

T he provinces of Cantabria and Asturias are historic lands that lay claim to attractions ranging from fishing villages along the coastlines to the Picos de Europa, a magnificent stretch of snowcapped mountains.

Cantabria was settled in prehistoric times and later colonized by the Romans. The Muslims were less successful in their invasion. Protected by the mountains, many Christians found refuge here during the long centuries of Moorish domination. Much religious architecture remains from this period, particularly Romanesque. Cantabria was once part of the Castilla y León district of Spain, but is now an autonomous region.

Most tourism is confined to the northern coastal strip; much of the mountainous inland is poor and unpopulated. Away from the coast, you'll need a rental car because public transport is inadequate at best. **Santander,** a rail terminus, makes the best center for touring the region; it also has the most tourist facilities. From Santander, you can get nearly anywhere in the province within a 3-hour drive.

The principality of Asturias lies between Cantabria in the east and Galicia in the west. It reaches its scenic (and topographical) summit in the **Picos de Europa,** where the first Spanish national park was inaugurated. With green valleys, fishing villages, and forests, Asturias is a land for all seasons.

The coastline of Asturias constitutes one of the major sightseeing attractions in northern Spain. Called the **Costa Verde ★★**, it begins in the east at San Vicente de la Barquera and stretches almost 145km (90 miles) to Gijón. Allow about 6 hours to drive it without stops. The western coast, beginning at Gijón, goes all the way to Ribadeo, a border town with Galicia—a distance of 180km (112 miles). This rocky coastline, studded with fishing villages and containing narrow estuaries and small beaches, is one of the most spectacular stretches of scenery in Spain. It takes all day to explore.

Asturias is an ancient land, as prehistoric cave paintings in the area demonstrate. Iron Age Celtic tribes resisted the Romans, as Asturians proudly point out to this day. Residents of the region also resisted the Moors, who subjugated the rest of Spain. The Battle of Covadonga in 722 represented the Moors' first major setback in Iberia. Asturians are still staunchly independent. In 1934, Francisco Franco, then an ambitious young general, arrived with his Moroccan troops to suppress an uprising by miners who had declared an independent Socialist republic. His Nationalist forces returned again and again to destroy such Asturian cities as Gijón for their fierce resistance during the Spanish Civil War.

SANTANDER ★

393km (244 miles) N of Madrid, 116km (72 miles) NW of Bilbao

Santander has always been a rival of San Sebastián in the east, but it has never attained the premier status of that Basque resort. It did, however, become a

FACING PAGE: **World-famous Cabrales cheese for sale in Las Arenas de Cabrales.**

royal residence from 1913 to 1930, after city officials presented an English-style Magdalena Palace to Alfonso XIII and his queen, Victoria Eugenia.

An ancient city, Santander was damaged by a 1941 fire, which destroyed the Old Quarter and most of its dwellings. It was rebuilt along original lines, with wide boulevards, a waterfront promenade, sidewalk cafes, shops, restaurants, and hotels.

Most visitors to Santander head for **El Sardinero ★★**, a resort less than 2.5km (1½ miles) from the city. Buses and trolleys make the short run between the city center and El Sardinero both day and night. Besides hotels and restaurants, Santander has three **beaches,** Playa de Castaneda, Playa del Sardinero, and Playa de la Concha. If they become too crowded, take a 15-minute boat ride to **El Puntal,** a beautiful beach that is rarely crowded, even in August.

If you don't like crowds or beaches, go up to the lighthouse, a little more than 2km (1¼ miles) from El Sardinero, where the views are wide-ranging. A restaurant serves snacks both indoors and outdoors. Here, you can hike along the green cliffs or loll in the grass.

Essentials

GETTING THERE Five to 10 daily **flights** from Madrid and Barcelona land at **Aeropuerto de Santander** (✆ **90-240-47-04;** www.aena.es), a little more than 6.5km (4 miles) from the town center. It's accessible by taxi and

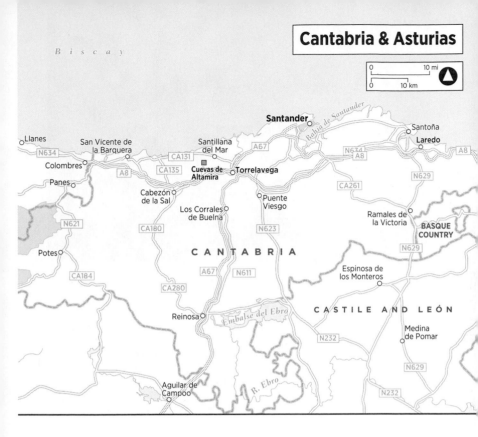

costs 20€. Much cheaper is the regular bus service that runs between the airport and the train station (2€ one-way). The local office of **Iberia** is at the airport (© **90-240-05-00;** www.iberia.com).

There are three **trains** daily from Madrid (trip time: 5½–9 hr.); a one-way fare costs 46€ to 71€. For rail information, call © **90-224-02-02** (www.renfe.es).

Buses arrive at Calle Navas de Tolosa (© **94-221-19-95;** www.alsa.es). There are 26 connections a day to and from Bilbao (trip time: 1½ hr.); a one-way ticket costs 6.70€. Six to nine buses a day arrive from Madrid (trip time: 5½ hr.), costing from 32€.

N-634 continues west from Laredo to the intersection with N-635, which you follow into Santander.

VISITOR INFORMATION The **tourist information office** is at Jardines de Pereda (© **94-220-30-00;** www.ayto-santander.es). It's open September to June Monday to Friday 8:30am to 7pm, Saturday 10am to 2pm; and July to August Monday to Saturday 9am to 9pm.

SPECIAL EVENTS The **Music and Dance Festival** in August is one of the most important artistic events in Spain. Occasionally, this festival coincides with religious celebrations honoring Santiago (St. James), the patron saint of Spain.

El Sardinero beach in Santander.

Exploring Santander

Biblioteca Menéndez y Pelayo Located in the same building as the Municipal Museum is this 50,000-volume library amassed by historian/writer Marcelino Menéndez y Pelayo (1856–1912), Santander's most illustrious man of letters, and left to Santander upon his death in 1912. Guided tours are available. Nearby is the Casa Museo, which displays this great man's study and shows how modestly he lived.

Calle Rubio 6. © **94-223-45-34.** www.bibliotecademenendezpelayo.org. Free admission. Mon–Sat 9am–1:30pm and 4:30–9pm.

Catedral Greatly damaged in the 1941 fire, this restored, fortresslike 13th-century cathedral holds the tomb of Menéndez y Pelayo (see above). The 12th-century crypt with a trio of low-slung aisles can be entered through the south portico. The Gothic cloister was restored after the fire. Roman ruins were discovered beneath the north aisle in 1983.

Plaza José Equino Trecu, Somorrostro s/n. © **94-222-60-24.** Free admission. Daily 10am–1pm and 4–7:30pm. Closed during Mass 11–11:30am and 6:30–7pm.

Museo Municipal de Bellas Artes Located near the Ayuntamiento (Town Hall), the Municipal Museum of Fine Arts has some interesting Goya paintings, notably his portrait of Ferdinand VII, commissioned by the city, and his series of etchings called *Disasters of War.* You can also see some of his continuing series of *Caprichos (Whims).* See also Zurbarán's *Mystic Scene* and an array of works by Flemish, Spanish, and Italian artists, many of them contemporary.

Calle Rubio 6. © **94-223-94-85.** www.museosdesantander.com. Free admission. June 16–Sept 14 Mon–Fri 11:15am–1pm and 5:30–9pm, Sat 10:30am–1pm; Sept 15–June 15 Mon–Fri 10am–1pm and 5:30–9pm, Sat 10am–1pm.

Museo Regional de Prehistoria y Arqueología de Cantabria ★ This museum has some interesting artifacts discovered in the Cantabrian province—not only Roman but unusual prehistoric finds. Since it is unlikely you'll be allowed to visit the Cuevas de Altamira (see "Santillana & Altamira Caves," below), come here to see objects and photographs from these prehistoric caves with their remarkable paintings. Some of the items on display date from 15,000 years ago.

Calle Casimiro Sáinz 4. © **94-220-71-09.** www.museosdecantabria.com. Free admission. June 16–Sept 16 Tues–Sat 10am–1pm and 4–7pm, Sun 11am–2pm; Sept 17–June 15 Tues–Sat 9am–1pm and 4–7pm, Sun 11am–2pm.

Shopping

True aficionados of pottery and the nuances of ceramics usually drive from Santander to **Santillana del Mar,** 29km (18 miles) away, where handcrafted ceramics are in great abundance. But if you want to stay in Santander's city limits and see a pared-down version of what's available in Santillana del Mar, head for any of the retailers on the Calle Arrabal, in the city's commercial center.

An antiques gallery well stocked with old furniture and paintings with rich veneers is **Fundación Marcellino Botín,** Calle Pedrueca 1 (© **94-222-60-72**). Ironically, many of Santander's boutiques and stores aren't in the city at all but within a 50-unit shopping center 3km (1¾ miles) from town, beside the road leading to the airport. Check out the **Centro Comercial Valle Real,** Carretera Bilbao Km 2.

Where to Stay in & Around Santander

Santander is loaded with good-value hotels, from year-round city hotels to summer villas at El Sardinero. It gets crowded, so try to reserve well in advance. Parking is readily available at or near any of the hotels listed.

IN TOWN

Abba Santander Hotel ★ ⚑ Steps from the rail station, this budget bet in the heart of the city is ideal for those without transportation. The hotel has been a Santander tradition since 1923. The exterior may not be too enticing, but the atmosphere improves inside this family-operated inn. Although it's in a congested area, street noises seem at a minimum. The midsize guest rooms, well cared for and comfortably furnished, are often in the old-fashioned style of northern Spain, with glassed-in balconies and high ceilings. Breakfast is offered in a formal room with Queen Anne chairs and oak wainscoting.

Calderón de la Barca 3, 39002 Santander. © **94-221-24-50.** Fax 94-222-92-38. www.abba santanderhotel.com. 37 units. 69€–157€ double. AE, DC, MC, V. Nearby parking 12€. **Amenities:** Restaurant; bar; room service; Wi-Fi (6€ per hour, in lobby). *In room:* A/C, TV, hair dryer, minibar.

Bahía ★★★ Even though it's not on the beach, this hotel, with style and personality, is the finest place to lay your head at night in all of Santander. An antique building with a colonial aura has been given a new lease on life after extensive modernization. Surrounded by century-old pine gardens and palms, it lies near Pagurea Beach. Modern decor and old-style furniture combine to form a harmonious whole, with many original and contemporary paintings adorning the walls. Each room opens onto a small terrace. A creative, Mediterranean-influenced cuisine is based on quality, market-fresh ingredients, the best in any season.

Av. Alfonso XIII no. 6. © **94-220-50-00.** www.hotelbahia.com. 188 units. 80€–160€ double. AE, DC, MC, V. Parking 13€. **Amenities:** Restaurant; bar; exercise room; room service; spa. *In room:* A/C, TV, Wi-Fi (free).

Hotel Central ★ 🎁 The blue Beaux Arts facade of this hotel was built around 1900 and is one of the most attractive and ornate in its neighborhood. Inside, the hotel is known for its original decor and cozy atmosphere. The rooms are midsize and done in a comfortable modern style, with many cozy, homelike touches like bedside reading lamps and armchairs. The location is about a block from the Plaza Fortificada and the sea-fronting Jardines de Pereda.

General Mola 5, 39004 Santander. © **94-222-24-00.** Fax 94-236-38-29. www.elcentral.com. 41 units. 60€–155€ double; 142€–198€ suite. AE, DC, MC, V. Nearby parking 13€. **Amenities:** Restaurant; bar; babysitting; room service. *In room:* A/C, TV, hair dryer, Wi-Fi (free).

NH Ciudad de Santander ★ About 8 blocks north of Santander's busiest seaside promenade (Paseo de Pereda) in the center of the city's commercial and shopping heartland, this white-sided five-story rectangular hotel dates from 1989. A big-windowed lobby here has marble floors, honey-colored wooden paneling, and modern accessories. The midsize rooms are monochromatic like the lobby, with convenient writing desks.

Menéndez Pelayo 13–15, 39006 Santander. © **94-231-99-00.** Fax 94-221-73-03. www.nh-hotels.com. 62 units. 74€–195€ double; 155€–215€ suite. AE, DC, MC, V. Parking 13€ indoors; 9.50€ outdoors. Bus: 5. **Amenities:** Restaurant; bar; babysitting; room service. *In room:* A/C, TV, hair dryer, minibar, Wi-Fi (13€ per 24 hr.).

AT EL SARDINERO

Hotel Real ★★★ This grande dame is the most splendid and luxurious hotel in the El Sardinero area. Architecturally noteworthy—it was the first building in the region constructed of reinforced concrete—the Real was built in 1917 to house the entourage of courtiers who accompanied King Alfonso XIII on his midsummer vacations to Santander. Purchased and completely renovated by the prestigious HUSA chain, it is once again one of the most elegant hotels in northern Spain, filled with updated reminders of a more gracious age. Located about 3km (1¾ miles) east of the commercial center of town, near the site of the Royal Palace on a hillside above Magdalena Beach, the Real contains richly conservative and spacious rooms, most with views of the sea. The hotel also has a thalassotherapy center.

Paseo Pérez Galdós 28, 39005 Santander. © **94-227-25-50.** Fax 94-227-45-73. www.hotelreal.es. 123 units. 160€–285€ double; from 344€ junior suite; from 454€ suite. AE, DC, MC, V. Free parking. Bus: 1, 2, 5, or 7. **Amenities:** Restaurant; bar; babysitting; exercise room; room service; spa. *In room:* A/C, TV, hair dryer, minibar, Wi-Fi (free).

Las Brisas ★ 🎁 A mansion from the 1920s, this building has been successfully converted into a well-run family-style hotel by Teresa and Jesús García, the friendly and hospitable owners. It's an upmarket cottage-style hotel opening onto the often chilly waters of northern Spain. Las Brisas features rooms in a wide range of sizes, from singles to family-size duplexes. Flowery curtains and blankets and dark wood furniture predominate. Try for one of the units with views over the water. The cozy breakfast room is a snug retreat.

Calle la Braña 14, 39005 Santander. © **94-227-50-11.** Fax 94-228-11-73. www.hotellasbrisas.net. 13 units. 70€–100€ double; 70€–120€ triple. AE, DC, MC, V. Parking 12€. *In room:* TV, hair dryer.

Palacio del Mar ★ One of the city's most modern hotels dates from the mid-1990s, when it was built near the La Sardinero beaches, a short drive north of Santander's commercial core. The decor features a sinuous series of postmodern lines that might have been inspired by a Joan Miró painting, accented with winding staircases and walls made from glass blocks. Many of the units are spacious suites, each with comfortable and contemporary-looking furniture, three phone extensions, and cheerful upholstery.

Av. de Cantabria 5, El Sardinero, 39012 Santander. © **94-239-24-00.** Fax 94-239-22-20. www. hotel-palaciodelmar.com. 67 units. 64€–210€ double; 220€–320€ suite. AE, DC, MC, V. Parking 14€. **Amenities:** Restaurant; bar; babysitting; access to nearby health club; room service. *In room:* A/C, TV, hair dryer, minibar, Wi-Fi (3€ per hour).

Where to Dine in Santander

Most visitors to Santander dine at their hotels or boardinghouses, which sometimes offer better value for the money and more efficient service than city restaurants. For variety, however, below are a few suggestions.

Bodega del Riojano SPANISH Dating from the 1500s, this was once a wine cellar, the evidence of which can still be seen today in its time-blackened wooden beams and old tables. Locals call the bodega the "Round Museum" (Museo Redondo) because of its display of paintings on the ends of old wine barrels. Since 1940, this has been a favorite local tavern for both food and drink. Dishes are frequently changed on the menu—in fact, they're adjusted daily, and there are major seasonal variations. Always-reliable fresh fish can be grilled or baked to your specifications. Succulent pork chops also come from the grill. One of the best dishes likely to be featured is sweet red peppers stuffed with ground beef. The desserts are homemade daily.

Río de la Pila 5. © **94-221-67-50.** Reservations recommended. Main courses 14€–19€. MC, V. July–Aug daily 1:30–4pm and 8:30pm–midnight; Sept–June Tues–Sat 1:30–4pm and 8:30pm–midnight, Sun 1:30–4pm.

El Serbal ★★★ CANTABRIAN/SPANISH The market leader of all restaurants in the area is this Michelin-starred candidate, a citadel of elegance and fine cuisine prepared with market-fresh ingredients. The chef is a *cuisinier* of rare professionalism and a dedicated gastronome who sets out to please the most discerning of palates—and succeeds. Against a backdrop of contemporary design, the menu features delectable items that make choosing difficult. The sirloin of venison served with foie gras, peaches, and blueberry sauce is a standout. You might also enjoy the ox sirloin roasted with fresh rosemary and served in a port-wine sauce. Baked skate appears with black olives, and anglerfish is grilled to perfection and served with cuttlefish-laced noodles. The sumptuous desserts are made fresh daily.

Calle Andrés del Río 7. © **94-222-25-15.** www.restaurantesdesantander.es. Reservations required. Main courses 17€–24€; tasting menu 52€. AE, MC, V. Mon–Fri and Sun 1:30–4pm and 8:30–11:30pm. Closed Sat and Feb 1–2. Bus: 7.

Zacarías ★★ 🍴 CANTABRIAN/SPANISH Zacarías Puente Herboso is the best-known chef in Santander. Although he's a geologist by profession, his growing interest in gourmet food led to his opening of this first-class restaurant. As a well-known food writer, he is the local authority on Cantabrian recipes, which he fashions to his own specifications instead of slavishly following the originals. The fresh flavors of the local countryside are enticingly showcased here. Try his fisherman's stew, a delectable kettle made with *merluza* (hake), clams, and potatoes. His *alubias rojas* (red beans with sausage) is another favorite. Enjoying local renown is *guiso pescadores*, boiled potatoes sautéed in garlic, olive oil, onion,

Lunch at Gaudí's Summer Palace

The town of Comillas lies 49km (30 miles) to the west of Santander and only a short drive to the west of Santillana del Mar. It makes the perfect luncheon stopover, especially if you go to its major attraction, **El Capricho de Gaudí,** Barrio de Sobrellano (© **94-272-03-65;** www.elcaprichodegaudi.com), the summer palace of Gaudí, the fabled Catalan architect. You can't tour the palace, but you can take in its gingerbread windows and swirling turrets. The tile-covered villa was built in 1883. You can have a meal in its dining hall most days from 1 to 3:30pm and 9 to 11pm. It is closed Sunday night and Monday, and from January 12 to February. Main courses cost 18€ to 25€. Well-prepared specialties include grilled *merluza* with baby clams, along with such Continental dishes as duck magret in a port-wine

sauce with a confit of apples, or crepes filled with foie gras and served with grapes and applesauce.

fresh parsley, and red chile peppers. Nothing is quite as alluring as his *manganos encebollados,* or calamari and caramelized onion. Most main courses are at the low to middle range of prices below.

Hernán Cortés 38. © **94-221-23-33.** www.restaurantezacarias.com. Reservations recommended. Main courses 15€–30€. AE, DC, MC, V. Daily 1–4pm and 8pm–12:30am.

Santander After Dark

The most exciting thing to do in the evening is head for the gaming tables of the **Gran Casino del Sardinero,** Plaza de Italia (© **94-227-60-54;** www.grancasinosardinero.es), which has a cover charge of 4€. It's open daily from 5pm to 4am; be sure to bring your passport for entry. In the same complex is a bar/restaurant/cafe called **Lisboa** (© **94-227-10-20**), a good place to celebrate your winnings or try to forget what you've lost. It serves moderately priced meals, and some locals even drop in for breakfast. In summer it's especially crowded. Lisboa is open daily from 9am to 2am (closed Mon in winter).

Laredo's Puebla Vieja.

LAREDO

60km (37 miles) W of Bilbao, 48km (30 miles) E of Santander, 427km (265 miles) N of Madrid

To an American, "the streets of Laredo" means the gun-slinging Old West. To a Spaniard it means an ancient maritime town on the eastern Cantabrian coast that is now a major summer resort, with hundreds of apartments and villas along its 5km (3 miles) of beach. Playa de la Salvé is to the west and Playa de Oriñón is to the east.

The medieval quarter, **Puebla Vieja,** retains the traditional atmosphere of Laredo. It was walled on the orders of Alfonso VIII of Castile, who wanted to protect the town from pirate raids along the coast. The hillside **Iglesia de la Asunción,** dating from the 13th century, overlooks the harbor. It has five naves and rather bizarre capitals.

If you're driving west to Santoña, note the big monument honoring native son Juan de la Cosa, the cartographer who sailed with Columbus on his first voyage to America.

Essentials

GETTING THERE From Bilbao, head west along the coastal highway (identified at various points as the A-8 or the E-70), and follow the signs to Laredo.

Bus service is available from both Bilbao and Santander. The station is in the town center at Av. de José Antonio s/n (✆ **94-260-49-67;** www. alsa.es). There are at least 18 buses per day coming into Laredo from Bilbao, and as many as 31 per day coming into Laredo from Santander. Travel time to Laredo from Bilbao is 40 minutes, and the one-way fare is 3.80€. Travel time from Santander is 45 minutes, and the one-way fare is 3.75€.

VISITOR INFORMATION The **tourist information office,** Alameda de Miramar s/n (✆ **94-261-10-96;** www.laredo.es), is open July 1 to September 15 daily 9am to 9pm. The rest of the year, hours are daily 9:30am to 1:30pm and 4 to 7pm.

SPECIAL EVENTS On the last Friday of August, the annual **Battle of Flowers** draws thousands of visitors to watch bloom-adorned floats parade through the Old Town.

Where to Stay in Laredo

El Ancla del Laredo Although hardly a thrill, this is the best place to stay in Laredo. In a residential area a short stroll from the beach, the hotel has operated successfully since 1965. The architectural style evokes an English chalet, and the interior is cozy, with nautical motifs and sea paraphernalia. (*Ancla* means "anchor.") The guest rooms' decor is light and airy, with wooden beams and fittings, along with rattan furniture and carpeted floors.

Calle González Gallego 10, 39770 Laredo. ✆ **94-260-55-00.** Fax 94-261-16-02. www.hotelel ancla.com. 32 units. 73€–132€ double. AE, DC, MC, V. Free parking. **Amenities:** Restaurant; bar; babysitting; room service; Wi-Fi (free, in lobby). *In room:* A/C, TV, hair dryer, minibar.

Risco On a hillside overlooking Laredo, .8km (½ mile) southeast of the center, this aging 1960s hotel opens onto impressive views of both the Old Town and a nearby beach. It offers simple, functionally furnished rooms, each clean and comfortable, with a neat bathroom. In the garden are tables for the hotel's **restaurant** (see below).

La Arenosa 2, 39770 Laredo. © **94-260-50-30.** Fax 94-260-50-55. 25 units. 85€–105€ double; 111€–130€ suite. Rates include continental breakfast. AE, DC, MC, V. Free parking. **Amenities:** Restaurant; bar; room service. *In room:* TV, Wi-Fi (free).

Where to Dine in Laredo

Camarote SEAFOOD The owner of Camarote (in the center of town) is Felipe Manjarrés, and his *chef de cuisine* specializes in seafood, especially fresh fish. The decor is tasteful and attractive, and the outdoor terrace is a pleasant alternative to the indoor dining room. The spinach with crayfish and the cheese tarts are truly excellent. Original recipes are used for salads with ham and shrimp as well as for those with tuna and fresh fruit. Try the grilled sea bream or a filet steak Rossini.

Av. Vitoria s/n. © **94-260-67-07.** Reservations recommended. Main courses 14€–28€. AE, MC, V. Daily 1–4pm and 9pm–midnight.

Casa Conrado ASTURIAN/BASQUE Almost as solidly established as the cathedral nearby, this restaurant offers good-tasting, hearty Asturian stews, seafood platters, seafood soups, several preparations of hake (including one cooked in cider), scallops of veal with champagne, and a full range of desserts. The restaurant is a local favorite and a long-established culinary tradition. The service is attentive.

Argüelles 1. © **98-522-39-19.** Reservations recommended. Main courses 15€–24€. AE, DC, MC, V. Mon–Sat 1–4pm and 9pm–midnight. Closed Aug. Bus: 1.

Risco ★ SEAFOOD This is Laredo's most appealing restaurant, known for innovative seafood dishes. The chef prepares such items as marinated salmon with pink peppercorns, scrambled eggs with lobster, and peppers stuffed with minced pigs' trotters or crabmeat. For dessert, try a fresh-fruit sorbet. Some tables are set up in the garden, or you can dine in a traditional room with views of the sea. The restaurant is on the ground floor of the Risco hotel (see above).

At the Risco, La Arenosa 2. © **94-260-50-30.** Reservations recommended. Main courses 12€–25€; *menú del día* 18€. AE, DC, MC, V. Tues–Sun 1–4pm; Tues–Sat 8:30–11pm.

SANTILLANA & ALTAMIRA CAVES ★★

29km (18 miles) SW of Santander, 393km (244 miles) N of Madrid

The Village of Santillana

Among the most perfectly preserved medieval villages in Europe, **Santillana del Mar** is now a famous Spanish national landmark. A monastery houses the relics of St. Juliana, a martyr in Asia Minor who refused to surrender her virginity to her husband. The name Santillana is a contraction of "Santa Juliana." The "del Mar" is misleading, as Santillana is not on the water but inland.

Jean-Paul Sartre called Santillana "the prettiest village in Spain," and we wouldn't want to dispute his esteemed judgment. In spite of all the tour buses, Santillana retains its medieval atmosphere and is very much a village of dairy farmers to this day.

Wander on foot throughout the village, taking in its principal sites, including **Plaza de Ramón Pelayo** (sometimes called Plaza Mayor). Here the Parador de Santillana (p. 658) has been installed in the old Barreda Bracho residence.

A 15th-century tower, facing Calle de Juan Infante, is known for its pointed arched doorway. A walk along Calle de las Lindas (Street of Beautiful Women) may not live up to its promise, but it does include many of the oldest buildings in Santillana and two towers dating from the 14th and 15th centuries. Calle del Río gets its name from a stream running through town to a central fountain.

Santillana del Mar is the traditional base for visiting the **Caves of Altamira** (see below), which contain some of the most famous Stone Age paintings in the world. However, the government has closed the caves. Instead of the original caves, you can visit an amazing facsimile, well worth your while.

ESSENTIALS

GETTING THERE La Cantábrica (✆ 94-272-08-22) operates four to seven **buses** a day from Santander but cuts back to four between September and June. Trip time is 45 minutes, and a one-way fare costs 6€.

If you're driving, take the N-611 out of Santander to reach the C-6316 cutoff to Santillana.

VISITOR INFORMATION The **tourist information office** is at Av. Escultor Jesús Otero 20 (✆ 94-281-88-12; www.santillana-del-mar.com). It's open daily 9:30am to 1:30pm and 4 to 7pm.

EXPLORING SANTILLANA

Visit the 800-year-old cathedral, **Colegiata de Santa Juliana** ★, Calle Santo Domingo (✆ 94-281-80-04), which shelters the tomb of the village's patron saint, Juliana, and walk through its ivy-covered cloister. Among the treasures displayed are 1,000-year-old documents and a 17th-century Mexican silver altarpiece. It's open Tuesday to Sunday 10am to 1:30pm and 4 to 7:30pm. In winter, it closes at 6:30pm. The 3€ admission includes the Convent of the Poor Clares.

At the other end of the main street, the 400-year-old Convento de Regina Coelí, also called the **Convent of the Poor Clares** (Museo Diocesano; ✆ 94-281-80-04), houses a rich art collection inspired by a Madrid art professor who encouraged the nuns to collect and restore religious paintings and statues damaged or abandoned during the Spanish Civil War. The collection is constantly expanding. The convent is open Tuesday to Sunday 10am to 1:30pm and 4 to 8pm (until 6:30pm in winter).

WHERE TO STAY IN SANTILLANA
Moderate

Casa del Marqués ★★ This *antigua casa sensorial* (old manor house) is the second-best place to stay in town. It houses you in style, comfort, and atmosphere in the heart of town near Plaza Mayor. The present building stands on the foundation of a manor dating from the 12th century. Dripping with antiquity, the building has its original stone walls. The midsize guest rooms are furnished comfortably but with a kind of rustic decor to honor the building's long history. From the terraces or balconies of the hotel, panoramic views unfold.

Cantón 26, 39330 Santillana del Mar. ✆/fax **94-281-88-88**. 15 units. 127€–200€ double; 254€–320€ suite. AE, DC, MC, V. Parking 12€. **Amenities:** Bar; babysitting; room service. *In room:* A/C, TV, hair dryer, minibar, Wi-Fi (free).

Parador de Santillana Gil Blas/Santillana del Mar ★★ The best places to stay in town are either of these two *paradores*. Although they occupy the same address, they are two different hotels, each with 28 units. The more expensive, with better rooms, is the government-rated four-star Parador de Santillana Gil Blas, followed by the government-rated three-star Parador de Santillana del Mar. Both hotels occupy a 400-year-old former palace with modern extensions, and both are filled with antiques and have hand-hewn plank floors, chandeliers, and refectory tables. Large portraits of knights in armor hang in the main gallery. Most of the guest rooms are large, with antiques and windows on two sides, some with views of a garden. Several rooms in the three-star *parador* are much smaller. (These tend to be on the top floor.)

Plaza de Ramón Pelayo 11, 39300 Santillana del Mar. ℂ **94-202-80-28** for Parador de Santillana Gil Bas; ℂ **94-281-80-00** for Parador de Santillana del Mar. Fax 94-281-83-91 for both *paradores*. www.parador.es. 56 units. Santillana del Mar: 143€–155€ double; 172€–186€ suite. Santillana Gil Blas: 160€–171€ double; 208€–297€ suite. AE, DC, MC, V. Free parking. **Amenities:** Restaurant; bar; room service; sauna. *In room:* A/C, TV, hair dryer, minibar, Wi-Fi (free).

Inexpensive

Casa del Organista ★★ 🏨 This 18th-century manor is a little secret we're revealing to you. In the Old Town, this gem discreetly receives guests and does so with a certain style. Of all the hotels in town, this one is the most tranquil and scenically located. We liked our stay so much that we regretted packing up and shipping out to the next town. Most of the three-story structure has retained its original architecture, including wooden balconies and thick wooden beams evocative of a mountain house. Guest rooms are midsize, furnished with wood headboards under beamed ceilings.

Calle Los Hornos 4, 39330 Santillana del Mar. ℂ **94-284-03-52.** Fax 94-284-01-91. www.casa delorganista.com. 14 units. 56€–89€ double. MC, V. Free parking. **Amenities:** Bar; room service. *In room:* TV, hair dryer.

Hotel Altamira ★ This government-rated three-star hotel in the center of the village is a 400-year-old former palace. Although not as impressive as the *parador,* it often takes the overflow in its comfortable, well-maintained rooms. Two units have private lounges. The **restaurant** (see below) serves Cantabrian cuisine highlighted by seafood.

Calle Cantón 1, 39330 Santillana del Mar. ℂ **94-281-80-25.** Fax 94-284-01-36. www.hotel altamira.com. 32 units. 60€–120€ double. AE, DC, MC, V. Nearby parking 5€. **Amenities:** Restaurant; bar; room service. *In room:* A/C (in some), TV, hair dryer.

Hotel Siglo XVIII ★ 🏨 This small, cozy nest a 5-minute walk from the Old Town is a government-rated three-star. It has operated since 1996 in an old building behind a stone facade. Inside, the decor is cozy and homelike, with a lingering aura of the 18th century, dominated by carved wood, high beamed ceilings, white walls, and tiled floors. The guest rooms, some of which have balconies, are midsize with plenty of comfort and light.

Revolgo 38, 39330 Santillana del Mar. ℂ **94-284-02-10.** Fax 94-284-02-11. www.hotelsigloxviii. com. 16 units. 51€–75€ double. AE, DC, MC, V. Free parking. **Amenities:** Bar; room service. *In room:* A/C, TV, hair dryer.

Los Infantes ★ This government-rated three-star hotel is a comfortable choice, although not as charming as the Hotel Altamira (see above). Located in an 18th-century building on the main road leading into the village, Los Infantes has kept the old flavor of Santillana: beamed ceilings and lounges furnished with tapestries, antiques, and paintings. The small rooms are cozy and well kept, with wall-to-wall carpeting; two have balconies.

Av. L'Dorat 1, 39330 Santillana del Mar. © **94-281-80-11.** Fax 94-284-01-03. www.hotel-santillana.com. 28 units. 73€–128€ double; 95€–151€ suite. AE, DC, MC, V. Free parking. **Amenities:** Restaurant; bar; Wi-Fi (free, in lobby). *In room:* TV, hair dryer.

WHERE TO DINE IN SANTILLANA

Dining isn't one of the compelling reasons to visit Santillana del Mar. Most visitors dine in the hotels. However, **Parador de Santillana Gil Blas** (see above) is a fine choice.

Hotel Altamira Restaurant CANTABRIAN The restaurant is housed in a series of dining rooms known for regional specialties. Nonguests of the hotel often visit for a taste of Cantabrian cuisine, which specializes in freshly caught seafood. The decor is rustic, the service casual and polite, and the food fresh and well prepared. On a recent visit, the catch of the day was turbot, which came with a vinaigrette sauce and fresh tomatoes. Sea bass was another good choice, having been oven baked with fresh thyme. Meat eaters will gravitate to a delectable roast suckling pig or to *codido montañez* (a stew of beans, pork, and fresh vegetables).

Calle Cantón 1. © **94-281-80-25.** Reservations recommended. Main courses 12€–22€. AE, DC, MC, V. Daily 1:15–4pm and 8–11pm.

The Altamira Caves

About 2.5km (1½ miles) from Santillana del Mar are the **Cuevas de Altamira ★★★** (© **94-281-80-05**), famous for prehistoric paintings dating from the end of the Ice Age, paintings that have caused these caves to be called the "Sistine Chapel of prehistoric art." The cave paintings at Altamira are ranked among the finest prehistoric paintings ever discovered. These ancient depictions of bison and horses, painted vividly in reds and blacks on the caves' ceilings, were not discovered until the late 19th century. Once their authenticity was established, scholars and laypersons alike flocked to see these works of art, which provide a fragile link to our remote ancestors.

Severe damage was caused by the bacteria brought in by so many visitors, so now the Research Center and Museum of Altamira no longer allows visitors.

King Juan Carlos and Queen Sofía officially opened the **Museo de Altamira** (© **94-281-80-05**), located a few hundred feet from the original caves. On

---

Cave Painters from 15,000 Years Ago

Altamira is not the only ancient cave in the region. At Puente Viesgo you can visit **El Castillo ★**, found at Carretera N623 Km 28 from Santander (© **94-259-84-25**). Lying in a medieval hamlet in the Pas Valley, this cave was excavated under the 350m (1,150-ft.) peak of the mountain, Monte del Castillo. Decorated by artists 15,000 years ago, the cave has several different sections. The caves are open April to October Tuesday to Sunday 9am to noon and 3 to 6:30pm; November to March, hours are Wednesday to Sunday 9am to 2pm. Admission is 4€ for adults, 2€ for kids 4 to 12.

Cave paintings at Altamira.

exhibit is a perfect replica of the cave, complete with precisely realistic copies of the original murals. The replica was created by computerized digital-transfer technology; the so-called "neocave" contains every crack and indentation of the original. The highlight is the array of 21 red bison in the Polychrome Chamber.

If you don't have a car, you have to walk from Santillana del Mar, as there is no bus service. From May to October, hours are Tuesday to Saturday 9:30am to 8pm, and Sunday 9:30am to 3pm. November to April, hours are Tuesday to Saturday 9:30am to 6pm, and Sunday 9:30am to 3pm. Admission is 2.40€ for adults, 1.20€ for students, and free for those 18 and under and seniors 65 and over. Admission is free to all on Saturday and Sunday after 2:30pm. The center is closed January 1 and 6, May 5, and December 24, 25, and 31.

LOS PICOS DE EUROPA ★★★

Potes: 114km (71 miles) W of Santander, 398km (247 miles) N of Madrid. Cangas de Onís: 147km (91 miles) W of Santander, 419km (260 miles) N of Madrid

These mountains are technically part of the Cordillera Cantábrica, which runs parallel to the northern coastline of Spain. In the narrow and vertiginous band known as Los Picos de Europa, they are by far at their most dramatic.

These "European Peaks" are the most famous and most legend-riddled mountains in Spain. Rising more than 2,590m (8,500 ft.), they are not high by alpine standards, but their proximity to the sea makes their height especially awesome. During the Middle Ages, they were passable only with great difficulty. (The ancient Romans constructed a north-south road whose stones are still visible in some places.) An abundance of wildlife, the medieval battles that occurred here, and dramatically rocky heights have all contributed to the legends that are an essential part of the principality of Asturias.

Covering a distance of only 39km (24 miles) at their longest point, Los Picos are geologically and botanically different from anything else in the region. Thousands of years ago, glaciers created massive and forbidding limestone cliffs, which today challenge the most dedicated and intrepid rock climbers in Europe.

As you tour the majestic Picos de Europa, be on the lookout for some of the rarest **wildlife** remaining in Europe. On the beech-covered slopes of these mountains and in gorges laden with jasmine, you might spot the increasingly rare Asturcon, a shaggy, rather chubby wild horse so small it first looks like a toy pony. Another endangered species is the Iberian brown bear—but if you see one, keep your distance. The park is also home to the sure-footed chamois goat, rare butterflies, peregrine falcons, buzzards, and golden eagles. All wildlife is strictly protected by the government.

If you **hike** in this region, make sure you're well prepared. Many of the slopes are covered with loosely compacted shale, making good treads on hiking boots a must. Inexperienced hikers should stick to well-established paths. In summer, temperatures can get hot and humid, and sudden downpours sweeping in from the coastline are common in any season. Hiking is not recommended between October and May.

By far the best way to see this region is **by car.** Most drivers arrive in the region on the N-621 highway, heading southwest from Santander, or on the same highway northeast from the cities of north-central Spain (especially León and Valladolid). This highway connects many of the region's best vistas in a straight line. It also defines the region's eastern boundary. If you're driving east from Oviedo, you'll take the N-632, in which case the first town of any importance will be Cangas de Onís.

Travel by bus is much less convenient but possible if you have lots of time. The region's touristic hubs are the towns of Panes and Potes; both have bus service (two buses per day in summer, one per day in winter) from Santander and León (one bus per day in summer). The same buses come to Panes and Potes from the coastal town of Unquera. From Oviedo, there are two buses daily to the district's easternmost town of Cangas; they continue a short distance farther southeast to Covadonga. Within the region, a small local bus runs once a day, according to an erratic schedule, along the northern rim of the Picos, connecting Cangas de Onís with Las Arenas.

Exploring the Region

If you have a car, the number and variety of tours in this region are almost endless, but for this guide, we have organized the region into three driving tours. Any of them, with their side excursions, can fill an entire day; if you're rushed and omit some of the side excursions, you can spend a half-day.

DRIVING TOUR 1:

PANES TO POTES ★★

DISTANCE: **29km (18 miles); 45 minutes**

Except for one optional detour, this drive extends entirely along one of the region's best roads, N-621, which links León and Valladolid to Santander. The drive is most noteworthy for its views of the ravine containing the Deva River, a ravine so steep that direct sunlight rarely penetrates it.

About two-thirds of the way to Potes, signs point you on a detour to the village of:

1 Liébana

This village is .8km (½ mile) off the main road. Here you'll find the church of Nuestra Señora de Liébana, built in the 10th century in the Mozarabic style. Some people consider it the best example of Arabized Christian architecture in Europe, with Islamic-inspired geometric motifs. If it isn't open, knock at the door of the first house you see as you enter the village; it's the home of the guardian, who will unlock the church if she's around. For this, she will expect a tip. If she's not around, content yourself with admiring the church from the outside.

Continuing for about another 8km (5 miles), you'll reach the village of:

2 Potes

This is a charming place with well-kept alpine houses against a backdrop of jagged mountains.

Three kilometers (1¾ miles) southwest of Potes, near Turiano, stands the:

3 Monasterio de Santo Toribio de Liébana

The monastery dates from the 17th century. Restored to the transitional Romanesque style it enjoyed at the peak of its vast power, it contains what is reputed to be a splinter from the True Cross, brought from Jerusalem in the 8th century by the bishop of Astorga. The monastery is also famous as the former home of Beatus de Liébana, the 8th-century author of *Commentary on the Apocalypse,* one of Spain's most famous ecclesiastical documents. Ring the bell during daylight hours, and one of the brothers will let you enter if you are properly attired.

At the end of a winding and beautiful road to the west of Potes is the:

4 Parador de Fuente-Dé

You can spend the night here (p. 668) or just stop for lunch. The drive following the path of the Deva River for the most part will take you to:

5 Fuente-Dé

Once you're here, a **teleférico,** the third-largest cable-car system in the world (© **94-273-66-10;** www.cantur.com), carries you 800m (2,625 ft.) up to an observation platform above a wind-scoured rock face. The cable car operates July to August daily 9am to 8pm, September to June daily 10am to 6pm. A one-way fare costs 8€; round-trip is 14€. At the top you can walk

The Monasterio de Santo Toribio de Liébana.

Fuente-Dé's *teleférico.*

5km (3 miles) along a footpath to the rustic **Refugio de Aliva** (© **94-273-09-99**), open between June and September 15. Doubles cost 75€. If you opt for just a meal or a snack at the hostel's simple restaurant, remember to allow enough time to return to the *teleférico* before its last trip down.

DRIVING TOUR 2:
POTES TO CANGAS DE ONÍS ★

DISTANCE: **85km (53 miles); 2 hours**

This tour includes not only the Quiviesa Valley and some of the region's most vertiginous mountain passes, but also some of its most verdant fields and most elevated pastures. You might stop at an occasional village, but most of the time you will be going through deserted countryside. Your route will take you through several tunnels and high above mountain streams set deep into gorges. The occasional belvederes along the way always deliver on their promise of panoramic views.

The village of Potes (see "Driving Tour 1," above) is your starting point. Take N-621 southwest to Riaño. At Riaño, turn north for a brief ride on N-625. Then take a winding route through the heart of the region by driving northwest on N-637. Although it's beautiful all along the way, the first really important place you'll reach is:

1   Cangas de Onís

This is the westernmost town in the region, where you can get a hotel room and a solid meal after a trek through the mountains. The biggest attraction in Cangas de Onís is an ivy-covered **Roman bridge,** lying west of the center, spanning the Sella River. Also of interest is the **Capilla de Santa Cruz,** immediately west of the center. One of the earliest Christian sites in Spain, it was originally constructed in the 8th century over a Celtic dolmen and rebuilt in the 15th century.

About 1.5km (1 mile) northwest of Cangas de Onís, beside the road leading to Arriondas, stands the:

2 Monasterio de San Pedro

This is a Benedictine monastery in the village of **Villanueva.** The church that you see was originally built in the 17th century, when it enclosed the ruins of a much older Romanesque church. It has some unusual carved capitals showing the unhappy end of the medieval King Favila, supposedly devoured by a Cantabrian bear.

DRIVING TOUR 3:
CANGAS DE ONÍS TO PANES ★★

DISTANCE: **56km (35 miles); 1 hour**

This tour travels along the relatively straight C-6312 from the western to the eastern entrance to the Picos de Europa region. A number of unusual excursions can easily stretch this into an all-day outing.

From Cangas de Onís (see "Driving Tour 2," above), head west about 1.6km (1 mile). You'll reach the turnoff to:

1 Cueva del Buxu

Inside the cave is a limited number of prehistoric rock engravings and charcoal drawings, somewhat disappointingly small. Only 25 people per day are allowed inside (respiration erodes the drawings), so unless you arrive early, you won't get in. It's open Wednesday to Sunday from 10am to 2pm and 4 to 6:30pm. Admission is 3€.

The Roman bridge of Cangas de Onís.

Some 6.5km (4 miles) east, signs point south in the direction of:

2 Covadonga

Revered as the birthplace of Christian Spain, Covadonga is about 9.5km (6 miles) off the main highway. A battle here in A.D. 718 pitted a ragged band of Christian Visigoths against a small band of Muslims. The resulting victory established the first niche of Christian Europe in Moorish Iberia. The town's most important monuments are **La Santa Cueva,** a cave containing the sarcophagus of Pelayo (d. 737), king of the Visigothic Christians; and an enormous neo-Romanesque basilica, built between 1886 and 1901, commemorating the Christianization of Spain. At the end of the long boulevard that funnels into the base of the church stands a statue of Pelayo.

Return to the highway and continue east. You'll come to the village of Las Estazadas; then after another 11km (6¾ miles) you'll reach:

3 Las Arenas de Cabrales

Note that some maps refer to this town simply as Arenas. This is the headquarters of a cheese-producing region whose Cabrales, a blue-veined cheese made from ewes' milk, is avidly consumed throughout Spain.

Drive 5km (3 miles) south from Arenas, following signs to the village of:

4 Puente de Poncebos

This is shown on some maps simply as Poncebos. This village is several miles downstream from the source of Spain's most famous salmon-fishing river, the Cares, which flows through deep ravines from its source near the more southerly village of Cain.

Beginning at Poncebos, a footpath has been cut into the ravine on either side of the Cares River. It is one of the engineering marvels of Spain, known for centuries as the **Divine Gorge.** It crosses the ravine many times over footbridges and sometimes through tunnels chiseled into the rock face beside the water, making a hike along the banks of this river a memorable outing. You can climb up the riverbed from Poncebos, overland to the village of Cain, a total distance of 11km (6¾ miles). Allow between 3 and 4 hours. At Cain, you can take a taxi back to where you left your car in Poncebos if you don't want to retrace your steps.

After your trek up the riverbed, continue your drive to the village of:

5 Panes

This village lies at a distance of 23km (14 miles), to the eastern extremity of the Picos de Europa.

Where to Stay & Dine in the Region

Accommodations are extremely limited in these mountain towns. If you're planning an overnight stop, make sure you have a reservation. Most taverns will serve you food during regular opening hours without a reservation.

Directly north of Cangas de Onís, the unprepossessing little village of Arriondas has not only one but two Michelin-starred restaurants. Nowhere in the Picos de Europa area can you dine so well as you can here. In fact, these are two of the best restaurants along the entire north coast of Spain.

La Santa Cueva, built into the rock.

IN ARRIONDAS

Casa Marcial ★★ ASTURIAN Even though it's not quite as good as El Corral del Indiano (see below), this is one of the great restaurants along the northern coast of Spain, an unexpected discovery in this remote pueblo. Here Chef Nacho Manzano creates a superlative cuisine in an antique farmhouse fronting rolling green foothills. On our last visit, we arrived on a hot day and found the perfect dish for our palate: an icy cucumber soup poured around a sorbet made of green pepper with swirls of virgin green olive oil poured over it.

From the River Stella comes a salmon served in a "pool" of melon gazpacho with fresh asparagus. Manzano can take any dish, perhaps locally grown chicken, and turn it into a masterpiece—in this case by braising it to an elegant mahogany and folding fresh gizzards into a bravura meal. Each of his dishes could rate a star. One of his most devoted patrons told us he knew the secret of the chef's success: "He can blur the borders between the sea and the forest."

Carretera AS-342, La Salgar 10, 4.5km (2¾ miles) north of Arriondas. ✆ **98-584-09-91.** www.casamarcial.com. Reservations required. Main courses 20€–30€; fixed-price menu 30€–75€. AE, MC, V. Tues–Sat 1–4pm and 9–11:30pm; Sun 1–4pm. Closed 5 weeks in Jan–Feb (dates vary).

El Corral del Indiano ★★★ ASTURIAN Chef José Antonio Campo Viejo lures some of Europe's greatest gastronomes to this gem of a restaurant at the foot of Los Picos de Europa. However, this is no rustic mountain tavern. Modernist tableware adorns the stiff white tablecloths, which are set off against electric-blue walls. Although the chef draws inspiration from local recipes, he infuses every one of his sensational dishes with his own culinary creativity. Main courses are expensive; it's a better value to order the tasting menu. A sweet, briny soup might combine fresh clams with just-picked green peas, resulting in a velvety taste that makes you wish it were June year-round. Many local homes cook smoked sausages and beans, but no kettle is better than the one simmering on Viejo's stove. His *pote asturiano,* a blend of cabbage and pig parts, is the best version of that dish we've ever had.

Av. de Europa 14. ✆ **98-584-10-72.** www.elcorraldelindianu.com. Reservations required. Main courses 18€–28€; tasting menu 70€. AE, DC, MC, V. Fri–Wed 1:30–4pm; Fri–Sat and Mon–Tues 9–11pm.

IN CANGAS DE ONÍS

Hotel Aultre Naray ★ 🛏 A small hotel with character, this establishment is in an Asturian country house dating from 1873. Its robust masonry work is typical of the 19th century, and the entrance has a beautiful stone archway. The decor came from an interior-design workshop in Madrid, resulting in a harmonious blend of traditional architecture with current design trends. The hotel has well-furnished, midsize guest rooms, each with a tiled bathroom. There's a cozy sitting room with a fireplace for guests. The hotel is in the foothills of the Escapa mountain range and enjoys a panoramic view of the mountains and an oak forest on the banks of the River Sella. The area is a perfect place for fishing; hiking in the mountains and canoeing are other popular diversions.

Cangas de Onís, Peruyes, 33547 Asturias. ✆ **98-584-08-08.** Fax 98-584-08-48. www. aultrenaray.com. 10 units. 70€–115€ double; 113€–163€ family room for 4. AE, DC, MC, V. Free parking. **Amenities:** Restaurant; bar. *In room:* TV, hair dryer.

Wheels of Cabrales cheese.

La Palmera CANTABRIAN When the weather is right, you can dine outside here, enjoying mountain air with the food. Sometimes this place is overrun, but on other occasions you can have a meal in peace. The menu features game from the surrounding mountains, along with filet of beef, lamb chops, and salmon in green sauce. Try the local mountain cheese. La Palmera is 3km (1¾ miles) east of Cangas de Onís on the road to Covadonga.

Soto de Cangas, La Rotunda. ✆ **98-594-00-96.** Main courses 9€–21€. AE, DC, MC, V. Wed–Mon 10am–11pm. Closed Aug.

IN COSGAYA

Hotel del Oso This well-run little hotel in the valley of Liébana is located in two buildings next to the Deva River, beside the road leading from Potes to the *parador* and cable car at Fuente-Dé. The "Hotel of the Bear" is ringed with natural beauty. Its small rooms are well furnished and maintained. Meals are taken at the Mesón del Oso (see below).

Carretera Potes–Fuente-Dé Km 14, 39582 Cosgaya. ✆ **94-273-30-18.** Fax 94-273-30-36. www. hoteldeloso.com. 50 units. 65€–77€ double. MC, V. Free parking. Closed Jan 7–Feb 15. From Potes, take the road signposted to Espinama 15km (9⅓ miles) south. **Amenities:** Restaurant; bar; outdoor pool; outdoor tennis court. *In room:* TV, hair dryer, Wi-Fi (free).

Mesón del Oso CANTABRIAN Open to the public since 1981, this stone-built restaurant is named after the bear that supposedly devoured Favila, an 8th-century king of Asturias. Here, at the birthplace of the Christian warrior King Pelayo, you can enjoy Lebaniega cuisine, reflecting the bounty of mountain, stream, and sea. The portions are generous. Try trout from the Deva River, grilled tuna, roast suckling pig, or a mountain stew called *cocida lebaniego,* whose recipe derives from local lore and tradition. Dessert might be a fruit-based tart. There's an outdoor terrace.

Carretera Espinama s/n, in the Hotel del Oso. ℭ **94-273-30-18.** Main courses 10€–25€. MC, V. Daily 1–3:45pm and 9–10:45pm. Closed Jan 7–Feb 15. From Potes, take the route south toward Espinama for 15km (9⅓ miles).

IN FUENTE-DÉ

Parador de Fuente-Dé ★★ The finest place to stay in the area, this government-run *parador* faces the Picos de Europa. Opened in 1975 and renovated in 2009, it is at the end of the major road through the Liébana region. Hunters in autumn and mountain climbers in summer often fill its attractively decorated and comfortably furnished guest rooms, which are midsize to spacious.

At 3.5 Km de Espinama, 39588 Fuente-Dé. ℭ **94-273-66-51.** Fax 94-273-66-54. www.parador. es. 78 units. 104€–127€ double. AE, DC, MC, V. Free parking. Closed Nov–Feb. Drive 26km (16 miles) west of Potes. **Amenities:** Restaurant; bar; room service. *In room:* A/C, TV, hair dryer, minibar, Wi-Fi (free).

GIJÓN

473km (294 miles) N of Madrid, 192km (119 miles) W of Santander, 29km (18 miles) E of Oviedo

The major port of Asturias and its largest city is a summer resort and an industrial center rolled into one. As a port, Gijón (pronounced Hee-*hohn*) is said to predate the Romans. The Visigoths came through here, and in the 8th century the Moors wandered through the area, but none of those would-be conquerors made much of an impression.

The best part of the city to explore is the barrio of **Cimadevilla,** with its maze of alleys and leaning houses. This section, jutting into the ocean to the north of the new town, spills over an elevated piece of land known as Santa Catalina. Santa Catalina forms a headland at the west end of the **Playa San Lorenzo,** stretching for about 2.5km (1½ miles); this sandy beach has good facilities. After time at the beach, you can stroll through **Parque Isabel la Católica,** at its eastern end.

Gijón is short on major monuments. The city was the birthplace of Gaspar Melchor de Jovellanos (1744–1811), one of Spain's most prominent men of letters, as well as an agrarian reformer and liberal economist. Manuel de Godoy, the notorious minister, ordered that Jovellanos be held prisoner for 7 years in Bellver Castle on Majorca. In Gijón, his birthplace has been restored and turned into the **Museo-Casa Natal de Jovellanos,** Plaza de Jovellanos (ℭ **98-518-51-52;** www.jovellanos.net), open July to August Tuesday to Saturday from 11am to 1:30pm and 5 to 9pm, and Sunday 11am to 2pm; September to June, hours are Tuesday to Saturday 10am to 1pm and 5 to 8pm, and Sunday 11am to 2pm. Admission is free.

You can also visit the **Termas Romanas,** or Roman Baths, at Campos Valdés (ℭ **98-534-51-47**), which are underground at the end of the Old Town, opening onto Playa de San Lorenzo. Discovered in 1903, these baths are now fully excavated, and the town has opened a museum here. Near the baths are reconstructed parts of the old Roman wall. The baths are open July to August Tuesday to Saturday 11am to 1:30pm and 5 to 9pm, Sunday 11am to 2pm and 5 to 8pm. From September to June they are open Tuesday to Saturday 10am to 1pm and 5 to 8pm, Sunday 11am to 2pm and 5 to 7pm. Admission is 3€, free for children 15 and under.

After viewing the baths, you'll find yourself at **Playa San Lorenzo,** the city's best beach, which attracts sunbathers from the surrounding area. *Tip:* If this beach is too crowded, you can find more remote beaches strung along the bases of some cliffs farther on. The beaches here are more rock strewn, however, and the surf is a bit rougher.

Essentials

GETTING THERE Gijón doesn't have an airport, but **Iberia** flies to the airport at Ranón (✆ **98-512-76-07;** www.iberia.com), 42km (26 miles) away, a facility it shares with Oviedo-bound passengers.

Gijón has good rail links and makes a good gateway into Asturias. **RENFE trains** (✆ **90-224-02-02;** www.renfe.com) arrive from Madrid in 6 to 7 hours; the one-way trip costs 48€. There is also service from Oviedo (see the following section) every 30 minutes during the day. The trip takes 35 minutes from Oviedo to Gijón; a one-way ticket costs 11€.

There is frequent **bus service** (✆ **90-242-22-42** for information). Fifteen buses per day arrive from Madrid, taking 5½ hours and costing 49€ one-way. There is also service from Bilbao at the rate of 10 buses per day; the one-way trip takes 5 hours and costs 20€. Service is every hour from Oviedo; the one-way trip takes only an hour and costs 2€.

Driving from Santander in the east, head west along the N-634. At Ribadesella, you can take the turnoff to the N-632, the coastal road to Gijón. This is the scenic route. To save time, continue on N-634 until you reach the outskirts of Oviedo, and then cut north on A-66, the express highway to Gijón.

VISITOR INFORMATION The **tourist information office** is at Calle Rodríguez San Pedro (✆ **98-534-17-71;** www.gijon.info). It's open in summer daily 10am to 10pm, off season daily 10am to 2:30pm and 4:30 to 7:30pm.

SPECIAL EVENTS The most exciting time to be in Gijón is on **Asturias Day,** the first Sunday in August. This fiesta is celebrated with parade floats, traditional folk dancing, and lots of music. But summers here tend to be festive even without a festival. Vacationers are fond of patronizing the cider taverns (*chigres*), eating grilled sardines, and joining in singalongs in the portside *tascas*. Be aware that you can get as drunk on cider as you can on beer, maybe somewhat faster.

Where to Stay in Gijón
EXPENSIVE

Hotel Hernán Cortés ★★ About 1 block east of Plaza del 6 de Agosto, midway between Playa San Lorenzo and the harbor, this elegant and classic hotel named after the conquistador is one of the finest in town. Although it has been renovated, its midsize guest rooms retain a bit of yesteryear's allure and provide such thoughtful extras as shoeshine equipment. The Cortés doesn't have a restaurant, but the proprietors will serve you lunch or dinner in your room from a neighboring restaurant.

Fernández Vallín 5, 33205 Gijón. ✆ **98-534-60-00.** Fax 98-535-56-45. www.hotelhernancortes. es. 60 units. 95€–160€ double; 145€–250€ suite. AE, DC, MC, V. Nearby parking 14€. Bus: 4 or 11. **Amenities:** Bar; room service. *In room:* A/C, TV, hair dryer, minibar, Wi-Fi (free).

Parador Molino Viejo (Parador de Gijón) ★★★ 😊 Next to the verdant confines of Gijón's most visible park, about .8km (½ mile) east of the town center and an easy walk from the popular San Lorenzo beach, this is the premier place to stay. Awarded four stars by the government (which runs it), it was constructed around the core of an 18th-century cider mill. The *parador* is surrounded by a garden strewn with tables, beside a stream sheltering colonies of swans. It contains a marble-sheathed reception area, an unpretentious restaurant, and a cider bar that, on weekends, is quite popular with local residents. The guest rooms are somewhat cramped and surprisingly simple for a four-star hotel; however, they're tastefully restored with well-scrubbed wooden floors, thick shutters, and traditional furniture.

Parque Isabel la Católica s/n, 33203 Gijón. © **800/223-1356** in the U.S., or 98-537-05-11. Fax 98-537-02-33. www.parador.es. 40 units. 143€–179€ double. AE, DC, MC, V. Free parking. Bus: 4 or 11. **Amenities:** Restaurant; bar; children's center; room service; Wi-Fi (free, in lobby). *In room:* A/C, TV, hair dryer, minibar.

INEXPENSIVE

Hotel Begoña Centro This functional, modern hotel offers small rooms that are well furnished and comfortable, plus efficient chamber service to keep everything clean. Regional and national dishes, with many seafood concoctions, are served in the restaurant. The hotel is on the southern outskirts of the new town, 1 block north of Avenida Manuel Llaneza, the major traffic artery from the southwest.

Av. de la Costa 44, 33205 Gijón. © **98-514-72-11.** Fax 98-539-82-22. www.hotelesbegona. com. 249 units. 78€ double. AE, DC, MC, V. Parking 13€. Bus: 4 or 11. **Amenities:** Restaurant; bar; babysitting; room service. *In room:* TV, Wi-Fi (free).

La Casona de Jovellanos ★ 🍴 This venerable hotel was built on foundations 3 centuries old, on the rocky peninsula that was the site of the oldest part of fortified Gijón, a short distance south of Parque Santa Catalina. It contains only a few rooms, so reservations are imperative. The small rooms are attractively furnished and well maintained. In 1794, the writer Jovellanos established the Asturian Royal Institute of Marine Life and Mineralogy here, and it was later transformed into this hotel, within walking distance of the beach and yacht basin.

Plaza de Jovellanos 1, 33201 Gijón. © **98-534-12-64.** Fax 98-535-61-51. www.lacasonade jovellanos.com. 13 units. 50€–90€ double. AE, DC, MC, V. Nearby parking 13€. Bus: 4 or 11. **Amenities:** Restaurant; bar; room service. *In room:* TV, hair dryer, Wi-Fi (free).

Where to Dine in Gijón

Casa Tino 🍴 ASTURIAN Quality combined with quantity, at reasonable prices, is the hallmark of this restaurant near the police station, north of Manuel Llaneza and west of Paseo de Begoña. Each day the chef prepares a different stew—sometimes fish and sometimes meat. The place is packed with chattering diners every evening, many of them regulars. Sample the white beans of the region cooked with pork, stewed hake, or marinated beefsteak, perhaps finishing with one of the fruit tarts.

Alfredo Truan 9. © **98-534-13-87.** www.restaurantecasatino.com. Main courses 8€–20€; *menú del día* 9.95€. AE, DC, MC, V. Fri–Wed 1:15–3:30pm and 8:45–11:30pm. Bus: 4 or 11.

Casa Víctor SEAFOOD Owner and sometime-chef Víctor Bango is a bit of a legend. He oversees the buying and preparation of the fresh fish for which this place is famous. The successful young people of Gijón enjoy the tavernlike atmosphere here, as well as the imaginative dishes—a mousse made from the roe of sea urchins, for example, is all the rage in Asturias these days. Well-chosen wines accompany such other menu items as octopus served with fresh vegetables, or grilled steak. Casa Víctor is located by the dockyards.

Carmen 11. ✆ **98-535-00-93.** www.casavictor.com. Reservations recommended. Main courses 14€–30€; fixed-price dinner 45€; fixed-price lunch 18€. AE, DC, MC, V. Mon and Wed–Sat 1–3:30pm; Mon–Sat 8:30–11pm. Closed mid-Dec to mid-Jan. Bus: 10.

El Puerto CANTABRIAN Set directly on the waterfront, with very large windows that overlook the fishing boats and pleasure craft bobbing at anchor in the nearby harbor, this restaurant has emerged since its debut in 1990 as the finest in Gijón. Sheathed in hardwood paneling and accented with glittering crystal ornaments and lighting fixtures, it specializes in an upscale *cocina del mercado,* often based on very fresh fish, most of which was hauled out of nearby waters within a few hours of its preparation. An enduring specialty is sliced hake served with lobster claws, clams, and green sauce. Appropriate starters include homemade foie gras with grapes, and a succulent version of crepes stuffed with flake-fleshed spider crab. Most diners are accommodated on the street level, but additional seating is available on the floors immediately below and above.

Calle Claudio Alvarogonzález s/n. ✆ **98-534-90-96.** Reservations recommended. Main courses 12€–30€; *menú gastronómico* 49€. AE, DC, MC, V. Daily 1:30–4pm; Mon–Sat 9pm–midnight. Closed Easter week.

OVIEDO

203km (126 miles) W of Santander, 444km (276 miles) N of Madrid

Oviedo is the capital of Asturias. Only 26km (16 miles) from the coast, Oviedo is very pleasant in summer, when much of Spain is unbearably hot. It makes an ideal base for excursions along the Costa Verde. Despite its high concentration of industry and mining, the area has unspoiled scenery.

Razed in the 8th century during the Reconquest, it was rebuilt in an architectural style known as Asturian pre-Romanesque, which predated many of the greatest achievements under the Moors. Remarkably, this architectural movement was in flower when the rest of Europe lay under the black cloud of the Dark Ages.

As late as the 1930s, Oviedo was suffering violent upheavals. An insurrection in the mining areas on October 5, 1934, led to a seizure of the town by miners, who set up a revolutionary government. The subsequent fighting led to the destruction of many historical monuments. The cathedral was also damaged, and the university was set on fire. Even more destruction came during the Spanish Civil War. Despite Oviedo's long and violent history, it is a peaceful city today.

Essentials

GETTING THERE Oviedo doesn't have an airport. The nearest one is at Santiago del Monte, Ranón, 52km (32 miles) away, which it shares with Gijón-bound passengers. Call ✆ **98-512-75-00** for information.

RENFE (✆ **90-224-02-02;** www.renfe.es) offers three **trains** per day from Madrid; the one-way trip takes 9 hours and costs 48€. **FEVE** (✆ **91-453-38-00;** www.feve.es) runs trains from Bilbao; the one-way trip takes 7 hours and costs 22€. **ALSA** (✆ **90-242-22-42;** www.alsa.

jurassic park **IN ASTURIAS**

Dinosaur buffs from around the world flock to one of the most extensive dinosaur museums in the world, **Musée del Jurásico del Asturias ★★★**, San Juan de Duz at Colunga (*©* **90-230-66-00;** www.museojurasicoasturias.com), 32km (20 miles) east of Gijón and 40km (25 miles) northeast of Oviedo. The 209km (130-mile) stretch of sandy beaches and towering cliffs along this coast have produced so many dinosaur bones that the area is dubbed "the Dinosaur Coast." In all, 800 fossils, representing dinosaurs that inhabited the earth 65 million to 280 million years ago, are displayed in a trio of large exhibition spaces. The bones are presented in life-size versions, and the museum itself is built in the shape of a big hoof print. Admission is 6€ adults, 4€ children 4 to 11 and seniors 66 and up. From June 21 to September 21, hours are daily 10:30am to 2:30pm and 4 to 8pm. Off-season visits are possible Wednesday to Sunday 10:30am to 2:30pm and 4 to 7pm.

18

Oviedo

CANTABRIA & ASTURIAS

es) operates **buses** from Madrid; the trip one-way takes 5 hours and costs 30€. Driving from the east or west, take N-634 across the coast of northern Spain. From the south, take N-630 or A-66 from León.

VISITOR INFORMATION The **tourist information office** is at Plaza de La Constitución 4 (*©* **98-408-60-60**). Regular hours are daily from 10am to 2pm and 4:30 to 7pm. But from July to September hours are daily 9:30am to 7:30pm.

Exploring Oviedo

Oviedo has been rebuilt into a modern city around Parque de San Francisco. It still contains historical and artistic monuments, the most important being the **Catedral de San Salvador ★**, on the Plaza de Alfonso II el Casto (*©* **98-522-10-33**). The original church dates to the 8th century, but the Gothic church was begun in 1348 and completed at the end of the 15th century (except for the spire, which dates from 1556). Inside is an altarpiece in the florid Gothic style, dating from the 14th and 15th centuries. The cathedral's 9th-century **Cámara Santa (Holy Chamber)** is famous for the Cross of Don Pelayo, the Cross of the Victory, and the Cross of the Angels, the finest specimens of Asturian art in the world. Admission to the cathedral is free, but entrance to the Holy Chamber is 1.50€ for adults, 1€ for children 10 to 15, and free for children 9 and under. For 3€ for adults and 1.50€ for children, you can buy a package ticket to also visit the Museo de la Iglesia and the Claustro Gótico. Both are open July to September Monday to Friday 10am to 8pm, and Saturday 10am to 6pm. Off season, they're open Monday to Friday 10am to 1pm and 4 to 7pm, and Saturday 4 to 6pm. Take bus no. 1.

Standing above Oviedo, on Monte Naranco, are two of the most famous examples of Asturian pre-Romanesque architecture. **Santa María del Naranco ★★** (*©* **98-529-56-85**), originally a 9th-century palace and hunting lodge of Ramiro I, offers views of Oviedo and the snowcapped Picos de Europa. Once containing baths and private apartments, it was converted into a church in the 12th century. Intricate stonework depicts hunting scenes, and barrel vaulting rests on a network of blind arches. The open porticoes at both ends were architecturally 200 years ahead of their time. From April to September, the church is open Sunday and Monday 9:30am to 1pm, and Tuesday to Saturday 9:30am to

1pm and 3:30 to 7pm. Off-season hours are Sunday and Monday 10am to 1pm, Tuesday to Saturday 10am to 12:30pm and 3 to 4:30pm. Admission is 3€ and includes admission to San Miguel de Lillo. Entrance is free on Monday.

About 90m (295 ft.) away is **San Miguel de Lillo** ★ (© **98-529-56-85**). It, too, was built by Ramiro I as a royal chapel and was no doubt a magnificent specimen of Asturian pre-Romanesque architecture until 15th-century architects marred its grace. The stone carvings that remain, however, are exemplary. Most of the sculptures have been transferred to the archaeological museum in town. The church is open the same hours as Santa María del Naranco (see above). Ask the tourist office for its 45-minute walking tour from the center of Oviedo to the churches.

Shopping

Serious shoppers know that Oviedo offers some of Spain's best outlets for handbags and shoes. For a number of the finest boutiques, head for the intersection of **Uria** and **Gil de Jaz.** In this district, and on adjoining side streets, you'll find some of the country's best-known designer boutiques, selling the same merchandise that goes for far higher prices in such cities as Madrid and Barcelona. You'll also come across good sales on Asturian ceramic ware.

Where to Stay in Oviedo

EXPENSIVE

Hotel de la Reconquista ★★★ Named after a subject dear to the hearts of the Catholic monarchs—the ejection of the Muslims from Iberia—this is one of the most prestigious hotels in Spain. Originally built between 1754 and 1777 as an orphanage and hospital, it received visits from Queen Isabella II in 1858 and a reworking of its baroque stonework during a restoration in 1958. The Reconquista was converted into a hotel in 1973. Despite the subsequent growth of the city, the hotel remains the second-largest building in Oviedo. The interior boasts a combination of modern and reproduction furniture, as well as a scattering of ecclesiastical paintings and antiques. The spacious guest rooms are outfitted in antique styles, with views of the Old Town or of a series of elegantly antique interior courtyards. The hotel is 2 blocks north of the largest park in the town center, Campo San Francisco.

Gil de Jaz 16, 33004 Oviedo. © **98-524-11-00.** Fax 98-524-60-11. www.hoteldelareconquista. com. 142 units. 149€–240€ double; from 963€ suite. AE, DC, MC, V. Parking 24€. Bus: 1, 2, or 3. **Amenities:** 2 restaurants; bar; room service; sauna. *In room:* A/C, TV, DVD (in some), hair dryer, minibar, Wi-Fi (free).

MODERATE

El Magistral In the commercial district of Uria, this six-story hotel—rated three stars by the government—was built in 1997. The modern design in the public areas is dominated by glass and chrome with spot lighting and tiled floors. The midsize guest rooms are more traditional, with parquet floors and pastel walls. The hotel's **restaurant** is about 50m (165 ft.) from the main building and has a fine reputation locally for its regional cuisine.

Calle Jovellanos 3, 33003 Oviedo. © **98-520-42-42.** Fax 98-521-06-79. www.elmagistral.com. 34 units. 65€–110€ double. AE, DC, MC, V. Parking 10€. **Amenities:** Restaurant; bar; room service. *In room:* A/C (in some), TV, hair dryer, minibar.

Santa María del Naranco and a view of Oviedo.

Hotel Vetusta ★ 🛏 In the center of the city, just a 5-minute walk from the cathedral, this four-story hotel takes its name from an imaginary fictional city invented by the author Clarín. It has been in operation since 1997, following the successful renovation of an old structure of wood and brick, split by wooden balconies. The interior has steel and wood fittings and is done in an ultracontemporary style. The small guest rooms are very compact but comfortably furnished. Some have balconies, and eight contain a hydromassage.

Calle Covadonga 2, 33002 Oviedo. ✆ **98-522-22-29.** Fax 98-522-22-09. www.hotelvetusta. com. 16 units. 70€–120€ double. AE, DC, MC, V. Nearby parking 10€. **Amenities:** Bar; room service; Wi-Fi (free, in lobby). In room: A/C, TV, hair dryer, minibar.

Marcos This modern hotel in the Old Quarter is noted for its tasteful decor. The small guest rooms are comfortable, inviting, and well maintained, including the bathrooms with restored plumbing. The hotel stands right in the middle of the historic district, within walking distance of many attractions.

Calle Caveda 23, 33002 Oviedo. ✆ **98-522-72-72.** Fax 98-522-80-18. www.room-matehotels. com. 47 units. 64€–110€ double. AE, DC, MC, V. Nearby parking 10€. Bus: 1, 2, or 3. **Amenities:** Restaurant; bar; babysitting; room service. In room: A/C, TV, hair dryer, minibar, Wi-Fi (free).

Where to Dine in Oviedo

Casa Conrado ASTURIAN Almost as solidly established as the cathedral nearby, this restaurant offers good-tasting, hearty Asturian stews, seafood platters, seafood soups, several preparations of hake (including one cooked in cider), scalops of veal with champagne, and a full range of desserts. It is a local favorite and a long-established culinary tradition. The service is attentive.

Argüelles 1. ✆ **98-522-39-19.** www.casaconrado.com. Reservations recommended. Main courses 20€–27€; fixed-price menu 45€. AE, DC, MC, V. Mon–Sat 1–4pm and 9pm–midnight. Closed Aug. Bus: 1.

Casa Fermín ★ ASTURIAN/INTERNATIONAL The chef here prepares the town's best regional cuisine, in a building near the university and the cathedral. To order the most classic dish, ask for *fabada asturiana,* a bean dish with Asturian black pudding and Avilés ham. A tasty hake cooked in cider is another option. Venison is a specialty in season (Oct–Mar), but the most elegant dish is filet mignon with foie gras and a truffle sauce. Try the province's traditional Cabrales cheese. Although it's been around for half a century, Casa Fermín has a contemporary air to it (the decor is in pink and granite) because it's filled with plants and covered with skylights. The restaurant is directly east of Parque de San Francisco.

Calle San Francisco 8. ℂ **98-521-64-52.** www.casafermin.com. Reservations recommended. Main courses 23€–28€; fixed-price menus 36€–65€. AE, DC, MC, V. Mon–Sat 1:30–4pm and 9pm–midnight. Bus: 1 or 2.

El Raitán ★ 🍴 ASTURIAN This restaurant south of the cathedral serves a fixed-price menu and bases all its dishes on regional ingredients, with meals accompanied by wines from La Rioja. A large array of well-prepared choices is available for each course. Each day the chef presents about 10 classic regional dishes that change with the season. These might include hake cooked in cider or veal sirloin in a Cabrales cheese sauce, or even wild boar stew. For a starter, we'd recommend the cream of crab soup if featured. The tavern setting with overhead beams is atmospheric and intimate.

Trascorrales 6. ℂ **98-521-42-18.** www.elraitanroxu.com. Reservations recommended. Main courses 12€–25€; *menú asturiano* (Asturian tasting menu) 35€. AE, DC, MC, V. Wed–Mon 1–4pm; Mon and Wed–Sat 8pm–midnight. Bus: 1 or 2.

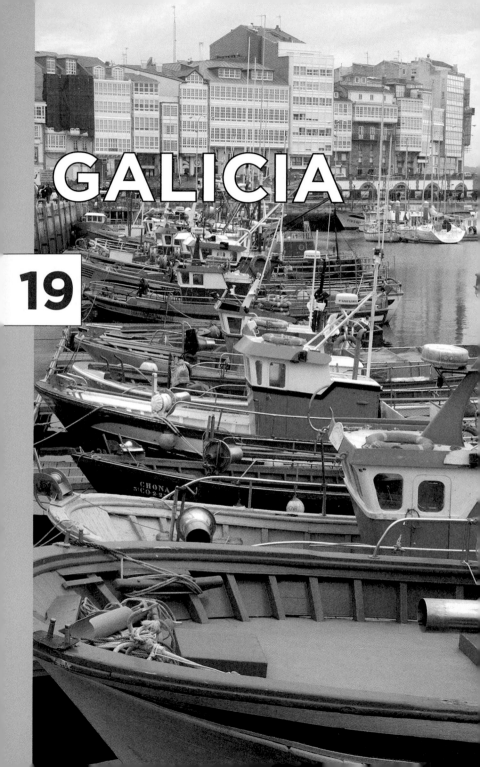

GALICIA

19

Extending above Portugal in the northwest corner of Spain, Galicia is a rain-swept land of grass and granite, much of its coastline gouged by fjordlike inlets. It is a land steeped in Celtic tradition—in many areas its citizens, called Gallegos, speak their own language (not a dialect of Spanish but a separate language, Gallego). Galicia consists of four provinces: A Coruña (including Santiago de Compostela), Pontevedra, Lugo, and Orense.

The Romans made quite an impression on the region. The walls around the city of **Lugo** and the Tower of Hercules at **A Coruña** are part of that legacy. The Moors came, too, and did a lot of damage along the way. But finding the natives none too friendly and other battlefields more promising, they moved on.

Nothing did more to put Galicia on the tourist map than **Camino de Santiago,** the route of religious pilgrims. It is the oldest, most traveled, and most famous route on the old Continent. To guarantee a place in heaven, pilgrims journeyed to the supposed tomb of Santiago (St. James), patron saint of Spain. They trekked across the Pyrenees by the thousands, risking their lives in transit. The Camino de Santiago contributed to the development and spread of Romanesque art and architecture across Spain. Pilgrimages to the shrine lessened as medieval culture began its decline.

A CORUÑA ★

604km (375 miles) NW of Madrid, 155km (96 miles) N of Vigo

Despite the fact that A Coruña is an ancient city, it does not have a wealth of historical and architectural monuments. Celts, Phoenicians, and Romans all occupied the port, and it is another of the legendary cities that claim Hercules as its founder.

The greatest event in the history of A Coruña occurred in 1588, when Philip II's "Invincible Armada" sailed from here to England. Only half the ships made it back to Spain. The following year, Sir Francis Drake and his ships attacked the port in reprisal.

Essentials

GETTING THERE There are seven flights a week from Madrid to A Coruña. Serviced only by **Iberia, Aeropuerto de Alvedro** (✆ 90-240-47-04; www.aena.es) lies 10km (6¼ miles) from the heart of the city.

Trains arrive at Estación San Cristóbal, Plaza San Cristóbal (✆ 90-224-02-02; www.renfe.es). Depending on the train, the one-way ride from Madrid lasts 8½ to 11 hours and costs 50€. **Monbus** (✆ 90-229-29-00) runs **buses** between A Coruña and Santiago de Compostela every hour. Trip time one-way is between 50 minutes and 1½ hours, and costs 11€.

FACING PAGE: **Fishing boats in A Coruña.**

By car, A Coruña is reached from Madrid by the N-VI. You can also follow the coastal highway, N-634, which runs all the way across the northern rim of Spain from San Sebastián to the east.

VISITOR INFORMATION The **tourist office** at Dársena de la Marina s/n (© **98-122-18-22;** www.turgalicia.es) is open Monday to Friday 10am to 2pm and 4 to 7pm, Saturday and Sunday 11am to 2pm.

Exploring A Coruña

A Coruña's Old Town is ideal for a stroll. **Plaza de María Pita** divides the Old Town from the newer city. María Pita, a local housewife, was said to have spotted the approach of Drake's troops. Risking her own life, she fired a cannon

A Coruña's seaside harbor.

shot to alert the citizens to an imminent invasion. For that act of heroism, she is revered to this day.

You can take a stroll through the **Jardines de Méndez Núñez,** between the harbor and Los Cantones (Cantón Grande and Cantón Pequeño). Facing the police station and overlooking the port, the gardens are in the very center of town and make for a restful interlude during your sightseeing.

The cobbled **Plazuela de Santa Bárbara**—a tiny, tree-shaded plaza flanked by old houses and the high walls of the Santa Bárbara convent—also merits a visit.

Jardín de San Carlos, along Paseo del Parrote, dates from 1843 and is near the Casa de la Cultura. This garden grew on the site of an old fortress that once guarded the harbor. It contains the tomb of Gen. John Moore, who fought unsuccessfully against the troops of Napoleon. He retreated with his British forces to A Coruña, where he was shot in a final battle. These gardens now make an ideal picnic spot.

Iglesia de Santa María del Campo, Calle de Santa María, is a 13th-century church with an elaborately carved west door, modeled in the traditional Romanesque-Gothic style. Beneath its rose window you'll see a Gothic portal from the 13th or 14th century. The tympanum is carved with a scene depicting the Adoration of the Magi.

Castillo de San Antón, a 16th-century fort, is now the **Museo Arqueológico e Histórico** (𝄐 98-118-98-50), on the southeast side of the peninsula. It's open July and August Tuesday to Saturday 10am to 9pm, and Sunday 10am to 3pm. From September to June, it is open Tuesday to Saturday 10am to 7:30pm and Sunday 10am to 2:30pm. Admission is 3€ adults, 2€ for seniors and children 11 and under. In addition to a panoramic location on its own islet, the museum has many unusual artifacts from A Coruña province. Take bus no. 3 or 3A.

The second-largest port in Spain, A Coruña is a popular vacation resort that gets very crowded in July and August. Riazor Beach, right in town, is a good, fairly wide beach, but the best one is Santa Cristina, about 5km (3 miles) outside town. There's regular round-trip bus service, but the best way to go is via the steamer (catch it next to Club Náutico) that plies the bay.

Where to Stay in A Coruña

EXPENSIVE

Hesperia Finisterre ★★ ☺ Immediately above the port, a short walk east of the tourist information office at the edge of the Old Town, this high-rise hotel is one of the finest and most panoramic in town. Guest rooms are small but comfortable, with wall-to-wall carpeting, lots of exposed wood, and bright contemporary upholstery. The hotel is the preferred choice of business travelers. Although it was built in 1947, it has been remodeled many times since.

Paseo del Parrote 20, 15001 A Coruña. ✆ **98-120-54-00.** Fax 98-120-84-62. www.hesperia-finisterre.com. 92 units. 69€–176€ double; from 123€ suite. AE, DC, MC, V. Parking 15€. Bus: 1, 2, 3, or 5. **Amenities:** Restaurant; bar; babysitting; bikes; children's programs; health club; Jacuzzi; 3 outdoor heated pools; room service; sauna; 2 outdoor tennis courts. *In room:* A/C, TV, hair dryer, minibar, Wi-Fi (free).

Meliá María Pita ★★★ On Orzan beach, close to the historic district, this graceful, government-rated four-star hotel is the city's finest. It's in an elegant building with extensive glass windows. A member of the Meliá chain, it offers a well-lit marble-floor interior and one of the city's most efficient staffs. Guest rooms are generally large and comfortable, with wooden floors and tasteful decor. The most desirable accommodations come with private balconies overlooking the ocean.

Av. Pedro Barrié de la Maza 1, 15003 A Coruña. ✆ **98-120-50-00.** Fax 98-120-55-65. www.solmelia.com. 167 units. 74€–285€ double; from 235€ suite. AE, DC, MC, V. Parking 15€. **Amenities:** Restaurant; bar; babysitting; room service; sauna. *In room:* A/C, TV, hair dryer, minibar, Wi-Fi (12€ per 24 hr.).

MODERATE

Ciudad de A Coruña On the northwestern tip of the peninsula, surrounded by sea grasses and dunes, this government-rated three-star establishment is cordoned off from the apartment-house complexes that surround it by a wide swath of green. Each attractively modern guest room has a private well-equipped bathroom. Accommodations are generally roomy and maintenance is excellent.

Juan Sebastián El Cano 13, Paseo de Adormideras s/n, 15002 A Coruña. ✆ **98-121-21-00.** Fax 98-122-46-10. www.eurostarshotels.com. 131 units. 49€–200€ double; 109€–399€ suite. AE, DC, MC, V. Free parking. Bus: 3, 3A, or 5. **Amenities:** Restaurant; bar; babysitting; exercise room; room service; sauna. *In room:* A/C, TV, hair dryer, minibar, Wi-Fi (free).

NH Atlántico This convenient, comfortable, and contemporary hotel contrasts with the ornate 19th-century park surrounding it, where crowds of Galicians gather in fine weather. The Atlántico is in the building that houses the city's casino. Well-furnished guest rooms are among the most appealing in town, thanks to spacious dimensions and comfortably contemporary furnishings a cut above less expensive competitors.

Jardines de Méndez Núñez s/n, 15006 A Coruña. ✆ **98-122-65-00.** Fax 98-120-10-71. www.nh-hoteles.com. 199 units. 109€–125€ double; 216€–600€ junior suite. AE, DC, MC, V. Parking 17€. Bus: 1, 2, or 3. **Amenities:** Restaurant; bar; babysitting; exercise room; room service; sauna. *In room:* A/C, TV, hair dryer, minibar, Wi-Fi (17€ per 24 hr.).

INEXPENSIVE

Almirante There are few amenities here—just good, clean rooms, all doubles, at good prices. Room dimensions are a bit skimpy, but the price is right. All units are equipped with neatly kept bathrooms with shower stalls. There is no restaurant, but a continental breakfast is served in the cafeteria (for an extra charge). The location is a bonus: just 1 minute from the beach.

Paseo de Ronda 54, 15011 A Coruña. ✆ **98-125-96-00.** Fax 98-125-96-08. www.hotel-almirante.com. 19 units. 40€–60€ double. AE, MC, V. Parking 9€. Bus: 7, 14, or 14A. **Amenities:** Bar; room service. *In room:* TV.

Hotel Riazor ★ 🍴 In the center of the city by the sea, this hotel is one of the most affordable of the top-rated places to stay. Just cross the busy promenade and you're on the beach. Most of the midsize to spacious bedrooms open onto panoramic views of the bay. The hotel has been frequently restored over the years, and offers personalized guest services in the well-equipped bedrooms. Riazor is suitable for both vacationers and business clients.

Av. Pedro Barrié de la Maza 29, 15004 A Coruña. © **98-125-34-00.** Fax 98-125-34-04. www. riazorhotel.com. 174 units. 50€–110€ double, 70€–130€ triple. AE, DC, MC, V. Parking 12€. **Amenities:** Restaurant/coffee shop; bar; room service. In room: A/C, TV, CD player, hair dryer, minibar, Wi-Fi (free).

Where to Dine in A Coruña

Two or so blocks from the waterfront, several restaurants specialize in Galician cuisine, all at competitive prices. It's customary to go window-shopping for food here. The restaurants along two of the principal streets—Calle de la Estrella and Calle de los Olmos—all have display counters up front.

Adega O Bebedeiró GALICIAN In business since the 1980s, this dining room looks much older and, in fact, evokes a rustic farmstead with its old stone walls, fireplace, and hardwood floors. Guests sit at pine tables and stools, taking in the backdrop of dust-covered wine bottles and farm equipment. In such a traditional setting, you expect old-fashioned, time-tested recipes—and that's what you get. The kitchen uses first-rate fresh ingredients in their hearty, regional fare such as local fish stuffed with shellfish and baked in a puff pastry. A side dish worth savoring is the mushrooms grown in the nearby countryside and served in olive oil with a green-pepper sauce. An unusual concoction is prawns stewed with fresh avocado. The kitchen also turns out one of the best shellfish-laced paellas in town.

Calle Angel Rebollo 34. © **98-121-06-09.** www.adegaobebedeiro.com. Main courses 21€–32€. AE, DC, MC, V. Tues–Sun 1–4pm; Tues–Sat 8pm–midnight. Closed 2 weeks in both June and Dec.

Casa Pardo ★★★ GALICIAN Near the bus station south of the Old Town, this restaurant is justly acclaimed as the finest dining room in the city. Under the direction of Eduardo Pardo Pereira, it offers both a traditional cuisine and innovative seafood dishes. Fresh shellfish and fish dishes, everything from oysters to salmon, are prepared here with skill. The Galician turbot is delectable. Seafood items aren't the only selections on the menu—fresh meat and vegetable dishes are also well prepared. Patrons of this entrenched dining room prefer such wines as Terras Gauda and Viña Costeira. The restaurant is elegant but unstuffy. The fact that the first-rate staff is alert and informed about the graceful service rituals of Old Spain makes the atmosphere subtle and relaxed, although undeniably formal.

Calle Novoa Santos 15. © **98-128-00-21.** www.casapardo-domus.com. Reservations recommended. Main courses 12€–30€; fixed-price menu 40€–95€. AE, DC, MC, V. Mon–Sat 1:30–4pm; Tues–Sat 9pm–midnight.

El Coral ★ GALICIAN/SEAFOOD/INTERNATIONAL This is our favorite and one of the most popular dining spots at the port. In business since 1954, it offers polite service, cleanliness, and Galician cookery prepared with distinction. The restaurant specializes in shellfish, fish, meats, and Galician wines. Popular main courses include *calamares rellenos* (stuffed squid) and *la lubina al horno* (sea bass). The front window forms an altar of shellfish in infinite varieties, a tapestry of crustaceans and mollusks. Inside, the atmosphere is intimate and elegant, with formally dressed waiters, crisp white linens, dark-wood-paneled walls, and glittering crystal chandeliers.

Av. de la Marina Callejón de la Estacada 9. © **98-120-05-69.** Fax 98-122-91-09. www. restaurantemarisqueriacoral.com. Reservations recommended. Main courses 17€–26€. AE, DC, MC, V. Mon–Sat 1–4pm and 9pm–midnight. Bus: 1, 2, 5, or 17.

A Coruña After Dark

Some of the most appealing bars in A Coruña are atmospheric holes in the wall with a local clientele and a decor that has remained virtually unchanged since the end of the Spanish Civil War. We like to start our evening at **A Roda,** Capitán Troncoso 8 (© **98-122-86-71;** daily 1–4pm and 8pm–midnight), which is rightly known for its tapas. A lively group of both locals and visitors can be found here devouring such selections as octopus in its own ink. If you want to go dancing after your drinks and tapas, and if it's after 11pm, consider a run into the town's most appealing and most popular disco, **Disco Playa Club,** Andén de Riazor (© **98-127-75-14;** www.playaclub.net). Set on an oceanfront terrace, a few feet from the waves of Playa Riazor, it's open year-round Thursday through Saturday.

SANTIAGO DE COMPOSTELA ★★★

614km (382 miles) NW of Madrid, 74km (46 miles) S of A Coruña

All roads in Spain once led to the northwestern pilgrimage city of Santiago de Compostela. A journey to the tomb of the beheaded apostle, St. James, was a high point for the medieval faithful—peasant and prince alike—who converged here from all over Europe.

Santiago de Compostela's link with legend began in A.D. 813, when an urn was discovered containing what were believed to be the remains of St. James, a disciple of Jesus who was beheaded in Jerusalem. A temple was erected over the spot, but in the 16th century, church fathers hid the remains of the saint, fearing they might be destroyed in raids along the coast by Sir Francis Drake. Somewhat amazingly, the alleged remains—subject of millions of pilgrimages from across Europe—lay relatively forgotten.

For decades no one was certain where they were. Then, in 1879, a workman making repairs on the church discovered what were supposed to be the remains, hidden since the 1500s. To prove it was the actual corpse of St. James, church officials brought back a sliver of the skull of St. James from Italy. They claimed that it fit perfectly, like a puzzle piece, into the recently discovered skeleton.

In addition to being the third-most-holy city of the Christian world (after Rome and Jerusalem), Santiago de Compostela is a university town and a marketplace for Galician farmers. With its flagstone streets, churches, and shrines, it is one of the most romantic and historic of Spain's great cities. Santiago also has the dubious distinction of being the rainiest city in Spain, but the showers tend to arrive and end suddenly. Locals claim that the rain only makes their city more beautiful, and the rain-slick cobblestones might prompt you to agree.

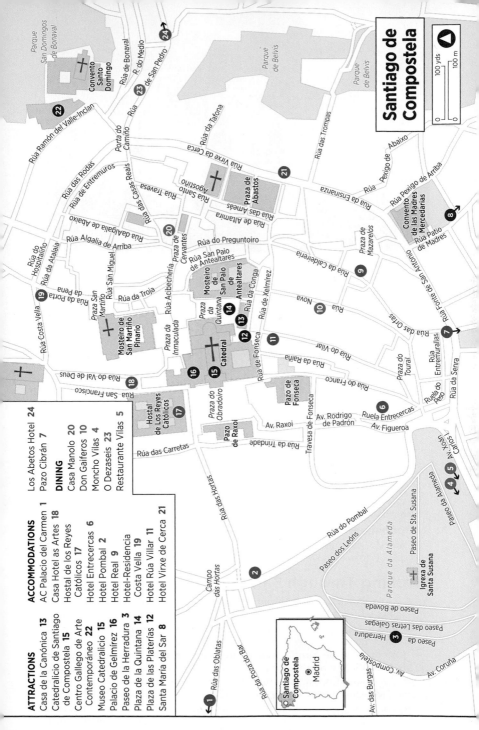

Santiago de Compostela

0 100 yds
0 100 m

ATTRACTIONS
Casa de la Canónica **13**
Catedralicio de Santiago
de Compostela **15**
Centro Gallego de Arte
Contemporáneo **22**
Museo Catedralicio **15**
Palacio de Gelmírez **16**
Paseo de la Herradura **3**
Plaza de la Quintana **14**
Plaza de las Platerías **12**
Santa María del Sar **8**

ACCOMMODATIONS
AC Palacio del Carmen **1**
Casa Hotel as Artes **18**
Hostal de los Reyes
Católicos **17**
Hotel Entrecercas **6**
Hotel Pombal **2**
Hotel Real **9**
Hotel-Residencia
Costa Vella **19**
Hotel Rúa Villar **11**
Hotel Virxe de Cerca **21**

Los Abetos Hotel **24**
Pazo Cibrán **7**

DINING
Casa Manolo **20**
Don Gaiferos **10**
Moncho Vilas **4**
O Dezaseis **23**
Restaurante Vilas **5**

683

The silhouette of the Catedralicio de Santiago de Compostela.

Essentials

GETTING THERE From Madrid, Iberia has five daily **flights** to Santiago, and there is one daily flight from Barcelona. The only international airport in Galicia is east of Santiago de Compostela at Lavacolla (𝄢 **98-154-75-01** for flight information), 11km (6¾ miles) from the center on the road to Lugo.

From A Coruña, 21 **trains** make the 1-hour trip daily at a cost of 4.60€ to 15€. Two trains arrive daily from Madrid; the 8-hour trip costs 47€. Call 𝄢 **90-224-02-02** for information (www.renfe.es).

Buses leave on the hour, connecting A Coruña with Santiago (trip time: 1 hr.), and cost 12€ one-way. For information, call **Monbus** (𝄢 **98-229-29-00;** www.monbus.es). Eight buses a day arrive in Santiago from Madrid, taking 8 hours and costing 60€ one-way. For information, call **Alsa** at 𝄢 **98-158-61-33** (www.alsa.es).

If you're driving, take the express highway (A-9/E-50) south from A Coruña to reach Santiago. From Madrid, N-VI runs to Galicia. From Lugo, head south along N-640.

VISITOR INFORMATION The **tourist office,** at Rúa del Villar 43 (𝄢 **98-158-40-81;** www.turgalicia.es), is open Monday to Friday 10am to 8pm, Saturday 11am to 2pm and 5 to 7pm, and Sunday 11am to 2pm.

Strolling Through Santiago

Santiago de Compostela's highlight is undoubtedly its storied cathedral, and you should take at least 2 hours to see it. Afterward, take a stroll through this enchanting town, which has a number of other interesting monuments as well as many stately mansions along Rúa del Villar and Rúa Nueva.

Catedralicio de Santiago de Compostela ★★★, Plaza del Obradoiro (𝄢 **98-156-05-27**), begun in the 11th century, is the crowning achievement of Spanish Romanesque architecture, even though it actually reflects a number of styles. Maestro Mateo's **Pórtico de la Gloria ★★★**, carved in 1188, ranks among the finest produced in Europe at that time. The three arches of the portico are carved with biblical figures from the Last Judgment. In the center, Christ is flanked by apostles and the 24 Elders of the Apocalypse. Below the Christ figure is a depiction of St. James himself. He crowns a carved column that includes a portrayal of Mateo at the bottom. If you observe this column, you will see that five deep indentations have been worn into it by pilgrims since the Middle Ages. Even today, pilgrims line up here to lean forward, place their hands on the pillar, and touch foreheads with Mateo.

The cathedral has three naves in cruciform shape and several chapels and cloisters. The altar, with its blend of Gothic simplicity and baroque decor, is extraordinary. In the crypt, a silver urn contains what are believed to be the remains of the Apostle St. James. A cathedral museum, **Museo Catedralicio ★**, displays tapestries and archaeological fragments. Next door, **Palacio de Gelmírez** (☏ **98-157-23-00**), an archbishop's palace built during the 12th century, is an outstanding example of Romanesque architecture.

Admission to the cathedral and to the Palacio de Gelmírez is free. Hours for the cathedral are daily 7am to 9pm. For the cloisters and the Palacio de Gelmírez, hours are from June to September, Monday to Saturday 10am to 2pm and 4 to 8pm, Sunday 10am to 2pm; from October to May, Monday to Saturday 10am to 1:30pm and 4 to 6:30pm, Sunday 10am to 1:30pm. Admission to the Museo Catedralicio costs 5€; hours are daily 10am to 2pm and 4 to 8pm.

Most of the other impressive buildings are on Plaza del Obradoiro, also called Plaza de España. Next to the cathedral is **Hostal de los Reyes Católicos ★**, now a *parador* (see below), formerly a royal hospice, and, in the 15th century, a pilgrims' hospice. It was designed by Enrique de Egas, Isabella and Ferdinand's favorite architect. Tourists may visit the cloistered courtyard with its beautiful 16th- to 18th-century fountains and the main chapel; however, you must have a guide from the cathedral in attendance (☏ **98-158-22-00** for information). Hours are daily from 10am to 1pm and 4 to 7pm.

One of the most important squares in the Old Town is **Plaza de la Quintana,** to the left of the cathedral's Goldsmith's Doorway. This is a favorite square with students, who often perch on the flight of broad steps that connect the rear of the cathedral to the walls of a convent. The square is dominated by **Casa de la Canónica,** the former residence of the canon.

South of the square is the Renaissance-style **Plaza de las Platerías (Silversmiths' Square),** which has an elaborate fountain.

Centro Gallego de Arte Contemporáneo, Rúa Valle-Inclán s/n (☏ **98-154-66-19;** www.cgac.org), is the Galician Center of Contemporary Art, highlighting artworks from regional, national, and international artists. The center's changing exhibits feature contemporary artists, and it hosts retrospectives. Until the opening of this center, contemporary art had virtually no place on the city's agenda, which emphasized the ancient or the antique. Among the several exhibition

A detail from the Cathedral's Pórtico de la Gloria.

The Plaza de las Platerías.

rooms is a terrace for open-air exhibits, affording a panoramic view of Santiago's Old Town. The admission-free museum is open Tuesday through Sunday from 11am to 8pm.

Farther afield, visit the Romanesque **Santa María del Sar,** on Calle Castron d'Ouro, .8km (½ mile) down Calle de Sar, which starts at the Patio de Madre. This collegiate church is one of the architectural gems of the Romanesque style in Galicia. Its walls and columns are on a 15-degree slant thought to be attributable to either a fragile foundation or an architect's fancy. Visit the charming cloister with its slender columns. The church is open Monday to Saturday 10am to 1pm and 4 to 7pm. Admission is 1€.

Cap off your day with a walk along **Paseo de la Herradura,** the gardens southwest of the Old Town, from where you have an all-encompassing view of the cathedral and the Old City.

Shopping

The artfully naive blue-and-white porcelain that is the town's trademark is available for sale at **Sargadelos,** Rúa Nueva 16 (© **98-158-19-05**). A competitor that stocks similar ceramics, plus a wide range of other regional handicrafts, is **Amboa,** Rúa Nueva 44 (© **98-158-33-59**).

A favorite of most tourists is *tarta Santiago,* a tart sold at virtually every pastry shop in the city. Also very popular is *queso de tetilla,* a local cheese shaped like breasts.

Many of the local wines, including assorted bottles of Ribeiro, Condado, and, most famous of all, Albariño, are sold without fanfare in grocery stores throughout Galicia. But for a specialist in the subtleties of Galician and other Spanish wines, head for **Charcuterías Seco,** San Pedro Mezonzo (© **98-159-12-67;** www.charcuteriasseco.com).

EUROPE'S oldest HOTEL

The oldest hotel in Europe has been giving travelers a place of rest for nearly 5 centuries. In 1499 the Catholic kings founded the Hospedaje Real (Royal Hospice) in Santiago de Compostela to serve as a respite for the hundreds of thousands of pilgrims who came to pay homage to the shrine of Saint James. Known today as the **Hostal de Los Reyes Católicos** (see review below), the same structure is Europe's most ancient hotel, and certainly one of its most luxurious.

During the Middle Ages, Santiago prevailed, together with Jerusalem and Rome, as one of the three holy cities of Christendom. The cult of Santiago (St. James) drew hordes of pilgrims trekking across northern Spain in search of the saint's tomb. The route to Santiago proved long, arduous, and dangerous. Having made the pilgrimage themselves, the Catholic monarchs experienced firsthand the dearth of accommodations along the way—hence the decision by Ferdinand and Isabella to construct monasteries and hospitals to house and protect visitors, the best effort culminating in this prominent structure.

Construction on the Hospital Real began in the 15th century and continued through the 18th century. Set on Obradoiro Plaza, this grand edifice shares the square with the impressive cathedral of Santiago. In addition to its luxury rooms, this government-rated five-star hotel boasts a concert and exhibition room surrounded by cloisters.

Architecturally, the old part of the city stopped developing in the baroque period and, as a result, its buildings exude an aura of impressive grandeur—in fact, a sense of mysticism permeates Santiago. It is fitting, then, that one of Spain's great monumental cities should be home to one of the country's most luxurious, historically significant hotels.

Where to Stay in & Around Santiago
EXPENSIVE

AC Palacio del Carmen ★ 🏢 Installed in a former convent, this is one of our favorite nests in Santiago, as the original architecture of the former convent was respected during its massive renovation into a hotel. It stands in the historic center near Plaza del Obradoiro. In spite of the building's age, all the small-to-midsize guest rooms have been comfortably styled and fitted with modern conveniences, including tiled bathrooms. The on-site **restaurant** serves an innovative Galician cuisine, with some haute cuisine dishes added to tempt the most demanding of palates.

Oblatas s/n, 15703 Santiago de Compostela. ✆ **98-155-24-44.** Fax 98-155-24-45. www.ac-hotels.com. 74 units. 80€–188€ double; 165€–315€ suite. AE, DC, MC, V. Parking 13€. **Amenities:** Restaurant; bar; babysitting; concierge; exercise room; indoor heated pool; room service. *In room:* A/C, TV, hair dryer, minibar, Wi-Fi (10€ per 24 hr.).

Hostal de los Reyes Católicos ★★★ This former 16th-century hospice, founded by Ferdinand and Isabella, is one of the most spectacular hotels in Europe. Next to the cathedral, it served as a resting place and hospital for pilgrims visiting the tomb of Saint James. Even if you don't stay here, you should take a guided tour (see the box above, "Europe's Oldest Hotel").

The hotel has four huge open-air courtyards, each with its own covered walk, gardens, and fountains. In addition, there are great halls, French grillwork, and a large collection of antiques. A Gothic chapel hosts weekly concerts. There's a range of accommodations, everything from Franco's former bedchamber to small rooms. Many of the palatial rooms have ornate canopied beds draped in embroidered red velvet. Hand-carved chests, gilt mirrors, and oil paintings enhance the air of luxury. The private bathrooms are quite sumptuous.

Plaza de Obradoido 1, 15705 Santiago de Compostela. ℂ **98-158-22-00.** Fax 98-156-30-94. www.parador.es. 137 units. 265€–281€ double; from 322€ suite. Rates include continental breakfast. AE, DC, MC, V. Parking 18€. **Amenities:** 2 restaurants; bar; babysitting; room service. *In room:* A/C, TV, hair dryer, minibar, Wi-Fi (free).

MODERATE

Hotel Rúa Villar ★ 🏠 One of the best examples of recycling an old building, this stellar guesthouse was converted from an 18th-century manor house into a small hotel. Compostelana hospitality is at its warmest at this inviting choice. Its exposed stone walls and mellow old wood beams evoke the past, but all the rooms and amenities are up-to-date. Much use is made of marble and wood—management calls these "noble materials." The art on display is often by such famous Spanish artists as Julio Romero de Torres or Miró. The hotel lies in the heart of the monumental zone of Santiago, only 15m (49 ft.) from the cathedral.

Rúa do Villar, 8–10, 15705 Santiago de Compostela. ℂ **98-151-98-58.** Fax 98-151-96-77. www. hotelruavillar.com. 14 units. 90€–150€ double. Rates include breakfast buffet. AE, DC, MC, V. No parking. **Amenities:** Bar; babysitting; room service. *In room:* A/C, TV/DVD, CD player, hair dryer, minibar, Wi-Fi (free).

Hotel Virxe de Cerca ★ A 10-minute walk from the cathedral, this is one of Santiago's leading hotels. Its owners converted an 18th-century structure (once both a banking house and the residence of the local Jesuit community) into today's hotel. The once "royal road" ran in front of the building. The facade opens toward the market in the historic part of town, where country vendors peddle their wares; the back opens toward Belvis Park. The hotel also has a private garden. Part of its charm is a glass-encased dining area, evoking an old cloister. All guest rooms have been tastefully and attractively furnished. The **restaurant's** Galician cuisine is first-rate.

Virxe da Cerca 27, 15703 Santiago de Compostela. ℂ **98-156-93-50.** Fax 98-158-69-25. www. pousadasdecompostela.com. 43 units. 90€–130€ double. AE, DC, MC, V. Limited free parking. **Amenities:** Restaurant; bar; babysitting; room service. *In room:* A/C, TV, hair dryer, minibar, Wi-Fi (free).

Los Abetos Hotel ★★ If you're seeking quaint charm from long ago, check into the Reyes Católicos *parador*. But if you want the best facilities in town and up-to-date comfort in a government-rated four-star hotel, make it Los Abetos. A favorite of business travelers, it works equally well for pilgrims to the Old City. Surrounded by private gardens, the hotel also has the best fitness facilities, with everything from a modern gym to a heated swimming pool. Fresh as tomorrow, guest rooms range from midsize to spacious, and each comes with a first-rate private bathroom with tub and shower.

San Lázaro, 15820 Santiago de Compostela. ✆ **98-155-70-26.** Fax 98-158-61-77. www.hotel losabetos.com. 148 units. 64€–150€ double. Children 9 and under stay free. AE, DC, MC, V. Free parking. **Amenities:** Restaurant; bar; exercise room; outdoor pool; sauna; outdoor tennis court. *In room:* A/C, TV, hair dryer, minibar, Wi-Fi (free).

INEXPENSIVE

Casa Hotel as Artes ★ 🎁 Lying in the vicinity of the cathedral, this hotel is a delight and a most inviting choice for those who can't afford the steep rates of Hostal de los Reyes Católicos. What makes the place so special is that each of its midsize, well-furnished rooms is named after a different international artist and decorated in the spirit of that artist. Rooms honor Rodin, Dante, Vivaldi, Gaudí, Picasso, and even Charlie Chaplin. The Picasso Room has two reproductions of his paintings, including one from his so-called "blue period." The accommodations are decorated in an old Spanish style, with hardwood floors, wrought-iron double beds, and recessed windows with beveled shutters.

Traversía de Dos Puertas 2, off Rúa San Francisco, 15707 Santiago de Compostela. ✆ **98-155-52-54.** Fax 98-157-78-23. www.asartes.com. 7 units. 55€–117€ double. AE, DC, MC, V. Parking 9€. **Amenities:** Bar; sauna. *In room:* TV, hair dryer, Wi-Fi (free).

Hotel Entrecercas 🛥 This modern property not only offers some of the city's most affordable accommodations, but lies 30m (98 ft.) from the cathedral itself, so it's in the most central location for exploring the medieval core on foot. The owner has sensitively restored the old building, retaining its ancient stonework and restoring exposed and time-blackened wood beams. The guest rooms are simply but comfortably decorated. In summer you should reserve as far in advance as possible.

Entrecercas 11, 15705 Santiago de Compostela. ✆ **98-157-11-51.** Fax 98-157-11-12. www. hotelentrecercas.es. 8 units. 75€–86€ double. Rates include continental breakfast. AE, DC, MC, V. Nearby parking 13€. **Amenities:** Cafeteria. *In room:* TV, hair dyer, Wi-Fi (free).

Hotel Pombal ★★ Across from Alameda Park, this is one of the newest inns of Santiago. It is part of the Pousadas de Compostela chain of hotels. Lying an 8- to 10-minute walk from the cathedral in the heart of the historic district, the hotel has both charm and grace. The midsize guest rooms have been tastefully and comfortably converted, with many traditional touches evocative of 19th-century Spain.

Rúa do Pombal 12, 15705 Santiago de Compostela. ✆ **98-156-93-50.** Fax 98-158-69-25. www. pousadasdecompostela.com. 15 units. 70€–110€ double. AE, DC, MC, V. No parking. **Amenities:** Bar; room service. *In room:* A/C, TV, hair dryer, minibar, Wi-Fi (free).

Hotel Real ★ 🎁 Only a few minutes' walk from the cathedral, this small hotel is a charmer. A former house for university students, it's been successfully converted to receive guests at large. Its guest rooms are distributed across three floors, all of them enjoying natural light and a balcony overlooking the medieval city. The guest rooms are small but tastefully furnished and comfortable, each with a tidy, immaculate bathroom. Breakfast, the only meal offered, is served in a delightful little salon.

Caldereria 49, 15700 Santiago de Compostela. ✆ **98-156-92-90.** Fax 98-156-92-91. www.hotel real.com. 13 units. 60€–78€ double. AE, MC, V. No parking. **Amenities:** Room service. *In room:* TV, Wi-Fi (free).

Hotel-Residencia Costa Vella This well-run hotel is on Porta de la Peña, which leads into the medieval sector of Santiago. The traditional, glass-fronted building is located at one of the loftiest points in the city. Midsize guest rooms have Galician styling, with carved wooden headboards and stone accents. The rooms manage to look classical yet modern. Breakfast, served with a view, features such Galician delights as cheese with honey, almond cake, and homemade toasted bread.

Rúa Porta de Peña 17, 15704 Santiago de Compostela. ✆ **98-156-95-30.** Fax 98-156-95-31. www. costavella.com. 14 units. 62€–87€ double. MC, V. Parking 9€, must be reserved in advance. Closed Dec 23–Jan 8. **Amenities:** Bar; room service. *In room:* TV, hair dryer.

Pazo Cibrán ★ 🎁 Sensitively restored, this farmhouse/manor dates from the 1700s. It's located 7km (4⅓ miles) to the south of Santiago, about 15 minutes by car if there's no traffic. You're welcomed by the hospitable proprietor, Mayka Iglesias, who offers six rooms in the main manor plus five more spacious accommodations in a converted stable. Guest rooms are beautifully and traditionally furnished, and come with handsome bathrooms. Madam Iglesias has maintained her ancestral family living room so that it's filled with antiques and interesting objects; it opens onto a stunning garden. There's even a "bamboo walk." Nearby, in another converted house, is the **Restaurant Roberto.** Traditional Galician dishes with homegrown products are served here.

San Xulián a de Sales, 15885 Verda. ✆ **98-151-15-15.** Fax 98-181-47-66. www.pazocibran.com. 11 units. 54€–99€ double. AE, DC, MC, V. Free parking. **Amenities:** Bar; babysitting; room service. *In room:* TV/DVD, no phone.

Where to Dine in Santiago

Casa Manolo 🍴 GALICIAN Set in the large but cozy dining room of a brick-built house that's at least a century old, this family-run restaurant offers one of the best dining values in Santiago. There's only one option here: a two-course fixed-price menu of different roasts and filets. Veal cutlets, either breaded in the "Milanese" style, or with cheese in the "Parmigiana" style, are enduringly popular, as are the pastas (especially cannelloni stuffed with a form of ricotta cheese). Filet steak, served *a la plancha* (grilled), and pork chops are also good. Don't expect glamour, as that's not what this place sells. Instead, you'll get generous portions of rib-sticking food more reasonably priced than virtually anywhere else.

Plaza Cervantes s/n. ✆ **98-158-29-50.** Fixed-price menu 9.50€. MC, V. Daily 1–4pm; Mon–Sat 8:30–11:30pm. Closed in Jan.

Don Gaiferos ★ GALICIAN Acclaimed as the best restaurant in this historic city, this winning choice is only 200m (656 ft.) from the cathedral and has been turning out a savory cuisine for 3 decades. The food is enjoyed as much by locals as by visitors. The decor is tasteful and inviting, and the location is right next to the Church of Santa María Salomé. The well-crafted cuisine is made from first-rate ingredients. Tuck into the freshly caught *merluza* (hake), which is served with a delectable sauce. The scallops with Spanish rice are a delight, as are the giant prawns filled with smoked salmon. The zesty kettle of fish stew is the city's finest. You can also order a well-flavored loin of beef or even steak tartare. To finish off the meal, the chef makes a smooth dessert. It could be an utterly delightful cheesecake studded with bilberries, or it could be an almond tart. You'll want to pay homage to the pastry chef.

Rúa Nova 23. © **98-158-38-94.** Reservations required. Main courses 6€–30€; set menu 36€. AE, DC, MC, V. Daily 1:15–3:45pm; Tues–Sat 8:15–11:30pm.

Moncho Vilas ★ GALICIAN You'll be greeted here by a view of a large and busy tapas bar, where the culinary temptations of the actual restaurant are made available in smaller versions. Farther inside, at tables surrounded by stained-glass windows, ceramic tiles, dark paneling, and memorabilia from the region, larger portions of serious dishes create happy memories. The place has been thriving as one of the town's most respected restaurants since 1975. The chef shines with such specialties as loin of pork with wine and herbs, and salads of tomatoes with cheese and anchovies; many different preparations of hake; pork chitterlings *(chicharrones)* with hot peppers and pimientos; and roasted octopus with herbs and olive oil.

Av. Vilagarcía 21. © **98-159-83-87.** Reservations recommended. Main courses 12€–28€. MC, V. Tues–Sun 1:30–4pm and Tues–Sat 8:30–11pm.

O Dezaseis ★ 🍴 TAPAS/GALICIAN The best place in town for tapas and empanadas lies slightly out of the city center and is well worth the trek. You can build an entire meal around these tapas, or else order one of the generous fixed-price menus. "Sixteen" (its English name) is in a subterranean, grottolike section with stone and wood that used to be a stable some 3 centuries ago. The empanadas are exceptional, especially slices from a huge wheel of tuna flavored with Spanish paprika. Octopus is another specialty, and it's cooked until tender and then tossed on the superhot grill and sprinkled with spices. Small plates of fish emerge from the grill or else you can have an omelet with ham and chorizo. The local ham, *lacón,* is about the best item on the menu.

Rúa San Pedro 16. © **98-156-48-80.** www.dezaseis.com. Reservations not needed. Tapas 4.60€–11€; main courses 11€–13€; fixed-price menus 20€–27€. MC, V. Mon–Sat 2–4pm and 8:30pm–midnight.

Restaurante Vilas ★ 🍴 SEAFOOD Located on the outskirts of the Old Town on the road to Pontevedra, this reliable Spanish tavern, housed in a three-story town house, enjoys a devoted clientele, many from industry, politics, and the arts. Beyond the large bar near the entrance and display cases filled with fresh fish, you'll find the baronial stone-trimmed dining room. A wide variety of fish is available—fresh sardines, three different preparations of salmon, a *zarzuela* (seafood stew), and eels. Two kinds of paella are served, and nonfish dishes such as partridge and rabbit are also on the menu. The restaurant was founded in 1915 as a small eating house. Back then, it was on the outskirts of town, but it was enveloped by the city long ago. Today, the restaurant is run by the grandsons of the original founders.

Calle Rosalía de Castro 88. © **98-159-21-70.** Reservations required. Main courses 10€–25€; set menu 19€. AE, DC, MC, V. Mon–Sat 1–5pm and Mon–Fri 8pm–midnight.

Santiago After Dark

In the religious center of Galicia, there's much more to do after dark than pray. An estimated 200 bars and *cafeterías* are found on the Rúa do Franco and its neighbor, Rúa da Raíña. The pavement along those streets on weekend evenings at around 11pm is mobbed. You can have a lot of fun ducking into any of the establishments, but particularly convivial is **Bar/Cafetería Dakar,** Rúa do Franco 13 (© **98-157-81-92**).

Beiro, Rúa da Raiña 3 (© **98-158-13-70;** www.obeiro.com), is one of the town's best wine bars, with a marvelous selection of vintages from throughout the country, especially wines from Galicia itself. Slices of Serrano ham, savory sausages, and homemade country terrines round out the food offerings, along with one of the best selections of Galician cheese in town; try the breast-shaped *queso de tetilla,* a local favorite.

One of the town's hot spots is **Modus Vivendi,** Piazza Feixoó 1 (© **98-157-61-09;** www.pubmodusvivendi.net), where rock music blasts the night away in a cozy but too crowded interior. It's very psychedelic in decor and attracts local students and young visiting foreigners Sunday to Thursday 6:30pm to 3am, Friday and Saturday 6:30pm to 4:30am. Techno, house, pop, and rock music are played at the garishly decorated **Retablo Café Concerto,** Rúa Nova 13 (© **98-156-48-51**). It's open daily 3pm to 5am.

RÍAS ALTAS ★

In Norway they're called fjords; in Brittany, abers; in Scotland, lochs; and in Galicia, *rías.* These inlets have been cut into the Galician coastline by the turbulent Atlantic Ocean pounding against its shores. Rías Altas is a relatively modern name applied to all the estuaries on the northern Galician coast, from Ribadeo (the gateway to Galicia on the border with Asturias) to A Coruña (the big Atlantic seaport of northwest Spain). The part that begins at Ribadeo, part of Lugo province, is also called Marina Lucense. Four estuaries form the Artabro Gulf: A Coruña, Betanzoa, Ares, and Ferrol. All four converge on a single point, where the Marola crag rises.

On the Road from Ribadeo to A Coruña

From Ribadeo, take the corniche road west (N-634) until you reach the Ría de Foz. About 2.5km (1½ miles) south of the Foz-Barreiros highway, perched somewhat in isolation on a hill, stands **Iglesia de San Martín de Mondoñeda,** part

---

Sleeping in Historic Places

A marvelous new way of staying in Galicia is a web of historic inns, manor houses, and even convents that welcome visitors. It's organized through **Pazos de Galicia** (www.pazosdegalicia.com).

You can obtain a map on the Web showing historic homes around the cities you plan to visit in Galicia, with A Coruña, Santiago de Compostela, and Pontevedra being the most preferred choices. Of course, you'll need a car to reach these places, which lie outside cities or towns of historic interest.

Just to get you started and to show what's available, here's a preview of the offerings.

Pazo La Buzaca, Lugar de San Lorenzo 36, 36668 Morana (© **98-655-36-84;** www.pazolabuzaca.com), is a 13-room 17th-century structure that houses guests luxuriously behind a stone wall. Part of the complex was a former hunting lodge. It is a good base for exploring attractions in and around Pontevedra.

A restored, rustic manor house, **Pazo do Souto,** La Toree 1, 106 Yessamo Carballo, makes an ideal base for exploring the maritime city of A Coruña. Guests live in style and luxury at this long-abandoned property, which today has a restaurant and an outdoor swimming pool.

Vicedo, in the Rías Altas.

of a monastery that dates from 1112. Please keep in mind that while corniche roads are sinuous and panoramic, they are often located high above the major roads and have steep, usually dangerous drop-offs on the other side.

The little town of **Foz** is a fishing village and a summer resort with beaches separated by a cliff. You might stop here for lunch.

From Foz, cut northwest along the coastal highway (C-642), going through **Burela,** another fishing village. You can make a slight detour south to **Sargadelos,** a ceramics center. You can purchase the famous Galician pottery here much more cheaply than elsewhere in Spain.

Back on the coastal road (C-642) at Burela, continue west, approaching Ría de Viveiro and the historic village of **Viveiro.** Part of its medieval walls and an old gate, Puerta de Carlos V, have been preserved. The town has many old churches of interest, including the Gothic-style Iglesia San Francisco. Viveiro is a summer resort, attracting vacationers to its beach, Playa Covas, and it makes a good lunch stop.

The road continues northwest to **Vicedo,** passing such beaches as Xillo and Aerealong. Excellent vistas greet you, and oxen can be seen plowing the cornfields.

Driving on, you'll notice the coastline becoming more saw-toothed. Eventually you reach **Ortigueira,** a major fishing village at the head of the *ría* (estuary) from which it takes its name. A Celtic folk festival is staged here at the end of August.

From here you can continue south along C-642 to **El Ferrol,** which used to be called El Caudillo, in honor of the late dictator Francisco Franco, who was born here and who used to spend part of his summers in this area. El Ferrol is one of the major shipbuilding centers of Spain, and since the 18th century it has been a center of the Spanish navy. It's a grimy town, but it lies on one of the region's most beautiful *rías*. Despite its *parador,* few tourists linger at El Ferrol (also spelled O Ferrol).

From El Ferrol, C-642 continues south, passing through the small town of **Puentedeume** (also spelled Pontedeume), on the Rías Ares. Historically, it was the center of the counts of Andrade. The remains of their 14th-century palace can be seen, along with the ruins of a 13th-century castle, rising to the east.

Shortly below Betanzos, head west along N-VI until you reach A Coruña. The entire trip from Ribadeo is roughly 242km (150 miles) and takes at least 4 hours.

Where to Dine Along the Coast

Nito ★ SEAFOOD Established in the early 1970s, this restaurant is in the center of Viveiro, only 90m (295 ft.) from the beach, with a sweeping view of the Atlantic. It starts serving dinner early (for Spain, that is; 8:30pm) and maintains a nice balance between prices and quality of its ingredients. The food is unpretentious but flavorful. Shellfish is the specialty, but you can order grilled sea bream or perhaps a house-style beefsteak. Most diners begin their meal with a bowl of *caldo gallego,* a traditional soup of meat, beans, and vegetables. A full range of wines is offered. Diners wanting to eat outside can sit on a gardenview terrace.

Playa de Area, Viveiro. © **98-256-09-87.** Reservations recommended. Main courses 23€–50€. MC, V. Daily 1–4pm and 8pm–midnight.

Exploring the Rias Altas on Two Wheels

Some of the best biking in Spain is found in the Rías Altas. Much of south and central Spain is too hot for biking, but here temperatures are generally cool, and an interesting vista unfolds at every turn. The **tourist office** at Viveiro, Av. Ramón Canosa s/n (© **98-256-08-79;** www.viveiro.es), can give you a map and some suggested routes. The office is open Monday to Saturday 11am to 2pm and 4:30 to 7:30pm; July to August it's also open Sunday from noon to 2pm.

From Viveiro, the most scenic route is to the west, along the C-642 to El Ferrol on the sea. A particularly dramatic stretch awaits you if you head north along a secondary road when you come to the junction with the little town of Mera. Signs point north to another little town, Carino, opening onto views of Cabo Ortegal. To the east is a sheltered body of water, Ría de Santa María, and to the west the Atlantic Ocean. From Viveiro you can also go inland, heading south along Route 640, and following the signs to the hamlet of Oral. Or you can take the coastal road east from Viveiro, signposted RIBADEO. Ribadeo is too built up to interest most cyclists but, depending on your stamina, you can cycle to the seaside villages of San Ciprian, Burela, and Foz.

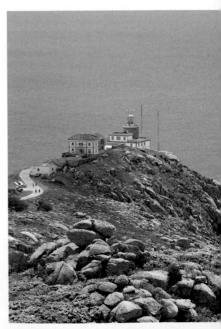

From A Coruña to Cape Fisterra

This next section, the drive "to the end of the world," takes you from A Coruña to **Cabo Fisterra** ★ (called Fisterra or Finisterre on most maps). The 145km (90-mile) trip takes at least 3 hours. For the ancients, Cape Fisterra was the end of the world as they knew it.

Cabo Fisterra, the end of the world.

This route takes you along **A Costa da Morte** (the **Coast of Death;** in Castilian, La Costa de la Muerte), so called because of the numerous shipwrecks that have occurred here.

Leaving A Coruña, take the coastal road west (Hwy. 552), heading first to the road junction of **Carballo,** a distance of 36km (22 miles). From this little town, many of the small coastal harbors are within an easy drive. **Malpica,** to the northwest, is the most interesting, with its own beach. An offshore seabird sanctuary exists off this former whaling port. From Malpica, continue to the tiny village of **Corme** at Punta Roncudo. This sheltered fishing village draws summer beach fans to its isolated sand dunes.

From Corme, continue along the winding roads to the whitewashed village of **Camariñas,** which stands on the *ría* of the same name. Camariñas is known as a village of expert lace makers, and you'll see their work for sale at many places. A road here leads all the way to the lighthouse at Cabo Vilán.

The road now leads to **Mugia** (shown on some maps as Muxia), below which stands the lighthouse at Cabo Touriñan. Continue driving south along clearly marked coastal roads that are sometimes perched precariously on cliff tops overlooking the sea. They will lead you to **Corcubión,** a village with a Romanesque church. From here, follow signs that lead you along a lonely south-bound secondary road to the end of the line, **Cabo Fisterra,** for a panoramic view. The sunsets from here are among the most spectacular in the world. The Roman poet Horace said it best: "The brilliant skylight of the sun drags behind it the black night over the fruitful breasts of earth."

RÍAS BAJAS ★★

After Cabo Fisterra, some of the most dramatic coastal scenery in Spain flanks coastal N-550, following the edge of one of the most tortuous shorelines in Europe. Four estuaries, collectively called the Rías Bajas, face the Atlantic from Cape Silleiro to Baiona to Point Louro in Muros. Two of these are in the province of Pontevedra (Ría de Pontevedra and Ría de Vigo); one is in the province of A Coruña (Ría de Muros y Noya); and one (Ría de Arousa) divides its shores between the two provinces. The 32km (20-mile) Vigo estuary is the longest, stretching from Ponte Sampasio to Baiona.

Driving from Muros to Santa Uxea de Ribeira

The seaside town of **Muros** has many old houses and a harbor, but **Noya** (also spelled Noia), to the southeast, is more impressive. If you don't have a car but would like to see at least one or two *ría* fishing villages, you can do so at either Noya or Muros: Both are on a bus route connecting them with Santiago de Compostela. **Monbus** (✆ **98-229-29-00;** www.monbus.es) runs 11 buses per day from Santiago for Noya, and 9 to Muros. Some of the tiny villages and beaches are connected by bus routes. Rates are in the 12€ to 14€ range.

If you do drive, the entire trip is only 76km (47 miles); at a leisurely pace it should take you 2 hours. Noya has a number of interesting, handsome old churches, including the 14th-century **Igrexa de Santa María** (with tombstones dating from the 10th c.) and **Igrexa de San Francisco.** A lot of good beaches lie on the northern bank of the *ría* near Muros. Noya is your best bet for a lunch stop.

From Noya, the coast road (N-550) continues west to **Porto do Son.** You can take a detour to Cabo de Corrubedo, with its lighthouse, before continuing on to Santa Uxea de Ribeira at the southern tip. Ribeira is a fishing port and a canning center. At **Santa Uxea de Ribeira** you'll see Ría de Arousa, the largest and deepest of the inlets.

From Ribeira, continue east along the southern coastal road to **A Puebla de Caramiñal.** From here, take a marked route 10km (6¼ miles) inland into the mountains, to admire the most magnificent panorama in all of *rías* country—the **Mirador de la Curota ★★★**, at 498m (1,634 ft.). The four inlets of the Rías Bajas can, under the right conditions, be seen from the belvedere. In clear weather you can view Cape Fisterra.

Back on N-550, drive as far as Padrón, where, it is claimed, the legendary sea vessel arrived bringing Santiago (St. James) to Spain. Padrón was also the home of romantic poet Rosalía de Castro (1837–85), sometimes called the Emily Dickinson of Spain. Her house, **Casa Museo de Rosalía de Castro,** Carretera de Hebrón (✆ 98-181-12-04; www.rosaliadecastro.org), is open Tuesday to Saturday 10am to 1:30pm and 4 to 7pm, and Sunday 10am to 1:30pm. Admission is 1.50€. Padrón makes a good lunch stop.

From Padrón, follow the alleged trail of the body of St. James north along N-550 to Santiago de Compostela, or take N-550 south to Pontevedra.

Where to Stay & Dine

Chef Rivera ★ 🎁 GALICIAN/SPANISH The owner's name, to everyone in town, is simply El Chef. His innovative cuisine is based on traditional Continental recipes. His wife, Pierrette, attends to service in the dining room, which resembles an English pub with its dark, warm colors and leather upholstery. Try the shellfish soup or stew, or the house-style monkfish. The restaurant is known for its *pimientos de Padrón,* which are tiny green peppers sautéed in olive oil. The trick is that about one in five of those peppers is very spicy. You might finish your meal with lemon mousse.

The couple also rents 17 simply furnished **guest rooms** equipped with neatly kept bathrooms containing shower stalls. Double rooms range from 45€ to 60€.

Enlace Parque 7, Padrón. ✆ **98-181-04-13.** Fax 98-181-14-54. www.chefrivera.com. Reservations recommended. Main courses 14€–24€. AE, DC, MC, V. Daily 1–4pm and 9–11pm. Closed Sun–Mon nights in winter.

PONTEVEDRA ★

58km (36 miles) S of Santiago de Compostela, 839km (521 miles) NW of Madrid

An aristocratic old Spanish town on the Lérez River and the capital of Pontevedra province, the city of Pontevedra still has vestiges of an ancient wall that once encircled the town. In medieval days, the town was called Pontis Veteris (Old Bridge).

Sheltered at the end of the Pontevedra Ría, the city was a bustling port, and foreign merchants mingled with local traders, seamen, and fishers. It was the home of Pedro Sarmiento de Gamboa, the 16th-century navigator and cosmographer who wrote *Voyage to the Magellan Straits.* In the 18th century, the Lérez delta silted up and the busy commerce moved elsewhere, mainly to Vigo. Pontevedra entered a period of decline, which may account for its significant old section. Had it been a more prosperous town, the people might have torn down the ancient structures to rebuild.

The old barrio, a maze of colonnaded squares and cobbled alleyways, is between Calle Michelena and Calle del Arzobispo Malvar, stretching to Calle Cobián and the river. The old mansions, called *pazos*, evoke former marine glory, since it was the sea that provided the money to build them. Seek out such charming squares as Plaza de la Leña, Plaza de Mugártegui, and Plaza de Teucro.

Essentials

GETTING THERE From Santiago de Compostela in the north, 14 to 17 **trains** per day make the 1½-hour one-way trip to Pontevedra at a cost of 5.50€. **RENFE** has an office on Plaza Calvo Sotelo s/n (✆ **90-224-02-02;** www. renfe.es), where you can get information. The actual rail and bus stations are .8km (½ mile) from the town center on Alféreces Provisionales.

Pontevedra has good links to major Galician cities. From Vigo in the south, **bus** travel time is only 1 hour if you take one of the 12 inland expresses leaving from Vigo daily; the one-way fare is 6€. From Santiago de Compostela in the north, a bus leaves every hour during the day for Pontevedra (1 hr.); the one-way trip costs 9€. For information, call ✆ **98-229-29-00** (www.monbus.es).

From Santiago de Compostela, head south along N-550 to reach Pontevedra.

VISITOR INFORMATION The **tourist office,** at Xral. Gutiérrez Mellado 1 (✆ **98-685-08-14;** fax 98-684-81-23; www.turgalicia.es), is open July to September, Monday to Saturday 10am to 2pm and 4:30 to 7:30pm, and Sunday 10am to 2pm. From October to June, it is open Monday to Friday 10am to 2pm and 4 to 6pm, and Saturday 10am to 12:30pm.

SPECIAL EVENTS The town is host to two popular festivals, including the weeklong **La Virgen de la Peregrina (the Pilgrim's Virgin),** which takes place in the historic Old Town beginning the second Sunday in August. The celebration features religious street processions, live entertainment, food vendors, and kiosks selling handicrafts and antiques. An entrance charge may be applied for certain cultural performances, but concerts sponsored by the city are free. Another good time to visit is for the medieval fair, **Feria Franca,** occurring in the historic district on the first Friday afternoon in September and extending to Saturday night. People dress up in Middle Ages costumes and enjoy live music, parades, and food (some recipes are medieval).

Exploring Pontevedra

In the **Old Quarter** ★, the major attraction is the **Basílica de Santa María la Mayor** ★, Calle del Arzobispo Malvar (✆ 98-686-61-85), with its avocado green patina, dating from the 16th century. Its most remarkable feature is its west front, carved to resemble an altarpiece, with a depiction of the Crucifixion at the top. The church is open daily 10am to 1pm and 5 to 9pm.

The **Museo de Pontevedra,** Pasantería 10 (✆ **98-685-14-55;** fax 98-684-006-93; www.museo.depontevedra.es), with a hodgepodge of everything from the Pontevedra attic, contains displays ranging from prehistoric artifacts to a still life by Zurbarán. Many of the exhibits are maritime oriented, and there is a valuable collection of jewelry. The museum is open Tuesday to Saturday 10am to

2pm and 4 to 7pm, Sunday 11am to 2pm. Free admission. The museum opens onto a major square in the Old Town, Plaza de Leña (Square of Wood).

Iglesia de San Francisco, Plaza de la Herrería, is another church of note. Its Gothic facade opens onto gardens. It was founded in the 14th century and contains a sculpture of Don Payo Gómez Charino, noted for his part in the 1248 Reconquest of Seville, when it was wrested from Muslim domination.

Directly south, the gardens lead to the 18th-century **Capilla de la Peregrina,** Plaza Peregrina, with a narrow half-moon facade connected to a rotunda and crowned by a pair of towers. It was constructed by followers of the cult of the Pilgrim Virgin, which was launched in Galicia sometime in the 17th century.

The Old Quarter of Pontevedra.

Where to Stay in Pontevedra

Hotel Rías Bajas On a busy street corner near Plaza de Galicia in the commercial center, this 1960s hotel is more comfortable than you might expect, judging from the outside. The largest hotel in town, it is often used for community political meetings and press conferences. The lobby, with stone and wood paneling, has been designed to look like an English club. The midsize guest rooms are comfortable and well maintained.

Daniel de la Sota 7, 36001 Pontevedra. © **98-685-51-00.** Fax 98-685-51-50. www.hotelrias bajas.com. 100 units. 55€–98€ double; 75€–116€ triple. AE, DC, MC, V. Parking 10€. **Amenities:** Restaurant; bar; room service. *In room:* TV, minibar, Wi-Fi (free).

Hotel Virgen del Camino On a relatively quiet street off Highway C-531, at the edge of the suburbs, this balconied stucco hotel contains comfortable English-style sitting rooms. The midsize guest rooms have wall-to-wall carpeting and first-rate bathrooms. The best doubles contain separate salons and sitting rooms.

Virgen del Camino 55, 36001 Pontevedra. © **98-685-59-00.** Fax 98-685-09-00. www.hotel virgendelcamino.com. 52 units. 67€–96€ double; 105€–135€ suite. Rates include continental breakfast. AE, DC, MC, V. Parking 11€. **Amenities:** Restaurant; bar; room service. *In room:* A/C, TV, hair dryer.

Parador de Pontevedra ★★ This *parador* is in the Old Quarter of Pontevedra, in a well-preserved 16th-century palace near the Basílica de Santa María la Mayor. Built on either 13th- or 14th-century foundations, this hotel became one of Spain's first *paradores* when it opened in 1955. The interior has been maintained very much as the old *pazo* (manor house) looked. It includes a quaint old kitchen, or *lar* (heart), typical of Galician country houses and furnished with characteristic items. Off the vestibule is a courtyard dominated by a large old stone staircase. Many of the attractively furnished accommodations are large enough to include sitting areas. Many also overlook the walled-in formal garden.

Calle Barón 19, 36002 Pontevedra. ☎ **98-685-58-00.** Fax 98-685-21-95. www.parador.es. 47 units. 127€–184€ double; 191€–240€ suite. AE, DC, MC, V. Limited free parking. **Amenities:** Restaurant; bar; babysitting; room service. *In room:* A/C, TV, hair dryer, minibar, Wi-Fi (free).

Where to Dine in Pontevedra

Alameda GALICIAN/SEAFOOD Set within a 70-year-old stone-sided building in the town's historic core, this is a restaurant known by virtually everyone in town as a well-managed, straightforward refuge of comfort and fresh, well-prepared food. Come here for seafood such as a salad of wild greens and braised filet of lubina, a ragout of shrimp and barnacles studded with strips of turbot, and breast and thigh of duckling served *en confit* in a style that might remind you of something you'd find in France. Dining areas evoke old Spain, with exposed stone, woodwork, and a hardworking staff.

Alameda 10. ☎ **98-685-7412.** Reservations recommended. Main courses 15€–30€; fixed-price menu 48€. AE, DC, MC, V. Mon–Sat 1–4pm; Mon and Wed–Sat 9–11:30pm.

Casa Román GALICIAN Known for the quality of its food, this long-established restaurant is on the street level of a brick apartment building in a leafy downtown development known as Campolongo, near Plaza de Galicia. To reach the dining room, you pass through a tavern. In addition to lobster (which you can see in the window), a wide array of well-prepared fish and shellfish dishes is served here, including sea bass, squid, sole, crab, and tuna.

Augusto García Sánchez 12. ☎ **98-684-35-60.** Main courses 14€–25€; fixed-price menu 19€. AE, DC, MC, V. Tues–Sun 1:30–3:45pm; Tues–Sat 9–11:45pm.

Casa Solla ★★★ 🍴 GALICIAN In business for nearly half a century, this is an old-time favorite that showcases the culinary imagination of its owner and chef, Pepe Solla, who is acclaimed as the best chef in Galicia. He calls his cuisine *comida de autur,* which means he creates his own recipes, inspired by the Galician kitchen. Whatever he serves Solla imbues with his own taste, style, and flavor. He cooks freshly caught Galician sole and a filet mignon in an Albariño wine sauce—both are delights. Foodies drive for miles around to sample two of his specialties, including hake that's steamed at a low temperature and served with an almond-flavored cream sauce, or else wild Iberian boar that's roasted at a low temperature for 12 hours before it's taken off the bone and "finished" on a charcoal grill. One of the most delightful finishes to a meal is the fresh figs of summer served with Cabrales cheese.

Av. Sineiro 7 Km 2, San Salvador de Poio, 2km (1¼ miles) from the center of town, toward El Grove. ☎ **98-687-28-84.** www.restaurantesolla.com. Reservations recommended. Main courses 19€–35€. AE, DC, MC, V. Tues–Wed and Fri–Sat 12:30–4pm and 9–11:30pm; Thurs and Sun 1:30–4pm. Closed Dec 20–Jan 4.

Pontevedra After Dark

The cool temperatures that descend over the hot, sultry plain surrounding Pontevedra seem to incite local residents into after-dark promenades through the Old City. You'll find pubs and bars sprawled on either side of the streets that interconnect Plaza Santa María la Mayor, in the northwestern quadrant of the town's historic core, with the very central Plaza de la Herrería. By midnight on the weekends, rhythmic electronic music emanates from the town's most popular disco, **Disco Carabas,** Calle Cobian Rolfignac 6 (☎ **98-686-26-95;**

www.carabasdisco.com). Disco Carabas appeals to high-energy dance freaks in their early 20s. Don't even think of heading off to a Pontevedra disco before midnight, as it's likely to be locked until then (but the music keeps pumping until 4am). Expect entrance fees of around 10€, depending on the night of the week.

EL GROVE & LA TOJA ★

636km (395 miles) NW of Madrid, 32km (20 miles) W of Pontevedra, 73km (45 miles) S of Santiago de Compostela

A summer resort and fishing village with some 8km (5 miles) of beaches of varying quality, El Grove is on a peninsula west of Pontevedra. It juts into the Ría de Arousa, a large inlet at the mouth of the Ulla River. The village has become more commercial than many visitors would like, but it is still renowned for its fine cuisine. A shellfish festival is held here every October.

La Toja (A Toxa in Galician), an island linked to El Grove by bridge, is a famous spa and the most fashionable resort in Galicia, known for its sports and leisure activities. The casino and the golf course are both very popular. The island is covered with pine trees and surrounded by some of the finest scenery in Spain.

La Toja first became known for health-giving properties when, according to legend, the owner of a sick donkey left it on the island to die. The donkey recovered, and its cure was attributed to the waters of an island spring.

Essentials

GETTING THERE   The **train** from Santiago de Compostela goes as far as Vilagarcía de Arousa; take the bus from there. For train schedules, call ✆ **90-224-02-02** (www.renfe.es).

From Pontevedra, **buses** heading for Ponte Vilagarcía de Arousa stop at La Toja. Call Monbus at ✆ **98-229-29-00** (www.monbus.es) for details. A one-way fare costs 6€.

If you're driving, head east from Pontevedra on the 550 coastal road via Sanxenxo. From Santiago de Compostela, expressway A-9 leads to Caldas de Reis, where you turn off onto the 550, heading west to the coast.

VISITOR INFORMATION   The **tourist information office,** Plaza Do Corgo s/n (✆ **98-673-14-15;** www.turismogrove.com), is open in winter Monday and Wednesday to Friday 10am to 2pm and 4 to 6pm, Tuesday and Sunday 11am to 2pm (closed Mon in summer).

Where to Stay & Dine in El Grove

Hotel Amandi   This stylish and tasteful family-run hotel is a brisk 10-minute walk from the bridge that connects El Grove with La Toja. The midsize rooms are decorated with antique reproductions; most have tiny terraces with ornate cast-iron balustrades and sea views. Breakfast is the only meal served.

Castelao 94, 36980 El Grove. ✆ **98-673-19-42.** Fax 98-673-16-43. www.hotelamandi.com. 30 units. 25€–45€ per person double. Rates include continental breakfast. MC, V. Parking 8€. Closed Jan. **Amenities:** Outdoor pool; Wi-Fi (free, in lobby). *In room:* TV.

La Posada del Mar   SEAFOOD   This warm, inviting place near the bridge leading to La Toja is the best dining spot outside those at the hotels. At times you can watch women digging for oysters in the river in front. The chef, naturally, specializes in fish, including a wide selection of shellfish. Among the specialties are a savory soup, outstanding shellfish paella, Galician-style hake, and fresh grilled salmon. For dessert, try the *flan de la casa.*

Castelao 202. © **98-673-01-06.** Reservations required July–Aug. Main courses 10€–21€; fixed-price menus 30€–100€. AE, DC, MC, V. Tues–Sun 1–4pm; Tues–Sat 8:30pm–midnight. Closed mid-Dec to Jan.

Where to Stay in La Toja

Gran Hotel de La Toja ★★ Enveloped by pine trees on well-landscaped grounds, this classic spa hotel is one of the finest in Galicia. Government-rated at five stars, the completely renovated resort lies on a breeze-swept island off El Grove. The guest rooms—try for one with a view—are both modern and functional, as well as immaculately kept. They come with some of the best bathrooms in the area, with both tub and shower. A year-round resort, the Gran has some of the best facilities and amenities in the area, ranging from a first-rate spa to a 9-hole golf course and even a casino. The food, a **Galician cuisine** with elaborate **Continental dishes,** is worthy of the setting; the chefs specialize in fresh fish and shellfish harvested off the coast of northwest Spain. Try one of the Albariño wines, which pair well with most dishes.

Isla de la Toja, 36991, Pontevedra. © **98-673-00-25.** Fax 98-673-00-26. www.granhotel hesperia-latoja.com. 197 units. 90€–340€ double; 240€–390€ suite. AE, DC, MC, V. Free parking. **Amenities:** 2 restaurants; bar; 9-hole golf course (nearby); health club; 2 pools (1 heated indoor); room service; spa; 3 outdoor tennis courts. *In room:* TV, hair dryer, minibar, Wi-Fi (free).

Hotel Louxo Set on flatlands a few paces from the town's ornate casino is this modern white building, sheltered from the Atlantic winds. It offers clean, stylish, and modern accommodations; most rooms are midsize. Each comes with a neatly kept bathroom. The many ground-floor public rooms have rows of comfortable seating areas and sweeping views over the nearby tidal flats.

O Grove, 36991 Isla de la Toja, Pontevedra. © **98-673-02-00.** Fax 98-673-27-91. www.louxo latoja.com. 116 units. 88€–158€ double; 120€–200€ suite. Rates include continental breakfast. AE, DC, MC, V. Free parking. **Amenities:** Restaurant; bar; babysitting; exercise room; 2 freshwater pools (1 heated indoor); room service; sauna. *In room:* A/C, TV, hair dryer, minibar, Wi-Fi (free).

TÚY ★

29km (18 miles) S of Vigo, 48km (30 miles) S of Pontevedra

A frontier town first settled by the Romans, Túy (Tui) is a short distance from Portugal, near the two-tiered road-and-rail bridge (over the Miño River) that links the two countries. The bridge was designed by Alexandre-Gustave Eiffel. (He designed a tower in Paris you may have heard of.) If you're driving from Portugal's Valença do Minho, Túy is your introduction to Spain.

Essentials

GETTING THERE Trains make the 1½- to 2-hour trip daily from Vigo to Túy (2.35€). From Vigo, **buses** run south to Túy hourly, taking 1 hour (2.75€).

If you're driving from Vigo, head south along the A-9 expressway until you see the turnoff for Túy.

The Eiffel bridge outside Túy.

VISITOR INFORMATION The **tourist office,** at Rua Colón s/n, Edificio Sampaio (© **98-660-17-89**), is open Monday to Friday 9:30am to 1:30pm and 4:30 to 6:30pm, Saturday 10am to noon.

Exploring Túy

The winding streets of the Old Quarter lead to the **Catedral** ★, a national art treasure that dominates the *zona monumental*. The acropolis-like cathedral/fortress, built in 1170, wasn't used for religious purposes until the early 13th century. Later architects respected the original Romanesque and Gothic styles and didn't make changes in its design. If you have time, you may want to visit the Romanesque-style **Iglesia de San Bartolomé** on the outskirts of town, and the **Iglesia de Santo Domingo,** a beautiful example of Gothic style. (Look for the bas-reliefs in the cloister.) The churches are open to the public in summer. The latter church stands next to Santo Domingo Park. Walls built over Roman fortifications surround Túy.

Where to Stay & Dine in Túy

Parador de Tui ★★ ☺ Advance reservations are essential if you want to stay in this elegant, fortress-style hacienda four streets north of the Miño River crossing. Built in 1968, the inn was designed to blend with the architectural spirit of the province, emphasizing local stone and natural woods. Brass chandeliers, paintings by well-known Gallegos, and antiques combined with reproductions furnish the public rooms. In the main living room are a large inglenook fireplace, a tall banjo-shaped grandfather clock, hand-knotted rugs, hand-hewn benches, and comfortable armchairs. The midsize guest rooms are sober in style, but are comfortable and offer views across a colonnaded courtyard to the river and hills. They are furnished with Castilian-style pieces.

Av. de Portugal s/n, 36700 Túy. © **98-660-03-00.** Fax 98-660-21-63. www.parador.es. 30 units. 127€–276€ double; 191€–332€ suite. AE, DC, MC, V. Free parking. **Amenities:** Restaurant; babysitting; children's center; outdoor pool; room service; outdoor tennis court. *In room:* TV, hair dryer, minibar, Wi-Fi (2€ per hour).

THE
BALEARIC
ISLANDS

The Balearic Islands (Los Baleares)—an archipelago composed of the major islands of Majorca, Minorca, and Ibiza, plus the diminutive Formentera, Cabrera, and uninhabited Dragonera—lie off the coast of Spain, between France and the coast of northern Africa. The islands have known many rulers and occupying forces: Carthaginians, Greeks, Romans, Vandals, and Moors. But despite a trove of Bronze Age megaliths and some fine Punic artifacts, the invaders who have left the largest imprint on Balearic culture are the hordes of sun-seeking vacationers who descend every year.

After the expulsion of the Moors by Jaume I in 1229, the islands flourished as the kingdom of Majorca. When they were integrated into the kingdom of Castile in the mid–14th century, they experienced a massive decline. The early 19th century provided a renaissance for the islands; artists such as George Sand and her lover, Chopin, and, later, the poet Robert Graves established the islands, especially Majorca and Ibiza, as a haven for musicians, writers, and artists. (Read Sand's book *A Winter in Majorca*.) Gradually the artists' colony attracted tourists of all dispositions.

Today, the Balearics are administered by an autonomous government, Govern Balear. **Majorca,** the largest island, is the most commercial and touristy. Many of its scenic expanses have given way to sprawling hotels and fast-food joints, although parts remain beautiful indeed. Freewheeling **Ibiza** attracts the international party crowd, as well as visitors who come to the island for its tamer offerings, such as white-sand beaches and sky-blue waters. The smallest of the major islands, **Minorca,** is also the most serene. It is less touristy than Majorca and Ibiza, and for that reason, it is now experiencing an "anti-tourist" tourist boom.

The government of the islands has finally awakened to the damage caused by overdevelopment of Majorca and Ibiza. Under new guidelines, some 35% of this island group is now safeguarded from exploitation by builders.

Very few visitors have time to explore all three islands, so you'll have to decide early which one is for you. Many vacationers include one of the Balearic Islands as an add-on to a visit to Barcelona or the Costa Brava, while others view them as destinations in themselves.

MAJORCA ★★★

Majorca (Mallorca in Spanish) is the most popular of Spain's Mediterranean islands, drawing millions of visitors each year. About 209km (130 miles) from Barcelona and 145km (90 miles) from Valencia, Majorca has a coastline 500km (311 miles) long. The beautiful island is an explorer's paradise in its exterior, although it's horribly overbuilt along certain coastal regions. The north is mountainous; the fertile southern flatlands offer a landscape of olive and almond groves, occasionally interrupted by windmills.

PREVIOUS PAGE: **Cala'n Porter beach, on Minorca.**

THE BALEARIC ISLANDS | Majorca

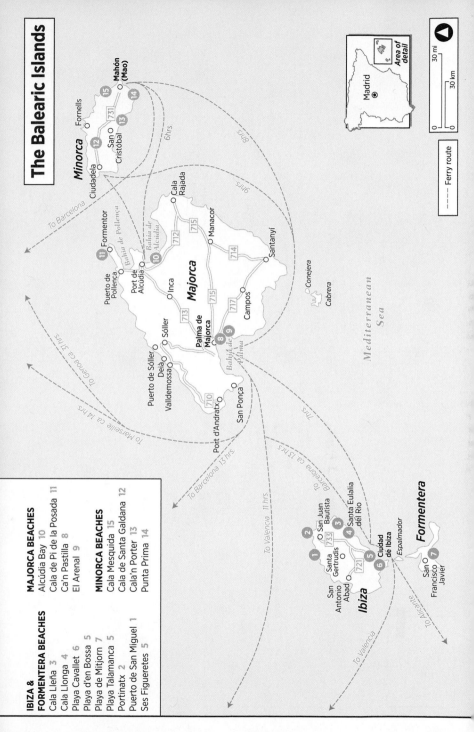

The Balearic Islands

Minorca

Fornells
Ciudadela
San Cristóbal
Mahón (Mao)
Formentor
Puerto de Pollença
Port d'Alcúdia
Bahía de Pollença
Bahía de Alcúdia
Cala Rajada
Manacor
Santanyí
Inca
Sóller
Deià
Puerto de Sóller
Valldemossa
Palma de Majorca
Bahía de Palma
San Ponça
Port d'Andratx
Campos

Majorca

712
715
714
713
715
717
710

Conejera
Cabrera

Mediterranean Sea

To Barcelona
8 hrs.
6 hrs.
9 hrs.

To Genoa ca 3 ⅓ hrs.
To Marseille ca. 14 hrs.
To Barcelona 13 hrs.
To Valencia 11 hrs.
To Valencia
To Alicante
7 hrs.

San Antonio Abad
Santa Gertrudis
San Juan Bautista
Santa Eulalia del Río
Ciudad de Ibiza
Espalmador
San Francisco Javier

Ibiza
Formentera

733
722

Area of detail

Madrid

0   30 mi
0   30 km

----- Ferry route

IBIZA & FORMENTERA BEACHES
Cala Lleña 3
Cala Llonga 4
Playa Cavallet 6
Playa d'en Bossa 5
Playa de Mitjorn 7
Playa Talamanca 5
Portinatx 2
Puerto de San Miguel 1
Ses Figueretes 5

MAJORCA BEACHES
Alcúdia Bay 10
Cala de Pi de la Posada 11
Ca'n Pastilla 8
El Arenal 9

MINORCA BEACHES
Cala Mesquida 15
Cala de Santa Galdana 12
Cala'n Porter 13
Punta Prima 14

705

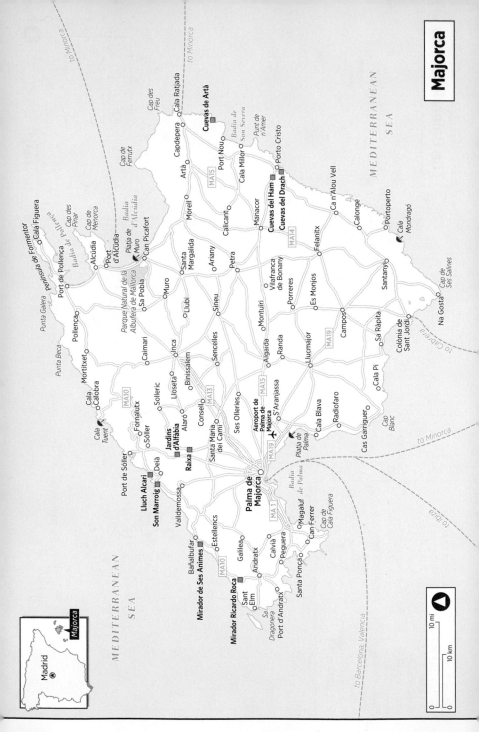

Majorca

The golden sands of Majorca are famous, with lovely beaches such as Ca'n Pastilla and El Arenal, but they tend to be overcrowded with sun worshipers on package tours. Tourist facilities line the shores of Cala Mayor and Sant Agustí; both have good beaches, including Playa Magaluf, the longest beach on the Calvía coast. Cala de San Vicente, 6.5km (4 miles) north of Pollença, is a beautiful beach bordered by a pine grove and towering cliffs. Stretches of golden-sand beach lie between Cala Pi and Cala Murta in Formentor near the tip of the northern coast.

Island Essentials

GETTING THERE At certain times of the year, the trip by boat or plane can be pleasant, but in August these routes to Palma must surely qualify as the major bottleneck in Europe. Don't travel without advance reservations, and be sure you have a return plane ticket if you come in August—otherwise you may not get off the island until September!

Iberia (☎ **90-240-05-00;** www.iberia.com) flies to Palma's **Aeroport Son San Joan** (☎ **97-178-90-00**) from Barcelona, Valencia, and Madrid. There are daily planes from Madrid and Valencia, and several daily flights from Barcelona in summer. **Spanair** (☎ **90-213-14-15;** www.spanair. com) flies into Palma from Barcelona (up to three times a day year-round). **Air Europa** (☎ **90-240-15-01;** www.aireuropa.com) flies to Palma from Barcelona a maximum of two times a day during peak season and, to a lesser extent, it also flies to Palma from Madrid and Seville.

British and other European travelers should consult a travel agent and look into the available package tours, which combine airfare and accommodations; they can save you a ton of money.

Countless charter flights also make the run. Bookings are very tight in August, and delays of at least 24 hours (or more) are common. If you're flying—say, Iberia—on a transatlantic flight from New York to Madrid or Barcelona, you should have Majorca written into your ticket before your departure if you plan to visit the Balearics as part of your Spanish itinerary.

From the airport, bus no. 1 takes you to Plaça Espanya in the center of Palma from 5:30am to 2:15pm daily; the cost is 2€. A metered cab charges from 25€ for the 25-minute drive into the city.

Trasmediterránea, Estació Marítim in Palma (☎ **90-245-46-45;** www.trasmediterranea.es), operates a daily **ferry** from Barcelona (trip time: 3½ hr.), from 67€ one-way. There are six ferries per week from Valencia, Monday to Saturday, taking 7 hours and costing 69€ one-way. (A faster boat takes 4–6 hr. and costs 120€). In Barcelona, tickets can be booked at the Trasmediterránea office at Estació Marítim (☎ **90-245-46-45**), and in Valencia at the office at Terminal Trasmediterráneo Muelle Deponiente, Estacio Marítima (☎ **90-245-46-45**). Any travel agent in Spain can also book you a seat. Schedules and departure times (subject to change) should always be checked and double-checked.

GETTING AROUND At the tourist office in Palma, you can pick up a

---

Not an Island for All Seasons

July and August are high season for Majorca; don't even think of coming then without a reservation. It's possible to swim comfortably from June to October; after that, it's prohibitively cold.

bus schedule that explains island routes. Or call **Empresa Municipal de Transportes** (© 90-070-07-10; www.emtpalma.es). This company runs city buses from its main terminal, Estació Central D'Autobus, Plaça Espanya. The standard one-way fare is 1.25€ within Palma; at the station you can buy a booklet good for 10 rides, costing 8€. Some of the most frequented bus routes include transportation from Palma to the Coves del Drac; the one-way trip takes 1 hour and costs 9.50€. Other popular routes go to Dexa (45 min.; 6€ one-way), and to Valldemossa (30 min.; 4€ one-way).

Ferrocarril de Sóller, Carrer Eusebio Estada 1 (© **97-175-20-51;** www.trendesoller.com), off Plaça Espanya, has **train** service through majestic mountain scenery to Sóller. Trains run from 8am to 7pm; a one-way ticket costs 10€. A "tourist train" leaves daily at 10:50am and 12:15pm and costs 10€. The only thing special about this route is a 10-minute stop at Mirador del Pujol d'en Banya. A ride on the tourist train itself, however, is a worthwhile experience. Privately owned, it was constructed by orange growers in the early 1900s and still uses the carriages of the Belle Epoque days.

Another train runs to Inca; it's often called "the Leather Express" because most passengers are on board to buy inexpensive leather goods in the Inca shops. **Servicios Ferroviarios de Mallorca** leaves from Plaça Espanya (© **97-175-22-45** for more information and schedules). The train ride is only 40 minutes, with 40 departures per day Monday through Saturday and 32 per day on Sunday. A one-way fare costs 7€. For a radio **taxi,** call © **97-175-54-40.**

If you plan to stay in Palma, you don't need a car. The city is extremely traffic clogged, and parking is scarce. If you'd like to take our driving tour (see "Exploring Majorca by Car: The West Coast," p. 725), you can rent cars at such companies as **Europcar,** at the airport terminal (© **90-210-50-55;** www.europcar.com), where rentals range from 86€ to 295€ per day. **Avis** at the airport terminal (© **97-178-91-87;** www.avis.com) is well stocked with cars; its rates range from 58€ to 180€ per day. Reservations should always be made in advance.

Palma de Majorca ★★

Palma, on the southern tip of the island, is the seat of the autonomous government of the Balearic Islands, as well as the center for most of Majorca's hotels, restaurants, and nightclubs. The Moors constructed Palma in the style of a casbah, or walled city. Its foundations are still visible, although obscured by the high-rise hotels that have cropped up.

Old Palma is typified by the area immediately surrounding the cathedral. Mazes of narrow alleys and cobblestone streets recall the era when Palma was one of the chief ports in the Mediterranean. Today Palma is a bustling city whose massive tourist industry has more than made up for its decline as a major seaport. It's estimated that nearly half the island's population lives in Palma. The islanders call Palma simply Ciutat ("City"); it is the largest of the Balearic ports, its bay often clogged with yachts. Arrival by sea is the most impressive, with the skyline characterized by Bellver Castle and the cathedral's bulk.

ESSENTIALS

VISITOR INFORMATION The **National Tourist Office** is in Palma at Plaça Reina 2 (© **97-171-22-16**). It's open Monday to Friday 9am to 8pm, and Saturday 9am to 2pm.

GETTING AROUND In Palma, you can get around the Old Town and the Paseo on foot. Otherwise, you can make limited use of taxis, or take one of the buses that cut across the city. Out on the island, you'll have to depend mainly on buses or rented cars.

Where to Get Those Phone Cards

Local newsstands and tobacco shops sell phone cards valued between 3€ and 15€. They can be used in any public telephone booth, and they allow you to make both domestic and international calls.

FAST FACTS The **U.S. Consulate,** Edificio Reina Constanza, Porto Pi, B, 9D (© 97-140-37-07), is open from 10:30am to 1:30pm Monday to Friday. The **British Consulate,** Carrer Convent dels Caputxins, 4 (© **97-171-24-45**), is open from 8:30am to 1:30pm Monday to Friday.

In case of an **emergency,** dial © **112.** If you fall ill, head to **Clínica Rotger,** Calle Santiago Rusiñol 9 (© **97-144-85-00;** www.clinicarotger. es), or **Clínica Juaneda,** Calle Son Espanyolet 55 (© **97-173-16-47**). Both clinics are open 24 hours.

For **Internet access,** go to **Babaloo,** Calle Verja 2 (© **97-195-77-25;** www.babaloointernet.com), just off Calle Sant Magi. It charges 2€ per hour and is open Monday to Saturday 10am to 10pm and Sunday 3 to 10pm.

Majorca observes the same **holidays** as the rest of Spain but also celebrates June 29, the Feast of St. Peter, the patron saint of all fishers.

The central **post office** is at Constitución 6 (© **97-172-70-54** or 90-219-71-97). Hours are Monday to Friday 8:30am to 8:30pm, and Saturday 9:30am to 2pm.

FUN ON & OFF THE BEACH

There is a beach fairly close to the cathedral in Palma, but some readers have been discouraged from swimming here because of foul-smelling, albeit covered, sewers nearby. The closest public beach is **Playa Nova,** a 35-minute bus ride from downtown Palma. Some hotels, however, have private beaches. If you head east, you reach the excellent beaches of **Ca'n Pastilla.** The golden-sand beaches at **El Arenal** are very well equipped with tourist facilities. Going to the southwest, you find good but often crowded beaches at **Cala Mayor** and **Sant Agustí.**

Take note: You can swim from late June to October; don't believe the promoters who try to sell you on mild Majorcan winters in January and February—it can get downright cold. Spring and fall can be heaven sent, and in summer the coastal areas are pleasantly cooled by sea breezes.

GOLF Majorca is a golfer's dream. The best course is **Son Vida Club de Golf,** Urbanización Son Vida, about 13km (8 miles) east of Palma along the Andrade Highway. This 18-hole course is shared by the guests of the island's two best hotels, Arabella Sheraton Golf Hotel and Castillo Hotel Son Vida. However, the course is open to all players who call for reservations (© **97-179-12-10;** www.sonvidagolf.com). Greens fees are 70€ for hotel guests and 95€ for nonguests for 18 holes. Golf cart rentals are also available for 45€. There are many golf courses on the island. For information about them, contact **Federación Balear de Golf,** Av. Jaime III no. 17, in Palma (© **97-172-27-53;** www.fbgolf.com).

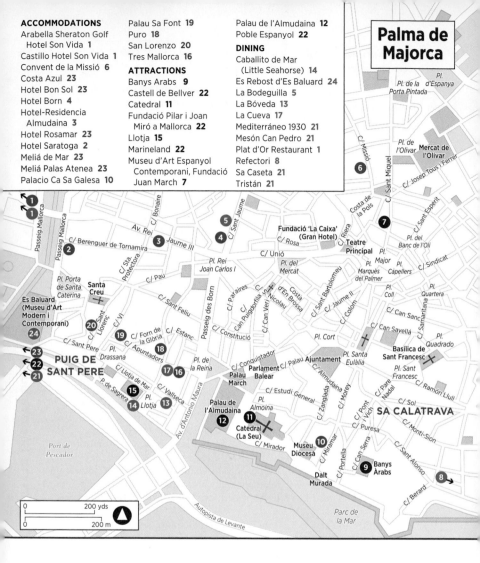

Palma de Majorca

ACCOMMODATIONS
Arabella Sheraton Golf Hotel Son Vida **1**
Castillo Hotel Son Vida **1**
Convent de la Missió **6**
Costa Azul **23**
Hotel Bon Sol **23**
Hotel Born **4**
Hotel-Residencia Almudaina **3**
Hotel Rosamar **23**
Hotel Saratoga **2**
Meliá de Mar **23**
Meliá Palas Atenea **23**
Palacio Ca Sa Galesa **10**
Palau Sa Font **19**
Puro **18**
San Lorenzo **20**
Tres Mallorca **16**

ATTRACTIONS
Banys Arabs **9**
Castell de Bellver **22**
Catedral **11**
Fundació Pilar i Joan Miró a Mallorca **22**
Llotja **15**
Marineland **22**
Museu d'Art Espanyol Contemporani, Fundació Juan March **7**
Palau de l'Almudaina **12**
Poble Espanyol **22**

DINING
Caballito de Mar (Little Seahorse) **14**
Es Rebost d'Es Baluard **24**
La Bodeguilla **5**
La Bóveda **13**
La Cueva **17**
Mediterráneo 1930 **21**
Mesón Can Pedro **21**
Plat d'Or Restaurant **1**
Refectori **8**
Sa Caseta **21**
Tristán **21**

HIKING Because of the hilly terrain in Majorca, this sport is better pursued here than on Ibiza or Minorca. The mountains of the northwest, the Serra de Tramuntana, are best for exploring. The tourist office (see above) will provide you with a free booklet called *20 Hiking Excursions on the Island of Majorca.* For hiking information, contact **Grup Excursionista de Mallorca,** the Majorcan Hiking Association, at C/dels Horts, 1 Baixos, in Palma (© **87-194-79-00;** www.gemweb.org).

TENNIS If your hotel doesn't have a court, head for the **Club de Tenis,** Av. Son Rigo s/n (© **97-126-12-89**).

A view of Playa Nova, in Palma.

WATERSPORTS Most beaches have outfitters who will rent you Windsurfers and dinghies. The best outfitter is **Escola d'Esports Nàutics,** Paseo Playa d'en Repic, at Port de Sóller (© **60-935-41-32;** www.nauticsoller.com).

SHOPPING

Stores in Palma offer handicrafts, elegant leather goods, Majorcan pearls, and fine needlework. The best shopping is on the following streets: San Miguel, Carrer Sindicato, Jaume II, Jaume III, Carrer Platería, Vía Roman, and Passeig des Borne, plus the streets radiating from the Borne all the way to Plaça Cort, where the city hall stands. Most shops close on Saturday afternoon and Sunday.

Loewe, Av. Jaume III no. 1 (© **97-171-52-75**), offers fine leather, elegant accessories for men and women, luggage, and chic apparel for women.

An Unspoiled Mediterranean Island

Declared a National Reserve in 1991, **Illa de Cabrera ★★** lies off the south coast of Majorca. It is the largest of the 19 islands that form the Archipelago of Cabrera. With its lush vegetation, dramatic coastline, and abundant life, it makes for the most intriguing day trip from Majorca. Large colonies of birds and marine fauna await visitors.

In the 13th and 14th centuries, Cabrera was used by pirates as a base from which to attack Majorca. The ruins of a castle built in the 14th century can be seen at the entrance to the port.

Excursions à Cabrera (© **97-164-90-34;** www.excursionsacabrera.com) operates tours from Colonia de Sant Jordi, 47km (29 miles) southeast of Palma around 9:30am daily, returning at 6pm; the round-trip fare is 32€. Trip time is 30 minutes.

For high-quality artificial pearls, head for **Mediterráneo,** Av. Jaume III no. 11, Centro (© **97-172-45-39**). Since 1719, **Gordiola,** Carrer de la Victoria 2 (© **97-171-15-41**), has been making the best glass products on the island.

SEEING THE SIGHTS

Most visitors don't spend much time exploring the historic sights in Palma, but there are a number of places to see if you've had too much sun.

Viajes Sidetours, Av. Gabriel Roca 19 (© **97-145-35-11**), offers numerous full- and half-day excursions throughout Palma and the surrounding countryside. The full-day excursion to Valldemossa and Sóller takes visitors through the monastery where former island residents Chopin and his lover, George Sand, spent their scandalous winter. After leaving the monastery, the tour explores the peaks of the Sierra Mallorquina and then makes its way to the seaside town of Sóller. Call ahead for ticket prices. Tours are reserved for groups with a minimum of 37 people.

Another full-day tour of the mountainous western side of the island is conducted by train and boat, including a ride on one of Europe's oldest railways to the town of Sóller and the Monasterio de Lluch, as well as a boat ride between the port of Sóller and La Calobra. The eastern coast of Majorca is explored in the "Caves of Drach and Hams" tour. A concert on the world's largest underground lake (Lake Martel), tours through the caves, a stop at an olive-wood works, and a visit to the Majorica Pearl Factory are all covered. Times of departure may vary.

Balearic Discovery, Calle Jaime Solivellas 11, Selva (© **97-187-53-95;** www.balearicdiscovery.com), offers tailor-made travel services to people who want a unique experience during their time in Majorca. The company can arrange everything from art tours to windsurfing excursions.

Banys Arabs You can spend hours exploring the narrow streets of the medieval quarter (Barri Gòtic) east of the cathedral. Along the way, you may want to visit these Moorish baths that date from the 10th century. They are the only complete remaining Moorish-constructed buildings in Palma. One room contains a dome supported by 12 columns.

Carrer Serra 7. © **97-172-15-49.** Admission 2€. Apr–Sept daily 9am–7pm; Oct–Mar daily 9am–6pm. Bus: 15.

Castell de Bellver ★ Erected in 1309, this hilltop round castle was once the summer palace of the kings of Majorca—during the short period when there were kings of Majorca. The castle, which was a fortress with a double moat, is well preserved and now houses the Museu Municipal, which is devoted to archaeological objects and old coins. It's really

The Castell de Bellver.

La Seu's altar and *baldachin*.

the view from here, however, that is the chief attraction. In fact, the name, Bellver, means "beautiful view."

Btw. Palma and Son Armadams. ℭ **97-173-06-57.** Admission 3€ adults; 1€ children 14–18, students, and seniors; free for children 13 and under. Apr–Sept Mon–Sat 8am–8:30pm, Sun 10am–5pm; Oct–Mar Mon–Sat 8am–7:15pm, Sun 10am–5pm. Museum closed Sun. Bus: 3 or 15.

Catedral (La Seu) ★★ This Catalonian Gothic cathedral, called La Seu, stands in the Old Town overlooking the seaside. It was begun during the reign of Jaume II (1276–1311) and completed in 1601. Its central vault is 43m (141 ft.) high, and its columns rise 20m (66 ft.). There is a wrought-iron *baldachin* (canopy) by Gaudí over the main altar. The treasury contains pieces said to be part of the True Cross, and relics of San Sebastián, patron saint of Palma. Museum and cathedral hours often change; call ahead to make sure they're accepting visitors before you go.

Carrer Palau Reial. ℭ **97-172-31-30.** Free admission to cathedral; museum and treasury 3.50€. Apr–May and Oct Mon–Fri 10am–5:15pm; Nov–Mar Mon–Fri 10am–3:15pm; June–Sept Mon–Fri 10am–6:15pm; Sat year-round 10am–2:15pm. Bus: 15.

Fundació Pilar I Joan Miró a Mallorca ★ The great artist and his wife, Pilar Juncosa, donated four workshops in which the artist carried out his creative work on the island from 1956 until his death in 1983. At Miró's former estate, rotating exhibitions devoted to his life and work are presented along with a permanent collection of his art and sculptures. You can also see his studio as it was at the time of his death.

Carrer Joan de Saridakis 29. ℭ **97-170-14-20.** Admission 6€ adults, 3€ children and seniors. Mid-May to mid-Sept Tues–Sat 10am–7pm; off season Tues–Sat 10am–6pm; year-round Sun 10am–3pm. Bus: 3 or 6.

Llotja ★ This 15th-century Gothic structure is a leftover from the wealthy mercantile days of Majorca. La Lonja (its Spanish name) was, roughly, an exchange or guild. Exhibitions here are announced in local newspapers.

Plaza de la Llotja. ℭ **97-171-17-05.** Free admission. Tues–Sat 11am–2pm and 5–9pm; Sun 11am–2pm. Bus: 15.

Marineland Eighteen kilometers (11 miles) west of Palma, just off the coast road en route to Palma Nova, this attraction offers a variety of amusements—dolphin, sea lion, and parrot shows. The daily dolphin shows are at 11:30am and 3:30pm; the parrot shows, daily at 10:30am, 12:30, and 4:30pm. There's a Polynesian pearl-diving demonstration and a small zoo. You'll find a cafeteria, picnic area, and children's playground, as well as beach facilities.

Costa d'en Blanes. ℂ **97-167-51-25.** www. marineland.es. Admission 22€ adults, 16€ children 3–12, free for children 2 and under. Feb 23–Nov 16 Mon–Fri 9:30am–4:30pm; Sat–Sun 9:30am–5:30pm. Direct bus, marked MARINELAND, from Palma rail station.

Museu d'Art Espanyol Contemporani, Fundació Juan March ★ The Juan March Foundation's Museum of Spanish Contemporary Art reopened in 1997, with newly acquired modern paintings. The works represent one of

A sculpture outside the Fundació Pilar I Joan Miró a Mallorca.

the most fertile periods of 20th-century art, with canvases by Picasso, Miró, Dalí, and Juan Gris, as well as by Antoni Tàpies, Carlos Saura, Miquel Barceló, Lluis Gordillo, Susana Solano, and Jordi Teixidor. A room devoted to temporary exhibits was added to the restored museum. One series, for example, featured 100 Picasso engravings from the 1930s. The oldest and best-known work in the museum is Picasso's *Head of a Woman,* from his cycle of paintings known as *Les Demoiselles d'Avignon.* These works form part of the collection that the Juan March Foundation began to amass in 1973.

Carrer Sant Miquel 11. ℂ **97-171-35-15.** www.march.es. Free admission. Mon–Fri 10am–6:30pm; Sat 10:30am–2pm.

Palau de l'Almudaina Long ago, Muslim rulers erected this splendid fortress surrounded by Moorish-style gardens and fountains opposite the cathedral. During the short-lived reign of the kings of Majorca, it was converted into a royal residence that evokes the Alcázar at Málaga. Now it houses a museum displaying antiques, artwork, suits of armor, and Gobelin tapestries. Panoramic views of Palma's harbor can be seen from here.

Carrer Palau Reial. ℂ **97-121-41-34.** www.patrimonionacional.es. Admission 4€ adults, 2.70€ children, free for all Wed. Apr–Sept Mon–Fri 10am–5:45pm, Sat 10am–1:15pm; Oct–Mar Mon–Fri 10am–1:15pm and 4–5:15pm, Sat 10am–1:15pm. Closed holidays. Bus: 15.

Poble Espanyol ★ This is a touristy collection of buildings evoking Spain in miniature and is similar to the Poble Espanyol in Barcelona (p. 514). Bullfights are held in its *corrida* on summer Sundays. There are representations of such famous structures as the Alhambra in Granada, Torre de Oro in Seville, and El Greco's House in Toledo.

Carrer Pueblo Español s/n. ✆ **97-173-70-75.** www.poble-espanyol.com/pemsa/en.html. Admission 8.50€ adults, 6.50€ students, 5.50€ children 7–12. Mon 9am–8pm; Tues–Thurs 9am–2pm; Fri 9am–4am; Sat 9am-5pm; Sun 9am–midnight. Bus: 5.

WHERE TO STAY IN PALMA

If you go in high season, reserve well in advance—Majorca's staggering number of hotels are still not enough to hold the August crowds. Some of our hotel recommendations are in El Terreno, the heart of local nightlife. Don't book into one of these hotels unless you like plenty of action, continuing until late at night.

Palma's suburbs, notably Cala Mayor, about 4km (2½ miles) from the center, and San Agustín, about 5km (3 miles) from town, continue to sprawl. In El Arenal, part of Playas de Palma, there is a huge concentration of hotels. The beaches at El Arenal are quite good but have a Coney Island atmosphere.

Very Expensive

Arabella Sheraton Golf Hotel Son Vida ★★★ ☺ Castillo Hotel Son Vida (see below) is more highly rated and elegant, but Arabella is more scenically located. The ecology of the area has been fiercely protected. Don't come here expecting raucous good times on the beach; the resort is elegant and rather staid. There's no health club and no shuttle to the beach; many visitors drive to the several nearby beaches. Arabella does boast one of the only hotel bullrings in Spain. The low-rise complex is intensely landscaped and offers views over the lush green grounds (not of the sea) from many of its good-size rooms. Accommodations have white walls, dark-stained furnishings, carpeting, and, in the more expensive accommodations, balconies or verandas. The hotel's golfing facilities are among the best in Spain, and room rates include greens fees. Guests can patronize the Arabella courses of Son Vida, Son Muntaner, Son Quint—all 18-hole courses—or the 9-hole Son Quint Executive Course. Guests have free shuttle transfer to all four courses.

Carrer de la Vinagrella, 07013 Palma de Majorca. ✆ **800/325-3535** in the U.S., or 97-178-71-00. Fax 97-178-72-00. www.mallorca-resort.com. 93 units. 330€–500€ double; 1,100€–1,400€ suite. Rates include buffet breakfast. AE, DC, MC, V. Free parking. Bus: 7. **Amenities:** 2 restaurants; bar; babysitting; bikes; children's center; concierge; exercise room; 18-hole golf course; 2 pools (1 heated indoor); room service; spa; 3 tennis courts (lit); Wi-Fi (free, in lobby). *In room:* A/C, TV, hair dryer, minibar.

Castillo Hotel Son Vida ★★★ Set in a 13th-century castle in the Son Vida Hills, on a secluded hilltop overlooking Palma, this hotel, a member of the Leading Hotels of the World, commands the most panoramic views on the island. It recently underwent massive renovations. Several rooms are in a modern wing, a pleasing reproduction of a Spanish hacienda. Inside, the public rooms are swathed in sumptuous fabrics, Oriental rugs, and chandeliers. Guest rooms in the new building are not quite as distinctive as those in the castle. Many rooms have private balconies or terraces.

Carrer Raixa 2, 07013 Palma de Majorca. ✆ **888/625-5144** in the U.S., or 97-149-34-93. Fax 97-149-34-94. www.hotelsonvida.com. 167 units. 250€–840€ double; from 1,090€ suite. Rates include buffet breakfast. AE, DC, MC, V. Free parking. Bus: 7. **Amenities:** 2 restaurants; bar; babysitting; concierge; exercise room; 2 nearby golf courses; 3 pools (1 heated indoor); room service; spa. *In room:* A/C, TV/DVD, hair dryer, kitchenette, minibar, Wi-Fi (free).

Palacio Ca Sa Galesa ★★ 🎁 Although not in the same league as the Arabella and Son Vida (both reviewed above), this place is a delight and less expensive. For generations this 15th-century town house languished as a decaying apartment building facing the side of the cathedral. In 1993, an entrepreneurial couple from Cardiff, Wales, began restoring the place, salvaging the original marble floors and stained-glass windows, sheathing the walls of the public areas with silk, and adding modern amenities. Today the place is loaded with English and Spanish antiques and paintings. Most rooms overlook an enclosed courtyard draped with potted plants and climbing vines. The guest rooms are quite opulent, with antiques and Persian rugs.

Carrer de Miramar 8, 07001 Palma de Majorca. ✆ **97-171-54-00.** Fax 97-172-15-79. www. palaciocasagalesa.com. 12 units. 180€–348€ double; 350€–503€ suite. AE, MC, V. Parking 17€. **Amenities:** Jacuzzi; room service. *In room:* A/C, TV, hair dryer, minibar.

Expensive

Convent de la Missió ★ 🎁 In Palma's Old Town, next to a church of the same name, this 17th-century convent stands amid narrow streets and plant-filled courtyards. No longer educating missionaries, it has been massively restored and turned into a hotel with many amenities, including a solarium and a whirlpool. The guest rooms range from small to spacious. Suites are equipped with Jacuzzis. The guest rooms are comfortably furnished, very inviting, and cozy in their minimalist style, with white and sand the predominant colors.

Carrer de la Missió, 07003 Palma de Majorca. ✆ **97-122-73-47.** Fax 97-122-73-48. www.convent delamissio.com. 14 units. 225€–258€ double; 258€ junior suite; 340€–391€ suite. Rates include buffet breakfast. AE, DC, MC, V. Parking 15€. **Amenities:** Restaurant; bar; babysitting; room service; sauna. *In room:* A/C, TV, hair dryer, minibar.

Palau Sa Font ★ 🎁 This 16th-century palace was successfully converted into one of Majorca's most charming boutique hotels. It's a 3-minute walk from the harbor, and a 15-minute walk from the cathedral. The atmosphere is a bit funky (unless you like jelly bean colors). Distressed iron and island stone add more traditional notes. Especially popular with English visitors, this has been called by some London tabloids the hippest place to stay in the Old Town. The place is imbued with atmosphere. Designers transformed the guest rooms into a blend of modern and traditional.

Carrer Apuntadores 38, Barrio Antiguo, 07017 Palma de Majorca. ✆ **97-171-22-77.** Fax 97-171-26-18. www.palausafont.com. 19 units. 155€–205€ double; 220€ junior suite. Rates include buffet breakfast. AE, DC, MC, V. No parking. Closed Jan. **Amenities:** Bar; babysitting; outdoor pool; Wi-Fi (free, in lobby). *In room:* A/C, TV, hair dryer, minibar.

Puro ★★★ The hottest, chicest address to open in Palma's Old Town is this inn, hailed as a "nirvana for trendoids" in the press. Mats Wahlström, an entrepreneur and globe-trotter based in Stockholm, discovered the building and set out to create a hotel that evokes Miami's South Beach with a touch of Barcelona. An all-white lobby flows up a flight of steps to an all-white bar leading to an all-white restaurant, where you dine inside "tents" decked with tassels. The hotel restaurant, **Opio,** is a cherished dining ticket, with a Swedish chef cooking Mediterranean and Asian fusion cuisine. A young, professional staff member will show you to your midsize-to-spacious room. The rooms have a touch of whimsy, with everything from mirror-studded cushions from Rajasthan to feathered hats from Cameroon. Our favorite spot is the roof deck with its plunge pool, sun beds, and tents.

Montenegro 12, 07012 Palma de Majorca. ☎ **97-142-54-50.** Fax 97-142-54-51. www.purohotel. com. 23 units. 212€–315€ double; 255€–345€ junior suite; 352€–515€ suite. Rates include buffet breakfast. AE, MC, V. Parking 18€. **Amenities:** Restaurant; bar; babysitting; concierge; room service. *In room:* A/C, TV/DVD, hair dryer, minibar, movie library, Wi-Fi (free).

Tres Mallorca ★★ 🛎 This little gem of a boutique hotel lies at the crossroads of elegance and comfort. Two palaces from 1576 were blended with a modern structure, and a rustic island style was seamlessly paired with contemporary design. Many of the original architectural features have been preserved. The result is a winning choice for those who seek a one-of-a-kind hotel of character in the heart of Palma's Old Town. The most unusual feature of the present hotel: Two roof terraces are linked by a bridge. In this space guests enjoy an infinity splash pool, as well as sweeping vistas of Palma and its port. The midsize bedrooms are minimalist in decor but comfortably and attractively furnished, with wood floors and plush sofas in flamboyant colors.

Calle Apuntadores 3, 07012 Palma de Mallorca. ☎ **97-171-73-33.** Fax 97-171-73-72. www.hoteltres.com. 41 units. 251€–283€ double; 283€–304€ junior suite. Rates include buffet breakfast. AE, DC, MC, V. No parking. **Amenities:** Restaurant; bar; babysitting; outdoor pool; room service; sauna. *In room:* A/C, TV/DVD, CD player, hair dryer, minibar, Wi-Fi (in some; free).

Moderate

Hotel-Residencia Almudaina Located on the main commercial street in Palma, this simple hotel offers comfortable, clean, basic rooms. Although small, the units are well maintained and have neatly kept bathrooms. Because of the street location, many of the rooms are quite noisy; the quietest are in the rear. Some have terraces and glass doors letting in ample sunlight.

Av. Jaume III no. 9, 07012 Palma de Majorca. ☎ **97-172-73-40.** Fax 97-172-25-99. www.hotel almudaina.com. 77 units. 110€–140€ double. Rates include buffet breakfast. AE, DC, MC, V. Nearby parking 17€. Bus: 1, 13, or 15. **Amenities:** Bar; room service. *In room:* A/C, TV, hair dryer, minibar, Wi-Fi (free).

Hotel Saratoga ★ Under an arcade beside the Old City's medieval moat is the entrance to the Hotel Saratoga. Constructed in 1962, the hotel features bright, well-furnished guest rooms, many with balconies or terraces with views of the bay and city of Palma. The mostly midsize guest rooms include well-maintained and tiled bathrooms. One of the hotel's most attractive features is a cafe/bar on the seventh floor, with views over the bay.

Passeig Majorca 6, 07012 Palma de Majorca. ☎ **97-172-72-40.** Fax 97-172-73-12. www.hotel saratoga.es. 187 units. 140€–190€ double; 220€–250€ suite. Rates include buffet breakfast. AE, DC, MC, V. Parking 16€. Bus: 3, 7, or 15. **Amenities:** Restaurant; bar; exercise room; 2 outdoor pools; room service; sauna. *In room:* A/C, TV, hair dryer, minibar, Wi-Fi (free).

Meliá Palas Atenea ★ A member of the Sol chain, this modern hotel offers extensive leisure facilities for vacationers, while still catering to business travelers. It overlooks the Bay of Palma, within walking distance of the town's major restaurants and shops. Spacious guest rooms have terraces, many overlooking the harbor or Bellver Castle. Furnishings are standardized, but the rooms are exceedingly comfortable, ranging from midsize to spacious.

Passeig Ing. Gabriel Roca 29, 07014 Palma de Majorca. ☎ **97-128-14-00.** Fax 97-145-19-89. www. solmelia.com. 361 units. 101€–200€ double; 157€–215€ suite. AE, DC, MC, V. Parking 14€. Bus: 1. **Amenities:** 2 restaurants; bar; babysitting; concierge; exercise room; 2 pools (1 heated indoor); room service; spa. *In room:* A/C, TV, hair dryer, minibar, Wi-Fi (12€ per 24 hr.).

San Lorenzo ★★ This antique hotel and romantic oasis occupies the center of the maze of winding streets that form Palma's Old City. The building is from the 18th century, and the decor is a pleasant mix of traditional Majorcan and modern. The airy guest rooms are painted white and have beamed ceilings. While some have balconies, the more luxurious ones offer fireplaces and private terraces. This hotel is perfect for relaxing after a day of sightseeing or shopping. The fixtures in its Art Deco bar once decorated a saloon in Paris.

San Lorenzo 14, 07012 Palma de Majorca. ℂ **97-172-82-00.** Fax 97-171-19-01. www.hotel sanlorenzo.com. 6 units. 150€–190€ double; 240€ suite. AE, DC, MC, V. No parking. **Amenities:** Bar; babysitting; outdoor pool; room service. *In room:* A/C, TV, hair dryer, minibar, Wi-Fi (free).

Inexpensive

Costa Azul ⚓ Head here for a bargain—despite the reasonable rates, you'll get views of the yachts in the harbor. This place isn't glamorous, but it does offer good value. A short taxi ride will deposit you on the Plaça Gomila in El Terreno with its after-dark diversions. Barren, well-worn rooms here are clean and furnished very modestly.

Passeig Marítim 7, 07014 Palma de Majorca. ℂ **97-173-19-40.** Fax 97-173-19-71. www.esperanza-hoteles.com. 126 units. 80€–145€ double. AE, DC, MC, V. Parking 16€. Bus: 1, 3, or 21. **Amenities:** Restaurant; bar; babysitting; indoor heated pool; room service; sauna; Wi-Fi (free, in lobby). *In room:* A/C, TV.

Hotel Born ★ ⚓ If you'd like to stay within the city of Palma itself, there is no better bargain than this government-rated two-star hotel in the city's exact center. A 16th-century palace, which once belonged to the marquis of Ferrandell, was vastly altered and extended in the 18th century with a Majorcan courtyard. Today it's been converted into a small, cozy inn with all the modern amenities; at the same time, it retains many of its original architectural features, such as Romanesque arches. Guest rooms are, for the most part, spacious and well equipped. Off Plaça Rei Juan Carlos, the hotel opens onto a tranquil side street.

Carrer Sant Jaume 3, 07012 Palma de Mallorca. ℂ **97-171-29-42.** Fax 97-171-86-18. www.hotel-born.com. 30 units. 76€–97€ double; 120€ suite. Rates include continental breakfast. AE, DC, MC, V. No parking. **Amenities:** Bar; bikes. *In room:* A/C, TV.

Hotel Rosamar Hotel Rosamar, right on the main road in the boomtown El Terreno district, is popular with gay men and women. Fresh and clean small rooms have well-maintained bathrooms and balconies overlooking a front patio surrounded by tall palm trees. The focus of social life is the young, lively crowd that frequents the Rosamar.

Joan Miró 74, 07015 Palma de Majorca. ℂ **97-173-27-23.** Fax 97-128-38-28. www.rosamar-palma.com. 40 units. 45€–65€ double; 75€ triple; 95€–100€ suite. Rates include continental breakfast. AE, MC, V. Nearby parking 15€. Closed Oct–Mar. Bus: 3, 4, 21, or 22. **Amenities:** Bar. *In room:* Ceiling fan, Wi-Fi (free).

WHERE TO STAY AT ILLETAS

This suburb of Palma lies immediately west of the center.

Hotel Bon Sol ★ ☺ Set across from a beach, about 6.5km (4 miles) west of Palma, this government-rated four-star hotel was built in 1953 and renovated frequently since then. It charges less than other hotels with similar amenities, and the nearby beach makes it quite popular with vacationing families, who dine within the airy, somewhat spartan dining room. The core is a four-story, white-sided masonry tower; some of the suites are clustered into simple, outlying villas.

The hotel overlooks a garden, adjacent to the sea. The midsize rooms are efficient but comfortable and well suited to beachfront vacations.

Paseo de Illetas 30, 07181 Illetas, Majorca. (C) **97-140-21-11.** Fax 97-140-25-59. www.ila-chateau. com/bonsol. 147 units. 170€ double; 205€ suite. Rates include continental breakfast. AE, DC, MC, V. Free parking. Closed Nov 6–Dec 20. **Amenities:** 2 restaurants; bar; babysitting; children's center; exercise room; Jacuzzi; 2 outdoor heated pools; room service; sauna; 2 outdoor tennis courts (lit); Wi-Fi (free, in lobby). *In room:* A/C, TV, hair dryer, minibar.

Meliá de Mar ★★ Originally built in 1964, Meliá de Mar is one of the most comfortable (albeit expensive) hotels in Palma. This seven-story hotel is close to the beach and sports a large garden. The marble-floored lobby and light, summery furniture offer a cool refuge from the hot sun. The calm, deliberately uneventful setting is evocative of spa hotels in central Europe. Guest rooms, mainly midsize, have many fine features, including excellent beds.

Paseo de Illetas 7, 07015 Calvia, Majorca. (C) **97-140-25-11.** Fax 97-140-58-52. www.solmelia. com. 144 units. 175€–450€ double; from 474€ suite. Rates include buffet breakfast in summer. AE, DC, MC, V. Free parking. Closed Oct–Mar. **Amenities:** 3 restaurants; bar; babysitting; concierge; exercise room; 2 freshwater pools (1 heated indoor, 1 outdoor); room service; spa; outdoor tennis court (lit); Wi-Fi (free, in lobby). *In room:* A/C, TV, hair dryer, minibar.

WHERE TO STAY AT SANTA MARÍA DEL CAMI

Reads Hotel & Spa ★★ 🏆 Peacefully located in beautiful countryside, this hotel is only 18km (11 miles) from Palma on the way to Inca Alcúdia. The 16th-century Majorcan villa has been renovated and furnished with good-quality reproduction furniture as well as antiques. An unspoiled view of the Tramuntana Mountains forms the backdrop to the hotel, which is surrounded by gardens. Beamed ceilings and wooden shutters add an authentically traditional touch to the rooms, which were all refurbished and painted in subtle Mediterranean colors. The deluxe doubles and suites have French doors opening onto terraces with stunning views. Four reception rooms include an extraordinary blue room with *trompe l'oeil* clouds painted on the walls, and what was previously the olive-pressing room, the *tafona*. Children 11 and under are not admitted.

Ca'n Moragues, 07320 Santa María, Majorca. (C) **97-114-02-61.** Fax 97-114-07-62. www.reads hotel.com. 23 units. 195€–340€ double; 245€–390€ junior suite; 285€–680€ suite. Rates include buffet breakfast. AE, DC, MC, V. Free parking. **Amenities:** 2 restaurants; bar; babysitting; bikes; exercise room; 2 freshwater heated pools (1 indoor); room service; spa; outdoor tennis court (lit); Wi-Fi (free, in lobby). *In room:* A/C, TV/DVD, hair dryer.

WHERE TO STAY AT PUIGPUNENT

Gran Hotel Son Net ★★★ This 17th-century manor house next to a nature reserve nestles in a lush mountain valley 15km (9⅓ miles) from Palma. It was converted from a private residence by David Stein, a California tycoon and art collector. Apart from the setting, the hotel boasts works by artists such as Hockney, Stella, and Christoph, and there's even a small Chagall on one wall. A classical Majorcan aristocratic sense of decoration has been followed faithfully, with white walls, stone floors, and dark wood beams and shutters. The rooms are spacious, and the most idyllic corner units on the top floor have a southern exposure.

Castillo Son Net, 07194 Puigpunent, Majorca. (C) **97-114-70-00.** Fax 97-114-70-01. www.sonnet. es. 24 units. 215€–740€ double; 535€–1,750€ suite. AE, DC, MC, V. Free parking. **Amenities:** 2 restaurants; bar; babysitting; outdoor pool; room service. *In room:* A/C, TV/DVD, CD player, hair dryer, minibar, Wi-Fi (free).

WHERE TO STAY AT LA BONANOVA

Valparaíso Palace ★★ This magnificently situated hotel is directly west of Palma and south of the sprawling grounds of Castell de Bellver, the round hilltop castle crowning Palma. Only minutes from the center of town and 2km (1¼ miles) from a good beach, this seven-story luxury property has been in business since 1976. The architecture is extremely modern and the entrance is set in the midst of landscaped gardens and an artificial lake. The impressive lobby, with its marble floors and pristine decor, has an efficient, helpful staff. The guest rooms are spacious and handsomely furnished.

Calle Francisco Vidal Sureda 23, 07016 Palma de Majorca. © **97-140-03-00.** Fax 97-140-59-04. www.grupotelvalparaiso.com. 174 units. 272€–320€ double; 420€–630€ suite. Rates include buffet breakfast. AE, DC, MC, V. Free parking. **Amenities:** 2 restaurants; 2 bars; babysitting; health club; Internet (free, in lobby); 3 freshwater heated pools (1 indoor); room service; spa; outdoor tennis court (lit). *In room:* A/C, TV, hair dryer, minibar, Wi-Fi (6€ per hour).

WHERE TO STAY AT PALMANOVA

Hotel Punta Negra ★★ A 10-minute drive west from the center of Palma, this hotel enjoys a privileged position in Costa d'en Blanes. In an exclusive area, this two-story hotel is surrounded by two Mediterranean beaches and an array of golf courses. Elegant and posh, it's constructed in classic Majorcan style with white walls, antique furnishings, carpeted floors, and panoramic views of either the sea or pine forests. The hotel is only 1.5km (1 mile) from the yachting port of Puerto Portals. Spacious and beautifully furnished rooms are equipped with elegant bathrooms.

Carretera Andaitz Km 12, 07181 Costa d'en Blanes, Majorca. © **97-168-07-62.** Fax 97-168-39-19. www.h10.es. 137 units. 95€–255€ double; 129€–285€ suite. Rates include continental breakfast. AE, DC, MC, V. Free parking. **Amenities:** 2 restaurants; bar; babysitting; bikes; concierge; exercise room; nearby 18-hole golf course; Jacuzzi; 3 freshwater pools (1 heated indoor); room service; sauna; outdoor tennis court (lit). *In room:* A/C, TV, hair dryer, minibar, Wi-Fi (free).

WHERE TO STAY AT BINISSALEM

Scott's Hotel ★★ 🎖 This handsomely restored 18th-century mansion is in the little town of Binissalem, in the center of Majorca. It's not for beach buffs, but if you have a car and want a retreat, you'll find this nugget 20km (12 miles) from Palma and a 20-minute drive to a sandy beach. The beautifully furnished and rather elegant guest rooms come in a wide variety of sizes, ranging from two singles to two full suites, with units "in between" consisting of king-size doubles, twins, queen-size doubles, or junior suites. You feel as though you're living in a country manor house instead of staying in a hotel. Antiques, handmade beds, and Persian rugs form just a backdrop for the grand tranquillity. Children 11 and under are not admitted.

Plaza de la Iglesia 12, 07350 Binissalem, Majorca. © **97-187-01-00.** Fax 97-187-02-67. www. scottshotel.com. 17 units. 175€–325€ double; 270€–410€ suite. 3-night minimum stay. No children 11 and under. AE, MC, V. Free parking. **Amenities:** Indoor heated pool. *In room:* A/C, hair dryer.

WHERE TO DINE IN & AROUND PALMA

Majorca's most typical main dish is *lomo,* or pork loin, the specialty in any restaurant offering Majorcan cuisine. *Lomo con col* is a method of preparation wherein the loin is enveloped in cabbage leaves and served with a sauce made with tomatoes, grapes, pine nuts, and bay leaf.

A local sausage, *sabrosada*, is made with pure pork and red peppers. Paprika gives it its characteristic bright red color. *Sopas mallorquinas* can mean almost anything, but basically they consist of mixed greens in soup flavored with olive oil and thickened with bread. When garbanzos (chickpeas) and meat are added, these become a meal in themselves.

The best-known vegetable dish is *el tumbet*, a kind of cake with a layer of potato and another of lightly sautéed eggplant. Everything is covered with a tomato sauce and peppers, and then boiled for a while. Eggplant, often served stuffed with meat or fish, is one of the island's vegetable mainstays. *Frito mallorquín* might include anything but basically is a dish of fried onions and potatoes, mixed with red peppers, diced lamb liver, "lights" (lungs), and fennel. It's zesty, to say the least.

In the Balearic Islands, only Majorca produces wine, but this wine isn't exported. The red wine bottled around Felanitx and Binissalem adds Franja Roja and Viña Paumina to your wine list. Most of the wine, however, comes from mainland Spain. *Café carajillo*—coffee with cognac—is a Spanish specialty particularly enjoyed by Majorcans.

Expensive

Es Rebost d'Es Baluard ★★ MAJORCAN   This "glass box" attached to the El Baluard modern art museum is the best place in town to sample new Majorcan cookery. The talented chef, Joan Torrens, takes traditional recipes of the island and modernizes them based on seasonal produce. Dishes are delicately crafted and harmonious in flavor and are backed up with an impressive wine list. For starters, try an innovative dish: sticky rice with rabbit, mushrooms, and snails; or perhaps cream of artichokes with Iberian ham. Fish is a specialty, including a ragout of prawns and scallops with a citrus vinaigrette, or else you can try such meat dishes as a crystallized suckling pig or a loin of lamb stuffed with eggplant.

9 Plaza Santa Catalina. ☏ **97-171-96-09.** Reservations required. Main courses 15€–22€. AE, DC, MC, V. Mon–Sat 1:30–3:30pm and 8–10:30pm. Closed last 2 weeks of Jan and last 2 weeks of Aug.

Mediterráneo 1930 ★ MEDITERRANEAN   Named after the Art Deco, 1930s-era styling that fills its interior, this is a well-managed, artfully hip restaurant adjacent to Hotel Meliá Victoria. One of the top restaurants in Palma, with a sense of chic defined by its cosmopolitan owner Juan Martí, it has a beige-and-white decor accented by verdant plants and Art Deco sculptures. The menu relies heavily on seafood, with special emphasis on fish slowly baked in a salt crust, a process that adds a light-textured flakiness to even the most aromatic fish. Another specialty is beefsteak cooked on a hot stone carried directly to your table and served with such sauces as béarnaise, pepper, or port.

Passeig Marítim 33. ☏ **97-173-03-77.** www.mediterraneo1930.com. Reservations recommended. Main courses 18€–23€; fixed-price menus 20€–31€. AE, DC, MC, V. Daily 1–3:30pm and 7:30–11:30pm.

Plat d'Or Restaurant ★★★ MEDITERRANEAN   This deluxe restaurant in the Arabella Sheraton Golf Hotel Son Vida serves arguably the grandest gourmet cuisine on the island. The award-winning chef, Rafel Sánchez, blends traditional recipes with modern ones. From the windows, views open onto the pool area and the golf course. Every night of the week in summer there's a different themed evening. The chef is extraordinarily attentive to details, and you might relish such starters as langoustines with couscous or fresh pasta filled with lobster and herby cheese with white truffled butter. Main fish lures include sea bass with squid and a wonton of vegetable or else Majorcan lamb with a cashew nut juice and a flavoring of fresh bay leaves.

In the Arabella Sheraton Golf Hotel Son Vida (p. 715), Carrer de la Vinagrella. ℂ **97-178-71-00.** Reservations required. 3-course menu 68€, excluding wine. AE, DC, MC, V. Daily 7:30–10:30pm. Closed Nov 17–Dec 21.

Refectori ★★★ INTERNATIONAL No chef is more celebrated in Palma than Jaime Oliver—no relation to *The Naked Chef.* His splendid kitchen, located on the ground floor of the previously recommended Convent de la Missió (p. 716), offers the island's most creative cuisine. To enjoy it, reserve well in advance, especially if you want a table on the open-air terrace. The best of seasonal produce—backed up by a varied wine list—awaits diners, who can also sit in the main room decorated with black-and-white photographs of Majorcan salt mounds. The fish of the day is one of the most requested dishes, though you may opt instead for the ostrich steak with a mild orange and ginger sauce. Various imaginative specialties include braised beef cheeks with sun-dried tomatoes, black olives, and basil; potato-and-Parmesan gnocchi with young spinach and wild mushrooms; and filet of mackerel with a saffron-laced bouillabaisse sauce.

Carrer de la Missió. ℂ **97-122-73-47.** Reservations required far in advance. Main courses 26€–29€. AE, DC, MC, V. Mon–Fri 1–3:30pm; Mon–Sat 7:30–10:30pm. Closed Nov–Mar.

Tristán ★★★ CONTEMPORARY SPANISH/MAJORCAN Several miles southwest of Palma, Tristán overlooks the marina of Port Portals. This is the finest restaurant in the Balearics, winning a coveted two stars from Michelin, a designation previously unheard of in the archipelago. The sophisticated menu varies, depending on what's best in the market each day. Some of the best dishes might include Iberian pork braised in red wine and served with foie gras, or else fried quail with braised onions. John Dory is another specialty; it's served with a tarragon-laced tomato sauce. But this recitation doesn't prepare you for the exceptional bursts of flavor you'll sample in the chef's creations.

Port Portals 1, Portals Nous. ℂ **97-167-55-47.** Reservations required. Main courses 39€–57€; 4-course menu 145€; 6-course menu 175€. AE, DC, MC, V. Daily 8–10:30pm. Closed Jan 7–Feb 28.

Moderate

Caballito del Mar (Little Seahorse) SEAFOOD Although there are several outdoor tables here, many guests prefer to dine inside because of the lively spirit of this popular place along the seafront. The decor is vaguely nautical, and the activity is sometimes frenzied, but that's part of its charm. The food is well prepared from fresh ingredients; specialties include a Majorcan version of bouillabaisse, *zarzuela* (fish stew), assorted grilled fish (our favorite), oysters in season, or grilled monkfish with scallops and potato purée. The chef also shines with other specialties, including ravioli filled with duck liver and wild mushrooms; baked turbot with potatoes, mussels, clams, and prawns; and spider-crab stew.

Passeig de Sagrera 5. ℂ **97-172-10-74.** www.caballitodemar.info. Reservations recommended. Main courses 20€–32€. AE, DC, MC, V. June–Sept daily 1–4pm and 8pm–midnight; off season Tues–Sun 1–4pm and 8pm–midnight. Bus: 6 or 15.

La Bodeguilla ★★ MAJORCAN/SPANISH For regional food and wine, it's hard to beat the skillful chefs at this regional tavern in the center of town. The wine carte of some 300 bottles from all over Spain first drew us here. We'd recommend a local wine, a smooth red Godegues Ribas Sió. The menu of fresh regional products (when available) is adroitly prepared and full of flavor. On a glass-topped barrel you can dine on *carpaccio de pulpo* (octopus) or *ravioli de morcilla* (fennel-flavored blood sausage tucked into a delicate noodle pouch). The chef's specialty is a duxelle sirloin of venison with foie gras and fresh mushrooms in a puff pastry crust. Other delights from various regions of Spain include Castilian young lamb, deer Wellington, cod with garlic and chili peppers, and fresh anchovies from Andalusia.

Carrer San Jaume 3. ℂ **97-171-82-74.** www.la-bodeguilla.com. Reservations required. Main courses 15€–40€. AE, MC, V. Daily noon–midnight.

La Cueva ★★ MAJORCAN/SEAFOOD We delight in constantly discovering places that locals often guard for themselves. It is not our aim to spoil these establishments, but we operate on the theory that visitors deserve the chance to sample the best even if it's in an unpretentious, nontouristy atmosphere. This place is decorated like a regional tavern, with slabs of meat hanging from the ceiling. The fish tapas here are the best on the island, and you can order platter after platter until you are full. Try the *pescaditos fritos* (fried fish). The chefs work culinary miracles with *pulpo* (octopus). All the fish and shellfish dishes we've sampled here are really, really fresh and are deftly handled in the kitchen. Of course, the menu can depend on the catch of the day.

5 Calle Apuntadores. ℂ **97-172-44-22.** Reservations recommended. Main courses 6€–20€. AE, MC, V. Mon–Sat noon–midnight.

Sa Caseta ★ 📷 MAJORCAN For some of the best-tasting regional cuisine, and to escape the heat of Palma, we like to head directly west of the city to the satellite village of Gènova. Here, in the attractive dining rooms of a hacienda, you can enjoy typical local cuisine served by a helpful staff. *Sopas mallorquinas* (the island's famed vegetable soup) begins many a meal here. The chef obviously loves cod, and he cooks it superbly in at least 10 different preparations. You might want to order some of the best suckling pig or roast baby lamb in Majorca. Paella is served with dried salt cod and vegetables, an unusual variation on this classic dish.

Carrer Alférez Martínez Vaquer 1, Gènova. ℂ **97-140-42-81** or 97-140-26-40. www.sacaseta. com. Reservations recommended. Main courses 12€–30€; tasting menu 35€. AE, DC, MC, V. Mon–Thurs 1:30–4:30pm and 7:30pm–midnight; Fri–Sun 1:30pm–midnight. Closed Wed Oct–Feb.

Inexpensive

La Bóveda SPANISH Set in the oldest part of Palma, a few steps from the cathedral, this rustic-looking restaurant maintains a busy tapas bar near the entrance, and no more than 14 tables set near the bar or in the basement. The menu lists predictable Spanish staples, each well prepared, including roasted or fried veal, pork, chicken, and fish, served with fresh greens, potatoes, or rice. Any of the roster of tapas from the bar (fava beans with strips of ham, spinach tortillas, grilled or deep-fried calamari, and shrimp with garlic sauce) can be served while you're at your table, along with bottles of full-bodied red or more delicate white wines. A worthy and particularly refreshing dessert consists of freshly made sorbet, sometimes garnished with a shot of vodka or bourbon, depending on the flavor of the sorbet.

Calle Botería 3. ℂ **97-171-48-63.** www.restaurantelaboveda.com. Reservations recommended for a table in the restaurant, not necessary for the tapas bar. Main courses 14€–22€. AE, MC, V. Mon–Sat 1:30–4pm and 8:30pm–midnight. Closed Feb. Bus: 7 or 13.

Mesón Can Pedro MAJORCAN This restaurant has thrived since the early 1970s and is still going strong from a location in a hilltop suburb (Gènova) overlooking Palma. A completely unpretentious local favorite, it has a bustling, animated atmosphere enhanced by aromas wafting from kitchens known for succulent grilled lamb chops. Also worthwhile are tenderloin steaks, roasted pork, spicy kabobs, and different preparations of veal. One regional dish worth sampling is savory snails prepared with fennel and garlic and served with dollops of aioli.

Carrer Rector Vives 4 and 14, Gènova. ☎ **97-140-24-79.** www.mesoncanpedro.com. Reservations recommended. Main courses 15€–28€. AE, DC, MC, V. Tues–Sun 12:30–4:30pm and 7pm–midnight. Bus: 4.

PALMA AFTER DARK

Palma is packed with bars and dance clubs. Sure, there are some fun hangouts along the island's northern tier, but for a rocking laser- and strobe-lit club, you'll have to boogie in Palma.

Set directly on the beach, close to a dense concentration of hotels, **Tito's,** Passeig Marítim (☎ **97-173-00-17;** www.titosmallorca.com), charges a cover of 15€ to 18€, including the first drink. A truly international crowd mingles on a terrace overlooking the Mediterranean. This club is the most popular, panoramic, and appealing disco on Majorca. If you visit only one nightclub during your time on the island, this should be it. Between June and September, it's open every night of the week from 11pm to at least 6am. The rest of the year, it's open Thursday to Sunday 11pm to 6am.

On the side of a cliff fronting the bay, **Abraxas,** Passeig Marítim 42 (☎ **97-145-59-08**), is a cavelike club with a crowded dance floor. To escape head for the open-air terrace. The disco balls, the go-go dancers, and the strobes will transport you back to the '60s. Cover ranges from 12€ to 21€ and includes (depending on the night) one or two drinks. It's open daily 10pm to 6am.

Costa Galana, Av. Argentina 45 (☎ **97-145-46-58**), is an elegant bar with white leather chairs. Electric jazz and deep house music rule the night. It's a great place to chill out. Upstairs is a bustling cafe; the lounge downstairs pulsates at night. Open Monday to Thursday and Sunday 8am to 2am, Friday and Saturday 8am to 4am. Beer costs from 2.50€, mixed drinks from 5€.

SoHo Bar, Av. Argentina 5 (☎ 97-145-47-19), is an urban bar and a meeting place for indie-music lovers, some of whom spill out onto the terrace on a warm summer night. Its decor is retro—very '70s—with comfortable armchairs and sofas. Seating is divided so that the bar appears to be several different lounges. Beer costs from 2€, mixed drinks from 5€. Open daily 6:30pm to 2:30am.

ABACO, Carrer Sant Joan 1 (☎ **97-171-49-39**), just might be the most opulently decorated nightclub in Spain—a cross between a harem and a czarist Russian church. The bar is adorned with a trove of European decorative artworks. The place is always packed, with many customers congregating in a beautiful courtyard, which contains exotic caged birds, fountains, more sculpture than the eye can absorb, extravagant bouquets, and hundreds of flickering candles. All this exoticism is enhanced by the lushly romantic music (for example, we heard Ravel's *Boléro*) piped in through the sound system. Whether you view this as a bar, a museum, or a sociological survey, be sure to go. The bar is open Sunday to Thursday 8pm to 1am, Friday and Saturday 8pm to 3am, from February to December only. Wandering around is free; drinks cost 7€ to 13€.

Casino de Mallorca lies on the harborfront promenade at Av. Gabriel Roca 4 (☎ **97-113-00-00;** www.casinodemallorca.com). It's the place to go in search of Lady Luck. You'll need a passport—plus a shirt and tie for men—to enter, and you must pay a 4.50€ entrance charge. Inside, you can play American or French roulette, blackjack, or dice, or simply pull the lever on one of the many slot machines. The casino is open daily 4pm to 5am.

The best beer hall is **Lorien,** Carrer de les Caputxines 5 (✆ **97-172-32-02**), and its bartenders offer you some 100 types of beer from some two dozen countries, notably Belgium, Germany, Holland, and England. Ever had beer made from bananas?

Exploring Majorca by Car: The West Coast

Mountainous Majorca has the most dramatic scenery in the Balearics. It's best appreciated if you have your own car and can explore easily on your own. Below, we outline a good daylong outing of about 142km (88 miles) that begins and ends in Palma.

Leave Palma heading west on C-719, passing through some of the most beautiful scenery of Majorca. Just a short distance from the sea rises the Sierra de Tramontana. The road passes the heavy tourist development of Palma Nova before coming to **Santa Ponça,** a town with a fishing harbor divided by a promontory. A fortified Gothic tower and a watchtower are evidence of the days when this small harbor suffered repeated raids and attacks. It was in a cove here that Jaume I's troops landed on September 12, 1229, to begin the Reconquest of the island from the Muslims.

From Santa Ponça, continue along the highway, passing Paguera, Cala Fornells, and Camp de Mar, all beautiful spots with sandy coves. Between Camp de Mar and Port D'Andratx are corniche roads, a twisting journey to **Port D'Andratx.** Summer vacationers mingle with fishermen in this natural port, which is set against a backdrop of pines. The place was once a haven for smugglers.

Leaving the port, continue northeast along C-719 to reach **Andratx,** 5km (3 miles) away. Because of frequent raids by Turkish pirates, this town moved inland. Located 31km (19 miles) west of Palma, Andratx is one of the loveliest towns on the island, surrounded by fortifications and boasting a Gothic parish church and the mansion of Son Mas.

After leaving Andratx, take C-710 N, a winding road that runs parallel to the island's jagged northwestern coast. It's the highlight of the trip; most of the road is perched along the cliff edge and shaded by pine trees. It's hard to drive and pay attention to the scenery at the same time. Stop at the **Mirador Ricardo Roca** for a panoramic view of a series of coves. These coves can be reached only from the sea.

The road continues to **Estallenchs,** a town of steep slopes surrounded by pine groves, olive and almond trees, and fruit orchards (especially apricot). Estallenchs sits at the foot of the Galatzo mountain peak. Stop and explore some of its steep, winding streets on foot. From the town, you can walk to Cala de Estallenchs cove, where a spring cascades down the high cliffs.

The road winds on to **Bañalbufar,** 8km (5 miles) from Estallenchs and about 26km (16 miles) west from Palma—one of the most scenic spots on the island. Set 100m (328 ft.) above sea level, it seems to perch directly over the sea. **Mirador de Ses Animes ★**, a belvedere constructed in the 17th century, offers a panoramic view of the coastline.

Many small excursions are possible from here. You might want to venture over to **Port d'es Canonge,** reached by a road branching out from the C-710 to the north of Bañalbufar. It has a beach, a simple restaurant, and some old fishermen's houses. The same road takes you inland to **San Granja,** a mansion originally constructed by the Cistercians as a monastery in the 13th century.

Back on C-710, continue to **Valldemossa,** the town where the composer Frédéric Chopin and the French writer George Sand spent their now-famous winter. After a visit to the **Cartuja (Carthusian monastery)** where they lived, you can wander at leisure through the steep streets of the Old Town. The cloister of **Ses Murteres** provides a romantic garden. Note the pharmacy where Chopin, who was often ill during that winter, spent much time. The **Carthusian Church** is from the late 18th and early 19th centuries. Goya's father-in-law, Bayeu, painted the dome's frescoes.

Beyond Valldemossa, the road runs along cliffs some 395m (1,300 ft.) high until they reach **San Marroig,** the former residence of Archduke Lluis Salvador (see "Valldemossa & Deià [Deyá]," below), which is actually within the town limits of Deià. He erected a small neoclassical temple on a slope overlooking the sea to give visitors a panoramic vista. Son Marroig, his former mansion, has been turned into a museum. From an arcaded balcony, you can enjoy a view of the famous pierced rock, the Foradada, rising out of the water.

By now you have reached **Deià,** where small tile altars in the streets reproduce scenes from the Calvary. This was the home for many years of the English writer Robert Graves. He is buried at the **Campo Santo,** the cemetery, which you may want to visit for its panoramic view, if nothing else. Many other foreign painters, writers, and musicians have found inspiration in Deià, which is a virtual Garden of Eden.

Continue north along the highway. You come first to **Lluch Alcari,** which Archduke Salvador considered one of the most beautiful spots on earth. Picasso retreated here for a short period in the 1950s. The settlement was once the victim of pirate raids, and you can see the ruins of several defense towers.

C-710 continues to **Sóller,** just 10km (6¼ miles) from Deià. The urban center has five 16th-century facades, an 18th-century convent, and a parish church of the 16th and 17th centuries. It lies in a broad basin where citrus and olive trees are abundant. Many painters, including Rusiñol, settled here and found inspiration.

Travel 5km (3 miles) north on C-711 to reach the coast and **Port de Sóller,** one of the best natural shelters along the island. It lies at the back of a bay that is almost round. A submarine base is here today, but it is also a harbor for pleasure craft. It has a lovely beach. The **Sanctuary of Santa Catalina** dominates one of the best views of the inlet.

After leaving the Sóller area, you face a choice: If you've run out of time, you can cut the tour in half here and head back along C-711 to Palma with two stops along the way. Your other option is to continue north, following the C-710 and local roads, to **Cape Formentor,** where even more spectacular scenery awaits you. Among the highlights of this coastal detour: **Fornalutx,** a lofty

---

Take the Train

If you're not driving, you can still reach Sóller aboard a turn-of-the-20th-century narrow-gauge railroad train from Palma. You can catch the train at the Palma Terminal on Calle Eusebio Estada, near Plaça d'Espanya. It runs daily at 8, 10:50, 11:50am, 12:15, 1:30, 3:10, and 7:30pm; the fare is 17€ one-way. Call ✆ **97-175-20-51** for information.

mountain village with steep cobbled streets, Moorish-tiled roofs, and groves of almond trees; the splendid, hair-raising road to the harbor village of **Sa Calobra,** plunging to the sea in one area and then climbing arduously past olive groves, oaks, and jagged boulders in another area; and the 13th-century **Monasterio de Lluch,** some 45km (28 miles) north of Palma, which is home to the Black Virgin of Lluch, the island's patron saint. The well-known "boys' choir of white voices" sings there daily at noon and again at twilight.

Those not taking the coastal detour can head south along C-711 with a stop at **Jardins d'Alfàbia** (© 97-161-31-23; www.jardinesdealfabia.com), Carretera Palma–Sóller Km 17, a former Muslim residence. This estate in the sierra foothills includes a palace and romantic gardens. In the richly planted gardens, you can wander among pergolas, a pavilion, and ponds. Inside the palace you can see a good collection of Majorcan furniture and an Arabic coffered ceiling. The gardens are open April to October Monday to Saturday 9:30am to 6:30pm; and November to March Monday to Friday 9:30am to 5:30pm, and Saturday 9:30am to 1pm. Admission is 5€.

From Alfàbia, the highway becomes straight and Palma is just 18km (11 miles) away. But before reaching the capital, consider a final stop at **Raixa,** another charming place, built on the site of an old Muslim hamlet. It stands 1.5km (1 mile) outside the village of Buñola ("Small Vineyard"). The present building was once the estate of Cardinal Despuif and his family, who constructed it in the Italian style near the end of the 1700s. Ruins from Roman excavations are found on the grounds. Rusiñol came here, painting the place several times. Raixa keeps the same hours as Jardins d'Alfàbia (see above).

After Raixa, the route leads directly to the northern outskirts of Palma.

Valldemossa & Deià ★★

Valldemossa is the site of the **Cartoixa Reial ★**, Plaça de las Cartujas s/n (© 97-161-21-06), where George Sand and the tubercular Frédéric Chopin wintered in 1838 and 1839. The monastery was founded in the 14th century, but the present buildings are from the 17th and 18th centuries. After monks abandoned the dwelling, the cells were rented to guests, which led to the appearance of Sand and Chopin, who managed to shock the conservative locals. They occupied cells 2 and 4. The only belongings left are a small painting and a French piano. The peasants, fearing they'd catch Chopin's tuberculosis, burned most of the rest after the couple returned to the mainland. The cells may be visited November to February, Monday to Saturday 9:30am to 4:30pm, Sunday 10am to 1:30pm; and March to October, Monday to Saturday 9:30am to 6pm. Admission is 7.50€ adults, free for children 9 and under.

It's also possible to visit **Palau del Rei Sancho,** next door to the monastery, on the same ticket. This is a Moorish retreat built by one of the island kings. You'll be given a guided tour of the palace by a woman in Majorcan dress.

From Valldemossa, continue through the mountains, following the signposts for 11km (6¾ miles) to Deià. Before the village, consider a stopover at **Son Marroig** (© 97-163-91-58; www.sonmarroig.com), at Km 26 on the highway. Now a museum, this was once the estate of Archduke Luis Salvador. Born in 1847, the archduke fled court life and found refuge here with his young bride in 1870. A tower on the estate is from the 1500s. Many of the archduke's personal furnishings and mementos, such as photographs and his ceramic collection, are still here. The estate is surrounded by lovely gardens, and the property has many panoramic views. It is open Monday to Saturday 9:30am to 6:30pm (to 5:30pm in winter). Admission is 3€.

Set against a backdrop of olive green mountains, **Deià (Deyá)** is peaceful and serene, with its stone houses and creeping bougainvillea. It has long had a special meaning for artists. Robert Graves, the English poet and novelist (*I, Claudius* and *Claudius the God*), lived in Deià, and died here in 1985. He is buried in the local cemetery.

It is now possible to visit Graves's home, where he once entertained such notables as Ava Gardner, Alec Guinness, and Peter Ustinov. **Ca N'Alluny ★**, Carretera de Soller Km 1 (© **97-163-61-85**), lies a 5-minute walk from the center of the town. Graves and his then companion, Laura Riding, built the house in 1932. The poet wrote: "I wanted to go where town was still town; and country, country."

Tomás Graves, the poet's son, told the press: "My father's legacy can be seen as something besides a tombstone." The house has been restored the way it was when Graves returned to the island in 1946, containing the original furnishings, even the electrical fittings. Visitors can explore the studies of both Laura and Robert Graves, as well as visit the kitchen and dining room.

Valldemossa lacks basic services, including a tourist office. It is connected to a bus service from Palma, however. **Bus Nord Balear** (© **97-149-06-80**) goes to Valldemossa 13 times daily for a one-way fare of 5€. Buses leave Palma at Plaza España (Calle Eusebio Estrada). To reach Deià by public transportation from Palma, 27km (17 miles) away, just stay on the bus that stops in Valldemossa. If you're driving from Palma, take the Carretera Valldemossa–Deià to Valldemossa; from there, you can continue to Deià. Those with cars might want to consider one of the idyllic accommodations offered in this little Majorcan village.

A courtyard of the Cartoixa Reial.

A winding road in Deià.

WHERE TO STAY

Deià offers some of the most tranquil and stunning retreats on Majorca—La Residencia and Es Molí—but it has a number of more affordable little boardinghouses as well.

Cases de Ca's Garriguer ★ 🎒 Set amid 101 hectares (250 acres) of olive groves, this restored manor appears as it was in the early 1800s, although it's been completely modernized. Originally, it was an old *finca* (farmhouse) lying on the outskirts of Valldemossa. Today, it's been turned into a miniresort with a swimming pool and a solarium (even parasols and deck chairs are set out for you). The guest rooms are individually decorated, spacious, and well furnished, some with a small sitting area. Modern art graces the otherwise old-fashioned setting of exposed wooden beams and heavy oak furnishings. Seven of the rooms open onto private terraces. ℂ **97-161-23-00.** Fax

Carretera Valldemossa a Andratx Km 2.5, 07170 Valldemossa, Majorca. ℂ **97-161-23-00.** Fax 97-161-25-83. www.vistamarhotel.es. 10 units. 120€–175€ double. Rates include continental breakfast. AE, V. Free parking. Closed Nov–Feb. **Amenities:** Restaurant; bar; babysitting; outdoor pool; room service; sauna. *In room:* A/C, TV, hair dryer, minibar.

Hotel Costa d'Or ★ ☺ This former villa, 1.5km (1 mile) north of Deià on the road to Sóller, offers the best possible view of the vine-covered hills and the rugged coast beyond. Surrounded by private gardens filled with fig trees, date palms, and orange groves, this hotel was upgraded to government-rated four-star status. Both its public areas and its private guest rooms have been totally refurbished and equipped with modern amenities such as air-conditioning. It doesn't have the charm of Es Molí or La Residencia (see below), but it is nonetheless inviting. The most desirable guest rooms open onto panoramic views of the area.

Lluch Alcari s/n, 07179 Deià, Majorca. ℂ **97-163-90-25.** Fax 97-163-93-47. www.hoposa.es. 41 units. 134€–255€ double; 223€–275€ suite. Rates include buffet breakfast. MC, V. Free parking. Closed Oct 26–Mar 13. **Amenities:** Restaurant; bar; babysitting; bikes; exercise room; 2 freshwater pools (1 heated indoor); room service; 2 outdoor tennis courts (lit). *In room:* A/C, TV, minibar.

Hotel Es Molí ★★ One of the best-recommended and most spectacular hotels on Majorca originated in the 1880s as a severely dignified manor house in the rocky highlands above Deià, home of the landowners who controlled access to the town's freshwater springs. In 1966 the manor house was augmented by two annexes, transforming it into this luxurious four-star hotel. Guest rooms are beautifully furnished and impeccably maintained, often with access to a private veranda overlooking the gardens or the faraway village. Some hardy souls make it a point to hike for 30 minutes to the public beach at Deià Bay; others wait for the shuttle bus to take them to the hotel's private beach, 6km (3¾ miles) away.

Carretera Valldemossa s/n, 07179 Deià, Majorca. ✆ **97-163-90-00.** Fax 97-163-93-33. www. esmoli.com. 87 units. 218€–294€ double; 340€–374€ junior suite; 407€–452€ suite. Rates include buffet breakfast; half-board 23€ extra per person per day. AE, DC, MC, V. Free parking. Closed Nov–Apr. **Amenities:** Restaurant; bar; airport transfers (56€); babysitting; exercise room; outdoor freshwater heated pool; room service; outdoor tennis court (lit). *In room:* A/C, TV/DVD, hair dryer, minibar; Wi-Fi (30€ per 24 hr.).

La Residencia ★★★ This is the most stylish, hip, elegant hotel on Majorca, a renowned hostelry that became even more famous in the early 1990s when it was acquired by British businessman and founder of Virgin Airlines, Richard Branson. This star-caliber secluded haunt describes itself as "your revenge on everyday life." The ambience is luxurious but unpretentious at these two tawny, 16th-century stone manor houses surrounded by 5.3 hectares (13 acres) of rocky Mediterranean gardens. Spacious guest rooms are outfitted with rustic antiques, terra-cotta floors, four-poster beds, and, in some cases, beamed ceilings, all with luxurious appointments. Open hearths, deep leather sofas, wrought-iron candelabra, and a supremely accommodating staff greet you.

Camino Son Canals s/n, 07179 Deià, Majorca. ✆ **97-163-90-11.** Fax 97-163-90-70. www.hotel-laresidencia.com. 59 units. 580€–750€ double; 925€ junior suite; 1,250€ suite; 1,425€–3,050€ suite with private pool. Rates include buffet breakfast. AE, DC, MC, V. Free parking. **Amenities:** 2 restaurants; 2 bars; babysitting; exercise room; 3 freshwater pools (1 heated indoor); room service; spa; 2 outdoor tennis courts (lit). *In room:* A/C, TV/DVD, hair dryer, Wi-Fi (free).

Valldemossa Hotel ★ 📠 The owners rightly claim they are not hoteliers but hosts welcoming you into their private home, which was once part of the local Carthusian monastery. The 19th-century stone-built house on a hill has been sensitively restored and turned into this idyllic retreat set in acres of olive and orange trees, and opening onto Palma Bay. Bedrooms have been modernized with just enough antique touches to give them charm. Guests meet fellow guests in the courtyard shaded by swaying palms, and later they dine in a well-run restaurant, serving excellent Mediterranean dishes.

Carretera Valldemossa s/n, 17170 Valldemossa, Majorca. ✆ **97-161-26-26.** Fax 97-161-26-25. www.valldemossahotel.com. 12 units. 303€–345€ double; 386€–450€ suite. Rates include buffet breakfast. AE, MC, V. Free parking. **Amenities:** Restaurant; bar; babysitting; 2 freshwater pools (1 heated indoor); spa. *In room:* A/C, TV/DVD, minibar, Wi-Fi (free).

WHERE TO DINE IN VALLDEMOSSA

Ca'n Costa MAJORCAN/INTERNATIONAL This restaurant specializes in Majorcan cuisine but includes some international dishes to please the mostly foreign patronage. The owner has selected only the finest of wines from the island itself, which he has wisely combined with some good vintages from Rioja. The hearty regional fare includes roast pork loin with mushrooms from the fields, and even thrush enveloped in cabbage. Try for a seat on the outdoor patio, which offers a panoramic vista of the coast.

Carretera Valldemossa–Deià Km 2.5. ✆ **97-161-22-63.** www.cancostavalldemossa.com. Reservations recommended. Main courses 11€–26€. AE, DC, MC, V. Wed–Mon 12:30–4pm and 7:30–11pm.

Ca'n Quet ★ INTERNATIONAL This restaurant, belonging to the Hotel Es Molí (p. 729), is one of the most sought-after dining spots on the island. Set on a series of terraces above a winding road leading out of town, the building is modern and stylish, with an undeniably romantic air. Cascades of pink geraniums adorn its terraces, and if you wander along the sloping pathways you'll find groves of orange and lemon trees, roses, and a swimming pool ringed with neoclassical balustrades.

There's a spacious and sunny bar, an elegant indoor dining room with a blazing fire in winter, and alfresco dining on the upper terrace under an arbor. The food is well prepared, and the portions are generous. Meals can include a salad of marinated fish, terrine of fresh vegetables, fish crepes, shellfish stew, duck with sherry sauce, and an ever-changing selection of fresh fish.

Carretera Valldemossa–Sóller. © **97-163-91-96.** Reservations required. Main courses 20€–40€. AE, MC, V. Tues–Sun 1–4pm and 7:30–11pm. Closed Nov–Apr.

WHERE TO DINE IN DEIÀ

El Olivo ★★ INTERNATIONAL/MEDITERRANEAN This is one of the island's most elegant and upscale restaurants. It's set within what was built several centuries ago as an olive press, a thick-walled outbuilding of La Residencia Hotel (p. 730). Much of the illumination comes from theatrical-looking candelabra placed on every table, whose flickering light throws shadows against thick ceiling beams, antique accessories, and very formal table settings. The cuisine is modern and subtly flavored. The chefs know how to take classic dishes and add inventive touches. Some tempting starters include tuna fish in a sesame oil served with a gazpacho sorbet, and a fish-and-seafood broth swimming with ravioli under a lemon foam. Main-dish delights might include market-fresh fish seasoned with herbs and served with candied garlic, and breast of duckling poached in *cueva* and served with fresh figs and a fig mustard.

In La Residencia Hotel, San Canals. © **97-163-93-92.** Reservations recommended. Main courses 36€–42€; fixed-price menu 95€; 6-course vegetarian menu 74€. AE, DC, MC, V. Summer daily 1–3pm and 8–11pm; winter daily 1–3pm and 7:30–9:30pm.

Es Racó d'es Teix ★★★ MEDITERRANEAN Though chef Josef Sauerschell is a celebrity favorite, mere mortals will also appreciate his sublime dishes that are classic Mediterranean fare modernized with lighter textures and less fat. He's avid about using only the freshest market ingredients. All his dishes reflect his culinary imagination, beginning with his carpaccio of tuna with sesame, honey, coriander, and mango, or his parfait of foie gras with apricots, brioche, and mange-tout. Sauerschell's luminous cooking is also reflected in his main dishes, especially his fresh Mediterranean fish soup or his John Dory with a ragout of squid and sautéed vegetables. The special of specials is Majorcan suckling pig with foie gras served with cabbage and truffle sauce.

Calle de sa Vinya Veia 6. © **97-163-95-01.** www.esracodesteix.es. Reservations required. Main courses 28€–38€. Tasting menu without wine 95€, tasting menu with wine 160€. MC, V. Wed–Sun 1–3pm and 8–11pm. Closed mid-Nov to late Jan.

Inca

About 27km (17 miles) north of Palma is Inca, the island's second-largest city and Majorca's market and agricultural center.

Thursday is market day for farming equipment and livestock, but visitors will be more interested in the variety of low-priced leather goods—shoes, purses, jackets, and coats—sold here. In general, stores in Inca selling these leather goods are open Monday to Friday 9:30am to 7pm and Saturday 9:30am to noon.

Modernization has deprived Inca of its original charm, but the parish church of Santa María la Mayor and the convent of San Jerónimo hold some interest, as does the original Son Fuster Inn, a reminder of an earlier, simpler era. From Palma, **trains** (© 97-150-00-59) run Monday to Friday at the rate of 40 per day and 36 on Saturday and Sunday. Trip time is only 40 minutes. A one-way ticket costs 5€. Inca lies on C-713, the road leading to the Pollença-Formentor region.

WHERE TO DINE

Cellar Ca'n Amer ★ 💼 MAJORCAN If you can stay in Inca for lunch or dinner, we recommend this charming spot. In a building dating from 1850, you'll find the most authentic *cueva* (cave) dining on the island. A container of local wine, which everyone here seems to drink, is tapped from one of the dozens of casks that line the stone walls of the vaults. The interconnected dining rooms are furnished with wooden tables and rustic artifacts. A polite staff serves large portions of Majorcan specialties, including shoulder of lamb stuffed with eggplant and regional sausage, thrush wrapped in cabbage leaves, and the chef's version of roast suckling pig with a bitter but tasty sauce. There is an array of fresh seafood and fish.

Carrer Pau 39. © **97-150-12-61.** Main courses 12€–23€; set menu without wine 24€. AE, MC, V. May–Sept Mon–Fri 1–4pm and 7:30pm–midnight; Oct–Apr daily 1–4pm and Mon–Sat 7:30pm–midnight.

Lloseta

Away from the madding crowds (but also from the beaches), the hamlet of Lloseta nestles in the north-central Raiguer region, close to the city of Inca and 31km (19 miles) northeast of Palma, at the foot of the Serra de Tramuntana mountain range. This is one of the most beautiful regions in the land, a sector known for its handicrafts, pottery, wine, and glassmaking.

WHERE TO STAY

Ca's Comte ★ 💼 This *casa sensorial* (nobleman's house) dates from the 18th century and has been beautifully preserved and restored. It's like a journey back into the past, although the building is completely up-to-date. Take the lounge, for example. In the off season, its traditional wood-burning fireplace is ablaze. In contrast, in summer you can enjoy refreshing mountain breezes. Each of the guest rooms—half doubles, half suites—is individually decorated and cozily furnished with taste and your comfort in mind. Decorated in traditional Majorcan style, the dining room is warm and welcoming; it's complemented by an outdoor terrace and an inner courtyard.

Comte d'Aiamans 11, 07360 Lloseta, Majorca. © **97-187-30-77.** Fax 97-151-91-92. www.petit hotelcascomte.com. 8 units. 139€ double; 171€ suite. Rates include buffet breakfast. AE, DC, MC, V. No parking. **Amenities:** Restaurant; bar; babysitting; concierge; room service; spa. *In room:* A/C, TV, hair dryer, minibar.

Port de Pollença/Formentor

Beside a sheltered bay and between Cape Formentor to the north and Cape del Pinar to the south lies Port de Pollença, 65km (40 miles) north of Palma. The town is between two hills: **Calvary** to the west and **Puig** to the east. Calvary Chapel offers the best views of the resort and the bay, which provides excellent water-skiing and sailing.

The view from the Cabo de Formentor.

Low-rise hotels, private homes, restaurants, and snack bars line the very attractive beach, which is somewhat narrow at its northwestern end but has some of the island's finest, whitest sand and warmest, clearest water. For several miles along the bay there is a pleasant pedestrian promenade. There is only one luxury hotel in the area, however, out on the Formentor Peninsula.

Tons of fine white sand were imported to the beach at the southeastern end of Pollença Bay to create a broad ribbon of sunbathing space that stretches for several miles along the bay. Windsurfing, water-skiing, and scuba diving are among the watersports offered in the area.

Cabo de Formentor ★, "the devil's tail," can be reached from Port de Pollença via a spectacular road, twisting along to the lighthouse at the cape's end. Formentor is Majorca's fjord country—a dramatic landscape of mountains, pine trees, rocks, and sea, plus some of the best beaches in Majorca. In Cape Formentor, you'll see *miradores*, or lookout windows, which provide panoramic views.

ESSENTIALS

GETTING THERE Five **buses** a day leave the Plaça Espanya in Palma, pass through Inca, and continue on to Port de Pollença; a one-way fare costs 7€. If you're driving, you can continue on from Deià (see earlier) along C-710, or from Inca on C-713, all the way to Pollença.

VISITOR INFORMATION The **tourist information office,** on Passeig de Saralegui s/n (© **97-186-54-67**), is open Monday to Saturday 8am to 3pm and 5 to 7pm.

EXPLORING THE COAST

The plunging cliffs and rocky coves of Majorca's northwestern coast are a stunning prelude to Port de Pollença. The **Mirador de Colomer** provides an expansive view of the striking California-like coast that stretches from Punta de la Nau to Punta de la Troneta and includes El Colomer (Pigeon's Rock), named for the nests in its cave.

But it is the 20km (12-mile) stretch of winding, at times vertiginous road leading from Port de Pollença to the tip of the **Formentor Peninsula** that delivers the island's most intoxicating scenic views. Cliffs more than 200m (656 ft.) high and spectacular rock-rimmed coves embrace intense turquoise waters. About halfway along this road is **Cala de Pi de la Posada,** where you will find a lovely bathing beach. Continuing on to the end, you'll come to the lighthouse at **Cabo de Formentor.**

Wednesday is **market day** in Port de Pollença, so head for the town square (there's only one) between 8am and 1pm and browse through the fresh produce, leather goods, embroidered tablecloths, ceramics, and more. Bargaining is part of the fun. Sunday is market day in the town of Pollença.

Alcúdia Bay is a long stretch of narrow, sandy beach with beautiful water backed by countless hotels, whose crowds rather overwhelm the area in peak season. The nightlife is more abundant and varied here than in Port de Pollença.

Between Port de Alcúdia and Ca'n Picafort is the **Parc Natural de S'Albufera,** Carretera Alcúdia–Artá Km 27, 07458 C'an Picafort (© **97-189-22-50**). A wetlands area of lagoons, dunes, and canals covering some 800 hectares (1,977 acres), it attracts bird-watchers and other nature enthusiasts. To date, more than 200 species of birds have been sighted here, among them herons, owls, ospreys, and warblers. The best times to visit are spring and fall, when migratory birds abound. Spring, too, offers a marvelous display of flora. The park is open daily (except Christmas) October to March from 9am to 5pm and April to September from 9am to 7pm. Visits are free, but you must get a permit at the reception center, where all motorized vehicles must be left. Binoculars are available for rent. The reception center has further information.

In the town of Pollença, about 6km (3¾ miles) from Port Pollença, is an 18th-century stairway leading up to an *ermita* (hermitage). Consisting of 365 stairs, it is known as the **Monte Calvario (Calvary),** but you can also reach the top by car via Carrer de las Cruces, which is lined with 3m-high (9¾-ft.) concrete crosses.

The marshes of the Parc Natural de S'Albufera.

Cala San Vicente, between Pollença and Port de Pollença, is a pleasant, small, sandy cove with some notable surf. Several small hotels and restaurants provide the necessary amenities.

Various companies offer tours of Pollença Bay, and many provide glass-bottom boats for viewing the varied aquatic creatures and plants. Many of these boats leave from Port de Pollença's Estació Marítim several times daily during the summer months, with less frequent departures in winter. Your hotel concierge or the marina can provide you with a schedule.

WHERE TO STAY IN PORT DE POLLENÇA & FORMENTOR

Barceló Formentor ★★★ In Formentor, on the northern tier of the island, this cliffside hotel is one of the most famous in the Balearic Islands, having hosted everyone from Sir Winston Churchill to Charlie Chaplin. The building is long and spread out, but it blends well with its garden landscaping. It lies next to one of the island's best beaches. The hotel is a year-round destination, unlike many other island resorts that close in winter. Its chefs deserve high praise for their combination of international and Mediterranean cuisine. The hotel opened in 1929 (in time to face a worldwide depression). Guest rooms are beautifully styled, comfortably furnished, and well maintained, coming in a variety of sizes and shapes.

Playa Formento, 07470 Port de Pollença, Majorca. ☏ **97-189-91-00.** Fax 97-186-51-55. www.barceloformentor.com. 125 units. 206€–478€ double; 528€–740€ junior suite. Rates include buffet breakfast. AE, DC, MC, V. Free parking. **Amenities:** 3 restaurants; 3 bars; bikes; children's center; exercise room; 2 outdoor pools; room service; sauna; 4 tennis courts (lit). *In room:* A/C, TV, hair dryer, minibar, Wi-Fi (free).

Hotel Illa d'Or ★ Originally built in 1929, and enlarged and improved several times since then, this four-story hotel sits at the relatively isolated northwestern edge of Pollença Bay—far from the heavily congested, touristed region around Palma. Decorated in a mixture of colonial Spanish and English reproductions, it offers a seafront terrace with a view of the mountains and airy, simply furnished spaces. Guest rooms are midsize to spacious, each with comfortable furnishings, including good beds and modern bathrooms. The beach is just a few steps away.

Passeig Colón 265, 07470 Port de Pollença, Majorca. ☏ **97-186-51-00.** Fax 97-186-42-13. www.hotelillador.com. 120 units. 110€–236€ double; 310€–500€ suite. Rates include buffet breakfast. DC, MC, V. Free parking. Closed Dec–Jan 9. **Amenities:** Restaurant; 2 bars; bikes; exercise room; Jacuzzi; 2 pools (1 heated indoor); room service; sauna; outdoor tennis court. *In room:* A/C, TV, hair dryer, minibar, Wi-Fi (free).

Hotel Miramar 🏊 Dating from 1912, this centrally located hotel is one of Port de Pollença's grand old-fashioned hostelries, in a desirable position across the coastal road from the beach. It has ornate front columns supporting a formal balustrade, tiled eaves, and several jardinieres. The lobby is furnished with antiques. Some rooms have private verandas overlooking the flower-filled courtyard in back. All the small-to-midsize guest rooms are comfortably furnished and well maintained.

Passeig Anglada Camarasa 39, 07470 Port de Pollença, Majorca. ☏ **97-186-64-00.** Fax 97-186-40-75. www.hotel-miramar.net. 84 units. 90€–154€ double. Rates include buffet breakfast. AE, DC, MC, V. No parking. Closed Nov–Mar. **Amenities:** Restaurant; babysitting; room service. *In room:* A/C, TV, hair dryer.

Hotel Pollentia ★ This hotel is .8km (½ mile) from the commercial center of the resort, behind a screen of foliage. It's our favorite hotel in Port de Pollença because of its cool, airy spaciousness and genial reception. The steps leading to the formal modern lobby are banked with dozens of terra-cotta pots overflowing with ivy and geraniums. The reception area has Majorcan glass chandeliers. Many of the well-furnished but small rooms have private terraces. Guests have access to a private terrace overlooking the Mediterranean.

Passeig de Londres s/n, 07470 Port de Pollença, Majorca. ✆ **97-186-52-00.** Fax 97-186-60-34. www.hoposa.es/pagingles/hpollentiai.htm. 70 units. 78€–116€ double. Rates include buffet breakfast. AE, DC, MC, V. No parking. Closed Nov–Apr. **Amenities:** Bar. *In room:* A/C, hair dryer.

Son Brull ★★★ 🎁 Barcelona architect Nacho Forteza took a decaying 18th-century monastery and turned it into one of the most charming 21st-century inns in Majorca, going, in the owner's words, from "abstinence to abundance." Urban chic has been combined with a Mediterranean lifestyle in this government-rated five-star hotel in the north of Majorca. The location is a 10-minute drive from some beautiful sandy coves idyllic for swimming. The public rooms combine modern decorations with century-old walls, with everything focused on the old mansion's beautiful inner courtyard. The spacious guest rooms are one of a kind, with contemporary technology and modern, comfortable furniture.

Carretera Palma-Pollença, 07460 Port de Pollença, Majorca. ✆ **97-153-53-53.** Fax 97-153-10-68. www.sonbrull.com. 23 units. 262€–744€ double; 423€–840€ junior suite. Rates include buffet breakfast. AE, DC, MC, V. Free parking. Closed Dec–Jan. **Amenities:** Restaurant; bar; babysitting; exercise room; 2 freshwater heated pools (1 indoor); room service; spa. *In room:* A/C, TV/DVD, CD player, hair dryer, Wi-Fi (free).

WHERE TO DINE IN PORT DE POLLENÇA

Stay Restaurant ★ SPANISH/INTERNATIONAL This restaurant offers a unique menu that changes about every 2 months, depending on what's available at the market. The superb cuisine respects tradition, and many classic dishes are served, including sea bream filet grilled or served with a white-wine sauce; or grilled salmon prepared and served the same way. A more exotic specialty is roasted veal kidneys with garlic and sherry sauce, with another option being sliced chicken breast in puff pastry with a cream sauce laced with fresh mushrooms.

Muelle Nuevo, Estació Marítim s/n. ✆ **97-186-40-13.** www.stayrestaurant.com. Reservations recommended July–Aug. Main courses 13€–38€; *menú del día* 32€. AE, MC, V. Daily noon–4pm and 7:30–10:30pm.

Majorca's East Coast: The Cava Route

The east coast of Majorca is often called the cava route because of the caves that stud the coastline. Although there are scores, we include only the most important ones. In general, Majorca's east coast does not have the dramatic scenery of its west coast, but it has worthy attractions in its own right.

Leave Palma on the freeway, but turn onto Carretera C-715 in the direction of Manacor. About 56km (35 miles) east of Palma, you come to your first stop, Petra.

PETRA

Petra was founded by Jaume II over the ruins of a Roman settlement. This was the birthplace of Father Junípero Serra (1713–84), the Franciscan priest who founded the missions in California that eventually grew into San Diego,

Monterey, and San Francisco. A statue commemorates him at the Capitol building in Washington, D.C., and you will also see a statue of Father Serra in this, his native village.

Museo Beato Junípero Serra, Carrer Barracar (𝄢 **97-156-11-49**), gives you an idea of how people lived on the island in the 18th century. The property was bought and fixed up by the Rotary Club of San Francisco, which then presented it as a gift to the citizens of Petra in 1972. The museum, 457m (1,500 ft.) from the center of the village, is open every day of the year but doesn't keep regular hours. Visits are by appointment only. Call at least 1 day in advance. Admission is free, but donations are encouraged.

CUEVAS DEL DRACH ★★★

After Petra, follow C715 southeast into Manacor, and from there take the road east toward the sea and the town of **Porto Cristo,** 61km (38 miles) east of Palma. Go .8km (½ mile) south of town to **Cuevas del Drach (Caves of the Dragon;** 𝄢 **97-182-07-53;** www.cuevasdeldrach.com). The caves contain an underground forest of stalactites and stalagmites, as well as five subterranean lakes, where you can listen to a concert and later go boating a la Jules Verne. The roof appears to glitter with endless icicles. Martel Lake, 176m (577 ft.) long, is the largest underground lake in the world. E. A. Martel, a French speleologist who charted the then-mysterious caves in 1896, described them better than anyone: "As far as the eye can see, marble cascades, organ pipes, lace draperies, pendants or brilliants, hang suspended from the walls and roof." From April to October, tours depart daily every hour from 10am to 5pm; from November to March, they depart daily at 10:45am, noon, 2, and 3:30pm. Admission is 11€.

If you don't have a car, you can take one of the four daily buses that leave from the railroad station in Palma. (Inquire at the tourist bureau in Palma for departure times.) The buses pass through Manacor on the way to Porto Cristo.

CUEVAS DEL HAM

Discovered in 1906, these caves, whose name means "fish hooks," are .8km (½ mile) from Porto Cristo on the road to Manacor. **Cuevas del Ham** (𝄢 **97-182-09-88**) are far less impressive than Cuevas del Drach and can be skipped if you're rushed. Tours depart every 10 minutes daily April to October 10am to 6pm, and November to March daily 10:30am to 5pm. Admission is 11€ for adults, free for children 11 and under. These caves contain white stalactites and follow the course of an underground river. The river links to the sea, so the water level inside the cave's pools rises and falls according to the tides.

CUEVAS DE ARTÀ ★★★

Near Platja de Canyamel (Playa de Cañamel, on some maps), **Cuevas de Artà** (𝄢 **97-184-12-93;** www.cuevasdearta.com) occupy a stretch of land closing Canyamel Bay to the north. These caves are said to be the inspiration for the Jules Verne tale *Journey to the Center of the Earth,* published in 1864. (Verne may have heard or read about the caves; it is not known if he ever actually visited them.) Formed by seawater erosion, the caves are about 32m (105 ft.) above sea level, and some of the chambers rise about 46m (151 ft.).

You enter an impressive vestibule and immediately see walls blackened by the torches used to light the caves for early tourists in the 1800s. The Reina de las Columnas (Queen of the Columns) rises about 22m (72 ft.) and is followed by a lower room whose Dante-esque appearance has led to it being called

Stalactites in the Cuevas del Drach.

"Inferno." It is followed by a field of stalagmites and stalactites (the "Purgatory Rooms"), which eventually lead to the "Theater" and "Paradise."

The caves were once used by pirates, and centuries ago they provided a haven for Spanish Moors fleeing the persecution of Jaume I. The stairs in the cave were built for Isabella II for her 1860 visit. In time, such luminaries as Sarah Bernhardt, Alexandre Dumas, and Victor Hugo arrived for the tour. Tours depart daily May to October, every half-hour from 10am to 6pm, off season 10am to 5pm. Admission is 10€.

IBIZA ★

Ibiza (Ee-*bee*-thah) was once a virtually unknown and unvisited island; Majorca, its bigger neighbor, got all the business. But in the 1950s, Ibiza's art colony began to thrive, and in the 1960s it became the European resort most favored by the flower children. A New York art student once wrote, "Even those who come to Ibiza for the 'wrong' reason (to work!) eventually are seduced by the island's easy life. Little chores like picking up the mail from the post office stretch into daylong missions." Today, Ibiza is overrun by middle-class package-tour visitors, mainly from England, France, Germany, and Scandinavia. It has become a major mecca for gay travelers as well, making Ibiza a wild combination of chic and middle-class.

At 585 sq. km (226 sq. miles), it is the third largest of the Balearic Islands. Physically, Ibiza has a jagged coastline, some fine beaches, whitewashed houses, secluded bays, cliffs, and hilly terrain dotted with fig and olive trees. Warmer than Majorca, it's a better choice for a winter vacation, but it can be sweltering in July and August. Thousands of tourists descend on the island in summer, greatly taxing the island's limited water supply.

Ciudad de Ibiza boasts Playa Talamanca in the north and Ses Figueretes and Playa d'en Bossa in the south, two outstanding white sandy beaches. Las Salinas, in the south, near the old salt flats, offers excellent sands. Playa Cavallet and Aigües Blanques attract the nude sunbathers. Other good beaches include Cala Bassa, Port des Torrent, Cala Tarida, and Cala Conta—all within a short bus or boat ride from San Antonio de Portmany. The long sandy cove of Cala Llonga, south of Santa Eulalia del Río, and the white sandy beach of El Cana to

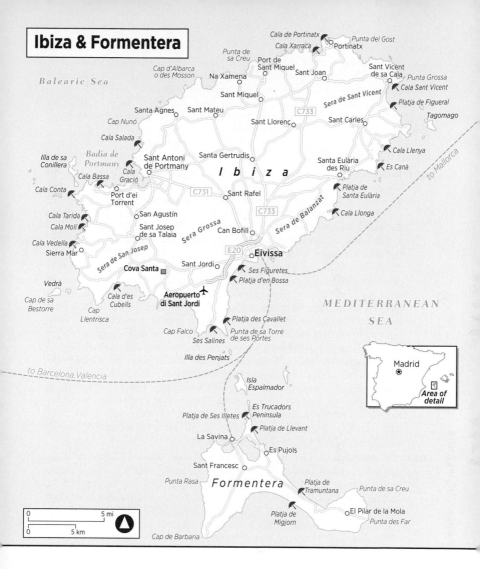

Ibiza & Formentera

Balearic Sea

Cap d'Albarca
o des Mosson

Punta de
sa Creu

Cala de Portinatx
Cala Xarraca
Portinatx
Punta del Gost

Port de
Sant Miquel
Sant Joan

Na Xamena

Sant Miquel

Sant Vicent
de sa Cala
Punta Grossa
Cala Sant Vicent

Sera de Sant Vicent

Platja de Figueral

Tagomago

Santa Agnes
Sant Mateu

Cap Nunó

Sant Llorenç

Sant Carles

Cala Salada

Illa de sa
Conillera

*Badia de
Portmany*

Sant Antoni
de Portmany

Santa Gertrudis

I b i z a

Santa Eulària
des Riu

Cala Llenya

Es Canà

Cala
Bassa

Cala
Gració

Cala Conta

Port d'ei
Torrent

Sant Rafel

C731

Platja de
Santa Eulària

Cala Tarida

Cala Moli

San Agustín

Sant Josep
de sa Talaia

C733

Sera Grossa

Can Bofill

Sera de Balanzat

Cala Llonga

Cala Vedella

Sierra Mar

Sera de San Josep

Sant Jordi

E20

Eivissa

Cova Santa

Vedrà

Cap de sa
Bestorre

Cala d'es
Cubells

**Aeropuerto
di Sant Jordi**

Ses Figuretes
Platja d'en Bossa

*MEDITERRANEAN
SEA*

Cap
Llentrisca

Cap Falco

Platja des Cavallet

Punta de sa Torre
de ses Pòrtes

Ses Salines

Illa des Penjats

to Barcelona, Valencia

Isla
Espalmador

Madrid

**Area of
detail**

Es Trucadors
Peninsula

Platja de Ses Illetes

Platja de Llevant

La Savina

Es Pujols

Sant Francesc

Punta Rasa

Formentera

Platja de
Tramuntana

Punta de sa Creu

Platja de
Migjorn

El Pilar de la Mola
Punta des Far

Cap de Barbaria

0 — 5 mi
0 — 5 km

the north are sacred to Ibiza's sun worshipers. In Formentera, Playa de Mitjorn stretches 5km (3 miles) and is relatively uncrowded. Set against a backdrop of pines and dunes, the pure white sand of Es Pujols makes it the most popular of Ibiza's beaches, and deservedly so.

Many travelers still arrive dreaming of soft drugs and hard sex. Both exist in great abundance, but there are dangers. It's common to pick up the local paper and read the list of the latest group of people deported because of *irresponsibilidad económica* (no money) or *conducta antisocial* (drunk and disorderly conduct). Some young travelers, frankly, have forsaken Ibiza, taking a ferry 40 minutes away (and just 5km/3 miles as the crow flies) to the tiny island of Formentera (see the following section), where they find less harassment (although anyone looking suspicious will be noticed out here too). Formentera is the most southern of the Balearic Islands, and because of limited accommodations, restaurants, and nightlife, it is most often visited on a day trip from Ibiza.

Eivissa is the local (Catalan) name for Ibiza. Catalan is the most common language of the island, but it is a dialectal variation—called Eivissenc or Ibicenco. The same language is spoken on Formentera.

Island Essentials

GETTING THERE As with Palma, if you come in July and August, be sure you have a return ticket and a reservation. Stories of passengers who were stranded for days in Ibiza in midsummer are legendary.

Iberia (✆ 90-240-05-00; www.iberia.com) flies into **Es Codolar International Airport** (✆ 90-240-47-04), 5.5km (3½ miles) from Ciudad de Ibiza. Seven daily flights connect Ibiza with Palma de Majorca, and three flights a day arrive from Barcelona. It's possible to take one of two daily flights from Valencia or one of three from Madrid. With the exception of charter flights winging in from virtually everywhere, Iberia is the main carrier servicing Ibiza. Its only other competitor on this route is **Air Europa** (✆ 90-240-15-01 in Ibiza; www.aireuropa.com), which offers flights to Ibiza from Barcelona (a maximum of two flights a day), as well as from Madrid, at intervals much less frequent than those offered aboard Iberia. The price of flights to Ibiza varies considerably because of season, promotion, and availability.

Trasmediterránea, Estación Marítim, Muelle Ibiza (✆ 90-245-46-45; www.trasmediterranea.es), operates a **ferry service** from Barcelona at the rate of four per week; a one-way ticket costs 72€. From Valencia to Ibiza, there is only one boat per week, costing 72€ one way. From Palma, there are four ferries per week, Tuesday to Friday; a one-way ride costs 56€. Check with travel agents in Barcelona, Valencia, or Palma regarding ferry schedules. You can book tickets through any agent.

GETTING AROUND If you land at Es Cordola Airport outside Ciudad de Ibiza, you will find **bus** service for the 5.5km (3½-mile) ride into town. Sometimes taxis are shared. In Ciudad de Ibiza, buses leave for the airport from Av. Isidor Macabich 24 (by the ticket kiosk), every hour on the hour, daily from 7am to 10pm.

Once in Ibiza, you'll have to walk, but the city is compact and can be covered on foot. There are buses, however, leaving for the nearby beaches. The two main bus terminals are at Av. Isidor Macabich 20 and 42 (✆ 97-131-20-75).

One of the most popular means of getting around the island, especially in the south, is moped or bicycle. Rental arrangements can be made through **Casa Valentín,** corner of Av. B. V. Ramón 19 (✆ 97-131-08-22). Mopeds cost from 25€ to 35€ per day. If you'd like to rent a car, both Hertz and Avis have offices at the airport.

VISITOR INFORMATION The **tourist information office** is at Antonio Riquer 2, in the port of Ciudad de Ibiza (✆ 97-119-19-51; www.ibiza.travel). It's open June to November Monday to Friday 9am to 9pm, Saturday 9:30am to 7:30pm; and December to May, Monday to Friday 8:30am to 3pm, Saturday 10:30am to 1pm. There is another office at the airport (✆ 97-180-91-18), which is open only May to October Monday to Saturday 9am to 2pm and 3 to 8pm, Sunday 9am to 2pm.

Ciudad de Ibiza

The island's capital, Ciudad de Ibiza, was founded by the Carthaginians 2,500 years ago. Today the town consists of a lively marina district around the harbor and an old town, **D'Alt Vila ★**, with narrow cobblestone streets and flat-roofed, whitewashed houses. The yacht-clogged marina and the district's main street, Vara de Rey, are constant spectacles—from old fishermen to the local Ibizan women swathed in black to the ubiquitous, scantily clad tourists. The marina district is fun to wander through with its art galleries, dance clubs, boutiques, bars, and restaurants.

Much of the Old Town's medieval character has been preserved, in spite of massive development elsewhere. Many houses have Gothic styling and open onto spacious courtyards. These houses, some of which are 500 years old, are often festooned with geraniums and bougainvillea. The Old Town is entered through the Puerta de las Tablas, flanked by Roman statues.

Plaça Desamparadors, crowded with open-air restaurants and market stalls, lies at the top of the town. Traffic leaves town through the Portal Nou.

FUN ON & OFF THE BEACH

BEACHES The most popular (and overcrowded) beaches are **Playa Talamanca** in the north and **Ses Figueretes** (also called Playa Figueretes) in the south. Don't be surprised to find a lot of nudity. The best beaches are connected by boats and buses. The remoter ones are accessed by a private car or private boat. Both Playa Talamanca and Ses Figueretes are near Ciudad de Ibiza, as is another popular beach, **Playa d'en Bossa,** to the south.

To avoid the hordes near Ciudad de Ibiza, continue past Playa d'en Bossa until you reach **Las Salinas,** near the old salt flats farther south. Here, beaches include **Playa Cavallet,** one of the officially designated nudist strands (though nudism doesn't always follow official designations laid down by Ibizan law).

The most horrendously over-crowded beach in Ibiza is **Playa San Antonio,** at San Antonio de

Ibiza's D'Alt Vila (Old Town).

The crystal-clear water of Talamanca beach.

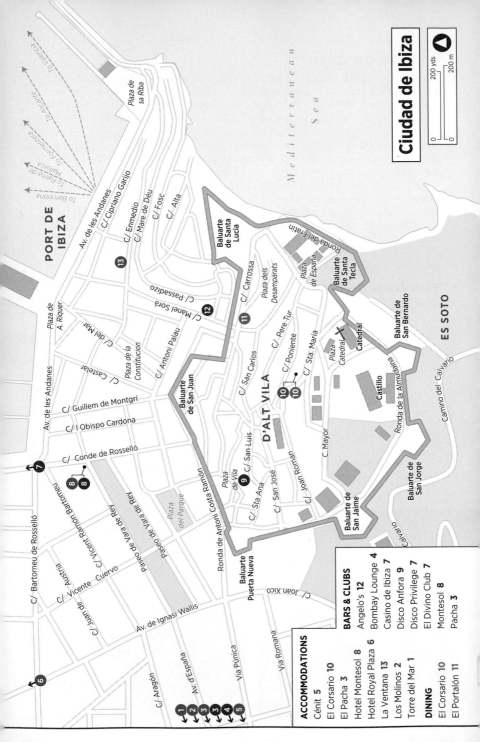

Ciudad de Ibiza

PORT DE IBIZA

Mediterranean Sea

0   200 yds
0   200 m

742

Plaza de sa Riba

To Valencia
To Alicante
To Palma de Mallorca
To Formentera
To Barcelona

Av. de les Andanes
C/ Cipriano Garijo
C/ Enmedio
C/ Mare de Déu
C/ Fosc
C/ Alta

Baluarte de Santa Lucia
Baluarte de Santa Tecla
Ronda del Frati
Plaza de España

ES SOTO

Baluarte de San Bernardo

Plaza de A. Riquer
C/ del Mar
Plaza de la Constitución
C/ Castelar
C/ Antoni Palau
C/ Manel Sorà
C/ Passedizo
Plaza dels Desamparats
C/ Carrossa

Catedral
Plaza Catedral
Castillo

Av. de les Andanes
C/ Guillem de Montgrí
C/ I Obispo Cardona
C/ Conde de Rosselló

Baluarte de San Juan
C/ San Carlos
C/ Pere Tur
C/ Poniente
C/ Sta. María
C/ Mayor

Ronda de la Almudaina
Baluarte de San Jorge

D'ALT VILA

C/ Bartomeu de Rosselló
C/ Juan de Austria
C/ Vicente Cuervo
C/ Vicent Ramón Cuervo
Paseo de Vara de Rey
Plaza del Parque
Ronda de Antoni Costa Ramón

C/ San Luis
Plaza de Vila
C/ San José
C/ Sta. Ana
C/ San José
C/ Joan Roman

Baluarte de San Jaime
Calvario
Camino del Calvario

Baluarte Puerta Nueva
C/ Joan Xico

Av. de Ignasi Wallis
C/ Aragón
Av. d'Espanya
Via Púnica
Via Romana

7
8 8
6
13
12
11
10 10
9
1 2 3 3 4 5

ACCOMMODATIONS
Cénit **5**
El Corsario **10**
El Pacha **3**
Hotel Montesol **8**
Hotel Royal Plaza **6**
La Ventana **13**
Los Molinos **2**
Torre del Mar **1**

DINING
El Corsario **10**
El Portalón **11**

BARS & CLUBS
Angelo's **12**
Bombay Lounge **4**
Casino de Ibiza **7**
Disco Anfora **9**
Disco Privilege **7**
El Divino Club **7**
Montesol **8**
Pacha **3**

Portmany—if it got any worse, you'd have to stand up instead of lie down! However, a boat or bus will take you to several beaches southwest of the town, all far less congested. These include **Cala Bassa, Port des Torrent, Cala Tarida,** and **Cala Conta.**

Santa Eulalia del Río, site of the third major tourist development in Ibiza, has a less crowded beach, but it's also less impressive. If you stay in this east-coast town, you can find a better beach at Cala Llonga in the south or at one of the beaches along the north, including **Playa d'es Caná** and **Cala Lleña.** These beaches are among the finest on Ibiza.

If you venture to the north coast, you'll discover more good beaches at the tourist developments of **Portinatx,** which is at the very northern tip, and at **Puerto de San Miguel,** north of the small town of San Miguel. The quickest way to reach San Miguel from Ciudad de Ibiza is to go inland via Santa Gertrudis, and then head north. Along the way, you'll pass Río de Santa Eulalia, the only river in the Balearics.

TENNIS You'll find five public tennis courts at **Port Sant Miguel** (© 97-133-46-02). Open during daylight hours, they're usually unsupervised. No appointments are necessary for access to these courts, but for information about their condition and whether players are waiting to use them, contact the Hotel Hacienda (© 97-133-45-00; www.hotelhacienda-ibiza.com).

SHOPPING

Fashion has been an important Ibiza industry since the late 1960s, when a non-conformist fashion philosophy took hold, combining elements of the traditional *pitiusa* (peasant dress) attire of the natives and the natural, free-flowing garments of the hippies who flocked here in the 1960s. In recent years, Ibizan designs have become much more sophisticated and complex, but the individualistic spirit has not wavered.

At the corner of Conde Rosselón, master artisan Pedro Planells creates hand-sewn, original leather goods at **Pedro's,** Carrer Aníbal 8 (© 97-131-30-26). Many items can be custom-made. Pedro creates stylish accessories and home furnishings in leather and silver. Well-heeled clients have included everyone from international celebrities to King Juan Carlos. Pedro's keeps conventional Spanish hours, but during the off season, his hours and days vary.

Sandal Shop, Plaça de Vila 2 (© 97-130-54-75), sells high-quality leather goods made by a cast of local artisans. One-of-a-kind accessories, including bejeweled belts and leather bags, are designed for individual clients. Custom-made sandals can be created to suit personal fashion tastes.

A JOURNEY INTO IBIZA'S PAST

Although Ibiza is primarily a destination for sun and fun, there's a sightseeing attraction worth a special visit.

Museo Arqueològic de Ibiza y Formentera (Museum of Archaeology) ★ Located in Ibiza's Old Town, this museum in a former arsenal houses the world's most important collection of Punic remains. It contains pottery and other artifacts from prehistoric sites in Formentera and Ibiza, and Punic terracotta figurines and other items from the sanctuaries of Illa Plana (7th–5th c. B.C.) and Cuieram (4th–2nd c. B.C.). Also on display are vases, figurines, and other Carthaginian artifacts found in the island's burial grounds. Examples of Roman epigraphs, sculpture, and small glass bottles are included in the exhibit. Other

Punic vases at Ibiza's Museum of Archaeology.

displays include Moorish artifacts (10th–13th c. A.D.), Christian wooden and stone sculptures, plus 14th- to 16th-century ceramics.

Plaça de Catedral 3. ℂ **97-130-12-31.** www.aamaef.org. Admission 3€ for adults, 1.50€ students, free for children 17 and under. Winter Tues–Sat 9am–3pm, Sun 10am–2pm; Apr–Sept Tues–Sat 10am–2pm and 6–8pm, Sun 10am–2pm. Closed holidays.

WHERE TO STAY IN & AROUND CIUDAD DE IBIZA

The chances of finding space in peak summer months are dismal, more so than in any Mediterranean resort in Spain. At other overcrowded resorts, such as those on the Costa Brava and Costa del Sol, a visitor faced with the NO VACANCY sign can always press on or go inland to find a room for the night. But in Ibiza, because of infrequent transportation, a visitor without a reservation in July and August can land in a trap. You may end up sleeping on the beach on an air mattress (if the police let you; alternatively, there are camping areas), even if your pockets are bulging with euros.

The island is not always prepared for its hordes of international tourists. The hotels can't be built fast enough. Many of the hastily erected ones sprouting up in San Antonio de Portmany, Santa Eulalia del Río—even on the outskirts of Ciudad de Ibiza—are more frame than picture.

Individual bookings in most establishments range from the horrifically difficult to the impossible. In many cases hoteliers don't bother to answer requests for space in summer. Armed with a nice fat contract from a British tour group, they're not interested in the plight of the stranded pilgrim. So if you're set on going to Ibiza during the summer, ***book through a package tour*** to ensure an ironclad reservation. You'll probably find a better bargain, anyway. Try booking with **Viajes Urbis,** Av. 8 d'Agost s/n, 07800 Ibiza (ℂ **97-131-44-12;** www.viajesurbis.com). In the less-busy months, using your credit card to reserve is enough to guarantee a hotel room upon your arrival.

In Town

In town, hotels are limited and often lack style and amenities, except for the following recommendations.

Cénit ⚓ This is the bargain place to stay here. Circular in shape, the hotel looks like a quartered wedding cake. In the pueblo style, each floor has been staggered to provide a terrace for the rooms above. The small accommodations are routine but comfortable, and the beds are firm. The Cénit is perched on a hillside a short walk from the beach.

Carrer Archiduque Lluis Salvador, 07800 Ibiza. ℂ **97-130-14-04.** Fax 97-130-07-54. www. ibiza-spotlight.com/cenit. 63 units. 52€–102€ double; 85€–140€ apt. Rates include continental breakfast (in double rooms only). AE, DC, MC, V. No parking. Closed mid-Oct to Apr. **Amenities:** Outdoor freshwater pool. *In room:* TV, fridge, kitchenette (in some).

El Corsario ★ 🎒 After your taxi deposits you near the church below, you'll have to walk the last 152m (500 ft.) uphill to reach this hotel, within a labyrinth of cobblestone pedestrian walkways. The house was built in 1570, and it is rumored that its terraces were built by corsairs. The modest rooms are pleasant and clean, often containing antiques. Some overlook an enclosed garden of trailing bougainvillea and cultivated flowers. No parking is available. The **dining room** here is noteworthy, especially for its fish dishes (see review below).

Carrer Ponent 5, 07800 Ibiza. ℂ **97-130-12-48.** Fax 97-139-19-53. www.ibiza-hotels.com/COR-SARIO. 15 units. 140€–170€ double; 235€–430€ suite. MC, V. **Amenities:** Restaurant; bar; babysitting; room service. *In room:* TV, hair dryer, minibar.

El Pachá ★★ If you like to sleep where you party, stay at this funky hotel, the hippest on the island; it's linked with Pachá, a legend among local dance clubs. The most famous boutique hotel in Ibiza, it has been thoroughly renovated and is the trendiest place in town, right on the Paseo Marítimo fronting the water. Rated four stars by the government, it is glitzy, evoking the designs of Philippe Starck. Its main color scheme is white. You can meet fellow guests at the pool, most of them wearing the skimpiest of beachwear, if that.

Paseo Marítimo, s/n, 07800 Ibiza. ℂ **97-131-59-63.** Fax 97-131-02-53. www.avantgardehotels. com. 57 units. 120€–395€ double; 770€–1,100€ suite. Rates include buffet breakfast. AE, DC, MC, V. **Amenities:** Restaurant; bar; babysitting; bikes; concierge; outdoor freshwater pool; room service; Wi-Fi (free, in lobby). *In room:* A/C, TV, DVD player (in some), hair dryer, minibar.

Hotel Montesol This old favorite enjoys a new lease on life after renovations. Its proximity to the marina affords panoramic views of the sea, and the small rooms are clean and comfortable, though sterile. Nonetheless, this is a good bargain for Ibiza, especially if you plan to spend most of your time outside of your room, exploring the island. There is no restaurant; however, many bistros are located nearby.

Vara de Rey 2, 07800 Ibiza. ℂ **97-131-01-61.** Fax 97-131-06-02. www.hotelmontesol.com. 55 units. 70€–110€ double. MC, V. No parking. **Amenities:** Bar; babysitting. *In room:* A/C, TV.

Hotel Royal Plaza ★★ Located 3 blocks from the port, this six-story modern hotel offers in-town convenience plus a casual, resortlike atmosphere. For those who want to stay within Ciudad de Ibiza, this is the premier choice. The marble reception lobby exudes elegance. Well-appointed accommodations with firm beds are midsize and carpeted; most have private terraces. The rooftop pool offers a sunbathing platform, with commanding views of the port and town of Ibiza.

Carrer Pedro Francés 27–29, 07800 Ibiza. ℂ **800/528-1234** in the U.S., or 97-131-00-00. Fax 97-131-40-95. www.hotelroyalplaza.net. 117 units. 129€–235€ double; 234€–442€ suite. AE, DC, MC, V. Free parking. **Amenities:** 2 restaurants; 2 bars; babysitting; exercise room; Jacuzzi; outdoor freshwater pool; room service; sauna. *In room:* A/C, TV, hair dryer, minibar, Wi-Fi (free).

La Ventana ★ This is a perfect name ("the Window") for what was once a castle and is now a hotel on the hillside of the Old City, overlooking the Mediterranean. What is more, the hotel, peaceful as it is in itself, is one of the best places to get tickets for clubs featuring music. The present owners have succeeded in decorating the hotel very stylishly with a mixture of clever lighting, beautiful fittings, and Asian objets d'art. The rooms are painted in wonderful, almost Indian colors and have great beds with floating canopies of white net. There's a terrace on the roof with wide Moroccan-style sofas and an amazing view of the Old City and the sea beyond.

Sa Carrossa 13, Dalt Vila, 07800 Ibiza. ✆ **97-139-08-57.** Fax 97-139-01-45. www.laventanaibiza. com. 14 units. Winter 85€–125€ double, 200€ suite; summer 165€–240€ double, 395€ suite. AE, MC, V. Free parking. **Amenities:** Restaurant; bar; babysitting; room service. *In room:* A/C, TV, hair dryer, minibar.

In Playa de Ses Figueretes

On the edge of town, a number of modern beach hotels have been erected that are far superior to the ones in the city. With few exceptions, most are booked solid in summer by tour groups.

Los Molinos ★ This modern resort is a favorite with snowbirds from the north of Europe. Situated less than a mile from Ciudad de Ibiza, it's nestled between the water and a medieval village. Los Molinos is the finest hotel in Ses Figueretes; it offers resort life combined with proximity to town. The midsize accommodations, most with private terraces facing the sea, are comfortably furnished, with twin beds pushed together European-style.

Ramón Muntaner 60, 07800 Ibiza. ✆ **97-130-22-50.** Fax 97-130-25-04. www.thbhotels.com. 168 units. 85€–297€ double. AE, DC, MC, V. Free parking. **Amenities:** 2 restaurants; 2 bars; exercise room; Jacuzzi; outdoor freshwater pool; room service; sauna. *In room:* A/C, TV, hair dryer, minibar, Wi-Fi (free).

In Es Vivé

Torre del Mar ★ This is the only modern hotel in the area to compete with the standards and luxury of the Royal Plaza (see above). Lying 2km (1¼ miles) from the center of the city, opening onto a wide sandy beach, it's like a Florida resort hotel with absolutely no island character. But you don't come here for that, as it attracts beach lovers who like lots of facilities and comfort. A government-rated four-star hotel, it's one of the best-accessorized hotels on the island, especially for those who are athletic. The beach, De'en Bossa, is its major attraction, as it is one of the largest on the island. Guest rooms are a bit small for such a luxury hotel, but they are nicely furnished and comfortable. The units open onto views of the surrounding mountains or the sea.

Platja D'en Bossa, 07819 Es Vivé, Ibiza. ✆ **97-130-30-50.** Fax 97-130-40-60. www.hoteltorre delmar.com. 213 units. 145€–330€ double; 235€–380€ junior suite. AE, DC, MC, V. Free parking. Closed mid-Oct to Apr. **Amenities:** Restaurant; 2 bars; babysitting; exercise room; Jacuzzi; 2 freshwater pools (1 heated indoor); room service; sauna; outdoor tennis court (lit). *In room:* A/C, TV, hair dryer, minibar, Wi-Fi (free).

WHERE TO DINE IN CIUDAD DE IBIZA

It's hard to find authentic Ibizan cuisine. The clientele and often the chefs are mainly from continental Europe, and the menu choices cater almost exclusively to their tastes.

Because of the lack of agriculture on some parts of the island, fish has always been the mainstay of the local Mediterranean diet. But budget travelers may be put off by the price of some of this fare. Once the cheapest item you could order on a menu, fish is now one of the most expensive. The fish is sautéed, baked, or broiled and might be blended into a rice dish called *arroz a la pescadora. Parrillada* and *zarzuela* are two stewlike dishes containing an assortment of fish.

As in Majorca, pork is important in the local diet. Some islanders feed figs to these animals to sweeten their meat, which is turned into such pungent cooked sausages as *sabrosadas* or *longanizas.*

A local dish occasionally offered on some menus is *sofrit pages,* a stew made with three kinds of meat and poultry—chicken, pork, and lamb—and then cooked with pepper, cloves, cinnamon, and garlic. One of the best seafood plates is *borrida de rajada,* crayfish in an almond sauce.

The most famous dessert is *flaó,* a kind of cheesecake to which mint and anisette are added for flavoring. *Greixonera* is a spiced pudding, and *maccarrones de San Juan* is cinnamon- and lemon-flavored milk baked with cheese.

El Corsario ★ MEDITERRANEAN The dining room at this hotel (p. 745), with its panoramic view, is so romantic it deserves special mention. This 400-year-old flower-draped villa is near the hilltop fortress. Your taxi deposits you about 152m (500 ft.) down the hill in a square fronting an old church, and you must climb the slippery cobblestones to reach the villa. There you'll find a stand-up bar, two pleasant dining rooms with a handful of neatly laid tables, and a view of the harbor. Menu specialties include various pastas, two different preparations of lamb, and especially fresh fish brought up from the harbor. The cookery is home-style and well prepared, especially if you stick to the fish dishes.

Carrer Ponent 5. (✆ **97-130-12-48.** Reservations required. Main courses 15€–30€. AE, DC, MC, V. Daily 8pm–midnight. Closed Nov–Apr.

El Portalón SPANISH/INTERNATIONAL Before you hit the bars (go very late, as is the fashion), dine here in the Old Town. Alfresco courtyard dining is a lure, as is the handsome crowd. El Portalón attracts gay as well as straight couples, usually European. The food is a combination of Spanish, Catalan, and Mediterranean. It's expensive, but worth the extra euros.

Plaça dels Desamparats 1-2. (✆ **97-130-39-01.** Reservations recommended. Main courses 18€–30€. AE, DC, MC, V. Easter–Oct daily noon–4pm and 8pm–1am; Nov–Easter daily 8pm–1am.

CIUDAD DE IBIZA AFTER DARK

In many ways, **El Divino Club,** Puerto Ibiza Nueva (✆ **97-131-83-38;** www.eldivino-ibiza.com), is the most physically beautiful disco on Ibiza. Open daily in summer only, it prides itself on the supermodels, celebs, and trendies who have graced its premises with their presence. Wear the most hip outfit you packed. The club doesn't open its doors until midnight; it remains open nightly until 6am. The cover charge is 25€ to 50€ (includes one drink); it tends to be more expensive in summer.

The crowd at the **Montesol** (p. 745) hotel bar, Vara de Rey 2 (✆ **97-131-01-61**), a short walk from the harbor on the main street, is likely to include expatriates, newly arrived social climbers, and Spaniards along for the view. In many ways this is the greatest circus in town, made more pleasant by the well-prepared tapas and the generous drinks. If you enjoy people-watching, sit at one of the sidewalk tables. Montesol is open daily from 8am to midnight.

Despite its age (it's one of the oldest discos on Ibiza, with a nightlife pedigree extending back to the 1960s), **Pachá,** Av. 8 de Agosto s/n (© **97-193-21-30;** www.pacha.com), a spacious split-level disco near the casino, is still hip. Made up of three separate bar areas and dance floors, and open only in the summer, it continues to attract the young and the not-so-young, the bored, the restless, and the jaded. In summer, overheated dancers can cool off in a swimming pool. The music, primarily droning disco and rap, has the cadence of jackhammers. The cover is a painful 20€ to 60€ (includes one drink).

Everyone from supermodels to soccer stars floods into the **Bombay Lounge,** Av. 8 Agosto 23 (© **97-193-12-37;** www.bombay-lounge.com), which is opposite Pachá. With a backdrop of jazz, soul, and house music, it is the most chic cocktail lounge in the city. It is the ultimate chill-out bar, decorated in warm, earthy tones with soft lighting along with Buddhas and plush cushions. If you like decadent lounges, you've come to the right place. When in Ibiza, you order fresh *caipirinhas.* If you don't know this drink, the bartender will explain. You can also try Wasabi martinis, mojitos, and classic daiquiris. Light bites and classic burger and fries are served nightly until 2:30am. The club opens at 10pm, but the A-list patrons show up after midnight. No cover.

Disco Privilege, Carretera Sant Antoni Km 7, Urbanización San Rafael (© **97-119-80-86;** www.privilegeibiza.com), is a sprawling nightclub built to entertain 5,000, many of whom seem to rush the dance floor simultaneously. Wander from room to room, stopping wherever you feel the urge, as the interior contains more bars, semisecluded patios, and romantic trysting spots than most hotels. Dance music, however, will conspire to keep you on the floor dancing, dancing, dancing. The club is open from June to September, daily from midnight to 8am. The cover is 45€ (includes one drink).

There's gambling in the modern **Casino de Ibiza,** Carrettera Ibiza-San Antonio at the Juan XXIII Roundabout (© **97-131-33-12;** www.casinoibiza. com). With the usual gaming tables and slot machines, it's open nightly 6pm to 5am. The adjoining nightclub and dining hall offer live cabaret entertainment between May and October, with shows that feature a relatively tame assortment of magicians, comedians, and pretty women in feathers and spangles whose fancy stepping begins at 11pm. Casino entrance is 5€. A passport is required for admission.

With the possible exception of Mykonos, few other islands in the Mediterranean cater to gay travelers as much as Ibiza. A stroll through Ciudad de Ibiza's Old Town reveals dozens of gay bars catering to international visitors; most are open from 9 or 10pm to 3am. Although many close and reopen with disconcerting frequency, one of the most deeply entrenched is **Disco Anfora,** Carrer San Carlos 5 (© **97-130-28-93;** www.disco-anfora.com), a haute electronic disco that blares away, to the dancing pleasure of a mostly gay clientele, between midnight and 6am every night in summer. The cover charge of 12€ to 17€ includes the first drink. Other gay sites include **Angelo's,** Carrer Alfonso XII no. 11 (© **97-131-09-68**), which serves drinks beginning around 10pm every evening.

San Antonio de Portmany

Known to the Romans as Portus Magnus and before that a Bronze Age settlement, this thriving town was discovered in the 1950s by foreigners and has remained popular ever since. Tourism here is "megamass." The town today goes by two names—San Antonio de Portmany for Spanish speakers or Sant Antoni de Portmany for Catalan speakers.

In summer you have as much chance of finding a room here as you would booking a reservation on the last flight to the moon if the earth were on fire. Virtually all the hotels have a direct pipeline to tour-group agencies in northern Europe, and the individual traveler probably won't get the time of day. If you're determined to stay in the area during peak travel season, your best bet is to arrange a package tour.

The resort, with a 14th-century parish church, is built on an attractive bay. Avoid the impossibly overcrowded narrow strip of sand at San Antonio itself. Take a ferry or bus to one of the major beaches, including Cala Gració, 1.5km (1 mile) to the north, set against a backdrop of pines; or Port des Torrent, 5km (3 miles) southwest. Cala Bassa in the south is also popular. San Antonio overlooks the Isla Conejera, an uninhabited rock island. With its hordes of visitors, San Antonio has an easygoing lifestyle, plus lots of mildly entertaining nightlife. Even if you're staying in Ciudad de Ibiza or Santa Eulalia, you may want to hop over for the day or evening.

Take note: When visiting hooligans have had too much cheap booze, San Antonio can get dangerous. In the earlier part of the evening, however, you may want to patronize one of the bars or open-air terraces around Avinguda Doctor Fleming.

ESSENTIALS

GETTING THERE **Buses** leave from Ciudad de Ibiza every 15 minutes; a one-way fare costs 2€.

VISITOR INFORMATION The **tourist information office** is at Passeig de Ses Fonts (*©* **97-134-33-63**). It's open May to October Monday to Friday 9:30am to 8pm, and Saturday and Sunday 9:30am to 1pm. Off-season hours are Monday to Friday 9:30am to 2:30pm and Saturday 9am to 1pm.

EXPLORING THE AREA

Throughout the day, boats leave from Passeig de Ses Fonts. They take you to **Cala Bassa,** a sandy beach on a thin strip, for 6€ one-way, or to **Cala Conta,** a slightly rocky beach, for 6€ one-way. If you negotiate, they will take you along the coastline northwest to the far point of Portinatx. This is virtually the only way to see the coastline, since there isn't a road running along it; most visitors agree it's Ibiza's most beautiful coastline.

North of the waterfront, the chief attraction is **Sa Cova de Santa Agnès,** a national monument and an object of eerie devotion. This has been a place of sacred worship ever since a sailor prayed to Santa Agnès during a rough storm and was saved. The sailor, to show his gratitude, placed a figure of the saint in this dark hole. It's become a place of pilgrimage ever since. You may view it free on Monday and again on Saturday from 9am to noon.

If you have rented a car, you can explore **Cueva de Ses Fontanelles,** north of Platja Calad Salada, where faintly colorful prehistoric paintings decorate the walls.

WHERE TO STAY IN & AROUND SAN ANTONIO

The prospect of finding a room here in July and August is bleak—some Brits reserve a year in advance. British package tourists virtually occupy the crescent beach and busy harbor all during the warm months. You stand a better chance of finding lodgings in Ciudad de Ibiza.

Hotel Tropical Located away from the port area in a commercial section of town, this hotel has a private recreation area that's like a small public park, with dozens of reclining chairs and some billiard tables. The hotel was built in the early 1960s with a russet-and-white-marbled lobby filled with armchairs. The Tropical is rated one of the best hotels in the center of San Antonio, with comfortably furnished, modernized, but rather bland rooms that are small to midsize.

Cervantes 28, 07820 San Antonio, Ibiza. 🕐 **97-134-00-50.** Fax 97-134-40-69. www.hotel-tropicalibiza.com. 142 units. 27€–53€ per person double; 33€–59€ half-board per person. Rates include buffet breakfast. AE, DC, MC, V. No parking. Closed Nov–Apr. **Amenities:** 2 restaurants; 2 bars; babysitting; bikes; concierge; exercise room; 2 freshwater pools (1 heated indoor); Wi-Fi (free, in lobby). *In room:* A/C, hair dryer, minibar.

Hotel Village ★ 🏨 Located 24km (15 miles) west of Ciudad de Ibiza, this small, elegant hotel is one of our favorite refuges on the island. The midsize guest rooms, done in white marble, have terraces, most facing the sea, but with several open onto the mountains. Each room is very comfortably furnished with adequate living space and has a tidy, tiled bathroom. A walkway leads down the hill to a rocky beach, where guests can sunbathe.

Apartado 27, Urbanización Caló den Real (along the road to Cala Vadella, 11km/6½ miles south of San Antonio), 07830 Sant Josep, Ibiza. 🕐 **97-180-80-01.** Fax 97-180-80-27. www.hotelvillage.net. 20 units. 134€–288€ double; 153€–320€ suite. Rates include buffet breakfast. MC, V. Free parking. **Amenities:** Restaurant; bar; babysitting; exercise room; outdoor freshwater pool; room service; sauna; 2 outdoor tennis courts. *In room:* A/C, TV, hair dryer, minibar.

Los Jardines de Palerm This intimate little hotel, outside the village of San José (11km/6¾ miles south of San Antonio), is constructed in the style of a 17th-century hacienda. Patios and garden terraces scattered throughout the grounds are ideal locations for sunbathing, enjoying a lazy Ibiza afternoon, and getting away from the noise and bustle of the street. The small guest rooms are rustic, with beamed ceilings, antiques, and good beds. Each unit has its own terrace. Prices change every month—the lowest price quoted below is charged in March, while the highest is for August.

Apartado 62, 07080 San José, Ibiza. 🕐 **97-180-03-18.** Fax 97-180-04-53. www.jardinsdepalerm.com. 9 units. 150€–245€ double; 199€–286€ minisuite; 246€–329€ junior suite; 270€–399€ suite. Rates include continental breakfast. AE, MC, V. No parking. **Amenities:** Restaurant; bar; babysitting; 2 outdoor freshwater pools. *In room:* A/C, TV, ceiling fans, hair dryer, no phone, Wi-Fi (free).

Pikes ★ Originally a *finca*, this 600-year-old compound is now a luxurious playground for well-heeled travelers and celebrities from around the world. Touted for its "sophisticated informality," Pikes boasts spacious rooms with sensuous interiors, including king-size beds. The hotel offers activities and entertainment for its guests, ranging from flamenco shows to costume balls. Pikes provides a VIP card that allows entrance to most of the area's clubs and casinos.

Camino Sa-Vorera 1, Apartado 104, 07820 San Antonio, Ibiza. 🕐 **97-134-22-22.** Fax 97-134-23-12. www.pikeshotel.com. 26 units. 170€–230€ double; 250€–775€ suite. Rates include buffet breakfast. AE, DC, MC, V. Free parking. **Amenities:** Restaurant; bar; babysitting; concierge; exercise room; Jacuzzi; outdoor freshwater pool; room service; sauna; outdoor tennis court; Wi-Fi (free, in lobby). *In room:* A/C, TV, hair dryer, kitchenette (in some), minibar.

WHERE TO DINE AROUND SAN ANTONIO

Sa Capella MEDITERRANEAN This restaurant is set in a 600-year-old chapel with stone vaulting, rose windows, radiating alcoves, balconies, and chandeliers that can be lowered on pulleys from the overhead masonry. You pass beneath an arbor of magenta bougainvillea and are ushered to your table by a waiter dressed in red-and-white traditional Ibizan costume. Meals are flavorful and well versed in the culinary traditions of the Mediterranean. The best items are grilled fresh fish; roast suckling pig in the style of Segovia; shepherd's-style lamb chops served with potatoes and carrots; marinated mussels; roasted rabbit; and steak served on a hot stone. Partly because of its historic setting, and partly because of its fine food, this dining choice has a deservedly devoted following.

Carretera de Santa Inés Km 1.2 (just to the north of San Antonio). © **97-134-00-57.** Reservations recommended. Main courses 18€–42€. DC, MC, V. Daily 8pm–midnight. Closed Nov–Mar.

The Northern Coast

The north remains largely untainted by the scourge of mass tourism, except for a handful of coves. Here you'll find some of the island's prettiest countryside, with fields of olive, almond, and carob trees and the occasional *finca* raising melons or grapes.

EXPLORING THE AREA

Off the road leading into Port de Sant Miquel (Puerto de San Miguel) is **Cova de Can Marça** (© **97-133-47-76;** www.covadecanmarsa.com), about 90m (295 ft.) from the Hotel Galeón (see below). There is a fine view of the bay from the hotel's snack bar. After a stunning descent down stairs clinging to the cliff's face, you enter a cave that's more than 100,000 years old and forms its stalactites and stalagmites at the rate of about .6 centimeter (¼ in.) per 100 years. A favored hiding place for smugglers and their goods in former days, it's now a beautifully orchestrated surrealistic experience—including a sound-and-light display—not unlike walking through a Dalí painting. Many of the limestone formations are delicate miniatures. The half-hour tour is conducted in several languages for groups of up to 70. From Holy Week to the end of October, tours are offered daily every half-hour from 11am to 6pm. Admission is 8€ for adults and 4.50€ for children.

At the island's northern tip is **Portinatx,** a pretty series of beaches and bays now marred by a string of shops and haphazardly built hotels. For a taste of its original, rugged beauty, go past all the construction to the jagged coast along the open sea.

Every Saturday year-round there is a **flea market** just beyond Sant Carles (San Carlos), on the road to Santa Eulalia. (You'll know where it is by all the cars parked along the road.) Open from about 10am until 8 or 9pm, it offers all kinds of clothing (both antique and new), accessories, crafts, and the usual odds and ends.

A beautiful drive leads from Sant Carles (San Carlos) along the coast to Cala Sant Vicent (San Vicente).

Deserted Benirras beach, outside Port de Sant Miquel.

WHERE TO STAY

Hotel offerings are more limited in the north than in the traditional pockets of tourism in the south and west. Nevertheless, the island's finest hotel, the five-star Hacienda, is here, above Na Xamena Bay. Port de Sant Miquel, Cala Sant Vicent, and Portinatx—once tranquil, seaside havens—have become increasingly pockmarked with package-tour hotels.

Hotel Galeón One of two hotels overlooking the little bay, this basic hotel offers simple, clean, and comfortable but small guest rooms, each equipped with a good bed and neatly kept bathrooms. Units have terraces with views of the sea.

Puerto de San Miguel, 07815 San Miguel, Ibiza. ☎ **97-133-45-34.** Fax 97-133-45-35. www.san miguelresort.com. 182 units. 52€–136€ double. Rates include buffet breakfast. AE, V. Free parking. Closed Nov–Apr. **Amenities:** Restaurant; 3 bars; bikes; exercise room; outdoor pool; sauna; outdoor tennis court (lit); watersports rentals; Wi-Fi (free, in lobby). *In room:* A/C, TV, hair dryer.

Hotel Hacienda Na Xamena ★★★ Located 23km (14 miles) northwest of Ciudad de Ibiza, this Moorish villa, set on a promontory overlooking Na Xamena Bay, is the top destination on Ibiza for well-heeled travelers and celebrities seeking leisure and sanctuary. Luxury, informality, privacy, and personal service—the Hacienda has it all. Public rooms are filled with cubbyholes, ideal for cozying up to a book or travel companion. Spacious guest rooms are decorated with four-poster beds, sumptuous carpets, and balconies overlooking the Mediterranean.

Na Xamena, 07815 San Miguel, Ibiza. ☎ **97-133-45-00.** Fax 97-133-45-14. www.hotelhacienda-ibiza.com. 65 units. 236€–574€ double; 451€–1,823€ suite. AE, DC, MC, V. Free parking. Closed Nov–Apr. **Amenities:** 4 restaurants; bar; babysitting; bikes; exercise room; 3 fresh-water pools (1 heated indoor); room service; spa; outdoor tennis court (lit). *In room:* A/C, TV, hair dryer, minibar, Wi-Fi (free).

Escaping from the Hordes

If you want to escape to a lovely beach that remains a stranger to hotel construction, head for **Playa Benirras,** just north of Port de Sant Miquel. An unpaved but passable road leads out to this small, calm, pretty cove, where lounge chairs are available and pedal boats are for rent. On the beach are snack bars and restaurants.

Santa Eulalio del Rio

Once patronized by expatriate artists from the capital, 15km (9⅓ miles) to the south, Santa Eulalia del Río now attracts mostly middle-class northern Europeans.

Santa Eulalia is at the foot of the Puig de Missa, on the estuary of the only river in the Balearics. The principal monument in town is a fortress church standing on a hilltop, or *puig*. Dating from the 16th century, it has an ornate Gothic altar screen.

Santa Eulalia is relatively free of the sometimes plastic quality of San Antonio. Visitors often have a better chance of finding accommodations here than in the other two major towns.

ESSENTIALS

GETTING THERE During the day, **buses** run between Ciudad de Ibiza and Santa Eulalia del Río every hour; a one-way fare costs 2€.

Seven **boats** a day run between Ciudad de Ibiza and Santa Eulalia del Río. The boats run on the hour, and the first leaves Ciudad de Ibiza at 10:30am and Santa Eulalia del Río at 9:30am. The boat ride takes 45 minutes. For information, call ℭ **61-649-66-06.**

VISITOR INFORMATION The **tourist information office,** at Marià Riquer Wallis 4 (ℭ **97-133-07-28**), is open Monday to Friday 9am to 2pm. In summer the office is open Sunday to Friday 9:30am to 1:30pm and 5 to 7:30pm, and Saturday 10am to 1pm.

EXPLORING THE AREA

You can reach the famous northern beaches from Santa Eulalia by bus or boat, departing from the harborfront near the boat basin. **Aigües Blanques** is one of the best beaches, just 10km (6¼ miles) north. (It's legal to go nude here.) It's reached by four buses a day. A long, sandy cove, **Cala Llonga,** is 5km (3 miles) south and is serviced by 12 buses a day. Cala Llonga fronts a bevy of package-tour hotels, so it's likely to be crowded. Boats depart Santa Eulalia for Cala Llonga every 30 minutes, from 9am to 6pm. **Es Caná** is a white-sand beach, 5km (3 miles) north of town; boats and buses leave every 30 minutes, from 8am to 9pm. Four buses a day depart for **Cala Llenya** and **Cala Nova.**

WHERE TO STAY

Hotel Catalonia Ses Estaques A much-favored hotel in this resort, close to the seashore at the edge of town, Ses Estaques is open only in the good-weather months. On the walk to the private beach, you will find a beautiful garden filled with roses, palms, and ivy. The swimming pool is edged with pines and a poolside snack bar. Inside, the hotel is filled with extra touches and hidden, charming corners. There's an aquarium in the spacious lobby, and a pleasant tropical restaurant on the beach a short walk away. Each of the comfortable terrazzo-floored rooms has a balcony with a view of the garden or the sea.

Ses Estaques s/n, 07840 Santa Eulalia del Río, Ibiza. ℭ **97-133-02-00.** Fax 97-133-04-86. www. hoteles-catalonia.es. 217 units. 160€–190€ double. Rates include buffet breakfast. AE, DC, MC, V. Free parking. Closed Nov–Apr. **Amenities:** 2 restaurants; 2 bars; babysitting; outdoor pool; outdoor tennis court; Wi-Fi (free, in lobby). *In room:* A/C, TV, hair dryer, minibar.

Quilibra Aguas de Ibiza ★★★ At the marina at Santa Eulalia, this government-rated five-star hotel is a pocket of posh. The epitome of modernity, it offers a wide variety of rooms, including corner suites with panoramic views. Most of the units have a sitting room (or living room) plus a private terrace. Bathrooms are elegant and chic, made of natural stone with iridescent, glass-tile walls and separate showers and bathtubs. In the sleek, contemporary lobby, a wide range of offerings are presented, everything from wine tastings to elaborate tapas. Traditional Ibizan food, along with Mediterranean specialties, is served in the restaurant.

Calla Salvador Camacho 9, 07840 Santa Eulalia del Río, Ibiza. © **97-113-99-91.** http://aguas deibiza.com. 112 units. 310€ double; 370€–660€ suite. AE, DC, MC, V. Free parking. **Amenities:** 2 restaurants; 2 bars; exercise room; pool (outdoors); room service; spa. *In room:* A/C, TV, hair dryer, minibar, Wi-Fi (free).

Sol Elite S'Argamassa ★ ☺ Three kilometers (1¾ miles) outside Santa Eulalia del Río, near Roman ruins, the Hotel S'Argamassa is a well-run, family-oriented resort. The hotel is a short walk from the beach and maintains its own small pier. All the midsize guest rooms have terraces with sea views. The hotel has no restaurant, but dining options are nearby.

Urbanización S'Argamassa, 07182 Santa Eulalia del Río, Ibiza. © **97-133-00-51.** Fax 97-133-00-76. www.solmelia.com. 217 units. 60€–200€ double. AE, DC, MC, V. No parking. Closed Oct–Apr. **Amenities:** Restaurant; bar; babysitting; children's center; exercise room; 2 outdoor freshwater pools; 2 outdoor tennis courts. *In room:* A/C, TV, hair dryer, minibar.

WHERE TO DINE

El Naranjo ★ CONTINENTAL This chic nighttime rendezvous has the most beautiful courtyard in town. Many refer to this place as "the Orange Tree," its name in English. The orange-tree patio, with its flowering bougainvillea vines, has such appeal that many diners don't mind its out-of-the-way location (in town, several blocks from the water). If your table isn't ready when you arrive, enjoy an aperitif in the cozy bar. The menu items are beautifully prepared and served. One newspaper called the chef "an artist." Dishes include fresh fish, as well as duckling in red-currant-and-pepper sauce. Begin with *las tres mousses* (three mousses) as an appetizer, and finish with the lemon tart for dessert.

Carrer San José 31. © **97-133-03-24.** Reservations required. Main courses 19€–27€. AE, DC, MC, V. Tues–Sun 1–3:30pm and 7:30–11:30pm. Closed Jan 7–Feb 2.

Santa Gertrudis de Fruitera

Don't blink or you'll pass right through this hamlet in central Ibiza, lying inland and to the west of Santa Eulalia del Río. Yet visitors have found their way here, evidenced by the little handicrafts shops and galleries in the central square, Plaça de l'Església. There are also fine bars here if you'd like to escape inland from the beaches one day and see what an island village looks like. All of these bars serve a tasty snack called *bocadillo completo* (a roll of tomato, cheese, and Serrano ham).

The main reason for coming here is to stay at one of the island's most enchanting retreats, Cas Gasi, reviewed below.

Cas Gasi ★ 🏨 A cozy nest, this little inn lies in a valley in the heart of Ibiza, a 12-minute drive from Ciudad de Ibiza and its major beaches. If you shun beach hotels and want an authentic island experience, consider this 19th-century manorial hacienda in a rural setting of olive groves, almond trees, and gardens. (They grow their own organic vegetables.) Guests sit on porches and terraces in summer

The specialty of Santa Gertrudis: *bocadillo completo.*

taking in the bucolic view, retreating in winter to the warm ambience of the living room with its roaring fireplace. The casa is like a country resort with its two swimming pools at different levels, each surrounded by garden terraces. Views from the property are of the 1,570m-high (5,150-ft.) Sa Talaiassa, the island's only mountain.

Under wooden beamed ceilings, the breezy and spacious guest rooms are immaculately kept and furnished, often with brass beds. Hand-painted wall tiles and handmade terra-cotta floor tiles add to the ambience. Bathrooms are cool, cozy, and up-to-date. Dinner can be served if requested in advance, and breakfast is offered on a terrace.

Cami Vell a Sant Mateu, Apartado 117, 07814 Santa Gertrudis, Ibiza. © **97-119-77-00.** Fax 97-119-78-99. www.casgasi.com. 10 units. 303€–399€ double; 560€–750€ suite. Rates include continental breakfast. MC, V. Free parking. **Amenities:** Restaurant; bar; babysitting; exercise room; 2 outdoor pools; spa; Wi-Fi (free, in lobby). *In room:* A/C, TV/DVD, CD player, hair dryer, minibar.

FORMENTERA ★

For years, Formentera was known as the "forgotten Balearic." The smallest island of the archipelago, it's a 78-sq.-km (30-sq.-mile) flat limestone plain. In the east it is flanked by La Mola, a peak rising 187m (614 ft.), and in the west it is protected by Berberia, at 96m (315 ft.).

The Romans called it Frumentaria (meaning "wheat granary") when they oversaw it as a booming little agricultural center. But that was then. A shortage of water, coupled with strong winds, has allowed only meager vegetation to grow, notably some fig trees and fields of wild rosemary (which are home to thousands of green lizards). A few hearty goats live on the island.

Like Ibiza, Formentera has a salt industry. Its year-round population of 5,000 swells in summer, mostly with day-trippers from Ibiza. Limited hotels have kept development in check, and most visitors come over for the day to enjoy the beaches, where they often swim without bathing suits and sunbathe along the excellent stretches of sand. Britons and Germans make up the majority of tourists who actually spend the night.

Island Essentials

GETTING THERE Formentera is serviced by up to 36 **boat** passages a day in summer and about 8 per day in winter. Boats depart from Ciudad de Ibiza, on Ibiza's southern coast, for La Savina (La Sabina), 3km (1¾ miles) north of the island's capital and largest settlement, Sant Francesc (San Francisco Javier). Depending on the design of the boat you select, passage across the 5km (3-mile) channel separating the islands takes between 35 minutes and

1 hour. A round-trip fare costs from 39€. For information on schedules, contact **Trasmapi** (✆ **97-131-44-33;** www.trasmapi.com), although it's usually easier to ask employees at almost any hotel on the island, who are usually well versed in the hours of ferryboats to and from Ibiza.

GETTING AROUND As ferryboats arrive at the quays of La Sabina, taxis line up at the pier. One-way passage to such points as Es Pujols and Playa de Mitjorn costs 10€ to 15€, but it's always wise to negotiate the fare before the journey begins. To call a taxi in Sant Francesc, dial ✆ **97-132-20-16;** and in La Sabina, ✆ **97-132-20-02.** Regardless of when and where you call for a taxi, be prepared to wait.

Car rentals can be arranged through **Formotor** (✆ **97-132-29-29;** www.formotor.com), whose kiosk is at La Sabina, close to where you disembark from the ferryboats.

If you want to enjoy seeing Formentera by bicycle or a motor scooter, you can rent them from **Moto-Rent Migjorn,** in La Sabina (✆ **97-132-23-06;** www.motorentmigjorn.com), or from **Moto-Rent Pujols,** in Pujols (✆ **97-132-21-38;** www.motorentpujols.com). Motor scooters rent for 25€ to 41€ per day, bicycles for around 6€ to 10€ per day.

VISITOR INFORMATION The **tourist office** in Formentera, Edo. de Servicios de Puerto s/n, in Port de la Sabina (✆ **97-132-20-57**), is open Monday to Friday 10am to 2pm and 5 to 7pm, Saturday 10am to 2pm.

HITTING THE BEACH

Beaches, beaches, and more beaches—that's why visitors come here. You can see the ocean from any point on the island. Some say the island has the best beaches in the Mediterranean—an opinion not without merit. Formentera has been declared a "World Treasure" by UNESCO, one of four places so honored because of its special character as an ecological and wildlife preserve. This implies indirect control by UNESCO of activities that could jeopardize the island's ecological well-being.

Meanwhile, day-trippers from Ibiza have fun sampling its long, sedate beaches and solitary coves before returning to Ibiza's ebullience in the evening. The island is ringed with beaches, so selecting the one you think will appeal to you is about the only problem you'll face—that and whether you should wear a bathing suit.

Playa de Mitjorn, on the southern coast, is 5km (3 miles) long; it has many uncrowded sections. This is the principal area for nude sunbathing. A few bars and hotels occupy the relatively undeveloped stretch of sand. You can make **Es Copinyars,** the name of one of the beachfronts, your stop for lunch, as it has a number of restaurants and snack bars.

At **Es Calo,** along the northern coast, west of El Pilar, there are some small boardinghouses, called *hostales.* From this point, you can see the lighthouse of La Mola, which was featured in Jules Verne's *Journey Round the Solar System* and, if weather conditions are right, Majorca.

The town of Sant Ferran serves the beach of **Es Pujols,** darling of the package-tour operators. This is the most crowded beach on Formentera, and you may want to avoid it. The beaches, however, are pure white sand, with a backdrop of dunes and pine trees. It's a good place to go windsurfing and is the site of several tourist amenities. The beach is protected by the Punta Prima headland.

Westward, **Cala Sahona** is another popular tourist spot, lying near the lighthouse on Cabo Berberia. Often pleasure vessels anchor here on what is the most beautiful cove in Formentera.

Playa de Mitjorn at dusk.

WHERE TO STAY ON FORMENTERA

Accommodations are scarce, so you must arrive with an ironclad reservation should you want to spend the night or a longer time.

Club Punta Prima ★★ Built in 1987 in a low-slung, two-story format hugging the coastline a short walk from the beach, this hotel attracts a loyal clientele from northern Europe. The good-size rooms are comfortably furnished and well maintained, each with an excellent bed. Great attention has been paid to the enhancement and preservation of the site's isolated natural beauty.

Punta Prima, 07871 Sant Ferran, Formentera. © **97-132-82-44.** Fax 97-132-82-69. www.hotel-formentera.com. 96 units. 105€ double; 135€–170€ suite. AE, DC, MC, V. No parking. Closed Nov–May. **Amenities:** Restaurant; bar; bikes; concierge; outdoor saltwater pool; room service; outdoor tennis court. *In room:* A/C, TV, hair dryer, Wi-Fi (free).

Hotel Riu La Mola Located at Es Arenals, this hotel is one of the best equipped on the island—and during the summer it is usually packed. Opening onto the longest beach on the island, Playa de Migjorn, La Mola is designed in the style of a Spanish village. The good-size rooms are comfortable and well furnished, each with a firm bed.

Apartado 23, 07840 Playa de Migjorn, Formentera. © **97-132-70-00.** Fax 97-132-70-01. www.riu.com. 328 units. 99€–317€ double. Rates include buffet breakfast and dinner. AE, DC, MC, V. No parking. Closed Nov–Apr. **Amenities:** Restaurant; 2 bars; babysitting; children's center; exercise room; 2 outdoor freshwater pools; 2 outdoor tennis courts (lit); limited watersports rentals. *In room:* A/C, TV, hair dryer, minibar.

Sa Volta This small, inexpensive *hostal* features good, clean, modest guest rooms and neatly kept bathrooms with shower stalls. It has no restaurant, but you are right in the tourist belt of Formentera, in the midst of many cafes, restaurants, and nightlife options. Reserve well in advance, as it's hard to get a room here.

Av. Miramar 94, 07871 Es Pujols, Formentera. ☎ **97-132-81-25.** Fax 97-132-82-28. www.savolta. com. 25 units. 88€–165€ double; 150€–250€ junior suite. Rates include buffet breakfast. AE, DC, MC, V. Free parking. Closed Jan–Feb. **Amenities:** Restaurant; bar; babysitting; bikes; outdoor freshwater pool. *In room:* A/C, TV, hair dryer, minibar, Wi-Fi (free).

WHERE TO DINE ON FORMENTERA

Juan y Andrea ★ SEAFOOD Right on the beach in a natural park, this restaurant attracts any visiting celebrity, and the staff will still be talking about Bill Clinton's summer 2004 visit a decade hence. The restaurant is secluded on a section of beach under the shelter of palm trees. The same local family has offered the same specialties here for more than a quarter century. After a patron selects a lobster from a big tank, it is cooked and served at one of the ramshackle beach tables. Grilled seafood and fresh fish are prepared to perfection here, as is the island's best paella, served sizzling hot. *Arroz negro* (rice with squid ink) and *labuna a la sal* (sea bass cooked in salt to preserve its juice) are two specialties. If you prefer, you can actually sit on the sand and eat at a low table.

Playa Illetas, Carretera la Savina, Es Pujols. ☎ **97-118-71-30.** www.juanyandrea.com. Reservations recommended June–Aug. Main courses 20€–35€. AE, MC, V. Daily 12:30–3:30pm and 7:30–11pm. Closed Oct 16–Apr 30.

Sa Palmera SPANISH/INTERNATIONAL Lying along the beach, Playa Es Pujols, this rustically decorated restaurant has been going strong ever since its opening in 1968. It is decorated with wood furniture inside, and on a chilly day you can enjoy that ambience, retreating outside when the weather is fair. The specialty is the fresh fish of the day, which can be grilled or served in an herb-flavored green sauce. Another specialty is a *zarzuela* of *mariscos*, a seafood stew flavored with tomatoes, white wine, and fish broth. Paella is yet another choice dish, as is Argentine-style barbecued beef. Beef loin is served with onions, tomatoes, and peppers on a skewer. Most entrees are in the low to midprice range.

Playa Es Pujols. ☎ **97-132-83-56.** Main courses 10€–25€. MC, V. Apr–Oct Tues–Sun 12:30–11pm. Closed Nov–Mar.

MINORCA ★★

Minorca (also written "Menorca") is one of the most beautiful islands in the Mediterranean; miles of lovely beaches have made it a longtime favorite vacation spot for Europeans.

The island is barely 15km (9⅓ miles) wide and less than 52km (32 miles) long. Its principal city is **Mahón** (also called Maó; pop. 25,000), set on a rocky bluff overlooking the great port, which was fought over for centuries by the British, French, and Spanish.

After Majorca, it is the second largest of the Spanish Balearic Islands, but it has more beaches than Majorca, Ibiza, and Formentera combined—they range from miles-long silver or golden crescents of sand to rocky bays, or *calas*, reminiscent of Norwegian fjords. Our favorite is **Cala'n Porter,** 11km (6¾ miles) west of Mahón. Towering promontories guard the slender estuary where this spectacular beach is found. Another of Minorca's treasures, **Cala de Santa Galdana,** is 23km (14 miles) south of Ciudadela. Its gentle bay and excellent sandy beach afford the most scenic spot on the island. Illa d'en Colom, an island in the Mahón bay, is bordered with great beaches but can be reached only by boat.

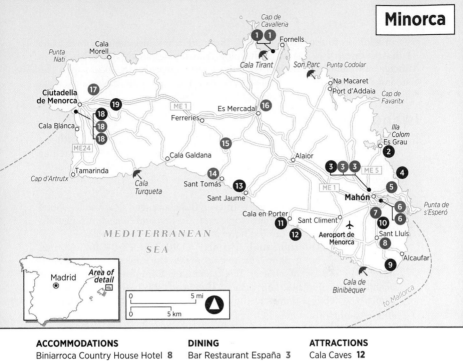

Minorca

ACCOMMODATIONS

Biniarroca Country House Hotel **8**
Hesperia Patricia **18**
Hotel Almirante Farragut **18**
Hotel del Almirante
(Collingwood House) **5**
Hotel Port Mahón **6**
Hotel RTM Capri **3**
Hotel Rural Sant Ignasi **17**
Hotel Santo Tomás **14**
Hotel Sol Menorca **14**
Hotels Cala Bona & Mar Blava **18**
Sant Joan de Binissaida **7**
Sol Gavilanes **14**

DINING

Bar Restaurant España **3**
Bar Triton **18**
Ca N'Olga **16**
Casa Manolo **18**
Cas Quintu **18**
Es Caliu Grill **18**
Es Pla **1**
Jàgaro **3**
La Minerva **6**
Molí d'es Reco **16**
Restaurant/Café Balear **18**
S'Algaret **1**
S'Engolidor **15**

ATTRACTIONS

Cala Caves **12**
Cala Mesquida **4**
Cala'n Porter **11**
Catedral **18**
Església de San Francisco **18**
Església de Santa María la Major **3**
Es Grau **2**
La Cova d'en Xoroi **12**
Naveta d'es Tudons **19**
Plaça d'Alfons III **18**
Punta Prima **9**
Torre d'en Gaumés **13**
Trepucó **10**
Xoriguer Gin Distillery **3**

The beaches along 217km (135 miles) of pine-fringed coastline are the island's greatest attraction, although many are not connected by roads. Nude bathing is commonplace, even though the practice is officially illegal. Golf, tennis, and sailing are available at reasonable fees, and windsurfing is offered at all major beaches.

With more than 60,000 permanent inhabitants, Minorca plays host to about half a million visitors a year. But it is not overrun with tourist developments and has none of the junky excess that has plagued Ibiza and Majorca for years.

Unlike those islands, Minorca is not utterly dependent on tourism; it has some industry, including leatherwork, costume-jewelry production, dairy farming, and even gin manufacturing. Life here is quiet and relaxed; it is not a place to go for glittering nightlife. Some clubs in Ibiza don't even open until 4am, but on Minorca nearly everybody, local and visitor alike, is in bed well before then.

In addition to trips to the beach, there are some fascinating things to do for those interested in history, archaeology, music, and art. Many artists live in Minorca, and exhibitions of their work are listed regularly in the local paper. The Catedral de Santa María in Mahón has one of Europe's great pipe organs, at which world-famous organists have given free concerts.

Island Essentials

GETTING THERE Minorca, lying off the eastern coast of Spain and northeast of Majorca, is reached by air or sea. The most popular method of reaching Minorca, and certainly the quickest, is to fly, but you can take a ferry from mainland Spain or from the other two major Balearic Islands, Ibiza and Majorca.

It is always good to arrive with everything arranged in advance—hotel rooms, car rentals, ferry, or airplane tickets. In July and August, reservations are vital because of the limited hotel and transportation facilities. **Minorca International Airport** (© 90-240-47-04 for information; www.aena.es) is 3km (1¾ miles) outside the capital city of Mahón. It receives dozens of charter flights, mainly from Germany, Italy, the Scandinavian countries, and Britain. **Iberia** (© 97-136-92-10) operates regularly scheduled domestic flights from Barcelona, Palma de Majorca, and even Madrid.

Regular **ferry service,** which operates frequently in the summer, connects Minorca with Barcelona, and Palma de Majorca. From Barcelona, the journey takes 9 hours aboard moderately luxurious lines. If you're on a real budget but still want a decent night's sleep, bunk in a four-person cabin, which is about the same price as a chair in the lounge. Meals can be purchased in a self-service restaurant on board or else brought along.

The ferry service is operated by **Trasmediterránea,** whose offices in Mahón are at Estació Marítim, along Moll (Andén) de Ponent (© 97-136-29-50; www.trasmediterranea.es); it's open Monday to Friday 8am to 1pm and 5 to 7pm. Saturday hours are 7 to 10pm, and Sunday 2:30 to 5pm, but only to receive the ferry from Valencia. However, any travel agency in Barcelona or Palma, even Ibiza, can book you a ticket; you need not go directly to one of the company's offices.

GETTING AROUND Transportes Menorca (TMSA), Cí Rodees 5, Maó (© 97-136-04-75; www.tmsa.es), operates **bus** service around the island. The tourist office (see Mahón's "Visitor Information," below) has complete bus schedules for the island.

The Spanish-owned **Atesa** (© 97-136-62-13; www.atesa.es) operates a rental-car desk at the airport, charging from 66€ to 117€ for its cheaper models. **Avis** (© 97-136-15-76; www.avis.com) operates out of the airport, asking from 58€ for its cheapest cars per day. Car-rental firms on the island will deliver a vehicle to the airport either upon your arrival or after you check into your hotel—but you must specify in advance.

To summon a local taxi, call © 97-138-28-96. The taxi stop is at Plaça s'Esplanada in Mahón. The typical one-way fare—say, from Mahón to the beaches at Cala'n Porter—is 15€.

THE BALEARIC ISLANDS | Minorca

Mahón

Mahón (Maó) and neighboring Villacarlos, in their gorgeous Georgian architecture and Chippendale reproductions, still show traces of British occupation. There's also Golden Farm, the magnificent mansion north of the capital, overlooking Mahón harbor, where in October 1799 Admiral Lord Nelson enjoyed a brief rest and, according to local legend, hid out with his ladylove, Emma Hamilton. In truth, Nelson was here alone working on *Sketches of My Life.*

The largest city on the island, Mahón is an east-coast port. In the Minorcan language, it is called Maó. Mahón has allegedly lent its name to one of the world's most popular sauces, mayonnaise.

Mahón was built on the site of an old castle standing on a cliff overlooking one of Europe's finest natural harbors, some 5.5km (3½ miles) long. The castle and the town wall erected to dissuade pirates are long gone, except for the archway of San Roque.

The first Christian king from the mainland, Alfonso II, established a base in the harbor in 1287. It became known as **Isla del Rey (Island of the King).** When the British constructed a hospital here to tend to wounded soldiers, it was called "Bloody Island." Since 1722, when the seat of government was moved here from Ciudadela, Mahón has been the capital of Minorca.

ESSENTIALS

GETTING THERE From the airport (see above), you must take a **taxi** into Mahón—there is no bus link. The approximate cost is 37€.

Mahón is the **bus** transport depot for the island, with departures from Calle José Anselmo Clave in the heart of town. The most popular run—seven buses per day in summer, four buses per day in winter—is to Ciudadela, but there are connections to other parts of the island. The tourist office (see "Visitor Information," below) distributes a list of schedules, and the list is published in the local newspaper, *Menorca Diario Insular.* Tickets cost 5€ and are purchased once you're aboard. Make sure you carry some change.

VISITOR INFORMATION The **tourist office,** at Nord 4 (© **90-292-90-15**), is open Monday to Friday 9am to 1pm and 5 to 7pm, Saturday 9am to 1pm.

CITY LAYOUT The heart of Mahón is the Plaça de la Constitució, with its Town Hall from the 18th century, constructed in an English Palladian style.

Plaça s'Esplanada, seat of the tourist office, is actually the main square. On Sunday, locals gather here to enjoy ice cream, the best in the Balearics. In summer, a market is held on Tuesday and Saturday 9am to 2pm. Artisans from all

The port of Mahón.

over the island sell their wares there. The northern boundary of the city is formed by **Puerto de Mahón,** which has many restaurants and shops along Muelle Comercial.

Mahón is not a beach town, but it has some accommodations and is the center of the best shopping and nightclubs. The closest beaches for swimming are those at **Es Grau** and **Cala Mesquida.**

Villacarlos stretches east along the port, a virtual extension of the capital, and it doesn't have beaches, either. Several good restaurants line the harbor leading toward Villacarlos. When the British founded this village, now a southeast suburb of Mahón, they called it Georgetown.

FUN ON & OFF THE BEACH

BEACHES **Cala'n Porter,** 11km (6¾ miles) west of Mahón, is one of the most spectacular beaches on the island. It's a sandy beach at a narrow estuary inlet protected by high promontories. Thinly scattered houses perch upon a cliff. You can drop by a bar here during the day. **La Cova d'en Xoroi,** ancient troglodyte habitations overlooking the sea from the upper part of the cliffs, can also be visited. (See "Central & Southern Minorca," p. 771.)

Going around the cliff face, you'll discover more caves at **Cala Caves.** People still live in some of these caves, and there are boat trips to see them from Cala'n Porter.

North of Mahón on the road to Fornells you'll encounter many beachside settlements. Close to Mahón, and already being exploited, is **Cala Mesquida,** one of the best beaches. To reach it, turn off the road to Cala Llonga and follow the signs to PLAYA.

The next fork in the road takes you to **Es Grau,** another fine beach. Along the way you see the salt marshes of S'Albufera, abundant in migrant birds. Reached by bus from Mahón, Es Grau, 8km (5 miles) north of Mahón, opens onto a sandy bay and gets very crowded in July and August. From Es Grau you can take a boat to **Illa d'en Colom,** an island in the bay with some good beaches. There are several bars at Es Grau for refueling.

South of Mahón is the little town of Sant Lluís and the large sandy beach to the east, **Punta Prima.** Patronized heavily by occupants of the local *urbanizaciones,* this beach is serviced by buses from Mahón, with six departures daily. The same buses will take you to an attractive necklace of beaches, the **Platges de Son Bou,** on the southern shore. Many tourist facilities are found here. (See "Central & Southern Minorca," p. 771.)

GOLF The only course is **Golf Son Parc** (© 97-118-88-75; www.golfson parc.com), a traditional 9-hole course that added another 9 holes in 2006.

WINDSURFING & SAILING The best spots are at Fornells Bay, which is 1.6km (1 mile) wide and several miles long. **Windsurfing Fornells,** Nov 33, Es Mercadal (© 97-118-81-50; www.windfornells.com), can supply you with gear.

SEEING MAHÓN'S SIGHTS

Most people don't take sightseeing too seriously in Mahón, as they are here mainly to enjoy the views of the port, to dine, or to shop. Even so, you may want to visit the **Església de Santa María la Major,** Plaça Constitució (© 97-136-39-49). The church was founded in 1287 by the Christian conqueror Alfonso III, who wanted to celebrate the Reconquest. Over the years, the original Gothic structure has been much altered, and it was rebuilt in 1772. It has a celebrated

A megalithic stone monument at Trepucó.

organ with four keyboards and more than 3,000 pipes, constructed in 1810 by Johan Kyburz, a Swiss artisan. Admiral Collingwood brought it to Mahón during the Napoleonic wars. A music festival in July and August showcases the organ, whose melodic sounds can be heard even as you sit drinking in a nearby cafe. The church is open daily 8am to 1pm and 6 to 8:30pm; donations are appreciated.

The best way to see the changing aspect of Mahón's port involves taking an hour-long **catamaran tour** offered by **Yellow Catamarans,** Moll de Llevant 12 (*© 63-967-63-51;* www.yellow catamarans.com). The cost is 10€ for adults, 5€ for children 10 and under. Because part of the sailing craft's hull contains glass windows below the water-line, you'll get views of underwater life that would otherwise be possible only with a submarine. Tours are conducted May to October at 10:30am, and then continue on the hour until 4pm. Departure time is not guaranteed, and the boat can leave up to 30 minutes later than scheduled.

You can visit the **Xoriguer Gin Distillery,** on the harborfront at Moll de Ponent 91 (*© 97-136-21-97*). Here, giant copper vats simmer over wood-fed fires. Later, after watching the process by which the famed Minorcan gin is made, you can taste more than a dozen brews. The distillery and a store selling the products, including potent liqueurs, is open Monday to Friday 8am to 7pm, and Saturday 9am to 1pm.

SIDE TRIPS BACK IN TIME

From Mahón you can take excursions to some of the prehistoric relics in the area. One of these, marked off the Mahón-Villacarlos highway, is **Trepucó,** where you'll find both a 4m (13-ft.) *taula* (huge T-shaped stone structure) and a *talayot* (circular stone tower). The megalithic monuments stand on the road to Sant Lluís, only about 1.6km (1 mile) from Mahón. Of all the prehistoric remains on the island, this site is the easiest to visit. It was excavated by Margaret Murray and a team from Cambridge University in the 1930s.

Another legacy of prehistoric people can be visited at Km 4 (a stone marker) off the Mahón-Ciudadela highway. The trail to **Talatí de Dalt** is marked. Your path will lead to this *taula* with subterranean caves.

Yet another impressive prehistoric monument is **Torre d'en Gaumés,** 15km (9⅓ miles) from Mahón off the route to Son Bou. (The path is signposted.) You can take a bus from Mahón to Son Bou if you don't have a car. This megalithic settlement spreads over many acres, including both *taulas* and *talayots,* along with ancient caves in which people once lived. The exact location is 3km (1¾ miles) south of Alayor off the road to Son Bou.

The restored **Naveta d'es Tudons** is accessible 5km (3 miles) east of Ciudadela, just to the south of the road to Mahón. This is the best-preserved and most significant prehistoric collection of megalithic monuments on Minorca. Its *naveta* (a boat-shaped monument thought to be a dwelling or a burial chamber) is said to be among the oldest monuments constructed by humans in Europe. Archaeologists have found the remains of many bodies at this site, along with a collection of prehistoric artifacts, including pottery, decorative jewelry, and weapons—but they have now been removed to museums. The site is more easily visited if you stay in Ciudadela (see below).

WHERE TO STAY

In Mahón

Hotel del Almirante (Collingwood House) ★ 🎁 This is an offbeat choice. Originally built in the late 18th century for Admiral Collingwood, a close friend of Lord Nelson, the hotel later served as a convent, as the home of a German sculptor, and, until the end of World War II, as the German embassy. Architecturally, it reflects a number of styles: Italianate, Georgian, and Minorcan. In 1964, it was restored and enlarged into a hotel. The reception area, with its 18th-century staircase, is decorated with numerous oil paintings and, like the rest of the public rooms, successfully mixes antiques with British memorabilia. Guests are housed in the main building or in one of the more modern bungalow accommodations. The rooms are a mixed bag—you don't really know what you get until the maid opens the door.

Carretera de Villacarlos s/n, 07700 Mahón, Minorca. ☎ **97-136-27-00.** Fax 97-136-27-04. www. hoteldelalmirante.com. 40 units. 65€–106€ double. Rates include buffet breakfast. DC, MC, V. Free parking. Closed Nov–Apr. **Amenities:** Restaurant; bar; babysitting; outdoor freshwater pool; room service; outdoor tennis court; Wi-Fi (free, in lobby). *In room:* A/C.

Hotel Port Mahón ★ Perched on a steep hillside above the harbor, this hotel looks like a large Georgian villa whose charms are largely of another era. Located in a residential neighborhood, it offers, without question, the most traditional accommodations in Minorca. It's one of the few large hotels that stays open year-round, and half of its rooms are usually reserved for tour groups. Some guests have been coming here since the 1950s, which indicates the age level of many of the patrons. There is a sense of calm and unhurried comfort in the airy, stone-floored public areas. The rooms overlook the harbor, the bougainvillea-filled garden, or the quiet street outside. Each unit has an ornate balcony with louvered shutters and potted flowers.

Av. Fort de L'Eau, 07701 Mahón, Minorca. ☎ **97-136-26-00.** Fax 97-135-10-50. www.sethotels. com. 82 units. 100€–200€ double; 160€–260€ suite. Rates include buffet breakfast. AE, DC, MC, V. No parking. **Amenities:** Restaurant; 2 bars; outdoor freshwater heated pool; room service. *In room:* A/C, TV, hair dryer, minibar, Wi-Fi (free).

Hotel RTM Capri If you don't stay at the more expensive and superior Hotel Port Mahón (see above), this comfortable, modern hotel, conveniently situated in the heart of Mahón, is the next best choice. Each of the simple rooms is comfortably but blandly furnished with conservative furniture, and each has a private balcony. It's well managed, with a sense of stewardship that derives from its long-term ownership and administration by a local family. Unlike many hotels on the island, this one is in the commercial core of Mahón and, as such, caters to business travelers from other parts of the Balearics and Europe; it has a more urban focus than hotels geared only to the resort trade.

Carrer Sant Esteve 8, 07703 Mahón, Minorca. © **97-136-14-00.** Fax 97-135-08-53. www.rtm
hotels.com. 75 units. 70€–188€ per person double. Rates include buffet breakfast. AE, DC, MC, V.
No parking. **Amenities:** Restaurant; bar; babysitting; exercise room; outdoor freshwater heated
pool; room service; spa. *In room:* A/C, TV, hair dryer, minibar, Wi-Fi (free).

On the Outskirts

Biniarroca Country House Hotel ★★★ 🛎 This is clearly the most romantic hotel on the island, and it's set in a flowery garden imbued with the scent of
lavender. Two Roman-style, green-tiled pools add a hedonistic note. The boutique hotel lies on the outskirts of Sant Lluís, directly to the south of Mahón.
Artworks, such as impressionist oil paintings, are harmoniously blended with
modern design to create a restful retreat, both rustic and luxurious—a blend of
the old and new. The garden rooms are individually decorated and contain private
terraces. Classic doubles lie in the main house. Dine at the acclaimed on-site
restaurant on freshly prepared food, some of it grown in the hotel garden. No
children 15 and under are allowed.

Cami Vella 57, 07710 Sant Lluís, Minorca. © **97-115-12-50.** http://biniarroca.com. 18 units. 80€–
295€ double; 215€–310€ junior suite; 240€–350€ suite. Rates include breakfast. MC, V. Closed
Nov–Mar. **Amenities:** Restaurant; bar; bikes; concierge; 2 pools (outdoor); room service. *In room:*
A/C, TV, TV/DVD (in some), fridge (in some), Wi-Fi (free).

Sant Joan de Binissaida ★★ 🛎 Approached on a roadway flanked by fig
trees and chinaberry, this is a beautifully restored antique farmhouse 15km (9⅓
miles) south of the capital of Mahón, between the villages of Sant Lluís and Es
Castell. Since the owner is an opera buff, he's named all the rooms after composers, including Bellini, Puccini, Verdi, Bach, Mozart, and Beethoven. The rooms
are tasteful, elegant, and harmoniously decorated, often with antiques. Stables
have been converted to accommodate more guests, but, in spite of their individual terraces, these are less desirable than units in the main house. There is much
of a house-party feel about the place in summer. The chef de cuisine concocts a
superb menu based on the day's fresh products.

Cami de Binissaida 108, 07720 Es Castell, Minorca. © **97-135-55-98.** Fax 97-135-50-01. http://
santjoan.binissaida.com. 12 units. 130€–260€ double; 160€–300€ junior suite; 200€–340€ suite.
Rates include buffet breakfast. MC, V. Closed Jan–Mar. **Amenities:** Restaurant; bar; pool (outdoor); room service. *In room:* A/C, TV, TV/DVD, fridge, Wi-Fi (free).

WHERE TO DINE

Fish and seafood form most of the basis of the Minorcan diet. The sea harvest is
abundant along the long coastline. The most elegant dish, *caldereta de langosta,*
consists of pieces of lobster blended with onion, tomato, pepper, and garlic, and
flavored with an herb liqueur. This is a favorite dish of King Juan Carlos when
he visits Minorca.

Shellfish paella is also popular, as is *escupinas* ("warty Venus"), a local shellfish. *Tordos con col* (thrushes with cabbage) are served in autumn. A peasant dish,
pa amb oli, often precedes a meal. This is bread flavored with salt and olive oil
and rubbed with fresh tomato.

Wine is brought in from mainland Spain, but gin is made on the island, a
legacy from the days of the British occupation. You can drink the gin by itself
or mix it with lemon and ice. For the latter, ask the bartender for *palloza* (pronounced pah-*yoh*-thah). Gin mixed with soda or lemonade is called a *pomada.*

Bar Restaurant España ⚜ SPANISH Originally established around 1938, this is one of the oldest continuously operating restaurants in Minorca, thanks to a solidly reliable clientele and well-prepared food served in generous portions at reasonable prices. Patrons include vacationing northern Europeans who tend to communicate with one another and the staff in English. Partly because of its cosmopolitan clientele, the menu is designed to appeal to a wide variety of palates. Examples include *cigales a la americana* (prawns in a spicy red sauce), shrimp with garlic, mussels marinara, baked fish (especially hake and cod), grilled veal and pork, and beefsteaks grilled and served with a decidedly Spanish flair.

Carrer Victori 48–50. ℂ **97-136-32-99.** Reservations recommended. Main courses 10€–25€. *Menú del día* 10€. MC, V. Daily 1–3:30pm and 7:30–11pm. Closed Dec 23–Feb 4.

Jàgaro ★★ SEAFOOD/MINORCAN The seafood menu here is Minorca's most eclectic and interesting. Begin with *ensalada templada con cigalitos y setas,* a mix of warm prawns and wild mushrooms served on a bed of lettuce; or Jàgaro's interpretation of gazpacho, flavored with shrimp and melon. The *mosaico de verduras,* a plate of grilled fresh vegetables, is an excellent choice. Main courses may include *carpaccio de mero* (grouper) served with a tangy green-mustard sauce, *caldereta de langosta,* or *ortigas* (sea anemones). Seafood offerings are extensive, although meat dishes, including duck *maigret* (breast) in orange sauce, and foie gras with sweet-and-sour sauce, are very appealing.

Moll de Llevant 334. ℂ **97-136-23-90.** Reservations recommended. Main courses 15€–50€. AE, DC, MC, V. Apr–Sept daily noon–4pm and 8pm–midnight; Oct–Mar Tues–Sun noon–4pm, Tues–Sat 8pm–midnight. Closed: Feb.

La Minerva ★★ CATALAN/MEDITERRANEAN This is the finest restaurant in Mahón. Located on the port, it is cozy and traditional, specializing in fresh seafood such as clams, mussels, and lobster. Opposite Isla Pinto, it's just east of the ferry terminal. Many nearby dining places offer lackluster, overpriced food, but this one is a winner. Imbued with a nautical decor, the restaurant feeds you well and lets you enjoy a view of the water and the comings and goings of patrons in their tenders. The cuisine is prepared in the main building on the other side of the road, and then rushed across by waiters long skilled in not getting run over by passing cars. You might enjoy the freshly made house special: a salad of prawns, avocado, black olives, radicchio, and hearts of palm. Some flavor-filled meat dishes appear on the menu: Pork loin with fresh plums is especially tantalizing, as are Ping-Pong-ball–size meatballs in an almond sauce. However, we prefer the seafood, including grouper baked with slices of garlic in an oil or vinegar sauce, served with an aromatic ratatouille.

Moll del Llevant 87. ℂ **97-135-19-95.** www.restaurantelaminerva.com. Reservations required. Main courses 18€–38€; tasting menu 20€. AE, DC, MC, V. Daily 1:30–3:30pm and 8–11:30pm.

Ciudadela ★

At the western end of the island, the town of Ciudadela (Ciutadella de Menorca) has a typically Mediterranean air about it. Lining the narrow streets of the Old City are noble mansions of the 17th and 18th centuries, as well as numerous churches. It was the capital until 1722, when the British chose Mahón instead, largely because its harbor channel is more navigable than the one at Ciudadela. Subsequently, the British built the main island road to link the two cities.

Like Mahón, Ciudadela perches high above its harbor, which is smaller than Mahón's. The seat of Minorca's bishopric, Ciudadela pontificates while Mahón administrates.

Known as Medina Minurka under the Muslims, Ciudadela retains Moorish traces despite the 1558 Turkish invasion and destruction of the city. An obelisk in memory of the city's futile defense against that invasion stands in the pigeon-filled **Plaça d'es Born (Plaza del Born),** the city's main square overlooking the port.

ESSENTIALS

GETTING THERE From the airport, you must take a taxi to Ciudadela, as there is no bus link. The cost is approximately 45€ each way.

From Mahón, six **buses** go back and forth every day; a one-way fare costs 4.50€. Departures are from Plaça s'Esplanada in Mahón.

Driving from Ciudella in the west to Mahón in the east coast, head east along C-721, which traverses through the center of Minorca and is the best road on the island.

VISITOR INFORMATION The **tourist office,** located at Plaça Catedral 5 (© 97-138-26-93), is open June to September daily 9am to 9pm; October to May, hours are Monday to Friday 9am to 1pm and 5 to 7pm, and Saturday 9am to 1pm.

EXPLORING CIUDADELA: THE BEACH & BEYOND

In Ciudadela, buses depart from Plaça d'Artrutx for most coastal destinations, including the best beaches. Of these, **Cala Santandria,** 3km (1¾ miles) to the south, is known for its white sands. This is a sheltered beach near a creek; in its background are rock caves, which were inhabited in prehistoric times. The coves of **En Forcat, Blanes,** and **Brut** are near Ciudadela.

Cala de Santa Galdana, not reached by public transport, is the most stunning in the area, lying 23km (14 miles) south of Ciudadela. The bay here is tranquil and ringed with a beach of fine golden sand. Tall, bare cliffs rise in the background, and the air is perfumed with the scent of pine trees. The road to this beach, unlike so many others on Minorca, is a good one.

The center of Ciudadela is **Plaça d'es Born,** site of tourist information. This was the center of life when the town was known to Jaume I. Back then Ciudadela was completely walled to protect itself from pirate incursions, which were a serious threat from the 13th century on. Much of the present look of this square, and of Ciudadela itself, is due to its demotion in 1722, when the capital was transferred to Mahón. For centuries, this checked urban development in Ciudadela, and many buildings now stand that might have been torn down to make way for progress.

Cala de Santa Galdana from afar.

The central Plaça d'es Born.

Plaça d'es Born looks over the port from the north. Once it was known as Plaza Generalísimo, honoring the dictator Franco. The square was built around the obelisk that remembers the hopeless struggle of the town against the invading Turks who entered the city in 1558 and caused much destruction. On the west side of the square is the **Ayuntamiento (Town Hall).**

To the southwest of the square stands **Església de San Francisco.** The 14th-century Gothic building has some excellent carved wood altars. The town once had a magnificent opera house, Casa Salort, but that cultural note sounds no more, as it's been turned into a somewhat seedy movie theater. Another once-splendid palace, Palacio de Torre-Saura, also opens onto the square. Still owner-occupied, it was constructed in the 1800s.

The **cathedral,** Plaça Pío XII, was ordered built by the conquering Alfonso III on the site of the former mosque. It is Gothic in style and fortresslike in appearance. The facade of the church, in the neoclassical style, was added in 1813. The church suffered heavy damage in 1936, during the Spanish Civil War, but it has since been restored.

Ciudadela is at its liveliest at the **port,** where you'll find an array of little shops, bars, restaurants, and sailboats, along with some impressive yachts in summer. **Carrer Quadrado,** lined with shops and arcades, is another street worth walking.

The Moorish influence lingers in a block of whitewashed houses in the **Voltes,** off the Plaça s'Esplanada. In Ciudadela the local people still meet at **Plaça d'Alfons III,** the square honoring their long-ago liberator.

WHERE TO STAY IN & AROUND CIUDADELA
Expensive
Hesperia Patricia ★ Built in 1988, this three-story building is centrally located, which business travelers find convenient. It is Ciudadela's most respected, most luxurious hotel. Near the Plaça d'es Born, about a half-mile from the nearest beach (Playa de La Caleta), it has a polite, hardworking staff well versed in the

island's facilities and geography. The spacious guest rooms are comfortable, carpeted, and outfitted pleasantly in pastels.

Passeig Sant Nicolau 90–92, 07760 Ciudadela, Minorca. ✆ **97-138-55-11.** Fax 97-148-11-20. www. hesperia-patricia.com. 44 units. 64€–206€ double; 130€–235€ junior suite. AE, DC, MC, V. Free parking on street. **Amenities:** Bar; outdoor freshwater pool; room service; Wi-Fi (free, in lobby). *In room:* A/C, TV, hair dryer, minibar.

Hotel Rural Sant Ignasi ★★ 🎒 For tranquillity seekers, this is a real discovery, as it lies outside town and is surrounded by gardens and woodland of oak and palm trees. This was once the private hacienda address of a prestigious Menorcan family before its successful conversion to a hotel of elegance and charm. The location is within an easy drive of all the beaches on the northern and southwestern coast of the island. The staff can also direct you to such activities as horseback riding, watersports, and cycling.

The restored home has a lot of style and personality in its midsize bedrooms. Each room on the ground level, where the floors are 2 centuries old, has a private garden. Units on the second landing open onto terraces with views of the countryside. For romantic escapists, there are rooms in the ancient loft of the house, with a lovely communal lounge and sloping wooden ceilings.

Carretera Cala Morell, Apartado 424, 07760 Ciudadela, Minorca. ✆ **97-138-55-75.** Fax 97-148-03-37. www.santignasi.com. 25 units. 105€–252€ double; 176€–378€ suite. MC, V. Free parking. Closed Oct–Mar. **Amenities:** Restaurant; bar; babysitting; 2 outdoor freshwater pools; room service. *In room:* A/C, TV, hair dryer, minibar.

Moderate

Hotel Almirante Farragut Five kilometers (3 miles) outside Ciudadela, beside a small rock-lined inlet, this four-story building is one of the best hotels in the development of Los Delfines, a cluster of resort hotels initiated in the 1970s and 1980s. Public rooms are airy, large, sparsely furnished, and appropriate to the hotel's role as a warm-weather beach resort with an international clientele, often from England and Germany. Guest rooms are pleasant, with standardized furnishings. Each has a balcony or terrace, usually overlooking either the rocky inlet or the open sea. Prices vary widely according to season, but lodgings that the hotel identifies as suites are nothing more than larger-than-usual double rooms.

Urbanización Los Delfines, Cala'n Forcat, 07760 Ciudadela, Minorca. ✆ **97-138-80-00.** Fax 97-138-81-07. www.hotelesglobales.com. 493 units. 63€–205€ double. Rates include buffet breakfast. MC, V. Free parking. Closed Nov–Apr. **Amenities:** Restaurant; 2 bars; babysitting; bikes; children's center; concierge; exercise room; 2 outdoor saltwater pools; 2 outdoor tennis courts (lit); extensive watersports equipment; Wi-Fi (free, in lobby). *In room:* A/C, TV, fridge (in some), hair dryer.

Inexpensive

Hotels Cala Bona & Mar Blava Set within a few paces of each other, these two hotels were both built in 1970 and share the same manager, owner, and facilities. Technically, the Cala Bona is categorized as a one-star hotel by the local tourist office, and the Mar Blava is a two-star hotel, but since the simple and angular rooms are almost identical, no one makes a big point about that. Once you register (within the lobby of the Mar Blava), you'll wonder why management doesn't combine them both into a single hotel with the same name. Stairs lead down to a small beach, and there's a larger beach just 5 minutes away. In both hotels, guest rooms are clean and comfortable, albeit very simple. Most have views of the sea. The hotels share an outdoor pool and an outdoor terrace. The in-house restaurant is used only for breakfast.

20

THE BALEARIC ISLANDS

Minorca

Av. del Mar 14–16, 07760 Ciudadela, Minorca. ☏ **97-138-00-16.** Fax 97-148-20-70. www.cala-bona.net. 40 units. 45€–80€ double. Rates include buffet breakfast. AE, DC, MC, V. Free parking nearby. Closed Nov–Mar. **Amenities:** Restaurant; bar; babysitting; outdoor freshwater pool; room service. *In room:* Ceiling fans, TV, hair dryer.

WHERE TO STAY NEAR CIUDADELA

Hotel Sol Menorca This hotel gives the impression of a large, well-maintained hacienda, complete with lacy iron balconies and louvered shutters. Surrounded by lawns and flowering shrubs, it has a private beach and a sweeping view of rocky islets. Many guests make their balconies an extension of their midsize rooms, reading, sitting, and talking within sight of the sea.

Playa Santo Tomás s/n, 07749 San Cristóbal (11km/6¾ miles southwest of Ciudadela), Minorca. ☏ **97-137-00-50.** Fax 97-137-03-48. www.solmelia.com. 188 units. 46€–240€ double. Rates include buffet breakfast. AE, DC, MC, V. Parking 10€. Closed early Oct to Apr 30. **Amenities:** Restaurant; bar; babysitting; exercise room; outdoor freshwater pool; room service. *In room:* A/C, TV, hair dryer, minibar.

WHERE TO DINE IN & AROUND CIUDADELA

The port of Ciudadela offers a wide selection of restaurants for all palates and prices. Beyond that, there are some commendable choices in and around town.

Bar Triton TAPAS The best place for tapas in the port, Triton offers a wide range of snacks, including sausages, *tortillas* (Spanish omelets), meatballs, and a dozen or so seafood tapas, among them octopus, stuffed squid, and *escupiñas* (Minorcan clams). On the wall inside are photos and illustrations of the port before it was a haven for vacationers. As in those days, fishers still make up an important part of the clientele, and you'll often find the locals engaged in a friendly afternoon game of cards. For generations, this bar has made it a point to open every day at 4am, presumably in time to serve coffee, snacks, and, in some cases, stiff drinks to fishermen headed out onto the nearby fishing banks. Now it also welcomes a coterie of fashionable night owls, who straggle in for a late-night (or early-morning) nightcap before tottering off to bed.

Marina 55. ☏ **97-138-00-02.** Tapas 3.50€–30€; combined platters 7€–20€. MC, V. Easter–Oct daily 4am–2am; Nov–Easter 4am–1am.

Casa Manolo ★ SPANISH/MINORCAN Located at the port, across from the spot where the larger yachts anchor, Casa Manolo is a favorite of the yachting crowd. You can dine indoors in a room carved out of stone, or alfresco on the intimate terrace. King Juan Carlos has been seen here enjoying the elegant atmosphere and outstanding cuisine. The menu consists mainly of fresh seafood and lobster dishes. The specialty of the house is *arroz de pescado caldoso,* a dish resembling paella, but with more focus on fish. The *caldereta de langosta,* a lobster-based bouillabaisse, is one of our favorites. The hardworking and affable owner, María Postores, supervises all aspects of your dining experience.

Marina 117. ☏ **97-138-00-03.** www.rtecasamanolo.com. Reservations required in summer. Main courses 18€–42€. AE, DC, MC, V. Daily 1–4pm and 8–11:30pm. Closed Feb–Mar.

Cas Quintu SPANISH/MINORCAN Thriving since the early 1960s from a position on an ornate square in the most historic core of town, Cas Quintu offers both indoor and outdoor tables that afford vantage points for people-watching. You can order drinks and light food in the cafe daily from 9am to 2pm. This establishment's selection of tapas is among the best in town. Full meals are served outdoors or in one of a pair of rooms in back. Specialties include a zesty squid sautéed in butter, several different preparations of beefsteak, a perfect sole meunière, and a mixed grill of fish based on the catch of the day.

Cami De Bax 8. ✆ **97-138-10-02.** Main courses 15€–25€; fixed-price menu 27€. AE, MC, V. Daily 1–4pm and 8–11:30pm.

Es Caliu Grill SPANISH About 2.5km (1½ miles) south of Ciudadela, along the main road between Cala Santandria and Cala Blanca, Es Caliu is the place to come when you've had your fill of seafood. Specializing in grilled meats of the freshest quality, it offers lamb, veal, pork, rabbit, quail, and spit-roasted suckling pig. But beyond fine food, you get a special ambience. Above the bar hang hams and garlic braids, and off to the side are stacked wine barrels. The family-style tables and benches are made of cut and polished logs. The outdoor terrace is roofed and festooned with cascading flowers; indoors are two rustic dining areas, one with a fireplace.

Carretera Cala Blanca. ✆ **97-138-01-65.** www.grillescaliu.com. Main courses 15€–28€. MC, V. May–Oct daily 1–4pm and 7pm–midnight; off season Fri 7–11:30pm, Sat–Sun 1–4pm and 7–11:30pm.

Restaurant/Café Balear ★ SEAFOOD The fishing boat carrying the catch of the day docks here to restock the fish tank. This cafe/restaurant arguably serves the best and freshest seafood on the island. Situated right on the water's edge, it offers excellent food prepared by the local personality-chef José Luis Ruesca. The *merluza* (hake) is an always worthy choice, as is the rice with fresh shrimp. The lobster stew is the island's best. Young waiters zoom around, serving the plentiful, fresh, and well-presented dishes to tanned people from all over the world.

Passeig Pla de Sant Joan 15. ✆ **97-138-00-05.** www.cafe-balear.com. Reservations required. Main courses 16€–20€; set menu 22€. AE, DC, MC, V. Summer Mon–Sat 1–4:30pm and 7pm–12:30am; off season Tues–Sun 1–4pm, Mon–Sat 7:30pm–midnight. Closed Nov.

CIUDADELA AFTER DARK

Café El Molino, Camino de Maó 7 (✆ **97-138-00-00**), is one of our favorite bars, a hangout near the Avinguda de la Constitució. It has attracted virtually every drinker in town since it was established in 1905 within the circular premises of a windmill built in 1794. It provides a rustic but richly international contrast to the busy square it borders and boasts the unusual distinction of having monumental walls and vaulted ceilings a lot older than those of the buildings surrounding it. The clientele includes visiting foreigners and local fishers, and the mood changes from that of an early-morning cafe, whose opening is timed to coincide with the departure of fishing boats, to a late-night bar. This place is earthy, regional, and brusque, yet invaluable for an insight into old-time Minorca.

Central & Southern Minorca

Topographically and climatically, this is the more tranquil part of the island. The beaches are more accessible, and the winds blow less—as a result, tourism has taken a firmer foothold here than in the north. Santo Tomás, Cala Galdana, Platges de Son Bou, Cala Bosch, and Punta Prima are some of the focal points for travelers.

Es Mercadal, a town of several thousand inhabitants at the foot of Monte Toro, is an ensemble of white houses with grace notes of color. Among its claims to local fame are two types of almond confectionery—*carquinyols* (small, hard

An alley in Es Mercadal.

cookies) and *amargos* (a kind of macaroon). The place to get both is **Pastelería Villalonga Ca's Sucrer,** Carrer Nou 46, Es Mercadal (℃ **97-1 15-41-44;** www. cassucrer.es), open Tuesday to Saturday 9:30am to 1:30pm and 5 to 8:30pm, and Sunday 11am to 2pm.

From Es Mercadal, you can take a road 4km (2½ miles) up to **Monte Toro,** the island's tallest mountain at 355m (1,165 ft.), crowned with a sanctuary that is a place of pilgrimage for Minorcans. The winding road leads to a panoramic view of the island's rolling green countryside dotted with *fincas,* trim fields, and stands of trees. From this vantage point you can clearly see the contrast between the flatter southern part of the island and the hilly northern region. The hilltop sanctuary includes a small, simple church with an ornate gilded altar displaying the image (reportedly found nearby in 1290) of the Virgin Mare de Déu d'el Toro, the island's patron saint. In 1936 the church was destroyed by fire, but the statue was saved from the flames and a new church built. The church is open daily from early morning to sunset; admission is free. In the courtyard of the sanctuary is a bronze monument to those Minorcans who left in the 18th century, while the island was still a British colony, to colonize Spanish settlements in North America. The large statue of Christ commemorates the dead in the Spanish Civil War. There is a snack bar with a pleasant terrace here.

Platges de Son Bou is a stunning beach scarred by two outsize hotels. Although still enchanting, the 1.6km-long (1-mile) narrow beach and clear turquoise waters are now often crowded, even in the off season; in July and August they're best avoided. At the eastern end of the beach just beyond the two monster hotels are the ruins of a Paleo-Christian basilica, most probably dating from the 5th or 6th century. Visible in the cliffs beyond are cave dwellings, some of which appear quite prosperous, with painted facades and shades to keep out the noonday sun.

WHERE TO STAY

Most of the hotels in this area cater almost exclusively to tour groups.

Hotel Santo Tomás ★ One of our favorite hotels on Minorca, Santo Tomás offers the best quality and comfort on the island; it's the only government-rated four-star hotel on the beach. Public areas are airy and spacious, and accommodations are comfortable. Most rooms open onto a terrace that faces the sea.

Playa Santo Tomás, 07749 Es Migjorn Gran, Minorca. ℃ **97-137-00-25.** Fax 97-137-02-04. www. sethotels.com. 85 units. 120€–290€ double; 170€–365€ suite. Rates include buffet breakfast and dinner. AE, DC, MC, V. Free parking. Closed Nov–Apr. **Amenities:** 2 restaurants; bar; babysitting; exercise room; 2 freshwater pools (1 heated indoor); room service; sauna; spa. *In room:* A/C, TV, hair dryer, minibar.

Sol Gavilanes A large resort hotel, Sol Gavilanes is fully equipped with swimming pools, discos, restaurants, and bars. It's atop a steep slope overlooking one of the most perfect beaches in the Mediterranean, surrounded by a grove of pines and palmettos. The original beauty of Cala Galdana has been substantially marred by construction, but you can enjoy the best end of its sandy, crescent-shaped beach and turquoise waters by staying here. Each of the sizable, functionally furnished units has a balcony.

Urbanización Cala Galdana s/n, 07750 Ferreries, Minorca. ✆ **97-115-45-45.** Fax 97-115-45-46. www.solmelia.com. 346 units. 51€–276€ double; 129€–322€ suite. Rates include buffet breakfast. MC, V. Free parking. Closed Nov–Apr. **Amenities:** 3 restaurants; bar; babysitting; children's center; exercise room; 2 outdoor freshwater pools; room service; spa; limited watersports equipment. *In room:* A/C, TV, hair dryer, minibar.

WHERE TO DINE

Some of the best dining in this area is offered in the inland villages rather than along the coast. **Es Mercadal,** in particular, has a few choice restaurants.

Ca N'Olga ★ MINORCAN/INTERNATIONAL A stylish, sophisticated spot that attracts a similar clientele, Ca N'Olga is warm, winsome, and intimate. Occupying a typical white-stucco Minorcan house that's some 150 years old, this restaurant offers dining on a pretty outdoor patio or at a handful of indoor tables.

The eclectic menu changes frequently with the market offerings. It is likely to include quail with onion-and-sherry vinegar and *osso buco*. Some standard dishes that tend to appear regularly are *cap roig* (scorpionfish), *cabrito* (baby goat), a fish terrine, and mussels au gratin. Among the homemade desserts you'll often find a velvety-smooth fig ice cream and chestnut pudding.

Pont Na Macarrana, Es Mercadal. ✆ **97-137-54-59.** Reservations recommended on weekends. Main courses 18€–32€. AE, DC, MC, V. Mid-Mar and Nov Wed–Mon 1:30–3:30pm and 8:30–11:30pm; Apr–May and Oct Wed–Sun 1:30–3:30pm and 8:30–11:30pm; June–Sept daily 1:30–3:30pm and 7:45–11:30pm. Closed Dec to mid-Mar.

Molí d'es Reco MINORCAN Easily spotted by the 300-year-old windmill that inspired the name of this 1982 creation, Molí d'es Reco offers a pleasant outdoor patio but a rather plain indoor dining area. Overall, the place is a bit touristy, but

---

Where the Flintstones Boogie the Night Away

Just .8km (½ mile) to the east in Cala'n Porter is a unique nightspot. Embedded in a series of caves within a sheer cliff face rising from the sea, **La Cova d'en Xoroi** (✆ **97-137-72-36;** www.cova denxoroi.com) is a conglomeration of bars, terraces, intimate nooks and crannies, and a disco floor. For sheer drama, the setting is without equal. As you walk down the entrance stairway, the magnificent setting opens before you. The dance floor overlooks the sea at the cliff's edge—there's no window, just a railing. Prehistoric vessels were found inside these caves that, according to legend, were once the refuge of a Moor called Xoroi, who had abducted a local maid and made his home here with her and their family. You can visit this unusual spot during the day as well, from 10:30am to 9pm. In the evening, from 11pm to 4am, La Cova d'en Xoroi transforms into a disco. Admission is 15€ to 25€, including your first drink.

The view from Monte Toro, outside Es Mercadal.

it offers hearty Minorcan fare including stuffed eggplant, *oliaigua amb tomatecs* (a soup with tomato, onion, parsley, green pepper, and garlic), snails with spider crab, partridge with cabbage, and *calamares a la menorquina* (stuffed squid with an almond cream sauce).

Calle Major 53, Es Mercadal. ✆ **97-137-53-92.** www.restaurantemolidesraco.com. Reservations recommended in summer. Main courses 15€–32€. AE, MC, V. Daily 1–4pm and 7–11pm.

S'Engolidor ★ 🏠 MINORCAN In the village of Es Migjorn Gran (San Cristóbal), between Es Mercadal and Santo Tomás, is this cozy and relatively undiscovered restaurant. Except for a small sign on the door, it could be mistaken for any other house on this quiet side street. The building dates from 1740, with sections added throughout the years. The interior is simple: stark white walls accented with artwork. The dining area consists of several small rooms, containing only a few tables each. You can dine outdoors in one of the small patio areas; many overlook the owner's compact vegetable garden. The menu consists of Minorcan specialties, including *olaigua* (eggplant stuffed with fish) and a particularly succulent version of roasted lamb. Owner José Luis maintains four simple **guest rooms** that, although clean and cozy, contain virtually no amenities other than private bathrooms and a sense of peace and quiet. A double room, with breakfast included, costs 45€ to 58€ per night.

Carrer Major 3, Es Migjorn Gran. ✆ **97-137-01-93.** www.sengolidor.com. Reservations recommended on weekends. Main courses 18€–28€. MC, V. May–Oct Tues–Sun 8–11pm. Closed Nov–Apr.

Fornells & the Northern Coast

The road leading north from Es Mercadal to Fornells runs through some of the island's finer scenery. Mass-tourism hotels, so far, have not discovered this place, but there are a few good dining choices. On the northern coast, the tiny town of Fornells snuggles around a bay filled with boats and windsurfers and lined with restaurants and a few shops. Built around four defense fortifications—the Talaia de la Mola (now destroyed), the Tower of Fornells at the harbor mouth, the fortress of the Island of Las Sargantanas ("the Lizards") situated in the middle of the harbor, and the now-ruined Castle of San Jorge or San Antonio—Fornells today is a flourishing fishing village noted for its upscale restaurants featuring savory lobster *calderetas.*

West of Fornells is **Platja Binimella,** a beautiful beach (unofficially nudist) easily accessible by car. Its long, curving, sandy cove is peacefully set against undulating hills. A snack bar is the sole concession to civilization.

By far the most splendid panorama here is from the promontory at **Cap de Cavalleria,** the northernmost tip of the island, marked by a lighthouse. Getting here requires some effort, however. At a bend in the road leading to Platja Binimella, a signpost indicates the turnoff to Cap de Cavalleria through a closed gate heading to a dirt road. The closed gate is typical of many of the roads leading to Minorca's undeveloped beaches. All the beaches in Spain, however, are public, so no one may impede access to them—although landowners might discourage visitors by making access difficult. The prevailing custom is simply to open the gate, go on through, and close it behind you. It is important that you close the gate because often they keep livestock confined to certain areas. As you follow the long dirt road (negotiable in a regular car or on a motorbike) out to Cap de Cavalleria, you come across several more sets of gates and travel through countryside reminiscent of the Scottish highlands, with cultivated fields and scattered grand *fincas.* Shortly before the lighthouse is a parking area down to the left. You'll have to pick your way across the scrub and rocks for the views. The best one is from a circular tower in ruins up to the right of the lighthouse. Now brace yourself for a vista encompassing the whole of Minorca—a symphony of dramatic cliffs and jewel-blue water.

WHERE TO DINE

Fornells is noted for its fine seafood restaurants specializing in Minorcan *calderetas.* King Juan Carlos has been known to sail in here when he wants to savor the seafood stew. In peak summer season, people call their favorite Fornells restaurant days in advance with their orders.

Es Pla ★ MINORCAN/SEAFOOD If any restaurant in Minorca deserves a comparison to the grand Roman watering holes of *La Dolce Vita,* it's this one, where King Juan Carlos and his family have come to dine several times. Stylish, airy, and elegant in a way that reflects the seagoing life of the island, Es Pla has thrived here since the 1960s, on a wood-floored porch that is only about 2m (6½ ft.) above the swell of the surf. Large and informal, it has a long stainless-steel bar area and an indoor/outdoor design. Menu items include a roster of perfectly prepared fish, meat, and shellfish, but the acknowledged culinary winner—and the most frequently ordered dish—is paella with crayfish. Only the shellfish dishes are high-priced.

Passeig des Pla, Fornells. ✆ **97-137-66-55.** Reservations recommended July–Aug. Main courses 10€–70€. AE, DC, MC, V. Daily 1–4pm and 7–10pm. Closed Jan–Mar.

S'Algaret SPANISH Adjacent to the *hostal* of the same name, S'Algaret is much frequented by locals and is one of the few economical alternatives in Fornells. (Here, you eat rather than dine.) The restaurant is sleepy, quiet, small in scale, and unpretentious. You can nibble on good-tasting tapas, sandwiches, a selection of tortillas, and a smattering of *platos combinados* (combination plates), the ingredients of which change daily.

Plaça S'Algaret 7, Fornells. ✆ **97-137-66-66.** Tapas 3€–8€ per *ración* (serving); *menú del día* 25€; platters 14€–24€. AE, MC, V. Daily 8am–midnight.

FAST FACTS

[FastFACTS] SPAIN

American Express The American Express number to call in Spain is ℰ **90-210-09-56.** A staff member will direct you to the nearest location to deal with your Amex needs.

Area Codes Dial **011** and then the country code for Spain **(34).** Drop the zero before dialing the city area code. See "Staying Connected," on p. 83.

Business Hours Banks are open Monday to Friday 9:30am to 2pm and Saturday 9:30am to 1pm. Most offices are open Monday to Friday 9am to 5 or 5:30pm; the longtime practice of early closings in summer seems to be dying out. In restaurants, lunch is usually 1 to 4pm and dinner 9 to 11:30pm or midnight. There are no set rules for the opening of bars and taverns; many open at 8am, others at noon. Most stay open until 1:30am or later. Major stores are open Monday to Saturday from 9:30am to 8pm; smaller establishments, however, often take a siesta, doing business 9:30am to 1:30pm and 4:30 to 8pm. Hours can vary from store to store.

Currency See "Money & Costs," on p. 71.

Drinking Laws The legal drinking age is 18. Bars, taverns, and cafeterias usually open at 8am, and many serve alcohol to 1:30am or later. Generally, you can purchase alcoholic beverages at almost any market.

Driving Rules See "Getting There & Getting Around," p. 65.

Drugstores To find an open pharmacy *(farmacia)* outside normal business hours, check the list of stores posted on the door of any drugstore. The law requires drugstores to operate on a rotating system of hours so that there's always a drugstore open somewhere, even Sunday at midnight.

Electricity The U.S. uses 110-volt electricity, Spain 220-volt. Most low-voltage electronics, such as laptops, iPods, and cellphone chargers, will do fine with 220-volt. It's still smart to check with the manufacturer to determine how your appliance will handle a voltage switch. If it can't, a voltage converter can be used; these are available at such outlets as Radio Shack. Small adaptors change a plug from a U.S. flat prong to a Spanish round prong so that you can fit it into a local socket, but they don't work as electrical converters. Adaptors are sold at most hardware stores *(ferreteria)* in Spain, but converters are hard to come by. Better purchase one before flying off to Spain.

Embassies & Consulates If you lose your passport, fall seriously ill, get into legal trouble, or have some other serious problem, your embassy or consulate can help. These are the Madrid addresses and hours: The **United States Embassy,** Calle de Serrano 75 (☎ **91-587-22-00;** http://madrid.usembassy.gov; Metro: Núñez de Balboa), is open Monday to Friday 9am to 6pm. The **Canadian Embassy,** Núñez de Balboa 35 (☎ **91-423-32-50;** http://canadaonline.about.com/od/travel/a/embspain.htm; Metro: Velázquez), is open Monday to Thursday 8:30am to 5:30pm, and Friday 8:30am to 2:30pm. The **British Embassy,** Calle Fernando el Santo 16 (☎ **91-700-82-00;** http://ukinspain.fco.gov.uk/en; Metro: Colón), is open Monday to Friday 9am to 1:30pm and 3 to 6pm. The **Republic of Ireland** has an embassy at Paseo Castellana 46 (☎ **91-436-40-93;** http://ireland.visahq.com/embassy/Spain; Metro: Serrano); it's open Monday to Friday 9am to 2pm. The **Australian Embassy,** Plaza Diego de Ordas 3, Edificio Santa Engracia 120 (☎ **91-353-66-00;** www.spain.embassy.gov.au; Metro: Ríos Rosas), is open Monday to Thursday 8:30am to 5pm and Friday 8:30am to 2:15pm. Citizens of **New Zealand** have an embassy at Plaza de la Lealtad 2 (☎ **91-523-02-26;** www.nzembassy.com/home.cfm?c=27; Metro: Banco de España); it's open Monday to Friday 9am to 2pm and 3 to 5:30pm.

Emergencies The national emergency number for Spain (except in the Basque Country) is ☎ **006;** in the Basque Country it is ☎ **088.**

Etiquette & Customs In Franco's day, many visitors would be arrested for the skimpy, revealing clothes worn around the city streets of Spain today. Nonetheless, it is considered extremely rude for men to go bare-chested except at the beach or poolside. Spaniards and church officials object to your visiting churches and cathedrals scantily clad, even on the hottest day of summer. Casual dress is acceptable, but you should "cover up" as much skin as possible.

In spite of what you've heard about days of yore, when Spaniards showed up for appointments 2 or 3 hours late, most nationals now show up on time as they do in the rest of the E.U. countries. It's always wise for men to wear a suit for business meetings. Spanish speakers should address strangers with the formal *usted* instead of the more familiar *tú.*

It is extremely offensive to make critical comments to Spaniards about their country—politics, religion, customs, their approval of same-sex marriages, whatever. Spaniards are rather formal in social matters. Spaniards are addressed as *Señor* for Mr., *Señora* for Mrs., and *Señorita* for Ms. It is customary to eat late in Spain, at least after 8:30pm. If you arrive in a dining room at 6pm, you'll be labeled a country bumpkin. It is polite to keep both hands visible during the course of a meal.

Gasoline (Petrol) Service stations abound on the major arteries of Spain and in such big cities as Madrid and Barcelona. They are open 24 hours a day. On secondary roads, most stations open at 7am daily, closing at 11pm or midnight, so plan accordingly. In today's Spain, stations are generally self-service. Prices are the same as at a full-service station. Newer models of automobiles take unleaded gas called *gasoline sin plomo.* The price of gasoline in Spain, especially in these uncertain times, varies from week to week, but always expect it to be expensive, far more so than in the States. Most stations will accept credit cards.

Holidays Holidays include January 1 (New Year's Day), January 6 (Feast of the Epiphany), March 19 (Feast of St. Joseph), Good Friday, Easter Monday, May 1 (May Day), June 10 (Corpus Christi), June 29 (Feast of St. Peter and St. Paul), July 25 (Feast of St. James), August 15 (Feast of the Assumption), October 12 (Spain's National Day), November 1 (All Saints' Day), December 8 (Immaculate Conception), and December 25 (Christmas).

No matter how large or small, every city or town in Spain also celebrates its local saint's day. In Madrid it's May 15 (St. Isidro). You'll rarely know what the local holidays are in your next destination in Spain. Try to keep money on hand, because you may arrive in town only to find banks and stores closed. In some cases, intercity bus services are suspended on holidays.

Insurance Medical Insurance For travel overseas, most U.S. health plans (including Medicare and Medicaid) do not provide coverage, and the ones that do often require you to pay for services upfront and reimburse you only after you return home.

As a safety net, you may want to buy travel medical insurance, particularly if you're traveling to a remote or high-risk area where emergency evacuation might be necessary. If you require additional medical insurance, try **MEDEX Assistance** (✆ 800/537-2029 or 410/453-6300; www.medexassist.com) or **Travel Assistance International** (✆ **800/821-2828;** www.travelassistance.com; for general information on services, call the company's **Worldwide Assistance Services, Inc.,** at ✆ **800/777-8710;** www.worldwideassistance.com).

Canadians should check with their provincial health plan offices or call **Health Canada** (✆ **866/225-0709;** www.hc-sc.gc.ca) to find out the extent of their coverage and what documentation and receipts they must take home in case they are treated overseas.

Travelers from the U.K. should carry their European Health Insurance Card (EHIC), which replaced the E111 form as proof of entitlement to free/reduced-cost medical treatment abroad (✆ **0845/605-0707;** www.ehic.org.uk). Note, however, that the EHIC covers only "necessary medical treatment."

Travel Insurance The cost of travel insurance varies widely, depending on the destination, the cost and length of your trip, your age and health, and the type of trip you're taking, but expect to pay between 5% and 8% of the vacation itself. You can get estimates from various providers through **InsureMyTrip.com** (✆ **800/487-4722**). Enter your trip cost and dates, your age, and other information for prices from more than a dozen companies.

U.K. citizens and their families who make more than one trip abroad per year may find that an annual travel insurance policy works out cheaper. Check **www.moneysuper market.com** (✆ **0845/345-5708**), which compares prices across a wide range of providers for single- and multitrip policies.

Most big travel agents offer their own insurance and will probably try to sell you their package when you book a holiday. Think before you sign. **Britain's Consumers' Association** recommends that you insist on seeing the policy and reading the fine print before buying travel insurance. The **Association of British Insurers** (✆ **020/7600-3333;** www.abi.org.uk) gives advice by phone and publishes *Holiday Insurance,* a free guide to policy provisions and prices. You might also shop around for better deals: Try **Columbus Direct** (✆ **0870/033-9988;** www.columbusdirect.com).

Trip-Cancellation Insurance Trip-cancellation insurance will help retrieve your money if you have to back out of a trip or depart early, or if your travel supplier goes bankrupt. Trip cancellation traditionally covers such events as sickness, natural disasters, and State Department advisories. The latest news in trip-cancellation insurance is the availability of **expanded hurricane coverage** and the **"any reason"** cancellation coverage—which costs more but covers cancellations made for any reason. You won't get back 100% of your prepaid trip cost, but you'll be refunded a substantial portion. **TravelSafe** (✆ **888/885-7233;** www.travelsafe.com) offers both types of coverage. Expedia also offers any-reason cancellation coverage for its air-hotel packages. For details, contact one of the following recommended insurers: **Access America** (✆ 866/807-3982; www.accessamerica.com); **Travel Guard International** (✆ 800/826-4919; www.travel guard.com); **Travel Insured International** (✆ 800/243-3174; www.travelinsured.com); and **Travelex Insurance Services** (✆ 800/228-9792; www.travelex-insurance.com).

For more information on insurance, visit www.frommers.com/planning.

Internet Access See "Staying Connected," on p. 83.

Language The official language in Spain is Castilian Spanish (or *castellano*). Although Spanish is spoken in every province of Spain, local tongues reasserted themselves with the restoration of democracy in 1975. After years of being outlawed during the Franco dictatorship, Catalan has returned to Barcelona and Catalonia, even appearing on street signs; this language and its derivatives are also spoken in the Valencia area and in the Balearic Islands, including Majorca (even though natives there will tell you they speak Mallorquín). The Basque language is widely spoken in the Basque region (the northeast, near France), which is seeking independence from Spain. Likewise, the Gallego language, which sounds and looks very much like Portuguese, has enjoyed a renaissance in Galicia (the northwest). Of course, English is spoken in most hotels, restaurants, and shops.

The best phrase book is *Spanish for Travellers* by Berlitz; it has a menu supplement and a 12,500-word glossary of both English and Spanish. See also "Useful Terms & Phrases," p. 784."

Legal Aid In case of trouble with the authorities, contact your local embassy or consulate, which will recommend an English-speaking lawyer in your area. You will, of course, be charged a typical attorney's fee for representation.

Lost & Found Be sure to tell all of your credit card companies the minute you discover your wallet has been lost or stolen, and file a report at the nearest police precinct. Your credit card company or insurer may require a police report number or record of the loss. Most credit card companies have an emergency toll-free number to call if your card is lost or stolen; they may be able to wire you a cash advance immediately or deliver an emergency credit card in a day or two.

To report a lost credit card, contact the following toll-free in Spain: American Express at ✆ **91-743-70-00;** Diners Club at ✆ **90-110-10-11;** MasterCard at ✆ **90-097-12-31;** or Visa at ✆ **90-099-11-24.**

If you need emergency cash over the weekend, when all banks and American Express offices are closed, you can have money wired to you via **Western Union** (✆ **800/325-6000;** www.westernunion.com).

Mail Airmail letters to the United States and Canada cost .78€ up to 15 grams, and letters to Britain or other E.U. countries cost .58€ up to 20 grams. Letters within Spain cost .29€. Postcards have the same rates as letters. Allow about 8 days for delivery to North America, generally less to the United Kingdom; in some cases, letters take 2 weeks to reach North America. Rates change frequently, so check at your local hotel before mailing anything. As for surface mail to North America, forget it. Chances are you'll be home long before your letter arrives.

Maps For one of the best overviews of the Iberian Peninsula (Spain and Portugal), get Michelin map no. 990 (folded version) or map no. 460 (spiral-bound version). For more detailed looks at Spain, Michelin has a series of six maps (nos. 441–446) showing specific regions, complete with many minor roads.

For extensive touring, purchase *Mapas de Carreteras—España y Portugal,* published by Almax Editores and available at most leading bookstores in Spain. This cartographic compendium of Spain provides an overview of the country and includes road and street maps of some of its major cities.

The **American Automobile Association** (www.aaa.com) publishes a regional map of Spain that's available free to members at most AAA offices in the United States. Incidentally, the AAA is associated with the **Real Automóvil Club de España** (**RACE;** ℂ **90-240-45-45;** www.race.es). This organization can supply helpful information about road conditions in Spain, including tourist and travel advice. It will also provide limited road service, in an emergency, if your car breaks down.

Measurements See the chart on the inside front cover of this book for details on converting metric measurements to nonmetric equivalents.

Newspapers & Magazines All cities and towns, of course, have Spanish-language newspapers and magazines. However, in the touristed areas of big cities, many kiosks sell editions of the *International Herald Tribune* along with *Newsweek* and *Time.*

Passports See www.frommers.com/planning for information on how to obtain a passport.

For Residents of Australia Contact the **Australian Passport Information Service** at ℂ **131-232,** or visit the government website at www.passports.gov.au.

For Residents of Canada Contact the central **Passport Office,** Department of Foreign Affairs and International Trade, Ottawa, ON K1A 0G3 (ℂ **800/567-6868;** www.ppt.gc.ca).

For Residents of Ireland Contact the **Passport Office,** Setanta Centre, Molesworth Street, Dublin 2 (ℂ **01/671-1633;** www.foreignaffairs.gov.ie).

For Residents of New Zealand Contact the **Passports Office** at ℂ **0800/225-050** in New Zealand or 04/474-8100, or log on to www.passports.govt.nz.

For Residents of the United Kingdom Visit your nearest passport office, major post office, or travel agency or contact the **United Kingdom Passport Service** at ℂ **0870/521-0410** or search its website at www.ukpa.gov.uk.

For Residents of the United States To find your regional passport office, either check the U.S. State Department website (http://travel.state.gov/passport) or call the **National Passport Information Center**'s toll-free number (ℂ **877/487-2778**) for automated information.

Police The national emergency number is ℂ **006** throughout Spain, except in the Basque Country, where it is ℂ **088.**

Smoking On January 1, 2006, Spain banned smoking in the workplace. Restaurants, bars, and nightclubs of a certain size have to designate certain areas as nonsmoking, and smoking is also banned on public transportation and in other areas such as cultural centers.

Taxes The internal sales tax (known in Spain as IVA) ranges from 7% to 33%, depending on the commodity being sold. Food, wine, and basic necessities are taxed at 7%; most goods and services (including car rentals), at 13%; luxury items (jewelry, all tobacco, imported liquors), at 33%; and hotels, at 7%.

If you are not a European Union resident and make purchases in Spain worth more than 90€, you can get a tax refund. To get this refund, you must complete three copies of a form that the store will give you, detailing the nature of your purchase and its value. Citizens of non-E.U. countries show the purchase and the form to the Spanish Customs Office. The shop is supposed to refund the amount due you. Inquire at the time of purchase how they will do so and discuss in what currency your refund will arrive.

Telephones See "Staying Connected," on p. 83.

Time Spain is 6 hours ahead of Eastern Standard Time in the United States. Daylight saving time is in effect from the last Sunday in March to the last Sunday in September.

Tipping Don't overtip. The government requires that restaurant and hotel bills include their service charges—usually 15% of the bill. However, that doesn't mean you should skip out of a place without dispensing an extra euro or two. Some guidelines: Your hotel porter should get .80€ per bag. Maids should be given 1€ per day, more if you're generous. Tip doormen .75€ for assisting with baggage and .50€ for calling a cab. Tipping a concierge depends on how much you have used his or her services. For example, some visitors never ask for anything from a concierge. In that case, you can tip nothing. Sometimes a concierge will submit a bill for services rendered, including making restaurant reservations, arranging a bus tour, or securing theater tickets. In that case, you can pay the bill and check out.

Should a concierge not submit a bill, and you have used his services only a couple of times, 5€ is a sufficient tip in most deluxe and first-class hotels. If you've used concierge services a lot, 20€ would be an appropriate tip. In less expensive hotels, you generally tip much less, perhaps 1€ or 2€ for some minor service rendered.

For cabdrivers, add about 10% to the fare as shown on the meter. At airports, such as Barajas in Madrid and major terminals, the porter who handles your luggage will present you with a fixed-charge bill.

Service is included in restaurant bills. But it is the custom to tip extra—in fact, the waiter will expect a tip. That tip is left at your discretion. Some Spanish diners leave nothing if the service was outright bad. Other, more generous diners tip as much as 5% to 10% if the service was good.

Barbers and hairdressers expect a 10% to 15% tip. Tour guides expect 2€, although a tip is not mandatory. Theater and bullfight ushers get from .50€.

Toilets In Spain they're called *aseos, servicios,* or *lavabos* and are labeled *caballeros* for men and *damas* or *señoras* for women. If you can't find any, go into a bar, but you should order something.

Visitor Information The Tourist Office of Spain's official website can be found at **www.spain.info/us/tourspain**. You can obtain information from any of the following tourist offices.

In Canada 2 Bloor St. W., Ste. 3402, Toronto, ON M4W 3E2 (✆ **416/961-3131;** fax 416/961-1992).

In the U.S. 666 Fifth Ave., 35th Floor, New York, NY 10103 (✆ **212/265-8822;** fax 212/265-8864); 845 N. Michigan Ave., Ste. 915E, Chicago, IL 60611 (✆ **312/642-1992;** fax 312/642-9817); 8383 Wilshire Blvd., Ste. 956, Beverly Hills, CA 90211 (✆ **323/658-7188;** fax 323/658-1061); 1395 Brickell Ave., Ste. 1130, Miami, FL 33131 (✆ **305/358-1992;** fax 305/358-8223).

In the U.K. 79 New Cavendish St., 2nd Floor, London W1W 6XB (✆ **020/7486-8077;** fax 020/7486-8034).

Water See "Health," on p. 73.

Websites For general info, check out **www.spain.info/us/tourspain**, the official page of the Tourist Office of Spain; **www.red2000.com**; or **www.cyberspain.com**. You'll find more details at **www.softguides.com**. If you're interested in the cultural treasures, go to **www.mcu.es**.

AIRLINE, HOTEL & CAR-RENTAL WEBSITES

MAJOR AIRLINES

Aeroméxico
www.aeromexico.com

Air Canada
www.aircanada.com

Air Europa
www.aireuropa.com

Air France
www.airfrance.com

Alitalia
www.alitalia.com

American Airlines
www.aa.com

British Airways
www.british-airways.com

Continental Airlines
www.continental.com

Delta Air Lines
www.delta.com

EgyptAir
www.egyptair.com

El Al Airlines
www.elal.co.il/elal/english

Finnair
www.finnair.com

Iberia Airlines
www.iberia.com

Lan Airlines
www.lanchile.com

Lufthansa
www.lufthansa.com

Northwest Airlines
www.nwa.com

South African Airways
www.flysaa.com

Swiss Air
www.swiss.com

Thai Airways International
www.thaiair.com

Turkish Airlines
www.thy.com

United Airlines
www.united.com

US Airways
www.usairways.com

Virgin Atlantic Airways
www.virgin-atlantic.com

BUDGET AIRLINES

Aer Lingus
www.aerlingus.com

AirTran Airways
www.airtran.com

Air Berlin
www.airberlin.com

BMI Baby
www.bmibaby.com

easyJet
www.easyjet.com

Frontier Airlines
www.frontierairlines.com

Ryanair
www.ryanair.com

Spirit Airlines
www.spiritair.com

MAJOR HOTEL & MOTEL CHAINS

Abba Hotels
www.abbahoteles.com

AC Hotels
www.ac-hotels.com

Barceló Hotels & Resorts
www.barcelo.es

Best Western International
www.bestwestern.com

Crowne Plaza Hotels
www.ichotelsgroup.com/
crowneplaza

Derby Hotels
www.derbyhotels.es

Four Seasons
www.fourseasons.com

Hesperia Hoteles
www.hoteles-hesperia.es

Hilton Hotels
www1.hilton.com

Holiday Inn
www.ichotelsgroup.com

Husa Hoteles
www.husa.es

Hyatt
www.hyatt.com

Iberostar Hotels & Resorts
www.iberostar.com

InterContinental Hotels & Resorts
www.ichotelsgroup.com

Macia Hotels
www.maciahoteles.com

Marriott
www.marriott.com

Mercure
www.mercure.com

Novotel
www.novotel.com

Radisson Hotels & Resorts
www.radisson.com

Ramada Worldwide
www.ramada.com

Riu Hotels & Resorts
www.riu.com

Sheraton Hotels & Resorts
www.starwoodhotels.com/sheraton

Sol Meliá
www.solmelia.com

Westin Hotels & Resorts
www.starwoodhotels.com/westin

CAR-RENTAL AGENCIES

Auto Europe
www.autoeurope.com

Avis
www.avis.com

Budget
www.budget.com

Dollar
www.dollar.com

Enterprise
www.enterprise.com

Hertz
www.hertz.com

Kemwel (KHA)
www.kemwel.com

National
www.nationalcar.com

Thrifty
www.thrifty.com

USEFUL TERMS & PHRASES

Most Spaniards are very patient with foreigners who try to speak their language. That said, you might encounter several difficult regional languages and dialects in Spain: In Catalonia, they speak **catálan** (the most widely spoken non-national language in Europe); in the Basque Country, they speak **euskera;** in Galicia, you'll hear **gallego.** However, Castilian Spanish (**castellano,** or simply **español**) is understood everywhere; for that reason, we've included a list of simple words and phrases in *castellano* to help you get by.

BASIC WORDS & PHRASES

English	Spanish	Pronunciation
Good day	Buenos días	**bweh-nohs dee-ahs**
How are you?	¿Cómo está?	**koh-moh es-tah**
Very well	Muy bien	**mwee byehn**
Thank you	Gracias	**grah-syahs**
You're welcome	De nada	**deh nah-dah**
Goodbye	Adiós	**ah-dyohs**
Please	Por favor	**pohr fah-vohr**

English	Spanish	Pronunciation
Yes	Sí	**see**
No	No	**noh**
Excuse me	Perdóneme	**pehr-*doh*-neh-meh**
Give me	Déme	***deh*-meh**
Where is . . . ?	¿Dónde está . . . ?	***dohn*-deh es-*tah***
the station	la estación	**lah es-tah-*syohn***
a hotel	un hotel	**oon oh-*tel***
a gas station	una gasolinera	***oo*-nah gah-so-lee-*neh*-rah**
a restaurant	un restaurante	**oon res-tow-*rahn*-teh**
the toilet	el baño	**el *bah*-nyoh**
a good doctor	un buen médico	**oon bwehn *meh*-dee-coh**
the road to . . .	el camino a/hacia . . .	**el cah-*mee*-noh ah/*ah*-syah**
To the right	A la derecha	**ah lah deh-*reh*-chah**
To the left	A la izquierda	**ah lah ees-*kyehr*-dah**
Straight ahead	Derecho	**deh-*reh*-choh**
I would like	Quisiera	**kee-*syeh*-rah**
I want . . .	Quiero . . .	***kyeh*-roh**
to eat	comer	**ko-*mehr***
a room	una habitación	***oo*-nah ah-bee-tah-*syohn***
Do you have . . . ?	¿Tiene usted . . . ?	**tyeh-neh oo-*sted***
a book	un libro	**oon *lee*-broh**
a dictionary	un diccionario	**oon deek-syoh-*na*-ryo**
How much is it?	¿Cuánto cuesta?	***kwahn*-toh *kwehs*-tah**
When?	¿Cuándo?	***kwahn*-doh**
What?	¿Qué?	**keh**
There is (Is there . . . ?)	(¿)Hay (. . . ?)	**aye**
What is there?	¿Qué hay?	**keh aye**
Yesterday	Ayer	**ah-*yehr***
Today	Hoy	**oy**
Tomorrow	Mañana	**mah-*nyah*-nah**
Good	Bueno	***bweh*-noh**
Bad	Malo	***mah*-loh**
Better (Best)	(Lo) Mejor	**(loh) meh-*hor***
More	Más	**mahs**
Less	Menos	***meh*-nohs**
No smoking	Se prohibe fumar	**seh proh-*ee*-beh foo-*mahr***

English	Spanish	Pronunciation
Postcard	Tarjeta postal	tar-*heh*-tah pohs-*tahl*
Insect repellent	Repelente contra insectos	reh-peh-*lehn*-teh *cohn*-trah een-*sehk*-tohs
Do you speak English?	¿Habla usted inglés?	*ah*-blah oo-*sted* een-*glehs*
Is there anyone here who speaks English?	¿Hay alguien aquí que hable inglés?	eye *ahl*-gyehn ah-*kee* keh ah-bleh een-*glehs*
I speak a little Spanish.	Hablo un poco de español.	*ah*-bloh oon *poh*-koh deh es-pah-*nyol*
I don't understand Spanish very well.	No (lo) entiendo muy bien el español.	noh (loh) ehn-*tyehn*-doh mwee byehn el es-pah-*nyol*
What time is it?	¿Qué hora es?	keh *oh*-rah es
May I see your menu?	¿Puedo ver el menú (la carta)?	*pweh*-do vehr el meh-*noo* (lah *car*-tah)
The check, please.	La cuenta por favor.	lah *kwehn*-tah pohr fah-*vohr*
What do I owe you?	¿Cuánto le debo?	*kwahn*-toh leh *deh*-boh
What did you say? (Colloquial)	¿Mande?	*mahn*-deh
What did you say? (Formal)	¿Cómo?	koh-moh
Do you accept traveler's checks?	¿Acepta usted cheques de viajero?	ah-*sehp*-tah oo-*sted* cheh-kehs deh byah-*heh*-roh

NUMBERS

English	Spanish	Pronunciation
1	uno	*oo*-noh
2	dos	dohs
3	tres	trehs
4	cuatro	*kwah*-troh
5	cinco	*seen*-koh
6	seis	says
7	siete	*syeh*-teh
8	ocho	*oh*-choh
9	nueve	*nweh*-beh
10	diez	dyehs
11	once	*ohn*-seh
12	doce	*doh*-seh
13	trece	*treh*-seh
14	catorce	kah-*tohr*-seh

English	Spanish	Pronunciation
15	quince	*keen*-seh
16	dieciséis	dyeh-see-*says*
17	diecisiete	dyeh-see-*syeh*-teh
18	dieciocho	dyeh-see-*oh*-choh
19	diecinueve	dyeh-see-*nweh*-beh
20	veinte	*bayn*-teh
30	treinta	*trayn*-tah
40	cuarenta	kwah-*rehn*-tah
50	cincuenta	seen-*kwehn*-tah
60	sesenta	seh-*sehn*-tah
70	setenta	seh-*tehn*-tah
80	ochenta	oh-*chehn*-tah
90	noventa	noh-*behn*-tah
100	cien	*syehn*
200	doscientos	doh-*syehn*-tohs
500	quinientos	kee-*nyehn*-tos
1,000	mil	meel

TRAVEL TERMS

Aduana Customs

Aeropuerto Airport

Avenida Avenue

Avión Airplane

Aviso Warning

Bus Bus

Calle Street

Cheques viajeros Traveler's checks

Correo(s) Mail, or post office

Dinero Money

Embajada Embassy

Embarque Boarding

Entrada Entrance

Equipaje Luggage

Este East

Frontera Border

Hospedaje Inn

Norte North

Oeste West

Pasaje Ticket

Pasaporte Passport

Puerta de salida Boarding gate

Salida Exit

Tarjeta de embarque Boarding card

Vuelo Flight

EMERGENCY TERMS

¡Auxilio! Help!

Ambulancia Ambulance

Bomberos Fire brigade

Clínica Clinic

Emergencia Emergency

Enfermo/a Sick

Enfermera Nurse

Farmacia Pharmacy

Fuego/Incendio Fire

Hospital Hospital

Ladrón Thief

Peligroso Dangerous

Policía Police

Médico Doctor

¡Váyase! Go away!

INDEX

PHOTO CREDITS

NOTES

PHOTO CREDITS